6e

Cost Accounting:
Foundations and Evolutions

Michael R. **Kinney**, *Texas A&M University*

Jenice **Prather-Kinsey**, *University of Missouri—Columbia*

Cecily A. **Raiborn**, *Loyola University New Orleans*

THOMSON

SOUTH-WESTERN

Australia · Canada · Mexico · Singapore · Spain · United Kingdom · United States

THOMSON

SOUTH-WESTERN

Cost Accounting: Foundations and Evolutions, Sixth Edition
Michael R. Kinney, Jenice Prather-Kinsey, and Cecily A. Raiborn

VP/Editorial Director:
Jack W. Calhoun

Publisher:
Rob Dewey

Senior Acquisitions Editor:
Sharon Oblinger

Developmental Editor:
Carol Bennet

Marketing Manager:
Keith Chasse

Production Editor:
Margaret M. Bril

Manager of Technology, Editorial:
Vicky True

Technology Project Editor:
Robin Browning

Manufacturing Coordinator:
Doug Wilke

Production House:
LEAP Publishing Services, Inc.

Printer:
Courier
Kendalville, Indiana

Art Director:
Michelle Kunkler

Internal Designer:
Ann Small Design

Cover Designer:
Ann Small Design

Cover Images:
© Getty Images

Photography Manager:
John Hill

Photo Researcher:
Stuart Kunkler

Library of Congress Control Number:
2004117233

For more information about our products,
contact us at:

Thomson Learning Academic Resource
Center
1-800-423-0563

Thomson Higher Education
5191 Natorp Boulevard
Mason, OH 45040
USA

Asia (including India)
Thomson Learning
5 Shenton Way
#01-01 UIC Building
Singapore 068808

Australia/New Zealand
Thomson Learning Australia
102 Dodds Street
Southbank, Victoria 3006
Australia

Canada
Thomson Nelson
1120 Birchmount Road
Toronto, Ontario
M1K 5G4
Canada

Latin America
Thomson Learning
Seneca, 53
Colonia Polanco
11560 Mexico
D.F.Mexico

UK/Europe/Middle East/Africa
Thomson Learning
High Holborn House
50/51 Bedford Row
London WC1R 4LR
United Kingdom

Spain (including Portugal)
Thomson Paraninfo
Calle Magallanes, 25
28015 Madrid, Spain

Brief Contents

Contents

Preface

Cost accounting is a dynamic discipline constantly responding to the needs of managers in a global and highly competitive business world. Managers need cost accounting tools to develop, implement, and evaluate strategy. Managers also need cost accounting methods to determine product costs for internal management and external financial reporting. The sixth edition of *Cost Accounting: Foundations and Evolutions* provides in-depth coverage of cost management concepts and procedures in a logically sequenced and reader-friendly framework.

Students will find cost accounting applicable to their business and personal lives when presented in a readable and interesting format. A text is useless if students do not understand the significance and relevancy of the subject to their professional and personal lives. We believe students and faculty will find the contents of this edition of cost management dynamic and fun to learn.

Improvements in the Sixth Edition

Better Chapter Content and Organization

The title of the sixth edition *Cost Accounting: Foundations and Evolutions* reflects the new topical organization of the text. The chapters are organized accordingly to include cost foundation topics in the first eleven chapters and cost management and evolutionary topics in the remaining chapters of the text. This revised organization required some topics that were positioned in the latter half of the fifth edition, such as "The Master Budget" and "Absorption and Variable Costing," to be moved to the first half of the book. Similarly, some topics in the first half of the fifth edition, for example, "Implementing Quality Concepts," and "Cost Management Systems," have been moved to the second half for this sixth edition. The revised organization of the text should correspond with a two-semester sequence where traditional cost concepts are taught in the first cost class and managerial and evolutionary topics are taught in the second cost course.

The chapter flows have also been sequenced to be more logical. For example, Chapter 2 now focuses on the cost terms that will be used throughout the textbook. This chapter represents the foundations of cost management terminology and will be useful to students in understanding the remainder of the textbook than a chapter that focuses on cost management systems.

Students find overhead costing to be a difficult concept. Overhead costing concepts are used in job order costing, activity-based-costing, and process costing. Hence, overhead costing is introduced early in the text (Chapter 3) to facilitate discussion of those very topics. Further, a chapter has been dedicated to computing overhead rates, hoping to give students the opportunity to learn the basics of overhead costing before applying it to inventory/product costing methods.

Standard costing and master budgeting are within the first half of the textbook and follow one another. Standard costing concepts are used in preparing the master budget and hence the sequencing of standard costing concepts first. Moreover, flexible budgets are introduced in Chapter 3 with the goal that all techniques needed to develop master budgets will have been introduced before the master budgeting chapter. Thus, the sequence should be more logical and easier to comprehend in this sixth edition.

Some of the material included in the fifth edition is covered in substantial depth in courses other than cost accounting. To minimize such duplication, coverage of some topics has been greatly reduced or even eliminated in the sixth edition. For example, the global environment of business in Chapter 1 of the fifth edition is reduced in the sixth edition, as it is generally presented in an International Accounting or Management course.

Unique Instructional Platform Designed for Student Success

Focus Companies Integrated Throughout

Introducing: Lays out each chapter's interaction with a unique, real-world company. This segment provides the background for a company whose underlying operations engage chapter content. With the framework in place, students immediately begin to see real applications of cost accounting.

Revisiting: Concludes the coverage of the focus company laid out by the Introducing segment. Using real cost accounting questions encountered by the focus company, students are presented with specific, real-world applications of the chapter's concepts.

Through these two features, students are provided with both the overall context and specific detail to grasp the real-world implementation of each chapter's key concepts. The focus companies were generally selected based on student appeal and include General Motors, Specialized Bike, JetBlue, Williamsburg Soap and Candle Company, and Ford Motor Company. Additionally, Chapter 1 focuses on Donna Krall, CPA, CMA, so that students may understand why cost accounting, rather than financial, might be selected as a career choice.

More Infographic and Explanatory Visuals

Because today's students are visual learners, more explanatory visuals have been added within each chapter. For example, in Chapter 1, the value chain exhibit has

EXHIBIT 1–6
COMPONENTS OF A VALUE CHAIN

been designed to look like a chain interlocking one link to another. Info-pictures have been provided within each link as an example of what research and development (R&D) or product design is. The team approach to solving management issues is illustrated with a circular chain rather than with a vertical listing of functions implying no cross-functional teams to cost management. Further, R&D does not stop once the product is designed or produced. Rather, R&D is constantly evolving. This is illustrated with a circular chain rather than a disjointed flat chain where one begins with R&D and ends with customer service. Chapter 1 also includes an organization chart of the focus company to convey the differences between line and staff functions and the accountant's role within an organization.

What factors create under- or over-applied overhead?

NEW! Inclusion of Pop-Up Questions

This text's pop-up questions are intended to get the students' attention without overwhelming them with lengthy learning objective questions. The pop-up questions are short and to the point in addressing critical concepts needed to understand chapter content and draw attention to the underlying reasons for the importance of the chapter material.

Many of the features of the fifth edition were retained as users indicated that they were the strength of this cost textbook above that of our competitors. Hence, the chapter focus company concept, solution strategies, demonstration problems and end-of-chapter material have been continued. These features of the fifth edition were pointed to as making this text easy to read and understand and easy for faculty to teach.

NEW! Comprehensive Review Module Pulls It All Together

This comprehensive review module includes the following:

- **Bulleted Chapter Summary:** Chapter summaries have been retained but the format has been changed for easier readability. Chapter summaries are now in outline format so that students can quickly visualize the main and subtopics of a chapter and how they interrelate. These summaries are directly related to the objectives stated at the beginning of the chapter and provide a quick review of the essential chapter elements

- **Solution Strategies Review:** Comprehensive solution strategies designed to earmark important journal entries, concepts, and mathematical formulae serve to aid in solving end-of-chapter exercises and problems. These are proven techniques, helpful in facilitating the learning process and preparing students for exams.

Solution Strategies

MANUFACTURING CYCLE EFFICIENCY

Cycle Time
= Value-Added Processing Time + Inspection Time + Transfer Time + Idle Time

MCE = Value-Added Processing Time ÷ Total Cycle Time

ACTIVITY-BASED COSTING

1. Determine the organization's activity centers.
2. Determine departmental activities and efforts needed to conduct those activities, that is, the cost drivers.
3. Determine departmental resources consumed in conducting activities and allocate costs of these resources to activity centers based on the cost drivers.

▪ **Demonstration Problems:** Studies have shown that students retain more when answers are provided immediately after solving a problem. Hence, the demonstration problem allows students to work a comprehensive problem and check the accuracy of their answers with the solution directly following. Further, demonstration problems are a comprehensive review of chapter content.

Better End-of-Chapter Material

As the old adage goes, "Practice makes perfect." Therefore, it is important to have a sufficient number of end-of-chapter items that cover all of the chapter materials and range in level of difficulty from easy to advanced. The sixth edition has reduced the number of questions but increased the number of exercises and problems. The sixth edition also presents short cases that require research on and discussion of issues associated with cost management techniques. Instead of the typical matching exercise for key terms, crossword puzzles for key chapter terms are available on the text's Web site. Enhanced Excel templates of selected exercises and problems are available on the Web.

Instructor Support Materials

A comprehensive instructor support package is provided for this text, including:

Instructor's Manual (0-324-31796-4). Prepared by Charles Russo, Ph.D., CPA of Bloomsburg University, this manual contains sample syllabi, terminology glossaries, and lecture outline summaries. Masters for teaching transparencies for each chapter are included at the end of this volume, providing additional perspectives on text materials and reflecting select PowerPoint presentation slides.

Instructor's Resource CD (0-324-31792-1). This CD contains PowerPoint Lecture Slides that provide entertaining and informative graphics and text for full-color, electronic presentations. ExamView Pro® Testing Software is easy-to-use software that allows you to customize exams, practice tests, and tutorials and deliver them over a network, on the web, or in printed form. Finally, the files for the Instructor's Manual, Test Bank, Solutions Manual, and Excel Spreadsheets will be included.

Solutions Manual (0-324-31789-1). Prepared by the authors and verified by Nat R. Briscoe, Ph.D., CPA of Northwestern State University, this volume has been independently reviewed and checked for accuracy. It contains solutions to all numerical end-of-chapter materials and many non-numerical items, with discussion points provided for many of the features in the book. The Solutions Manual also includes a copy of the Student Check Figures, which also have been verified.

Solution Transparency Acetates (0-324-31790-5). Acetates are provided from the Solutions Manual for all numerical end-of-chapter materials.

Test Bank (0-324-31791-3). Prepared by Edward Walker, Ph.D., CPA of McNeese State University and verified by Sanjay Gupta, Ph.D., CPA, CMA of Valdosta State University, the Test Bank contains thousands of multiple-choice, short exercise, and short discussion questions with related solutions with level of difficulty (easy, medium, difficult) identified for each question.

Web Resources. This text's supporting Web site at http://kinney.swlearning.com provides downloadable versions of key instructor supplements, as well as student features that enhance students' learning experience. (See Student Support Materials below.)

WebTutor Advantage for WebCT and WebTutor Advantage for Blackboard (Instructor's Versions). These items provide instructors with the class-management tools and features instructors need to facilitate online learning. (See Student Support Materials for learning features.)

Additional Instructor Support Materials

Cases in Cost Management: A Strategic Emphasis, 2nd edition, by John Shank: This book provides 35 proven cases focusing on strategic decision making. Helping students develop the ability to apply the concepts of managerial cost analysis in strategic decision making, the cases give particular attention to such topics as ABC, ABM, value chain, and target cost.

Building Business Spreadsheets with Excel, by Kathleen Adkins: This text teaches readers how to build business spreadsheets like a pro. Problem-based learning is used to build students' skills in completing real-life problems. In addition, students learn Excel's best features for working accurately and efficiently, how to find and solve common errors, give spreadsheets a professional look, solve printing problems, and structure spreadsheets to answer business's common "what-if" questions.

Student Support Materials

Student Study Guide (0-324-31788-3). Prepared by Alan Campbell and Sharie Dow of Saint Leo University Center for Online Learning and verified by Edward Walker, Ph.D., CPA of McNeese State University, this chapter-by-chapter manual makes it easy for students to reinforce content through independent review and self-examination. It features chapter overviews, detailed chapter notes, and self-test questions.

Personal Trainer. This feature boosts grades while reducing study time—allowing students to enhance skills with practice problems and complete assigned homework problems, all from their own computers.

Spreadsheet Templates. This package allows students to solve selected and icon-designated end-of-chapter exercises and problems using Excel®. Templates are available online at the text Web site or from the instructor.

Web Resources (0-324-31795-6). This text's supporting Web site at http://kinney.swlearning.com provides online quizzes, Excel templates to solve selected EOC problems, links to other cost accounting resources, and updates on URL cites in the text, and more.

WebTutor Advantage for WebCT and WebTutor Advantage for Blackboard (0-324-31794-8) and **WebCT** (0-324-31793-X). These features offer online learning features that make learning cost accounting easier and more portable. In addition to Personal Trainer access, enhanced quizzing and Problem Tutorials allow students to better prepare for assignments. Games like Quiz Bowl and Crossword Puzzles help students to be better prepared for assignments in a relaxed format. Selected videos with interactive questions give students valuable background about how actual companies employ management accounting techniques covered in the text. Discussion threads directly link each chapter's topics and its "Introducing" and "Revisiting" companies. In all, WebTutor Advantage gives students valuable advantages that make the course run smoothly.

Xtra! Available separately or as a free option when bundled with every new textbook, Xtra! gives students access to the following online learning tools: Problem Tutorials, Quiz Bowl, Crossword Puzzles, and the PowerPoint slides.

Acknowledgments

We would like to thank all the people who have helped us during the revision of this text. The constructive comments and suggestions made by the following reviewers were instrumental in developing, rewriting, reorganizing, and improving the quality, readability, and student orientation of *Cost Accounting: Foundations and Evolutions.*

Adrian Allen
Shaw University

Jerry Bennett
University of South Carolina

Tim Biggart
University of North Carolina at Greensboro

Nat R. Briscoe
Northwestern State University

Scott Butterfield
University of Colorado at Colorado Springs

Chiaho Chang
Montclair State University

David Dearman
University of Arkansas at Fort Smith

Michael Eames
Santa Clara University

Rafik Elias
California State University, Los Angeles

Lou Fowler
Missouri Western State College

Nashwa George
Montclair State University

Lyal Gustafson
University of Wisconsin, Whitewater

Sanjay Gupta
Valdosta State University

Dan Heitger
Auburn University

Carl Keller
*Indiana University-Purdue University
Fort Wayne*

Larry Killough
Virginia Polytech Institute

Thomas J. Krissek
Northeastern Illinois University

Sandra S. Lang
McKendree College

Chor Lau
*California State University at
Los Angeles*

Wallace R. Leese
*California State University,
Chico*

Robert Lin
*California State University,
Hayward*

Hugh Pforsich
*California State University,
Sacramento*

Tom Pressly
Indiana University of Pennsylvania

Celia Renner
Boise State University

George Schmelzle
*Indiana University-Purdue University
Fort Wayne*

Henry Schwarzbach
University of Rhode Island

Paul J. Shinal
Cayuga Community College

John Stancil
Florida Southern College

Gerald Thalmann
North Central College

We are grateful for the materials from the Institute of Management Accountants, the American Institute of CPAs, the various periodical publishers, and the featured organizations that have contributed significantly to making this text a truly useful learning tool for the students. Thanks go to Leslie Kauffman for her work on past editions. The authors also wish to thank all the people at South-Western College Publishing (Sharon Oblinger, acquisitions editor; Marge Bril, production editor) and those at Litten Editing and Production, Inc. who have helped us on this project. Special thanks go to Carol Bennett, developmental editor, for her time, effort, and expertise on this edition. Lastly, sincere gratitude goes to our families and friends who provided unending support and encouragement during this process.

Mike Kinney
Jenice Prather-Kinsey
Cecily Raiborn

Cost Accounting:

Foundations and Evolutions

1

Introduction to Cost Accounting

Objectives

AFTER COMPLETING THIS CHAPTER, YOU SHOULD BE ABLE TO ANSWER THE FOLLOWING QUESTIONS:

LO.1 WHAT ARE THE RELATIONSHIPS AMONG FINANCIAL, MANAGEMENT, AND COST ACCOUNTING?

LO.2 WHAT ARE TWO COMMON ORGANIZATIONAL STRATEGIES?

LO.3 WHAT IS A VALUE CHAIN, AND WHAT ARE THE MAJOR VALUE CHAIN FUNCTIONS?

LO.4 HOW IS A BALANCED SCORECARD USED TO IMPLEMENT AN ORGANIZATION'S STRATEGY?

LO.5 WHY MUST ACCOUNTANTS UNDERSTAND AN ORGANIZATION'S STRUCTURE TO PERFORM EFFECTIVELY IN THAT ORGANIZATION?

LO.6 WHAT ARE THE SOURCES OF ETHICAL STANDARDS FOR COST ACCOUNTANTS?

LO.7 WHAT ARE THE SOURCES OF AUTHORITATIVE PRONOUNCEMENTS FOR THE PRACTICE OF COST ACCOUNTING?

Introducing

Donna Krall, CPA, CMA

Donna Krall graduated with an undergraduate degree in accounting from Eastern Michigan University and went to work for Deloitte, one of the "Big Four" accounting firms. Like most new hires, she dreamed of becoming a partner with the firm, not realizing that the odds of that happening were less than 1 percent!

Krall took and passed the CPA Exam. On track with her dream objective, she soon attained the title of "experienced senior" at Deloitte. A senior has a high level of responsibility for client audit engagements in determining whether clients' financial statements were prepared in accordance with generally accepted accounting principles (GAAP). In their audit of financial statements, seniors must be up-to-date on the financial accounting pronouncements issued by the Financial Accounting Standards Board (FASB) because it prescribes methods for preparing client financial statements. However, it wasn't long before Krall realized that she wanted a job that was more challenging and creative than what she was doing in public accounting.

Krall returned to the academic life and earned an MBA from Wayne State University. In addition, she decided that she would enhance her managerial skills by becoming a Certified Management Accountant (CMA). This credential was one of the reasons that General Motors (GM) decided to recruit Krall into its internal audit department. She accepted the position because it offered new challenges and a great deal more flexibility than what she had been experiencing in public accounting.

The internal audit position gave Krall the opportunity to use her public accounting experience to audit GM value chain functions such as purchasing, research and development, and marketing. She also used her previously developed research skills to address various accounting questions and recommended solutions. So although she was in industry, she had a financial reporting function: auditing for compliance with GAAP.

After three years at GM, Krall was promoted to a quasi-project manager position. In this position, she focused less on financial accounting and became more involved with cost accounting. Today, Krall is in charge of improving the logistical movement of goods globally at GM and in turn controlling freight costs. GM has numerous supply chain subcontractors that provide logistics services involving shipping goods between intercontinental operations. Krall's challenge is to determine whether the subcontractors' freight charges are appropriate and which charges can be reduced through process automation.

Krall enjoys her position for several reasons. First, it allows her to be creative in finding ways to reduce freight costs. She can use many tools, including financial software, in the process. Second, Krall is empowered to identify and implement cost-cutting processes for subcontractor services and software vendors globally. This part of her job means that she travels to locations such as Brazil, Germany, and Mexico to seek solutions to supply chain freight payment problems. Because of her international experiences, she has realized that there is a skill she wished she had: the ability to speak a second language. For instance, she often works in Latin American countries but cannot speak Spanish; thus, she often finds it difficult to explain technical terms. Luckily, members on her team are native Spanish speakers, and they help her bridge the communication gaps. Third, Krall can see professional opportunities at GM beyond her current position. She knows that solid performance as a project coordinator will put her in line for a promotion to cost manager, bringing not only additional pay but also benefits such as a new company car each year. Krall's career aspirations are not limited to a one-level promotion; many cost accounting managers have become controllers and chief operating officers in large corporations.

Interestingly, most accounting graduates who begin their careers in public accounting are likely to leave that career path within five years. The next position for these individuals is often in an industry setting that welcomes not only the technical accounting skills that are honed in public accounting but also the management and business skills and knowledge needed to rise to the top of an organization. As Donna Krall's story indicates, the CMA credential is something that companies recognize as an indicator of management potential.

Source: E-mail interview with Donna Krall; http://www.gm.com.

Starting a career as a junior auditor with the goal of becoming partner in a public accounting firm is the dream of many accounting majors. However, a career goal of becoming a chief financial officer or controller is equally viable, and the end result can be equally rewarding. This text presents tools and techniques that cost and management accountants use and provides problem-solving methods that are useful in achieving corporate goals. Such knowledge will prove valuable to a student who wants to become a Certified Public Accountant (CPA) and/or a Certified Management Accountant (CMA). The first part of this text presents the traditional methods of cost and managerial accounting that are the building blocks of generating information used to satisfy internal and external user needs. The second part of the text presents innovative cost and managerial accounting topics and methods.

COMPARISON OF FINANCIAL, MANAGEMENT, AND COST ACCOUNTING

Accounting is called the language of business. As such, accounting can be viewed as having different "dialects." The financial accounting "dialect" is often characterized as the primary focus of accounting. This area of accounting focuses on preparing and reporting financial statements: the balance sheet, income statement, cash flow statement, and statement of changes in stockholders' equity. The second "dialect" of accounting is that of management and cost accounting. This area of accounting is concerned with providing information to parties inside an organization so that they can plan, control operations, make decisions, and evaluate performance.[1]

Financial Accounting

Are all types of accounting the same?

The objective of financial accounting is to provide useful information to external users, including investors and creditors. Financial accounting requires compliance with generally accepted accounting principles (GAAP), which are primarily issued by the Financial Accounting Standards Board (FASB) and the Securities and Exchange Commission (SEC). Financial accounting information is typically historical, quantitative, monetary, and verifiable. Such information usually reflects activities of the whole organization. Publicly held companies are required to have their financial statements audited by an independent auditing firm.

return on investment

In the early 1900s, financial accounting was the dominant source of information in evaluating business operations. Companies, including **General Motors**, often used **return on investment** (ROI) to allocate resources and evaluate divisional performance.[2] ROI is calculated as net income divided by total assets. Using a single measure such as ROI for decision making was considered reasonable when companies were engaged in one type of activity, operated only domestically, were primarily labor intensive, and were managed and owned by a small number of people who were very familiar with the operating processes. For example, when GM was incorporated in Detroit, Michigan, in 1899 as Olds Motor Works, the company had only $500,000 of capital.[3] The company manufactured a single type of product, conducted all business in U.S. dollars, had a labor-intensive production operation, and was managed by its owners. Company performance could be easily evaluated by management using financial accounting information to calculate ROI.

The dominance of financial accounting in management reporting can be attributed to the fact that growth in the securities market created an increased demand for audited financial reports. Preparing financial reports was a costly process, and information technology was limited. Developing a management accounting system separate from the financial accounting system would have been cost prohibitive given the limited benefits that would have accrued to managers and own-

---

[1] Other accounting "dialects," such as tax and auditing, are beyond the scope of this text.
[2] H. Thomas Johnson and Robert S. Kaplan, *Relevance Lost: The Rise and Fall of Management Accounting* (Boston, MA: Harvard Business School Press, 1987).
[3] General Motors Web site: *http://www.gm.com* under investors, corporate info, and corporate history (accessed 1/21/03); *http://www.gm.com/company/corp_info/history/?section=Company&layer=CorporateInfo&action=open&page=0* (accessed January 12, 2003).

ers who were intimately familiar with their company's singular operating activity. Collecting information and providing reports to management on a real-time basis would have been impossible given the technology available in that era.

Management Accounting

Management accounting comprises financial and nonfinancial information intended to meet internal users' needs. Managers are often concerned with fulfilling corporate goals, communicating and implementing strategy, and coordinating product design, production, marketing, and administration of business segments. Management accounting information commonly addresses individual or divisional concerns rather than those of the firm "as a whole." Management accounting is not required to adhere to GAAP but provides both historical and forward-looking information for managers' information needs.

By the mid-1900s, managers were often no longer owners but individuals chosen for their skills in accounting, finance, or law. These managers frequently lacked in-depth knowledge of a company's underlying operations and processes. Additionally, companies had begun to operate in multiple states and countries and to manufacture many products in a non-labor-intensive environment. Trying to manage by using only financial reporting figures and measures sometimes created dysfunctional behavior. Managers needed an accounting system that could help in implementing and monitoring a company's goals in a globally competitive, multiple product environment. Introduction of information technology that could be acquired at a reasonable cost allowed management accounting to develop into a discipline separate from financial accounting. Thus, under these new circumstances, management accounting evolved independently from financial accounting. The primary differences between financial and management accounting are shown in Exhibit 1–1.

Cost Accounting

cost accounting

Cost accounting acts as a bridge between financial and management accounting as illustrated in Exhibit 1–2. **Cost accounting** information addresses the demands of both financial and management accounting by providing product cost information to (1) external parties (stockholders, creditors, and various regulatory bodies) for

EXHIBIT 1–1

FINANCIAL AND MANAGEMENT ACCOUNTING DIFFERENCES

	Financial Accounting	Management Accounting
Primary users	External	Internal
Primary organizational focus	Whole (aggregated)	Parts (segmented)
Information characteristics	Must be • Historical • Quantitative • Monetary • Verifiable	May be • Current or forecasted • Quantitative or qualitative • Monetary or nonmonetary • Timely and, at a minimum, reasonably estimated
Overriding criteria	Generally accepted accounting principles	Situational relevance (usefulness)
	Consistency	Benefits in excess of costs
	Verifiability	Flexibility
Recordkeeping	Formal	Combination of formal and informal

EXHIBIT 1–2

RELATIONSHIP OF FINANCIAL, MANAGEMENT, AND COST ACCOUNTING

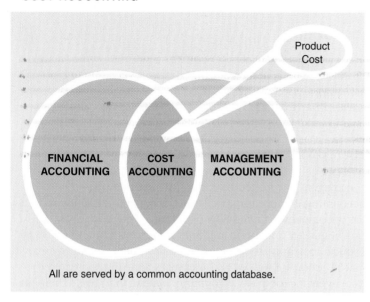

All are served by a common accounting database.

product cost
upstream cost
downstream cost

investment and credit decisions and (2) internal managers who are responsible for planning, controlling, decision making, and evaluating performance.

Product cost information is developed in compliance with GAAP for financial reporting purposes. As such, **product cost** is defined as comprising of the costs incurred in the factory to make a unit of product. But product cost information can also be developed outside of the constraints of GAAP to assist management in its needs for planning and controlling operations. For example, management could be interested in knowing the total cost associated with a unit of product to set product selling price. This information could include costs outside the factory area, such as research and development and distribution costs.

As companies grew and were organized across multiple locations, financial accounting became less appropriate for satisfying management's information needs. To prepare plans, evaluate performance, and make more complex decisions, management needed forward-looking information rather than the historical data provided by financial accounting. Companies began incurring significant **upstream** (research, development, and product design) and **downstream** (marketing, distribution, and customer service) **costs** that were becoming a larger percentage of total costs. Managers needed to add these upstream and downstream costs to product cost when making pricing decisions. The various types of cost items associated with products are shown in Exhibit 1–3.

To illustrate the change in current operations, consider that **GM** now operates around the world, with each country location having its own GAAP and its own currency. ROI and product costs are more complicated to compute, compare, and

EXHIBIT 1–3

ORGANIZATIONAL COSTS

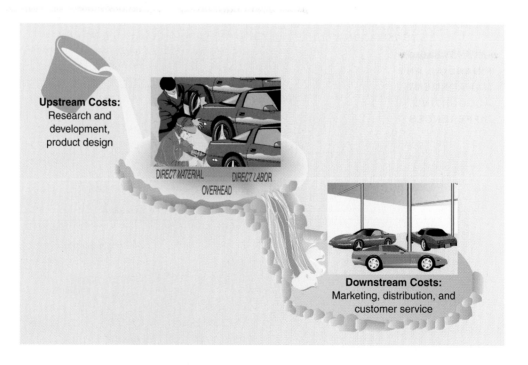

interpret in such a business environment than when the company was operating solely in Michigan. For example, GM's Asian operations could be highly labor intensive, whereas North American operations could be highly capital intensive. Product costs cannot be easily compared between the two locations because their production processes are not similar. Such complications have resulted in the evolution of the cost accounting database to include more than simply financial accounting measures.

Cost Management

cost management

Cost management reflects management's concern for continuously reducing costs while concurrently improving customer satisfaction. For example, **GM** management could be concerned with controlling freight costs or the amount of time it takes to manufacture an automobile. The longer the production time is, the higher are the production costs associated with labor, utilities, and supplies. Managers could want financial and nonfinancial information about alternative manufacturing processes that could reduce production time and costs without reducing product quality.

ORGANIZATIONAL STRATEGY AND THE COST ACCOUNTANT

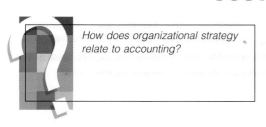

How does organizational strategy relate to accounting?

The cost accountant supplies information needed by financial accountants and management accountants. Although financial accounting must be prepared in compliance with GAAP, management accounting must be prepared in accordance with management needs. Managers desire information to use in developing mission statements, implementing strategy, measuring and controlling the value chain and managers' performance, and in setting balanced scorecard goals, objectives, and targets.

Developing Strategy

LO.2
WHAT ARE TWO COMMON ORGANIZATIONAL STRATEGIES?

mission statement

In responding to globalization challenges, managers must consider the underlying strategy that identifies how a company intends to achieve its mission. A **mission statement** expresses what an organization wants to accomplish and how its products and services can uniquely meet its targeted customers' needs. A mission statement indicates the purposes for which the organization exists and is used to develop the organization's strategy. Mission statements are generally modified over time to adapt to the ever-changing business environment. For instance, in 1999, **GM**'s mission was to introduce new products to the market, enhance global growth, and introduce in-vehicle communication products. Three years later, in 2002, the company's mission was dramatically different: GM wanted to be aggressive in the marketplace, reduce costs, improve quality, and generate more cash from operating activities.

strategy

After preparing its mission statement, a company develops a strategy to achieve a competitive advantage. **Strategy** is the plan that indicates how an organization will fulfill its goals and objectives by deploying its resources to create value for customers and shareholders. A strategic focus guides a company and its subunits toward the organizational mission. Small organizations frequently have a single strategy while large organizations often have an overall entity strategy as well as individual strategies for each business unit (such as a division). Business unit strategies should flow from the organization's overall strategy to ensure effective and efficient resource allocations that are compatible with corporate goals.

Managers are concerned with formulating strategy, and cost accountants are charged with providing management the information necessary to assess progression toward strategic achievement. For example, GM could seek to reduce production costs by redesigning its automobiles to require fewer parts and thus less assembly or production time. Management could also decide to reduce upstream costs by reducing the time it takes to advance a car from concept to production approval. Exhibit 1–4 provides one type of nonfinancial, competitive information that GM's managers might use to assist in formulating strategy.

Most companies employ either a "cost leadership" or "product differentiation" strategy. **Cost leadership** refers to a company's ability to maintain its competitive edge by undercutting competitor prices. Successful cost leaders sustain a large market share by focusing almost exclusively on manufacturing products or providing services at a low cost. For example, Wal-Mart, the Dodge Neon, and Bic pens compete in their markets based on prices. **Product differentiation** refers to a company's ability to offer superior quality products or more unique services than competitors; such products and services are, however, generally sold at premium prices. Neiman Marcus, the Chevrolet Corvette, and Mont Blanc pens compete on quality and features. Successful companies generally focus on one strategy or the other; however, many firms focus on both strategies at the same time, although one often dominates.

Cost accountants gather financial and nonfinancial information to help management achieve organizational strategy. Exhibit 1–5 provides a checklist of questions that help indicate whether an organization has a comprehensive strategy in place.

Deciding on a strategy is a difficult and often controversial process that should reflect the organization's core competencies. A **core competency** is any critical function or activity in which an organization seeks a higher proficiency than its competitors, making it the root of competitiveness and competitive advantage. "Core competencies are different for every organization; they are, so to speak, part of an organization's personality."[4] Technological innovation, engineering, product development, and after-sale service are examples of core competencies. The Japanese electronics industry is viewed as having a core competency in miniaturization of electronics. **Disney** believes it has a core competency in entertainment. **Porsche**

cost leadership

product differentiation

core competency

EXHIBIT 1–4

QUICKER CAR INFORMATION

Time it takes to develop new vehicle from concept approval to production

Auto Maker	Current Average (months)	Goal (months)	Record Time (Model)
Mazda	21	15–18	17 months (Capella)
Toyota	27*	18*	15 months (Ipsum. Starlet)
Mitsubishi	24	18	19 months (FTO)
Nissan	30	20	Not available
Honda	36*	24*	24 months* (CR-V)
Chrysler Corporation	29	24	24 months (Sebring)
Ford	37	24	18 months (European Escort restyling)
GM	46	38	26 months (Yukon, Tahoe)

*Includes design time before concept approval

Source: Valerie Reitman and Robert L. Simison, "Japanese Car Makers Speed Up Car Making," *The Wall Street Journal,* December 29, 1995, p. B1.

---

[4] Peter F. Drucker, "The Information Executives Truly Need," *Harvard Business Review* (January–February 1995), p. 60.

EXHIBIT 1–5

CHECKLIST OF STRATEGY QUESTIONS

1. Who are your five most important competitors?

2. Is your firm more or less profitable than these firms?

3. Do you generally have higher or lower prices than these firms, for equivalent product/service offerings? Is this difference due mainly to the mix of customers, to different costs, or to different requirements for profit?

4. Do you have higher or lower relative costs than your main competitors? Where in the cost structure (for example, cost of raw materials, cost of product, cost of selling, cost of distributing, cost of advertising and marketing) are the differences most pronounced?

5. [What are] the different business segments which account for 80 percent of your profits? [You will probably find that you are in many more segments than you thought and that their profit variability is much greater than you thought.] If you cannot define the segments that constitute 80 percent of your total profits, you need to conduct a detailed product line profitability review.

6. In each of the business segments defined above, how large are you relative to the largest of your competitors? Are you gaining or losing relative market share?

7. In each of your important business segments, what are your customers' and potential customers' most important purchase criteria?

8. How do you and your main competitors in each segment rate on these market purchase criteria?

9. What are the main strengths of the company as a whole, based on aggregating customers' views of your firm in the segments that comprise most of your profits? What other competencies do you believe the firm has, and why do they seem to be not appreciated by the market?

10. Which are your priority segments and where is it most important to the firm as a whole that you gain market share? How confident are you that you will achieve this, given that other firms may have targeted the same segments for share gain? What is your competitive advantage in these segments and how sure are you that this advantage is real rather than imagined? (If you are not gaining relative market share, the advantage is probably illusory.)

Source: *The Financial Times Guide to Management and Finance* (London: Financial Times/Pearson Education Limited, 1994), p. 359.

believes its core competencies are quality engineering and flexible, lean production work flow.

Value Chain

LO.3
WHAT IS A VALUE CHAIN, AND WHAT ARE THE MAJOR VALUE CHAIN FUNCTIONS?

value chain

The foundation of strategic management is the value chain, which is used to identify the processes that lead to cost leadership or product differentiation. The value chain is a set of value-adding functions or processes that convert inputs into products and services for company customers. For instance, **GM** acquires and then adds value to rubber, metal, paint, plastic, and glass by converting these inputs into automobiles. Following are definitions and examples of the functions contained in the generic value chain shown in Exhibit 1–6.

- *Research and Development*—experimenting to reduce costs or improve quality. GM can experiment with various paint formulas to produce the most lasting exterior paint finish.
- *Design*—developing alternative product, service, or process designs. In 1996, GM changed the Corvette design by moving the transmission to the back of the car; this change gave passengers more leg room. Many companies have redesigned plant layouts to reduce production time per unit of output.
- *Supply*—managing raw materials received from vendors. Companies often develop long-term alliances with suppliers to reduce costs and improve quality. GM might establish a long-term alliance with Delphi Automotive Systems to ensure the timing of shipments of auto components, adherence to established

EXHIBIT 1–6
COMPONENTS OF A VALUE CHAIN

parts specifications, and low purchase costs. In many instances, suppliers become extensions of a company's upstream operations.

■ *Production*—acquiring and assembling resources to produce a product or render a service. For GM, production reflects the acquisition of tires, metal, paint, fabric, glass, radios, brakes, and other inputs and the assembly of those items into an automobile.

■ *Marketing*—promoting a product or service to current and prospective customers. Promotion could involve developing a Super Bowl half-time commercial, placing automobiles on a showroom floor, designing a billboard advertisement, or recording a radio announcement to inform customers about the company's products or services.

■ *Distribution*—delivering a product or service to a customer. GM uses trains and trucks to deliver automobiles to dealerships. Other companies could use airlines to distribute their products.

■ *Customer Service*—supporting customers after the sale of a product or service. GM provides an 800 number for its customers to call if they have questions or need roadside service. Other companies could require customers to return the product so that they can repair it.

After developing a strategy, company managers must communicate that strategy to all members in the value chain so that the strategy can be effectively implemented. For example, if GM had developed the Saturn without input from marketing, the public might have been less aware of the car's features or quality when it was introduced. The product design team coordinated with the production area to ensure that GM had or could obtain the resources necessary to produce the Saturn as specified. The communication network needed for coordination between functions is designed in part with input from cost accountants who integrate the information needs of managers of each value chain function.

Balanced Scorecard

LO.4
HOW IS A BALANCED SCORECARD USED TO IMPLEMENT AN ORGANIZATION'S STRATEGY?

Accounting information is helpful to managers when they can use it to measure dimensions of performance that are important to accomplishing strategic goals. In the past, management spent a significant amount of time analyzing historical financial data to assess whether organizational strategy was effective. Today, firms use a portfolio of information to determine not only how the organization has performed in the past but also how it is likely to perform in the future. Historical financial data reflect **lag indicators** or outcomes that have resulted from past actions, such as installing a new production process or implementing a new software system. For example, an increase in operating profits (lag indicator) could occur after a new production process is installed. Unfortunately, lag indicators are often recognized and assessed too late to significantly improve current or future actions.

lag indicators

lead indicators

In contrast, **lead indicators** reflect future financial and nonfinancial outcomes (including opportunities and problems) and thereby help assess strategic progress and guide decision making before lag indicators are known. For example, a lead indicator would be the percentage of employees trained on a new paperless and efficient accounting information system that will soon be on-line. The expectation is that the higher the percentage of employees trained to use the new accounting system, the more rapidly orders will be processed, the more satisfied customers will be with turnaround time after placing an order, and the more quickly profits will be realized from the system's increased efficiency over that of the old system. If an insufficient percentage of employees are trained (lead indicator) compared to the planned percentage of those to be trained, future profits (lag indicator) will decrease (or not increase as expected) because some customers will be unhappy with sales order turnaround time.

Is there only one way to measure organizational success?

Lead and lag performance indicators can be developed for many dimensions of performance. Management often uses both lead and lag indicators in a balanced scorecard to assess strategy congruence. The **balanced scorecard** (BSC), developed by Robert Kaplan (Harvard University) and David Norton (Renaissance Solutions, Inc.), is a framework that restates an organization's strategy into clear and objective performance measures focused on customers, internal business processes, employees, and shareholders. Thus, the balanced scorecard provides a means by which actual business outcomes can be evaluated against performance targets.

balanced scorecard

The BSC includes long-term and short-term, internal and external, financial and nonfinancial measures to balance management's view and execution of strategy. As illustrated in Exhibit 1–7, this simplified balanced scorecard has four perspectives: learning and growth, internal business, customer value, and financial performance. Each of these perspectives has a unique set of goals and measures.

learning and growth perspective

The **learning and growth perspective** focuses on using the organization's intellectual capital to adapt to changing customer needs or to influence new customers' needs and expectations through product or service innovations. This perspective addresses whether a company can continue to progress and be seen by customers as adding value. For example, if **GM** planned to develop an affordable electric car by January 2007, it would have to establish goals and measures regarding technology implementation and the production flow that would be necessary to produce such a vehicle. GM would have to train employees to use new technology and then evaluate them on their achievements while managers would keep employee satisfaction, retention, and productivity in mind. For the learning and growth perspective, GM might target January 1, 2006, to have all production managers trained to use a particular technology system.

EXHIBIT 1–7

SIMPLISTIC BALANCED SCORECARD

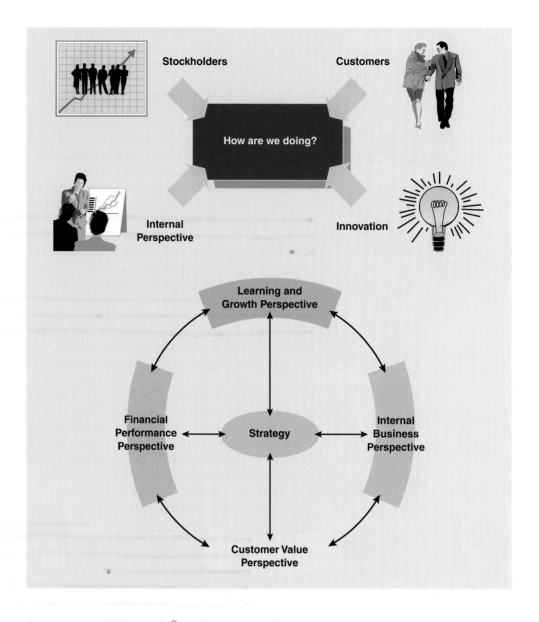

internal business perspective

The **internal business perspective** addresses those things that the organization needs to do well to meet customer needs and expectations. For example, to produce a low-cost electric car, GM might design the production work flow to maximize technology and minimize expensive labor costs. This technology would require setting dates for introducing new production schedules, purchasing assembly machinery, and finalizing long-term contracts with new suppliers.

customer value perspective

The **customer value perspective** addresses how well the organization is doing relative to important customer criteria such as speed (lead time), quality, service, and price (both purchase and after purchase). For example, GM could want to guarantee that the time needed to fill a customer order for an electric car is less than one month. Lead time is extremely important to GM, and it is important to the consumer. To illustrate, when the Impala was first introduced to the market, the company found that many customers complained about the three-month order-filling time. Additionally, to enhance after-purchase customer satisfaction, GM might decide to offer a free loaner vehicle during the first three years of ownership if the electric car is in the repair shop.

financial perspective

Finally, the **financial perspective** addresses the concerns of stockholders and other stakeholders about profitability and organizational growth. GM, could,

Company employees have a genuine interest in the company's profitability and organizational growth and are thus attuned to the financial perspective of the balanced scorecard.

GETTY IMAGES

for example, allow divisions to attain a lower ROI during the start-up phase of instituting new technologies and training personnel to produce the electric car, or the company could try to reduce start-up costs by outsourcing its technologies to lower labor-cost countries. Outsourcing is now quite common. For example, **IBM** plans to save $168 million per year by moving several thousand computer programming jobs to China where labor costs will be about $12.50 per hour rather than the $56 per hour incurred for a U.S. computer programmer.[5] Exhibit 1–8 illustrates a more complicated and more realistic balanced scorecard than Exhibit 1–7.

COMPETING IN A GLOBAL ENVIRONMENT

Most businesses participate in the global economy, which encompasses the international trade of goods and services, movement of labor, and flows of capital and information.[6] The world has essentially become smaller through improved technology and communication capabilities as well as trade agreements that promote international movement of goods and services among countries. Multinational corporation managers must achieve their organization's strategy within a global structure and under international regulations while exercising ethical behavior. One of the key responsibilities of top managers in organizing their businesses for global competition is the assignment of the authority and responsibilities to make decisions.

Organizational Structure

LO.5
WHY MUST ACCOUNTANTS UNDERSTAND AN ORGANIZATION'S STRUCTURE TO PERFORM EFFECTIVELY IN THAT ORGANIZATION?

organizational structure

authority

responsibility

line manager

staff employee

An organizational structure is composed of people, resources other than people, and commitments that are acquired and arranged to achieve organizational strategy and goals. An organization's structure normally evolves from its mission, strategies, goals, and managerial personalities. **Organizational structure** reflects the way in which authority and responsibility for making decisions are distributed in an organization. **Authority** refers to the right (usually by virtue of position or rank) to use resources to accomplish a task or achieve an objective. **Responsibility** is the obligation to accomplish a task or achieve an objective.

Every organization contains line and staff managers. **Line managers** work directly toward attaining organizational goals. Exhibit 1–9 indicates key line managers of **General Motors**. Persons in these positions will be held responsible for achieving targeted balanced scorecard measures or budgeted operating income for their divisions or geographic regions.

Staff employees give assistance and advice to line managers. For example, a GM line manager could consult engineering staff to determine which countries are in compliance with the International Standards Organization (ISO) 9000 quality management system regulation before deciding whether to outsource a production job to a particular South African company. Such staff could advise management

---

[5] William M. Bulkeley, "IBM Documents Five Rare Looks at Sensitive Plans of 'Offshoring,'" *The Wall Street Journal* (January 10, 2004), p. A1.

[6] Paul Krugman, *Peddling Prosperity,* quoted by Alan Farmham in "Global—or Just Globaloney," *Fortune* (June 27, 1994), p. 98.

EXHIBIT 1–8
BALANCED SCORECARD AND PERSPECTIVES

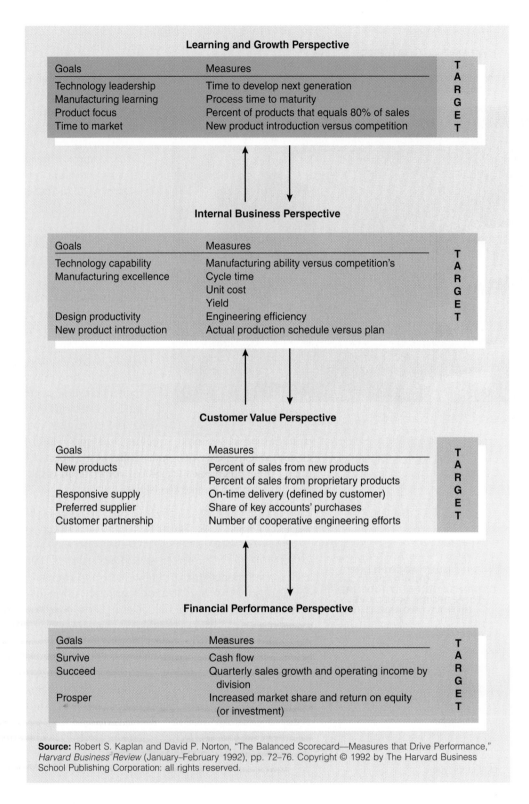

Learning and Growth Perspective

Goals	Measures	
Technology leadership	Time to develop next generation	T
Manufacturing learning	Process time to maturity	A R G E T
Product focus	Percent of products that equals 80% of sales	
Time to market	New product introduction versus competition	

Internal Business Perspective

Goals	Measures	
Technology capability	Manufacturing ability versus competition's	T
Manufacturing excellence	Cycle time	A
	Unit cost	R G
	Yield	E
Design productivity	Engineering efficiency	T
New product introduction	Actual production schedule versus plan	

Customer Value Perspective

Goals	Measures	
New products	Percent of sales from new products	T
	Percent of sales from proprietary products	A
Responsive supply	On-time delivery (defined by customer)	R G
Preferred supplier	Share of key accounts' purchases	E
Customer partnership	Number of cooperative engineering efforts	T

Financial Performance Perspective

Goals	Measures	
Survive	Cash flow	T
Succeed	Quarterly sales growth and operating income by division	A R G
Prosper	Increased market share and return on equity (or investment)	E T

Source: Robert S. Kaplan and David P. Norton, "The Balanced Scorecard—Measures that Drive Performance," *Harvard Business Review* (January–February 1992), pp. 72–76. Copyright © 1992 by The Harvard Business School Publishing Corporation: all rights reserved.

that South Africa is one of the 85 countries that have adopted the ISO 9000 standard.[7]

The treasurer and controller are also staff positions. Treasurers are generally responsible for achieving short- and long-term financing, investing, and cash management goals. The controller is responsible for delivering financial reports in

[7] *http://www.ch/iso/en/aboutiso/isomembers/MemberCountryList* (accessed 2/19/04).

EXHIBIT 1-9
ORGANIZATIONAL STRUCTURE OF GM

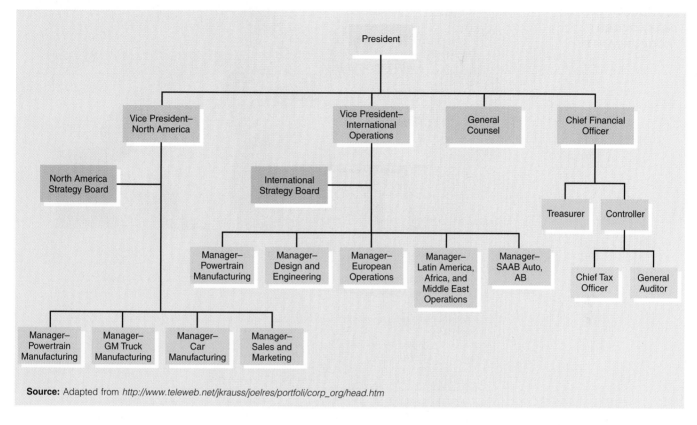

Source: Adapted from *http://www.teleweb.net/jkrauss/joelres/portfoli/corp_org/head.htm*

conformity with GAAP to management. Cost accountants are staff, usually under the authority of the controller.

Because accounting and other information is used to measure the organization's performance, managers can be tempted to manipulate the information to manage the perceptions of others about the performance of the organization. A strong organizational commitment to ethical behavior can curb deceptive uses of information.

Professional Ethics

LO.6
WHAT ARE THE SOURCES OF ETHICAL STANDARDS FOR COST ACCOUNTANTS?

Are ethics important to accountants and managers?

It is important that managers achieve their financial budgets and balanced scorecard targets; such achievement should be accomplished by focusing on targeted market share and desired levels of customer satisfaction. Recently, however, executives at many companies have exhibited unethical behavior in trying to "make their numbers." **WorldCom** (now **MCI**), **Enron**, **ImClone**, and **HealthSouth** are but a few of the many companies having managers who face criminal penalties from acting unethically within the parameters of their jobs. As a result, the U.S. Congress passed the Sarbanes-Oxley Act of 2002 to hold CEOs and CFOs personally accountable for the accuracy of their organization's financial reporting. In addition, the accounting profession promotes high ethical standards for accountants through several of its professional organizations. The Institute of Management Accountants (IMA) is a voluntary membership organization of accountants, finance specialists, academics, and others. The IMA administers the Certified Management Accountant (CMA) Exam and publishes the *Standards of Ethical Conduct for Management Accountants*. CMAs are required to adhere to the IMA's ethical standards. These standards (Exhibit 1–10) focus on competence, confidentiality,

EXHIBIT 1–10
STANDARDS OF ETHICAL CONDUCT FOR MANAGEMENT ACCOUNTANTS

COMPETENCE

Practitioners of management accounting and financial management have responsibility to:
- Maintain an appropriate level of professional competence by ongoing development of their knowledge and skills.
- Perform their professional duties in accordance with relevant laws, regulations, and technical standards.
- Prepare complete and clear reports and recommendations after appropriate analyses of relevant and reliable information.

CONFIDENTIALITY

Practitioners of management accounting and financial management have responsibility to:
- Refrain from disclosing confidential information acquired in the course of their work except when authorized, unless legally obligated to do so.
- Inform subordinates as appropriate regarding the confidentiality of information acquired in the course of their work and monitor their activities to assure the maintenance of that confidentiality.
- Refrain from using or appearing to use confidential information acquired in the course of their work for unethical or illegal advantage either personally or through third parties.

INTEGRITY

Practitioners of management accounting and financial management have responsibility to:
- Avoid actual or apparent conflicts of interest and advise all appropriate parties of any potential conflict.
- Refrain from engaging in any activity that would prejudice their ability to carry out their duties ethically.
- Refuse any gift, favor, or hospitality that would influence or would appear to influence their actions.
- Refrain from either actively or passively subverting the attainment of the organization's legitimate and ethical objectives.
- Recognize and communicate professional limitations or other constraints that would preclude responsible judgment or successful performance of an activity.
- Communicate unfavorable as well as favorable information and professional judgments or opinions.
- Refrain from engaging in or supporting any activity that would discredit the profession.

OBJECTIVITY

Practitioners of management accounting and financial management have responsibility to:
- Communicate information fairly and objectively.
- Disclose fully all relevant information that could reasonably be expected to influence an intended user's understanding of the reports, comments, and recommendations presented.

integrity, and objectivity. Adherence to these standards helps management accountants attain a high level of professionalism to facilitate the development of trust from people inside and outside the organization.

competence

Competence means that individuals will develop and maintain the skills needed to practice their profession. For instance, cost accountants working in companies involved in government contracts must be familiar with not only GAAP but also standards issued by the Cost Accounting Standards Board. **Confidentiality**

confidentiality

means that individuals will refrain from disclosing company information to inappropriate parties (such as competitors) that could be specifically defined in the company's code of ethics. **Integrity** means that individuals will not participate in

integrity

activities that would discredit their company or profession. For example, cost accountants should not accept supplier gifts because they could bias (or could be perceived to bias) the accountants' ability to evaluate the suppliers and their prod-

objectivity

ucts. **Objectivity** means that individuals will provide full and fair disclosure of all relevant information. For example, a cost accountant should not provide earnings numbers that materially misstate a company's financial operations.

Cost and management accountants can face instances in which others exhibit illegal or immoral behavior; such activities could include financial fraud, theft, environmental violations, or employee discrimination. The accountants should evaluate the situation and, if appropriate, "blow the whistle" on the activities by disclosing them to appropriate persons or agencies. Federal laws, including the Sarbanes-Oxley Act, provide for legal protection of whistle-blowers. In fact, the False Claims Act allows whistle-blowers to receive 15 to 20 percent of any settlement proceeds resulting from the identification of such activities.[8] If managers fail to blow the whistle and knowingly provide false information in public financial reports, they can be severely punished. For example, if the chief officer knowingly certifies false financial reports, he or she may be punished with a maximum penalty of a $5 million fine or 20 years in prison, or both under the Sarbanes-Oxley Act.[9]

The Institute of Management Accountants' (IMA) code of ethical conduct also provides guidance on what to do when confronted with ethical issues. Accountants should document what (if any) regulations have been violated, research and record the appropriate actions that should have been taken, and provide evidence of violation of such actions. This information should be kept confidential and reported and discussed with a superior who is not involved in the situation—meaning that it could be necessary to communicate up the corporate ladder, even as far as the audit committee. It is important to document each communication and finding in the process. If accountants cannot resolve the matter, their only recourse could be to resign and consult a legal adviser before reporting the matter to regulatory authorities.

Ethics in Multinational Corporations

Individuals working for multinational companies should be aware of not only their company's and the IMA's code of ethical conduct but also the laws and ethical parameters within countries in which the multinational operates. After many American companies were found to have given bribes in connection with business activities, the United States passed the Foreign Corrupt Practices Act (FCPA) in 1977. This law prohibits U.S. corporations from offering or giving bribes (directly or indirectly) to foreign officials to influence those individuals (or cause them to use their influence) to help businesses obtain or retain business. The act is directed at payments that cause officials to act in a way specified by the firm rather than in a way prescribed by their official duties. In December 2000, the SEC filed an action against **IBM**, arising from a contract given to IBM-Argentina (a wholly owned

[8] Grover L. Porter, "Whistleblowers a Rare Breed," *Strategic Finance* (August 2003), pp. 50–53.
[9] Utpal Bhattacharya, Peter Groznik, and Bruce Haslem, "Is CEO Certification Credible," *Regulation* (Fall 2003), pp. 8–10.

subsidiary) to update the computer systems of **Banco de la Nacion Argentina (BNA)**. During the course of this contract, about $4.5 million was "diverted" to certain BNA officials (the government-owned bank). The SEC determined that IBM violated certain provisions of the FCPA and ordered the company to pay a $300,000 civil penalty.[10] In addition to the FCPA in the United States, the Organization of Economic Cooperation and Development (OECD) issued a document to combat bribery in early February 1999. This document "makes it a crime to offer, promise or give a bribe to a foreign public official in order to obtain or retain international business deals."[11] As of the end of 2003, the 35 countries in Exhibit 1–11 had signed this document, and the U.S. has modified the FCPA to conform to several of the document's provisions. Signing the OECD convention illustrates that companies globally are beginning to acknowledge that bribery should not be considered an appropriate means of doing business.

Cost Accounting Standards

**LO.7
WHAT ARE THE SOURCES OF AUTHORITATIVE PRONOUNCEMENTS FOR THE PRACTICE OF COST ACCOUNTING?**

Although internal accounting reports need not comply with the GAAP established by the FASB and the SEC, three important bodies (the IMA, Society of Management Accountants of Canada, and Cost Accounting Standards Board) do issue cost accounting guidelines or standards.

**EXHIBIT 1–11

COUNTRIES SIGNING THE OECD BRIBERY CONVENTION (AS OF MARCH 10, 2004)**

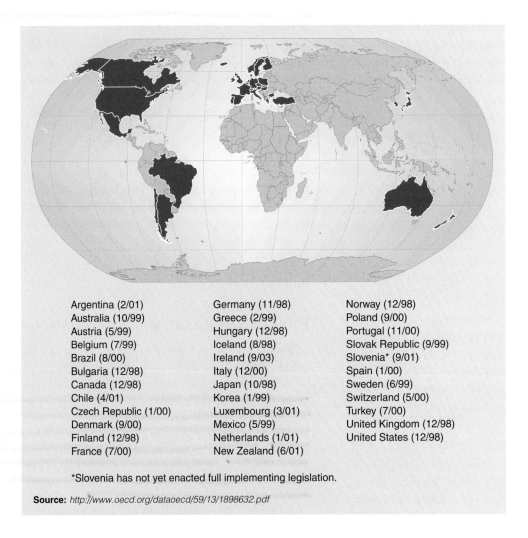

Argentina (2/01)	Germany (11/98)	Norway (12/98)
Australia (10/99)	Greece (2/99)	Poland (9/00)
Austria (5/99)	Hungary (12/98)	Portugal (11/00)
Belgium (7/99)	Iceland (8/98)	Slovak Republic (9/99)
Brazil (8/00)	Ireland (9/03)	Slovenia* (9/01)
Bulgaria (12/98)	Italy (12/00)	Spain (1/00)
Canada (12/98)	Japan (10/98)	Sweden (6/99)
Chile (4/01)	Korea (1/99)	Switzerland (5/00)
Czech Republic (1/00)	Luxembourg (3/01)	Turkey (7/00)
Denmark (9/00)	Mexico (5/99)	United Kingdom (12/98)
Finland (12/98)	Netherlands (1/01)	United States (12/98)
France (7/00)	New Zealand (6/01)	

*Slovenia has not yet enacted full implementing legislation.

Source: *http://www.oecd.org/dataoecd/59/13/1898632.pdf*

---

[10] *http://www.usdoj.gov:80/criminal/fraud/fcpa/Appendices/Appendix b.pdf.*
[11] *http://www.oecd.org.*

The IMA issues directives on the practice of management and cost accounting called *Statements on Management Accounting* (SMAs). SMAs are not legally binding standards, but they undergo a rigorous developmental and exposure process that ensures their wide support. The Society of Management Accountants of Canada, which is similar to the IMA, also issues guidelines on the practice of management accounting. These Management Accounting Guidelines (MAGs), like SMAs, are not mandatory for organizational accounting but are guidelines for high-quality accounting practices. Finally, the U.S. Congress established the Cost Accounting Standards Board (CASB), a public sector body, in 1970 to issue uniform cost accounting standards for defense contractors and federal agencies. The CASB produced 20 cost accounting standards (one of which has been withdrawn) from its inception until it was terminated in 1980. The CASB was recreated in 1988 as an independent board of the Office of Federal Procurement Policy to help ensure uniformity and consistency in government contracting. CASB standards do not constitute a comprehensive set of rules, but compliance is required for companies bidding on or pricing cost-related contracts to the federal government. Hence, CASB standards are legally binding, whereas SMAs are not.

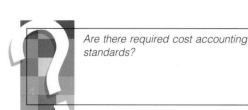

Are there required cost accounting standards?

Although the IMA, Society of Management Accountants of Canada, and CASB have been instrumental in standards development, much of the body of knowledge and practice in management accounting has been provided by industry practice and economic and finance theory. Thus, no "official" agency publishes generic management accounting standards for all companies, but there is wide acceptance of (and, therefore, authority for) the methods presented in this text.

Revisiting

Donna Krall, CPA, CMA

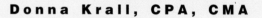

Donna Krall began her professional career, as many accounting graduates do, working in the audit and attest area of a large public accounting firm. In many cases, working as an auditor allows new entrants to the profession to get inside views of many different client firms. During the auditing process, auditors learn a great deal about the financial and operational details of client companies. Clients often offer the auditors involved in the audit engagement permanent jobs at the client company. After the passage of the Sarbanes-Oxley Act of 2002, however, members of the auditing staff are no longer able to enter client companies in upper-level positions until at least one year from the last time the auditors worked on the client engagement.

Other professionals like Krall decide to leave public accounting and earn additional academic and professional credentials, such as the MBA and CMA, that add breadth and depth to their professional qualifications. These new qualifi-

cations allow the accounting professionals to move into new organizations and pursue new career routes. Some of these transitions are from the financial to the operational side of the business.

General Motors is one of the largest business organizations in the world. As such, its demand for high-quality professionals in both line and staff positions is enormous. Krall is one of many professionals hired by the company to support its global operations of 300,000+ employees. In addition to producing a complete array of vehicles, GM owns a financing company, collaborates with other manufacturers to develop new technology, and is a major shareholder in another auto manufacturer. To generate the information necessary to coordinate and manage all of these activities in a complex global environment, GM will continue to hire bright, well-trained financial experts like Donna Krall.

Source: E-mail interview with Donna Krall; *http://www.gm.com.*

Comprehensive Review Module

Chapter Summary

1. Accounting

   - provides information to external parties (stockholders, creditors, and various regulatory bodies) for investment and credit decisions.

   - helps estimate the cost of products produced and services provided by the organization.

   - provides information useful to internal managers who are responsible for planning, controlling, decision making, and evaluating performance.

2. The purposes of financial, management, and cost accounting are that

   - financial accounting is designed to meet external information needs and to comply with generally accepted accounting principles.

   - management accounting attempts to satisfy internal users' information needs.

   - cost accounting creates an overlap between financial accounting and management accounting by providing product costing information for financial statements and quantitative, disaggregated, cost-based information that managers need to perform their responsibilities.

3. The organizational mission and strategy are important to cost accountants because they help

   - establish appropriate measures of accomplishment.

   - develop, implement, and monitor the necessary information systems.

4. Two common corporate strategies are

   - cost leadership, which refers to maintaining a competitive edge by undercutting competitor prices.

   - product differentiation, which refers to offering (generally at a premium price) superior quality products or more unique services than competitors.

5. The value chain is a set of value-adding functions or processes that convert inputs into products and services for company customers, and organizations add value through the value chain functions of

   - research and development

   - product design

   - supply

   - production

   - marketing

   - distribution

   - customer service

6. A balanced scorecard

   - is a four-perspective measure of critical goals and targets needed to operationalize strategy.

   - looks at success factors for learning and growth, internal business, customer satisfaction, and stockholder value.

   - includes financial and nonfinancial, internal and external, long-term and short-term, and lead and lag indicators.

7. The organizational structure

   - is composed of people, resources other than people, and commitments that are acquired and arranged relative to authority and responsibility to achieve organizational mission, strategy, and goals.

   - is used by cost accountants to understand how information is communicated between managers and departments as well as the authority and responsibility of each manager.

   - has line personnel who seek to achieve the organizational mission and strategy through balanced scorecard targets.

   - has staff personnel, such as cost accountants, who seek to advise and assist line personnel.

8. Some sources for professional ethics include the

   - IMA's Code of Ethics that refers to issues of competence, confidentiality, integrity, and objectivity.

   - Sarbanes-Oxley Act that requires corporate CEOs and CFOs to sign off on the accuracy of financial reports.

   - False Claims Act that provides for whistle-blowing protection.

- Foreign Corrupt Practices Act that prohibits U.S. corporations from offering or giving bribes to foreign officials to influence those individuals to help, obtain, or retain business.

9. Generally accepted cost accounting standards

- do not exist for companies that are not engaged in contracts with the federal government; however, the statements on management accounting and management accounting guidelines are well-researched suggestions related to management accounting practices.

- are prepared by the Cost Accounting Standards Board for companies engaged in federal government cost/bidding contracts.

Key Terms

authority (p. 13)
balanced scorecard (p. 11)
competence (p. 17)
confidentiality (p. 17)
core competency (p. 8)
cost accounting (p. 5)
cost leadership (p. 8)
cost management (p. 7)
customer value perspective (p. 12)
downstream cost (p. 6)

financial perspective (p. 12)
integrity (p. 17)
internal business perspective (p. 12)
lag indicator (p. 11)
lead indicator (p. 11)
learning and growth perspective (p. 11)
line manager (p. 13)
mission statement (p. 7)

objectivity (p. 17)
organizational structure (p. 13)
product cost (p. 6)
product differentiation (p. 8)
responsibility (p. 13)
return on investment (p. 4)
staff employee (p. 13)
strategy (p. 7)
upstream cost (p. 6)
value chain (p. 9)

Questions

1. Flexibility is said to be the hallmark of modern management accounting, whereas standardization and consistency describe financial accounting. Explain why the focus on these two accounting systems differs.
2. Why would operating in a global (rather than a strictly domestic) marketplace create a need for additional information for management? Discuss some of the additional information you think managers would need and why such information would be valuable.
3. Why is a mission statement important to an organization?
4. What is organizational strategy? Why would each organization have a unique strategy or set of strategies?
5. What is a core competency and how do core competencies impact the feasible set of alternative organizational strategies?
6. What is the value chain of an organization, and how does it interface with strategy?
7. What is a balanced scorecard, and how is it more useful than ROI in implementing and monitoring strategy in a global economy?
8. Differentiate between authority and responsibility. Can you have one without the other? Explain.
9. What ethical issues might affect a U.S. or Canadian company considering opening a business in Russia?

Exercises

10. (Accounting information) You are a partner in a local accounting firm that does financial planning and prepares tax returns, payroll, and financial re-

ports for medium-size companies. Business is good, and your monthly financial statements show that your organization is consistently profitable. Cash flow is becoming a small problem, however, and you could need to take a loan from the bank. You have also been receiving customer complaints about time delays and price increases.

   a. What accounting information do you think is most important to take with you to discuss a possible loan with your banker?

   b. What accounting information do you think is most important in ascertaining the business activities of your accounting firm in regard to addressing time delays and price increases? What nonaccounting information is important?

   c. Can the information in parts (a) and (b) be gathered from the accounting records directly? Indirectly? If not at all, where would you obtain such information?

11. (Organizational accountants) Use library and Internet resources to find how the jobs of management accountants have changed in the last 10 years.

   a. Prepare a "then-versus-now" comparison.

   b. What five skills do you believe are the most important for management accountants to possess? Discuss the rationale for your choices. Do you think these skills have changed over the past 10 years? Why or why not?

12. (Global operations) The 2000 annual report of **Nestlé** (headquartered in Switzerland) was slightly nontraditional in that the annual financial statements and management report were in English and French. International Financial Reporting Standards were used to prepare the financial statements.

   a. Discuss the costs and benefits of a Swiss-based company taking the time to provide such translations into English and French.

   b. What additional information would you want to have to assess how transactions and activities are related to Nestlé's strategic plans?

13. (Strategic information) Go to the World Wide Web and select the financial reports of a multinational manufacturing company. Assume that you have just been offered a position as this company's CEO. Use the information in the annual report (or 10-K) to develop answers to each of the following questions that should help you make your acceptance decision.

   a. What is the company's mission?

   b. What is the company's strategy? Does it differ from the strategy it had two years ago?

   c. What are the company's core competencies?

   d. What are the value chain processes for this company?

   e. What products does the company manufacture?

   f. What is the company's organizational structure? Prepare an organizational chart.

   g. What would be your top priorities for this company in the coming year?

   h. Based on your findings, would you accept this offer and why?

14. (Strategy) You are the manager of the local **Lowe's** home improvement store. What are the five factors that you believe to be most critical to the success of your organization? How would these factors influence your store's strategy?

15. (Strategy) You are the manager of a small restaurant in your hometown.

   a. What information would you obtain in making the decision whether to add quiche and spicy chicken wings to your menu?

   b. Why would each of the information items in part (a) be significant?

16. (Strategy) Choose a company that might use each of the following strategies relative to its competitors and discuss the benefits that might be realized

from that strategy. Indicate the industry in which the company does business, the company's primary competitors, and whether a code of conduct or corporate governance appears on its Web site.
   a. Differentiation
   b. Cost leadership

17. (Strategy) Select a major U.S. or non-U.S. automobile manufacturer. Use library, Internet, and other resources to answer as completely as possible the questions in Exhibit 1–5 about the auto manufacturer you have chosen.

18. (Mission statement) Obtain a copy of the mission statement of your college or university. Draft a mission statement for this cost accounting class that supports the school's mission statement.
   a. How does your mission statement reflect the goals and objectives of the college mission statement?
   b. How can you measure the successful accomplishment of your college objectives?

WebTUTOR Advantage

19. (Mission statement) You have managed Missouri's **Best Buy** franchise for 15 years and employ 100 employees. Business has been profitable, but you are concerned that Best Buy's Kansas City, Missouri, locations could soon experience a downturn in growth. You have decided to prepare for such an event by engaging in a higher level of strategic planning, beginning with a company mission statement.
   a. How does a mission statement add strength to the strategic planning process?
   b. Who should be involved in developing a mission statement and why?
   c. What factors should be considered in the development of a mission statement? Why are these factors important?
   d. Prepare a mission statement for Best Buy and discuss how your mission statement will provide benefits to strategic planning.

20. (Mission) Mission statements are intended to indicate what an organization does and why it exists. Some of them, however, are simply empty words with little or no substance used by few people to guide their activities.
   a. Does an organization need a mission statement? If so, why?
   b. How could a mission statement help an organization in its pursuit of ethical behavior from employees?
   c. How could a mission statement help an organization in its pursuit of the production of high-quality products and the provision of high levels of customer service?

21. (Core competencies) As a team, list the core competencies of your local public school district and explain why you believe these items to be core competencies. Make appointments with the principal of one of the high schools or the superintendent of the public school system and, without sharing your list, ask this individual what he or she believes the core competencies to be and why. Prepare a written or video presentation that summarizes, compares, and contrasts all competencies on your lists. Share copies of your presentation with the individuals whom you contacted.

22. (Value chain) You are the management accountant for an automobile manufacturer. You've been asked to prepare a presentation that will illustrate the company's value chain.
   a. What activities or types of companies would you include in the upstream (supplier) part of the value chain?
   b. What internal activities would you include in the value chain?
   c. What activities or types of companies would you include in the downstream (distribution and retailing) part of the value chain?

23. (Value chain) Strategic alliances represent an important value chain arrangement. In many organizations, suppliers are beginning to provide more and more input into customer activities.

   a. In the United States, when would a strategic alliance be considered illegal?

   b. What would you perceive to be the primary reasons for pursuing a strategic alliance?

   c. You are the manager of a catalog company that sells flowers and plants. With whom would you want to establish strategic alliances? What issues might you want to specify prior to engaging in the alliance?

24. (Organizational structure) Early this year, you started a financial planning services firm and now have 20 clients. Because of other obligations (including classes), you have hired three employees to help service the clients.

   a. What types of business activities would you empower these employees to handle and why?

   b. What types of business activities would you do yourself and why?

25. (Ethics) In pursuing organizational strategy, cost and management accountants want to instill trust between themselves and their constituents including other organizational members and the independent auditing firm. The IMA published a code of conduct for management accountants.

   a. List and explain each of the major guidelines of the IMA's code.

   b. What steps should a cost accountant who detects unethical behavior by his or her supervisor take before deciding to resign?

26. (Ethics) You are a senior manager at MegaMac Inc. All senior managers and the board of directors are scheduled to meet next week to discuss the questionable earnings management found by the outside independent auditors. The CEO has asked you to be prepared to start the discussion by developing questions that should be addressed before responding to the auditors.

   a. Why would the CEO be concerned about the questionable earnings management? After all, isn't it the auditor who attests to the accuracy of financial reporting?

   b. If the board of directors insisted on not further addressing the questionable earnings management and you decided to resign and blow the whistle, would you have any protection? (You might want to read an article by G. L. Porter entitled "Whistleblowers: A Rare Breed" in the August 2003 issue of *Strategic Finance*.)

WebTUTOR Advantage

27. (Ethics) The Foreign Corrupt Practices Act (FCPA) prohibits U.S. firms from giving bribes to officials in foreign countries, although bribery is customary in some countries. Non-U.S. companies operating in foreign countries are not necessarily similarly restricted; thus, adherence to the FCPA could make competing with non-U.S. firms more difficult in foreign countries. Do you think that bribery should be considered so ethically repugnant to Americans that companies are asked to forgo a foreign custom and, hence, the profits that could be obtained through observance of the custom? Prepare both a pro and a con position for your answer, assuming you will be asked to defend one position or the other.

28. (Ethics) "Few trends could so thoroughly undermine the very foundation of our free society," writes Milton Friedman in *Capitalism and Freedom*, "as the acceptance by corporate officials of a social responsibility other than to make as much money for their shareholders as possible."

WebTUTOR Advantage

a. Discuss your reactions to this quote from a legal standpoint.

b. Discuss your reactions to this quote from an ethical standpoint.

c. How would you resolve any ethical conflicts that exist between your two answers?

29. (Ethics) Accounting has a long history of being an ethical profession. In recent years, however, some companies have asked their accountants to help "manage earnings."

a. What does it mean to "manage earnings"?

b. List several accounting firms that have been accused of "managing earnings."

c. Who is more likely to be involved in such a situation, the financial accountant or the management accountant? Why?

d. Do you believe that "managing earnings" is ethical? Discuss the rationale for your answer.

30. (Code of conduct) Use library and Internet resources to research the names and countries of the stock exchanges on which **Sappi Fine Paper** lists. As a cost accountant, cite the sources you would use to study the code of conduct applicable to each of the stock exchanges. Write a short paper on the complexities relative to ethics of listing on stock exchanges across multiple countries.

31. (Interview) Call a local company and set up an interview with the firm's cost or management accountant. Use the following questions as starting points for your interview.

- What is your educational background?
- What was your career path to attain this position?
- What are your most recurring tasks?
- What aspects of your job do you find to be the most fun? The most challenging?
- What college courses do you think would be the most helpful in preparing a person for your job? Why were these courses chosen?

a. Compare and contrast your interview answers with those of other students in the class.

b. Which one or two items from the interview were of the most benefit to you? Why?

2

Cost Terminology and Cost Behaviors

Objectives

AFTER COMPLETING THIS CHAPTER, YOU SHOULD BE ABLE TO ANSWER THE FOLLOWING QUESTIONS:

LO.1 WHAT ASSUMPTIONS DO ACCOUNTANTS MAKE ABOUT COST BEHAVIOR, AND WHY ARE THESE ASSUMPTIONS NECESSARY?

LO.2 HOW ARE COSTS CLASSIFIED, AND WHY ARE SUCH CLASSIFICATIONS USEFUL?

LO.3 HOW DOES THE CONVERSION PROCESS OCCUR IN MANUFACTURING AND SERVICE COMPANIES?

LO.4 WHAT PRODUCT COST CATEGORIES EXIST, AND WHAT ITEMS COMPOSE THOSE CATEGORIES?

LO.5 HOW IS THE COST OF GOODS MANUFACTURED CALCULATED AND USED IN PREPARING AN INCOME STATEMENT?

Introducing

General Motors (GM) is the largest automobile manufacturer in the world. The company's brands are known throughout the world; they include Buick, Cadillac, Chevrolet, GMC, Holden, HUMMER, Olds, Opel, Pontiac, Saab, Saturn, and Vauxhall. In some countries, GM has alliances that allow it to distribute Isuzu, Suzuki, Subaru, and Daewoo products.

Of the many brands and car lines produced by GM, perhaps the Corvette has the most interesting history, which now spans more than 50 years. The Corvette was the first two-seater roadster in the United States, first made in 1952. At that time, two of the cars were produced to test the drive train at a cost of $55,000–$60,000 each. The next year, approximately 250 fiberglass-bodied Corvettes were manufactured as a test run of public demand for a $3,000+ automobile. Corvettes originally featured a V-6 engine with 150 horsepower, two-speed automatic transmission, white exterior, red interior, black canvas convertible top, AM radio, and heater. The cars were initially produced with the goal of gaining consumer interest and demand for speedy sports cars; thus, GM was not concerned about production cost. The sticker price, however, was a bit on the steep side: $3,498, or 42 percent of the Corvette engineer's annual salary!

Before the 1954 model year, the Corvette underwent numerous design changes and 12,300 of the cars were ordered. The company patented the "CORVETTE" trademark and designated the Union Boulevard plant in St. Louis as the only plant to assemble Corvettes. By mid-1954, St. Louis was producing 50 Corvettes a day, but sales began to dwindle.

During the early 1950s, Corvette production costs consisted mostly of labor costs. Manufacturing overhead costs were low because plants were not automated and power costs were minimal. During this period of labor-intensive production and low demand for Corvettes, GM lost thousands of dollars on each one sold.

GM then entered Corvettes in road races as a way to attract demand. However, in each race, the Corvette malfunctioned. For instance, a rod went through the engine block in the first leg of the Mexican Road Race. Even a Corvette engineer suggested that GM drop the car's production.

Another battery of design changes took place in the late 1950s. The redesign offered the option of either an automatic or a four-speed manual transmission, a more powerful engine, lighter weight, a top speed of more than 150 mph, and a restyled body with dual headlamps, aluminum radiators, and a dual carburetor. The new design worked because, by 1956, Corvette had won first place in both a Massachusetts 65-mile car race and the Seattle Seafair Class C/Production race. In 1957, a Corvette won first place in the Florida International 12-hour Grand Prix, and consumer interest in Corvettes reawakened.

The Corvette was shown at many of the most prestigious car shows, for example, the GM Motorama show at the Waldorf-Astoria in New York City and the Chicago auto show. Corvette Clubs, such as the Northern California Corvette Association, began developing. However, despite increased consumer interest, the Corvette did not generate a profit until 1958.[1]

Corvette production was moved from St. Louis, Missouri, to Bowling Green, Kentucky, in mid-1981. The Bowling Green plant has more than 1 million square feet and 7 miles of conveyors. It takes more than five days to build a Corvette, in part because high quality is one of the foremost concerns.

Source: *http://www.islandnet.com/~kpolsson/vettehis/* (downloaded on 4/19/2004); *http://www.gm.com* (downloaded on 4/19/2004).

cost

unexpired cost

expired cost

No product or service can be produced without the incurrence of costs for material, labor, and overhead. Cost reflects the monetary measure of resources given up to attain an objective such as making a good or delivering a service. However, the term *cost* must be defined more specifically before "the cost" can be determined and communicated. Thus, a clarifying adjective is generally used to specify the type of cost being considered. For example, an asset's balance sheet value is an unexpired cost, but the portion of an asset's value consumed or sacrificed during a period is an expense or expired cost, which is shown on the income statement.

To effectively communicate information to others, accountants must clearly understand the differences among the various types of costs, their computations, and their usage. This chapter provides the terminology that is necessary to understand and communicate cost and management accounting information. The chapter also presents cost flows and the process of cost accumulation in a production environment.

[1] Stephen J. Mrax, "40 Years and Counting," *Machine Design* (August 27, 1993), pp. 27–32.

COST TERMINOLOGY

A *cost management system* is a set of formal methods developed for planning and controlling an organization's cost-generating activities relative to its strategy, goals, and objectives. This system is designed to communicate with managers concerning all value chain functions about product costs, product profitability, cost management, strategy implementation, and management performance. Cost concepts and terms have been developed to facilitate this communication process. Some important types of costs are summarized in Exhibit 2–1.

EXHIBIT 2–1

COST CLASSIFICATION CATEGORIES

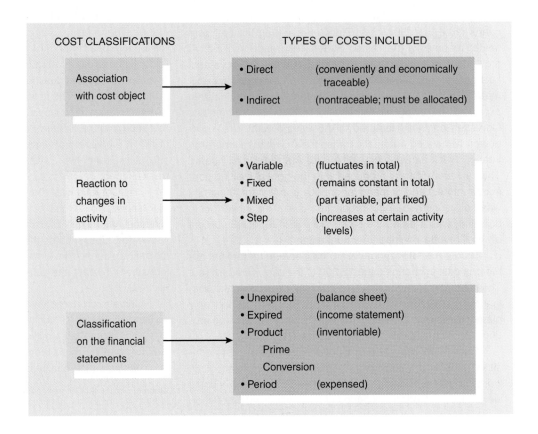

Direct and Indirect Costs

cost object

A **cost object** is anything for which management wants to collect or accumulate costs. Production operations and product lines are common cost objects. For example, **GM** could define its Bowling Green, Kentucky, Corvette plant as a cost object and desire information about operating costs for February 2006; alternatively, GM could define the Corvette Z06 as the cost object and want to know its production cost during the same month. Collecting these costs in different ways can help management make decisions regarding the efficiency of operations at the Bowling Green plant or the effectiveness of cost management in producing its Corvette Z06.

Costs related to the making of a product or delivery of a service are appropriately labeled product or service costs. The costs associated with any cost object can be classified according to their relationship to the cost object.

direct costs

Direct costs are conveniently and economically traceable to the cost object. If management requested cost data about the Corvette Z06, direct costs might include tires, fiberglass, CD player, leather, paint, and production line labor. Although glue is used in the Corvette Z06, trying to trace that material would not be cost effective because the cost amount is insignificant. In fact, the clerical and information-processing cost of trying to trace the glue cost would probably be significantly higher than either the glue cost or any benefits that management might obtain from the information. Thus, the cost of the glue used in each car would not be classified as direct.

indirect costs

Indirect costs cannot be economically traced to the cost object but instead must be allocated to the cost object. For example, the GM plant in Bowling Green incurs property tax, janitorial maintenance, cost accounting, and building depreciation costs each period. Because many models of Corvettes are produced in this plant, these costs are not directly traceable to the Corvette Z06 cost object. Additionally, it might not be important for GM to know how much janitorial labor cost is used to produce each kind of Corvette.

Why is it necessary to specify a cost object to define direct and indirect costs?

Classification of a cost as direct or indirect depends on the specification of the cost object. For example, if the Bowling Green plant is specified as the cost object, then the plant's depreciation cost is directly traceable. However, if the cost object is specified as the Corvette Z06, the plant's depreciation cost is not directly traceable, in which case the depreciation is classified as indirect and must be allocated to the cost object.

COST BEHAVIORS TO CHANGES IN ACTIVITY

LO.1
WHAT ASSUMPTIONS DO ACCOUNTANTS MAKE ABOUT COST BEHAVIOR, AND WHY ARE THESE ASSUMPTIONS NECESSARY?

In managing costs, accountants must understand how costs behave relative to changes in output volume. Accountants describe a cost's behavior pattern according to the way its *total* cost (rather than its *unit* cost) reacts to changes in a related activity measure. Every organizational cost will change if extreme shifts in activity levels occur or if enough time passes. However, a total cost can be observed to behave in a particular way within a given period in relation to limited changes in an associated activity measure. Common activity measures include production volume, service and sales volumes, hours of machine time used, pounds of material moved, and number of purchase orders sent.

To properly identify, analyze, and use cost behavior information, a time frame must be specified to indicate how far into the future a cost should be examined, and a particular range of activity must be assumed. For example, the purchase cost of each Corvette Z06 tire might be expected to increase by $0.75 next year but by $3.00 by the year 2010. When **GM** estimates production costs for next year, the $0.75 increase would be relevant, but the $3.00 increase would not be. The assumed range of activity that reflects the company's normal operating range is referred to as the **relevant range**. Within the relevant range, the two extreme cost behaviors are variable and fixed.

relevant range

variable cost

A cost that varies in total in direct proportion to changes in activity is a **variable cost**. Because total cost varies in direct proportion to activity changes, a variable cost is a constant amount per unit. Relative to activity volume of units of output or number of customers serviced, examples of variable costs include the costs of materials, hourly wages, and sales commissions. Variable costs are extremely important to a company's total profit picture because every time a product is produced or sold or a service is rendered, a corresponding amount of variable cost is incurred.

Why do accountants use approximations of a cost's real behavior?

Although accountants view variable costs as linear, economists view these costs as curvilinear as in Exhibit 2–2. The cost line slopes upward at a given rate until a range of activity is reached in which the average variable cost rate becomes fairly constant. Within this relevant range, the firm experiences benefits such as discounts on material prices, improved worker skill and productivity, and other operating efficiencies. Beyond this relevant range, the slope becomes quite steep as the entity

EXHIBIT 2-2

ECONOMIC REPRESENTATION OF A VARIABLE COST

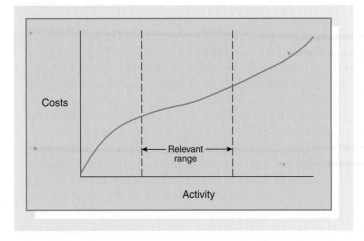

enters a range of activity in which certain operating factors cause the average variable cost to increase. In this range, the firm finds that costs rise rapidly due to worker crowding, equipment shortages, and other operating inefficiencies. Although the curvilinear graph is more correct, it is not as easy to use in planning or controlling costs. Accordingly, accountants choose the range in which these variable costs are assumed to behave as they are defined and, as such, the actual cost behavior is an approximation of reality.

To illustrate a variable cost, assume that the battery used in Corvettes costs $28 as long as purchases are made within the relevant production range of 0 to 40,000 cars annually. (At higher levels of activity, the price per battery could either decrease because of a volume discount from the supplier or increase because the supplier's capacity to produce batteries would be exhausted.) Within this relevant range, total battery cost can be calculated as $28 times the number of Corvettes produced. For instance, if 30,000 Corvettes were produced, total variable cost of batteries would be $840,000 ($28 × 30,000).

fixed cost

In contrast, a cost that remains constant in total within the relevant range of activity is considered a **fixed cost**. Many fixed costs are incurred to provide production capacity to a firm. Fixed costs include salaries (as opposed to hourly wages), depreciation (computed using the straight-line method), and insurance. On a per-unit basis, a fixed cost varies inversely with changes in the level of activity: The per-unit fixed cost decreases with increases in the activity level and increases with decreases in the activity level. If a higher volume is achieved, then fixed costs per unit are lower.

EXHIBIT 2-3

COMPARATIVE TOTAL AND UNIT COST BEHAVIOR DEFINITIONS

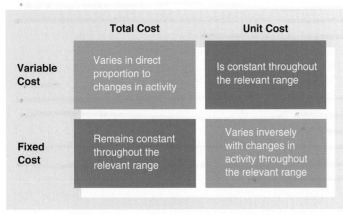

	Total Cost	Unit Cost
Variable Cost	Varies in direct proportion to changes in activity	Is constant throughout the relevant range
Fixed Cost	Remains constant throughout the relevant range	Varies inversely with changes in activity throughout the relevant range

To illustrate how to determine the total and unit amounts of a fixed cost, suppose that GM rents its Corvette manufacturing facilities for $1,200,000 annually. The facilities have a maximum annual output capacity of 40,000 Corvettes. If GM expects to produce 30,000 Corvettes per year, its total annual rent expense is a fixed cost of $1,200,000 and its rent expense per Corvette is $40 ($1,200,000 ÷ 30,000). However, if GM produces 40,000 Corvettes in a year, total annual rent expense remains at $1,200,000, but rent expense per Corvette decreases to $30 ($1,200,000 ÷ 40,000). In summary, total fixed facility rental cost remains the same as the level of activity changes within the relevant range of production, but fixed cost per unit varies inversely from $40 to $30 as the level of Corvettes produced increases from 30,000 to 40,000. The respective total cost and unit cost definitions for variable and fixed cost behaviors are presented in Exhibit 2–3.

In the long run, however, even fixed costs will not remain constant. Business will increase or decrease volume sufficiently that production capacity could be added or sold. Alternatively, management could decide to "trade" fixed and variable costs for one another. For example, if a company installs new highly computerized equipment, this generates an additional large fixed cost for depreciation and eliminates the variable cost of some hourly production workers.

Alternatively, if a company decides to outsource its data processing support function, the fixed costs of data processing equipment depreciation and personnel salaries can be traded for a variable cost that reflects transaction volume. Whether variable costs are traded for fixed costs or vice versa, a shift from one type of cost behavior to another type changes a company's basic cost structure and can have a significant impact on its profits.

Other costs exist that are not strictly variable or fixed. For example, a mixed cost has both a variable and a fixed component. On a per-unit basis, a mixed cost does not fluctuate in direct proportion to changes in activity, nor does it remain constant with changes in activity. An electric bill that is computed as a flat charge for basic service (the fixed component) plus a stated rate for each kilowatt hour of usage (the variable component) is an example of a mixed cost. Exhibit 2–4 shows a graph for Bowling Green's electricity charge from its power company, assuming a cost of $5,000 per month plus $0.018 per kilowatt hour (kwh) consumed. In a month when Bowling Green uses 80,000 kwhs of electricity, its total electricity bill is $6,440 [$5,000 + ($0.018 × 80,000)]. If it uses 90,000 kwhs, the electricity bill is $6,620.

Another type of cost shifts upward or downward when activity changes by a certain interval or "step." A step cost can be characterized as variable or fixed. Step variable costs have small steps and step fixed costs have large steps. For example, a water bill computed as $0.002 per gallon for up to 1,000 gallons, $0.003 per gallon for 1,001 to 2,000 gallons, and $0.005 per gallon for 2,001 to 3,000 gallons is a step variable cost. In contrast, the salary cost for airline reservations agents is a step fixed cost. Assume that each agent can serve 1,000 customers per month and is paid $3,200 per month. If airline volume increases from 3,500 customers to 6,000 customers, the airline will need six reservations agents rather than four. Each additional 1,000 passengers will result in an additional step fixed cost of $3,200.

Understanding the types of behavior exhibited by costs is necessary to make valid estimates of total costs at various activity levels. Although not all costs conform strictly to the aforementioned behavioral categories, these categories represent the types of cost behavior typically encountered in business. Cost accountants generally separate mixed costs into their variable and fixed components so that the behavior of these costs is more readily apparent.[2] When step variable or step fixed costs exist, accountants must choose a specific relevant range of activity that will allow step variable costs to be treated as variable and step fixed costs to be treated as fixed.

mixed cost

step cost

EXHIBIT 2–4
GRAPH OF A MIXED COST

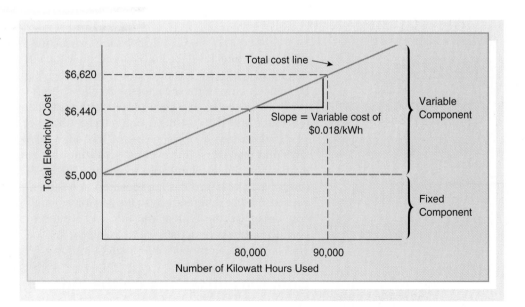

_____
[2] Separation of mixed costs is discussed in Chapter 3.

By separating mixed costs into their variable and fixed components and by specifying a time period and relevant range, cost accountants force all costs into either variable or fixed categories. Assuming a variable cost to be constant per unit and a fixed cost to be constant in total within the relevant range can be justified for two reasons. First, the assumed conditions approximate reality and, if the company operates only within the relevant range of activity, the cost behaviors selected are appropriate. Second, selection of a constant per-unit variable cost and a constant total fixed cost provides a convenient, stable measurement for use in planning, controlling, and decision making.

Accountants use predictors of cost changes to make these generalizations about variable and fixed costs. A **predictor** is an activity measure that, when changed, is accompanied by consistent, observable changes in a cost item. However, simply because the two items change together does not prove that the predictor causes the change in the other item. For instance, assume that every time you see a Corvette commercial on prime-time television, the following day's weather is sunny. If this is consistent, observable behavior, you can use a Corvette commercial to *predict* the following day's weather—but viewing the commercial does not *cause* the following day's weather!

predictor

cost driver

EXHIBIT 2–5
TOTAL RAW MATERIAL COST RELATIVE TO PRODUCTION VOLUME

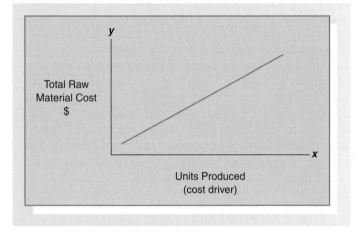

In contrast, a predictor that has an absolute cause-and-effect relationship to a cost is called a **cost driver**. For example, production volume has a direct effect on the total cost of raw material used and can be said to "drive" that cost. Exhibit 2–5 plots production volume on the *x*-axis and raw material cost on the *y*-axis to show the linear cause-and-effect relationship between production volume and total raw material cost. This exhibit also illustrates the variable cost characteristic of raw material cost: The same amount of raw material cost is incurred for each unit produced. If the raw material is assumed to be batteries and the units produced are assumed to be Corvettes, this illustration shows that as total Corvette production rises, total battery cost also rises. Thus, Corvette production volume could be used to predict total battery cost.

In most situations, however, the cause–effect relationship is less clear because multiple factors commonly cause cost incurrence. For example, factors including production volume, material quality, worker skill levels, and level of automation affect quality control costs. Although determining which factor actually caused a specific change in a quality control cost can be difficult, any of these factors could be chosen to predict that cost if confidence exists about the factor's relationship with cost changes. To be used as a predictor, the factor and the cost need only change together in a foreseeable manner.

Traditionally, a single predictor has often been used to predict costs. Accountants and managers, however, are realizing that single predictors do not necessarily provide the most reliable forecasts. This realization has caused a movement toward activity-based costing (covered in Chapter 4), which uses multiple cost drivers to predict different costs. Production volume, for instance, would be a valid cost driver for the cost of the metal Corvette emblem attached to each Corvette produced, but product size and weight would be more realistic drivers for **General Motors**' automobile shipping costs.

Cost Classifications on the Financial Statements

LO.2
HOW ARE COSTS CLASSIFIED, AND WHY ARE SUCH CLASSIFICATIONS USEFUL?

The balance sheet and income statement are two of a company's financial statements. The *balance sheet* is a statement of unexpired costs (assets) and liabilities and owners' capital; the *income statement* is a statement of revenues and expired costs (expenses and losses). The concept of matching revenues and expenses on the income statement is central to financial accounting. The matching concept provides a basis for deciding when an unexpired cost becomes an expired cost and is moved from an asset category to an expense or loss category.

Expenses and losses differ in that expenses are intentionally incurred in the process of generating revenues, but losses are unintentionally incurred in the context of business operations. Cost of goods sold and expired selling and administrative costs are examples of expenses. Costs incurred for damage related to fires, for abnormal production waste, and for the sale of a machine at below book value are examples of losses.

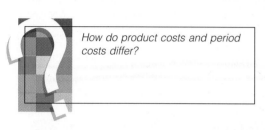

How do product costs and period costs differ?

When a specific product is specified as the cost object, all costs can be classified as either product or period. **Product costs** are related to making or acquiring the products or providing the services that directly generate the revenues of an entity; **period costs** are related to business functions other than production, such as selling and administration.

product costs

period costs

inventoriable costs

Product costs are also called **inventoriable costs** and include direct costs (direct material and direct labor) and indirect costs (overhead). Precise classification of some costs into one of these categories can be difficult and require judgment in the classification process, however, the following definitions (with Corvette examples) are useful. Any material that can be easily and economically traced to a product is a **direct material**. Direct material includes raw material (fiberglass), purchased components from contract manufacturers (batteries), and manufactured subassemblies (engines and transmissions). **Direct labor** refers to the time spent by individuals who work specifically on manufacturing a product or performing a service. At **GM**'s Bowling Green plant, the people welding the parts to the uniframe are considered direct labor and their wages are direct labor costs. Any factory or production cost that is indirect to the product or service is **overhead.** This cost element includes GM factory supervisors' salaries as well as depreciation, insurance, and utility costs on GM's production machinery, equipment, and facilities. The sum of direct labor and overhead costs is referred to as **conversion cost**—those costs that are incurred to convert materials into products.[3] The sum of direct material and direct labor cost is referred to as prime cost.

direct material

direct labor

overhead

conversion cost

Period costs are generally more closely associated with a particular time period rather than with making or acquiring a product or performing a service. Period costs that have future benefit are classified as assets, whereas those having no future benefit are expensed as incurred. Prepaid insurance on an administration building represents an unexpired period cost; when the premium period passes, the insurance becomes an expired or period cost (insurance expense). Salaries paid to the sales force and depreciation on computers in the administrative area are also period costs.

distribution cost

One particularly important type of period cost is that of distribution. A **distribution cost** is any cost incurred to warehouse, transport, or deliver a product or service. Financial accounting rules prescribe that distribution costs be expensed as incurred. However, managers should remember that these costs relate directly to products and services and should not adopt an "out-of-sight, out-of-mind" attitude about these costs simply because of the way they are handled under GAAP. Distribution costs must be planned for in relationship to product/service volume, and these costs must be controlled for profitability to result from sales. Thus, even though distribution costs are not technically considered part of product cost, they can have a major impact on managerial decision making.

---

[3] In the past, direct material and direct labor cost represented the largest percentage of production cost. The term *prime cost* was used to refer to the sum of these two items. In the current automated production environment, direct labor cost has become a very low percentage of product cost and, thus, "prime cost" has lost much of its significance.

THE CONVERSION PROCESS

To some extent, all organizations convert or change inputs into outputs. Inputs typically consist of material, labor, and overhead. In general, product costs are incurred in the production (or conversion) area and period costs are incurred in all nonproduction (or nonconversion) areas.[4] Conversion process output is usually either products or services. See Exhibit 2–6 for a comparison of the conversion activities of different types of organizations. Note that many service companies engage in a high degree of conversion. Firms of professionals (such as accountants, architects, attorneys, engineers, and surveyors) convert labor and other resource inputs (material and overhead) into completed jobs (audit reports, building plans, contracts, blueprints, and property survey reports).

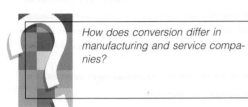

How does conversion differ in manufacturing and service companies?

Firms that engage in only low or moderate degrees of conversion can conveniently expense insignificant costs of labor and overhead related to conversion. The savings in clerical cost from expensing outweigh the value of any slightly improved information that might result from assigning such costs to products or services. For example, when employees open shipping containers, hang clothing on racks, and tag merchandise with sales tickets, a labor cost for conversion is incurred. Retail clothing stores, however, do not attach the stock people's wages to inventory; such labor costs are treated as period costs and are expensed when they are incurred. The major distinction of retail firms relative to service and manufacturing firms is that retailers have much lower degrees of conversion than the other two types of firms.

In contrast, in high-conversion firms, the informational benefits gained from accumulating the material, labor, and overhead costs incurred to produce output significantly exceed clerical accumulation costs. For instance, immediately expensing the labor costs incurred for production employees working on a Corvette assembly line as a period cost would be inappropriate. Similarly, when constructing a house, certain types of costs are quite significant (see Exhibit 2–7). The exhibit indicates that the clerical cost of accumulating direct labor costs is only $110, or less than 0.5 percent of direct labor costs. Direct labor costs of $25,000 are accumulated as a separate component of product costs because of the materiality of the amount and because they require management's cost-control attention. Furthermore, labor costs are inventoried as part of the cost of the construction job until the house is completed.

EXHIBIT 2–6
DEGREES OF CONVERSION IN FIRMS

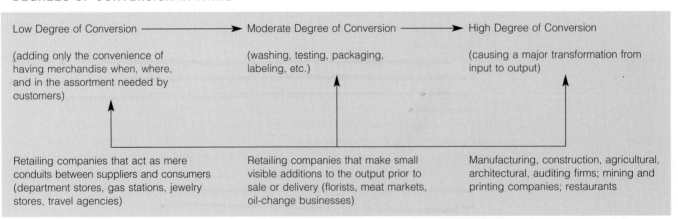

Low Degree of Conversion	Moderate Degree of Conversion	High Degree of Conversion
(adding only the convenience of having merchandise when, where, and in the assortment needed by customers)	(washing, testing, packaging, labeling, etc.)	(causing a major transformation from input to output)
Retailing companies that act as mere conduits between suppliers and consumers (department stores, gas stations, jewelry stores, travel agencies)	Retailing companies that make small visible additions to the output prior to sale or delivery (florists, meat markets, oil-change businesses)	Manufacturing, construction, agricultural, architectural, auditing firms; mining and printing companies; restaurants

[4] It is less common but possible for a cost incurred outside the production area to be in direct support of production and, therefore, considered a product cost. An example of this situation is the salary of a product cost analyst who is based at corporate headquarters; this cost is part of overhead.

EXHIBIT 2–7
BUILDING CONSTRUCTION COSTS

	Manufacturing Cost	Clerical Cost
Direct material	40%	34%
Manufacturing overhead	35	34
Direct labor	25	22
Total cost	$100,000	$500

manufacturer

service company

For convenience, a **manufacturer** is defined as any company engaged in a high degree of conversion of raw material input into a tangible output. Manufacturers typically use people and machines to convert raw material to output that has substance and can, if desired, be physically inspected. A **service company** refers to a firm engaged in a high or moderate degree of conversion using a significant amount of labor. A service company's output can be tangible (an architectural drawing) or intangible (insurance protection) and normally cannot be inspected prior to use. Service firms can be either profit-making businesses or not-for-profit organizations.

Firms engaging in only low or moderate degrees of conversion ordinarily have only one inventory account (Merchandise Inventory). In contrast, manufacturers normally use three inventory accounts: (1) Raw Material Inventory, (2) Work in Process Inventory (for partially converted goods), and (3) Finished Goods Inventory. Service firms have an inventory account for the supplies used in the conversion process and could have a Work in Process Inventory account, but these firms do not normally have a Finished Goods Inventory account because services typically cannot be warehoused. If collection is yet to be made for a completed service engagement, the service firm has a receivable from its client instead of Finished Goods Inventory.

Retailers versus Manufacturers/Service Companies

Retail companies purchase goods in finished or almost finished condition so those goods typically need little, if any, conversion before being sold to customers. Costs associated with such inventory are usually easy to determine, as are the valuations for financial statement presentation.

In comparison, manufacturers and service companies engage in activities that involve the physical transformation of inputs into, respectively, finished products and services. The materials or supplies and conversion costs of manufacturers and service companies must be assigned to output to determine the cost of inventory produced and cost of goods sold or services rendered. Cost accounting provides the structure and process for assigning material and conversion costs to products and services.

Exhibit 2–8 compares the input–output relationships of a retail company with those of a manufacturing/service company. This exhibit illustrates that the primary difference between retail companies and manufacturing/service companies is the absence or presence of the area labeled the "production center." In this business area, input factors such as raw material enter and are transformed and stored until the goods or services are completed. If the output is a product, it can be warehoused and/or displayed until it is sold. Service outputs are directly provided to the client commissioning the work. Retail companies normally incur very limited conversion time, effort, and cost compared to manufacturing or service companies. Thus, although a retailer could have a department (such as one that adds store name labels to goods) that might be viewed as a "mini" production center, most often retailers have no designated "production center."

EXHIBIT 2-8
BUSINESS INPUT/OUTPUT RELATIONSHIPS

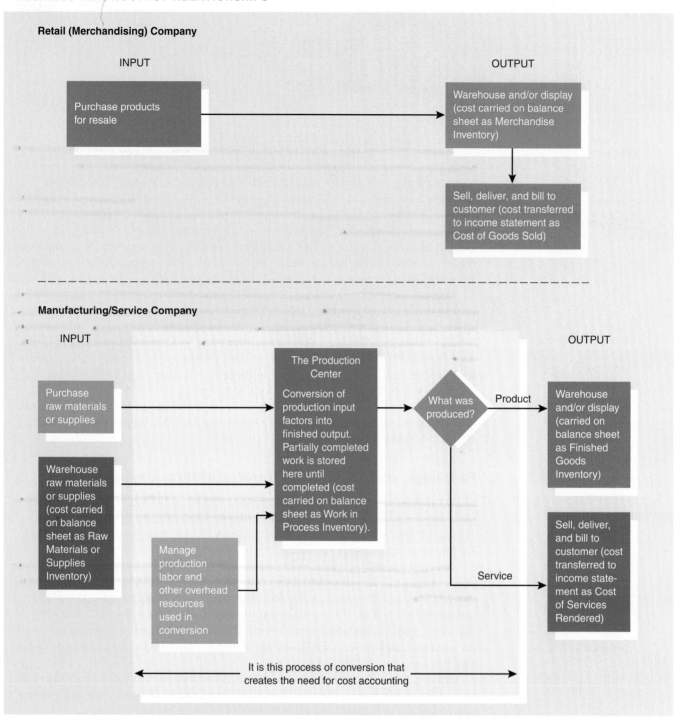

Exhibit 2–9 depicts an accrual-based accounting system in which costs flow from the various inventory accounts on the balance sheet through (if necessary) the production center. The cost accumulation process begins when raw materials or supplies are placed into production. As work progresses on a product or service, costs are accumulated in the firm's accounting records. Accumulating costs in appropriate inventory accounts allows businesses to match the costs of buying or manufacturing a product or providing a service with the revenues generated when

EXHIBIT 2-9
STAGES AND COSTS OF PRODUCTION

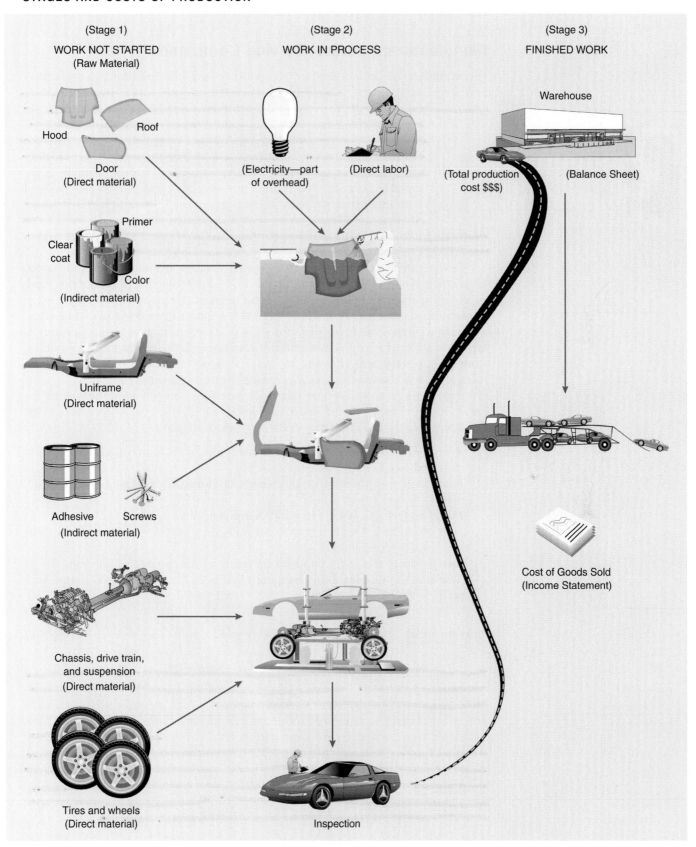

the goods or services are sold. At the point of sale, these product/service costs will flow from an inventory account to Cost of Goods Sold or Cost of Services Rendered on the income statement.

Manufacturers versus Service Companies

Several differences in accounting for production activities exist for a manufacturer and a service company. A manufacturer must account for raw material, work in process, and finished goods to maintain control over the production process. An accrual accounting system is essential for such organizations so that total production costs can be accumulated as goods flow through the manufacturing process. On the other hand, most service firms need only track their work in process (incomplete jobs). Such accounting is acceptable because service firms normally have few, if any, raw material costs other than supplies for work not started. Because services generally cannot be warehoused, costs of finished jobs are usually transferred immediately to the income statement to be matched against job revenues rather than being carried on the balance sheet in a finished goods account.

 *Why are service companies easier to account for than manufacturing companies?*

Despite the accounting differences among retailers, manufacturers, and service firms, each type of organization can use cost and management accounting concepts and techniques, although in different degrees. Managers in all firms engage in planning, controlling, evaluating performance, and making decisions. Thus, management accounting is appropriate for all firms. Cost accounting techniques are essential to all firms engaged in significant conversion activities. In most companies, managers are constantly looking for ways to reduce costs; cost accounting and management accounting are used extensively in this pursuit.

Regardless of how costs are classified, managers are continuously looking for new and better ways to reduce costs without sacrificing quality or productivity. Consider some of **DaimlerChrysler**'s cost-reduction plans:

- *Advanced technologies:* Eliminate overlapping research into fuel cells, electric cars, and advanced diesel engines.
- *Finance:* Reduce back-office costs and coordinate tax planning and other activities.
- *Purchasing:* Consolidate parts and equipment buying.
- *Joint production:* Use plants to make multiple types of vehicles through flexible manufacturing lines.
- *New products:* Possibly cooperate on future products such as minivans.
- *New markets:* Cooperate in emerging markets such as Latin America and Asia, perhaps with joint ventures.[5]

STAGES OF PRODUCTION

raw material
work in process
finished goods

The production or conversion process can be viewed in three stages: (1) work not started (**raw material**), (2) work started but not completed (**work in process**), and (3) units fully completed (**finished goods**). Costs are associated with each processing stage. The stages of production in a manufacturing firm and some costs associated with each stage are illustrated in Exhibit 2–9. In the first stage of processing, the costs incurred reflect the prices paid for raw materials and/or supplies. As work progresses through the second stage, accrual-based accounting requires that labor and overhead costs related to the conversion of raw materials or supplies be accumulated and attached to the goods. The total costs incurred in stages 1 and 2 equal the total production cost of finished goods in stage 3.

[5] Gregory White and Brian Coleman, "Chrysler, Daimler Focus on Value of Stock," *The Wall Street Journal* (September 21, 1998), p. A3.

Cost accounting uses Raw Material, Work in Process, and Finished Goods Inventory accounts to accumulate processing costs and assign them to the goods produced. The three inventory accounts relate to the three stages of production shown in Exhibit 2–9 and form a common database for cost, management, and financial accounting information.

In a service firm, the work not started stage of processing normally consists of the cost of supplies needed to perform the services (Supplies Inventory). When supplies are placed into work in process, labor and overhead are added to achieve finished results. Determining the cost of services provided is extremely important in both profit-oriented service businesses and not-for-profit entities. For instance, architectural firms accumulate the costs incurred for designs and models of each project, and hospitals accumulate the costs of an X-ray, an MRI, or outpatient surgery for each patient.

COMPONENTS OF PRODUCT COST

LO.4
WHAT PRODUCT COST CATEGORIES EXIST, AND WHAT ITEMS COMPOSE THOSE CATEGORIES?

Product costs are related to items that generate an entity's revenues. These costs can be separated into three components: direct material, direct labor, and production overhead.[6]

Direct Material

Any readily identifiable part of a product is called a *direct material*. Theoretically, direct material cost should include the cost of all materials used to manufacture a product or perform a service. However, some material costs are not conveniently or economically traceable. Such costs are treated and classified as *indirect costs*. For example, all of the items shown in stage 1 of Exhibit 2–8 are essential in producing a Corvette. However, the cost of the screws and adhesives could be neither easily traceable nor monetarily significant to Corvette's production cost. Thus, these costs can be classified and accounted for as indirect materials and included as part of overhead.

In a service business, direct materials are often insignificant or are not easily traced to a designated cost object. For instance, the cost of the paper on which an architect prepares building plans is very small relative to the overall value of the plans. Accordingly, even though the paper can easily be traced to the final product (the actual blueprints), paper cost is so insignificant that it does not justify the expense of tracking as a direct material.

Direct Labor

Direct labor refers to the individuals who work specifically on manufacturing a product or performing a service. Direct labor could also be considered work that directly adds value to the final product or service. The welder on the **GM** production line, the chef preparing the meals at the local restaurant, and the dental hygienist at the dental clinic represent direct labor personnel.

Direct labor cost consists of the wages or salaries paid to direct labor employees. Such wages and salaries must also be conveniently traceable to the product or service. Direct labor cost should include basic compensation, production efficiency bonuses, and the employer's share of Social Security and Medicare taxes. In addition, if a company's operations are relatively stable, direct labor cost should

---

[6] This definition of product cost is the traditional one and is referred to as *absorption cost*. Another product costing method, called *variable costing*, excludes the fixed overhead component. Absorption and variable costing are compared in Chapter 3.

include all employer-paid insurance costs, holiday and vacation pay, and pension and other retirement benefits.[7]

As with materials, some labor costs that theoretically should be considered direct are treated as indirect. The first reason for this treatment is that specifically tracing the particular labor costs to production can be inefficient. For instance, fringe benefit costs should be treated as direct labor cost, but the time, effort, and clerical cost of tracing this cost might not be worth the additional accuracy it would provide. Thus, the treatment of employee fringe benefits as indirect costs is often based on clerical cost efficiencies.

Second, treating certain labor costs as direct can result in erroneous information about product or service costs. Assume that the Corvette Division employs 20 assembly department workers who are paid $26 per hour and time and a half ($39) for overtime.[8] One week, the employees worked a total of 1,000 hours (including 200 hours of overtime) to complete all production orders. Of the total employee labor payroll of $28,600, only $26,000 (1,000 hours × $26 per hour) is classified as direct labor cost. The remaining $2,600 (200 hours × $13 per hour) is considered overhead. If the overtime cost were assigned to products made during the overtime hours, those products would appear to have a labor cost 50 percent higher than items made during regular working hours. Because products are assigned to regular or overtime shifts randomly, the items completed during overtime hours should not be forced to bear overtime charges. Therefore, costs for overtime or shift premiums are usually considered overhead rather than direct labor cost and are allocated among all units.

On some occasions, however, costs such as overtime should not be considered overhead. If a customer requests a job to be scheduled during overtime hours or is in a rush and requests overtime to be worked, overtime or shift premiums should be considered direct labor and attached to the job that created the costs. Assume that in July, a dealership requested five red Z06 Corvettes designed to accommodate basketball players Kevin Garnett, Shaq O'Neal, Dwight Howard, LeBron James, and Yao Ming to be delivered in two weeks. To produce this order, Corvette workers had to work overtime. The dealership's bill for the rush-ordered, oversized Corvettes should include the overtime charges.

The direct labor cost lost by replacing humans with robots is partly made up in depreciation costs for these robots.

Because laborers historically performed the majority of conversion activity, direct labor once represented a large portion of total manufacturing cost. For example, in 1953, a Corvette was manufactured entirely with direct labor; no automated production activity was used. Now, in highly automated work environments, direct labor often represents less than 10 to 15 percent of total manufacturing cost. For example, the Corvette division has replaced a significant percentage of direct labor with robotics or other machinery. Now managers can find that almost all direct labor cost is replaced with a new production cost: the depreciation cost associated with robots and other fully automated machinery.

[7] Institute of Management Accountants (formerly National Association of Accountants), *Statements on Management Accounting Number 4C: Definition and Measurement of Direct Labor Cost* (Montvale, N.J.: NAA, June 13, 1985), p. 4.
[8] Wage rates reflect information provided in "New Contract Delivers Solid Economic Gains for GM and Delphi Workers," *http://www.uaw.org/contracts/03/gm.*

Overhead

As previously defined, *overhead* is any factory or production cost that is indirect to manufacturing a product or providing a service. Accordingly, overhead does not include direct material and direct labor. Overhead does, however, include indirect material and indirect labor as well as all other costs incurred in the production area.[9] Automated and computerized technologies have made manufacturing more capital intensive. With direct labor becoming a progressively smaller proportion of product cost, overhead has become a progressively larger proportion, and such costs merit much more attention than they did in the past.

Overhead costs can be either variable or fixed based on how they behave in response to changes in production volume or some other activity measure. Variable overhead includes the costs of indirect material, indirect labor paid on an hourly basis (such as wages for forklift operators, material handlers, and other workers who support the production, assembly, and/or service process), lubricants used for machine maintenance, and the variable portion of factory electricity charges. Depreciation calculated using either the units-of-production or service life method is also a variable overhead cost; this depreciation method reflects a decline in machine utility based on usage rather than time passage and is appropriate in an automated plant.

Fixed overhead includes costs such as straight-line depreciation on factory assets, factory license fees, and factory insurance and property taxes. Fixed indirect labor costs include salaries for production supervisors, shift superintendents, and plant managers. The fixed portion of factory mixed costs (such as maintenance and utilities) is also part of fixed overhead. Investments in new equipment can create significantly higher fixed overhead costs but can also improve product or service quality—and, thus, reduce another overhead cost, that of poor quality.

Quality costs are an important component of overhead cost. Quality is a managerial concern for two reasons. First, high-quality products or services enhance a company's ability to generate revenues and produce profits. Consumers want the best quality they can find for the money they spend. Second, managers are concerned about production process quality because higher process quality leads to shorter production time and reduced costs for spoilage and rework. The level of customer satisfaction with a company's products or services is usually part of the customer perspective in the balanced scorecard.

Quality costs are usually referred to as either being costs of controlling quality or costs of failing to control quality. Control costs include prevention and appraisal costs. **Prevention costs** are incurred to improve quality by precluding product defects and improper processing from occurring. Amounts spent on implementing training programs, researching customer needs, and acquiring improved production equipment are prevention costs. Amounts incurred for monitoring or inspecting are called **appraisal costs**; these costs are incurred to find mistakes not eliminated through prevention.

Failure costs can be internal (such as scrap and rework) or external (such as costs of product returns caused by quality problems, resulting in warranty costs, and complaint department costs). Amounts spent for prevention costs minimize the costs incurred for appraisal and failure. Quality costs are discussed in greater depth in Chapter 17.

Quality costs exhibit different types of cost behaviors. Some quality costs are variable in relation to the quantity of defective output, some are step fixed with increases at specific levels of defective output, and some are fixed for a specific

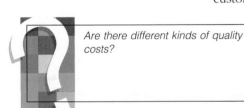

Are there different kinds of quality costs?

prevention costs
appraisal costs
failure costs

---

[9] Another term used for overhead is *burden.* Although this is the term under which the definition appears in *SMA No. 2, Management Accounting Terminology,* the authors believe that this term is unacceptable because it connotes costs that are extra, unnecessary, or oppressive. Overhead costs are essential to the conversion process but simply cannot be traced directly to output.

time. For example, rework cost approaches zero if the quantity of defective output is also nearly zero. However, these costs would be extremely high if the number of defective parts produced were high. In contrast, training expenditures are set by management and might not vary regardless of the quantity of defective output produced in a given period.

ACCUMULATION AND ALLOCATION OF OVERHEAD

Direct material and direct labor are easily traced to a product or service. Overhead, on the other hand, must be accumulated over a period and allocated to the products manufactured or services rendered during that time. **Cost allocation** refers to the assignment of an indirect cost to one or more cost objects using some reasonable allocation base or driver. Cost allocations can be made over several time periods or within a single time period. For example, in financial accounting, a building's cost is allocated through depreciation charges over its useful or service life. This process is necessary to satisfy the *matching principle*. In cost accounting, production overhead costs are allocated within a period through the use of allocation bases or cost drivers to products or services. This process reflects application of the *cost principle,* which requires that all production or acquisition costs attach to the units produced, services rendered, or units purchased.

Overhead costs are allocated to cost objects for three reasons: (1) to determine the full cost of the cost object, (2) to motivate the manager in charge of the cost object to manage it efficiently, and (3) to compare alternative courses of action for management planning, controlling, and decision making.[10] The first reason relates to financial statement valuations. Under generally accepted accounting principles (GAAP), the "full cost" of a cost object must include allocated production overhead. In contrast, the assignment of nonfactory overhead costs to products is not normally allowed under GAAP.[11] The other two reasons for overhead allocations are related to internal purposes and, thus, no hard-and-fast rules apply to the overhead allocation process.

Regardless of why overhead is allocated, the method and basis of allocation should be rational and systematic so that the resulting information is useful for product costing and managerial purposes. Traditionally, the information generated for satisfying the "full cost" objective was also used for the second and third objectives. However, because the first purpose is externally focused and the others are internally focused, different methods can be used to provide different costs for different needs.

Allocating overhead to products or services is done using several systems. In an **actual cost system**, actual direct material and direct labor costs are accumulated in Work in Process Inventory as the costs are incurred. Actual production overhead costs are accumulated separately in an Overhead Control account and are assigned to Work in Process Inventory at the end of a period or completion of production. Use of an actual cost system is generally considered to be difficult because all production overhead information must be available before any cost allocation can be made to products or services. For example, the cost of products and services produced in May could not be calculated until the May electricity bill is received in June.

An alternative to an actual cost system is a **normal cost system**, which combines actual direct material and direct labor costs with overhead that is assigned using a predetermined rate or rates. A **predetermined overhead rate** (or *overhead application rate*) is a charge per unit of activity that is used to allocate (or apply) overhead cost from the Overhead Control account to Work in Process In-

Margin terms:
cost allocation

actual cost system

normal cost system

predetermined overhead rate

---

[10] Institute of Management Accountants, *Statements on Management Accounting Number 4B: Allocation of Service and Administrative Costs* (Montvale, N.J.: NAA, June 13, 1985), pp. 9–10.
[11] Although potentially unacceptable for GAAP, certain nonfactory overhead costs must be assigned to products for tax purposes.

ventory for the period's production or services. Predetermined overhead rates are discussed in detail in Chapter 3.

Actual Cost System

Product costs can be accumulated using either a perpetual or a periodic inventory system. In a perpetual inventory system, all product costs flow through Work in Process Inventory to Finished Goods Inventory and, ultimately, to Cost of Goods Sold; this cost flow is diagrammed in Exhibit 2–10. The *perpetual inventory system continuously provides current information for financial statement preparation and for inventory and cost control*. Because the costs of maintaining a perpetual system have diminished significantly as computerized production, bar coding, and information processing have become more pervasive, this text assumes that all companies discussed use a perpetual system.

Earth Car Company is used to illustrate the flow of product costs in a manufacturing company's actual cost system. The April 1, 2006, inventory account balances for the company were as follows: Raw Material Inventory (all direct), $73,000; Work in Process Inventory, $145,000; and Finished Goods Inventory, $87,400. Earth Car uses separate variable and fixed accounts to record the incurrence of overhead.

EXHIBIT 2–10
ILLUSTRATION OF PERPETUAL INVENTORY ACCOUNTING SYSTEM

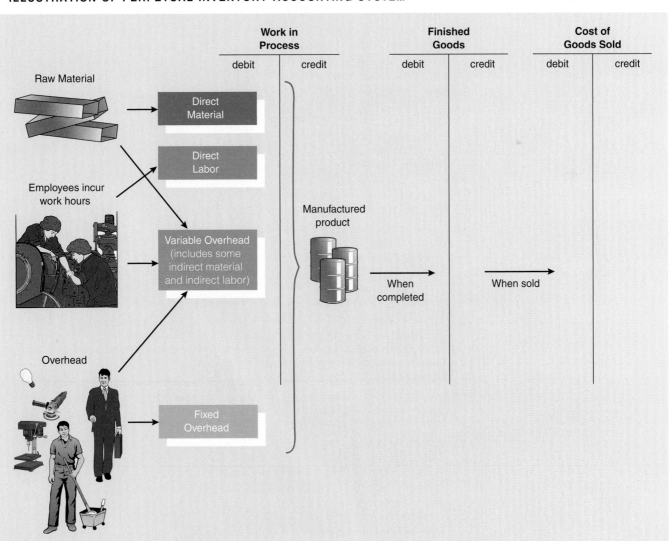

In this illustration, actual overhead costs are used to allocate overhead to Work in Process Inventory. The journal entries in Exhibit 2–11 are keyed to the following transactions representing Earth Car's activity for April.

During the month, Earth Car's purchasing agent bought $280,000 of direct material on account (entry 1), and the warehouse manager transferred $284,000 of material into the production area (entry 2). April's production wages totaled $530,000, of which $436,000 was for direct labor (entry 3). April salaries for the production supervisor were $20,000 (entry 4). April utility cost of $28,000 was accrued; an analysis of this cost indicated that $16,000 was variable and $12,000 was fixed (entry 5). Supplies costing $5,200 were removed from Supplies Inventory and placed into the production process (entry 6). Also, Earth Car paid $7,000 for April's property taxes on the factory (entry 7), depreciated the factory assets $56,880 (entry 8), and recorded

EXHIBIT 2–11

EARTH CAR COMPANY— APRIL 2006 JOURNAL ENTRIES

(1) Raw Material Inventory	280,000	
Accounts Payable		280,000
To record cost of direct material purchased on account.		
(2) Work in Process Inventory	284,000	
Raw Material Inventory		284,000
To record direct material transferred to production.		
(3) Work in Process Inventory	436,000	
Variable Overhead Control	94,000	
Salaries & Wages Payable		530,000
To accrue factory wages for direct and indirect labor.		
(4) Fixed Overhead Control	20,000	
Salaries & Wages Payable		20,000
To accrue production supervisor's salaries.		
(5) Variable Overhead Control	16,000	
Fixed Overhead Control	12,000	
Utilities Payable		28,000
To record mixed utility cost in its variable and fixed amounts.		
(6) Variable Overhead Control	5,200	
Supplies Inventory		5,200
To record supplies used.		
(7) Fixed Overhead Control	7,000	
Cash	7,000	
To record payment for factory property taxes for the period.		
(8) Fixed Overhead Control	56,880	
Accumulated Depreciation—Equipment		56,880
To record depreciation on factory assets for the period.		
(9) Fixed Overhead Control	3,000	
Prepaid Insurance		3,000
To record expiration of prepaid insurance on factory assets.		
(10) Work in Process Inventory	214,080	
Variable Overhead Control		115,200
Fixed Overhead Control		98,880
To record the assignment of actual overhead costs to Work in Process Inventory.		
(11) Finished Goods Inventory	1,058,200	
Work in Process Inventory		1,058,200
To record the transfer of work completed during the period.		
(12) Accounts Receivable	1,460,000	
Sales	1,460,000	
To record the selling price of goods sold on account during the period.		
(13) Cost of Goods Sold	1,054,000	
Finished Goods Inventory		1,054,000
To record cost of goods sold for the period.		

the expiration of $3,000 of prepaid insurance on the factory assets (entry 9). Entry 10 shows the assignment of actual overhead to Work in Process Inventory for, respectively, variable and fixed overhead for the company during April. During April, $1,058,200 of goods were completed and transferred to Finished Goods Inventory (entry 11). Sales of $1,460,000 on account were recorded during the month (entry 12); the goods that were sold had a total cost of $1,054,000 (entry 13). An abbreviated presentation of the cost flows is shown in selected T-accounts in Exhibit 2–12.

Cost of Goods Manufactured and Sold

LO.5
HOW IS THE COST OF GOODS MANUFACTURED CALCULATED AND USED IN PREPARING AN INCOME STATEMENT?

cost of goods manufactured

The T-accounts in Exhibit 2–12 provide detailed information about the cost of material used, goods transferred from work in process, and goods sold. This information is needed to prepare financial statements. Because most managers cannot access the detailed accounting records, they need to have the flow of costs and the calculation of important income statement amounts presented to them in a formalized manner. Therefore, a schedule of **cost of goods manufactured** (CGM) is prepared as a preliminary step to the determination of cost of goods sold (CGS).[12] CGM is the total production cost of the goods that were completed and transferred to Finished Goods Inventory during the period. This amount is similar to the cost of net purchases in the cost of goods sold schedule for a retailer.

How does cost of goods manufactured differ from cost of goods sold?

Formal schedules of cost of goods manufactured and cost of goods sold are presented in Exhibit 2–13 using the amounts shown in Exhibits 2–11 and 2–12. The schedule of cost of goods manufactured starts with the beginning balance of Work in Process (WIP) Inventory and details all product cost components. The cost of material used in production during the period is equal to the beginning balance of Raw Material Inventory plus raw material purchased minus the ending balance of Raw Material Inventory. If Raw Material Inventory includes both direct and indirect materials, the cost of direct material used is assigned to WIP Inventory and the cost of indirect material used is included in variable overhead. Because direct labor cannot

EXHIBIT 2-12

SELECTED T-ACCOUNTS FOR EARTH CAR'S APRIL PRODUCTION AND SALES

Raw Material Inventory				Variable Overhead Control			
Beg. bal.	73,000	(2)	284,000	(3)	94,000	(10)	115,200
(1)	280,000			(5)	16,000		
				(6)	5,200		
End. bal.	69,000						

Work in Process Inventory				Fixed Overhead Control			
Beg. bal.	145,000	(11)	1,058,200	(4)	20,000	(10)	98,880
(2) DM	284,000			(5)	12,000		
(3) DL	436,000			(7)	7,000		
(10) OH	214,080			(8)	56,880		
				(9)	3,000		
End. bal.	20,880						

Finished Goods Inventory				Cost of Goods Sold		
Beg. bal.	87,400	(13) CGS	1,054,000	(13)	CGS 1,054,000	
(11) CGM	1,058,200					
End. bal.	91,600					

[12] A service business prepares a schedule of cost of services rendered.

EXHIBIT 2–13

COST OF GOODS MANUFACTURED AND COST OF GOODS SOLD SCHEDULES

EARTH CAR COMPANY
Schedule of Cost of Goods Manufactured
For the Month Ended April 30, 2006

Beginning balance of Work in Process, 4/1/06			$ 145,000
Manufacturing costs for the period			
Raw materials (all direct)			
Beginning balance	$ 73,000		
Purchases of materials	280,000		
Raw materials available	$353,000		
Ending balance	(69,000)		
Total raw materials used		$284,000	
Direct labor		436,000	
Variable overhead			
Indirect labor	$ 94,000		
Utilities	16,000		
Supplies	5,200	115,200	
Fixed overhead			
Supervisor's salary	$ 20,000		
Utilities	12,000		
Factory property taxes	7,000		
Factory asset depreciation	56,880		
Factory insurance	3,000	98,880	
Total current period manufacturing costs			934,080
Total costs to account for			$1,079,080
Ending work in process, 4/30/06			(20,880)
Cost of goods manufactured			$1,058,200

EARTH CAR COMPANY
Schedule of Cost of Goods Sold
For the Month Ended April 30, 2006

Beginning finished goods, 4/1/06	$ 87,400
Cost of goods manufactured	1,058,200
Cost of goods available for sale	$1,145,600
Ending finished goods, 4/30/06	(91,600)
Cost of goods sold	$1,054,000

be warehoused, all charges for direct labor during the period are part of WIP Inventory. Variable and fixed overhead costs are added to direct material and direct labor costs to determine total manufacturing costs.

Beginning WIP Inventory cost is added to total current manufacturing costs to obtain a subtotal amount referred to as "total costs to account for." The value of ending WIP Inventory is calculated (through techniques discussed later in the text) and subtracted from the subtotal to provide the cost of goods manufactured during the period. The schedule of cost of goods manufactured is usually prepared only as an internal schedule and is not provided to external parties.

In the schedule of cost of goods sold, the cost of goods manufactured is added to the beginning balance of Finished Goods (FG) Inventory to find the cost of goods available for sale during the period. Ending FG Inventory is calculated by multiplying a physical unit count times a unit cost. If a perpetual inventory system is used, the actual amount of ending FG Inventory can be compared to the amount shown in the accounting records; any differences can be attributed to losses that could have arisen from theft, breakage, evaporation, or accounting errors. Ending FG Inventory is subtracted from the cost of goods available for sale to determine the cost of goods sold.

Some accountants prefer to streamline the presentation of the schedule of cost of goods manufactured and sold when perpetual inventory accounting is used. This alternative is presented in Exhibit 2–14.

EXHIBIT 2–14
ALTERNATIVE COST OF GOODS MANUFACTURED AND COST OF GOODS SOLD SCHEDULES

EARTH CAR COMPANY
Schedule of Cost of Goods Manufactured
For the Month Ended April 30, 2006

Beginning balance of Work in Process, 4/1/06		$ 145,000
Manufacturing costs for the period:		
Total raw materials used	$284,000	
Direct labor	436,000	
Variable overhead applied	115,200	
Fixed overhead applied	98,880	
Total current period manufacturing costs		934,080
Total costs to account for		$1,079,080
Ending Work in Process, 4/30/06		(20,880)
Cost of goods manufactured		$1,058,200

EARTH CAR COMPANY
Schedule of Cost of Goods Sold
For the Month Ended April 30, 2006

Beginning finished goods, 4/1/06	$ 87,400
Cost of goods manufactured	1,058,200
Cost of goods available for sale	$1,145,600
Ending finished goods, 4/30/06	(91,600)
Cost of goods sold	$1,054,000

General Motors

Revisiting

Although the original Corvettes were produced 100 percent by hand, today's Corvette is produced in a capital-intensive environment. The Corvette's rigid uniframe is constructed using 53 robotic welders, 1,200 spot welds, and 120 inches of hand welds. The steel cage gives the car its structural integrity. Panels are attached to the uniframe with hand-applied glue and through machinery-precise bonding that ensures exact fit and alignment.

Inspection points occur regularly through the production process. While the skeleton and body are being produced to form the Corvette frame, another department is producing and assembling each car's chassis, which includes the drive train, suspension, and engine. Finally, in the "marriage" department, the body and chassis are joined, and the wheels are attached to the Corvette. Tire integrity is tested, and the tires are balanced before they are placed on the automobile. The "start-up" department adds gasoline and the Vette is fired up; suspensions are settled and an extensive battery of perfor-

mance tests and checks are conducted. This series of painstaking and meticulous production activities result in one of five Corvette models: the LT1, LT4, LT5, C5, or the top-of-the-line Z06. The LT1 has a V-8 engine with 330 horsepower and a sticker price of approximately $45,000, whereas the Z06 has a LS6 V8 engine with 407 horsepower and a sticker price starting at approximately $53,000.

Corvette has selected the V8 engine because of its high power and controllability. Corvettes have raced in the Daytona Measured Mile Race, SCAA Race, and NASCAR Winston Cup Series Race. The power of the V8 also provides the control to operate under extreme weather conditions and with predictable throttle response. All of this power and quality have resulted in sales of more than 1 million cars since Corvette's inception and an expected demand of 36,000 Corvettes in 2004—a sales number that equals the Bowling Green Plant's capacity.

Source: Stephen Mraz, "40 Years and Counting," *Magazine Design* (August 27, 1993, pp. 27–32); and 1996 Corvette Owner's Manual.

Comprehensive Review Module

Chapter Summary

1. Costs are classified as

   - direct and indirect costs depending on their relationship to a cost object.

   - variable, fixed, or mixed depending on their reaction to changes in an activity level.

   - unexpired (assets) or expired (expenses and losses) depending on whether they have future value to the company.

   - product (inventoriable) or period (selling, administration, and financing) depending on their association with the revenue-generating items sold by the company.

2. To estimate production cost within a relevant range of activity, accountants assume that

   - variable costs are constant per unit and will change in direct proportion to changes in activity.

   - fixed costs are constant in total and will vary inversely on a per-unit basis with changes in activity.

   - step costs are either variable or fixed, depending on the size of the changes that occur with changes in activity.

   - mixed costs will fluctuate in total with changes in activity and can be separated into their variable and fixed components.

3. The conversion process differs in manufacturers, service companies, and retailers in that

   - manufacturers require extensive activity to convert raw material into finished goods; the primary costs in these companies are raw material, direct labor, and overhead; manufacturers use three inventory accounts (Raw Material, Work in Process, and Finished Goods).

   - service companies often require extensive activity to perform a service; the primary costs in these companies are direct labor and supplies; service companies may use Supplies Inventory and Work in Process Inventory accounts, but goods that are completed are usually transferred immediately to customers.

   - retailers require little, if any, activity to ready purchased goods for sale; the primary costs in these companies are generally purchase prices for goods and labor wages; retailers use a Merchandise Inventory account.

4. Three product cost categories are

   - direct material, which is physically and conveniently traceable to the product or service.

   - direct labor, which reflects people whose work is physically and conveniently traceable to the product or service.

   - overhead, which is any cost incurred in the production (or conversion) area that is not direct material or direct labor; overhead includes indirect material and indirect labor costs.

5. Cost of goods manufactured

   - reflects the costs that were in the production area at the beginning of the period plus those production costs (direct material, direct labor, and overhead) incurred during the period minus the costs of incomplete goods that remain in the production area at the end of the period.

   - is shown on an internal management report.

   - is added to beginning Finished Goods Inventory to determine the cost of goods available (CGA) for sale for the period; CGA is reduced by ending Finished Goods Inventory to determine cost of goods sold on the income statement.

Solution Strategies

PRODUCT COST

```
  Direct Material
+ Direct Labor
+ Overhead
= Total Product Cost
```

COST OF GOODS MANUFACTURED

Beginning balance of Work in Process Inventory			$XXX
Manufacturing costs for the period:			
Raw material (all direct):			
Beginning balance	$XXX		
Purchases of materials	XXX		
Raw material available for use	$XXX		
Ending balance	(XXX)		
Direct material used		$XXX	
Direct labor		XXX	
Variable overhead		XXX	
Fixed overhead		XXX	
Total current period manufacturing costs			XXX
Total costs to account for			$XXX
Ending balance of Work in Process Inventory			(XXX)
Cost of goods manufactured			$XXX

COST OF GOODS SOLD

Beginning balance of Finished Goods Inventory	$XXX
Cost of goods manufactured	XXX
Cost of goods available for sale	$XXX
Ending balance of Finished Goods Inventory	(XXX)
Cost of goods sold	$XXX

Demonstration Problem

Willie-Wonka Company had the following account balances as of August 1, 2006:

Raw Material (direct and indirect) Inventory	$20,300
Work in Process Inventory	7,000
Finished Goods Inventory	18,000

During August, the company incurred the following factory costs:

1. Purchased $164,000 of raw material on account.
2. Issued $180,000 of raw material, of which $134,000 was direct to the product.
3. Accrued factory payroll of $88,000; $62,000 was for direct labor and the rest was for supervisors' salaries.
4. Accrued utility costs of $7,000; of these costs, $1,600 were fixed.
5. Accrued property taxes on the factory in the amount of $2,000.
6. Had prepaid insurance of $1,600 on factory equipment that expired in August.
7. Had straight-line depreciation on factory equipment of $40,000.
8. Applied actual overhead to Work in Process Inventory.
9. Transferred goods costing $320,000 to Finished Goods Inventory.
10. Had total sales on account of $700,000.
11. Had cost of goods sold of $330,000.
12. Had selling and administrative costs of $280,000 (credit "Various Accounts").
13. Had ending Work in Process Inventory of $5,600.

Required:

a. Journalize the transactions for August.
b. Post transactions to the general ledger accounts for Work in Process Inventory, Finished Goods Inventory, and Cost of Goods Sold.
c. Prepare a schedule of cost of goods manufactured for August using actual costing.
d. Prepare an income statement, including a detailed schedule of cost of goods sold.

Solution to Demonstration Problem

a.

(1)	Raw Material Inventory		164,000	
	Accounts Payable			164,000
	Purchased raw material on account.			

(2)	Work in Process Inventory		134,000	
	Variable Overhead Control		46,000	
	Raw Material Inventory			180,000
	Transferred direct and indirect materials to production.			

(3)	Work in Process Inventory		62,000	
	Fixed Overhead Control		26,000	
	Salaries and Wages Payable			88,000
	To accrue factory wages and salaries.			

(4)	Variable Overhead Control		5,400	
	Fixed Overhead Control		1,600	
	Utilities Payable			7,000
	To accrue factory utility expenses.			

(5)	Fixed Overhead Control		2,000	
	Property Taxes Payable			2,000
	To accrue property tax expenses.			

(6)	Fixed Overhead Control		1,600	
	Prepaid Insurance			1,600
	To record expired insurance on factory equipment.			

(7)	Fixed Overhead Control		40,000	
	Accumulated Depreciation—Factory Equipment			40,000
	To record depreciation on factory equipment.			

(8)	Work in Process Inventory		122,600	
	Variable Overhead Control			51,400
	Fixed Overhead Control			71,200
	To apply or close overhead to Work in Process.			

(9)	Finished Goods Inventory		320,000	
	Work in Process Inventory			320,000
	To record cost of goods manufactured.			

(10)	Accounts Receivable		700,000	
	Sales			700,000
	To record sales on account.			

(11)	Cost of Goods Sold		330,000	
	Finished Goods Inventory			330,000
	To record cost of goods sold for the period.			

(12)	Selling & Administrative Expenses		280,000	
	Various accounts			280,000
	To record selling and administrative expenses.			

b.

Work in Process				**Finished Goods**				**Cost of Goods Sold**		
BB	7,000	(9)	320,000	BB	18,000	(11) 330,000		(11) 330,000	
(2)	134,000			(9)	320,000				
(3)	62,000								
(8)	122,600								
EB	5,600			EB	8,000				

where BB = beginning balance

EB = ending balance

c.

WILLIE-WONKA
Cost of Goods Manufactured Schedule
For Month Ended August 31, 2006

Balance of Work in Process Inventory, 8/1/06			$ 7,000
Manufacturing costs for the period			
Raw material			
Beginning balance		$ 20,300	
Purchases of materials		164,000	
Raw material available		$184,300	
Indirect material used	$46,000		
Ending balance	4,300	(50,300)	
Total direct material used		$134,000	
Direct labor		62,000	
Variable overhead		51,400	
Fixed overhead		71,200	
Total current period manufacturing costs			318,600
Total costs to account for			$325,600
Balance of Work in Process Inventory, 8/31/06			(5,600)
Cost of goods manufactured[a]			$320,000

[a]Notice the similarities between the schedule of cost of goods manufactured and the Work in Process T-account.

d.

WILLIE-WONKA
Income Statement
For the Month Ended August 31, 2006

Sales		$700,000
Cost of goods sold		
Finished goods, 8/1/06	$ 18,000	
Cost of goods manufactured	320,000	
Cost of goods available	$338,000	
Finished goods, 8/31/06	(8,000)	
Cost of goods sold		(330,000)
Gross margin		$370,000
Selling and administrative expenses		(280,000)
Income from operations		$ 90,000

Key Terms

actual cost system *(p. 42)*
appraisal cost *(p. 41)*
conversion cost *(p. 33)*
cost *(p. 27)*
cost allocation *(p. 42)*
cost driver *(p. 32)*
cost object *(p. 28)*
cost of goods manufactured
     (p. 45)
direct cost *(p. 28)*
direct labor *(p. 33)*
direct material *(p. 33)*

distribution cost *(p. 33)*
expired cost *(p. 27)*
failure cost *(p. 41)*
finished goods *(p. 38)*
fixed cost *(p. 30)*
indirect cost *(p. 29)*
inventoriable cost *(p. 33)*
manufacturer *(p. 35)*
mixed cost *(p. 31)*
normal cost system *(p. 42)*
overhead *(p. 33)*
period cost *(p. 33)*

predetermined overhead rate
     (p. 42)
predictor *(p. 32)*
prevention cost *(p. 41)*
product cost *(p. 33)*
raw material *(p. 38)*
relevant range *(p. 29)*
service company *(p. 35)*
step cost *(p. 31)*
unexpired cost *(p. 27)*
variable cost *(p. 29)*
work in process *(p. 38)*

Questions

1. When discussing a cost object, what is the distinction between a direct cost and an indirect cost?
2. Why is it necessary for a company to assume a relevant range of activity when making assumptions about cost behavior?
3. How do cost drivers and predictors differ, and why is the distinction important?
4. What is the distinction between a product cost and a period cost?
5. What are conversion costs? Why are they called this?
6. How does an actual costing system differ from a normal costing system? What advantages does a normal costing system offer?
7. What is meant by the term *cost of goods manufactured*? Why does this item appear on an income statement?

Exercises

8. (Direct vs. indirect costs) Krzyzewski Inc. manufactures stainless steel flatware (knives, spoons, and forks). Following are some costs incurred in the factory in 2006 for flatware production:

    Material costs
Stainless steel	$800,000
Equipment oil and grease	16,000
Plastic and fiberglass for handles	30,000
Flatware racks for customer storage	18,400

    Labor costs
Equipment operators	$400,000
Equipment mechanics	100,000
Factory supervisors	236,000

    a. What is the direct material cost for 2006?
    b. What is the direct labor cost for 2006?
    c. What are the total indirect material and indirect labor costs for 2006?

9. (Direct vs. indirect costs) Pitino State University's College of Business has five departments: Accounting, Finance, Management, Marketing, and Information Systems. Each department chairperson is responsible for the department's budget preparation. Indicate whether each of the following costs incurred in the Marketing Department is direct or indirect to the department:
    a. Marketing chairperson's salary
    b. Cost of computer time of campus mainframe used by members of the department

   c. Marketing faculty salaries

   d. Cost of equipment purchased by the department from allocated state funds

   e. Cost of travel by department faculty paid from externally generated funds contributed directly to the department

   f. Cost of secretarial salaries (secretaries are shared by the entire college)

   g. Depreciation allocation of the college building cost for the number of offices used by department faculty

   h. Cost of periodicals/books purchased by the department

10. (Direct vs. indirect costs) Following is a list of raw materials that might be used in the production of a laptop computer: touch pad and buttons, network connector, battery, AC adapter, CD drive, mother board, glue, screws, paper towels, and machinery and equipment oil. The laptops are produced using the same building and equipment used to produce desk top computers and servers. Classify each raw material as direct or indirect when the cost object is the

   a. Laptop

   b. Computer production plant

11. (Cost classifications) Indicate whether each of the following items is a variable (V), fixed (F), or mixed (M) cost and whether it is a product or service (PT) cost or a period (PD) cost. If some items have alternative answers, indicate the alternatives and the reasons for them.

   a. Wages of forklift operators who move finished goods from a central warehouse to the loading dock

   b. Paper towels used in factory restrooms

   c. Insurance premiums paid on the headquarters of a manufacturing company

   d. Columnar paper used in an accounting firm

   e. Cost of labels attached to shirts made by a company

   f. Wages of factory maintenance workers

   g. Property taxes on a manufacturing plant

   h. Salaries of secretaries in a law firm

   i. Freight costs of acquiring raw material from suppliers

   j. Cost of wax to make candles

   k. Cost of radioactive material used to generate power in a nuclear power plant

12. (Cost behavior) Self Company produces athletic logo caps. The company incurred the following costs to produce 4,000 caps last month:

Cardboard for the brims	$ 2,400
Cloth material	4,000
Plastic for headbands	3,000
Straight-line depreciation	3,600
Supervisors' salaries	9,600
Utilities	1,800
Total	$24,400

   a. What did each cap component cost on a per-unit basis?

   b. What is the probable type of behavior that each of the costs exhibits?

   c. The company expects to produce 5,000 caps this month. Would you expect each type of cost to increase or decrease? Why? Why can't the total cost of 5,000 caps be determined?

13. (Cost behavior) Thomason Company manufactures high-pressure basketballs. Costs are incurred in the production process for a rubber material used to make the balls, a steel mesh material used in the balls, depreciation on the factory building, and utilities to run production machinery. Graph the most likely cost behavior for each of these costs and show what type of cost behavior is indicated by each cost.

14. (Cost behavior) Your social fraternity/sorority has the opportunity to have Beyonce perform for free at the school's basketball arena on January 28, 2006, because one of the members won an Internet contest. Your school is located in Illinois; its basketball arena holds 25,000 people. The chancellor is charging your fraternity/sorority $80,000 for the facilities and $25 for each ticket sold. The fraternity/sorority asks you, their only numbers-astute member, to determine how much to charge for each ticket. The group wants to make a profit of $5 per ticket sold. You make the assumption that 10,000 tickets will be sold.

   a. What is the total cost if 10,000 tickets are sold?
   b. What price per ticket must be charged for the group to earn its desired profit margin?
   c. Suppose that on January 27, 2006, a major snow storm hit Illinois, bringing in 36 inches of snow and ice. Only 5,000 tickets are sold because most students were going to buy their tickets at the door. What is the total profit or loss to the fraternity/sorority?
   d. What assumptions did you make about your calculations that should have been conveyed to the fraternity/sorority?
   e. Suppose instead that no storm hit Illinois and, by showtime, 20,000 concert tickets had been sold. What is the total profit or loss to the fraternity/sorority?

15. (Total cost determination with mixed cost) Magarity Accounting Services pays $800 per month for a tax software license. In addition, variable charges average $6 for every tax return the firm prepares.

   a. Determine the total cost and the cost per unit if the firm expects to prepare the following number of tax returns in March 2006:
      1. 500
      2. 600
      3. 1,200
   b. Why does the cost per unit change in parts (1), (2), and (3)?

16. (Predictors and cost drivers; team activity) The IZZO accounting firm often uses factors that change in a consistent pattern with costs to explain or predict cost behavior.

   a. As a team of three or four, select factors to predict or explain the behavior of the following costs:
      1. Staff accountant's travel expenses
      2. Inventory of office supplies
      3. Laptops used to record audit findings
      4. Maintenance costs for a lawn service company
   b. Prepare a presentation of your chosen factors that also addresses whether the factors could be used as cost drivers in addition to cost predictors.

17. (Cost drivers) Assume that Ellis Hospital performs the following activities in providing outpatient service:
   1. Verifying patient's insurance coverage
   2. Scheduling patient's arrival date and time
   3. Scheduling staff to prepare patient's surgery room
   4. Scheduling doctors and nurses to perform surgery
   5. Ordering patient tests
   6. Moving patient to laboratory and administer lab tests
   7. Moving patient to the surgery room
   8. Administering anesthetic
   9. Performing surgery
   10. Moving patient to recovery room

11. Discharging patient after recovery

12. Billing the insurance company

Assume that the patient is the cost object and determine the appropriate cost driver or drivers for each activity.

18. (Financial statement classifications) Billy Donovan's Airboats purchased a plastics extruding machine for $200,000 to make boat hulls. During its first operating year, the machine produced 10,000 units; its depreciation was calculated to be $25,000. The company sold 8,000 of the hulls.

a. What part of the $200,000 machine cost is expired?

b. Where would each of the amounts related to this machine appear on the financial statements?

19. (Product and period costs) T. Smith Company incurred the following costs in May 2006:

- Paid a six-month premium for insurance of company headquarters, $24,000.
- Paid three months of property taxes on its factory building, $15,000.
- Paid an $80,000 bonus to the company president.
- Accrued $20,000 of utility costs, of which 40 percent was for the headquarters and the remainder was for the factory.

a. What expired period cost is associated with the May information?

b. What unexpired period cost is associated with the May information?

c. What product cost is associated with the May information?

d. Discuss why the product cost cannot be described specifically as expired or unexpired in this situation.

20. (Company type) Indicate whether each of the following terms is associated with a manufacturing (Mfg.), a retailing or merchandising (Mer.), or a service (Ser.) company. There can be more than one correct answer for each term.

a. Prepaid rent

b. Merchandise inventory

c. Cost of goods sold

d. Sales salaries expense

e. Finished goods inventory

f. Depreciation—factory equipment

g. Cost of services rendered

h. Auditing fees expense

i. Direct labor wages

21. (Degrees of conversion) Indicate whether each of the following types of organizations is characterized by a high, low, or moderate degree of conversion.

a. Bakery in a grocery store

b. Convenience store

c. Christmas tree farm

d. Textbook publisher

e. Sporting goods retailer

f. Auto manufacturer

g. Cranberry farm

h. Custom print shop

i. Italian restaurant

j. Concert ticket seller

WebTUTOR Advantage

22. (Labor cost classification) Fisher Homes Inc. produces a variety of household products. The firm operates 24 hours per day with three daily work shifts. The first-shift workers receive "regular pay." The second shift receives a 5 percent pay premium, and the third shift receives a 10 percent pay premium. In addition, when production is scheduled on weekends, the firm pays an overtime premium of 50 percent (based on the pay rate for first-shift employees). Labor premiums are included in overhead. The October 2006 factory payroll is as follows:

Total wages for October for 36,000 hours	$648,000
Normal hourly wage for first-shift employees	$16
Total regular hours worked, split evenly among the three shifts	30,000

a. How many overtime hours were worked in October?

b. How much of the total labor cost should be charged to direct labor? To overhead?

c. What amount of overhead was for second- and third-shift premiums? For overtime premiums?

23. (Essay on direct labor) A portion of the costs incurred by business organizations is designated as direct labor cost. As used in practice, the term *direct labor cost* has a wide variety of meanings. Unless the meaning intended in a given context is clear, misunderstanding and confusion are likely to ensue. If a user does not understand the elements included in direct labor cost, erroneous interpretations of the numbers can occur and could result in poor management decisions. In addition to understanding the conceptual definition of direct labor cost, management accountants must understand how direct labor cost should be measured. Write a paper that discusses the following issues:

a. Distinguish between direct labor and indirect labor.

b. Discuss why some nonproductive labor time (such as coffee breaks, personal time) can be and often is treated as direct labor whereas other nonproductive time (such as downtime or training) is treated as indirect labor.

c. Following are labor cost elements that a company has classified as direct labor, manufacturing overhead, or either direct labor or manufacturing overhead, depending on the situation.

- *Direct labor:* Included in the company's direct labor are cost production efficiency bonuses and certain benefits for direct labor workers such as FICA (employer's portion), group life insurance, vacation pay, and workers' compensation insurance.

- *Manufacturing overhead:* Included in the company's overhead are costs for wage continuation plans in the event of illness, the company-sponsored cafeteria, the personnel department, and recreational facilities.

- *Direct labor or manufacturing overhead:* Included in the "situational" category are maintenance expense, overtime premiums, and shift premiums.

Explain the rationale used by the company in classifying the cost elements in each of the three categories.

d. The two aspects of measuring direct labor costs are (1) the quantity of labor effort that is to be included, and (2) the unit price by which each of these quantities is multiplied to arrive at a monetary cost. Why are these considered separate and distinct aspects of measuring labor cost?

(CMA adapted)

24. (Journal entries—service industry) Hopkins & Bruder CPAs incurred the following costs in performing SEC audits during 2006. Prepare journal entries for each of the following transactions:

a. Paper and pencil supplies cost, $5,000; $2,000 was incurred for selling and administrative expenses.

    b. Depreciation of laptops used in the audit, $605,000.

    c. Depreciation on the Hopkins & Bruder Building, located in downtown New York, $1,800,000 of which 10 percent of the space is used to conduct audits.

    d. Partner salaries, $8,000,000.

    e. Audit junior staff salaries, $1,000,000.

    f. Manager salaries, $3,000,000.

    g. Travel costs to the client offices, $1,800,000.

    h. Insurance and property tax on the downtown building, $950,000.

25. (CGM and CGS) Bea Knight Company had the following inventory balances at the beginning and end of August 2006:

	August 1, 2006	**August 31, 2006**
Raw material inventory	$ 24,000	$ 32,000
Work in process inventory	136,000	168,000
Finished goods inventory	62,000	48,000

All raw material is direct to the production process. The following information is also available about August manufacturing costs:

Cost of raw material used	$256,000
Direct labor cost	324,000
Factory overhead	232,000

    a. Calculate the cost of goods manufactured for August.

    b. Determine the cost of goods sold for August.

26. (CGM and CGS) Boeheim Custom Clocks' August 2006 cost of goods sold was $4,600,000. August 31 work in process was 40 percent of the August 1 work in process. Overhead was 225 percent of direct labor cost. During August, $1,537,000 of direct material was purchased. Other August information follows:

Inventories	**August 1, 2006**	**August 31, 2006**
Direct material	$ 60,000	$ 84,000
Work in process	180,000	?
Finished goods	250,000	196,000

    a. Prepare a schedule of the cost of goods sold for August.

    b. Prepare the August cost of goods manufactured schedule.

    c. What was the amount of prime costs incurred in August?

    d. What was the amount of conversion costs incurred in August?

27. (Cost of services rendered) The following information is related to the Calipari Veterinary Clinic for April 2006, the firm's first month in operation:

Veterinarian salaries for April	$24,000
Assistants' salaries for April	8,400
Medical supplies purchased in April	3,600
Utilities for month (80 percent related to animal treatment)	1,800
Office salaries for April (20 percent related to animal treatment)	5,200
Medical supplies on hand at April 30	1,600
Depreciation on medical equipment for April	1,200
Building rental (70 percent related to animal treatment)	1,400

Compute the cost of services rendered.

Problems

28. (Cost behavior; advanced) L. Olson Ink makes stationery sets of 100 percent rag content edged in 24 karat gold. In an average month, the firm produces 40,000 boxes of stationery; each box contains 100 pages of stationery and 80 envelopes. Production costs are incurred for paper, ink, glue, and boxes.

The company manufactures this product in batches of 500 boxes of a specific stationery design. The following data have been extracted from the company's accounting records for June 2006:

Cost of paper for each batch	$10,000
Cost of ink and glue for each batch	1,000
Cost of 500 gold boxes for each batch	32,000
Direct labor for producing each batch	16,000
Labor costs for each batch design	40,000

Overhead charges total $408,000 per month and are considered fully fixed for purposes of cost estimation.

a. What is the cost per box of stationery based on average production volume?

b. If sales volume increases to 60,000 boxes per month, what will be the cost per box (assuming that cost behavior patterns remain the same as in June)?

c. If sales are 60,000 boxes per month but the firm does not want the cost per box to exceed its current level [based on part (a)], what amount can the company pay for labor design costs, assuming all other costs are the same as June levels?

d. Assume that L. Olson Ink is now able to sell, on average, each box of stationery at a price of $300. If the company is able to increase its volume to 60,000 boxes per month, what sales price per box will generate the same gross margin that the firm is now achieving on 40,000 boxes per month?

e. Would it be possible to lower total costs by producing more boxes per batch, even if the total volume of 40,000 is maintained? Explain.

29. (Cost behavior) Lute Olson Company's cost structure can contain a number of different cost behavior patterns. Following are descriptions of several different costs; match these to the appropriate graphs. On each graph, the vertical axis represents cost and the horizontal axis represents level of activity or volume.

Identify, by letter, the graph that illustrates each of the following cost behavior patterns. Each graph can be used more than once.

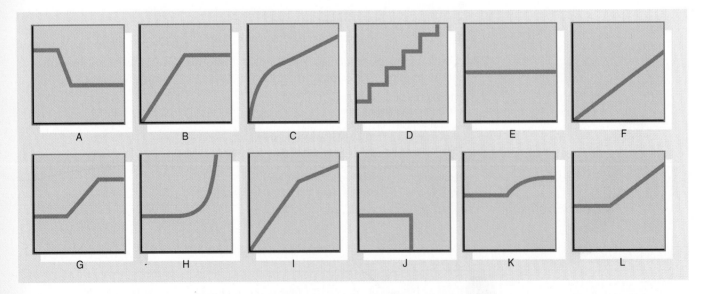

1. Cost of raw material, where the cost decreases by $0.06 per unit for each of the first 150 units purchased, after which it remains constant at $2.75 per unit.

2. City water bill, which is computed as follows: first 750,000 gallons or less, $1,000 flat fee; next 15,000 gallons, $0.002 per gallon used; next 15,000 gallons, $0.005 per gallon used; next 15,000 gallons, $0.008 per gallon used; and so on.

3. Salaries of maintenance workers, assuming one maintenance worker is needed for every 1,000 hours or less of machine time.

4. Electricity bill—a flat fixed charge of $250 plus a variable cost after 150,000 kilowatt hours are used.

5. Depreciation of equipment using the straight-line method.

6. Rent on a machine that is billed at $1,000 for up to 500 hours of machine time. After 500 hours of machine time, an additional charge of $1 per hour is paid up to a maximum charge of $2,500 per period.

7. Rent on a factory building donated by the county; the agreement provides for a monthly rental of $100,000 less $1 for each labor hour worked in excess of 200,000 hours. However, a minimum rental payment of $20,000 must be made each month.

8. Cost of raw materials used.

9. Rent on a factory building donated by the city with an agreement providing for a fixed-fee payment unless 250,000 labor hours are worked, in which case no rent needs to be paid.

(AICPA adapted)

30. (Cost classifications) Rick Majerus is a house painter who incurred the following costs during April 2006 when he painted four houses. He spent $1,200 on paint, $80 on mineral spirits, and $300 on brushes. He also bought two pairs of coveralls for $100 each; he wears coveralls only while he works. During the first week of April, Rick placed a $100 ad for his business in the classifieds. He hired an assistant for one of the painting jobs; the assistant was paid $25 per hour and worked 50 hours.

Being a very methodical person, Rick kept detailed records of his mileage to and from each painting job. His average operating cost per mile for his van is $0.70. He found a $30 receipt in his van for a metropolitan map that he purchased in April. He uses the map as part of a contact file for referral work and for bids that he has made on potential jobs. He also had $30 in receipts for bridge tolls ($2 per trip) for a painting job he did across the river.

Near the end of April, Rick decided to go camping, and he turned down a job on which he had bid $6,000. He called the homeowner long distance (at a cost of $3.20) to explain his reasons for declining the job.

Using the following headings, indicate how to classify each of the April costs incurred by Rick. Assume that the cost object is a house-painting job.

Type of Cost	Variable	Fixed	Direct	Indirect	Period	Product

31. (Journal entries) Advanced T. Davis Rags makes evening dresses. The following information has been gathered from the company records for 2006, the first year of company operations. Work in Process Inventory at the end of 2006 was $61,000.

Direct material purchased on account	$ 740,000
Direct material issued to production	596,000
Direct labor payroll accrued	430,000
Indirect labor payroll accrued	124,000
Factory insurance expired	4,000
Factory utilities paid	28,600
Depreciation on factory equipment recorded	43,400
Factory rent paid	168,000
Sales on account	1,908,000

The company's gross profit rate for the year was 35 percent.

a. Compute the cost of goods sold for 2006.

b. What was the total cost of goods manufactured for 2006?

c. If net income was $100,600, what were total selling and administrative expenses for the year?

d. Prepare journal entries to record the flow of costs for the year, assuming the company uses a perpetual inventory system.

32. (Journal entries) The following transactions were incurred by O'Brien Company during April 2006:

1. Direct material issued to production, $350,000.

2. Direct labor cost paid, 70,000 hours at $16 per hour.

3. Indirect labor cost accrued, 15,500 hours at $10 per hour.

4. Depreciation on factory assets recorded, $75,400.

5. Supervisors' salaries paid, $28,000.

6. Indirect materials issued to production, $19,200.

7. Goods costing $1,680,000 were completed and transferred to finished goods.

a. Prepare journal entries for these transactions using a single overhead account for both variable and fixed overhead and assuming that the Raw Material Inventory account contains only direct material.

b. If Work in Process Inventory had a beginning balance of $107,560, what is its ending balance?

33. (CGM and CGS) Billy Tubbs Inc. began business in July 2006. The firm makes an exercise machine for home and gym use. Following are data taken from the firm's accounting records that pertain to its first year of operations.

Direct material purchased on account	$450,000
Direct material issued to production	424,000
Direct labor payroll accrued	236,000
Indirect labor payroll paid	90,600
Factory insurance expired	6,000
Factory utilities paid	17,800
Factory depreciation recorded	35,800
Ending Work in Process Inventory (96 units)	111,000
Ending Finished Goods Inventory (30 units)	91,200
Sales on account ($3,700 per unit)	740,000

a. How many units did the company sell in its first year? How many units were completed in the first year?

b. What was the cost of goods manufactured?

c. What was the per-unit cost of goods manufactured?

d. What was the cost of goods sold in the first year?

e. What was the company's first-year gross margin?

34. (Product and period costs; CGM and CGS) At the beginning of August 2006, Bob Hubble Corporation had the following account balances:

Raw Material Inventory (both direct and indirect)	$24,000
Work in Process Inventory	36,000
Finished Goods Inventory	8,000

During August, the following transactions took place.

1. Raw material was purchased on account, $190,000.

2. Direct material ($40,400) and indirect material ($5,000) were issued to production.

3. Factory payroll consisted of $60,000 for direct labor employees and $14,000 for indirect labor employees.

4. Office salaries totaled $48,200 for the month.

5. Utilities of $13,400 were accrued; 70 percent of the utilities cost is for the factory area.

6. Depreciation of $20,000 was recorded on plant assets; 80 percent of the depreciation is related to factory machinery and equipment.

7. Rent of $22,000 was paid on the building. The factory occupies 60 percent of the building.

8. At the end of August, the Work in Process Inventory balance was $16,600.

9. At the end of August, the balance in Finished Goods Inventory was $17,800.

Bob Hubble Corporation uses an *actual* cost system and debits actual overhead costs incurred to Work in Process.

a. Determine the total amount of product cost (cost of goods manufactured) and period cost incurred during August 2006.

b. Compute the cost of goods sold for August 2006.

35. (CGM and CGS) Billy Tubbs' Collectibles produces collectible pieces of art. The company's Raw Material Inventory account includes the costs of both direct and indirect materials. Account balances for the company at the beginning and end of July 2006 follow.

	July 1, 2006	July 31, 2006
Raw Material Inventory	$46,600	$34,800
Work in Process Inventory	73,200	60,000
Finished Goods Inventory	36,000	52,400

During the month, the company purchased $164,000 of raw material; direct material used during the period amounted to $128,000. Factory payroll costs for July were $197,000 of which 85 percent was related to direct labor.

Overhead charges for depreciation, insurance, utilities, and maintenance totaled $150,000 for July.

a. Prepare a schedule of cost of goods manufactured.

b. Prepare a schedule of cost of goods sold.

36. (Missing data) Mike Montgomery Company suffered major losses in a fire on June 18, 2006. In addition to destroying several buildings, the blaze destroyed the company's work in process for an entire product line. Fortunately, the company was insured; however, it needs to substantiate the amount of the claim. To this end, the company has gathered the following information that pertains to production and sales of the affected product line:

1. The company's sales for the first 18 days of June amounted to $460,000. Normally, this product line generates a gross profit equal to 30 percent of sales.

2. Finished Goods Inventory was $58,000 on June 1 and $85,000 on June 18.

3. On June 1, Work in Process Inventory was $96,000.

4. During the first 18 days of June, the company incurred the following costs:

Direct material used	$152,000
Direct labor	88,000
Manufacturing overhead applied	84,000

a. Determine the value of Work in Process Inventory that was destroyed by the fire.

b. What other information might the insurance company require? How would management determine or estimate this information?

37. (Cost management; ethics) An extremely important and expensive variable cost per employee is health care provided by the employer. This cost is expected to rise each year as more and more expensive technology is used on patients and as the costs of that technology are passed along through the insurance company to the employer.

One simple way to reduce these variable costs is to cut back on employee insurance coverage.

a. Discuss the ethical implications of reducing employee health care coverage to reduce the variable costs incurred by the employer.

b. Assume that you are an employer with 600 employees. You are forced to cut back on some insurance benefits. Your coverage currently includes the following items: mental health coverage, long-term disability, convalescent facility care, nonemergency but medically necessary procedures, dependent coverage, and life insurance. Select the two you would eliminate or dramatically reduce and provide reasons for your selections.

c. Prepare a plan that might allow you to "trade" some variable employee health care costs for a fixed or mixed cost.

38. (Production cost management) A large percentage of U.S. companies outsource some part of their business processes, which include accounting, customer service, engineering, human resources, information technology, marketing, procurement, and sales. Moreover, many firms are outsourcing operations to other countries where labor rates are much lower in order to stay competitive. Some of the favorite offshore destinations are India, China, the Philippines, Eastern Europe, Costa Rica, Malaysia, and Mexico because these countries provide astronomical savings in costs. For example, India is the leading offshore market for IT development, customer care, engineering, and payroll processing because it provides the highest quality services at the lowest cost worldwide. The trend to outsource mission-critical activities is growing exponentially and will continue to grow in today's wireless and high-technology business environment.

a. Discuss some benefits and drawbacks to outsourcing the following activities: (1) finance, (2) data processing, and (3) travel arrangements.

b. How might outsourcing of manufacturing functions affect the (1) prevention, (2) appraisal, and (3) failure costs of a company?

c. What effects might outsourcing of each of the activities in part (a) have on an organization's employees and their work relationships?

3

Predetermined Overhead Rates, Flexible Budgets, and Absorption/Variable Costing

Objectives

AFTER COMPLETING THIS CHAPTER, YOU SHOULD BE ABLE TO ANSWER THE FOLLOWING QUESTIONS:

LO.1 WHY AND HOW ARE OVERHEAD COSTS ALLOCATED TO PRODUCTS AND SERVICES?

LO.2 WHAT CAUSES UNDERAPPLIED OR OVERAPPLIED OVERHEAD, AND HOW IS IT TREATED AT THE END OF A PERIOD?

LO.3 WHAT IMPACT DO DIFFERENT CAPACITY MEASURES HAVE ON SETTING PREDETERMINED OVERHEAD RATES?

LO.4 HOW ARE THE HIGH-LOW METHOD AND LEAST SQUARES REGRESSION ANALYSIS USED IN ANALYZING MIXED COSTS?

LO.5 HOW DO MANAGERS USE FLEXIBLE BUDGETS TO SET PREDETERMINED OVERHEAD RATES?

LO.6 HOW DO ABSORPTION AND VARIABLE COSTING DIFFER?

LO.7 HOW DO CHANGES IN SALES OR PRODUCTION LEVELS AFFECT NET INCOME COMPUTED UNDER ABSORPTION AND VARIABLE COSTING?

Introducing

Batavia, a small village in Ohio, is the setting for a unique Web-based business owned by Dee Griffis. This mother of four worked part-time most of her life so that she could be involved in her children's sports, school, or church functions. Like many homemakers, she experienced "empty-nest syndrome" when her grown children left for college or marriage.

She began her entrepreneurial experiences by making crafts and selling them at craft shows, but she quickly determined that there was no real positive relationship between the time she was spending and the money she was earning. Griffis knew that she possessed solid business and people skills from her years of working for others. It didn't take her long to recognize that she could combine her love for children and her office talents into establishing a viable commercial enterprise.

Born in August 2002, Baby Gifts-N-Treasures was based on one overarching concept: Babies are unique but most baby products aren't! Thus, Griffis put her craft talents to work and began designing and creating her own products; she prepared a color catalog of her creations and distributed it free at craft shows. She soon recognized that the catalog was "free" for customers, not for her! Her advertising investment was, for her as well as other retailers, a high overhead cost. The mixed cost of designing (fixed) and printing (vari-able) the catalog was not being covered by the sales it generated. Another option needed to open up quickly or Griffis would be closing up shop!

That option was clear, but the solution was a little fuzzy. The Internet offered the opportunity to be seen worldwide without huge printing or mailing costs, but how did a company get to be "seen" on search engines? With help from her Web site host, Griffis found out that exchanging links with other Web sites that have similar products helps a company get to the top of the search engine list rapidly. Thus, the Web site for Baby Gifts-N-Treasures now has about 200 other stores listed on exchange links. Griffis' networking paid off: The company is now listed on the first page of most search engines . . . a must for generating high sales volume!

Griffis is extremely cost conscious and, because of her creativity, saved a significant amount of money by designing her own stationery, catalog pages, business cards, invoices, gift certificates, and shipping labels. Baby Gifts-N-Treasures is located in Griffis' home, which means that her overhead costs are minimal. Her most significant overhead expense is for her 1-800 line, fax line, and long-distance charges when the 800-number is in use.

Source: Interview with Dee Griffis, June 22, 2004.

Any cost of doing business that is not incurred for direct material or direct labor is *overhead*. Some overhead costs are incurred in the production area; others, as in most retail businesses, are incurred in selling and administrative departments. Manufacturers previously considered direct material and direct labor as the primary production costs; similarly, a retailer's primary costs were for inventory and sales salaries. In the past, overhead was often an "additional" cost that was necessary but not exceptionally significant. However, many manufacturing firms recently have invested heavily in automation, and many retailers have been pressured by customers to provide more customer service and product variety. These changes have significantly increased the amount of production and nonproduction overhead costs incurred.

Regardless of where costs are incurred, a simple fact exists: For a company to be profitable, product or service selling prices must cover all direct and indirect costs. Direct material and labor costs can be easily traced to output and, as such, create few accounting difficulties. In contrast, indirect costs cannot be traced directly to separately distinguishable outputs.

Chapter 2 discusses actual cost systems in which actual direct material, direct labor, and production overhead are assigned to products. This chapter discusses normal costing and its use of predetermined overhead rates to determine product cost. Separation of mixed costs into variable and fixed elements, flexible budgets, and various production capacity measures are also discussed.

In addition, this chapter discusses two methods of presenting information on financial statements: absorption and variable costing. *Absorption costing* is commonly used for external reporting; *variable costing* is commonly used for internal reporting. Each method uses the same basic data but structures and processes the data differently. Either method can be used in job order or process costing and with actual, normal, or standard costs.

NORMAL COSTING AND PREDETERMINED OVERHEAD

Normal costing is an alternative costing system to actual costing. As shown in Exhibit 3–1, normal costing assigns actual direct material and direct labor to products but allocates production overhead to products using a predetermined overhead rate. Many accounting procedures are based on allocations. Cost allocations can be made over several time periods or within a single time period. For example, in financial accounting, a building's cost is allocated through depreciation charges over its useful or service life. This process is necessary to fulfill the *matching principle.* In cost accounting, production OH costs are allocated within a period through the use of predictors or cost drivers to products or services. This process reflects the application of the *cost principle,* which requires that all production or acquisition costs attach to the units produced, services rendered, or units purchased.

> *Why are predetermined OH rates used?*

There are four primary reasons for using predetermined overhead rates in product costing. First, a predetermined rate allows overhead to be assigned during the period to the goods produced or sold and to services rendered. Thus, a predetermined overhead rate improves the timeliness of information although simultaneously reducing the precision of information.

Second, predetermined overhead rates adjust for variations in actual overhead costs that are unrelated to activity. Overhead can vary monthly because of seasonal or calendar (days in a month) factors. For example, factory utility costs could be highest in the summer because of the necessity to run air conditioning. If monthly production were constant and actual overhead were assigned to production, the increase in utilities would cause product cost per unit to be higher in the summer than during the rest of the year. Assume that a company produces 3,000 units of its sole product each month. Utility costs for April and June were $600 and $900, respectively. The average actual April utility cost per unit would be $0.20 ($600 ÷ 3,000 units), but $0.30 ($900 ÷ 3,000) in June. Although this single cost difference is not necessarily significant, numerous differences of this type could cause a large distortion in unit cost.

Third, predetermined overhead rates overcome the problem of fluctuations in activity levels that have no impact on actual fixed overhead costs. Even if total production overhead were the same for each period, changes in activity would cause a per-unit change in cost because of the fixed cost element of overhead. If a company incurred $600 of utility cost in both October and November but produced 3,750 units in October and 3,000 units in November, the average actual unit utility cost would be $0.16 ($600 ÷ 3,750 units) in October and $0.20 ($600 ÷

LO.1
WHY AND HOW ARE OVERHEAD COSTS ALLOCATED TO PRODUCTS AND SERVICES?

EXHIBIT 3–1
ACTUAL VERSUS NORMAL COSTING

	Actual Cost System	Normal Cost System
Direct material	Assigned to product/service	Assigned to product/service
Direct labor	Assigned to product/service	Assigned to product/service
Overhead	Assigned to product/service	Assigned to overhead (OH) control account; predetermined OH rate is used to allocate overhead to product/service

Focus on Quality

Investments In Shipping Equipment Provide Rewards

An important concern for e-tailers is packaging. Packaging problems include high labor costs, high shipping costs, and high rates of return caused by damage. To correct these problems, companies need to be certain that the equipment in their packaging operations is designed to promote faster delivery, fewer returns, enhanced customer satisfaction, and lower fulfillment costs.

Such requirements may suggest mechanization, automation, or a combination of both. Most companies use a hybrid. When machines are introduced, labor costs, errors, and injury claims decline dramatically, but material handling costs (generally through equipment depreciation) rise significantly—possibly even to more than the labor costs. However, the cost of lost sales also declines; one study by **PricewaterhouseCoopers** reported that 31 percent of customers returned on-line purchases because they were broken or damaged upon receipt. Thus, the lack of returns can more than offset the investment in equipment.

An important and cost-efficient change for a distribution center is to improve the speed of the goods in the packaging area. The volume requirements of a packaging operation must accommodate "peak periods" to eliminate the possibility of bottlenecks. When a volume of 50,000 to 60,000 packages a day is reached, companies should definitely consider automated equipment.

E-commerce companies should remember that customer satisfaction is a key to success, and poorly designed or messy packaging dilutes the customer's first impression of quality. Packages should protect goods, contain easily disposable material, and should be easy to reuse in the event of a return. A **3M** Packaging Systems Division survey found that customers were extremely irritated by oversized packaging surrounded by a mass of filler. Clearly, installing a packaging process that reduces costs, protects the product, and enhances company image should receive significant attention from cost-conscious managers.

Sources: Adapted from Paul B. Hogan, "Packaging: Fast Way to Improve Customer Satisfaction and Reduce Cost of Fulfillment," *Material Handling Management* (October 2001), pp. 59–60 and Mary Aichlmayr, "Making a Case for Automation," *Transportation and Distribution* (June 2001), pp. 85–97.

3,000 units) in November. As mentioned earlier, many such overhead cost differences could create major variations in unit cost. By establishing a uniform annual predetermined overhead rate for all units produced during the year, the problems shown by these examples are overcome.

Finally, using predetermined overhead rates—especially when the bases for those rates truly reflect the drivers of costs—often allows managers to be more aware of individual product or product line profitability as well as the profitability of doing business with a particular customer or vendor. For instance, assume that **Baby Gifts-N-Treasures** purchases a product that retails for $40 from Vendor X for $20. If Dee Griffis has determined that a reasonable overhead rate per hour for vendor telephone conferences is $5 and that she often spends three hours on the phone with Vendor X because of customer complaints or shipping problems, Griffis could decide that the $5 profit on the product [$40 selling price minus $20 product cost plus $15 in overhead] does not make it cost beneficial to continue working with Vendor X.

Formula for Predetermined Overhead Rate

With one exception, normal cost system journal entries are identical to those made in an actual cost system. In both systems, overhead is debited during the period to a manufacturing overhead account and credited to the various accounts that "created" the overhead costs. An actual cost system then transfers the total amount of actual overhead cost from the overhead account to Work in Process Inventory.

Alternatively, a normal cost system assigns overhead cost to Work in Process Inventory through the use of a predetermined overhead rate.

To calculate a predetermined overhead rate, total budgeted overhead (OH) cost at a specific activity level is divided by the related activity level:

$$\text{Predetermined OH rate} = \frac{\text{Total Budgeted OH Cost at a Specified Activity Level}}{\text{Volume of Specified Actitity Level}}$$

Overhead cost and its related activity measure are typically budgeted for one year, although a longer or shorter period would be more appropriate to the organization's production cycle. For example, a longer period is more appropriate in a company that constructs ships, bridges, or high-rise office buildings.

A construction company that builds bridges will likely budget overhead cost for a period longer than one year.

GETTY IMAGES

Companies should use an activity base that is logically related to actual overhead cost incurrence. Although production volume might be the first activity base considered, this base is reasonable only if the company manufactures one type of product or renders just one type of service. If it makes or performs multiple products or services, production volumes cannot be summed to determine "activity" because of the heterogeneous nature of the items.

To effectively allocate overhead to heterogeneous products or services, a measure of activity that is common to all output must be selected. The activity base should be a cost driver that directly causes the incurrence of overhead costs. Direct labor hours and direct labor dollars are common activity measures; however, these bases could be deficient if a company is highly automated. Using any direct labor measure (hours or dollars) to allocate overhead costs in automated plants results in extremely high overhead rates because the costs are applied over a relatively small activity base. In automated plants, machine hours could be a more appropriate base for allocating overhead. Other possible measures include the number of purchase orders, product-related physical characteristics such as tons or gallons, number or amount of time of machine setups, number of parts, material handling time, and number of product defects.

Applying Overhead to Production

Once calculated, the predetermined overhead rate is used throughout the period to apply overhead to Work in Process Inventory using the predetermined rate and the actual level of activity. Thus, applied overhead is the dollar amount of overhead assigned to WIP Inventory using the activity that was employed to develop the application rate. Overhead can be applied when goods or services are transferred out of Work in Process Inventory or at the end of each month if financial statements are to be prepared. Or, under the real-time systems currently in use, overhead can be applied continuously as production occurs.

For convenience, both actual and applied overhead are recorded in a single general ledger account.[1] Debits to the account represent actual overhead costs, and

applied overhead

---

[1] Some companies may use separate overhead accounts for actual and applied overhead. In such cases, the actual overhead account has a debit balance and the applied overhead account has a credit balance. The applied overhead account is closed at the end of the year against the actual overhead account to determine the amount of underapplied or overapplied overhead.

credits represent applied overhead. Variable and fixed overhead may also be recorded in a single account or in separate accounts. Maintaining separate variable and fixed overhead accounts provides better information. Exhibit 3–2 presents the alternative overhead recording possibilities.

EXHIBIT 3–2

COST ACCOUNTING SYSTEM POSSIBILITIES FOR MANUFACTURING OVERHEAD

Single overhead account for variable and fixed overhead:

Manufacturing Overhead Control

Total actual OH incurred $VVFF	Total OH applied $AABB

Separate overhead accounts for variable and fixed overhead:

Manufacturing Variable Overhead (VOH) Control

Total actual VOH incurred $VV	Total VOH applied $AA

Manufacturing Fixed Overhead (FOH) Control

Total actual FOH incurred $FF	Total FOH applied $BB

If separate rates are used to apply variable and fixed overhead, the general ledger would have separate variable and fixed overhead accounts. Because overhead represents an ever-larger part of product cost in automated factories, the benefits of separating overhead according to its variable or fixed behavior is thought to be greater than the time and effort needed to make that separation. Separation of mixed costs is discussed later in the chapter.

Regardless of the number of predetermined overhead rates used, actual overhead is debited to the general ledger overhead account and credited to the source of the overhead cost. Overhead is applied to Work in Process Inventory as the activity designated as the denominator in the predetermined overhead rate formula actually occurs. Applied overhead is debited to Work in Process Inventory and credited to the overhead general ledger account.

Assume that Elmer Inc., a manufacturer of children's car seats, budgeted the following amounts for 2006: 50,000 machine hours, $375,000 of variable overhead costs, and $630,000 of fixed overhead costs. Elmer has decided to compute separate predetermined overhead rates using machine hours as the allocation base. Thus, the company's variable and fixed rates are, respectively, $7.50 ($375,000 ÷ 50,000) and $12.60 ($630,000 ÷ 50,000) per machine hour. During March 2006, the company incurred 4,300 machine hours, $31,385 of actual variable overhead costs, and $55,970 of actual fixed overhead costs. Using the predetermined overhead rates, Elmer would apply $32,250 (4,300 × $7.50) of variable overhead and $54,180 (4,300 × $12.60) of fixed overhead to the month's production. March 2006 journal entries to record actual and applied overhead are

Variable Manufacturing Overhead	31,385	
Fixed Manufacturing Overhead	55,970	
Various accounts		87,355
To record actual manufacturing overhead.		
Work in Process Inventory	86,430	
Variable Manufacturing Overhead		32,250
Fixed Manufacturing Overhead		54,180
To apply variable and fixed manufacturing overhead to WIP.		

*What factors create under- or over-
applied overhead?*

underapplied overhead

overapplied overhead

At year-end, total actual overhead will differ from total applied overhead. The difference is called *underapplied* or *overapplied overhead*. **Underapplied overhead** means that the overhead applied to Work in Process Inventory is less than the actual overhead incurred; **overapplied overhead** means that the overhead applied to Work in Process Inventory is more than actual overhead incurred. Underapplied or overapplied overhead must be closed at year-end because a single year's activity level was used to determine the overhead rate(s).

Under- or overapplication is caused by two factors that can work independently or simultaneously. These two factors are cost differences and utilization differences. If actual fixed overhead (FOH) cost differs from expected FOH cost, a fixed manufacturing overhead spending variance is created. If actual capacity utilization differs from expected utilization, a volume variance arises.[2] The independent effects of these differences are as follows:

$$\text{Actual FOH Cost} > \text{Expected FOH Cost} = \text{Underapplied FOH}$$
$$\text{Actual FOH Cost} < \text{Expected FOH Cost} = \text{Overapplied FOH}$$
$$\text{Actual Utilization} > \text{Expected Utilization} = \text{Overapplied FOH}$$
$$\text{Actual Utilization} < \text{Expected Utilization} = \text{Underapplied FOH}$$

In most cases, however, both costs and utilization differ from estimates. When this occurs, no generalizations can be made as to whether FOH will be underapplied or overapplied.

Disposition of Underapplied and Overapplied Overhead

Disposition of underapplied or overapplied overhead depends on the materiality of the amount involved. If the amount is immaterial, it is closed to Cost of Goods Sold. As in Exhibit 3–3, when overhead is underapplied (debit balance), an insufficient amount of overhead was applied to production and the closing process causes Cost of Goods Sold to increase. Alternatively, overapplied overhead (credit balance) reflects the fact that too much overhead was applied to production, so closing overapplied overhead causes Cost of Goods Sold to decrease.

EXHIBIT 3–3
**EFFECTS OF
UNDERAPPLIED AND
OVERAPPLIED OVERHEAD**

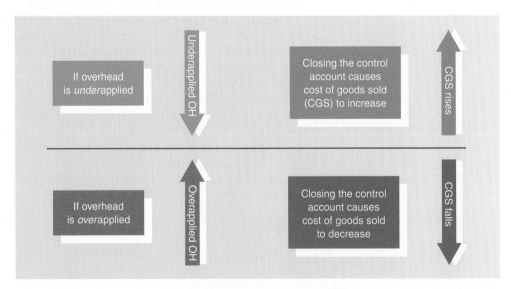

[2] These variances are covered in depth in Chapter 7.

To illustrate the closing process, assume that Elmer Inc. had $383,000 and $657,000, respectively, of actual variable and fixed overhead costs during 2006. The company used 51,500 machine hours during the year, and, thus, applied variable overhead (VOH) was $386,250 (51,500 × $7.50) and applied fixed OH was $648,900 (51,500 × $12.60). At year-end, the Variable Manufacturing Overhead account has a credit, or overapplied, balance of $3,250 ($383,000 − $386,250), and the Fixed Manufacturing Overhead account has a debit, or underapplied, balance of $8,100 ($657,000 − $648,900). Each amount is immaterial, so the journal entries to close these amounts are:

Variable Manufacturing Overhead	3,250	
Cost of Goods Sold		3,250
To close overapplied VOH.		
Cost of Goods Sold	8,100	
Fixed Manufacturing Overhead		8,100
To close underapplied FOH.		

If the amount of underapplied or overapplied overhead is significant, it should be prorated among the accounts in which applied overhead is recorded: Work in Process Inventory, Finished Goods Inventory, and Cost of Goods Sold. A significant amount of underapplied or overapplied overhead means that the overhead account balance is quite different than it would have been if actual overhead costs had been assigned to production. Proration makes the account balances conform more closely to actual historical cost as required for external reporting by generally accepted accounting principles. Exhibit 3–4 uses assumed data for Elmer Inc. to illustrate prorating a significant amount of overapplied fixed overhead to the

EXHIBIT 3–4
PRORATION OF OVERAPPLIED FIXED OVERHEAD

Fixed Manufacturing Overhead		Account Balances	
Actual FOH	$220,000	Work in Process Inventory	$ 45,640
Applied FOH	260,000	Finished Goods Inventory	78,240
Overapplied FOH	$ 40,000	Cost of Goods Sold	528,120

1. Add balances of accounts and determine proportional relationships:

	Balance	Proportion	Percentage
Work in Process	$ 45,640	$45,640 ÷ $652,000	7
Finished Goods	78,240	$78,240 ÷ $652,000	12
Cost of Goods Sold	528,120	$528,120 ÷ $652,000	81
Total	$652,000		100

2. Multiply percentages by the overapplied overhead amount to determine the adjustment amount needed:

Account	%	×	Overapplied FOH	=	Adjustment Amount
Work in Process	7	×	$40,000	=	$ 2,800
Finished Goods	12	×	$40,000	=	$ 4,800
Cost of Goods Sold	81	×	$40,000	=	$32,400

3. Prepare the journal entry to close manufacturing overhead account and assign adjustment amount to appropriate accounts:

Fixed Manufacturing Overhead	40,000	
Work in Process Inventory		2,800
Finished Goods Inventory		4,800
Cost of Goods Sold		32,400
To close overapplied fixed overhead.		

accounts based on their year-end account balances.[3] If the overhead had been underapplied, the accounts debited and credited in the journal entry would be reversed.

Alternative Capacity Measures

LO.3
WHAT IMPACT DO DIFFERENT CAPACITY MEASURES HAVE ON SETTING PREDETERMINED OVERHEAD RATES?

The two primary causes of underapplied or overapplied overhead are (1) a difference between budgeted and actual costs and (2) a difference in the activity level chosen to compute the predetermined overhead and the actual activity level experienced. The activity level used in setting the predetermined overhead rate generally reflects a consideration of organizational capacity.

theoretical capacity

The estimated maximum potential activity for a specified time is the **theoretical capacity**. This measure assumes that all production factors are operating perfectly. Theoretical capacity disregards realities such as machinery breakdowns and reduced or stopped plant operations on holidays. Choosing this activity level for setting a predetermined overhead rate provides a probable outcome of a significant amount of underapplied overhead cost.

practical capacity

normal capacity

Reducing theoretical capacity by ongoing, regular operating interruptions (such as holidays, downtime, and start-up time) provides the **practical capacity** that could be achieved during regular working hours. Consideration of historical and estimated future production levels and the cyclical fluctuations provides a **normal capacity** measure that encompasses the firm's long-run (5 to 10 years) average activity. This measure represents an attainable level of activity but will not result in applied overhead costs that are most similar to actual overhead costs. Thus, many firms use expected capacity as the selected measure of activity.

expected capacity

Expected capacity is a short-run concept that represents the firm's anticipated activity level for the upcoming period based on projected product demand. Expected capacity level is determined during the budgeting process, which is discussed in Chapter 8. If actual results are close to budgeted results (in both dollars and volume), this measure should result in product costs that most closely reflect actual costs and, thus, an immaterial amount of underapplied or overapplied overhead.[4]

See Exhibit 3–5 for a visual representation of capacity measures. Although expected capacity is shown in this diagram as much smaller than practical capacity, it is possible for expected and practical capacity to be more equal—especially in a highly automated plant.

Regardless of the capacity level chosen for the denominator in calculating a predetermined overhead rate, if individual overhead rates are to be developed for variable and fixed costs, any mixed overhead costs must be separated into their variable and fixed components.

SEPARATING MIXED COSTS

LO.4
HOW ARE THE HIGH-LOW METHOD AND LEAST SQUARES REGRESSION ANALYSIS USED IN ANALYZING MIXED COSTS?

As discussed in Chapter 2, a mixed cost contains both a variable and fixed component. For example, the cost for a cell phone plan that has a flat charge for basic service (the fixed component) plus a stated rate for each minute of use (the variable component) is a mixed cost. A mixed cost does not remain constant with changes in activity, nor does it fluctuate on a per-unit basis in direct proportion to changes in activity.

---

[3] *Theoretically,* underapplied or overapplied overhead should be allocated based on the amounts of applied overhead contained in each account rather than on total account balances. Use of total account balances could cause distortion because they contain direct material and direct labor costs that are not related to actual or applied overhead. In spite of this potential distortion, use of total balances is more common *in practice* for two reasons. First, the theoretical method is complex and requires detailed account analysis. Second, overhead tends to lose its identity after leaving Work in Process Inventory, thus making more difficult the determination of the amount of overhead in Finished Goods Inventory and Cost of Goods Sold account balances.
[4] Except where otherwise noted in the text, expected capacity has been chosen as the basis to calculate the predetermined fixed manufacturing overhead rate because it is believed to be the most prevalent practice. This choice, however, may not be the most effective for planning and control purposes as is discussed further in Chapter 7 with regard to standard cost variances.

EXHIBIT 3–5
MEASURES OF CAPACITY

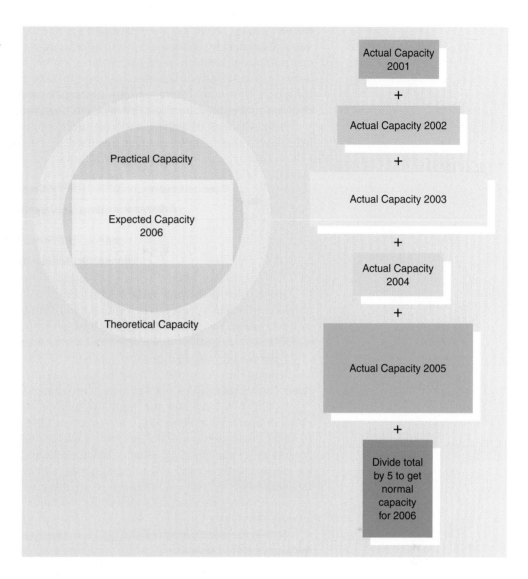

Accountants typically assume that costs are linear rather than curvilinear. Because of this assumption, the general formula for a straight line can be used to describe any type of cost within a relevant range of activity. The straight-line formula is

$$y = a + b\mathrm{X}$$

where y = total cost (dependent variable)
a = fixed portion of total cost
b = unit change of variable cost relative to unit changes in activity
X = activity base to which y is being related (the predictor, cost driver, or independent variable)

If a cost is entirely variable, the a value in the formula is zero. If the cost is entirely fixed, the b value in the formula is zero. If a cost is mixed, it is necessary to determine formula values for both a and b. Two methods of determining these values—and thereby separating a mixed cost into its variable and fixed components—are the high-low method and regression analysis.

High-Low Method

high-low method

The **high-low method** analyzes a mixed cost by first selecting the highest and lowest levels of activity in a data set if these two points are within the relevant range. Activity levels are used because activities cause costs to change, not vice versa. Occasionally, operations occur at a level outside the relevant range (a special rush order could require excess labor or machine time), or distortions could occur in a cost within the relevant range (a leak in a water pipe goes unnoticed for a period of time). Such nonrepresentative or abnormal observations are called **outliers** and should be disregarded when analyzing a mixed cost.

outliers

Next, changes in activity and cost are determined by subtracting low values from high values. These changes are used to calculate the *b* (variable unit cost) value in the $y = a + bX$ formula as follows:

$$b = \frac{\text{Cost at High Activity Level} - \text{Cost at Low Activity Level}}{\text{High Activity Level} - \text{Low Activity Level}}$$

$$b = \frac{\text{Change in Total Cost}}{\text{Change in Activity Level}}$$

The *b* value is the unit variable cost per measure of activity. This value is multiplied by the activity level to determine the amount of total variable cost contained in total cost at either the high or the low level of activity. The fixed portion of a mixed cost is found by subtracting total variable cost from total cost.

Total mixed cost changes with changes in activity. The change in total mixed cost equals the change in activity times the unit variable cost. By definition, the fixed cost element does not fluctuate with changes in activity.

Exhibit 3–6 illustrates the high-low method using machine hours and utility cost information for Elmer Inc. In November 2005, the company wants to determine its predetermined overhead rate to use in calendar year 2006. It gathered information for the prior 10 months' machine hours and utility costs. During 2005, the department's normal operating range of activity was between 3,500 and 9,000 machine hours per month. Because it is substantially in excess of normal activity levels, the May observation is viewed as an outlier and should not be used in the analysis of utility cost.

One potential weakness of the high-low method is that outliers can inadvertently be used in the calculation. Estimates of future costs calculated from a line drawn using such points will not indicate actual costs and probably are not good predictions. A second weakness is that this method considers only two data points. A more precise method of analyzing mixed costs is least squares regression analysis.

Least Squares Regression Analysis

least squares regression analysis

Least squares regression analysis is a statistical technique that analyzes the relationship between dependent and independent variables. The least squares method is used to develop an equation that predicts an unknown value of a **dependent variable** (cost) from the known values of one or more **independent variables** (activities). When multiple independent variables exist, least squares regression also helps to select the independent variable that is the best predictor of the dependent variable. For example, managers can use least squares to decide whether machine hours, direct labor hours, or pounds of material moved best explain and predict changes in a specific overhead cost.[5]

dependent variable

independent variables

Simple regression analysis uses one independent variable to predict the dependent variable based on the $y = a + bX$ formula for a straight line. In **multiple regression**, two or more independent variables are used to predict the dependent variable. All text examples use simple regression and assume that a lin-

simple regression

multiple regression

[5] Further discussion of finding independent variable(s) that best predict the value of the dependent variable can be found in most textbooks on statistical methods treating regression analysis under the headings of dispersion, coefficient of correlation, coefficient of determination, or standard error of the estimate.

EXHIBIT 3–6

ANALYSIS OF MIXED COST FOR ELMER INC.

The following machine hours and utility cost information is available:

Month	Machine Hours	Utility Cost
January	7,260	$2,960
February	8,850	3,410
March	4,800	1,920
April	9,000	3,500
May	11,000	3,900 *Outlier*
June	4,900	1,860
July	4,600	2,180
August	8,900	3,470
September	5,900	2,480
October	5,500	2,310

STEP 1: Select the highest and lowest levels of activity within the relevant range and obtain the costs associated with those levels. These levels and costs are 9,000 and 4,600 hours, and $3,500 and $2,180, respectively.

STEP 2: Calculate the change in cost compared to the change in activity.

	Machine Hours	Associated Total Cost
High activity	9,000	$3,500
Low activity	4,600	2,180
Changes	4,400	$1,320

STEP 3: Determine the relationship of cost change to activity change to find the variable cost element.

$$b = \$1,320 \div 4,400 \text{ MH} = \$0.30 \text{ per machine hour}$$

STEP 4: Compute total variable cost (TVC) at either level of activity.

High level of activity: TVC = $0.30(9,000) = $2,700
Low level of activity: TVC = $0.30(4,600) = $1,380

STEP 5: Subtract total variable cost from total cost at the associated level of activity to determine fixed cost.

High level of activity: $a = \$3,500 - \$2,700 = \$800$
Low level of activity: $a = \$2,180 - \$1,380 = \$800$

STEP 6: Substitute the fixed and variable cost values in the straight-line formula to get an equation that can be used to estimate total cost at any level of activity within the relevant range.

$$y = \$800 + \$0.30X$$

where X = machine hours

ear relationship exists between variables so that each one-unit change in the independent variable produces a constant unit change in the dependent variable.[6]

regression line

A **regression line** is any line that goes through the means (or averages) of the independent and dependent variables in a set of observations. As in Exhibit 3–7, numerous straight lines can be drawn through any set of data observations,

[6] Curvilinear relationships between variables also exist. For example, quality defects (dependent variable) tend to increase at an increasing rate in relationship to machinery age (independent variable).

EXHIBIT 3–7

ILLUSTRATION OF LEAST SQUARES REGRESSION LINE

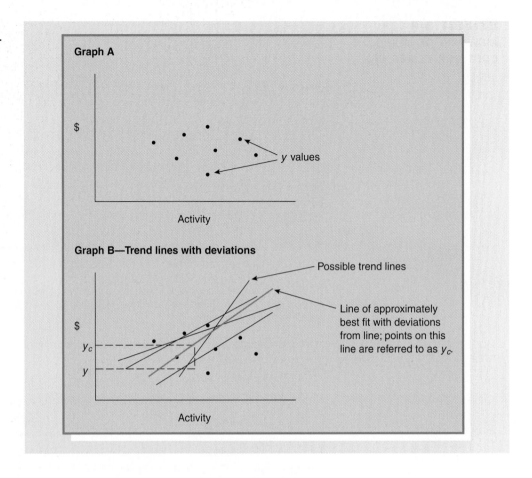

but most of these lines would provide a poor fit to the data. Actual observation values are designated as *y* values; these points do not generally fall directly on a regression line. The least squares method mathematically fits the best possible regression line to observed data points. The method fits this line by minimizing the sum of the squares of the vertical deviations between the actual observation points and the regression line. The regression line represents computed values for all activity levels, and the points on the regression line are designated as y_c values.

The regression line of best fit is found by predicting the *a* and *b* values in a straight-line formula using the actual activity and cost values (*y* values) from the observations. The equations necessary to compute *b* and *a* values using the method of least squares are as follows[7]:

$$b = \frac{\sum xy - n(\bar{x})(\bar{y})}{\sum x^2 - n(\bar{x})^2}$$

$$a = \bar{y} - b\bar{x}$$

where $\bar{x}$ = mean of the independent variable
       $\bar{y}$ = mean of the dependent variable
       n = number of observations

Using the machine hour and utility cost data for Elmer Inc. (presented in Exhibit 3–6 and excluding the May outlier), the following calculations can be made:

---

[7] These equations are derived from mathematical computations beyond the scope of this text but can be found in many statistics books. The symbol Σ means "the summation of."

x	y	xy	x^2
7,260	$ 2,960	$ 21,489,600	52,707,600
8,850	3,410	30,178,500	78,322,500
4,800	1,920	9,216,000	23,040,000
9,000	3,500	31,500,000	81,000,000
4,900	1,860	9,114,000	24,010,000
4,600	2,180	10,028,000	21,160,000
8,900	3,470	30,883,000	79,210,000
5,900	2,480	14,632,000	34,810,000
5,500	2,310	12,705,000	30,250,000
59,710	$24,090	$169,746,100	424,510,100

The mean of x (or $\bar{x}$) is 6,634.44 (59,710 ÷ 9), and the mean of y (or $\bar{y}$) is $2,676.67 ($24,090 ÷ 9). Thus,

$$b = \frac{\$169,746,100 - 9(6,634.44)(\$2,676.67)}{424,510,100 - 9(6,634.44)(6,634.44)} = \frac{\$9,922,241}{\$28,367,953} = \underline{\$0.35}$$

$$a = \$2,676.67 - \$0.35(6,634.44) = \$2,676.67 - \$2,322.05 = \underline{\$354.62}$$

The b (variable cost) and a (fixed cost) values for the department's utility costs are $0.35 and $354.62, respectively. These values are close to, but not exactly the same as, the values computed using the high-low method.

By using these values, predicted costs (y_c values) can be computed for each actual activity level. The line that is drawn through all of the y_c values will be the line of best fit for the data. Because actual costs do not generally fall directly on the regression line and predicted costs naturally do, these two costs differ at their related activity levels. It is acceptable for the regression line not to pass through any or all of the actual observation points because the line has been determined to mathematically "fit" the data.

Like all mathematical models, regression analysis is based on certain assumptions that produce limitations on the use of the model. Three of these assumptions follow; others are beyond the scope of the text. First, for regression analysis to be useful, the independent variable must be a valid predictor of the dependent variable; the relationship can be tested by determining the coefficient of correlation. Second, like the high-low method, regression analysis should be used only within a relevant range of activity. Third, the regression model is useful only as long as the circumstances existing at the time of its development remain constant; consequently, if significant additions are made to capacity or if there is a major change in technology usage, the regression line will no longer be valid.

Once a method has been selected and mixed overhead costs have been separated into fixed and variable components, a flexible budget can be developed to indicate the estimated amount of overhead at various levels of the denominator activity.

Flexible Budgets

LO.5
HOW DO MANAGERS USE FLEXIBLE BUDGETS TO SET PREDETERMINED OVERHEAD RATES?

flexible budget

A **flexible budget** is a planning document that presents expected variable and fixed overhead costs at different activity levels. The activity levels shown on a flexible budget usually cover the contemplated range of activity for the upcoming period. If all activity levels are within the relevant range, costs at each successive level should equal the previous level plus a uniform monetary increment for each variable cost factor. The increment is equal to variable cost per unit of activity times the quantity of additional activity.

Expected cost information from the flexible budget is used for the numerator in computing the predetermined overhead rate. See Exhibit 3–8 for a flexible overhead budget for Elmer Inc. at selected levels of activity. Except for the information for utilities (which was taken from the previous high-low method computations of $0.35 variable and $800 per month fixed), all amounts have been assumed. Note that the variable overhead cost per machine hour (MH) does not change within the relevant range, but the fixed overhead cost per machine hour varies inversely with the level of activity. Given that the company selected 50,000 machine hours as the denominator level of annual activity, the variable and fixed predetermined overhead rates were $7.50 and $12.60, respectively.

EXHIBIT 3–8

FLEXIBLE OVERHEAD BUDGET FOR ELMER INC.

	Number of Machine Hours (MH)				
	40,000	45,000	50,000	55,000	75,000
Variable OH (VOH)					
Indirect material	$ 60,000	$ 67,500	$ 75,000	$ 82,500	$112,500
Indirect labor	120,000	135,000	150,000	165,000	225,000
Utilities	14,000	15,750	17,500	19,250	26,250
Other	106,000	119,250	132,500	145,750	198,750
Total	$300,000	$337,500	$375,000	$412,500	$562,500
VOH rate per MH	$7.50	$7.50	$7.50	$7.50	$7.50
FOH					
Factory salaries	$215,000	$215,000	$215,000	$215,000	$215,000
Depreciation	300,000	300,000	300,000	300,000	300,000
Utilities	9,600	9,600	9,600	9,600	9,600
Other	105,400	105,400	105,400	105,400	105,400
Total	$630,000	$630,000	$630,000	$630,000	$630,000
FOH rate per MH	$15.75	$14.00	$12.60	$11.45	$8.40

Plantwide versus Departmental Overhead Rates

Because most companies produce many different kinds of products, calculation of a plantwide predetermined overhead rate generally does not provide the most useful information. For example, assume that Elmer Inc. has two departments, Assembly and Finishing. Assembly is highly automated, but Finishing requires significant direct labor. As such, it is highly probable that machine hours would be the more viable overhead allocation base for Assembly, and direct labor hours would be for Finishing.

Exhibit 3–9 uses a single product (Part #AB79Z) to show the cost differences that can be created by using a plantwide overhead rate. Production of this part requires 1 hour of machine time in Assembly and 5 hours of direct labor time in Finishing. The departmental cost amounts shown in Exhibit 3–9 have been assumed so that they will balance with information provided in Exhibit 3–8. Notice that the $20.10 plantwide rate using machine hours is the same total rate calculated in Exhibit 3-8: a variable rate of $7.50 per MH plus a fixed rate of $12.60 per MH. For purposes of this illustration, the use of separate variable and fixed overhead rates is ignored.

Exhibit 3–9 shows the tremendous difference that can be created in product cost depending on the overhead application rate. A company with multiple departments that use significantly different types of work effort (such as automated versus manual) as well as diverse material that require considerably different times

EXHIBIT 3–9

PLANTWIDE VERSUS DEPARTMENTAL OVERHEAD RATE FOR ELMER INC.

	Plantwide	Assembly	Finishing
Budgeted annual overhead	$1,005,000	$724,500	$280,500
Budgeted annual direct labor hours (DLHs)	13,000	3,000	10,000
Budgeted annual machine hours (MHs)	50,000	45,000	5,000

Departmental overhead rates

   Assembly (automated): $724,500 ÷ 45,000 = $16.10 per MH

   Finishing (manual): $280,500 ÷ 10,000 = $28.05 per DLH

Plantwide overhead rates

   Using DLHs: $1,005,000 ÷ 13,000 = $77.31 per DLH

   Using MHs: $1,005,000 ÷ 50,000 = $20.10 per MH

Part #AB79Z

Overhead assigned using departmental rates

Assembly	1 MH × $16.10	$ 16.10
Finishing	5 DLHs × $28.05	140.25
Total		$156.35

Total overhead assigned using plantwide rates

Based on DLHs	5 DLHs × $77.31	$386.55
Based on MHs	1 MH × $20.10	20.10

Using assumed direct material and direct labor costs, the total cost of Part AB79Z is:

	Using Departmental OH Rates	Using a Plantwide Rate Based on DLHs	Using a Plantwide Rate Based on MHs
Direct material	$110.00	$110.00	$110.00
Direct labor	36.00	36.00	36.00
Overhead	156.35	386.55	20.10
Total cost	$302.35	$532.55	$166.10

in those departments should use separate departmental predetermined overhead rates to attach overhead to products to derive the most rational product cost. Homogeneity is more likely to occur within a department than among departments; thus, separate departmental rates generally provide better information for management planning, control, and decision making than do plantwide rates. Computing departmental rates allows each department to select the most appropriate measure of activity (or cost driver) relative to its operations.

Additionally, the use of variable and fixed categories within each department lets management understand how costs react to changes in activity. The use of variable and fixed categories also makes it easier to generate different reports for external and internal reporting purposes.

OVERVIEW OF ABSORPTION AND VARIABLE COSTING

LO.6

HOW DO ABSORPTION AND VARIABLE COSTING DIFFER?

In preparing reports on financial information, costs can be accumulated and presented in different ways. Choice of cost accumulation method determines which costs are recorded as part of product cost and which are considered period costs. In contrast, choice of the cost presentation method determines how costs are shown on external financial statements or internal management reports. Accumulation and presentation procedures are accomplished using one of two methods, absorption costing or variable costing. Each method structures or processes the same basic data differently, and either method can be used in job order or process costing and with actual, normal, or standard costs. Although one approach is required for external reporting, that approach is not necessarily appropriate for internal decision making.

absorption costing

Absorption costing treats the costs of all manufacturing components (direct material, direct labor, variable overhead, and fixed overhead) as inventoriable, or product, costs in accordance with generally accepted accounting principles. Absorption costing, also known as **full costing**, has been used exclusively in the previous chapters that introduced product costing systems and valuation. In fact, the product cost definition given in Chapter 2 specifically fits the absorption costing method. Under absorption costing, costs incurred in the nonmanufacturing areas of the organization are considered period costs and are expensed in a manner that properly matches them with revenues. Exhibit 3–10 depicts the absorption costing model.

full costing

functional classification

In addition, absorption costing presents expenses on an income statement according to their functional classifications. A **functional classification** is a group of costs that were all incurred for the same principal purpose. Functional classifications generally include cost of goods sold, selling expense, and administrative expense.

variable costing

In contrast, **variable costing** is a cost accumulation method that includes only direct material, direct labor, and variable overhead as product costs. This method

EXHIBIT 3–10
ABSORPTION COSTING MODEL

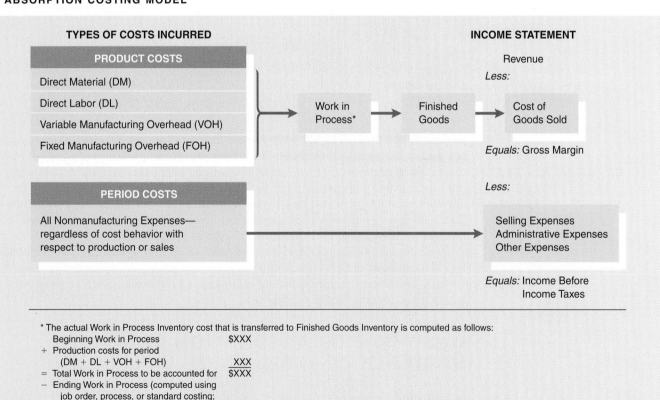

TYPES OF COSTS INCURRED	**INCOME STATEMENT**

PRODUCT COSTS

Direct Material (DM)

Direct Labor (DL)

Variable Manufacturing Overhead (VOH)

Fixed Manufacturing Overhead (FOH)

Work in Process* → Finished Goods → Cost of Goods Sold

Revenue
Less:
Cost of Goods Sold
Equals: Gross Margin

PERIOD COSTS

All Nonmanufacturing Expenses— regardless of cost behavior with respect to production or sales

Less:
Selling Expenses
Administrative Expenses
Other Expenses

Equals: Income Before Income Taxes

* The actual Work in Process Inventory cost that is transferred to Finished Goods Inventory is computed as follows:

Beginning Work in Process	$XXX
+ Production costs for period (DM + DL + VOH + FOH)	XXX
= Total Work in Process to be accounted for	$XXX
− Ending Work in Process (computed using job order, process, or standard costing; also appears on end-of-period balance sheet)	(XXX)
= Cost of Goods Manufactured	$XXX

direct costing

treats fixed manufacturing overhead (FOH) as a period cost. Like absorption costing, variable costing treats costs incurred in the organization's selling and administrative areas as period costs. Variable costing income statements typically present expenses according to cost behavior (variable and fixed), although expenses can also be presented by functional classifications within the behavioral categories. Variable costing is also known as **direct costing**. See Exhibit 3–11 for the variable costing model.

Two differences exist between absorption and variable costing: One relates to cost accumulation and the other relates to cost presentation. The cost accumulation difference is that absorption costing treats fixed overhead as a product cost; variable costing treats it as a period cost. Absorption costing advocates contend that products cannot be made without the production capacity provided by fixed manufacturing costs and, therefore, these costs "belong" to the product. Variable costing advocates contend that fixed manufacturing costs would be incurred whether or not any products are manufactured; thus, such costs are not caused by production and cannot be product costs.

The cost presentation difference is that absorption costing classifies expenses by function on the income statement and on management reports while variable

EXHIBIT 3–11

VARIABLE COSTING MODEL

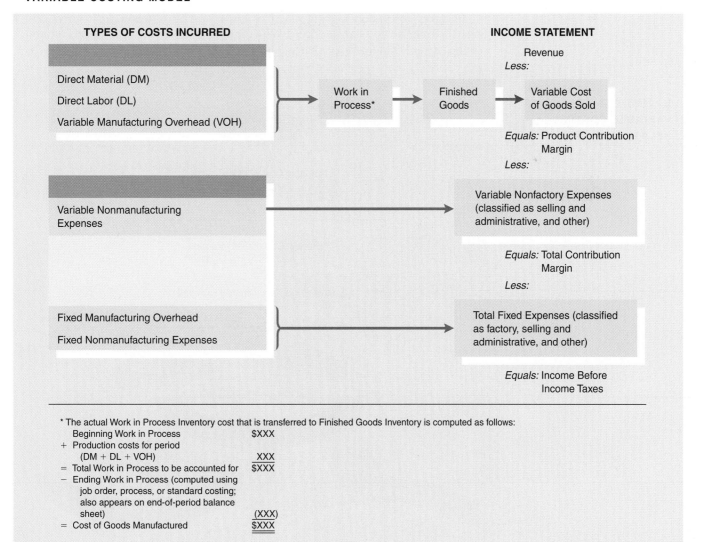

costing categorizes expenses first by behavior and then, possibly, by function. Under variable costing, cost of goods sold is more appropriately called *variable cost of goods sold* because it is composed only of variable production costs. Sales minus variable cost of goods sold is called **product contribution margin**; it indicates how much revenue is available to cover all period expenses and to provide net income.

product contribution margin

Variable, nonmanufacturing period expenses, such as sales commissions set at 10 percent of product selling price, are deducted from product contribution margin to determine the amount of total contribution margin. Total **contribution margin** is the difference between total revenues and total variable expenses. This amount indicates the dollar amount available to "contribute" to cover all fixed expenses, both manufacturing and nonmanufacturing. After fixed expenses are covered, any remaining contribution margin provides income. A variable costing income statement is also referred to as a *contribution income statement*. See Exhibit 3–12 for a diagram of these variable costing relationships.

contribution margin

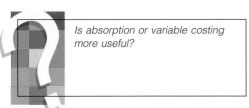

Is absorption or variable costing more useful?

Major authoritative bodies of the accounting profession, such as the Financial Accounting Standards Board and the Securities and Exchange Commission, require the use of absorption costing to prepare external financial statements; absorption costing is also required for filing tax returns with the Internal Revenue Service. The accounting profession has, in effect, disallowed the use of variable costing as a generally accepted inventory method for external reporting purposes.

Because absorption costing classifies expenses by functional category, cost behavior (relative to changes in activity) cannot be observed from an absorption costing income statement or management report. Understanding cost behavior is

EXHIBIT 3–12
VARIABLE COSTING RELATIONSHIPS

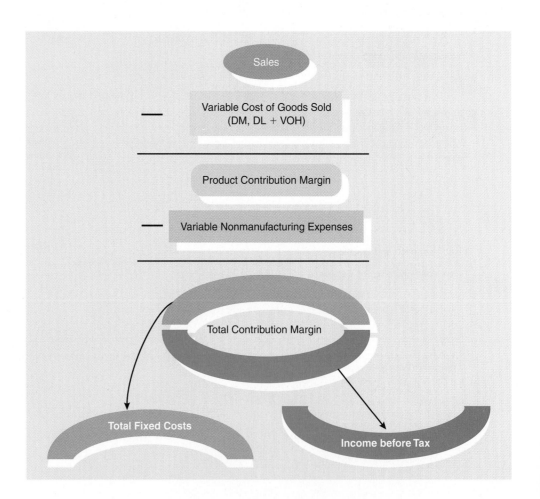

extremely important for many managerial activities including budgeting, cost-volume-profit analysis, and relevant costing.[8] Thus, internal financial reports distinguishing costs by behavior are often prepared for use in management decision making and analysis. The next section provides a detailed illustration using both absorption and variable costing.

ABSORPTION AND VARIABLE COSTING ILLUSTRATIONS

Renaldo Company began operations in 2006 and has been hired by Elmer Inc. to make car seat cushions. Product specifications are likely to continue at least until model year 2009. Data for this product are used to compare absorption and variable costing procedures and presentations.

The company uses standard costs for material and labor and predetermined rates for variable and fixed overhead. See Exhibit 3–13 for unit production costs, annual budgeted nonmanufacturing costs, and other basic operating data for Renaldo Company. The fixed manufacturing overhead application rate of $0.54 per unit is computed by dividing budgeted annual FOH ($162,000) by expected capacity (300,000 units). All costs are assumed to remain constant over the three years 2006 through 2008, and for simplicity, Renaldo is assumed to complete all units started and, therefore, will have no work in process inventory at the end of

EXHIBIT 3–13
RENALDO BASIC DATA FOR 2006, 2007, AND 2008

Sales price per unit	$6.00
Standard variable cost per unit	
Direct material	$2.04
Direct labor	1.50
Variable manufacturing overhead	0.18
Total variable manufacturing cost per unit	$3.72

$$\text{Standard Fixed Factory Overhead Rate} = \frac{\text{Budgeted Annual Fixed Factory Overhead}}{\text{Budgeted Annual Capacity in Units}}$$

FOH rate = $162,000 ÷ 300,000 = $0.54

Total absorption cost per unit	
Standard variable manufacturing cost	$ 3.72
Standard fixed manufacturing overhead (SFOH)	0.54
Total absorption cost per unit	$ 4.26
Budgeted nonproduction expenses	
Variable selling expenses per unit	$ 0.24
Fixed selling and administrative expenses	$2,340

Total budgeted nonproduction expenses = ($0.24 per unit sold + $2,340)

	2006	2007	2008	Total
Actual units made	300,000	290,000	310,000	900,000
Actual unit sales	300,000	270,000	330,000	900,000
Change in Finished Goods inventory	0	+ 20,000	(20,000)	0

[8] These topics are covered in Chapters 8 (budgeting), 9 (cost-volume-profit analysis), and 10 (relevant costing).

a period.[9] Also, all actual costs are assumed to equal the standard and budgeted costs for the years presented. The bottom section of Exhibit 3–13 is a comparison of actual unit production with actual unit sales to determine the change in inventory for each of the three years.

Because Renaldo began operations in 2006, that year has no beginning finished goods inventory. The next year, 2007, also has no beginning inventory because all units produced in 2006 were also sold in 2006. In 2007 and 2008, production and sales quantities differ, which is a common situation because production frequently "leads" sales so that inventory can be stockpiled for a later period. Refer to Exhibit 3–14 for the operating results for Renaldo for the years 2006 through 2008 using both absorption and variable costing. This example assumes that Renaldo had no beginning inventory as well as having equal cumulative units of production and sales for the three years. Under these conditions, the data in Exhibit 3–14 demonstrate that, regardless of whether absorption or variable costing is used, the cumulative income before tax will be the same ($1,279,800). Also, as in 2006, for any year in which there is no change in inventory from the beginning to the end of the year, both methods will result in the same net income.

EXHIBIT 3–14

RENALDO ABSORPTION AND VARIABLE COSTING INCOME STATEMENTS FOR 2006, 2007, AND 2008

ABSORPTION COSTING PRESENTATION				
	2006	**2007**	**2008**	**Total**
Sales ($6 per unit)	$1,800,000	$1,620,000	$1,980,000	$5,400,000
Cost of goods sold (CGS) ($4.26 per unit)	(1,278,000)	(1,150,200)	(1,405,800)	(3,834,000)
Standard gross margin	$ 522,000	$ 469,800	$ 574,200	$1,566,000
Volume variance (U)	0	(5,400)	5,400	0
Adjusted gross margin	$ 522,000	$ 464,400	$ 579,600	$1,566,000
Selling and administrative expenses	(95,400)	(88,200)	(102,600)	(286,200)
Income before tax	$ 426,600	$ 376,200	$ 477,000	$1,279,800

VARIABLE COSTING PRESENTATION				
	2006	**2007**	**2008**	**Total**
Sales ($6 per unit)	$1,800,000	$1,620,000	$1,980,000	$5,400,000
Variable CGS ($3.72 per unit)	(1,116,000)	(1,004,400)	(1,227,600)	(3,348,000)
Product contribution margin	$ 684,000	$ 615,600	$ 752,400	$2,052,000
Variable selling expenses				
($0.24 x units sold)	(72,000)	(64,800)	(79,200)	(216,000)
Total contribution margin	$ 612,000	$ 550,800	$ 673,200	$1,836,000
Fixed expenses				
Manufacturing	$ 162,000	$ 162,000	$ 160,200	$ 486,000
Selling and administrative	23,400	23,400	23,400	70,200
Total fixed expenses	$ (185,400)	$ (185,400)	$ (185,400)	$ (556,200)
Income before tax	$ 426,600	$ 365,400	$ 487,800	$1,279,800
Differences in income before tax	$ 0	$ 10,800	$ (10,800)	$ 0

[9] Actual costs can also be used under either absorption or variable costing. Standard costing was chosen for these illustrations because it makes the differences between the two methods more obvious. If actual costs had been used, production costs would vary each year, and such variations would obscure the distinct differences caused by the use of one method, rather than the other, over a period of time. Standard costs are also treated as constant over time to more clearly demonstrate the differences between absorption and variable costing and to reduce the complexity of the chapter explanations.

volume variance

Actual production and operating costs have been assumed to equal the standard and budgeted costs for years 2006 through 2008. However, differences in actual and budgeted capacity utilization occurred for 2007 and 2008, which create a volume variance for each of those years under absorption costing. A **volume variance** reflects the monetary impact of a difference between the budgeted capacity used to determine the fixed overhead application rate and the actual capacity at which the company operates. Thus, for Renaldo Company, there is no volume variance for 2006 because the budgeted and actual production levels were 300,000 units. For 2007, the volume variance is calculated as [$0.54 × (290,000 − 300,000)], or $5,400 unfavorable. For 2008, it is calculated as [$0.54 × (310,000 − 300,000)], or $5,400 favorable. Each of these amounts is considered immaterial and is shown as an adjustment to the year's gross margins. No volume variances are shown under variable costing because fixed manufacturing overhead is not applied to products using a budgeted capacity measure; the FOH is deducted in its entirety as a period expense.

The income statements in Exhibit 3–14 show that absorption and variable costing provide different income figures in some years. Comparing the two sets of statements indicates that the difference in income arises solely from the different treatment of fixed overhead. If no beginning or ending inventories exist, cumulative total income under both methods will be identical. Over the three-year period, Renaldo Company produced and sold 900,000 units. Thus, all the costs incurred (whether variable or fixed) are expensed in one year or another under either method. The income difference in each year is caused solely by the timing of the expensing of fixed manufacturing overhead.

In Exhibit 3–14, absorption costing income before tax for 2007 exceeds that of variable costing by $10,800. This difference is caused by the fixed overhead assigned to the 20,000 units made but not sold ($0.54 × 20,000) and, thus, placed in inventory in 2007. Critics of absorption costing refer to this phenomenon as one that creates illusionary or phantom profits. **Phantom profits** are temporary absorption costing profits caused by producing more inventory than is sold. When previously produced inventory is sold, the phantom profits disappear. In contrast, variable costing expenses all fixed manufacturing overhead in the year it is incurred.

phantom profits

In 2008, inventory decreased by 20,000 units. This decrease, multiplied by the fixed overhead rate of $0.54, explains the $10,800 by which 2008 absorption costing income falls short of variable costing income in Exhibit 3–14. For 2008, not only is all current year fixed manufacturing overhead expensed through cost of goods sold, but also the $10,800 of fixed overhead that was retained in 2007's ending inventory is shown in the 2008 cost of goods sold. Only 2008 fixed manufacturing overhead is shown on the variable costing income statement.

COMPARISON OF THE TWO APPROACHES

LO.7
HOW DO CHANGES IN SALES OR PRODUCTION LEVELS AFFECT NET INCOME COMPUTED UNDER ABSORPTION AND VARIABLE COSTING?

Whether absorption costing income is more or less than variable costing income depends on the relationship of production to sales. In all cases, to determine the effect on income, it must be assumed that variances from standard are immaterial and that unit product costs are constant over time. See Exhibit 3–15 for the possible relationships between production and sales levels and the effects of these relationships on income. These relationships are as follows:

When and how will absorption and variable costing incomes differ?

- If production equals sales, absorption costing income will equal variable costing income.
- If production is more than sales, absorption costing income is greater than variable costing income. This result occurs because some fixed manufacturing overhead cost is deferred as part of inventory cost on the balance sheet under absorption costing whereas the total

EXHIBIT 3–15

PRODUCTION/SALES RELATIONSHIPS AND EFFECTS ON INCOME AND INVENTORY

where P = Production and S = Sales
AC = Absorption Costing and VC = Variable Costing

	Absorption vs. Variable Income Statement Income before Taxes	Absorption vs. Variable Balance Sheet Ending Inventory
P = S	AC = VC No difference from beginning inventory $FOH_{EI} - FOH_{BI} = 0$	No additional difference $FOH_{EI} = FOH_{BI}$
P > S (Stockpiling inventory)	AC > VC By amount of fixed OH in ending inventory minus fixed OH in beginning inventory $FOH_{EI} - FOH_{BI} = +$ amount	Ending inventory increased (by fixed OH in additional units because P > S) $FOH_{EI} > FOH_{BI}$
P < S (Selling off beginning inventory)	AC < VC By amount of fixed OH released from balance sheet beginning inventory $FOH_{EI} - FOH_{BI} = -$ amount	Ending inventory difference reduced (by fixed OH from BI charged to cost of goods sold) $FOH_{EI} < FOH_{BI}$

*The effects of the relationships presented here are based on two qualifying assumptions:
 (1) that unit costs are constant over time
 (2) that any fixed cost variances from standard are written off when incurred rather than being prorated to
     inventory balances.

amount of fixed manufacturing overhead cost is expensed as a period cost under variable costing.

If production is less than sales, income under absorption costing is less than income under variable costing. In this case, absorption costing expenses all of the current period fixed manufacturing overhead costs and releases some fixed manufacturing overhead cost from the beginning inventory where it had been deferred from a prior period.

This process of deferring and releasing fixed overhead costs into and from inventory makes it possible to manipulate income under absorption costing by adjusting levels of production relative to sales. For this reason, some people believe that variable costing is more useful for external purposes than absorption costing. For internal reporting, variable costing information provides managers information about the behavior of the various product and period costs. To carry out their planning, controlling, and decision-making functions, managers need to understand and be able to project how costs will change in reaction to changes in activity levels. Variable costing, through its emphasis on cost behavior, provides that necessary information.

Revisiting

When Griffis decided to establish her Internet business, she was shocked to learn that a skilled Web site designer would cost between $3,000 and $5,000, depending on the number of pages and products. Lacking the funds, she sought the answer to that problem at a bank where she found that women who start businesses are considered "high risk" and getting a loan would be more difficult than she had thought. The banker suggested that she pay someone to write a business plan that could be reviewed by a bank committee to determine whether she qualified for a loan. This suggestion would create yet another cost that she could ill afford, so Griffis decided that she'd just have to learn a new skill: Web site design. Several months later, her ability to upload her Web site was cause for celebration.

Needing products for her Web site required Griffis to spend a large amount of time in Web research and in phone calls to locate wholesale specialty stores that could provide the distinctive baby products she wanted to sell. Most suppliers, however, required a minimum purchase of $300 to $500 and upfront payment because Baby Gifts-N-Treasures was a new customer. Because she'd never gotten her bank loan, Griffis used personal credit cards and bought inventory that she had to store until a sale occurred.

With debts rising, Griffis engaged in more investigative research until she came across the perfect solution to her purchasing problem: drop-shipping. Baby Gifts-N-Treasures now receives orders and relays them to vendors; the vendors ship goods to customers and invoice Griffis' company at wholesale; the company then invoices the customer and never has to physically keep the goods in stock! Thus, Griffis now keeps very few items in stock. She stays in touch with vendors on the status of customer orders and, because of the relationships that have been established, vendors are generally very willing to accommodate her special requests.

Concentrated effort and getting to know her vendors personally have given Griffis a wide selection of companies that are happy to provide high-quality, personalized keepsakes for her to showcase at Baby Gifts-N-Treasures. As of mid-2004, just two years after its beginning, the company's primary customers are large corporate entities doing repeat business on high-end products. Griffis is thrilled with the way her business has turned out! According to her, anyone who has a good idea, is willing to work hard, can gain proficiency at new tasks, is a bit of a risk taker, and has the support of family and friends can become a successful entrepreneur. Owning a business is the best job in the world: It provides the freedom to do something you love and earn money while doing it. Additionally, for Dee Griffis, there's that extra benefit of knowing that her products give customers a lifetime of memories.

Source: Interview with Dee Griffis, June 22, 2004.

Comprehensive Review Module

Chapter Summary

1. Overhead costs are allocated to products to

   - eliminate the problems caused by delays in obtaining actual cost data.

   - make the overhead allocation process more effective.

   - allocate a uniform amount of overhead to goods or services based on related production efforts.

   - allow managers to be more aware of individual product or product line profitability as well as the profitability of doing business with a particular customer or vendor.

2. Underapplied (actual is more than applied) or overapplied (actual is less than applied) overhead is

   - caused by a difference between budgeted and actual overhead costs and/or a difference between budgeted and actual level of activity chosen to compute the predetermined overhead rate.

   - closed at the end of each period (unless normal capacity is used for the denominator level of activity) to

     ➤ Cost of Goods Sold (CGS) if the amount of underapplied or overapplied overhead is immaterial (underapplied will cause CGS to increase and overapplied will cause CGS to decrease)

     or

     ➤ Work in Process Inventory, Finished Goods Inventory, and Cost of Goods Sold (based on their proportional balances) if the amount of underapplied or overapplied overhead is material.

3. Capacity measures affect the setting of predetermined overhead rates because the use of

   - expected capacity (the budgeted capacity for the upcoming year) will result in a predetermined overhead rate that would probably be most closely related to an actual overhead rate.

   - practical capacity (the capacity that allows for normal operating interruptions) will generally result in a predetermined overhead rate that is substantially lower than an actual overhead rate would be.

   - normal capacity (the capacity that reflects a long-run average) can result in an overhead rate that is higher or lower than an actual overhead rate, depending on whether capacity has been over- or underutilized during the years under consideration.

   - theoretical capacity (the estimated maximum potential capacity) will result in a predetermined overhead rate that is exceptionally lower than an actual overhead rate; however, this rate reflects a company's true ability to use its capacity.

4. Mixed costs can be separated into their variable and fixed components by using

   - the high-low method, which considers the change in cost between the highest and lowest activity levels in the data set (excluding outliers) and determines a variable cost per unit based on that change; fixed cost is then determined by subtracting total variable cost at either the highest or lowest activity level from total cost at that level.

   - regression analysis, which uses the costs and activity levels in the entire data set (excluding outliers) as input to mathematical formulas that allow the determination first of variable cost and, subsequently, of fixed cost.

5. Flexible budgets are used by managers to help set predetermined overhead rates by

   - allowing managers to understand what manufacturing overhead costs are incurred and what the behaviors (variable, fixed, or mixed) of those costs are.

   - allowing managers to separate mixed costs into their variable and fixed elements.

   - providing information on the budgeted costs to be incurred at various levels of activitiy.

   - providing a visualization of the impacts on the predetermined fixed overhead rate (or on a plantwide rate) from changing the denominator level of activity.

6. Absorption and variable costing differ in that

   - absorption costing

➢ includes all manufacturing costs, both variable and fixed, as product costs.

➢ presents nonmanufacturing costs according to functional areas on the income statement: standard gross margin, adjusted gross margin, and operating income.

- variable costing

➢ includes only the variable costs of production (direct material, direct labor, and variable manufacturing overhead) as product costs.

➢ presents both nonmanufacturing and manufacturing costs according to cost behavior on the income statement: product contribution margin, total contribution margin, and operating income.

7. Differences between sales and production volume result in differences in income between absorption and variable costing because

- absorption costing requires fixed costs are written off as a function of the number of units sold;

➢ Thus, if production volume is higher than sales volume, some fixed costs will be deferred in inventory at year-end, making net income higher than under variable costing.

➢ Conversely, if sales volume is higher than production volume, the deferred fixed costs from previous periods will be written off as part of cost of goods sold, making net income lower than under variable costing.

- variable costing requires that all fixed costs are written off in the period incurred, regardless of when the related inventory is sold;

➢ Thus, if production volume is higher than sales volume, all fixed manufacturing costs will be expensed in the current period and not be deferred until sold, making net income lower than under absorption costing.

➢ Conversely, if sales volume is higher than production volume, only current period fixed manufacturing costs will be expensed in the current period, making net income higher than under absorption costing.

Solution Strategies

PREDETERMINED OVERHEAD RATE

$$\text{Predetermined OH rate} = \frac{\text{Total Budgeted OH Cost at a Specified Activity Level}}{\text{Volume of Specified Activity Level}}$$

(Can be separate variable and fixed rates or a combined rate)

HIGH-LOW METHOD

(Using assumed amounts)

	(Independent Variable) Activity	(Dependent Variable) Associated Total Cost	−	Total Variable Cost (Rate × Activity)	=	Total Fixed Cost
"High" level	14,000	$18,000	−	$11,200	=	$6,800
"Low" level	9,000	14,000	−	7,200	=	6,800
Differences	5,000	$ 4,000				

$0.80
variable cost per unit of activity

LEAST SQUARES REGRESSION ANALYSIS

The equations necessary to compute *b* and *a* values using the method of least squares are as follows:

$$b = \frac{\sum xy - n(\overline{x})(\overline{y})}{\sum x^2 - n(\overline{x})^2}$$

$$a = \overline{y} - b\overline{x}$$

where $\bar{x}$ = mean of the independent variable

$\bar{y}$ = mean of the dependent variable

n = number of observations

UNDERAPPLIED AND OVERAPPLIED OVERHEAD

Overhead Control	XXX	
Various accounts		XXX
Actual overhead is debited to the overhead		
general ledger account.		
Work in Process Inventory	YYY	
Overhead Control		YYY
Applied overhead is debited to WIP and		
credited to the overhead general ledger account.		

A debit balance in Manufacturing Overhead at the end of the period is underapplied overhead; a credit balance is overapplied overhead. The debit or credit balance in the overhead account is closed at the end of the period to Cost of Goods Sold or prorated to Work in Process Inventory, Finished Goods Inventory, and Cost of Goods Sold.

FLEXIBLE BUDGET

To prepare a flexible budget,

1. separate mixed costs into variable and fixed elements
2. determine the $a + bX$ cost formula for each item of the budget category (for example, all items creating manufacturing overhead)
3. select several potential levels of activity within the relevant range
4. use the cost formulas to determine the total cost expected at each of the selected levels of activity

ABSORPTION AND VARIABLE COSTING

1. Determine which method is being used (absorption or variable). The following abbreviations are used: VOH, variable manufacturing overhead; FOH, fixed manufacturing overhead; DM, direct material; DL, direct labor.
   a. If absorption:
      - Determine the (FOH) application rate.
      - Determine the denominator capacity used in determining manufacturing FOH.
      - Determine whether production was equal to the denominator capacity. If not, a fixed overhead (FOH) volume variance must be properly assigned to cost of goods sold and, possibly, inventories.
      - Determine the cost per unit of product, which consists of (DM + DL + VOH + FOH).
   b. If variable:
      - Determine the cost per unit of product, which consists of (DM + DL + VOH).
      - Determine the total fixed manufacturing OH and assign that amount to the income statement as a period expense.
2. Determine the relationship of production to sales.
   a. If Production = Sales, then Absorption Costing Income = Variable Costing Income.
   b. If Production > Sales, then Absorption Costing Income > Variable Costing Income.
   c. If Production < Sales, then Absorption Costing Income < Variable Costing Income.

3. The dollar difference between absorption costing income and variable costing income equals (FOH application rate × change in inventory units).

Demonstration Problem

Lacer Company management uses predetermined variable and fixed rates to apply overhead to its product. For 2006, the company budgeted production at 27,000 units, which would require 54,000 direct labor hours (DLHs) and 27,000 machine hours (MHs). At that level of production, total variable and fixed manufacturing overhead costs were expected to be $13,500 and $105,300, respectively. Variable overhead is applied to production using direct labor hours, and fixed overhead is applied using machine hours. During 2006, Lacer Company produced 23,000 units and experienced the following operating statistics and costs: 46,000 direct labor hours; 23,000 machine hours; $11,980 actual variable manufacturing overhead; and $103,540 actual fixed manufacturing overhead. By the end of 2006, all 23,000 units that were produced were sold; thus, the company began 2007 with no beginning finished goods inventory.

In 2007 and 2008, Lacer Company management decided to apply manufacturing overhead to products using units of production (rather than direct labor hours and machine hours). The company produced 25,000 and 20,000 units, respectively, in 2007 and 2008. Lacer's budgeted and actual fixed manufacturing overhead for both years was $100,000. Production in each year was projected at 25,000 units. Total variable production cost (including variable manufacturing overhead) is $3 per unit. The following absorption costing income statements and supporting information are available:

	2007	2008
Net sales (20,000 units and 22,000 units)	$300,000	$330,000
Cost of goods sold (a)	(140,000)	(154,000)
Volume variance (0 and 5,000 units @ $4)	0	(20,000)
Gross margin	$160,000	$156,000
Operating expenses (b)	(82,500)	(88,500)
Income before tax	$ 77,500	$ 67,500
(a) Cost of goods sold		
Beginning inventory	$ 0	$ 35,000
Cost of goods manufactured[a]	175,000	140,000
Goods available for sale	$175,000	$175,000
Ending inventory[b]	(35,000)	(21,000)
Cost of goods sold	$140,000	$154,000

[a]CGM
   25,000 units × $7 (of which $3 are variable) = $175,000
   20,000 units × $7 (of which $3 are variable) = $140,000
[b]EI
   25,000 − 20,000 = 5,000 units; 5,000 × $7 = $ 35,000
   5,000 + 20,000 − 22,000 = 3,000 units; 3,000 × $7 = $ 21,000

(b) Analysis of operating expenses		
Variable	$ 50,000	$ 55,000
Fixed	32,500	33,500
Total	$ 82,500	$ 88,500

Required:
a. Determine the variable and fixed predetermined overhead rates for 2006, and calculate how much underapplied or overapplied overhead existed at the end of that year.
b. Recast the 2007 and 2008 income statements on a variable costing basis.
c. Reconcile income for 2007 and 2008 between absorption and variable costing.

Solution to Demonstration Problem

a. VOH rate = $13,500 ÷ 54,000 DLHs = $0.25 per DLH
    FOH rate = $105,300 ÷ 27,000 MHs = $3.90 per MH

Actual VOH	$11,980	Actual FOH	$103,540
Applied VOH (46,000 × $0.25)	(11,500)	Applied FOH (23,000 × $3.90)	(89,700)
Underapplied VOH	$ 480	Underapplied FOH	$ 13,840

Note that the large underapplication of fixed overhead was caused mainly by a difference between the number of machine hours used to set the rate (27,000) and the number of machine hours that were actually used (23,000): 4,000 × $3.90 = $15,600. The underapplication of fixed overhead was constrained by the fact that the company incurred only $103,540 of fixed overhead rather than the $105,300 the company expected to incur. The total underapplication is the combination of the negative machine hour effect and the positive total expenditure effect: $15,600 − ($105,300 − $103,540) = $13,840.

b.

	2007	2008
Net sales	$ 300,000	$ 330,000
Variable cost of goods sold	(60,000)	(66,000)
Product contribution margin	$ 240,000	$ 264,000
Variable operating expenses	(50,000)	(55,000)
Total contribution margin	$ 190,000	$ 209,000
Fixed costs		
Manufacturing	$ 100,000	$ 100,000
Operating	32,500	33,500
Total fixed costs	$(132,500)	$(133,500)
Income before tax	$ 57,500	$ 75,500

c. Reconciliation 2007

Absorption costing income before tax	$77,500
− Fixed manufacturing overhead in ending inventory ($4.00 × 5,000)	(20,000)
Variable costing income before tax	$57,500

Reconciliation 2008

Absorption costing income before tax	$67,500
+ Fixed manufacturing overhead released from beginning inventory ($4.00 × 2,000)	8,000
Variable costing income before tax	$75,500

Key Terms

absorption costing *(p. 80)*
applied overhead *(p. 68)*
contribution margin *(p. 82)*
dependent variable *(p. 74)*
direct costing *(p. 81)*
expected capacity *(p. 72)*
flexible budget *(p. 77)*
full costing *(p. 80)*
functional classification
   (p. 80)

high-low method *(p. 73)*
independent variable *(p. 74)*
least squares regression analysis
   (p. 74)
multiple regression *(p. 74)*
normal capacity *(p. 72)*
outlier *(p. 74)*
overapplied overhead
   (p. 70)
phantom profit *(p. 85)*

practical capacity *(p. 72)*
product contribution margin
   (p. 82)
regression line *(p. 75)*
simple regression *(p. 74)*
theoretical capacity *(p. 72)*
underapplied overhead
   (p. 70)
variable costing *(p. 80)*
volume variance *(p. 85)*

Questions

1. What is the difference between a variable and a mixed cost, considering that each changes in total with changes in activity levels?
2. The high-low method of analyzing mixed costs uses only two observation points: the high and the low points of activity. Are these always the best points for prediction purposes? Why or why not?
3. Discuss the reasons a company would use a predetermined overhead rate rather than apply actual overhead to products or services.
4. Why are departmental overhead rates more useful for managerial decision making than plantwide rates? What is the reason for using separate variable and fixed rates rather than total rates?
5. Why would regression analysis provide a more accurate cost formula for a mixed cost than the high-low method would?
6. How does absorption costing differ from variable costing in cost accumulation and income statement presentation?
7. What is meant by classifying costs (a) functionally and (b) behaviorally? Why would a company be concerned about functional and behavioral classifications?
8. Is variable or absorption costing generally required for external reporting? Why is this method required compared to the alternative?
9. Why does variable costing provide more useful information than absorption costing for making internal decisions?
10. What are the income relationships between absorption and variable costing when production differs from sales? What causes these relationships to occur?

Exercises

11. (Predetermined OH rates) Warlaski Corp. prepared the following 2007 abbreviated flexible budget for different levels of machine hours:

	10,000	11,000	12,000	13,000
Variable factory overhead	$ 40,000	$ 44,000	$ 48,000	$ 52,000
Fixed factory overhead	164,700	164,700	164,700	164,700

Each product requires 2 hours of machine time, and the company expects to produce 5,490 units in 2007. Production is expected to be evenly spread throughout the year.
   a. Calculate separate variable and fixed overhead rates using as the basis of application (1) units of product and (2) machine hours.
   b. Calculate the combined overhead rate using (1) units of product and (2) machine hours.

c. All actual overhead costs are equal to expected overhead costs in 2007, but Warlaski Corp. produced 5,600 units of product. If the separate rates based on units of product calculated in part (a) were used to apply overhead, what amounts of underapplied or overappled variable and fixed overhead exist at year-end 2007?

12. (OH application) Use the information in Exercise 11 and assume that Warlaski Corp. has decided to use units to apply overhead to production. In April 2007, the company produced 4,420 units and had $32,980 and $163,800, of variable and fixed overhead, respectively.

    a. What amount of variable factory overhead should be applied to production in April 2007?

    b. What amount of fixed factory overhead should be applied to production in April 2007?

    c. Calculate the under- or overapplied variable and fixed overhead for April 2007.

WebTUTOR Advantage

13. (Predetermined OH rate) Rachel Company has a monthly overhead cost formula of $42,900 + $6 per direct labor hour for 2007. The firm's 2007 expected annual capacity is 156,000 direct labor hours, to be incurred evenly each month. Making one unit of the company's product requires 3 direct labor hours.

    a. Determine the total overhead to be applied to each unit of product in 2007.

    b. Prepare journal entries to record the application of overhead to Work in Process Inventory and the incurrence of $128,550 of actual overhead in January 2007 when 12,780 direct labor hours were worked.

    c. Given the information in part (b), how many units should have been produced in January?

14. (Predetermined OH rates) Cairo Products applies overhead using a combined rate for fixed and variable overhead. The rate has been established at 175 percent of direct labor cost. During the first three months of the current year, actual costs were incurred as follows:

	Direct Labor Cost	Actual Overhead
January	$360,000	$640,000
February	330,000	570,400
March	340,000	600,000

    a. What amount of overhead was applied to production in each of the three months?

    b. What was the underapplied or overapplied overhead for each of the three months and for the first quarter?

15. (Underapplied or overapplied overhead) At the end of 2006, Westmeier Corporation's accounts showed a $66,000 credit balance in Manufacturing Overhead. In addition, the company had the following account balances:

Work in Process Inventory	$384,000
Finished Goods Inventory	96,000
Cost of Goods Sold	720,000

    a. Prepare the necessary journal entry to close the overhead account if the balance is considered immaterial.

    b. Prepare the necessary journal entry to close the overhead account if the balance is considered material.

    c. Which method do you believe is more appropriate for the company and why?

16. (Underapplied or overapplied overhead) At year-end 2006, Zwylia Co. has a $50,000 debit balance in its Manufacturing Overhead Control account. Relevant account balance information at year-end follows:

	Work in Process	Finished Goods	Cost of Goods Sold
Direct material	$ 40,000	$ 80,000	$120,000
Direct labor	20,000	40,000	50,000
Factory overhead	40,000	80,000	100,000
	$100,000	$200,000	$270,000

  a. What overhead rate was used during the year?

  b. Provide arguments to be used for deciding whether to prorate the balance in the overhead account at year-end.

  c. Prorate the overhead account balance based on the relative balances of the appropriate accounts.

  d. Prorate the overhead account balance based on the relative overhead components of the appropriate account balances.

  e. Identify some possible reasons that the company had a debit balance in the overhead account at year-end.

17. (Predetermined OH rates; capacity measures) Stir'em makes blenders and uses a normal cost system that applies overhead based on machine hours. The following 2007 budgeted data are available:

Variable factory overhead at 100,000 machine hours $435,000
Variable factory overhead at 150,000 machine hours   652,500
Fixed factory overhead at all levels between 10,000 and 180,000 machine hours   405,000

Practical capacity is 180,000 machine hours; expected capacity is two-thirds of practical.

  a. What is Stir'em's predetermined variable overhead rate?

  b. What is the predetermined fixed overhead rate using practical capacity?

  c. What is the predetermined fixed overhead rate using expected capacity?

  d. During 2007, the firm incurs 115,000 machine hours and $900,000 of overhead costs. How much variable overhead is applied? How much fixed overhead is applied using the rate found in part (b)? How much fixed overhead is applied using the rate found in part (c)? Calculate the total under- or overapplied overhead for 2007 using both fixed overhead rates.

18. (Product costing and pricing) Chaney Tool Company is bidding on a contract with the government of Manatuka. The cost-plus contract includes an add-on markup of 50 percent of production cost. Direct material and direct labor are expected to total $15 per unit. Variable overhead is estimated at $4 per unit. Total fixed overhead to produce the 50,000 units needed by the government is $1,400,000. By acquiring the machinery and supervisory support needed to produce the 50,000 units, Chaney Tool will obtain the actual capacity to produce 80,000 units.

  a. Should the price bid by Chaney Tool include a fixed overhead cost of $28 per unit or $17.50? How were these two amounts determined? Which of these two amounts would be more likely to cause Chaney Tool to obtain the contract? Why?

  b. Assume that Chaney Tool set a bid price of $54.75 per unit and obtained the contract. After producing the units, the firm submitted an invoice to the government of Manatuka for $3,525,000. Manatuka's minister of finance requests an explanation. Can you provide one?

c. Chaney Tool uses the excess capacity to produce an additional 30,000 units while making the units for Manatuka. It sold these units to another buyer. Is it ethical to present a $3,525,000 bill to Manatuka? Discuss.

d. Chaney Tool does not use the excess capacity while making the units for Manatuka. However, several months after it completed that contract, the company begins production of additional units. Was it ethical to present a $3,525,000 bill to Manatuka? Discuss.

e. Chaney Tool does not use the excess capacity because no other buyer exists for units of this type. Was it ethical to make a bid based on a fixed overhead rate per unit of $54.75? Discuss.

WebTUTOR Advantage

19. (High-low method) Information about Larson Inc.'s utility cost for the last six months of 2006 follows. The high-low method will be used to develop a cost formula to predict 2007 utility charges, and the number of machine hours has been found to be an appropriate cost driver. Data for the first half of 2006 are not being considered because the utility company imposed a significant rate change as of July 1, 2006.

Month	Machine Hours	Utility Cost
July	33,750	$6,500
August	34,000	6,100
September	33,150	5,070
October	32,000	5,980
November	31,250	5,750
December	31,000	5,860

a. What is the cost formula for utility expense?

b. What would be the budgeted utility cost for September 2007 if 33,175 machine hours are projected?

20. (High-low method) Historic Abodes Corp. builds replicas of residences of famous and infamous people. The company is highly automated, and the new accountant owner has decided to use machine hours as the basis for predicting maintenance costs. The following data are available from the company's most recent eight months of operations:

Machine Hours	Maintenance Costs
4,000	$735
7,000	600
3,500	840
6,000	550
3,000	980
9,000	440
8,000	510
5,500	600

a. Using the high-low method, determine the cost formula for maintenance costs with machine hours as the basis for estimation.

b. What aspect of the estimated equation is bothersome? Provide an explanation for this situation.

c. Within the relevant range, can the formula be reliably used to predict maintenance costs? Can the *a* and *b* values in the cost formula be interpreted as fixed and variable costs? Why or why not?

21. (Least squares) Huppernan Supply has gathered the following data on the number of shipments received and the cost of receiving reports for the first seven weeks of 2007.

Number of Shipments Received	Cost of Receiving Reports
100	$175
87	162
80	154
70	142
105	185
115	200
120	202

a. Using the least squares method, develop the equation for predicting weekly receiving report costs based on the number of shipments received.

b. What is the predicted amount of receiving report costs for a month (assume a month is exactly four weeks) in which 340 shipments are received?

22. (Least squares) Wynona Products has complied the following data to analyze utility costs:

Month	Machine Hours	Utility Cost
January	200	$150
February	325	220
March	400	240
April	410	245
May	525	310
June	680	395
July	820	420
August	900	450

Use the least squares method to develop a formula for budgeting utility cost.

23. (Flexible budget; variances; cost control) The Birmingham plant of Katz Corp. prepared the following flexible overhead budget for three levels of activity within the plant's relevant range.

	12,000 Units	16,000 Units	20,000 Units
Variable overhead	$48,000	$64,000	$ 80,000
Fixed overhead	32,000	32,000	32,000
Total overhead	$80,000	$96,000	$112,000

After discussion with the home office, the plant expected to produce 16,000 units of its single product during 2007. However, demand for the product was exceptionally strong, and actual production for 2007 was 17,600 units. Actual variable and fixed overhead costs incurred in producing the 17,600 units were $69,000 and $32,800, respectively.

The production manager was upset because the company planned to incur $96,000 of costs and actual costs were $101,800. Prepare a memo to the production manager regarding the following questions.

a. Should the $101,800 actual cost be compared to the $96,000 expected cost for control purposes? Explain the rationale for your answer.

b. Analyze the costs and explain where the company did well or poorly in controlling its costs.

24. (High-low method; flexible budget) Denver Company has gathered the following information on its utility costs for the past six months.

Machine Hours	Utility Cost
2,600	$ 940
3,400	1,075
2,500	900
3,600	1,132
3,800	1,160
3,000	990

a. Using the high-low method, determine the cost formula for utility costs.
b. Prepare a flexible budget with separate variable and fixed categories for utility costs at 2,000, 3,000, and 4,000 machine hours.

25. (Flexible budget) Cheryl's Pet Salon provides dog grooming services. Analysis of monthly costs revealed the following cost formulas when direct labor hours are used as the basis of cost determination:

Supplies: $y = \$0 + \$4.00X$
Production labor: $y = \$500 + \$7.00X$
Utilities: $y = \$350 + \$5.40X$
Rent: $y = \$450 + \$0.00X$
Advertising: $y = \$75 + \$0.00X$

a. Prepare a flexible budget at 250, 300, 350, and 400 direct labor hours.
b. Calculate a total cost per direct labor hour at each level of activity.
c. The company is normally open 350 direct labor hours per month. Each grooming job takes an average of 1.25 hours. The owner wants to earn 40 percent on her costs. What should be the average charge for each grooming, rounded to the nearest dollar?

26. (Plantwide versus department OH rates) Jameel Corp. has gathered the following information to develop predetermined overhead rates for 2007. The company produces a wide variety of products that run through two departments, Assembly (automated) and Finishing (labor intensive).

Budgeted total overhead: $300,200 in Assembly and $99,800 in Finishing
Budgeted total direct labor hours: 5,000 in Assembly and 20,000 in Finishing
Budgeted total machine hours: 38,000 in Assembly and 2,000 in Finishing

a. Compute a plantwide overhead rate using direct labor hours.
b. Compute a plantwide overhead rate using machine hours.
c. Compute departmental overhead rates using machine hours for Assembly and direct labor hours for Finishing.
d. Determine the amount of overhead that would be assigned to a product that required 5 machine hours in Assembly and 1 direct labor hour in Finishing using the answers developed in parts (a), (b), and (c).

27. (Ending inventory valuation; absorption vs. variable costing) Pena Royals Company produces baseball caps. In May 2006, the company manufactured 18,000 caps and sold 16,560 caps. The cost per unit for the 18,000 caps produced was as follows:

Direct material	$4.00
Direct labor	2.00
Variable overhead	1.00
Fixed overhead	1.50
Total	$8.50

There was no beginning inventory for May.
a. What is the value of ending inventory using absorption costing?
b. What is the value of ending inventory using variable costing?
c. Which accounting method, variable or absorption, would have produced the higher net income for May?

WebTUTOR Advantage

28. (Absorption vs. variable costing) The MAZZILLI Juicer Company uses variable costing. The following data relate to the company's first year of operation when it produced 50,000 units and sold 46,000 units.

Variable costs per unit	
Direct material	$50
Direct labor	30
Variable overhead	14
Variable selling costs	12
Fixed costs	
Selling and administrative	$750,000
Manufacturing	500,000

How much higher (or lower) would the company's first-year net income have been if absorption costing had been used rather than variable costing? Show computations.

29. (Production cost; absorption vs. variable costing) Torodova Ltd. began business in 2006, during which it produced 104,000 quarts of olive oil. In 2006 it sold 98,000 quarts. Costs incurred during the year were as follows:

Ingredients used	$224,000
Direct labor	104,000
Variable overhead	192,000
Fixed overhead	93,600
Variable selling expenses	40,000
Fixed selling and administrative expenses	112,000
Total actual costs	$765,600

a. What was the actual production cost per quart under variable costing? Under absorption costing?

b. What was variable cost of goods sold for 2006 under variable costing?

c. What was cost of goods sold for 2006 under absorption costing?

d. What was the value of ending inventory under variable costing? Under absorption costing?

e. How much fixed overhead was charged to expense in 2006 under variable costing? Under absorption costing?

30. (Net income; absorption vs. variable costing) Francona Company produces softball bats. In 2007, fixed overhead was applied to products at the rate of $8 per unit. Variable cost per unit remained constant throughout the year. In July 2007, income before tax using variable costing was $94,000. July's beginning and ending inventories were 10,000 and 5,200 units, respectively.

a. Calculate income before tax under absorption costing assuming no variances.

b. Assume instead that the company's July beginning and ending inventories were 5,000 and 6,000 units, respectively. Calculate income before tax under absorption costing.

31. (Convert variable to absorption) The April 2006 income statement for Kick'in Sportswear has just been received by Bobby Cox, vice president of marketing. The firm uses a variable costing system for internal reporting purposes.

KICK'IN SPORTSWEAR
Income Statement
For the Month Ended April 30, 2006

Sales		$7,200,000
Variable standard cost of goods sold		(3,600,000)
Product contribution margin		$3,600,000
Fixed expenses		
Manufacturing (budget and actual)	$2,250,000	
Selling and administrative	1,200,000	(3,450,000)
Income before tax		$ 150,000

The following notes were attached to the statements:
- Unit sales price for April averaged $72.
- Unit manufacturing costs for the month were:

Variable cost	$36
Fixed cost	15
Total cost	$51

- The predetermined unit rate for fixed manufacturing costs was based on normal monthly production of 150,000 units.
- April production was 7,500 units in excess of sales.
- April ending inventory consisted of 12,000 units.

a. The marketing vice president is not familiar with variable costing.

   1. Recast the April income statement on an absorption costing basis.

   2. Reconcile and explain the difference between the variable costing and the absorption costing income figures.

b. Explain the features of variable costing that should appeal to the marketing vice president.

(CMA adapted)

32. (Variable and absorption costing) Defeet Remedy manufactures athletes' foot powder. Data pertaining to the company's 2007 operations follow:

Production for the year	90,000 units
Sales for the year (sales price per unit, $3)	97,500 units
Beginning 2007 inventory	17,500 units

Costs to Produce 1 Unit	
Direct material	$1.80
Direct labor	1.00
Variable overhead	0.15
Fixed overhead	0.32

Selling and Administrative Costs	
Variable (per unit sold)	$0.28
Fixed (per year)	$75,000

Fixed manufacturing overhead is assigned to units of production based on a predetermined rate using an expected production capacity of 100,000 units per year.

a. What is budgeted annual fixed manufacturing overhead?

b. If budgeted fixed overhead equals actual fixed overhead, what is underapplied or overapplied overhead in 2007 under absorption costing? Under variable costing?

c. What is the product cost per unit under absorption costing? Under variable costing?

d. How much total expense is charged against revenues in 2007 under absorption costing? Under variable costing?

e. Is pre-tax income higher under absorption or variable costing? By what amount?

33. (Essay) Because your professor is scheduled to address a national professional meeting at the time your class ordinarily meets, the class has been divided into teams to discuss selected issues. Your team's assignment is to prepare a report arguing whether manufacturing fixed overhead should be justifiably included as a product cost. You are also expected to draw your own conclusion about this issue and provide the rationale for your conclusion in your report.

Problems

34. (Predetermined OH rates; flexible budget; capacity) Lightening Company budgeted the following factory overhead costs for the upcoming year to help calculate variable and fixed predetermined overhead rates.

Indirect material: $1.25 per unit produced
Indirect labor: $1.00 per unit produced
Factory utilities: $3,000 plus $0.02 per unit produced
Factory machine maintenance: $10,000 plus $0.17 per unit produced
Material handling charges: $8,000 plus $0.06 per unit produced
Machine depreciation: $0.03 per unit produced
Building rent: $25,000
Supervisors' salaries: $72,000
Factory insurance: $6,000

The company produces only one type of product that has a theoretical capacity of 100,000 units of production during the year. Practical capacity is 80 percent of theoretical, and normal capacity is 95 percent of practical. The company's expected production for the upcoming year is 72,000 units.

a. Prepare a flexible budget for Lightening Company using each level of capacity.

b. Calculate the predetermined variable and fixed overhead rates for each capacity measure (round to the nearest cent when necessary).

c. Lightening Company decides to apply overhead to products using expected capacity as the budgeted level of activity. The firm actually produces 70,000 units during the year. All actual costs are as budgeted.

    1. Prepare journal entries to record the incurrence of actual overhead costs and to apply overhead to production. Assume cash is paid for costs when appropriate.

    2. What is the amount of underapplied or overapplied fixed overhead at year-end?

d. Which measure of capacity would be of most benefit to management and why?

35. (Plant vs. departmental OH rates) Sutton Industries has two departments, Fabrication and Finishing. Three workers oversee the 25 machines in Fabrication. Finishing uses 35 crafters to hand polish output, which is then run through buffing machines. Sutton's Product CG9832-09 uses the following amounts of direct labor and machine time in each department:

	Fabrication	Finishing
Machine hours	8.00	0.15
Direct labor hours	0.02	2.00

Following are the budgeted overhead costs and volumes for each department for the upcoming year:

	Fabrication	Finishing
Budgeted overhead	$635,340	$324,000
Budgeted machine hours	72,000	9,300
Budgeted direct labor hours	4,800	48,000

a. What is the plantwide rate for overhead application based on machine hours for the upcoming year? How much overhead will be assigned to each unit of Product CG9832-09 using this rate?

b. Sutton's auditors inform management that departmental rates using machine hours in Fabrication and direct labor hours in Finishing would be more appropriate than a plantwide rate. What would the rates be for each department? How much overhead would have been assigned to each unit of Product CG9832-09 using departmental rates?

c. Discuss why departmental rates are more appropriate than plantwide rates for Sutton Industries.

36. (Plant vs. departmental OH rates) Thompson Manufacturing makes a wide variety of products, all of which must be processed in the Cutting and the Assembly Departments. For the year 2007, Thompson has budgeted total overhead of $969,020, of which $383,400 will be incurred in Cutting and the remainder will be incurred in Assembly. Budgeted direct labor and machine hours are as follows:

	Cutting	Assembly
Budgeted direct labor hours	27,000	3,000
Budgeted machine hours	2,100	65,800

Two products made by Thompson are the RW22SKI and the SD45ROW. The following cost and production time information on these items have been gathered:

	RW22SKI	SD45ROW
Direct material	$34.85	$19.57
Direct labor rate in Cutting	$14.00	$14.00
Direct labor rate in Assembly	$6.50	$6.50
Direct labor hours in Cutting	6.00	4.80
Direct labor hours in Assembly	0.03	0.05
Machine hours in Cutting	0.06	0.15
Machine hours in Assembly	5.90	9.30

a. What is the plantwide rate for overhead application based on (1) direct labor hours and (2) machine hours for the upcoming year? Round all computations to the nearest cent.
b. What are the departmental rates for overhead application in Cutting and Assembly using the most appropriate base in each department? Round all computations to the nearest cent.
c. What are the costs of products RW22SKI and the SD45ROW using (1) a plantwide rate based on direct labor hours, (2) a plantwide rate based on machine hours, and (3) departmental rates calculated in (b)?
d. A competitor manufactures a product that is extremely similar to RW22SKI and sells each unit of it for $270. Discuss how Thompson's management might be influenced by the impact of the different product costs calculated in part (c).

37. (Under/Overapplied OH; OH disposition) Keller Co. budgeted the following variable and fixed overhead costs for 2007:

Variable indirect labor	$100,000
Variable indirect materials	20,000
Variable utilities	80,000
Variable portion of other mixed costs	120,000
Fixed machinery depreciation	62,000
Fixed machinery lease payments	13,000
Fixed machinery insurance	16,000
Fixed salaries	75,000
Fixed utilities	12,000

The company has decided to allocate overhead to production using machine hours. For 2007, machine hours have been budgeted at 100,000.

a. Determine the variable and fixed overhead application rates for Keller Company. The company uses separate variable and fixed manufacturing overhead control accounts.
b. During 2007, Keller Co. used 103,000 machine hours during production and incurred a total of $273,600 of variable overhead costs and

$185,680 of fixed overhead costs. Prepare journal entries to record the incurrence of the actual overhead costs and the application of overhead to production.

c. What amounts of underapplied or overapplied overhead exist at year-end 2007 for Keller?

d. Keller management believes that the fixed overhead amount calculated in part (c) should be considered immaterial. Prepare the entry to close the Fixed Overhead Control account at the end of the year.

e. Keller management believes that the variable overhead amount calculated in part (c) should be considered material and should be prorated to the appropriate accounts. At year-end, Keller had the following balances in its inventory and Cost of Goods Sold accounts:

Raw Material Inventory	$ 25,000
Work in Process Inventory	234,000
Finished Goods Inventory	390,000
Cost of Goods Sold	936,000

Prepare the entry to close the Variable Overhead Control account at the end of the year.

38. (Analyzing mixed costs) Hendry Dairy determined that the total overhead rate for costing purposes is $13.40 per cow per day (referred to as an *animal day*). Of this, $12.60 is the variable portion. Overhead cost information for two levels of monthly activity within the relevant range follow:

	4,000 Animal Days	6,000 Animal Days
Indirect materials	$12,800	$19,200
Indirect labor	28,000	40,000
Maintenance	5,200	6,800
Utilities	4,000	6,000
All other	7,600	10,800

a. Determine the fixed and variable values for each of the preceding overhead items and determine the total overhead cost formula.

b. Assume that the total overhead rate is based on expected annual capacity. What is this level of activity for the company?

c. Determine expected overhead costs at the expected annual capacity.

d. If the company raises its expected capacity by 3,000 animal days above the present level, calculate a new total overhead rate for product costing.

39. (Flexible budgets; predetermined OH rates) Cool Dip Enterprises makes large fiberglass swimming pools and uses machine hours and direct labor hours to apply overhead in the Production and Installation departments, respectively. The monthly overhead cost formula in Production is $y = \$7,950 + \$4.05$ *MH*; in Installation, the overhead cost formula is $y = \$6,150 + \$14.25$ DLH. These formulas are valid for a relevant range of activity to 6,000 machine hours in Production and 9,000 direct labor hours in Installation.

Each pool is estimated to require 25 machine hours in Production and 60 hours of direct labor in Installation. Expected capacity for the year is 120 pools.

a. Prepare a flexible budget for Production at possible annual capacities of 2,500, 3,000, and 3,500 machine hours. Prepare a flexible budget for Installation at possible annual capacities of 6,000, 7,000, and 8,000 machine hours.

b. Prepare a budget for next month's variable, fixed, and total overhead costs for each department assuming that expected production is 8 pools.

c. Calculate the total predetermined overhead cost to be applied to each pool scheduled for production in the coming month if expected capacity is used to calculate the predetermined overhead rates.

40. (High-low; least squares regression) LaSalle Company manufactures insulated windows. The firm's repair and maintenance (R&M) cost is mixed and varies most directly with machine hours worked. The following data have been gathered from recent operations:

Month	MHs	R&M Cost
May	1,400	$ 9,000
June	1,900	10,719
July	2,000	10,900
August	2,500	13,000
September	2,200	11,578
October	2,700	13,154
November	1,700	9,525
December	2,300	11,670

a. Use the high-low method to estimate a cost formula for repairs and maintenance.
b. Use least squares regression to estimate a cost formula for repairs and maintenance.
c. Does the answer to part (a) or (b) provide the better estimate of the relationship between repairs and maintenance costs and machine hours? Why?

41. (Least squares) Gulf Coast Breezes provides charter cruises into the Gulf of Mexico from a base in south Texas. Emily Lantz, the owner, wants to understand how her labor costs change per month. She recognizes that the cost is neither strictly fixed nor strictly variable. Thus, she has gathered the following information and has identified two potential predictive bases, number of charters and gross receipts:

Month	Labor Costs	Number of Charters	Gross Receipts
January	$16,000	10	$ 12,000
February	18,400	14	18,000
March	24,000	22	26,000
April	28,400	28	36,000
May	37,000	40	60,000
June	56,000	62	82,000
July	68,000	100	120,000
August	60,000	90	100,000
September	48,000	80	96,000

Using the least squares method, develop a labor cost formula using
a. number of charters
b. gross receipts

42. (Convert variable to absorption) Salado Corp. produces small outdoor sheds. The company began operations in 2006, produced 1,750 sheds and sold 1,500. A variable costing income statement for 2006 follows. During the year, variable production costs per unit were $800 for direct material, $300 for direct labor, and $200 for overhead.

SALADO CORP.
Income Statement (Variable Costing)
For the Year Ended December 31, 2006

Sales		$3,750,000
Variable cost of goods sold		
Beginning inventory	$ 0	
Cost of goods manufactured	2,275,000	
Cost of goods available for sale	$2,275,000	
Less ending inventory	(325,000)	(1,950,000)
Product contribution margin		$1,800,000
Less variable selling and administrative expenses		(270,000)
Total contribution margin		$1,530,000
Less fixed expenses		
Fixed factory overhead	$1,505,000	
Fixed selling and administrative expenses	190,000	(1,695,000)
Income before taxes		$ (165,000)

The company president is upset about the net loss because he wanted to borrow funds to expand capacity.

a. Prepare an absorption costing pre-tax income statement.

b. Explain the source of the difference between the net income and the net loss figures under the two costing systems.

c. Would it be appropriate to present an absorption costing income statement to the local banker considering the company president's knowledge of the net loss determined under variable costing? Explain.

d. Assume that during the second year of operations, Salado produced 1,750 sheds, sold 1,850, and experienced the same total fixed costs as in 2006. For the second year:

1. Prepare a variable costing pre-tax income statement.

2. Prepare an absorption costing pre-tax income statement.

3. Explain the difference between the incomes for the second year under the two systems.

43. (Income statements for two years, both methods) D-Tect manufactures radar detectors. Each unit contains product cost of $20 for direct material, $60 for direct labor, and $20 for variable overhead. The company's annual fixed cost is $750,000; it uses expected capacity of 25,000 units produced as the basis for applying fixed overhead to products. A commission of 10 percent of selling price is paid on each unit sold. Annual fixed selling and administrative expenses are $180,000. The following additional information is available:

	2006	2007
Selling price per unit	$200	$200
Number of units sold	20,000	24,000
Number of units produced	25,000	22,000
Beginning inventory (units)	15,000	20,000
Ending inventory (units)	20,000	?

Prepare pre-tax income statements under absorption and variable costing for the years ended 2006 and 2007, with any volume variance being charged to Cost of Goods Sold. Reconcile the differences in income for the two methods.

44. (Absorption costing versus variable costing) Riveting Manufacturing builds light aircraft engines and, since opening in 2005, has quickly gained a reputation for reliable and quality products. Factory overhead is applied to production using direct labor hours and any underapplied or overapplied overhead is closed at year-end to Cost of Goods Sold. The company's inventory balances for the last three years and income statements for the last two years follow.

Inventory Balances	12/31/05	12/31/06	12/31/07
Direct material	$22,000	$30,000	$10,000
Work in process			
Costs	$40,000	$48,000	$64,000
Direct labor hours	1,335	1,600	2,100
Finished goods			
Costs	$25,000	$18,000	$14,000
Direct labor hours	1,450	1,050	820

	COMPARATIVE INCOME STATEMENTS			
		2006		2007
Sales		$840,000		$1,015,000
Cost of goods sold				
Finished goods, 1/1	$ 25,000		$ 18,000	
Cost of goods manufactured	548,000		657,600	
Total available	$573,000		$675,600	
Finished goods, 12/31	(18,000)		(14,000)	
CGS before overhead adjustment	$555,000		$661,600	
Underapplied factory overhead	36,000		14,400	
Cost of goods sold		(591,000)		(676,000)
Gross margin		$249,000		$ 339,000
Selling expenses	$ 82,000		$ 95,000	
Administrative expenses	70,000		75,000	
Total operating expenses		(152,000)		(170,000)
Operating income		$ 97,000		$ 169,000

The same predetermined overhead rate was used in applying overhead to production orders in both 2006 and 2007. The rate was based on the following estimates:

Fixed factory overhead	$ 25,000
Variable factory overhead	$155,000
Direct labor cost	$150,000
Direct labor hours	25,000

In 2006 and 2007, actual direct labor hours expended were 20,000 and 23,000, respectively. The cost of raw material put into production was $292,000 in 2006 and $370,000 in 2007. Actual fixed overhead was $37,400 for 2006 and $42,300 for 2007, and the planned direct labor rate was equal to the actual direct labor rate.

For both years, all of the reported administrative costs were fixed. The variable portion of the reported selling expenses results from a commission of 5 percent of sales revenue.

a. For the year ended December 31, 2007, prepare a revised income statement using the variable costing method.

b. Prepare a numerical reconciliation of the difference in operating income between the 2006 absorption and variable costing statements.

c. Describe both the advantages and disadvantages of using variable costing.

(CMA adapted)

45. (Comprehensive) Royals Fashions Company produces and sells cotton jerseys. The firm uses variable costing for internal purposes and absorption costing for external purposes. At year-end, financial information must be converted from variable costing to absorption costing to satisfy external requirements.

At the end of 2006, management anticipated that 2007 sales would be 20 percent above 2006 levels. Thus, production for 2007 was increased by 20 percent to meet the expected demand. However, economic conditions in 2007 kept sales at the 2006 unit level of 40,000. The following data pertain to 2006 and 2007:

	2006	2007
Selling price per unit	$20	$20
Sales (units)	40,000	40,000
Beginning inventory (units)	4,000	4,000
Production (units)	40,000	48,000
Ending inventory (units)	4,000	?

Per-unit production costs (budgeted and actual) for 2006 and 2007 were:

Material	$2.25
Labor	3.75
Overhead	1.50
Total	$7.50

Annual fixed costs for 2006 and 2007 (budgeted and actual) were

Production	$117,000
Selling and administrative	125,000
Total	$242,000

The overhead rate under absorption costing is based on an annual capacity of 60,000 units. Any volume variance is assigned to Cost of Goods Sold. Taxes are to be ignored.

a. Present the income statement based on variable costing for 2007.

b. Present the income statement based on absorption costing for 2007.

c. Explain the difference, if any, in the income figures. Assuming that there is no work in process inventory, provide the entry necessary to adjust the book income amount to the financial statement income amount if an adjustment is necessary.

d. The company finds it worthwhile to develop its internal financial data on a variable costing basis. What advantages and disadvantages are attributed to variable costing for internal purposes?

e. Many accountants believe that variable costing is appropriate for external reporting; many others oppose its use for external reporting. List the arguments for and against the use of variable costing in external reporting.

(CMA adapted)

4

Job Order Costing

Objectives

AFTER COMPLETING THIS CHAPTER, YOU SHOULD BE ABLE TO ANSWER THE FOLLOWING QUESTIONS:

LO.1 HOW DO JOB ORDER AND PROCESS COSTING SYSTEMS AS WELL AS THEIR RELATED VALUATION METHODS DIFFER?

LO.2 WHAT CONSTITUTES A "JOB" FROM AN ACCOUNTING STANDPOINT?

LO.3 WHAT PURPOSES ARE SERVED BY THE PRIMARY DOCUMENTS USED IN A JOB ORDER COSTING SYSTEM?

LO.4 WHAT JOURNAL ENTRIES ARE USED TO ACCUMULATE COSTS IN A JOB ORDER COSTING SYSTEM?

LO.5 HOW DO TECHNOLOGICAL CHANGES IMPACT THE GATHERING AND USE OF INFORMATION IN JOB ORDER COSTING SYSTEMS?

LO.6 HOW ARE STANDARD COSTS USED IN A JOB ORDER COSTING SYSTEM?

LO.7 HOW DOES INFORMATION FROM A JOB ORDER COSTING SYSTEM SUPPORT MANAGEMENT DECISION MAKING?

LO.8 HOW ARE LOSSES TREATED IN A JOB ORDER COSTING SYSTEM?

Shoes. People buy them, wear them, and never think about them unless the shoes hurt their feet. But if you were wearing shoes made by "Shoe," you'd certainly know it! Mr. Calvin Dayes is not merely a cobbler; he is a craftsman from the old school. Originally from Jamaica, Dayes arrived in New Orleans around 1950 with less than $50 in his pocket. Since that time, he has come to call the city his own and has integrated the city's Mardi Gras tradition into his work life. Dayes makes boots for numerous monarchs and officers of Carnival parade organizations, known as *krewes*—and these "royalty" members now no longer groan at the prospect of standing on floats and throwing beads for hours.

Calvin Dayes, a night-owl by choice, works 12-hour shifts starting in the mid-to-late afternoon. His process has been honed by years of experience. First, he consults with his clients as to a basic shoe design; this process helps him determine the softness of the leather with which he will work. Dayes then prepares a working pattern, carefully sketching the client's feet onto a paper bag and taking length and width measurements, not forgetting to detail the placement and height of the client's arch. His garage is his manufacturing plant, which contains a variety of shoemaking machinery. Shoes and boots are formed on a "last," or wooden former in the shape of a foot. The shoes and boots are sewed and completed in his second manufacturing area—an old easy chair in his house with a board on his knees for a workspace. Soles and heels are added. Then the client comes in for a try-on, and the compliments spill forth. Clients often remark, "They're so soft and comfortable; they're like butter."

Calvin Dayes learned his craft from his father and made his first pair of shoes before he was seven years old. He is creative and imaginative, an impish man with a waxed Salvador Dali-like mustache. Dayes has the highest standards for his work, but unfortunately, many of his trade secrets may die with him because he has yet to find anyone to figuratively fill his own shoes!

Source: Adapted from John Pope's "Cobbler Crafts Boots Fit for Carnival Kings," (New Orleans) *Times-Picayune*, February 3, 2004, pp. B1, B3.

cost-plus contract

Customer manufacturers typically price their goods using two methods. A **cost-plus contract** may be used that allows producers, such as Calvin Dayes, to cover all direct costs and some indirect costs and to generate an acceptable profit margin. In other cases, producers may use a competitive bidding technique. In such instances, the company must accurately estimate the costs of making the unique products associated with each contract; otherwise, the company can incur significant losses when actual costs exceed those that were estimated during the bidding process.

Use of cost-plus contracts or competitive bidding is complicated by the nature of custom manufacturing, in which each job may be uniquely different from the next. In such circumstances, pricing and cost control cannot be based on an accounting system that aggregates costs across contracts. Thus, job order costing is used to accumulate the costs of each job (contract) separately from all other jobs.

A primary role for cost accounting is to determine the cost of an organization's products or services. Just as various methods (first-in, first-out; last-in, first-out; average; specific identification) exist to determine inventory valuation and cost of goods sold for a retailer, different methods are available to value inventory and calculate product cost in a manufacturing or service environment. The method chosen depends on the good or service produced and the company's conversion processes. A cost flow assumption is required for processes in which costs cannot be identified with and attached to specific units of production.

As the first in a sequence of product costing chapters, this chapter distinguishes between two primary costing systems (job order and process) and then discusses three methods of valuation that can be used within these systems (actual, normal, and standard). The chapter then focuses specifically on a job order costing system, such as that used by Calvin Dayes.

METHODS OF PRODUCT COSTING

Before product cost can be computed, a determination must be made about the (1) cost accumulation system and (2) valuation method to be used. The product

LO.1
HOW DO JOB ORDER AND PROCESS COSTING SYSTEMS AS WELL AS THEIR RELATED VALUATION METHODS DIFFER?

costing system defines the cost object and method of assigning costs to production. The valuation method specifies how product costs will be measured.

Companies must have both a cost system and a valuation method; six possible combinations exist as shown in Exhibit 4–1.[1]

Costing Systems

job order costing system

Job order and process costing are the two primary cost systems. A **job order costing system** is used by companies that make relatively small quantities or distinct batches of identifiable, tailor-made products that conform to specifications designated by the purchaser. Services in general are typically user specific, so such businesses commonly use job order costing systems. Thus, job order costing is appropriate for a cobbler making custom shoes and boots, a publishing company producing educational textbooks, an accountant preparing tax returns, an architectural firm designing commercial buildings, and a research firm performing product development studies. In these various settings, the word "job" is synonymous with client, engagement, project, or contract.

Why are different cost systems necessary?

process costing systems

In contrast, **process costing systems** (covered in Chapter 6) are used by companies that make large quantities of homogeneous goods such as breakfast cereal, candy bars, detergent, gasoline, and bricks. Given the mass manufacturing process, one unit of output cannot be readily identified with specific input costs within a given period—making the use of either a weighted average or FIFO cost flow assumption necessary. Cost flow assumptions provide a way for accountants to assign costs to products without regard for the actual physical flow of units.

EXHIBIT 4–1
COSTING SYSTEMS AND INVENTORY VALUATION

COST ACCUMULATION SYSTEM	METHOD OF VALUATION		
	Actual	**Normal**	**Standard**
JOB ORDER	Actual Direct Material Actual Direct Labor Actual Overhead (assigned to job after end of period)	Actual Direct Material Actual Direct Labor Overhead applied using predetermined rates at completion of job or end of period (predetermined rates times actual input)	Standard Direct Material Standard Direct Labor Overhead applied using predetermined rates when goods are completed or at end of period (predetermined rates times standard input)
PROCESS	Actual Direct Material Actual Direct Labor Actual Overhead (assigned to job after end of period using FIFO or weighted average cost flow)	Actual Direct Material Actual Direct Labor Overhead applied using predetermined rates (using FIFO or weighted average cost flow)	Standard Direct Material Standard Direct Labor Standard Overhead using predetermined rates (will always be FIFO cost flow)

[1] A third and fourth dimension (cost accumulation and cost presentation) are also necessary in this model. These dimensions relate to the use of absorption or variable costing and are covered in Chapter 3.

Valuation Methods

As indicated in Exhibit 4–1, the three valuation methods are actual, normal, and standard costing. Actual cost systems use the actual costs of direct material, direct labor, and overhead to determine work in process inventory cost. Service businesses that have few customers and/or low volume may use an actual cost system. However, because of the reasons discussed in Chapter 3, many companies prefer to use a normal cost system that combines actual direct material and direct labor costs with predetermined overhead (OH) rates. If the predetermined OH rate is substantially equivalent to what the actual OH rate would have been for an annual period, its use provides acceptable and useful costs.

standard cost system

Companies using either job order or process costing may employ standards (or predetermined benchmarks) for costs to be incurred and/or quantities to be used. In a **standard cost system**, unit norms or standards are developed for direct material and direct labor quantities and/or costs. Overhead is applied to production using a predetermined rate that is considered the standard. These standards can then be used to plan for future activities and cost incurrence and to value inventories. Both actual and standard costs are recorded in the accounting records to provide an essential element of cost control—having norms against which actual operating costs can be compared. A standard cost system allows companies to quickly recognize deviations or variances from expected production costs and to correct problems resulting from excess usage and/or costs. Actual costing systems do not provide this benefit, and normal costing systems cannot provide it in relation to material and labor.

Because the use of predetermined overhead rates is more common than the use of actual overhead costs, this chapter addresses a job order, normal cost system and describes several job order, standard cost combinations.[2]

JOB ORDER COSTING SYSTEM

LO.2
WHAT CONSTITUTES A "JOB" FROM AN ACCOUNTING STANDPOINT?

job

Product costing is concerned with (1) cost identification, (2) cost measurement, and (3) product cost assignment. In a job order costing system, costs are accumulated individually on a per-job basis. A **job** is a single unit or group of units that is identifiable as being produced to distinct customer specifications.[3] Each job is treated as a unique cost entity or cost object. Costs of different jobs are maintained in separate subsidiary ledger accounts and are not added together in the ledger.

The logic of separating costs for individual jobs is illustrated by an example for Carnival Krewe Shoes. During February, the company produced three pairs of boots; each pair required a different quantity and type of material, number of labor hours, and conversion operations. Exhibit 4–2 provides the Carnival Krewe Shoes' Work in Process Inventory control and subsidiary ledger accounts at the end of February. Because each job is distinctive, costs of the products cannot logically be averaged—a unique cost must be determined for each job.

Isn't it possible to compute an average cost for every job?

Actual direct material and actual direct labor costs are combined with an overhead cost that is computed as a predetermined overhead rate multiplied by some actual cost driver (such as cost or quantity of materials used or number of direct labor hours required). Normal cost valuation is used

---

[2] Although actual overhead may be assigned to jobs, such an approach would be less customary because total overhead would not be known until the period was over, causing an unwarranted delay in overhead assignment. Activity-based costing can increase the validity of tracing overhead costs to specific products or jobs.
[3] To eliminate the need for repetition, *units* should be read to mean either products or services because job order costing is applicable to both manufacturing and service companies. For the same reason, *produced* can mean *manufactured* or *performed*.

EXHIBIT 4–2
SEPARATE SUBSIDIARY LEDGER ACCOUNTS FOR JOBS

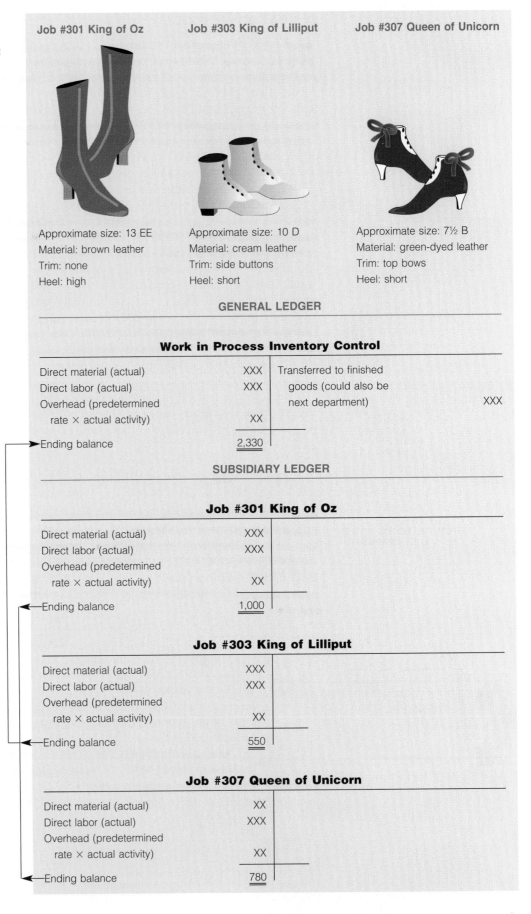

Job #301 King of Oz

Approximate size: 13 EE
Material: brown leather
Trim: none
Heel: high

Job #303 King of Lilliput

Approximate size: 10 D
Material: cream leather
Trim: side buttons
Heel: short

Job #307 Queen of Unicorn

Approximate size: 7½ B
Material: green-dyed leather
Trim: top bows
Heel: short

GENERAL LEDGER

Work in Process Inventory Control

Direct material (actual)	XXX	Transferred to finished	
Direct labor (actual)	XXX	goods (could also be	
Overhead (predetermined		next department)	XXX
rate × actual activity)	XX		
Ending balance	2,330		

SUBSIDIARY LEDGER

Job #301 King of Oz

Direct material (actual)	XXX
Direct labor (actual)	XXX
Overhead (predetermined	
rate × actual activity)	XX
Ending balance	1,000

Job #303 King of Lilliput

Direct material (actual)	XXX
Direct labor (actual)	XXX
Overhead (predetermined	
rate × actual activity)	XX
Ending balance	550

Job #307 Queen of Unicorn

Direct material (actual)	XX
Direct labor (actual)	XXX
Overhead (predetermined	
rate × actual activity)	XX
Ending balance	780

because, although actual direct material and direct labor costs are fairly easy to identify and associate with a particular job, overhead costs are usually not traceable to specific jobs and must be allocated to production. For example, Carnival Krewe Shoes' February utility costs are related to all jobs worked on during that month. Accurately determining which jobs created the need for a given amount of water, heat, or electricity would be impossible.

The output of any job can be a single unit or multiple similar or dissimilar units. If multiple outputs are produced, a per-unit cost can be computed only if the units are similar or if costs are accumulated for each separate unit (such as through an identification number). For example, **Aerosoles** produces many different styles of women's shoes. The company could determine the average cost per pair of "Ball Park," "Park Way," or "Lady Bug" shoe by accumulating the total costs per batch of homogeneous products in different production runs and treating each production run as a separate job. In such cases, an average production cost can be determined for each pair of shoes within each batch because the company considers the units, regardless of shoe size, within the batch as indistinguishable. If, however, the output consists of dissimilar units for which individual cost information is not gathered, no cost per unit can be determined although it is still possible to know the total job cost.

JOB ORDER COSTING: DETAILS AND DOCUMENTS

LO.3
WHAT PURPOSES ARE SERVED BY THE PRIMARY DOCUMENTS USED IN A JOB ORDER COSTING SYSTEM?

A job can be categorized by the stage of its production cycle. There are three stages of production: (1) contracted for but not yet started, (2) in process, and (3) completed.[4]

Because a company using job order costing makes products to user specifications, jobs occasionally require unique raw material. Thus, some raw material may not be acquired until a job is under contract and it is known that production will occur. The raw material acquired, although often separately distinguishable and related to specific jobs, is accounted for in a single general ledger control account (Raw Material Inventory) with subsidiary ledger backup. The material may, however, be designated in the storeroom and possibly in the subsidiary records as being "held for use in Job #303." Such designations should keep the material from being used on a job other than the one for which it was acquired.

Material Requisitions

LO.4
WHAT JOURNAL ENTRIES ARE USED TO ACCUMULATE COSTS IN A JOB ORDER COSTING SYSTEM?

material requisition form

When material is needed to begin a job, a **material requisition form** (shown in Exhibit 4–3) is prepared so the material can be released from the warehouse and sent to the production area. This source document indicates the types and quantities of material to be placed into production or used to perform a service job. Such documents are usually prenumbered and come in multiple-copy sets so that completed copies can be maintained in the warehouse, in the production department, and with each job. Completed material requisition forms verify material flow from the warehouse to the requisitioning department and allow responsibility for material cost to be traced to users. Although hard copy material requisition forms may still be used, it is increasingly common for this document to exist only electronically.

---

[4] In concept, there could be four categories. The third and fourth categories would distinguish between products completed but not sold and products completed and sold. However, the usual case is that firms using a job order costing system produce only products for which there is a current demand. Consequently, there is usually no inventory of finished products that await sale.

EXHIBIT 4–3
MATERIAL REQUISITION FORM

							No. 341
Date _____				Department _____			
Job Number _____				Issued by _____			
Authorized by _____				Inspected by _____			
Received by _____							

Item No.	Part No.	Description	Unit of Measure	Quantity Required	Quantity Issued	Unit Cost	Total Cost

The Raw Material Inventory account may contain the costs of both direct and indirect materials. When material is issued, its cost is released from Raw Material Inventory. If the material is considered direct to a job, the cost is sent to Work in Process Inventory; if the material is indirect, the cost is assigned to Manufacturing Overhead. Thus, the journal entry is as follows:

Work in Process Inventory (for direct material)	XXX	
Manufacturing Overhead (for indirect material)	XXX	
Raw Material Inventory		XXX
To issue direct and indirect material to production.		

When the first direct material associated with a job is issued to production, that job moves to the second stage of its production cycle—work in process. When a job enters this stage, cost accumulation must begin using the primary accounting document in a job order system—the job order cost sheet (or job cost record).

Job Order Cost Sheet

job order cost sheet

Why are job order cost sheets necessary?

The source document that provides virtually all financial information about a particular job is the **job order cost sheet**. The set of job order cost sheets for all incomplete jobs composes the Work in Process Inventory subsidiary ledger. Total costs contained on the job order cost sheets for all incomplete jobs should reconcile to the Work in Process Inventory control account balance in the general ledger (as shown in Exhibit 4–2).

The top portion of a job order cost sheet includes a job number, a description of the task, customer identification, various scheduling information, delivery instructions, and contract price. The remainder of the form details actual costs for material, labor, and applied overhead.

The form also might include budgeted cost information, especially if such information is used to estimate the job's selling price or support a bid price. In bid pricing, budgeted and actual costs should be compared at the end of a job to determine any deviations from estimates. Like the material requisition form, the job cost sheet exists only electronically in many companies today.

Exhibit 4–4 illustrates a job order cost sheet for Carnival Krewe Shoes. This company comprises a group of cordwainers who practice the traditional skills of

EXHIBIT 4–4
CARNIVAL KREWE SHOES' JOB ORDER COST SHEET

Job Number _____ 315 _____

Customer Name and Address:

Krewe of Desdemona
3801 N. Pine Ave.
New Orleans, LA

Contract Agreement Date: *6/01/06*
Scheduled Starting Date: *7/01/06*
Agreed Completion Date: *1/24/07*
Actual Completion Date:
Delivery Instructions: *Will be picked up by Krewe members*

Description of Job:

50 pairs of leather boots made to fit
per specifications in contract
dated 6/01/06

Contract Price *$46,000*

CUTTING & FORMING

DIRECT MATERIAL			DIRECT LABOR			OVERHEAD BASED ON					
						# OF LABOR HOURS			# OF MACHINE HOURS		
(EST. $5,000)			(EST. $10,200)			(EST. $3,000)			(EST. $200)		
Date	Source	Amount	Date	Source	Amount	Date	Source	Amount	Date	Source	Amount

ASSEMBLY
(SAME FORMAT AS ABOVE BUT WITH DIFFERENT OH RATES)

FINISHING
(SAME FORMAT AS ABOVE BUT WITH DIFFERENT OH RATES)

SUMMARY

	CUTTING & FORMING		ASSEMBLY		FINISHING	
	Actual	Budget	Actual	Budget	Actual	Budget
Direct material		$ 5,000		$ 0		$ 50
Direct labor		10,200		1,800		400
Overhead (labor)		3,000				
Overhead (machine)		200		2,000		850
Totals		$18,400		$3,800		$1,300

		Actual	Budget
Final Costs:	Cutting & Forming		$18,400
	Assembly		3,800
	Finishing		1,300
	Totals		$23,500

shoemaking for individual customers.[5] The company has contracted to produce 50 pairs of shoes for the Krewe of Desdemona. Although the shoes will be of different sizes, the company has agreed to make them for a lump-sum price. All of Carnival Krewe Shoes' job order cost sheets include a section for budgeted data so that budget-to-actual comparisons can be made for planning and control purposes. Direct material and direct labor costs are assigned and posted to jobs as work on the job is performed. Direct material information is gathered from the material

[5] The distinction between a cordwainer and a cobbler is that the former works only with new leather, whereas a cobbler commonly works with old leather.

requisition forms, and direct labor information is found on employee time sheets or employee labor tickets. (Employee time sheets are discussed in the next section.)

Overhead is applied to production at Carnival Krewe Shoes based on departmental rates. Each department may have more than one rate. For example, in the Cutting & Forming Department, the overhead rates for 2005–2006 are as follows:

Labor-related costs: $3 per direct labor hour
Machine-related costs: $4 per machine hour

Employee Time Sheets

employee time sheet

An **employee time sheet** indicates the jobs on which each employee worked and the direct labor time consumed. Exhibit 4–5 provides an illustration of a time sheet that would be completed manually by employees; such time sheets are most reliable if the employees fill them in as the day progresses. Work arriving at an employee station is accompanied by a tag or bar code specifying its job order number. The time work is started and stopped are noted on the time sheet.[6] These time sheets should be collected and reviewed by supervisors to ensure that the information is accurate.

Large businesses often use electronic time-keeping software rather than manual time sheets. Employees simply swipe their employee ID cards and job cards through an electronic scanner when they switch from one job to another. This software allows labor costs to be accumulated by job and department. In highly automated factories, employee time sheets may not be used because of the low proportion of direct labor cost to total cost. However, machine time can be tracked through the use of machine clocks or counters in the same way as human labor is tracked. As jobs are transferred from one machine to another, the clock or counter can be reset to mark the start and stop times. Machine times can then be equated to employee-operator time. Another convenient way to track employee time is through bar codes that can be scanned as products pass through individual workstations. There are also numerous time-and-attendance software tools.

Transferring employee time sheet (or alternative source document) information to the job order cost sheet requires knowledge of employee labor rates. Wage rates are found in employee personnel files. Time spent on the job is multiplied by the employee's wage rate, and the amounts are summed to find total direct labor cost for the period. The summation is recorded on the job order cost sheet. Time sheet information is also used for payroll preparation; the journal entry to record the labor cost is

Work in Process Inventory (for direct labor)	XXX	
Manufacturing Overhead (for indirect labor)	XXX	
Salaries and Wages Payable		XXX
To record direct and indirect labor wages.		

After these uses, time sheets are filed and retained so they can be referenced if necessary for any future information needs. If total actual labor costs for the job differ significantly from the original estimate, the manager responsible for labor cost control may be asked to explain the discrepancy. In addition, if a job is to be billed on a cost-plus basis, the number of hours worked may be audited by the buyer. This situation is quite common and especially important when dealing with government contracts. Hours not worked directly on the contracted job cannot be arbitrarily or incorrectly charged to the cost-plus job without the potential for detection. Last, time sheets provide information on overtime hours. Under the Fair

---

[6] Alternatives to daily time sheets are job time tickets that supervisors give to employees as they are assigned new jobs and supervisors' records of which employees worked on what jobs for what period of time. The latter alternative is extremely difficult if a supervisor is overseeing a large number of employees or if employees are dispersed through a large section of the plant.

EXHIBIT 4–5
EMPLOYEE TIME SHEET

For Week Ending _____

Department _____

Employee Name _____

Employee ID No. _____

Type of Work		Job Number	Start Time	Stop Time	Day (circle)	Total Hours
Code	Description					
					M T W Th F S	
					M T W Th F S	
					M T W Th F S	
					M T W Th F S	
					M T W Th F S	
					M T W Th F S	

_____   _____
Employee Signature   Supervisor's Signature (for overtime)

Labor Standards Act, overtime must generally be paid at a time-and-a-half rate to all nonmanagement employees when they work more than 40 hours in a week.

Overhead

Overhead costs can be substantial in manufacturing and service organizations. Actual overhead incurred during production is included in the Manufacturing Overhead control account. If actual overhead is applied to jobs, the cost accountant will wait until the end of the period and divide the actual overhead incurred in each designated cost pool by a related measure of activity or cost driver. Actual overhead would be applied to jobs by multiplying the actual overhead rate by the actual measure of activity associated with each job.

More commonly, normal costing is used, and overhead is applied to jobs with one or more annualized predetermined overhead application rates. Overhead is assigned to jobs by multiplying the predetermined rate by the actual measure of the activity base that was incurred for each job during the period. If a job is completed within a period, overhead is applied at completion of production so that a proper product cost can be transferred to Finished Goods Inventory. If, however, a job is not complete at the end of a period, overhead must be applied at that time so that Work in Process Inventory on the period-end balance sheet contains costs for all three product elements (direct material, direct labor, and overhead). The journal entry to apply overhead to WIP follows.

Work in Process Inventory XXX
    Manufacturing Overhead XXX
To apply overhead to WIP.

Completion of Production

When a job is completed, its total cost is debited to Finished Goods Inventory and removed from (credited to) Work in Process Inventory. Job order cost sheets for completed jobs are removed from the WIP subsidiary ledger and become the subsidiary ledger for the Finished Goods Inventory control account. When a job is sold, its cost is transferred from Finished Goods Inventory to Cost of Goods Sold.

Finished Goods Inventory	XXX	
Work in Process Inventory		XXX
To transfer completed goods to FG inventory.		
Cost of Goods Sold	XXX	
Finished Goods Inventory		XXX
To transfer goods sold from FG inventory to cost of goods sold.		

This cost transfer presumes the use of a perpetual inventory system, which is common in a job order costing environment because goods are generally easily identified and tracked.

Job order cost sheets for completed jobs are kept in a company's permanent files. A completed job order cost sheet provides management with an historical summary about total costs and, if appropriate, the cost per finished unit for a given job. The cost per unit may be helpful for planning and control purposes as well as for bidding on future contracts. If a job was exceptionally profitable, management might decide to pursue additional similar jobs. If a job was unprofitable, the job order cost sheet may indicate areas in which cost control was lax. Such areas are more readily identifiable if the job order cost sheet presents the original, budgeted cost information.

Unlike retailers and wholesalers, most businesses that use job order costing have little finished goods inventory. Production occurs only when a specific customer contracts for a particular good or service. Upon completion, the product or service cost may flow immediately to Cost of Goods Sold.

JOB ORDER COSTING AND TECHNOLOGY

LO.5
HOW DO TECHNOLOGICAL CHANGES IMPACT THE GATHERING AND USE OF INFORMATION IN JOB ORDER COSTING SYSTEMS?

The trend in job order costing is to automate data collection and data entry functions supporting the accounting system. Automating recordkeeping functions relieves production employees of that task, and electronically stored data can be accessed to serve many purposes. For example, data from a completed job can be used as input for projecting the costs of a future job on which a bid is to be made, the client's purchasing habits, or profit for next year. However, regardless of whether the data entry process is automated, virtually all product costing software, even very inexpensive off-the-shelf programs, contains a job costing module.

Has technology affected job order costing systems?

intranet

Many companies have created intranets to manage information, especially that pertaining to jobs produced. An **intranet** is a restricted network for sharing information and delivering data from corporate databases to local-area network (LAN) desktops. Exhibit 4–6 indicates some types of information that can be accessed on an intranet.

As shown in Exhibit 4–6, much information relevant to managing the production of a particular job is available on-line to managers. Data related to contract information and technical specifications, cost budgets, actual costs incurred, and stage of production measurements are instantly available to managers. Because input functions are automated, the intranet data become more closely correlated with real time.

In any job order costing system, the individual job is the cost object. The next section presents a comprehensive job order costing situation using information from Carnival Krewe Shoes, the company introduced earlier.

JOB ORDER COSTING ILLUSTRATION

Carnival Krewe Shoes establishes prices based on costs incurred. Over the long term, the company's goal is to realize a gross profit equal to 30 percent of sales revenue. This level of gross profit is sufficient to generate a reasonable profit af-

EXHIBIT 4–6

PROJECT MANAGEMENT SITE CONTENT

Project Management Library
- Instructions on how to use the project intranet site
- Project manager manuals
- Policy and procedure manuals
- Templates and forms
- Project management training exercises

General Project Information
- Project descriptions
- Photos of project progress
- Contract information
- Phone and e-mail directories
- Project team rosters
- Document control logs
- Scope documents
- Closure documents
- Links to project control tools
- Links to electronic document retrieval systems

Technical Information
- Drawing logs
- Detailed budgets and physical estimates
- Specifications
- Bill of materials by department
- Punch lists
- Links to drawing databases

Management Information
- Meeting minutes
- Daily logs
- Project schedules
- Task and resource checklists
- Shutdown and look-ahead reports
- Work-hour estimates
- Change notices
- Labor hours worked
- Earned value

Financial Information
- Project cost sheet
- Funding requests for each cost account
- Cash flow projections and budgets
- Original cost budgets and adjustments
- Contract status reports
- Departmental budget reports
- Links to mainframe sessions for requisitions and purchase order tracking
- Companywide financial statements

Source: Lawrence Barkowski, "Intranets for Project and Cost Management in Manufacturing," *Cost Engineering* (June 1999), p. 36. Reprinted with permission of AACE International, 209 Prairie Ave., Suite 100, Morgantown, WV 25601 USA. Internet: *http://www.aacei.org*. E-mail: *info@aacei.org*

ter covering selling and administrative costs. In more competitive circumstances, such as when a company has too much unused capacity, prices may not include such a large gross profit margin to increase the likelihood of gaining job contracts. Carnival Krewe Shoes has little unused capacity, so it sets prices somewhat higher to reduce the possibility of successfully obtaining too many contracts.

To help in establishing the price for the Krewe of Desdemona's shoes, Carnival Krewe Shoes' cost accountant provided the vice president of sales with the budgeted cost information shown earlier in Exhibit 4–4. The vice president of sales believed that a selling price slightly above normal levels was possible because of the noncompetitive nature of this market. Accordingly, the vice president set the sales price to yield a gross margin of roughly 49 percent [($46,000 − $23,500) ÷ $46,000]. The customers agreed to this sales price in a contract dated June 1, 2006. Carnival Krewe Shoes scheduled the job to begin on July 1, 2006, and to be completed by January 24, 2007. The job is assigned the number 315 for identification purposes.

The following journal entries illustrate the flow of costs for the Cutting & Forming Department of Carnival Krewe Shoes during July 2006. Work on several jobs, including Job #315, was performed in Cutting & Forming during that month. In entries 1, 2, and 4 that follow, separate WIP inventory accounts are shown for costs related to Job #315 and to other jobs. In practice, the Work in Process control account for a given department would be debited only once for all costs assigned to it. The details for posting to the individual job cost records would be presented in the journal entry explanations.

1. During July 2006, material requisition forms #L40–L55 indicated that raw materials costing $5,420 were issued from the warehouse to the Cutting & Forming Department. This amount included $4,875 of direct materials used on Job

Focus on Quality

Technology: Lower Meal Program Cost, Raise Service Quality

Theoretically, processing a federal school-meal application is simple: the child's name, identification number, and family food stamp number and income are entered into a computer software program that uses federal guidelines to determine the appropriate level of financial support. The process becomes more complicated when multiplied by 35,000—the number of East Baton Rouge (EBR) Parish (LA) children who are eligible to receive free or reduced price meals. During peak time, about 1,300 applications per day are filed. Data-entry mistakes and sloppy filing complicated meeting the 10-day turnaround deadline. Nine temporary workers were hired each fall to help the three full-time employees handle the load. Meanwhile, applicants paid full price for meals pending application approval.

However, since 1992, EBR has invested nearly $2 million in technology, software and support. Its annual technology budget hovers between $150,000 to $250,000. Decreased labor needs have reduced staff from 900 to 550 full-time employees.

The most successful purchase was a character-reading scanner that eliminated the fall-term application data-entry. The scanner reduced turnaround time from 10 to 3 days, boosted efficiency by 300%, and made filing-cabinet paper chases obsolete. Three employees now handle the work once done by 12.

System implementation cost $8,000 for the screen-capture software, $3,500 in annual maintenance fees, and $60 per month per school for software support. Although the department has saved $8,000 per year by eliminating temporary workers, the biggest savings has been in time. It's hard to financially quantify the time savings for students who receive meal benefits in 3 days, or for managers who don't have to search to find a student's status, or for supervisors who don't have to check rosters to confirm proper processing of students.

After application processing and approval, letter notifications must be sent. Some EBR schools faced print jobs of 1,500 to 3,000 pages—at the rate of 18 pages per minute on an overworked laser-jet printer. Two staffers worked overtime to pack letters into mailbags for distribution to kids to take home to parents. So, EBR foodservice rented its own network copier that completes the 3,000-page job in under an hour for $0.01 per page (not including supplies). Office staff now has plenty of time to prepare the mailbags before quitting time.

Source: Adapted from Janice Matsumoto, "Buying Into Efficiency," *Restaurants & Institutions* (April 1, 2001), pp. 103–108.

#315 and $520 of direct materials used on other jobs. The remaining $25 of raw materials issued during July were indirect materials.

Work in Process Inventory—Cutting & Forming (Job #315)	4,875	
Work in Process Inventory—Cutting & Forming (other jobs)	520	
Manufacturing Overhead—Cutting & Forming (indirect materials)	25	
Raw Material Inventory		5,420

To record direct and indirect materials issued per requisitions during July.

2. The July time sheets and payroll summaries for the Cutting & Forming Department workers were used to trace direct and indirect labor to that department. Total labor cost for the Cutting & Forming Department for July was $4,306. Job #315 required $4,200 of direct labor cost combining the two biweekly pay periods in July. The remaining jobs in process required $96 of direct labor cost, and indirect labor cost for the month totaled $10.

Work in Process Inventory—Cutting & Forming (Job #315)	4,200	
Work in Process Inventory—Cutting & Forming (other jobs)	96	
Manufacturing Overhead—Cutting & Forming (indirect labor)	10	
Wages Payable		4,306

To record wages associated with Cutting & Forming during July.

3. The Cutting & Forming Department incurred overhead costs in addition to indirect materials and indirect labor during July. Factory building and equipment depreciation of $1,500 was recorded. Insurance on the factory building ($200) for the month had been prepaid and had expired. The $1,200 bill for factory utility costs was received and would be paid in August. Repairs and maintenance costs of $50 were paid in cash. Additional miscellaneous overhead costs of $80 were incurred; these costs are credited to "Various accounts" for illustrative purposes. The following entry summarizes the accumulation of these other actual overhead costs for July.

Manufacturing Overhead—Cutting & Forming	3,030	
Accumulated Depreciation		1,500
Prepaid Insurance		200
Utilities Payable		1,200
Cash		50
Various accounts		80

To record actual overhead costs of the Cutting & Forming Department during July exclusive of indirect materials and indirect nonsalaried labor.

4. Carnival Krewe Shoes prepares financial statements at the end of each month. To do so, Work in Process Inventory must include all production costs: direct material, direct labor, and overhead. The company allocates overhead to the Cutting & Forming Work in Process Inventory based on two predetermined overhead rates: $3 per direct labor hour and $4 per machine hour. In July, the employees committed 350 hours of direct labor time to Job #315, and 15 machine hours were consumed on that job. The other jobs advanced during the month received total applied overhead of $32 [8 direct labor hours (assumed) × $3 + 2 machine hours (assumed) × $4].

Work in Process Inventory—Cutting & Forming (Job #315)	1,110	
Work in Process Inventory—Cutting & Forming (other jobs)	32	
Manufacturing Overhead—Cutting & Forming		1,142

To apply overhead to Cutting & Forming work in process for July using predetermined application rates.

Notice that the actual amount of June overhead in the Cutting & Forming Department, $3,030, is not equal to the amount of overhead applied to that department's Work in Process Inventory ($1,110). This $1,920 difference is the underapplied overhead for the month. Because the predetermined rates were based on annual estimates, differences in actual and applied overhead accumulate during the year. Underapplied or overapplied overhead will be closed at year-end (as shown in Chapter 3) either to Cost of Goods Sold (if the amount is immaterial) or to Work in Process Inventory, Finished Goods Inventory, and Cost of Goods Sold (if the amount is material).

The preceding entries for the Cutting & Forming Department would be similar to the entries made in each of the other departments of Carnival Krewe Shoes. Direct material and direct labor data are posted to each job order cost sheet frequently (usually daily); entries are posted to the general ledger control accounts for longer intervals (usually monthly).

Job #315 will pass consecutively through the three departments of Carnival Krewe Shoes. In other types of job shops, different departments may work on the same job concurrently. Similar entries for Job #315 are made throughout the production process, and Exhibit 4–7 shows the cost sheet at the job's completion. Note that direct material requisitions, direct labor cost, and applied overhead shown previously in entries 1, 2, and 4 are posted on the job cost sheet. Other entries are not detailed.

When the job is completed, its costs are transferred to Finished Goods Inventory. The journal entries related to completion and sale are as follows:

EXHIBIT 4–7
CARNIVAL KREWE SHOES' COMPLETED JOB ORDER COST SHEET

Job Number _____ 315 _____

Customer Name and Address:

Krewe of Desdemona
3801 N. Pine Ave.
New Orleans, LA

Contract Agreement Date: *6/01/06*
Scheduled Starting Date: *7/01/06*
Agreed Completion Date: *1/24/07*
Actual Completion Date:
Delivery Instructions: *Will be picked up by Krewe members*

Description of Job:

50 pair of leather boots made to fit
per specifications in contract
dated 6/01/06

Contract Price *$46,000*

CUTTING & FORMING

DIRECT MATERIAL			DIRECT LABOR			OVERHEAD BASED ON					
						# OF LABOR HOURS			# OF MACHINE HOURS		
(EST. $5,000)			(EST. $10,200)			(EST. $3,000)			(EST. $200)		
Date	Source	Amount	Date	Source	Amount	Date	Source	Amount	Date	Source	Amount
7/31	MR L40-L55	$4,875	7/31	payroll	$4,200	7/31	payroll	$1,050	7/31	Machine hour meters	$60
- - -	- - -	- - -	- - -	- - -	- - -	- - -	- - -	- - -	- - -	- - -	- - -

ASSEMBLY
(SAME FORMAT AS ABOVE BUT WITH DIFFERENT OH RATES)

FINISHING
(SAME FORMAT AS ABOVE BUT WITH DIFFERENT OH RATES)

SUMMARY

	CUTTING & FORMING		ASSEMBLY		FINISHING	
	Actual	Budget	Actual	Budget	Actual	Budget
Direct material	$ 4,875	$ 5,000	$ 0	$ 0	$ 52	$ 50
Direct labor	11,060	10,200	1,815	1,800	385	400
Overhead (labor)	3,100	3,000	0		0	
Overhead (machine)	246	200	2,114	2,000	803	850
Totals	$19,281	$18,400	$3,929	$3,800	$1,240	$1,300

		Actual	Budget
Final Costs:	Cutting & Forming	$19,281	$18,400
	Assembly	3,929	3,800
	Finishing	1,240	1,300
	Totals	$24,450	$23,500

Finished Goods Inventory—Job #315	24,450	
Work in Process Inventory—Cutting & Forming		19,281
Work in Process Inventory—Assembly		3,929
Work in Process Inventory—Finishing		1,240
To transfer completed goods to FG Inventory.		
Accounts Receivable—Krewe of Desdemona	46,000	
Sales		46,000
To record the sale of goods on account.		
Cost of Goods Sold—Job #315	24,450	
Finished Goods Inventory—Job #315		24,450
To record the related CGS for the above sale.		

Managers in all departments can use the completed job order cost sheet to determine how well costs were controlled. Overall, costs were slightly above the budgeted level. The Cutting & Forming Department experienced slightly higher costs than amounts budgeted in all categories. Assembly also incurred slightly higher than budgeted costs. Finishing Department costs, however, were slightly under budget. Costs in total were fairly well controlled on this job (especially given the complex nature of the job) because total actual costs were only 3.9 percent above the budgeted amounts.

In the remainder of the chapter, the use of job order costing data to support management decision making and improve cost control is discussed. The next section discusses how standard costs, rather than actual costs, can be used to improve cost management.

JOB ORDER COSTING USING STANDARD COSTS

LO.6

HOW ARE STANDARD COSTS USED IN A JOB ORDER COSTING SYSTEM?

The Carnival Krewe Shoes example illustrates the use of actual historical cost data for direct material and direct labor in a job order costing system. However, using actual direct material and direct labor costs may cause the costs of similar units to fluctuate from period to period or job to job because of changes in component costs. Use of standard costs for direct material and direct labor can minimize the effects of such cost fluctuations in the same way that predetermined rates do for overhead costs.

When are standard costs used in job order costing?

A standard cost system determines product cost by using predetermined norms in the inventory accounts for prices and/or quantities of cost components. After production is complete, standard production cost is compared to actual production cost to determine production efficiency. A difference between the actual quantity, price, or rate and its related standard is called a **variance**.

variance

Standards can be used in a job order system only if a company typically engages in jobs that produce fairly similar products. One type of standard job order costing system uses standards only for input prices of material or only for labor rates. Such a process is reasonable if all output relies on similar kinds of material or labor. If standards are used for price or rate amounts only, the debits to Work in Process Inventory become a hybrid of actual and standard information: actual quantities at standard prices or rates.

The output of painting companies is heterogeneous, with no set standard of quantity of paint determined for a particular job.

Macaluso Brothers, a house-painting company located in New Mexico, illustrates the use of price and rate standards. Management has decided that, because of the climate, one specific brand of paint (costing $30 per gallon) is the best to use. Painters employed by the company are paid $12 per hour. These two amounts can be used as price and rate standards for Macaluso Brothers. No standards can be set for the quantity of paint that will be used on a job or the amount of time that will be spent on the job. These items will vary based on the quantity and texture of wood of the structure as well as on the size of the structure being painted.

GETTY IMAGES

Assume that Macaluso Brothers paints a house requiring 50 gallons of paint and 80 hours of labor time. The standard paint and labor costs, respectively, are $1,500 (50 × $30) and $960 (80 × $12). The paint was purchased on sale for $1,350, or $27 per gallon. A comparison of this price to the standard results in a $150 favorable material price variance (50 gallons at $3 per gallon). If the actual labor rate paid to painters was $11 per hour, there would be an $80 favorable (80 hours at $1 per hour) labor rate variance.

Other job order companies produce output that is homogeneous enough to allow standards to be developed for both quantities and prices of material and labor. Such companies usually use distinct production runs for numerous similar products. In such circumstances, the output is homogeneous for each run, unlike the heterogeneous output of Macaluso Brothers.

Green Manufacturing, Inc., is a job order manufacturer that uses both price and quantity material and labor standards. Green manufactures wooden flower boxes that are retailed through several chains of garden supply stores. The boxes are contracted for on a job order basis because the garden store chains demand changes in style, color, and size with each spring gardening season. Green produces the boxes in distinct production runs each month for each retail chain. Price and quantity standards for direct material and direct labor have been established and are used to compare the estimated and actual costs of monthly production runs for each type of box produced.

Material and labor standards set for the boxes sold to Mountain Gardens are as follows: 8 linear feet of 1″ × 10″ redwood plank at $0.60 per linear foot and 1.4 direct labor hours at $9.00 per direct labor hour (DLH). In June, 2,000 boxes were produced for Mountain Gardens. Actual wood used was 16,300 linear feet, which was purchased at $0.58 per linear foot. Direct labor employees worked 2,700 hours at an average labor rate of $9.10.

Given this information, Green used 300 linear feet of redwood above the standard quantity for the job [16,300 − (8 × 2,000)]. This excess usage caused an unfavorable material quantity variance of $180 at the $0.60 standard price ($0.60 × 300 linear feet). The actual redwood used was purchased at $0.02 below the standard price per linear foot, which results in a $326 ($0.02 × 16,300) favorable material price variance.

The actual DLHs used were 100 less than standard [2,700 − (1.4 hours × 2,000)], which results in a favorable labor quantity variance of $900 ($9 standard rate × 100 hours). The work crew earned $0.10 per hour above standard, which gives a $270 unfavorable labor rate variance ($0.10 × 2,700). A summary of variances follows:

Direct material quantity variance	$ 180 unfavorable
Direct material price variance	(326) favorable
Direct labor quantity variance	(900) favorable
Direct labor rate variance	270 unfavorable
Net variance (cost less than expected)	$(776) favorable

From a financial perspective, Green controlled its total material and labor costs well on the Mountain Garden job.

Variances can be computed for actual-to-standard differences regardless of whether standards have been established for both quantities and prices or for prices or rates only. Standard costs for material and labor provide the same types of benefits as predetermined overhead rates: more timely information and comparisons against actual amounts. In fact, a predetermined overhead rate is simply a type of standard. It establishes a constant amount of overhead assignable as a component of product cost and eliminates any immediate need for actual overhead information in the calculation of product cost. More is presented on standards and variances in Chapter 7.

Standard cost job order systems are reasonable substitutes for actual or normal costing systems as long as the standards provide managers with useful information. Any type of product costing system is acceptable in practice if it is effective and efficient in serving the company's unique production needs, provides information desired by management, and can be maintained at a cost that is reasonable when compared to the benefits received. These criteria apply equally well to both manufacturers and service companies.

JOB ORDER COSTING TO ASSIST MANAGERS

LO.7
HOW DOES INFORMATION FROM A JOB ORDER COSTING SYSTEM SUPPORT MANAGEMENT DECISION MAKING?

Managers are interested in controlling costs in each department as well as for each job. Actual direct material, direct labor, and factory overhead costs are accumulated in departmental accounts and are periodically compared to budgets so that managers can respond to significant deviations. Transactions must be recorded in a consistent, complete, and accurate manner to have information on actual costs available for periodic comparisons.

How can managers use information from a job order system?

Managers in different types of job order organizations may stress different types of cost control. Companies such as **Aston Martin** are extremely concerned about labor hours and their related costs: Unlike most cars that are built on a moving assembly line, each Aston Martin DB9 takes about 200 labor-hours to hand make in a series of workstations at the Gaydon, England, plant.[7] Other companies, such as **CustomFineJewelry.com**, exert significant cost control for direct materials that include platinum, gold, diamonds, and Australian black opals. Hospitals must be careful to control overhead costs created by long waiting periods or delays in recording and communicating patient information.

One primary difference between job order costing for manufacturing and service organizations is that most service organizations use a fairly insignificant amount of materials relative to the value of labor for each job. In such cases, only direct labor may be traced to each job and all materials may be treated (for the sake of convenience) as part of overhead. Overhead then needs to be allocated to the various jobs, most commonly using a predetermined rate per direct labor hour or direct labor dollar. Other cost drivers that can effectively assign overhead to jobs may also be found.

Knowing the costs of individual jobs allows managers to better estimate future job costs and establish realistic bids and selling prices. Using budgets and standards in a job order costing system also provides information against which actual costs can be compared at regular time intervals for control purposes. These comparisons can also furnish some performance evaluation information. The following two examples demonstrate the usefulness of job order costing to managers.

Custom Engineering

Custom Engineering specializes in concrete structures. The firm has a diverse set of clients and types of jobs. Its president, Josh Bradley, wants to know which of the firm's clients are the most profitable and which are the least profitable. To determine this information, he requested a breakdown of profits per job measured on both a percentage and an absolute dollar basis.

Bradley found that no records of costs for each client's job were kept. Costs had been accumulated only by type—travel, entertainment, and so forth. Stan Tobias, the sales manager, was certain that the largest profits came from Custom's

[7] *http://www.astonmartin.com/companynews*; accessed 2/25/04.

largest accounts. Careful job cost analysis found that the largest accounts contributed most of the firm's revenue but the smallest percentage and absolute dollars of incremental profits. Until Bradley requested this information, no one had totaled the costs of recruiting each client or the travel, entertainment, and other costs associated with maintaining each client.

A company that has a large number of jobs that vary in size, time, or effort may not know which jobs are responsible for disproportionately large costs. Job order costing can assist in determining which jobs are truly profitable and can help managers to better monitor costs. As a result of the cost analysis, Bradley changed the company's marketing strategy. The firm began concentrating its efforts on smaller clients who were located closer to the primary office, causing a substantial increase in profits because significantly fewer costs were incurred for travel and entertainment. A job order costing system was implemented to track each client's per-period and total costs. Unprofitable accounts were dropped, and account managers felt more responsibility to monitor and control costs related to their particular accounts.

J. Madison's Custom Boats

J. Madison is a unique individual, a female boat builder. She and her employees custom manufacture small wooden boats to customer specifications. Before completing her MBA and learning about job order costing, Madison had merely "guesstimated" the costs associated with each boat's production. She would estimate selling prices by using vague information from past jobs and specifications for the new design and adding what she considered a reasonable profit margin. Often customers who indicated they thought the selling price was too high could talk Madison into price reductions.

After implementing a job order costing system, Madison had better cost control over the jobs that were in process, maintained better inventory valuations for financial statements, and had available better information with which to prevent part stockouts (not having parts in inventory) and production stoppages. The use of material requisitions helped make certain that materials acquired for a particular custom boat actually were used for that job. The job order cost sheets also gave her more up-to-date information that enhanced her ability to judge whether to accept additional work and when current work would be completed. Most importantly, the job order costing system gave Madison an informed means by which to understand how costs were spent on jobs, estimate costs that would be incurred on future jobs, and be able to justify price quotes on future jobs.

Whether an entity is a manufacturer or service organization that tailors its output to customer specifications, company management will find that job order costing techniques help in performing managerial functions. This cost system is useful for determining the cost of goods produced or services rendered in companies that are able to attach costs to specific jobs. As product variety increases, the size of production lots for many items shrinks, and job order costing becomes more applicable. Custom-made goods may become the norm rather than the exception in an environment that relies on flexible manufacturing systems and computer-integrated manufacturing.

PRODUCT AND MATERIAL LOSSES IN JOB ORDER COSTING

The production processes may result in losses of materials or partially completed products. Some losses, such as evaporation, leakage, or oxidation, are inherent in the manufacturing process; such reductions are called **shrinkage**. Modifying the

shrinkage

What happens if all units don't make it through production?

defects

spoilage

normal loss

abnormal loss

production process to reduce or eliminate the causes of shrinkage may be difficult, impossible, or simply not cost beneficial. At other times, production process errors (either by humans or machines) cause a loss of units through rejection at inspection for failure to meet appropriate quality standards or designated product specifications. Such units are considered either **defects** if they can be economically reworked and sold or **spoilage** if this cannot be done.

If units do not meet quality specifications, they may be reworked to meet product specifications or sold as irregulars. *Rework cost* is a product or period cost depending on whether the rework is considered to be normal or abnormal. A **normal loss** of units falls within a tolerance level that is expected during production. For example, if a company sets its quality goal as 99 percent of goods produced, the company would expect a normal loss of 1 percent. Any loss in excess of this expectation is considered an **abnormal loss**. Thus, the difference between normal and abnormal loss is merely one of degree and is determined by management.

In a job order situation, the accounting treatment for lost units depends on two issues: (1) Is a loss generally incurred for most jobs, or is it specifically identified with a particular job? (2) Is the loss considered normal or abnormal?

Generally Anticipated on All Jobs

If a normal loss is anticipated on all jobs, the predetermined overhead application rate should include an amount for the net cost of the loss, which is equal to the cost of defective or spoiled work less the estimated disposal value, if any, of that work. This approach assumes that losses are naturally inherent and unavoidable in the production of good products and the estimated loss should be allocated to the good products produced.

Assume that Kyndo Corp. produces special order cleaning compounds for different manufacturers. Regardless of the job, however, some shrinkage always occurs because of the mixing process. In computing the predetermined overhead rate related to the custom compounds, the following estimates are made:

Overhead costs other than spoilage		$121,500
Estimated spoilage cost	$10,300	
Sales of improperly mixed compounds to foreign distributors	(4,300)	6,000
Total estimated overhead		$ 127,500
Estimated gallons of production during the year		÷ 150,000
Predetermined overhead rate per gallon		$ 0.85

During the year, Kyndo Corp. accepted a job (#38) from Husserl Co. to manufacture 500 gallons of cleaning compound. Direct material cost for this job was $4,660, direct labor cost totaled $640, and applied overhead was $425 ($0.85 × 500 gallons), for a total job cost of $5,725. Kyndo Corp. put 500 gallons of compounds into production. Five gallons (or 1 percent) of the compounds became defective during the production process when a worker accidentally added a thickening agent meant for another job into a container of Kyndo's cleaning compound. Actual cost of the defective mixture was $57.25 (0.01 × $5,725), and it can be sold for $22. The following entry is made to account for the actual defect cost:

Disposal Value of Defective Work	22.00	
Manufacturing Overhead	35.25	
Work in Process Inventory—Job #38		57.25
To record disposal value of defective work incurred on Job #38 for Husserl Co.		

The estimated cost of spoilage was originally included in determining the predetermined overhead rate. Therefore, as defects or spoilage occur, the disposal value of the nonstandard work is included in an inventory account (if salable), and the net cost of the normal nonstandard work is charged to the Manufacturing Overhead account as is any other actual overhead cost.

Specifically Identified with a Particular Job

If defects or spoilage are not generally anticipated but are occasionally experienced on specific jobs *because of job-related characteristics,* the estimated cost should *not* be included in setting the predetermined overhead application rate. Because the defects/spoilage cost attaches to the job, disposal value of such goods reduces the cost of the job that created those goods. If no disposal value exists for the defective/spoiled goods, the cost of those lost units remains with the job that caused the defects/spoilage.

Assume that Kyndo Corp. did not typically experience spoilage in its production process. The company's predetermined overhead would have been calculated as $0.81 per gallon ($121,500 ÷ 150,000). Thus, the total cost for the Husserl Co. job would have been $5,705 [$4,660 + $640 + ($0.81 × 500)]. A greater than normal quantity of ammonia was added to 5 gallons of the batch at Husserl Co.'s request. However, after inspecting those 5 gallons, Husserl Co. asked Kyndo Corp. to keep the original formula for the remaining gallons. The 5 gallons could be sold to another company for $22; this amount would reduce the cost of the Husserl Co. job as shown in the following entry:

Disposal Value of Defective Work	22	
Work in Process Inventory—Job #38		22
To record disposal value of defective work		
incurred on Job #38 for Husserl Co.		

Abnormal Spoilage

LO.8
HOW ARE LOSSES TREATED
IN A JOB ORDER COSTING
SYSTEM?

The cost of all abnormal losses (net of any disposal value) should be written off as a period cost. This treatment is justified because asset cost should include only those costs that are necessary to acquire or produce inventory; unnecessary costs should be written off in the period in which they are incurred. Abnormal losses are not necessary to the production of good units and the cost is avoidable in the future. This cost should be separately identified and investigated for the cause so as to determine how to prevent future similar occurrences.

The following entry assumes that Kyndo Corp. normally anticipates some loss of partially completed products on its custom orders and that the estimated cost of those products was included in the development of a predetermined overhead application rate. Assume that on Job #135, the cost of defective units was $198, but that $45 of disposal value was associated with those units. Of the remaining $153 of cost, $120 was related to normal defects and $33 was related to abnormal defects. The following journal entry records these facts.

Disposal Value of Defective Work	45	
Manufacturing Overhead	120	
Loss from Abnormal Spoilage	33	
Work in Process Inventory—Job #135		198
To record reassignment of cost of defective		
and spoiled work on Job #135.		

The first debit represents the defective inventory's disposal value; the debit to Manufacturing Overhead is for the net cost of normal spoilage. The debit to Loss from Abnormal Spoilage is for the portion of the net cost of spoilage that was unnecessary and unanticipated in setting the predetermined application rate.

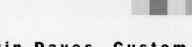

Revisiting

Calvin Dayes, Custom Shoemaker

"Shoe" says that he could take a person's foot measurements and have a pair of shoes made the next day. Unfortunately, based on his standards, that pair of shoes wouldn't be wearable. Slowly and carefully, he measures, fits, cuts, shapes, assembles, and sews leather into soft, supple creations that would make any foot dance.

Production output is limited to only about 48 pairs of shoes and boots per year; thus, Dayes chooses his customers carefully. Some are well-known; for instance, Dayes made a pair of boots for Kirk Douglas when he reigned in 1984 as Bacchus. Other clients are local New Orleanians. But the clients he is proudest to work for are those for whom he makes orthopedic shoes—his craft helped one gentleman whose foot had been sliced off by a lawn mower to walk again.

Calvin Dayes incurs all of the same costs that the big companies do; he simply incurs those costs in a different manner.

■ Direct material: leather rather than the big companies' canvas or plastic. Leather quality is exceptionally impor-

tant: It has to be soft enough to mold to one's legs and calves but strong enough not to be flimsy. To make certain that he obtains the proper quality of material at the most reasonable price, Dayes goes to New York and purchases all he expects to need in one bulk purchase.

■ Direct labor: lots of it rather than the big companies' automated production lines. All of the stitching in the shoes, however, is not by hand: Calvin Dayes knows the value of a good sewing machine.

■ Overhead: machinery and building depreciation, insurance, utilities, and supplies, but in significantly smaller amounts than the big companies. Dayes works in his garage and his home—both slightly disorganized and cluttered to an outsider, but not to the man who works the magic.

The end product made by Calvin Dayes is a pair of shoes that makes you wonder how soon you have to get in line to get another pair!

Source: Adapted from John Pope's "Cobbler Crafts Boots Fit for Carnival Kings," (New Orleans) *Times-Picayune*, February 3, 2004, pp. B1, B3.

Comprehensive Review Module

Chapter Summary

1. Job order and process costing systems differ in that job order costing

   - is used in companies that make limited quantities of customer-specified products or perform customer-specific services; process costing is used in companies that make mass quantities of homogeneous output on a continuous flow basis.

   - requires the use of a job order cost sheet to track the direct material, direct labor, and actual or applied overhead to each customer-specific job; process costing simply accounts for direct materials, direct labor, and actual or applied overhead by batch of goods per department.

   - does not allow for the computation of a cost per unit unless all units within the job are similar in nature; process costing can and does create a cost per unit for each cost element.

   - may use either an actual cost system (combining actual direct material, direct labor, and overhead), a normal cost system (combining actual direct material and direct labor, as well as applied overhead using a predetermined overhead rate), or a standard cost system (combining budgeted norms for direct material, direct labor, and overhead); process costing may use the same type of cost valuation systems but standard cost systems are significantly more prevalent in process costing than job order costing.

2. From an accounting standpoint, a "job"

   - is the cost object for which costs are accumulated.

   - can consist of one or more units of output.

   - has its costs accumulated on a job order cost sheet.

3. The primary documents used in a job order costing system are the

   - job order cost sheets which, for incomplete jobs, serve as the Work in Process Inventory subsidiary ledger; cost sheets for completed jobs not yet delivered to customers constitute the Finished Goods Inventory subsidiary ledger; and cost sheets for completed and sold jobs compose the Cost of Goods Sold subsidiary ledger.

   - material requisition forms, which trace the issuance of raw materials to the specific jobs in

Work in Process Inventory so that direct material can be included on the job order cost sheets.

   - employee time sheets, which record the hours worked and jobs worked on by employees so that direct labor can be included on the job order cost sheets.

4. The typical journal entries used to accumulate costs in a job order costing system record the

   - purchase, for cash or on credit, of raw materials for use in production.

   - issuance of direct material to Work in Process Inventory.

   - incurrence of direct labor hours and pay.

   - incurrence of actual overhead costs.

   - application of predetermined overhead to jobs in process.

   - completion of jobs and transfer of those jobs to Finished Goods Inventory.

   - sale of the products for cash or credit.

   - removal of products from Finished Goods Inventory upon sale and the expensing of the total production cost to Cost of Goods Sold.

5. Technological changes have impacted the gathering and use of information in job order costing systems by

   - including a job order costing module in even basic accounting software.

   - aiding the product management of jobs through software programs that allow operational and financial data about jobs to be shared throughout the firm, often disseminated on company intranets.

   - tracking job costs because more accurate and timely data are gathered and employees are relieved of the recurring burden of logging data.

   - allowing mechanical tracking, through scanners and bar codes, of employee work information and flow of parts and components.

6. Standard costs may be used in a job order costing system by

- establishing standards for quantities and/or costs of production inputs.

- providing a basis for managers to evaluate the efficiency of operations through comparisons of actual and standard costs. Differences between actual costs and standard costs are captured in variance accounts, and by analyzing the variances, managers gain an understanding of the factors that cause costs to differ from the expected amounts.

7. Job order costing information helps support management decision making by

- assisting managers in their planning, controlling, decision making, and performance evaluating functions.

- allowing managers to trace costs associated with specific current jobs to better estimate costs for future jobs.

- providing a way by which managers can better control the costs associated with current production, especially if comparisons with budgets or standards are used.

- attaching costs correctly to jobs that are contracted on a cost-plus basis.

- highlighting those jobs or types of jobs that are most profitable to the organization.

8. Both normal and abnormal losses may occur in a job order system and they are accounted for in the following manner

- normal losses that are generally anticipated on all jobs are estimated and included in the development of the predetermined overhead rate.

- normal losses that are associated with a particular job are charged to that job (net of any disposal value of the spoiled items).

- abnormal losses are always charged to a loss account in the period they are incurred.

Solution Strategies

BASIC JOURNAL ENTRIES IN A JOB ORDER COSTING SYSTEM

Raw Material Inventory	XXX	
Accounts Payable		XXX
To record the purchase of raw materials.		
Work in Process Inventory—Dept. (Job #)	XXX	
Manufacturing Overhead	XXX	
Raw Material Inventory		XXX
To record the issuance of direct and indirect materials requisitioned for a specific job.		
Work in Process Inventory—Dept. (Job #)	XXX	
Manufacturing Overhead	XXX	
Wages Payable		XXX
To record direct and indirect labor payroll for production employees.		
Manufacturing Overhead	XXX	
Various accounts		XXX
To record the incurrence of actual overhead costs. (Account titles to be credited must be specified in an actual journal entry.)		
Work in Process Inventory—Dept. (Job #)	XXX	
Manufacturing Overhead		XXX
To apply overhead to a specific job. (This may be actual OH or OH applied using a predetermined rate. Predetermined OH is applied at job completion or end of period, whichever is earlier.)		
Finished Goods Inventory (Job #)	XXX	
Work in Process Inventory		XXX
To record the transfer of completed goods from WIP to FG.		
Accounts Receivable	XXX	
Sales		XXX
To record the sale of goods on account.		
Cost of Goods Sold	XXX	
Finished Goods Inventory		XXX
To record the cost of the goods sold.		

Demonstration Problem

Custom Recreation builds recreational vehicles to clients' specifications. The firm has two departments: Chassis and Interior. The Chassis Department designs and configures the major components of the vehicle and is highly automated. The Interior Department selects and installs the furniture and accessories; this department is highly labor intensive. The Interior Department can begin work on RV interiors (such as staining or painting cabinets and sewing cushions) prior to the completion of the vehicle.

In its first month of operations (March 2006), Custom Recreation obtained contracts for three vehicles:

Job 1: A 30-foot mobile food bank
Job 2: A 35-foot slide-out motor home
Job 3: A 37-foot dressing room for a motion picture studio

Custom Recreation bills its customers on a cost-plus basis, with profit equal to 30 percent of costs. The firm uses a job order costing system based on normal costs. Overhead is applied in the Chassis Department at a predetermined rate of $95 per machine hour (MH). In the Interior Department, overhead is applied at a predetermined rate of $30 per professional labor hour (PLH). The following significant transactions occurred in March 2006.

1. Direct materials were purchased on account: $110,000.
2. Direct materials were requisitioned by Chassis for use in the three jobs: Job #1, $40,000; Job #2, $28,000; and Job #3, $18,000. Materials were issued to the Interior Department: Job #1, $3,000; Job #2, $6,000; and Job #3, $9,600.
3. Time sheets and payroll summaries indicated that the following direct labor costs were incurred:

	Chassis Department	Interior Department
Job #1	$8,000	$4,000
Job #2	6,000	9,000
Job #3	7,000	6,500

4. The following indirect costs were incurred in each department:

	Chassis Department	Interior Department
Labor	$ 9,200	$4,500
Utilities/Fuel	5,900	1,300
Depreciation	13,300	1,600

5. Overhead was applied based on the predetermined overhead rates in effect in each department. The Chassis Department had 360 MHs (90 MHs on Job #1, 170 MHs on Job #2, and 100 MHs on Job #3), and Interior worked 230 PLHs (50 PLHs on Job #1, 140 PLHs on Job #2, and 40 PLHs on Job #3) for the month.
6. Job #1 was completed and cash was collected for the agreed upon selling price. At month-end, Jobs #2 and #3 were only partially complete.
7. Any underapplied or overapplied overhead is assigned to Cost of Goods Sold at month-end.

Required:
a. Record the journal entries for transactions 1 through 7.
b. As of the end of March 2006, determine the total cost assigned to Jobs #2 and #3.

Solution to Demonstration Problem

a. 1. Raw Material Inventory   110,000
            Accounts Payable   110,000
        To record purchase of direct materials.

    2. WIP Inventory—Chassis (Job #1)   40,000
        WIP Inventory—Chassis (Job #2)   28,000
        WIP Inventory—Chassis (Job #3)   18,000
            Raw Material Inventory   86,000
        *To record requisition and issuance of materials to
        Chassis Department.*

        WIP Inventory—Interior (Job #1)   3,000
        WIP Inventory—Interior (Job #2)   6,000
        WIP Inventory—Interior (Job #3)   9,600
            Raw Material Inventory   18,600
        *To record requisition and issuance of materials to
        Interior Department.*

    3. WIP Inventory—Chassis (Job #1)   8,000
        WIP Inventory—Chassis (Job #2)   6,000
        WIP Inventory—Chassis (Job #3)   7,000
            Wages Payable   21,000
        To record direct labor costs for Chassis Department.

        WIP Inventory—Interior (Job #1)   4,000
        WIP Inventory—Interior (Job #2)   9,000
        WIP Inventory—Interior (Job #3)   6,500
            Wages Payable   19,500
        To record direct labor costs for Interior Department.

    4. Overhead—Chassis   28,400
        Overhead—Interior   7,400
            Wages Payable   13,700
            Utilities/Fuel Payable   7,200
            Accumulated Depreciation   14,900
        To record various overhead costs.

    5. WIP Inventory—Chassis (Job #1)   8,550
        WIP Inventory—Chassis (Job #2)   16,150
        WIP Inventory—Chassis (Job #3)   9,500
            Overhead—Chassis   34,200
        To record application of overhead to Chassis Department.

        WIP Inventory—Interior (Job #1)   1,500
        WIP Inventory—Interior (Job #2)   4,200
        WIP Inventory—Interior (Job #3)   1,200
            Overhead—Interior   6,900
        To record application of overhead to Interior Department.

    6. Finished Goods Inventory*   65,050
            WIP Inventory—Chassis   56,550
            WIP Inventory—Interior   8,500
        To record completion of Job #1.

        Cash   84,565
            Sales Revenue†   84,565
        To record sale of Job #1.

        Cost of Goods Sold   65,050
            Finished Goods Inventory   65,050
        To record cost of sales for Job #1.

    7. Overhead—Chassis   5,800
            Overhead—Interior   500
            Cost of Goods Sold   5,300
        *To assign underapplied and overapplied overhead
        to cost of goods sold.*

*Job #1 costs = $40,000 + $8,000 + $8,550 + $3,000 + $4,000 + $1,500 = $65,050
†Revenue, Job #1 = $65,050 × 1.30 = $84,565

b.

	Job #2	Job #3
Direct material—Chassis	$28,000	$18,000
Direct labor—Chassis	6,000	7,000
Overhead—Chassis	16,150	9,500
Direct material—Interior	6,000	9,600
Direct labor—Interior	9,000	6,500
Overhead—Interior	4,200	1,200
Totals	$69,350	$51,800

Key Terms

abnormal loss (p. 127)
cost-plus contract (p. 109)
defect (p. 127)
employee time sheet (p. 116)
intranet (p. 118)

job (p. 111)
job order cost sheet (p. 114)
job order costing system (p. 110)
material requisition form (p. 113)
normal loss (p. 127)

process costing system (p. 110)
shrinkage (p. 126)
spoilage (p. 127)
standard cost system (p. 111)
variance (p. 123)

Questions

1. In choosing a product costing system, what are the two choices available for a cost accumulation system? How do these systems differ?

2. In choosing a product costing system, what are the three valuation method alternatives? Explain how these methods differ.

3. In a job order costing system, what key documents support the cost accumulation process?

4. In a standard costing system, discuss how information about variances can be used to improve cost control.

5. If normal spoilage is generally anticipated to occur on all jobs, how should the cost of that spoilage be treated?

6. Why are normal and abnormal spoilage accounted for differently? Typically, how does one determine which spoilage is normal or abnormal?

Exercises

7. (Classifying) For each of the following firms, determine whether it is more likely to use job order or process costing. This firm
    a. is a health care clinic.
    b. makes custom jewelry.
    c. manufactures hair spray and hand lotion.
    d. provides public accounting services.
    e. manufactures paint.
    f. cans vegetables and fruits.
    g. is an automobile repair shop.
    h. provides landscaping services for corporations.
    i. manufactures baby food.
    j. provides property management services for a variety of real estate developments.
    k. designs custom software.
    l. produces candles.

8. (Journal entries) Clara Inc. produces custom-made floor tiles. During April 2006, the following information was obtained relating to operations and production:
   1. Direct material purchased on account, $174,000.
   2. Direct material issued to jobs, $163,800.
   3. Direct labor hours incurred, 3,400. All direct factory employees were paid $15 per hour.
   4. Actual factory overhead costs incurred for the month totaled $68,700. This overhead consisted of $18,000 of supervisory salaries, $21,500 of depreciation charges, $7,200 of insurance, $12,500 of indirect material, and $9,500 of utilities. Salaries, insurance, and utilities were paid in cash, and indirect material was taken from supplies inventory.
   5. Overhead is applied to production at the rate of $20 per direct labor hour. Beginning balances of Raw Material Inventory and Work in Process Inventory were, respectively, $4,300 and $22,400. Ending Work in Process Inventory was $4,700.
   a. Prepare journal entries for Transactions 1–5.
   b. Determine the balance in Raw Material Inventory at the end of the month.
   c. Determine the cost of the goods completed during April. If 10,000 similar units were completed, what was the cost per unit?
   d. What is the amount of underapplied or overapplied overhead at the end of April?

9. (Journal entries; cost flows) The following costs were incurred in February 2006 by Store-It-All, which produces customized storage buildings.

Direct material purchased on account		$ 38,000
Direct material used for jobs:		
Job #217	$22,400	
Job #218	3,600	
Other jobs	26,800	52,800
Direct labor costs for month:		
Job #217	$ 5,200	
Job #218	7,000	
Other jobs	9,800	22,000
Actual overhead costs for February		110,000

The balance in Work in Process Inventory on February 1 was $8,400, which consisted of $5,600 for Job #217 and $2,800 for Job #218. The February beginning balance in Direct Material Inventory was $12,300.

Actual overhead is applied to jobs on the basis of direct labor cost. Job #217 was completed and transferred to finished goods during February. It was then sold for cash at 135 percent of cost.
   a. Prepare journal entries to record the preceding information.
   b. Determine the February ending balance in Work in Process Inventory. How much of this balance relates to Job #218?

WebTUTOR Advantage

10. (Cost flows) Brooke Landscapes began operations on May 1, 2006. Its Work in Process Inventory account on May 31 appeared as follows:

Work in Process Inventory

Direct material	554,400	Cost of completed jobs	??
Direct labor	384,000		
Applied overhead	422,400		

The company applies overhead on the basis of direct labor cost. Only one job was still in process on May 31. That job had $132,600 in direct material and $93,600 in direct labor cost assigned to it.

a. What was the predetermined overhead application rate?

b. What was the balance in Work in Process Inventory at the end of May?

c. What was the total cost of jobs completed in May?

11. (Cost flows) For 2006, Brown Mfg. decided to apply overhead to units based on direct labor hours. The company's Work in Process Inventory account on January 31 appeared as follows:

Work in Process Inventory

Beginning balance	136,000		
Direct material	261,400	Cost of completed jobs	??
Direct labor	175,000		
Applied overhead	124,600		

The beginning balance of $136,000 contained 5,000 direct labor hours. During January, 14,000 direct labor hours were recorded. Only one job was still in process on January 31. That job had $41,500 in direct material and 3,700 direct labor hours assigned to it.

a. What was the predetermined overhead application rate for 2006?

b. What was the average direct labor rate per hour?

c. What was the balance in Work in Process Inventory at the end of January?

d. What was the total cost of jobs completed in January?

12. (Cost flows) Integrated Decisions Corp. applies overhead to jobs at a rate of 120 percent of direct labor cost. On December 31, 2006, a flood destroyed many of the firm's cost records, leaving only the following information:

Direct Material Inventory

Beg. balance	12,300		?
Purchases	?		
4,100			

Work in Process Inventory

Beg. balance	28,000		?
Direct material	?		
Direct labor	90,000		
Overhead	?		
24,000			

Finished Goods Inventory

Beg. balance	45,000		
Goods completed	?	685,000	
42,000			

Cost of Goods Sold

?	

As the cost accountant of Integrated Decisions, you must find the following for 2006:

a. Cost of goods sold.

b. Cost of goods manufactured.

c. Amount of overhead applied to production.

d. Cost of direct material used.

e. Cost of direct material purchased.

13. (Cost flows) On March 18, 2006, a fire destroyed Weymann World's work-in-process inventory, which consisted of two in-process custom jobs (B325 and Q428). The following information had, however, been contained in some off-site records:

- Weymann World applies overhead at the rate of 85 percent of direct labor cost.
- The cost of goods sold for the company averages 75 percent of selling price. Sales from January 1 to the date of the fire totaled $637,000.
- The company's wage rate for production employees is $8.90 per hour.
- As of March 18, $21,000 of direct material and 28 hours of direct labor had been recorded for Job B325. Also at that time, $14,700 of direct material and 40 hours of direct labor had been recorded for Job Q428.
- January 1, 2006, inventories were as follows: $19,500 of Direct Material, $? of Work in Process, and $68,900 of Finished Goods. Jobs B325 and Q428 were not in process on January 1.
- One job, R91, was completed and in the warehouse awaiting shipment on March 18. The total cost of this job was $53,600.

Determine the following amounts:

- **a.** Cost of goods sold for the year.
- **b.** Cost of goods manufactured during the year.
- **c.** Amount of applied overhead contained in each job in Work in Process Inventory.
- **d.** Cost of the WIP inventory destroyed by the fire.

14. (Job costs) Koontz & Assc., LLP, is a law firm that currently has four cases in process. Following is information related to those cases as of the end of March 2006:

	Case #1	Case #2	Case #3	Case #4
Direct materials	$120	$2,400	$1,350	$210
Direct labor hours ($90 per hour)	10	25	18	3
Estimated court hours	3	45	150	20

Koontz allocates overhead to cases based on a predetermined rate of $100 per estimated court hour. Determine the total cost assigned to each case as of March 31, 2006.

15. (Departmental overhead rates) Chalmette Company uses a normal cost, job order costing system. In the Mixing Department, overhead is applied using machine hours; in Paving, overhead is applied using direct labor hours. In December 2005, the company estimated the following data for its two departments for 2006:

	Mixing Department	Paving Department
Direct labor hours	3,000	7,000
Machine hours	15,000	3,000
Budgeted overhead cost	$120,000	$196,000

- **a.** Compute the predetermined overhead rate for each department of Chalmette Company.
- **b.** Job #116 was started and completed during March 2006. The job cost sheet shows the following information:

	Mixing Department	Paving Department
Direct material	$11,600	$1,400
Direct labor cost	$120	$1,050
Direct labor hours	24	120
Machine hours	160	44

Compute the overhead applied to Job #116 for each department and in total.

c. If the company had computed a companywide overhead rate rather than departmental rates, would such a rate have indicated the actual overhead cost of each job? Explain.

16. (Job cost and pricing) Jen Bernardi is an attorney who uses a job order costing system to collect costs relative to client engagements. Bernardi is currently working on a case for Joe Lundy. During the first three months of 2006, Bernardi logged 105 hours on the Lundy case.

In addition to direct hours spent by Bernardi, her secretary has worked 25 hours typing and copying 1,450 pages of documents related to the Lundy case. Bernardi's secretary works 160 hours per month and is paid a salary of $3,920 per month. The average cost per copy is $0.04 for paper, toner, and machine rental. Telephone charges for long-distance calls on the case totaled $265.50. Last, Bernardi has estimated that total office overhead for rent, utilities, parking, and so on, amount to $7,200 per month and that, during a normal month, she is at the office 120 hours.

a. Bernardi desires to earn, at a minimum, $90 per hour, and she wishes to cover all direct and allocated indirect costs related to a case. What minimum charge per hour (rounded to the nearest $10) should Bernardi charge Lundy? (*Hint:* Be sure to include office overhead.)

b. All the hours that Bernardi spends at the office are not necessarily billable hours. In addition, Bernardi did not consider certain other expenses such as license fees, country club dues, automobile costs, and other miscellaneous expenses when she determined the amount of overhead per month. Therefore, to cover nonbillable time as well as other costs, Bernardi desires to bill each client for direct costs plus allocated indirect costs plus 50 percent margin on her time and overhead. What will Bernardi charge Lundy in total for the time spent on his case?

17. (Underapplied or overapplied overhead) For 2006, Wilhem Co. applied overhead to jobs using a predetermined overhead rate of $18.40 per machine hour. This rate was derived by dividing the company's total budgeted overhead by the 48,000 machine hours anticipated for the year.

At the end of 2006, the company's manufacturing overhead control account had debits totaling $889,070. Actual machine hours for the year totaled 48,850.

a. How much was total budgeted overhead for 2006?

b. What amount of overhead was applied to Work in Process Inventory during 2006?

c. During 2006, 950 machine hours were used to complete Job #47. How much overhead should be assigned to this job for the year?

d. Is overhead underapplied or overapplied and by how much?

e. Describe the disposition of the underapplied or overapplied overhead determined in part (d).

f. If Wilhem Co. had used an actual cost system in 2006, what would have been the overhead rate per hour?

18. (Assigning costs to jobs) Kilhenny Co. uses a job order costing system and applies overhead to jobs at a predetermined rate of $2.20 per direct labor dollar. During April 2006, the company spent $14,800 on direct materials and $23,900 on direct labor for Job #344. Budgeted factory overhead for the company for the year was $660,000.

a. How did Kilhenny Co. compute the predetermined overhead rate for 2006?

b. Give the journal entry to apply overhead to all jobs, assuming that April's total direct labor cost was $30,700.

c. How much overhead was assigned to Job #344 during April?

d. If Job #344 had a balance of $18,350 on April 1, what was the balance on April 30?

19. (Assigning costs to jobs; cost flows) TORI'S, an interior decorating firm, uses a job order costing system and applies overhead to jobs using a predetermined rate of 60 percent of direct labor cost. On June 1, 2006, Job #918 was the only job in process. Its costs included direct material of $8,250, direct labor of $1,200, and applied overhead of $720. During June, the company began work on Jobs #919, #920, and #921. Direct material used for June totaled $17,350. June's direct labor cost totaled $6,300. Job #920 had not been completed at the end of June, and its direct material and direct labor charges were $3,350 and $650, respectively. All other jobs were completed in June.

a. What was the total cost of Job #920 as of the end of June 2006?

b. What was the cost of goods manufactured for June 2006?

c. If actual overhead for June was $4,350, was the overhead underapplied or overapplied for the month? By how much?

20. (Assigning costs to jobs) Tina Wheels is an advertising consultant; she tracks costs for her jobs using a job order costing system. During September, Tina and her staff worked on and completed jobs for the following companies:

	Brandon Company	Walker Manufacturing	Robbye Inc.
Direct material cost	$3,900	$7,100	$9,900
Direct labor cost	$2,790	$9,000	$14,175
Number of ads designed	3	10	8

Direct materials can be traced to each job because these costs are typically associated with photography and duplicating. Based on historical data, Tina has calculated an overhead charge of $58 per direct labor hour. The normal labor cost per hour is $45.

a. Determine the total cost for each of the advertising accounts for the month.

b. Determine the cost per ad developed for each client.

c. Tina charges $4,300 per ad developed. What was her net income for the month, assuming actual overhead for the month was $25,000?

d. You suggest to Tina that she bill ads on a cost-plus basis and suggest a mark-up of 30 percent on cost. How would her income have compared to her income computed in part (c) if she had used this method? How would her clients feel about such a method?

21. (Standard costing) Fine Print, Inc., incurred the following direct material costs in November 2006 for high-volume routine print jobs:

Actual unit purchase price	$0.016 per sheet
Standard unit price	$0.018 per sheet
Quantity purchased and used in November	490,000 sheets
Standard quantity allowed for good production	492,000 sheets

Calculate the material price variance and the material quantity variance.

22. (Standard costing) Delaware Inc. uses a standard cost system. The company experienced the following results related to direct labor in December 2006:

Actual hours worked	49,500
Standard hours for production	46,200
Actual direct labor rate	$9.25
Standard direct labor rate	$9.75

a. Calculate the total actual payroll.

b. Determine the labor rate variance.

c. Determine the labor quantity variance.

d. What concerns do you have about the variances in parts (b) and (c)?

23. (Cost control) Fabricated Steel Products makes steel storage containers for various chemical products. The company uses a job order costing system and obtains jobs based on competitive bidding. For each project, a budget is developed.

One of the firm's products is a 55-gallon drum. In the past year, the company made this drum on four separate occasions for four different customers. Financial details for the four orders follow.

Date	Job No.	Quantity	Bid Price	Budgeted Cost	Actual Cost
Jan. 17	2118	30,000	$150,000	$120,000	$145,000
Mar. 13	2789	25,000	125,000	100,000	122,000
Oct. 20	4300	40,000	200,000	160,000	193,000
Dec. 3	4990	35,000	175,000	140,000	174,000

Assume that you are the company's controller. Write a memo to management describing any problems that you perceive in the data presented and the steps that should be taken to eliminate recurrence of these problems.

24. (Job order costing; rework) Oehlke Rigging manufactures pulley systems to customer specifications and uses a job order system. Mary Sue Co. recently ordered 10,000 pulleys, and the job was assigned number BA468. Information for Job #BA468 revealed the following:

Direct material	$20,400
Direct labor	24,600
Overhead	18,400

Final inspection of the pulleys revealed that 230 were defective. In correcting the defects, an additional $850 of cost was incurred ($150 for direct material and $700 for direct labor). After the defects were corrected, the pulleys were included with the other good units and shipped to the customer.

a. Prepare the journal entry to record incurrence of the rework costs if rework is normal but specific to this job.

b. Prepare the journal entry to record incurrence of the rework costs if Oehlke Rigging's predetermined overhead rate includes normal rework costs.

c. Prepare the journal entry to record incurrence of the rework costs, assuming that all rework is abnormal.

25. (Labor time) Choose a Web search engine and type in "time-and-attendance software." Numerous sites will be displayed. Go to the Web sites of four companies that produce or sell such software. Prepare a brief report that compares and contrasts the software items. Choose one product that appeals to you more than the others and discuss the reasons for your choice.

26. (Process differences) Go to the Web site for **Green Design Furniture**. Prepare a report that reviews and explains the design and manufacturing process of this company. Why would it be necessary for Green Design Furniture to use a job order costing system? How does this company's production process differ from that of companies that manufacture furniture for sale at high-volume discount stores? What cost differences would you expect between the two companies?

27. (Strategic alliances) According to a *Wall Street Journal* article (Wei, "Accounting Alliances Gain Popularity," February 11, 2004, p. B4A), many large public accounting firms are establishing alliances with smaller firms. Such alliances allow the smaller entities to use the larger firms' research, training, and client-service capabilities. Such alliances are seen to be needed, given the Sarbanes-Oxley Act rules that limit the types of nonaudit services that firms can provide to audit clients.

a. Review the Sarbanes-Oxley Act of 2002 and write a brief synopsis of the provisions related to nonaudit services.

b. How does the contemporary use of joint ventures and other cooperative arrangements with other firms add complexity to the accounting function for a business managing its costs?

c. Why must managers and accountants not only look inside but also outside the firm to manage costs?

d. Why might a large CPA firm in such an alliance want to establish a job order system that would reflect the services used by smaller firms within the alliance? Would such a system necessarily involve the use of financial information?

28. (Ethics) Companies use time sheets for two primary reasons: to know how many hours an employee works and, in a job order production situation, to trace work hours to products. An article ("Altering of Worker Time Cards Spurs Growing Number of Suits" by Steven Greenhouse) in the *New York Times* on April 4, 2004, described a recent corporate practice of deleting worker hours to increase organizational profitability. Read this article and discuss the following:

a. What companies were mentioned as having been found to engage in this practice?

b. Why is it easier now than in the past to engage in this practice?

c. As a member of upper management, how would you respond to finding out that this practice was being used in some of your stores? Provide an answer that addresses both the short run and the long run.

Problems

29. (Journal entries) Shady Time installs awnings on residential and commercial structures. The company had the following transactions for February 2006:
- Purchased $195,000 of building (raw) material on account.
- Issued $185,000 of building (direct) material to jobs.
- Issued $30,000 of building (indirect) material for use on jobs.
- Accrued wages payable of $297,000, of which $237,000 could be traced directly to particular jobs.
- Applied overhead to jobs on the basis of 55 percent of direct labor cost.
- Completed jobs costing $333,000. For these jobs, revenues of $421,000 were collected.

Make all appropriate journal entries for the above transactions.

30. (Journal entries) Singer Refrigeration uses an actual cost, job order system. The following transactions are for August 2006. At the beginning of the month, Direct Material Inventory was $8,000, Work in Process Inventory was $25,000, and Finished Goods Inventory was $11,000.
- Direct material purchases on account totaled $90,000.
- Direct labor cost for the period totaled $75,600 for 8,000 direct labor hours; these costs were paid in cash.
- Actual overhead costs were $82,000 and are applied to production based on direct labor hours.
- The ending inventory of Direct Material Inventory was $3,000.
- The ending inventory of Work in Process Inventory was $11,500.
- Goods costing $243,700 were sold for $346,050.

a. What was the actual overhead rate per direct labor hour?
b. Prepare all journal entries for the preceding transactions.
c. Determine the ending balance in Finished Goods Inventory.

31. (Journal entries; assigning costs to jobs) Omega Engineers uses a job order costing system. On September 1, 2006, the company had the following account balances:

Raw Material Inventory	$ 166,200
Work in Process Inventory	756,300
Cost of Goods Sold	2,432,000

On September 1, the three jobs in Work in Process Inventory had the following balances:

Job #75	$293,200
Job #78	116,800
Job #82	346,300

The following transactions occurred during September:

Sept. 1 Purchased $970,000 of raw material on account.
     4 Issued $950,000 of raw material as follows: Job #75, $144,800; Job #78, $126,300; Job #82, $496,100; Job #86, $156,200; indirect material, $26,600.
    15 Prepared and paid the $378,500 factory payroll for Sept. 1–15. Analysis of this payroll showed the following information:

Job #75	4,830 hours	$ 42,300
Job #78	13,160 hours	133,600
Job #82	10,150 hours	101,500
Job #86	5,140 hours	55,400
Indirect wages		45,700

    15 On each payroll date, Omega Engineers applies manufacturing overhead to jobs at a rate of $8.50 per direct labor hour.
    15 Job #75 was completed and accepted by the customer and billed at a selling price of cost plus 25 percent. Selling prices are rounded to the nearest whole dollar.
    20 Paid the following monthly factory bills: utilities, $19,800; rent, $35,300; and accounts payable (accrued in August), $98,400.
    24 Purchased raw material on account, $312,000.
    25 Issued raw material as follows: Job #78, $77,400; Job #82, $106,300; Job #86, $174,500; and indirect material, $27,900.
    30 Recorded additional factory overhead costs as follows: depreciation, $104,500; expired prepaid insurance, $32,700; and accrued taxes and licenses, $16,200.
    30 Recorded and paid the factory payroll for Sept. 16–30 of $357,200. Analysis of the payroll follows:

Job #78	8,940 hours	$ 88,700
Job #82	13,650 hours	114,200
Job #86	9,980 hours	121,800
Indirect wages		32,500

    30 Applied overhead for the second half of the month to jobs.

a. Prepare journal entries for the transactions for September 2006.
b. Use T-accounts to post the information from the journal entries in part (a) to the job cost subsidiary accounts and to general ledger accounts.
c. Reconcile the September 30 balances in the subsidiary ledger with the Work in Process Inventory account in the general ledger.
d. Determine the amount of underapplied or overapplied overhead for September.

32. (Journal entries; cost flows) Excellent Components began 2006 with three jobs in process:

	TYPE OF COST			
Job No.	Direct Material	Direct Labor	Overhead	Total
247	$ 77,200	$ 91,400	$ 34,732	$ 203,332
251	176,600	209,800	79,724	466,124
253	145,400	169,600	64,448	379,448
Totals	$399,200	$470,800	$178,904	$1,048,904

During 2006, the following transactions occurred:

1. The firm purchased and paid for $542,000 of raw material.

2. Factory payroll records revealed the following:
- Indirect labor incurred was $54,000.
- Direct labor incurred was $602,800 and was associated with the jobs as follows:

Job No.	Direct Labor Cost
247	$ 17,400
251	8,800
253	21,000
254	136,600
255	145,000
256	94,600
257	179,400

3. Material requisition forms issued during the year revealed the following:
- Indirect material issued totaled $76,000.
- Direct material issued totaled $466,400 and was associated with jobs as follows:

Job No.	Direct Material Cost
247	$ 12,400
251	6,200
253	16,800
254	105,200
255	119,800
256	72,800
257	133,200

4. Overhead is applied to jobs on the basis of direct labor cost. Management budgeted overhead of $240,000 and total direct labor cost of $600,000 for 2006. Actual total factory overhead costs (including indirect labor and indirect material) for the year totaled $244,400.

5. Jobs #247 through #255 were completed and delivered to customers C.O.D. The revenue on these jobs was $2,264,774.

a. Prepare journal entries for all preceding events.

b. Determine ending balances for jobs still in process.

c. Determine cost of jobs completed, adjusted for underapplied or overapplied overhead.

33. (Simple inventory calculation) Production data for the first week in November 2006 for Bryan Machinery were as follows:

WORK IN PROCESS INVENTORY				
Date	Job No.	Material	Labor	Machine Time (Overhead)
Nov. 1	411	$950	18 hours	25 hours
1	412	620	5 hours	15 hours
7	417	310	4 hours	8 hours

Finished Goods Inventory, Nov. 1: $11,900
Finished Goods Inventory, Nov. 7: $ 0

MATERIAL RECORDS

Type	Inv. 11/1	Purchases	Issuances	Inv. 11/7
Aluminum	$4,150	$49,150	$29,350	$?
Steel	6,400	13,250	17,100	$?
Other	2,900	11,775	12,950	$?

Direct labor hours worked: 340. Labor cost is $15 per direct labor hour. Machine hours worked: 600.

Overhead for first week in November:

Depreciation	$ 4,500
Supervisor salaries	7,200
Indirect labor	4,175
Insurance	1,400
Utilities	1,125
Total	$18,400

Overhead is charged to production at a rate of $30 per machine hour. Underapplied or overapplied overhead is treated as an adjustment to Cost of Goods Sold at year-end. (All company jobs are consecutively numbered, and all work not in ending Finished Goods Inventory has been completed and sold.)

What is the value at November 7 of (1) the three material accounts, (2) Work in Process Inventory, and (3) Cost of Goods Sold?

34. (Job cost sheet analysis) As a candidate for a cost accounting position with Romano Construction, you have been asked to take a quiz to demonstrate your knowledge of job order costing. Romano's job order costing system is based on normal costs and overhead is applied based on direct labor cost. The following records pertaining to May have been provided to you:

Job No.	Direct Material	Direct Labor	Applied Overhead	Total Cost
167	$ 17,703	$ 6,920	$7,960	$32,583
169	54,936	7,240	8,328	70,504
170	1,218	2,000	2,300	5,518
171	154,215	28,500	?	?
172	28,845	2,200	2,532	33,577

To explain the missing job number, you are informed that Job #168 had been completed in April. You are also told that Job #167 was the only job in process at the beginning of May. At that time, the job had been assigned $12,900 for direct material and $3,600 for direct labor. At the end of May, Job #171 had not been completed; all others had. You are to provide answers to the following questions:

a. What predetermined overhead rate does Romano Construction use?
b. What was the total cost of beginning Work in Process Inventory?
c. What were total direct manufacturing costs incurred for May?
d. What was cost of goods manufactured for May?

35. (Departmental rates) Elegant Style Tile Corporation has two departments, Mixing and Drying. All jobs go through each department, and the company uses a job order costing system. Overhead is applied to jobs based on labor hours in Mixing and on machine hours in Drying. In December 2005, corporate management estimated the following production data for 2006 in setting its predetermined overhead rates:

	Mixing	Drying
Machine hours	14,400	208,000
Direct labor hours	176,000	24,800
Departmental overhead	$748,000	$988,000

Two jobs completed during 2006 were #2296 and #2297. The job order cost sheets showed the following information about these jobs:

	Job #2296	Job #2297
Direct material cost	$9,750	$12,600
Direct labor hours—Mixing	850	1,020
Machine hours—Mixing	80	90
Direct labor hours—Drying	40	46
Machine hours—Drying	220	250

Direct labor workers are paid $8 per hour in the Mixing Department and $20 per hour in Drying.

a. Compute the predetermined overhead rates used in Mixing and Drying for 2006.

b. Compute the direct labor cost associated with each job for both departments.

c. Compute the amount of overhead assigned to each job in each department.

d. Determine the total cost of Jobs #2296 and #2297.

e. Actual data for 2006 for each department follow.

	Mixing	Drying
Machine hours	14,600	215,600
Direct labor hours	172,800	25,200
Departmental overhead	$724,000	$1,024,000

What is the amount of underapplied or overapplied overhead for each department for the year ended December 31, 2006?

36. (Comprehensive) Gary Construction Company uses a job order costing system. In May 2006, Gary made a $1,650,000 bid to build a pedestrian overpass over the beach highway in Gulfport, Mississippi. Gary won the bid and assigned #515 to the project. Its completion date was set at December 15, 2006. The following costs were estimated for completion of the overpass: $620,000 for direct material, $335,000 for direct labor, and $201,000 for overhead.

During July, direct material cost assigned to Job #515 was $60,900, and direct labor cost associated with it was $87,520. The firm uses a predetermined overhead rate of 60 percent of direct labor cost. Gary Construction also worked on several other jobs during July and incurred the following costs:

Direct materials (including Job #515)	$289,650
Direct labor (including Job #515)	292,000
Indirect labor	27,900
Administrative salaries and wages	19,800
Depreciation on construction equipment	13,200
Depreciation on office equipment	3,900
Client entertainment (on accounts payable)	5,550
Advertising for firm (paid in cash)	3,300
Indirect material (from supplies inventory)	9,300
Miscellaneous expenses (design related; to be paid in the following month)	5,100
Accrued utilities (for office, $900; for construction, $2,700)	3,600

During July, Gary Construction completed several jobs that had been in process before the beginning of the month. These completed jobs generated $612,000 of revenues for the company. The related job cost sheets showed costs associated with those jobs of $414,500. At the beginning of July, Gary Construction had Work in Process Inventory of $435,900.

a. Prepare a job order cost sheet for Job #515, including all job details, and post the appropriate cost information for July.

b. Prepare journal entries for the preceding information.

c. Prepare a schedule of cost of goods manufactured for July for Gary Construction Company.

d. Assuming that the company pays income tax at a 40 percent rate, prepare an income statement for Gary Construction Company.

37. (Comprehensive) Safety First, Inc., designs and manufactures perimeter fencing for large retail and commercial buildings. Each job goes through three stages: design, production, and installation. Three jobs were started and completed during the first week of May 2006. No jobs were in process at the end of April 2006. Information for the three departments for the first week in May follows:

	DEPARTMENT		
Job #2019	**Design**	**Production**	**Installation**
Direct labor hours	200	NA	140
Machine hours	NA	180	NA
Direct labor cost	$20,400	$8,500	$2,520
Direct material	$ 2,400	$29,100	$2,600
Job #2020	**Design**	**Production**	**Installation**
Direct labor hours	170	NA	160
Machine hours	NA	600	NA
Direct labor cost	$17,340	$14,900	$2,880
Direct material	$2,050	$67,200	$9,200
Job #2021	**Design**	**Production**	**Installation**
Direct labor hours	180	NA	820
Machine hours	NA	240	NA
Direct labor cost	$18,360	$5,900	$3,800
Direct material	$4,400	$58,000	$2,600

Overhead is applied using departmental rates. Design and Installation use direct labor cost as the base, with rates of 30 and 90 percent, respectively. Production uses machine hours as the base, with a rate of $15 per hour. Actual overhead for the month was $26,400 in Design, $15,000 in Production, and $7,300 in Installation.

a. Determine the overhead to be applied to each job. By how much is the overhead underapplied or overapplied in each department? For the company?

b. Assume that no journal entries have been made to Work in Process Inventory. Make all necessary entries to both the subsidiary ledger and general ledger accounts.

c. Calculate the total cost for each job.

38. (Standard costing) MaMo Corp. specializes in making robotic conveyor systems to move materials within a factory. Model #89 accounts for approximately 60 percent of the company's annual sales. Because the company has produced and expects to continue to produce a significant quantity of this model, MaMo uses the following standard costs to account for Model #89 production costs.

Direct material (14,000 pounds)	$28,000
Direct labor (860 hours at $20 per hour)	17,200
Overhead	38,000
Total standard cost	$83,200

For the 200 units of Model #89 produced in 2006, the actual costs were

Direct material (3,000,000 pounds)	$ 5,800,000
Direct labor (178,400 hours)	3,478,800
Overhead	7,400,000
Total actual cost	$16,678,800

a. Compute a separate variance between actual and standard cost for direct material, direct labor, and manufacturing overhead for the Model #89 units produced in 2006.

b. Is the direct material variance found in part (a) driven primarily by the price per pound difference between standard and actual or the quantity difference between standard and actual? Explain.

39. (Standard costing) During July 2006, Haul-It, Inc., worked on two production runs (Jobs #918 and #2002) of the same product, a trailer hitch component. Job #918 consisted of 1,200 units of the product, and Job #2002 contained 2,000 units. The hitch components are made from ½″ sheet metal. Because this component is routinely produced for one of Haul-It's long-term customers, standard costs have been developed for its production. The standard cost of material for each unit is $4.50; each unit contains 6 pounds of material. The standard direct labor time per unit is 6 minutes for workers earning a rate of $20 per hour. The actual costs recorded for each job were as follows:

	Direct Material	Direct Labor
Job #918	(7,500 pounds) $5,250	(130 hours) $2,470
Job #2002	(11,800 pounds) 9,440	(230 hours) 4,255

a. What is the standard direct cost of each trailer hitch component?

b. What was the total standard direct cost assigned to each of the jobs?

c. Compute the variances for direct material and for direct labor for each job.

d. Why should variances be computed separately for each job rather than for the aggregate annual trailer hitch component production?

40. (Defective units and rework) Hoffus Corporation produces plastic pipe to customer specifications. Losses of less than 5 percent are considered normal because they are inherent in the production process. The company applies overhead to products using machine hours. Hoffus Corporation used the following information in setting its predetermined overhead rate for 2006:

Expected overhead other than rework	$425,000
Expected rework costs	37,500
Total expected overhead	$462,500
Expected machine hours for 2006	50,000

During 2006, the following production and cost data were accumulated:

Total good production completed	2,000,000 feet of pipe
Total defects	40,000 feet of pipe
Ending inventory	75,000 feet of pipe
Total cost of direct material for Job #B316	$343,550
Total cost of conversion for Job #B316	$78,875
Total machine hours for Job #B316	1,540
Cost of reworking defects during 2006	$37,750
Total actual overhead cost for 2006	$431,000

a. Determine the overhead application rate for 2006.

b. Determine the cost for Job #B316 in 2006.

c. Assume that the rework is normal and those units can be sold for the regular selling price. How will Hoffus Corporation account for the $37,750 of rework cost?

d. Assume that Hoffus does not include rework costs in developing the overhead application rate because rework is related to specific jobs. Determine the cost of Job #B316.

e. Using the information from part (d), assume that 20 percent of the rework cost was specifically related to 200 feet of pipe produced for Job #B316. The reworked pipe can be sold for $1.50 per foot. What is the total cost of Job #B316?

41. (Comprehensive; job cost sheet) Jefferson Construction Company builds bridges. In October and November 2006, the firm worked exclusively on a bridge spanning the Niobrara River in northern Nebraska. Jefferson Construction's Precast Department builds structural elements of the bridges in temporary plants located near the construction sites. The Construction Department operates at the bridge site and assembles the precast structural elements. Estimated costs for the Niobrara River Bridge for the Precast Department were $1,550,000 for direct material, $220,000 for direct labor, and $275,000 for overhead. For the Construction Department, estimated costs for the Niobrara River Bridge were $350,000 for direct material, $130,000 for direct labor, and $214,500 for overhead. Overhead is applied on the last day of each month. Overhead application rates for the Precast and Construction Departments are $25 per machine hour and 165 percent of direct labor cost, respectively.

TRANSACTIONS FOR OCTOBER

Oct. 1	Purchased $1,150,000 of material (on account) for the Precast Department to begin building structural elements. All of the material was issued to production; of the issuances, $650,000 was considered direct.
5	Installed utilities at the bridge site at a total cost of $25,000. This amount will be paid at a later date.
8	Paid rent for the temporary construction site housing the Precast Department, $5,000.
15	Completed bridge support pillars by the Precast Department and transferred to the construction site.
20	Paid machine rental expense of $60,000 incurred by the Construction Department for clearing the bridge site and digging foundations for bridge supports.
24	Purchased additional material costing $985,000 on account.
31	Paid the following bills for the Precast Department: utilities, $7,000; direct labor, $45,000; insurance, $6,220; and supervision and other indirect labor costs, $7,900. Departmental depreciation was recorded, $15,200. The company also paid bills for the Construction Department: utilities, $2,300; direct labor, $16,300; indirect labor, $5,700; and insurance, $1,900. Departmental depreciation was recorded on equipment, $8,750.
31	Issued a check to pay for the material purchased on October 1 and October 24.
31	Applied overhead to production in each department; 6,000 machine hours were worked in the Precast Department in October.

TRANSACTIONS FOR NOVEMBER

Nov. 1	Transferred additional structural elements from the Precast Department to the construction site. The Construction Department incurred a cash cost of $5,000 to rent a crane.
4	Issued $1,000,000 of material to the Precast Department. Of this amount, $825,000 was considered direct.
8	Paid rent of $5,000 in cash for the temporary site occupied by the Precast Department.
15	Issued $425,000 of material to the Construction Department. Of this amount, $200,000 was considered direct.
18	Transferred additional structural elements from the Precast Department to the construction site.
24	Transferred the final batch of structural elements from the Precast Department to the construction site.
29	Completed the bridge.
30	Paid final bills for the month in the Precast Department: utilities, $15,000; direct labor, $115,000; insurance, $9,350; and supervision and other indirect labor costs, $14,500. Depreciation was recorded, $15,200. The company also paid bills for the Construction Department: utilities, $4,900; direct labor, $134,300; indirect labor, $15,200; and insurance, $5,400. Depreciation was recorded on equipment, $18,350.
30	Applied overhead in each department. The Precast Department recorded 3,950 machine hours in November.
30	Billed the state of Nebraska for the completed bridge at the contract price of $3,450,000.

a. Prepare all necessary journal entries for the preceding transactions. For purposes of this problem, it is not necessary to transfer direct material and direct labor from one department into the other.

b. Post all entries to T-accounts.

c. Prepare a job order cost sheet, which includes estimated costs, for the construction of the bridge.

d. Discuss Jefferson Construction Company's estimates relative to its actual costs.

42. (Comprehensive) Tiny Tots Corp. is a manufacturer of furnishings for infants and children. The company uses a job order cost system. Tiny Tots' Work in Process Inventory on April 30, 2006, consisted of the following jobs:

Job No.	Items	Units	Accumulated Cost
CBS102	Cribs	20,000	$ 900,000
PLP086	Playpens	15,000	420,000
DRS114	Dressers	25,000	1,570,000

The company's finished goods inventory, carried on a FIFO basis, consists of five items:

Item	Quantity and Unit Cost	Total Cost
Cribs	7,500 units @ $64	$ 480,000
Strollers	13,000 units @ $23	299,000
Carriages	11,200 units @ $102	1,142,400
Dressers	21,000 units @ $55	1,155,000
Playpens	19,400 units @ $35	679,000
Total		$3,755,400

Tiny Tots applies factory overhead on the basis of direct labor hours. The company's factory overhead budget for the year ending May 31, 2006, totals $4,500,000, and the company plans to expend 600,000 direct labor hours during this period. Through the first 11 months of the year, a total of 555,000 direct labor hours was worked, and total factory overhead amounted to $4,273,500.

At the end of April, the balance in Tiny Tots' Raw Material Inventory account, which includes both raw material and purchased parts, was $668,000. Additions to and requisitions from the material inventory during May included the following:

	Raw Material	Parts Purchased
Additions	$242,000	$396,000
Requisitions:		
Job #CBS102	51,000	104,000
Job #PLP086	3,000	10,800
Job #DRS114	124,000	87,000
Job #STR077 (10,000 strollers)	62,000	81,000
Job #CRG098 (5,000 carriages)	65,000	187,000

During May, Tiny Tots' factory payroll consisted of the following:

Job No.	Hours	Cost
CBS102	12,000	$122,400
PLP086	4,400	43,200
DRS114	19,500	200,500
STR077	3,500	30,000
CRG098	14,000	138,000
Indirect	3,000	29,400
Supervision		57,600
Total		$621,100

The jobs that were completed in May and the unit sales for May follow:

Job No.	Items	Quantity Completed
CBS102	Cribs	20,000
PLP086	Playpens	15,000
STR077	Strollers	10,000
CRG098	Carriages	5,000

Items	Quantity Shipped
Cribs	17,500
Playpens	21,000
Strollers	14,000
Dressers	18,000
Carriages	6,000

a. Describe when it is appropriate for a company to use a job order costing system.

b. Calculate the dollar balance in Tiny Tots' Work in Process Inventory account as of May 31, 2006.

c. Calculate the dollar amount related to the playpens in Tiny Tots' Finished Goods Inventory as of May 31, 2006.

d. Explain the treatment of underapplied or overapplied overhead when using a job order costing system.

(CMA adapted)

43. (Missing amounts; challenging) Riveredge Manufacturing Company realized too late that it had made a mistake locating its controller's office and its electronic data processing system in the basement. Because of the spring thaw, the Mississippi River overflowed its banks on May 2 and flooded the company's basement. Electronic data storage was destroyed, and the company had not provided off-site storage of data. Some of the paper printouts were located but were badly faded and only partially legible. On May 3, when the flooding subsided, company accountants were able to assemble the following factory-related data from the debris and from discussions with various knowledgeable personnel. Data about the following accounts were found:

- Raw Material (includes indirect material) Inventory: Balance April 1 was $4,800.
- Work in Process Inventory: Balance April 1 was $7,700.
- Finished Goods Inventory: Balance April 30 was $6,600.
- Total company payroll cost for April was $29,200.
- Accounts payable balance April 30 was $18,000.
- Indirect material used in April cost $5,800.
- Other nonmaterial and nonlabor overhead items for April totaled $2,500.

Payroll records, kept at an across-town service center that processes the company's payroll, showed that April's direct labor amounted to $18,200 and represented 4,400 labor hours. Indirect factory labor amounted to $5,400 in April.

The president's office had a file copy of the production budget for the current year. It revealed that the predetermined manufacturing overhead application rate is based on planned annual direct labor hours of 50,400 and expected factory overhead of $151,200.

Discussion with the factory superintendent indicated that only two jobs remained unfinished on April 30. Fortunately, the superintendent also had copies of the job cost sheets that showed a combined total of $2,400 of direct material and $4,500 of direct labor. The direct labor hours on these jobs totaled 1,072. Both of these jobs had been started during April.

A badly faded copy of April's Cost of Goods Manufactured and Sold schedule showed cost of goods manufactured was $48,000, and the April 1 Finished Goods Inventory was $8,400.

The treasurer's office files copies of paid invoices chronologically. All invoices are for raw material purchased on account. Examination of these files revealed that unpaid invoices on April 1 amounted to $6,100; $28,000 of purchases had been made during April; and $18,000 of unpaid invoices existed on April 30.

  a. Calculate the cost of direct material used in April.

  b. Calculate the cost of raw material issued in April.

  c. Calculate the April 30 balance of Raw Material Inventory.

  d. Determine the amount of underapplied or overapplied overhead for April.

  e. What is the Cost of Goods Sold for April?

44. (Ethics) One of the main points of using a job order costing system is to achieve profitability by charging a price for each job that is proportionate to the related costs. The fundamental underlying concept is that the buyer of the product should be charged a price that exceeds all costs related to the job contract; thus, the price reflects the cost.

However, there are settings in which the price charged to the consumer does not reflect the costs incurred by the vendor to serve that customer. This is the situation in a recent case heard by the U.S. Supreme Court. The case involves the University of Wisconsin, which charges all students a user fee and then redistributes these fees to student organizations.

The purpose of collecting the fee is to ensure that money is available to support diversity of thought and speech in student organizations. The user fee supports even unpopular causes so that the students would hear many voices. In total, the fee subsidized about 125 student groups. However, a group of students filed suit, claiming that students should not be required to fund causes that are inconsistent with their personal beliefs.

  a. In your opinion, how would diversity of thought be affected if a student were allowed to select the organizations that would receive the student's user fee (e.g., as with dues)?

  b. Is the University of Wisconsin treating its students ethically by charging them to support student organizations supporting causes that conflict with students' personal beliefs?

45. (Ethics) Two types of contracts are commonly used when private firms contract to provide services to governmental agencies: cost-plus and fixed-price contracts. The cost-plus contract allows the contracting firm to recover the costs associated with providing the product or service plus a reasonable profit. The fixed-price contract provides for a fixed payment to the contractor. When a fixed-price contract is used, the contractor's profits are based on its ability to control costs relative to the price received.

In recent years, a number of contractors have either been accused or found guilty of improper accounting or fraud in accounting for contracts with the government. One deceptive accounting technique that is sometimes the subject of audit investigations involves cases in which a contractor is suspected of shifting costs from fixed-priced contracts to cost-plus contracts. In shifting costs from the fixed-priced contract, the contractor not only influences costs assigned to that contract but also receives a reimbursement plus an additional amount on the costs shifted to the cost-plus contract.

  a. Why would a company that conducts work under both cost-plus and fixed-price contracts have an incentive to shift costs from the fixed-price to the cost-plus contracts?

  b. From an ethical perspective, do you believe such cost shifting is ever justified? Explain.

46. (Research) **Timbuk2** is a San Francisco company that makes a variety of messenger, cyclist, and laptop bags. The company's Web site allows customers to design their own size, color, and fabric bags with specific features and accessories; then the company sews the bags to the customers' specifications.

    a. Visit the company's Web site and custom design a bag. Compare the quoted price with a bag of similar quality and features at a local store. Explain whether you think the Timbuk2 bag is a good value.

    b. Why would Timbuk2 be able to produce custom-made messenger bags for almost the same cost as mass-produced ones?

    c. Would you expect the quality of the custom-produced messenger bags to be higher or lower than the mass-produced ones? Discuss the rationale for your answer.

    d. Why would the custom-made messenger bags show a high profit margin?

5

Activity-Based Management and Activity-Based Costing

Objectives

AFTER COMPLETING THIS CHAPTER, YOU SHOULD BE ABLE TO ANSWER THESE QUESTIONS:

LO.1 ON WHAT ITEMS DOES ACTIVITY-BASED MANAGEMENT FOCUS?

LO.2 WHY DO NON-VALUE-ADDED ACTIVITIES CAUSE COSTS TO INCREASE UNNECESSARILY?

LO.3 WHY MUST COST DRIVERS BE DESIGNATED IN AN ACTIVITY-BASED COSTING SYSTEM?

LO.4 HOW DOES ACTIVITY-BASED COSTING DIFFER FROM A TRADITIONAL COST ACCOUNTING SYSTEM?

LO.5 WHAT NEW TYPES OF INFORMATION DOES AN ACTIVITY-BASED COSTING/MANAGEMENT SYSTEM OFFER MANAGEMENT?

LO.6 WHEN IS ACTIVITY-BASED COSTING APPROPRIATE IN AN ORGANIZATION?

Introducing

Formed in 1993 and located in New Orleans, Louisiana, **DynMcDermott** (DM) has one customer, the Department of Energy (DOE) of the U.S. federal government. DM is simply a "management" company; it has no assets or liabilities. It generates cash based on service performance results, and the annual performance fee reflects how well the company met the DOE's mission objectives for the period. DM's task is to manage and operate the DOE's Strategic Petroleum Reserve (SPR). The SPR is the largest emergency crude oil reserve in the world, having at least 90 days of the country's net oil imports on hand (based on the prior year). DM employs the maintenance and operations workforce responsible for the SPR's infrastructure of pipelines, pumps, motors, and other equipment.

Among other things, the company's mission statement refers to delivering cost-effective SPR operational readiness. DM's integration of industry best practices, cost-reduction initiatives, continuous process improvements, operational benchmarking, and safety have been instrumental factors in its ability to obtain and retain five-year contracts from DOE. The company employs a successful and contractually based business model that was derived from the Malcolm Baldrige National Quality Award criteria. DM is considered one of the top-performing federal contractors by DOE and the U.S. Office of Management and Budget and is the only company in Louisiana to win the Baldrige-based Louisiana Quality Award

three times (1996, 2001, and 2003). DM's health and safety programs have achieved world-class performance status as determined by OSHA and the company's environmental program has won national awards. DM has not received an environmental violation relating to the clean air, clean water, and hazardous waste since 1995.

DM has obtained significant cost savings and avoided many costs from the elimination of redundant and non-value-added work practices that occurred after implementing techniques such as activity-based management, total quality management, and Lean and Six Sigma tools, all of which are part of the Integrated Continuous Performance Improvement System. This type of system empowers employees to innovate and improve processes and complete their work in teams, often cross-functional in nature. One obvious benefit of cost reduction at DM is that renewal of the company's DOE contract will allow employees to retain their jobs; another benefit is reflected in increased employee profit sharing. With employees constantly on the lookout for ways to streamline processes and save the company time and money, DynMcDermott is proud of its abilities to effectively and efficiently beat out competitors for the job of overseeing an oil supply that is critical to national security.

Source: DynMcDermott 2004 Malcolm Baldrige National Quality Award application and discussions with Ron Schulingkamp, Strategic Systems Coordinator for DynMcDermott.

Because of its unique nature, **DynMcDermott** is not comparable in many respects to what could be considered "traditional" businesses. However, like other companies, DM must be both competent at its work product and competitive in its cost structure to retain its DOE contract. Generating cost efficiencies requires a solid knowledge of why costs are incurred, so implementing an activity-based management system to pinpoint human and mechanical processes that were not adding value to DM's customer was a realistic business option.

This chapter presents two topics that can improve management information and enhance the competitive advantage of an organization. First, the chapter discusses the reasons that companies now focus on value-added and non-value-added activities and explains how activities (rather than volume measures) can be used to determine product and service costs and to measure performance. Then the chapter discusses and illustrates basics of activity-based costing and discusses some criticisms of this technique.

ACTIVITY-BASED MANAGEMENT

Although specifically designated as an accounting function, determination of product cost is of major concern to all managers. The profitability of a particular product or market, product pricing implications, and investments to support production are issues that extend beyond accounting to the areas of corporate strategy, marketing, and finance. In theory, the cost to produce a product or perform a service would not matter if enough customers were willing to buy that product or service at a price high enough to cover its cost and provide a reasonable profit margin. In reality, customers purchase a product or service only if they perceive that it provides acceptable value for the price.

Management, then, should be concerned about whether customers perceive an equitable relationship between selling price and value. **Activity-based management** (ABM) focuses on controlling the activities incurred during the production or performance process to improve customer value and enhance profitability. ABM includes a variety of topics discussed in this and other chapters in the text. See Exhibit 5–1 for concepts that can be seen as part of activity-based management. These concepts help companies to produce more efficiently, determine costs more accurately, and control and evaluate performance more effectively. A primary component of activity-based management is **activity analysis**, which is the process of studying activities to classify them and to devise ways to minimize or eliminate non-value-added activities.

LO.1
ON WHAT ITEMS DOES ACTIVITY-BASED MANAGEMENT FOCUS?

activity-based management

activity analysis

activity

value-added activity

non-value-added activity

Value-Added versus Non-Value-Added Activities

In a business context, an **activity** is defined as a repetitive action performed in fulfillment of business functions. If one takes a black-or-white perspective, activities are either value added or non-value added. A **value-added** (VA) **activity** increases the worth of a product or service to a customer and is one for which the customer is willing to pay. Alternatively, a **non-value-added** (NVA) **activity** increases the time spent on a product or service but does not increase its worth.

EXHIBIT 5–1
COMPONENTS OF ACTIVITY-BASED MANAGEMENT

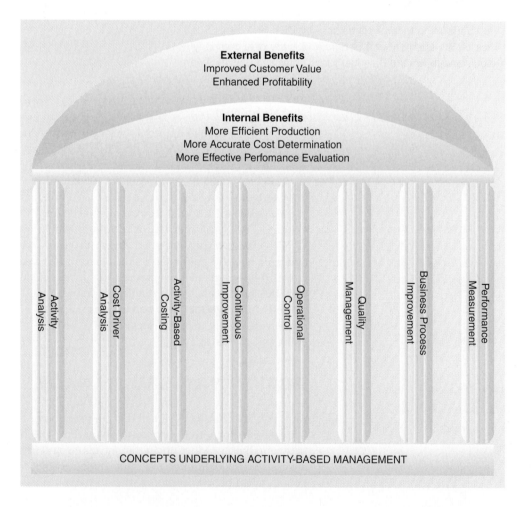

Why do managers view activities through the eyes of their customers in sorting value-added from non-value-added activities?

business-value-added activities

Non-value-added activities are unnecessary from the customer's perspective. Therefore, NVA activities can be reduced, redesigned, or eliminated without affecting the market value or quality of the product or service. Often an easy way to determine the value provided by an activity is to ask "why" five times: if a viable business answer can be gained, the activity generally adds value; otherwise, it adds no value.

Businesses can also engage in some activities that are essential (or appear to be essential) to business operations but for which customers would not willingly choose to pay (refer to Exhibit 5–2). These activities are known as **business-value-added activities**. For instance, companies must prepare invoices to document sales and collections. Customers realize this activity must occur, that it creates costs, and that product selling prices must be set to cover the costs of this activity. However, because invoice preparation adds no direct value to products and services, customers would prefer not to pay for this activity.

From a management perspective, the cost of serving customers must be determined so that the company can charge a satisfactory price and produce profits. Activities drive the consumption of resources, which in turn drives costs. Because most prices are set by the marketplace rather than by individual companies based on their costs, companies that can reduce or eliminate NVA activities can obtain a

EXHIBIT 5–2

CLASSIFICATIONS OF ACTIVITIES

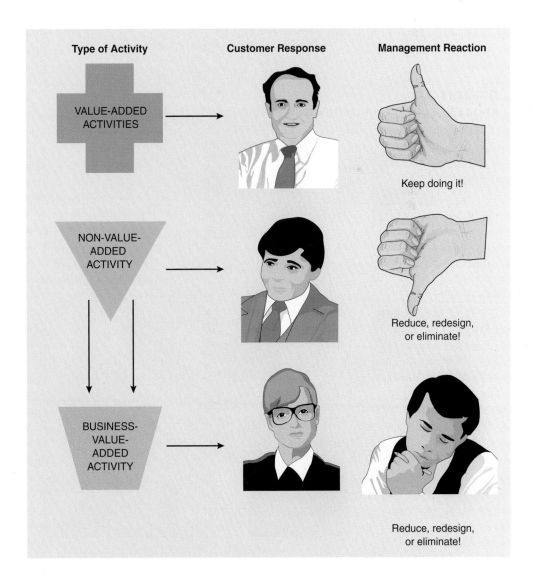

larger profit margin when selling at market price than those companies with higher costs. Additionally, if a company can reduce the "going" market price because costs have declined, it could be able to obtain a larger market share.

To begin activity analysis, managers should first identify organizational processes. A **process** is a series of activities that, when performed together, satisfy a specific objective. Thus, companies engage in processes for production, distribution, selling, administration, and other company functions. Processes should be defined before a company tries to determine what activities are related. Most processes occur horizontally across organizational functions and, thus, overlap multiple functional areas. For example, a production process also affects engineering, purchasing, receiving, warehousing, accounting, human resources, and marketing (see Exhibit 5–3). This depiction does not include the sales process for the product. From this illustration, it should be easy to see why a process should be defined in a more limited manner than "production."

process

process map

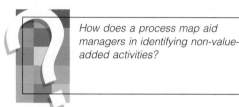

How does a process map aid managers in identifying non-value-added activities?

For each distinct process, a unique **process map** (or detailed flow-chart) should be prepared to indicate *every* step in *every* area that goes into making or doing something. Some of the steps included on the process map will be necessary and some will be unnecessary. Necessary steps are those activities that *must* be performed for the process to be completed; unnecessary steps are those activities for which a valid business answer to the question 'why" cannot be found. For example, one necessary step in making a pizza crust is to mix flour and water, but storing flour until it is needed would be considered unnecessary as indicated by the following manager-employee "conversation."

EXHIBIT 5–3
PROCESS FLOW IN AN ORGANIZATION

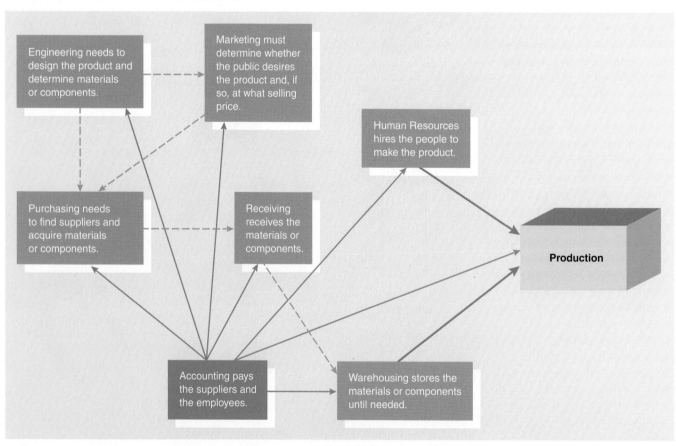

■ Why are we storing flour? Because it was acquired before it was actually needed.

■ Why was it acquired prior to use? Because the flour was acquired in a bulk shipment.

■ Why was the flour bought in bulk? Because flour is cheaper that way.

■ Why is it cheaper if buying in bulk creates costs for storing and moving the flour as well as possible costs of spilling or spoilage of the flour? Hmmm; that thought never occurred to me; maybe there's a better process.

LO.2
WHY DO NON-VALUE-ADDED ACTIVITIES CAUSE COSTS TO INCREASE UNNECESSARILY?

value chart

processing (service) time

inspection time

transfer time

idle time

cycle (lead) time

After a process map has been developed, a **value chart** can be constructed to identify the stages and time spent in those stages from the beginning to the end of a process. Time is usually classified in four ways: processing (or service), inspection, transfer, and idle. The actual time that it takes to perform all *necessary* functions to manufacture the product or perform the service is called the **processing (or service) time**; this use of time adds value. Performing quality control other than what is internal to the process results in **inspection time**; moving products or components from one place to another constitutes **transfer time**. Storage time and time spent waiting at a production operation for processing are considered **idle time**. Inspection time, transfer time, and idle time all add no value. Thus, the **cycle (or lead) time** from the receipt to completion of an order for a product or service is equal to value-added processing time plus non-value-added time.

Although viewing inspection time and transfer time as non-value-added activities is theoretically correct, few companies can completely eliminate all quality control functions and all transfer time. Understanding the non-value-added nature of these functions, however, should help managers strive to minimize such activities to the extent possible. Thus, companies should view value-added and non-value-added activities as occurring on a continuum and concentrate on attempting to eliminate or minimize those activities that add the most time and cost *and* the least value.

See Exhibit 5–4 for a value chart for a chemical product made by Thom Oil Company. Note the excessive time consumed by storing and moving materials. Value is added to products only during the times that production actually occurs; thus, Thom Oil's entire production sequence has only 11 days of value-added time.

Packaging may be a value-added activity for some companies and a non-value-added activity for others. Some products, such as liquids, require packaging; other products need little or no packaging. Because packaging takes up about a third of the U.S. landfills and creates a substantial amount of cost, companies and consumers are beginning to focus their attention on reducing or eliminating packaging.

Manufacturing Cycle Efficiency

manufacturing cycle efficiency

Dividing total value-added processing time by total cycle time results in a measurement referred to as **manufacturing cycle efficiency** (MCE). (A service company would compute service cycle efficiency by dividing total actual service time by total cycle time.) Using the information from Exhibit 5–4, Thom Oil Company's manufacturing cycle efficiency is 16 percent (11 ÷ 67) if the company operates with the least amount of NVA time or 11 percent (11 ÷ 97) if it operates with the greatest amount of NVA time.

Although 100 percent efficiency can never be achieved, most production processes add value to products only approximately 10 percent of the time from the receipt of the raw material until shipment to the customer. In other words, about 90 percent of manufacturing cycle time is waste. But, as in Exhibit 5–5, products act like magnets in regard to costs: The longer the cycle time to make a product, the more time the product has to "pull" costs to it.

EXHIBIT 5–4

VALUE CHART FOR THOM OIL COMPANY

Assembling									
Operations	Receiving	Quality control	Storage	Move to production	Waiting for use	Setup of machinery	Assembly	Move to inspection	Move to finishing
Average time (days)	4	2	20–30	1	6	1	6	1	1

Finishing									
Operations	Receiving	Move to production	Waiting for use	Setup of machinery	Finishing	Inspection	Packaging	Move to dockside	Storage	Ship to customer
Average time (days)	1	1	10–24	1	4	1	1	1	3	2–8

Total time in Assembling:	42 – 52 days	Assembling value-added time:	6 days
Total time in Finishing:	25 – 45 days	Finishing value-added time:	5 days
Total processing time:	67 – 97 days	**Total value-added time:**	**11 days**
Total value-added time:	11 – 11 days		
Total non-value-added time:	**56 – 86 days**		

Non-value-added activities

Value-added activities

A just-in-time (JIT) manufacturing process seeks to achieve substantially higher efficiency by producing components and goods at the precise time they are needed by either the next production station or the consumer.[1] Thus, use of JIT eliminates a significant amount of idle time (especially in storage) and increases manufacturing cycle efficiency. JIT also often relies on the use of automated technologies, such as flexible manufacturing systems, which reduce processing time and increase MCE.

In a retail environment, *cycle time* relates to the length of time from ordering to selling an item. Non-value-added activities in retail include shipping time from the supplier, delays in receiving to count merchandise, and any storage time between receipt and sale. In a service company, *cycle time* refers to the time between the service order and service completion. All time spent on activities that

EXHIBIT 5–5

RELATIONSHIP BETWEEN PRODUCT COST AND CYCLE TIME

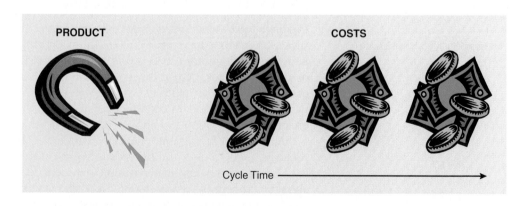

[1] JIT is discussed in greater depth in Chapter 18.

are not actual service performance or are "non-activities" (such as delays in beginning a job) are considered non-value-added activities for that job.

| What factors in an organization create non-value-added activities? |

NVA activities can be attributed to systemic, physical, and human factors. For example, a systemic cause is the need to manufacture products in large batches to minimize setup cost or the need to take service jobs in order of urgency. Physical factors often contribute to non-value-added activities because the plant and machine layout do not provide the most efficient transfer of products. This factor is especially apparent in multistory buildings in which receiving and shipping are on the ground floor, but storage and production are on upper floors. People can also be responsible for non-value-added activities because they have improper skills, received inadequate training, or need to be sociable.

Attempts to reduce non-value-added activities should be directed at all of these causes, but it is imperative that the "Willie Sutton" rule be applied. This rule is named for the bank robber who, when asked why he robbed banks, replied, "That's where the money is." The NVA activities that create the highest costs should be the ones on which management concentrates its efforts to reduce or eliminate. The system must be changed to reflect a new management philosophy regarding performance measures and determination of product cost. Physical factors must be changed as much as possible to eliminate layout difficulties and machine bottlenecks, and people must accept and work toward total quality control. Focusing attention on eliminating NVA activities should cause product/service quality to increase and cycle time and cost to decrease.

Constructing a value chart for every product or service would be extremely time consuming, but a few such charts can quickly indicate where a company is losing time and money through non-value-added activities. The cost of NVA activities can be approximated by using estimates for storage facility depreciation, property taxes and insurance charges, wages for employees who handle warehousing, and the cost of capital on working capital funds tied up in stored inventory. Summing these estimates in the value chart will indicate the amount by which costs could be reduced by eliminating non-value-added activities.

COST DRIVER ANALYSIS

LO.3
WHY MUST COST DRIVERS BE DESIGNATED IN AN ACTIVITY-BASED COSTING SYSTEM?

Companies engage in many activities that consume resources and cause costs to be incurred. All activities have *cost drivers,* defined in Chapter 2 as factors having direct cause–effect relationships to a cost. Many cost drivers can be identified for an individual business unit. For example, cost drivers for factory insurance are number of employees; value of property, plant, and equipment; and number of accidents or claims during a specified time period. Cost drivers affecting the entire plant include inventory size, physical layout, and number of different products produced. Cost drivers are classified as volume related (such as machine hours) and non-volume related, which generally reflect the incurrence of specific transactions (such as setups, work orders, or distance traveled).

More cost drivers can generally be identified for a given activity than should be used for cost accumulation or activity elimination. Management should limit the cost drivers selected to a reasonable number and make certain that the cost of measuring a driver does not exceed the benefit of using it. A cost driver should be easy to understand, directly related to the activity being performed, and appropriate for performance measurement. Thus, the cost driver for shipping cost that is the easiest to track and most measurable in Exhibit 5–6 is length of trip.

Costs have traditionally been accumulated into one or two cost pools (total factory overhead or variable factory overhead and fixed factory overhead), and one or two drivers (direct labor hours and/or machine hours) have been used to assign costs to products. These procedures cause few, if any, problems for financial

EXHIBIT 5–6
POTENTIAL COST DRIVERS FOR SHIPPING COST

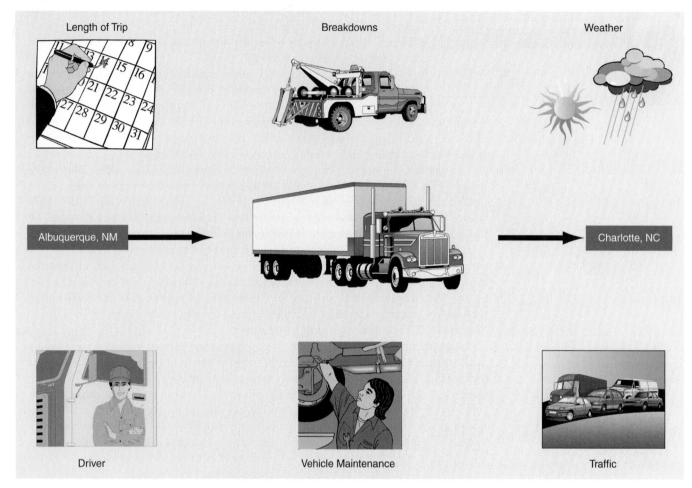

statement preparation. However, the use of single cost pools and single drivers can produce illogical product or service costs for internal managerial use in complex production (or service) environments.

Exhibit 5–7 indicates how activity analysis is combined with cost driver analysis to create a tool for managing costs. Cost driver analysis identifies the activities

EXHIBIT 5–7
ABC DATA AND COST MANAGEMENT

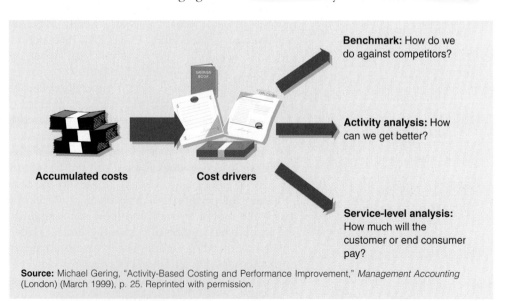

Source: Michael Gering, "Activity-Based Costing and Performance Improvement," *Management Accounting* (London) (March 1999), p. 25. Reprinted with permission.

causing costs to be incurred, activity analysis highlights the activities that do not add value and, as such, can be targeted for elimination to reduce costs and increase profitability.

To reflect more complex environments, the accounting system must first recognize that costs are created and incurred because their drivers occur at different levels.[2] This realization necessitates using **cost driver analysis**, which investigates, quantifies, and explains the relationships of drivers to their related costs. Traditionally, cost drivers were viewed as existing only at the unit level; for example, how many hours of labor or machine time were expended to produce a product or render a service? These drivers create **unit-level costs**, meaning that they are caused by the production or acquisition of a single unit of product or the delivery of a single unit of service. Other drivers and their costs are incurred for broader-based categories or levels of activity. These broader-based activity levels have successively wider scopes of influence on products and product types. The levels are batch, product or process, and organizational or facility. See Exhibit 5–8 for examples of the kinds of costs that occur at the various levels.

Costs that are caused by a group of things being made, handled, or processed at a single time are referred to as **batch-level costs**. An example of a batch-level cost is the cost of setting up a machine. Assume that machine setup to cast product parts costs $900. Two different parts are to be manufactured during the day; therefore, two setups will be needed at a total cost of $1,800. After the first setup, production will generate 3,000 Type A parts; the machine will then be reset to generate 600 Type B parts. These specific numbers of parts are needed for

cost driver analysis

unit-level costs

batch-level costs

EXHIBIT 5–8
LEVELS OF COSTS

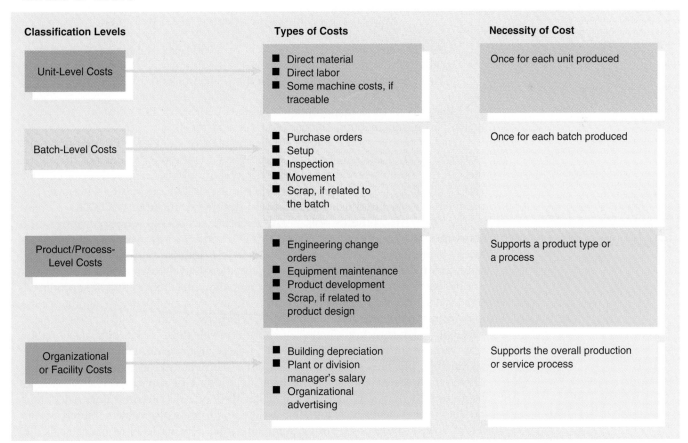

Classification Levels	Types of Costs	Necessity of Cost
Unit-Level Costs	■ Direct material ■ Direct labor ■ Some machine costs, if traceable	Once for each unit produced
Batch-Level Costs	■ Purchase orders ■ Setup ■ Inspection ■ Movement ■ Scrap, if related to the batch	Once for each batch produced
Product/Process-Level Costs	■ Engineering change orders ■ Equipment maintenance ■ Product development ■ Scrap, if related to product design	Supports a product type or a process
Organizational or Facility Costs	■ Building depreciation ■ Plant or division manager's salary ■ Organizational advertising	Supports the overall production or service process

[2] This hierarchy of costs was introduced by Robin Cooper in "Cost Classification in Unit-Based and Activity-Based Manufacturing Cost Systems," *Journal of Cost Management* (Fall 1990), p. 6.

production because the company is on a just-in-time production system. Computation of a cost per unit if setup cost were considered unit-based is as follows:

$$\text{Setup cost: } \$1,800 \div 3,600 \text{ parts } = \$0.50 \text{ per part}$$

Total setup cost assigned to Type A parts $= 3,000$ units $\times$ \$0.50 $= \$1,500$
Total setup cost assigned to Type B parts $= 600$ units $\times$ \$0.50 $= \$300$

This method assigns the majority of the cost to Type A parts even though one machine setup was needed for each production run.

Because the cost is actually created by a batch-level driver, the following cost assignments are more appropriate:

$$\text{Type A parts: } \$900 \div 3,000 \text{ units } = \$0.30 \text{ per unit}$$
$$\text{Type B parts: } \$900 \div 600 \text{ units } = \$1.50 \text{ per unit}$$

Using a batch-level perspective reveals the commonality of the cost to the units within the batch and is more indicative of the relationship between the activity (setup) and the driver (different production runs).

A cost caused by the development, production, or acquisition of different items is called a **product-level** (or **process-level**) **cost**. To illustrate this cost, assume that the engineering department of Thom Oil Company issued five engineering change orders (ECOs) during May. Of these ECOs, four relate to Product R, one relates to Product S, and none relates to Product T. Each ECO costs \$6,000 to issue. During May, the company produced a total of 7,500 units of product: 1,000 units of Product R, 1,500 units of Product S, and 5,000 units of Product T. If ECO costs are treated as unit-level costs, the following allocations would occur:

margin note: product-level (process-level) cost

$$\text{ECO cost: } \$30,000 \div 7,500 \text{ parts } = \$4.00 \text{ per unit}$$

Total ECO cost assigned to Product R $= 1,000$ units $\times$ \$4.00 $= \$4,000$
Total ECO cost assigned to Product S $= 1,500$ units $\times$ \$4.00 $= \$6,000$
Total ECO cost assigned to Product T $= 5,000$ units $\times$ \$4.00 $= \$20,000$

Note that this method inappropriately assigns \$20,000 of ECO cost to Product T, which had no engineering change orders issued for it!

Using a product/process-level driver (number of ECOs) for ECO costs would assign \$24,000 of costs to Product R and \$6,000 to Product S, but not merely to the current month's production. The ECO cost should be allocated to all current and future R and S units produced while these ECOs are in effect because the products manufactured using the changed design benefit from the ECOs.

Certain costs at the organizational level are incurred for the sole purpose of supporting facility operations. These **organizational-level costs** are common to many different activities and products or services and can be prorated to products only on an arbitrary basis. Although organizational-level costs should theoretically not be assigned to products at all, some companies attach them to goods produced or services rendered because the amounts are insignificant relative to all other costs.

margin note: organizational-level costs

Accountants have traditionally (and incorrectly) assumed that if costs did not vary with changes in production at the unit level, those costs were fixed rather than variable. In reality, batch, product/process, and organizational level costs are all variable, but they vary for reasons other than changes in production volume. Therefore, to determine a valid estimate of product or service cost, costs should be accumulated at each successively higher level of costs. Because unit, batch, and product/process level costs are all associated with units of products (merely at different levels), these costs can be summed at the product level to match with the revenues generated by product sales. Organizational-level costs are not product related, so they should be subtracted only in total from net product revenues.

Refer to Exhibit 5–9 for an illustration of how costs collected at the unit, batch, and product/process levels can be used to generate a total product cost. Each product cost is multiplied by the number of units sold, and that amount of cost

EXHIBIT 5–9

DETERMINING PRODUCT PROFITABILITY AND COMPANY PROFIT

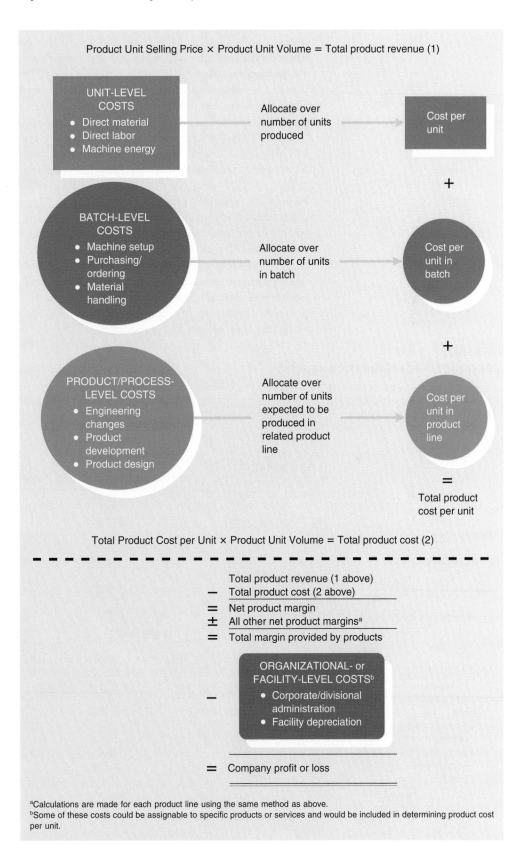

Product Unit Selling Price × Product Unit Volume = Total product revenue (1)

UNIT-LEVEL COSTS
- Direct material
- Direct labor
- Machine energy

Allocate over number of units produced → Cost per unit

+

BATCH-LEVEL COSTS
- Machine setup
- Purchasing/ordering
- Material handling

Allocate over number of units in batch → Cost per unit in batch

+

PRODUCT/PROCESS-LEVEL COSTS
- Engineering changes
- Product development
- Product design

Allocate over number of units expected to be produced in related product line → Cost per unit in product line

=

Total product cost per unit

Total Product Cost per Unit × Product Unit Volume = Total product cost (2)

- -

Total product revenue (1 above)
— Total product cost (2 above)
= Net product margin
± All other net product margins[a]
= Total margin provided by products

— **ORGANIZATIONAL- or FACILITY-LEVEL COSTS[b]**
- Corporate/divisional administration
- Facility depreciation

= Company profit or loss

[a]Calculations are made for each product line using the same method as above.
[b]Some of these costs could be assignable to specific products or services and would be included in determining product cost per unit.

of goods sold is subtracted from total product revenues to obtain a product line profit or loss item. These computations would be performed for each product line and summed to determine net product income or loss from which the unassigned organizational-level costs would be subtracted to find company profit or loss for internal management use. In this model, the traditional distinction between product and period costs (discussed in Chapter 2) can be and is ignored. The emphasis is on modfiying product profitability analysis for a focus on internal management purposes rather than external reporting. Because the product/period cost distinction required by generally accepted accounting principles is not recognized, the model in Exhibit 5–9 is not currently acceptable for external reporting.

Data for a sample manufacturing company with three products are presented in Exhibit 5–10 to illustrate the difference in information that would result from recognizing multiple cost levels. Before recognizing that some costs were incurred at the batch, product, and organizational levels, the company accumulated and allocated its factory overhead costs among its three products on a machine hour (MH) basis. Each product requires 1 machine hour, but Product D is a low-volume, special-order line. As in the first section of Exhibit 5–10, cost information indicated that Product D was a profitable product. After analyzing its activities, the company began capturing costs at the different levels and assigning them to products based on appropriate cost drivers. The individual details for this overhead assignment are not shown, but the final assignments and resulting product profitability figures are presented in the second section of Exhibit 5–10. This more refined approach to assigning costs shows that Product D is actually unprofitable.

EXHIBIT 5–10
PRODUCT PROFITABILITY ANALYSIS

Total overhead cost = $1,505,250
Total machine hours = 111,500
Overhead rate per machine hour = $13.50

	PRODUCT C (5,000 UNITS)		PRODUCT D (1,500 UNITS)		PRODUCT E (105,000 UNITS)		
	Unit	Total	Unit	Total	Unit	Total	Total
Product revenue	$50.00	$250,000	$45.00	$67,500	$40.00	$4,200,000	$4,517,500
Product costs							
Direct	$20.00	$100,000	$20.00	$30,000	$ 9.00	$ 945,000	
OH per MH	13.50	67,500	13.50	20,250	13.50	1,417,500	
Total	$33.50	$167,500	$33.50	$50,250	$22.50	$2,362,500	(2,580,250)
Net income		$ 82,500		$17,250		$1,837,500	$1,937,250

	PRODUCT C (5,000 UNITS)		PRODUCT D (1,500 UNITS)		PRODUCT E (105,000 UNITS)		
	Unit	Total	Unit	Total	Unit	Total	Total
Product revenue	$50	$250,000	$45	$ 67,500	$40	$4,200,000	$4,517,500
Product costs							
Direct	$20	$100,000	$20	$ 30,000	$ 9	$ 945,000	
Overhead							
Unit level	8	40,000	12	18,000	6	630,000	
Batch level	9	45,000	19	28,500	3	315,000	
Product level	3	15,000	15	22,500	2	210,000	
Total	$40	$200,000	$66	$ 99,000	$20	$2,100,000	(2,399,000)
Product line income or (loss)		$ 50,000		$(31,500)		$2,100,000	$2,118,500
Organizational-level costs							(181,250)
Net income							$1,937,250

Costs are incurred because firms engage in activities that consume resources. Accountants have traditionally accumulated costs as transactions occurred and thus have focused on the cost's amount rather than its source. However, this lack of consideration for underlying causes of costs has often resulted in both a lack of ability to control costs and flawed product cost data. Traditional cost allocations tend to subsidize low-volume specialty products by misallocating overhead to high-volume, standard products. This problem occurs because costs of the extra activities needed to make specialty products are assigned using the one or very few drivers of traditional costing—and usually these drivers are volume based. Interestingly, in 1954, William J. Vatter noted that when cost accounting could no longer fulfill the management information needs it was developed to meet, it would either have to change or it would be replaced with something else.[3] The time may have come for cost accounting to change by adopting new bases on which to collect and assign costs. Those bases are the activities that drive or create the costs.

ACTIVITY-BASED COSTING

activity-based costing (ABC)

Recognizing that several levels of costs exist, accumulating costs into related cost pools, and using multiple cost drivers to assign costs to products and services are the three fundamental components of **activity-based costing (ABC)**. ABC is a cost accounting system that focuses on the various activities performed in an organization and collects costs on the basis of the underlying nature and extent of those activities. This costing method focuses on attaching costs to products and services based on the activities conducted to produce, perform, distribute, or support those products and services.

LO.4
HOW DOES ACTIVITY-BASED COSTING DIFFER FROM A TRADITIONAL COST ACCOUNTING SYSTEM?

Managers in many manufacturing companies are concerned about the product costing information being provided by traditional cost accounting systems. Such product costs are reasonable for use in preparing financial statements but often have limited value for management decision making. Activity-based costing, on the other hand, is helpful in companies having the following characteristics:

1. production or performance of a wide variety of products or services;
2. high overhead costs that are not proportional to the unit volume of individual products;
3. significant automation that has made it increasingly difficult to assign overhead to products using the traditional direct labor or machine-hour bases;
4. profit margins that are difficult to explain; and
5. difficult-to-make products that show big profits and easy-to-make products that show losses.[4]

Companies having these characteristics could want to reevaluate their cost systems and implement activity-based costing.

Two-Step Allocation

activity center

After being recorded in the general ledger and subledger accounts, costs in an ABC system are accumulated in activity center cost pools. An **activity center** is any segment of the production or service process for which management wants a separate report on the costs of activities performed. In defining these centers, management should consider the following issues: geographical proximity of equipment, defined centers of managerial responsibility, magnitude of product costs, and need to keep the number of activity centers manageable. Costs having the same driver

---

[3] William J. Vatter, "Tailor-Making Cost Data for Specific Uses," in L. S. Rosen, ed., *Topics in Managerial Accounting* (Toronto: McGraw-Hill Ryerson Ltd., 1954), p. 194.
[4] Robin Cooper, "You Need a New Cost System When . . . ," *Harvard Business Review* (January–February 1989), pp. 77–82.

are accumulated in pools reflecting the appropriate level of cost incurrence (unit, batch, or product/process). The fact that a relationship exists between a cost pool and a cost driver indicates that, if the cost driver can be reduced or eliminated, the related cost should also be reduced or eliminated.

Gathering costs in pools having the same cost drivers allows managers to view an organization's activities cross-functionally. Some companies not using an ABC system accumulate overhead in departmental, rather than plantwide, cost pools, reflecting a vertical-function approach to cost accumulation, but, production and service activities are horizontal by nature. A product or service flows through an organization, affecting numerous departments as it goes. Using a cost driver approach to develop cost pools allows managers to more clearly focus on the various cost impacts created in making a product or performing a service than was possible traditionally.

activity driver

After accumulation, costs are allocated out of the activity center cost pools and assigned to products and services by use of a second driver. These drivers are often referred to as *activity drivers*. An **activity driver** measures the demands placed on activities and, thus, the resources consumed by products and services. An activity driver selected often indicates an activity's output. The process of cost assignment is the same as the overhead application process illustrated in Chapter 3. See Exhibit 5–11 for an illustration of this two-step allocation process of tracing costs to products and services in an ABC system.

EXHIBIT 5–11
TRACING COSTS IN AN ACTIVITY-BASED COSTING SYSTEM

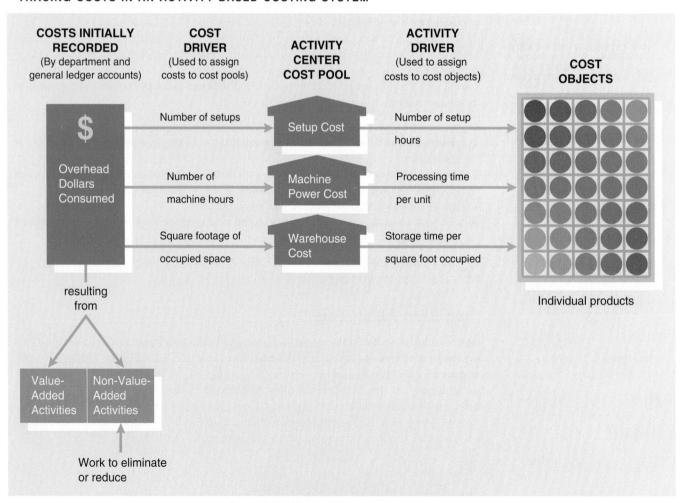

As noted in Exhibit 5–11, the cost drivers for the collection stage can differ from the activity drivers used for the allocation stage because some activity center costs are not traceable to lower levels of activity. Costs at the lowest (unit) level of activity should be allocated to products by use of volume- or unit-based drivers. Costs incurred at higher (batch and product/process) levels can also be allocated to products by use of volume-related drivers, but the volume measure should include only those units associated with the batch or the product/process—not with total production or service volume. See Exhibit 5–12 for some common drivers for various activity centers.

EXHIBIT 5–12

ACTIVITY DRIVERS

Activity Center	Activity Drivers
Accounting	Reports requested; dollars expended
Personnel	Job change actions; hiring actions; training hours; counseling hours
Data processing	Reports requested; transactions processed; programming hours; program change requests
Production engineering	Hours spent in each shop; job specification changes requested; product change notices processed
Quality control	Hours spent in each shop; defects discovered; samples analyzed
Plant services	Preventive maintenance cycles; hours spent in each shop; repair and maintenance actions
Material services	Dollar value of requisitions; number of transactions processed; number of personnel in direct support
Utilities	Direct usage (metered to shop); space occupied
Production shops	Fixed per-job charge; setups made; direct labor; machine hours; number of moves; material applied

Source: Michael D. Woods, "Completing the Picture: Economic Choices with ABC," *Management Accounting* (December 1992), p. 54. Reprinted from *Management Accounting.* Copyright by Institute of Management Accountants, Montvale, N.J.

Activity-Based Costing Illustrated

See Exhibit 5–13 for an ABC example. The process gathers information about the activities and costs for a factory maintenance department. Costs are then assigned to specific products based on activities. This department allocates its total personnel cost among the three activities performed in that department based on the number of employees in those areas. This allocation reflects the fact that occurrences of a specific activity, rather than volume of production or service, drive work performed in the department. One of the products manufactured by the company is Product Z, a rather complex unit with relatively low demand. Note that the cost allocated to it with the activity-based costing system is 132 percent higher than the cost allocated with the traditional allocation system ($1.564 versus $0.675)!

What are the typical patterns for changes in costs of products observed with the adoption of ABC?

Discrepancies in costs between traditional and activity-based costing methods are not uncommon. Activity-based costing systems indicate that significant resources are consumed by low-volume products and complex production operations. Studies have shown that, after the implementation of activity-based costing, the costs of high-volume standard products have often been too high and, using ABC, have declined anywhere from 10 to 30 percent. Low-volume complex specialty product costs tend to increase from 100 to 500 percent, although in some cases, these costs have risen by 1,000 to 5,000 percent![5] Thus, activity-based costing typically shifts a substantial amount of overhead cost from standard high-volume products to premium

[5] Peter B. B. Turney, *An Introduction to Activity-Based Costing* (ABC Technologies, 1990), video.

EXHIBIT 5–13

ILLUSTRATION OF ACTIVITY-BASED COSTING ALLOCATION

Factory Maintenance Department: The company's conventional system assigns the personnel costs of this department to products using direct labor hours (DLHs); the department has 9 employees and incurred $450,000 of personnel costs in the current year or $50,000 per employee. Expected DLHs are 200,000.

ABC ALLOCATION

Stage 1
Trace costs from general ledger and subsidiary ledger accounts to activity center pools according to number of employees:

- Regular maintenance—uses 5 employees; $250,000 is allocated to this activity; second-stage allocation to be based on machine hours (MHs)
- Preventive maintenance—uses 2 employees; $100,000 is allocated to this activity; second-stage allocation to be based on number of setups
- Repairs—uses 2 employees; $100,000 is allocated to this activity; second-stage allocation is based on number of machine starts

Stage 2
Allocate activity center cost pools to products using cost drivers chosen for each cost pool.

2001 activity of second-stage drivers: 500,000 MHs; 5,000 setups; 100,000 machine starts

Step 1:   Allocate costs per unit of activity of second-stage cost drivers.

- Regular maintenance—$250,000 ÷ 500,000 MHs = $0.50 per MH
- Preventive maintenance—$100,000 ÷ 5,000 setups = $20 per setup
- Repairs—$100,000 ÷ 100,000 machine starts = $1 per machine start

Step 2:   Allocate costs to products using quantity of second-stage cost drivers consumed in making these products. The following quantities of activity are relevant to Product Z: 30,000 MHs; 30 setups; 40 machine starts; and 3,000 DLHs out of a total of 200,000 DLHs in 2001. Ten thousand units of Product Z were manufactured during 2001.

ABC Allocation to Product Z = (30,000 × $0.50) + (30 × $20) + (40 × $1) = $15,640 for 10,000 units, or $1.564 per unit

Traditional Allocation to Product Z = $450,000 ÷ 200,000 DLHs = $2.25 per DLH; (3,000 × $2.25) = $6,750 for 10,000 units, or $0.675 per unit

special-order low-volume products, as in Exhibit 5–14. The ABC costs of moderately complex products and services (those that are neither extremely simple nor complex nor are produced in extremely low or high volumes) tend to remain approximately the same as the costs calculated using traditional costing methods.

Although the preceding discussion addresses costs normally considered product costs, activity-based costing is just as applicable to service department costs. Many companies use an activity-based costing system to allocate corporate overhead costs to their revenue-producing units based on the number of reports, documents, customers, or other reasonable measures of activity.

Short-Term and Long-Term Variable Costs

The traditional definition of *variable cost* is that it increases or decreases with a corresponding change in activity volume. Costs that do not move in relation to volume have conventionally been termed *fixed*. However, in many cases, as a business grows, "costs tend to be far more variable than they should be, and when it contracts, they are far more fixed than they should be."[6] Professor Robert Kaplan of Harvard University considers the ability of "fixed" costs to change under what he refers to as the "Rule of One," which means that possessing or using more than

---

[6] B. Charles Ames and James D. Hlavacek, "Vital Truths About Managing Your Costs," *Harvard Business Review* (January–February 1990), p. 145.

EXHIBIT 5–14
TRADITIONAL VERSUS ABC OVERHEAD ALLOCATIONS

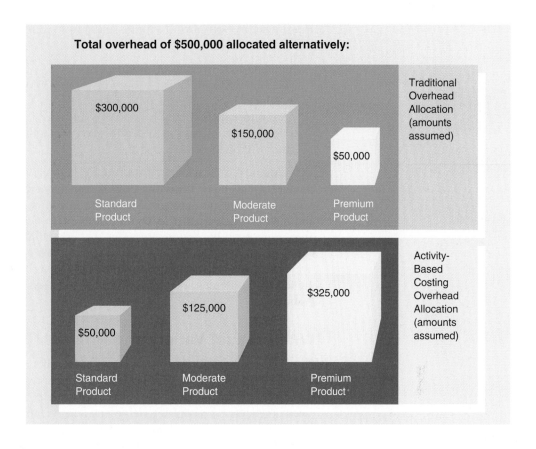

Total overhead of $500,000 allocated alternatively:

$300,000 — Standard Product
$150,000 — Moderate Product
$50,000 — Premium Product

Traditional Overhead Allocation (amounts assumed)

$50,000 — Standard Product
$125,000 — Moderate Product
$325,000 — Premium Product

Activity-Based Costing Overhead Allocation (amounts assumed)

long-term variable costs

product variety

product complexity

process complexity

one unit of a resource is evidence that the resource is variable.[7] Because of this logic, many fixed costs have come to be viewed as **long-term variable costs,** for which suitable (usually non-volume-related) cost drivers need to be identified.

Two significant cost drivers that cause long-term variable costs to change but that traditionally have been disregarded are variety and complexity. **Product variety** refers to the number of different types of products made; **product complexity** refers to the number of components included in a product; **process complexity** refers to the number of processes through which a product flows. These characteristics create additional overhead costs for things such as warehousing, purchasing, setups, and inspections—all of which can be seen as long-term variable costs because they will increase as the number and types of products increase. Therefore, managers should consider using items such as number of product types, number of components, and number of necessary processes as the cost drivers for applying ABC.

DETERMINING WHETHER ABC IS APPROPRIATE

LO.5
WHAT NEW TYPES OF INFORMATION DOES AN ACTIVITY-BASED COSTING/MANAGEMENT SYSTEM OFFER MANAGEMENT?

LO.6
WHEN IS ACTIVITY-BASED COSTING APPROPRIATE IN AN ORGANIZATION?

Although not every accounting system using direct labor or machine hours as the cost driver provides inadequate or inaccurate cost information, a great deal of information can be lost in the accounting systems of companies that ignore activity and cost relationships. Some general indicators can alert managers to the need to review the relevance of the cost information their system is providing. Several of these clues are more relevant to manufacturing entities, while others are equally

[7] Patrick L. Romano, "Activity Accounting: An Update—Part 2," *Management Accounting* (June 1989), p. 63.

appropriate to both manufacturing and service businesses. Factors to consider include the:

▪ number and diversity of products or services produced,
▪ diversity and differential degree of support services used for different products,
▪ extent to which common processes are used,
▪ effectiveness of current cost allocation methods,
▪ rate of growth of period costs.[8]

Additionally, if activity-based costing is developed, the new information will change management decisions only if management is free to set product/service prices, there are no strategic constraints in the company, and there is a climate and culture (such as that at **DynMcDermott**) of cost reduction in the company. Two primary underlying assumptions that companies must consider before adopting ABC are that the costs in each cost pool are (1) driven by homogeneous activities and (2) strictly proportional to the activity.[9] If these assumptions are met, the following circumstances could indicate the need to consider using activity-based costing.

With Product Variety and Product Complexity

Product variety is commonly associated with the need to consider activity-based costing. Products can be variations of the same product line (such as **Hallmark**'s different types of greeting cards), or they can be in numerous product families (such as **Procter & Gamble**'s detergents, diapers, fabric softeners, and shampoos). In either case, product additions cause numerous overhead costs to increase.

mass customization

In the quest for product variety, many companies are striving for **mass customization** of products through the use of flexible manufacturing systems. Such personalized production can often be conducted at a relatively low cost. Although such customization can please some customers, it has some drawbacks. First, there could be too many choices. For instance, at one point, **Nissan** reportedly had 87 different varieties of steering wheels, but customers did not want many of them and disliked having to choose from so many options.[10] Second, mass customization creates a tremendous opportunity for errors. Third, most companies have found that customers, given a wide variety of choices, typically make selections from a rather small percentage of the total. At **Toyota**, investigation of purchases revealed that 20 percent of the product varieties accounted for 80 percent of the sales.[11]

Pareto principle

This 20:80 ratio is fairly common and is referred to as the **Pareto principle**, after the Italian economist Vilfredo Pareto.[12]

Companies with complex products, services, or processes should investigate ways to reduce that complexity. Management could review the design of the company's products and processes to standardize them and reduce the number of different components, tools, and processes required. Products should be designed to consider the Pareto principle and take advantage of commonality of parts. For instance, if a company finds that 20 percent of its parts are used in 80 percent of its products, the company may need to consider two other factors. First, are the remaining components used in key products? If so, could equal quality be achieved by using the more

---

[8] T. L. Estrin, Jeffrey Kantor, and David Albers, "Is ABC Suitable for Your Company?" *Management Accounting* (April 1994), p. 40. Copyright Institute of Management Accountants, Montvale, N.J.

[9] Harold P. Roth and A. Faye Borthick, "Are You Distorting Costs by Violating ABC Assumptions?" *Management Accounting* (November 1991), pp. 39–40.

[10] B. Joseph Pine II, Bart Victor, and Andrew C. Boynton, "Making Mass Customization Work," *Harvard Business Review* (September–October 1993), p. 110.

[11] Ibid, p. 108.

[12] Pareto found that about 85 percent of Milan's wealth was held by about 15 percent of the people. The term *Pareto principle* was coined by Joseph Juran in relationship to quality problems. Juran found that a high proportion of such problems were caused by a small number of process characteristics (the vital few) whereas the majority of process characteristics (the trivial many) accounted for only a small proportion of quality problems.

common parts? If not, can the products be sold for a premium price to cover the costs associated with the use of low-volume components? Second, are the parts specified for product use purchased by important customers who are willing to pay a premium price for the products? If so, the benefits from the complexity could be worth the cost. However, would customers be equally satisfied if more common parts were used and product prices were reduced? Complexity is acceptable only if it adds value from the customer's point of view; consider the situation in Exhibit 5–15.

Process complexity can develop over time, or it can exist because of a lack of sufficient planning in product development. Processes are complex when they create difficulties for the people attempting to perform production operations (physical straining, awkwardness of motions, and wasted motions) or for the people using manufacturing machinery (multiple and/or detailed setups, lengthy transfer time between machine processes, recalibration of instruments, and so on). Process complexity reflects numerous non-value-added activities, causing time delays and cost increases.

simultaneous (concurrent) engineering

A company can employ simultaneous engineering to reduce both product and process complexity. **Simultaneous** (or **concurrent**) **engineering** refers to the continuous involvement of all primary functions and personnel contributing to a product's origination and production from the beginning of a project. Multifunctional teams design products by considering customer expectations, vendor capabilities, parts commonality, and production process compatibility. This type of integrated design effort is referred to as *design for manufacturability*. Simultaneous engineering helps companies to shorten the time to market for new products and minimize complexity and cost.

Many traditional cost systems are not designed to account for information such as how many different parts are used in a product, so management cannot identify products made with low-volume or unique components. Activity-based costing systems are flexible and can gather such details so that persons involved in reengineering efforts have information about relationships among activities and cost drivers. With these data, reengineering efforts can be focused on the primary causes of process complexity and on the causes that create the highest levels of waste.

With Lack of Commonality in Overhead Costs

Certain products and services create substantially more overhead costs than others do. Although some of these additional overhead costs are caused by product variety or product/process complexity, others are related to support services. For instance,

EXHIBIT 5–15
PRODUCT COMPLEXITY

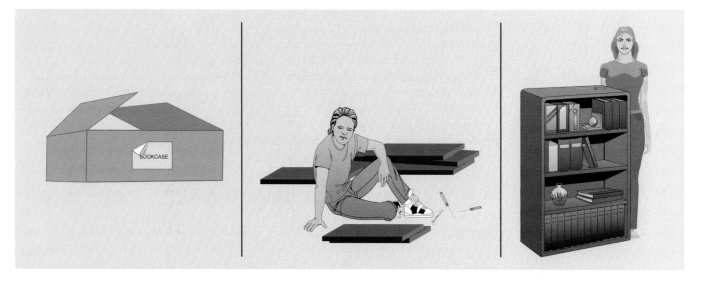

some products require high levels of advertising; some use high-cost distribution channels; and some require the use of high-technology machinery. If only one or two overhead pools are used, overhead related to specific products will be spread over all products. The result will be increased costs for products that are not responsible for the increased overhead.

With Problems in Current Cost Allocations

If a company has undergone one or more significant changes in its products or processes (such as increased product variety or business process reengineering), managers and accountants need to investigate whether the existing cost system still provides a reasonable estimate of product or service cost. After automating their production processes, many companies have experienced large reductions in labor cost with equal or greater increases in overhead cost. In such companies, using direct labor as an overhead allocation base produces extraordinarily high application rates. Consider the fact that some companies are using predetermined overhead rates that range from 500 to 2,000 percent of the direct labor cost. Products made using automated equipment tend to be charged an insufficient amount of overhead whereas products made using high proportions of direct labor tend to be overcharged.

Traditional overhead cost allocations also generally emphasize the assignment of product costs to products at the same time the majority of period costs are expensed as incurred. Activity-based costing recognizes that some period costs (such as R&D and distribution) are distinctly and reasonably associated with specific products and, therefore, should be traced and allocated to those products. This recognition changes the traditional view of product versus period cost.

With Changes in Business Environment

A change in a company's competitive environment could also require better cost information. Increased competition can occur because (1) other companies have recognized the profit potential of a particular product or service, (2) the product or service has become cost feasible to make or perform, or (3) an industry has been deregulated. If many new companies are competing for old business, the best estimate of product or service cost must be available to management so that reasonable profit margins can be maintained or obtained.

Changes in management strategy can also signal the need for a new cost system. For example, if management wants to start a new production operation, the cost system must be capable of providing information on how costs will change. Showing costs as conforming only to the traditional variable and fixed classifications might not allow usable information to be developed. Viewing costs as short-term variable versus long-term variable focuses on cost drivers and on the changes the planned operations will have on activities and costs.

continuous improvement

Continuous improvement recognizes the concepts of eliminating non-value-added activities to reduce cycle time, making products (or performing services) with zero defects, reducing product costs on an ongoing basis, and simplifying products and processes. Activity-based costing, by promoting an understanding of cost drivers, allows the non-value-added activities to be identified and their causes eliminated or reduced.

CRITICISMS OF ACTIVITY-BASED COSTING

Realistically assessing new models and accounting approaches for what they can help managers accomplish is always important. However, no currently existing accounting technique or system provides management exact cost information for every product or the information needed to make consistently perfect decisions.

Activity-based costing, though typically providing better information for certain types of companies than was generated under a traditional overhead allocation process, is not a cure-all for all managerial concerns. Following are some shortcomings of ABC.

First, activity-based costing requires a significant amount of time and, thus, cost to implement. If implementation is to be successful, substantial support is needed throughout the firm. An environment for change that requires overcoming a variety of individual, organizational, and environmental barriers must be created. Individual barriers are typically related to (1) fear of the unknown or shift in status quo, (2) potential loss of status, or (3) a necessity to learn new skills. Organizational barriers are often related to "territorial," hierarchical, or corporate culture issues. Environmental barriers are often built by employee groups (including unions), regulatory agencies, or other stakeholders of interest.

To overcome these barriers, a firm must recognize that these barriers exist, investigate their causes, and communicate information about the "what," "why," and "how" of ABC to all concerned parties. As was the case at DynMcDermott, top management must be involved with and support the implementation process; a shortfall in this area will make any progress toward the new system slow and difficult. Additionally, everyone in the company must be educated in new terminology, concepts, and performance measurements. Even if both of these conditions (support and education) are met, substantial time is needed to properly analyze the activities taking place in the activity centers, trace costs to those activities, and determine the cost drivers.

Activity-based costing leans toward allocating research & development costs to product cost.

GETTY IMAGES

Another problem with ABC is that it does not conform specifically to generally accepted accounting principles (GAAP). ABC suggests that some non-product costs (such as those for research and development) should be allocated to products whereas certain other traditionally designated product costs (such as factory building depreciation) should not be allocated to products. Therefore, most companies have used ABC for internal reporting, but continue to prepare their external financial statements on the more traditional system—requiring even more costs to be incurred. As ABC systems become more widely accepted, more companies could choose to refine how ABC and GAAP determine product cost to make those definitions more compatible and, thereby, eliminate the need for two costing systems.

Under what circumstances would it be appropriate to use ABC for both internal and external reporting?

One final criticism that has been leveled at activity-based costing is that it does not truly promote total quality management (TQM) and continuous improvement. For example, Dr. H. Thomas Johnson (Retzlaff Professor of Quality Management at Portland State University) has stated that merely having improved cost information available does not mean that a company will "change its commitment to mass-produce output at high speed, to control costs by encouraging people to manipulate processes, and to persuade customers to buy output the company has produced to cover its costs."[13] It is true that no cost accounting system

---

[13] H. Thomas Johnson, "It's Time to Stop Overselling Activity-Based Concepts," *Management Accounting* (September 1992), pp. 31, 33.

can change management decisions, but such a criticism reflects a problem with management decision making rather than the system producing the information.

Companies attempting to implement ABC as a cure-all for product failures, volume declines, or financial losses will quickly find that the system is ineffective for these purposes. However, companies can implement ABC and its related management techniques in support of and in conjunction with TQM, JIT, or any of the other world-class methodologies. Companies doing so will provide the customer the best variety, price, quality, service, and lead time of which they are capable. Not coincidentally, they might even find their businesses booming. Activity-based costing and activity-based management are effective in supporting continuous improvement, short lead times, and flexible manufacturing by helping managers to

- identify and monitor significant technology costs;
- trace many technology costs directly to products;
- increase market share;
- identify the cost drivers that create or influence cost;
- identify activities that do not contribute to perceived customer value (i.e., non-value-added activities or waste);
- understand the impact of new technologies on all elements of performance;
- translate company goals into activity goals;
- analyze the performance of activities across business functions;
- analyze performance problems; and
- promote standards of excellence.

In summary, ABC is a cost accounting tool that allocates overhead to products and services in a different manner than a traditional system does. ABC does not, by its implementation, cause the amount of overhead incurred by a company to be reduced; that outcome results from the implementation of activity-based management through its focus on identifying and reducing or eliminating non-value-added activities. Together, ABM and ABC help managers operate in the top right quadrant of the graph in Exhibit 5–16, so that they can produce products and perform services most efficiently and effectively and, thus, be highly competitive in the global business environment.

EXHIBIT 5–16
EFFICIENCY AND EFFECTIVENESS OF OPERATIONS

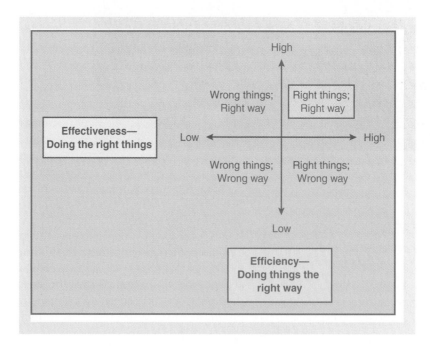

Revisiting

DynMcDermott Petroleum Operations Company

Although DynMcDermott is contractually prohibited from working for other customers, competitors are not prohibited from trying to take the DOE work away from DM. It is therefore imperative that the company not only meet but also exceed the DOE's expectations. Regular face-to-face meetings are held between DM and its DOE counterparts to define project requirements, identify areas for change, and agree on tasks. It is this high level of interaction that gives DM the ability to respond to new requirements such as those that were put into effect after September 11, 2001.

Process improvement teams are assembled with goals to improve process efficiency, solve problems, and make breakthrough improvements in both techniques and costs. For instance, one key performance goal for the company is $64.6 million in cost savings by 2008! Standardization of operating processes and the use of common equipment across storage sites are two important methods of reducing costs. Additionally, maintaining a highly trained group of employees dedicated to the elimination of process errors minimizes costs associated with inspections and testing.

In 2001 the company developed a plan to improve its performance system and identified ABM as a critical element in ensuring that there was a valid basis on which to begin the statistical evaluation of a process. To measure costs associated with inspection and testing, a team reviewed the audits and assessment process measures in the ABM system. Since 1993, internal and external audits and assessments have played a role in DM's effective governance system. Internal audits addressed all facets of DM including, among other things, safety, environmental issues, security, physical inventories, vehicle inspections, and property.

From January 2001 to April 2003, DM conducted a total of 11,052 quality control (QC) inspections at five locations in five different areas of activities. These inspections expended more than 13,000 person hours to identify, conduct, and process but did not document or identify any discrepancies in quality or procedural requirements, nor did they provide any opportunities for improvement. An evaluation showed that the focus of the inspections ranged from truly important, high-risk, mission-critical activities to completely meaningless activities, such as inspecting the limestone in security dog kennels and replacing lawn mower pulleys. Some of the latter were performed only to meet contractual targets related to number of inspections performed. During the fourth quarter of 2003, the QC inspection program took DM 5,570 person hours. Teams identified improvement opportunities and, with the support of the DOE, implemented a program to generate a 93 percent reduction in person hours at one location. These results were achieved by redesigning the goals of the QC process and eliminating non-value-added inspections. During the second quarter of 2004, the initial results of the new process have shown an overall cost reduction of 71 percent, providing a savings of $56,500 a year.

Because of the numerous recognitions it had already received, DynMcDermott management has now taken its performance to the next level by applying for the 2004 Malcolm Baldrige National Quality Award. Given the company's attention to detail, in-depth interaction with its customer, and highly trained and motivated workforce, the Baldrige Award is certainly an achievable goal.

Source: DynMcDermott 2004 Malcolm Baldrige National Quality Award application and discussions with Ron Schulingkamp, Strategic Systems Coordinator for DynMcDermott.

Comprehensive Review Module

Chapter Summary

1. Activity-based management focuses on

   - analyzing activities and identifying the cost drivers of those activities.

   - classifying activities as value-added or non-value-added (which includes business-value-added) and striving to eliminate or minimize the non-value-added costs.

   - making certain that customers perceive an equitable relationship between product selling price and value.

   - improving processes and controlling operations.

   - analyzing performance problems.

   - translating company goals into organizational activities.

2. Non-value-added (NVA) activities, such as inspection, transfer, and idleness, increase costs because

   - production or performance time is lengthened.

   - workers are engaged in activities for which customers are not willing to pay.

   - time is money.

3. Cost drivers are designated in an activity-based costing system to

   - identify what causes a cost to be incurred so that it can be controlled.

   - indicate at what level (unit, batch, product/process, or organizational) a cost occurs.

   - allow costs with similar drivers to be pooled together and a single, appropriate activity basis be used to allocate those costs to products or services.

   - manage costs more effectively and efficiently.

   - identify the costs related to product variety and product/process complexity.

4. Activity-based costing differs from a traditional cost accounting system in that it

   - identifies several levels of costs rather than the traditional concept that costs are fixed unless they vary specifically at the unit level.

   - collects costs in cost pools based on the underlying nature and extent of activities.

   - assigns costs within the multiple cost pools to products or services using multiple drivers (both volume and non-volume related) that best reflect the factor causing the costs to occur.

   - does not consider some product costs for internal purposes that are considered product costs for external reporting.

   - provides a more realistic picture of actual production cost than has traditionally been available.

5. Installation of an activity-based management/costing system will allow management to

   - recognize the cost impact of cross-functional activities in an organization.

   - recognize that fixed costs are, in fact, long-run variable costs that change based on an identifiable driver.

   - recognize the value of preparing process maps and value charts.

   - recognize that the traditional bases (direct labor and machine hours) might not produce the most logical costs of products/services.

   - recognize that standard products/services often support premium products/services.

   - set prices that are more reflective of the activities needed to produce special or premium products or to decide that such products are not profitable for the company.

   - calculate manufacturing cycle efficiency and use it to measure organizational performance.

   - recognize that the most effective way to control costs is to minimize or eliminate non-value-added activities.

   - engage in simultaneous engineering using multifunctional teams to accelerate the time to market of new products and reduce their complexity and costs.

   - recognize that all customers should not necessarily be retained at the current relationship.

6. Activity-based costing is appropriate in an organization that has

   - a large variety of products being produced and sold.

   - products that can be customized to customer specifications.

   - wide diversity in manufacturing needs for its products.

   - a lack of commonality in overhead costs related to products.

   - problems with its current overhead allocation system.

   - been affected by significant changes in its business environment, including widespread adoption of new technologies.

Solution Strategies

MANUFACTURING CYCLE EFFICIENCY

Cycle Time
= Value-Added Processing Time + Inspection Time + Transfer Time + Idle Time

$$MCE = \text{Value-Added Processing Time} \div \text{Total Cycle Time}$$

ACTIVITY-BASED COSTING

1. Determine the organization's activity centers.
2. Determine departmental activities and efforts needed to conduct those activities, that is, the cost drivers.
3. Determine departmental resources consumed in conducting activities and allocate costs of these resources to activity centers based on the cost drivers.
4. Determine activities needed to manufacture products or provide revenue-producing services, that is, the activity drivers.
5. Allocate costs to products and services based on activities and cost drivers involved.

Demonstration Problem

Potter Inc. manufactures wizard figurines. All figurines are approximately the same size, but some are ceramic and others are fancy, with purple leather capes and a prism-headed wand. Management is considering producing only the fancy figurines because the rate of return on sales is so much higher than it is on the ceramic figurines. The company's total production overhead is $5,017,500. Some additional data follow:

	Ceramic	Fancy
Revenues	$15,000,000	$16,800,000
Direct costs	$8,250,000	$8,750,000
Production (units)	1,500,000	350,000
Machine hours	200,000	50,000
Direct labor hours	34,500	153,625
Number of inspection	1,000	6,500

Required:

a. Potter Inc. has consistently used machine hours to allocate overhead. Determine the profitability of each line of figurines, and decide whether the company should stop producing the ceramic figurines.

b. The cost accountant has determined that production overhead costs can be assigned to separate cost pools. Pool #1 contains $1,260,000 of overhead costs for which the most appropriate cost driver is machine hours; Pool #2 contains $2,257,500 of overhead costs for which the most appropriate cost driver is direct labor hours; and Pool #3 contains $1,500,000 of overhead costs for which the most appropriate cost driver is number of inspections. Compute the overhead cost that should be allocated to each type of figurine using this methodology.

c. Discuss what management's decision should be.

Solution to Demonstration Problem

a. Overhead rate per MH = $5,017,500 ÷ 250,000 = $20.07 per MH

	Ceramic		Fancy	
		Ceramic		Fancy
Revenue		$15,000,000		$16,800,000
Direct costs	$8,250,000		$8,750,000	
Overhead	4,014,000		1,003,500	
Total costs		(12,264,000)		(9,753,500)
Gross margin		$ 2,736,000		$ 7,046,500
Rate of return on sales (rounded)		18%		42%

b.

	Ceramic	Fancy	Total
Machine hours	200,000	150,000	350,000
Rate per MH ($1,260,000 ÷ 350,000)	× $3.60	× $3.60	× $3.60
Pool #1 OH cost allocations	$720,000	$540,000	$1,260,000
Direct labor hours	34,500	153,625	188,125
Rate per DLH ($2,257,500 ÷ 188,125)	× $12	× $12	× $12
Pool #2 OH cost allocations	$414,000	$1,843,500	$2,257,500
Number of inspections	1,000	6,500	7,500
Rate per inspection ($1,500,000 ÷ 7,500)	× $200	× $200	× $200
Pool #3 OH cost allocations	200,000	$1,300,000	$1,500,000
Total allocated overhead costs	$1,334,000	$3,683,500	$5,017,500

	Ceramic		Fancy	
Revenue		$15,000,000		$16,800,000
Direct costs	$8,250,000		$8,750,000	
Overhead	1,334,000		3,683,500	
Total costs		(9,584,000)		(12,433,500)
Gross margin		$ 5,416,000		$ 4,366,500
Rate of return on sales		36%		26%

c. Given the new allocations, management should continue to produce both types of figurines because both appear to be profitable. However, the cost accountant could consider developing additional overhead pools because of the large number of costs charged to Pool #2.

Key Terms

Questions

1. What is activity-based management (ABM), and what are the specific management tools that fall beneath its umbrella?

2. Why are value-added activities defined from a customer viewpoint?

3. In a televised football game, what activities are value added? What activities are non-value added? Would everyone agree with your choices? Why or why not?

4. Do cost drivers exist in a traditional accounting system? Are they designated as such? How, if at all, does the use of cost drivers in a traditional accounting system differ from those in an activity-based costing system?

5. What is activity analysis, and how is it used in concert with cost driver analysis to manage costs?

6. Why do the more traditional methods of overhead assignment "overload" standard high-volume products with overhead costs, and how does ABC improve overhead assignments?

7. Are all companies likely to benefit to an equal extent from adopting ABC? Discuss.

8. Significant hurdles, including a large time commitment, are often encountered in adopting ABC. What specific activities associated with ABC adoption require large investments of time?

Exercises

9. (VA or NVA) Choose an activity related to this class, such as attending class or doing homework. Write down the answers to the question "why" five times to determine whether your activity is value added or non-value added.

10. (VA or NVA) Your boss wants to know whether quality inspections at your company add value. Use the "why" methodology to help your boss make this determination if you work at (a) a clothing manufacturer that sells to a discount chain and (b) a pharmaceutical manufacturer.

11. (VA or NVA) Go to a local department or grocery store.
   a. List five packaged items for which it is readily apparent that packaging is essential and, therefore, would be considered value added.
   b. List five packaged items for which it is readily apparent that packaging is nonessential and therefore adds no value.
   c. For each item listed in part (b), indicate why you think the item was packaged rather than left unpackaged.

12. (VA and NVA) Lawrence Co. is experiencing a problem with schedule changes in its Toledo plant. To help assess the financial impact of the problem, you have gathered the following information on the activities, estimated times, and average costs required for a single schedule change.

Activity	Est. Time	Average Cost
Review impact of orders	30 min–2 hrs	$ 300
Reschedule orders	15 min–24 hrs	800
Reschedule production orders	15 min–1 hr	75
Stop production and change over	10 min–3 hrs	150
Return and locate material (excess inventory)	20 min–6 hrs	1,500
Generate new production paperwork	15 min–4 hrs	500
Change purchasing schedule	10 min–8 hrs	2,100
Collect paperwork from the floor	15 min	75
Review new line schedule	15 min–30 min	100
Overtime premiums	3 hrs–10 hrs	1,000
Total		$6,600

a. Which of these, if any, are value-added activities?
b. What is the cost driver in this situation?
c. How can the cost driver be controlled and the activities eliminated?

13. (Cycle time and MCE) ZAM produces creole seasoning using the following process for each batch.

Function	Time (Minutes)
Receiving ingredients	60
Moving ingredients to stockroom	40
Storing ingredients in stockroom	3,580
Moving ingredients from stockroom	40
Mixing ingredients	180
Packaging ingredients	75
Moving packaged seasoning to warehouse	50
Storing packaged seasoning in warehouse	10,000
Moving packaged seasoning from warehouse to trucks	60

a. Calculate the cycle time of this manufacturing process.
b. Which of the functions add value?
c. Calculate the manufacturing cycle efficiency of this process.
d. What could ZAM do to improve its MCE?

14. (Cycle time and MCE) Billy Bubbly is the manager of Mill House Inc., which makes flavored fruit beverages. Company employees perform the following functions when preparing the beverages:

	Hours
Receiving and transferring ingredients to storage	2
Storing ingredients	36
Transferring the ingredients from storage	1
Mixing and cooking the ingredients	3
Bottling the beverages	2
Transferring the beverages to trucks for customer shipment	2

a. Calculate the cycle time of this manufacturing process.
b. Calculate the manufacturing cycle efficiency of this process.

15. (Cost drivers) The following costs are commonly incurred in manufacturing companies. For each cost, identify a cost driver and explain why it is appropriate.
a. Computer operations
b. Material handling
c. Factory depreciation
d. Engineering changes
e. Freight costs for materials
f. Equipment maintenance
g. Quality control
h. Material storage
i. Setup cost
j. Building utilities
k. Advertising expense

16. (Cost drivers) The following list shows the cost pools at Menard Company. For each pool, identify a cost driver and explain why it is appropriate.
a. Maintenance
b. Utilities
c. Information technology
d. Quality control
e. Material handling
f. Material storage
g. Factory costs, including rent, property taxes, insurance, etc.

WebTUTOR Advantage

17. (Identifying cost drivers) Cruise-IN fast-food restaurant relies on computer-controlled equipment to prepare food for customers. Classify each of the following costs as unit level (U), batch level (B), product/process level (P), or organizational level (O).
  a. Napkins
  b. Oil for the deep-fat fryer
  c. Store manager's salary
  d. Electricity expense for the pizza oven
  e. Maintenance of the restaurant building
  f. Refrigeration of raw materials
  g. Property taxes
  h. Wages of employees who clear and clean tables
  i. Frozen french fries
  j. Depreciation on kitchen equipment

18. (Value chart) Gonzales Manufacturing produces special-order desk nameplate stands. Production time is two days, but the average cycle time for any order is three weeks. The company president has asked you, as the new controller, to discuss missed delivery dates. Prepare an oral presentation for the executive officers in which you address the following:
  a. Possible causes of the problem.
  b. How a value chart could be used to address the problem.

19. (Cost allocation using cost drivers) Blanco Worldwide Industries has decided to implement an activity-based costing system for its in-house legal department. The principal expense in the legal department is professional salaries, and the estimated cost of professional salaries associated with each activity follow:

Reviewing supplier or customer contracts (Contracts)	$360,000
Reviewing regulatory compliance issues (Regulation)	500,000
Court actions (Court)	825,000

Management has determined that the appropriate cost allocation base for Contracts is the number of pages in the contract reviewed, for Regulation is the number of reviews, and for Court is professional hours. For 2007, the legal department reviewed 300,000 pages of contracts, responded to 500 regulatory review requests, and logged 5,000 professional hours in court.
  a. Determine the allocation rate for each activity in the legal department.
  b. What amount would be charged to a producing department that had 8,000 pages of contracts reviewed, made 25 regulatory review requests, and consumed 210 professional hours in court services during the year?
  c. How can the developed rates be used for evaluating output relative to cost incurred in the legal department? What alternative does the firm have to maintaining an internal legal department and how might this choice affect costs?

20. (Activity-based costing) Barbizon Enterprises is in the process of instituting an activity-based costing project in its 10-person purchasing department. Annual departmental overhead costs are $390,000. Because finding the best supplier takes the majority of effort in the department, most of the costs are allocated to this activity area. Many purchase orders are received in a single shipment.

Activity	Allocation Measure	Quantity	Total Cost
Find best suppliers	Number of telephone calls	200,000	$200,000
Issue purchase orders	Number of purchase orders	25,000	100,000
Review receiving reports	Number of receiving reports	15,000	90,000

One special order product manufactured by the company required the following purchasing department activities: 150 telephone calls, 40 purchase orders, and 20 receipts.

a. What amount of purchasing department cost should be assigned to this product?

b. If 80 units of the product are manufactured during the year, what is the purchasing department cost per unit?

21. (Activity-based costing) Eloquence Publishing is concerned about the profitability of its paperback dictionaries. Company managers are considering producing only the top-quality, hand-sewn dictionaries with gold-edged pages. Eloquence is currently assigning the $1,000,000 of overhead costs to both types of dictionaries based on machine hours. Of the overhead, $400,000 is utilities related and the remainder is primarily related to quality control inspectors' salaries. The following information about the products is also available:

	Regular	Hand-Sewn
Number produced	1,000,000	700,000
Machine hours	85,000	15,000
Inspection hours	5,000	25,000
Revenues	$3,200,000	$2,800,000
Direct costs	$2,500,000	$2,200,000

a. Determine the total overhead cost that is being assigned to each type of dictionary using the current allocation system.

b. Determine the total overhead cost that would be assigned to each type of dictionary if more appropriate cost drivers were used.

c. Should the company stop producing the regular dictionaries? Explain.

22. (Product profitability) Moldthan Systems manufactures lawn mowers and garden tractors. Lawn mowers are relatively simple to produce and are made in large quantities. Garden tractors are customized to individual wholesale customer specifications. The company sells 200,000 lawn mowers and 20,000 garden tractors annually. Revenues and costs incurred for each product are as follows:

	Lawn Mowers	Garden Tractors
Revenue	$13,000,000	$11,900,000
Direct material	2,000,000	1,800,000
Direct labor ($20 per hour)	1,200,000	4,000,000
Overhead	?	?

Manufacturing overhead totals $2,211,000, and administrative expenses equal $3,612,000.

a. Calculate the profit (loss) in total and per unit for each product if overhead is assigned to product using a per-unit basis.

b. Calculate the profit (loss) in total and per unit for each product if overhead is assigned to products using a direct labor hour basis.

c. Assume that manufacturing overhead can be divided into two cost pools as follows: $1,300,000, which has a cost driver of direct labor hours (totaling 260,000) and $911,000, which has a cost driver of machine hours (totaling 100,000). Lawn mower production uses 60,000 direct labor hours and 30,000 machine hours; garden tractor production uses 200,000 direct labor hours and 70,000 machine hours. Calculate the profit (loss) in total and per unit for each product if overhead is assigned to products using these two overhead bases.

d. Does your answer in part (a), (b), or (c) provide the better representation of the profit contributed by each product? Explain.

23. (Controlling overhead) Flagship Company is in the process of analyzing and updating its cost information and pricing practices. Since the company's product line changed from general paints to specialized marine coatings, there has been tremendous overhead growth, including costs in customer service, production scheduling, inventory control, and laboratory work. Factory overhead has essentially doubled since the shift in product lines. Although some large orders are still received, most current business is generated from products designed and produced in small lot sizes to meet specifically detailed environmental and technical requirements. Management believes that large orders are being penalized and small orders are receiving favorable cost (and, thus, selling price) treatment.

  a. Indicate why the shift in product lines would have caused such major increases in overhead.

  b. Is it possible that management is correct in its belief about the costs of large and small orders? If so, why?

  c. Write a memo to management suggesting how it might change the cost accounting system to reflect the changes in the business.

24. (Traditional vs. ABC methods) The cost systems at many companies selling multiple products have become less than adequate in today's global competition. Managers often make important product decisions based on distorted cost information because the cost systems have been primarily designed to focus on inventory measurement. Current literature suggests that many manufacturing companies should have at least three cost systems, one each for inventory measurement, operational control, and activity-based costing.

  a. Identify the purpose and characteristics of each of the following cost systems:

    1. Inventory measurement

    2. Activity-based costing

  b. Discuss why a cost system developed for inventory valuation could distort product cost information.

  c. Describe the benefits that management can obtain from using activity-based costing.

  d. List the steps that a company using a traditional cost system would take to implement activity-based costing.

(CMA adapted)

25. (Ethics) Many manufacturers are deciding to service only wholesalers or retailers that buy $10,000 or more of products from the manufacturers annually. Manufacturers defend such policies by stating that they can provide better service to customers that handle more volume and more diverse product lines.

  a. Relate the concepts in the chapter to the decision of manufacturers to drop small customers.

  b. Are there any ethical implications of eliminating groups of customers that could be less profitable than others?

  c. Does activity-based costing adequately account for all costs that are related to a decision to eliminate a particular customer base? (*Hint:* Consider opportunity costs such as those related to reputation.)

Problems

26. (Identifying non-value-added activities) Mark Dickenson plans to build a concrete walkway for his home during his vacation. The following schedule shows how project time will be allocated:

	Hours
Purchase materials	5
Obtain rental equipment	3
Remove sod and level site	10
Build forms for concrete	12
Mix and pour concrete into forms	5
Level concrete and smooth	2
Let dry	22
Remove forms from concrete	1
Return rental tools	1
Clean up	2

a. Identify the value-added activities. How much of the total is value-added time?

b. Identify the non-value-added activities. How much total time is spent performing non-value-added activities?

c. Calculate the manufacturing cycle efficiency.

27. (Activity analysis; MCE) Log Cabins Unlimited constructs vacation houses in the North Carolina mountains. The company has developed the following value chart:

Operations	Average Number of Days
Receiving materials	1
Storing materials	5
Measuring and cutting materials	3
Handling materials	7
Setting up and moving scaffolding	6
Assembling materials	7
Building fireplace	9
Pegging logs	4
Cutting and framing doors and windows	2
Sealing joints	4
Inspecting property (county inspectors)	3

a. What are the value-added activities and their total time?

b. What are the non-value-added activities and their total time?

c. Calculate the manufacturing cycle efficiency of the process.

d. Prepare a one-minute presentation explaining the difference between value-added and non-value-added activities.

28. (Activity-based costing) Outdoor Living makes umbrellas, gazebos, and lawn chairs. The company uses a traditional overhead allocation scheme and assigns overhead to products at the rate of $20 per direct labor hour. In 2006, the company produced 200,000 umbrellas, 20,000 gazebos, and 60,000 lawn chairs and incurred $8,000,000 of manufacturing overhead costs. The cost per unit for each product group in 2006 was as follows:

	Umbrellas	**Gazebos**	**Lawn Chairs**
Direct material	$ 8	$ 80	$ 8
Direct labor	12	90	30
Overhead	16	120	40
Total	$36	$290	$78

Because profitability has been lagging and competition has been getting more intense, Outdoor Living is considering implementing an activity-based costing system for 2007. In analyzing the 2006 data, management determined that all $8,000,000 of factory overhead could be assigned to four basic activities: quality control, setups, material handling, and equipment operation. Data from 2006 on the costs associated with each of the four activities follows:

Quality Control	**Setups**	**Material Handling**	**Equipment Operation**	**Total Costs**
$400,000	$400,000	$1,200,000	$6,000,000	$8,000,000

Management determined that the following allocation bases and total 2006 volumes for each allocation base could have been used for ABC:

Activity	Base	Volume
Quality control	Number of units produced	280,000
Setups	Number of setups	2,000
Material handling	Pounds of material used	4,000,000
Equipment operation	Number of machine hours	2,000,000

Volume measures for 2006 for each product and each allocation base were as follows:

	Umbrellas	Gazebos	Chaise Lounges
Number of units	200,000	20,000	60,000
Number of setups	400	800	800
Pounds of material	800,000	2,000,000	1,200,000
Number of machine hours	400,000	800,000	800,000

a. For 2006, determine the total overhead allocated to each product group using the traditional allocation based on direct labor hours.

b. For 2006, determine the total overhead that would have been allocated to each product group if activity-based costing were used. Compute the cost per unit for each product group.

c. Outdoor Living has a policy of setting sales prices based on product costs. How would the sales prices using activity-based costing differ from those obtained using the traditional overhead allocation?

29. (Activity-based costing; advanced) Stylish Components manufactures two products. Following is a production and cost analysis for each product for the year 2007.

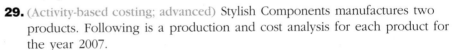

Cost Component	Product A	Product B	Both Products	Cost
Units produced	10,000	10,000	20,000	
Raw material used (units)				
X	50,000	50,000	100,000	$ 800,000
Y		100,000	100,000	$ 200,000
Labor hours used				
Department 1				$ 681,000
Direct labor	20,000	5,000	25,000	$ 375,000
Indirect labor				
Inspection	2,500	2,500	5,000	
Machine operations	5,000	10,000	15,000	
Setups	200	200	400	
Department 2				$ 462,000
Direct labor	5,000	5,000	10,000	$ 200,000
Indirect labor				
Inspection	2,500	5,000	7,500	
Machine operations	1,000	4,000	5,000	
Setups	200	400	600	
Machine hours used				
Department 1	5,000	10,000	15,000	$ 400,000
Department 2	5,000	20,000	25,000	$ 800,000
Power used (kw hours)				$ 400,000
Department 1			1,500,000	
Department 2			8,500,000	
Other activity data				
Building occupancy				$1,000,000
Purchasing				$ 100,000
Number of purchase orders				
Material X			200	
Material Y			300	
Square feet occupied				
Purchasing			10,000	
Power			40,000	
Department 1			200,000	
Department 2			250,000	

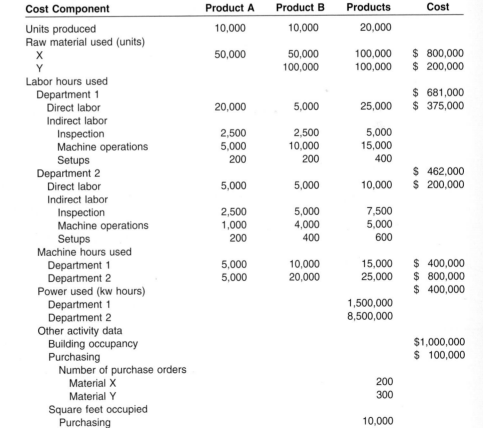

Peter Yound, the firm's cost accountant, has just returned from a seminar on activity-based costing. To apply the concepts he has learned, he decides to analyze the costs incurred for Products A and B from an activity basis. In doing so, he specifies the following first and second allocation processes:

FIRST STAGE: ALLOCATIONS TO DEPARTMENTS

Cost Pool	Cost Object	Activity Allocation Base
Power	Departments	Kilowatt hours
Purchasing	Material	Number of purchase orders
Building occupancy	Departments	Square feet occupied

SECOND STAGE: ALLOCATIONS TO PRODUCTS

Cost Pool	Cost Object	Activity Allocation Base
Departments		
Indirect labor	Products	Hours worked
Power	Products	Machine hours
Machinery-related	Products	Machine hours
Building occupancy	Products	Machine hours
Material		
Purchasing	Products	Materials used

Source: Adapted from Harold P. Roth and A. Faye Borthick, "Getting Closer to Real Product Costs," *Management Accounting* (May 1989), pp. 28–33. Reprinted from *Management Accounting*. Copyright by Institute of Management Accountants, Montvale, N.J.

a. Determine the total overhead for Stylish Components.

b. Determine the plantwide overhead rate for the company, assuming the use of direct labor hours.

c. Determine the cost per unit of Product A and Product B, using the overhead application rate found in part (b).

d. Using the step-down approach, determine the cost allocations to departments (first-stage allocations). Allocate in the following order: building occupancy, purchasing, and power.

e. Using the allocations found in part (d), determine the cost allocations to products (second-stage allocations).

f. Determine the cost per unit of Product A and Product B using the overhead allocations found in part (e).

30. 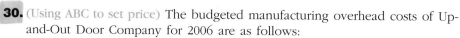 (Using ABC to set price) The budgeted manufacturing overhead costs of Up-and-Out Door Company for 2006 are as follows:

Type of Cost	Cost Amount
Electric power	$ 500,000
Work cells	3,000,000
Material handling	1,000,000
Quality control inspections	1,000,000
Product runs (machine setups)	500,000
Total budgeted overhead costs	$6,000,000

For the last five years, the cost accounting department has been charging overhead production costs based on machine hours. The estimated budgeted capacity for 2006 is 1,000,000 machine hours.

The president of Up-and-Out Door recently attended a seminar on activity-based costing. She now believes that ABC results in more reliable cost data that, in turn, will give the company an edge in pricing over its competitors. At the president's request, the production manager provided the following data regarding expected 2006 activity for the cost drivers of the preceding budgeted overhead costs.

Type of Costs	Activity Drivers
Electric power	100,000 kilowatt hours
Work cells	600,000 square feet
Material handling	200,000 material moves
Quality control inspections	100,000 inspections
Product runs (machine setups)	50,000 product runs

Peter Reed, the VP of marketing, received an offer to sell 5,000 doors to a local construction company. Peter asked the head of cost accounting to prepare cost estimates for producing the 5,000 doors. The head of cost accounting accumulated the following data concerning production of 5,000 doors:

Direct material cost	$100,000
Direct labor cost	$300,000
Machine hours	10,000
Direct labor hours	15,000
Electric power—kilowatt hours	1,000
Work cells—square feet	8,000
Number of material handling moves	100
Number of quality control inspections	50
Number of product runs (setups)	25

Source: Adapted from Nabil Hassa, Herbert E. Brown, and Paul M. Saunders, "Management Accounting Case Study: Beaver Window Inc.," *Management Accounting Campus Report* (Fall 1990). Copyright Institute of Management Accountants, Montvale, N.J.

a. What is the predetermined overhead rate if the traditional measure of machine hours is used?

b. What is the manufacturing cost per door as presently accounted for?

c. What is the manufacturing cost per door under the proposed ABC method?

d. If the two cost systems will result in different cost estimates, which cost accounting system is preferable as a pricing base and why?

31. (Activity driver analysis and decision making) Elsinore Manufacturing is concerned about its ability to control factory labor-related costs. The company has recently finished an analysis of these costs for 2006. Following is a summary of the major categories of labor costs identified by the company's accounting department:

Category	Amount
Base wages	$42,000,000
Health care benefits	7,000,000
Payroll taxes	3,360,000
Overtime	5,800,000
Training	1,250,000
Retirement benefits	4,600,000
Workers' compensation	800,000

Following are some of the potential cost drivers identified by the company for labor-related costs, along with their 2006 volume levels.

Potential Activity Driver	2006 Volume Level
Average number of factory employees	1,400
Number of new hires	200
Number of regular labor hours worked	2,100,000
Number of overtime hours worked	192,000
Total factory wages	$47,800,000
Volume of production in units	8,000,000
Number of production process changes	400
Number of production schedule changes	250

a. For each cost pool, determine the cost per unit of the activity driver using the activity driver that you believe has the closest relationship to the cost pool.

b. Based on your judgments and calculations in part (a), which activity driver should receive the most attention from company managers in their efforts to control labor-related costs? How much of the total labor-related cost is attributable to this activity driver?

c. In the contemporary environment, many firms ask their employees to work record levels of overtime. What activity driver does this practice suggest is a major contributor to labor-related costs? Explain.

32. (Activity-based costing and pricing) Orlando Community Hospital has been under increasing pressure to be accountable for the charges it assesses its patients. Its current pricing system is ad hoc, based on pricing norms for the geographical area, and it explicitly considers direct costs only for surgery, medication, and other treatments. Orlando's controller has suggested that the hospital improve its pricing policies by seeking a tighter relationship between costs and pricing. This approach would make prices for services less arbitrary. As a first step, the controller has determined that most costs can be assigned to one of three cost pools. The three cost pools follow along with the estimated amounts and activity drivers.

Activity Center	Amount	Activity Driver	Quantity
Professional salaries	$1,800,000	Professional hours	30,000 hours
Building costs	900,000	Square feet used	15,000 sq. ft.
Risk management	640,000	Patients served	1,000 patients

The hospital provides service in three broad categories. The services follow with their volume measures for the activity centers.

Service	Professional Hours	Square Feet	Number of Patients
Surgery	6,000	1,200	400
Housing patients	20,000	12,000	1,000
Outpatient care	4,000	1,800	600

a. Determine the allocation rates for each activity center cost pool.
b. Allocate the activity center costs to the three services provided by the hospital.
c. What bases might be used as cost drivers to allocate the service center costs among the patients served by the hospital? Defend your selections.

33. (Determining product cost) Grand Forks Corp. has identified activity centers to which overhead costs are assigned. The cost pool amounts for these centers and their selected activity drivers for 2006 are as follows.

Activity Centers	Costs	Activity Drivers
Utilities	$1,200,000	60,000 machine hours
Scheduling and setup	1,092,000	780 setups
Material handling	2,560,000	1,600,000 pounds of material

The company's products and other operating statistics follow:

	PRODUCTS		
	A	B	C
Direct costs	$80,000	$80,000	$90,000
Machine hours	30,000	10,000	20,000
Number of setups	130	380	270
Pounds of material	500,000	300,000	800,000
Number of units produced	40,000	20,000	60,000
Direct labor hours	32,000	18,000	50,000

a. Determine unit product cost using the appropriate cost drivers for each product.
b. Before it installed an ABC system, the company used a traditional costing system that allocated factory overhead to products using direct labor hours. The firm operates in a competitive market and sets product prices at cost plus a 20 percent markup.
   1. Calculate unit costs based on traditional costing.
   2. Determine selling prices based on unit costs for traditional costing and for ABC costs.
c. Discuss the problems related to setting prices based on traditional costing and explain how ABC improves the information.

34. (Product complexity) Superior Electronics is a world leader in the production of electronic test and measurement instruments. The company experienced almost uninterrupted growth through the 1990s, but in the 2000s, the low-priced end of the Portables Division's product line was challenged by the aggressive low-price strategy of several Japanese competitors. These Japanese companies set prices 25 percent below Superior's prevailing prices. To compete, the division needed to reduce costs and increase customer value by increasing operational efficiency.

The division took steps to implement just-in-time delivery and scheduling techniques as well as a total quality control program and to involve people techniques that moved responsibility for problem solving down to the operating level of the division. The results of these changes were impressive: substantial reductions in cycle time, direct labor hours per unit, and inventory levels as well as increases in output dollars per person per day and operating income. The cost accounting system was providing information, however, that did not seem to support the changes.

Total overhead cost for the division was $10,000,000; of this, part (55%) seemed to be related to materials and the remainder (45%) to conversion. Material-related costs pertain to procurement, receiving, inspection, stockroom personnel, and so on. Conversion-related costs pertain to direct labor, supervision, and process-related engineering. All overhead was applied on the basis of direct labor.

The division decided to concentrate efforts on revamping the application system for material-related overhead. Managers believed the majority of material overhead (MOH) costs were related to the maintenance and handling of each different part number. Other types of MOH costs were driven by the value of parts, absolute number of parts, and each use of a different part number.

At this time, the division used 8,000 different parts and in extremely different quantities. For example, annual usage of one part was 35,000 units; usage of another part was only 200 units. The division decided that MOH costs would decrease if a smaller number of different parts were used in the products.

Source: Adapted from Michael A. Robinson, ed., *Cases from Management Accounting Practice*, No. 5 (Montvale, N.J.: National Association of Accountants, 1989), pp. 13–17. Copyright by Institute of Management Accountants (formerly National Association of Accountants), Montvale, N.J.

a. Give some reasons that MOH would decrease if parts were standardized.

b. Using the numbers given, develop a cost allocation method for MOH to quantify and communicate the strategy of parts standardization.

c. Explain how the use of the method developed in part (b) would support the strategy of parts standardization.

d. Is any method that applies the entire MOH cost pool on the basis of one cost driver sufficiently accurate for complex products? Explain.

e. Are MOH product costing rates developed for management reporting appropriate for inventory valuation for external reporting? Why or why not?

35. (Activity-based costing) X-tra Sturdy Co. manufactures several different types of printed circuit boards; however, two of the boards account for the majority of the company's sales. The first of these boards, a television (TV) circuit board, has been a standard in the industry for several years. The market for this type of board is competitive and, therefore, price sensitive. X-tra Sturdy plans to sell 65,000 of the TV circuit boards in 2007 at a price of $150 per unit. The second high-volume product, a personal computer (PC) circuit board, is a recent addition to X-tra Sturdy's product line. Because the PC board incorporates the latest technology, it can be sold at a premium price; the 2007 plans include the sale of 40,000 PC boards at $300 per unit.

X-tra Sturdy's management group is meeting to discuss strategies for 2007, and the current topic of conversation is how to spend the sales and promotion dollars for next year. The sales manager believes that the market share for the TV board could be expanded by concentrating X-tra Sturdy's promotional efforts in this area. In response to this suggestion, the production manager said, "Why don't you go after a bigger market for the PC board? The cost sheets that I get show that the contribution from the PC board is more than double the contribution from the TV board. I know we get a premium price for the PC board; selling it should help overall profitability." X-tra Sturdy uses a standard cost system, and the following data apply to the TV and PC boards.

	TV Board	PC Board
Direct material	$80	$140
Direct labor	1.5 hours	4.0 hours
Machine time	0.5 hours	1.5 hours

Variable factory overhead is applied on the basis of direct labor hours. For 2007, variable factory overhead is budgeted at $1,120,000, and direct labor hours are estimated at 280,000. The hourly rates for machine time and direct labor are $10 and $14, respectively. X-tra Sturdy applies a material handling charge at 10 percent of material cost; this material handling charge is not included in variable factory overhead. Total 2007 expenditures for materials are budgeted at $10,800,000.

Drew Ciulla, X-tra Sturdy's controller, believes that before the management group proceeds with the discussion about allocated sales and promotional dollars to individual products, it might be worthwhile to look at these products on the basis of the activities involved in their production. As she explained to the group, "Activity-based costing integrates the cost of all activities, known as cost drivers, into individual product costs rather than including these costs in overhead pools." Ciulla has prepared the following schedule to help the management group understand this concept.

	Budgeted Cost	Cost Driver	Annual Activity for Cost Driver
Material overhead			
Procurement	$ 400,000	Number of parts	4,000,000 parts
Production scheduling	220,000	Number of boards	110,000 boards
Packaging and shipping	440,000	Number of boards	110,000 boards
	$1,060,000		
Variable overhead			
Machine setup	$ 446,000	Number of setups	278,750 setups
Hazardous waste disposal	48,000	Pounds of waste	16,000 pounds
Quality control	560,000	Number of inspections	160,000 inspections
General supplies	66,000	Number of boards	110,000 boards
	$1,120,000		
Manufacturing			
Machine insertion	$1,200,000	Number of parts	3,000,000 parts
Manual insertion	4,000,000	Number of parts	1,000,000 parts
Wave soldering	132,000	Number of boards	110,000 boards
	$5,332,000		

	REQUIRED PER UNIT	
	TV Board	PC Board
Parts	25	55
Machine insertions of parts	24	35
Manual insertions of parts	1	20
Machine setups	2	3
Hazardous waste	0.02 lb.	0.35 lb.
Inspections	1	2

"Using this information," Ciulla explained, "we can calculate an activity-based cost for each TV board and each PC board and then compare it to the standard cost we have been using. The only cost that remains the same for both cost methods is the cost of direct materials. The cost drivers will replace the direct labor, machine time, and overhead costs in the standard cost system."

a. Identify at least four general advantages associated with activity-based costing.

b. On the basis of standard costs, calculate the total contribution expected in 2007 for X-tra Sturdy Co.'s
   1. TV board
   2. PC board

c. On the basis of activity-based costs, calculate the total contribution expected in 2007 for X-tra Sturdy Co.'s
   1. TV board
   2. PC board

d. Explain how the comparison of the results of the two costing methods could impact the decisions made by X-tra Sturdy Co.'s management group.

(CMA adapted)

36. (Activity-based costing) Kingston Inc. provides a wide range of engineering and architectural consulting services through its three branch offices in Sky, Ruene, and Wayne. The company allocates resources and bonuses to the three branches based on the net income reported for the period. The following presents the results of 2007 performance.

	Sky	Ruene	Wayne	Total
Sales	$1,500,000	$1,419,000	$1,067,000	$ 3,986,000
Less: Direct labor	(382,000)	(317,000)	(317,000)	(1,016,000)
Direct material	(281,000)	(421,000)	(185,000)	(887,000)
Overhead	(710,000)	(589,000)	(589,000)	(1,888,000)
Net income	$ 127,000	$ 92,000	$ (24,000)	$ 195,000

Overhead items are accumulated in one overhead pool and allocated to the branches based on direct labor dollars. For 2007, this predetermined overhead rate was $1.859 for every direct labor dollar incurred by an office. The overhead pool includes rent, depreciation, taxes, and so on regardless of which office incurred the expense. This method of accumulating costs forces the offices to absorb a portion of the overhead incurred by other offices.

Management is concerned with the results of the 2007 performance reports. During a review of the overhead, it became apparent that many items of overhead are not correlated to the movement in direct labor dollars as previously assumed. Management decided that applying overhead based on activity-based costing and direct tracing, when possible, should provide a more accurate picture of the profitability of each branch. An analysis of the overhead revealed that the following dollars for rent, utilities, depreciation, and taxes could be traced directly to the office that incurred the overhead.

	Sky	Ruene	Wayne	Total
Direct overhead	$180,000	$270,000	$177,000	$627,000

Activity pools and activity drivers were determined from the accounting records and staff surveys as follows:

Activity Pools		Activity Driver	NUMBER OF ACTIVITIES BY LOCATION		
			Sky	Ruene	Wayne
General administration	$ 409,000	Direct labor $	382,413	317,086	317,188
Project costing	48,000	# of timesheet entries	6,000	3,800	3,500
Accounts payable/receiving	139,000	# of vendor invoices	1,020	850	400
Accounts receivable	47,000	# of client invoices	588	444	96
Payroll/Mail sort & delivery	30,000	# of employees	23	26	18
Personnel recruiting	38,000	# of new hires	8	4	7
Employee insur. processing	14,000	# of insur. claims filed	230	260	180
Proposals	139,000	# of proposals	200	250	60
Sales meetings, sales aids	202,000	Contracted sales	1,824,439	1,399,617	571,208
Shipping	24,000	# of projects	99	124	30
Ordering	48,000	# of purchase orders	135	110	80
Duplicating costs	46,000	# of copies duplicated	162,500	146,250	65,000
Blueprinting	77,000	# of blueprints	39,000	31,200	16,000
	$1,261,000				

a. How much overhead cost should be assigned to each branch based on activity-based costing concepts?

b. What is the contribution of each branch before subtracting the results obtained in part (a)?

c. What is the profitability of each branch office using activity-based costing?

d. Evaluate the concerns of management regarding the traditional costing technique currently used.

(IMA adapted)

37. (Activity-based costing and pricing) Black West owns and manages a commercial cold-storage warehouse. He stores a vast variety of perishable goods for his customers. Historically, he has charged customers using a flat rate of $0.08 per pound per month for goods stored. His cold-storage warehouse has 100,000 cubic feet of storage capacity.

In the past two years, West has become dissatisfied with the profitability of the warehouse operation. Despite the fact that the warehouse remains relatively full, revenues have not kept pace with operating costs. Recently, West approached his accountant, Kathy Kirby, about using activity-based costing to improve his understanding of the causes of costs and revise the pricing formula. Kirby has determined that most costs can be associated with one of four activities. Those activities and their related costs, volume measures, and volume levels for 2006 follow:

Activity	Cost	Monthly Volume Measure
Send/receive goods	$12,000	Weight in pounds—500,000
Store goods	8,000	Volume in cubic feet—80,000
Move goods	10,000	Volume in square feet—5,000
Identify goods	4,000	Number of packages—500

Source: Adapted from Harold P. Roth and Linda T. Sims, "Costing for Warehousing and Distribution," *Management Accounting* (August 1991), pp. 42–45. Reprinted from *Management Accounting*. Copyright by Institute of Management Accountants, Montvale, N.J.

a. Based on the activity cost and volume data, determine the amount of cost assigned to the following customers, whose goods were all received on the first day of last month.

Customer	Weight of Order in Pounds	Cubic Feet	Square Feet	Number of Packages
Jones	40,000	3,000	300	5
Hansen	40,000	2,000	200	20
Assad	40,000	1,000	1,000	80

b. Determine the price to be charged to each customer under the existing pricing plan.

    c. Determine the price to be charged using ABC, assuming West would base the price on the cost determined in part (a) plus a markup of 40 percent.

    d. How well does West's existing pricing plan capture the costs incurred to provide the warehouse services? Explain.

38. (Essay) Companies that want to be more globally competitive can consider the implementation of activity-based management (ABM). Such companies have often used other initiatives that involve higher efficiency, effectiveness, or output quality. These same initiatives are typically consistent with and supportive of ABM.

    a. In what other types of "initiatives" might such global companies engage?

    b. How might ABM and activity-based costing (ABC) help a company in its quest to achieve world-class status?

    c. For any significant initiative, senior management commitment is generally required. Would it be equally important to have top management support if a company was instituting ABC rather than ABM? Justify your answer.

    d. Assume that you are a member of top management in a large organization. Do you think implementation of ABM or ABC would be more valuable? Explain the rationale for your answer.

39. (Decision making; ethics; essay) As the chief executive officer of a large corporation, you have decided after discussion with production and accounting personnel to implement activity-based management concepts. Your goal is to reduce cycle time and, in turn, costs. A primary way to accomplish this goal is to install highly automated equipment in your plant, which would then displace approximately 60 percent of your workforce. Your company is the major employer in the area of the country where it is located.

    a. Discuss the pros and cons of installing the equipment from the perspective of your (1) stockholders, (2) employees, and (3) customers.

    b. How would you explain to a worker that his or her job is a non-value-added activity?

    c. What alternatives might you have that could accomplish the goal of reducing cycle time but not create economic havoc for the local area?

6

Process Costing

Objectives

AFTER COMPLETING THIS CHAPTER, YOU SHOULD BE ABLE TO ANSWER THE FOLLOWING QUESTIONS:

LO.1 HOW DOES PROCESS COSTING DIFFER FROM JOB ORDER COSTING?

LO.2 FOR WHAT REASONS ARE EQUIVALENT UNITS OF PRODUCTION USED IN PROCESS COSTING?

LO.3 HOW ARE EQUIVALENT UNITS OF PRODUCTION, UNIT COSTS, AND INVENTORY VALUES DETERMINED USING THE WEIGHTED AVERAGE METHOD OF PROCESS COSTING?

LO.4 HOW ARE EQUIVALENT UNITS OF PRODUCTION, UNIT COSTS, AND INVENTORY VALUES DETERMINED USING THE FIFO METHOD OF PROCESS COSTING?

LO.5 HOW CAN STANDARD COSTS BE USED IN A PROCESS COSTING SYSTEM?

LO.6 WHY WOULD A COMPANY USE A HYBRID COSTING SYSTEM?

LO.7 *(APPENDIX 1)* WHAT ALTERNATIVE METHODS CAN BE USED TO CALCULATE EQUIVALENT UNITS OF PRODUCTION?

LO.8 *(APPENDIX 2)* HOW ARE NORMAL AND ABNORMAL SPOILAGE LOSSES TREATED IN AN EUP SCHEDULE?

Introducing

Williamsburg Soap and Candle Company

Williamsburg Soap and Candle (WSAC) Company began in 1964, when founder John Barnett Jr. started dipping bayberry tapers as a retail tourist attraction for visitors to Colonial Williamsburg, Virginia. The company established a wholesale "arm" as gift shops in other locations started purchasing WSAC bayberry candles for resale and requests were received for tapers of other colors and fragrances. The product line grew to include molded and container candles as well as cold process soap.

WSAC makes three distinct types of candles: (1) dipped tapers, (2) molded or pillar candles, and (3) container candles. Dipped tapers are made by stringing a candle frame with wick, dipping the candle several times in wax (with cooling time between dips), and then allowing the warm tapers to cool completely before cutting them off the frame. Tapers are then sized to the correct height, finished on the bottom, graded for quality, boxed, and labeled. Dipped candles are the most labor-intensive product made by WSAC.

Molded candles are made by pouring wax into a prewarmed metal mold, cooling the candles in a water bath, adding more wax to the candle during the cooling process, and removing the candle from the mold after it has cooled

completely. Wicks can either be tied to the mold before pouring the wax (prewicked method) or inserted using a metal rod after the candle has cooled (after wicking).

Container candles are made by pouring wax into a glass, metal, or ceramic vessel. A paper core wick with a metal tab base is glued to the container bottom, the container is then warmed, and wax is added to the container. The container size dictates how many times wax must be poured. Smaller containers may require only one repour, while larger containers may require two or three repours.

For these three types of candles, WSAC uses process costing to determine product cost. After looking at the off-the-shelf computer programs designed for this purpose, company management decided that the available programs did not fit organizational needs. Thus, the computer program used at the company was written by in-house computer experts—but determining equivalent units of production and allocating period costs to goods transferred out and goods still in ending inventory are still essential elements of the system.

Source: Ms. Virginia Hartmann, president, Williamsburg Soap and Candle Company, April 2004.

At **Williamsburg Soap and Candle Company**, products are manufactured in a continuous flow process. Within a batch of output, each unit is basically identical to all others, although they may be of different scents or colors. Because Williamsburg Soap and Candle Company's production differs so dramatically from the products made by a company tailoring unique products to individual customer specifications, the product costing systems for the two types of companies also differ.

Job order costing is appropriate for companies making products or providing services in limited quantities that conform to customer specifications. In contrast, Williamsburg Soap and Candle Company uses process costing to accumulate and assign costs to units of production. Manufacturers of candy bars, bricks, gasoline, and paper, among many other types of firms also use this costing method.

LO.1
HOW DOES PROCESS COSTING DIFFER FROM JOB ORDER COSTING?

Both job order and process costing systems accumulate costs by cost component in each production department. However, the two systems assign costs to departmental output differently. In a job order system, costs are assigned to specific jobs and then, if possible, to units contained within the job. Process costing uses an averaging technique to assign costs directly to units produced during the period. In both systems, unit costs are transferred as goods are moved from one department to the next so that a total production cost can be accumulated.

This chapter first illustrates the weighted average and first-in, first-out (FIFO) methods of calculating unit cost in a process costing system. These two methods differ only in the treatment of beginning inventory units and costs. After unit cost has been determined, total costs are assigned to the units transferred out of a department and to that department's ending inventory. The chapter also describes a standard cost process costing system, which is an often-used simplification of the FIFO process costing system. Appendix 2 to this chapter provides a brief introduction to the issue of spoilage in a process costing production system.

INTRODUCTION TO PROCESS COSTING

Assigning costs to units of production is an averaging process. In the easiest situation, a product's actual unit cost is found by dividing a period's departmental production costs by that period's departmental production quantity. This average is expressed by the following formula:

$$\text{Unit Cost} = \text{Production Costs} \div \text{Production Quantity}$$

This formula is appropriate, however, only if all goods are fully complete at the end of a period.

The Numerator

The formula numerator is obtained by accumulating departmental costs incurred in a single period. Because most companies make more than one type of product, costs must be accumulated by product within each department. The accumulation can occur by using either separate Work in Process Inventory accounts for each product or a single Work in Process Inventory control account that is supported by detailed subsidiary ledgers containing specific product information.

Cost accumulation in a process costing system differs from that in a job order costing system in two ways: (1) the *quantity* of production for which costs are accumulated at any one time and (2) the *cost object* to which the costs are assigned. **Williamsburg Soap and Candle Company** occasionally contracts to make custom candles for a company's special promotion or for a particular client. For these orders, the company typically uses job order costing. Direct material and direct labor costs associated with each specialty order would be accumulated and assigned directly to the individual buyer's job. After each job is completed, the total material, labor, and allocated overhead costs are known and job cost can be determined.

In contrast, for its basic product lines, WSAC would use a process costing system to accumulate periodic costs for each department and each product. Because it manufactures several types of candles (mini-taper, tiny-taper, slim, traditional, and pillar) each period, the costs assignable to each product type must be individually designated and attached to the specific production runs. These costs are then assigned to the units worked on during the period.

Exhibit 6–1 presents the source documents used to make initial cost assignments to production departments during a period. Costs are reassigned at the end of the period (usually each month) from the departments to the units produced. As goods are transferred from one department to the next, related departmental production costs are also transferred. When products are complete, their costs are transferred from Work in Process Inventory to Finished Goods Inventory.

As in job order costing, direct material and direct labor components of product cost present relatively few problems for cost accumulation and assignment. Direct material cost can be measured from material requisition slips; direct labor cost can be determined from employee time sheets and wage rates for the period.

Overhead, however, must be indirectly assigned to output. If total overhead costs are relatively constant from period to period and production volume is relatively steady over time, actual overhead costs may be used for product costing. If such conditions do not exist, using actual overhead for product costing would result in fluctuating unit costs and, therefore, predetermined application rates are more appropriate. As managers find new ways to structure production activities and develop new management methods, the bases on which overhead is assigned to production may change. For example, as a production plant becomes less labor intensive and more automated, management should change from a labor-based to a machine-based overhead allocation.

EXHIBIT 6–1
COST FLOWS AND COST ASSIGNMENT

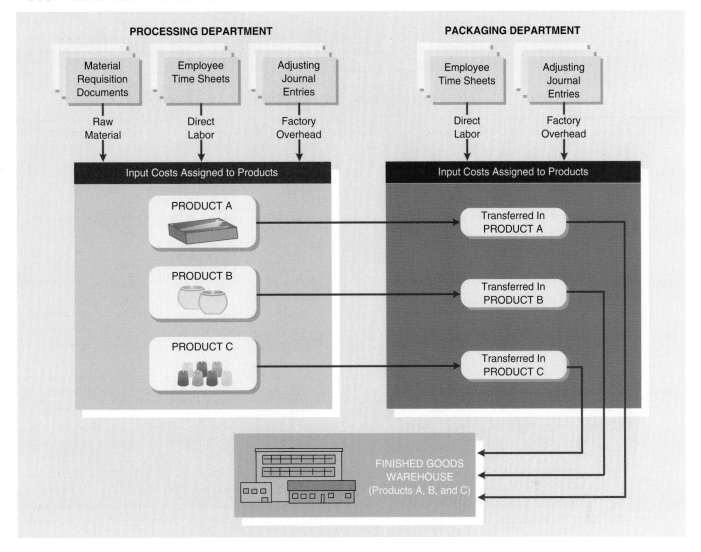

The Denominator

The denominator in the unit cost formula represents total departmental production for the period. If all units were 100 percent complete at the end of each accounting period, units could simply be counted to obtain the denominator. In most production processes, however, partially completed units compose Work in Process (WIP) Inventory at the end of one period and become the partially completed beginning inventory of the next period. Process costing assigns costs to both fully and partially completed units by mathematically converting partially completed units to equivalent whole units.

Units in beginning WIP Inventory were started last period but will be completed during the current period. This two-period production sequence means that some costs for these units were incurred last period and additional costs will be incurred in the current period. Additionally, the partially completed units in ending WIP Inventory were started in the current period but will not be completed until next period. Therefore, current period production efforts on ending WIP Inventory units cause some costs to be incurred in this period, and more costs will need to be incurred next period. This production sequence is illustrated in Exhibit 6–2.

EXHIBIT 6-2
TWO-PERIOD PRODUCTION SEQUENCE

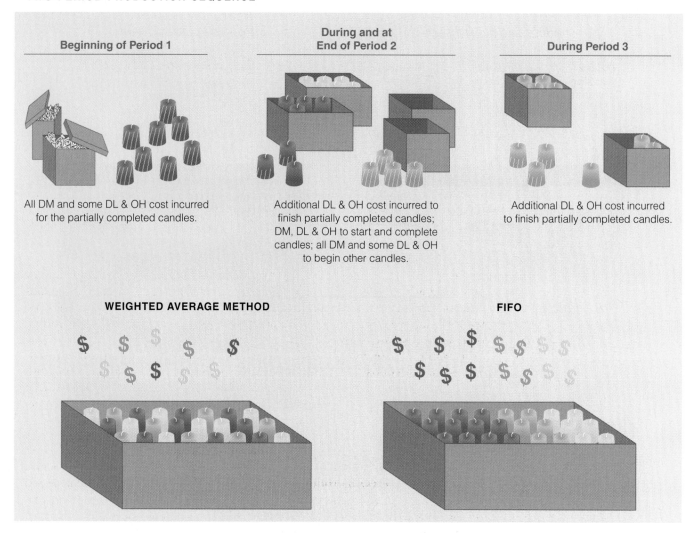

Beginning of Period 1	During and at End of Period 2	During Period 3
All DM and some DL & OH cost incurred for the partially completed candles.	Additional DL & OH cost incurred to finish partially completed candles; DM, DL & OH to start and complete candles; all DM and some DL & OH to begin other candles.	Additional DL & OH cost incurred to finish partially completed candles.

WEIGHTED AVERAGE METHOD

FIFO

Physical inspection of ending inventory units is needed to determine the proportion of direct material, direct labor, and overhead work that was completed during the current period. One hundred percent minus this proportion represents the proportion of work that needs to be completed next period. Inspection at the end of last period provided information on the proportion of work that needed to be completed this period on beginning inventory.

Equivalent Units of Production

LO.2
FOR WHAT REASONS ARE EQUIVALENT UNITS OF PRODUCTION USED IN PROCESS COSTING?

Units typically flow through a production department in first-in, first-out order. Goods that were incomplete at the end of the previous period are completed first in the current period; then units are started and completed during the current period; and, finally, some units are begun but not completed during the current period. Because manufacturing efforts benefit a variety of different units, production cannot be measured by counting whole units. Accountants use a concept known as *equivalent units of production* to measure the quantity of production achieved during a period.

equivalent units of production (EUP)

Equivalent units of production (EUP) are approximations of the number of whole units of output that could have been produced during a period from the actual effort expended during that period. EUPs are calculated by multiplying the

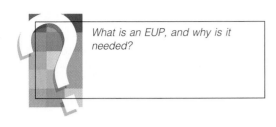

What is an EUP, and why is it needed?

number of actual, but incomplete, units produced by the respective percentage degree of completion. The following simple example indicates how equivalent units are calculated.

Assume a company had no beginning inventory in November. During November, the department worked on 220,000 units: 200,000 units were completed and 20,000 units were 40 percent complete at the end of the period. The EUP for the period are 208,000 [(200,000 × 100%) + (20,000 × 40%)].

WEIGHTED AVERAGE AND FIFO PROCESS COSTING METHODS

The two methods of accounting for cost flows in process costing are (1) weighted average and (2) FIFO. These methods relate to the manner in which cost flows are assumed to occur in the production process. In a very general way, these process costing approaches can be related to the cost flow methods used in financial accounting.

Retail businesses use the weighted average method to determine an average cost per unit of inventory. This cost is computed by dividing the total cost of goods available for sale by total units available for sale. Total cost and total units are found by adding purchases to beginning inventory. Costs and units of the current period are not distinguished in any way from those on hand at the end of the prior period. In contrast, the FIFO method of accounting for merchandise inventory separates goods according to when they were purchased and at what cost. The costs of beginning inventory are the first costs sent to Cost of Goods Sold, with other costs following in the order in which they were incurred; units remaining in the ending inventory are assigned costs based on the most recent purchases.

weighted average method

FIFO method

Use of these methods for costing the production of a manufacturing firm is similar to their use by a retailer. The weighted average method computes a single average cost per unit of the combined beginning inventory and current period production. The FIFO method separates beginning inventory and current period production and their costs so that a current period cost per unit can be calculated. The denominator used in the cost formula to determine unit cost differs, depending on which of the two methods is used.[1]

Some quantity of direct material must generally be introduced at the start of the production process or there would be no need for labor or overhead to be incurred. For example, to make its various products, **Williamsburg Soap and Candle Company**'s production process begins with candle wax. Any material added at the start of production is 100 percent complete throughout the process *regardless* of the percentage of completion of labor and overhead.

Most production processes require multiple direct materials. Additional materials may be added at any point or even continuously during processing. A material, such as a box or a glass container, may even be added at the end of processing. Until the end of the production process, the product would be 0 percent complete as to the box but may be totally complete with regard to other materials. The production flow for candles in Exhibit 6–3 visually illustrates the need for separate EUP computations for each cost component. The materials wicks and wax are 100 percent complete at any point in the process after the start of production; no additional quantities of these materials are added later in

---

[1] Note that the term *denominator* is used here rather than equivalent units of production. Based on its definition, EUPs are related to current period productive activity. Thus, for any given set of production facts, there is only one true measure of equivalent units produced—regardless of the cost flow assumption used—and that measure is FIFO EUP. However, this fact has been obscured over time due to continued references to the "EUP" computation for weighted average. Thus, the term *EUP* has taken on a generic use to mean "the denominator used to compute the unit cost of production for a period in a process costing system." EUP is used in this generic manner throughout the process costing discussion.

EXHIBIT 6–3

CANDLE MANUFACTURING PROCESS—PRODUCTION DEPARTMENT

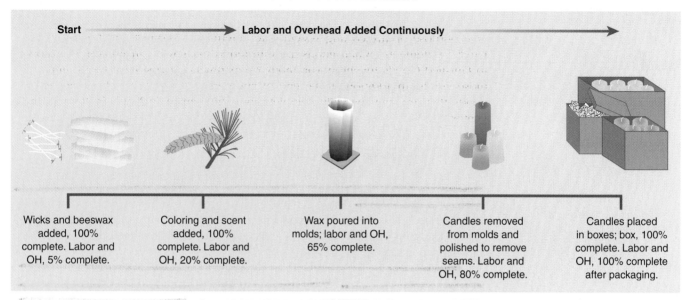

Wicks and beeswax added, 100% complete. Labor and OH, 5% complete.	Coloring and scent added, 100% complete. Labor and OH, 20% complete.	Wax poured into molds; labor and OH, 65% complete.	Candles removed from molds and polished to remove seams. Labor and OH, 80% complete.	Candles placed in boxes; box, 100% complete. Labor and OH, 100% complete after packaging.

production. When enough labor and overhead have been added to reach the 20 percent completion point, additional materials (color and scent) are added. Prior to 20 percent completion, these materials were 0 percent complete; after the 20 percent point, these materials are 100 percent complete. When labor and overhead processing are 99 percent finished, the candles are placed in boxes, after which the product is 100 percent complete. Thus, boxes are 0 percent complete throughout production; when the candles are boxed, the product is complete and transferred to the finished goods warehouse or directly to customers.

Assume that enough wicks and wax are started to make 8,000 candles. At period-end, the process is 75 percent complete as to labor and overhead. The candles would be 100 percent complete as to wicks, wax, color, and scent, but 0 percent complete as to boxes. The materials EUP calculations would indicate that there are 8,000 EUP for wicks, wax, color and scent and zero EUP for boxes. The labor and overhead (conversion) cost components would have an equivalency of 6,000 candles because the product is 75 percent complete and labor and overhead are added continuously during the process.[2]

When overhead is applied on a direct labor basis, or when direct labor and overhead are added to the product at the same rate, a single percentage of completion estimate can be made and used for both conversion cost components. However, because cost drivers other than direct labor are increasingly being used to apply overhead costs, single computations for "conversion EUP" will be made less often. For example, the cost driver for the utilities portion of overhead cost may be machine hours; the cost driver for the materials handling portion of overhead cost may be pounds of material. The increased use of multiple cost pools and/or activity-based costing concepts makes it less likely that the degrees of completion for the direct labor and overhead components of processing will be equal.

Calculation of equivalent units of production requires that a process cost flow method be specified. A detailed example of the calculations of equivalent units of production and cost assignment for each of the cost flow methods is presented in the next section.

---

[2] Although the same number of equivalent units results for wicks, wax, color, and scent and for labor and overhead, separate calculations of unit cost may be desirable for each component. These separate calculations would give managers more information for planning and control purposes. Managers must weigh the costs of making separate calculations against the benefits from having the additional information. For illustrative purposes, however, single computations will be made when cost components are at equal percentages of completion.

EUP CALCULATIONS AND COST ASSIGNMENTS

One purpose of any costing system is to determine a product cost for use on financial statements. When goods are transferred from Work in Process Inventory to Finished Goods Inventory (or another department), a cost must be assigned to those goods. In addition, at the end of any period, a value must be assigned to goods that are only partially complete and still remain in Work in Process Inventory. Exhibit 6–4 outlines the steps necessary in a process costing system to

EXHIBIT 6–4
STEPS IN PROCESS COSTING

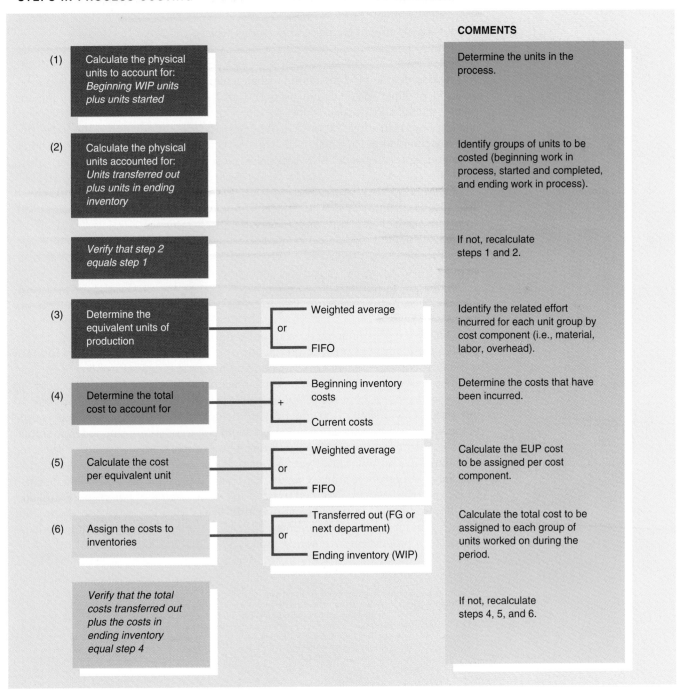

		COMMENTS
(1)	Calculate the physical units to account for: *Beginning WIP units plus units started*	Determine the units in the process.
(2)	Calculate the physical units accounted for: *Units transferred out plus units in ending inventory*	Identify groups of units to be costed (beginning work in process, started and completed, and ending work in process).
	Verify that step 2 equals step 1	If not, recalculate steps 1 and 2.
(3)	Determine the equivalent units of production — Weighted average or FIFO	Identify the related effort incurred for each unit group by cost component (i.e., material, labor, overhead).
(4)	Determine the total cost to account for + Beginning inventory costs / Current costs	Determine the costs that have been incurred.
(5)	Calculate the cost per equivalent unit — Weighted average or FIFO	Calculate the EUP cost to be assigned per cost component.
(6)	Assign the costs to inventories — Transferred out (FG or next department) or Ending inventory (WIP)	Calculate the total cost to be assigned to each group of units worked on during the period.
	Verify that the total costs transferred out plus the costs in ending inventory equal step 4	If not, recalculate steps 4, 5, and 6.

determine the costs assignable to the units completed and to those still in ending inventory at the end of a period. Each of these steps is discussed, and then a complete example is provided for both weighted average and FIFO costing.

total units to account for

The first step is to calculate the **total units to account for** or the total physical units for which the department is responsible. This amount is equal to the sum of whole and partial units worked on in the department during the current period. It is equal to actual beginning inventory units plus actual units started.

Second, determine what happened to the units to account for during the period. This step also requires the use of physical units. Units fit into one of two categories: (1) completed and transferred or (2) partially completed and remaining in ending Work in Process Inventory.[3]

At this point, verify that the total units for which the department was accountable are equal to the total units that were accounted for. If these amounts are not equal, any additional computations will be incorrect.

Third, choose either the weighted average or FIFO method to determine the equivalent units of production for each cost component. If all materials are added at the same degree of completion, a single computation for direct materials can be made. If multiple materials are used and are placed into production at different points, multiple EUP calculations for direct materials may be necessary. If overhead is based on direct labor or if these two factors are always at the same degree of completion, a single EUP can be computed for conversion. If neither condition exists, separate EUP schedules must be prepared for labor and overhead.[4]

total cost to account for

Fourth, find the **total cost to account for**. This amount is the summation of the balance in Work in Process Inventory at the beginning of the period plus all current costs for direct material, direct labor, and overhead.

Fifth, compute the cost per equivalent unit for each cost component using either the weighted average or FIFO equivalent units of production calculated in step 3.

Sixth, use the costs computed in step 5 to assign costs from the production process to units completed and transferred and to units remaining in Work in Process Inventory.

Quality Candle Company is used to demonstrate the steps involved in the computation of equivalent units of production and cost assignment for both methods of process costing. Quality Candle Company makes a variety of candles, including a 7-inch unscented pillar candle, popular with restaurants and hotels because of allergy concerns of customers. The company views the manufacturing process of this product as a single department with a single direct material, beeswax. Costs of the wicks and coloring are considered overhead. Candles are shipped in reusable containers to a central warehouse. From there, candles are distributed to wholesalers and retailers. Because wax is added at the start of processing, all inventories are 100 percent complete as to this material as soon as processing begins. Labor and overhead are assumed to be at the same degree of completion throughout the production process. Actual overhead is assigned to production at the end of each period. Exhibit 6–5 presents information for April 2006 regarding the candle maker's production inventories and costs.

---

[3] A third category (spoilage/breakage) does exist. It is assumed at this point that such happenings do not occur. Appendix 2 to this chapter describes the accounting for spoilage in process costing situations.

[4] As discussed in Chapter 5, overhead can be applied to products using a variety of traditional (direct labor hours or machine hours) or nontraditional (such as number of machine setups, pounds of material moved, and/or number of material requisitions) bases. The number of equivalent unit computations that need to be made results from the number of different cost pools and overhead allocation bases established in a company. Some highly automated manufacturers may not have a direct labor category. The quantity of direct labor may be so nominal that it is included in a conversion category and not accounted for separately.

EXHIBIT 6–5

PRODUCTION AND COST INFORMATION— APRIL 1, 2006

Candles in beginning inventory (40% complete as to labor and overhead or conversion)		5,000
Candles started during current period		200,700
Candles completed and transferred to finished goods		203,000
Candles in ending inventory (80% complete as to labor and overhead or conversion)		2,700
Costs of beginning inventory		
Direct material	$ 5,943	
Direct labor	1,800	
Overhead	14,958	$ 22,701
Current period costs		
Direct material	$321,120	
Direct labor	172,686	
Overhead	487,584	$981,390

Although figures are given for candles transferred out and for those in ending inventory, both figures are not essential. The number of candles remaining in ending inventory can be calculated by subtracting the candles that were completed and transferred during April from the total candles to account for. Alternatively, the number of candles transferred can be computed as the total candles to account for minus the candles in ending inventory. Quality Candle Company information is used to illustrate each step listed in Exhibit 6–4.

Weighted Average Method

LO.3
HOW ARE EQUIVALENT UNITS OF PRODUCTION, UNIT COSTS, AND INVENTORY VALUES DETERMINED USING THE WEIGHTED AVERAGE METHOD OF PROCESS COSTING?

STEP 1: CALCULATE THE TOTAL UNITS TO ACCOUNT FOR

Candles in beginning inventory	5,000
Candles started during current period	200,700
Candles to account for	205,700

STEP 2: CALCULATE THE TOTAL UNITS ACCOUNTED FOR

Candles completed and transferred out	203,000
Candles in ending WIP inventory	2,700
Candles accounted for	205,700

The items detailed in this step indicate the categories to which costs will be assigned in the final step. The number of candles accounted for in step 2 equals the number of candles to account for in step 1.

STEP 3: DETERMINE THE EQUIVALENT UNITS OF PRODUCTION

units started and completed

The weighted average EUP computation uses the number of candles in beginning inventory and the number of candles started and completed during the period. Units started and completed during a period equal units completed during the period minus units in beginning inventory. Units started and completed can also be computed as units started during the period minus the units in ending inventory. For Quality Candle Company, the candles started and completed in April are 198,000 (203,000 − 5,000) or (200,700 − 2,700). Exhibit 6–6 illustrates the concepts of total units to account for, total units accounted for, and units started and completed.

Ending inventory is 100 percent complete as to material because all material is added at the start of production. The ending inventory is 80 percent complete as to labor and overhead (conversion); one EUP computation can be made because these cost elements are assumed to be added at the same rate throughout

EXHIBIT 6–6
UNIT CONCEPTS

Total Units to Account For	Total Units Accounted For	Units Started and Completed
Beginning Inventory Units	Units Completed	Units Completed
+ Units Started	+ Ending Inventory Units	− Beginning Inventory Units
		or
		Units Started
		− Ending Inventory Units

the production process. The weighted average computation for equivalent units of production is as follows[5]:

	DM	Conversion (Labor & Overhead)
Beginning inventory (whole units)	5,000	5,000
Candles started and completed	198,000	198,000
Ending inventory (candles × % complete)	2,700	2,160
Equivalent units of production	205,700	205,160

STEP 4: DETERMINE THE TOTAL COST TO ACCOUNT FOR

Total cost to account for equals beginning inventory cost plus current period costs. Note that information is provided in Exhibit 6–5 on the cost for each element of production—direct material, direct labor, and overhead. Production costs can be determined from transfers of direct material from the warehouse, incurrence of direct labor, and either actual or applied overhead amounts. The sum of direct labor and overhead costs is the conversion cost. For Quality Candle Company, the total cost to account for is $1,004,091 ($22,701 + $981,390).

	DM	DL	OH	Total
Beginning inventory costs	$ 5,943	$ 1,800	$ 14,958	$ 22,701
Current period costs	321,120	172,686	487,584	981,390
To account for	$327,063	$174,486	$502,542	$1,004,091

The total cost to account for must be assigned to the goods transferred to Finished Goods Inventory (or, if appropriate, to the next department) and to ending Work in Process Inventory. Assignments are made in relation to the whole or equivalent whole units contained in each category.

STEP 5: CALCULATE THE COST PER EQUIVALENT UNIT OF PRODUCTION

A cost per equivalent unit of production must be computed for each cost component for which a separate calculation of EUP is made. Under the weighted average method, the costs of beginning inventory and those of the current period are summed for each cost component and averaged over that component's weighted average equivalent units of production. This calculation for unit cost for each cost component at the end of the period follows:

$$\text{Unit Cost} = \frac{\text{Beginning Inventory Cost} + \text{Current Period Cost}}{\text{Weighted Average Equivalent Units of Production}}$$

$$= \frac{\text{Total Cost Incurred}}{\text{Total Equivalent Units of Effort}}$$

[5] Different approaches exist to compute equivalent units of production and unit costs under weighted average and FIFO. In addition to the computations shown in the chapter, two other valid and commonly used approaches for computing and reconciling weighted average and FIFO equivalent units of production and unit costs are presented in Appendix 1 to this chapter.

This computation divides total cost by total units—the common weighted average approach that produces an average component cost per unit. Because labor and overhead are at the same degree of completion, their costs can be combined and shown as a single conversion cost per equivalent unit. Quality Candle Company's weighted average calculations for cost per EUP for material and conversion follow:

	Direct Material	+ Conversion	= Total
Beginning inventory costs	$ 5,943	$ 16,758	$ 22,701
Current period costs	321,120	660,270	981,390
Total cost per component	$327,063	$677,028	$1,004,091
Divided by EUP (step 3)	÷ 205,700	÷ 205,160	
Cost per EUP	$1.59	$3.30	$4.89

The amounts for the product cost components (material and conversion) are summed to find the total production cost of $4.89 for equivalent whole candles completed during April by Quality Candle Company.

STEP 6: ASSIGN COSTS TO INVENTORIES

This step assigns total production costs to units of product by determining the cost of (1) goods completed and transferred during the period and (2) units in ending Work in Process Inventory.

Using the weighted average method, the cost of goods transferred is found by multiplying the total number of units transferred by the total cost per EUP. Because this method is based on an averaging technique that combines both prior and current period work, it does not matter in which period the transferred units were started. All units and all costs are assumed to have been commingled. The total cost transferred for Quality Candle Company for April is $992,670 (203,000 × $4.89).

Ending WIP Inventory cost is calculated by multiplying the EUP for each cost component by the component cost per unit computed in step 5. Cost of ending inventory using the weighted average method is as follows:

Ending inventory		
Direct material (2,700 × $1.59)	$ 4,293	
Conversion (2,160 × $3.30)	7,128	
Total cost of ending inventory	$11,421	

The total costs assigned to units transferred out and to units in ending inventory must equal the total cost to account for. For the Quality Candle Company, total cost to account for (step 4) was determined as $1,004,091, which equals transferred-out cost ($992,670) plus cost of ending Work in Process Inventory ($11,421).

cost of production report

The steps just discussed can be combined into a **cost of production report**, which details all manufacturing quantities and costs, shows the computation of cost per EUP, and indicates the cost assignment to goods produced during the period. Exhibit 6–7 shows Quality Candle Company's cost of production report using the weighted average method.

The information contained on the cost of production report indicates the actual flow of goods and dollar amounts through the general ledger accounting system. The following T-accounts show how the highlighted information in Exhibit 6–7 "moves" through the Work in Process and Finished Goods Inventory accounts. The total cost to account for must either be transferred out of WIP or remain as the ending balance.

EXHIBIT 6–7
QUALITY CANDLE
COMPANY'S COST OF
PRODUCTION REPORT
FOR THE MONTH ENDED
APRIL 30, 2006
(WEIGHTED AVERAGE
METHOD)

		EQUIVALENT UNITS OF PRODUCTION	
Production Data	**Whole Units**	**Direct Material**	**Conversion**
Beginning inventory*	5,000		
Candles started	200,700		
Candles to account for	205,700		
Beginning inventory (completed)	5,000	5,000	5,000
Started and completed	198,000	198,000	198,000
Candles completed	203,000		
Ending WIP inventory	2,700	2,700	2,160
Candles accounted for†	205,700	205,700	205,160

Cost Data	**Total**	**Direct Material**	**Conversion**
Costs in beginning inventory	$ 22,701	$ 5,943	$ 16,758
Current period costs	981,390	321,120	660,270
Total cost to account for	$1,004,091	$327,063	$677,028
Divided by EUP		÷ 205,700	÷ 205,160
Cost per EUP	$4.89	$1.59	$3.30

Cost Assignment

Transferred out (203,000 × $4.89)		$ 992,670	
Ending inventory			
Direct material (2,700 × $1.59)	$4,293		
Conversion (2,700 × 80% × $3.30)	7,128	11,421	
Total cost accounted for		$1,004,091	

*Fully complete as to material; 40% complete as to conversion.
†Fully complete as to material; 80% complete as to conversion.

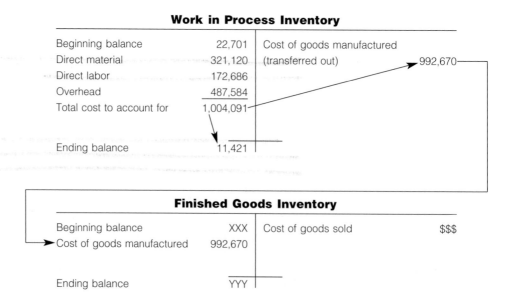

Work in Process Inventory

Beginning balance	22,701	Cost of goods manufactured	
Direct material	321,120	(transferred out)	992,670
Direct labor	172,686		
Overhead	487,584		
Total cost to account for	1,004,091		
Ending balance	11,421		

Finished Goods Inventory

Beginning balance	XXX	Cost of goods sold	$$$
Cost of goods manufactured	992,670		
Ending balance	YYY		

FIFO Method

Steps 1 and 2 are the same for the FIFO method as for the weighted average method because these two steps involve the use of physical units.

STEP 3: DETERMINE THE EQUIVALENT UNITS OF PRODUCTION

Using the FIFO method, the work performed last period is *not* commingled with work of the current period. The EUP schedule for FIFO is:

	DM	Conversion
Candles in beginning inventory completed in the current period	0	3,000
Candles started and completed	198,000	198,000
Ending inventory (candles × % complete)	2,700	2,160
Equivalent units of production	200,700	203,160

Under FIFO, only the work performed on the beginning inventory during the current period is shown in the EUP schedule; this work equals the whole units in beginning inventory times (1 − % work done in the prior period). No additional material is needed in April to complete the 5,000 candles in the beginning inventory. Because beginning inventory was 40 percent complete as to labor and overhead, the company needs to do 60 percent of the conversion work on the goods in the current period or the equivalent of 3,000 candles (5,000 × 60%).

Except for the different treatment of units in beginning inventory, the remaining amounts in the FIFO EUP schedule are the same as those for the weighted average method. Thus, the only difference between the EUPs of the two methods is equal to the number of candles in beginning inventory times the percentage of work performed in the prior period, as shown here:

	DM	Conversion
FIFO EUP	200,700	203,160
+ Beginning inventory (5,000 units × % work done in prior period: 100% material, 40% conversion)	5,000	2,000
= WA EUP	205,700	205,160

STEP 4: DETERMINE THE TOTAL COST TO ACCOUNT FOR

This step is the same as it was for the weighted average method; the total cost to account for is $1,004,091.

STEP 5: CALCULATE THE COST PER EQUIVALENT UNIT OF PRODUCTION

Because the FIFO EUP calculation ignores the work performed on beginning inventory in the prior period, the FIFO cost per EUP computation also ignores prior period costs. Because the EUP computations and the costs used to compute cost per EUP both differ, different cost per EUP results will be obtained for the weighted average and FIFO methods. The FIFO cost per EUP calculation is:

	Direct Material	+ Conversion	= Total
Current period costs	$321,120	$660,270	$981,390
Divided by EUP (step 3)	÷ 200,700	÷ 203,160	
Cost per EUP	$1.60	$3.25	$4.85

It is useful to understand the underlying difference between the weighted average (WA) and FIFO total cost computations. The WA total cost of $4.89 is the average cost of each candle completed during April, regardless of when production began. The FIFO total cost of $4.85 is the average cost of each candle completed (started and completed) solely during the current period. The $0.04 difference is caused by the difference in treatment of beginning work in process costs.

STEP 6: ASSIGN COSTS TO INVENTORIES

The FIFO method assumes that the units in beginning inventory are the first units completed during the current period and, thus, are the first units transferred. The remaining units transferred out during the period were both started and completed in the current period. As shown in the cost of production report in Exhibit 6–8, the two-step computation needed to determine the cost of goods transferred out distinctly presents this FIFO logic.

The first part of the cost assignment for units transferred out relates to beginning inventory units. At the start of April, these units had all material cost and some labor and overhead cost in Work in Process Inventory. These costs were not

EXHIBIT 6–8

QUALITY CANDLE COMPANY'S COST OF PRODUCTION REPORT FOR MONTH ENDED APRIL 30, 2006 (FIFO METHOD)

		EQUIVALENT UNITS OF PRODUCTION	
Production Data	Whole Units	Direct Material	Conversion
Beginning inventory*	5,000		
Candles started	200,700		
Candles to account for	205,700		
Beginning inventory completed†	5,000	0	3,000
Started and completed	198,000	198,000	198,000
Candles completed	203,000		
Ending WIP inventory‡	2,700	2,700	2,160
Candles accounted for	205,700	200,700	203,160

Cost Data	Total	Direct Material	Conversion
Costs in beginning inventory	$ 22,701		
Current period costs	981,390	$321,120	$660,270
Total cost to account for	$1,004,091		
Divided by EUP		÷ 200,700	÷ 203,160
Cost per EUP	$ 4.85	$ 1.60	$3.25

Cost Assignment

Transferred out		
Beginning inventory costs	$22,701	
Cost to complete		
Conversion (3,000 × $3.25)	9,750	$ 32,451
Started and completed (198,000 × $4.85)		960,300
Total cost transferred		$ 992,751
Ending inventory		
Direct material (2,700 × $1.60)	$ 4,320	
Conversion (2,700 × 80% × $3.25)	7,020	11,340
Total cost accounted for		$1,004,091

*Fully complete as to material; 40% complete as to conversion.
†0% additional material added; 60% additional conversion required.
‡Fully complete as to material; 80% complete as to conversion.

included in the EUP cost calculations in step 5. The costs to finish these units were incurred in the current period and, thus, completion is shown using current period costs. Total cost of producing the units contained in beginning inventory is equal to beginning inventory costs plus the current period costs of completion. Next, the cost of units started and completed in the current period is computed using current period costs. This cost assignment process for Quality Candle Company is as follows:

Transferred out	
(1) Beginning inventory (prior period costs)	$ 22,701
Completion of beginning inventory	
Direct material (0 × $1.60)	0
Conversion (5,000 × 60% × $3.25)	9,750
Total cost of beginning inventory transferred	$ 32,451
(2) Candles started and completed (198,000 × $4.85)	960,300
Total cost transferred	$992,751

The total cost for all units completed and transferred to Finished Goods Inventory for April is $992,751.[6]

The process of calculating the FIFO cost of ending Work in Process Inventory is the same as under the weighted average method. Ending work in process cost using FIFO is as follows:

Ending inventory	
Direct material (2,700 × $1.60)	$ 4,320
Conversion (2,160 × $3.25)	7,020
Total cost of ending inventory	$11,340

The total cost of the candles transferred ($992,751) plus the cost of the candles in ending inventory ($11,340) equals the total cost to be accounted for ($1,004,091).

Summary journal entries and T-accounts for Quality Candle Company for April are given in Exhibit 6–9. It is assumed that the company began April with no Finished Goods Inventory, 200,000 candles were sold on account for $9 each, and a perpetual FIFO inventory system is in use. Weighted average amounts are shown where they would differ from FIFO.

PROCESS COSTING IN A MULTIDEPARTMENT SETTING

Most companies have multiple, rather than single, department processing facilities. In a multidepartment production environment, goods are transferred from a predecessor (upstream) department to a successor (downstream) department. For example, if the candles at Quality Candle Company were boxed in-house, the company's manufacturing activities could be viewed as occurring in two departments, Processing and Packaging.

---

[6] Because of FIFO's two-step process to determine cost of units transferred, a question exists as to how to calculate a per-unit cost for the units that were in beginning inventory and those that were started and completed in the current period. The resolution of this question is found in the use of either the strict or the modified FIFO method.

If *strict FIFO* is used, beginning inventory units are transferred out at their total completed cost; the units started and completed during the current period are transferred at a separate and distinct current period cost. For Quality Candle Company, use of strict FIFO means that the 5,000 candles in beginning inventory are transferred at an approximate cost per unit of $6.49 ($32,451 ÷ 5,000). The candles started and completed in April are transferred at the current period cost of $4.85 (computed in step 5). If strict FIFO is used, the costs of these two groups should be reported separately, not added together to get a total transferred cost.

However, unless the difference between the unit costs of beginning inventory and of units started and completed is significant, there is no need to maintain the distinction. The costs of the two groups can be combined and averaged over all of the units transferred in a process known as the *modified FIFO method*. For Quality Candle Company, modified FIFO assigns an approximate average cost of $4.88 per candle ($992,951 ÷ 203,000) to all candles transferred from the department. Modified FIFO allows the next department or Finished Goods Inventory to account for all units received during the period at the same cost per unit. This method is useful when products are processed through several departments so that the number of separate unit costs to be accounted for does not become excessive.

EXHIBIT 6–9

**PROCESS COSTING
JOURNAL ENTRIES AND
T-ACCOUNTS**

1.	Work in Process Inventory		321,120	
	Raw Material Inventory			321,120

*To record issuance of material to production
(Exhibit 6–5).*

2.	Work in Process Inventory		172,686	
	Wages Payable			172,686

To accrue wages for direct labor (Exhibit 6–5).

3.	Manufacturing Overhead		487,584	
	Various accounts			487,584

To record actual overhead costs (Exhibit 6–5).

4.	Work in Process Inventory		487,584	
	Manufacturing Overhead			487,584

To apply actual overhead to production.

5.	Finished Goods Inventory		992,751	
	Work in Process Inventory			992,751

*To transfer cost of completed candles to finished
goods (Exhibit 6–8). (Entry would be for $992,670
if weighted average were used—Exhibit 6–7.)*

6.	Accounts Receivable		1,800,000	
	Sales			1,800,000

*To record sales on account (200,000 candles ×
$9.00).*

	Cost of Goods Sold		978,201	
	Finished Goods Inventory			978,201

To transfer cost of goods sold, using strict FIFO:

First 5,000 units	*$ 32,451*
Remaining 195,000 units at $4.85	*945,750*
	$978,201

*(Entry would be for $978,000 if weighted average
were used: 200,000 × $4.89.)*

Work in Process Inventory

Beginning balance	22,701	Cost of goods	
Direct material	321,120	manufactured	992,751
Direct labor	172,686		
Applied overhead	487,584		
Ending balance	11,340		

Finished Goods Inventory

Beginning balance	0	Cost of goods sold	978,201
Cost of goods			
manufactured	992,751		
Ending balance			
(3,000 @ $4.85)	14,550		

Cost of Goods Sold

April CGS	978,201	

Manufacturing costs *always* follow the physical flow of goods. Therefore, costs of the completed units of predecessor departments are treated as input costs in successor departments. Such a sequential treatment requires the use of an additional cost component element called *transferred in cost* or *prior department cost.* This element always has a percentage of completion factor of 100 percent because the goods would not have been transferred out of the predecessor department if they had not been fully complete. The transferred-in element is handled the same as any other cost element in the calculations of EUP and cost per EUP.

A successor department might add additional raw material to the units transferred in or might simply provide additional labor with a corresponding incurrence of overhead. Anything added in the successor department requires its own cost element column for calculating equivalent units of production and cost per equivalent unit (unless the additional elements have the same degree of completion, in which case they can be combined).

Occasionally, successor departments might change the unit of measure used in predecessor departments. For example, when Quality Candle Company produces candles, the measure in the Processing Department would be number of candles; the measure in the Packaging Department might be number of 24-unit cases of candles.

The demonstration problem at the end of the chapter provides a complete example of predecessor and successor department activities.

PROCESS COSTING WITH STANDARD COSTS

LO.5
HOW CAN STANDARD COSTS BE USED IN A PROCESS COSTING SYSTEM?

Do standard costs make process costing easier?

Companies may prefer to use standard rather than actual historical costs for inventory valuation purposes. Actual costing requires that a new production cost be computed each period. Once a production process is established, however, the "new" costs are often not materially different from the "old" costs, so standards for each cost element can be developed and used as predetermined cost benchmarks to simplify the costing process and eliminate periodic cost recomputations. Standards need to be reviewed, and possibly revised, at a minimum of once per year to keep quantities and amounts current. Consider, for example, when **Unilever** decided in 2002 to reduce package sizes of All®, Surf®, and Wisk®, any production quantity and cost standards that were in effect for those brands would have required adjustment.[7]

Calculations for equivalent units of production for standard process costing are identical to those of FIFO process costing. Unlike the weighted average method, the emphasis of both standard costing and FIFO are on the measurement and control of current production activities and current period costs. The weighted average method commingles prior and current period units and costs, which reduces the emphasis on current effort that standard costing is intended to represent and measure.

Use of standard quantities and costs allows material, labor, and overhead variances to be measured during the period. To illustrate the differences between using actual and standard process costing, the Quality Candle Company example is continued. The company's April production and standard cost information is given in Exhibit 6–10. Beginning inventory cost data have been restated from the original to reflect standard costs and to demonstrate the effect of consistent use of standard costs over successive periods. Beginning inventory consisted of 5,000 units that were fully complete as to material and 40 percent complete as to conversion. Therefore, the standard cost of beginning inventory is as follows:

---

[7] Jack Neff, "Unilever Cedes Laundry War," *Advertising Age* (May 27, 2003), pp. 1–2.

EXHIBIT 6–10

QUALITY CANDLE COMPANY'S PRODUCTION AND COST DATA FOR APRIL 2006 (STANDARD COSTING)

Production data

Beginning inventory (BI) (100%, 40%)	5,000
Candles started	200,700
Ending inventory (EI) (100%, 80%)	2,700

Standard cost of production

Direct material	$1.59
Direct labor	0.85
Overhead	2.35
Total	$4.79

Equivalent units of production (repeated from Exhibit 6–8):

	DM	Conversion
BI (candles × % not complete at start of period)	0	3,000
Candles started and completed	198,000	198,000
EI (candles × % complete at end of period)	2,700	2,160
Equivalent units of production	200,700	203,160

Material (5,000 × 100% × $1.59)	$ 7,950
Labor (5,000 × 40% × $0.85)	1,700
Overhead (5,000 × 40% × $2.35)	4,700
Total	$14,350

Exhibit 6–11 presents the cost of production report using the Quality Candle Company's standard cost information.[8]

When a standard cost system is used, inventories are stated at standard rather than actual costs. Summary journal entries for Quality Candle Company's April production, assuming a standard cost FIFO process costing system and amounts from Exhibit 6–11, are as follows:

1. WIP Inventory is debited for $319,093: the standard cost ($314,820) of material used to complete 198,000 units started in April plus the standard cost ($4,293) for the material used to produce ending work in process. Raw Material Inventory is credited for the actual cost of the material withdrawn during April ($321,120).

Work in Process Inventory	319,113	
Direct Material Variance	2,007	
Raw Material Inventory		321,120

To record issuance of material at standard and variance from standard.

2. WIP Inventory is debited for the standard cost of labor allowed based on the equivalent units produced in April. The EUPs for the month reflect the production necessary to complete the beginning inventory candles (3,000), the candles started and completed (198,000), and the work performed on the ending inventory candles (2,160), or a total of 203,160 EUP. Multiplying this equivalent production by the standard labor cost per candle of $0.85 gives a total of $172,686.

Work in Process Inventory	172,686	
Wages Payable		172,686

To accrue direct labor cost and assign labor cost to WIP Inventory at standard; there was no direct labor variance.

---

[8] Total material, labor, and overhead variances are shown for Quality Candle Company in Exhibit 6–11. Additionally, variances from actual costs must be closed at the end of a period. If the variances are immaterial, they can be closed to Cost of Goods Sold; otherwise, they should be allocated among the appropriate inventory accounts and Cost of Goods Sold.

3. Actual factory overhead incurred in April is $487,584.

Manufacturing Overhead	487,584	
Various accounts		487,584
To record actual overhead cost for April.		

4. WIP Inventory is debited for the standard cost of overhead based on the EUPs produced in April. Because labor and overhead are considered at the same percentage of completion, equivalent production is the same as in entry 2 or 203,160 EUPs. Multiplying the EUPs by the standard overhead application rate of $2.35 per candle gives $477,426.

Work in Process Inventory	477,426	
Manufacturing Overhead Variance	10,158	
Manufacturing Overhead		487,584
To apply overhead to WIP Inventory and record the overhead variance.		

5. Finished Goods Inventory is debited for the total standard cost ($972,370) of the 203,000 candles completed during the month (203,000 × $4.79).

Finished Goods Inventory	972,370	
Work in Process Inventory		972,370
To transfer standard cost of completed candles to FG Inventory.		

EXHIBIT 6–11

QUALITY CANDLE COMPANY'S COST OF PRODUCTION REPORT FOR MONTH ENDED APRIL 30, 2006 (STANDARD COSTING)

Costs to Be Accounted for	Direct Material	Direct Labor	Overhead	Total
Total costs				
Beginning WIP (at standard)	$ 7,950	$ 1,700	$ 4,700	$ 14,350
Current period (actual)	321,120	172,686	487,584	981,390
(1) Total	$329,070	$174,386	$492,284	$995,740
Cost Assignment (at standard)				
Transferred out				
Beginning inventory cost*	$ 7,950	$ 1,700	$ 4,700	$ 14,350
Cost to complete				
DL (3,000 × $0.85)		2,550		
OH (3,000 × $2.35)			7,050	
Total cost to complete				9,600
Started and completed				
DM (198,000 × $1.59)	314,820			
DL (198,000 × $0.85)		168,300		
OH (198,000 × $2.35)			465,300	
Total started and completed				948,420
Ending Inventory				
DM (2,700 × $1.59)	4,293			
DL (2,160 × $0.85)		1,836		
OH (2,160 × $2.35)			5,076	
Total WIP ending				11,205
(2) Total standard cost assigned	$327,063	$174,386	$482,126	$983,575
Variances from actual (1 − 2)*	2,007	0	10,158	12,165
Total costs accounted for	$329,070	$174,386	$492,284	$995,740

NOTE: Favorable variances would have been shown in parentheses.
*Beginning work in process is carried at standard costs rather than actual. Therefore, no portion of the variance is attributable to beginning WIP. Any variance that might have been associated with beginning WIP was measured and identified with the prior period.

A standard costing system eliminates the need to be concerned about differentiating between the per-unit cost of the beginning inventory units that were completed and the per-unit cost of the units started and completed in the current period. All units flowing out of a department are costed at the standard or "normal" production cost for each cost component: direct material, direct labor, and overhead. Thus, recordkeeping is simplified, and variations from the norm are highlighted in the period of incurrence. Standard cost systems are discussed in depth in Chapter 7.

Standard costing not only simplifies the cost flows in a process costing system but also provides a useful tool to control costs. By developing standards, managers have a benchmark against which actual costs can be compared. Managers may also use these standards as targets for the balanced scorecard. For example, meeting standard costs 98 percent of the time may be set as a performance measurement for the internal business process perspective. Variances serve to identify differences between the benchmark (standard) cost and the actual cost. By striving to control variances, managers control costs. Managers should also benchmark, to the extent possible, their firm's costs against costs incurred by other firms. Such information may help indicate the organization's cost strengths and weaknesses.

HYBRID COSTING SYSTEMS

LO.6
WHY WOULD A COMPANY USE A HYBRID COSTING SYSTEM?

hybrid costing system

Many companies are now able to customize what were previously mass-produced items. In such circumstances, neither job order nor process costing techniques are perfectly suited to attach costs to output. Thus, companies may choose to use a hybrid costing system that is appropriate for their particular processing situation. A **hybrid costing system** combines characteristics of both job order and process costing systems. A hybrid system would be used, for example, in a manufacturing environment in which various product lines have different direct materials but similar processing techniques.

> *How do companies account for customized "standard units"?*

To illustrate the need for hybrid systems, assume that you order an automobile with the following options: leather seats, a Bose stereo system and compact disk player, cruise control, and pearlized paint. The costs of all these options need to be traced specifically to your car, but the assembly processes for all cars produced by the plant are similar. The job order costing feature of tracing direct materials to specific jobs is combined with the process costing feature of averaging labor and overhead costs over all homogeneous production to derive the total cost of your automobile. It would not be feasible to try to use a job order costing system to trace labor or overhead cost to your car individually, and it would be improper to average the costs of your options over all the cars produced during the period.

A hybrid costing system may be appropriate for companies producing items such as furniture, clothing, or jam. In each instance, numerous kinds of raw materials could be used to create similar output. A table may be made from oak, teak, or mahogany; a blouse may be made from silk, cotton, or polyester; and jam may be made from peaches, strawberries, or apricots. The material cost for a batch run would need to be traced separately, but the production process of the batch is repetitive.

A table manufacturer likely would use a hybrid costing system due to its varying raw materials, such as teak, oak, pine, mahogany, etc.

GETTY IMAGES

Focus on Quality

Analyzing Root Causes

How much time, effort, and money do companies lose dealing with problems that continually resurface and disrupt the organization? This is known as the "price of nonconformance"—the failure to identify a problem's root cause, fix the process, measure results, and follow up.

Estimates of the price of nonconformance are as much as 25 to 40% of operating costs. However, by focusing on the process—not the people—organizations can correct the underlying causes of problems so they don't recur.

By preventing the recurrence of errors in service delivery or manufacturing processes, significant improvements in both productivity and quality are assured. By eliminating nonconformance in the system through zero defects and anticipating and preventing errors prior to process implementation, significant cost savings may be realized to positively impact the organization's profit margin. With an understanding of the environment necessary to create quality, organizations will identify solutions to costly, recurring problems.

The implementation of a system process improvement model . . . utilizing step-by-step root cause analysis will create an effective continuous quality improvement culture in an organization. Utilizing a step-by-step root cause analysis process, organizations can improve product quality, improve service quality, reduce operating costs, and impact operating profits positively.

The "root cause" is the reason for a nonconformance within a process. It is the underlying cause of a problem, not just the apparent cause. It is a focus on the process, not the people.

The root cause is a factor that, when changed or eliminated, will eliminate the nonconformance and prevent the problem. It is about designing prevention solutions into how work is done. Prevention solutions are not about reworking, redesigning, modifying, or fixing things; they are not about correction. Prevention solutions are about determining why the rework was required, why we must redesign the product, and why we must fix the item. It is about determining how to keep the problem from ever occurring again. It is about designing prevention into the process.

Root cause analysis is a formal, structured, disciplined approach to problem solving. Many root cause analysis processes have been developed to approach problem solving: some have three steps, some four, some six, or as many as 12 steps in the process.

Simply, root cause analysis is a systematic process of defining the problem, gathering and prioritizing data about the nonconformance, analyzing solutions to the problem, and evaluating the benefits versus the cost-effectiveness of all available prevention options.

Source: Charles C. Handley, "Quality Improvement through Root Cause Analysis," *Hospital Material Management Quarterly* (May 2000), pp. 74–75. Originally published and copyrighted by APICS–The Educational Society for Resource Management, © 1999 APICS International Conference Proceedings.

Hybrid costing systems provide a more accurate accounting picture of the actual type of manufacturing activities in certain companies. Job order costing and process costing are two ends of a continuum and, as is typically the case for any continuum, neither end is necessarily the norm. As the use of flexible manufacturing processes increase, so will the use of hybrid costing systems.

Revisiting

Williamsburg Soap and Candle Company

Over the years, the processes and products of **WSAC Company** have changed. For instance, since production activities were very labor intensive, John Barnett began designing and building machines to help with the candle-making processes. Later, the company was forced to discontinue making soap: Although people loved the look of the hand-rolled soaps, they weren't willing to pay a price that was sufficient to cover escalating processing costs and generate a reasonable profit margin.

While contracting in one product area, the company has expanded in another. In addition to making its traditional lines of candles, WSAC also does custom candle processing. One custom line takes "regular" dipped candles and adds private label packing, extra labeling, or different colors for the candles. Custom candles are also made in the container line; for example, WSAC makes container candles for a perfume manufacturer using that company's distinctive fragrances. Job order numbers track the custom work because of the additional materials and labor involved. Larger orders will naturally reduce the cost per candle ordered since fewer setups are involved.

Product quality is important at WSAC, and the need to maintain high standards caused a change in the production process of molded candles. Originally, the company used the "prewicked" method and found that it was very difficult to ensure that the candle would have a straight center wick—resulting in poor candle burn performance. The afterwicking (insertion) method was developed and is now used because it produces a higher quality product with no additional cost.

Currently, about 50 percent of revenues comes from the manufacturing/wholesale side of the company and the other 50 percent is generated through the six gift shops and the restaurant located at the Williamsburg site. WSAC also has two Web sites: One is designed solely for wholesale customers; the other (candlefactory.com) is for retail sales. The retail site opened only in late 2003 and is not a "significant" portion of the company business as of yet.

Management attributes company longevity to three important items: producing high-quality products at reasonable prices, paying attention to cost control and product profitability, and listening to customer feedback. In doing these things well, Williamsburg Soap and Candle Company is burning up the competition!

Source: Ms. Virginia Hartmann, president, Williamsburg Soap and Candle Company, April 2004.

Appendix 1

Alternative Calculations of Weighted Average and FIFO Methods

LO.7
WHAT ALTERNATIVE
METHODS CAN BE USED TO
CALCULATE EQUIVALENT
UNITS OF PRODUCTION?

Various methods are used to compute equivalent units of production under the weighted average and FIFO methods. One of the most common variations is the following EUP calculation for weighted average:

Units transferred out (whole units)
+ Ending work in process (equivalent units)
= Weighted average EUP

Once the weighted average EUP figure is available, the FIFO equivalent units can be quickly derived by subtracting the equivalent units in beginning work in process inventory that had been produced in the previous period:

Weighted average EUP
− Beginning work in process (equivalent units)
= FIFO EUP

This computation is appropriate because the weighted average method concentrates on units that were completed during the period as well as units started but not completed during the period. Unlike FIFO, the weighted average method does not exclude the equivalent units that were in beginning inventory. Thus, converting from weighted average to FIFO requires removal of the equivalent units produced in the previous period from beginning work in process.

Quality Candle Company's April production data presented in the chapter are repeated here to illustrate these alternative calculations for the weighted average and FIFO methods.

Candles in beginning work in process (100% complete as to material; 40% complete as to conversion costs)	5,000
Candles started during the month	200,700
Candles completed during the month	203,000
Candles in ending work in process (100% complete as to material; 80% complete as to conversion costs)	2,700

Using these data, the EUP are computed as follows:

	DM	Conversion
Candles transferred	203,000	203,000
+ Ending work in process equivalent units (2,700 × 100%; 2,700 × 80% complete)	2,700	2,160
= **Weighted average EUP**	205,700	205,160
− Beginning work in process equivalent units produced in previous period (5,000 × 100%; 5,000 × 40% complete)	(5,000)	(2,000)
= **FIFO EUP**	200,700	203,160

The distinct relationship between the weighted average and FIFO costing models can also be used in another manner to generate equivalent units of production. This method begins with the total number of units to account for in the period. From this amount, the EUPs to be completed next period are subtracted to give the weighted average EUP. Next, as in the method just shown, the equivalent units completed in the prior period (the beginning Work in Process Inventory) are deducted to give the FIFO equivalent units of production. Using Quality Candle Company data, these computations are as follows:

	DM	Conversion
Total units to account for	205,700	205,700
− EUP to be completed next period (ending inventory × % not completed: 2,700 × 0%; 2,700 × 20%)	0	(540)
= **Weighted average EUP**	205,700	205,160
− EUP completed in prior period (beginning inventory × % completed last period: 5,000 × 100%; 5,000 × 40%)	(5,000)	(2,000)
= **FIFO EUP**	200,700	203,160

These alternative calculations can be used either as a confirmation of answers found by using beginning inventory units, units started and completed, and ending inventory units or as a shortcut to initially compute equivalent units of production.

Appendix 2

Spoilage

The chapter examples assumed that all units to be accounted for have either been transferred out or are in ending work in process inventory. However, almost every process produces some units that do not meet production specifications. In other situations, addition or expansion of materials after the start of the process may cause the number of units accounted for to be higher than those to be accounted for originally or in a previous department. This appendix addresses two very simplistic examples of these more complex issues of process costing.

continuous loss

discrete loss

Losses in a production process may occur continuously or at a specific point. For example, the weight loss in roasting coffee beans would be considered a continuous loss because it occurs fairly uniformly through the process. In contrast, a discrete loss is assumed to occur at a specific point and is detectable only when a quality check is performed. Units that have passed an inspection point should be good units (relative to the specific characteristics inspected), whereas units that have not yet passed an inspection point may be good or may be defective/spoiled. Control points can be either built into the system or performed by inspectors.

Several methods can be used to account for units lost during production. Selection of the most appropriate method depends on whether the loss is considered normal or abnormal and whether the loss occurred continuously in the process or at a discrete point.[9] Exhibit 6–12 summarizes the accounting for the cost of lost units.

method of neglect

The costs of normal shrinkage and normal *continuous* losses in a process costing environment are handled through the **method of neglect**, which simply excludes the spoiled units in the equivalent units schedule. Ignoring the spoilage results in a smaller number of equivalent units of production (EUP), and dividing production costs by a smaller EUP raises the cost per equivalent unit. Thus, the cost of lost units is spread proportionately over the good units transferred and those remaining in Work in Process Inventory.

Alternatively, the cost of normal, *discrete* losses should be assigned only to units that have passed the inspection point. Such units should be good units (relative to the inspected characteristic), whereas the units prior to this point may be good or may be defective/spoiled. Assigning loss costs to units that may be found to be defective/spoiled in the next period would not be reasonable.

The cost of all abnormal losses should be accumulated and treated as a loss in the period in which those losses occurred. Abnormal loss cost is always accounted for on an equivalent unit basis.

EXHIBIT 6–12
CONTINUOUS VERSUS DISCRETE LOSSES

Type	Assumed to Occur	May Be	Cost Handled How?	Cost Assigned To?
Continuous	Uniformly throughout process	Normal	Absorbed by all units in ending inventory and transferred out on an EUP basis	Product
		or		
		Abnormal	Written off as a loss on an EUP basis	Period
Discrete	At inspection point or at end of process	Normal	Absorbed by all units past inspection point in ending inventory and transferred out on an EUP basis	Product
		or		
		Abnormal	Written off as a loss on an EUP basis	Period

[9] Normal and abnormal losses are defined in Chapter 4.

Hanks, Inc., will be used to illustrate the method of neglect for a normal loss and an abnormal loss. Hanks produces glass jars in a single department; the jars are then sold to candle manufacturers. All materials are added at the start of the process, and conversion costs are applied uniformly throughout the production process. Breakage commonly occurs after the jars are formed when a machine pushes air into them to form their openings. The company expects a maximum of 5 percent of the material started into production to be "lost" during processing. For convenience, quantities will be discussed in terms of jars rather than raw material inputs. Recyclable shipping containers are provided by buyers and, therefore, are not a cost to Hanks, Inc. The company uses the weighted average method of calculating equivalent units. Exhibit 6–13 provides the basic information for June 2006.

The department is accountable for 102,000 jars: 12,000 in beginning inventory plus 90,000 started into processing during June. Only 94,200 jars (79,200 completed and 15,000 in ending inventory) are accounted for prior to considering the processing loss. The 7,800 "spoiled" jars are included to balance the total 102,000 jars. Hanks, Inc., considers 4,500 (90,000 × 0.05) of the spoiled jars as normal spoilage; the remaining 3,300 (7,800 − 4,500) are considered abnormal spoilage. Under the method of neglect, the normal spoilage is not extended into the computation of equivalent units of production. This method simply allows the normal spoilage to "disappear" in the EUP schedule. Therefore, the cost per equivalent "good" jar made during the period is higher for each cost component.[10]

Exhibit 6–14 presents the cost of production report for Hanks, Inc., for June 2006. Had FIFO process costing been used, there would have been a difference in the number of equivalent units of production, the cost per equivalent unit, and the cost assignment schedule.[11]

EXHIBIT 6–13
PRODUCTION AND COST DATA FOR HANKS, INC., FOR JUNE 2006

Jars		
Beginning inventory (60% complete)	12,000	
Started during month	90,000	
Jars completed and transferred	79,200	
Ending inventory (75% complete)	15,000	
Spoiled jars	7,800	
Costs		
Beginning inventory		
Material	$ 16,230	
Conversion	3,459	$ 19,689
Current period		
Material	$101,745	
Conversion	19,041	120,786
Total costs		$140,475

[10] There is a theoretical problem with the use of the method of neglect when a company uses weighted average process costing. Units in ending Work in Process Inventory have spoiled unit cost assigned to them in the current period and will have lost unit cost assigned *again* in the next period. But even with this flaw, this method provides a reasonable measure of unit cost if the rate of spoilage is consistent from period to period.

[11] For FIFO costing, the EUP would be 85,500 and 86,550, respectively, for DM and Conversion. Cost per EUP would be $1.19 and $0.22, respectively for DM and Conversion. Total cost transferred out would be $115,497; total cost of ending Work in Process Inventory would be $20,325; and cost of abnormal loss would be $4,653.

EXHIBIT 6–14

**HANKS, INC., COST OF
PRODUCTION REPORT
FOR MONTH ENDED
JUNE 30, 2006 (NORMAL
AND ABNORMAL LOSS)**

		EQUIVALENT UNITS	
Production Data	**Whole Units**	**Material**	**Conversion**
Beginning inventory (100%; 60%)	12,000		
Jars started	90,000		
Jars to account for	102,000		
Beginning inventory (completed)	12,000	12,000	12,000
Jars started and completed	67,200	67,200	67,200
Total jars completed	79,200		
Ending inventory (100%; 75%)	15,000	15,000	11,250
Normal spoilage (not extended)	4,500		
Abnormal spoilage (100%; 100%)	3,300	3,300	3,300
Jars accounted for	102,000	97,500	93,750
Cost Data	**Total**	**Material**	**Conversion**
Beginning inventory costs	$ 19,689	$ 16,230	$ 3,459
Current costs	120,786	101,745	19,041
Total costs	$140,475	$117,975	$22,500
Divided by EUP		÷ 97,500	÷ 93,750
Cost per WA EUP	$ 1.45	$ 1.21	$0.24

Cost Assignment			
Transferred (79,200 × $1.45)		$114,840	
Ending inventory			
Material (15,000 × $1.21)	$18,150		
Conversion (11,250 × $0.24)	2,700	20,850	
Abnormal loss (3,300 × $1.45)		4,785	
Total costs accounted for		$140,475	

Comprehensive Review Module

Chapter Summary

1. Process costing

   - is similar to job order costing in that they both are averaging techniques used to assign costs to output in manufacturing companies.

   - differs from job order costing in that process costing is used in companies making large quantities of homogeneous products; job order costing is used in companies making smaller quantities of distinctive, custom-ordered products.

   - differs from job order costing in that process costing uses either the weighted average or FIFO method to compute equivalent units of production; job order costing does not use either type of cost flow assumption and does not compute equivalent units of production.

2. Equivalent units of production are used in process costing to

   - approximate the number of whole units of output that could have been produced during a period from the actual effort expended during that period.

   - assign production costs for material, labor, and overhead to completed and incomplete output of the period.

3. The weighted average method of process costing

   - combines the beginning inventory and current period production activity.

   - determines

     ➤ equivalent units of production by adding to the units in beginning inventory the units started and completed plus the equivalent units in ending inventory.

     ➤ unit cost (per cost component) by dividing total (beginning plus current) cost by equivalent units.

     ➤ transferred-out value by multiplying total units transferred out by the total cost per equivalent unit.

     ➤ ending inventory value by multiplying the equivalent units of each cost component by the related cost per equivalent unit.

4. The FIFO method of process costing

   - does *not* commingle the beginning inventory and current period production activity.

   - determines

     ➤ equivalent units of production by adding to the equivalent units of the beginning inventory completed in the current period the units started and completed plus equivalent units in the ending inventory.

     ➤ unit cost (per cost component) by dividing current cost by equivalent units.

     ➤ transferred-out value by adding to the cost of beginning inventory the cost necessary to complete the beginning inventory plus the cost of the units started and completed in the current period.

     ➤ ending inventory value by multiplying the equivalent units of each cost component by the related cost per equivalent unit.

5. Standard costs can be used in a process costing system in combination with the FIFO method to

   - assign a "normal" production cost to the equivalent units of output each period.

   - allow managers to quickly recognize and investigate significant deviations from expected production costs.

6. A hybrid costing system allows companies to

   - combine the characteristics of both job order and process costing systems.

   - trace direct material and/or direct labor that is related to a particular batch of goods to those specific goods using job order costing.

   - use process costing techniques to account for cost components that are common to numerous batches of output.

Solution Strategies

STEPS IN PROCESS COSTING COMPUTATIONS

1. Compute the total units to account for (in physical units):

    > Beginning inventory in physical units
    > + Units started (or transferred in) during period

2. Compute units accounted for (in physical units). This step involves identifying the groups to which costs are to be assigned (transferred out of or remaining in ending inventory).

    > Units completed and transferred
    > + Ending inventory in physical units

3. Compute equivalent units of production per cost component. The cost components include transferred in (if multidepartmental), direct material, direct labor, and overhead. In cases of multiple materials having different degrees of completion, each material is considered a separate cost component. If overhead is applied on a direct labor basis or is incurred at the same rate as direct labor, labor and overhead can be combined as one cost component and referred to as *conversion*.

    a. Weighted average

    > Beginning inventory in physical units
    > + Units started and completed*
    > + (Ending inventory × % complete)

    b. FIFO

    > (Beginning inventory × % not complete at start of period)
    > + Units started and completed*
    > + (Ending inventory × % complete)

    *Units started and completed = (Units transferred − Units in beginning inventory).

4. Compute total cost to account for:

    > Costs in beginning inventory
    > + Costs of current period

5. Compute cost per equivalent unit for each cost component:

    a. Weighted average

    > Cost of component in beginning inventory
    > + Cost of component for current period
    > = Total cost of component
    > ÷ EUP for component

    b. FIFO

    > Cost of component for current period
    > ÷ EUP for component

6. Assign costs to inventories using the weighted average or FIFO method. The total costs assigned to units transferred and to units in ending work in process inventory must equal the total cost to account for.

    a. Weighted average

    (1) Transferred:

    > Units Transferred × Total Cost per EUP for All Components

    (2) Ending inventory:

    > EUP for Each Component × Cost per EUP for Each Component

b.   FIFO

(1) Transferred:

> Beginning inventory costs
> + (Beginning inventory × % not complete at beginning of period for each
>   component × Cost per EUP for each component)
> ÷ (Units started and completed × Total cost per EUP for all components)

(2) Ending inventory:

> EUP for Each Component × Cost per EUP for Each Component

Demonstration Problem

Plaid-Clad manufactures golf bags in a two-department process, Assembly and Finishing. The Assembly Department uses weighted average costing; the percentage of completion of overhead in this department is unrelated to direct labor. The Finishing Department adds hardware to the assembled bags and uses FIFO costing; overhead is applied in this department on a direct labor basis. For June, the following production data and costs have been gathered:

Assembly Department: Units

Beginning work in process (100% complete for material; 40% complete for labor; 30% complete for overhead)	250
Units started	8,800
Ending work in process (100% complete for material; 70% complete for labor; 90% complete for overhead)	400

Assembly Department: Costs

	Material	Direct Labor	Overhead	Total
Beginning inventory	$ 3,755	$ 690	$ 250	$ 4,695
Current	100,320	63,606	27,681	191,607
Totals	$104,075	$64,296	$27,931	$196,302

Finishing Department: Units

Beginning work in process (100% complete for transferred in; 15% complete for material; 40% complete for conversion)	100
Units transferred in	8,650
Ending work in process (100% complete for transferred in; 30% complete for material; 65% complete for conversion)	200

Finishing Department: Costs

	Transferred In	Direct Material	Conversion	Total
Beginning inventory	$ 2,176	$ 30	$ 95	$ 2,301
Current	188,570	15,471	21,600	225,641
Totals	$190,746	$15,501	$21,695	$227,942

Required:

a.   Prepare a cost of production report for the Assembly Department.

b.   Prepare a cost of production report for the Finishing Department.

c.   Prepare T-accounts to show the flow of costs through the Assembly and Finishing Departments.

d.   Prepare the journal entries for the Finishing Department for June.

Solution to Demonstration Problem

a.

	Whole Units	EQUIVALENT UNITS OF PRODUCTION		
		Direct Material	Direct Labor	Overhead
Beginning inventory	250			
Units started	8,800			
Units to account for	9,050			
BI (completed)	250	250	250	250
Started and completed	8,400	8,400	8,400	8,400
Units completed	8,650			
Ending inventory	400	400	280	360
Units accounted for	9,050			
Weighted average EUP		9,050	8,930	9,010

Cost Data	Whole Units Total	Direct Material	Direct Labor	Overhead
BI costs	$ 4,695	$ 3,755	$ 690	$ 250
Current period costs	191,607	100,320	63,606	27,681
Total costs	$196,302	$104,075	$64,296	$27,931
Divided by EUP		÷ 9,050	÷ 8,930	÷ 9,010
Cost per EUP	$ 21.80	$11.50	$7.20	$3.10

Cost Assignment

Transferred out (8,650 × $21.80)		$188,570
Ending inventory		
Direct material (400 × $11.50)	$4,600	
Direct labor (280 × $7.20)	2,016	
Overhead (360 × $3.10)	1,116	7,732
Total cost accounted for		$196,302

b.

	Whole Units	EQUIVALENT UNITS OF PRODUCTION		
		Transferred In	Direct Material	Conversion
Beginning inventory	100			
Units started	8,650			
Units to account for	8,750			
BI (completed)	100	0	85	60
Started and completed	8,450	8,450	8,450	8,450
Units completed	8,550			
Ending inventory	200	200	60	130
Units accounted for	8,750			
FIFO EUP		8,650	8,595	8,640

Cost Data	Total			
BI costs	$ 2,301			
Current period costs	225,641	$188,570	$15,471	$21,600
Total costs	$227,942			
Divided by EUP		÷ 8,650	÷ 8,595	÷ 8,640
Cost per EUP	$ 26.10	$21.80	$1.80	$2.50

Cost Assignment

Transferred out		
Beginning inventory cost	$2,301	
Cost to complete		
Transferred in (0 × $21.80)	0	
Direct material (85 × $1.80)	153	
Conversion (60 × $2.50)	150	$ 2,604
Started and completed (8,450 × $26.10)		220,545
Ending inventory		
Transferred in (200 × $21.80)	$4,360	
Direct material (60 × $1.80)	108	
Conversion (130 × $2.50)	325	4,793
Total cost accounted for		$227,942

c.

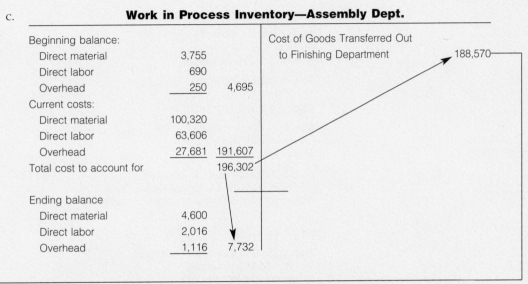

Work in Process Inventory—Assembly Dept.

Beginning balance:			Cost of Goods Transferred Out
Direct material	3,755		to Finishing Department
Direct labor	690		
Overhead	250	4,695	188,570
Current costs:			
Direct material	100,320		
Direct labor	63,606		
Overhead	27,681	191,607	
Total cost to account for		196,302	
Ending balance			
Direct material	4,600		
Direct labor	2,016		
Overhead	1,116	7,732	

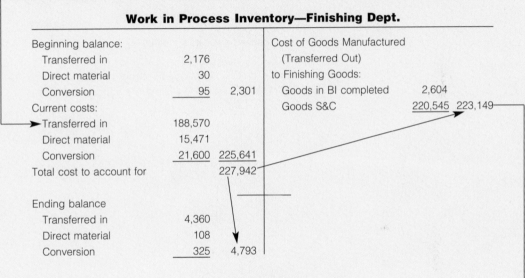

Work in Process Inventory—Finishing Dept.

Beginning balance:			Cost of Goods Manufactured		
Transferred in	2,176		(Transferred Out)		
Direct material	30		to Finishing Goods:		
Conversion	95	2,301	Goods in BI completed	2,604	
Current costs:			Goods S&C	220,545	223,149
Transferred in	188,570				
Direct material	15,471				
Conversion	21,600	225,641			
Total cost to account for		227,942			
Ending balance					
Transferred in	4,360				
Direct material	108				
Conversion	325	4,793			

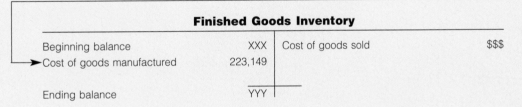

Finished Goods Inventory

Beginning balance	XXX	Cost of goods sold	$$$
Cost of goods manufactured	223,149		
Ending balance	YYY		

d. Assembly Dept.

Work in Process Inventory—Assembly	100,320	
Raw Material Inventory		100,320
To transfer in direct material.		
Work in Process Inventory—Assembly	63,606	
Wages Payable		63,606
To record direct labor costs for month.		
Work in Process Inventory—Assembly	27,681	
Overhead Control		27,681
To apply overhead costs to WIP for month.		
Work in Process Inventory—Finishing	188,570	
Work in Process Inventory—Assembly		188,570
To transfer completed goods to next department.		

Finishing Dept.

Work in Process Inventory—Finishing	15,471	
Raw Material Inventory		15,471
To transfer in direct material.		
Work in Process Inventory—Finishing	21,600	
Various Accounts		21,600
To record conversion costs for month.		
Finished Goods Inventory	223,149	
Work in Process Inventory—Finishing		223,149
To transfer completed goods to inventory.		

Key Terms

continuous loss *(p. 220)*
cost of production report *(p. 207)*
discrete loss *(p. 220)*
equivalent units of production
    (EUP) *(p. 200)*

FIFO method (of process costing)
    (p. 201)
hybrid costing system *(p. 216)*
method of neglect *(p. 220)*
total cost to account for *(p. 204)*

total units to account for *(p. 204)*
units started and completed
    (p. 205)
weighted average method (of
    process costing) *(p. 201)*

Questions

1. What are the characteristics of a company that would be more likely to use process costing rather than job order costing?

2. How do the weighted average and FIFO methods of process costing differ in the manner in which beginning work in process inventory is treated?

3. What is an "equivalent unit of production," and why is it a necessary concept to employ a process costing sytem?

4. Describe the six steps of process costing. What is the objective to be achieved by applying the six steps?

5. Which cost pool can be found in a downstream department that will not be present in the most upstream department? Discuss.

6. Why does standard costing make process costing more clerically and computationally efficient?

7. What is a hybrid costing system? In what circumstances are hybrid costing systems typically employed?

8. (Appendix 2) In a process costing system, how are normal and abnormal spoilage typically treated? Why are normal and abnormal spoilage treated differently?

Exercises

9. (EUP; weighted average) Newton Inc. uses a weighted average process costing system. All material is added at the start of the production process. Direct labor and overhead are added at the same rate throughout the process. Newton's records indicate the following production for October 2006:

Beginning inventory (70% complete as to conversion)	360,000 units
Started during October	510,000 units
Completed during October	780,000 units

Ending inventory for October is 40 percent complete as to conversion.
  a. What are the equivalent units of production for direct material?
  b. What are the equivalent units of production for conversion?

WebTUTOR *Advantage*

10. (EUP; FIFO) Assume that Newton Inc. in Exercise 9 uses the FIFO method of process costing.
  a. What are the equivalent units of production for direct material?
  b. What are the equivalent units of production for conversion?

11. (EUP; weighted average & FIFO) Shannon Inc. makes metal toy soldiers in a one-department production process. All metal is added at the beginning of the process. Paint for the toys and plastic bags for packaging are considered indirect materials. The following information is available relative to September 2006 production activities:

Beginning inventory: 25,000 toys (70% complete as to labor; 75% complete as to overhead)
Started into production: metal for 280,000 toys, which were cast during the month
Ending inventory: 30,000 toys (40% complete as to labor; 60% complete as to overhead)

a. Compute the EUP for direct material, direct labor, and overhead using weighted average process costing.

b. Compute the EUP for direct material, direct labor, and overhead using FIFO process costing.

c. Reconcile the calculations in parts (a) and (b).

12. (EUP; weighted average & FIFO) Clean-Up Corp. produces outdoor brooms. On April 30, 2006, the firm had 3,600 units in process that were 60 percent complete as to material, 40 percent complete as to direct labor, and 20 percent complete as to overhead. During May, 187,000 brooms were started. Records indicate that 184,200 units were transferred to Finished Goods Inventory in May. Ending units in process were 40 percent complete as to material, 25 percent complete as to direct labor, and 10 percent complete as to overhead.

a. Calculate the physical units to account for in May.

b. How many units were started and completed during May?

c. Determine May's EUP for each category using the weighted average method.

d. Determine May's EUP for each category using the FIFO method.

e. Reconcile your answers to parts (c) and (d).

13. (EUP; weighted average & FIFO) Matisse Company produces steel and uses a process costing system to assign production costs. During March 2006, the firm had a beginning Work in Process Inventory of 60,000 tons of steel that were 100 percent complete as to material and 40 percent complete as to conversion. During the month, raw material needed to produce 800,000 tons of steel was started in process. At month-end, 35,000 tons remained in Work in Process Inventory; these units were 90 percent complete as to material and 60 percent complete as to conversion.

a. Compute the total units to account for.

b. Determine how many units were started and completed.

c. Determine the equivalent units of production using the weighted average method.

d. Determine the equivalent units of production using the FIFO method.

WebTUTOR Advantage

14. (Cost per EUP; weighted average) Hogg Inc. manufactures pillar candles. In October 2006, company production is 26,800 equivalent units for direct material, 24,400 equivalent units for labor, and 21,000 equivalent units for overhead. During October, direct material, conversion, and overhead costs incurred are as follows:

Direct material	$ 78,880
Conversion	122,400
Overhead	42,600

Beginning inventory costs for October were $14,920 for direct material, $36,200 for labor, and $9,900 for overhead. What is the October weighted average cost per equivalent unit for direct material, direct labor, and overhead?

15. (Cost per EUP; FIFO) Assume that Hogg Inc. in Exercise 14 had 3,600 EUP for direct material in October's beginning inventory, 4,000 EUP for direct labor, and 3,960 EUP for overhead. What was the October FIFO cost per equivalent unit for direct material, direct labor, and overhead?

16. (Cost per EUP; weighted average & FIFO) Fantastic Borders manufactures concrete garden border sections. May 2006 production and cost information are as follows:

WA EUP
Direct material	80,000 sections
Direct labor	76,000 sections
Overhead	75,000 sections

FIFO EUP
Direct material	60,000 sections
Direct labor	62,000 sections
Overhead	66,000 sections

BI costs
Direct material	$ 9,800
Direct labor	3,160
Overhead	5,010

Current period costs
Direct material	$27,000
Direct labor	17,360
Overhead	42,240

All material is added at the beginning of processing.

a. What is the total cost to account for?

b. Using weighted average process costing, what is the cost per equivalent unit for each cost component?

c. Using FIFO process costing, what is the cost per equivalent unit for each cost component?

d. How many units were in beginning inventory and at what percentage of completion was each cost component?

17. (EUP; cost per EUP; weighted average) Ouch! manufactures canisters of mace. On August 1, 2006, the company had 9,800 units in beginning Work in Process Inventory that were 100 percent complete as to canisters, 60 percent complete as to other materials, 40 percent complete as to direct labor, and 20 percent complete as to overhead. During August, Ouch! started 81,500 units in the manufacturing process. Ending Work in Process Inventory included 4,600 units that were 100 percent complete as to canisters, 30 percent complete as to other materials, 25 percent complete as to direct labor, and 10 percent complete as to overhead.

Cost information for the month follows:

Beginning inventory
Canisters	$ 7,382
Other direct materials	6,188
Direct labor	3,963
Overhead	3,432

August costs
Canisters	65,658
Other direct materials	86,296
Direct labor	78,616
Overhead	157,814

Prepare a schedule showing the Ouch! August 2006 computation of weighted average equivalent units of production and cost per equivalent unit.

18. (EUP; cost per EUP; FIFO) Roll-Along makes skateboards and uses a FIFO process costing system. The company began April 2006 with 1,000 boards in process that were 70 percent complete as to material and 85 percent complete as to conversion. During the month, 3,800 additional boards were started. On April 30, 800 boards were still in process (40 percent complete as to material and 60 percent complete as to conversion). Cost information for April 2006 is as follows:

Beginning inventory costs	
Direct material	$13,181
Conversion	6,732
Current period costs	
Direct material	66,970
Conversion	29,040

a. Calculate EUP for each cost component using the FIFO method.
b. Calculate cost per EUP for each cost component.

WebTUTOR Advantage

19. (Cost assignment; weighted average) The following production and cost per EUP information are available for Degas Co. for January 2006:

Units transferred out during month	520,000
Units in ending inventory (100% complete as to direct material;	
30% complete as to direct labor; 45% complete as to overhead)	74,000
Direct material cost per EUP	$3.75
Direct labor cost per EUP	4.50
Overhead cost per EUP	5.10

a. What is the cost of the goods transferred during January?
b. What is the cost of the goods in ending inventory at January 31, 2006?
c. What is the total cost to account for during January?

20. (Cost assignment; FIFO) In November 2006, Monet Corporation computed its equivalent unit costs under FIFO process costing as follows:

Direct material	$12.75
Packaging	1.50
Direct labor	6.42
Overhead	3.84

Direct material and packaging are added, respectively, at the start and end of processing.

Beginning inventory cost was $513,405 and consisted of
- $344,520 direct material cost for 27,000 EUP.
- $95,931 direct labor cost for 8,100 EUP.
- $72,954 overhead cost for 9,450 EUP.

Monet transferred a total of 185,000 units to finished goods during November and had 6,000 units in ending inventory. The EI units were 40 percent complete as to direct labor and 55 percent complete as to overhead.

a. What percentage complete were the beginning inventory units as to direct material? Packaging? Direct labor? Overhead?
b. What was the total cost of the completed beginning inventory units?
c. What was the cost of the units started and completed in November?
d. What was the cost of November's ending inventory?

21. (EUP; cost per EUP; cost assignment; FIFO & weighted average) Manet Company mass-produces miniature speakers for portable CD players. The following T-account presents the firm's cost information for February 2006:

Work in Process Inventory

2/1 Direct material cost in BI	1,927	
2/1 Conversion cost in BI	437	
Feb. DM received	31,464	
Feb. DL incurred	6,535	
Feb. OH applied to production	5,178	

The company had 500 units in process on February 1. These units were 60 percent complete as to material and 30 percent complete as to conversion.

During February, the firm started 4,200 units and ended the month with 150 units still in process. The units in ending WIP Inventory were 80 percent complete as to material and 70 percent complete as to conversion.

a. Compute the unit costs for February under the FIFO method for direct material and for conversion.

b. Determine the total costs transferred to Finished Goods Inventory during February using the FIFO method.

c. Compute the unit costs for February under the weighted average method for direct material and for conversion.

d. Determine the cost of ending inventory using the weighted average method.

22. (EUP; weighted average & FIFO; two departments) Dali Metals has two processing departments, Fabrication and Assembly. Metal is placed into production in the Fabrication Department, where it is cut and formed into various components. These components are transferred to Assembly, where they are welded, polished, and coated with sealant. Production data follow for these two departments for March 2006:

Fabrication

Beginning WIP inventory (100% complete as to material; 25% complete as to conversion)	5,000
Units started during month	40,000
Ending WIP inventory (100% complete as to material; 60% complete as to conversion)	6,800

Assembly

Beginning WIP inventory (0% complete as to sealant; 35% complete as to conversion)	2,000
Units started during month	?
Ending WIP inventory (0% complete as to sealant; 15% complete as to conversion)	6,100

a. Determine the equivalent units of production for each cost component for each department under the weighted average method.

b. Determine the equivalent units of production for each cost component for each department under the FIFO method.

23. (Standard process costing; variances) DiskCity Products manufactures CDs and uses a standard process costing system. All material is added at the start of production, and labor and overhead are incurred equally throughout the process. The standard cost of one CD is as follows:

Direct material	$0.10
Direct labor	0.02
Overhead	0.07
Total cost	$0.19

The following production and cost data are applicable to April 2006:

Beginning inventory (45% complete)	18,000 units
Started in April	130,000 units
Ending inventory (65% complete)	14,400 units
Current cost of direct material	$18,400
Current cost of direct labor	2,698
Current cost of overhead	15,200

a. What cost is carried as the April beginning balance of Work in Process Inventory?

b. What cost is carried as the April ending balance of Work in Process Inventory?

c. What cost is transferred to Finished Goods Inventory for April?

d. Using the FIFO method, what are the total direct material, direct labor, and overhead variances for April?

e. Record the journal entries to recognize the direct material, direct labor, and overhead variances.

24. (Standard process costing) Renoir Company uses a standard costing system to account for its pita bread manufacturing process. The pita bread is packaged and sold by the dozen. The company has set the following standards for production of each package:

Direct material—ingredients	$0.45
Direct material—package	0.05
Direct labor	0.07
Overhead	0.11
Total cost	$0.68

On June 1, the company had 6,000 individual pita breads in process; these were 100 percent complete as to ingredients, 0 percent complete as to packaging, and 70 percent complete as to labor and overhead. During June, 155,000 pitas were started and 157,000 were finished. Ending inventory was 100 percent complete as to ingredients, 0 percent complete as to the packaging, and 60 percent complete as to labor and overhead.

a. What were the equivalent units of production for June?

b. What was the cost of the packages transferred to Finished Goods Inventory during June?

c. What was the cost of the ending Work in Process Inventory for June?

25. (Hybrid costing; advanced) Windy City Co. makes capes (one size fits most). Each cape goes through the same conversion process, but three types of fabric (Dacron, denim, and cotton) are available. The company uses a standard costing system, and standard costs for each type of cape follow:

	Dacron	Denim	Cotton
Material (2 yards)	$10	$ 8	$12
Direct labor (1 hour)	12	12	12
Overhead (based on 1.5 machine hours)	9	9	9
Total	$31	$29	$33

Material is added at the start of production. In March 2006, there was no beginning Work in Process Inventory and 2,500 capes were started into production. Of these, 300 were Dacron, 500 were denim, and 1,700 were cotton. At the end of March, 100 capes (20 Dacron, 30 denim, and 50 cotton) were not yet completed. The stage of completion for each cost component for the 100 unfinished capes is as follows:

Material	100% complete
Direct labor	25% complete
Overhead	35% complete

a. Determine the total cost of the capes completed and transferred to Finished Goods Inventory.

b. Determine the total cost of the capes in ending Work in Process Inventory.

26. (Internet) Search the Internet to identify a vendor of process costing software. Read the on-line literature provided by the vendor regarding the software. Then briefly describe the major features of the software in the areas of product costing, cost budgeting, and cost control.

27. (Research) In a team of three or four people, choose a company whose mass production process you would like to learn. Use the library, the Internet, and (if possible) personal resources to gather information. Prepare a visual representation (similar to Exhibit 6–3) of that production process. In this illustration, indicate the approximate percentage of completion points at which various materials are added and where/how labor and overhead flow into and through the process.

Assume that 1,000 units of product are flowing through your production process and are now at the 60 percent completion point as to labor. Prepare a written explanation about the quantity of direct material equivalent units that are included in the 1,000 units. Also explain how much overhead activity and cost have occurred and why the overhead percentage is the same as or different from the percentage of completion for labor.

28. (Appendix; EUP computations; normal loss) Southeastern Corp. produces paint in a process in which spoilage occurs continually. Spoilage of 1 percent or fewer of the gallons of raw material placed into production is considered normal. The following operating statistics are available for June 2006:

Beginning inventory (60% complete as to material; 70% complete as to conversion)	8,000 gallons
Started during June	180,000 gallons
Ending inventory (40% complete as to material; 20% complete as to conversion)	4,000 gallons
Spoiled	1,400 gallons

a. How many gallons were transferred out?

b. What are the FIFO equivalent units of production for material? For conversion?

29. (Appendix; normal vs. abnormal spoilage; WA) Weezer Plastics uses a weighted average process costing system, and company management has specified that the normal loss from shrinkage cannot exceed 5 percent of the units started in a period. All raw material is added at the start of the production process. March processing information follows:

Beginning inventory (30% complete as to conversion)	10,000 units
Started during March	60,000 units
Completed during March	58,200 units
Ending inventory (20% complete as to conversion)	8,000 units

a. How many total units are there to account for?

b. How many units should be treated as normal loss?

c. How many units should be treated as abnormal loss?

d. What are the equivalent units of production for direct material? For conversion?

e. How are costs associated with the normal spoilage handled?

f. How are costs associated with the abnormal spoilage handled?

30. (Appendix; EUP computation; normal loss; cost per EUP; FIFO; advanced) Rodin Inc. produces small plastic toys. As the raw material is heated, shrinkage occurs. Management believes that shrinkage of less than 8 percent is normal. All direct material is entered at the beginning of the process. March 2006 data follow:

Beginning inventory (30% complete as to conversion)	18,000 pounds
Started during month	60,000 pounds
Transferred	63,000 pounds
Ending inventory (20% complete as to conversion)	10,800 pounds
Loss	? pounds

The following costs are associated with March production:

Beginning inventory:		
Material	$ 7,000	
Conversion	5,400	$12,400
Current period:		
Material	$19,530	
Conversion	17,928	37,458
Total costs		$49,858

Prepare a March 2006 cost of production report for Rodin Inc. using FIFO process costing.

31. (Appendix; EUP computation; normal and abnormal loss; FIFO; advanced) Waykita Foods manufactures corn meal in a continuous, mass production process. Corn is added at the beginning of the process. Losses are few and occur only when foreign materials are found in the corn meal. Inspection occurs at the 95 percent completion point as to conversion.

During May, a machine malfunctioned and dumped salt into 8,000 pounds of corn meal. This abnormal loss occurred when conversion was 70 percent complete on those pounds of product. The error was immediately noticed, and those pounds of corn meal were pulled from the production process. An additional 2,000 pounds of meal were detected as unsuitable at the inspection point. These lost units were considered well within reasonable limits. May production data follow:

Beginning work in process (85% complete)	40,000 pounds
Started during the month	425,000 pounds
Ending work in process (25% complete)	10,000 pounds

a. Determine the number of equivalent units for direct material and for conversion assuming a FIFO cost flow.

b. If the costs per equivalent unit are $2.40 and $4.70 for direct material and conversion, respectively, what is the cost of ending inventory?

c. What is the cost of abnormal loss? How is this cost treated in May?

Problems

32. (Weighted average) Wyeth Products manufactures electronic language translators. Analysis of beginning Work in Process Inventory for February 2006 revealed the following for 800 units:

800 Units	Percent Complete	Costs Incurred
Material	45	$ 6,748
Direct labor	65	2,484
Overhead	40	5,710
Total beginning inventory		$14,942

During February, Wyeth Products started production of another 11,400 translators and incurred $259,012 for material, $58,316 for direct labor, and $188,210 for overhead. On February 28, the company had 400 units in process (70 percent complete as to material, 90 percent complete as to direct labor, and 80 percent complete as to overhead).

a. Prepare a cost of production report for February using the weighted average method.

b. Journalize the February transactions.

c. Prepare T-accounts to represent the flow of costs for Wyeth Products for February. Use XXX where amounts are unknown and identify what each unknown amount represents.

33. (FIFO) Use the information from Problem 32 for Wyeth Products.

a. Prepare a cost of production report for February using the FIFO method.

b. In general, what differences exist between the weighted average and FIFO methods of process costing and why do these differences exist?

34. (Weighted average) Lei Enterprises manufactures belt buckles in a single-step production process. To determine the proper valuations for inventory balances and Cost of Goods Sold, you have obtained the following information for August 2006:

	Whole Units	Cost of Material	Cost of Labor
Beginning work in process	400,000	$ 400,000	$ 576,000
Units started during period	2,000,000	2,600,000	3,204,000
Units transferred to finished goods	1,800,000		

Beginning inventory units were 100 percent complete as to material but only 80 percent complete as to labor and overhead. The ending inventory units were 100 percent complete as to material and 50 percent complete as to conversion. Overhead is applied to production at the rate of 60 percent of direct labor cost.

a. Prepare a schedule to compute equivalent units of production by cost component assuming the weighted average method.

b. Determine the unit production costs for material and conversion.

c. Calculate the costs assigned to completed units and ending inventory for August 2006.

35. (Weighted average) Sun Valley Micro produces computer cases. In the production process, materials are added at the beginning of production and overhead is applied to each product at the rate of 70 percent of direct labor cost. No Finished Goods Inventory existed at the beginning of July. A review of the firm's inventory cost records provides the following information:

	Units	DM Cost	DL Cost
Work in process 7/1/06			
(70% complete as to labor and overhead)	100,000	$ 750,000	$ 215,000
Units started in production	1,500,000		
Costs for July		5,650,000	4,1055,000
Work in process 7/31/06			
(60% complete as to labor and overhead)	400,000		

At the end of July, the cost of Finished Goods Inventory was determined to be $124,000.

a. Compute the following:

1. Equivalent units of production using the weighted average method.

2. Unit production costs for material, labor, and overhead.

3. Cost of goods sold.

b. Prepare the journal entries to record the July transfer of completed goods and the July cost of goods sold.

(CPA adapted)

36. (FIFO cost per EUP) Zack's Corp. makes a variety of snacks. The following information for August 2006 relates to a cashew and dried mango mix. Materials are added at the beginning of processing; overhead is applied on a direct labor basis. The mix is transferred to a second department for packaging. Zack's uses a FIFO process costing system.

Beginning WIP inventory (40% complete as to direct labor)	5,000 pounds
Mix started in August	80,400 pounds
Ending WIP inventory (80% complete as to labor)	4,000 pounds
Material cost incurred in August	$388,332
Conversion cost incurred in August	$107,380

Beginning inventory cost totaled $26,790. For August 2006, compute the following:

a. Equivalent units of production by cost component.

b. Cost per equivalent unit by cost component.

c. Cost of mix transferred to the packaging department in August.

d. Cost of August's ending inventory.

37. (Cost assignment; FIFO) Fresh Seasons Processors is a contract manufacturer for Delectable Dressing Company. Fresh Seasons uses a FIFO process costing system to account for its salad dressing production. All ingredients are added at the start of the process. Delectable provides reusable vats to Fresh Seasons for the completed product to be shipped to Delectable for bottling, so Fresh Seasons incurs no packaging costs. April 2006 production and cost information for Fresh Seasons Processors is as follows:

Gallons of dressing in beginning inventory	36,000
Gallons transferred out during April	242,000
Gallons of dressing in ending inventory	23,500
Costs of beginning inventory	
Direct material	$ 178,000
Direct labor	39,100
Overhead	81,740
Costs incurred in April	
Direct material	$1,136,025
Direct labor	451,450
Overhead	723,195

The beginning and ending inventories had the following degrees of completion each for labor and overhead:

	Beginning Inventory	**Ending Inventory**
Direct labor	55%	15%
Overhead	70%	10%

a. How many gallons of dressing ingredients were started in April?

b. What is the total cost of the completed beginning inventory?

c. What is the total cost of goods completed during April?

d. What is the average cost per gallon of all goods completed during April?

e. What is the cost of April's ending WIP inventory?

38. (Weighted average & FIFO) In a single-process production system, Nile Queen Corporation produces press-on fingernails. For October 2006, the company's accounting records reflected the following:

Beginning Work in Process Inventory	
(100% complete as to material; 30% complete as to direct labor;	
60% complete as to overhead)	6,000 units
Units started during the month	45,000 units
Ending Work in Process Inventory (100% complete as to material;	
40% complete as to direct labor; 80% complete as to overhead)	10,000 units

Cost Component	**Beginning Inventory**	**October**
Material	$6,510	$45,000
Direct labor	954	22,896
Overhead	2,318	35,412

a. For October, prepare a cost of production report, assuming that the company uses the weighted average method.

b. For October, prepare a cost of production report, assuming that the company uses the FIFO method.

39. (WA and FIFO) Starbing Paints makes quality paint sold at premium prices in one production department. Production begins with the blending of various chemicals, which are added at the beginning of the process, and ends with the canning of the paint. Canning occurs when the mixture reaches the 90 percent stage of completion. The gallon cans are then transferred to the Shipping Department for crating and shipment. Labor and overhead are added continuously throughout the process. Factory overhead is applied at the rate of $3 per direct labor hour.

Prior to May, when a change in the process was implemented, work in process inventories were insignificant. The change in process enables more production but results in large amounts of work in process. The company has always used the weighted average method to determine equivalent production and unit costs. Now production management is considering changing from the weighted average method to the first-in, first-out method.

The following data relate to actual production during May:

Costs for May

Work in process inventory, May 1

Direct material—chemicals	$ 45,600
Direct labor ($10 per hour)	6,250
Factory overhead	1,875

Current month

Direct material—chemicals	$228,400
Direct material—cans	7,000
Direct labor ($10 per hour)	35,000
Factory overhead	10,500

Units for May (Gallons)

Work in process inventory, May 1 (25% complete)	4,000
Sent to Shipping Department	20,000
Started in May	21,000
Work in process inventory, May 31 (80% complete)	5,000

a. Prepare a cost of production report for each cost element for May using the weighted average method.

b. Prepare a cost of production report for each cost element for May using the FIFO method.

c. Discuss the advantages and disadvantages of using the weighted average method versus the FIFO method, and explain under what circumstances each method should be used.

(CMA adapted)

40. (FIFO; second department; advanced) Xena Corp. makes porcelain sinks in a process requiring operations in three separate departments: Molding, Curing, and Finishing. Materials are introduced in Molding; additional material is added in Curing. The following information is available for the Curing Department for May 2006:

Beginning WIP Inventory (degree of completion: transferred in, 100%; direct material, 80%; direct labor, 40%; overhead, 30%)	8,000 units
Transferred in from Molding	40,000 units
Ending WIP Inventory (degree of completion: transferred in, 100%; direct material, 70%; direct labor, 50%; overhead, 40%)	4,000 units
Transferred to Finishing	? units

Cost Component	Beginning Inventory	Current Period
Transferred in	$154,000	$760,000
Direct material	24,960	161,600
Direct labor	20,080	256,800
Overhead	6,970	129,600

Prepare, in good form, a FIFO cost of production report for the Curing Department for May 2006.

41. (Two departments; weighted average; advanced) Big Piney Corporation makes plastic Christmas trees in two departments, Cutting and Boxing. In the Cutting Department, wire wrapped with green "needles" is placed into production at the beginning of the process and is cut to various lengths, depending on the size of the trees being made at that time. The "branches"

are then transferred to the Boxing Department where the lengths are separated into the necessary groups to make a tree. These are then placed in boxes and immediately sent to Finished Goods.

The following data are available related to the October 2006 production in each of the two departments:

		PERCENT OF COMPLETION		
	Units	Transferred In	Material	Conversion
Cutting Department				
Beginning inventory	8,000	N/A	100	30
Started in process	36,000			
Ending inventory	3,600	N/A	100	70
Boxing Department				
Beginning inventory	2,500	100	0	55
Transferred in	?			
Ending inventory	1,200	100	0	60

	COSTS		
	Transferred In	Material	Conversion
Cutting Department			
Beginning inventory	N/A	$ 73,250	$ 20,000
Current period	N/A	344,750	323,360
Boxing Department			
Beginning inventory	$41,605	$ 0	$ 2,100
Current period	?	95,910	61,530

a. Prepare a cost of production report for the Cutting Department assuming a weighted average method.

b. Using the data developed from part (a), prepare a cost of production report for the Boxing Department, also using the weighted average method.

42. (Cost flows: multiple departments) Sharp Corporation produces accent stripes for automobiles in 50-inch rolls. Each roll passes through three departments (Striping, Adhesion, and Packaging) before it is ready for shipment to automobile dealers and detailing shops. Product costs are tracked by department and assigned using a process costing system. Overhead is applied to production in each department at a rate of 80 percent of the department's direct labor cost.

The following T-account information pertains to departmental operations for June 2006:

Work in Process—Striping

Beginning	20,000		
DM	90,000		
DL	80,000	?	?
Overhead	?		
Ending	17,000		

Work in Process—Adhesion

Beginning	70,000		
Transferred in	?		
DM	22,600	?	480,000
DL	?		
Overhead	?		
Ending	20,600		

Work in Process—Packaging

Beginning	150,000		
Transferred in	?		
DM	?	CGM	?
Overhead	90,000		
Ending	40,000		

Finished Goods

Beginning	185,000		
TI	880,000	?	720,000
Ending	?		

a. What was the cost of goods transferred from the Striping Department to the Adhesion Department for the month?

b. How much direct labor cost was incurred in the Adhesion Department? How much overhead was assigned to production in the Adhesion Department for the month?

c. How much direct material cost was charged to products in the Packaging Department?

d. Prepare the journal entries for all interdepartmental transfers of products and the cost of the units sold during June 2006.

43. (Comprehensive; two dep artments; advanced) Safe-N-Sound makes a backyard fencing system for pet owners in a two-stage production system. In process 1, wood is cut and assembled into 6-foot fence sections. In process 2, the sections are pressure treated to resist the effects of weather and then coated with a wood preservative. The following production and cost data are available for March 2006 (units are 6-foot fence sections):

Units	Cutting Process	Pressure Process
Beginning WIP Inventory (March 1)	1,300	900
Complete as to material	80%	0%
Complete as to conversion	75%	60%
Units started in March	4,800	?
Units completed in March	?	4,500
Ending WIP Inventory (March 31)	1,100	?
Complete as to material	40%	0%
Complete as to conversion	20%	40%

Costs		
Beginning WIP Inventory		
Transferred in		$11,840
Material	$ 8,345	0
Conversion	7,720	1,674
Current		
Transferred in		$?
Material	$35,200	4,932
Conversion	21,225	11,300

a. Prepare EUP schedules for both the cutting and pressure processes. Use the FIFO method.

b. Determine the cost per equivalent unit for the cutting process assuming a FIFO method.

c. Assign costs to goods transferred and to inventory in the cutting process on a FIFO basis.

d. Transfer the FIFO costs to the pressure process. Determine cost per EUP on a modified FIFO basis. (See footnote 6, page 211.)

e. Assign costs to goods transferred out and to inventory in the pressure process on a modified FIFO basis.

f. Assuming there was no beginning or ending inventory of Finished Goods Inventory for March, what was Cost of Goods Sold for March?

44. (Standard process costing) Dark Out manufactures sunglass and ski goggle lenses. The company uses a standard process costing system and carries inventories at standard. In May 2006, the following data were available:

Standard Cost of 1 Unit	
Direct material	$ 5.50
Conversion	12.50
Total manufacturing cost	$18.00
Beginning WIP Inventory	10,000 units (100% DM; 70% conversion)
Started in May	180,000 units
Completed in May	160,000 units
Ending WIP Inventory	? units (100% DM; 60% conversion)
Actual costs for May	
Direct material	$ 981,000
Conversion	2,145,000
Total actual cost	$3,126,000

a. Prepare an equivalent units of production schedule.
b. Prepare a cost of production report and assign costs to goods transferred and to inventory.
c. Calculate and label the variances and close them to Cost of Goods Sold.

45. (Multiproduct; hybrid costing) Be-at-Ease Industries manufactures a series of three models of molded plastic chairs: standard (without arms), deluxe (with arms), and executive (with arms and padding). All are variations of the same design. The company uses batch manufacturing and has a hybrid costing system.

Be-at-Ease has an extrusion operation and subsequent operations to form, trim, and finish the chairs. Plastic sheets are produced by the extrusion operation, some of which are sold directly to other manufacturers. During the forming operation, the remaining plastic sheets are molded into chair seats and the legs are added; the standard model is sold after this operation. During the trim operation, the arms are added to the deluxe and executive models, and the chair edges are smoothed. Only the executive model enters the finish operation where the padding is added. All units produced receive the same steps within each operation.

The July production run had a total manufacturing cost of $898,000. The units of production and direct material costs incurred were as follows:

	Units Produced	Extrusion Materials	Form Materials	Trim Materials	Finish Materials
Plastic sheets	5,000	$ 60,000			
Standard model	6,000	72,000	$24,000		
Deluxe model	3,000	36,000	12,000	$ 9,000	
Executive model	2,000	24,000	8,000	6,000	$12,000
Totals	16,000	$192,000	$44,000	$15,000	$12,000

Manufacturing costs applied during July were as follows:

	Extrusion Operation	Form Operation	Trim Operation	Finish Operation
Direct labor	$152,000	$60,000	$30,000	$18,000
Factory overhead	240,000	72,000	39,000	24,000

a. For each product produced by Be-at-Ease during July, determine the
   1. Unit cost.
   2. Total cost.
   Be sure to account for all costs incurred during the month, and support your answer with appropriate calculations.
b. Without prejudice to your answer in part (a), assume that only 1,000 units of the deluxe model remained in Work in Process Inventory at the end of the month. These units were 100 percent complete as to material and 60 percent complete as to conversion in the trim operation. Determine the value of the 1,000 units of the deluxe model in Be-at-Ease's Work in Process Inventory at the end of July.

(CMA adapted)

46. (Appendix; shrinkage; weighted average) Burger Babies produces frozen hamburgers. In the Forming Department, ground beef is formed into patties and cooked; an acceptable shrinkage loss for this department is 3 percent of the pounds started. The patties are then transferred to the Finishing Department where they are placed on buns, boxed, and frozen.

Burger Babies uses a weighted average process costing system and has the following production and cost data for the Forming Department for May 2006:

Beginning inventory (80% complete as to conversion)	1,000 pounds
Started	125,000 pounds
Transferred to Finishing (357,300 patties)	119,100 pounds
Ending inventory (30% complete as to conversion)	3,000 pounds
Beginning inventory cost of ground beef	$953
May cost of ground beef	$113,962
Beginning inventory conversion cost	$75
May conversion cost	$11,940

a. What is the total shrinkage (in pounds)?

b. How much of the shrinkage is classified as normal? How is it treated for accounting purposes?

c. How much of the shrinkage is classified as abnormal? How is it treated for accounting purposes?

d. What are the May 2006 equivalent units of production in the Forming Department for direct materials and conversion?

e. What is the total cost of the patties transferred to the Finishing Department? Cost of ending inventory? Cost of abnormal spoilage?

f. How might Burger Babies reduce its shrinkage loss? How, if at all, would your solution(s) affect costs and selling prices?

47. (Appendix; normal and abnormal spoilage; FIFO; advanced) Robbin Darrell Company produces door pulls that are inspected at the end of production. Spoilage may occur because the door pull is improperly stamped or molded. Any spoilage in excess of 3 percent of the completed good units is considered abnormal. Material is added at the start of production. Labor and overhead are incurred evenly throughout production.

The company's May 2006 production and cost data follow:

Beginning inventory (50% complete)	5,600
Units started	74,400
Good units completed	70,000
Ending inventory (1/3 complete)	7,500

	Material	Conversion	Total
Beginning inventory	$ 6,400	$ 1,232	$ 7,632
Current period	74,400	31,768	106,168
Total	$80,800	$33,000	$113,800

Calculate the equivalent units schedule, prepare a FIFO cost of production report, and assign all costs.

48. (Appendix; normal and abnormal spoilage; weighted average; advanced) Use the Robbin Darrell Company data given in Problem 47. Prepare a May 2006 cost of production report using the weighted average method.

49. (Appendix; normal and abnormal discrete spoilage; WA) Shelley Brian Tools manufactures one of its products in a two-department process. A separate Work in Process account is maintained for each department, and the company uses a weighted average process costing system. The first department is Molding; the second is Grinding. At the end of production in Grinding, a quality inspection is made and then packaging is added. Overhead is applied in the Grinding Department on a machine-hour basis. Production and cost data for the Grinding Department for August 2006 follow:

Production Data

Beginning inventory (% complete: material, 0%; labor, 30%; overhead, 40%)	1,000 units
Transferred in from Molding	50,800 units
Normal spoilage (found at the end of processing during quality control)	650 units
Abnormal spoilage (found at end of processing during quality control)	350 units
Ending inventory (% complete: material, 0%; labor, 40%; overhead, 65%)	1,800 units
Transferred to finished goods	? units

Cost Data

Beginning inventory		
Transferred in	$ 6,050	
Material (label and package)	0	
Direct labor	325	
Overhead	980	$ 7,355
Current period		
Transferred in	$149,350	
Material (label and package)	12,250	
Direct labor	23,767	
Overhead	50,190	235,557
Total cost to account for		$242,912

a. Prepare a cost of production report for the Grinding Department for August.

b. Prepare the journal entry to dispose of the cost of abnormal spoilage.

50. (Appendix; normal and abnormal spoilage) Grand Monde Company manufactures various lines of bicycles. Because of the high volume of each type of product, the company employs a process cost system using the weighted average method to determine unit costs. Bicycle parts are manufactured in the Molding Department and transferred to the Assembly Department where they are partially assembled. After assembly, the bicycle is sent to the Packing Department.

Cost-per-unit data for the 20-inch dirt bike has been completed through the Molding Department. Annual cost and production figures for the Assembly Department follow.

PRODUCTION DATA

Beginning inventory (100% complete as to transferred in; 100% complete as to material; 80% complete as to conversion)	3,000 units
Transferred in during the year (100% complete as to transferred in)	45,000 units
Transferred to Packing	40,000 units
Ending inventory (100% complete as to transferred in; 50% complete as to material; 20% complete as to conversion)	4,000 units

COST DATA

	Transferred In	Direct Material	Conversion
Beginning inventory	$ 82,200	$ 6,660	$ 13,930
Current period	1,237,800	96,840	241,430
Totals	$1,320,000	$103,500	$255,360

Damaged bicycles are identified on inspection when the assembly process is complete. The normal rejection rate for damaged bicycles is 5 percent of those reaching the inspection point. Any damaged bicycles above the 5 percent quota are considered to be abnormal. Damaged bikes are removed from the production process and, when possible, parts are reused on other bikes. However, such salvage is ignored for the purposes of this problem.

Grand Monde does not want to assign normal spoilage cost to either the units in ending inventory (because they have not yet been inspected) or the bikes that are considered "abnormal spoilage." Thus, the company includes both normal and abnormal spoilage in the equivalent units schedule (at the appropriate percentage of completion). The cost of the normal spoilage is then added to the bikes transferred to the Packing Department. Abnormal spoilage is treated as a period loss.

a. Compute the number of damaged bikes that are considered to be

  1. A normal quantity of damaged bikes.

  2. An abnormal quantity of damaged bikes.

    b. Compute the weighted average equivalent units of production for the year for

        1. Bicycles transferred in from the Molding Department.

        2. Bicycles produced with regard to Assembly material.

        3. Bicycles produced with regard to Assembly conversion.

    c. Compute the cost per equivalent unit for the fully assembled dirt bike.

    d. Compute the amount of total production cost that will be associated with the following items:

        1. Normal damaged units.

        2. Abnormal damaged units.

        3. Good units completed in the Assembly Department.

        4. Ending Work in Process Inventory in the Assembly Department.

    e. What amount will be transferred to the Packing Department?

    f. Discuss some potential reasons for spoilage to occur in this company. Which of these reasons would you consider important enough to correct and why? How might you attempt to correct these problems?

(CMA adapted)

7

Standard Costing and Variance Analysis

Objectives

AFTER COMPLETING THIS CHAPTER, YOU SHOULD BE ABLE TO ANSWER THE FOLLOWING QUESTIONS:

LO.1 HOW ARE STANDARDS FOR MATERIAL, LABOR, AND OVERHEAD SET?

LO.2 WHAT DOCUMENTS ARE ASSOCIATED WITH STANDARD COST SYSTEMS, AND WHAT INFORMATION DO THOSE DOCUMENTS PROVIDE?

LO.3 HOW ARE MATERIAL, LABOR, AND OVERHEAD VARIANCES CALCULATED AND RECORDED?

LO.4 WHY ARE STANDARD COST SYSTEMS USED?

LO.5 HOW WILL STANDARD COSTING BE AFFECTED IF A SINGLE CONVERSION ELEMENT IS USED RATHER THAN THE TRADITIONAL LABOR AND OVERHEAD ELEMENTS?

LO.6 *(APPENDIX)* HOW DO MULTIPLE MATERIAL AND LABOR CATEGORIES AFFECT VARIANCES?

PHOTO: GETTY IMAGES

Introducing

Quality and cost are two key success factors in determining the success of bicycle manufacturers. Specialized Bicycle Components, Inc. has achieved high marks on both of these critical factors and, in doing so, has attained a top-four ranking in mountain bike production for several years, including 2004.

Mike Sinyard has been a bicycle enthusiast since he was eight. After receiving a BS in Business from San Jose State University in 1973, Sinyard took a bicycle tour of Europe where he met first-class bike manufacturers. Upon returning to the United States, he founded Specialized in Morgan Hill, California, with $1,000, using a small trailer attached to the back of his bike to sell Italian bicycle parts. He believed that Americans had a demand for a scarce product: high-tech, high-quality, affordable mountain bikes.

By 1977, Specialized's sales were approximately $275,000, but then they started to decline because Americans found the mountain bike uncomfortable and prone to flat tires. But in 1980, Specialized produced the $750 Stumpjumper, which put the company on the map. Sales escalated from $10.5 million in 1981 to $14 million by 1989. These high-end bikes, which were not in direct competition with bikes sold at Kmart or Wal-Mart, were sold at specialty shops.

Sinyard acquired the services of bike enthusiasts and bike designers to produce his premier bicycles. For instance, Robert Egger, a renowned designer, styled three popular Specialized bikes: the ManGo bike that looks similar to a Vespa scooter; the Cobra 427 that was inspired by the classic Schwinn Stingray; and the children's Hardlock that had an exceptionally good braking system and tough locks that made it very difficult to steal.

While the company was successfully designing and marketing desirable, high-end bicycles, the boss was losing his business focus. Sinyard began treating the company as a hobby. Its annual R&D budget was increased to $5 million and Sinyard kept "tinkering" with product designs. He was trying to increase sales with lower-priced, lower-quality bikes, but the company's reputation began to suffer. To "get back on track," Sinyard needed to rebuild product quality but at a lower production cost.

The company used computer-aided design systems to reduce the design-to-test-run time from 14 to 9 months, thus reducing design costs per unit. Specialized also found that building quality into the process was less expensive than correcting problems at the end of production. Investing in Internet commerce also lowered costs because of a 60 percent reduction in the customer service workforce. Internet commerce allowed Specialized to interface directly with customers rather than through dealers. Specialized addressed common customer queries on its Web site, so employees spent less time calling or e-mailing customers. A joint venture with DuPont and Uma Ibeerica resulted in a wheel that was half the weight and cost of the one used in the original 1974 models. These and many other cost-cutting strategies enabled Specialized to produce a bike enthusiast's dream machine within a desired cost structure.

Sources: *http://www.specialized.com/sbcHistory.jsp?a=b*, and Steve Kaufman, "Specialized Bicycle Founder Wheels Firm Back to Profitable Course," *Knight Ridder/Tribune Business News* (December 9, 1996).

The top five manufacturers of mountain bikes maintain that they offer the highest quality racing machine; however, they must do so in a price-competitive manner. For example, Specialized offers a line of premier mountain bikes starting at $975, which represents a target for all competitors in setting the allowable cost of producing the bike. The industry then follows common performance measures, such as cost per bicycle, frame, or wheel, as benchmarks for actual performance evaluation. Accountants and other financial professionals help explain the financial consequences of exceeding the target performance levels or failing to achieve them. Without a predetermined performance measure, managers have no way to know what level of performance is expected. And, without comparing the actual result to the predetermined measure, managers have no way of knowing whether the company met expectations and no way to exercise control.

Organizations develop and use standards for almost all tasks. For example, businesses set standards for employee sales expenses; hotels set standards for performing housekeeping tasks and delivering room service; casinos set standards for revenue to be generated per square foot of playing space. McDonald's standards state that 1 pound of beef will provide 10 hamburger patties, a bun will be toasted for 17 seconds, and one packet of sanitizer will be used for every 2.5 gallons of water when cleaning the shake machine.[1] Until 2003, the U.S. Department of Agriculture

[1] Daniel Kruger, "You Want Data with That?" *Forbes* (March 29, 2004), pp. 58–59.

had standards that dictated frozen meat pizza ingredients: "a crust, cheese, a tomato-based sauce and at least 10–12 percent meat by weight," which meant that a 12″ pepperoni pizza would have about 20 pepperoni slices![2]

Because of the variety of organizational activities and information objectives, no single standard costing system is appropriate for all situations. Some systems use standards for prices but not for quantities; other systems (especially in service businesses) use standards for labor but not material. This chapter discusses a traditional standard cost system that provides price and quantity standards for each cost component: direct material (DM), direct labor (DL), and factory overhead (OH). The chapter discusses how standards are developed, how variances are calculated, and what information can be gained from detailed variance analysis. It also presents journal entries used in a standard cost system. The chapter appendix covers mix and yield variances that can arise from using multiple materials or groups of labor.

DEVELOPMENT OF A STANDARD COST SYSTEM

Although manufacturing companies initiated standard cost systems, service and not-for-profit organizations can also use standards. A standard cost system records both standard and actual costs in the accounting records. This dual recording provides an essential element of cost control: having norms against which actual operations can be compared. Standard cost systems use **standard costs**, which are the budgeted costs to manufacture a single unit of product or perform a single service. Developing a standard cost involves judgment and practicality in identifying the material and labor types, quantities, and prices as well as understanding the types of organizational overhead and how they behave.

standard cost

What information is needed to set a standard cost?

A primary objective in manufacturing a product is to minimize unit cost while achieving certain quality specifications. Almost all products can be manufactured with a variety of inputs that would generate the same basic output and output quality. The input choices that are made affect the standards that are set.

Some possible input resource combinations are not necessarily practical or efficient. For instance, a work team might consist only of craftspersons or skilled workers, but such a team might not be cost beneficial if a large differential in the wage rates of skilled and unskilled workers existed. Also, providing high-technology equipment to unskilled labor is possible, but to do so would not be an efficient use of resources.

After management has established the desired output quality and determined the input resources needed to achieve that quality at a reasonable cost, it can develop quantity and price standards. Experts from cost accounting, industrial engineering, personnel, data processing, purchasing, and management help develop standards. To ensure credibility of the standards and to motivate people to operate as close to the standards as possible, standard-setting involvement of managers and workers whose performance will be compared to the standards is vital. The discussion of the standard-setting process begins with material.

Material Standards

LO.1
HOW ARE STANDARDS FOR
MATERIAL, LABOR, AND
OVERHEAD SET?

The first step in developing material standards is to identify and list the specific direct materials used to manufacture the product. This list is often available on product specification documents prepared by the engineering department prior to

[2] Associated Press, "Pizza May Get Sliced from Federal Rule Book," (New Orleans) *Times-Picayune* (November 9, 2001), p. C-5. The standards contained in 9 CFR 3119.500 were eliminated on July 31, 2003, and new ones took effect October 22, 2003; see *http://www.fsis.usda.gov.*

initial production. In the absence of such documentation, material specifications can be determined by observing the production area, querying production personnel, inspecting material requisitions, and reviewing the cost accounts related to the product. Three things must be known about material inputs: type, quantity, and quality. For example, in producing the wheel sets for a mountain bike, the bill of materials could include a rear wheel, front wheel, two mountain tubes, and two trail tires.

In making quality decisions, managers should remember that as the material grade rises, so generally does cost; decisions about material inputs usually seek to balance the relationships of cost, quality, and projected selling prices with company objectives. The resulting trade-offs affect material mix, material yield, finished product quality and quantity, overall product cost, and product salability. Thus, quantity and cost estimates become direct functions of quality decisions. Because of the quality selected for each component, estimates of the physical quantity of weight, size, volume, or some other measure can be made. These estimates are based on the results of engineering tests, opinions of managers and workers using the material, past material requisitions, and review of the cost accounts.

Specifications for materials, including quality and quantity, are compiled on a bill of materials. Data for Zoom Bike Company, which manufactures several product lines of bicycles including mountain bikes, are used to illustrate the details of standard costing. See Exhibit 7–1 for the company's bill of materials for one of its mountain bikes.

Even companies without formal standard cost systems develop bills of materials for products as guides for production activity. When converting quantities on the bill of materials into costs, companies often make allowances for normal waste

Are specific types of documents used in a standard costing system?

LO.2
WHAT DOCUMENTS ARE ASSOCIATED WITH STANDARD COST SYSTEMS, AND WHAT INFORMATION DO THOSE DOCUMENTS PROVIDE?

bill of materials

EXHIBIT 7–1

ZOOM BIKE COMPANY'S BILL OF MATERIALS

Product Name: <u>Mountain Bike (unassembled)</u>
Product # <u>15</u>
Date Established: <u>January 10, 2006</u>

COMPONENT ID#	QUANTITY REQUIRED	DESCRIPTION	COMMENTS
WF-05	1	Front wheel, tire & tube	Stumpjumper
WR-05	1	Rear wheel, tire & tube	Stumpjumper
B-05	2	Front & rear brakes	Includes derailleur, levers, and calipers
HB-05	1	Handlebar and stem	Stainless steel
B-21	16	2.5" x 5/16" bolts	Includes nuts and flat washers
S-18	12	3" clamps	Stainless steel
SPS-05	1	Seat post and seat	Nylon and black
P-05	2	Pedals	Black rubber
F-05	1	Frame	Fiberglass

of components.[3] After standard quantities have been developed, component prices that reflect quantity discounts allowed and freight/receiving costs must be determined. Purchasing agents can often influence prices by being aware of the company's purchasing habits and of alternative suppliers that can provide the most appropriate material in the most reasonable time at the most reasonable cost. Incorporating such information into price standards should make it easier for the purchasing agent to later determine the causes of any significant differences between actual and standard prices.

When all quantity and price information is available, component quantities are multiplied by unit prices to obtain the total cost of each component. (Remember that the price paid for the material becomes the *cost* of the material.) These totals are summed to determine the total standard material cost of one unit of product.

Labor Standards

Developing labor standards requires the same basic procedures as those used for material. Each production operation performed by workers (such as bending, reaching, lifting, moving material, and packing) or by machinery (such as drilling, cooking, and attaching parts) should be identified. In specifying operations and movements, activities such as cleanup, setup, and rework are considered. All unnecessary movements of workers and of material should be disregarded when time standards are set. Exhibit 7–2 indicates that a manufacturing worker's day is not spent entirely in productive work.

To develop usable standards, a company must obtain quantitative information for each production operation. The company can perform time and motion stud-

EXHIBIT 7–2

WHERE DID THE DAY GO?

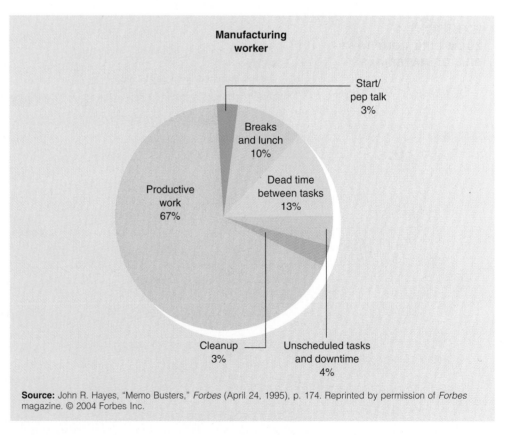

Source: John R. Hayes, "Memo Busters," *Forbes* (April 24, 1995), p. 174. Reprinted by permission of *Forbes* magazine. © 2004 Forbes Inc.

---

[3] Although such allowances are often made, they do not result in the most effective use of a standard cost system. Problems arising from their inclusion are discussed later in this chapter.

ies or can use times developed by industrial engineering studies for various movements.[4] Time standards can also be set by using the average time needed to manufacture a product during the past year as calculated from employee time sheets. A problem with this method is that such historical data can include inefficiencies. To compensate, management and supervisory personnel normally make subjective adjustments to the available data.

operations flow document

After all labor tasks have been analyzed a company can prepare an **operations flow document** that lists all operations necessary to make one unit of product or perform a specific service. When products are manufactured individually, the operations flow document shows the time necessary to produce one unit. In a flow process that produces goods in batches, individual times cannot be specified accurately. See Exhibit 7–3 for the operations flow document for Zoom Bike Company.

Labor rate standards should reflect employee wages and the related employer costs for fringe benefits, FICA (Social Security), and unemployment taxes. In the simplest situation, all departmental personnel would be paid the same wage rate as, for example, when wages are job specific or tied to a labor contract. If employees performing the same or similar tasks are paid different wage rates, a weighted average rate (total wage cost per hour divided by the number of workers) must be computed and used as the standard. Differences in rates could be caused by length of employment or skill level.

Overhead Standards

Overhead standards are predetermined factory overhead application rates. To provide the most appropriate costing information, overhead should be assigned to separate cost pools based on the cost drivers, and allocations to products should be made using different activity drivers.

standard cost card

After the bill of materials, operations flow document, and predetermined overhead rates per activity measure have been developed, a **standard cost card** is prepared. This document (see Exhibit 7–4) summarizes the standard quantities and costs needed to assemble one bike. For simplicity, it is assumed that the company uses only two rates to apply overhead: one for variable costs and one for fixed costs.

EXHIBIT 7–3

ZOOM BIKE COMPANY'S OPERATIONS FLOW DOCUMENT

Product: Mountain Bike
Product # 15
Date Established: January 10, 2006

Operation ID#	Department	Standard Time	Description of Task
009	Painting	3 hours	Spray primer, clear coat, and paint on frame
012	Assembly	5 hours	Assemble bike
015	Oiling	1 hour	Oil all gear parts
018	Testing	0.50 hour	Inspect and test bike
210	Packaging	0.25 hour	Place bike in corrugated packaging

[4] In performing internal time and motion studies, observers need to be aware that employees could engage in "slowdown" tactics when they are being clocked. The purpose of such tactics is to establish a longer time as the standard, which would make employees appear more efficient when actual results are measured. Employees also could slow down because they are being observed and want to be sure they are doing the job correctly.

EXHIBIT 7–4

ZOOM BIKE'S STANDARD COST CARD FOR MOUNTAIN BIKES

Product: Mountain Bike
Product # 15
Date Established: January 10, 2006

DIRECT MATERIAL

Component ID#	Quantity Required	Unit Cost	Total Cost
WF-05	1	$20.00	$ 20
WR-05	1	25.00	25
B-05	2	20.00	40
HB-05	1	23.00	23
B-21	16	0.75	12
S-18	12	1.25	15
SPS-05	1	17.00	17
P-05	2	14.00	28
F-05	1	200.00	200
Total cost			$380

DIRECT LABOR

ID#	Wage Rate/Hr	Total Hrs	Painting	Assembling	Oiling	Testing	Packaging	Total Cost
009	$12	3.00	36					$ 36
012	15	5.00		75				75
015	8	1.00			8			8
Testing	20	0.50				10		10
Packaging	8	0.25					2	2
Totals		9.75	36	75	8	10	2	$131

MANUFACTURING OVERHEAD

Variable overhead ($14 per labor hour) (9.75 direct labor hours)	$136.50
Fixed overhead ($24 per bike produced)*	24.00
Total overhead	$160.50

*Based on expected annual production of 5,000 mountain bikes

Data from the standard cost card are used to assign costs to inventory accounts. Both actual and standard costs are recorded in a standard cost system. Standard, rather than actual, production costs are debited to Work in Process Inventory.[5] A difference between an actual and a standard cost is a variance.

VARIANCE COMPUTATIONS

total variance

A **total variance** is the difference between total actual cost incurred and total standard cost applied to the output of the period. This variance can be diagrammed as follows:

---

[5] The standard cost of each cost element (direct material, direct labor, variable overhead, and fixed overhead) is said to be applied or allocated to the goods produced. This terminology is the same as that used when overhead is assigned to inventory based on a predetermined rate.

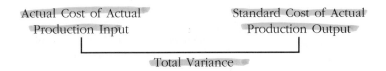

Actual Cost of Actual Production Input	Standard Cost of Actual Production Output

Total Variance

Total variances do not provide useful information for determining why cost differences occurred. For example, the preceding variance does not indicate whether it was caused by price or quantity factors, or both. To provide additional information, total variances are subdivided into price and usage components. The total variance diagram can be expanded to provide a general model indicating the two subvariances as follows:

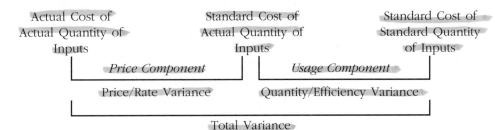

Actual Cost of Actual Quantity of Inputs	Standard Cost of Actual Quantity of Inputs	Standard Cost of Standard Quantity of Inputs

Price Component   *Usage Component*

Price/Rate Variance   Quantity/Efficiency Variance

Total Variance

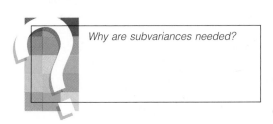

Why are subvariances needed?

This general variance analysis model will be referred to throughout the chapter as the *model.*

A price variance shows the difference between what was paid for inputs and what should have been paid for inputs. The price variance is calculated as the difference between the actual price (AP) and the standard price (SP) per unit of input multiplied by the actual input quantity (AQ):

$$\text{Price Element} = (AP - SP)(AQ)$$

The diagram of the general model moves from actual cost of actual input quantity in the left column to standard cost of standard input quantity in the right column. The middle column of the measure of input is a hybrid of actual quantity and standard price. The change from input to output reflects the fact that a specific quantity of production input will not necessarily produce the standard quantity of output.

How is standard quantity allowed computed?

A usage variance is calculated by multiplying the difference between the actual quantity of input and the standard quantity of input allowed for the output of the period times the standard input price. This computation provides a monetary measure that can be recorded in the accounting records. Usage variances focus on the efficiency of results or the relationship of input to output. The far right column in the general model shows a total standard cost. This cost reflects a measure of output known as the **standard quantity allowed**. This quantity, depicted in Exhibit 7–5, translates actual production output into the standard input quantity that should have been needed to achieve that output. The monetary amount shown in the right-hand column of the model is computed as the standard quantity allowed times the standard price of the input. The usage variance portion of the total variance is calculated as the difference between the actual input quantity and standard quantity of input (SQ) allowed multiplied by the standard price per unit of input:

standard quantity allowed

$$\text{Usage Element} = (AQ - SQ)(SP)$$

The following sections illustrate variance computations for each cost element.

EXHIBIT 7–5
DEPICTION OF STANDARD QUANTITY ALLOWED

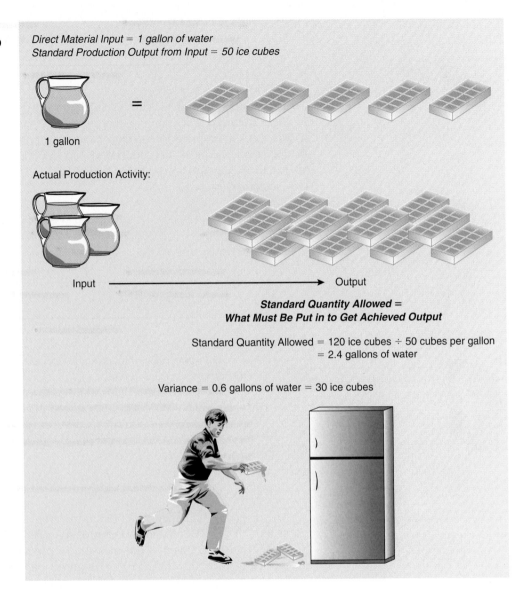

Direct Material Input = 1 gallon of water
Standard Production Output from Input = 50 ice cubes

1 gallon

Actual Production Activity:

Input ⟶ Output

Standard Quantity Allowed =
What Must Be Put in to Get Achieved Output

Standard Quantity Allowed = 120 ice cubes ÷ 50 cubes per gallon
= 2.4 gallons of water

Variance = 0.6 gallons of water = 30 ice cubes

MATERIAL AND LABOR VARIANCE COMPUTATIONS

LO.3
HOW ARE MATERIAL, LABOR, AND OVERHEAD VARIANCES CALCULATED AND RECORDED?

The standard costs of production for January 2006 for producing 400 mountain bikes (the actual quantity made) are shown in the top half of Exhibit 7–6. The lower half of the exhibit shows actual material, labor, and overhead quantities and cost data for January 2006. This standard and actual cost information is used to compute the January variances.

Material Variances

The general variance analysis model introduced earlier is used to compute price and quantity variances for materials. A price and quantity variance can be computed for each type of material. To illustrate the calculations, direct material item WF-05 is used.

EXHIBIT 7–6

STANDARD AND ACTUAL COST DATA FOR ZOOM BIKE COMPANY'S MOUNTAIN BIKES, JANUARY 2006

STANDARD COST FOR 400 MOUNTAIN BIKES			
Direct Material Component ID#	Quantity	Unit Cost	Total Cost
WF-05	400	$ 20.00	$ 8,000
WR-05	400	25.00	10,000
B-05	800	20.00	16,000
HB-05	400	23.00	9,200
B-21	6,400	0.75	4,800
S-18	4,800	1.25	6,000
SPS-05	400	17.00	6,800
P-05	800	14.00	11,200
F-05	400	200.00	80,000
Total standard direct material cost			$152,000

Direct Labor Department	Total Hours	Rate	Total Cost
Painting	1,200	$12.00	$14,400
Assembling	2,000	15.00	30,000
Oiling	400	8.00	3,200
Testing	200	20.00	4,000
Packaging	100	8.00	800
Total standard direct labor hours and cost	3,900		$52,400

Variable overhead ($14.00 × 3,900)		$54,600
Fixed overhead [($24.00 × 5,000) ÷ 12]		10,000
Total standard overhead cost		$64,600

ACTUAL JANUARY COST FOR 400 MOUNTAIN BIKES			
Direct Material Component ID#	Quantity	Unit Cost	Total Cost
WF-05	413	$ 19.00	$ 7,847
WR-05	400	24.00	9,600
B-05	810	20.00	16,200
HB-05	400	24.00	9,600
B-21	6,700	0.74	4,958
S-18	4,850	1.20	5,820
SPS-05	400	18.00	7,200
P-05	800	15.00	12,000
F-05	400	197.00	78,800
Total actual direct material cost			$152,025

Direct Labor Department	Total Hours	Rate	Total Cost
Painting	1,100	$12.00	$13,200
Assembling	1,900	16.00	30,400
Oiling	390	7.90	3,081
Testing	200	19.50	3,900
Packaging	90	8.00	720
Total actual direct labor hours and cost	3,680		$51,301

Variable overhead ($13.80 × 3,680)		$50,784
Fixed overhead ($21.20 × 400)		8,480
Total actual overhead cost		$59,264

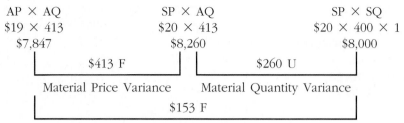

$$\text{AP} \times \text{AQ} \qquad\qquad \text{SP} \times \text{AQ} \qquad\qquad \text{SP} \times \text{SQ}$$
$$\$19 \times 413 \qquad\qquad \$20 \times 413 \qquad\qquad \$20 \times 400 \times 1$$
$$\$7,847 \qquad\qquad\qquad \$8,260 \qquad\qquad\qquad \$8,000$$

| $413 F | $260 U |

Material Price Variance   Material Quantity Variance

$153 F

Total Material Variance

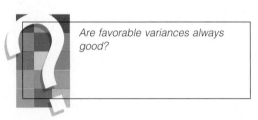

Are favorable variances always good?

material price variance

material quantity variance

If the actual price or quantity amounts used are higher than the standard price or quantity amounts, the variance is unfavorable (U); if the actual amounts are lower than the standard amounts used, the variance is favorable (F). *Unfavorable* is not equated with bad, nor is *favorable* equated with good. An unfavorable variance (higher actual cost or usage than standard) has a decreasing effect on income, and a favorable variance (lower actual cost or usage than standard) has an increasing effect on income. However, determination of "bad" or "good" must be made after identifying the cause of the variance and the implications that the variance had on other cost elements.

The **material price variance** (MPV) indicates whether the amount paid for material was less than or more than standard price. For item WF-05, the price paid was $19 versus a standard cost of $20 per unit. The $1 price variance per unit will increase income. The favorable MPV of $413 can also be calculated as [($20 − $19)(413) = ($1)(413) = $413]. This variance is favorable because the actual price is less than the standard. The purchasing manager should be able to explain why the price paid for item WF-05 was less than standard.

The **material quantity variance** (MQV) indicates whether the actual quantity used was less than or more than the standard quantity allowed for the actual output. This difference is multiplied by the standard price per unit of material. Production used 13 more units of WF-05 than the standard allowed, resulting in an unfavorable material quantity variance [($20)(400 − 413) = ($20)(−13) = −$260]. The unfavorable MQV will cause income to decrease. The production manager should be able to explain why so many additional WF-05 components were used in January.

The total material variance ($153 F) can be calculated by subtracting the total standard cost ($8,000) for component WF-05 input from the total actual cost ($7,847) of input. The total variance also represents the summation of the individual variances: ($413 F + $260 U) = $153 favorable variance.

To find the total direct material cost variances, price and quantity variances would be repeated for each direct material component WF-05 through F-05. The price and quantity variances then would be summed across items to obtain the total price and quantity variances.

Point of Purchase Material Variance Model

A total variance for a cost component generally equals the sum of the price and usage variances. An exception to this rule occurs when the quantity of material purchased is not the same as the quantity of material placed into production. Because the material price variance relates to the purchasing (rather than the production) function, the *point of purchase model* calculates the material price variance using the quantity of materials purchased (Q_p) rather than the quantity of materials used (Q_u). The general variance analysis model is altered slightly to isolate the variance as early as possible to provide more rapid information for management control purposes.

Zoom Bike Company used 413 WF-05s to make 400 mountain bikes (see Exhibit 7–6). However, assume that the company purchased 450 WF-05s at $19 per unit. Using this information, the material price variance is calculated as:

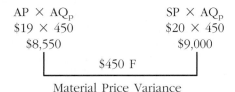

$$AP \times AQ_p \qquad\qquad SP \times AQ_p$$
$$\$19 \times 450 \qquad\qquad \$20 \times 450$$
$$\$8,550 \qquad\qquad\qquad \$9,000$$

$$\$450 \text{ F}$$
Material Price Variance

The format for the point of purchase model follows.

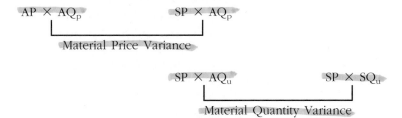

$$AP \times AQ_p \qquad\qquad SP \times AQ_p$$
Material Price Variance

$$SP \times AQ_u \qquad\qquad SP \times SQ_u$$
Material Quantity Variance

The material quantity variance is still computed for the actual quantity used and, thus, remains at $260 U. Because the price and quantity variances have been computed using different bases, they should not be summed, and no total material variance can be meaningfully determined.

Labor Variances

The labor variances for mountain bicycle production in January 2006 would be computed on a departmental basis and then summed across departments. To illustrate the computations, the Painting Department data are applied as follows:

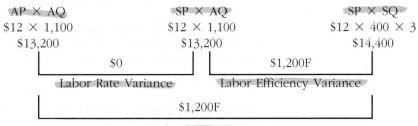

$$AP \times AQ \qquad\qquad SP \times AQ \qquad\qquad SP \times SQ$$
$$\$12 \times 1,100 \qquad\qquad \$12 \times 1,100 \qquad\qquad \$12 \times 400 \times 3$$
$$\$13,200 \qquad\qquad\qquad \$13,200 \qquad\qquad\qquad \$14,400$$

$$\$0 \qquad\qquad\qquad\qquad \$1,200F$$
Labor Rate Variance   Labor Efficiency Variance

$$\$1,200F$$
Total Labor Variance

labor rate variance

The **labor rate variance** (LRV) shows the difference between the actual wages paid to labor for the period and the standard wages for all hours worked. The LRV can also be computed as [($12 − $12)(1,100) = ($0)(1,100) = $0]. Multiplying the standard labor rate by the difference between the number of standard hours for the production achieved and the number of actual hours worked results in the **labor efficiency variance** (LEV): [(1,200 − 1,100)($12) = (100)($12) = $1,200 F].

labor efficiency variance

OVERHEAD VARIANCES

Because total variable overhead changes in direct relationship with changes in activity and fixed overhead per unit changes inversely with changes in activity, a specific activity level must be chosen to determine budgeted overhead costs and to develop an overhead application rate. Capacity refers to a level of activity and, as discussed in Chapter 3, the most common capacity measures are theoretical, practical, normal and expected capacity. Flexible budgets provide a means of determining the expected overhead costs at different activity levels.[6]

Exhibit 7–7 provides a flexible budget for annual mountain bike production at four alternative activity levels: 3,000, 4,000, 5,000, and 6,000 units. The flexible budget indicates that total unit cost for overhead declines as volume increases because the per-unit cost of fixed overhead moves inversely with volume changes. Managers of Zoom Bike Company selected 5,000 mountain bikes as a basis for determining the overhead application rates shown in Exhibit 7–4. At this activity level, expected direct labor hours are 48,750 (5,000 bikes at 9.75 hours each); total variable overhead is $682,500 ($14 × 48,750); and fixed overhead is $120,000. The fixed overhead application rate is then $120,000 divided by 5,000 bikes, resulting in $24 per bike.

Because Zoom Bike Company uses separate variable and fixed overhead application rates, separate price and usage variances are computed for each type of overhead. Such a four-variance approach provides managers the greatest detail and, thus, the greatest flexibility for control and performance evaluation.

Variable Overhead

The general variance analysis model can be used to calculate the price and usage subvariances for variable overhead (VOH) as follows:

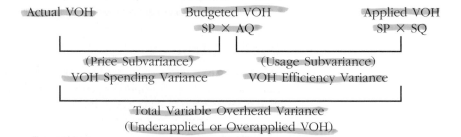

Actual VOH cost is debited to the Variable Manufacturing Overhead account with appropriate credits to various accounts. Applied VOH is debited to Work in Process Inventory and credited to Variable Manufacturing Overhead. Applied VOH reflects the standard overhead application rate multiplied by the standard quantity of activity for the period's actual output. The total VOH variance is the balance in the variable overhead account at period-end and equals the amount of underapplied or overapplied VOH.

Using the information in Exhibit 7–6, the variable overhead variances for mountain bike production are calculated as follows:

EXHIBIT 7–7

FLEXIBLE OVERHEAD BUDGET FOR ZOOM BIKE COMPANY'S ANNUAL MOUNTAIN BIKE PRODUCTION

Units of Production	3,000	4,000	5,000	6,000
Total labor hours allowed	29,250	39,000	48,750	58,500
Hourly overhead rate	× $14	× $14	× $14	× $14
Total variable overhead	$409,500	$546,000	$682,500	$819,000
Fixed overhead	120,000	120,000	120,000	120,000
Total overhead	$529,500	$666,000	$802,500	$939,000
Total OH cost per bike	$ 176.50	$ 166.50	$ 160.50	$ 156.50

[6] Flexible budgets are discussed in Chapter 3.

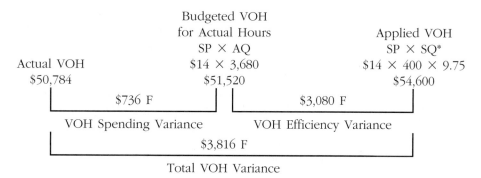

*Standard hours allowed = 400 bikes × 9.75 hours per bike = 3,900 hours

variable overhead spending
variance

    The difference between actual VOH and budgeted VOH based on actual hours is the **variable overhead spending variance**. Variable overhead spending variances are often caused by price differences—paying higher or lower prices than the standard prices allowed. Such fluctuations can occur because, over time, changes in variable overhead prices have not been included in the standard rate. For example, average indirect labor wage rates or utility rates could have changed since the predetermined variable overhead rate was computed. Managers usually have little control over prices charged by external parties and should not be held accountable for variances arising because of such price changes. In these instances, the standard rates should be adjusted.

    Another possible cause of a VOH spending variance is using a quantity of the items in variable overhead that differs from the quantity on which the standard is based. Such a difference can be associated with waste or shrinkage of production inputs (such as indirect materials). For example, deterioration of materials during storage or from lack of proper handling can be recognized only after those materials are placed into production. Such occurrences usually have little relationship to the input activity basis used, but they do affect the VOH spending variance. If waste or spoilage is the cause of the VOH spending variance, managers should be held accountable and encouraged to implement more effective controls.

variable overhead efficiency
variance

    The difference between budgeted VOH for actual hours and standard VOH is the **variable overhead efficiency variance**. This variance quantifies the effect of using more or less overhead-based inputs (e.g., labor hours, machine hours) than the standard allowed for the production achieved. When actual input exceeds standard input allowed, production operations are considered to be inefficient. Excess input also indicates that an increased VOH budget is needed to support the additional input.

Fixed Overhead

The total fixed overhead (FOH) variance is divided into its price and usage subvariances by inserting budgeted fixed overhead as a middle column into the general variance analysis model as follows:

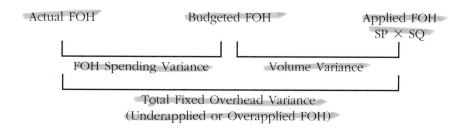

In the general variance analysis model, the left column is simply labeled "actual fixed overhead" and is not computed as a price multiplied by a quantity measure because FOH is incurred in lump sums. Actual FOH is debited to Fixed Manufacturing Overhead and credited to various accounts. Budgeted FOH is a constant amount throughout the relevant range; thus, the middle column is a constant figure regardless of the actual quantity of input or the standard quantity of input allowed. This concept is a key element in computing FOH variances. The $120,000 budgeted amount of fixed overhead can also be shown as the result of multiplying the standard FOH application rate by the capacity measure that was used to compute that standard rate ($24 per unit times 5,000 units for Zoom Bike's mountain bicycles).

fixed overhead spending variance

The difference between actual and budgeted FOH is the fixed overhead spending variance. This amount normally represents the price variance of the multiple FOH components, although it can also reflect resource mismanagement. Individual FOH components are shown in the flexible budget, and individual spending variances should be calculated for each component.

As with variable overhead, applied FOH is related to the standard application rate and the standard hours allowed for the actual production level. In regard to fixed overhead, the standard input allowed for the achieved production level measures the capacity utilization for the period. Applied fixed overhead is debited to Work in Process Inventory and credited to Fixed Manufacturing Overhead.

volume variance

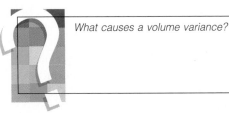

What causes a volume variance?

The fixed overhead volume variance is the difference between budgeted and applied fixed overhead. This variance is caused solely by producing at a level that differs from that used to compute the predetermined overhead rate. A volume variance occurs because, by using an application rate per unit of activity, FOH is treated as if it were variable cost even though it is not.

Although capacity utilization is controllable to some degree, the volume variance is the one over which managers have the least influence and control, especially in the short run. Thus, a volume variance is also called a

noncontrollable variance

noncontrollable variance. Although they cannot control the capacity level chosen to compute the predetermined FOH rate, managers do have the ability to control capacity utilization. The level of capacity utilization should always be viewed in relation to inventory and sales. Managers must understand that underutilization of capacity is not always undesirable; it is more appropriate for managers to regulate production than to produce goods that will end up in inventory stockpiles. Although it serves to utilize capacity, unneeded inventory production generates substantially more costs for materials, labor, and overhead (including storage and handling costs). The positive impact that such unneeded production will have on the volume variance is insignificant because this variance is of little or no value for managerial control purposes.

The difference between actual FOH and applied FOH is the total fixed overhead variance and equals the amount of underapplied or overapplied fixed overhead.

Using the data from Exhibit 7–6 for mountain bike production into the general variance analysis model gives the following:

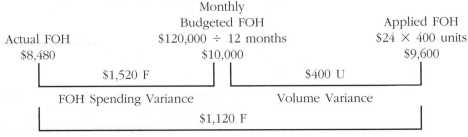

The FOH application rate is $24 per unit because a capacity level of 5,000 units was chosen for the year. Had any other capacity level been chosen, the FOH application rate would have differed, even though the total amount of budgeted monthly fixed overhead ($10,000) would have remained the same. If actual capacity usage differs from that used in determining the application rate used to apply FOH, a volume variance will occur. For example, if the department had chosen 4,800 units as the denominator level of activity to set the predetermined FOH rate, there would be no volume variance for January 2006—expected volume for the month (4,800 ÷ 12, or 400 units) would equal actual production volume.

Management is usually aware, as production occurs, of capacity utilization even if a volume variance is not reported. The volume variance merely translates under- or overutilization into a dollar amount. An unfavorable volume variance indicates lower-than-expected utilization of capacity. If available capacity is commonly being used at a level higher (or lower) than that which was anticipated or is available, managers should recognize that condition, investigate the reasons for it, and (if possible and desirable) initiate appropriate action. Managers can sometimes influence capacity utilization by modifying work schedules, taking measures to relieve any obstructions to or congestion of production activities, and carefully monitoring the movement of resources through the production process. Preferably, such actions should be taken before production rather than after it. Efforts made after production is completed might improve next period's operations but will have no impact on past production.

Alternative Overhead Variance Approaches

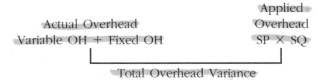

How are OH variances computed when a combined OH rate is used?

If the accounting system does not distinguish between variable and fixed costs, a four-variance approach is unworkable. Use of a combined (variable and fixed) overhead rate requires alternative overhead variance computations. A one-variance approach calculates only a **total overhead variance** as the difference between total actual overhead and total overhead applied to production. The amount of applied overhead is found by multiplying the combined rate by the standard input activity allowed for the actual production achieved. The one-variance approach is diagrammed as follows:

total overhead variance

Actual Overhead		Applied Overhead
Variable OH + Fixed OH		SP × SQ

Total Overhead Variance

Like other total variances, the total overhead variance provides limited information to managers.

Two-variance analysis is performed by inserting a middle column in the one-variance model:

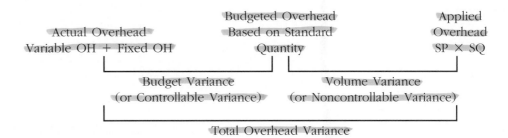

The middle column indicates the expected total overhead cost based on the standard quantity for the period's actual output. This amount represents total budgeted variable overhead at standard hours plus budgeted fixed overhead, which is constant at all activity levels in the relevant range.

budget variance

controllable variance

The **budget variance** equals total actual overhead minus budgeted overhead based on the standard quantity for the period's production. This variance is also referred to as the **controllable variance** because managers are somewhat able to control and influence this amount during the short run. The difference between total applied overhead and budgeted overhead based on the standard quantity is the volume variance; it will be the same as would be computed under the four-variance approach.

A modification of the two-variance approach provides a three-variance analysis. Inserting another column between the left and middle columns of the two-variance model separates the budget variance into spending and efficiency variances. The new column represents the flexible budget based on the actual hours. The three-variance model is as follows:

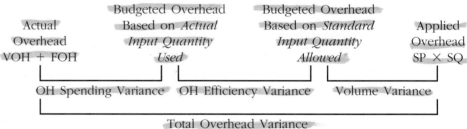

overhead spending variance

The spending variance shown in the three-variance approach is a total **overhead spending variance**. It is computed as total actual overhead minus total budgeted overhead at the actual activity level; this amount equals the sum of the VOH and FOH spending variances of the four-variance approach. The **overhead efficiency variance** is related solely to variable overhead and is the difference between total budgeted overhead at the actual activity level and total budgeted overhead at the standard activity level. This variance measures at standard cost the approximate amount of variable overhead caused by using more or fewer inputs than is standard for the actual production. The sum of the overhead spending and overhead efficiency variances of the three-variance analysis equals the budget variance of the two-variance analysis. The volume variance amount is the same as that calculated using the two-variance or the four-variance approach.

overhead efficiency variance

If variable overhead and fixed overhead are applied using a combined rate, the one-, two-, and three-variance approaches will have the interrelationships shown in Exhibit 7–8. The amounts in the exhibit represent the data provided earlier for

EXHIBIT 7–8

INTERRELATIONSHIPS OF OVERHEAD VARIANCES

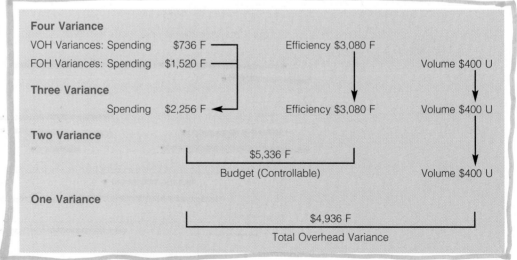

Zoom Bike Company. (The demonstration problem at the end of the chapter shows computations for each of the overhead variance approaches.) Managers should select the method that provides the most useful information and that conforms to the company's accounting system. As more companies begin to recognize the existence of multiple cost drivers for overhead and to use multiple bases for applying overhead to production, computation of the one-, two-, and three-variance approaches will diminish.

STANDARD COST SYSTEM JOURNAL ENTRIES

See Exhibit 7–9 for selected journal entries using Zoom Bike's mountain bike production data for January 2006. The following explanations apply to the numbered journal entries.

1. The debit to Raw Material Inventory is for the standard price of the actual quantity of component WF-05 purchased in January. The credit to Accounts Payable is for the actual price of the actual quantity of component WF-05 purchased. The variance credit reflects the favorable material price variance for that component. Similar entries would be made for purchases of all other components.

EXHIBIT 7–9

SELECTED JOURNAL ENTRIES FOR MOUNTAIN BIKE PRODUCTION, JANUARY 2006

(1)	Raw Material Inventory ($20 × 450)	9,000	
	Material Purchase Price Variance [($20 − $19) × 450]		450
	Accounts Payable		8,550
	To record the acquisition of 450 WF-05s.		
(2)	Work in Process Inventory ($20 × 400 × 1)	8,000	
	Material Quantity Variance {$20 × [(400 × 1) − 413]}	260	
	Raw Material Inventory ($20 × 413)		8,260
	To record issuance of WF-05s to production.		
(3)	Work in Process Inventory [$12 × (400 × 3)]	14,400	
	Labor Rate Variance [($12 − $12) × 1,100]	0	
	Labor Efficiency Variance {$12 × [(400 × 3) − 1,100]}		1,200
	Wages Payable ($12 × 1,100)		13,200
	To record incurrence of direct labor costs by the Painting Department.		
(4)	Variable Manufacturing Overhead	50,784	
	Fixed Manufacturing Overhead	8,480	
	Various accounts		59,264
	To record the incurrence of actual overhead costs for the company.		
(5)	Work in Process Inventory	64,200	
	Variable Manufacturing Overhead ($14 × 400 × $9.75)		54,600
	Fixed Manufacturing Overhead ($24 × 400 × 1)		9,600
	To apply standard overhead cost to the month's production.		
(6)	Variable Manufacturing Overhead ($54,600 − $50,784)	3,816	
	Variable Overhead Spending Variance		736
	Variable Overhead Efficiency Variance		3,080
	To close the variable overhead account and recognize the variable overhead variances for the month.		
(7)	Fixed Manufacturing Overhead	1,120	
	Volume Variance [($24 × 400 × 1) − ($120,000 ÷ 12)]	400	
	Fixed Overhead Spending Variance [$8,480 − ($120,000 ÷ 12)]		1,520
	To close the fixed overhead account and recognize the fixed overhead variances for the month.		

2. The debit to Work in Process Inventory is for the standard price of the standard quantity of the WF-05 component used in January; the Raw Material Inventory credit is for the standard price of the actual quantity of WF-05 components used in production. The debit to the Material Quantity Variance account reflects the overuse of WF-05s, valued at the standard price. Similar entries would be made for issuances of all other components to production.

3. The debit to Work in Process Inventory is for the standard hours allowed in the Painting Department to produce 400 mountain bikes multiplied by the standard wage rate. The Wages Payable credit is for the actual amount of direct labor wages paid to painters during the period. The Labor Efficiency Variance credit reflects the number of fewer than standard hours allowed multiplied by the standard wage rate. Similar entries would be made for wages incurred and standard direct labor wages allowed for all other departments.

4. During January, actual costs incurred for the variable and fixed overhead are debited to the manufacturing overhead accounts. These costs are caused by a variety of transactions including indirect material and labor usage, depreciation, and utility costs. This entry reflects the incurrence of all company overhead for the month.

5. Overhead is applied to production using the predetermined rates multiplied by the standard input allowed. Overhead application is recorded at completion of production or at the end of the period, whichever occurs first. The difference between actual debits and applied credits in each overhead account represents the total variable and fixed overhead variances and is also the underapplied or overapplied overhead for the period. For January, variable overhead and fixed overhead are applied at the respective $14 and $24 predetermined rates.

6. & 7. These entries assume an end-of-month closing of the Variable Manufacturing Overhead and Fixed Manufacturing Overhead accounts. These entries close the manufacturing overhead accounts and recognize the overhead variances. The balances in the accounts are reclassified to the appropriate variance accounts. This entry is provided for illustration only. This process would typically not be performed at month-end but at year-end because an annual period is used to calculate the overhead application rates.

Note that all unfavorable variances have debit balances and favorable variances have credit balances. Unfavorable variances represent excess production costs; favorable variances represent savings in production costs. Standard production costs are shown in inventory accounts (which have debit balances); therefore, excess costs are also debits.

Although standard costs are useful for internal reporting, they can be used in financial statements only if amounts are substantially equivalent to those that would have resulted from using an actual cost system. If standards are realistically achievable and current, this equivalency should exist. Standard costs in financial statements should provide fairly conservative inventory valuations because effects of excess prices and/or inefficient operations are eliminated.

At year-end, adjusting entries are made to eliminate standard cost variances. The entries depend on whether the variances are, in total, insignificant or significant. If the combined impact of the variances is insignificant, unfavorable variances are closed as debits to Cost of Goods Sold; favorable variances are credited to Cost of Goods Sold. Thus, unfavorable variances negatively affect operating income because of the higher-than-expected costs whereas favorable variances positively affect operating income because of the lower-than-expected costs. Even if the year's entire production has not been sold yet, this variance treatment is based on the immateriality of the amounts involved.

In contrast, large variances are prorated at year-end among ending inventories and Cost of Goods Sold so that the balances in those accounts approximate actual costs. Proration is based on the relative size of the account balances. Disposition of significant variances is similar to the disposition of large amounts of underapplied or overapplied overhead shown in Chapter 3.

To illustrate the disposition of significant variances, assume that Nailz Company has a $20,000 unfavorable (debit) year-end Material Purchase Price Variance. The company considers this amount significant. Nailz makes one type of product, which requires a single raw material input. Other relevant year-end account balances for Nailz Company are as follows:

Raw Material Inventory	$ 49,126
Work in Process Inventory	28,072
Finished Goods Inventory	70,180
Cost of Goods Sold	554,422
Total of affected accounts	$701,800

The theoretically correct allocation of the material purchase price variance would use actual material cost in each account at year-end. However, as was mentioned in Chapter 3 with regard to overhead, after the conversion process has begun, cost elements within account balances are commingled and tend to lose their identity. Thus, unless a significant misstatement would result, disposition of the variance can be based on the proportions of each account balance to the total, as follows:

Raw Material Inventory	7%	($49,126 ÷ $701,800)
Work in Process Inventory	4	($28,072 ÷ $701,800)
Finished Goods Inventory	10	($70,180 ÷ $701,800)
Cost of Goods Sold	79	($554,422 ÷ $701,800)
Total	100%	

Applying these percentages to the $20,000 material price variance gives the amounts in the following journal entry to assign to the affected accounts:

Raw Material Inventory ($20,000 × 0.07)	1,400	
Work in Process Inventory ($20,000 × 0.04)	800	
Finished Goods Inventory ($20,000 × 0.10)	2,000	
Cost of Goods Sold ($20,000 × 0.79)	15,800	
Material Purchase Price Variance		20,000

To dispose of the material price variance at year-end.

All variances other than the material price variance occur as part of the conversion process. Because conversion includes raw materials put into production (rather than raw materials purchased), all remaining variances are prorated only to Work in Process Inventory, Finished Goods Inventory, and Cost of Goods Sold. The preceding discussion about standard setting, variance computations, and year-end adjustments indicates that a substantial commitment of time and effort is required to implement and use a standard cost system. Companies are willing to make such a commitment for a variety of reasons.

WHY STANDARD COST SYSTEMS ARE USED

What are the benefits of using a standard cost system?

Standard cost systems are designed to provide information to management in performing its functions. The first reason for its use is that a standard cost system allows management to plan for expected costs to be incurred in performing production or service activities. Second, the system collects information on the actual costs incurred. Third, the system allows management to control operations by comparing expected costs with actual costs and to evaluate performance based on the size and explanations for the period's variances. These basic functions result in six distinct benefits of standard cost systems.

Clerical Efficiency

Less clerical time and effort are required in a standard cost system than in an actual cost system. A standard cost system assigns costs to inventory and Cost of Goods Sold accounts at predetermined amounts per unit regardless of actual conditions. With an actual cost system, actual unit costs must be continuously recalculated because of changing conditions. A standard cost system holds unit costs constant for some period.

Motivation

Standards help communicate management's expectations to workers. When standards are achievable and rewards for attaining them are available, workers are likely to be motivated to strive to meet them. The standards used, however, must require a reasonable amount of effort on the workers' part.

Planning

Planning generally requires estimates about the future. Managers can use current standards to estimate future quantity needs and costs. These estimates help determinate purchasing needs for material, staffing needs for labor, and capacity needs related to overhead that, in turn, will aid in planning for company cash flows. In addition, use of a standard simplifies budget preparation because a standard is, in fact, a budget for one unit of product or service. Standards are also used to provide the cost basis needed to analyze relationships among the organization's costs, sales volume, and profits.

Controlling

variance analysis

Are variances used to establish responsibility for poor results?

The control process begins with the establishment of standards as a basis against which actual costs can be measured and variances can be calculated. **Variance analysis** is the process of categorizing the nature (favorable or unfavorable) of the differences between actual and standard costs and seeking explanations for those differences. A well-designed variance analysis system computes variances as early as possible subject to cost-benefit assessments. The system should help managers determine who or what is responsible for each variance and who is best able to explain it. An early measurement and reporting system allows managers to monitor operations, take corrective action if necessary, evaluate performance, and motivate workers to achieve standard production.

In implementing control, managers must recognize that they have a specific scarce resource: their time. They must distinguish between situations that can be ignored and those that need attention. To do this, managers establish upper and lower tolerance limits of acceptable deviations from standard. If variances are small and within an acceptable range, no managerial action is required. If a variance is significantly different from standard, the manager responsible for the cost is expected to determine the variance cause(s). If the cause(s) can be found and corrective action is possible, such action should be taken so that future operations will adhere more closely to established standards.

Setting upper and lower tolerance limits for deviations (as illustrated in Exhibit 7–10) allows managers to implement the management by exception concept. In the exhibit, the only significant deviation from standard occurred on Day 5, when the actual cost exceeded the upper limit of acceptable performance. An exception report should be generated on this date so that the manager can investigate the underlying variance causes.

EXHIBIT 7–10

ILLUSTRATION OF MANAGEMENT BY EXCEPTION CONCEPT

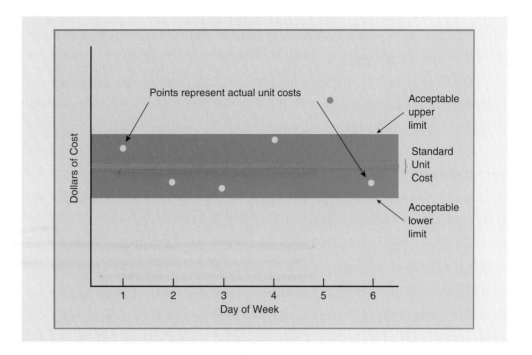

Variances large enough to fall outside the acceptability ranges often indicate problems. However, a variance does not reveal the problem's cause nor the person or group responsible for it. To determine variance causality, managers must investigate significant variances through observation, inspection, and inquiry. The investigation involves people at the operating level as well as accounting personnel. Operations personnel should spot variances as they occur and record the reasons for the variances to the extent that those reasons are discernable. For example, operating personnel could readily detect and report causes such as machine downtime or material spoilage.

One important point about variances must be made: An extremely favorable variance is not necessarily a good variance. Although people often want to equate the "favorable" designation with good, an extremely favorable variance could mean that an error was made when the standard was set or that a related, offsetting unfavorable variance exists. For example, if low-grade material is purchased, a favorable price variance can exist, but additional material might have to be used to overcome defective production. Also, an unfavorable labor efficiency variance might result because more time was required to complete a job as a result of using the inferior material. Another common situation begins with labor rather than material. Using lower-paid workers will result in a favorable rate variance but can cause excessive use of raw material and labor time. Managers must be aware that such relationships exist and that variances cannot be analyzed in isolation.

The time frame for which variance computations are made is being shortened. Monthly variance reporting is still common, but there is movement toward shorter reporting periods. As more companies integrate total quality management and just-in-time production into their operations, variance reporting and analysis will become more frequent.[7] Additionally, standards must be updated as an organization implements changes in production technology.

Decision Making

Standard cost information facilitates decision making. For example, managers can compare a standard cost with a quoted price to determine whether an item should

---

[7] Total quality management is discussed in Chapter 17 and just-in-time production is discussed in Chapter 18.

be manufactured in-house or purchased. Using actual cost information in such a decision could be inappropriate because the actual cost could fluctuate each period. Also, in deciding whether to offer a special price to customers, managers can use standard product cost to determine the lower price limit. Similarly, a company bidding on contracts must have some idea of estimated product costs. Bidding too low and winning the contract could cause substantial operating income (and, possibly, cash flow) problems; bidding too high could be noncompetitive and cause the contract to be awarded to another company.

Performance Evaluation

When they receive variance reports, managers should analyze them for both positive and negative information. Management needs to know when costs were and were not controlled and by which managers. Such information allows management to provide feedback to subordinates, investigate areas of concern, and make performance evaluations about who needs additional supervision, who should be replaced, and who should be promoted. For proper performance evaluations to be made, variance responsibility must be traced to specific managers.[8]

CONSIDERATIONS IN ESTABLISHING STANDARDS

When standards are established, the issues of appropriateness and attainability should be considered. Appropriateness, in relation to a standard, refers to the basis on which the standards are developed and how long they will be expected to last. Attainability refers to management's belief about the degree of difficulty or rigor that should be incurred in achieving the standard.

Appropriateness

Although standards are developed from past and current information, they should reflect relevant future technical and environmental factors. Consideration should be given to factors such as material quality, normal material-ordering quantities, expected employee wage rates, expected degree of plant automation and facility layout, and mix of employee skills. Once standards have been set, they will not remain useful forever. Current operating performance should *not* be compared to out-of-date standards. Standards must evolve to reflect an organization's changing methods and processes. Out-of-date standards produce variances that do not provide logical bases for planning, controlling, decision making, or evaluating performance.

Attainability

Standards provide a target level of performance and can be set at various levels of rigor. This level affects motivation; one reason for using standards is to motivate employees. Similar to the capacity levels discussed in Chapter 3, standards can be classified as expected, practical, and ideal. Depending on the type of standard in effect, the acceptable ranges used to apply the management by exception principle will differ. This difference is especially notable on the unfavorable side.

expected standard   **Expected standards** reflect what is actually expected to occur. Such standards anticipate future waste and inefficiencies and allow for them. As such, expected standards are not of significant value for motivation, control, or performance evaluation. A company using expected standards should set a very small range of ac-

---

[8] Cost control relative to variances is discussed in greater depth in Chapter 16. Performance evaluation is discussed in greater depth in Chapter 20.

ceptable variances because actual costs should conform closely to standards. In addition, expected standards tend to generate favorable variances.

practical standard

Standards that can be reached or slightly exceeded approximately 60 to 70 percent of the time with reasonable effort are called **practical standards**. These standards allow for normal, unavoidable time problems or delays such as machine downtime and worker breaks. Practical standards represent an attainable challenge and traditionally have been thought to be the most effective in motivating workers and determining their performance levels. Both favorable and unfavorable variances result from the use of such moderately rigorous standards.

ideal standard

Standards that provide for no inefficiency of any type are called **ideal** (or theoretical) **standards**; they encompass the highest level of rigor and do not allow for normal operating delays or human limitations such as fatigue, boredom, or misunderstanding. Unless a plant is entirely automated (and then the possibility of human error or power failure still exists), ideal standards are impossible to attain. Applying such standards traditionally resulted in discouraged and resentful workers who ultimately ignored the standards. Variances from ideal standards will always be unfavorable and were commonly not considered useful for constructive cost control or performance evaluation. Such a perspective has begun to change, however.

CHANGES IN STANDARDS USAGE

Many accountants and managers believe that variances are not being used correctly for control and performance evaluation purposes. For example, material standards generally include a factor for waste, and labor standards are commonly set at the expected level of attainment even though this level compensates for downtime and human error. Use of standards that are not aimed at the highest possible (ideal) level of attainment are now being questioned in business environments concerned with world-class operations.

Use of Ideal Standards and Theoretical Capacity

The Japanese influence on Western management philosophy and production techniques has been significant. Both total quality management (TQM) and just-in-time (JIT) production systems evolved as a result of an upsurge in Japanese productivity. These two concepts are inherently based on ideal standards. Rather than including waste and inefficiency in the standards and then accepting additional waste and spoilage deviations under a management by exception principle, both TQM and JIT begin with the premises of zero defects, zero inefficiency, and zero downtime. Under TQM and JIT, ideal standards become expected standards and there is no (or only a minimal allowable) level of acceptable deviation from standards.

When a standard is set at a less-than-ideal level, managers are allowing and encouraging inefficient resource utilization. Ideal standards result in the most useful information for managerial purposes as well as the highest quality products and services at the lowest possible cost. If no inefficiencies are built into or tolerated in the system, deviations from standard should be minimized and overall organizational performance improved. Workers can, at first, resent the introduction of standards set at a "perfection" level, but it is in their and management's best long-run interest to have such standards. Higher standards for efficiency automatically mean lower costs because of the elimination of non-value-added activities such as waste, idle time, and rework.

Implementation of ideal standards requires substantial organization communication and teamwork. First, determine current problems and causes of those problems. For example, where and why are variances occurring? Second, use the answers to the previous questions to determine what needs to change. For example, if variances are caused by the equipment, facility, or workers, management must be ready to invest in plant and equipment items, equipment rearrangements, or worker training so that the standards are amenable to the operations. Training is essential if workers are to perform at the high levels of efficiency demanded by theoretical standards. If variances are related to external sources (such as poor-quality material), management must be willing to change suppliers and/or pay higher prices for higher grade input. Third, setting standards at the ideal level in part assigns the responsibility for quality to workers; thus, management must also give those workers the authority to react to problems. Fourth, requiring people to work at their maximum potential demands recognition, which means that management must provide rewards for achievement.

In addition to ideal standards, world-class companies can also use theoretical capacity in setting fixed overhead rates. If a company were totally automated or if people consistently worked at their fullest potential, such a capacity measure would provide the lowest and most appropriate overhead application rate. Any underapplied overhead resulting from a difference between theoretical and actual capacity would indicate capacity that should be either used or eliminated; it could also indicate human capabilities that have not been fully developed. Also, any end-of-period underapplied overhead would be viewed as a period cost and closed to a loss account (such as Loss from Inefficient Operations) on the income statement. Showing the underapplied overhead in this manner should attract managerial attention to the inefficient and ineffective use of resources.

Whether setting standards at the ideal level and using theoretical capacity to determine fixed overhead rates will become norms of non-Japanese companies cannot be determined at this time. However, standards will slowly move from the expected or practical and closer to the ideal if only because of competition. A competitor that produces goods based on the highest possible standards and the highest level of capacity is more likely to have lower costs and higher quality—which, in turn, will often result in lower prices.

Adjusting Standards

Standards are generally set after comprehensive investigation of prices and quantities for the various cost elements. Traditionally, these standards were retained for at least one year and, sometimes, for multiple years.[9] Currently, the business environment (which includes suppliers, technology, competition, product design, and manufacturing methods) changes so rapidly that a standard can no longer be useful for management control purposes for an entire year.

Company management must consider whether to modify standards during a year in which significant cost or quantity changes occur. Ignoring the changes is a simplistic approach that allows the same type of cost to be recorded at the same amount all year. Thus, for example, any material purchased during the year would be recorded at the same standard cost regardless of when it was purchased. Although making recordkeeping easy, this approach eliminates any opportunity to adequately control costs or evaluate performance. Additionally, such an approach could create large differentials between standard and actual costs, making standard costs unacceptable for external reporting.

Changing the standards to reflect price or quantity changes would make some aspects of management control and performance evaluation more effective and others more difficult. For instance, budgets prepared using the original standards

---

[9] According to a 1999 Institute of Management Accountants' survey, 54 percent of companies update their standards annually and another 20 percent update them on an as-needed basis. See Kip R. Krumwiede, "Results of 1999 Cost Management Survey: The Use of Standard Costing and Other Costing Practices," *Cost Management Update* (December 1999/January 2000), pp. 1–4.

would need to be adjusted before appropriate actual comparisons could be made against them. Changing standards also creates a problem for recordkeeping and inventory valuation. Should products be valued at the standard cost in effect when they were produced or the standard cost in effect when the financial statements are prepared? Although production-point standards would be more closely related to actual costs, their use might undermine many of the benefits discussed earlier in the chapter.

If possible, management should consider combining these two choices in the accounting system. The original standards can be considered "frozen" for budget purposes and a revised budget can be prepared using the new current standards. Differences between these two budgets would reflect variances related to business environment cost changes. These variances could be designated as uncontrollable (such as those related to changes in the market price of raw material) or internally initiated (such as changes in standard labor time resulting from employee training or equipment rearrangement). Comparing the budget based on current standards with actual costs would provide variances that more adequately reflect internally controllable causes, such as excess material and/or labor time usage caused by inferior material purchases.

Material Price Variance Based on Purchases Rather Than on Usage

The material price variance computation has traditionally been based on purchases rather than on usage to calculate the variance as quickly as possible relative to the cost incurrence. Although calculating the material price variance at the purchase point allows managers to see the impact of buying decisions more rapidly, such information might not be most relevant in a just-in-time environment. Buying material that is not needed for current production requires that the material be stored and moved, both of which are non-value-added activities. The trade-off in price savings should be measured against the additional costs to determine the cost-benefit relationship of such a purchase.

Additionally, computing a material price variance on purchases rather than on usage can reduce the probability of recognizing a relationship between a favorable material price variance and an unfavorable material quantity variance. If a favorable price variance resulted from buying low-grade material, effects of that purchase will not be known until the material is actually used.

Decline in Direct Labor

As the proportion of product cost related to direct labor declines, the necessity for direct labor variance computations is minimized. Direct labor can be combined with overhead to become viewed as the "conversion cost" of a product. Alternatively, the increase in automation often relegates labor to an indirect category because workers become machine overseers rather than product producers.

CONVERSION COST AS AN ELEMENT IN STANDARD COSTING

LO.5
HOW WILL STANDARD COSTING BE AFFECTED IF A SINGLE CONVERSION ELEMENT IS USED RATHER THAN THE TRADITIONAL LABOR AND OVERHEAD ELEMENTS?

As discussed in Chapter 2, conversion cost consists of direct labor and manufacturing overhead. The traditional view of separating product cost into three categories (direct material, direct labor, and overhead) is appropriate in a labor-intensive production setting. However, in more highly automated factories, direct labor cost

Advanced automation in factories translates into lower direct labor cost as a percentage of total product cost.

GETTY IMAGES

generally represents only a small part of total product cost. In such circumstances, one worker might oversee a large number of machines and deal more with troubleshooting machine malfunctions than with converting raw material into finished products. These new conditions mean that workers are probably considered indirect rather than direct labor and, therefore, their wages should be considered overhead.

Many highly automated companies have adapted their standard cost systems to provide for only two elements of product cost, direct material and conversion. In these situations, conversion costs are likely to be separated into variable and fixed components. Conversion costs can also be separated into direct and indirect categories based on the ability to trace such costs to a machine rather than to a product. Overhead can be applied under an activity-based costing methodology using a variety of cost drivers such as number of machine hours, material cost, number of production runs, number of machine setups, or throughput time.

Variance analysis for conversion cost in automated plants normally focuses on the following: (1) spending variances for overhead costs, (2) efficiency variances for machinery and production costs rather than labor costs, and (3) a volume variance for production. These types of analyses are similar to the traditional three-variance overhead approach. In an automated system, managers are likely to be able to better control not only the spending and efficiency variances but also the volume variance. The idea of planned output is essential in a just-in-time system. Variance analysis under a conversion cost approach is illustrated in Exhibit 7–11. Regardless of how variances are computed, managers must analyze those variances and use them for cost control purposes to the extent that such control can be exercised.

Assume that Zoom Bike makes a bike frame in a new facility that is fully automated; all labor required for this product is considered indirect. For simplicity, it is assumed that all overhead is applied on the basis of budgeted machine hours. Necessary 2006 production and cost information for bike frames follows:

Expected production	12,000 units
Actual production	13,000 units
Actual machine time	25,000 MHs
Budgeted machine time (at 2 hours per unit)	24,000 MHs
Budgeted variable conversion cost	$96,000
Budgeted fixed conversion cost	$192,000
Actual variable conversion cost	$97,500
Actual fixed conversion cost	$201,000

Variable conversion rate: $96,000 ÷ 24,000 = $4 per MH
Fixed conversion rate: $192,000 ÷ 24,000 = $8 per MH
Standard machine hours allowed: 13,000 units × 2 hours per unit = 26,000 MHs

The variance computations for conversion costs follow.

EXHIBIT 7–11

VARIANCES UNDER CONVERSION APPROACH

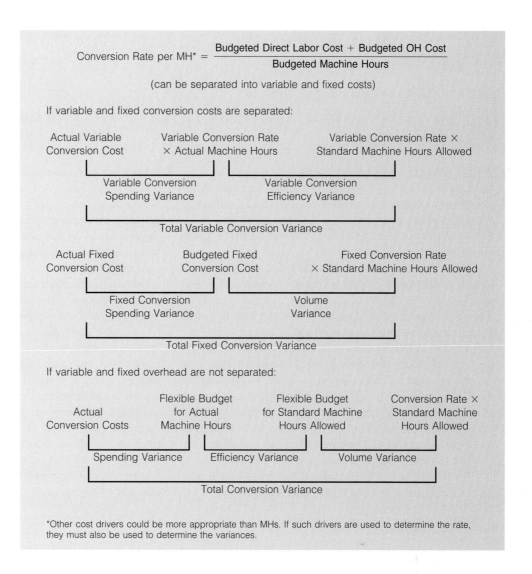

$$\text{Conversion Rate per MH*} = \frac{\text{Budgeted Direct Labor Cost} + \text{Budgeted OH Cost}}{\text{Budgeted Machine Hours}}$$

(can be separated into variable and fixed costs)

If variable and fixed conversion costs are separated:

Actual Variable Conversion Cost	Variable Conversion Rate × Actual Machine Hours	Variable Conversion Rate × Standard Machine Hours Allowed

Variable Conversion Spending Variance   Variable Conversion Efficiency Variance

Total Variable Conversion Variance

Actual Fixed Conversion Cost	Budgeted Fixed Conversion Cost	Fixed Conversion Rate × Standard Machine Hours Allowed

Fixed Conversion Spending Variance   Volume Variance

Total Fixed Conversion Variance

If variable and fixed overhead are not separated:

Actual Conversion Costs	Flexible Budget for Actual Machine Hours	Flexible Budget for Standard Machine Hours Allowed	Conversion Rate × Standard Machine Hours Allowed

Spending Variance   Efficiency Variance   Volume Variance

Total Conversion Variance

*Other cost drivers could be more appropriate than MHs. If such drivers are used to determine the rate, they must also be used to determine the variances.

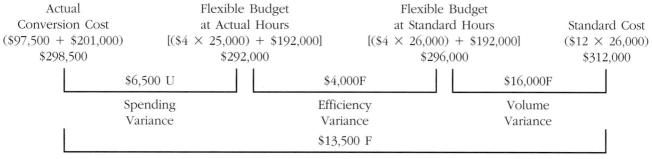

Actual Conversion Cost ($97,500 + $201,000) $298,500	Flexible Budget at Actual Hours [($4 × 25,000) + $192,000] $292,000	Flexible Budget at Standard Hours [($4 × 26,000) + $192,000] $296,000	Standard Cost ($12 × 26,000) $312,000

$6,500 U $4,000F $16,000F

Spending Variance   Efficiency Variance   Volume Variance

$13,500 F

Total Conversion Cost Variance

Revisiting
Specialized Bicycle Components, Inc.

Bicycle production has become extremely competitive. The specialty bike industry focuses on people who really *ride* (rather than just pedal around!); thus, high quality, durability, value for price, and innovation are extremely important. Equally important is the ability to achieve a reasonable profit margin from sales.

Market price represents a target measure for all competitors in setting the allowable cost to produce a bike. For example, if Specialized Bicycle Components, Inc., desires a gross margin of 30 percent for a mountain bike priced at $1,200, the target production cost should not exceed $840. This amount includes the costs for direct materials, direct labor, and overhead. The company would develop standard or benchmark costs for the various cost elements and measure actual production costs against those standards as a means of evaluating performance. In some cases, such as the bicycle wheel, Specialized could realize that the "old" standard is no longer acceptable and use product design and innovation to make the wheel lighter as well as less expensive.

From 1988 to 1997, Specialized lost more than 5 percent of its market share. During this time, the company faced many specialty competitors such as Trek, Gary Fisher, Giant, and Raleigh. Increased competition resulted in decreased selling prices, which put pressure on all bike manufacturers, including Specialized, to focus on producing bikes at a lower target cost. To do this effectively means that standard costs had to be developed and variances from them should be favorable rather than unfavorable. Additionally, to meet the lower target production cost, many companies are leaving the United States and going offshore to countries that have lower wage rates and often higher production efficiencies.

In 2004, raw material costs in the bicycle industry escalated tremendously and many manufacturers became concerned with their cost standards. Managers could find that they must adjust material cost standards to reflect current market prices rather than consistently face unfavorable price variances. Cost control in the bike manufacturing industry has been and continues to be an ongoing issue. In its plans to grow market share, Specialized must not lose sight of the need to meet its cost standards while continuing to produce the high-quality bicycles on which the company's reputation was built.

Source: Industry information based on e-mail response from Fred Clements from National Bike Dealers Association on May 3, 2004; Specialized information from *http://www.specialized.com* on May 3, 2004.

Appendix

Mix and Yield Variances

**LO.6
HOW DO MULTIPLE MATERIAL
AND LABOR CATEGORIES
AFFECT VARIANCES?**

Most companies combine many materials and various classes of direct labor to produce goods. In such settings, the material and labor variance computations presented in the chapter are insufficient.

When a product is made from more than one material, a goal is to combine the materials in a way that produces the desired quality in the most cost-beneficial manner. Sometimes materials can be substituted for one another without affecting product quality. In other instances, only one specific material or type of material can be used. For example, a furniture manufacturer might use either oak or maple to build a couch frame and still have the same basic quality. A perfume manufacturer, however, could be able to use only a specific fragrance oil to achieve a desired scent.

Labor, like materials, can be combined in many different ways to make the same product. Some combinations are less expensive or more efficient than others. As with materials, some amount of interchangeability among labor categories is assumed. However, all potential combinations could not be viable; for example, unskilled workers could not be substituted for skilled craftspeople to cut Baccarat or Waterford crystal. The goal is to find the most effective and efficient selection of workers to perform specific tasks.

mix

Each possible combination of materials or labor is called a **mix**. Experience, judgment, and experimentation are used to set the standards for the materials mix and labor mix. Mix standards are used to calculate mix and yield variances for materials and labor. An underlying assumption in product mix situations is that the potential for substitution among the material and labor components exists. If this assumption is invalid, changing the mix cannot improve the yield and could even prove wasteful. In addition to mix and yield variances, price and rate variances are still computed for materials and labor.

The Fish Place is used to illustrate the computation of price/rate, mix, and yield variances. The company recently began packaging a frozen 1-pound Gumbo-combo that contains processed crab, shrimp, and oysters. To some extent, one ingredient can be substituted for the other. In addition, it is assumed that the company uses two direct labor categories (A and B). There is a labor rate differential between these two categories. Exhibit 7–12 provides standard and actual information for the company for December 2006.

Material Price, Mix, and Yield Variances

material mix variance

material yield variance

A material price variance shows the dollar effect of paying prices that differ from the raw material standard. The **material mix variance** measures the effect of substituting a nonstandard mix of materials during the production process. The **material yield variance** is the difference between the actual total quantity of input and the standard total quantity allowed based on output; this difference reflects standard mix and standard prices. Summing the material mix and yield variances provides a material quantity variance similar to the one discussed in the chapter; the difference is that the sum of the mix and yield variances is attributable to multiple ingredients rather than to a single one. A company can have a mix variance without experiencing a yield variance.

yield

The standard materials mix is 30 percent crab, 45 percent shrimp, and 25 percent oysters. Process **yield** is the output quantity that results from a specified input. For Gumbo-combo, the yield from 60 pounds of crab, 90 pounds of shrimp, and 50 pounds of oysters is one lot of 200 one-pound packages. Computations for the price, mix, and yield variances are given in a format similar to that used in the chapter:

EXHIBIT 7–12

STANDARD AND ACTUAL INFORMATION FOR DECEMBER 2006

Material standards for one lot (200 1-pound packages):

Crab	60 pounds at $7.20 per pound	$ 432
Shrimp	90 pounds at $4.50 per pound	405
Oysters	50 pounds at $5.00 per pound	250
Total	200 pounds	$1,087

Labor standards for one lot (200 1-pound packages):

Category A workers	20 hours at $10.50 per hour	$210
Category B workers	10 hours at $14.30 per hour	143
Total	30 hours	$353

Actual production and cost data for December:

Production   40 lots

Material:

Crab	Purchased and used	2,285.7 pounds at $7.50 per pound
Shrimp	Purchased and used	3,649.1 pounds at $4.40 per pound
Oysters	Purchased and used	2,085.2 pounds at $4.95 per pound
Total		8,020.0 pounds

Labor:

Category A workers	903 hours at $10.50 per hour	$9,481.50
Category B workers	387 hours at $14.35 per hour	$5,553.45
Total	1,290 hours	

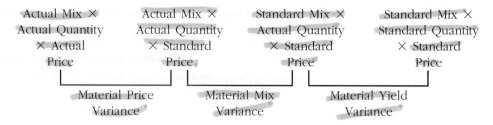

Assume that The Fish Place used 8,020 total pounds of ingredients to make 40 lots of Gumbo-combo. The standard quantity necessary to produce this quantity of Gumbo-combo is 8,000 total pounds of ingredients. The actual mix of crab, shrimp, and oysters was 28.5, 45.5, and 26.0 percent, respectively:

Crab   (2,285.7 pounds of 8,020) = 28.5%
Shrimp (3,649.1 pounds of 8,020) = 45.5%
Oysters (2,085.2 pounds of 8,020) = 26.0%

Computations necessary for the material variances are shown in Exhibit 7–13. These amounts are then used to compute the variances.

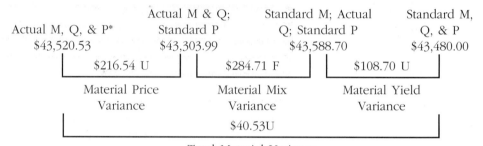

*Note: M = mix, Q = quantity, and P = price.

These computations show a single price variance being calculated for materials. To be more useful to management, separate price variances can be calculated for each material used. For example, the material price variance for crab is $685.71 U ($17,142.75 − $16,457.04), for shrimp is $364.91 F ($16,056.04 − $16,420.95), and for oysters is $104.26 F ($10,321.74 − $10,426.00). The savings on shrimp and

EXHIBIT 7–13

COMPUTATIONS FOR MATERIAL MIX AND YIELD VARIANCES

(1) Total actual data (mix, quantity, and prices):		
Crab—2,285.7 pounds at $7.50	$17,142.75	
Shrimp—3,649.1 pounds at $4.40	16,056.04	
Oysters—2,085.2 pounds at $4.95	10,321.74	$43,520.53
(2) Actual mix and quantity; standard prices:		
Crab—2,285.7 pounds at $7.20	$16,457.04	
Shrimp—3,649.1 pounds at $4.50	16,420.95	
Oysters—2,085.2 pounds at $5.00	10,426.00	$43,303.99
(3) Standard mix; actual quantity; standard prices:		
Crab—30% × 8,020 pounds × $7.20	$17,323.20	
Shrimp—45% × 8,020 pounds × $4.50	16,240.50	
Oysters—25% × 8,020 pounds × $5.00	10,025.00	$43,588.70
(4) Total standard data (mix, quantity, and prices):		
Crab—30% × 8,000 pounds × $7.20	$17,280.00	
Shrimp—45% × 8,000 pounds × $4.50	16,200.00	
Oysters—25% × 8,000 pounds × $5.00	10,000.00	$43,480.00

oysters was less than the added cost for crab, so the total price variance was unfavorable. Also, less than the standard proportion of the most expensive ingredient (crab) was used, so it is reasonable that there would be a favorable mix variance. The company also experienced an unfavorable yield because total pounds of material allowed for output (8,000) was less than actual total pounds of material used (8,020).

Labor Rate, Mix, and Yield Variances

The two labor categories used by The Fish Place are unskilled (A) and skilled (B). When labor standards are prepared, the labor categories needed to perform various tasks and the amount of time each task is expected to take are established. During production, variances will occur if workers are not paid the standard rate, do not work in the standard mix on tasks, or do not perform those tasks in the standard time.

labor mix variance

labor yield variance

The labor rate variance is a measure of the cost of paying workers at other than standard rates. The **labor mix variance** is the financial effect associated with changing the proportionate amount of higher or lower paid workers in production. The **labor yield variance** reflects the monetary impact of using a higher or lower number of hours than the standard allowed. The sum of the labor mix and yield variances equals the labor efficiency variance. The diagram for computing labor rate, mix, and yield variances is as follows:

Actual Mix ×	Actual Mix ×	Standard Mix ×	Standard Mix ×
Actual Hours ×	Actual Hours ×	Actual Hours ×	Standard Hours ×
Actual Rate	Standard Rate	Standard Rate	Standard Rate

Labor Rate Variance Labor Mix Variance Labor Yield Variance

Standard rates are used to make both the mix and yield computations. For Gumbo-combo, the standard mix of A and B labor shown in Exhibit 7–12 is two-thirds and one-third (20 and 10 hours), respectively. The actual mix is 70 percent (903 of 1,290 total hours) A and 30 percent (387 of 1,290) B. See Exhibit 7–14 for the labor computations for Gumbo-combo production. Because 30 hours is the standard to produce 1 lot of Gumbo-combo, the standard number of hours allowed for production of 40 lots is 1,200 (800 hours of A and 400 hours of B).

EXHIBIT 7–14

COMPUTATIONS FOR LABOR MIX AND YIELD VARIANCES

(1) Total actual data (mix, hours, and rates):		
Category A—903 hours at $10.50	$9,481.50	
Category B—387 hours at $14.35	5,553.45	$15,034.95
(2) Actual mix and hours; standard rates:		
Category A—903 hours at $10.50	$9,481.50	
Category B—387 hours at $14.30	5,534.10	$15,015.60
(3) Standard mix; actual hours; standard rates:		
Category A—2/3 × 1,290 × $10.50	$9,030.00	
Category B—1/3 × 1,290 × $14.30	6,149.00	$15,179.00
(4) Total standard data (mix, hours, and rates):		
Category A—2/3 × 1,200 × $10.50	$8,400.00	
Category B—1/3 × 1,200 × $14.30	5,720.00	$14,120.00

Using the amounts from Exhibit 7–14, the labor variances for Gumbo-combo production in December are calculated in diagram form:

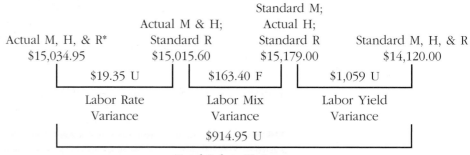

*Note: M = mix, H = hours, and R = rate.

As with material price variances, separate rate variances can be calculated for each class of labor. Because category A does not have a labor rate variance, the total rate variance for December relates solely to category B.

The Fish Place saved $163.40 by using the actual mix of labor rather than the standard. A higher proportion of the less expensive class of labor (category A) than specified in the standard mix was used. One result of substituting a higher proportion of lower paid workers seems to be that an unfavorable yield occurred because total actual hours (1,290) were higher than standard (1,200).

Because there are trade-offs in mix and yield when component qualities and quantities are changed, management should observe the integrated nature of price, mix, and yield. The effects of changes of one element on the other two need to be considered for managing cost efficiency and output quality. If mix and yield can be increased by substituting less expensive resources while maintaining quality, managers and product engineers should change the standards and the proportions of components. If costs are reduced but quality is maintained, selling prices could also be reduced to gain a larger market share.

Comprehensive Review Module

Chapter Summary

1. Setting standards for

   - material requires that management identify the

     ➢ types of material inputs needed to make the product or perform the service.

     ➢ quality of material inputs needed to make the product or perform the service.

     ➢ quantity of material inputs needed to make the product or perform the service.

     ➢ prices of the material inputs, given normal purchase quantities.

   - labor requires that management identify the

     ➢ types of labor tasks needed to make the product or perform the service.

     ➢ times of labor tasks needed to make the product or perform the service.

     ➢ skill levels of personnel needed to make the product or perform the service.

     ➢ wage rates or salary levels for the level of labor skills needed.

   - overhead requires that management identify the

     ➢ various variable and fixed overhead costs incurred in the organization.

     ➢ estimated level of activity to be used in computing the predetermined overhead rate(s).

     ➢ estimated variable and fixed overhead costs at the estimated level of activity.

     ➢ predetermined overhead rate(s) used to apply overhead to production or service performance.

2. The documents used in a standard cost system include the

   - bill of materials, which contains all quantity and quality raw material specifications to make one unit (or batch) of output.

   - operations flow document, which contains all labor operations necessary to make one unit (or batch) of output or perform a particular service.

   - standard cost card, which summarizes the standard quantities and costs needed to complete one unit of product or perform a particular service.

3. A variance is the difference between an actual and a standard cost. Standard costs are recorded in the Work in Process Inventory account, and variances are recorded as either debit (unfavorable) or credit (favorable) differences between the standard cost and the actual cost incurred. In general, variances are calculated as follows for

   - direct material:

     ➢ Material Price Variance = (Actual Price × Actual Quantity) − (Standard Price × Actual Quantity)

     ➢ Material Quantity Variance = (Standard Price × Actual Quantity) − (Standard Price × Standard Quantity)

     ➢ Total Material Variance = Material Price Variance + Material Quantity Variance

   - direct labor

     ➢ Labor Rate Variance = (Actual Price × Actual Quantity) − (Standard Price × Actual Quantity)

     ➢ Labor Efficiency Variance = (Standard Price × Actual Quantity) − (Standard Price × Standard Quantity)

     ➢ Total Labor Variance = Labor Rate Variance + Labor Efficiency Variance

   - variable overhead

     ➢ VOH Spending Variance = Actual VOH − (Standard Price × Actual Quantity)

     ➢ VOH Efficiency Variance = (Standard Price × Actual Quantity) − Applied VOH

     ➢ Total VOH Variance = VOH Spending Variance + VOH Efficiency Variance

   - fixed overhead

     ➢ FOH Spending Variance = Actual FOH − Budgeted FOH

     ➢ Volume Variance = Budgeted FOH − Applied FOH

➤ Total FOH Variance = FOH Spending Variance + Volume Variance

4. A standard cost system is used to

• provide clerical efficiency

• assist management in its planning, controlling, decision making, and performance evaluation functions

• motivate employees when the standards are

➤ set at a level to encourage high-quality production and promote cost control.

➤ seen as expected performance goals.

➤ updated periodically so that they reflect actual economic conditions.

5. In highly automated companies, the standard cost system can use

• only two elements of production cost, direct material and conversion.

• ideal standards rather than expected or practical standards.

• fixed overhead rates based on theoretical capacity rather than expected, normal, or practical capacity.

Solution Strategies

ACTUAL COSTS (AC)

1. Direct material:

$$\text{Actual Price (AP)} \times \text{Actual Quantity Purchased or Used (AQ)}$$
$$\text{DM: AP} \times \text{AQ} = \text{AC}$$

2. Direct labor:

$$\text{Actual Price (Rate)} \times \text{Actual Quantity of Hours Worked}$$
$$\text{DL: AP} \times \text{AQ} = \text{AC}$$

STANDARD COSTS (SC)

1. Direct material:

$$\text{Standard Price} \times \text{Standard Quantity Allowed}$$
$$\text{DM: SP} \times \text{SQ} = \text{SC}$$

2. Direct labor:

$$\text{Standard Price (Rate)} \times \text{Standard Quantity of Hours Allowed}$$
$$\text{DL: SP} \times \text{SQ} = \text{SC}$$

GENERAL VARIANCE FORMAT

$AP \times AQ$	$SP \times AQ$	$SP \times SQ$

Material Price Variance	Material Quantity Variance
Labor Rate Variance	Labor Efficiency Variance
VOH Spending Variance	VOH Efficiency Variance

VARIANCES IN FORMULA FORMAT

The following abbreviations are used:

AFOH = actual fixed overhead
AM = actual mix
AP = actual price or rate
AQ = actual quantity or hours
AVOH = actual variable overhead
BFOH = budgeted fixed overhead (remains at constant amount regardless of activity level as long as within the relevant range)
SM = standard mix
SP = standard price
SQ = standard quantity allowed
TAOH = total actual overhead

$$\text{Material price variance} = (AP \times AQ) - (SP \times AQ)$$
$$\text{Material quantity variance} = (SP \times AQ) - (SP \times SQ)$$
$$\text{Labor rate variance} = (AP \times AQ) - (SP \times AQ)$$
$$\text{Labor efficiency variance} = (SP \times AQ) - (SP \times SQ)$$

Four-variance approach:

Variable OH spending variance = $AVOH - (VOH \text{ rate} \times AQ)$
Variable OH efficiency variance = $(VOH \text{ rate} \times AQ) - (VOH \text{ rate} \times SQ)$
Fixed OH spending variance = $AFOH - BFOH$
Volume variance = $BFOH - (FOH \text{ rate} \times SQ)$

Three-variance approach:

Spending variance = $TAOH - [(VOH \text{ rate} \times AQ) + BFOH]$
Efficiency variance = $[(VOH \text{ rate} \times AQ) + BFOH)] - [(VOH \text{ rate} \times SQ) + BFOH]$
Volume variance = $[(VOH \text{ rate} \times SQ) + BFOH] - [(VOH \text{ rate} \times SQ) +$
$(FOH \text{ rate} \times SQ)]$ (This is equal to the volume variance of the four-variance approach.)

Two-variance approach:

Budget variance = $TAOH - [(VOH \text{ rate} \times SQ) + BFOH]$
Volume variance = $[(VOH \text{ rate} \times SQ) + BFOH] - [(VOH \text{ rate} \times SQ) +$
$(FOH \text{ rate} \times SQ)]$ (This is equal to the volume variance of the four-variance approach.)

One-variance approach:

$$\text{Total OH variance} = TAOH - (\text{Combined OH rate} \times SQ)$$

MULTIPLE MATERIAL

Material price variance = $(AM \times AQ \times AP) - (AM \times AQ \times SP)$
Material mix variance = $(AM \times AQ \times SP) - (SM \times AQ \times SP)$
Material yield variance = $(SM \times AQ \times SP) - (SM \times SQ \times SP)$

MULTIPLE LABOR CATEGORIES

Labor rate variance = $(AM \times AQ \times AP) - (AM \times AQ \times SP)$
Labor mix variance = $(AM \times AQ \times SP) - (SM \times AQ \times SP)$
Labor yield variance = $(SM \times AQ \times SP) - (SM \times SQ \times SP)$

VARIANCES IN DIAGRAM FORMAT

Direct Material

Point of Purchase

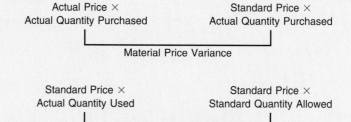

Actual Price ×	Standard Price ×
Actual Quantity Purchased	Actual Quantity Purchased

Material Price Variance

Standard Price ×	Standard Price ×
Actual Quantity Used	Standard Quantity Allowed

Material Quantity Variance

Point of Usage

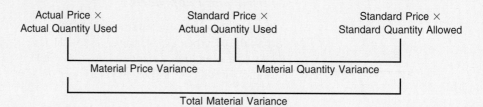

Actual Price ×	Standard Price ×	Standard Price ×
Actual Quantity Used	Actual Quantity Used	Standard Quantity Allowed

Material Price Variance   Material Quantity Variance

Total Material Variance

Direct Labor

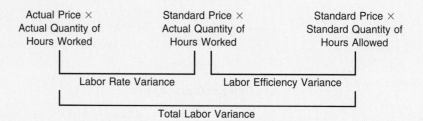

Actual Price ×	Standard Price ×	Standard Price ×
Actual Quantity of	Actual Quantity of	Standard Quantity of
Hours Worked	Hours Worked	Hours Allowed

Labor Rate Variance   Labor Efficiency Variance

Total Labor Variance

Overhead four-variance approach:

Variable Overhead

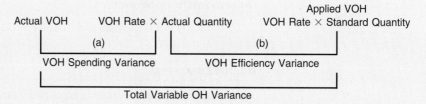

		Applied VOH
Actual VOH	VOH Rate × Actual Quantity	VOH Rate × Standard Quantity
	(a)	(b)

VOH Spending Variance   VOH Efficiency Variance

Total Variable OH Variance

Fixed Overhead

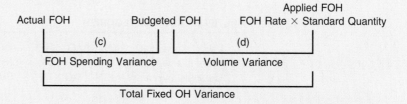

		Applied FOH
Actual FOH	Budgeted FOH	FOH Rate × Standard Quantity
	(c)	(d)

FOH Spending Variance   Volume Variance

Total Fixed OH Variance

Overhead one-, two-, and three-variance approaches:

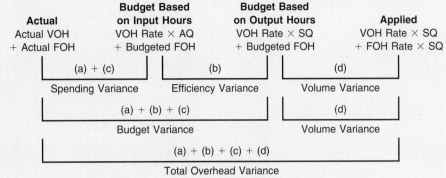

Mix and Yield Variances

MULTIPLE MATERIALS

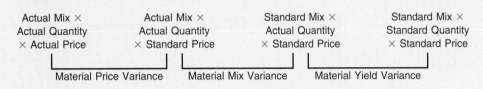

MULTIPLE LABOR CATEGORIES

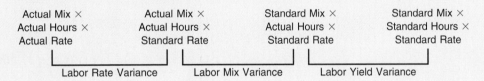

Demonstration Problem

Sprewell Containers makes 300-gallon plastic water tanks for a variety of commercial uses. The standard per unit material, labor, and overhead costs are as follows:

Direct material: 80 pounds @ $2	$160
Direct labor: 1.25 hours @ $16 per hour	20
Variable overhead: 30 minutes of machine time @ $50 per hour	25
Fixed overhead: 30 minutes of machine time @ $40 per hour	20

The overhead application rates were developed using a practical capacity of 6,000 units per year. Production is assumed to occur evenly throughout the year.

During May 2006, the company produced 525 tanks. Actual data for May 2006 are as follows:

Direct material purchased: 46,000 pounds @ $1.92 per pound
Direct material used: 43,050 pounds (all from May's purchases)
Total labor cost: $10,988.25 for 682.5 hours
Variable overhead incurred: $13,770 for 270 hours of machine time
Fixed overhead incurred: $10,600 for 270 hours of machine time

Required:
a. Calculate the following:
    1. Material price variance based on purchases
    2. Material quantity variance

3. Labor rate variance
4. Labor efficiency variance
5. Variable overhead spending and efficiency variances
6. Fixed overhead spending and volume variances
7. Overhead variances using a three-variance approach
8. Overhead variances using a two-variance approach
9. Overhead variance using a one-variance approach
b. Record the entries to recognize the variances

Solution to Demonstration Problem

a.   1.

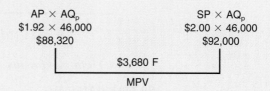

AP × AQ$_p$
$1.92 × 46,000
$88,320

SP × AQ$_p$
$2.00 × 46,000
$92,000

$3,680 F
MPV

2.   SQ = 525 × 80 pounds = 42,000 pounds

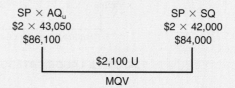

SP × AQ$_u$
$2 × 43,050
$86,100

SP × SQ
$2 × 42,000
$84,000

$2,100 U
MQV

3. & 4.   AR = $10,988.25 ÷ 682.5 hours = $16.10 per hour
          SQ = 525 × 1.25 hours = 656.25 hours

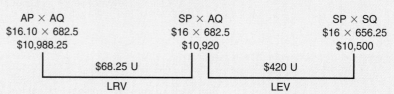

AP × AQ
$16.10 × 682.5
$10,988.25

SP × AQ
$16 × 682.5
$10,920

SP × SQ
$16 × 656.25
$10,500

$68.25 U
LRV

$420 U
LEV

5.   SQ = 525 × 0.5 = 262.5 hours

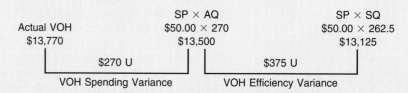

Actual VOH
$13,770

SP × AQ
$50.00 × 270
$13,500

SP × SQ
$50.00 × 262.5
$13,125

$270 U
VOH Spending Variance

$375 U
VOH Efficiency Variance

6.   BFOH, annually = 6,000 × $20 = $120,000
     BFOH, monthly = $120,000 ÷ 12 months = $10,000

     SQ = 262.5 hours [from part (5)].

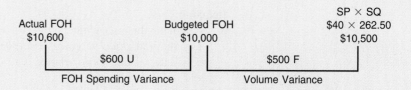

Actual FOH
$10,600

Budgeted FOH
$10,000

SP × SQ
$40 × 262.50
$10,500

$600 U
FOH Spending Variance

$500 F
Volume Variance

7., 8., & 9.   Combined overhead application rate = $50 + $40 = $90 per MH; SQ = 262.5 hours [from part (5)].

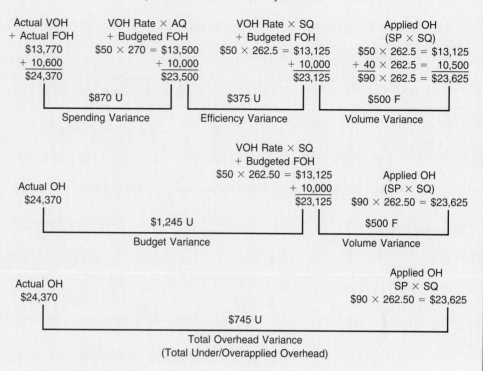

b. All amounts are taken from the computations shown in part (a).

Raw Material Inventory	92,000.00	
Material Price Variance		3,680.00
Accounts Payable		88,320.00
To record the acquisition of material.		
Work in Process Inventory	84,000.00	
Material Quantity Variance	2,100.00	
Raw Material Inventory		86,100.00
To record distribution of material to production.		
Work in Process Inventory	10,500.00	
Labor Rate Variance	68.25	
Labor Efficiency Variance	420.00	
Wages Payable		10,988.25
To record incurrence of direct labor costs in all departments.		
Variable Overhead Efficiency Variance	375.00	
Variable Overhead Spending Variance	270.00	
Variable Manufacturing Overhead		645.00
To close the variable overhead account.		
Fixed Overhead Spending Variance	600.00	
Fixed Manufacturing Overhead		100.00
Volume Variance		500.00
To close the fixed overhead account.		

Key Terms

bill of material *(p. 249)*
budget variance *(p. 262)*
controllable variance *(p. 262)*
expected standard *(p. 268)*
fixed overhead spending variance
     (p. 260)
ideal standard *(p. 269)*
labor efficiency variance *(p. 257)*
labor mix variance *(p. 277)*
labor rate variance *(p. 257)*
labor yield variance *(p. 277)*
material mix variance *(p. 275)*

material price variance *(p. 256)*
material quantity variance *(p. 256)*
material yield variance *(p. 275)*
mix *(p. 275)*
noncontrollable variance *(p. 260)*
operations flow document *(p. 251)*
overhead efficiency variance
     (p. 262)
overhead spending variance
     (p. 262)
practical standard *(p. 269)*
standard cost *(p. 248)*

standard cost card *(p. 251)*
standard quantity allowed *(p. 253)*
total overhead variance *(p. 261)*
total variance *(p. 252)*
variable overhead efficiency
     variance *(p. 259)*
variable overhead spending
     variance *(p. 259)*
variance analysis *(p. 266)*
volume variance *(p. 260)*
yield *(p. 275)*

Questions

1. What is a standard cost card? What information does it contain? How does it relate to a bill of materials and an operations flow document?

2. Why are the quantities shown in the bill of materials not always the same quantities shown in the standard cost card? How is the material standard developed?

3. A total variance can be calculated for each cost component of a product. Into what variances can this total be separated and to what does each relate? (Discuss separately for material and labor.)

4. What is meant by the term *standard hours*? Does the term refer to inputs or outputs?

5. Why are the overhead spending and overhead efficiency variances said to be controllable? Is the volume variance controllable? Why or why not?

6. How are actual and standard costs recorded in a standard cost system?

7. How are insignificant variances closed at the end of an accounting period? How are significant variances closed at the end of an accounting period? Why is there a difference in treatment?

8. What are the three primary uses of a standard cost system? In a business that routinely manufactures the same products or performs the same services, why are standards helpful?

9. What is meant by the process of *management by exception*? How do managers use a standard cost system in their efforts to control costs?

10. Why do managers care about the utilization of capacity? Are they controlling costs when they control utilization?

11. *(Appendix)* What variances can be computed for direct material and direct labor when some materials or labor inputs are substitutes for others? What information does each of these variances provide?

Exercises

12. (Direct material variances) Belichick Patio makes wrought iron table and chair sets. During April, the purchasing agent bought 12,800 pounds of scrap iron at $0.89 per pound. During the month, 10,700 pounds of scrap iron

were used to produce 300 table and chair sets. Each set requires a standard quantity of 35 pounds at a standard cost of $0.85 per pound.

a. For April, compute the direct material price variance (based on the quantity purchased) and the direct material quantity variance.

b. Identify the titles of individuals in the firm who would be responsible for each of the variances.

c. Provide some possible explanations for the variances computed in part (a).

WebTUTOR Advantage

13. (Direct material variances) In November, Gruden Publishing Company's costs and quantities of paper consumed in manufacturing its 2007 Executive Planner and Calendar were as follow:

Actual unit purchase price	$0.075 per page
Standard quantity allowed for good production	195,800 pages
Actual quantity purchased during November	230,000 pages
Actual quantity used in November	200,000 pages
Standard unit price	$0.080 per page

a. Calculate the total cost of purchases for November.

b. Compute the material price variance (based on quantity purchased).

c. Calculate the material quantity variance.

14. (Direct labor variances) The accounting firm of Reid and Associates set the following standard for its inventory audit of DelRio Co.: 300 hours at an average billing rate of $145. The firm actually worked 270 hours during the inventory audit process. The total labor variance for the audit was $500 unfavorable.

a. Compute the total actual payroll. Record the entry to accrue payroll costs.

b. Compute the labor efficiency variance.

c. Compute the labor rate variance.

d. Write a memo to the appropriate personnel regarding feedback about the labor efficiency variance. The memo should also offer a brief explanation that is consistent with the labor rate and efficiency variances.

WebTUTOR Advantage

15. (Direct labor variances) Snyder Lumber builds standard prefabricated wooden frames for apartment walls. Each frame requires 10 direct labor hours at an average standard hourly rate of $22. During May, the company produced 630 frames in 6,200 direct labor hours. Payroll records indicate that workers earned $139,500.

a. What were the standard hours allowed for May construction?

b. Calculate the direct labor variances.

16. (Direct material and direct labor variances) In December, Billie Parcells, president of Parcells Co., received the following information from Joe Gibbs, the new controller, in regard to November production of gym bags:

November production	2,400 gym bags
Actual cost of material purchased and used	$21,875
Standard material allowed	0.5 square yard per bag
Material quantity variance	$800 U
Actual hours worked	5,000 hours
Standard labor time per gym bag	2 hours
Labor rate variance	$650 F
Standard labor rate per hour	$17
Standard price per yard of material	$16

Ms. Parcells asked Mr. Gibbs to provide her the following information:

a. Standard quantity of material allowed for November production.

b. Standard direct labor hours allowed for November production.

c. Material price variance.

d. Labor efficiency variance.

e. Standard prime (direct material and direct labor) cost to produce one bag.

f. Actual cost to produce one gym bag in November.

g. An explanation for the difference between standard and actual cost. Be sure that the explanation is consistent with the pattern of the variances.

17. (Direct material and labor variances) Steve Spurrier Cottonworks produces 100 percent cotton T-shirts. For each T-shirt, standard direct material and labor costs follow:

Direct material   2.0 yards @ $3.00
Direct labor   0.7 hour @ $2.50

Actual March production and costs for the company to produce 5,000 T-shirts are:

	Quantity	Cost
Direct material		
Purchased	15,000 yards	$44,850
Requisitioned into production	11,500 yards	34,950
Direct labor	4,750 hours	12,000

a. Compute the direct material and direct labor variances.

b. How might the sales and production managers explain the direct material variances?

c. How might the production and personnel managers explain the direct labor variances?

d. Record the year-end adjusting entry to close the material and labor variances.

18. (Missing information for materials and labor) For each independent case, fill in the missing figures.

	Case A	Case B	Case C	Case D
Units produced	800	?	240	1,500
Standard hours per unit	3	0.8	?	?
Standard hours allowed	?	600	480	?
Standard rate per hour	$7	?	$9.50	$6
Actual hours worked	2,330	675	?	4,875
Actual labor cost	?	?	$4,560	$26,812.50
Labor rate variance	$466 F	$1,080 F	$228 U	?
Labor efficiency variance	?	$780 U	?	$2,250 U

19. (Overhead variances) Wannstedt Corp. has a fully automated bicycle production facility in which almost 97 percent of conversion costs are driven by machine hours. Gregg Williams, the company's cost accountant, has computed the following overhead variances for January:

Variable overhead spending variance $37,000 F
Variable overhead efficiency variance   20,060 F
Fixed overhead spending variance   14,000 U
Fixed overhead volume variance   17,000 U

Williams has gone on vacation, so the company president asks you to show her how the variances were computed and to answer several other questions. You know that budgeted fixed overhead is $500,000; the predetermined variable and fixed overhead rates are $10 and $20 per machine hour, respectively, and budgeted capacity is 10,000 units.

a. Using the four-variance approach, prepare the analysis in diagram format similar to that on page 282 with as much detail as possible.

b. What is the standard number of machine hours allowed for each unit of output?

c. What is the number of actual hours worked?

d. What is the total spending variance?

e. What additional information about the manufacturing overhead variances is gained by inserting detailed computations into the variable and fixed manufacturing overhead variance analysis?

f. How would the overhead variances be closed if the three-variance approach were used?

20. (Computation of all overhead variances) The manager of Missouri's Department of Transportation has determined that it typically takes 30 minutes for the department's employees to register a new car. In Boone County, the fixed overhead rate computed on an estimated 4,000 direct labor hours is $8 per direct labor hour, whereas the variable overhead rate is estimated at $3 per direct labor hour.

During July, 7,600 cars were registered in Boone County and 3,700 direct labor hours were worked in registering those vehicles. For the month, variable overhead was $10,730 and fixed overhead was $29,950.

a. Compute overhead variances using a four-variance approach.

b. Compute overhead variances using a three-variance approach.

c. Compute overhead variances using a two-variance approach.

21. (Four-variance approach; journal entries) Vermeil Manufacturing set 60,000 direct labor hours as the 2006 capacity measure for computing its predetermined variable overhead rate. At that level, budgeted variable overhead costs are $270,000. Vermeil will apply budgeted fixed overhead of $118,800 on the basis of 3,300 budgeted machine hours for the year. Both machine hours and fixed overhead costs are expected to be incurred evenly each month.

During March 2006, Vermeil incurred 4,900 direct labor hours and 250 machine hours. Variable and fixed overhead were $21,275 and $10,600, respectively. The standard times allowed for March production were 4,955 direct labor hours and 240 machine hours.

a. Using the four-variance approach, determine the overhead variances for March 2006.

b. Prepare all journal entries related to overhead for Vermeil Manufacturing for March 2006.

22. (Missing data; three-variance approach) Jeff Fisher Corporation's flexible budget formula for total overhead is $720,000 plus $16 per direct labor hour. The combined overhead rate is $40 per direct labor hour. The following data have been recorded for the year:

Actual total overhead	$1,160,000
Total overhead spending variance	32,000 U
Volume variance	48,000 U

Use a three-variance approach to determine the number of the following:

a. Standard hours allowed

b. Actual direct labor hours worked

23. (Variances and cost control) Cowher Dimension applies overhead using machine hours. The total overhead application rate is $40 per hour based on a normal monthly capacity of 24,000 machine hours. Overhead is 30 percent variable and 70 percent fixed. Each unit of product requires 12 machine hours.

During September, Cowher Dimension produced 2,300 units of product and incurred 25,000 machine hours. Actual overhead cost for September was $1,000,000.

a. What number of standard hours was allowed for September?

b. What is total annual budgeted fixed overhead cost?

c. What is the controllable overhead variance?

d. What is the noncontrollable overhead variance?

24. (Journal entries) Dungy Chemical had the following balances in its trial balance at year-end.

	Debit	Credit
Direct Material Inventory	$ 36,600	
Work in Process Inventory	43,920 *6.32%*	
Finished Goods Inventory	65,880 *9.47%*	
Cost of Goods Sold	585,600 *84.21*	
Material Price Variance	7,250	
Material Quantity Variance		$10,965
Labor Rate Variance		1,100
Labor Efficiency Variance	4,390	
VOH Spending Variance		3,600
VOH Efficiency Variance	300	
FOH Spending Variance	650	
Volume Variance	1,475	

Assume that taken together, the variances, are believed to be significant. Prepare the journal entries to close the variances at year-end.

25. (Variances and conversion cost category) Billick Brake manufactures brake rotors. Until recently, the company applied overhead to production using direct labor hours. However, company facilities were recently automated, and the accounting system was revised to show only two cost categories, direct material and conversion. Estimated variable and fixed conversion costs for the current month were $170,000 and $76,000, respectively. Expected output for the current month was 5,000 rotors and the estimated number of machine hours was 10,000. During the month, the firm actually used 9,000 machine hours to make 4,800 rotors while incurring $228,000 of conversion costs. Of this amount, $150,000 was variable cost.

a. Using the four-variance approach, compute the variances for conversion costs.

b. Evaluate the effectiveness of the firm in controlling the current month's costs.

26. (Developing standard cost card and discussion) Johnna Fox Desserts Company produces fruit-flavored frozen desserts. Company products have typically had strong regional sales, but recently other companies have begun marketing similar products in the area. Price competition has become increasingly important. Butch Davis, the company's controller, is in the process of implementing a standard cost system because of its usefulness in cost control and in making better pricing decisions.

The company's most popular product is raspberry sherbet, which is produced in 10-gallon batches. Each batch requires 6 quarts of raspberries. The raspberries are sorted by hand before entering the production process. Because of imperfections in the raspberries, 1 quart of berries is discarded for every 4 quarts of acceptable berries. The standard direct labor sorting time to obtain 1 quart of acceptable raspberries is 3 minutes. The acceptable raspberries are then blended with other ingredients; blending requires 12 minutes of direct labor time per batch. During blending, some material is lost. After blending, the sherbet is packaged in quart containers. Davis has gathered the following cost information:

- Raspberries are purchased for $0.80 per quart.
- All other ingredients cost a total of $0.45 per gallon.
- Direct labor is paid $9.00 per hour.
- The total cost of material and labor required to package the sherbet is $0.38 per quart.

a. Develop the standard cost for the direct cost components of a 10-gallon batch of raspberry sherbet. The standard cost should identify standard quantity, standard price/rate, and standard cost per batch for each direct cost component.

b. As part of implementing the company's standard cost system, Davis plans to train those responsible for maintaining the standards on how to use variance analysis. He is particularly concerned with the causes of unfavorable variances.

1. Discuss the possible causes of unfavorable material price variances, and identify the individual(s) who should be held responsible for these variances.

2. Discuss the possible causes of unfavorable labor efficiency variances, and identify the individual(s) who should be held responsible for these variances.

(CMA adapted)

27. (Behavioral implications of standard costing) Contact a local company that uses a standard cost system. Make an appointment with a manager at that company to interview her or him on the following issues:
- the characteristics that should be present in a standard cost system to encourage positive employee motivation
- how a standard cost system should be implemented to positively motivate employees
- the meaning of *management by exception* and how variance analysis often results in the use of this concept
- how employee behavior could be adversely affected when "actual to standard" comparisons are used as the basis for performance evaluation

Prepare a paper and an oral presentation based on your interview.

28. (Standard setting; team project) As a four-person team, choose an activity that is commonly performed every day, such as taking a shower/bath, preparing a meal, or doing homework. Have each team member time himself/herself performing that activity for two days and then develop a standard time for the team. Now have the team members time themselves performing the same activity for the next five days.

a. Using an assumed hourly wage rate of $12, calculate the labor efficiency variance for your team.

b. Prepare a list of reasons for the variance.

c. How could some of the variance have been avoided?

29. (Cost control evaluation) The Jim Haslett Concrete Company makes precast concrete steps for use with manufactured housing. The company had the following 2007 budget based on expected production of 3,200 units:

	Standard Cost	Amount Budgeted
Direct material	$22.00	$ 70,400
Direct labor	12.00	38,400
Variable overhead		
Indirect material	4.20	13,440
Indirect labor	1.75	5,600
Utilities	1.00	3,200
Fixed overhead		
Supervisory salaries		40,000
Depreciation		15,000
Insurance		9,640
Total		$195,680

Cost per unit = $195,680 ÷ 3,200 = $61.15

Actual production for 2007 was 3,500 units, and actual costs for the year were as follows:

Direct material used	$ 80,500
Direct labor	42,300
Variable overhead	
Indirect material	14,000
Indirect labor	6,650
Utilities	3,850
Fixed overhead	
Supervisory salaries	41,000
Depreciation	15,000
Insurance	8,800
Total	$212,100

$$\text{Cost per unit} = \$212,100 \div 3,500 = \$60.60$$

The plant manager, Leslie Martz, whose annual bonus includes (among other factors) 20 percent of the net favorable cost variances, states that she saved the company $1,925 [($61.15 − $60.60) × 3,500]. She has instructed the plant cost accountant to prepare a detailed report to be sent to corporate headquarters comparing each component's actual per-unit cost with the per-unit amounts in the preceding annual budget to prove the $1,925 cost savings.

a. Is the actual-to-budget comparison proposed by Martz appropriate? If her comparison is not appropriate, prepare a more appropriate comparison.

b. How would you, as the plant cost accountant, react if Martz insisted on her comparison? Suggest what alternatives are available to you.

30. (Ethics essay) Jack Austin is a plant manager who has done a good job of controlling some overhead costs during the current period and a poor job of controlling others. Austin's boss has asked him for a variance report for the period.

a. Discuss the ethics of using a two-variance approach to report the overhead variances rather than a three- or four-variance approach.

b. If Austin does not provide his boss detailed information on the individual cost components and their related variances, can the boss judge Austin's performance during the period? Defend your answer.

31. (Direct labor variances; advanced) Many companies face the prospect of paying workers overtime wages; some of these payments are at time-and-a-half wages.

a. How does overtime pay affect direct labor cost? Variable overhead?

b. Obviously, paying overtime to already employed workers makes better financial business sense than does hiring additional workers. If workers would prefer not to work overtime but do so to maintain their jobs, how does overtime affect the ethical contract between employers and employees?

c. What effects might overtime have on job efficiency? On job effectiveness (such as quality of production)?

d. Would you be in favor of limiting allowable hours of overtime to have more individuals employed? Discuss this question from the standpoint of (1) the government, (2) the employer, (3) a currently employed worker, and (4) an unemployed individual.

32. (Essay; ethics) An HMO medical program began reimbursing hospitals according to diagnostic-related groups (DRGs). Each DRG has a specified standard "length of stay." If a patient leaves the hospital early, the hospital is favorably financially impacted, but a patient staying longer than the specified time costs the hospital money.

a. From the hospital administrator's point of view, would you want favorable length-of-stay variances? How might you go about trying to obtain such variances?

b. From a patient's point of view, would you want favorable length-of-stay variances? Answer this question from the point of view of (1) a patient who has had minor surgery and (2) a patient who has had major surgery.

c. Would favorable length-of-stay variances necessarily equate to high-quality care?

33. (Appendix) Herman Edwards Company produces 12-ounce cans of mixed pecans and cashews. Standard and actual information follows.

Standard Quantities and Costs (12-oz. can)

Pecans: 6 ounces at $3.00 per pound	$1.125
Cashews: 6 ounces at $4.00 per pound	1.500

Actual Quantities and Costs for Production of 18,000 Cans

Pecans: 7,473 pounds at $2.90 per pound
Cashews: 6,617 pounds at $4.25 per pound

Determine the material price, mix, and yield variances.

34. (Appendix) Mike Shanahan Ltd. is a mechanical engineering firm that employs both engineers and draftspeople. The average hourly rates are $80 for engineers and $40 for draftspeople. For one project, the standard was set at 375 hours of engineer time and 625 hours of draftsperson time. Actual hours worked on this project were:

Engineers—500 hours at $85 per hour
Draftspeople—33 hours at $42.00 per hour

Determine the labor rate, mix, and yield variances for this project.

35. (Appendix) Holly Sherman Legal Services has three labor classes: secretaries, paralegals, and attorneys. Standard wage rates are as follows: secretaries, $25 per hour; paralegals, $40 per hour; and attorneys, $85 per hour. The firm has established a standard of 0.5 hours of secretarial time and 2.0 hours of paralegal time for each hour of attorney time in probate cases. For October, the numbers of actual direct labor hours worked and of standard hours allowed for probate cases were as follows:

	Actual DLHs	**Number of Standard Hours Allowed**
Secretarial	500	500
Paralegal	1,800	2,000
Attorney	1,100	1,000

a. Calculate October's direct labor efficiency variance and decompose the total into the following components:

1. Direct labor mix variance

2. Direct labor yield variance

b. Prepare a memo addressing whether management used an efficient mix of labor.

(CMA adapted)

Problems

36. (Material and labor variances) Jim Mora Marine uses a standard cost system for materials and labor in producing fishing boats. Production requires three materials: fiberglass, paint, and a prepurchased trim package. The standard costs and quantities for materials and labor are as follows:

Standards for One Fishing Boat

2,500 pounds of fiberglass @ $0.80 per pound	$2,000
6 quarts gel coat paint @ $60.00 per gallon	90
1 trim package	400
40 hours of labor @ $25.00 per hour	1,000
Standard cost for DM and DL	$3,490

The following actual data related to the production of 300 boats was recorded for July:

Material Purchased

Fiberglass—820,000 pounds @ $0.83 per pound
Paint—500 gallons @ $55.50 per gallon
Trim packages—320 @ $405 per package

Material Used

Fiberglass—790,000 pounds
Paint—462 gallons
Trim packages—304

Direct Labor Used

12,100 hours @ $23.50 per hour

Calculate the material and labor variances for Jim Mora Marine for July. Base the material price variance on the quantity of material purchased.

37. (Variance calculation and journal entries) DomCapers Toy Co. makes small plastic toys having the following material and labor standards:

	Standard Quantity	Standard Cost
Material	0.5 pound	$4.00 per pound ($2.00 per unit of output)
Labor	12 minutes	16.00 per hour ($3.20 per unit of output)

During October, 29,000 pounds of material were acquired at $4.15 per pound; only 25,300 pounds of that was used in production during the month to make 50,000 toys. Factory payroll for October showed 10,300 direct labor hours at a total cost of $160,680.

a. Compute material and labor variances, basing the material price variance on the quantity of material purchased.
b. Assuming a perpetual inventory system is used, prepare the relevant general journal entries for October.

38. (Incomplete data) Schottenheimer Medical Supply manufactures latex surgical gloves. Most processing is done by machines, which can produce 400 pairs of gloves per hour. Each pair of gloves requires 0.85 square foot of latex, which has a standard price of $0.80 per square foot. Machine operators are considered direct labor and are paid $25 per hour.

During one week in May, Schottenheimer produced 30,000 pairs of gloves and experienced a $1,500 unfavorable material quantity variance. The company had purchased 1,500 more square feet of material than had been used in production that week. The unfavorable material price variance for the week was $570. A $104 favorable total labor variance was generated based on 77 total actual labor hours to produce the gloves. Determine the following amounts:

a. Standard quantity of material for production achieved
b. Actual quantity of material used
c. Actual quantity of material purchased
d. Actual price of material purchased
e. Standard hours allowed for production
f. Labor efficiency variance
g. Labor rate variance
h. Actual labor rate

39. (Incomplete data) Capers Home Study Products makes wooden lap desks. A small fire on October 1 partially destroyed the records relating to September's production. The charred remains of the standard cost card appears here.

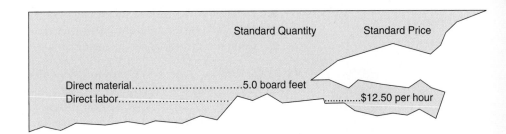

	Standard Quantity	Standard Price
Direct material................................	5.0 board feet	
Direct labor................................		............$12.50 per hour

From other fragments of records and several discussions with employees, you learn the following:

- The standard quantity of material allowed for September's production was 4,000 board feet.
- The September payroll for direct labor was $19,220 based on 1,550 actual hours worked.
- The production supervisor distinctly remembered being held accountable for 50 more hours of direct labor than should have been worked. She was upset because top management failed to consider that she saved several hundred board feet of material by creative efforts that required extra time.
- The purchasing agent's files showed that 4,300 board feet had been purchased in September at $2.05 per board foot. She was proud of the fact that this price was $0.05 below standard cost per foot. All purchased material had been used during the month.

a. How many units were produced during September?
b. Calculate all variances for direct material and direct labor for September.
c. What is the standard number of hours allowed for the production of each unit?
d. Prepare general journal entries reflecting direct material and direct labor activity and variances for September, assuming a standard cost, perpetual inventory system.

40. (Adjusting standards) Lovie Corp., started in early 2000, manufactures traditional Hawaiian dresses. At that time, the following material and labor standards were developed:

Material	3.0 yards at $6 per yard
Labor	1.5 hours at $10 per hour

In May 2006, Lovie Corp. hired a new cost accountant, David Anulu. At the end of the month, Anulu was reviewing the production variances and was amazed to find that the company's material and labor standards had never been revised. Actual material and labor data for May 2006 when 17,200 muumuus were produced follow:

Material	Purchased, 50,000 yards at $7.00
	Used 50,000 yards
Labor	17,800 hours at $13.50 per hour

Material prices have risen 4 percent each year since 2000, but the company can now buy at 94 percent of regular price due to increased purchase volume. Also, direct material waste has been reduced from 1/4 yard to 1/8 yard per muumuu; waste has always been included in the standard material quantity. Beginning in 2001, each annual labor contract has specified a 5 percent cost-of-living adjustment. Revision of the plant layout and acquisition of more efficient machinery has decreased the labor time per muumuu by one-third since the company began.

a. Determine the material and labor variances based on the company's original standards.

b. Determine the new standards against which Anulu should measure the May 2006 results. (Round adjustments annually to the nearest cent.)

c. Compute the variances for material and labor using the revised standards.

41. (Calculation of four variances) Murlarkey's Ceramics has an expected monthly capacity of 3,000 units but only 1,900 units were produced and 2,000 direct labor hours were used during October 2006 due to a fire on the production floor. Actual variable overhead for October was $16,000 and actual fixed overhead was $44,000.

Standard cost data follow:

	Standard Cost per Unit (One Unit Takes One Labor Hour)
Direct material	$ 9.00
Direct labor	15.00
Variable overhead	8.00
Fixed overhead	16.00
Total	$48.00

a. Compute and compare the actual overhead cost per unit with the expected overhead cost per unit.

b. Calculate overhead variances using the four-variance method.

42. (Four-variance approach; journal entries) Mike Tice Products makes picnic tables, swings, and benches. Standard hours allowed for each product are as follows:

Picnic table	10 standard direct labor hours
Swing	3 standard direct labor hours
Bench	12 standard direct labor hours

The standard variable overhead rate is $4 per direct labor hour; the standard fixed overhead application rate at expected annual capacity is $2 per direct labor hour. Expected monthly capacity is 3,000 direct labor hours.

June production was 100 picnic tables, 400 swings, and 60 benches; production required 3,020 actual direct labor hours. Actual variable and fixed overhead for June were $11,800 and $6,200, respectively.

a. Prepare a variance analysis using the four-variance approach. (*Hint:* Convert the production of each type of product into standard hours allowed for all work accomplished for the month.)

b. Prepare journal entries to record the incurrence of actual overhead, application of overhead to production, and closing of the overhead variance accounts (assuming those variances are immaterial).

c. Evaluate the effectiveness of the managers in controlling costs.

43. (Variance analysis with unknowns) Dennis Green Co. produces neon signs. The company's standard costs for labor and overhead follow:

Direct labor (4 hours @ $12 per hour)	$ 48
Factory overhead (10,000 DLH expected capacity)	
Variable (4 hours @ $16 per direct labor hour)	64
Fixed (4 hours @ $8 per direct labor hour)	32
Total unit conversion cost	$144

The following information is available for December when 8,000 standard labor hours were used:

Labor rate variance	$ 4,500 U
Labor efficiency variance	12,000 U
Actual variable overhead	154,000
Actual fixed overhead	79,000

Calculate the amounts for the following unknowns:

a. Total applied factory overhead
b. Volume variance
c. Variable overhead spending variance
d. Variable overhead efficiency variance
e. Total actual overhead
f. Number of units manufactured

44. (Combined overhead rates) Kwan and Yamaguchi Industries manufactures a down-filled sleeping bag with the following standard cost information for 2007:

- Each sleeping bag requires 1 hour of machine time to produce.
- Variable overhead is applied at the rate of $9 per machine hour.
- Fixed overhead is applied at the rate of $12 per machine hour, based on an expected annual capacity of 30,000 machine hours.

Production Statistics for 2007

Number of sleeping bags produced	31,000 units
Actual number of machine hours	33,300 hours
Variable overhead cost incurred	$265,400
Fixed overhead cost incurred	$354,500

a. Using a combined overhead rate, calculate variances using the two-variance approach.
b. Using a combined overhead rate, calculate variances using the three-variance approach.

45. (Comprehensive) Tom Coughlin Co. manufactures metal screen doors with the following standard quantity and cost information:

Direct Material

Aluminum	4 sheets at $2	$ 8
Copper	3 sheets at $4	12
Direct labor	7 hours at $8	56
Variable overhead	5 machine hours at $3	15
Fixed overhead	5 machine hours at $2	10

Overhead rates were based on normal monthly capacity of 6,000 machine hours.

During November, the company produced only 850 doors because of a labor strike that occurred during union contract negotiations. After the dispute was settled, the company scheduled overtime to try to meet regular production levels. The following costs were incurred in November:

Material

Aluminum	4,000 sheets purchased at $2; used 3,500 sheets
Copper	3,000 sheets purchased at $4.20; used 2,600 sheets

Direct Labor

Regular time	5,200 hours at $8.00 (pre-contract settlement)
Regular time	900 hours at $8.50 (post-contract settlement)

Variable Overhead

$11,650 (based on 4,175 machine hours)

Fixed Overhead

$9,425 (based on 4,175 machine hours)

Determine the following:
a. Total material price variance
b. Total material usage (quantity) variance
c. Labor rate variance
d. Labor efficiency variance
e. Variable overhead spending variance
f. Variable overhead efficiency variance
g. Fixed overhead spending variance
h. Volume variance
i. Budget variance

46. (Comprehensive; all variances; all methods) B. Callahan Painting Services paints interiors of residences and commercial structures. The firm's management has established cost standards per 100 square feet based on the amount of area to be painted.

Direct material ($18 per gallon of paint)	$1.50
Direct labor	2.00
Variable overhead	0.60
Fixed overhead (based on 600,000 square feet per month)	1.25

Management has determined that 400 square feet can be painted by the average worker each hour. During May, the company painted 600,000 square feet of space and incurred the following costs:

Direct material (450 gallons purchased and used)	$ 8,300.00
Direct labor (1,475 hours)	12,242.50
Variable overhead	3,480.00
Fixed overhead	7,720.00

a. Compute the direct material variances.
b. Compute the direct labor variances.
c. Use a four-variance approach to compute overhead variances.
d. Use a three-variance approach to compute overhead variances.
e. Use a two-variance approach to compute overhead variances.
f. Reconcile your answers for parts (c) through (e).
g. Discuss other cost drivers that could be used as a basis for measuring activity and computing variances for this company.

47. (Variance disposition) Dennis Erickson Manufacturing had the following variances at year-end 2006:

Material price variance	$23,400 U
Material quantity variance	24,900 F
Labor rate variance	5,250 F
Labor efficiency variance	36,900 U
Variable overhead spending variance	3,000 U
Variable overhead efficiency variance	1,800 F
Fixed overhead spending variance	6,600 F
Volume variance	16,800 U

In addition, the following inventory and Cost of Goods Sold account balances existed at year-end 2006:

Raw Material Inventory	$ 338,793
Work in Process Inventory	914,277
Finished Goods Inventory	663,663
Cost of Goods Sold	2,724,267

a. Prepare the journal entry at December 31 to dispose of the variances, assuming that all are insignificant.

b. After posting your entry in part (a), what is the balance in Cost of Goods Sold?

c. Prepare the journal entries at December 31 to dispose of the variances, assuming that all are significant.

d. After posting your entries in part (c), what are the balances in each inventory account and in Cost of Goods Sold?

48. (Conversion cost variances) The May budget for Mia Hamm Mfg. shows $1,080,000 of variable conversion costs, $360,000 of fixed conversion costs, and 72,000 machine hours for the production of 24,000 units of product. During May, 76,000 machine hours were worked and 24,000 units were produced. Variance and fixed conversion costs for the month were $1,128,800 and $374,500, respectively.

a. Calculate the four conversion cost variances assuming that variable and fixed costs are separated.

b. Calculate the three conversion cost variances assuming that fixed and variable costs are combined.

49. (Standards revision) Mariucci Company uses a standard cost system for its aircraft component manufacturing operations. Recently, the company's direct material supplier went out of business, but Mariucci's purchasing agent found a new source that produces a similar material. The price per pound from the original supplier was $7.00; the new source's price is $7.77. The new source's material reduces scrap and, thus, each unit requires only 1.00 pound rather than the previous standard of 1.25 pounds per unit. In addition, use of the new source's material reduces direct labor time from 24 to 22 minutes per unit because there is less machine setup time. At the same time, the recently signed labor contract increased the average direct labor wage rate from $12.60 to $14.40 per hour.

The company began using the new direct material on April 1, the same day that the new labor agreement went into effect. However, Mariucci Company is still using the following standards that were set at the beginning of the calendar year:

Direct material	1.2 pounds at $6.80 per pound	$ 8.16
Direct labor	20 minutes at $12.30 per DLH	4.10
Standard DM and DL cost per unit		$12.26

Dan Reeves, cost accounting supervisor, had been examining the following April 30 variance report.

PERFORMANCE REPORT
STANDARD COST VARIANCE ANALYSIS FOR APRIL 2006

Standard		Price Variance		Quantity Variance		Actual
DM	$ 8.16	($0.97 × 1.0)	$0.97 U	($6.80 × 0.2)	$1.36 F	$ 7.77
DL	4.10	[$2.10 × (22/60)] 0.77 U		[$12.30 × (2/60)] 0.41 U		5.28
	$12.26					$13.05

COMPARISON OF 2006 ACTUAL COSTS

	Average 1st Quarter Costs	April Costs	Percent Increase (Decrease)
DM	$ 8.75	$ 7.77	(11.2)
DL	5.04	5.28	4.8
	$13.79	$13.05	(5.4)

Tessa Marchibroda, assistant controller, came into Reeves' office. Reeves said, "Tessa, look at this performance report! Direct material price increased 11 percent, and the labor rate increased over 14 percent during April. I expected greater variances, yet prime costs decreased over 5 percent from the $13.79 we experienced during the first quarter of this year. The proper message just isn't coming through."

Tessa said, "This has been an unusual period. With all the unforeseen changes, perhaps we should revise our standards based on current conditions and start over."

Reeves replied, "I think we can retain the current standards but expand the variance analysis. We could calculate variances for the specific changes that have occurred to direct material and direct labor before we calculate the normal price and quantity variances. What I really think would be useful to management right now is to determine the impact the changes in direct material and direct labor had in reducing our prime costs per unit from $13.79 in the first quarter to $13.05 in April—a reduction of $0.74."

a. Discuss the advantages of (1) immediately revising the standards and (2) retaining the current standards and expanding the analysis of variances.

b. Prepare an analysis that reflects the impact of the new direct material and new labor contract on reducing Mariucci Company's standard costs per unit from $13.79 to $13.05. The analysis should show the changes in direct material and direct labor costs per unit that are caused by (1) the use of the new direct material and (2) the labor rates of the new contract. This analysis should be in sufficient detail to identify the changes due to direct material price, direct labor rate, the effect of direct material quality on direct material usage, and the effect of direct material quality on direct labor usage.

(CMA adapted)

50. (Variances and variance responsibility) Linda Walters Co. produces miniature footballs with the following standard costs per unit:

Material: one square foot of leather at $2.00	$ 2.00
Direct labor: 1.6 hours at $4.00	6.40
Variable overhead cost	3.00
Fixed overhead cost	1.45
Total cost per unit	$12.85

Per-unit overhead cost was calculated from the following annual overhead budget for 60,000 footballs.

Variable Overhead Cost

Indirect labor—30,000 hours at $4.00	$120,000	
Supplies (oil)—60,000 gallons at $0.50	30,000	
Allocated variable service department costs	30,000	
Total variable overhead cost		$180,000

Fixed Overhead Cost

Supervision	$ 27,000	
Depreciation	45,000	
Other fixed costs	15,000	
Total fixed overhead cost		87,000
Total budgeted overhead cost at 60,000 units		$267,000

Following are the charges to the manufacturing department for November when 5,000 units were produced:

Material (5,300 square feet at $2.00)	$10,600
Direct labor (8,200 hours at $4.10)	33,620
Indirect labor (2,400 hours at $4.10)	9,840
Supplies (oil) (6,000 gallons at $0.55)	3,300
Allocated variable service department costs	3,200
Supervision	2,475
Depreciation	3,750
Other fixed costs	1,250
Total	$68,035

Purchasing normally buys about the same quantity as is used in production during a month. In November, it purchased 5,200 square feet of material at a price of $2.10 per foot.

a. Calculate the following variances from standard costs for the data given:
  1. Material purchase price
  2. Material quantity
  3. Direct labor rate
  4. Direct labor efficiency
  5. Overhead budget
b. The company has divided its responsibilities so that the Purchasing Department is responsible for the purchase price of materials and the Manufacturing Department is responsible for the quantity of materials used. Does this division of responsibilities solve the conflict between price and quantity variances? Explain your answer.
c. Prepare a report detailing the overhead budget variance. The report, which will be given to the Manufacturing Department manager, should show only that part of the variance that is her responsibility and should highlight the information in ways that would be useful to her in evaluating departmental performance and when considering corrective action.
d. Assume that the departmental manager performs the timekeeping function for this manufacturing department. From time to time, analyses of overhead and direct labor variances have shown that the manager has deliberately misclassified labor hours (that is, listed direct labor hours as indirect labor hours and vice versa) so that only one of the two labor variances is unfavorable. It is not feasible economically to hire a separate timekeeper. What should the company do, if anything, to resolve this problem?

(CMA adapted)

51. (Appendix) Venus Williams Food Industries produces three-topping, 18-inch frozen pizzas and uses a standard cost system. The three pizza toppings (in addition to cheese) are onions, olives, and mushrooms. To some extent, discretion may be used to determine the actual mix of these toppings. The company has two classes of labor, and discretion also may be used to determine the mix of the labor inputs. The standard cost card for a pizza follows:

Onions	3 ounces at $0.10 per ounce
Olives	3 ounces at $0.35 per ounce
Mushrooms	3 ounces at $0.50 per ounce
Labor category 1	5 minutes at $12 per hour
Labor category 2	6 minutes at $8 per hour

During May 2006, the company produced 12,000 pizzas and used the following inputs:

Onions	2,000 pounds
Olives	3,000 pounds
Mushrooms	2,000 pounds
Labor category 1	1,300 hours
Labor category 2	1,000 hours

During the month there were no deviations from standards on material prices or labor rates.

a. Determine the material quantity, mix, and yield variances.

b. Determine the labor efficiency, mix, and yield variances.

c. Prepare the journal entries to record the above mix and yield variances.

52. (Appendix) Dave McGinnis Products makes NOTAM, a new health food. For a 50-pound batch, standard material and labor costs are as follows:

	Quantity	Unit Price	Total
Wheat	25.0 pounds	$ 0.20 per pound	$5.00
Barley	25.0 pounds	0.10 per pound	2.50
Corn	10.0 pounds	0.05 per pound	0.50
Skilled labor	0.8 hour	12.00 per hour	9.60
Unskilled labor	0.2 hour	8.00 per hour	1.60

During June, the following materials and labor were used in producing 600 batches of NOTAM:

Wheat	18,000 pounds at $0.22 per pound
Barley	14,000 pounds at $0.11 per pound
Corn	10,000 pounds at $0.04 per pound
Skilled labor	400 hours at $12.25 per hour
Unskilled labor	260 hours at $8.00 per hour

a. Calculate the material quantity, mix, and yield variances.

b. Calculate the labor efficiency, mix, and yield variances.

8

The Master Budget

Objectives

AFTER COMPLETING THIS CHAPTER, YOU SHOULD BE ABLE TO ANSWER THE FOLLOWING QUESTIONS:

LO.1 WHY IS BUDGETING IMPORTANT?

LO.2 HOW IS STRATEGIC PLANNING RELATED TO BUDGETING?

LO.3 WHAT IS THE STARTING POINT OF A MASTER BUDGET AND WHY?

LO.4 HOW ARE THE VARIOUS COMPONENTS IN A MASTER BUDGET PREPARED, AND HOW DO THEY RELATE TO ONE ANOTHER?

LO.5 WHY IS THE CASH BUDGET SO IMPORTANT IN THE MASTER BUDGETING PROCESS?

LO.6 WHAT BENEFITS ARE PROVIDED BY A BUDGET?

LO.7 *(APPENDIX)* HOW DOES A BUDGET MANUAL FACILITATE THE BUDGETING PROCESS?

Founded in 1932 by Walter Stevenson, S & S Hinge Company is located outside of Chicago in Bloomingdale, Illinois. The company has grown from its original 10,000-square foot location to a 50,000-square-foot state-of-the-art facility first occupied in 1994. Management has retained its entrepreneurial roots; Walter's son Al is now president. He has been with the company since 1946 and, in 2004, celebrated his 85th birthday. Grandson Chris is general manager and vice president of sales/marketing.

S & S Hinge's current facility uses progressive carbide tool technology that pulls a metal strip through the system into several die-stamping operations that split the strip, create and bend metal "teeth," add wire, and close the metal teeth. Other stamping operations such as hole patterns, notching, and staking can be performed on-line if the correct dies are available in addition to a compatible customer application. The cut-off press then cuts the hinge to the desired length. The stamping department produces the company's standard, continuous (or "piano") hinges that are a minimum of 2 inches long. S & S produces more than 200 different types of standard hinges in various combinations of metals, widths, lengths, thickness gauges, and pin diameters.

Additional operations in the secondary department at the company are used to modify hinges to customer specifications that cannot be performed at the work center. In this department, hinges can be cut to length and patterns of holes can be punched into the hinges. Customization can also involve bending operations that allow the hinges to fit into allotted spaces and applications.

By dividing tasks into two departments, the company can streamline production operations. The "no-frills" standard hinges pass through only the first department and then go either directly to customers operating in a just-in-time environment or to finished goods inventory. Alternatively, made-to-order hinges pass through both departments, with the additional operations in the secondary department creating no production bottlenecks for hinges that do not require the extra machine operations.

Source: Information provided at *http://www.sandshinge.com* and from Warren Moss, S & S Hinge Company accounting manager.

In virtually any endeavor, intelligent behavior involves visualizing the future, imagining what results one wishes to occur, and determining the activities and resources needed to achieve those results. If the process is complex, the means of obtaining results should be documented because of the human tendency to forget and the difficulty of mentally processing many facts and relationships at the same time.

Planning is the cornerstone of effective management, and effective planning requires that managers must predict, with reasonable precision, the key variables that affect company performance and conditions. These predictions provide management a foundation for effective problem solving, control, and resource allocation. Planning (especially in financial terms) is important when future conditions are expected to be approximately the same as current ones, and it is *critical* when conditions are expected to change.

During the strategic planning process, managers come to an agreement on organizational goals and objectives and how to achieve them. Typically, goals are stated as desired abstract achievements (such as "to become a market leader for a particular product"), and objectives are stated as desired quantifiable results for a specified time (such as "to manufacture 200,000 units of a particular product with fewer than 1 percent defects next year"). The process of achieving goals and objectives requires complex activities, diverse resources, and formalized planning.

A plan should include qualitative narratives of goals, objectives, and means of accomplishment. However, if plans consisted only of qualitative narratives, comparisons between actual results and expectations could be only in the form of vague generalizations, and there would be no way to measure how well the organization met its specified objectives. The process of formalizing plans and translating qualitative narratives into a documented, quantitative format is called **budgeting**. The end result of this process is a **budget**, which quantitatively expresses an organization's commitment to planned activities and to resource acquisition and use.

budgeting

budget

This chapter covers the budgeting process and preparation of the master budget. Budgeting is important for organizations of all sizes, especially those that have a large amount of monetary, human, and physical resources.

THE BUDGETING PROCESS

**LO.1
WHY IS BUDGETING
IMPORTANT?**

Budgeting is an important part of an organization's entire planning process, in part because it determines a direction or path chosen from many alternatives. Inclusion of quantifiable amounts provides specific criteria against which future performance (also recorded in accounting terms) can be compared. Thus, a budget is a type of standard that allows variances to be computed and feedback about those variances to be given to appropriate individuals.

Strategic Planning

**LO.2
HOW IS STRATEGIC
PLANNING RELATED TO
BUDGETING?**

Although budgets are typically expressed in financial terms, they must begin with nonquantitative factors. The budgeting and planning processes are concerned with all organizational resources—raw material, inventory, supplies, personnel, and facilities—and can be viewed from a long-term or a short-term perspective.

Are planning and budgeting the same activity?

Managers who plan on a long-range basis (5 to 10 years) are engaged in strategic planning. Top-level management conducts this process, often with the assistance of several key staff members. The result is a statement of long-range organizational goals and the strategies and policies that will help achieve those goals. Strategic planning is not concerned with day-to-day operations, although the strategic plan is the foundation on which short-term planning is based. Managers engaging in strategic planning should identify key variables that are believed to be the direct causes of the achievement or nonachievement of organizational goals and objectives. Key variables can be internal (under the control of management) or external (normally noncontrollable by management). Effective strategic planning requires that managers build plans and budgets that integrate external considerations and influences with the firm's internal factors.

Approximately half of all planning time is currently spent on analyzing external factors. In one study, U.S. respondents viewed critical external factors as follows:

- competitor actions,
- U.S. market conditions,
- political/regulatory climate (United States),
- emerging technology issues,
- consumer trends and attitudes,
- international market conditions,
- demographics, and
- political/regulatory climate (international).[1]

Tactical Planning

After identifying key variables, management should gather information related to them. Much of this information is historical and qualitative and provides a useful starting point for tactical planning activities. Tactical planning determines how the strategic plans will be achieved. Some tactical plans, such as corporate policy statements, exist for the long term and address repetitive situations. Most tactical plans, however, are short term (1 to 18 months); they are considered "single-use" plans

---

[1] "Extrovert or Introvert," *Public Utilities Fortnightly* (November 1, 1998), p. 70ff.

and are developed to address a given set of circumstances or to cover a specific period of time.

The annual budget is an example of a single-use tactical plan. Although this budget is typically prepared for a one-year period, shorter horizon (quarterly and monthly) plans should also be included for the budget to work effectively. The budget is the quantified end-product that results from the predictions and assumptions that were made about achieving both financial and nonfinancial goals and objectives. Financial goals could include targets for net income, earnings per share, or sales revenue. Nonfinancial performance goals and objectives could include a designated customer satisfaction level, defect reduction rates, and percentage of on-time deliveries. By quantifying potential difficulties in achieving organizational goals and objectives and by making those difficulties visible, budgets can help stimulate managers to think of ways to overcome those difficulties before they are realized.

> *Who should be involved in the budgeting process?*

Budgets are also effective devices to communicate objectives, constraints, and expectations to all organizational personnel. Such communication promotes understanding of what is to be accomplished, how those accomplishments are to be achieved, and the manner in which resources are to be allocated. Determination of resource allocations is made, in part, from a process of obtaining information, justifying requests, and negotiating compromises.

Employee participation is needed to effectively integrate necessary information from various sources as well as to obtain individual managerial commitment to the resulting budget. Participation helps to produce a spirit of cooperation, motivate employees, and instill a feeling of teamwork. At the same time, the greater the degree of participation by all personnel affected in the budgeting process, the greater the time and cost involved. Traditionally, to say that a company uses a large degree of participation has implied that budgets have been built from the bottom of the organization upward.

A well-prepared budget translates a company's strategic and tactical plans into usable guides for company activities. Exhibit 8–1 illustrates the relationships among strategic planning, tactical planning, and budgeting. Both strategic planning and tactical planning require that the latest information regarding the economy, environment, technological developments, and available resources be incorporated into the setting of goals and objectives. This information is used to adjust the previously gathered historical information for any changes in the key variables for the

EXHIBIT 8–1

RELATIONSHIPS AMONG PLANNING PROCESSES

Who?	What?	How?	Why?
Top management	Strategic planning	Statement of organizational mission, goals, and strategies; long range (5–10 years)	Establish a long-range vision of the organization and provide a sense of unity of and commitment to specified purposes
Top management and midmanagement	Tactical planning	Statement of organizational plans; short range (1–18 months)	Provide direction for achievement of strategic plans; state strategic plans in terms on which managers can act; furnish a basis against which results can be measured
Top management, midmanagement, and operational management	Budgeting	Quantitative and monetary statements that coordinate company activities for a year or less	Allocate resources effectively and efficiently; indicate a commitment to objectives; provide a monetary control device

planning period. The planning process also demands that, as activity takes place and plans are implemented, a monitoring system is in place to provide feedback so that the control function can be put into operation.

Management reviews the budget prior to approving and implementing it to determine whether the forecasted results are acceptable. The budget could indicate that results expected from the planned activities do not achieve the desired objectives. In this case, planned activities are reconsidered and revised so that they more effectively achieve the desired outcomes expressed during the tactical planning stage.

After a budget has been accepted, it is implemented and considered a standard against which performance can be measured. The budget sets the resource constraints under which managers must operate for the upcoming budget period. Thus, the budget becomes the basis for controlling activities and resource usage. The control phase includes making actual-to-budget comparisons, determining variances, investigating variance causes, taking necessary corrective action, and providing feedback to operating managers. Feedback, both positive and negative, is essential to the control process and, to be useful, must be provided in a timely manner. This cyclical process is illustrated in Exhibit 8–2.

The preceding discussion describes a budgeting process, but, as with many other business practices, budgeting can be unique to individual countries. For example, the lengthy and highly specific budgeting process used by many U.S. companies differs dramatically from that used by many Japanese companies. Japanese companies view the budget more as a device to help focus personnel and resources on achieving group and firm-level targets than as a control device by which to gauge individual performance.

Regardless of the specific budgeting process, it results in a **master budget**. This budget is a comprehensive set of budgets, budgetary schedules, and pro forma organizational financial statements.

master budget

THE MASTER BUDGET

operating budget

LO.3
WHAT IS THE STARTING POINT OF A MASTER BUDGET AND WHY?

As shown in Exhibit 8–3, operating and financial budgets compose the master budget. An **operating budget** is a budget that is expressed in both units and dollars. When an operating budget relates to revenues, the units presented are expected

EXHIBIT 8–2
CYCLICAL NATURE OF BUDGETING PROCESS

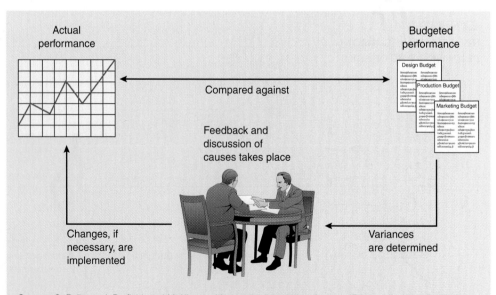

Source: C. Raiborn, J. Barfield, and M. Kinney, *Managerial Accounting*, 2nd ed. (Eagan, MN: West Publishing, 1996), Exhibit 10–12, p. 515.

EXHIBIT 8–3

COMPONENTS OF A MASTER BUDGET

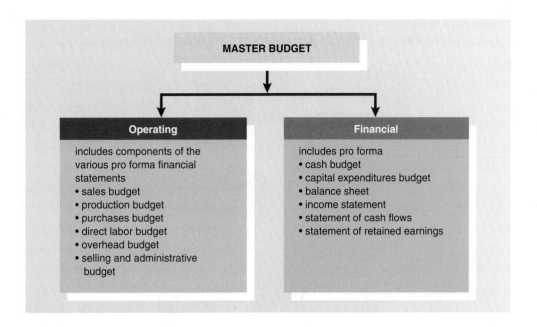

to be sold, and the dollars reflect selling prices. In contrast, when an operating budget relates to costs, the input units presented are expected to be either transformed into output units or consumed, and the dollars reflect costs.

financial budget

Monetary details from the various operating budgets are combined to prepare **financial budgets**, which indicate the funds to be generated or consumed during the budget period. Financial budgets include cash and capital budgets as well as the projected, or pro forma, financial statements that are the ultimate focal points for top management.

The master budget is prepared for a specific period and is static in the sense that it is based on a single level of output demand.[2] Developing the budget using a single demand level is necessary to facilitate the many time-consuming tasks that must occur before starting the budget period's operations. Such arrangements include making certain that an adequate number of personnel are hired, that needed production and/or storage space is available, and that suppliers, prices, delivery schedules, and quality of resources are confirmed.

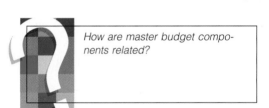

How are master budget components related?

The sales demand level selected for use in the master budget affects all other budget components. Because of the many budgetary relationships, all departmental budgets must interact in a coordinated manner. A budget developed by one department is often an essential ingredient in developing another department's budget.

The budgetary process shown in Exhibit 8–4 illustrates how the various functional areas of a manufacturing organization interact and are involved with master budget preparation. The process begins with the Sales Department's estimates of the types, quantities, and timing of demand for the company's products. The budget is typically prepared for a year and then subdivided into quarterly and monthly periods.

A production manager combines sales estimates with additional information from Purchasing, Personnel, Operations, and Capital Facilities; the combined information allows the production manager to specify the types, quantities, and timing of products to be manufactured. Sales estimates, in conjunction with esti-

---

[2] Companies can engage in contingency planning, providing for multiple budgeting paths. For example, a company could construct three budgets, respectively, for a high level of activity, an expected level of activity, and a low level of activity. If actual activity turns out to be either higher or lower than expected, management has a budget ready.

EXHIBIT 8–4

THE BUDGETARY PROCESS IN A MANUFACTURING ORGANIZATION

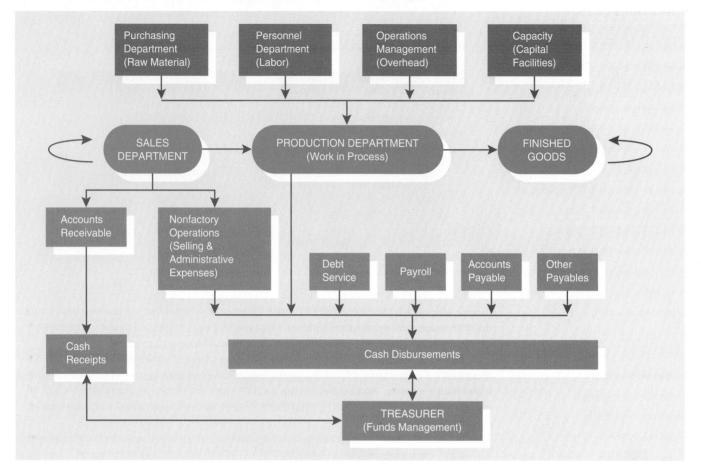

mated collection patterns, are used to determine the amounts and timing of cash receipts.

For the treasurer to properly manage organization funds, cash receipts and disbursements information must be matched from all areas so that cash is available when needed and in the amount needed.

Departments involved in the budgeting process both generate and consume information. For example, the Sales Department must receive finished goods information to know whether goods are in stock (or can be produced) before selling products. In addition, the treasurer must *receive* continual cash information as well as *provide* information to various organizational units on funds availability so that proper funds management can be maintained.

If top management encourages participation by lower-level managers in the budgeting process, each department either prepares its own budget or provides information for inclusion in a budget. Exhibit 8–5 presents an overview of the budget preparation sequence, indicates departmental budget preparation responsibility, and illustrates how the budgets interface.

The master budget begins with a sales budget derived from forecasted or expected demand. Next, production and cash flows are budgeted based on the sales budget. The budgeting process ends with the preparation of pro forma financial statements. Exhibit 8–5 depicts information flow but not necessary details; thus, the chapter next discusses the specifics of preparing a master budget.

EXHIBIT 8–5
THE MASTER BUDGET: AN OVERVIEW

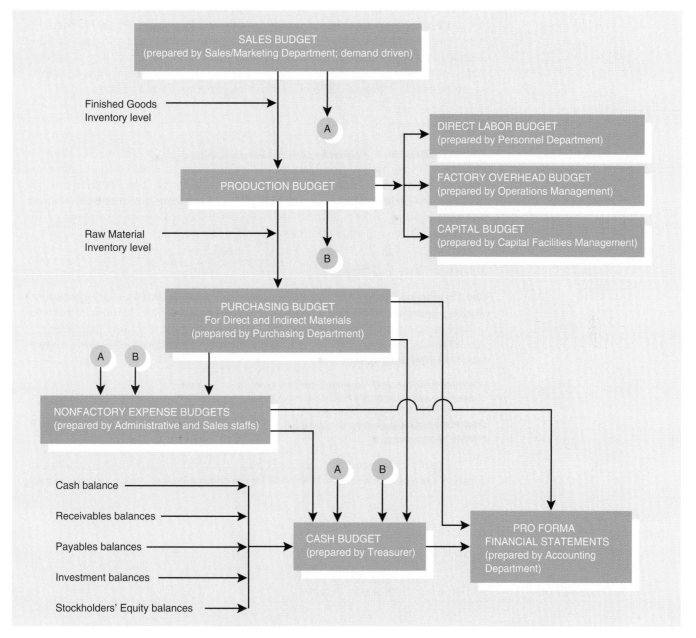

THE MASTER BUDGET ILLUSTRATED

LO.4
HOW ARE THE VARIOUS COMPONENTS IN A MASTER BUDGET PREPARED, AND HOW DO THEY RELATE TO ONE ANOTHER?

This illustration uses information from Miracle Mile Metal (MMM) Company, an illustrative company that has been in business for several years. The company, which produces a single type of 6-foot, made-to-stock steel hinge, is preparing its 2006 budget and has estimated total annual sales at 350,000 hinges. Although annual sales would be detailed on a monthly basis, the MMM Company illustration focuses on the budgets for only the first quarter of 2006. The process of developing the master budget is the same regardless of whether the time frame is one year or one quarter.

The December 31, 2005, balance sheet presented in Exhibit 8–6 provides account balances needed to begin preparation of the master budget. The December 31, 2005, balances are really estimates rather than actual figures because the budget process for 2006 must begin significantly before December 31, 2005. The company's budgetary time schedule depends on many factors, including its size and degree of forecasting sophistication. Assume that MMM Company begins its budgeting process in November 2005, when the 2006 sales forecast is received by management or a committee designated to oversee the budgeting process.

Sales Budget

The sales budget is prepared in both units and sales dollars. The selling price set for 2006 is $5 per hinge, regardless of sales territory or customer. Monthly demand and its related revenue impact for the first four months of 2006 are shown in Exhibit 8–7. Dollar sales figures are computed by multiplying sales quantities by product selling prices. April information is presented because some elements of the March budget require the subsequent month's information.

Production Budget

The production budget follows from the sales budget and uses information regarding the type, quantity, and timing of units to be sold. Sales information is used in conjunction with beginning and ending inventory information so that managers can schedule necessary production. The following formula provides the computation for units to be produced:

Number of units to be sold (from sales budget)	XXX
+ Number of units desired in ending inventory	XXX
= Total units needed during period	XXX
− Number of units in beginning inventory	(XXX)
= Units to be produced	XXX

Company management determines any policy on units desired in ending inventory. Desired ending inventory balance is generally a function of the quantity

EXHIBIT 8–6
BEGINNING BALANCE SHEET FOR MMM COMPANY

Miracle Mile Metal Company
Balance Sheet
December 31, 2005

ASSETS			LIABILITIES & STOCKHOLDERS' EQUITY		
Current Assets			**Current Liabilities**		
Cash		$ 10,000	Accounts Payable		$ 42,504
Accounts Receivable	$ 69,840		Dividends Payable (payment		
Less Allowance for Uncollectibles	(1,248)	68,592	scheduled for March 31)		45,000
Inventories			Total Current Liabilities		$ 87,504
Raw Material (3,443 pounds)	$ 7,919*				
Finished Goods (1,500 units)	4,800	12,719			
Total Current Assets		$ 91,311			
Plant Assets			**Stockholders' Equity**		
Property, Plant, and Equipment	$370,000		Common Stock	$180,000	
Less Accumulated Depreciation	(90,000)	280,000	Retained Earnings	103,807	283,807
			Total Liabilities and		
Total Assets		$371,311	Stockholders' Equity		$371,311

*This amount is actually $7,918.90, or 3,443 pounds of steel multiplied by $2.30 per pound. It has been rounded for simplicity in this exhibit. Retained Earnings has been similarly rounded.

EXHIBIT 8–7

SALES BUDGET FOR THE THREE MONTHS AND QUARTER ENDING MARCH 31, 2006

	January	February	March	Total for Quarter	April*
Sales in units	30,000	28,000	33,000	91,000	32,000
Sales in dollars	$150,000	$140,000	$165,000	$455,000	$160,000

*Information for April is needed for subsequent computations.

and timing of demand in the upcoming period as related to the firm's capacity and speed to produce particular units. Frequently, management stipulates that ending inventory be equal to a given percentage of the next period's projected sales. Other alternatives include a constant amount of inventory, a buildup of inventory for future high-demand periods, or near-zero inventory under a just-in-time system. The decision about ending inventory levels results from the consideration of whether a firm wants to have constant production with varying inventory levels or variable production with constant inventory levels.

Why don't budgeted number of units to be sold equal budgeted number of units to be produced?

Managers should consider the high costs of stockpiling inventory before making a decision about how much inventory to keep on hand. Demand for MMM Company's products is relatively constant year-round. Because most sales are to recurring customers, MMM's policy is that ending finished goods inventory should be 5 percent of the next month's unit sales. Considering this policy and using the sales information from Exhibit 8–7, the production budget shown in Exhibit 8–8 is prepared.

January's beginning inventory is the 1,500 units on hand at December 31, 2005, or 5 percent of January's estimated sales of 30,000 units. Desired March ending inventory is 5 percent of the April sales of 32,000 hinges (given in Exhibit 8–7). MMM does not have any work in process inventory because all units placed into production are assumed to be fully completed each period.[3]

Purchases Budget

Direct material must be purchased each period in sufficient quantities to meet production needs. In addition, the quantities of direct material purchased must conform with the company's desired ending inventory policies. Miracle Mile Metal Company's management ties its policy for ending direct material inventory to its production needs for the following month. Because of occasional difficulty in obtaining the high quality of material needed, MMM's ending inventory for direct material is set at 10 percent of the quantity needed for the following month's production.

Companies may have different policies for the direct material associated with different products or for different seasons of the year. For example, a company

EXHIBIT 8–8

PRODUCTION BUDGET FOR THE THREE MONTHS AND QUARTER ENDING MARCH 31, 2006

	January	February	March	Total
Sales in units (from Exhibit 8–7)	30,000	28,000	33,000	91,000
+ Desired ending inventory	1,400	1,650	1,600	1,600
= Total needed	31,400	29,650	34,600	92,600
− Beginning inventory	(1,500)	(1,400)	(1,650)	(1,500)
= Units to be produced	29,900	28,250	32,950	91,100

[3] Most manufacturing entities do not produce only whole units during the period. Normally, partially completed beginning and ending work in process inventories will exist. These inventories create the need to use equivalent units of production when computing the production budget.

may maintain only a minimal ending inventory of a direct material that is consistently available in the quantity and quality desired. Alternatively, if a material is difficult to obtain at certain times of the year, a company may stockpile that material for use in future periods.

The purchases budget is first stated in whole units of finished products and then converted to direct material component requirements and dollar amounts. Production of an MMM hinge requires only one direct material: 6 feet of steel. Steel cost has been estimated by the purchasing agent at $2.30 per pound, and it takes 1.1 pounds of steel to produce one 6-foot hinge. Exhibit 8–9 shows MMM's purchases cost for each month of the first quarter of 2006. Note that beginning and ending inventory quantities are expressed first in terms of hinges and then are converted to the appropriate quantity measure (pounds of steel). Total budgeted cost of direct material purchases for the quarter is $231,292.60.

EXHIBIT 8-9
PURCHASES BUDGET FOR THE THREE MONTHS AND QUARTER ENDING MARCH 31, 2006

	January	February	March	Quarter
Units to be produced (from Exhibit 8–8)	29,900	28,250	32,950	91,100
+ EI (10% of next month's production)	2,825	3,295	3,450*	3,450
= Total whole units needed	32,725	31,545	36,400	94,450
– Beginning inventory	(3,130)†	(2,825)	(3,295)	(3,130)
= Finished units for which purchases are required	29,595	28,720	33,105	91,420
STEEL PURCHASES				
Finished units	29,595	28,720	33,105	91,420
× Pounds needed per unit	× 1.1	× 1.1	× 1.1	× 1.1
= Total pounds to be purchased	32,554.5	31,592	36,415.5	100,562
× Price per pound	× $2.30	× $2.30	× $2.30	× $2.30
= Total cost of steel purchases	$74,875.35	$72,661.60	$83,755.65	$231,292.60

*April production is assumed to be 34,500 units.
†BI of raw materials (RM) was 3,443 pounds; each unit requires 1.1 pounds, so there was enough RM for 3,130 units, or 10% of the following month's production.

Personnel Budget

Given expected production, the Engineering and Personnel Departments can work together to determine the necessary labor requirements for the factory, sales force, and office staff. Labor requirements are stated in terms of total number of people, specific number of worker types (skilled laborers, setup helpers, salespeople, clerical personnel, etc.), and production hours needed for factory employees. Labor costs are computed from items such as union labor contracts, minimum wage laws, fringe benefit costs, payroll taxes, and bonus arrangements. The various personnel amounts are shown, as appropriate, in either the direct labor budget, manufacturing overhead budget, or selling and administrative budget.

Direct Labor Budget

Miracle Mile Metal Company's management has reviewed the staffing requirements and has developed the direct labor cost estimates shown in Exhibit 8–10 for the first quarter of 2006. Factory direct labor costs are based on standard hours of labor needed to produce the units in the production budget. The average wage rate

EXHIBIT 8–10
DIRECT LABOR BUDGET
FOR THE THREE MONTHS
AND QUARTER ENDING
MARCH 31, 2006

	January	February	March	Total
Units to be produced	29,900	28,250	32,950	91,100
× Standard hours allowed	× .025	× .025	× .025	× .025
= Total hours allowed	747.50	706.25	823.75	2,277.50
× Average wage rate (including fringe benefits)	× $6.80	× $6.80	× $6.80	× $6.80
= Direct labor cost	$ 5,083	$ 4,803	$ 5,601	$ 15,487

Note: The cost for February has been rounded up to the next whole dollar, and the cost for March has been rounded down to balance to the appropriate quarter total.

includes the direct labor payroll rate, payroll taxes, and fringe benefits; these items usually add between 25 and 30 percent to the base labor cost. All compensation is paid in the month in which it is incurred.

Overhead Budget

Overhead costs are the third production cost that must be budgeted by month and for the quarter. MMM Company has determined that machine hours are the best predictor of overhead costs and has prepared the overhead budget shown in Exhibit 8–11.

In estimating overhead, all fixed and variable costs must be specified, and mixed costs must be separated into their fixed (a) and variable (b) components. Each overhead amount shown is calculated using the $y = a + bX$ formula discussed in Chapter 3. For example, March maintenance cost is $575 fixed cost plus $988.50 ($0.30 × 3,295 estimated machine hours) variable cost for a total of $1,563 (rounded). Both total cost and cost net of depreciation are shown in the budget. The net of depreciation cost is expected to be paid in cash during the month and will affect the cash budget.

EXHIBIT 8–11
OVERHEAD BUDGET
FOR THE THREE MONTHS
AND QUARTER ENDING
MARCH 31, 2006

			January	February	March	Total
Estimated machine hours (X) (assumed)			2,990	2,825	3,295	9,110
	Value of					
	(fixed) a	**(variable)** b				
Overhead item						
Depreciation	$1,700	$0	$ 1,700	$ 1,700	$ 1,700	$ 5,100
Indirect material	0	0.20	598	565	659	1,822
Indirect labor	6,000	1.50	10,485	10,238	10,942	31,665
Utilities	500	0.10	799	783	829	2,411
Property tax	500	0	500	500	500	1,500
Insurance	450	0	450	450	450	1,350
Maintenance	575	0.30	1,472	1,423	1,563	4,458
Total cost (y)	$9,725	$2.10	$16,004	$15,659	$16,643	$48,306
Total cost net of depreciation			$14,304	$13,959	$14,943	$43,206

Note: The costs for February have been rounded up to the next whole dollar, and the costs for March have been rounded down to balance to the appropriate quarter total.

Selling and Administrative Budget

Selling and administrative (S&A) expenses can be predicted in the same manner as overhead costs. Exhibit 8–12 presents the first-quarter 2006 Miracle Mile Metal Company's S&A budget. Sales figures, rather than production levels, are the activity measure used to prepare this budget. The company has two salespeople who receive $1,000 per month plus a 2 percent commission on sales. Administrative salaries total $9,000 per month.

EXHIBIT 8–12

SELLING AND ADMINISTRATIVE BUDGET FOR THE THREE MONTHS AND QUARTER ENDING MARCH 31, 2006

			January	February	March	Total
Predicted sales (from Exhibit 8–7)			$150,000	$140,000	$165,000	$455,000
	Value of					
	(fixed) *a*	**(variable)** *b*				
S&A item						
Supplies	$ 0	$0.02	$ 3,000	$ 2,800	$ 3,300	$ 9,100
Depreciation	500	0	500	500	500	1,500
Miscellaneous	100	0.01	1,600	1,500	1,750	4,850
Compensation						
Salespeople	2,000	0.02	5,000	4,800	5,300	15,100
Administrative	9,000	0	9,000	9,000	9,000	27,000
Total cost (*y*)	$11,600	$0.05	$19,100	$18,600	$19,850	$57,550
Total cost net of depreciation			$18,600	$18,100	$19,350	$56,050

Capital Budget

The master budget focuses on the short-term or upcoming fiscal period. Managers, however, must also assess long-term needs such as plant and equipment purchases and budget for those expenditures. This assessment is referred to as capital budgeting and is discussed in Chapter 15. The capital budget is prepared separately from the master budget, but because current expenditures are involved, capital budgeting does affect the master budgeting process.

How is accrual-based information translated into cash-based information?

As shown in Exhibit 8–13, MMM Company's managers have decided to purchase a new $28,000 piece of machinery in January and to pay for it in February. The machinery will be placed into service in April after installation, testing, and employee training. Depreciation on the new machinery will not be included in the overhead calculation until installation is complete.

EXHIBIT 8–13

CAPITAL BUDGET FOR THE THREE MONTHS AND QUARTER ENDING MARCH 31, 2006

	January	February	March	Total
Acquisition—machinery	$28,000	$ 0	$0	$28,000
Cash payment for machinery	0	28,000	0	28,000

Cash Budget

LO.5
**WHY IS THE CASH BUDGET
SO IMPORTANT IN THE
MASTER BUDGETING
PROCESS?**

After the preceding budgets have been developed, a cash budget can be constructed. The cash budget could be the most important schedule prepared during the budgeting process because, without cash, a company cannot survive.

The following model can be used to summarize cash receipts and disbursements in a way that assists managers to devise appropriate financing measures to meet company needs.

Cash Budget Model

Beginning cash balance		XXX
+ Cash receipts (collections)		XXX
= Cash available for disbursements exclusive of financing		XXX
− Cash needed for disbursements (purchases, direct labor, overhead, S&A, taxes, bonuses, etc.)		(XXX)
= Cash excess or deficiency (*a*)		XXX
− Minimum desired cash balance		(XXX)
= Cash needed or available for investment or loan repayment		XXX
Financing methods		
± Borrowing (repayments)	XXX	
± Issue (reacquire) capital stock	XXX	
± Sell (acquire) investments	XXX	
± Sell (acquire) plant assets	XXX	
± Receive (pay) interest or dividends	XXX	
Total impact (+ or −) of planned financing (*b*)		XXX
= Ending cash balance (*c*), where [(*c*) = (*a*) ± (*b*)]		XXX

CASH RECEIPTS AND ACCOUNTS RECEIVABLE

Because not all sales are made on a cash basis, managers must translate sales information into cash receipts through the use of an expected collection pattern. This process considers the collection patterns experienced in the recent past and management's judgment about changes that could disturb current collection patterns. For example, changes that could weaken current collection patterns include recessionary conditions, increases in interest rates, less strict credit-granting practices, and ineffective collection practices.

In specifying collection patterns, managers should recognize that different types of customers pay in different ways. Any sizable, unique category of clientele should be segregated. MMM Company has two types of customers: (1) cash customers who never receive a discount and (2) credit customers. Of the credit customers, manufacturers and wholesalers are allowed a 2 percent cash discount; retailers are not allowed the discount.

MMM Company has determined from historical data that the collection pattern diagrammed in Exhibit 8–14 is applicable to its customers. Of each month's sales, 20 percent will be for cash, and 80 percent will be on credit. The 40 percent of the credit customers who are allowed the discount pay in the month of the sale. Collections from the remaining credit customers are as follows: 20 percent in the month of sale, 50 percent in the month following the sale, and 29 percent in the second month following the sale. Uncollectible accounts amount to 1 percent of the credit sales that do not take a discount.

Using the sales budget, information on November and December 2005 sales, and the collection pattern, management can estimate cash receipts from sales during the first three months of 2006. Management must have November and December sales information because collections for credit sales extend over three months, meaning that collection of some of the previous year's sales occur early in the current year. MMM Company's November and December sales were $125,000 and $135,000, respectively. Using MMM's expected collection pattern, projected monthly collections in the first quarter of 2006 are shown in Exhibit 8–15.

EXHIBIT 8–14
MIRACLE MILE METAL COMPANY'S COLLECTION PATTERN FOR SALES

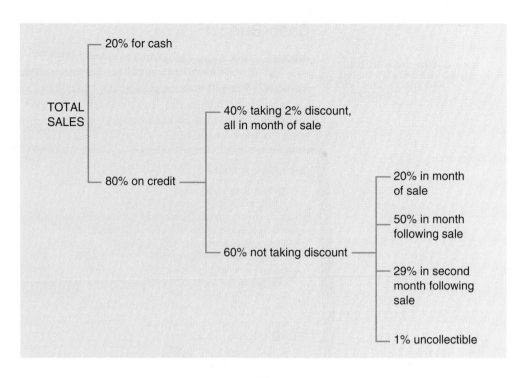

EXHIBIT 8–15
CASH COLLECTIONS FOR THE THREE MONTHS AND QUARTER ENDING MARCH 31, 2006

	January	February	March	Total	Disc.	Uncoll.
From						
November 2005 sales						
$125,000(0.8)(0.6)(0.29)	$ 17,400			$ 17,400		
$125,000(0.8)(0.6)(0.01)						$ 600
December 2005 sales						
$135,000(0.8)(0.6)(0.5)	32,400			32,400		
$135,000(0.8)(0.6)(0.29)		$ 18,792		18,792		
$135,000(0.8)(0.6)(0.01)						648
January 2006 sales						
$150,000(0.2)	30,000			30,000		
$150,000(0.8)(0.4)(0.98)	47,040N			47,040	$ 960	
$150,000(0.8)(0.6)(0.2)	14,400			14,400		
$150,000(0.8)(0.6)(0.5)		36,000		36,000		
$150,000(0.8)(0.6)(0.29)			$ 20,880	20,880		
$150,000(0.8)(0.6)(0.01)						720
February 2006 sales						
$140,000(0.2)		28,000		28,000		
$140,000(0.8)(0.4)(0.98)		43,904N		43,904	896	
$140,000(0.8)(0.6)(0.2)		13,440		13,440		
$140,000(0.8)(0.6)(0.5)			33,600	33,600		
March 2006 sales						
$165,000(0.2)			33,000	33,000		
$165,000(0.8)(0.4)(0.98)			51,744N	51,744	1,056	
$165,000(0.8)(0.6)(0.2)			15,840	15,840		
Totals	$141,240	$140,136	$155,064	$436,440	$2,912	$1,968

N stands for "net of discount." To determine the gross amount, divide the net amount by 0.98 (i.e., 100% − 2%).

The amounts for November and December collections can be reconciled to the 12/31/05, balance sheet (Exhibit 8–6), which indicated a balance of $69,840 in Accounts Receivable. This amount appears in the collection schedule as follows:

December 31, 2005, Balance in Accounts Receivable

January collections of November sales	$17,400
Estimated November bad debts	600
January collections of December sales	32,400
February collections of December sales	18,792
Estimated December bad debts	648
December 31, 2005, Accounts Receivable balance	$69,840

January 2006 sales of $150,000 are used to illustrate the collection calculations in Exhibit 8–15. The first line for January represents cash sales of 20 percent of total sales, or $30,000. The next line represents the 80 percent of the customers who buy on credit and who take the discount:

Sales to credit customers (80% of $150,000)	$120,000

Sales to customers allowed discount (40% × $120,000)	$ 48,000
− Discount taken by customers (0.02 × $48,000)	(960)
= Net collections from customers allowed discount	$ 47,040

The third line reflects the 60 percent of credit customers who paid in the month of sale but were not allowed the discount. The remaining amounts in Exhibit 8–15 are computed similarly.

After the cash collections schedule has been prepared, balances for Accounts Receivable, Allowance for Uncollectibles, and Sales Discounts can be projected. These T-accounts for Miracle Mile Metal Company follow. Balances will be used to prepare pro forma, quarter-end 2006 financial statements. For illustrative purposes only, all sales are initially recorded as Accounts Receivable. Immediate cash collections are then deducted from the Accounts Receivable balance.

Accounts Receivable

12/31/05 Balance (Exhibit 8–6)	69,840		Collections in January from beginning A/R ($17,400 + $32,400)	49,800
January 2006 sales (Exhibit 8–7)	150,000		Cash sales in January (Exh. 8–15)	30,000
			Credit collections subject to discount (cash received, $47,040)	48,000
			Credit collections not subject to discount	14,400
February 2006 sales (Exhibit 8–7)	140,000		Collections in February from beginning A/R	18,792
			Cash sales in February (Exh. 8–15)	28,000
			Collections in Feb. from Jan. sales	36,000
			Credit collections subject to discount (cash received, $43,904)	44,800
			Credit collections not subject to discount	13,440
March 2006 sales (Exhibit 8–7)	165,000		Cash sales in March (Exh. 8–15)	33,000
			Collections in Mar. from Jan. sales	20,880
			Collections in Mar. from Feb. sales	33,600
			Credit collections subject to discount (cash received, $51,744)	52,800
			Credit collections not subject to discount	15,840
3/31/06 Balance	85,488			

Allowance for Uncollectible Accounts

12/31/05 Balance (Exhibit 8–6)	1,248
January estimate (Exhibit 8–15)	720
February estimate	
[$140,000(80%)(60%)(1%)]	672
March estimate	
[$165,000(80%)(60%)(1%)]	792
3/31/06 Balance	3,432

Sales Discounts

January discounts	960
February discounts	896
March discounts	1,056
3/31/06 Balance	2,912

Note that the estimated uncollectible accounts from November 2005 through March 2006 have not been written off as of the end of the first quarter of 2006. Companies continue to make collection efforts for a substantial period before accounts are acknowledged as truly worthless. Thus, these receivables may remain on the books six months or more from the original sales date. When accounts are written off, Accounts Receivable and the Allowance for Uncollectibles will both decrease; however, there will be no income statement impact relative to the write-off.

CASH DISBURSEMENTS AND ACCOUNTS PAYABLE

Using the purchases information from Exhibit 8–9, management can prepare a cash disbursements schedule for Accounts Payable. Miracle Mile Metal Company buys all raw material on account. It pays for 40 percent of each month's purchases in the month of purchase and is allowed a 2 percent discount for prompt payment. The remaining 60 percent is paid in the month following purchase, and no discounts are taken.

Exhibit 8–16 presents the first-quarter 2006 cash disbursements information for purchases. The December 31, 2005, Accounts Payable balance of $42,504 (Exhibit

EXHIBIT 8–16

CASH DISBURSEMENTS FOR ACCOUNTS PAYABLE FOR THE THREE MONTHS AND QUARTER ENDING MARCH 31, 2006

Payment for Purchases of	January	February	March	Total	Discount
December 2005	$42,504			$ 42,504	
January 2006 (from Exhibit 8–9)					
$74,875.35(0.40)(0.98)	29,351N			29,351	$ 599
$74,875.35(0.60)		$44,925		44,925	
February 2006 (from Exhibit 8–9)					
$72,661.60(0.40)(0.98)		28,483N		28,483	581
$72,661.60(0.60)			$43,597	43,597	
March 2006 (from Exhibit 8–9)					
$83,755.65(0.40)(0.98)			32,832N	32,832	670
Total disbursements for A/P	$71,855	$73,408	$76,429	$221,692	$1,850

N stands for "net of discount." The total amount of gross purchases paid for in the month of purchase is the sum of the net of discount payment plus the amount shown on the same line in the Discount column.

8–6) represents 60 percent of December purchases of $70,840. All amounts have been rounded to whole dollars.

Accounts payable activity is summarized in the following T-account. The March 31 balance represents 60 percent of March purchases that will be paid during April.

Accounts Payable

		12/31/05 Balance (Exhibit 8–6)	42,504
January payments for December purchases (Exhibit 8–16)	42,504	January purchases (Exhibit 8–9)	74,875
January payments for January purchases subject to discount (cash paid, $29,351)	29,950	February purchases (Exhibit 8–9)	72,661
February payments for January purchases (Exhibit 8–16)	44,925	March purchases (Exhibit 8–9)	83,756
February payments for February purchases subject to discount (cash paid, $28,483)	29,064		
March payments for February purchases (Exhibit 8–16)	43,597		
March payments for March purchases subject to discount (cash paid, $32,832)	33,502		
		3/31/06 Balance	50,254

Purchases Discounts

	January discounts	599
	February discounts	581
	March discounts	670
	3/31/06 Balance	1,850

Given the cash receipts and disbursements information for MMM Company, the cash budget model is used to formulate the cash budget shown in Exhibit 8–17. The company has established $10,000 as its desired minimum cash balance. There are two primary reasons for having a desired minimum cash balance: One is internal; the other is external. The first reason reflects the uncertainty associated with the budgeting process. Because managers cannot budget with absolute precision, they maintain a "cushion" to protect the company from potential errors in forecasting collections and payments. The second reason is that the company's banks may require a minimum cash balance in relation to an open line of credit.

For simplicity, it is assumed that any investments or sales of investments are made in end-of-month $1,000 increments. Interest on company investments at 6 percent per annum or .005 percent per month is added to the company's bank account at month's end.

Exhibit 8–17 indicates that Miracle Mile Metal Company has a $41,398 excess of cash available over disbursements in January. Such an excess, however, does not consider the need for the $10,000 minimum balance. Thus, the company has $31,398 available. It used $31,000 of that amount to purchase temporary investments at the end of January.

In February, MMM Company again will have enough cash to meet its desired minimum cash balance, pay for the machinery, and make an additional $2,000 temporary investment. In March, MMM has enough excess cash available, coupled with the liquidation of $6,000 of investments, to pay the $45,000 dividend that is due.

EXHIBIT 8–17

**CASH BUDGET FOR
THE THREE MONTHS
AND QUARTER ENDING
MARCH 31, 2006**

	January	February	March	Total
Beginning cash balance	$ 10,000	$ 10,398	$ 10,419	$ 10,000
Cash collections (Exhibit 8–15)	141,240	140,136	155,064	436,440
Cash available exclusive of financing	$151,240	$150,534	$165,483	$446,440
Disbursements				
Accounts payable (for purchases, Ex. 8–16)	$ 71,855	$ 73,408	$ 76,429	$221,692
Direct labor (Ex. 8–10)	5,083	4,803	5,601	15,487
Overhead (Ex. 8–11)*	14,304	13,959	14,943	43,206
S&A expenses (Ex. 8–12)*	18,600	18,100	19,350	56,050
Total disbursements	$109,842	$110,270	$116,323	$336,435
Cash excess (inadequacy)	$ 41,398	$ 40,264	$ 49,160	$110,005
Minimum balance desired	(10,000)	(10,000)	(10,000)	(10,000)
Cash available (needed)	$ 31,398	$ 30,264	$ 39,160	$100,005
Financing				
Borrowings (repayments)	$ 0	$ 0	$ 0	$ 0
Issue (reacquire) stock	0	0	0	0
Sell (acquire) investments	(31,000)	(2,000)	6,000	(27,000)†
Sell (acquire) plant assets	0	(28,000)	0	(28,000)
Receive (pay) interest‡	0	155	165	320
Receive (pay) dividends	0	0	(45,000)	(45,000)
Total impact of planned financing	$ (31,000)	$ (29,845)	$ (38,835)	$ (99,680)
Ending cash balance	$ 10,398	$ 10,419	$ 10,325	$ 10,325

*These amounts are the net of depreciation figures.
†This is the net result of investments and disposals of investments.
‡Interest is calculated assuming a 6 percent annual rate (.005 percent per month) and investments and disposals of investments are made at the end of the month in $1,000 increments.

Cash flow provides the short-run source of power in a business to negotiate and act. In addition to preparing and executing a sound cash budget, a business can take other measures. Exhibit 8–18 offers some suggestions in this regard for small businesses, although the same prescriptions are applicable to businesses of all sizes.

Budgeted Financial Statements

The final step in the budgeting process is the development of budgeted (pro forma) financial statements for the period. These financial statements reflect the results that will be achieved if the estimates and assumptions used for all previous budgets actually occur. Such statements allow management to determine whether the predicted results are acceptable. If results are not acceptable, management has the opportunity to change and adjust items before the beginning of the period for which the budget is being prepared.

When expected net income is not considered reasonable, management can investigate the possibility of raising selling prices or finding ways to decrease costs. Any specific changes considered by management might have related effects that must be included in the revised projections. For example, raising selling prices

EXHIBIT 8–18
TEN WAYS TO IMPROVE SMALL BUSINESS CASH FLOW

Cash flow is the lifeblood of any small business. A healthy stream is essential if a business is to succeed. In general, the key is to accelerate the flow of money coming in and delay what goes out. Having written credit and collection policies can also help. Here are 10 tips a business can use to improve cash flow.

1. **Establish sound credit practices.** Before dealing with a new customer, always get at least three trade references and one bank reference. Credit reports, available from Dun and Bradstreet and others, report on a company's general financial health as well as how quickly—or slowly—it pays its bills. Never give credit until you are comfortable with a customer's ability to pay.

2. **Expedite fulfillment and shipping.** Fill orders accurately and efficiently, and then use the quickest means available to deliver products and services to customers. Unnecessary delays can add days or weeks to customer payments.

3. **Bill promptly and accurately.** The faster you mail an invoice, the faster you will be paid. When possible, send an invoice with the order. If deliveries do not automatically trigger an invoice, establish a set billing schedule, preferably weekly. Check invoices for accuracy before mailing them. All invoices should include a payment due date. An invoice without payment terms may fall to the bottom of a customer's pile of bills.

4. **Offer discounts for prompt payment.** Given an incentive, some customers will pay sooner rather than later. Trade discounts typically give 1 percent to 2 percent off the total amount due if customers pay in 10 days.

5. **Aggressively follow up on past due accounts.** As soon as a bill becomes overdue, call the customer and ask when you can expect payment. Keep a record of the conversation and the customer's response. Set a follow-up date in the event the promised payment is not received. Ask delinquent customers with genuine financial problems to try to pay at least a small amount every week. When necessary, don't hesitate to seek professional help from an attorney or collection agency.

6. **Deposit payments promptly.** Don't let checks sit in a drawer waiting to be deposited. The sooner you make a deposit, the sooner you can put the money to work for your business. If you are really serious about speeding up your cash flow, a post office box or bank lockbox can accelerate receipt of checks.

7. **Seek better payment terms from suppliers and banks.** Better payment terms from suppliers are the simplest way to slow down a company's cash outflow. While most suppliers provide 30-day terms, 60 or 90 days are sometimes available, though it might mean changing suppliers. Better credit terms translate into borrowing money interest free. Some banks also could be willing to restructure business loans to make them easier to repay.

8. **Keep a tight control on inventory.** Less cash tied up in inventory generally means better cash flow. While some suppliers offer deeper discounts on volume purchases, if inventory sits on the shelf too long, it ties up money that could be put to better use elsewhere.

9. **Review and reduce expenses.** Take a critical look at all expenses. If you're not sure an expense is necessary, hold back until you are confident it will have a favorable impact on the bottom line. Consider ways to decrease operating costs, such as switching from a weekly to a biweekly payroll to reduce payroll processing costs. Be careful not to cut costs that could hurt profits. For instance, rather than cutting the marketing budget, redirect the money to areas where it will have a more positive impact.

10. **Pay bills on time, but never before they are due.** The basic rule is to take as long as you are allowed to pay bills—without incurring late fees or interest charges. Make an exception to this rule only when you are offered a trade discount for early payment.

Source: "10 Ways to Improve Small Business Cash Flow," New York State Society of CPAs, New York: *http://www.nysscpa.org*. Reprinted with permission.

could decrease volume. Alternatively, reductions in costs from using lower-grade material could increase spoilage during production or cause a decline in demand. With the availability of the computer, changes in budget assumptions and their resultant effects can be simulated quickly and easily.

COST OF GOODS MANUFACTURED SCHEDULE

In a manufacturing environment, management must prepare a schedule of cost of goods manufactured before it can prepare an income statement. This schedule is necessary to determine cost of goods sold. Using information from previous budgets, Miracle Mile Metal Company's budgeted cost of goods manufactured schedule is shown in Exhibit 8–19. Because it was assumed that no beginning or ending work in process inventories existed, cost of goods manufactured equals the period's manufacturing costs of the period. Had partially completed work in process inventory existed, the computations would be more complex and would have involved the use of equivalent units of production.

EXHIBIT 8–19

PRO FORMA COST OF GOODS MANUFACTURED SCHEDULE

Miracle Mile Metal Company
Pro Forma Cost of Goods Manufactured Schedule
For Quarter Ending March 31, 2006

Beginning work in process inventory			$ 0
Cost of raw material used			
Beginning balance (Exhibit 8–6)		$ 7,919	
Net purchases (from Accounts Payable			
and Purchases Discounts, p. 321)		229,442	
Total raw material available		$237,361	
Ending balance of raw material (Note A)		(8,729)	
Cost of raw material used		$228,632	
Direct labor (Exhibit 8–10)		15,487	
Factory overhead (Exhibit 8–11)		48,306	
Total costs to be accounted for			292,425
Ending work in process inventory			(0)
Cost of goods manufactured			$292,425
Note A: Steel			
Ending balance (Exhibit 8–9) required for finished goods	3,450		
Pounds per unit	× 1.1		
Total pounds of raw material required	3,795		
Price per pound	× $2.30		
Ending balance of raw material	$8,728.50		

INCOME STATEMENT

MMM Company's projected income statement for the first quarter of 2006 is presented in Exhibit 8–20. This statement uses much of the information previously developed in determining the revenues and expenses for the period.

BALANCE SHEET

On completion of the income statement, a March 31, 2006, balance sheet (Exhibit 8–21, p. 326) can be prepared.

STATEMENT OF CASH FLOWS

The information found on the income statement, balance sheet, and cash budget is also used to prepare a statement of cash flows (SCF). This statement can assist managers in judging the company's ability to handle fixed cash outflow commitments, adapt to adverse changes in business conditions, and undertake new commitments. Furthermore, because the SCF identifies the relationship between net income and net cash flow from operations, it assists managers in judging the quality of the company's earnings.

Whereas the cash budget is essential to current cash management, the budgeted SCF gives managers a more global view of cash flows by rearranging them into three distinct major activities (operating, investing, and financing). Such a rearrangement permits management to judge whether the specific anticipated flows are consistent with the company's strategic plans. In addition, the SCF would incorporate a schedule or narrative about significant noncash transactions if any have occurred, such as an exchange of stock for land, that are disregarded in the cash budget.

EXHIBIT 8–20
PRO FORMA INCOME
STATEMENT

Miracle Mile Metal Company
Pro Forma Income Statement
For Quarter Ending March 31, 2006

Sales (Exhibit 8–7)			$455,000
Less sales discounts (p. 320)			(2,912)
Net sales			$452,088
Cost of goods sold			
Finished goods—12/31/05 (Exhibit 8–6)		$ 4,800	
Cost of goods manufactured (Exhibit 8–19)		292,425	
Cost of goods available for sale		$297,225	
Finished goods—3/31/06 (Note A)		(5,120)	(292,105)
Gross margin			$159,983
Expenses			
Uncollectible accounts expense (Note B)		$ 2,184	
S&A expenses (Exhibit 8–12)		57,550	(59,734)
Income from operations			$100,249
Other revenue—interest earned (Exhibit 8–17)			320
Income before income taxes			$100,569
Income taxes (assumed rate of 40%)			(40,228)
Net income			$ 60,341

Note A

Beginning finished goods units	1,500	
Production (Exhibit 8–8)	91,100	
Units available for sale	92,600	
Sales (Exhibit 8–7)	(91,000)	
Ending finished goods units	1,600	
Cost per unit:		
Material	$2.53	
Conversion (assumed)	0.67	× $3.20
Cost of ending inventory		$ 5,120

Note B

Total sales	$455,000
× % credit sales	× 0.80
= Credit sales	$364,000
× % not taking discount	× 0.60
= Potential bad debts	$218,400
× % estimated uncollectible	× 0.01
= Estimated bad debts	$ 2,184

The operating section of the SCF prepared on either a direct or an indirect basis is acceptable for external reporting. The direct basis uses pure cash flow information (cash receipts and cash disbursements) for operating activities. The operating section of a SCF prepared on an indirect basis begins with net income and makes reconciling adjustments to arrive at cash flow from operations. Exhibit 8–22 provides a statement of cash flows for Miracle Mile Metal Company using the information from the cash budget in Exhibit 8–17; the second, indirect presentation of the operating section uses the information from the income statement in Exhibit 8–20 and the balance sheets in Exhibits 8–6 and 8–21.

EXHIBIT 8–21
PRO FORMA BALANCE SHEET

Miracle Mile Metal Company
Pro Forma Balance Sheet
March 31, 2006

ASSETS			LIABILITIES AND STOCKHOLDERS' EQUITY		
Current Assets			**Current Liabilities**		
Cash (Exhibit 8–17)		$ 10,325	Accounts Payable (p. 321)		$ 50,254
Accounts Receivable (p. 319)	$ 85,488		Income Tax Payable		
Less Allowance for Uncollectibles			(Exhibit 8–20)		40,228
(p. 320)	(3,432)	82,056			
Inventories			Total Current Liabilities		$ 90,482
Raw Material (3,795 pounds)					
(Exhibit 8–19, Note A)	$ 8,729*				
Finished Goods (1,600 units)					
(Exhibit 8–20, Note A)	5,120	13,849			
Investment		27,000			
Total Current Assets		$133,230			
Plant Assets			**Stockholders' Equity**		
Property, Plant, and Equipment					
(Note A)	$398,000		Common Stock	$180,000	
Less Accumulated Depreciation			Retained Earnings	164,148	344,148
(Note B)	(96,600)	301,400	Total Liabilities and Stockholders' Equity		$434,630
Total Assets		$434,630			

Note A		
Beginning balance (Exhibit 8–6)	$370,000	
Purchased new machine	28,000	
Ending balance	$398,000	

Note B		
Beginning balance (Exhibit 8–6)	$ 90,000	
Factory depreciation (Exhibit 8–11)	5,100	
S&A depreciation (Exhibit 8–12)	1,500	
Ending balance	$ 96,600	

Note C		
Beginning balance (Exhibit 8–6)	$103,807	
Net income (Exhibit 8–20)	60,341	
Ending balance	$164,148	

Miracle Mile Metal Company generates a rather low cash flow from operations ($100,325) compared to net sales revenue as well as a rather low net income per net sales dollar (13.3 percent). These two items suggest that MMM Company could want to review its hinge sales price and its production costs. Another issue that could be discussed is why such a high proportion of retained earnings was paid out as dividends.

EXHIBIT 8–22
PRO FORMA STATEMENT
OF CASH FLOWS

Miracle Mile Metal Company
Pro Forma Statement of Cash Flows
For Quarter Ending March 31, 2006

Operating activities			
Cash collections from sales		$436,440	
Interest earned		320	
Total		$436,760	
Cash payments			
For inventory:			
Raw material	$221,692		
Direct labor	15,487		
Overhead	43,206	(280,385)	
For S&A costs		(56,050)	
Net cash inflow from operating activities			$100,325
Investing activities			
Purchase of plant asset		$ (28,000)	
Short-term investment		(27,000)	
Net cash outflow from investing activities			(55,000)
Financing activities			
Dividends paid		$ (45,000)	
Net cash outflow from financing activities			(45,000)
Net increase in cash			$ 325
Beginning balance of cash (1/1/06)			10,000
Ending balance of cash (12/31/06)			$ 10,325
Alternative (indirect) basis for operating activities			
Net income		$ 60,341	
+ Depreciation (Exhibit 8–11 and Exhibit 8–12)	$ 6,600		
− Increase in net Accounts Receivable ($68,592 − $82,056)	(13,464)		
− Increase in total inventory ($12,719 − $13,849)	(1,130)		
+ Increase in Taxes Payable ($0 − $40,228)	40,228		
+ Increase in Accounts Payable ($42,504 − $50,254)	7,750	39,984	
= Net cash inflow from operating activities		$100,325	

CONCLUDING COMMENTS

LO.6
**WHAT BENEFITS ARE
PROVIDED BY A BUDGET?**

The benefits of a well-prepared budget are that the document can act as:

1. a guide to help managers align activities and resource allocations with organizational goals;

2. a vehicle to promote employee participation, cooperation, and departmental coordination;

3. a tool to enhance conduct of the managerial functions of planning, controlling, problem solving, and performance evaluating;

4. a basis on which to sharpen management's responsiveness to changes in both internal and external factors; and

5. a model that provides a rigorous view of future performance of a business in time to consider alternative measures.

What details are important in the budgeting process?

Sales forecasts should specify type and quantity of product to be sold, geographic locations of sales, buyer types, and when sales are to be made.

Because of its fundamental nature in the budgeting process, demand must be predicted as accurately and with as many details as possible. Sales forecasts should indicate type and quantity of products to be sold, geographic locations of the sales, types of buyers, and when the sales are to be made. Such detail is necessary because different products require different production and distribution facilities, different customers have different credit terms and payment schedules, and different seasons or months can necessitate different shipping schedules or methods.

Estimated sales demand has a pervasive impact on the master budget. To arrive at a valid prediction, managers use as much information as is available and can combine several estimation approaches. Combining prediction methods provides managers a way to confirm estimates and reduce uncertainty. Some ways of estimating future demand are (1) canvassing sales personnel for a subjective consensus, (2) making simple extrapolations of past trends, (3) using market research, and (4) employing statistical and other mathematical models.

Care should be taken to use realistic, rather than optimistic or pessimistic, forecasts of revenues and costs. Firms can develop computer models that allow repetitive simulations to be run after changes are made to one or more factors. These simulations permit managers to review results that would be obtained under various circumstances.

continuous budgeting

The master budget is normally prepared for a year and is detailed by quarters and months within those quarters. Some companies use a process of **continuous budgeting**, which means that an ongoing 12-month budget is presented by successively adding a new budget month (12 months into the future) as each current month expires. Such a process allows management to work, at any time, within the present 1-month component of a full 12-month annual budget. Continuous budgets make the planning process less sporadic. Rather than having managers "go into the budgeting period" at a specific time, they are continuously involved in planning and budgeting.

If actual results differ from plans, managers should find the causes of the differences and then consider budget revisions. Arrangements usually cannot be made rapidly enough to revise the current month's budget. However, under certain circumstances and if they so desire, managers could revise future months' budgets. If actual performance deviates substantially from what was expected, management could adjust the budget, depending on the variance causes.

If the causes are beyond the organization's control and are cost related, management can decide to revise budget cost estimates upward or downward to be more realistic. If the causes are internal (such as the sales staff not selling the product), management can leave the budget in its original form so that the effects of operational control are visible in the comparisons. Regardless of whether the budget is revised, managers should commend those individuals responsible for positive performance and communicate the effects of such performance to other related departments. For example, if the sales force has sold significantly higher quantities of product than expected in the original budget, production and purchasing will need to be notified to increase the number of units manufactured and amount of raw material purchased.

budget slack

participatory budget

imposed budget

When budgets are used for performance evaluations, management often encounters the problem of **budget slack**, which is the intentional underestimation of revenues and/or overestimation of expenses. Slack can be incorporated into the budget during the development process in a participatory budget. A **participatory budget** is developed through joint decision making by top management and operating personnel. However, slack is not often found in **imposed budgets**, which top management prepares with little or no input from operating personnel. After the budget has been developed, operating personnel are informed of the budget goals and constraints. The budgeting process can be represented by a continuum with participatory budgets on one end and imposed budgets on the other. Only rarely is a budget either purely participatory or purely imposed. The budget process in a particular company is usually defined by the degree to which the process is either participatory or imposed.

Having budget slack allows subordinate managers to achieve their objectives with less effort than would be necessary without the slack. Slack also creates problems because of the significant interaction of the budget factors. For example, if sales volumes are understated or overstated, problems in the production, purchasing, and personnel areas can arise.

Top management can try to reduce slack by tying actual performance to the budget through a bonus system. Operating managers are rewarded with large bonuses for budgeting relatively high performance levels and achieving those levels. If performance is set at a low or minimal level, achievement of that performance is either not rewarded or only minimally rewarded. Top management must be aware that budget slack has a tremendous negative impact on organizational effectiveness and efficiency.

Managers could want to consider expanding their budgeting process to recognize the concepts of activities and cost drivers in a manner consistent with activity-based management. An activity budget can be created by mapping the line items in the conventional budget to a list of activities. This type of budget can help management become more aware of the budgeted costs of proposed non-value-added activities and make managers question why such costs are being planned. Based on this enhanced awareness, managers can plan to reduce or eliminate some of these non-value-added activities.

Revisiting

S & S Hinge Company

At S & S Hinge, one of the primary budgeting issues for the company is product pricing. Steel, stainless steel, and aluminum raw material prices have skyrocketed in the recent past, and S & S must pass such raw material price increases along to customers to maintain its profitability. Customers, however, are aware that the price increases that have occurred are related to problems outside the control of the company. S & S prides itself on its customer relationships and has instituted numerous controls to contain nonmaterial costs so that the company's prices remain competitive.

Although many metal-working production operations have gone offshore, this company wants to make certain that its high standards will not cause a customer to turn to an alternative, less expensive, lower-quality source. Company management and employees are dedicated to total quality management concepts; it guarantees 100 percent defect-free products and minimizes lead times from order to shipment. The company has the largest stock of continuous hinges in the industry so that customers can be provided next-day shipping. For continual, blanket-order customers, S & S also provides free inventory management services, one of the reasons that the company is tops in industry customer service. In budgeting, management estimates that 40–45 percent of total sales will be from standard (or made-to-stock) hinges and the remainder will be from made-to-order hinges.

Direct material accounts for more than half of total production cost, and the company refuses to compromise its quality beliefs by purchasing lower-grade metals simply to generate cost savings. Only prime metals (steel, stainless steel, aluminum, and preplated brass) that meet the company's tolerance, hardness, and finish standards are purchased from mills around the world. Occasionally, the company has difficulty obtaining the proper grade of raw materials, causing the need to stockpile when accessibility exists.

Direct labor accounts for less than 10 percent of product cost. The die-stamping, hole-punching, and cutting machines are automated and require only one person to set up and run a line, although a second person is sometimes used to help perform setup operations when production changes are made.

The company's recycling program has generated a secondary revenue stream. By its very nature, the manufacturing process creates scrap; the quantity depends on the raw material being used and the hinges being produced. Estimates of this revenue source are that recycled aluminum and stainless steel generate about 40 percent of their original values; steel generates only about 25 percent.

The company is currently reviewing potential changes to its accounting system. One is the implementation of a new methodology called "lean accounting"; another is a review of the budgeting process. However, any changes will be made with the following goal in mind: to be profitable and proud of product quality. That way, when Chris celebrates *his* 85th birthday, he'll know that he's kept up a strong family tradition!

Source: Information provided at *http://www.sandshinge.com* and from Warren Moss, S & S Hinge Company accounting manager.

Appendix

LO.7
**HOW DOES A BUDGET
MANUAL FACILITATE THE
BUDGETING PROCESS?**

budget manual

Budget Manual

To be useful, a budget requires a substantial amount of time and effort from the persons who prepare it. This process can be improved by the availability of an organizational **budget manual**, which is a detailed set of information and guidelines about the budgetary process. The manual should include

1. statements of the budgetary purpose and its desired results;
2. a listing of specific budgetary activities to be performed;
3. a calendar of scheduled budgetary activities;
4. sample budgetary forms; and
5. original, revised, and approved budgets.

The statements of budgetary purpose and desired results communicate the reasons behind the process. These statements should flow from general to specific details. An example of a general statement of budgetary purpose is this: "The cash budget provides a basis for planning, reviewing, and controlling cash flows from and for various activities; this budget is essential to the preparation of a pro forma statement of cash flows." Specific statements could include references to minimum desired cash balances and periods of intense cash needs.

Budgetary activities should be listed by position rather than person because the responsibility for actions should be assigned to the individual holding the designated position at the time the budget is being prepared. The manual's activities section should indicate who has the final authority for revising and approving the budget. Budget approval can be delegated to a budget committee or reserved by one or several members of top management.

The budget calendar helps coordinate the budgetary process; it should indicate a timetable for all budget activities and be keyed directly to the activities list. The timetable for the budget process is unique to each organization. The larger the organization, the more time will be consumed to gather and coordinate information, identify weak points in the process or the budget itself, and take corrective action. The calendar should also indicate control points for the upcoming periods at which budget-to-actual comparisons are to be made and feedback provided to managers who are responsible for operations.

Sample forms are extremely useful because they provide for consistent presentations of budget information from all individuals, making summarization of information easier and quicker. The sample forms should be easy to understand and may include standardized worksheets that allow managers to update historical information to arrive at budgetary figures. This section of the budget manual may also provide standard cost tables for items on which the organization has specific guidelines or policies. For example, in estimating employee fringe benefit costs, the company rule of thumb could be 25 percent of base salary. Or, if company policy states that each salesperson's per diem meal allowance is $30, meal expenses would be budgeted as estimated travel days multiplied by $30.

The final section of the budget manual contains the budgets generated during the budgeting process. Numerous budgets probably will be submitted and revised prior to actual budget implementation. Understanding this revision process and why changes were made is helpful for future planning. The final approved master budget is included in the budget manual as a control document.[4]

---

[4] In the event of changes in economic conditions or strategic plans, the "final" budget can be revised during the budget period.

Comprehensive Review Module

Chapter Summary

1. Budgeting is important so that companies

   - can visualize the future and move in a focused direction.

   - plan effectively.

   - agree on and communicate organizational goals and objectives.

   - develop quantitative translations of their goals and objectives.

   - commit resources to desired activities.

   - establish financial performance indicators of success.

   - engage people to participate in the planning process.

   - produce a spirit of cooperation among employees and organizational departments or divisions.

   - control operations and resource usage.

2. Strategic planning and budgeting are related because they

   - tie the long-term and short-term (tactical) plans together.

   - use the same underlying key variables to identify success.

   - harmonize external considerations and internal factors.

   - require current information regarding the economy, environment, technological developments, and available resources.

3. The starting point of a master budget

   - reflects a single level of output demand.

   - is static to facilitate the numerous arrangements (employees, suppliers, prices, resource quality, capacity availability, etc.) that must be in place before beginning operations.

   - affects all other organizational activities and budgets.

4. Master budget components

   - include the

     - ➢ Sales budget, which reflects units and dollars.

     - ➢ Production budget, which adds sales and desired finished goods ending inventory and subtracts finished goods beginning inventory.

     - ➢ Purchases budget, which adds production and desired raw material or component ending inventory and subtracts raw material or component beginning inventory; purchases quantities are then multiplied by raw material or component costs.

     - ➢ Direct labor budget, which multiples production by standard hours allowed and then by average wage rate.

     - ➢ Overhead budget, which adds (variable factory OH costs multiplied by the quantity of the cost driver) plus fixed factory OH costs.

     - ➢ Selling and administrative budget, which adds (variable nonfactory costs multiplied by the quantity of the cost driver) plus fixed nonfactory costs.

     - ➢ Capital budget, which contains fixed asset purchases and payment points.

     - ➢ Cash budget, which reflects all cash received from and spent on items included in the other budgets.

   - are combined to prepare pro forma financial statements for management review and assessment.

5. The cash budget is critical to the master budgeting process because it

   - is essential for an organization to have cash to survive.

   - translates accrual-based information (such as sales revenues) into actual cash flows.

   - can help indicate whether credit practices are effective (i.e., whether customers are paying for purchases within the designated credit period).

   - allows the organization to forecast when cash borrowings could be necessary or when cash investments could be made (and for how long).

   - can be used to help prepare the pro forma statement of cash flows.

6. Budgets benefit organizations by

   - guiding management to align organizational goals with activities and resource commitments.

   - promoting employee participation and departmental coordination.

   - enhancing the managerial functions of planning, controlling, and problem solving.

   - allowing management to forecast future performance to determine acceptability and, if necessary, provide an opportunity for change.

   - providing a benchmark against which to judge how effectively and efficiently organizational goals were met.

Solution Strategies

Sales Budget
  Units of sales
× Selling price per unit
= Dollars of sales

Production Budget
  Units of sales
+ Units desired in ending inventory
− Units in beginning inventory
= Units to be produced

Purchases Budget
  Units to be produced
+ Units desired in ending inventory
− Units in beginning inventory
= Units to be purchased

Direct Labor Budget
  Units to be produced*
× Standard time allowed per unit
= Standard labor time allowed
× Per hour direct labor cost
= Total direct labor cost

*Converted to direct material component requirements, if necessary

Overhead Budget
  Predicted activity base
× Variable overhead rate per unit of activity
= Total variable overhead cost
+ Fixed overhead cost
= Total overhead cost

Selling and Administrative Budget
  Predicted sales dollars (or other variable measure)
× Variable S&A rate per dollar (or other variable measure)
= Total variable S&A cost
+ Fixed S&A cost
= Total S&A cost

Schedule of Cash Receipts (Collections) from Sales
  Dollars of credit sales for month
× Percent collection for month of sale
= Credit to accounts receivable for month's sales
− Allowed and taken sales discounts
= Receipts for current month's credit sales
+ Receipts from cash sales
+ Current month's cash receipts for prior months' credit sales
= Cash receipts for current month

Schedule of Cash Payments for Purchases
   Units to be purchased
$\times$ Cost per unit
= Total cost of purchases
$\times$ Percent payment for current purchases
= Debit to accounts payable for month's purchases
− Purchase discounts taken
= Cash payments for current month's purchases
+ Cash purchases
+ Current month's payments for prior months' purchases
= Cash payments for accounts payable for current month

Cash Budget
   Beginning cash balance
+ Cash receipts (collections)
= Cash available for disbursements
− Cash needed for disbursements:
     Cash payments for accounts payable for month
     Cost of compensation
     Total cost of overhead minus depreciation
     Total S&A cost minus depreciation
= Cash excess or deficiency
− Minimum desired cash balance
= Cash needed or available for investment or financing
$\pm$ Various financing measures
= Ending cash balance

Demonstration Problem

Bass Lighting Fixtures' July 31, 2006, balance sheet includes the following:

Cash	$30,000 debit
Accounts Receivable	92,000 debit
Allowance for Uncollectible Accounts	2,044 credit
Merchandise Inventory	12,266 debit

The firm's management has designated $30,000 as the firm's monthly minimum cash balance. Other information about Bass follows:

- Revenues of $200,000 and $240,000 are expected for August and September, respectively. All goods are sold on account.
- The collection pattern for accounts receivable is 55 percent in the month of sale, 44 percent in the month following the sale, and 1 percent uncollectible.
- Cost of goods sold approximates 60 percent of sales revenues.
- Management wants to end each month with 10 percent of that month's cost of sales in merchandise inventory.
- All accounts payable for inventory are paid in the month of purchase.
- Other monthly expenses are $26,000, which includes $4,000 of depreciation but does not include uncollectible accounts expense.

Required:
a. Forecast the August cash collections.
b. Forecast the August and September cost of purchases.
c. Prepare the cash budget for August including the effects of financing (borrowing or investing).

Solution to Demonstration Problem

a. **August Collections**

From July ($92,000 − $2,044)	$ 89,956
From August ($200,000 $\times$ 0.55)	110,000
Total	$199,956

b.

	August	September
Sales	$200,000	$240,000
Cost of goods sold (60%)	$120,000	$144,000
Add desired ending balance	12,000	14,400
Total needed	$132,000	$158,400
Less beginning balance	(12,266)	(12,000)
Cost of purchases	$119,734	$146,400

c. **August Cash Budget**

Beginning cash balance		$ 30,000
August collections		199,956
Total cash available for disbursements		$229,956
Disbursements		
Purchase of merchandise	$119,734	
Other monthly expenses ($26,000 − $4,000)	22,000	(141,734)
Cash excess or deficiency (*a*)		$ 88,222
Less minimum cash balance desired		(30,000)
Cash available or needed		$ 58,222
Financing:		
Acquire investment (*b*)		(58,222)
Ending cash balance (*c*); (*c = a − b*)		$ 30,000

Key Terms

budget *(p. 305)*
budgeting *(p. 305)*
budget manual *(p. 331)*
budget slack *(p. 329)*

continuous budgeting *(p. 328)*
financial budget *(p. 309)*
imposed budget *(p. 329)*
master budget *(p. 308)*

operating budget *(p. 308)*
participatory budget *(p. 329)*

Questions

1. Why is the master budget an important source of information for managers and operating personnel?

2. How does the strategic plan influence preparation of the master budget?

3. Distinguish between a tactical plan and a strategic plan. How are these plans related?

4. After a master budget has been prepared, what is its role in managerial control?

5. Differentiate between the operating and financial budgets that are contained in a master budget. Why are both types needed?

6. Discuss the sequence in which the major components of the master budget are prepared. Why is it necessary to prepare the components in such a sequence?

7. Why is a firm's production budget influenced by the finished goods inventory policy?

8. Assume that in preparing the cash budget, the accountant discovers that a cash shortage will likely occur in a specific month. What actions might the accountant recommend to management to deal with the cash shortage?

9. The cash budget and the pro forma statement of cash flows both provide information about cash. What information about cash is common to these two sources, and what information is unique to the two sources?

10. What is budgetary slack, and what actions might top managers take to rid their firms' budgets of slack?

11. (Appendix) Why is it necessary for a company to prepare a budget manual?

Exercises

12. (Revenue budget) In 2006, the Teachers' Credit Union (TCU) had $2,000,000 in business loans at an average interest rate of 5.5 percent as well as $1,600,000 in consumer loans with an average rate of 10 percent. The credit union also has $500,000 invested in government securities that pay interest at an average rate of 2 percent.

For 2007, TCU estimates that its business loan portfolio will rise to $3,000,000, and the interest rate will rise to 6.5 percent. It projects that consumer loans will be $2,000,000 and have an average interest rate of 13 percent. The credit union's government security investment will be $800,000 and will bear an average interest rate of 3.5 percent. What is TCU's projected revenue for 2006?

WebTUTOR Advantage

13. (Production budget) Jessica Corp. has the following projected sales, in units, for the first four months of 2006:

January	25,600
February	24,000
March	32,000
April	38,400

The company desires to have an ending inventory each month equal to one-half of next month's estimated sales; however, this criterion was not in effect at the end of 2005. Ending inventory at that time was 7,400 units. Determine the company's production requirements for each month of the first quarter of 2006.

14. (Production budget) David Company's sales budget has the following unit sales projections for each quarter of calendar year 2006:

January–March	540,000
April–June	680,000
July–September	490,000
October–December	550,000
Total	2,260,000

Sales for the first quarter of 2007 are expected to be 600,000 units. Ending inventory of finished goods for each quarter is scheduled to equal 10 percent of the next quarter's budgeted sales. The company is expected to be in compliance with this policy as of December 31, 2005. Develop a quarterly production budget for 2006 and for the year in total.

15. (Material purchases budget) San Angelo Co. has projected sales of 42,960 pairs of cowboy boots in October. Each pair of boots requires 2.5 linear feet of leather. The beginning inventory of leather and boots, respectively, are 2,000 yards and 2,152 pairs. San Angelo Co. wants to have 3,000 yards of leather and 5,800 pair of boots on hand at the end of October due to high sales projections for the holiday season. To convert linear feet of leather to yards, simply divide by 3 because the leather comes in a standard width. If San Angelo Co. has no beginning or ending work in process inventory, how many yards of leather must the company purchase in October?

16. (Material purchases budget) King Culvert Company has budgeted sales of 380,000 feet of its concrete culvert products for June 2006. Each foot of product requires 8 pounds of concrete ($0.11 per pound) and 15 pounds of gravel ($0.05 per pound). Actual beginning inventories and projected ending inventories are shown below.

	June 1	June 30
Finished goods inventory (in feet)	24,500	20,000
Concrete (in pounds)	82,000	68,600
Gravel (in pounds)	65,300	92,500

a. How many pounds of concrete does King Culvert plan to purchase in June? What will be the cost of those purchases?

b. How many pounds of gravel does King Culvert plan to purchase in June? What will be the cost of those purchases?

17. (Production and related schedules) Lewis Corp. manufactures and sells plastic boxes and trays. Sales are projected to be evenly spread over the annual period. Estimated product sales and material needs for each unit of product follow:

	Boxes	Trays
Annual sales	84,000	60,000
Material A	2.0 pounds	1.0 pound
Material B	3.0 pounds	4.0 pounds
Direct labor	2.0 hours	0.5 hour

Overhead is applied at a rate of $1.60 per direct labor hour.

	Expected Beginning Inventories	Desired Ending Inventories
Material A	2,000 pounds	2,500 pounds
Material B	5,000 pounds	3,400 pounds
Boxes	1,000 units	1,200 units
Trays	300 units	450 units

Material A costs $0.05 per pound, and Material B costs $0.08 per pound. Prepare the following information:

a. Production schedule by product and in total.

b. Purchases budget in units by product and in total as well as in dollars.

c. Direct labor budget in hours by product and in total.

d. Overhead to be charged to production by product and in total.

18. (Cash collections) Clark Inc. is preparing its first-quarter monthly cash budget for 2006. The following information is available about actual and expected sales:

November	December	January	February	March
$41,500	$38,000	$39,500	$44,000	$29,500

Tracing collections from prior year monthly sales and discussions with the credit manager helped develop a profile of collection behavior patterns.

Of a given month's sales, 40 percent is typically collected in the month of sale. Because the company terms are 1 percent (end of month) net 30, all collections within the month of sale are net of the 1 percent discount. Of a given month's sales, 30 percent is collected in the month following the sale. The remaining 30 percent is collected in the second month following the month of the sale. Bad debts are negligible and should be ignored.

a. Prepare a schedule of cash collections for Clark Inc. by month for January, February, and March.

b. Calculate the Accounts Receivable balance at March 31.

19. (Cash budget) The October 1, 2006, Accounts Receivable balance for Rosa Architectural Company is $607,500. Of that balance, $450,000 represents remaining accounts receivable from September billings. The normal collection pattern for the firm is 20 percent of billings in the month of service, 55 percent in the month after service, and 22 percent in the second month following service. The remaining billings are uncollectible. October billings are expected to be $900,000.

a. What were August billings for Rosa Architectural Company?

b. What amount of September billings is expected to be uncollectible?

c. What are the firm's projected cash collections in October?

WebTUTOR Advantage

20. (Cash collections, accounts receivable) Leon's Club is developing a forecast for June 2006 cash receipts from sales. Total sales for June 2006 are expected to be $850,000. Of each month's sales, 75 percent is expected to be on credit. The Accounts Receivable balance at May 31 is $173,250 of which $135,000 represents the rémainder of May credit sales. There are no receivables from months prior to April 2006. Leon's Club's collection pattern for credit sales is 60 percent in the month of sale, 25 percent in the month following the sale, and 15 percent in the second month following the sale. Leon's Club has no uncollectible accounts.

a. What were total sales for April 2006?

b. What were credit sales for May 2006?

c. What are projected cash collections for June 2006?

d. What will be the balance of Accounts Receivable at June 30, 2006?

21. (Cash balance) Some projected information for May 2006 for Elaine Corp. follows:

Income after income tax	$560,000
Accrued income tax expense	41,000
Decrease in accounts receivable for month	4,000
Decrease in accounts payable for month	3,500
Depreciation expense	23,100
Estimated bad debts expense	2,050
Dividends paid	20,000

Using this information, what is the company's projected increase in cash for May 2006?

22. (Cash disbursements) Use the following information to determine Larose Co.'s projected cash disbursements for May 2006.

Sales for May	$2,000,000
Gross profit on sales	40%
Wages expense for May	$512,500
Other cash expenses for May	$235,250
Decrease in accounts payable during May	$40,000
Decrease in merchandise inventory during May	$33,750

23. (Cash budget) The following cash budget is for the second quarter of next year. Complete the missing numbers on the cash budget, assuming that the accountant has requested a minimum cash balance of $3,500 at the start of each month. All borrowings, repayments, and investments are made in even $500 amounts. No borrowings or investments exist at the beginning of April.

	April	May	June	Total
Beginning cash balance	$ 3,700	$?	$?	$?
Cash receipts	8,200	10,100	?	?
Total cash available	$?	$?	$20,500	$38,900
Cash disbursements				
Payments on account	$?	$ 3,900	$ 5,700	$?
Wages expense	5,000	?	6,200	17,300
Overhead costs	4,000	4,600	?	13,000
Total disbursements	$10,300	$?	$16,300	$?
Cash excess (deficiency)	$?	$?	$?	$?
Minimum cash balance	(3,500)	(3,500)	?	?
Cash available (needed)	$?	$ (4,400)	$?	$ (5,800)
Financing				
Borrowings (repayments)	$ 2,000	$?	$ (500)	$?
Acquire (sell) investments	0	0	?	?
Receive (pay) interest	0	0	?	(10)
Ending cash balance	$ 3,600	$?	$?	$ 3,690

24. (Various budgets) Compute the required answer for each of the following independent situations.

a. For next year, Harrington Suits projects $20,000,000 of sales and total fixed manufacturing costs of $5,000,000. Variable manufacturing costs are estimated at 40 percent of sales. Assuming no change in inventory, what is the company's projected cost of goods sold?

b. Bea Company has projected the following information for October:

Sales	$900,000
Gross profit (based on sales)	35%
Increase in merchandise inventory in October	$40,000
Decrease in accounts payable for October	$34,000

What are expected cash disbursements for inventory purchases for October?

25. (Projected income statement) Last year's income statement for Joyner Company follows.

Sales (50,000 × $10)		$ 500,000
Cost of goods sold		
Direct material	$200,000	
Direct labor	100,000	
Overhead	50,000	(350,000)
Gross profit		$ 150,000
Expenses		
Selling	$ 50,000	
Administrative	60,000	(110,000)
Income before taxes		$ 40,000

This year, sales in units are expected to increase by 20 percent; material and labor costs are expected to increase by 10 percent. Overhead is applied to production based on a percentage of direct labor costs. Fixed selling expenses total $12,000; the remainder varies with sales dollars. All administrative costs are fixed.

Management desires to earn 10 percent on sales this year and will adjust the unit selling price if necessary. Develop a pro forma income statement for the year for Joyner Company that incorporates the indicated changes.

26. (Budgeted income; cash; accounts receivable) In preparing its budget for July, Dynamic Inc. has the following accounts receivable information available:

Accounts receivable at June 30	$750,000
Estimated credit sales for July	900,000
Estimated collections in July for credit sales in July and prior months	660,000
Estimated write-offs in July for uncollectible credit sales	27,000
Estimated provision for uncollectible accounts for credit sales in July	20,000

a. What is the projected balance of Accounts Receivable at July 31?

b. Which of these amounts (if any) will affect the cash budget?

c. Which of these amounts (if any) will affect the pro forma income statement for July?

(CPA adapted)

27. (Pro forma income statement) The following budget information is available for Global Company for May.

- Sales are expected to be $400,000. All sales are on account, and a provision for bad debts is made monthly at 2.5 percent of sales.
- Inventory was $35,000 on April 30 and an increase of $10,000 is planned for May.
- All inventory is marked to sell at cost plus 60 percent.
- Estimated cash disbursements for selling and administrative expenses for the month are $55,000.
- Depreciation for May is projected at $8,000.

Prepare a pro forma income statement for Global Co. for May.

(CPA adapted)

28. (Pro forma income) You have been asked to determine whether the purchase of a new piece of production machinery can be cost justified for your company. The machine will increase fixed overhead by $350,000 per year but reduce variable expenses per unit by 35 percent. Budgeted 2006 sales of the company's products are 120,000 units at an average selling price of $25. Variable expenses are currently 75 percent of sales, and fixed costs total $400,000 per year.

a. Prepare an income statement assuming that the new machine is not purchased.

b. Prepare an income statement assuming that the new machine is purchased.

c. Should the machine be acquired?

29. (Essay) Many managers believe that if all amounts in their spending budgets are not spent during a period, they will lose allocations in future periods and that they will receive little or no recognition for the cost savings.

Prepare an essay that discusses the behavioral and ethical issues involved in a spend-it-or-lose-it attitude. Include in your discussion the issue of negotiating budget allocation requests prior to the beginning of the period.

30. (Continuous budgeting) You own a small boat manufacturing company. At a recent manufacturers' association meeting, you overheard one of the other company owners say that he liked using a continuous budgeting process. Discuss what you believe are the advantages and disadvantages of continuous budgeting for your company in a report to your top management group.

31. (Research) Find the Web page for a charitable organization that operates internationally as well as domestically.

a. Prepare a list of activities in which this organization is currently involved.

b. What would be the greatest challenges in budgeting for such an organization?

c. Do you think not-for-profits need to be as concerned with budgeting as do for-profit organizations? Explain the rationale for your answer.

32. (Planning) High-level executives have often indicated that competitors' actions are the top external factor impacting their businesses and their business plans.

a. Why do you believe that competitors' actions are so important to business planning?

b. How would competitors' actions affect a business's internal planning?

c. What other internal and external factors do you think are key elements in a business's budgeting process?

Problems

33. (Production and purchases budgets) Schorg Products has prepared the following unit sales forecast for 2006:

	January–June	July–December	Total
Sales	580,000	720,000	1,300,000

Estimated ending finished goods inventories are 25,000 units at December 31, 2005; 36,000 units at June 30, 2006; and 60,000 units at December 31, 2006.

In manufacturing each unit of this product, Schorg Products uses 4 pounds of material A and 3 gallons of material B. Materials A and B cost, respectively, $1.25 per pound and $0.80 per gallon.

The company carries no work in process inventory. Ending inventories of direct material are projected as follows:

	December 31, 2005	June 30, 2006	December 31, 2006
Material A (in pounds)	120,000	135,000	142,000
Material B (in gallons)	45,000	35,000	38,000

Prepare a production and purchases budget for each semiannual period of 2006.

34. (Production; purchases; cash disbursements) Brenda's Tea Company has budgeted sales of 300,000 cans of iced tea mix during June 2006 and 375,000 cans during July. Production of the mix requires 14 ounces of tea and 2 ounces of sugar. June 1 inventories of tea and sugar are as follows:

Iced tea mix	12,300 cans of finished product
Tea	750 pounds
Sugar	200 pounds

The company generally carries an inventory of 5 percent of the following month's needs for finished goods. Raw materials are stocked in relation to finished goods ending inventory. Assuming that the desired ending inventory stock is achieved, answer the following questions.

a. How many cans of iced tea mix need to be produced in June?

b. How many pounds of tea need to be purchased in June?

c. How many pounds of sugar need to be purchased in June?

d. If tea and sugar cost $3.50 and $0.40 per pound, respectively, what dollar amount of purchases is budgeted for June?

e. If the company normally pays for 30 percent of its budgeted purchases during the month of purchase and takes a 2 percent discount, what are budgeted cash disbursements for June purchases during June?

35. (Production; purchases; cash budgets) King Hats expects sales and collections for the first three months of 2006 to be as follows:

	January	February	March	Total
Sales quantity	3,200	2,600	3,700	9,500
Revenue	$57,600	$46,800	$66,600	$171,000
Collections	$58,080	$48,960	$62,640	$169,680

The December 31, 2005, balance sheet revealed the following selected account balances: Cash, $18,760; Raw Materials Inventory, $3,812.50; Finished Goods Inventory, $10,500; and Accounts Payable, $3,800. The Raw Materials Inventory balance represents 457.50 yards of felt and 12,200 inches of ribbon. The Finished Goods Inventory consists of 800 hats.

Ending finished goods inventory should be sufficient to satisfy 25 percent of the subsequent month's sales. In this regard, the company predicts both production and sales of 3,600 hats in April. King Corp. completes all work in the month it is started; so, no work in process exists.

Each hat requires 3/4 of a yard of felt and 20 inches of ribbon. Felt costs $5 per yard, and ribbon costs $0.15 per inch. Ending inventory policy for raw materials is 20 percent of the next month's production.

The company normally pays for 80 percent of a month's purchases of raw materials in the month of purchase (on which it takes a 2 percent cash discount). The remaining 20 percent is paid in full in the month following the month of purchase.

Direct labor is budgeted at $4 per hat produced and is paid in the month of production. Total out-of-pocket factory overhead can be predicted as $5,200 per month plus $1.25 per hat produced. Total nonfactory cash costs equal $2,800 per month plus 10 percent of sales revenue. All factory and nonfactory cash expenses are paid in the month of incurrence. In addition, the company plans to make an estimated quarterly tax payment of $5,000 and pay executive bonuses of $15,000 in January 2006.

Management wants to have a minimum cash balance of $12,000 at the end of each month. If the company has to borrow funds, it will do so in $1,000 multiples at the beginning of a month at a 12 percent annual interest rate. Loans are to be repaid at the end of a month in multiples of $1,000. Interest is paid only when a repayment is made. Investments are made in $1,000 multiples at the end of a month, and interest is earned at 8 percent per year.

a. Prepare a production budget by month and in total for the first quarter of 2006.

b. Prepare a raw material purchases budget by month and in total for the first quarter of 2006.

c. Prepare a schedule of cash payments for purchases by month and in total for the first quarter of 2006. The Accounts Payable balance on December 31, 2005, represents the unpaid 20 percent of December purchases.

d. Prepare a combined payments schedule for factory overhead and nonfactory cash costs for each month and in total for the first quarter of 2006.

e. Prepare a cash budget for each month and in total for the first quarter of 2006.

36. (Budgeted sales and S&A; other computations) Larson Mfg. has projected cost of goods sold (CGS) for June 2006 of $1,200,000. Of this amount, $75,000 represents fixed overhead costs. Total variable costs for the company each month average 70 percent of sales. The company's cost to retail (CGS to sales) ratio is 60 percent, and the company normally shows a 15 percent rate of net income on sales. All purchases and expenses (except depreciation) are paid in cash: 65 percent in the month incurred and 35 percent in the following month. Depreciation is $37,500 per month.

a. What are Larson's expected sales for June?

b. What are Larson's expected variable selling and administrative costs for June?

c. What are Larson's total fixed costs? How much of this is selling and administrative fixed cost?

d. Larson normally collects 55 percent of its sales in the month of sale and the rest in the next month. What are expected cash receipts and disbursements related only to June's transactions?

37. (Cash budget) The January 31, 2006, balance sheet of Weymann World follows:

Assets		Liabilities and Stockholders' Equity		
Cash	$ 12,000	Accounts Payable		$ 70,200
Accounts Receivable (net of Allowance for Uncollectibles of $1,440)	34,560			
Inventory	52,400	Common Stock	$25,000	
Plant Assets (net of Accumulated Depreciation of $60,000)	36,000	Retained Earnings)	39,760	64,760
		Total Liabilities and		
Total Assets	$134,960	Stockholders' Equity		$134,960

Additional information about the company follows:

- Expected sales for February and March are $120,000 and $130,000, respectively.
- The collection pattern from the month of sale forward is 50 percent, 48 percent, and 2 percent uncollectible.
- Cost of goods sold is 65 percent of sales.
- Purchases each month are 60 percent of the current month's sales and 30 percent of the next month's projected sales. All purchases are paid for in full in the month following purchase.
- Selling and administrative expenses each month are $21,500, of which $4,000 is depreciation.

a. What are budgeted cash collections for February 2006?
b. What will be the Inventory account balance at February 28, 2006?
c. What will be the projected balance in the Retained Earnings account at February 28, 2006?
d. If the company wishes to maintain a minimum cash balance of $8,000, how much will be available for investment or need to be borrowed at the end of February 2006?

38. (Cash budget; challenging) Jud's Department Store typically makes 80 percent of its sales on credit. It bills sales twice monthly, on the 10th of the month for the last half of the prior month's sales and on the 20th of the month for the first half of the current month's sales. All sales are made with terms of 2/10, n/30. Based on past experience, accounts receivable are collected as follows:

Within the discount period	80%
On the 30th day	18%
Uncollectible	2%

Sales for May 2006 were $600,000, and projected sales for the next four months are

June	$800,000
July	700,000
August	800,000
September	600,000

Jud's average profit margin on its products is 30 percent of selling price.

Jud's purchases merchandise to meet the current month's sales demand and to maintain a desired monthly ending inventory of 25 percent of the next month's sales. All purchases are on account with terms of n/30. Jud's pays for one-half of a month's purchases in the month of purchase and the other half in the month following the purchase. All sales and purchases occur evenly throughout the month.

a. How much cash can Jud's plan to collect from credit sales during July 2006?

b. How much cash can Jud's plan to collect in September 2006 from sales made in August?

c. What will be the budgeted dollar value of Jud's inventory on August 31, 2006?

d. How much merchandise should Jud's plan to purchase during June 2006?

e. What are Jud's budgeted cash payments for merchandise during August 2006?

(CMA adapted)

39. (Cash budget; challenging) Freeman Manufacturing has incurred substantial losses for several years and has decided to declare bankruptcy. The company petitioned the court for protection from creditors on March 31, 2006, and submitted the following balance sheet:

FREEMAN MANUFACTURING
Balance Sheet
March 31, 2006

	Book Value	Liquidation Value
Assets		
Accounts Receivable	$100,000	$ 50,000
Inventories	90,000	40,000
Plant Assets (net)	150,000	160,000
Totals	$340,000	$250,000

Freeman's liabilities and stockholders' equity at this date follow:

Accounts Payable—General Creditors	$600,000
Common Stock	60,000
Retained Earnings Deficit	(320,000)
Total	$340,000

Freeman's management informed the court that the company has developed a new product and that a prospective customer is willing to sign a contract for the purchase of 10,000 units of this product during the year ending March 31, 2007, 12,000 units during the year ending March 31, 2008, and 15,000 units during the year ending March 31, 2009, at a price of $90 per unit. This product can be manufactured using Freeman's present facilities. Monthly production with immediate delivery is expected to be uniform within each year. Receivables are expected to be collected during the calendar month following sales. Unit production costs of the new product are estimated as follows:

Direct material	$20
Direct labor	30
Variable overhead	10

Fixed costs of $130,000 (excluding depreciation) are estimated per year. Purchases of direct material will be paid during the calendar month following purchase. Fixed costs, direct labor, and variable overhead will be paid as incurred. Inventory of direct material will equal 60 days' usage. After the first month of operations, 30 days' usage will be ordered each month.

The general creditors have agreed to reduce their total claims to 60 percent of their March 31, 2006, balances under the following conditions:

- Existing accounts receivable and inventories are to be liquidated immediately, with the proceeds turned over to the general creditors.

- The reduced balance of accounts payable is to be paid as cash is generated from future operations but no later than March 31, 2008. No interest will be paid on these obligations.

Under this proposed plan, the general creditors would receive $110,000 more than the current liquidation value of Freeman's assets. The court has engaged you to determine the feasibility of this plan.

Ignoring any need to borrow and repay short-term funds for working capital purposes, prepare a cash budget for the years ending March 31, 2007 and 2008, showing the cash expected to be available to pay the claims of the general creditors, payments to general creditors, and the cash remaining after payment of claims.

(CPA adapted)

40. (Cash budget; advanced) Collegiate Management Education (CME), Inc., is a nonprofit organization that sponsors a wide variety of management seminars throughout the Southwest. In addition, it is heavily involved in research into improved methods of teaching and motivating college administrators. Its seminar activity is largely supported by fees, and the research program is supported by membership dues.

CME operates on a calendar-year basis and is finalizing the budget for 2006. The following information has been taken from approved plans, which are still tentative at this time:

Seminar Program

Revenue:

The scheduled number of programs should produce $12,000,000 of revenue for the year. Each program is budgeted to produce the same amount of revenue. The revenue is collected during the month the program is offered. The programs are scheduled during the basic academic year and are not held during June, July, August, or December. Of the revenue, 12 percent is generated in each of the first five months of the year and the remainder is distributed evenly during September, October, and November.

Direct expenses:

The seminar expenses are made up of three types:

- Instructors' fees are paid at the rate of 70 percent of seminar revenue in the month following the seminar. The instructors are considered independent contractors and are not eligible for CME employee benefits.
- Facilities fees total $5,600,000 for the year. They are the same for each program and are paid in the month the program is given.
- Annual promotional costs of $1,000,000 are spent equally in all months except June and July when there is no promotional effort.

Research Program

Research grants:

The research program has a large number of projects nearing completion. The main research activity this year includes feasibility studies for new projects to be started in 2007. As a result, the total grant expense of $3,000,000 for 2006 is expected to be paid out at the rate of $500,000 per month during the first six months of the year.

Salaries and Other CME Expenses

- Office lease—annual amount of $240,000 paid monthly at the beginning of each month.
- General administrative expenses—$1,500,000 annually, or $125,000 per month, paid in cash as incurred.
- Depreciation expense—$240,000 per year.
- General CME promotion—annual cost of $600,000, paid monthly.
- Salaries and benefits are as follows:

Number of Employees	Annual Cash Salary	Total Annual Salaries
1	$50,000	$ 50,000
3	40,000	120,000
4	30,000	120,000
15	25,000	375,000
5	15,000	75,000
22	10,000	220,000
50		$960,000

Employee benefits amount to $240,000, or 25 percent of annual salaries. Except for the pension contribution, the benefits are paid as salaries are paid. The annual pension payment of $24,000, based on 2.5 percent of total annual salaries, is due on April 15, 2006.

Other Information
- Membership income—CME has 100,000 members, each of whom pays a $100 annual fee. The fee for the calendar year is invoiced in late June.
- Collection schedule—July, 60 percent; August, 30 percent; September, 5 percent; and October, 5 percent.
- Capital expenditures—This program calls for a total of $510,000 in cash payments to be spread evenly over the first five months of 2006.
- Cash and temporary investments at January 1, 2006, are estimated at $750,000.
- **a.** Prepare a budget of the annual cash receipts and disbursements for 2006.
- **b.** Prepare a cash budget for CME for January 2006.
- **c.** Using the information developed in parts (a) and (b), identify two important operating problems of CME.

(CMA adapted)

41. (Pro forma results) Katherine Company has decided to reprice its sole product, a metal desk, for the upcoming year. Current variable production cost is $50 per unit, and total fixed costs are $2,000,000. Fixed manufacturing costs are 80 percent of total fixed costs and are allocated to the product based on the number of units produced. There are no variable selling or administrative costs. Variable and fixed costs are expected to increase by 15 and 8 percent, respectively, next year. Estimated production and sales are 300,000 units. Selling price is normally set at full production cost plus 25 percent, rounded to the nearest dollar.
- **a.** What is the expected full production cost per unit of Katherine Company's desks for next year?
- **b.** What is the product's expected selling price?
- **c.** What is pro forma income before tax using the selling price computed in part (b)?
- **d.** What would be the required selling price (rounded to the nearest dollar) for the company to earn income before tax equal to 25 percent of sales?

42. (Comprehensive) Moonbeam Co. produces and sells upscale mixers and breadmakers. In October 2006, Moonbeams's budget department gathered the following data to meet budget requirements for 2006.

2006 PROJECTED SALES

Product	Units	Price
Mixers	60,000	$ 90
Breadmakers	40,000	140

2006 INVENTORIES (UNITS)

Product	Expected 1/1/06	Desired 12/31/06
Mixers	15,000	20,000
Breadmakers	4,000	5,000

To produce one unit of each product, the following major internal components are used (in addition to the plastic housing for products, which is subcontracted in a subsequent operation):

Component	Mixer	Breadmaker
Motor	1	1
Beater	2	4
Fuse	2	3

Projected data for 2006 with respect to components are as follows:

Component	Anticipated Purchase Price	Expected Inventory 1/1/06	Desired Inventory 12/31/06
Motor	$18.00	2,000	3,600 units
Beater	1.75	21,000	24,000 units
Fuse	2.40	6,000	7,500 units

Projected direct labor requirements for 2006 and rates are as follows:

Product	Hours per Unit	Rate per Hour
Mixers	2	$ 8
Breadmakers	3	10

Overhead is applied at a rate of $5 per direct labor hour.

Based on these projections and budget requirements for 2006 for mixers and breadmakers, prepare the following budgets for 2006:

a. Sales budget (in dollars).
b. Production budget (in units).
c. Internal components purchases budget (in units and dollars).
d. Direct labor budget (in dollars).
e. What is the total production cost, excluding subsequent departments, per mixer and per breadmaker?

(CPA adapted)

43. (Master budget preparation; advanced) Color Blaze Company manufactures a red industrial dye. The company is preparing its 2006 master budget and has presented you with the following information.

1. The December 31, 2005, balance sheet for the company follows.

COLOR BLAZE COMPANY
Balance Sheet
December 31, 2005

Assets			Liabilities and Stockholders' Equity		
Cash		$ 5,080	Notes Payable		$ 25,000
Accounts Receivable		26,500	Accounts Payable		2,148
Raw Materials Inventory		800	Dividends Payable		10,000
Finished Goods Inventory		2,104	Total Liabilities		$ 37,148
Prepaid Insurance		1,200	Common Stock	$100,000	
Building	$300,000		Paid-in Capital	50,000	
Accum. Depreciation	(20,000)	280,000	Retained Earnings	128,536	278,536
			Total Liabilities and		
Total Assets		$315,684	Stockholders' Equity		$315,684

2. The Accounts Receivable balance at 12/31/05 represents the remaining balances of November and December credit sales. Sales were $70,000 and $65,000, respectively, in those two months.

3. Estimated sales in gallons of dye for January through May 2006 follow.

January	8,000
February	10,000
March	15,000
April	12,000
May	11,000

Each gallon of dye sells for $12.

4. The collection pattern for accounts receivable is as follows: 70 percent in the month of sale, 20 percent in the first month after the sale, and 10 percent in the second month after the sale. Color Blaze expects no bad debts and gives no cash discounts.

5. Each gallon of dye has the following standard quantities and costs for direct materials and direct labor:

1.2 gallons of direct material (some evaporation occurs during processing) @ $0.80 per gallon	$0.96
0.5 hour of direct labor @ $6 per hour	3.00

Variable overhead (VOH) is applied to the product on a machine-hour basis. Processing 1 gallon of dye takes 5 hours of machine time. The variable overhead rate is $0.06 per machine hour; VOH consists entirely of utility costs. Total annual fixed overhead is $120,000; it is applied at $1 per gallon based on an expected annual capacity of 120,000 gallons. Fixed overhead per year is composed of the following costs:

Salaries	$78,000
Utilities	12,000
Insurance—factory	2,400
Depreciation—factory	27,600

Fixed overhead is incurred evenly throughout the year.

6. There is no beginning inventory of work in process. All work in process is completed in the period in which it is started. Raw materials inventory at the beginning of the year consists of 1,000 gallons of direct material at a standard cost of $0.80 per gallon. There are 400 gallons of dye in finished goods inventory at the beginning of the year carried at a standard cost of $5.26 per gallon: direct material, $0.96; direct labor, $3.00; variable overhead, $0.30; and fixed overhead, $1.00.

7. Accounts Payable relates solely to raw material and is paid 60 percent in the month of purchase and 40 percent in the month after purchase. No discounts are given for prompt payment.

8. The dividend will be paid in January 2006.

9. A new piece of equipment costing $9,000 will be purchased on March 1, 2006. Payment of 80 percent will be made in March and 20 percent in April. The equipment has a useful life of three years and will have no salvage value.

10. The note payable has a 12 percent interest rate; interest is paid at the end of each month. The principal of the note is repaid as cash is available to do so.

11. Color Blaze's management has set a minimum cash balance at $5,000. Investments and borrowings are made in even $100 amounts. Investments will earn 9 percent per year.

12. The ending finished goods inventory should include 5 percent of the next month's needs. This is not true at the beginning of 2006 due to a miscalculation in sales for December. The ending inventory of raw materials also should be 5 percent of the next month's needs.

13. Selling and administrative costs per month are as follows: salaries, $18,000; rent, $7,000; and utilities, $800. These costs are paid in cash as they are incurred.

Prepare a master budget for each month of the first quarter of 2006 and pro forma financial statements as of the end of the first quarter of 2006.

44. (Preparing and analyzing a budget) Randazzo Ridenour & Co., LLP, a local accounting firm, has a formal budgeting system. The firm has five partners, two managers, four seniors, two secretaries, and two bookkeepers. The budgeting process has a bottom-line focus; that is, the budget and planning process continues to iterate and evolve until an acceptable budgeted net income is obtained. The determination of an acceptable level of net income is based on two factors: (1) the amount of salary the partners could generate if they were employed elsewhere and (2) a reasonable return on the partners' investment in the firm's net assets.

For 2006, after careful consideration of alternative employment opportunities, the partners agreed that the best alternative employment would generate the following salaries:

Partner 1	$150,000
Partner 2	225,000
Partner 3	110,000
Partner 4	90,000
Partner 5	125,000
Total	$700,000

The second input to determining the desired net income level is more complex. This part of the desired net income is based on the value of the net assets owned by the accounting firm. The partners have identified two major categories of assets: tangible and intangible. The partners have agreed that the net tangible assets are worth $230,000. The intangible assets, consisting mostly of the accounting practice itself, are worth 1.1 times gross fees billed in 2006. In 2006, the firm's gross billings totaled $1,615,000. The partners have also agreed that a reasonable rate of return on the net assets of the accounting firm is 12 percent. Thus, the partners' desired net income from return on investment is as follows:

Tangible assets	$ 230,000
Intangible assets ($1,615,000 × 110%)	1,776,500
Total investment	$2,006,500
Rate of return	× 0.12
Required dollar return	$ 240,780

The experience of the accounting firm indicates that other operating costs are incurred as follows:

Fixed expenses (per year)

Salaries (other than partners)	$300,000
Overhead	125,000

Variable expenses

Overhead	15% of gross billings
Client service	5% of gross billings

Source: Adapted from Jerry S. Huss, "Better Budgeting for CPA Firms," *Journal of Accountancy* (November 1977), pp. 65–72. Reprinted with permission from the *Journal of Accountancy*. Copyright © 2000 by American Institute of CPAs. Opinions of the authors are their own and do not necessarily reflect policies of the AICPA.

a. Determine the minimum level of gross billings that would allow the partners to realize their net income objective. Prepare a budget of costs and revenues at that level.

b. If the partners believe that the level of billings you have projected in part (a) is not feasible given the time constraints at the partner, manager, and senior levels, what changes can they make to the budget to preserve the desired level of net income?

45. (Revising and analyzing an operating budget) Lopez Agency, a division of Chalmette Industries (CI), offers consulting services to clients for a fee. CI's corporate management is pleased with the performance of Lopez Agency for the first nine months of the current year and has recommended that Lopez's division manager, Sara Kross, submit a revised forecast for the remaining quarter because the division has exceeded the annual year-to-date plan by

20 percent of operating income. An unexpected increase in billed hour volume over the original plan is the main reason for this gain in income. The original operating budget for the first three quarters for Lopez Agency follows.

2006 OPERATING BUDGET

	1st Quarter	2nd Quarter	3rd Quarter	Total 9 Months
Consulting fees				
Management consulting	$ 315,000	$ 315,000	$ 315,000	$ 945,000
EDP consulting	421,875	421,875	421,875	1,265,625
Total	$ 736,875	$ 736,875	$ 736,875	$ 2,210,625
Other revenue	10,000	10,000	10,000	30,000
Total	$ 746,875	$ 746,875	$ 746,875	$ 2,240,625
Expenses				
Consultant salaries	$(386,750)	$(386,750)	$(386,750)	$(1,160,250)
Travel and entertainment	(45,625)	(45,625)	(45,625)	(136,875)
Administrative	(100,000)	(100,000)	(100,000)	(300,000)
Depreciation	(40,000)	(40,000)	(40,000)	(120,000)
Corporate allocation	(50,000)	(50,000)	(50,000)	(150,000)
Total	$(622,375)	$(622,375)	$(622,375)	$(1,867,125)
Operating income	$ 124,500	$ 124,500	$ 124,500	$ 373,500

When comparing the actuals for the first three quarters to the original plan, Kross analyzed the variances and will reflect the following information in her revised forecast for the fourth quarter.

The division currently has 25 consultants on staff, 10 for management consulting and 15 for EDP consulting, and has hired 3 additional management consultants to start work at the beginning of the fourth quarter to meet the increased client demand.

The hourly billing rates for consulting revenues will remain at $90 for each management consultant and $75 for each EDP consultant. However, due to the favorable increase in billing hour volume when compared to the plan, the hours for each consultant will be increased by 50 hours per quarter. New employees are equally as capable as current employees and will be billed at the same rates.

The annual budgeted salaries and actual salaries, paid monthly, are $50,000 for a management consultant and 8 percent less for an EDP consultant. Corporate management has approved a merit increase of 10 percent at the beginning of the fourth quarter for all 25 existing consultants, but the new consultants will be compensated at the planned rate.

The planned salary expense includes a provision for employee fringe benefits amounting to 30 percent of the annual salaries; however, the improvement of some corporatewide employee programs will increase the fringe benefit allocation to 40 percent.

The original plan assumes a fixed hourly rate for travel and other related expenses for each billing hour of consulting. These expenses are not reimbursed by the client, and the previously determined hourly rate has proven to be adequate to cover these costs.

Other revenues are derived from temporary rentals and interest income and remain unchanged for the fourth quarter.

Administrative expenses have been favorable at 7 percent below the plan; this 7 percent savings on fourth-quarter expenses will be reflected in the revised plan.

Depreciation for office equipment and computers will stay constant at the projected straight-line rate.

Due to the favorable experience for the first three quarters and the division's increased ability to absorb costs, CI corporate management has increased the corporate expense allocation by 50 percent.

a. Prepare a revised operating budget for the fourth quarter for Lopez Agency that Sara Kross will present to Chalmette Industries. Be sure to furnish supporting calculations for all revised revenue and expense amounts.

b. Discuss the reasons that an organization would prepare a revised forecast.

c. Discuss your feelings about the 50 percent increase in corporate expense allocations.

(CMA adapted)

9

Break-Even Point and Cost-Volume-Profit Analysis

Objectives

AFTER COMPLETING THIS CHAPTER, YOU SHOULD BE ABLE TO ANSWER THE FOLLOWING QUESTIONS:

LO.1 WHY IS VARIABLE COSTING MORE USEFUL THAN ABSORPTION COSTING IN DETERMINING THE BREAK-EVEN POINT AND DOING COST-VOLUME-PROFIT ANALYSIS?

LO.2 HOW IS THE BREAK-EVEN POINT DETERMINED USING THE FORMULA APPROACH, GRAPH APPROACH, AND INCOME STATEMENT APPROACH?

LO.3 HOW CAN A COMPANY USE COST-VOLUME-PROFIT (CVP) ANALYSIS?

LO.4 HOW DO BREAK-EVEN AND CVP ANALYSIS DIFFER FOR SINGLE-PRODUCT AND MULTIPRODUCT FIRMS?

LO.5 HOW ARE MARGIN OF SAFETY AND OPERATING LEVERAGE CONCEPTS USED IN BUSINESS?

LO.6 WHAT ARE THE UNDERLYING ASSUMPTIONS OF CVP ANALYSIS?

Introducing

Ford Motor Company was founded in Detroit, Michigan, in June 1903 by Henry Ford and 11 business associates. Within the first month of operations, Ford had shipped its first vehicle to its first customer. These early vehicles were named using letters of the alphabet, such as the Model 'T' first produced in 1908. Because Henry Ford sought to produce and sell a high volume of cars, the company was the first to develop a production line on which an employee could stay at the same location and perform the same task repetitively as the vehicle moved past the employee.

Henry Ford's mass production strategy required him to make Fords to meet the needs of many people at affordable prices. In 1925, Ford purchased Lincoln Motor Company to offer luxury automobiles. Ford's entry into the mid-sized market occurred when it produced the Mercury in the 1930s. The Thunderbird of the 1950s tapped the luxury sports car group; a more affordable sports car was the Mustang produced in the 1960s. The North American Opel of 1971 was a "multigeographic" car, being sold in Canada, Mexico, and the United States.

In 1956, the company went public with 350,000 initial shareholders. In 1967, Ford established Ford of Europe and entered the global market. The company was successful in growing market share by producing cars for people around the world.

Ford's strategy of increasing market share by selling a high volume of trucks and cars is illustrated by the Taurus. In 1993, each Taurus was sold at a $2,600 discount from list price to beat the price of a Honda Accord. Profit margin was of little concern to the company because it was still operating under Henry Ford's strategy of focusing on the number of cars sold. In fact, the company sold Taurus models to car rental companies at deeply discounted prices and made bulk deliveries. These tactics allowed Ford to continue producing the Taurus even when consumer demand was dropping. The rental cars could also be returned to Ford Motor Company within a year. When Ford sold the used rental cars, the trade-in values of cars owned by other customers were undercut. Ford's high-volume strategy did not enhance earnings.

Perhaps the most difficult challenge faced by Ford Motor Company was to grow market share while maintaining stringent financial discipline. For example, when the Taurus was launched, Ford had to answer several difficult questions. How much would each car cost to manufacture? At what price would the cars be sold? What amounts of discounts or rebates could be given and still achieve break-even sales volume? How many cars must be sold to cover costs (break even)? How sensitive was the break-even point to selling price per unit, variable cost per unit, and fixed cost per unit? What percentage of total cost was fixed? What financial implications existed for sales volumes if inflation were high or if a new facility were needed to accommodate the company's growth in sales? Answers to these questions would give Ford Motor Company an indication of the risk taken when it launched the Taurus. The ability to answer such questions has been a core focus of Ford's business strategy.

Source: Joseph B. White and Norihiko Shirouzu, "At Ford Motor, High Volume Takes Backseat to Profits," *The Wall Street Journal* (May 7, 2004), pp. A1, A12.

Planning and controlling are two essential management functions. Planning is oriented on the *future*, which means that uncertainty exists; information helps reduce that uncertainty. In contrast, controlling is performed by comparing *current* performance to preestablished plans. Information allows such comparisons to be made. Much of the information that is used to plan and control reflects the relationships among product costs, selling prices, and volumes. Changing one of these essential ingredients in the income mix can affect the other amounts. For example, before increasing advertising, **Ford Motor Company** would need to estimate whether an additional advertising campaign would generate a sufficient increase in sales volume and contribution margin to compensate for the increased fixed cost.

This chapter focuses on understanding how costs, volume, and profits interact. Changes in one component (such as an increase in volume) will cause changes in other components (such as an increase in variable costs). Understanding these relationships can help in predicting future conditions (planning) and explaining, evaluating, and acting on past results (controlling). Before generating profits, a company must first reach its break-even point, which means that it must generate sufficient sales revenue to cover all costs. Then, by linking cost behavior and sales volume, managers can use the cost-volume-profit model to plan and control.

The chapter also presents the concepts of margin of safety and degree of operating levels. Information provided by these models helps managers focus on the impacts of volume changes on organizational profitability.

THE BREAK-EVEN POINT

LO.1
WHY IS VARIABLE COSTING MORE USEFUL THAN ABSORPTION COSTING IN DETERMINING THE BREAK-EVEN POINT AND DOING COST-VOLUME-PROFIT ANALYSIS?

As discussed in Chapter 3, absorption costing is the traditional approach to product costing and is primarily used for external reporting. Alternatively, variable costing is more commonly used for internal purposes because it makes cost behavior more transparent. The variable costing presentation of separating variable from fixed costs facilitates the use of this chapter's models: break-even point, cost-volume-profit, margin of safety, and degree of operating leverage.

A variable costing income statement for Clearsig Company is presented in Exhibit 9–1. Assume that **Ford Motor Company** has hired Clearsig Company to make automobile antennas for the Taurus. Product specifications have been established for several years and will continue at least until model year 2010. In addition to the traditional income statement information, per-unit amounts are shown for sales revenue, variable costs, and contribution margin. The company is seen to have a total variable cost of production of 62 percent, a variable selling expense of 4 percent, and a contribution margin ratio of 34 percent. These Clearsig Company data will be used throughout the chapter to illustrate break-even and cost-volume-profit computations.

LO.2
HOW IS THE BREAK-EVEN POINT DETERMINED USING THE FORMULA APPROACH, GRAPH APPROACH, AND INCOME STATEMENT APPROACH?

A company's **break-even point** (BEP) is that level of activity, in units or dollars, at which total revenues equal total costs. At breakeven, a company's revenues exactly cover its costs; thus, the company incurs neither a profit nor a loss on operating activities. Companies, however, do not wish merely to "break even" on operations. The BEP is calculated to establish a point of reference. Knowing BEP, managers are better able to set sales goals that should generate income from operations rather than produce losses.

break-even point

Why would a manager want to know break-even point?

Finding the break-even point first requires understanding company revenues and costs. A short summary of revenue and cost assumptions is presented at this point to provide a foundation for BEP calculation and cost-volume-profit (CVP) analysis. These assumptions, and some challenges to them, are discussed in more detail at the end of the chapter.

EXHIBIT 9–1

CLEARSIG COMPANY INCOME STATEMENT FOR 2006

	Total	Per Unit	Percentage
Sales (300,000 units)	$1,800,000	$ 6.00	100
Variable costs			
Production	$1,116,000	$ 3.72	62
Selling	72,000	0.24	4
Total variable cost	(1,188,000)	$(3.96)	(66)
Contribution margin	$ 612,000	$ 2.04	34
Fixed costs			
Production	$ 160,200		
Selling and administrative	23,400		
Total fixed cost	(183,600)		
Income before income tax	$ 428,400		

- *Relevant range:* The company is assumed to be operating within the relevant range of activity specified in determining the revenue and cost information used in each of the following assumptions.[1]
- *Revenue:* Revenue per unit is assumed to remain constant; fluctuations in per-unit revenue for factors such as quantity discounts are ignored. Thus, total revenue fluctuates in direct proportion to level of activity or volume.
- *Variable costs:* On a per-unit basis, variable costs are assumed to remain constant. Therefore, total variable costs fluctuate in direct proportion to level of activity or volume. Variable production costs include direct material, direct labor, and variable overhead; variable selling costs include charges for items such as commissions and shipping. Variable administrative costs can exist in areas such as purchasing.
- *Fixed costs:* Total fixed costs are assumed to remain constant and, as such, per-unit fixed cost decreases as volume increases. (Fixed cost per unit increases as volume decreases.) Fixed costs include both fixed manufacturing overhead and fixed selling and administrative expenses.
- *Mixed costs:* Mixed costs are separated into their variable and fixed elements before they are used in BEP or CVP analysis. Any method (such as regression analysis) that validly separates these costs in relation to one or more predictors can be used.

An important concept in break-even analysis is contribution margin (CM), which can be defined on either a per-unit or total basis. CM per unit equals selling price per unit minus total variable cost per unit, which includes both production and selling and administrative costs. Unit contribution margin is constant because revenue and variable cost have been defined as being constant per unit. Total CM is the difference between total revenues and total variable costs for all units sold. This amount fluctuates in direct proportion to sales volume. On either a per-unit or total basis, contribution margin indicates the amount of revenue remaining after all variable costs have been covered.[2] This amount contributes to the coverage of fixed costs and the generation of profits.

Breakeven can be demonstrated using the formula, graph, and income statement approaches. Data needed to compute the break-even point and perform CVP analysis are given in the income statement shown in Exhibit 9–1 for Clearsig Company.

FORMULA APPROACH TO BREAKEVEN

The formula approach to break-even analysis uses an algebraic equation to calculate the break-even point. In this analysis, sales volume, rather than production activity, is the focus of the relevant range. The equation represents the variable costing income statement and shows the relationships among revenue, fixed cost, variable cost, volume, and profit as follows:

$$R(X) - VC(X) - FC = P$$

where
$$R = \text{revenue (selling price) per unit}$$
$$X = \text{volume (number of units)}$$
$$R(X) = \text{total revenue}$$
$$VC = \text{variable cost per unit}$$
$$VC(X) = \text{total variable cost}$$
$$FC = \text{total fixed cost}$$
$$P = \text{profit}$$

---

[1] Relevant range is the range of activity over which a variable cost will remain constant per unit and a fixed cost will remain constant in total.

[2] Contribution margin refers to the total contribution margin. Product contribution margin is the difference between revenues and total variable *production* costs included in cost of goods sold.

Because this equation is simply a formula representation of an income statement, P can be set equal to zero so that the formula indicates a break-even situation. At the point where P = $0, total revenues are equal to total costs, and break-even point (BEP) in units can be found by solving the equation for X.

$$R(X) - VC(X) - FC = \$0$$
$$R(X) - VC(X) = FC$$
$$(R - VC)(X) = FC$$
$$X = FC \div (R - VC)$$
$$X = FC \div CM$$

Break-even volume equals total fixed cost divided by contribution margin per unit (revenue per unit minus the variable cost per unit). Using the operating information in Exhibit 9–1 for Clearsig Company ($6.00 selling price per antenna, $3.96 variable cost per antenna, and $183,600 of total fixed costs), the BEP for the company is calculated as

$$\$6.00(X) - \$3.96(X) - \$183,600 = \$0$$
$$\$6.00(X) - \$3.96(X) = \$183,600$$
$$\$2.04(X) = \$183,600$$
$$X = \$183,600 \div \$2.04$$
$$X = 90{,}000 \text{ antennas}$$

Break-even point can be expressed either in units or dollars of revenue. One way to convert a unit break-even point to dollars is to multiply the number of units by the selling price per unit. For Clearsig, break-even point in sales dollars is $540,000 (90,000 antennas × $6 per antenna).

contribution margin ratio

Another method of computing BEP in sales dollars requires the computation of a **contribution margin** (CM) **ratio**, which is calculated as contribution margin divided by revenue; it indicates what proportion of revenue remains after variable costs have been covered. The contribution margin ratio represents that portion of the revenue dollar remaining to go toward covering fixed costs and increasing profits. The CM ratio can be calculated using either per-unit or total revenue and variable cost information. Dividing total fixed cost by the CM ratio gives the BEP in sales dollars. The contribution margin ratio allows the break-even point to be determined even if unit selling price and unit variable cost are not known. Subtracting the CM ratio from 100 percent gives the **variable cost** (VC) **ratio**, which represents the variable cost proportion of each revenue dollar.[3]

variable cost ratio

The contribution margin ratio for Clearsig Company is given in Exhibit 9–1 as 34 percent ($2.04 ÷ $6.00). Thus, break-even sales dollars are ($183,600 ÷ 0.34), or $540,000. BEP in units can be determined by dividing the BEP in sales dollars by the unit selling price, or $540,000 ÷ $6.00 = 90,000 antennas.

The break-even point provides a starting point for planning future operations. Managers want to earn operating profits rather than simply cover costs. Substituting an amount other than zero for the profit (P) term in the break-even formula converts break-even analysis to cost-volume-profit analysis.

---

[3] Derivation of the contribution margin ratio formula follows:

$$\text{Sales} - [(VC\%)(\text{Sales})] = FC$$
$$(1 - VC\%)\text{Sales} = FC$$
$$\text{Sales} = FC \div (1 - VC\%)$$
$$\text{because } (1 - VC\%) = CM\%$$
$$\text{then Sales} = FC \div CM\%$$

where VC% = the % relationship of variable cost to sales
CM% = the % relationship of contribution margin to sales

Thus, the variable cost ratio plus the contribution margin ratio is equal to 100 percent.

CVP ANALYSIS

cost-volume-profit analysis

Because profit cannot be achieved until the break-even point is reached, the starting point of CVP analysis is the break-even point. Examining shifts in costs and volume and the resulting effects on profits is called **cost-volume-profit** (CVP) **analysis**. It can be used to calculate the sales volume necessary to achieve a desired target profit, stated as either a fixed or variable amount on a before- or after-tax basis.

Managers can use CVP to effectively plan and control because they can concentrate on the relationships among revenues, costs, volume changes, taxes, and profits. The CVP model can be expressed mathematically or graphically. The CVP model considers all costs, regardless of whether they are product, period, variable, or fixed. The analysis is usually performed on a companywide basis. The same basic CVP model and calculations can be applied to a single- or multiproduct business.

Using Cost-Volume-Profit Analysis

LO.3
HOW CAN A COMPANY USE COST-VOLUME-PROFIT (CVP) ANALYSIS?

CVP analysis requires substitution of known amounts in the formula to determine an unknown amount. The formula mirrors the income statement when known amounts are used for selling price per unit, variable cost per unit, volume of units, and fixed costs to find the amount of profit generated under given conditions. Because CVP analysis is concerned with relationships among the elements affecting continuing operations, in contrast with nonrecurring activities and events, profits—as used in this chapter—refer to operating profits before extraordinary and other nonoperating, nonrecurring items. The following quote indicates the pervasive usefulness of the CVP model:

> Cost Volume Profit analysis (CVP) is one of the most hallowed, and yet one of the simplest, analytical tools in management accounting. [CVP] allows managers to examine the possible impacts of a wide range of strategic decisions [in] such crucial areas as pricing policies, product mixes, market expansions or contractions, outsourcing contracts, idle plant usage, discretionary expense planning, and a variety of other important considerations in the planning process. Given the broad range of contexts in which CVP can be used, the basic simplicity of CVP is quite remarkable. Armed with just three inputs of data—sales price, variable cost per unit, and fixed costs—a managerial analyst can evaluate the effects of decisions that potentially alter the basic nature of a firm.[4]

Why would a company use CVP analysis?

An important application of CVP analysis is to set a desired target profit and focus on the relationships between it and other known income statement amounts to find an unknown. One common unknown in such applications is volume because managers want to know what sales quantity needs to be generated to produce a particular profit amount.

Selling price is not assumed to be as common an unknown as volume because selling price is often market related and is not a management decision variable. Additionally, because selling price and volume are often directly related and certain costs are considered fixed, managers can use CVP to determine how high variable cost can be yet still allow the company to produce a desired amount of profit. Variable cost can be affected by modifying product specifications or material quality as well as by being more efficient or effective in the production, service, and/or distribution processes. Profit can be stated as either a fixed or variable amount and on either a before-tax or after-tax basis. The following examples continue using the Clearsig Company data with different amounts of target profit.

Fixed Amount of Profit

Because contribution margin represents the amount of sales dollars remaining after variable costs are covered, each dollar of CM generated by product sales goes first to cover fixed costs and then to produce profits. *After the break-even point is reached, each dollar of contribution margin is a dollar of before-tax profit.*

BEFORE TAX

Profit is treated in the break-even formula as an additional cost to be covered. Inclusion of a target profit changes the break-even formula to a CVP equation.

$$R(X) - VC(X) - FC = PBT$$
$$R(X) - VC(X) = FC + PBT$$
$$X = (FC + PBT) \div (R - VC)$$

or

$$X = (FC + PBT) \div CM$$

where PBT = fixed amount of profit before tax

Clearsig's management desires a $255,000 before-tax profit. The calculations in Exhibit 9–2 show that to achieve this profit before tax, the company must sell 215,000 antennas and generate $1,290,000 of revenue.

AFTER TAX

In choosing a target profit amount, managers must recognize that income tax represents a significant influence on business decision making. A company wanting a particular amount of income after tax must first determine, given the applicable tax rate, the amount of income that must be earned on a before-tax basis. The CVP formulas that designate a fixed after-tax income amount follow.

$$PBT - [(TR)(PBT)] = PAT$$

EXHIBIT 9–2
CLEARSIG CVP ANALYSIS—FIXED AMOUNT OF PROFIT BEFORE TAX

In units:

Profit before tax (PBT) desired = $255,000

$$R(X) - VC(X) = FC + PBT$$
$$CM(X) = FC + PBT$$
$$(\$6.00 - \$3.96)X = \$183,600 + \$255,000$$
$$\$2.04X = \$438,600$$
$$X = \$438,600 \div \$2.04 = 215,000 \text{ antennas}$$

In sales dollars:

$$\text{Sales} = (FC + PBT) \div CM \text{ ratio}$$
$$\text{Sales} = \$438,600 \div 0.34$$
$$\text{Sales} = \$1,290,000$$

and

$$R(X) - VC(X) - FC - [(TR)(PBT)] = PAT$$

where PBT = fixed amount of profit before tax
PAT = fixed amount of profit after tax
TR = tax rate

PAT is further defined so that it can be integrated into the original CVP formula:

$$PBT(1 - TR) = PAT$$

or

$$PBT = PAT \div (1 - TR)$$

Substituting into the formula,

$$R(X) - VC(X) - FC = PBT$$
$$R(X) - VC(X) = FC + PBT$$
$$(R - VC)(X) = FC + [PAT \div (1 - TR)]$$
$$CM(X) = FC + [PAT \div (1 - TR)]$$

Assume the managers at Clearsig Company want to earn $244,800 of profit after tax and the company's marginal tax rate is 20 percent. The number of antennas and dollars of sales needed is calculated in Exhibit 9–3.

Set Amount of Profit Per Unit

Managers could wish to analyze profit as a set amount per unit. Stating profits in this manner means they act similarly to a variable cost. A set amount of profit can also be stated on either a before-tax or after-tax basis or as either a percentage of

EXHIBIT 9–3
CLEARSIG CVP ANALYSIS—FIXED AMOUNT OF PROFIT AFTER TAX

In units:

PAT desired = $244,800; tax rate = 20%
PBT = PAT ÷ (1 − TR)
PBT = $244,800 ÷ (1 − 0.20)
PBT = $244,800 ÷ 0.80
PBT = $306,000 necessary profit before tax

CM(X) = FC + PBT
$2.04X = $183,600 + $306,000
$2.04X = $489,600
X = $489,600 ÷ $2.04
X = 240,000 antennas

In sales dollars:

Sales = (FC + PBT) ÷ CM ratio
Sales = ($183,600 + $306,000) ÷ 0.34
Sales = $489,600 ÷ 0.34
Sales = $1,440,000

revenues or a per-unit amount. For these alternatives, the CVP formula must be adjusted to recognize that profit is related to volume of activity.

BEFORE TAX

This example assumes that profit is a set amount per unit. The adjusted CVP formula for computing the necessary unit sales volume to earn a specified amount of profit before tax per unit is

$$R(X) - VC(X) - FC = P_uBT(X)$$

where P_uBT = amount of profit per unit before tax

Solving for X (volume) gives the following:

$$R(X) - VC(X) - P_uBT(X) = FC$$
$$CM(X) - P_uBT(X) = FC$$
$$X = FC \div (CM - P_uBT)$$

The unit profit is treated in the CVP formula as if it were an additional variable cost to be covered. This treatment effectively "adjusts" the original contribution margin and contribution margin ratio. When setting the desired profit as a percentage of selling price, the profit percentage cannot exceed the contribution margin ratio. If it does, an infeasible problem is created because the "adjusted" contribution margin is negative. In such a case, the variable cost percentage plus the desired profit percentage would exceed 100 percent of the selling price, and such a condition cannot exist.

Assume that Clearsig's president wants to know what level of sales (in antennas and dollars) would be required to earn a 16 percent before-tax profit on sales. This rate of return translates into a set amount of profit per unit of $0.96. The calculations shown in Exhibit 9–4 provide the answers to these questions.

EXHIBIT 9–4

CLEARSIG CVP ANALYSIS—SET AMOUNT OF PROFIT PER UNIT BEFORE TAX

In units:

$$P_uBT \text{ desired} = 16\% \text{ of sales revenue}$$
$$P_uBT = 0.16(\$6.00)$$
$$P_uBT = \$0.96$$

$$CM(X) - P_uBT(X) = FC$$
$$\$2.04X - \$0.96X = \$183,600$$
$$\$1.08X = \$183,600$$
$$X = \$183,600 \div \$1.08$$
$$X = 170,000 \text{ antennas}$$

In sales dollars, the following relationships exist:

	Per Antenna	Percentage
Selling price	$ 6.00	100
Variable costs	(3.96)	(66)
Set amount of profit before tax	(0.96)	(16)
"Adjusted" contribution margin	$ 1.08	18

$$\text{Sales} = FC \div \text{"Adjusted" CM ratio*}$$
$$\text{Sales} = \$183,600 \div 0.18$$
$$\text{Sales} = \$1,020,000$$

*It is not necessary to have per-unit data; all computations can be made with percentage information only.

AFTER TAX

Adjustment to the CVP formula to determine unit profit on an after-tax basis involves stating profit in relation to both volume and the tax rate. Algebraically, the formula is:

$$R(X) - VC(X) - FC - \{(TR)[P_uBT(X)]\} = P_uAT(X)$$

where P_uAT = amount of profit per unit after tax

P_uAT is further defined so that it can be integrated into the original CVP formula:

$$P_uAT(X) = P_uBT(X) - \{(TR)[P_uBT(X)]\}$$
$$P_uAT(X) = P_uBT(X)[(1 - TR)]$$
$$P_uBT(X) = [P_uAT \div (1 - TR)](X)$$

Thus, the following relationship exists:

$$R(X) - VC(X) = FC + [P_uAT \div (1 - TR)](X)$$
$$CM(X) = FC + P_uBT(X)$$
$$CM(X) = FC + P_uBT(X)$$
$$CM(X) - P_uBT(X) = FC$$
$$X = FC \div (CM - P_uBT)$$

Clearsig wishes to earn an after-tax profit of 16 percent of revenue and has a 20 percent tax rate. The necessary sales in units and dollars are given in Exhibit 9–5.

Each of the preceding CVP illustrations used a variation of the formula approach. The graph approach is an alternative method of presenting CVP solutions.

EXHIBIT 9–5

CLEARSIG CVP ANALYSIS—SET AMOUNT OF PROFIT PER UNIT AFTER TAX

In units:

$$P_uAT \text{ desired} = 16\% \text{ of revenue; tax rate} = 20\%$$
$$P_uAT = 0.16(\$6.00)$$
$$P_uAT = \$0.96$$

$$P_uBT = \$0.96 \div (1.00 - 0.20)$$
$$P_uBT = \$0.96 \div 0.80$$
$$P_uBT = \$1.20$$

$$CM(X) - P_uBT(X) = FC$$
$$\$2.04X - \$1.20X = \$183,600$$
$$\$0.84X = \$183,600$$
$$X = \$183,600 \div \$0.84$$
$$X = 218,582 \text{ antennas (rounded)}$$

	Per Antenna	Percentage
Selling price	$6.00	100
Variable costs	(3.96)	(66)
Set amount of profit before tax	(1.20)	(20)
"Adjusted" contribution margin	$0.84	14

$$\text{Sales} = FC \div \text{"Adjusted" CM ratio}$$
$$\text{Sales} = \$183,600 \div 0.14$$
$$\text{Sales} = \$1,311,438.50$$

THE GRAPH APPROACH TO BREAKEVEN

Although solutions to break-even and CVP problems can be determined using equations, sometimes the information is more effectively conveyed to managers in a visual format. Exhibit 9–6 graphically presents each income statement item for Clearsig Company's original data (see Exhibit 9–1) to provide visual representations of revenue, costs, and contribution margin behaviors.

break-even chart

While illustrating individual behaviors, the graphs presented in Exhibit 9–6 are not very useful for determining the relationships among the income statement amounts. A **break-even chart** can be prepared to graph the relationships among revenue, volume, and costs. The BEP on a break-even chart is located at the point where the total cost and total revenue lines intersect. Two graph approaches can be used to prepare break-even charts: the traditional or CVP approach and the profit-volume graph approach.

EXHIBIT 9–6
CLEARSIG GRAPH PRESENTATION OF INCOME STATEMENT ITEMS

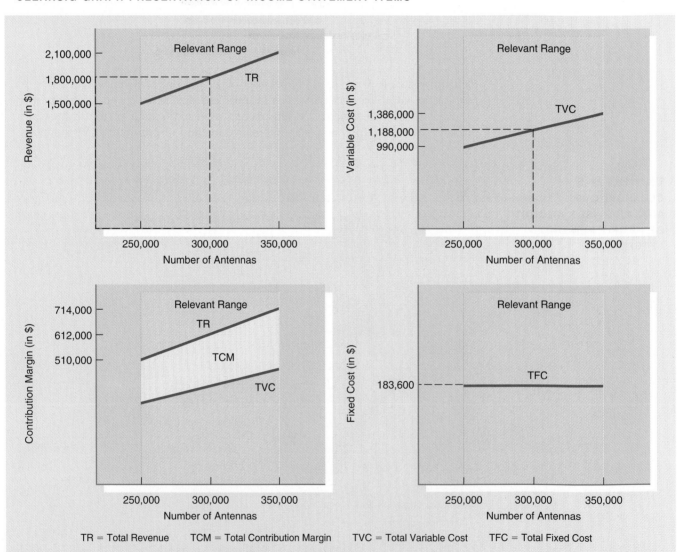

TR = Total Revenue　　TCM = Total Contribution Margin　　TVC = Total Variable Cost　　TFC = Total Fixed Cost

Note: Linear functions are always assumed for total revenue, total variable cost, and total fixed cost. These functions are reflected in the basic assumptions given on p. 372.

Traditional Approach

The traditional approach to graphing breakeven focuses on the relationships among revenues, costs, and profits (or losses). This approach does not show contribution margin. A traditional break-even chart for Clearsig Company is prepared as follows.

Step 1: As shown in Exhibit 9–7, label each axis and graph the cost lines. The total fixed cost is drawn parallel to the *x*-axis (volume). The variable cost line begins at the point where the total fixed cost line intersects the *y*-axis. The slope of the variable cost line is the per-unit variable cost. The resulting line represents total cost. The distance between the fixed cost and the total cost lines represents total variable cost at each activity volume level.

EXHIBIT 9–7
CLEARSIG GRAPH OF TOTAL AND VARIABLE COSTS

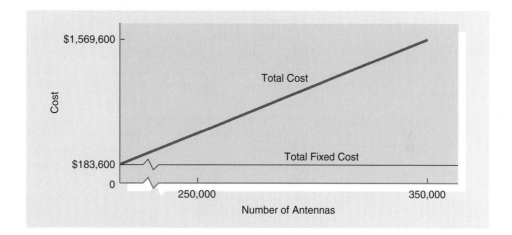

Step 2: Chart the revenue line, beginning at $0. The break-even point is located at the intersection of the revenue line and the total cost line. The vertical distance to the right of the BEP and between the revenue and total cost lines represents a profit; the distance between the revenue and total cost lines to the left of the break-even point represents a loss. If exact readings could be taken on the graph in Exhibit 9–8, the break-even point for Clearsig Company would be $540,000 of sales, or 90,000 antennas.

EXHIBIT 9–8
CLEARSIG TRADITIONAL APPROACH OF GRAPHING BREAKEVEN

VC and TC should be parallel, the vertical distance between the two is the fixed cost.

B/E: TR=TC

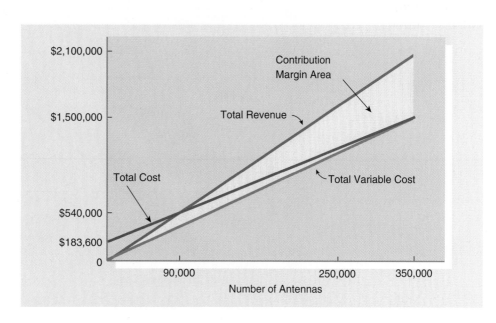

Profit-Volume Graph

profit-volume graph

The **profit-volume** (PV) **graph** provides a depiction of the amount of profit or loss associated with each sales level. The horizontal or *x*-axis on the PV graph represents sales volume; the vertical or *y*-axis represents dollars of profit or loss. Amounts shown above the *x*-axis are positive and represent profits; amounts shown below the *x*-axis are negative and represent losses.

Two points can be located on the graph: total fixed cost and break-even point. Total fixed cost is shown on the *y*-axis below the sales volume line as a negative amount. If no products were sold, the fixed cost would still be incurred and a loss of that amount would result. Location of the BEP in units may be determined algebraically and is shown at the point where the profit line intersects the *x*-axis; at that point, there is no profit or loss. The amount of profit or loss for any sales volume can be read from the *y*-axis. The slope of the profit (diagonal) line is determined by the unit contribution margin, and the points on the line represent the contribution margin earned at each volume level. The line shows that no profit is earned until total contribution margin covers total fixed cost.

The PV graph for Clearsig Company is shown in Exhibit 9–9. Total fixed cost is $183,600 and break-even point is 90,000 antennas. The diagonal line reflects the original Exhibit 9–1 income statement data indicating a profit of $428,400 at a sales level of 300,000 antennas.

The graph approach to breakeven provides a detailed visual display of the break-even point. It does not, however, provide a precise solution because exact points cannot be determined on a graph. A definitive computation of the break-even point can be found algebraically using the formula approach or a computer software application. A third approach to illustrating breakeven is the income statement approach.

THE INCOME STATEMENT APPROACH

The income statement approach to CVP analysis allows accountants to prepare pro forma (budgeted) statements using available revenue information. Income statements can also be used to prove the accuracy of computations made using the

EXHIBIT 9–9
CLEARSIG PROFIT-VOLUME GRAPH

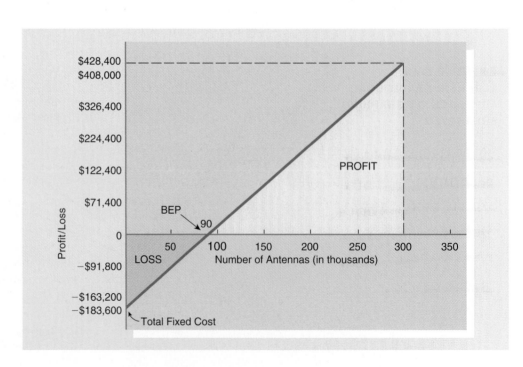

CVP formula, or the statements can be prepared merely to determine the impact of various sales levels on profit after tax (net income). The income statement approach can be readily adapted to computerized spreadsheets, which can be used to quickly obtain the results of many different combinations of the CVP factors.

Because the formula, graph, and income statement approaches are based on the same relationships, each should align with the other. Exhibit 9–10 proves each of the computations made in Exhibits 9–2 through 9–5 for Clearsig Company. The answers provided by break-even or CVP analysis are valid only in relation to specific selling prices and cost relationships. Changes that occur in the company's selling price or cost structure will cause a change in the BEP or in the sales needed to obtain a desired profit. However, the effects of revenue and cost changes on a company's break-even point or sales volume can be determined through incremental analysis.

INCREMENTAL ANALYSIS FOR SHORT-RUN CHANGES

The break-even point can increase or decrease, depending on revenue and cost changes. Other things being equal, the BEP will increase if there is an increase in the total fixed cost or a decrease in the unit (or percentage) contribution margin. A decrease in contribution margin could arise because of a reduction in selling price, an increase in variable cost per unit, or a combination of the two. The break-even point will decrease if total fixed cost decreases or unit (or percentage) contribution margin increases. A change in the BEP will also cause a shift in total profit or loss at any level of activity.

Incremental analysis

Incremental analysis is a process that focuses only on factors that change from one course of action or decision to another. As related to CVP situations, incremental analysis is based on changes occurring in revenues, costs, and/or volume. Following are some examples of changes that could occur in a company and the

EXHIBIT 9–10
CLEARSIG'S INCOME STATEMENT APPROACH TO CVP—PROOF OF COMPUTATIONS

Previous computations:

Break-even point: 90,000 antennas

Fixed profit ($255,000) before tax: 215,000 antennas

Fixed profit ($244,800) after tax: 240,000 antennas

Set amount of profit (16% on revenues) before tax: 170,000 antennas

Set amount of profit (16% on revenues) after tax: 218,582 antennas

R = $6.00 per antenna; VC = $3.96 per antenna; FC = $183,600;

Tax rate = 20% for Exhibits 9–3 and 9–5

Antennas sold	Basic Data 90,000	Ex. 9–2 215,000	Ex. 9–3 240,000	Ex. 9–4 170,000	Ex. 9–5 218,582
Sales	$ 540,000	$1,290,000	$1,440,000	$1,020,000	$1,311,492
Total variable cost	(356,400)	(851,400)	(950,400)	(673,200)	(865,585)
Contribution margin	$ 183,600	$ 438,600	$ 489,600	$ 346,800	$ 445,907
Total fixed cost	(183,600)	(183,600)	(183,600)	(183,600)	(183,600)
Profit before tax	$ 0	$ 255,000	$ 306,000	$ 163,200*	$ 262,461
Tax (20%)			(61,200)		(52,307)
Profit after tax (NI)			$ 244,800		$ 209,846†

*Desired profit before tax = 16% on revenue; 0.16 × $1,020,000 = $163,200
†Desired profit after tax = 16% on revenue; 0.16 × $1,311,492 = $209,839 (rounded)

incremental computations that can be used to determine the effects of those changes on the BEP or on profit. In most situations, incremental analysis is sufficient to determine the feasibility of contemplated changes, and a complete income statement need not be prepared. The basic facts presented for Clearsig Company in Exhibit 9–1 are continued. All of the following examples use before-tax information to simplify the computations. After-tax analysis would require the application of the (1 − tax rate) adjustment to all profit figures.

Case 1

Clearsig Company wants to earn a before-tax profit of $102,000. How many antennas must the company sell to achieve that profit? The incremental analysis relative to this question addresses the number of antennas above the break-even point that must be sold. Because each dollar of contribution margin after BEP is a dollar of profit, the incremental analysis focuses only on the profit desired:

$$\$102,000 \div \$2.04 = 50,000 \text{ antennas above BEP}$$

Because the BEP has already been computed as 90,000 antennas, the company must sell a total of 140,000 antennas.

Case 2

Clearsig Company estimates that it can sell an additional 36,000 antennas if it spends an additional $15,300 on advertising. Should the company incur this extra fixed cost? The contribution margin from the additional antennas must first cover the additional fixed cost before additional profits can be generated.

Increase in contribution margin (36,000 antennas × $2.04 CM per antenna)	$73,440
− Increase in fixed cost	(15,300)
= Net incremental benefit	$58,140

Because there is a net incremental profit of $58,140, the company should undertake the advertising campaign.

An alternative computation is to divide the additional fixed cost of $15,300 by the $2.04 contribution margin. The result indicates that 7,500 antennas would be required to cover the additional cost. Because the company expects to sell 36,000 antennas, the remaining 28,500 antennas would produce $2.04 of profit per antenna, or $58,140.

Case 3

Clearsig Company estimates that, if an antenna's selling price is reduced to $5.40, an additional 20,000 antennas per year can be sold. Should the company take advantage of this strategy? Current sales volume, given in Exhibit 9–1, is 300,000 antennas. If the selling price is reduced, the contribution margin per unit will decrease to $1.44 per antenna ($5.40 SP − $3.96 VC). Sales volume will increase to 320,000 antennas (300,000 + 20,000).

Total new contribution margin (320,000 antennas × $1.44 CM per antenna)	$ 460,800
− Total fixed cost (unchanged)	(183,600)
= New profit before tax	$ 277,200
− Current profit before tax (from Exhibit 9–1)	(428,400)
= Net incremental loss	$(151,200)

Because it will go from being profitable to incurring a loss, Clearsig should not reduce its selling price. The company, however, might want to investigate the possibility that a reduction in price could, in the long run, increase demand to more than the additional 20,000 antennas per year and, thus, make the price reduction a profitable action.

Case 4

Clearsig Company has an opportunity to sell 100,000 antennas to a customer other than Ford for $5 per antenna. The antennas will be packaged and sold using the customer's own logo. Packaging costs will increase by $0.28 per antenna, but the company will not incur any other variable selling costs. If Clearsig accepts the job, it will pay a $10,000 commission to the salesperson calling on this customer. This sale will not interfere with current sales to Ford and is within the company's relevant range of activity. Should Clearsig make this sale?

The new variable cost per antenna is $4.00 ($3.96 total current variable costs + $0.28 additional variable packaging cost − $0.24 current variable selling costs). The $5 selling price minus the $4 new total variable cost provides a contribution margin of $1 per antenna sold to the contractor.

Total additional contribution margin (100,000 antennas × $1 CM per antenna)	$100,000
− Additional fixed cost (commission) related to this sale	(10,000)
= Net incremental benefit	$ 90,000

The total CM generated by the sale more than covers the additional fixed cost. Thus, the sale produces a net incremental profit and, therefore, should be made.

As with all proposals, this one should be evaluated on the basis of its long-range potential. Is the commission a one-time payment? Will sales to the customer continue for several years? Will such sales not affect regular business in the future? Is the sales price to the new customer a legal one?[5] If all of these questions can be answered "yes," Clearsig should seriously consider this opportunity. In addition, referral business by the new customer could also increase sales.

The incremental approach is often used to evaluate alternative pricing strategies in economic downturns. In such stressful times, companies must confront the reality that they could be unable to sell a normal volume of goods at normal prices. With this understanding, they can choose to maintain normal prices and sell a lower volume of goods or reduce prices and attempt to maintain market share and normal volume.

CVP ANALYSIS IN A MULTIPRODUCT ENVIRONMENT

LO.4
HOW DO BREAK-EVEN AND CVP ANALYSIS DIFFER FOR SINGLE-PRODUCT AND MULTIPRODUCT FIRMS?

Companies typically produce and sell a variety of products, some of which could be related (such as dolls and doll clothes or sheets, towels, and bedspreads). To perform CVP analysis in a multiproduct company, one must assume either a constant product sales mix or an average contribution margin ratio. The constant mix assumption can be referred to as the "bag" (or "basket") assumption. The analogy is that the sales mix represents a bag of products that are sold together. For example, when some product A is sold, a set amount of products B and C is also sold. Use of an assumed constant sales mix allows a weighted average contribution margin ratio to be computed for the bag of products being sold. Without the assumption of a constant sales mix, break-even point cannot be calculated, nor can CVP analysis be used effectively.[6]

In a multiproduct company, the CM ratio is weighted by the quantities of each product included in the "bag." This weighting process means that the contribution margin ratio of the product making up the largest proportion of the bag has the greatest impact on the average contribution margin of the product mix.

---

[5] The Robinson-Patman Act addresses the legal ways in which companies can price their goods for sale to different purchasers.

[6] After the constant percentage contribution margin in a multiproduct firm has been determined, all situations regarding profit points can be treated in the same manner as they were earlier in the chapter. One must remember, however, that the answers reflect the "bag" assumption.

What changes are made in CVP analysis if a company sells a variety of products?

Suppose that, because of the success of the antennas, Clearsig management has decided to produce antenna mounting kits. The vice president of marketing estimates that, for every three antennas sold, the company will sell one antenna mounting kit. Therefore, the "bag" of products has a 3:1 product ratio. Clearsig will incur an additional $46,800 in fixed plant asset costs (depreciation, insurance, and so forth) to support a higher relevant range of production. Exhibit 9–11 provides relevant company information and shows the break-even computations.

EXHIBIT 9–11

CLEARSIG CVP ANALYSIS—MULTIPLE PRODUCTS

	Antennas		Antenna Kits	
Product Cost Information				
Selling price	$6.00	100%	$2.00	100%
Total variable cost	(3.96)	(66)%	(0.92)	(46)%
Contribution margin	$2.04	34%	$1.08	54%

Total fixed costs (FC) = $183,600 previous + $46,800 additional = $230,400

	Antennas	Antenna Kits	Total	Percentage
Number of products per bag	3	1		
Revenue per product	$6.00	$2.00		
Total revenue per "bag"	$18.00	$2.00	$20.00	100
Variable cost per product	(3.96)	(0.92)		
Total variable cost per "bag"	(11.88)	(0.92)	(12.80)	(64)
Contribution margin—product	$2.04	$1.08		
Contribution margin—"bag"	$ 6.12	$1.08	$ 7.20	36

BEP in units (where B = "bags" of products)

$$CM(B) = FC$$
$$\$7.20B = \$230,400$$
$$B = 32,000 \text{ bags}$$

Note: Each "bag" consists of 3 antennas and 1 antenna kit; therefore, it will take 96,000 antennas and 32,000 antenna kits to break even, assuming the constant 3:1 mix.

BEP in sales dollars (where CM ratio = weighted average CM per "bag"):

$$B = FC \div CM \text{ ratio}$$
$$B = \$230,400 \div 0.36$$
$$B = \$640,000$$

Note: The break-even sales dollars also represent the assumed constant sales mix of $18 of sales of antennas to $2 of sales of antenna kits to represent a 90% to 10% ratio. Thus, the company must have $576,000 ($640,000 × 90%) in sales of antennas and $64,000 in sales of antenna kits to break even.

Proof of these computations using the income statement approach:

	Antennas	Antenna Kits	Total
Sales	$576,000	$64,000	$640,000
Variable costs	(380,160)	(29,440)	(409,600)
Contribution margin	$195,840	$34,560	$230,400
Fixed costs			(230,400)
Income before tax			$ 0

Any shift in the product sales mix will change the weighted average contribution margin and the break-even point. If the sales mix shifts toward a product with a lower dollar contribution margin, the BEP will increase and profits will decrease unless there is a corresponding increase in total revenues. A shift toward higher dollar margin products without a corresponding decrease in revenues will cause a lower break-even point and increase profits. The financial results shown in Exhibit 9–12 indicate that a shift toward the product with the lower dollar contribution margin (antenna kits) causes a higher break-even point and lower profits (in this case, a loss). This exhibit assumes that Clearsig sells 32,000 "bags" of product, but the mix was not in the exact proportions assumed in Exhibit 9–11. Instead of a 3:1 ratio, the sales mix was 2.5 antennas to 1.5 antenna kits. A loss of $15,360 resulted because the company sold a higher proportion of the antenna kits, which have a lower dollar contribution margin than the antennas.

MARGIN OF SAFETY

LO.5
HOW ARE MARGIN OF SAFETY AND OPERATING LEVERAGE CONCEPTS USED IN BUSINESS?

margin of safety

When making decisions about business opportunities and changes in sales mix, managers often consider the **margin of safety** (MS), which is the excess of budgeted or actual sales over break-even sales. It is the amount that sales can drop before reaching the break-even point and, thus, it provides a measure of the amount of "cushion" against losses.

The margin of safety can be expressed in units, in dollars, or a percentage. The following formulas are applicable:

EXHIBIT 9–12
CLEARSIG'S EFFECTS OF PRODUCT MIX SHIFT

	Antennas	Antenna Kits	Total	Percentage
Number of products per bag	2.5	1.5		
Revenue per product	$6.00	$2.00		
Total revenue per "bag"	$15.00	$3.00	$18.00	100.0
Variable cost per product	(3.96)	(0.92)		
Total variable cost per "bag"	(9.90)	(1.38)	(11.28)	(62.7)
Contribution margin—product	$2.04	$1.08		
Contribution margin—"bag"	$ 5.10	$1.62	$ 6.72	37.3

BEP in units (where B = "bags" of products)

$$CM(B) = FC$$
$$\$6.72B = \$230,400$$
$$B = 34,286 \text{ bags}$$

Actual results: 32,000 "bags" with a sales mix ratio of 2.5 antennas to 1.5 antenna kits; thus, the company sold 80,000 antennas and 48,000 antenna kits.

	80,000 Antennas	48,000 Antenna Kits	Total
Sales	$480,000	$96,000	$576,000
Variable costs	(316,800)	(44,160)	(360,960)
Contribution margin	$163,200	$51,840	$215,040
Fixed cost			(230,400)
Net loss			$(15,360)

$$\text{Margin of safety in units} = \text{Actual sales in units} - \text{Break-even sales in units}$$
$$\text{Margin of safety in \$} = \text{Actual sales in \$} - \text{Break-even sales in \$}$$
$$\text{Margin of safety \%} = \text{Margin of safety in units} \div \text{Actual unit sales}$$

or

$$\text{Margin of safety \%} = \text{Margin of safety in \$} \div \text{Actual sales \$}$$

How is the margin of safety calculated?

The break-even point for Clearsig (using the original, single-product data) is 90,000 units, or $540,000 of sales. The company's income statement presented in Exhibit 9–1 shows actual sales for 2006 of $1,800,000 for 300,000 antennas. Clearsig's margin of safety is quite high because the company is operating far above its break-even point (see Exhibit 9–13).

Margin of safety calculations allow management to determine how close to a "danger level" the company is operating and, as such, provides an indication of risk. The lower the margin of safety, the more carefully management must watch sales and control costs so that it will not generate a net loss. At low margins of safety, managers are less likely to take advantage of opportunities that, if incorrectly analyzed or forecasted, could send the company into a loss position.

EXHIBIT 9–13
CLEARSIG'S MARGIN OF SAFETY

In units: 300,000 actual − 90,000 BEP = 210,000 antennas

In sales $: $1,800,000 actual sales − $540,000 BEP sales = $1,260,000

As a percentage: 210,000 ÷ 300,000 = 70%

or

$1,260,000 ÷ $1,800,000 = 70%

OPERATING LEVERAGE

operating leverage

Another measure that is closely related to the margin of safety and provides useful management information is the company's degree of operating leverage. The relationship between a company's variable and fixed costs is reflected in its **operating leverage**. Typically, highly labor-intensive organizations have high variable costs and low fixed costs; thus, these organizations have low operating leverage. (An exception to this rule is a sports team, which is highly labor intensive, but its labor costs are fixed rather than variable.)

Conversely, organizations that are highly capital intensive or automated have cost structures that include low variable and high fixed costs, providing high operating leverage. Because variable costs are low relative to selling prices, the contribution margin is high. However, high fixed costs mean that BEP also tends to be high. If the market predominantly sets selling prices, volume has the primary impact on profitability. As companies become more automated, they will face this type of cost structure and become more dependent on volume to add profits. Thus, a company's cost structure strongly influences the degree to which its profits respond to changes in volume.

Companies with high operating leverage have high contribution margin ratios. Although such companies have to establish fairly high sales volumes to initially cover fixed costs, once those costs are covered, each unit sold after breakeven produces large profits. Thus, a small increase in sales can have a major impact on a company's profits.

degree of operating leverage

The **degree of operating leverage** (DOL) measures how a percentage change in sales from the current level will affect company profits. In other words, it indicates how sensitive the company is to sales volume increases and decreases. The computation for degree of operating leverage follows.

$$\text{Degree of Operating Leverage} = \text{Contribution Margin} \div \text{Profit before Tax}$$

This calculation assumes that fixed costs do not increase when sales increase.

Assume that Clearsig Company is currently selling 200,000 antennas. The income statement in Exhibit 9–14 reflects this sales level and shows that the company has an operating leverage factor of 1.818. If Clearsig increases sales by 20 percent, the 36.36 percent change in profits equals the degree of operating leverage multiplied by the percentage change in sales or (1.818 × 20%). If sales decrease by the same 20 percent, the impact on profits is a negative 36.36 percent. These amounts are confirmed in Exhibit 9–14.

EXHIBIT 9–14
CLEARSIG'S DEGREE OF OPERATING LEVERAGE

	Current (200,000 antennas)	20% Increase (240,000 antennas)	20% Decrease (160,000 antennas)
Sales	$1,200,000	$1,440,000	$960,000
Variable costs ($3.96 per antenna)	(792,000)	(950,400)	(633,600)
Contribution margin	$ 408,000	$ 489,600	$326,400
Fixed costs	(183,600)	(183,600)	(183,600)
Profit before tax	$ 224,400	$ 306,000*	$142,800†

Degree of operating leverage = Contribution margin ÷ Profit before tax

($408,000 ÷ $224,400)	1.818	
($489,600 ÷ $306,000)		1.600
($326,400 ÷ $142,800)		2.286

*Profit increase = $306,000 − $224,400 = $81,600 (or 36.36% of the original profit)
†Profit decrease = $142,800 − $224,400 = $(81,600) (or −36.36% of the original profit)

The degree of operating leverage decreases the further a company moves from its break-even point. Thus, when the margin of safety is small, the degree of operating leverage is large. In fact, at the BEP, the degree of operating leverage is infinite because any increase from zero is an infinite percentage change. If a company is operating close to BEP, each percentage increase in sales can make a dramatic impact on net income. As a company moves away from break-even sales, its margin of safety increases but the degree of operating leverage declines. The relationship between the margin of safety and degree of operating leverage follows.

$$\text{Margin of Safety \%} = 1 \div \text{Degree of Operating Leverage}$$
$$\text{Degree of Operating Leverage} = 1 \div \text{Margin of Safety \%}$$

This relationship is proved in Exhibit 9–15 using the 200,000-antenna sales level information for Clearsig. Therefore, if one of the two measures is known, the other can be easily calculated.

EXHIBIT 9–15
CLEARSIG'S MARGIN OF SAFETY AND DEGREE OF OPERATING LEVERAGE RELATIONSHIP

Margin of Safety % = Margin of Safety in Units ÷ Actual Sales in Units
= [(200,000 − 90,000) ÷ 200,000] = 0.55, or 55%

Degree of Operating Leverage = Contribution Margin ÷ Profit before Tax
= $408,000 ÷ $224,400 = 1.818

Margin of Safety = (1 ÷ DOL) = (1 ÷ 1.818) = 0.55, or 55%

Degree of Operating Leverage = (1 ÷ MS %) = (1 ÷ 0.55) = 1.818

UNDERLYING ASSUMPTIONS OF CVP ANALYSIS

CVP analysis is a short-run model that focuses on relationships among selling price, variable costs, fixed costs, volume, and profits. This model is a useful planning tool that can provide information about the impact on profits when changes are made in the cost structure or in sales level. However, the CVP model, like other models, is an abstraction of reality and, as such, does not reveal all forces at work. It reflects, but does not duplicate, reality. Although limiting the accuracy of the results, several important but necessary assumptions are made in the CVP model. These assumptions follow.

What assumptions affect the use of CVP analysis?

1. All revenue and variable cost behavior patterns are constant per unit and linear within the relevant range.
2. Total contribution margin (total revenue − total variable cost) is linear within the relevant range and increases proportionally with output. This assumption follows directly from assumption 1.
3. Total fixed cost is constant within the relevant range. This assumption, in part, indicates that no capacity additions will be made during the period under consideration.
4. Mixed costs can be accurately separated into their fixed and variable elements. Although accuracy of separation can be questioned, reliable estimates can be developed from the use of regression analysis or the high-low method (as discussed in Chapter 3).
5. Sales and production are equal; thus, there is no material fluctuation in inventory levels. This assumption is necessary because fixed cost can be allocated to inventory at a different rate each year. Thus, variable costing information must be available. Because CVP and variable costing both focus on cost behavior, they are distinctly compatible with one another.
6. In a multiproduct firm, the sales mix remains constant. This assumption is necessary so that a weighted average contribution margin can be computed.
7. Labor productivity, production technology, and market conditions will not change. If any of these changes were to occur, costs would change correspondingly, and selling prices might change. Such changes would invalidate assumptions 1 through 3.

These assumptions limit the activity volume for which the calculations can be made as well as the time frame for the usefulness of the calculations. Changes in selling prices or costs will require that new computations be made for break-even and CVP analyses.

The preceding seven assumptions are the traditional ones associated with cost-volume-profit analysis. An additional assumption must be noted with regard to the distinction between variable and fixed costs. Accountants have generally assumed that cost behavior, once classified, remains constant as long as operations remain within the relevant range. Thus, for example, once a cost was determined to be "fixed," it would be fixed next year, the year after, and 10 years from now.

It is more appropriate, however, to regard fixed costs as long-term variable costs. Over the long run, through managerial decisions, companies can lay off supervisors and sell plant and equipment items. Fixed costs are not fixed forever. Generating cost information in a manner that yields a longer-run perspective is presented in Chapter 5 on activity-based costing/management. Part of the traditional "misclassification" of fixed costs has been caused by improperly specifying drivers of costs. As production and sales volumes are less often viewed as cost drivers, companies will begin to recognize that a "fixed cost" exists only in a short-term perspective.

Because companies can lay off supervisors and sell plant and equipment over the long run, these costs may be more accurately regarded as long-term variable costs, rather than fixed costs.

GETTY IMAGES

Such a reclassification of costs simply means that cost drivers for long-term variable costs have to be specified in break-even and CVP analyses. The formula will need to be expanded to include these additional drivers, and more information and a longer time frame will be needed to make the calculations. No longer will sales volume necessarily be the overriding nonmonetary force in the computations.

These adjustments to the CVP formula will force managers to take a long-run, rather than a short-run, view of product opportunities. Such a perspective could produce better organizational decisions. As the time frame is extended, both the time value of money and life-cycle costing become necessary considerations. Additionally, the traditional income statement becomes less useful for developing projects that will take several years to mature. A long-run perspective is important in a variety of circumstances, such as when variable or fixed costs arise only in the first year that a product or service is provided to customers.

Revisiting

Today, Ford Motor Company is a global family of automotive brands consisting of Aston Martin, Ford, Jaguar, Land Rover, Lincoln, Mazda, Mercury, and Volvo. Ford is beginning its second century of existence with a new strategy of increasing profits, not number of cars sold. Since the end of October 2001, Ford's new chairman and chief executive officer has been William Clay Ford, Jr., who believes that chasing market share has caused Ford numerous problems. In 2002, the company suffered a net loss of $1 billion, and in March 2003, stock prices plunged to $6.60 per share. Standard and Poor's downgraded Ford's debt to triple-B-minus, or almost junk-bond level. Cost-volume-profit analysis could have revealed that increased sales resulted in mounting long-term variable costs from which Ford could not recover. Now Ford wants to be the best, not the biggest. For example, Mr. Ford is targeting a pre-tax profit of $7 billion a year. CVP analysis will be useful in setting product sales and downsizing goals.

Ford's strategy of steering away from high volume is evidenced in its most recent capacity-cutting efforts. For example, Ford stopped producing the low-margin Ford Taurus and Mercury Sable fleets at its Chicago plant. Ford has closed two factories that built low-profit Ranger trucks and is consolidating all production of the Focus into one factory. Mr. Ford is reducing the company's production of slow-selling models such as gas-guzzling SUVs. Sales of luxury SUVs have also suffered as a result of rising gasoline prices. Ford has reduced vehicle discounts to realize $900+ of increased revenue per vehicle. By 2003, the company had downsized its rental fleet by 70,000 vehicles and planned a 40,000–50,000 further vehicle reduction in 2004. Ford believes that short-run sales volume reductions will result in long-run profit increases.

Ford is also implementing cost-cutting strategies to enhance the bottom line. It is making factories more flexible so they can be used to build multiple types of vehicles rather than running high volumes of a single model. Ford is following the just-in-time philosophy of producing to meet demand, not to meet massive capacities. Costs, prices, and sales of each model are closely monitored in hopes of maximizing revenue. Ford has beefed up its accounting information system so that consolidated and product/geographic-segmented sales and cost data can be obtained on a weekly basis; the old information system took months to extract these kinds of data. From the new information system, Ford learned that California and the Sun Belt states were very interested in 4-wheel drive pickups. The company then motivated dealers to sell the 4-wheel-drive F-150 series trucks to consumers in these locations because they have higher profit margins and less discounted pricing. Multiproduct CVP analysis would be useful to Ford in developing the product mix needed to achieve the new CEO's targeted profit.

Finally, cost-volume-profit analysis would be most helpful to Ford in launching its hybrid gasoline/electric powered SUV, the Escape Hybrid, which was scheduled to be available in August 2004. The company believes the timing is right for this vehicle as the average price of regular gasoline in the United States soared over $2 per gallon in mid-2004. The selling price for the Escape is estimated between $35,000 to $36,000 and for the 4-wheel drive about $41,000 to $42,000. In setting the Escape's price, Ford can use CVP analysis to make a wide range of decisions such as product mix, production or parts outsourcing, discretionary expense planning, production process alternatives, and plant locations. After all, Ford wants to set a selling price that will help meet the company's overall $7 billion pre-tax profit target.

Source: Adapted from Jeremy Cato, "Ford Is First Auto Maker to Market Hybrid SUV," *http://www.GlobeandMail.com* (May 20, 2004).

Comprehensive Review Module

Chapter Summary

1. Variable costing is more useful than absorption costing in determining break-even point and doing cost-volume-profit analysis because variable costing

   - shows costs separated by cost behavior in variable and fixed categories rather than by functional classification as in absorption costing.

   - shows fixed costs in lump-sum amounts rather than being allocated to products on a per-unit basis as in absorption costing.

   - does not allow for the deferral or release of fixed costs to or from inventory when production and sales volumes differ as happens in absorption costing.

2. Break-even point can be determined using the

   - formula approach by solving the following formulas for *X*:

     - X = Fixed Cost ÷ Contribution Margin; where X = BEP in units

     - X = Fixed Cost ÷ Contribution Margin Ratio; where X = BEP in sales dollars

   - graph approach

     - by reading the y-axis at the point where the total revenue and total cost lines intersect using the traditional cost-volume-profit graph.

     - by reading where the profit line intersects the x-axis using the profit-volume graph.

   - income statement approach which

     - requires developing complete income statements showing total revenue minus total costs as being equal to a profit figure.

     - is often used to prove the solutions found with other approaches.

3. Cost-volume-profit (CVP) analysis can be used by a company to

   - determine break-even point by assigning a zero value to the profit figure.

   - study the interrelationships of

     - prices,

     - volumes,

   - fixed and variable costs, and

   - contribution margins.

   - calculate the level of sales volume necessary to achieve specific before- or after-tax target profit objectives.

   - enhance a manager's ability to positively influence current operations and to predict future operations, thereby reducing the risk of uncertainty.

4. In a multiproduct environment, break-even and CVP analysis

   - require that a constant product sales mix or "bag" assumption be used for the various products.

   - require that a weighted average contribution margin or CM ratio be calculated for each "bag" of product sold.

   - state solutions in terms of "bags" of product, which means the solutions must be converted (using the original product sales mix) to actual units (or sales dollars) of individual products.

5. Companies use the margin of safety (MS) and degree of operating leverage (DOL) concepts as follows:

   - the MS indicates how far (in units, in sales dollars, or as a percentage) a company is operating from its break-even point; the MS percentage is equal to (1 − degree of operation leverage).

   - the DOL shows the percentage change that would occur in profit given a specified percentage change in sales from the current level; the DOL is equal to (1 − MS%).

6. The break-even and CVP models are based on several assumptions that limit their ability to reflect reality. Underlying assumptions are that

   - revenue and variable cost per unit are constant and linear within the relevant range.

   - contribution margin is linear within the relevant range.

   - total fixed cost is constant within the relevant range.

   - mixed costs can be accurately separated into their variable and fixed components.

- sales and production levels are equal.

- sales mix is constant in a multiproduct setting.

- labor productivity, production technology, and market conditions will not change during the period under consideration.

Solution Strategies

COST-VOLUME-PROFIT (CVP)

The basic equation for break-even and CVP problems is

$$\text{Total Revenue} - \text{Total Cost} = \text{Profit}$$

CVP problems can also be solved by using a numerator/denominator approach. All numerators and denominators and the types of problems that each relates to follow. The formulas relate to both single- and multiproduct firms, but results for multiproduct firms are per bag and should be converted to units of individual products.

Problem Situation	Numerator	Denominator
Simple BEP in units	FC	CM
Simple BEP in dollars	FC	CM%
CVP with fixed profit in units	FC + P	CM
CVP with fixed profit in dollars	FC + P	CM%
CVP with specified profit in units	FC	$CM - P_U$
CVP with profit specified as a % of sales	FC	$CM\% - P_U\%$

where   FC = fixed cost
CM = contribution margin per unit
CM% = contribution margin percentage
P = total profit (on a before-tax basis)
P_U = profit per unit (on a before-tax basis)
$P_U\%$ = profit percentage per unit (on a before-tax basis)

To convert after-tax profit to before-tax profit, divide after-tax profit by $(1 - \text{tax rate})$.

MARGIN OF SAFETY (MS)

Margin of Safety in Units = Actual Sales in Units − Break-Even Sales in Units
Margin of Safety in Dollars = Actual Sales $ − Break-Even Sales $
Margin of Safety % = (Margin of Safety in Units or $) ÷ (Actual Sales in Units or $)

DEGREE OF OPERATING LEVERAGE (DOL)

Degree of Operating Leverage = Contribution Margin ÷ Profit Before Tax
Predicted Profit = [1 + (DOL × Percent Change in Sales)] × Current Profit

Demonstration Problem

Flyin' High makes small bird houses that sell for $25 each. The company's annual level of production and sales is 120,000 units. In addition to $430,500 of fixed manufacturing overhead and $159,050 of fixed administrative expenses, the following per-unit costs have been determined for each bird house:

Direct material	$ 6.00
Direct labor	3.00
Variable manufacturing overhead	0.80
Variable selling expense	2.20
Total variable cost	$12.00

Required:

a. Prepare a variable costing income statement at the current level of production and sales.

b. Calculate the unit contribution margin in dollars and the contribution margin ratio for a bird house.

c. Determine the break-even point in number of bird houses.

d. Calculate the dollar break-even point using the contribution margin ratio.

e. Determine Flyin' High's margin of safety in units, in sales dollars, and as a percentage.

f. Compute the company's degree of operating leverage. If sales increase by 25 percent, by what percentage will before-tax income increase?

g. How many bird houses will the company need to sell to earn $996,450 in before-tax income?

h. If the company wants to earn $657,800 after tax and is subject to a 20 percent tax rate, how many units must be sold?

i. How many bird houses would need to be sold to break even if Flyin' High's fixed manufacturing costs increased by $7,865? (Use the original data.)

j. The company has received an offer from a Brazilian company to buy 4,000 bird houses at $20 per unit. The per-unit variable selling cost of the additional units will be $2.80 (rather than $2.20), and $18,000 of additional fixed administrative cost will be incurred. This sale would not affect domestic sales or their costs. Based on quantitative factors alone, should Flyin' High accept this offer?

Solution to Demonstration Problem

a.

Flyin' High
Variable Costing Income Statement

Sales (120,000 × $25.00)		$3,000,000
Variable production costs		
Direct material (120,000 × $6.00)	$720,000	
Direct labor (120,000 × $3.00)	360,000	
Overhead (120,000 × $0.80)	96,000	
Variable selling expenses (120,000 × $2.20)	264,000	(1,440,000)
Contribution margin		$1,560,000
Fixed costs		
Manufacturing overhead	$430,500	
Administrative	159,050	(589,550)
Income before income tax		$ 970,450

b. CM = SP − VC = $25 − $12 = $13 per unit
CM% = CM ÷ SP = $13 ÷ $25 = 52%

c. BEP = FC ÷ CM = $589,550 ÷ $13 = 45,350 bird houses

d. BEP = FC ÷ CM% = $589,550 ÷ 0.52 = $1,133,750 in sales

e. MS = Current unit sales − BEP unit sales = 120,000 − 45,350 = 74,650 bird houses
MS = Current sales in dollars − BEP sales in dollars = $3,000,000 − $1,133,750 = $1,866,250
MS = MS in units ÷ Current unit sales = 74,650 ÷ 120,000 = 62% (rounded)

f.   DOL = Current CM ÷ Current Pre-Tax Income = $1,560,000 ÷ $970,450 = 1.61 (rounded)

Increase in Income = DOL × % Increase in Sales = 1.61 × 0.25 = 40.25%

Proof:

New Sales = 120,000 × 1.25 = 150,000

New CM = 150,000 × $13.00 = $1,950,000

New Pre-Tax Profit = New CM − FC = $1,950,000 − $589,550 = $1,360,450

Increase = New Pre-Tax Profit − Old Pre-Tax Profit = $1,360,450 − $970,450 = $390,000

Increase in % Terms = $390,000 ÷ $970,450 = 40.19% (rounded)

g. $13X = $589,550 + $996,450

X = $1,586,000 ÷ $13

X = 122,000 bird houses

h.   PBT = PAT ÷ (1 − tax rate) = $657,800 ÷ (1 − 0.20) = $657,800 ÷ 0.80 = $822,250

$13X = $589,550 + $822,250

X = $1,411,800 ÷ $13

X = 108,600 bird houses

i.   X = Increase in FC ÷ CM

X = $7,865 ÷ $13

X = 605 units

New BEP = 45,350 + 605 = 45,955 bird houses

j.   New CM for Each Additional Unit = $20.00 − $12.60 = $7.40

Total New CM = $7.40 × 4,000 = $29,600

Increase in Pre-Tax Profit = Increase in CM − Increase in FC = $29,600 − $18,000 = $11,600

Yes, the company should accept the offer.

Key Terms

break-even chart *(p. 362)*
break-even point *(p. 354)*
contribution margin ratio *(p. 356)*
cost-volume-profit analysis *(p. 357)*

degree of operating leverage
    (p. 370)
incremental analysis *(p. 365)*
margin of safety *(p. 369)*

operating leverage *(p. 370)*
profit-volume graph *(p. 364)*
variable cost ratio *(p. 356)*

Questions

1. What information is provided by a variable costing income statement that is useful in computing the break-even point? Is this information on an absorption costing income statement? Explain your answer.

2. How is break-even point defined? What are the differences among the formula, graph, and income statement approaches for computing breakeven?

3. What is the contribution margin ratio? How is it used to calculate the break-even point?

4. Why is CVP analysis generally used as a short-run tool? Would CVP ever be appropriate as a long-run model?

5. What does the "bag" assumption mean, and why is it necessary in a multi-product firm? What additional assumption must be made in multiproduct CVP analysis that doesn't pertain to a single-product CVP situation?

6. A multiproduct company has a sales mix of nine widgees to three squigees. Widgees have a contribution margin ratio of 45 percent, and squigees have a contribution margin ratio of 80 percent. If the sales mix changes to six widgees to six squigees, will the company have a higher or lower weighted average contribution margin ratio and a higher or lower break-even point (in sales dollars)? Explain the rationale for your answer.

7. Define and explain the relationship between margin of safety and operating leverage.

Exercises

8. (Variable costing income statement) Gatorsip Beverages began business in 2006 selling bottles of a thirst-quenching drink. Production for the first year was 52,000 bottles of Gatorsip, and sales were 49,000 bottles. The selling price per bottle was $3.10. Costs incurred during the year were as follows:

Ingredients used	$28,000
Direct labor	13,000
Variable overhead	24,000
Fixed overhead	2,600
Variable selling expenses	5,000
Fixed selling and administrative expenses	14,000
Total actual costs	$86,600

a. What was the production cost per bottle under variable costing?
b. What was variable cost of goods sold for 2006?
c. What was the contribution margin per bottle?
e. What was the contribution margin ratio?

9. (Variable costing income statement) AEC manufactures automotive distributor caps. The following information is available for 2006, the company's first year in business when it produced 75,000 caps. Revenue of $360,000 was generated by the sale of 45,000 caps.

	Variable Costs	Fixed Costs
Production		
Direct material	$150,000	
Direct labor	225,000	
Overhead	37,500	$ 56,250
Selling and administrative	90,000	150,000

  a. What is the variable production cost per unit?
  b. What is the total contribution margin per unit?
  c. Prepare a variable costing income statement.

10. (Cost and revenue behavior) The following financial data have been determined from analyzing the records of Red Sox Gloves (a one-product firm):

Contribution margin per unit	$ 25
Variable costs per unit	21
Annual fixed cost	90,000

How does each of the following measures change when product volume goes up by one unit at Red Sox Gloves?
  a. Total revenue
  b. Total cost
  c. Income before tax

11. (Break-even point) Braves Company has the following revenue and cost functions:

$$\text{Revenue} = \$60 \text{ per unit}$$
$$\text{Costs} = \$120,875 + \$35 \text{ per unit}$$

  a. What is the break-even point in units?
  b. What is the break-even point in dollars?

12. (Break-even point) HST makes and sells class rings for local schools. Operating information follows:

Selling price per ring	$250
Variable costs per ring	
Rings and stones	$90
Sales commissions	18
Overhead	8
Annual fixed costs	
Selling expenses	$42,000
Administrative expenses	56,000
Manufacturing	30,000

  a. What is HST's break-even point in rings?
  b. What is HST's break-even point in sales dollars?
  c. What would HST's break-even point be if sales commissions increased to $22?
  d. What would be HST's break-even point if selling expenses decreased by $5,000?

13. (Sales price computation) Sportswear Inc. has designed a new athletic suit. The company plans to produce and sell 60,000 units of the new product in the coming year. Annual fixed costs are $1,200,000, and variable costs are 70 percent of selling price. If the company wants a pre-tax profit of $600,000, at what minimum price must it sell its product?

14. (CVP) HG Industries makes children's playhouses that sell for $3,000 each. Costs are as follows:

	Per Unit	**Total**
Direct material	$1,400	
Direct labor	200	
Variable production overhead	125	
Variable selling and administrative cost	75	
Fixed production overhead		$200,000
Fixed selling and administrative		82,000

a. How many playhouses must HG Industries sell to break even?

b. If HG Industries' management wants to earn a pre-tax profit of $78,000, how many playhouses must it sell?

c. If HG Industries' management wants to earn a pre-tax profit of $258,000, how many playhouses must it sell?

15. (CVP; taxes) Use the information for HG Industries in Exercise 14 and assume a tax rate for the company of 35 percent.

a. If HG Industries' management wants to earn an after-tax profit of $265,785, how many playhouses must it sell?

b. How much revenue is needed to yield an after-tax profit of 13 percent of revenue? How many playhouses does this revenue amount represent?

16. (CVP) Houston Corp. sells a product for $180 per unit. The company's variable costs per unit are $30 for direct material, $25 per unit for direct labor, and $17 per unit for overhead. Annual fixed production overhead is $37,400, and fixed selling and administrative overhead is $25,240.

a. What is contribution margin per unit?

b. What is the contribution margin ratio?

c. What is break-even point in units?

d. Using the contribution margin ratio, what is the break-even point in sales dollars?

e. If Houston Corp. wants to earn a pre-tax profit of $25,920, how many units must the company sell?

17. (CVP; taxes) Use the information for Houston Corp. in Exercise 16 and assume a tax rate for the company of 30 percent.

a. If Houston Corp. wants to earn an after-tax profit of $67,900, how many units must the company sell?

b. If Houston Corp. wants to earn an after-tax profit of $2.80 on each unit sold, how many units must the company sell?

18. (Incremental sales) Marlins Industries has annual sales of $1,250,000 with variable expenses of 60 percent of sales and fixed expenses per month of $25,000. By how much must annual sales increase for Marlins Industries to have pre-tax income equal to 30 percent of sales?

19. (CVP; taxes) Jack McDeonary has a small plant that makes gasoline-powered golf carts. The selling price is $4,000 each, and costs are as follows:

Costs	**Per Unit**	**Total**
Direct material	$1,600	
Direct labor	500	
Variable overhead	250	
Variable selling	25	
Fixed production overhead		$200,000
Fixed selling and administrative		80,420

McDeonary's income is taxed at a 35 percent rate.

a. How many golf carts must McDeonary sell to earn $500,000 after tax?

b. What level of revenue is needed to yield an after-tax income equal to 20 percent of sales?

20. (Volume and pricing) Rae Ditzy is the county commissioner of Geismer. She had decided to institute tolls for local ferry boat passengers. After the tolls had been in effect for four months, Astra Astute, county accountant, noticed that collecting $725 in tolls incurred a daily cost of $900. The toll is $0.25 per passenger.

   a. How many people are using the ferry boats each day?

   b. If the $900 cost is entirely fixed, how much must each passenger be charged for the toll process to break even? How much must each passenger be charged for the toll process to make a profit of $250 per day?

   c. Assume that only 80 percent of the $900 is fixed and the remainder varies by passenger. If the toll is raised to $0.30 per person, passenger volume is expected to fall by 10 percent. If the toll is raised and volume falls, will the county be better or worse off than it is currently and by what amount?

   d. Assume that only 80 percent of the $900 is fixed and the remainder varies by passenger. If passenger use will decline by 5 percent for every $0.10 increase from the current $0.25 rate, at what level of use and toll amount would the county first make a profit?

   e. Discuss the saying "We may be showing a loss, but we can make it up in volume."

21. (Comprehensive) Compute the answers to each of the following independent situations.

   a. Orlando Ray sells liquid and spray mouthwash in a sales mix of 2:4, respectively. The liquid mouthwash has a contribution margin of $10 per unit; the spray's CM is $5 per unit. Annual fixed costs for the company are $100,000. How many units of spray mouthwash would Orlando Ray sell at the break-even point?

   b. Piniella Company has a break-even point of 4,000 units. At BEP, variable costs are $6,400 and fixed costs are $1,600. If one unit over break-even is sold, what will be the company's pre-tax income?

   c. Montreal Company's product sells for $10 per bottle. Annual fixed costs are $216,000 and variable cost is 40 percent of selling price. How many units would Montreal Company need to sell to earn a 25 percent pre-tax profit on sales?

   d. York Mets Company has a BEP of 2,800 units. The company currently sells 3,200 units at $65 each. What is the company's margin of safety in units, in sales dollars, and as a percentage?

22. (Formula; graph; income statement) Lou & Art Inc. had the following income statement for 2007.

Sales (30,000 gallons @ $4)		$120,000
Variable costs		
Production (40,000 gallons @ $1.50)	$60,000	
Selling (40,000 gallons @ $0.25)	10,000	(70,000)
Contribution margin		$ 50,000
Fixed costs		
Production	$23,000	
Selling and administrative	3,100	(26,100)
Income before tax		$ 23,900
Income tax (40%)		(9,560)
Net income		$ 14,340

   a. Compute the break-even point using the equation approach.

   b. Prepare a CVP graph to reflect the relationships among costs, revenues, profit, and volume.

   c. Prepare a profit-volume graph.

  d. Prepare a short explanation for company management about each of the graphs.

  e. Prepare an income statement at break-even point using variable costing.

WebTUTOR Advantage

23. (CVP; multiproduct) Howe Wholesalers sells baseball products. Its Little League Division handles both bats and gloves. Historically, the firm's sales have averaged six bats for every two gloves. Each bat has a $4 contribution margin, and each glove has a $5 contribution margin. The fixed cost of operating the Little League Division is $170,000 per year. The selling prices of bats and gloves, respectively, are $10 and $15. The corporatewide tax rate is 40 percent.

  a. How much revenue is needed to break even? How many bats and gloves does this represent?

  b. How much revenue is needed to earn a pre-tax profit of $132,222?

  c. How much revenue is needed to earn an after-tax profit of $132,222?

  d. If Little League Division earns the revenue determined in part (b) but does so by selling five bats for every two gloves, what would be the pre-tax profit (or loss)? Why is this amount *not* $132,222?

24. (Multiproduct) Whee-Go makes three types of scooters. The company's total fixed costs are $1,080,000,000. Selling prices, variable costs, and sales percentages for each type of scooter follow.

	Selling Price	Variable Cost	Percent of Total Sales
Mod	$2,200	$1,900	30%
Rad	3,700	3,000	50
X-treme	6,000	5,000	20

  a. What is Whee-Go's break-even point in units and sales dollars?

  b. If the company has an after-tax income goal of $1 billion and the tax rate is 50 percent, how many units of each type of scooter must be sold for the goal to be reached at the current sales mix?

  c. Assume the sales mix shifts to 50 percent Mod, 40 percent Rad, and 10 percent X-treme. How does this change affect your answer to part (b)?

  d. If Whee-Go sold more X-treme scooters and fewer Mod scooters, how would your answers to parts (a) and (b) change? No calculations are needed.

WebTUTOR Advantage

25. (CVP; margin of safety) Harry Potted grows corn in Nebraska. He currently sells his corn at $2.25 per bushel. Variable costs associated with growing and selling a bushel of corn is $1.80. Annual fixed costs are $74,250.

  a. What is the break-even point in sales dollars and bushels of corn? If Potted's farm is 1,200 acres, how many bushels must he produce per acre to break even?

  b. If the business is currently producing and selling 180,000 bushels, what is the margin of safety in bushels, in dollars, and as a percentage?

26. (CVP; operating leverage) Brenda's Nail Salon provides sculptured nail manicures for $40. Variable cost per set is $10 and monthly fixed cost is $1,050.

  a. What is the break-even point in units and sales dollars?

  b. If Brenda Boudreaux, the owner, wants the business to earn a pre-tax profit of 40 percent of revenues, how many manicures must be done in a month?

  c. If the salon currently has 40 customers per month, what is the degree of operating leverage?

  d. If the salon can increase sales by 35 percent above the current level, what will be the increase in net income? What will be the new net income? Prove your calculations with an income statement.

27. (Operating leverage; margin of safety) Tampa Packing makes a protein drink, Bottled Energy. The selling price per half-gallon is $3.60, and variable cost of production is $2.16. Total fixed costs per year are $316,600. The company is currently selling 250,000 half-gallons per year.
  a. What is the margin of safety in half-gallons?
  b. What is the degree of operating leverage?
  c. If the company can increase sales in half-gallons by 30 percent, what percentage increase will it experience in income? Prove your answer using the income statement approach.
  d. If the company increases advertising by $41,200, sales in half-gallons will increase by 15 percent. What will be the new break-even point? The new degree of operating leverage?

28. (Leverage factors; essay) A group of prospective investors has asked for your help in understanding the comparative advantages and disadvantages of building a company that is either labor intensive or, in contrast, one that uses significant cutting-edge technology and is therefore capital intensive. Prepare a report addressing the issues. Include discussions regarding cost structure, BEP, CVP, MS, DOL, risk, customer satisfaction, and the relationships among these concepts.

29. (Product cost; essay) A friend of yours, attending another university, states that she learned that CVP is a short-run-oriented model and is, therefore, of limited usefulness. Your professor, however, has often discussed CVP in presentations about long-run planning to your cost accounting class. You decide to investigate your friend's allegation by preparing a report addressing your friend's contention. Your professor is also asking you to prepare a separate report for internal management's use that addresses how the CVP model could be adapted to become more useful for making long-run decisions. Prepare these two reports, one for your friend's understanding and one for your professor.

30. (Ethics; essay) Valdez Chemical Company's new president has learned that, for the past four years, the company has been dumping its industrial waste into the local river and falsifying reports to authorities about the levels of suspected cancer-causing materials in that waste. The plant manager says that there is no proof that the waste causes cancer and that only a few fishing villages are within 100 miles downriver. If the company must treat the substance to neutralize its potentially injurious effects and then transport it to a legal dump site, the company's variable and fixed costs would rise to a level that might make the firm uncompetitive. If the company loses its competitive advantage, 10,000 local employees could become unemployed and the town's economy could collapse.
  a. What specific variable and fixed costs can you identify that would increase (or decrease) if the waste were treated rather than dumped? How would these costs affect product contribution margin?
  b. What ethical conflicts does the president face?
  c. What rationalizations can you detect that plant employees have devised?
  d. What options and suggestions can you offer the president?

31. (Essay; Internet) A significant trend in business today is the increasing use of outsourcing. Go to the Internet and search Web sites with the objective of gaining an understanding for the vast array of outsourcing services that are available. Prepare a presentation in which you discuss the extensive use of outsourcing today and how it could be used as a tool to manage a firm's cost structure and in CVP planning.

Problems

32. (CVP decision alternatives) Dusty Baker owns a sports brokerage agency and sells tickets to major league baseball, football, and basketball games. He also sells sports travel packages that include game tickets, airline tickets, and hotel accommodations. Revenues are commissions based as follows:

Game ticket sales	8% commission
Airline ticket sales	10% commission
Hotel bookings sales	20% commission

Monthly fixed costs include advertising ($1,100), rent ($900), utilities ($250), and other costs ($2,200). There are no variable costs.

A typical month generates the following sales amounts that are subject to the stated commission structure:

Game tickets	$30,000
Airline tickets	4,500
Hotel bookings	7,000
Total	$41,500

a. What is Baker's normal monthly profit or loss?
b. Baker estimates that airline bookings can be increased by 40 percent if he increases advertising by $600. Should he increase advertising?
c. Baker's friend Ozzi has asked him for a job in the travel agency. Ozzi has proposed that he be paid 50 percent of whatever additional commissions he can bring to the agency plus a salary of $400 per month. Baker has estimated that Ozzi can generate the following additional bookings per month:

Game tickets	$10,000
Airline tickets	1,500
Hotel bookings	4,000
Total	$15,500

Hiring Ozzi would also increase fixed costs by $400 per month for his salary. Should Baker hire Ozzi?
d. Baker hired Ozzi and in the first month Ozzi generated an additional $8,000 of bookings for the agency. The bookings, however, were all airline tickets. Was the decision to hire Ozzi a good one? Why or why not?

33. (CVP) Abraham Inc., in business since 1995, makes swimwear for professional athletes. Analysis of the firm's financial records for the current year reveals the following:

Average swimsuit selling price	$ 140
Variable swimsuit expenses	
Direct material	56
Direct labor	24
Variable overhead	16
Annual fixed costs	
Selling	20,000
Administrative	48,000

The company's tax rate is 40 percent. Louise Abraham, company president, has asked you to help her answer the following questions.
a. What is the break-even point in number of swimsuits and in dollars?
b. How much revenue must be generated to produce $80,000 of pre-tax earnings? How many swimsuits would this level of revenue represent?
c. How much revenue must be generated to produce $80,000 of after-tax earnings? How many swimsuits would this represent?
d. What amount of revenue would be necessary to yield an after-tax profit equal to 20 percent of revenue?

e. Abraham is considering purchasing a new faster sewing machine, which will save $12 per swimsuit in cost but will raise annual fixed costs by $8,000. She expects to make and sell an additional 5,000 swimsuits. Should she make this investment?

f. A marketing consultant told Abraham that she could increase the number of swimsuits sold by 30 percent if she would lower the selling price by 10 percent and spend $20,000 on advertising. She has been selling 3,000 swimsuits. Should she make these two related changes?

34. (CVP) CSP Inc. makes a child's jumper chair that sells for $60. Variable manufacturing and variable selling costs are, respectively, $35 and $10 per unit. Annual fixed costs are $975,000.

a. What is the contribution margin per unit and the contribution margin ratio?

b. What is the break-even point in units?

c. How many units would need to be sold for the company to earn a pre-tax income of $900,000?

d. If the company's tax rate is 60 percent, how many units would need to be sold to earn an after-tax profit of $1,500,000?

e. If labor costs are 60 percent of the variable manufacturing costs and 40 percent of the fixed costs, how would a 10 percent decrease in both variable and fixed labor costs affect the break-even point?

f. Assume that the total market for jumper chairs is 500,000 units per year and that CSP Inc. currently has 18 percent of the market. CSP wants to obtain a 25 percent market share but cannot raise selling prices. If the company also wants to earn a pre-tax profit of $1,600,000, by how much will variable costs need to be reduced? Provide some suggestions for variable cost reductions.

35. (CVP single product; comprehensive) Speedy Gonzalez Inc. makes baseballs that sell for $12.50. Annual production and sales are 240,000 balls. Costs for each ball are as follows:

Direct material	$3.00
Direct labor	1.50
Variable overhead	0.40
Variable selling expenses	1.10
Total variable cost	$6.00
Total fixed overhead	$589,550

a. Calculate the unit contribution margin in dollars and the contribution margin ratio for the company.

b. Determine the break-even point in number of baseballs.

c. Calculate the dollar break-even point using the contribution margin ratio.

d. Determine the company's margin of safety in number of baseballs, in sales dollars, and as a percentage.

e. Compute the company's degree of operating leverage. If sales increase by 25 percent, by what percentage would before-tax income increase?

f. How many balls must the company sell if it desires to earn $996,450 in before-tax profit?

g. If the company wants to earn $657,800 after tax and is subject to a 20 percent tax rate, how many balls must be sold?

h. How many balls would the company need to sell to break even if its fixed costs increased by $7,865? (Use original data.)

i. Speedy Gonzalez Inc. has received an offer to provide a one-time sale of 8,000 baseballs at $10 each to a network of sports superstores. This sale would not affect other sales, nor would the cost of those sales change. However, the variable cost of the additional units would increase by $0.30 for shipping, and fixed costs would increase by $18,000. Based solely on financial information, should the company accept this offer? Show your calculations. What other factors might the company wish to consider in accepting or rejecting this offer?

36. (Graph) Thunderbird Club has the following monthly cost and fee information: monthly membership fee per member, $25; monthly variable cost per member, $12; and monthly fixed cost, $1,800. Costs are extremely low because volunteers provide almost all services and supplies.
  a. Prepare a break-even chart for Thunderbird Club.
  b. Prepare a profit-volume graph for Thunderbird Club.
  c. At this time, Thunderbird Club has only 120 members. Which of the preceding items would you use in a speech to the membership to solicit volunteers to help with a fund-raising project? Why?

37. (Multiproduct firm) Techno Sounds, Inc., makes portable refrigerators, ice trays, and batteries that sell in a normal sales mix of 1:3:6. The following financial information is available:

	Refrigerators	Ice Trays	Batteries
Variable product costs	$ 62.00	$1.20	$0.22
Variable selling expenses	14.00	0.50	0.10
Variable administrative expenses	3.00	0.05	0.03
Selling price	140.00	5.00	0.50

Annual fixed factory overhead	$110,000
Annual fixed selling expenses	60,000
Annual fixed administrative expenses	16,920

The firm is in a 40 percent tax bracket.
  a. What is the annual break-even point in revenues?
  b. How many refrigerators, ice trays, and batteries are expected to be sold at the break-even point?
  c. If the firm desires pre-tax income of $114,640, how much total revenue is required, and how many units of each product must be sold?
  d. If the firm desires net income of $103,176, how much total revenue is required, and how many units of each product must be sold?
  e. If the firm achieves the revenue determined in part (d), what is its margin of safety in dollars and as a percentage?

38. (Multiproduct firm) Decoy Inc. makes small pressed resin roosters and hens. For every rooster sold, the company sells two hens. The following information is available about the company's selling prices and costs:

	Rooster	Hen
Selling price	$12	$6
Variable cost	4	4

Annual fixed costs	$144,000

  a. What is the average contribution margin ratio?
  b. Calculate the monthly break-even point if fixed costs are incurred evenly throughout the year. At BEP, indicate how many units of each product will be sold.
  c. If the company wants to earn $48,000 pre-tax profit monthly, how many units of each product must it sell?
  d. Company management has specified $27,000 as monthly net income, and the company is in a 40 percent tax bracket. However, marketing information has indicated that the sales mix has changed to one rooster to five hens. How much total revenue and what number of products must be sold to achieve the company's profit objective?

e. If the company can reduce variable cost per unit (regardless of product) to $3 by raising monthly fixed costs by $3,000, how will the break-even point change? Should the company make these changes? Use original data.

39. (Multiproduct firm) Anaheim Company produces and sells V8 car engines and lawn mower engines in a sales mix of three V8s to five lawn mower engines. Selling prices for the V8 and lawn mower engines are $1,200 and $240, respectively; respective variable costs are $480 and $160. The company's annual fixed costs are $1,800,000. Compute the sales volume of each engine type needed to:

a. Break even.

b. Earn $800,000 of income before tax.

c. Earn $800,000 of income after tax, assuming a 30 percent tax rate.

d. Earn 12 percent on sales revenue in before-tax income.

e. Earn 12 percent on sales revenue in after-tax income, assuming a 30 percent tax rate.

40. (Comprehensive; multiproduct) Greenbacks Flooring makes three types of artificial turf: astro, golf, and lawn. The company's tax rate is 40 percent. The following costs are expected for 2006:

	Astro	Golf	Lawn
Variable costs (on a per-square-yard basis)			
Direct material	$10.40	$6.50	$17.60
Direct labor	3.60	0.80	12.80
Production overhead	2.00	0.30	3.50
Selling expense	1.00	0.50	4.00
Administrative expense	0.40	0.20	0.60

Fixed overhead	$760,000
Fixed selling expense	240,000
Fixed administrative expense	200,000

Per-yard expected selling prices are as follows: astro, $32.80; golf, $16.00; and lawn, $50.00. The expected sales mix is as follows:

	Astro	Golf	Lawn
Square yards	9,000	72,000	6,000

a. Calculate the break-even point for 2006.

b. How many square yards of each product are expected to be sold at the break-even point?

c. If the company wants to earn pre-tax profits of $800,000, how many square yards of each type of turf would it need to sell? How much total revenue would be required?

d. If the company wants to earn an after-tax profit of $680,000, determine the revenue needed using the contribution margin percentage approach.

e. If the company achieves the revenue determined in part (d), what is the margin of safety (1) in dollars and (2) as a percentage?

41. (CVP analysis) Jim Tracy owns Sportsday Hotel, a luxury hotel with 60-two bedroom suites for coaches and their players. Capacity is 10 coaches and 50 players. Each suite is equipped with extra long king-sized beds, supertall and extended shower heads, extra tall bath room vanities, a laptop, and a printer. Each suite has a Pacific Ocean view. Hotel services include airport limousine pickup and drop off, a daily fruit basket, champagne on the day of arrival, and a Hummer for transportation. Coaches and players are interviewed about their dietary restrictions and room service requirements before arrival. The hotel's original cost was $1,920,000, and depreciation is $160,000 per year. Other hotel operating costs include:

Labor	$320,000 per year plus $5 per suite per day
Utilities	$158,000 per year plus $1 per room per day
Miscellaneous	$100,000 per year plus $6 per suite per day

In addition to these costs, costs are incurred for food and beverage for each guest. These costs are strictly variable and (on average) run $40 per day for coaches and $15 per day for players.

a. Assuming that the hotel is able to maintain an average annual occupancy of 80 percent in both the coach and player suites (based on a 360-day year), determine the minimum daily charge that must be assessed per suite per day to generate $240,000 of income before tax.

b. Assume that the per-day price Tracy charges is $240 day for coaches and $200 for players. If the sales mix is 12 to 48 (12 coach days of occupancy for every 48 player days of occupancy), compute the following:

   1. The break-even point in total occupancy days.

   2. Total occupancy days required to generate $400,000 of income before tax.

   3. Total occupancy days to generate $400,000 of after-tax income. Jim's personal tax rate is 35 percent.

c. Tracy is considering adding a massage service for guests to complement current hotel services. He has estimated that the costs of providing such a service would largely be fixed because all necessary facilities already exist. He would, however, need to hire five certified masseurs at a cost of $500,000 per year. If Tracy decides to add this service, how much would he need to increase his daily charges (assume equal dollar increases to coach and player room fees) to maintain the break-even point computed in part (b)?

42. (CVP analysis; advanced) Piratrac Railways is a luxury passenger carrier in South Africa. All seats are first class, and the following data are available.

Number of seats per passenger train car	120
Average load factor (percentage of seats filled)	75%
Average full passenger fare	$70
Average variable cost per passenger	$30
Fixed operating costs per month	$1,200,000

a. What is the break-even point in passengers and revenues?

b. What is the break-even point in number of passenger train cars?

c. If Piratrac raises its average passenger fare to $85, it is estimated that the load factor will decrease to 60 percent. What will be the break-even point in number of passenger cars?

d. (Refer to original data.) Fuel cost is a significant variable cost to any railway. If fuel charges increase by $8 per barrel, it is estimated that variable cost per passenger will rise to $40. What would be the new break-even point in passengers and in number of passenger train cars?

e. Piratrac has experienced an increase in variable cost per passenger to $35 and an increase in total fixed costs to $1,500,000. The company has decided to raise the average fare to $80. If the tax rate is 40 percent, how many passengers are needed to generate an after-tax profit of $400,000?

f. (Use original data.) Piratrac is considering offering a discounted fare of $50, which the company believes would increase the load factor to 80 percent. Only the additional seats would be sold at the discounted fare. Additional monthly advertising costs would be $80,000. How much pretax income would the discounted fare provide Piratrac if the company has 40 passenger train cars per day, 30 days per month?

g. Piratrac has an opportunity to obtain a new route that would be traveled 15 times per month. The company believes it can sell seats at $75 on the route, but the load factor would be only 60 percent. Fixed costs would increase by $100,000 per month for additional crew, additional passenger train cars, maintenance, and so on. Variable cost per passenger would remain at $30.

1. Should the company obtain the route?
2. How many passenger train cars would Piratrac need to earn pre-tax income of $50,500 per month on this route?
3. If the load factor could be increased to 75 percent, how many passenger train cars would be needed to earn pre-tax income of $50,500 per month on this route?
4. What qualitative factors should be considered by Piratrac in making its decision about acquiring this route?

43. (Incremental analysis) Fair Winds Co. makes portable hair dryers. You have been asked to predict the potential effects of some proposed company changes. The following information is available:

Variable costs per unit	
Direct material	$4.60
Direct labor	3.25
Production overhead	2.15
Selling expenses	1.15
Administrative expenses	0.75
Annual fixed costs	
Production overhead	$300,000
Selling	240,000
Administrative	120,000

The selling price is $23.50 per unit, and expected sales volume for the current year is 150,000 units. Following are some changes proposed by various members of the company.

1. Engineers suggest that adding a radio headset to each unit at a cost of $3.60 would increase product sales by 20 percent.
2. The sales manager suggests that a $130,000 increase in advertising will increase sales by 15 percent.
3. The sales force believes that lowering the price by 5 percent will increase demand in units by 10 percent.

a. Compute the current break-even point in units and dollars.
b. Compute the current margin of safety in dollars, in units, and as a percentage.
c. Compute the independent effects on profit and dollar break-even point of each of the suggestions. For each proposal, advise company management about acceptability.

44. (MS; DOL; PV graph) You are considering buying one of two local firms (VPI and TECH). VPI uses a substantial amount of direct labor in its manufacturing operations and its salespeople work on commission. TECH uses the latest automated technology in manufacturing; its salespeople are salaried. The following financial information is available for the two companies:

	VPI		TECH	
	2005	**2006**	**2005**	**2006**
Sales	$600,000	$960,000	$600,000	$840,000
Expenses including taxes	(528,000)	(823,200)	(528,000)	(667,200)
Net income	$ 72,000	$136,800	$ 72,000	$172,800

After examining cost data, you find that the fixed costs for VPI are $60,000; the fixed costs for TECH are $300,000. The tax rate for both companies is 40 percent.

a. Recast the income statements into a variable costing format.

b. What is break-even sales for each firm for each year?

c. Assume that you could acquire either firm for $1,200,000, and you want an after-tax return of 12 percent on your investment. Determine what sales level for each firm would allow you to reach your goal.

d. What is the margin of safety for each firm for each year? What is the degree of operating leverage?

e. Assume that product demand for 2007 is expected to rise by 15 percent from the 2006 level. What will be the expected net income for each firm?

f. Assume that product demand for 2007 is expected to fall by 20 percent from the 2006 level. What will be the expected net income for each firm?

g. Prepare a profit-volume graph for each firm.

45. (CVP; DOL; MS—two quarters; comprehensive) Following is information pertaining to Tigers Company's operations of the first and second quarter of 2007:

	QUARTER	
	First	**Second**
Units		
Production	70,000	60,000
Sales	60,000	70,000
Expected activity level	65,000	65,000
Unit selling price	$37.50	$37.50
Unit variable costs		
Direct material	$17.25	$17.25
Direct labor	8.25	8.25
Factory overhead	3.90	3.90
Selling and administrative	2.85	2.85
Fixed costs		
Factory overhead	$97,500	$97,500
Selling and administrative	21,400	21,400

Additional Information

- There were no finished goods at January 1, 2007.
- Tigers writes off any quarterly underapplied or overapplied overhead as an adjustment to Cost of Goods Sold.
- Tigers' income tax rate is 35 percent.

a. Prepare a variable costing income statement for each quarter.

b. Calculate each of the following for 2007 if 260,000 units were produced and sold:

  1. Unit contribution margin.
  2. Contribution margin ratio.
  3. Total contribution margin.
  4. Net income.
  5. Degree of operating leverage.
  6. Annual break-even unit sales volume.
  7. Annual break-even dollar sales volume.
  8. Annual margin of safety as a percentage.
  9. Annual margin of safety in units.

10

Relevant Information
for Decision Making

Objectives

AFTER COMPLETING THIS CHAPTER, YOU SHOULD BE ABLE TO ANSWER THE FOLLOWING QUESTIONS:

LO.1 WHAT FACTORS ARE RELEVANT IN MAKING DECISIONS AND WHY?

LO.2 WHAT ARE SUNK COSTS, AND WHY ARE THEY NOT RELEVANT IN MAKING DECISIONS?

LO.3 WHAT ARE THE RELEVANT CONSIDERATIONS IN OUTSOURCING?

LO.4 HOW CAN MANAGEMENT MAKE THE BEST USE OF A SCARCE RESOURCE?

LO.5 HOW DOES SALES MIX PERTAIN TO RELEVANT COSTING PROBLEMS?

LO.6 HOW ARE SPECIAL PRICES SET, AND WHEN ARE THEY USED?

LO.7 HOW IS SEGMENT MARGIN USED TO DETERMINE WHETHER A PRODUCT LINE SHOULD BE RETAINED OR ELIMINATED?

LO.8 *(APPENDIX)* HOW IS A LINEAR PROGRAMMING PROBLEM FORMULATED?

Satyam Computer Services, Ltd., organized in Secunderabad, India, in 1987, competes in the software and information technology support industry and provides services to clients in a diverse array of industries. Satyam offers software development, systems maintenance, packaged software integration, engineering design, and business process outsourcing. The company has grown rapidly since its formation: As of 2003, Satyam employed more than 12,000 people globally and was the fourth largest provider of IT services in India based on the amount of export revenues generated for the year.

Satyam is the beneficiary of a global movement to outsource goods and services. Many U.S. firms are currently outsourcing work to foreign companies including Satyam in a trend known as *offshoring*. Satyam and other India-based firms have found an edge in the global marketplace due in part to the highly educated, English-speaking workforce and to the lower wage structure in India relative to that in highly developed nations.

The strength of the offshoring movement is evident in the fact that Satyam derived 77 percent of its revenues for fiscal year 2003 from North America; 26 percent was generated from work performed for only two U.S. customers. The significance of Satyam's customer base is indicated by the fact that most of the company's revenues are generated in U.S. dollars compared to the majority of its expenses denominated in Indian rupees. The company projected its 2004 growth at more than 10 percent in employment and 20 percent in revenues, a rate completely uncommon among North American and European companies. To support its growth, Satyam has established development centers around the globe including four in the United States, one in Canada, two in Australia, and one combined office for China and Japan.

Source: Satyam Computer Services, Limited, Form 6-K,
*http://www.sec.gov/Archives/edgar/data/1106056/000114554904000196/u92
288e6vk.htm#003.*

Accounting information can improve but cannot perfect management's understanding of the consequences of decision alternatives. To the extent that accounting information can reduce management's uncertainty about economic facts, outcomes, and relationships involved in various courses of action, such information is valuable for decision-making purposes.

relevant costing

This chapter introduces the topic of **relevant costing**, which focuses managerial attention on a decision's relevant (or pertinent) facts. Relevant costing techniques are applied in virtually all business decisions in both short-term and long-term contexts. The chapter examines the application of relevant costing techniques to common types of business decisions, such as replacing an asset, outsourcing a product or part, allocating scarce resources, determining the appropriate sales/production mix, and accepting specially priced orders. Discussion of analysis tools that are applied to longer-term decisions is deferred to Chapter 14. Long-term decisions generally require consideration of costs and benefits that are mismatched in time; that is, the cost is incurred currently but the benefit is derived in future periods.

THE CONCEPT OF RELEVANCE

**LO.1
WHAT FACTORS ARE
RELEVANT IN MAKING
DECISIONS AND WHY?**

Why does the passage of time affect the relevance of specific costs?

In choosing among the available alternatives, managers should consider all relevant costs and revenues associated with each alternative. One of the most important concepts for managers to recognize is the relationship between time and relevance. As the decision time horizon gets shorter, fewer costs and revenues are relevant because only a limited set of them is subject to change by short-term management actions. Over the long term, management action can influence virtually all costs. Regardless of whether the decision is a short- or long-term one, all decision making requires analysis of relevant information.

For information to be relevant, it must possess three characteristics: (1) be associated with the decision under consideration, (2) be important to the decision maker, and (3) have a connection to or bearing on some future endeavor.

Association with Decision

Cost accountants can assist managers in determining which costs and revenues are decision relevant. Costs or revenues are relevant when they are logically related to a decision and vary from one decision alternative to another by being either incremental or differential. **Incremental revenue** is the amount of revenue that differs across decision choices; **incremental** (or **differential**) **cost** is the amount of cost that varies across the decision choices. For example, if the operating costs of an existing machine is $10,000 yearly and the operating cost of a potential replacement machine is $6,000, the incremental cost to operate the existing machine is $4,000 ($10,000 − $6,000).

To the extent possible and practical, relevant costing compares the incremental revenues and incremental costs of alternative choices. Although incremental costs can be variable or fixed, a general guideline is that most variable costs are relevant but most fixed costs are not. The logic of this guideline is that, as an activity measure (such as sales or production volume) changes within the relevant range, total variable cost changes, but total fixed cost does not. However, as is often the case, there are exceptions to this general rule.

The difference between the incremental revenue and the incremental cost of a particular alternative is the positive or negative incremental benefit (incremental profit or incremental loss) of that course of action. Management can compare incremental benefits of alternatives in deciding on the most profitable (or least costly) alternative. Although such a comparison can sound simple, often it is not for two reasons. First, the concept of relevance is an inherently individual determination and, second, the amount of information available to make decisions is increasing. One challenge is to get as much information as possible that reflects relevant costs and benefits.

Some relevant factors, such as sales commissions or direct production costs, are easily identified and quantified because the accounting system captures them. Other factors are relevant and quantifiable but are not part of the accounting system. Such factors cannot be overlooked simply because they are more difficult to obtain or require the use of estimates. For instance, **opportunity costs** represent the benefits forgone because one course of action is chosen over another. These costs are extremely important in decision making but are not included in the accounting records.

To illustrate the concept of opportunity cost, assume that on August 1, Brittany bought a ticket for $70 to attend a play in November. In October, Brittany's friend asks to buy the ticket for $120. The $120 price offered by Brittany's friend is an opportunity cost, a benefit that Brittany will sacrifice if she chooses to attend the play rather than sell the ticket.

Importance to Decision Maker

The need for specific information depends on how important that information is relative to the achievement of managerial objectives. Additionally, managers give more weight to more precise information than to less precise information in the decision process. However, if information is extremely important but less precise, a manager must weigh importance against precision.

Bearing on the Future

Information can be *based* on past or present data but is relevant only if it pertains to a future decision choice. All managerial decisions are made to affect future

incremental revenue

incremental cost

differential cost

opportunity cost

events, so the information on which decisions are based should reflect future conditions. The future can be the short run (2 hours from now or next month) or the long run (three years from now).

Future costs are the only costs that can be avoided, and a longer time horizon equates to more costs that are controllable, avoidable, and relevant. *Only information that has a bearing on future events is relevant in decision making.* People too often forget this mandate, however, and try to make decisions using inapplicable data. One common error is using a sunk cost, such as a previously purchased asset's acquisition cost or book value, in current decision making. This error reflects the misconception that sunk costs are relevant costs.

SUNK COSTS

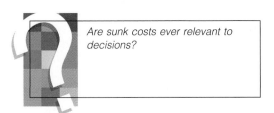

Are sunk costs ever relevant to decisions?

sunk cost

Costs incurred in the past to acquire an asset or a resource are called **sunk costs**. They cannot be changed no matter what future course of action is taken because past expenditures are not recoverable regardless of current circumstances.

After acquiring an asset or a resource, managers could find that it is no longer adequate for the intended purposes, does not perform to expectations, is technologically out of date, or is no longer marketable. Managers then must decide of whether to keep or dispose of the old asset. This decision considers the current or future selling price that can be obtained for the old asset, but such a price is the result of current or future conditions and does not "recoup" the historical or sunk cost. The historical cost is irrelevant to the decision.

Although asset-acquisition decisions are covered in depth in Chapter 14, they provide an excellent introduction to the concept of relevant information. The following illustration makes some simplistic assumptions regarding asset acquisitions but demonstrates why sunk costs are not relevant costs.

Assume that Capricorn Electronics purchases a B2B buy-side purchasing system for $3,000,000 on January 6, 2006. This ("original") system is expected to have a useful life of five years and no salvage value. Five days later, on January 11, Trisha Black, vice president of production, notices an advertisement for a similar system for $2,800,000. This "new" system also has an estimated life of five years and no salvage value, but its features enable it to perform as well as the original system, and it has additional analysis features that will save $100,000 per year in operating costs over the original system. On investigation, Ms. Black discovers that the original system can be sold for only $1,900,000. See Exhibit 10–1 for data on the original and new B2B purchasing systems.

Capricorn Electronics has two options: (1) use the original system or (2) sell it and buy the new system. See Exhibit 10–2 for the relevant costs Ms. Black should consider in making her decision. As the computations show, the original system's $3,000,000 purchase price does not affect the decision process. This amount was "gone forever" when the company bought the system. However, by selling the original system, the company will effectively reduce the net cash outlay for the

EXHIBIT 10–1

CAPRICORN ELECTRONICS: B2B SYSTEM REPLACEMENT DECISION DATA

	Original System (Purchased Jan. 6)	New System (Available Jan. 11)
Cost	$3,000,000	$2,800,000
Life in years	5	5
Salvage value	$0	$0
Current resale value	$1,900,000	Not applicable
Annual operating cost	$355,000	$255,000

EXHIBIT 10–2
RELEVANT COSTS
RELATED TO CAPRICORN
ELECTRONICS'
ALTERNATIVES

Alternative (1): Use original system		
Operating cost over life of original system ($355,000 × 5 years)		$ 1,775,000
Alternative (2): Sell original system and buy new		
Cost of new system	$ 2,800,000	
Resale value of original system	(1,900,000)	
Effective net outlay for new system	$ 900,000	
Operating cost over life of new system ($255,000 × 5 years)	1,275,000	
Total cost of new system		(2,175,000)
Benefit of keeping the old system		$ (400,000)
The alternative incremental calculation follows:		
Savings from operating the new system for 5 years		$ 500,000
Less effective incremental outlay for new system		(900,000)
Incremental advantage of keeping the old system		$ (400,000)

new system to $900,000 because of the $1,900,000 generated from selling the old system. Using either system, Capricorn Electronics will incur operating costs over the next five years, but it will spend $500,000 less using the new system ($100,000 savings per year × 5 years).

A common analylical tendency is to include the $3,000,000 cost of the old system. However, this cost is not differential for the decision alternatives. If it keeps the original system, Capricorn Electronics will deduct the $3,000,000 as depreciation expense over the system's life. Alternatively, if it sells the system, it will charge the $3,000,000 against the revenue realized from the system's sale. Thus, the $3,000,000 depreciation charge or its equivalent loss is the same in magnitude whether the company retains the original system or disposes of it and buys the new one. Because the amount is the same under both alternatives, it is not relevant to the decision process.

Ms. Black must condition herself to make decisions considering her set of *future* alternatives. The relevant factors in deciding whether to purchase the new system are the

1. cost of the new system ($2,800,000)
2. current resale value of the original system ($1,900,000)
3. annual savings of the new system ($100,000) and the number of years (5) such savings would be enjoyed[1]

This example demonstrates the difference between relevant and irrelevant costs, including sunk costs. The next section shows how the concepts of relevant costing, incremental revenues, and incremental costs are applied in making some common managerial decisions.

RELEVANT COSTS FOR SPECIFIC DECISIONS

Managers routinely choose one course of action from a set of alternatives that have been identified as feasible solutions to problems. In doing so, the costs and benefits of the alternatives are calculated to find the net benefit of each alternative. In

---

[1] In addition, two factors that were not discussed are important: the potential tax effects of the transactions and the time value of money. The authors have chosen to defer consideration of these items to Chapter 14, which covers capital budgeting. Because of the time value of money, both systems were assumed to have zero salvage values at the end of their lives—a fairly unrealistic assumption.

making decisions, managers must also find a way to include any inherently non-quantifiable considerations. Inclusion can be made by attempting to quantify those items or by simply making instinctive value judgments about nonmonetary benefits and costs.

In evaluating courses of action, managers should select the alternative that provides the highest incremental benefit to the company. In doing so, they must compare the net benefits of all courses of action against a baseline alternative. One course of action that is often used as the baseline alternative is the "change nothing" or "do nothing" option.

Although certain incremental revenues and incremental costs are associated with other alternatives, the "change nothing" alternative has a zero incremental benefit because it is the status quo. Some situations involve specific government regulations or mandates in which a "change nothing" alternative does not exist. For example, if a duly licensed governmental regulatory agency issued an injunction against a company polluting river water, the company would be forced to correct the pollution problem (assuming that it wishes to continue in business). It could delay the installation of pollution control devices at the risk of fines or closure. Management should consider such fines as incremental costs; closure would create an opportunity cost amounting to the income that would have been generated had sales continued.

Rational decision-making behavior includes a comprehensive evaluation of the monetary effects of all alternative courses of action. The chosen course should be one that will make the business better off than it is currently. Decision choices can be evaluated using relevant costing techniques.

OUTSOURCING DECISIONS

LO.3
WHAT ARE THE RELEVANT CONSIDERATIONS IN OUTSOURCING?

A common question that managers must answer is whether the necessary components and services will be available at the right time to ensure that production can occur. Additionally, the inputs must be of the appropriate quality and be obtainable at a reasonable price. Traditionally, many companies ensured the availability of parts and services as well as the desired level of quality by controlling all functions internally. However, there is an increasing trend by companies to purchase a higher percentage of required materials, components, and services through an outsourcing process. **Outsourcing** refers to having work performed for one company by an off-site non-affiliated supplier; it allows a company to buy a product (or service) from an outside supplier rather than making the product or performing the service in-house.

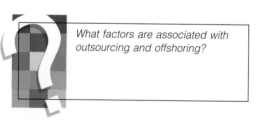

What factors are associated with outsourcing and offshoring?

outsourcing

offshoring

The outsourcing trend is global in scope and has become a hotly debated topic in the United States. Central to the debate is the effect on U.S. employment that outsourcing has when it involves **offshoring**, which sends jobs formerly performed in the home country to foreign countries. However, a careful analysis of outsourcing suggests that more work is outsourced to U.S. firms from other countries than is exported from the United States to foreign firms.[2] Information technology work is the most common work taken offshore followed by manufacturing and back-office processing work (e.g., customer service).[3]

outsourcing decision
make-or-buy decision

The **outsourcing** (or **make-or-buy**) **decision** is made only after performing an analysis that compares internal production and opportunity costs with purchase cost and assesses the best uses of facilities. Having an insourcing (make) option implies that the company has the capacity available for that purpose or has considered

---

[2] See Michael M. Phillips, "More Work Is Outsourced to U.S. Than Away From It, Data Show," *The Wall Street Journal*, April 3, 2004, p. A1.
[3] See Kate O'Sullivan and Don Durfee, "Offshoring by the Numbers," *CFO*, June 2004, pp. 51 ff.

the cost of obtaining the necessary capacity. Relevant information for this type of decision includes both quantitative and qualitative factors. See Exhibit 10–3 for the primary motivations for companies to pursue outsourcing.

As shown in the graphic on the next page, most outsourcing is not related to an organization's strategic core but to the management of operating costs.[4] Thus, more often routine activities such as information processing are outsourced rather than activities that constitute core competencies or new strategies.

EXHIBIT 10–3
REASONS TO OUTSOURCE

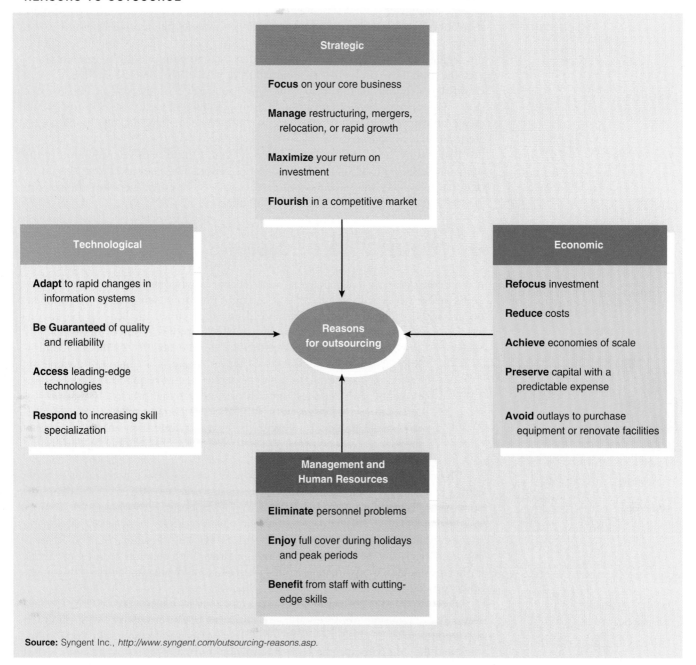

Source: Syngent Inc., *http://www.syngent.com/outsourcing-reasons.asp.*

---

[4] See Jerry Bowles, "Outsourcing for Competitive Advantage," *Forbes,* June 7, 2004, p. 101.

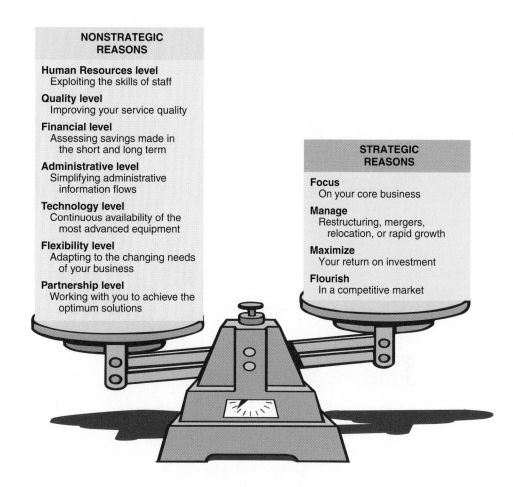

Numerous factors, such as those included in Exhibit 10–4, should be considered in the outsourcing decision. Several quantitative factors, such as incremental direct material and direct labor costs per unit, are known with a high degree of certainty. Other factors, such as the variable overhead per unit and the opportunity cost associated with production facilities, must be estimated. The qualitative factors should be evaluated by more than one individual so personal biases do not cloud valid business judgment.

Although companies can gain the best knowledge, experience, and methodology available in a process through outsourcing, they also lose some control. Thus, company management should carefully evaluate the activities to be outsourced. The pyramid in Exhibit 10–5 is one model for assessing outsourcing risk. Factors to consider include whether (1) a function is considered critical to the organization's long-term viability (such as product research and development), (2) the organization is pursuing a core competency relative to this function, or (3) issues such as product/service quality, time of delivery, flexibility of use, or reliability of supply cannot be resolved to the company's satisfaction.

Refer to Exhibit 10–6 for information about computer keyboards that Capricorn Electronics produces. The total cost to manufacture one keyboard is $7.90, or one keyboard can be purchased externally for $7.00. Capricorn's cost accountant is preparing an analysis to determine whether the company should continue making the keyboards or buy them from the outside supplier.

Production of each keyboard requires a cost outlay of $6.20 per unit for material, labor, and variable overhead. In addition, $0.50 of the fixed overhead is considered direct product cost because it specifically relates to the manufacture of

EXHIBIT 10–4
OUTSOURCE DECISION CONSIDERATIONS

Relevant Quantitative Factors	Relevant Qualitative Factors

Relevant Quantitative Factors

- Incremental production costs for each unit
- Unit cost of purchasing from outside supplier (price less any discounts available plus shipping, etc.)
- Number of available suppliers
- Production capacity available to manufacture components
- Opportunity costs of using facilities for production rather than for other purposes
  * Amount of space available for storage
  * Costs associated with carrying inventory
  * Increase in throughput generated by buying components

Relevant Qualitative Factors

- Reliability of supply sources
- Ability to control quality of inputs purchased from outside
- Nature of the work to be subcontracted (such as the importance of the part to the whole)
- Impact on customers and markets
- Future bargaining position with supplier(s)
- Perceptions regarding possible future price changes
- Perceptions about current product prices (are the prices appropriate or, in some cases with international suppliers, is product dumping involved?)

keyboards. This $0.50 is an incremental cost because it could be avoided if Capicorn does not produce the keyboards. The remaining fixed overhead ($1.20) is not relevant to the outsourcing decision. This amount is a common cost incurred by general production activity that is unassociated with the cost object (keyboards). Therefore, because this portion of the fixed cost would continue under either alternative, it is not relevant.

EXHIBIT 10–5
OUTSOURCING RISK PYRAMID

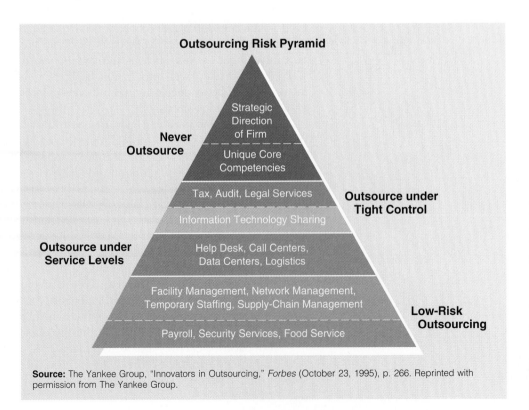

Source: The Yankee Group, "Innovators in Outsourcing," *Forbes* (October 23, 1995), p. 266. Reprinted with permission from The Yankee Group.

EXHIBIT 10–6

CAPRICORN ELECTRONICS— OUTSOURCE DECISION COST INFORMATION

	Present Manufacturing Cost per Keyboard	Relevant Cost of Manufacturing per Keyboard
Direct material	$2.40	$2.40
Direct labor	3.00	3.00
Variable factory overhead	0.80	0.80
Fixed factory overhead*	1.70	0.50
Total unit cost	$7.90	$6.70
Quoted price from supplier		$7.00

*Of the $1.70 fixed factory overhead, only $0.50 is actually caused by keyboard production and could be avoided if the firm chooses not to produce keyboards. The remaining $1.20 of fixed factory overhead is allocated indirect (common) costs that would continue even if keyboard production ceases.

The relevant cost for the insource alternative is $6.70—the cost that would be avoided if the company does not make the keyboard. This amount should be compared to the $7.00 cost quoted by the supplier under the outsource alternative. The amounts are the incremental costs of making and buying, respectively. All else being equal, management should choose to make the keyboards rather than purchase them because the company will save $0.30 on each keyboard made rather than purchased. Relevant costs, regardless of whether they are variable or fixed, are avoidable because one decision alternative was chosen over another. In an outsourcing decision, variable production costs are relevant. Fixed production costs are relevant *only* if they can be avoided when production is discontinued.

The opportunity cost of the facilities being used by production is also relevant in this decision. Choosing to outsource a product component rather than to make it allows the company to use its facilities for an alternative purpose. If a more profitable alternative is available, management should consider diverting the capacity to this use. Assume that Capicorn Electronics can rent out the physical space now used to produce keyboards for $360,000 per year. If the company produces 600,000 keyboards annually, it has an opportunity cost of $0.60 per unit ($360,000 ÷ 600,000 keyboards) from using rather than renting the production space. Existence of this opportunity cost makes the outsource alternative more attractive: The opportunity cost would be added to the production cost since the company is forgoing this amount by choosing to make the keyboards. Sacrificing potential revenue is as much a relevant cost as is the incurrence of expenses. See Exhibit 10–7 for calculations relating to this decision on both a per-unit and a total cost basis. Under either format, the comparison indicates that there is a $0.30 per-unit advantage to outsourcing over insourcing.

Another opportunity cost that can be associated with insourcing is an increase in plant production activity (or throughput) that is sacrificed because a component is being made. Assume that keyboard production uses a resource that has been determined to be a bottleneck in the manufacturing plant. Management calculates that plant throughput can be increased by 1 percent per year on all products if the company buys the keyboards rather than making them. Assume that this increase in throughput would provide an estimated additional annual contribution margin of $210,000 (with no incremental fixed costs). Dividing this amount by the 600,000 keyboards currently being produced results in a $0.35 per-unit opportunity cost related to manufacturing. When added to the previously calculated relevant costs of $7.30, the relevant cost of manufacturing keyboards becomes $7.65.

Based on the information in Exhibit 10–7 (even without the inclusion of the throughput opportunity cost), Capicorn Electronics' cost accountant should inform company management that it is more economical to purchase keyboards for $7

EXHIBIT 10–7

**CAPRICORN
ELECTRONICS'
OPPORTUNITY COST AND
OUTSOURCE DECISION**

	Insource	Outsource	
Per unit			
Direct production costs	$ 6.70		
Opportunity cost (revenue)	0.60		
Purchase cost		$ 7.00	
Cost per case	$ 7.30	$ 7.00	
			Difference in Favor of Outsourcing
In total			
Revenue from renting capacity	$ 0	$ 360,000	$360,000
Cost for 600,000 cases	(4,020,000)	(4,200,000)	(180,000)
Net cost	$(4,020,000)	$(3,840,000)	$180,000*

*The $180,000 represents the net purchase benefit of $0.30 per unit multiplied by the 600,000 units to be purchased during the year.

than to manufacture them. This analysis—determining which alternative is preferred based on the *quantitative* considerations—is the typical starting point of the decision process. Managers then use judgment to assess the decision's qualitative aspects.

Assume that Capricorn Electronics' purchasing agent read a newspaper article that the keyboard supplier being considered is in poor financial condition and would likely file for bankruptcy. In this case, management would decide to insource rather than to outsource the keyboards from this supplier. In this instance, quantitative analysis supports the purchase of the units, but qualitative considerations suggest this would not be a wise action because the stability of the supplying source is questionable.

This additional consideration also indicates that a theoretically short-run decision can have many potential long-run effects. If Capricorn had stopped keyboard production and rented out its facilities and the supplier had then gone bankrupt, Capricorn would face high start-up costs to reestablish its keyboard production process. This was essentially the situation faced several years ago by Stonyfield Farm, a New Hampshire–based yogurt company. Stonyfield Farm subcontracted its yogurt production, and one day found its supplier bankrupt, making Stonyfield unable to fill customer orders. It took Stonyfield two years to acquire the necessary production capacity and regain market strength.

This long-run view is also expressed in Chapter 5, which suggested that the term *fixed cost* is really a misnomer because, while it does not vary with volume in the short run, it *does* vary in the long run. Thus, fixed costs should more appropriately be referred to as long-run variable costs. As such, they are relevant for long-run decision making.

To illustrate this reasoning, assume that a company manufactures a particular part (rather than outsourcing it) and expects demand for that item to increase in the next few years. If the company has the need to expand capacity in the future, it will incur additional "fixed" capacity costs. In turn, these additional costs would likely cause product costs to increase because of the need to allocate the new larger amount of overhead to production. To suggest that products made before capacity is added would cost less than those made afterward is a short-run view. The long-run viewpoint should consider both the current and long-run variable costs over the product life cycle: Capacity costs were "fixed" only until the relevant range of productive capacity changed. However, many firms actively engage in cooperative efforts with their suppliers to control costs and reduce prices. Strong supplier relationships are required for companies using JIT technologies.

Many doctors' offices, especially if space is an issue, opt to out-source blood testing to independent labs.

GETTY IMAGES

Outsourcing decisions are not confined solely to manufacturing entities. Many service organizations also make such decisions. For example, accounting and law firms must decide whether to prepare and present in-house continuing education programs or to outsource them. Many schools have decided whether to bus their students themselves or use independent contractors to do so. Doctors investigate the differences in cost, quality of results, and convenience to patients from having blood samples drawn and tested in the office or at an independent lab facility. Outsourcing can include product and process design activities, accounting and legal services, utilities, engineering services, and employee health services.

As discussed earlier, outsourcing decisions include the opportunity costs of facilities. If capacity is occupied in one way, it cannot be used at the same time for another purpose. Limited capacity is only one type of scarce resource that managers need to consider when making decisions.

Scarce Resources Decisions

LO.4
HOW CAN MANAGEMENT MAKE THE BEST USE OF A SCARCE RESOURCE?

scarce resource

Managers frequently must confront the short-run problem of making the best use of scarce resources that are essential to production activity but are available only in limited quantity. **Scarce resources** including machine hours, skilled labor hours, raw materials, production capacity, and other inputs create limitations on producing goods or providing services. In the long run, company management could obtain a higher quantity of a scarce resource, such as by purchasing additional machines to increase machine hours' availability. However, in the short run, management must make the most efficient use of the currently available scarce resources.

Determining the best use of a scarce resource requires management to recognize and pursue company objectives. If an objective is to maximize company profits, a scarce resource is best used to produce and sell the product having the highest contribution margin *per unit of the scarce resource*. This strategy assumes that the company must ration only one scarce resource.

See Exhibit 10–8 for information on two products that Capricorn Electronics manufactures, desktop computers and notebook computers. Each desktop computer manufactured requires 1 chip, and each notebook computer requires 3 chips. Currently, Capricorn has access to only 6,200 chips per month to make desktops, notebooks, or some combination of both. Because Capricorn's demand for chips (which reflects customer product demand) is more than 6,200 per month, the purchased chip is a scarce resource for the company. The contribution margin of the desktop is $130 per unit, and of the notebook is $270 per unit (Exhibit 10–8). Fixed annual overhead related to these two product lines totals $9,220,000 and is allocated to products for purposes of inventory valuation. Fixed overhead, however, does not change with production levels within the relevant range and, accordingly, is not relevant in a short-run scarce resource decision. No variable selling or administrative costs are related to either product.

EXHIBIT 10–8

**CAPRICORN
ELECTRONICS—DESKTOP
AND NOTEBOOK
COMPUTER INFORMATION**

	Desktop	Notebook
Selling price per unit (*a*)	$800	$1,200
Variable production cost per unit:		
Direct material	$450	$ 600
Direct labor	125	150
Variable overhead	95	180
Total variable cost (*b*)	$670	$ 930
Unit contribution margin [(*c*) = (*a*) − (*b*)]	$130	$ 270
Number of chips required per unit (*d*)	÷ 1	÷ 3
Contribution margin per chip [(*c*) ÷ (*d*)]	$130	$ 90

Because fixed overhead per unit is not relevant in the short run, unit contribution margin rather than unit gross margin is the appropriate measure of profitability of the two products.[5] Unit contribution margin is divided by the input quantity of the scarce resource to obtain the contribution margin per unit of scarce resource. The last line in Exhibit 10–8 shows the $130 contribution margin per chip for the desktop compared to $90 for the notebook. Thus, it is more profitable for Capricorn Electronics to produce desktop computers than notebooks.

At first glance, it appears that the notebook would by a substantial margin be the more profitable of the two products because its contribution margin per unit ($270) is significantly higher than that of the desktop ($130). However, because the notebook requires three times as many chips as the desktop, production of the desktop generates a higher contribution margin per chip. If Capricorn Electronics makes only these two types of product and wants to achieve the highest possible profit, it would dedicate all available data chips to the production of desktops. If it sells all units produced, this strategy would provide a total contribution margin of $806,000 per month (6,200 × $130).

When one limiting factor is involved, the outcome of a scarce resource decision indicates which single type of product should be manufactured and sold. Most situations, however, involve several limiting factors that compete in striving to attain business objectives. Linear programming, discussed in the appendix to this chapter, is one method used to solve problems with several limiting factors.

In addition to considering the monetary effects related to scarce resource decisions, managers must remember that all factors cannot be readily quantified and that the qualitative aspects of the situation must be evaluated in addition to the quantitative ones. For example, before choosing to produce only desktops, Capricorn Electronics' managers should assess the potential damage to the firm's reputation and customer markets if the company were to limit its product line to a single item. Such a choice severely restricts its customer base and is especially important if the currently manufactured products are competitively related. For example, if Hewlett-Packard began making only home printers, many business printer buyers would not find that product appropriate for their needs and would buy printers from another company.

Concentrating on a single product can also create market saturation or company stagnation. Customers infrequently purchase some products, such as refrigerators and **Rolex** watches, or purchase items in single units. Making such a product limits the company's opportunity for repeat business. If a company concentrates on the *wrong* single product (such as "slap" bracelets or laser video disks), that exclusionary choice can be the beginning of the company's end.

---

[5] Gross margin (or gross profit) is unit selling price minus total production cost per unit. Total production cost includes allocated fixed overhead.

In some cases, the revenues and expenses of a group of products must be considered as a set of decisions in allocating scarce resources. Multiple products could be complementary or part of a package in which one product cannot be used effectively without another product or is the key to revenue generation in future periods. To illustrate these possibilities, consider the following products: **Cross**'s well-known ballpoint pen and mechanical pencil sets, **Gillette**'s Atra razor and razor blades, and **Mattel**'s Barbie "family" of products. Would it be reasonable for Cross to make only pens, Gillette to make only razors, or Mattel to make only Barbie dolls? In the case of Gillette, the company is known for giving away its razors to 18-year-old males. Mattel's management would probably choose to manufacture and sell Barbie dolls at zero contribution margin because of the profits that Barbie accessories earn.

Thus, company management could decide that production and sale of some number of less profitable products is necessary to maintain either customer satisfaction or sales of other products. Production mix translates on the revenue side into sales mix, which the next section addresses.

Sales Mix Decisions

LO.5
HOW DOES SALES MIX PERTAIN TO RELEVANT COSTING PROBLEMS?

How can managers influence company sales mix?

sales mix

Managers continuously strive to achieve a variety of company objectives such as profit maximization, improvement of its relative market share, and generation of customer goodwill and loyalty. Selling products or performing services accomplishes these objectives. Regardless of whether the company is a retailer, manufacturer, or service organization, **sales mix** refers to the relative product quantities composing a company's total sales. Some important factors affecting a company's sales mix are product selling prices, sales force compensation, and advertising expenditures. Because a change in one or all of these factors could cause sales mix to shift, managing it is fundamental to managing profit.

See Exhibit 10–9 for information on Capricorn Electronics' home printer line that illustrates the effects of the three factors—selling prices, sales compensation, and advertising—on sales mix. The product line includes student, commercial, and professional printers, each with different features and targeted at a different market segment.

SALES PRICE CHANGES AND RELATIVE PROFITABILITY OF PRODUCTS

A company must continually monitor the sales prices of its products, both with respect to each other and to competitors. Such monitoring can provide information that causes management to change one or more sales prices. Factors that might influence price changes include fluctuations in demand or production/distribution cost, economic conditions, and competition. Any shift in the selling price of one product in a multiproduct firm normally causes a change in sales mix of that firm because of the economic law of demand elasticity with respect to price.[6]

Capricorn Electronics' management has set profit maximization as the primary corporate objective. This strategy does not necessarily translate to maximizing unit sales of the product with the highest selling prices and minimizing unit sales of the product with the lowest selling price because the highest selling price per unit does not necessarily yield the highest contribution margin per unit or per dollar of sales. In Capricorn Electronics' case, the printer with the highest sales price (the professional model) yields the second highest unit contribution margin of the three

---

[6] The law of demand elasticity indicates how closely price and demand are related. Product demand is highly elastic if a small price reduction generates a large demand increase. If demand is less elastic, large price reductions are needed to bring about moderate sales volume increases. In contrast, if demand is highly elastic, a small price increase results in a large drop in demand.

EXHIBIT 10–9

CAPRICORN ELECTRONICS—PRINTER PRODUCT INFORMATION

	Student	Commercial	Professional
Unit selling price (SP)	$80	$450	$900
Variable costs			
Direct material	$33	$185	$425
Direct labor	12	75	245
Variable factory overhead	15	45	90
Total variable production cost	$60	$305	$760
Product contribution margin	$20	$145	$140
Variable selling expense (10% of SP)	(8)	(45)	(90)
Contribution margin per unit	$12	$100	$ 50

Total fixed costs:	
Production	$4,200,000
Selling & administrative	1,100,000
Total	$5,300,000

products but the lowest contribution margin as a percent of sales. The company generates more profit by selling a dollar's worth of the commercial printer than a dollar's worth of either the student or professional model. A dollar of sales of the commercial printer yields $0.22 (rounded) of contribution margin compared to $0.12 for the student and $0.056 (rounded) for the professional.

If profit maximization is a company's goal, management should consider each product's sales volume and unit contribution margin. Total company contribution margin is the sum of the contribution margins provided by the sale of all products. See Exhibit 10–10 for information on product sales volumes; the data indicate the respective total contribution margins from the three printer types. To maximize profits from the printers, Capricorn's management must maximize total contribution margin rather than per-unit contribution margin.

A product's sales volume is almost always directly related to its sales price. Generally, when the price of a product or service is increased and demand is elastic with respect to price, demand for that product decreases.[7] Thus, in an attempt

EXHIBIT 10–10

CAPRICORN ELECTRONICS— RELATIONSHIP BETWEEN CONTRIBUTION MARGIN, SALES VOLUME, AND PROFIT

	Unit Contribution Margin (from Exhibit 10–9)	Current Sales Volume in Units	Income Statement Information
Student printers	$ 12	52,000	$ 624,000
Commercial printers	100	39,000	3,900,000
Professional printers	50	15,000	750,000
Total contribution margin of product sales mix			$ 5,274,000
Fixed expenses (from Exhibit 10–9)			(5,300,000)
Product line income at present volume and sales mix			$ (26,000)

[7] Such a decline in demand would generally not occur when the product in question has no close substitutes or is not a major expenditure in consumers' budgets.

to increase profits, if Capricorn Electronics' management raises the student printer price to $100, the company should experience some decline in demand. Assume that consultation with the marketing research personnel indicates that this price increase would cause demand for that product to drop from 52,000 to 30,000 printers per period. See Exhibit 10–11 for the effect of this pricing decision on Capricorn Electronics' printer product line income.

Because contribution margin per unit of the student printer increased, the total dollar contribution margin generated by sales of that product increased despite the decrease in unit sales. This example assumed that customers did not switch their purchases from the student printer to other Capricorn Electronics products when its price went up. When some product prices in a product line remain stable while others increase, customers might substitute one product for another. This instance ignored switching within the company, but some customers would likely purchase one of the more expensive printers after the price of the student printer increased. For example, customers might believe that the difference in functionality between the student and commercial printers is worth the price difference and make such a purchasing switch.

In making decisions to raise or lower prices, relevant quantitative factors include (1) new contribution margin per unit of product, (2) short-term and long-term changes in product demand and production volume because of the price change, and (3) best use of the company's scarce resources. Some relevant qualitative factors involved in pricing decisions are (1) impact of changes on customer goodwill toward the company, (2) customer loyalty toward company products, and (3) competitors' responses to the firm's new pricing structure.[8] Also, changes in the competitive environment create opportunities to produce new products; exploiting such opportunities leads to sales mix changes.

When pricing proposed new products, management should take a long-run view of the product's life cycle. This view should include assumptions about consumer behavior, competitor behavior, pace of technology changes, government posture, environmental concerns, size of the potential market, and demographic changes. These considerations would affect product price estimates at the various stages in the product's life cycle.

SALES COMPENSATION CHANGES

Many companies compensate salespeople by paying a fixed rate of commission on gross sales dollars. This approach motivates salespeople to sell the highest priced

EXHIBIT 10–11

CAPRICORN ELECTRONICS— RELATIONSHIP BETWEEN SALES PRICE CHANGE, SALES VOLUME, AND PROFIT

	Unit Contribution Margin (from Exhibit 10–9)	New Sales Volume in Units	Income Statement Information
Student printers	$ 30*	30,000	$ 900,000
Commercial printers	100	39,000	3,900,000
Professional printers	50	15,000	750,000
Total contribution margin of product sales mix			$ 5,550,000
Fixed expenses (from Exhibit 10–9)			(5,300,000)
Product line income at new volume and sales mix			$ 250,000

*New price of $100 minus [total variable production costs of $60 plus variable selling expense of $10 (10% of new selling price)].

---

[8] With regard to the actions of competitors, consider what occurs when one airline lowers its fares on a particular route. It typically does not take very long for all other airlines flying that route to adjust their fares accordingly. Thus, any competitive advantage is only for a short time span.

product rather than the product providing the highest contribution margin to the company. If the company has a profit-maximization objective, such a compensation policy will not be effective in achieving that objective.

Assume that Capricorn Electronics has a price structure for its printers as follows: student, $100; commercial, $450; and professional, $900. The company's current policy is to pay sales commissions equal to 10 percent of selling price. This commission structure encourages sales of professional printers rather than commercial or student printers. Capricorn is considering a new sales force compensation structure that would provide base salaries for all salespeople totaling $925,000 per period.[9] In addition, it would pay salespeople a 15 percent commission on product contribution margin (selling price minus total variable production cost). The per-unit product contribution margins of the printers are $40, $145, and $140 for student, commercial, and professional printers, respectively. The new compensation policy should motivate sales personnel to sell more of the printers that produce the highest commission, which would correspondingly be the company's most profitable products.[10]

Refer to Exhibit 10–12 for a comparison of Capricorn Electronics' total contribution margin using the current sales mix and commission structure with that of the new compensation structure focused on total contribution margin. The new structure would increase profits because it shifts sales from the printers with a lower contribution margin ratio to those with the higher contribution margin ratio. Salespeople also benefit from the new pay structure, which will significantly increase their income composed of base salary and commission. Reflected in the sales mix change is the fact that student printers can be sold with substantially less salesperson effort per unit than that required for the other models.

Fixed expenses would not be considered in setting compensation structures unless those expenses were incremental relative to the new policy or to changes in sales volumes. The new base salaries were an incremental cost of Capricorn Electronics' proposed compensation plan.

EXHIBIT 10–12
CAPRICORN ELECTRONICS—IMPACT OF CHANGE IN COMMISSION STRUCTURE

Product Contribution Margin	−	Commission	=	Contribution Margin after Commission	×	Volume	=	Total Contribution Margin
Old Policy—Commissions Equal 10% of Selling Price								
Student	$ 40	(0.1 × $100) = $10		$ 30.00		30,000		$ 900,000
Commercial	145	(0.1 × $450) = $45		100.00		39,000		3,900,000
Professional	140	(0.1 × $900) = $90		50.00		15,000		750,000
Total contribution margin for product sales						84,000		$5,550,000
New Policy—Commissions Equal 15% of Product Contribution Margin per Unit and Incremental Base Salaries of $925,000								
Student	$ 40	(0.15 × $40) = $6.00		$ 34.00		40,000		$1,360,000
Commercial	145	(0.15 × $145) = $21.75		123.25		49,000		6,039,250
Professional	140	(0.15 × $140) = $21.00		119.00		10,000		1,190,000
Total contribution margin for product sales						99,000		$8,589,250
Less sales force base salaries								(925,000)
Contribution margin adjusted for sales force base salaries								$7,664,250

[9] The revised compensation structure should allow the sales personnel to achieve the same or higher income as before the change given a similar level of effort.

[10] This statement relies on the assumption that the salespersons' efforts are more highly correlated with unit sales than dollar sales. If this assumption is accurate, the commission structure should encourage sales of products with higher contribution margin ratios.

ADVERTISING BUDGET CHANGES

Adjusting the advertising budgets respective to each company product or increasing the company's total advertising budget could lead to shifts in the sales mix. This section uses the data for Capricorn Electronics from Exhibit 10–11 and examines a proposed increase in the company's total advertising budget.

Capricorn Electronics' advertising manager, Merry Market, has proposed increasing the advertising budget from $500,000 to $650,000 per year. She believes the increased advertising will result in the following additional printer sales during the coming year: student, 2,500; commercial, 1,500; and professional, 750. Company management wants to know whether spending the additional $150,000 for advertising to generate the additional 4,750 units of sales will produce higher profits than the printer line is currently generating.

The original fixed costs, as well as the contribution margin generated by the current sales levels, are irrelevant to the decision. The relevant items are the increased sales revenue, increased variable costs, and increased fixed cost—the incremental effects of the advertising change. The difference between incremental revenues and incremental variable costs is the incremental contribution margin from which the incremental fixed cost is subtracted to provide the incremental benefit (or loss) of the decision.[11]

See Exhibit 10–13 for calculations of the expected increase in contribution margin if the company makes the increased advertising expenditure. The $262,500 of additional contribution margin is more than the $150,000 incremental cost for advertising, indicating that company management should increase its advertising by $150,000.

Increased advertising can cause changes in the sales mix or in the number of units sold by targeting advertising efforts at specific products. Sales can also be influenced by opportunities that allow companies to obtain business at a sales price that differs from the normal price.

Special Order Decisions

LO.6
HOW ARE SPECIAL PRICES SET, AND WHEN ARE THEY USED?

special order decision

A **special order decision** requires management to compute a reasonable sales price for production or service jobs not part of the company's normal realm of operations. Special order situations include jobs that require a bid, are accepted during slack periods, or are made to a particular buyer's specifications. Typically, the sales price quoted on a special order job should be high enough to cover the job's variable and incremental fixed costs and generate a profit.

Sometimes companies depart from their price-setting routine and bid on jobs at "low-ball" selling prices. A low-ball bid could cover only costs and produce no profit or could even be below cost. The rationale of low-ball bids is to obtain the job and have the opportunity to introduce company products or services to a particular market segment. Special pricing of this nature could provide work for a period of time, but it cannot be continued over the long run. To remain in business,

EXHIBIT 10–13

CAPRICORN ELECTRONICS—ANALYSIS OF INCREASED ADVERTISING COST

	Student	Commercial	Professional	Total
Increase in volume	2,500	1,500	750	4,750
Contribution margin per unit	× $30	× $100	× $50	
Incremental contribution margin	$75,000	$150,000	$37,500	$ 262,500
Incremental fixed cost of advertising				(150,000)
Incremental benefit from increased advertising expenditure				$ 112,500

[11] This same type of incremental analysis is shown in Chapter 9 in relation to CVP computations.

a company must set selling prices to cover total costs and provide a reasonable profit margin.[12]

Another type of special pricing job is that of private-label orders in which the buyer's name (rather than the producer's) is attached to the product. Companies could accept these jobs during slack periods to more effectively use available capacity. Fixed costs of such jobs are typically not allocated to special order, private-label products. Some variable costs (such as sales commissions) can be reduced or eliminated by the very nature of the private-label process. Prices on these special orders are typically set high enough to cover actual variable costs and contribute to overall profits.

Special prices can also be justified when orders are of an unusual nature (because of the quantity, method of delivery, or packaging) or because the products are being tailormade to customer instructions. Last, special pricing is used when goods are produced for a one-time job, such as an overseas order that will not affect domestic sales.

Assume that Capricorn Electronics has the opportunity to bid on a special order for 60,000 private-label printers for a major electronics retailer. Company management wants to obtain the order if the additional business will provide a satisfactory contribution to profit. The company currently has unused production capacity available, and can obtain the necessary components and raw material from suppliers. Also, the company has no immediate opportunity to apply its currently unused capacity in another way, so there is no opportunity cost.

Management has gathered information (Exhibit 10–14) to determine a price to bid on the private-label printers. Direct material and components, direct labor, and variable factory overhead costs are relevant to setting the bid price because these costs will be incurred for each printer produced. Although all variable costs are normally relevant to a special pricing decision, the variable selling expense is irrelevant in this instance because no sales commission will be paid on this sale. Fixed manufacturing overhead and fixed selling and administrative expenses are not expected to increase because of this sale, so these expenses are not considered in the pricing decision.

Using the available cost information, the relevant cost for determining the bid price for each printer is $150 (direct material and components, direct labor, and variable overhead). This cost is the *minimum* price at which the company should sell one printer. Any price higher than $150 will provide some profit on the sale.

Assume that Capricorn Electronics' printer line is currently experiencing a $3,100,000 net loss and company managers want to set a bid price that would cover the net loss and create $200,000 of before-tax profit. In this case, Capricorn would spread the total $3,300,000 desired contribution margin over the 60,000-unit

EXHIBIT 10–14

CAPRICORN ELECTRONICS—PRIVATE-LABEL PRINTER PRODUCT INFORMATION

	Normal Costs	Relevant Costs
Per-unit cost for printers:		
Direct material and components	$ 90	$ 90
Direct labor	25	25
Variable overhead	35	35
Variable selling expense (commission)	20	0
Total variable cost	$170	$150
Fixed factory overhead (allocated)	30	
Fixed selling & administrative expense	20	
Total cost per printer	$220	

[12] An exception to this general rule can occur when a company produces related or complementary products. For instance, an electronics company can sell a video game at or below cost and allow the ancillary software program sales to be the primary source of profit.

special order at $55 per printer. This decision would be a bid price of $205 per printer ($150 variable cost + $55). However, *any* price above the $150 variable cost will contribute toward reducing the $3,100,000 product line loss.

In setting the bid price, management must decide what it considers a "reasonable" profit on the special order. Assume that Capricorn's management believes that a normal profit margin of $25 per printer, or 11.4 percent (rounded) of the $220 full cost is reasonable. Setting the special order bid price at $167.10 would cover the variable production costs of $150 and provide the 11.4 percent profit margin ($17.10) on incremental unit cost. This computation illustrates a simplistic cost-plus approach to pricing but ignores both product demand and market competition. Capricorn's bid price should also reflect these considerations. In addition, its management should consider any effects that the additional job will have on normal company activities and whether this job will create additional, unforeseen costs. As discussed in Chapter 5, activities create costs, so management must be aware of the cost drivers of the company's costs.

When setting a special order price, management must consider qualitative as well as quantitative issues. For instance, management should answer questions such as the following in setting the special order price. Will setting a low bid price cause this customer (or others) to believe that the company has established a precedent for future prices? Will the contribution margin on a bid, set low enough to acquire the job, be sufficient to justify the additional burdens placed on management and employees by this activity? Will the additional production activity require the use of bottleneck resources and reduce company throughput? How, if at all, will special order sales affect the company's normal sales? If the special order is scheduled during a period of low business activity (off-season or recession), is management willing to take the business at a lower contribution or profit margin simply to keep a trained workforce employed?

Robinson-Patman Act

A final consideration in making special pricing decisions in the United States is the **Robinson-Patman Act**, which prohibits companies from pricing the same product at different levels when those amounts do not reflect related cost differences. Cost differences must result from actual variations in the cost to manufacture, sell, or distribute a product because of different methods of production or quantities sold.

ad hoc discount

Companies may, however, give **ad hoc discounts**, which are price concessions that relate to real (or imagined) competitive pressures rather than to location of the merchandising chain or volume purchased. Such discounts are not usually subject to detailed justification because they are based on a competitive market environment. Although ad hoc discounts do not require intensive justification under the law, other types of discounts do because they could reflect some type of price discrimination. Prudent managers must understand the legalities of special pricing and the factors that allow for its implementation. For normally stocked merchandise, the only support for pricing differences is a difference in distribution costs.

In making pricing decisions, managers typically first analyze the market environment, including the degree of industry competition and competitors' prices. Then managers normally consider full production cost in setting normal sales prices. Full production cost includes an allocated portion of the fixed costs of the production process, which in a multiproduct environment could include common costs of production relating to more than one type of product. Allocations of common costs can distort the results of operations shown for individual products.

Product Line and Segment Decisions

LO.7
HOW IS SEGMENT MARGIN USED TO DETERMINE WHETHER A PRODUCT LINE SHOULD BE RETAINED OR ELIMINATED?

Operating results of multiproduct environments are often presented in a disaggregated format that shows results for separate product lines within the organization or division. In reviewing these disaggregated statements, managers must distinguish relevant from irrelevant information regarding individual product lines. If all costs (variable *and* fixed) are allocated to product lines, a product line or segment could be perceived to be operating at a loss when actually it is not. The commingling of relevant and irrelevant information on the statements could cause such perceptions.

See Exhibit 10–15 for basic earnings information for the Speaker Division of Capricorn Electronics, which manufactures three speaker lines: automotive, residential, and band. The data in the exhibit make it appear that the band line is operating at a net loss of $165,000. Managers reviewing such results might reason that the firm would be $165,000 more profitable if they eliminate band speakers. Such a conclusion could be premature because of the mixture of relevant and irrelevant information in the income statement presentation.

All fixed expenses have been allocated to the individual product lines in Exhibit 10–15. Such allocations are traditionally based on one or more measures of "presumed" equity, such as the following for each product line: square footage of the manufacturing plant occupied, number of machine hours incurred for production, and number of employees directly associated with it. In all cases, however, allocations could force fixed expenses into specific product line operating results even though some of those expenses were not actually incurred for the benefit of the specific product line.

Exhibit 10–16 segregates the Speaker Division's fixed expenses into three subcategories: (1) avoidable if the particular product line is eliminated (these expenses can also be referred to as *attributable expenses*), (2) directly associated with a particular product line but not avoidable, and (3) incurred for the benefit of the company as a whole (common expenses) and that are allocated to the individual product lines. The latter two subcategories are irrelevant in deciding whether to eliminate a product line. An unavoidable expense merely shifts to another product line if the one with which it is associated is eliminated. Common expenses will be incurred regardless of which product lines are eliminated. An example of a common cost is the insurance premium on a manufacturing facility that houses all product lines.

If the band line is eliminated, total divisional profit will decline by $350,000, the segment margin of the band product line. **Segment margin** represents the excess of revenues over direct variable expenses and avoidable fixed expenses. It is the amount remaining to cover unavoidable direct fixed expenses and common expenses and to provide profits.[13] Segment margin is the appropriate figure on which to base the continuation or elimination decision because it measures the segment's contribution to the coverage of indirect and unavoidable expenses. The

How is segment margin used in deciding whether to keep or discontinue a product line or business segment?

segment margin

EXHIBIT 10–15

SPEAKER DIVISION OF CAPRICORN ELECTRONICS PRODUCT LINE INCOME STATEMENTS (IN $000S)

	Automotive	Residential	Band	Total
Sales	$ 8,000	$ 9,800	$ 3,000	$ 20,800
Total direct variable expenses	(5,400)	(5,700)	(2,200)	(13,300)
Total contribution margin	$ 2,600	$ 4,100	$ 800	$ 7,500
Total fixed expenses	(2,100)	(3,700)	(965)	(6,765)
Net income (loss)	$ 500	$ 400	$ (165)	$ 735
Details of fixed expenses				
(1) Avoidable fixed expenses	$ 1,200	$ 3,000	$ 450	$ 4,650
(2) Unavoidable fixed expenses	600	420	300	1,320
(3) Allocated common expenses	300	280	215	795
Total	$ 2,100	$ 3,700	$ 965	$ 6,765

[13] All common expenses are assumed to be fixed; this is not always the case. Some common costs could be variable, such as expenses of processing purchase orders or computer time-sharing expenses for payroll or other corporate functions.

EXHIBIT 10–16

SPEAKER DIVISION OF CAPRICORN ELECTRONICS SEGMENT MARGIN INCOME STATEMENTS (IN $000S)

	Automotive	Residential	Band	Total
Sales	$ 8,000	$ 9,800	$ 3,000	$ 20,800
Total direct variable expenses	(5,400)	(5,700)	(2,200)	(13,300)
Total contribution margin	$ 2,600	$ 4,100	$ 800	$ 7,500
(1) Avoidable fixed expenses	(1,200)	(3,000)	(450)	(4,650)
Segment margin	$ 1,400	$ 1,100	$ 350	$ 2,850
(2) Unavoidable fixed expenses	(600)	(420)	(300)	(1,320)
Product line result	$ 800	$ 680	$ 50	$ 1,530
(3) Allocated common expenses	(300)	(280)	(215)	(795)
Net income (loss)	$ 500	$ 400	$ (165)	$ 735

new net income of $385,000 that would result from having only two product lines (automotive and residential) is in the following alternative computations.

	(In $000)
Current net income	$ 735
Decrease in income due to elimination of band (segment margin)	(350)
New net income	$ 385
Proof:	
Total contribution margin of automotive and residential lines	$ 6,700
Less avoidable fixed expenses of the automotive and residential lines	(4,200)
Segment margin of automotive and residential lines	$ 2,500
Less all remaining unavoidable and allocated expenses	
in Exhibit 10–16 ($1,320 + $795)	(2,115)
Remaining income with two product lines	$ 385

Based on the information in Exhibit 10–16, the Speaker Division should not eliminate the band product line because it is generating a positive segment margin and covering its relevant expenses.

In classifying product line costs, managers should be aware that some costs can appear to be avoidable but are actually not. For example, the salary of a supervisor working directly with a product line appears to be an avoidable fixed cost if the product line is eliminated. However, if this individual has significant experience, the company often retains the supervisor, whom it transfers to another area when product lines are cut. These types of determinations must be made before costs can be appropriately classified in product line elimination decisions.

Depreciation on factory equipment used to manufacture a specific product is an irrelevant cost in product line decisions. But if the equipment can be sold, the selling price is relevant to the decision because selling it would increase the marginal benefit of the decision to discontinue the product line. Even if the equipment will be kept in service and used to produce other products, the depreciation expense is unavoidable and irrelevant to the decision.

Before making spontaneous decisions to discontinue a product line, management should carefully consider what it would take to turn the product line around and what long-term ramifications the elimination decision would have. For example, the elimination of a product line shrinks market assortment, which could cause some customers to seek other suppliers that maintain a broader market assortment. And, as in other relevant costing situations, this decision has qualitative as well as quantitative factors that must be analyzed. Individual customers also should be analyzed (in the same manner as product lines) for profitability. When necessary, ways to improve the cost–benefit relationship should be determined.

Management's task is to effectively and efficiently allocate its finite stock of resources to accomplish its chosen set of objectives. A cost accountant must learn what uses management will make of information requested to ensure that the information provided is relevant and in the appropriate form. Managers must have a reliable quantitative basis on which to analyze problems, compare viable solutions, and choose the best course of action. Because management is a social rather than a natural science, it has no fundamental "truths," and few related problems are susceptible to black-or-white solutions. Relevant costing is a process of making human approximations of the costs of alternative decision results.

Revisiting

Satyam Computer Services, Ltd.

Many Indian companies have been prospering as a result of the outsourcing trend, particularly when businesses "offshore" from the United States. In addition to lower wages, high education levels, and an ability to communicate fluently in our native tongue, another reason for U.S. companies to outsource to firms in India is the time difference. While U.S. business sleeps, India is at work. Thus, a U.S. firm can submit work to an Indian firm at the end of one business day and potentially have it completed by the beginning of the next! Leading U.S. technology firms such as IBM, Microsoft, Oracle, and Lucent Technologies have partnered with Satyam Computer Services at a significant cost savings. For example, in the area of software development, the ratio of U.S. labor cost to Indian labor cost is 8 to 1. This important ratio translates into cost advantages for U.S. firms competing in the global marketplace. Complementing the labor cost of advantage in India is the declining cost to communicate internationally. To illustrate, in 2004 the estimated cost of leasing a phone line for calls and data transmission from Los Angeles to Bangalore was less than one-third of the estimated cost

for 2000. This change dramatically reduced the transactions costs of communicating and transferring information.

Many of Satyam's partners are software vendors that rely on it to custom install and integrate software with other clients' systems. At first glance, it is tempting to conclude that Satyam's phenomenal growth is attributable to its huge labor cost advantage. However, even though Satyam does enjoy a significant labor cost advantage relative to competitors in the United States, it enjoys no such advantage in competing with other Indian firms. The company must distinguish itself on the basis not only of cost but also quality and breadth of services. Certainly Satyam has done exactly that. Because of its tremendous success in attracting clients and partners, Satyam has grown in a few short years to become the third largest information technology company on the Indian bourse or stock exchange.

Source: Satyam Computer Services, Limited, Form 6-K, *http://www.sec.gov/Archives/edgar/data/1106056/000114554904000196/u92288e6vk.htm#003*. See also Jesse Drucker, "Global Talk Gets Cheaper," *The Wall Street Journal*, March 11, 2004, pp. B1, B2.

Appendix

Linear Programming

LO.8
HOW IS A LINEAR PROGRAMMING PROBLEM FORMULATED?

Some factors restrict the immediate attainment of almost any objective. For example, assume that the objective of Washington Hospital's board of directors is to care for more sick people during the coming year. Factors restricting the attainment of that objective include the number of beds in the hospital, size of its staff, hours per week the staff is allowed to work, and number of charity patients the hospital can accept. Each factor reflects a limited or scarce resource; to achieve its objective, Washington Hospital must find a way to allocate its limited resources efficiently and effectively.

Managers are always concerned about allocating scarce resources among competing uses. If a company has only one scarce resource, managers will schedule production or other measures of activity in a way that maximizes the scarce resource's use. Most situations, however, involve several limiting factors that compete with one another during the process of striving to attain business objectives. Solving problems having several limiting factors requires the use of **mathematical programming**, which refers to a variety of techniques used to allocate limited resources among activities to achieve a specific goal or purpose. This appendix introduces linear programming, which is one form of mathematical programming.[14]

mathematical programming

Basics of Linear Programming

Linear programming (LP) is a method used to find the optimal allocation of scarce resources in a situation involving *one objective* and *multiple limiting factors*.[15] The objective and restrictions on achieving that objective must be expressible as linear equations.[16] The equation that specifies the objective is called the **objective function**, which typically is to maximize or to minimize some measure of performance, such as maximizing contribution margin or minimizing product cost.

linear programming

objective function

A **constraint** is any type of limiting factor that hampers management's pursuit of the objective. Resource constraints involve limited availability of labor time, machine time, raw material, space, or production capacity. Demand or marketing constraints restrict the quantity of product that can be sold during a time period. Constraints can also be in the form of technical product requirements. For example, requirements as to calories or vitamin content could constrain the production of frozen meals.

constraint

A final constraint in all LP problems is a **non-negativity constraint**, which is a limiting factor that states that negative values for physical quantities cannot exist in a solution. Constraints represent the limits imposed on optimizing the objective function and like the objective function, are specified in mathematical equations.

non-negativity constraint

Almost every allocation problem has multiple **feasible solutions** that do not violate any problem constraints. Different solutions generally give different values for the objective function, although some problems have several solutions that provide the same value for the objective function. Solutions in fractional values can be generated. If solutions must be restricted to whole numbers, **integer programming** techniques must be used to add constraint to the problem. The **optimal solution** to a maximization or minimization goal provides the best answer to the allocation problem.

feasible solution

integer programming

optimal solution

Formulating a LP Problem

Linear programming techniques commonly applied to production scheduling and combination of ingredients. Management's goal in determining production mix in a multiproduct environment is to find the product mix that, when sold, maximizes the company's contribution margin. The goal in determining the mix of ingredients for a specific product is to find the mix providing the specified level of quality at the minimum variable cost.

Each LP problem contains one dependent variable, two or more independent (or decision) variables, and one or more constraints. A **decision variable** is the

decision variable

---

[14] This chapter discusses basic linear programming concepts; it is not an all-inclusive presentation. Any standard management science text should be consulted for an in-depth presentation of the subject.

[15] Finding the best allocation of resources when multiple goals exist is called *goal programming*. This text does not address this topic.

[16] If the objective and/or restrictions cannot be expressed in linear equations, the technique of nonlinear programming must be used. No general method has been developed that can solve all types of nonlinear programming problems.

unknown element, such as number of units, for which the problem is being solved. The first and most important step in solving linear programming problems is to set up the information in mathematical equation form. The objective function and each constraint must be identified. The objective function is frequently stated in such a way that the solution either maximizes contribution margin or minimizes variable costs. Basic objective function formats for maximization and minimization problems follow.

Maximization problem

$$\text{Objective function: MAX CM} = CM_1X_1 + CM_2X_2$$

Minimization problem

$$\text{Objective function: MIN VC} = VC_1X_1 + VC_2X_2$$

where   CM = contribution margin
CM_1 = contribution margin per unit of the first product
CM_2 = contribution margin per unit of the second product
X_1 = number of units of the first product
X_2 = number of units of the second product
VC = variable cost
VC_1 = variable cost per unit of the first product
VC_2 = variable cost per unit of the second product

Resource constraints are usually expressed as inequalities.[17] The following is the general formula for a less-than-or-equal-to resource constraint:

$$\text{Resource constraint(1): } A_1X_1 + A_2X_2 \leq \text{Resource 1}$$

where X_1 = number of units of the first product
X_2 = number of units of the second product

input–output coefficient

The coefficients (A_1 and A_2) are **input–output coefficients** that indicate the rate at which each decision variable uses or depletes the scarce resource.

Machine time is an example of a resource constraint. Assume that Capricorn Electronics has only 10,000 machine hours available to produce disk drives and external modems. Producing one disk drive unit requires 0.50 machine hour, and producing one modem requires 0.25 hour. The resource constraint is shown as:

$$0.5X_1 + 0.25X_2 \leq 10,000$$

where X_1 = number of disk drive units
X_2 = number of modem units

If Capricorn Electronics manufactured only one of the two types of products, it could produce 20,000 (10,000 ÷ 0.5) disk drives or 40,000 modems. In manufacturing both products, the company must recognize that producing one disk drive precludes manufacturing two modems. The contribution margin of each product and the other constraints under which the company operates determine the mix of units to be produced.

All general concepts of formatting a linear programming problem are illustrated in the following maximization problem using data for Modern Office Solutions (MOS), which sells two office storage products, file cabinets and storage shelves.

---

[17] It is also possible to have strict equality constraints. For example, in producing a 10-pound bag of dog food, ingredients could be combined in a variety of ways, but total weight is required to be 10 pounds.

See Exhibit 10–17 for information on these products and the constraints that must be considered. MOS managers want to know the mix of products that will generate the maximum contribution margin. The company produces the items for future sale and must store them for the near term in its warehouse. The problem is composed of the following factors: (1) the objective is to maximize contribution margin (CM), (2) the decision variables are the file cabinet (X_1) and storage shelves (X_2), and (3) the constraints are labor time, machine time, and warehouse storage space.

Equations used to express objective functions should indicate the purpose of the problem and how that purpose is to be realized. MOS's purpose (objective) is to maximize its contribution margin by producing and selling the combination of file cabinets and storage shelves that provide contribution margins of $25 and $9, respectively. The objective function is stated as

$$MAX\ CM = 25X_1 + 9X_2$$

The constraint inequalities represent the demands made by each decision variable on scarce resource availability. Total labor time for producing the two products must be less than or equal to 2,100 hours per month. Each file cabinet and storage shelf produced takes 3 and 2 labor hours, respectively. The labor constraint is expressed as

$$3X_1 + 2X_2 \leq 2,100$$

Expressing the machine time constraint equation is similar to that of the labor time constraint: 2 hours of machine time for each file cabinet and 1 hour for each storage shelf. Total machine time available per month is 850 hours. This resource constraint is

$$2X_1 + 1X_2 \leq 850$$

The file cabinets and storage shelves produced cannot exceed available warehouse storage space. Each file cabinet consumes substantially more space than each storage shelf. The production constraint is expressed as

$$8X_1 + 3X_2 \leq 4,000$$

EXHIBIT 10–17

MODERN OFFICE SOLUTIONS PRODUCT INFORMATION AND CONSTRAINTS

File cabinet	
Contribution margin per unit	$25
Labor hours to manufacture 1 unit	3
Machine hours to assemble 1 unit	2
Cubic feet of warehouse space per unit	8
Storage shelves	
Contribution margin per unit	$ 9
Labor hours to manufacture 1 unit	2
Machine hours to assemble 1 unit	1
Cubic feet of warehouse space per unit	3
Constraints	
Total labor time available each month	2,100 hours
Total machine time available each month	850 hours
Warehouse space available	4,000 cubic feet

Although not shown in Exhibit 10–17, non-negativity constraints exist for this problem. They state that production of either product cannot be less than zero units and are shown as

$$X_1 \geq 0$$
$$X_2 \geq 0$$

See Exhibit 10–18 for the mathematical formulas needed to solve the Modern Office Solutions LP production problem. Next a method for solving the problem must be chosen.

Solving a LP Problem

Linear programming problems can be solved by a graphical approach or by the simplex method. Graphs are simple to use and provide a visual representation to solve linear programming problems. Graphical methods are useful, however, only when the problem has two decision variables and few constraints or two constraints and few decision variables.

The graphical method of solving a linear programming problem consists of five steps:

1. State the problem in terms of a linear objective function and linear constraints.
2. Graph the constraints and determine the **feasible region**, which is the graphical space contained within and on all of the constraint lines.
3. Determine the coordinates of each corner (or **vertex**) of the feasible region.
4. Calculate the value of the objective function at each vertex.
5. Select the optimal solution. The optimal solution for a maximization problem is the one with the highest objective function value and in a minimization problem is the one with the lowest objective function value.

feasible region

vertex

Labeled constraint lines and the corner values are identified in Exhibit 10–19.

The feasible region whose corners are A–B–C is shaded. Only the machine hours constraint is binding; the other two constraint line fall outside the machine hour constraint and, therefore, do not impact the solution. The total contribution margin at each corner is calculated as follows:

Corner	VALUES		
	X_1	X_2	
A	0	0	CM = $25(0) + $9(0) = $0
B	425	0	CM = $25(425) + $9(0) = $10,625
C	0	850	CM = $25(0) + $9(850) = $7,650

Inspection reveals that the contribution margin is at its highest ($10,625) at point B. The corners that are not part of the feasible region are not evaluated because they do not satisfy all of the constraints of the problem.

EXHIBIT 10–18
MODERN OFFICE
SOLUTIONS LP PROBLEM
STATEMENT

Objective Function: MAX CM = $25X_1 + 9X_2$

Constraints (subject to):

$3X_1 + 2X_2 \leq 2,100$	(labor time in hours)
$2X_1 + 1X_2 \leq 850$	(machine time in hours)
$8X_1 + 3X_2 \leq 4,000$	(warehouse storage space)
$X_1 \geq 0$	(non-negativity of file cabinets)
$X_2 \geq 0$	(non-negativity of storage shelves)

EXHIBIT 10–19
MODERN OFFICE
SOLUTIONS PRODUCTION
CONSTRAINTS

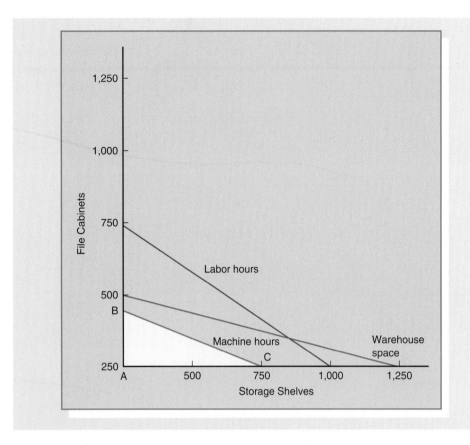

The **simplex method** is a more efficient way to handle complex linear programming problems. It is an iterative (sequential) algorithm that solves multivariable, multiconstraint linear programming problems. An **algorithm** is a logical step-by-step problem-solving technique (generally utilizing a computer) that continuously searches for an improved solution from the one previously computed. The simplex method does not check *every* feasible solution but only those occurring at the corners of the feasible region. Because corners always represent the extremities of the feasible region, a corner is where the maximum or minimum value of the objective function is always located.

The simplex method begins with a mathematical statement of the objective function and constraints. The inequalities in the constraints must be expressed as equalities to solve the problems algebraically. Expressing inequalities as equalities is accomplished by introducing slack or surplus variables (S) into constraint equations. A **slack variable** represents the unused amount of a resource at any level of operation. The amount of the slack variable can range from zero to the total amount of the constrained resource. Slack variables are associated with "less than or equal to" ($\leq$) constraints and are added to the left side of the constraint equation. A **surplus variable** represents overachievement of a minimum requirement and is associated with "greater than or equal to" ($\geq$) constraints. Surplus variables are subtracted from the left side of a constraint equation. The formulas for Modern Office Solutions in Exhibit 10–18 are repeated here with the inclusion of slack variables ($S1$, $S2$, and $S3$) for each constrained resource. There are no surplus variables for Modern Office Solutions because all constraints were "less than or equal to" constraints.

simplex method

algorithm

slack variable

surplus variable

Objective Function: MAX CM $= 25X_1 + 9X_2$

Constraints (subject to):

$$3X_1 + 2X_2 + S_1 = 2,100 \text{ (labor time in hours)}$$
$$2X_1 + 1X_2 + S_2 = 850 \text{ (machine time in hours)}$$
$$8X_1 + 3X_2 + S_3 = 4,000 \text{ (warehouse storage in cubic feet)}$$

Solving a linear programming problem using the simplex method requires either the use of matrix algebra or a computer.

Comprehensive Review Module

Chapter Summary

1. Because of their association with the decision, importance to the decision maker, and bearing on the future, the following items are relevant in decision making:

   - incremental or differential costs that vary between decision choices.

   - opportunity costs, which represent the benefits sacrificed by pursuing one decision choice rather than another; opportunity costs, however, are not included in the accounting records.

2. Sunk costs

   - are costs incurred in the past to acquire assets or resources.

   - are not relevant to making decisions because they cannot be changed regardless of which future course of action is taken.

   - are not recoverable regardless of current circumstances.

3. Relevant considerations in outsourcing (or offshoring) decisions include

   - quantitative factors such as

     ➤ incremental/differential production costs.

     ➤ opportunity costs.

     ➤ external purchase costs.

     ➤ cash flow.

   - qualitative factors such as

     ➤ capacity availability.

     ➤ quality control.

     ➤ technology availability.

     ➤ organizational core competencies.

     ➤ employee skill levels in-house and externally.

     ➤ business risk.

     ➤ supplier availability and reliability.

4. A scarce resource

   - is essential to production activity but is available only in limited quantity.

   - includes machine hours, skilled labor hours, raw materials, and production capacity.

   - requires management to make decisions using the contribution margin per unit of scarce resource; organizational profitability will be maximized by producing and selling that product/service that has the highest contribution margin per unit of scarce resource.

5. Sales mix is important in relevant costing problems because it will be affected by changes in

   - sales prices.

   - sales compensation methods.

   - advertising budgets.

6. Special prices

   - are generally set based on relevant variable production and selling costs and, if any, incremental fixed costs.

   - may or may not include a profit amount.

   - are used when companies bid on special order jobs, such as those that

     ➤ require a bid.

     ➤ are accepted during slack periods.

     ➤ are made to a particular buyer's specifications.

     ➤ are of an unusual nature because of the order quantity, method of delivery, or packaging.

7. Segment margin

   - represents the excess of revenues over direct variable expenses and avoidable fixed expenses of a specific product/service line.

   - measures the segment's contribution to the coverage of indirect and unavoidable expenses.

   - is used to decide whether a product line should be retained or eliminated; a positive segment margin indicates retention and a negative segment margin indicates elimination.

Solution Strategies

General rule of decision making: Choose the alternative that yields the greatest incremental benefit.

Incremental (additional) revenues
− Incremental (additional) costs
Incremental benefit (positive or negative)

RELEVANT COSTS

- Direct material
- Direct labor
- Variable production overhead
- Variable selling expenses related to *each* alternative (can be greater or less than under the "change nothing" alternative)
- Avoidable fixed production overhead
- Avoidable fixed selling/administrative costs (if any)
- Opportunity cost of choosing some other alternative (either increases the cost of one alternative or reduces the cost of another alternative)

RELEVANT COST ANALYSIS IN SPECIFIC DECISIONS

Single Scarce Resource

1. Determine the scarce resource.
2. Determine the production per unit of the scarce resource.
3. Determine the contribution margin per unit of the scarce resource.
4. Multiply production (step 2) by contribution margin (step 3) to obtain total contribution margin provided by the product per unit of the scarce resource. Production and sale of the product with the highest contribution margin per unit of scarce resource maximizes profits.

Product Line Analysis

Sales
− Direct variable expenses
= Product line contribution margin
− Avoidable fixed expenses
= Segment (product line) margin*
− Unavoidable fixed expenses
= Product line operating results

*Make decision to retain or eliminate based on this line item.

Demonstration Problem

Home Cinema produces various equipment for home theatres and home sound systems. One key component in all of its products is a speaker module. Each speaker module requires two specific speakers and is configured from a custom combination of the speaker modules. The firm currently incurs these costs to make each speaker module:

Direct material	$48
Direct labor	32
Variable overhead	20
Fixed overhead	20

Of the per-unit fixed overhead, the firm could avoid $8 if it did not make the modules but purchased them from another company that has offered to sell an equivalent module for $112. Home Cinema produces 20,000 modules annually.

Required: (Consider each requirement to be independent of the others.)

a. Should Home Cinema outsource the production of the module? Show calculations.

b. Home Cinema's vice president, Fred Flick, estimates that the company can rent out the facilities used to make the modules for $120,000 annually. What should the company do? Show calculations.

c. What are some qualitative factors that Home Cinema should consider in making this speaker module outsourcing decision?

Solution to Demonstration Problem

a. Relevant cost of making:

Direct material	$ 48
Direct labor	32
Variable overhead	20
Avoidable fixed overhead	8
Total	$108
Cost to outsource	$112

Therefore, Home Cinema should continue to make the speaker module.

b. $120,000 rental income ÷ 20,000 modules = $6 opportunity cost per module

Relevant cost to insource [part (a)]	$108
Opportunity cost	6
Total	$114

The cost to insource now exceeds the cost to outsource. Therefore, Home Cinema should purchase the item.

c. Some qualitative factors include the following:
- Home Cinema's future control of quality, supply, cost, and price of the speaker module
- Supplier's long-run going concern prospects
- Existence and number of other suppliers
- Impact on customers and markets
- Impact on employees
- Reaction of financial and business press

Key Terms

ad hoc discount *(p. 411)*
algorithm *(p. 419)*
constraint *(p. 415)*
decision variable *(p. 415)*
differential cost *(p. 394)*
feasible region *(p. 418)*
feasible solution *(p. 415)*
incremental cost *(p.394)*
incremental revenue *(p. 394)*
input–output coefficients *(p. 416)*
integer programming *(p. 415)*

linear programming *(p. 415)*
make-or-buy decision *(p. 397)*
mathematical programming
    (p. 415)
non-negativity constraint *(p. 415)*
objective function *(p. 415)*
offshoring *(p. 397)*
opportunity cost *(p. 394)*
optimal solution *(p. 415)*
outsourcing *(p. 397)*
outsourcing decision *(p. 397)*

relevant costing *(p. 393)*
Robinson-Patman Act *(p. 411)*
sales mix *(p. 405)*
scarce resource *(p. 403)*
segment margin *(p. 412)*
simplex method *(p. 419)*
slack variable *(p. 419)*
special order decision *(p. 409)*
sunk cost *(p. 395)*
surplus variable *(p. 419)*
vertex *(p. 418)*

Questions

1. What does the term *relevance* mean in the context of cost analysis for making management decisions?

2. How does the passage of time affect the set of costs that is relevant to a decision?

3. What are opportunity costs and why are they arguably the most difficult set of costs to analyze in making a decision?

4. Describe sunk costs. Are there circumstances in which sunk costs are relevant to decisions? Discuss.

5. What is outsourcing? Why is it heatedly debated?

6. What is a scarce resource? Why is the most scarce resource in an organization likely to change from time to time?

7. What is the objective of managing the sales mix of products? What are the major factors that influence sales mix?

8. What is a special order decision? Under what circumstances would a company refuse to accept a special order?

9. What is segment margin? How is segment margin used in the quantitative analysis of a decision to drop or keep a product line?

10. (*Appendix*) Under what circumstances is linear programming needed to analyze a scarce resource decision?

Exercises

11. (Relevant costs) Assume that you are about to graduate from your university. You are trying to decide whether to apply for graduate school or enter the job market. To help make the decision, you have gathered the following data:

Costs incurred for the bachelor's degree	$103,000
Out-of-pocket costs for the master's degree	$72,000
Estimated starting salary with B.A.	$40,400
Estimated starting salary with M.A.	$48,800
Estimated time to complete master's degree	2 years
Estimated time from the present to retirement	40 years

a. Which of these factors are relevant to your decision?
b. What is the opportunity cost associated with earning the master's degree?

---

c. What is the out-of-pocket cost to obtain the master's degree?

d. What other factors should you consider before making a decision?

12. (Relevant costs) Because of a monumental error committed by its purchasing department, JC's Grocery ordered 50,000 heads of lettuce rather than the 500 that should have been ordered. The company paid $0.60 per head for the lettuce. Although management is confident that it can sell 5,000 units through regular sales, the market is not large enough to absorb the other 45,000 heads. Management has identified two ways to dispose of the excess heads. First, a wholesaler has offered to purchase them for $0.35 each. Second, a restaurant chain has offered to purchase the heads if JC's will agree to convert them into packaged lettuce for salads. This option would require JC's to incur $10,000 for conversion and the heads could then be sold for the equivalent of $0.48 each.

a. Which costs are sunk in this decision?

b. Actually, JC's can consider three alternatives. Describe the alternative that is not mentioned in the problem.

c. What are the relevant costs of each decision alternative, and what should the company do?

13. (Relevant vs. sunk costs) Your roommate, Sara Canfield, purchased a new cordless telephone just before this school term for $70. Shortly after the semester began, Sara's phone was crushed by an errant "flying plant" during a party at her apartment. Returning the equipment to her retailer, Sara was informed that the estimated cost of repairs was $55 because the damage was not covered by the manufacturer's warranty.

Pondering the figures, Sara was ready to decide to make repairs; after all, she had recently paid $70 for the equipment. However, before making a decision, Sara asked for your advice.

a. Using concepts from this chapter, prepare a brief presentation outlining factors that Sara should consider in making her decision.

b. Continue the presentation in part (a) by discussing the options Sara should consider in making her decision. Start by defining a base case against which alternatives can be compared.

14. (Asset replacement) Certain production equipment used by Westside Manufacturing has become obsolete relative to current technology. The company is considering whether it should keep or replace its existing equipment. To aid in this decision, the company's controller gathered the following data:

	Old Equipment	New Equipment
Original cost	$75,000	$99,000
Remaining life	5 years	5 years
Accumulated depreciation	$39,500	$0
Annual cash operating costs	$17,000	$4,000
Current salvage value	$22,000	NA
Salvage value in 5 years	$0	$0

a. Identify any sunk costs in the data.

b. Identify any irrelevant (nondifferential) future costs.

c. Identify all relevant costs to the equipment replacement decision.

d. What are the opportunity costs associated with the alternative of keeping the old equipment?

e. What is the incremental cost to purchase the new equipment?

f. What qualitative considerations should be considered before making any decision?

WebTUTOR Advantage

15. (Asset replacement) On April 1, 2006, Panther Hydraulics purchased new computer-based production scheduling software for $120,000. On May 15,

2006, a representative of a computerized manufacturing technology company demonstrated new software that was clearly superior to that purchased by the firm in April. The price of this software is $270,000. Corporate managers estimate that the new software would save the company $28,000 annually in schedule-related costs compared to the recently installed software. Both software packages should last 10 years (the expected life of the computer hardware) and have no salvage value at that time. The company can sell its existing software for $48,000 if it chooses to purchase the new one. Should the company keep and use the software purchased earlier or buy the new one?

16. (Outsourcing) Highland Technologies manufactures fiberglass housings for portable generators. One part of a housing is a metal latch. Currently, the company produces the 120,000 metal latch units required annually. Company management is considering purchasing the part from an external vendor. The following data are available for making the decision:

Cost per Unit to Manufacture

Direct material	$0.40
Direct labor	0.34
Variable overhead	0.18
Fixed overhead—applied	0.28
Total cost	$1.20

Cost per Unit to Purchase

Purchase price	$0.98
Freight charges	0.02
Total cost	$1.00

a. Assuming that all of Highland Technologies' internal production costs are avoidable if it purchases rather than makes the latch, what would be the net annual cost advantage to purchasing the latches?

b. Assume that some of Highland Technologies' fixed overhead costs could not be avoided if it purchases rather than makes the latches. How much of the fixed overhead must be avoidable for the company to be indifferent as to making or buying the latches?

17. (Outsourcing) Lincoln Steel Co. produces pickup truck bumpers that it sells on a wholesale basis to new car retailers. The average bumper sales price is $120. Normal annual sales volume is 150,000 units, which is maximum production capacity. At this capacity, the company's per-unit costs are as follows:

Direct material	$42 (including mounting hardware @ $12 per unit)
Direct labor	14
Overhead (2/3 is fixed)	36
Total	$92

A key component in producing bumpers is the mounting hardware used to attach the bumpers to the vehicles. Indiana Mechanical has offered to sell Lincoln Steel as many mounting units as the company needs for its bumper production for $16 per unit. If Lincoln Steel accepts the offer, the released facilities currently used to produce mounting hardware could be used to produce an additional 4,800 bumpers. What alternative is more desirable and by what amount? (Assume that the company is currently operating at its capacity of 150,000 units.)

18. (Outsourcing) Pneumatic Shoe Company manufactures various types of shoes for sports and recreational use. Several types require a built-in air pump. Presently, the company makes all air pumps it requires. However, management is evaluating an offer from Cloud Supply Co. to provide air pumps at a cost of $3.60 each. Pneumatic's management has estimated that the variable production costs of the air pump total $2.75 per unit and that the company could avoid $23,000 per year in fixed costs if it purchased rather than produced the air pumps.

a. If Pneumatic requires 25,000 pumps per year, should it make them or buy them from Cloud Supply Co.?

b. If Pneumatic requires 60,000 pumps per year, should it make them or buy them?

c. Assuming that all other factors are equal, at what level of production would the company be indifferent as to making and buying the pumps?

WebTUTOR Advantage

19. (Allocation of scarce resources) Because the employees of one of the company's plants are on strike, the Elkhorn Digital plant is operating at peak capacity. It makes two electronic products, MP3 players and PDAs. Presently, the company can sell as many of each product as can be made, but making a PDA takes twice as long in production labor time as an MP3 player. Elkhorn's production capacity is only 120,000 labor hours per month. Data on each product follow:

	MP3 players	PDAs
Sales	$ 36	$ 64
Variable costs	(30)	(54)
Contribution margin	$ 6	$ 10
Labor hours required	1	2

Fixed costs are $240,000 per month.

a. How many of each product should Elkhorn make? Explain your answer.

b. What qualitative factors would you consider in making this product mix decision?

20. (Allocation of scarce resources) Latoya Jones received her accounting degree in 1976. Since graduating, she has obtained significant experience in a variety of job settings. Her skills include auditing, income and estate taxation, and business consulting. Jones currently has her own practice, and her skills are in such demand that she limits her practice to taxation issues. Most of her engagements are one of three types: individual income taxation, estate taxation, or corporate taxation. Following are data pertaining to the revenues and costs of each tax area (per tax return):

	Individual	Estate	Corporate
Revenue	$350	$1,200	$750
Variable costs	$50	$200	$150
Hours per return of Jones' time	2	8	5

Fixed costs of operating the office are $50,000 per year. Jones has such significant demand for her work that she must ration her time. She desires to work no more than 2,500 hours in the coming year. She can allocate her time so that she works only on one type of tax return or on any combination of the three types.

a. How should Jones allocate her time in the coming year to maximize her income?

b. Based on the optimal allocation, what is Jones' projected pre-tax income for the coming year?

c. What other factors should Jones consider in allocating her time?

d. What could Jones do to overcome the scarce resource constraint?

21. (Special order) Farmer's Wire Co. produces 15-gauge barbed wire that is retailed through farm supply companies. Presently, the company has the capacity to produce 50,000 tons of wire per year. It is operating at 85 percent of annual capacity, and at this level of operations, the cost per ton of wire is as follows:

Direct material	$440
Direct labor	60
Variable overhead	50
Fixed overhead	160
Total	$710

The average sales price for the output produced by the firm is $800 per ton. The state of Texas has approached the firm to supply 200 tons of wire for the state's prisons for $580 per ton FOB Farmer's Wire Co. plant. No production modifications would be necessary to fulfill the order from the state of Texas.

a. What costs are relevant to the decision to accept this special order?

b. What would be the dollar effect on pre-tax income if this order were accepted?

22. (Special order) Classic Wood Products produces solid-oak umbrella stands. Each stand is handmade and hand finished using the finest materials available. The firm has been operating at capacity for the past three years (2,000 stands per year). Based on the capacity level operations, the firm's costs per stand are as follows:

Material	$ 75
Direct labor	55
Variable overhead	15
Fixed overhead	30
Total cost	$175

All selling and administrative expenses incurred by the firm are fixed. The average selling price of stands is $275.

Recently, a large retailer approached Sam Tirade, the president of Classic Wood Products, about supplying three special stands to give as gifts to CEOs of key suppliers. These stands would require approximately twice as much material as the typical one now made. Mr. Tirade estimates that the following per-unit costs would be incurred to make the three stands:

Material	$450
Direct labor	350
Variable overhead	60
Total direct costs	$860

To accept the special order, the firm would have to sacrifice production of 20 regular units.

a. Identify all relevant costs that Tirade should consider in deciding whether to accept the special order.

b. Assume the large retailer offers a total of $3,600 for the three stands. How would accepting this offer affect Classic Wood Products' pre-tax income?

23. (Sales mix) Canine Challet provides two types of services to dog owners, grooming and training. All company personnel can perform each service equally well. To expand sales and market share, Canine Challet's manager, Brenda Bulldog, relies heavily on radio and billboard advertising, but the 2006 advertising budget is expected to be very limited. Information on projected operations for 2006 follows:

	Grooming	Training
Revenue per billable hour	$30	$50
Variable cost of labor	$8	$18
Material cost per billable hour	$4	$6
Allocated fixed cost per year	$200,000	$180,000
Projected billable hours for 2006	20,000	16,000

a. What is Canine Challet's projected pre-tax profit or (loss) for 2006?

b. If $1 spent on advertising could increase grooming revenue by $20 or training revenue by $20, on which service should each advertising dollar be spent?

c. If $1 spent on advertising could increase either grooming billable or training billable time by 1 hour, on which service should each advertising dollar be spent?

24. (Sales mix) One product produced and sold by Ohio Outdoors is an ATV gun rack for which 2006 projections follow:

Projected volume in units	90,000
Sales price per unit	$50
Variable production cost per unit	$9
Variable selling cost per unit	$7
Fixed production cost	$225,000
Fixed selling and administration costs	$75,000

a. Compute the projected pre-tax profit to be earned on the ATV gun rack during 2006.

b. Corporate management estimates that unit volume could be increased by 20 percent if sales price were decreased by 10 percent. How would such a change affect the profit level projected in part (a)?

c. Rather than cutting the sales price, management is considering holding the sales price at the projected level and increasing advertising by $220,000. Such a change would increase volume by 25 percent. How would the level of profit under this alternative compare to the profit projected in part (a)?

25. (Product line) Operations of Tanner Oil Drilling Services are separated into two geographical divisions: United States and Mexico. The operating results of each division for 2006 follow.

	United States	Mexico	Total
Sales	$ 7,200,000	$ 3,600,000	$10,800,000
Variable costs	(4,740,000)	(2,088,000)	(6,828,000)
Contribution margin	$ 2,460,000	$ 1,512,000	$ 3,972,000
Direct fixed costs	(900,000)	(480,000)	(1,380,000)
Segment margin	$ 1,560,000	$ 1,032,000	$ 2,592,000
Corporate fixed costs	(1,800,000)	(900,000)	(2,700,000)
Operating income (loss)	$ (240,000)	$ 132,000	$ (108,000)

Corporate fixed costs are allocated to the divisions based on relative sales. Assume that all of a division's direct fixed costs could be avoided by eliminating that division. Because the U.S. Division is operating at a loss, Tanner's president is considering eliminating it.

a. If the U.S. Division had been eliminated at the beginning of the year, what would have been Tanner's pre-tax income?

b. Recast the income statements into a more meaningful format than the one given. Why would total corporate operating results go from a $108,000 loss to the results determined in part (a)?

26. (Product line) Support Services provides outsourcing services for three areas: payroll, general ledger (GL), and tax compliance. The company is currently contemplating the elimination of the GL area because it is showing a pre-tax loss. An annual income statement follows:

SUPPORT SERVICES
Income Statement by Service Line
For the Year Ended July 31, 2006
(in thousands)

	Payroll	GL	Tax	Total
Sales	$ 2,200	$ 1,600	$ 1,800	$ 5,600
Cost of sales	(1,400)	(1,000)	(1,080)	(3,480)
Gross margin	$ 800	$ 600	$ 720	$ 2,120
Avoidable fixed and variable costs	$ 630	$ 725	$ 520	$ 1,875
Allocated fixed costs	90	80	105	275
Total fixed costs	$ 720	$ 805	$ 625	$ 2,150
Operating profit	$ 80	$ (205)	$ 95	$ (30)

a. Should corporate management drop the GL area? Support your answer with appropriate schedules.

b. How would the decision affect the company's pre-tax profit?

27. (Appendix) The contribution margins for three different products are $9.50, $5.00, and $1.50. State the objective function in equation form to maximize the contribution margin.

28. (Appendix) The variable costs for four different products are $0.65, $0.93, $1.39, and $0.72. State the objective function in equation form to minimize the variable costs.

29. (Appendix) California Fashions makes three items: pants, shorts, and shirts. The contribution margins are $3.25, $2.05, and $2.60 per unit, respectively. The manager must decide what mix of clothes to make. The company has 800 labor hours and 4,000 yards of material available. Additional information for labor and material requirements follows.

	Sewing Time	Fabric Needed
Pants	2.5 hours	2.5 yards
Shorts	1.0 hour	2.0 yards
Shirts	2.5 hours	1.0 yard

Write the objective function and constraints for the clothes manufacturer.

30. (Appendix) Josie Galvez is a college student with a food budget of $120 per month. She wants to get a certain level of nutritional benefits from the food she buys. The following table lists the foods she can buy with the nutritional information per serving.

	Carbohydrates	Protein	Potassium	Calories	Cost
Pizza	38 g.	10 g.	0	500	$3.99
Tuna	1 g.	13 g.	0	60	1.29
Cereal	35 g.	7 g.	120 mg.	190	0.93
Macaroni & cheese	23 g.	3 g.	110 mg.	110	2.12
Spaghetti	42 g.	8 g.	100 mg.	210	3.42
Recommended daily allowance	50 g.	10 g.	100 mg.	2,000	

Write the objective function and constraints to minimize the cost yet meet the recommended daily nutritional allowances.

Problems

31. (Asset replacement) Clarion Tools recently created a new product, a computer-controlled, laser-precise lathe, and Midwest Ornamental Metals is considering purchasing one. Midwest's CFO received the following information from the accounting department regarding the company's existing lathe and the new Clarion lathe. The savings in operating costs offered by the new lathe would mostly derive from reduced waste, reduced labor, and energy cost savings:

Old Machine

Original cost	$575,000
Present book value	$250,000
Annual cash operating costs	$350,000
Market value now	$100,000
Market value in 5 years	$0
Remaining useful life	5 years

New Machine

Cost	$700,000
Annual cash operating costs	$220,000
Market value in 5 years	$0
Useful life	5 years

a. Based on financial considerations alone, should Midwest purchase the new lathe? Show computations to support your answer.

b. What qualitative factors should Midwest consider before making a decision about purchasing the new lathe?

32. (Asset replacement) Northern Plains Energy Company provides electrical services to several rural counties in Nebraska and South Dakota. Its efficiency has been greatly affected by changes in technology. The company is currently considering the replacement of its main steam turbine, which was put in place in the 1970s but is now obsolete. The turbine's operation is very reliable, but it is much less efficient than newer, computer-controlled ones. The controller presented the following financial information to corporate management:

	Old Turbine	New Turbine
Original cost	$3,000,000	$2,000,000
Market value now	$400,000	$2,000,000
Remaining life	8 years	8 years
Quarterly operating costs	$120,000	$45,000
Salvage value in 8 years	$0	$0
Accumulated depreciation	$1,000,000	N/A

a. Identify the costs that are relevant to the company's equipment replacement decision.

b. Determine whether it is more financially sound to keep the old turbine or replace it. Provide your own computations based on relevant costs only.

c. For this part only, assume that the cost of the new technology is unknown. What is the maximum amount that Northern could pay for the new technology and be in the same financial condition as it is currently?

d. What other considerations would come into play if, rather than a new turbine, the company was considering solar-powered technology to replace the old turbine system?

33. (Outsourcing) Handy Grab Inc. manufactures handles for suitcases and other luggage. Attaching each handle to the luggage requires two to six standard fasteners, which the company has historically produced. The costs to produce one fastener (based on capacity operation of 4,000,000 units per year) are:

Direct material	$0.04
Direct labor	0.03
Variable factory overhead	0.02
Fixed factory overhead	0.07
Total	$0.16

The fixed factory overhead includes $200,000 of depreciation on equipment for which there is no alternative use and no market value. The balance of the fixed factory overhead pertains to the salary production supervisor who has a lifetime employment contract and skills that could be used to displace the supervisor of floor maintenance who draws a salary of $50,000 per year but is due to retire from the company.

CarryAll Corp. recently approached Handy Grab with an offer to supply all required fasteners for $0.13 per unit. Anticipated sales demand for the coming year will require 4,000,000 fasteners.

a. Identify the costs that are relevant in this outsourcing decision.

b. What is the total annual advantage or disadvantage (in dollars) of outsourcing the fasteners rather than making them?

c. What qualitative factors should be taken into account in making this decision?

34. (Outsourcing) Modern Building Systems manufactures steel buildings for agricultural and commercial applications. Currently, it is trying to decide between two alternatives regarding a major overhead door assembly for the company's buildings. The alternatives are as follows:

#1: Purchase new equipment with a five-year life and no salvage value at a cost of $5,000,000. Modern Building Systems uses straight-line depreciation and allocates that amount on a per unit of production basis.

#2: Purchase the assemblies from an outside vendor who will sell them for $240 each under a five-year contract.

Following is Modern Building System's present cost to produce one door assembly based on current and normal activity of 50,000 units per year.

Direct material	$139
Direct labor	66
Variable overhead	43
Fixed overhead*	36
Total	$284

*The fixed overhead includes $7 supervision cost, $9 depreciation, and $20 general company overhead.

The new equipment would be more efficient than the old equipment and would reduce direct labor costs and variable overhead costs by 25 percent. Supervisory costs of $350,000 would be unaffected. The new equipment would have a capacity of 75,000 assemblies per year. Modern Building Systems could lease the space occupied by current assembly production to another firm for $114,000 per year if the company decides to buy from the outside vendor.

a. Show an analysis, including relevant unit and total costs, for each alternative of producing or buying the assemblies. Assume 50,000 assemblies are needed each year.

b. How would your answer differ if 60,000 assemblies were needed?

c. How would your answer differ if 75,000 assemblies were needed?

d. In addition to quantitative factors, what qualitative factors should be considered?

35. (Sales mix with scarce resources) EuroCycles makes wholly by hand three unique bicycle models: racing, touring, and basic. All products are made by skilled craftspeople experienced in making all three models. Because it takes about a year to train each craftsperson, labor is a fixed production constraint over the short term. For 2006, the company expects to have available 34,000 labor hours. The average hourly labor rate is $25. Data regarding the current product line follow:

	Racing	Touring	Basic
Selling price	$1,800	$1,360	$480
Variable costs			
Direct material	$440	$320	$120
Direct labor	600	550	150
Variable factory overhead	360	240	82
Variable selling	40	30	20
Fixed costs			
Factory	$300,000		
Selling and administrative	150,000		

The company pays taxes at the rate of 50 percent of operating income.

a. If the company can sell an unlimited amount of any of the products, how many of each product should it make? What pre-tax income will the company earn given your answer?

b. How many of each product must the company make if it has the policy to devote no more than 50 percent of its available skilled labor capacity to any one product but at least 20 percent to every product? What pre-tax income will the company earn given your answer?

c. Given the nature of the three products, is it reasonable to believe that there are market constraints on the mix of products that can be sold? Explain.

d. How does the company's tax rate enter into the calculation of the optimal labor allocation?

36. (Sales mix) Lassiter Leather produces leather belts and key fobs that sell for $40 and $10, respectively. The company currently sells 100,000 units of each type with the following operating results:

Belts

Sales (100,000 × $40)		$ 4,000,000
Variable costs		
Production (100,000 × $22)	$2,200,000	
Selling (100,000 × $6)	600,000	(2,800,000)
Contribution margin		$ 1,200,000
Fixed costs		
Production	$ 400,000	
Selling and administrative	180,000	(580,000)
Income		$ 620,000

Key Fobs

Sales (100,000 × $10)		$1,000,000
Variable costs		
Production (100,000 × $5)	$ 500,000	
Selling (100,000 × $1)	100,000	(600,000)
Contribution margin		$ 400,000
Fixed costs		
Production	$ 100,000	
Selling and administrative	80,000	(180,000)
Income		$ 220,000

Corporate management has expressed its disappointment with the income being generated from the sales of these two products. Managers have asked for your help in analyzing three alternative plans to improve operating results.

1. Change the sales commission to 11 percent of sales price less variable production costs for each product from the current 5 percent of selling price. The marketing manager believes that the sales of the belts will decline by 5,000 units but those of key fobs will increase by 15,000 units.

2. Increase the advertising budget for belts by $25,000. The marketing manager believes this will increase the sales of the belts by 19,000 units but will decrease the sales of the key fobs by 9,000 units.

3. Raise the per-unit price of the belts by $5 and of the key fobs by $3. The marketing manager believes this will cause a decrease in the sales of the belts by 6,000 units and of the key fobs by 10,000 units.

  a. Determine the effects on the income of each product line and the company in total if each alternative plan is put into effect.

  b. What is your recommendation to the management of Lassiter Leather?

37. (Product line) Birnberg Food Service sells quality ice cream and steaks via home delivery. Income statements showing revenues and costs of fiscal year 2006 for each product line follow:

	Ice Cream	Steaks
Sales	$ 8,000,000	$ 3,600,000
Less: Cost of merchandise sold	(4,800,000)	(2,600,000)
Commissions to salespeople	(800,000)	(300,000)
Delivery costs	(1,200,000)	(240,000)
Depreciation on equipment	(400,000)	(200,000)
Salaries of division managers	(160,000)	(150,000)
Allocated corporate costs	(200,000)	(200,000)
Net income (loss)	$ 440,000	$ (90,000)

Management is concerned about profitability of steaks and is considering dropping the line. Management estimates that it could rent the equipment currently used to process steaks to a competitor for $17,000 annually. If the steaks line is dropped, allocated corporate costs would decrease from a total of $400,000 to $370,000, and all employees, including the manager of the product line, would be dismissed. The depreciation would be unaffected by the decision, but $210,000 of the delivery costs charged to the steaks line could be eliminated if it is dropped.

  a. Recast the preceding income statements in a format that provides more information in making this decision regarding the steaks product line.

  b. What is the net advantage or disadvantage (change in total company pre-tax profits) of continuing sales of steaks?

  c. Should the company be concerned about losing sales of ice cream products if it drops the steaks line? Explain.

  d. How would layoffs that would occur as a consequence of dropping the steaks line adversely affect the whole company?

38. (Product line) You have been hired to assist the management of Posture Perfect Chair Company in resolving certain issues. Posture Perfect has its home office in Tennessee and leases facilities in Tennessee, Georgia, and Florida, where it produces a high-quality bean bag chair designed for residential use. Posture Perfect management has provided you a projection of operations for fiscal 2007, the forthcoming year, as follows:

	Total	Tennessee	Georgia	Florida
Sales	$ 8,800,000	$ 4,400,000	$ 2,800,000	$ 1,600,000
Fixed costs				
Factory	$ 2,200,000	$ 1,120,000	$ 560,000	$ 520,000
Administration	700,000	420,000	220,000	60,000
Variable costs	2,900,000	1,330,000	850,000	720,000
Allocated home office costs	1,000,000	450,000	350,000	200,000
Total costs	$(6,800,000)	$(3,320,000)	$(1,980,000)	$(1,500,000)
Pre-tax profit from operations	$ 2,000,000	$ 1,080,000	$ 820,000	$ 100,000

The sales price per unit is $50.

Due to the marginal results of operations in Florida, Posture Perfect has decided to cease its operations there and sell that factory's machinery and equipment by the end of 2007. Managers expect proceeds from the sale of these assets to exceed their book value by enough to cover termination costs.

However, Posture Perfect would like to continue serving its customers in that area if it is economically feasible. It is considering the following three alternatives:

1. Expand the operations of the Georgia factory by using space that is currently idle. This move would result in the following changes in that factory's operations:

	Increase over Factory's Current Operations
Sales	50%
Fixed costs	
Factory	20%
Administration	10%

Under this proposal, variable costs would be $16 per unit sold.

2. Enter into a long-term contract with a competitor who will serve that area's customers and will pay Posture Perfect a royalty of $8 per unit based on an estimate of 30,000 units being sold.

3. Close the Florida factory and not expand the operations of the Georgia factory.

*Total home office costs of $500,000 will remain the same under each situation.

To assist the company's management in determining which alternative is most economically feasible, prepare a schedule computing its estimated pre-tax profit from total operations that would result from each of the following methods:

a. Expansion of the Georgia factory.

b. Negotiation of a long-term contract on a royalty basis.

c. Close the Florida operations with no expansion at other locations.

(AICPA adapted)

39. (Comprehensive) Jersey Glass Products has processing plants in Ohio and New Jersey. Both plants use recycled glass to produce jars that a variety of food processors use in food canning. The jars sell for $10 per hundred units. Budgeted revenues and costs for the year ending December 31, 2006, in thousands of dollars, are:

	Ohio	New Jersey	Total
Sales	$1,100	$2,000	$3,100
Variable production costs			
Direct material	$ 275	$ 500	$ 775
Direct labor	330	500	830
Factory overhead	220	350	570
Fixed factory overhead	350	450	800
Fixed regional promotion costs	50	50	100
Allocated home office costs	55	100	155
Total costs	$1,280	$1,950	$3,230
Operating income (loss)	$ (180)	$ 50	$ (130)

Home office costs are fixed and are allocated to manufacturing plants on the basis of relative sales levels. Fixed regional promotional costs are discretionary advertising costs needed to obtain budgeted sales levels.

Because of the budgeted operating loss, Jersey Glass is considering ceasing operations at its Ohio plant. If it does so, proceeds from the sale of plant assets will exceed asset book values and exactly cover all termination costs; fixed factory overhead costs of $25,000 would not be eliminated. Jersey Glass is considering the following three alternative plans:

PLAN A: Expand Ohio's operations from its budgeted 11,000,000 units to a budgeted 17,000,000 units. It is believed that this can be accomplished by increasing Ohio's fixed regional promotional expenditures by $120,000.

PLAN B: Close the Ohio plant and expand the New Jersey operations from the current budgeted 20,000,000 units to 31,000,000 units to fill Ohio's budgeted production of 11,000,000 units. The Ohio region would continue to incur promotional costs to sell the 11,000,000 units. All sales and costs would be budgeted by the New Jersey plant.

PLAN C: Close the Ohio plant and enter into a long-term contract with a competitor to serve the Ohio region's customers. This competitor would pay a royalty of $1.25 per 100 units sold to Jersey Glass, which would continue to incur fixed regional promotional costs to maintain sales of 11,000,000 units in the Ohio region.

a. Without considering the effects of implementing Plans A, B, and C, compute the number of units that the Ohio plant must produce and sell to cover its fixed factory overhead costs and fixed regional promotional costs.

b. Prepare a schedule by plant and in total of Jersey Glass's budgeted contribution margin and operating income resulting from the implementation of each of the following:

   1. Plan A.
   2. Plan B.
   3. Plan C.

(AICPA adapted)

40. (Sales and profit improvement) Pink Passion is a retail organization that sells upscale clothing to girls and young women in the Northeast. Each year, store managers in consultation with their supervisors establish financial goals, and then a monthly reporting system captures actual performance.

One of the firm's sales districts, District A, has three stores but has historically been a very poor performer. Consequently, the district supervisor has been searching for ways to improve the performance of her three stores. For May, she set performance goals with the managers of Stores 1 and 2. They will receive bonuses if the stores exceed certain performance measures. The manager of Store 3 decided not to participate in the bonus scheme. Because the district supervisor is unsure what type of bonus will encourage better performance, she offered the manager of Store 1 a bonus based on sales in excess of budgeted sales of $570,000; she offered the manager of Store 2 a bonus based on net income in excess of budgeted net income. The company's net income goal for each store is 12 percent of sales. The budgeted sales for Store 2 are $530,000.

Other pertinent data for May follow:

- At Store 1, sales were 40 percent of total District A sales; sales at Store 2 were 35 percent of total District A sales. The cost of goods sold at both stores was 42 percent of sales.
- Variable selling expenses (sales commissions) were 6 percent of sales for all stores and districts.
- Variable administrative expenses were 2.5 percent of sales for all stores and districts.
- Maintenance cost including janitorial and repair services is a direct cost for each store. The store manager has complete control over this outlay; however, it should not be below 1 percent of sales.
- Advertising is considered a direct cost for each store and is completely under the store manager's control. Store 1 spent two-thirds of District A's total outlay for advertising, which was 10 times more than Store 2 spent on advertising.
- The rental expense at Store 1 is 40 percent of District A's total and at Store 2 is 30 percent of District A's total.

- District A expenses are allocated to the stores based on sales.
  a. Which store, Store 1 or Store 2, appears to generate more profit under the new bonus scheme?
  b. Which store, Store 1 or Store 2, appears to generate more revenue under the new bonus scheme?
  c. Why would Store 1 have an incentive to spend so much more on advertising than Store 2?
  d. Which store manager has the most incentive to spend money on regular maintenance? Explain.
  e. Which bonus scheme appears to offer the most incentive to improve the profit performance of the district in the short term? Long term?

(CMA adapted)

41. (Special order) Clean-N-Brite is a multiproduct company with several manufacturing plants. The Cincinnati plant manufactures and distributes two household cleaning and polishing compounds, regular and heavy duty, under the HouseSafe label. The forecasted operating results for the first six months of 2006, when 100,000 cases of each compound are expected to be manufactured and sold, are presented in the following statement:

HOUSESAFE COMPOUNDS—CINCINNATI PLANT
Forecasted Results of Operations
For the Six-Month Period Ending June 30, 2006

	Regular	Heavy-Duty	Total
		(IN $000)	
Sales	$ 2,000	$ 3,000	$ 5,000
Cost of sales	(1,600)	(1,900)	(3,500)
Gross profit	$ 400	$ 1,100	$ 1,500
Selling and administrative expenses			
Variable	$ 400	$ 700	$ 1,100
Fixed*	240	360	600
Total selling and administrative expenses	$ (640)	$(1,060)	$(1,700)
Income (loss) before taxes	$ (240)	$ 40	$ (200)

*The fixed selling and administrative expenses are allocated between the two products on the basis of dollar sales volume on the internal reports.

The sales price per case for the regular compound is $20 and for the heavy duty is $30 during the first six months of 2006. The manufacturing costs by case of product follow.

	COST PER CASE	
	Regular	Heavy-Duty
Raw material	$ 7.00	$ 8.00
Direct labor	4.00	4.00
Variable manufacturing overhead	1.00	2.00
Fixed manufacturing overhead*	4.00	5.00
Total manufacturing cost	$16.00	$19.00
Variable selling and administrative costs	$ 4.00	$ 7.00

*Depreciation charges are 50 percent of the fixed manufacturing overhead of each line.

Each product is manufactured on a separate production line. Annual normal manufacturing capacity is 200,000 cases of each product. However, the plant is capable of producing 250,000 cases of regular compound and 350,000 cases of heavy-duty compound annually.

The following schedule reflects top management consensus regarding the price/volume alternatives for the HouseSafe products for the last six months of 2006, which are essentially the same as those during its first six months.

REGULAR COMPOUND		HEAVY-DUTY COMPOUND	
Alternative Prices (per case)	Sales Volume (in cases)	Alternative Prices (per case)	Sales Volume (in cases)
$18	120,000	$25	175,000
20	100,000	27	140,000
21	90,000	30	100,000
22	80,000	32	55,000
23	50,000	35	35,000

Top management believes the loss for the first six months reflects a tight profit margin caused by intense competition and that many competitors will be forced out of this market by next year, so the company's profits should improve.

a. What unit selling price should Clean-N-Brite select for each HouseSafe compound for the remaining six months of 2006? Support your answer with appropriate calculations.

b. Without prejudice to your answer for requirement (a), assume that the optimum price/volume alternatives for the last six months were a selling price of $23 and volume level of 50,000 cases for the regular compound and a selling price of $35 and volume of 35,000 cases for the heavy-duty compound.

   1. Should Clean-N-Brite consider closing its operations until 2007 to minimize its losses? Support your answer with appropriate calculations.

   2. Identify and discuss the qualitative factors that should be considered in deciding whether the Cincinnati plant should be closed during the last six months of 2006.

(CMA adapted)

42. (Special order) Hydraulic Engineering, located in Toronto, manufactures a variety of industrial valves and pipe fittings sold to customers in the United States. Currently, the company is operating at 70 percent of capacity and is earning a satisfactory return on investment.

Prince Industries Ltd. of Scotland has approached Hydraulic's management with an offer to buy 120,000 units of a pressure valve. Prince manufactures an almost identical valve pressure valve, but a fire in Prince's valve plant has closed its manufacturing operations. Prince needs the 120,000 valves over the next four months to meet commitments to its regular customers; the company is prepared to pay $19 each for the valves, FOB shipping point.

Hydraulic Engineering's product cost for the pressure valve based on current attainable standards is

Direct material	$ 5
Direct labor	6
Manufacturing overhead	9
Total cost	$20

Manufacturing overhead is applied to production at the rate of $18 per standard direct labor hour. This overhead rate is made up of the following components:

Variable factory overhead	$ 6
Fixed factory overhead—direct	8
Fixed factory overhead—allocated	4
Applied manufacturing overhead rate	$18

Additional costs incurred in connection with sales of the pressure valve include 5 percent sales commissions and $1 freight expense per unit. However, the company does not pay sales commissions on special orders that come directly to management.

In determining selling prices, Hydraulic adds a 40 percent markup to product cost, which provides a $28 suggested selling price for the pressure valve. The marketing department, however, has set the current selling price at $27 to maintain market share.

Production management believes that it can handle the Prince Industries order without disrupting its scheduled production. The order would, however, require additional fixed factory overhead of $12,000 per month in the form of supervision and clerical costs.

If management accepts the order, Hydraulic will manufacture 30,000 pressure valves and ship them to Prince Industries each month for the next four months. Shipments will be made in weekly consignments, FOB shipping point.

   a. Determine how many additional direct labor hours would be required each month to fill the Prince Industries order.

   b. Prepare an incremental analysis showing the impact of accepting the Prince Industries order.

   c. Calculate the minimum unit price that Hydraulic Engineering's management could accept for the Prince Industries order without reducing net income.

   d. Identify the factors, other than price, that Hydraulic Engineering should consider before accepting the Prince Industries order.

(CMA adapted)

43. (Ethics essay) Karlson Computers manufactures computers and all components. Its purchasing agent informed the company owner, Alberta Karlson, that another company had offered to supply keyboards for Karlson's computers at prices below the variable costs at which Karlson can make them. Incredulous, Ms. Karlson hired an industrial consultant to explain how the supplier could offer the keyboards at less than Karlson's variable costs. It seems that the consultant suspects the competitor supplier of using many illegal aliens to work in its plant. These people are poverty stricken and will take work at substandard wages. The purchasing agent and the plant manager decide that Karlson should buy the competitor's keyboards because "no one can blame us for his hiring practices and will not even be able to show that we knew of those practices."

   a. What are the ethical issues involved in this case?

   b. What are the advantages and disadvantages of buying from this competitor supplier?

   c. What do you think Ms. Karlson should do and why?

11

Allocation of Joint Costs and Accounting for By-Products

Objectives

AFTER COMPLETING THIS CHAPTER, YOU SHOULD BE ABLE TO ANSWER THE FOLLOWING QUESTIONS:

LO.1 HOW ARE THE OUTPUTS OF A JOINT PROCESS CLASSIFIED?

LO.2 AT WHAT POINT IN A PROCESS ARE JOINT PRODUCTS IDENTIFIABLE?

LO.3 WHAT MANAGEMENT DECISIONS MUST BE MADE BEFORE BEGINNING A JOINT PROCESS?

LO.4 HOW IS THE JOINT COST OF PRODUCTION ALLOCATED TO JOINT PRODUCTS?

LO.5 HOW ARE BY-PRODUCTS AND SCRAP ACCOUNTED FOR?

LO.6 HOW SHOULD NOT-FOR-PROFIT ORGANIZATIONS ACCOUNT FOR JOINT COSTS?

Perdue Farms Incorporated is a U.S.–based company that produces poultry and poultry-related products. Arthur W. Perdue founded the company in the 1920s as a small table-egg business and it is still privately owned and controlled by the Perdue family. Perdue now generates more than $2.7 billion in annual sales and employs 20,000 associates across five continents. *Forbes* magazine lists Perdue as one of the 100 largest family-owned businesses.

The company's chickens feed on high-quality corn and soy, which helps them have more breast meat and a higher meat-to-bone ratio than competitors' chickens have. In 1974, the company first developed the roaster and, due to continuous improvements in quality goals, now confidently advertises that product as being far superior to roasters offered by competitors.

Perdue is vertically integrated, operating its own grain division and feed mills to ensure the quality of the food for its poultry as well as hatcheries and selective breeding operations to ensure the quality of its poultry. Research labs conduct diagnostics to ensure the company's poultry flocks are disease free. After the flock has been quality approved, it is transported by company-owned Perdue Transportation trucks to the nearest processing plant. In the United States, Perdue has processing plants in Alabama, Connecticut, Delaware, Florida, Indiana, Kentucky, Maryland, New Jersey, North Carolina, Tennessee, Virginia, and West Virginia.

Processing begins by plucking the feathers from the birds' carcasses. Then the legs, feet, and internal organs are removed. A goal of processing is to perform all operations without damage to the carcass at least 95 to 100 percent of the time. Then the chickens are washed inside and outside.

At this time, the chickens are separated into the following categories: delicatessen, whole, parts, or ground. After classification is complete, some chickens are sold as is; others are processed further. For example, chickens in the "delicatessen" category are fully cooked and frozen and then sold to delicatessens and food service channels. Some of the chicken meat is made into chicken nuggets or breaded chicken cutlets. After the chickens have been fully processed, Perdue Transportation trucks deliver the poultry and poultry products to wholesale and middle-market customers.

In addition to processing poultry for human consumption, Perdue also recycles poultry litter into organic fertilizer. *Poultry litter* is defined as the ground materials, including waste matter, that is found in hatcheries and breeding operations. For sanitary reasons and odor control, the litter is gathered and transported by company trucks to plants where it is heated and pasteurized to destroy bacteria. The litter is then reduced to a powder and made into pellets. This recycling process protects the soil around company hatcheries and breeding operations from becoming overly saturated with the nutrients (including ammonia) contained in the litter while generating pellets that can be used to enhance "nutrient-deficient" regions.

Since its beginnings, Perdue's objectives have always included customer satisfaction, cost control, and profitability. The high level of quality of its poultry and poultry products and the diversity of its product lines illustrate the company's focus on customer satisfaction. Company efforts to recycle poultry litter provide a way to reduce waste management costs and increase revenues. As with many food processors, Perdue Farms has recognized that, within product safety parameters, the "old-time" and environmentally acceptable philosophy of total product utilization is both cost and revenue beneficial.

Source: *http://www.perdue.com* and *http://www.koami.or.kr/bbs/jck99/sp_3_033.pdf.*

Almost every company produces and sells more than one type of product. Some companies engage in multiple production processes to manufacture a variety of products. Other companies, such as Perdue Farms, have a single process that simultaneously generates different outputs such as whole chicken, chicken parts, ground chicken, and fertilizer from a single input. Similarly, refining crude oil can produce gasoline, motor oil, heating oil, and kerosene, and mining gold can produce copper, silver, and ore.

joint process

A single process in which one product cannot be manufactured without producing others is known as a **joint process**. Such processes are common in the extractive, agricultural, food, and chemical industries. Additionally, the process of producing first-quality merchandise and factory seconds in a single operation can be viewed as a joint process. This situation is valid if the manufacturing process is unstable and is "unable to maintain output at a uniform quality level, and the products that emerge from the [process] vary across one or more quality dimensions."[1] Given this definition, joint processes are pervasive within the manufacturing sector.

This chapter discusses joint manufacturing processes, their related product outputs, and the accounting treatment of the costs of those processes. Costs incurred for material, labor, and overhead during a joint process are referred to as the **joint cost** of the production process. Joint cost is allocated only to the primary products of a joint process using either a physical or monetary measure. Although joint cost allocations are necessary to determine financial statement valuations, such allocations should not be used in making internal decisions.[2] Although, for financial reporting purposes allocation of joint costs to joint products is necessary, these costs must be interpreted carefully for purposes of making internal decisions. For example, in evaluating the profitability of a specific joint product, the decision maker must keep in mind that the profitability of the product will be determined largely by the choice of method used to allocate the joint costs and there will always be an extent to which the allocation of joint costs is arbitrary. Following incurrence of the joint cost, additional **separate costs** can be incurred in later stages of production that are assignable to specific primary products.

In addition, advertising can be a joint cost in retail or service businesses and not-for-profit (NFP) organizations. In retail or service businesses, for example, an ad can publicize different product lines or different locations. A NFP could produce a brochure that serves the concurrent purposes of providing public service information and requesting donations. Joint costs for nonmanufacturing operations are covered in the last section of the chapter.

joint cost

separate cost

OUTPUTS OF A JOINT PROCESS

LO.1
HOW ARE THE OUTPUTS OF A JOINT PROCESS CLASSIFIED?

joint product

A joint process simultaneously produces more than one product line. A product that has a sales value resulting from a joint process is classified as (1) a joint product, (2) a by-product, or (3) scrap. **Joint products** are the *primary* outputs of a joint process; each joint product has substantial revenue-generating ability. Joint products are the primary reason for entering into the production process. These products are also called *primary products, main products,* or *coproducts.*

How are the categories of joint process outputs determined?

Joint products are not necessarily totally different products. The definition of joint products has been extended to include similar products of differing quality that result from the same process. For example, even the whole chickens resulting from the Perdue Farms process could be of different grades: Some will be sold as roasters, some will be deemed "delicatessen" variety and sold frozen, and some will be sold fresh to supermarkets.

by-product

scrap

In contrast, **by-products** and **scrap** are incidental outputs of a joint process. Both are salable, but their sales values alone would not be sufficient for management to justify undertaking the joint process. For example, Perdue Farms would never undertake chicken processing simply to generate the by-products that it further processes into fertilizer or that it sells to pet food manufacturers. **Krispy Kreme** would never undertake doughnut manufacturing to generate the doughnut holes that it sells to customers. **Sunpine Forest Products** would never undertake lumber production to generate the sawdust that it sells as livestock bedding. By-products are distinguished from scrap by their higher sales value.

waste

A final output from a joint process is **waste**, which is a residual output that has no sales value. A normal amount of waste can create a production cost that

---

[1] James F. Gatti and D. Jacque Grinnell, "Joint Cost Allocations: Measuring and Promoting Productivity and Quality Improvements," *Journal of Cost Management* (July–August 2000), pp. 13–21.

[2] Sometimes correctly pricing a product depends on knowledge of the full cost of making the product, particularly when contractual agreements require cost-plus pricing. Joint cost allocation is also necessary to the costing of products for financial reporting.

Companies can try to minimize waste by reclassifying it as scrap or by-products, such as turning chicken litter and bones into usable organic fertilizer.

GETTY IMAGES

cannot be avoided in some industries. Alternatively, many companies have learned either to minimize their production waste by changing their processing techniques or to reclassify waste as a by-product or scrap by finding uses for the materials that generate some minimal amount of revenue.

Over time, a company can change a product classification because of changes in technology, consumer demand, or ecological factors. Some products originally classified as by-products can be reclassified as joint products, and some joint products can be reduced to the by-product category. Even products originally viewed as scrap or waste can be upgraded to joint product status. Years ago, for example, chicken litter, bones, beaks, and feet were considered waste and discarded. These items are now recycled and processed further to produce organic fertilizer. Therefore, depending on the company, these items can be classified as by-products or scrap.

Classification of joint process output is based on management judgment, normally after considering the relative sales values of the outputs. Classifications are unique to each company. For example, poultry company A could classify whole chickens and breast meat as the only joint products and all other chicken parts as by-products, but poultry company B could classify whole chickens, thighs, legs, and wings as joint products and all other chicken parts as by-products. These classifications can result from the fact that company A's processing facilities are large enough only to clean the chickens and remove the breast meat; any additional processing would require a capital investment that would not be cost–beneficial. Poultry company B could have significantly larger facilities that allow further processing at costs substantially less than the sales value of the multiple products.

THE JOINT PROCESS

LO.2
AT WHAT POINT IN A PROCESS ARE JOINT PRODUCTS IDENTIFIABLE?

Joint products are typically manufactured in companies using mass production processes and a process costing accounting method.[3] The outputs of a chicken processing plant, for example, can include whole chickens and edible chicken pieces (joint products), damaged chicken for grinding (by-product), chicken feet and litter (scrap) for fertilizer, and chicken entrails (waste) that are discarded. See Exhibit 11–1 for the output of such a joint process.

split-off point

The point at which joint process outputs are first identifiable as individual products is called the **split-off point**. A joint process can have one or more split-off points, depending on the number and types of output produced. Output can be sold at the split-off point if a market exists for products at that degree of completion. Alternatively, some or all of the products can be processed further after exiting the joint process.

Joint cost includes all direct material, direct labor, and overhead costs incurred up to the split-off point. For financial reporting purpose, the cost principle requires that all necessary and reasonable costs of production should be attached to prod-

---

[3] For simplicity, Chapter 6 on process costing included examples in which calculating equivalent units was relatively straightforward.

EXHIBIT 11–1

ILLUSTRATION OF JOINT PROCESS OUTPUT

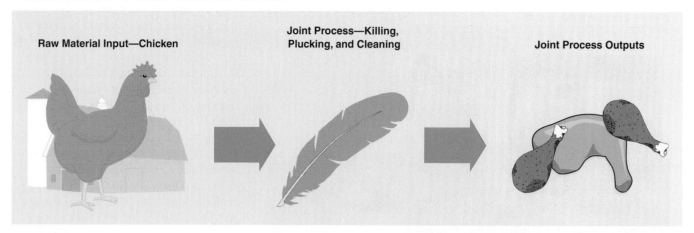

Raw Material Input—Chicken	Joint Process—Killing, Plucking, and Cleaning	Joint Process Outputs

Why is joint process cost assigned only to joint products?

ucts. Thus, at split-off, the joint cost must be allocated to products. The joint cost is allocated solely to the joint products because their creation was the reason that management undertook the joint production process; allocation of joint cost to the "extra" by-products, scrap, or waste would be both improper and not cost beneficial. Although the joint cost allocation is necessary for financial statement valuation purposes, that allocation is not relevant to internal decision making. After reaching the split-off, the joint cost has already been incurred and is a sunk cost that cannot be changed regardless of what future course of action is taken.

If any of the joint process outputs are processed further, additional costs after split-off will be incurred. Any costs incurred after split-off are assigned to the separate products for which those costs were incurred. See Exhibit 11–2 for a depiction of a joint process with multiple split-off points and the allocation of costs to products. For simplicity, all output of this joint process is considered primary output; there are no by-products, scrap, or waste. Note that two of the joint product outputs of joint process 1 (products B and C) become direct material for joint process 2. For accounting purposes, the joint cost allocations will follow products B and C into joint process 2, but these allocated costs should not be used in making decisions about further processing in that department or in department 4. Such decisions should be made *only after* considering whether the expected additional revenues from further processing are higher than the expected additional costs of further processing.

THE JOINT PROCESS DECISION

LO.3
WHAT MANAGEMENT DECISIONS MUST BE MADE BEFORE BEGINNING A JOINT PROCESS?

Before committing resources to a joint production process, management must first decide whether the total expected revenues from the sale of the joint process output are likely to exceed the total expected processing costs. Both joint cost, additional separate processing costs after split-off, and selling or disposal costs should be included in this estimate. Because the joint process results in a "basket" of products, some additional processing costs might need to be incurred to make products salable, or some disposal costs might be necessary for waste materials. After joint process costs have been incurred, they become sunk costs regardless of whether the output is salable at the end of the joint process or at what amount.

If total anticipated revenues from the basket of products exceed the anticipated joint and separate costs, managers must compare the income from this use of re-

EXHIBIT 11-2
MODEL OF A JOINT PROCESS

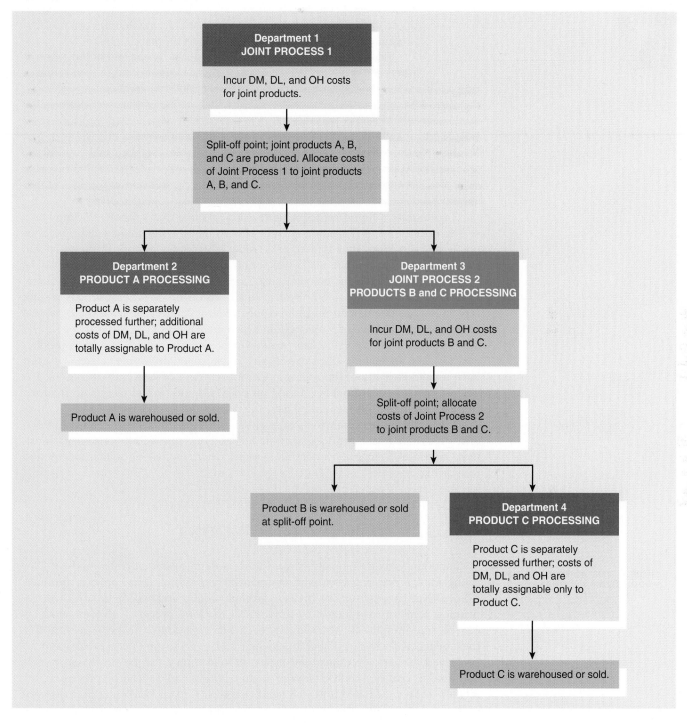

sources to that provided by the best alternative use of company resources. If joint process income exceeds that from other uses, management would decide that this joint production process is the best use of capacity and would begin production; thus, managers next decide whether to engage in the joint production process or to apply organizational resources elsewhere.

The next two decisions are made at split-off. The third decision is to determine how to classify outputs of the joint process. Some output will be primary;

Why is the split-off point in a joint process important?

other will be by-product, scrap, or waste. This classification decision is necessary for the joint cost to be allocated because *joint cost is assigned only to joint products.* However, before allocation, joint cost can be reduced by the value of the by-products and scrap. Determination of by-product and scrap value is discussed later in the chapter.

The fourth decision is the most complex. Management must decide whether to sell any (or all) of the joint process output at split-off or to process it further. If primary products are marketable at split-off, further processing should be undertaken only if the value added to the product, as reflected by the incremental revenue, exceeds the incremental cost. If a primary product is not marketable at split-off, additional costs *must* be incurred to make that product marketable. For nonprimary output, management must also estimate whether the incremental revenue from additional processing will exceed additional processing cost. If additional processing provides no net benefit, the nonmarketable output should be disposed of without further processing after the split-off point.

To illustrate a further processing decision, assume that a whole chicken has a selling price of $0.48 per pound at split-off and that the minimum selling price for edible chicken parts after further processing is $0.53 per pound. If the additional processing cost is less than $0.05 per pound, the $0.05 incremental revenue ($0.53 − $0.48) exceeds the incremental cost, and additional processing should occur. Note that the joint cost is not used in this decision process because it is a sunk cost after it has been incurred, and the only relevant items in the decision to process further are the incremental revenue and incremental cost.[4]

See Exhibit 11–3 for the four management decision points in a joint production process. In making decisions at any potential point of sale, managers must have a valid estimate of the selling price of each type of joint process output. Expected selling prices should be based on both cost and market factors. In the long run and assuming that demand exists, the selling prices and volumes of products must be sufficient to cover their total costs. However, immediate economic influences on setting selling prices, such as competitors' prices and consumers' sensitivity to price changes, cannot be ignored when estimating selling prices and forecasting revenues.

ALLOCATION OF JOINT COST

LO.4
HOW IS THE JOINT COST OF PRODUCTION ALLOCATED TO JOINT PRODUCTS?

Scrumptious Turkey Company is used to demonstrate alternative methods of allocating joint processing cost. The company manufactures three primary products from a joint process: turkey breasts, ground turkey, and whole turkeys. (All remaining parts are considered by-products of the joint process.) All joint products can be sold at split-off. Alternatively, each turkey product can be processed further, which will create additional separate costs for the products. Breasts can be processed further to produce deli meats; ground turkey can be processed further and used as part of a turkey sausage mixture; whole turkeys can be processed further to make precooked and marinated roasters. Certain marketing and disposal costs for advertising, commissions, and transportation are incurred regardless of when the products are sold. Refer to Exhibit 11–4 for assumed information on Scrumptious Turkey's processing operations and joint products for October 2006. The company started 10,000 tons of turkey during that month; approximately 10 percent of the tonnage started will become a by-product used in fertilizer pellets. Thus, an input of 10,000 tons results in 9,000 tons of joint product output and 1,000 tons of by-product.

---

[4] See Chapter 10 for a detailed discussion of incremental or relevant costs.

EXHIBIT 11–3

DECISION POINTS IN A JOINT PRODUCTION PROCESS

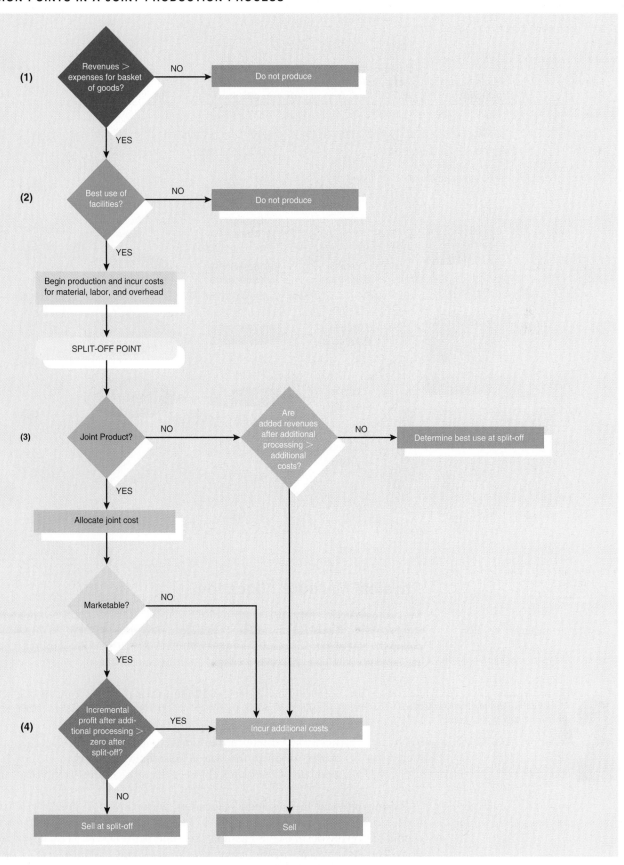

EXHIBIT 11–4
JOINT COST INFORMATION FOR SCRUMPTIOUS TURKEY

Joint processing cost for period: $5,400,000

(1) Joint Product	(2) Tons Produced	(3) Sales Price per Ton at Split-Off	(4) Selling Cost per Ton Regardless of When Sold	(5) Separate Cost per Ton if Processed Further	(6) Final Sales Price per Ton
Breast	3,800	$2,800	$200	$100	$3,200
Ground	2,400	1,800	100	100	2,100
Whole	2,800	1,200	50	60	1,500

Diagram of problem assuming products are sold at split-off.

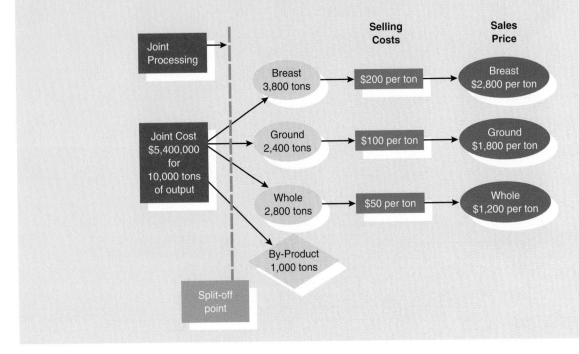

Physical Measure Allocation

physical measurement allocation

An easy, objective way to prorate joint cost at the split-off point is to use a physical measure. **Physical measurement allocation** uses a common physical characteristic of the joint products as the proration base. All joint products must be measurable by the same characteristic, such as one of these:

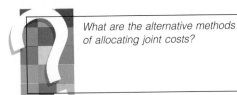

What are the alternative methods of allocating joint costs?

- tons of meat, bone, and hide in the meat packing or chicken processing industry
- tons of ore in the mining industry
- linear board feet in the lumber milling industry
- barrels of oil in the petroleum refining industry
- number of computer chips in the semiconductor industry

Using physical measurement allocation, Scrumptious Turkey's $5,400,000 of joint cost is assigned as in Exhibit 11–5. This allocation process treats each unit of output as equally desirable and assigns the same per-unit cost to each. For Scrumptious Turkey, physical measurement allocation would assign a cost of approximately $600 ($5,400,000 ÷ 9,000 tons) per ton of turkey, regardless of type.

EXHIBIT 11–5

SCRUMPTIOUS TURKEY'S JOINT COST ALLOCATION BASED ON PHYSICAL MEASUREMENT

Cost per Physical Measure = Total Joint Cost ÷ Total Units of Physical Measurement

= $5,400,000 ÷ 9,000 tons = $600 per ton

Joint Product	Tons Produced	Cost per Ton	Total Allocated Cost	Gross Profit per Ton at Split-Off		
				Revenue	Cost	Profit
Breast	3,800	$600	$2,280,000	$2,800	$600	$2,200
Ground	2,400	600	1,440,000	1,800	600	1,200
Whole	2,800	600	1,680,000	1,200	600	600
Total	9,000		$5,400,000			

The entries to recognize the joint processing cost, allocate it to the joint products, and recognize separate processing cost (assuming that all joint products are processed further) follow.

Work in Process Inventory—Turkey Processing	5,400,000	
Various accounts		5,400,000
To record joint processing cost.		
Work in Process Inventory—Breast	2,280,000	
Work in Process Inventory—Ground	1,440,000	
Work in Process Inventory—Whole	1,680,000	
Work in Process Inventory—Turkey Processing		5,400,000
To allocate joint processing cost.		
Work in Process Inventory—Breast (3,800 tons × $100)	380,000	
Work in Process Inventory—Ground (2,400 tons × $100)	240,000	
Work in Process Inventory—Whole (2,800 tons × $60)	168,000	
Various accounts		788,000
To record separate processing costs.		

The selling costs per ton would be recorded at the point of sale of the products.

Unlike monetary measures, physical measures provide an unchanging yardstick of output.[5] Assuming that "ton" has the same definition, a ton of output produced from a process 10 years ago is the same measurement as a ton produced from that process today. Physical measures are useful in allocating joint cost to products that have extremely unstable selling prices. These measures are also necessary in rate-regulated industries that use cost to determine selling prices. For example, assume that a rate-regulated company has the right to set selling price at 20 percent above cost. It is circular logic to allocate joint cost using selling prices that were set based on cost to produce the output.

Allocating joint cost based on a physical measure, however, ignores the revenue-generating ability of individual joint products. Products that weigh the most or that are produced in the largest quantity will receive the highest proportion of joint cost allocation—regardless of their ability to bear that cost when they are sold. In the case of Scrumptious Turkey, each ton of whole turkey has been assigned a cost of $600. Computations in Exhibit 11–5 show that this product generates the lowest gross profit per ton of the three joint products yet is being assigned the same joint cost per ton as the breast meat and ground turkey.

Monetary Measure Allocation

All commonly used allocation methods employ a process of proration. Because this physical measure allocation process is so simple, a detailed proration scheme

---

[5] There are occasional exceptions to the belief that physical measures provide an unchanging yardstick of output. To illustrate, many grocery products have been downsized in recent years. For example, if a coffee producer used "bags of coffee" as a physical measure, production of several years ago could not be equated with current production because coffee was formerly sold in 1-pound containers and now is customarily sold in 13-ounce packages.

is unnecessary. However, the following steps can be used to prorate joint cost to joint products in more complex monetary measure allocations.

1. Choose a monetary allocation base.
2. List the values that compose the base for each joint product.
3. Sum the values in step 2 to obtain a total value for the list.
4. Divide each individual value in step 2 by the total in step 3 to obtain a numerical proportion for each value. The sum of these proportions should total 1.00, or 100 percent.[6]
5. Multiply the joint cost by each proportion to obtain the amount to be allocated to each product.
6. Divide the prorated joint cost for each product by the number of equivalent units of production (EUP) for each product to obtain a cost per EUP for valuation purposes.

The primary benefit of monetary over physical measure allocations is that the former recognizes the relative ability of each product to generate a profit at sale.[7] A problem with monetary measure allocations is that the basis used is dynamic. Because of fluctuations in general and specific price levels, a dollar's worth of output today is different from a dollar's worth of output from the same process five years ago. However, accountants customarily ignore price level fluctuations when recording or processing data, so this particular flaw of monetary measures is not usually considered significant.

Three of the many monetary measures that can be used to allocate joint cost to primary output are presented in this text. These measures are sales *value at split-off, net realizable value at split-off,* and *approximated net realizable value at split-off.*

SALES VALUE AT SPLIT-OFF

sales value at split-off allocation

The **sales value at split-off allocation** method assigns joint cost to joint products based on the relative sales values of the products at the split-off point. To use this method, all joint products must be marketable at split-off. Scrumptious Turkey assigns joint cost to production using the allocation method in Exhibit 11–6. The low selling price per ton of whole turkeys relative to the other joint products results in a lower allocated cost per ton than resulted from the physical measure alloca-

EXHIBIT 11–6
SCRUMPTIOUS TURKEY'S JOINT COST ALLOCATION BASED ON SALES VALUE AT SPLIT-OFF

Joint Product	Tons Produced	Selling Price	Total Revenue	Proportion	Joint Cost	Amount Allocated	Cost per Ton
Breast	3,800	$2,800	$10,640,000	0.58[a]	$5,400,000	$3,132,000	$824.21
Ground	2,400	1,800	4,320,000	0.24[b]	5,400,000	1,296,000	540.00
Whole	2,800	1,200	3,360,000	0.18[c]	5,400,000	972,000	347.14
Total	9,000		$18,320,000	1.00		$5,400,000	

Proportions = Total Revenue of Respective Joint Product ÷ Total Revenue

[a]$10,640,000 ÷ $18,320,000 = 0.58 (rounded)
[b]$4,320,000 ÷ $18,320,000 = 0.24 (rounded)
[c]$3,360,000 ÷ $18,320,000 = 0.18 (rounded)

[6] Using decimal fractions often requires rounding. Greater precision can be obtained by dividing each step 2 value by the step 3 value, and multiplying that resulting value by the total joint cost.
[7] Monetary measures are more reflective of the primary reason a joint process is undertaken: profit. Physical base allocations are sometimes of dubious value because they are based on the flawed assumption that all physical units are equally desirable.

tion technique. This process uses a weighting technique based on both quantity produced and selling price of production. The account titles for the entries to recognize joint processing cost, allocate it to the joint products, and recognize separate processing cost are the same as those used earlier; however, the amounts allocated will differ.

NET REALIZABLE VALUE AT SPLIT-OFF

net realizable value at split-off allocation

How do you know whether to process joint products beyond split-off?

net realizable value (NRV)

The **net realizable value at split-off allocation** method assigns joint cost based on the proportional net realizable values of the joint products at the split-off point. **Net realizable value (NRV)** is equal to product sales revenue at split-off minus any costs necessary to prepare and dispose of the product. This method requires that all joint products be marketable at the split-off point and considers the additional costs that must be incurred at split-off to realize the estimated sales revenue. The selling costs for Scrumptious Turkey's products (in the fourth column of Exhibit 11–4) will be incurred whether the product is sold at split-off or after further processing. Joint cost is assigned based on each product's relative proportion of total NRV (Exhibit 11–7). Results in Exhibits 11–6 and 11–7 are very similar because selling costs incurred for each primary product are relatively low. When disposal costs are relatively high, cost allocations based on sales value at split-off and net realizable value can differ substantially.

APPROXIMATED NET REALIZABLE VALUE AT SPLIT-OFF

approximated net realizable value at split-off allocation

Often, some or all of the joint products are not salable at the split-off point. For these products to be sold, they must be processed additionally after split-off, which causes additional costs to be incurred. This lack of marketability at split-off means that neither the sales value at split-off nor the net realizable value at split-off approach can be used. **Approximated net realizable value at split-off allocation** requires that a *simulated* NRV at the split-off point be calculated to distribute the joint cost proportionately.[8] This value is computed on a per-product basis as final sales price minus incremental separate costs. Incremental separate cost refers to all processing and disposal costs that are incurred between the split-off point and the

EXHIBIT 11–7

SCRUMPTIOUS TURKEY'S JOINT COST ALLOCATION BASED ON NET REALIZABLE VALUE AT SPLIT-OFF

Joint Product	Tons Produced	Unit NRV per Ton	Total NRV	Proportion	Joint Cost	Amount Allocated	Cost per Ton
Breast	3,800	$2,600[a]	$ 9,880,000	0.57[d]	$5,400,000	$3,078,000	$810.00
Ground	2,400	1,700[b]	4,080,000	0.24[e]	5,400,000	1,296,000	540.00
Whole	2,800	1,150[c]	3,220,000	0.19[f]	5,400,000	1,026,000	366.43
Total	9,000		$17,180,000	1.00		$5,400,000	

Unit NRV per Ton = Sales Value at Split-Off − Selling Expenses at Split-Off

[a]Unit NRV per ton = $2,800 − $200 = $2,600
[b]Unit NRV per ton = $1,800 − $100 = $1,700
[c]Unit NRV per ton = $1,200 − $50 = $1,150

Proportions = Total Revenue of Respective Joint Product ÷ Total Revenue

[d]$9,880,000 ÷ $17,180,000 = 0.57 (rounded)
[e]$4,080,000 ÷ $17,180,000 = 0.24 (rounded)
[f]$3,220,000 ÷ $17,180,000 = 0.19 (rounded)

[8]Another name for this method is the *artificial net realizable value at split-off allocation*.

point of sale. An underlying assumption of this method is that the incremental revenue from further processing is equal to or greater than the incremental costs of further processing and selling. Using the information in Exhibit 11–4, approximated NRVs at split-off are determined for each Scrumptious Turkey product.

Joint Product	Final Sales Price per Ton	Separate Cost per Ton after Split-Off	Approximated NRV at Split-Off
Breast	$3,200	$300[a]	$2,900
Ground	2,100	200[b]	1,900
Whole	1,500	110[c]	1,390

Separate Cost after Split-Off = Separate Processing Cost + Selling Cost at Split-Off:
[a]$200 + $100 = $300
[b]$100 + $100 = $200
[c]$60 + $50 = $110

Further processing should be undertaken only if the incremental revenues will exceed the incremental costs based on the following computations.

Joint Product	Final Sales Price	Sales Price at Split-Off	Separate Cost per Ton at Split-Off	Separate Cost per Ton after Split-Off
Breasts	$3,200	$2,800	$200	$300
Ground	2,100	1,800	100	200
Whole	1,500	1,200	50	110

Joint Product	Incremental Revenue	Incremental Cost	Incremental Profit
Breasts	$400	$100	$300
Ground	300	100	200
Whole	300	60	240

For all products, the incremental revenues from further processing exceed the incremental costs beyond split-off. Thus, the company will be better off if it processes all joint products further than if it sells them at split-off. The same conclusion can be reached by comparing the net realizable values at split-off with the approximated net realizable values at split-off, as follows:

Joint Product	Net Realizable Value at Split-Off	Approximated Net Realizable Value at Split-Off	Difference
Breast	$2,600	$2,900	$300
Ground	1,700	1,900	200
Whole	1,150	1,390	240

The decisions made about further processing affect the values used to allocate joint cost in the approximated net realizable value method. If it is uneconomical to process one or more products further, the value base used for allocation of joint cost will be a mixture of actual and approximated NRVs at split-off. Products that will not be processed further will be valued at their actual net realizable values at split-off; products that will be processed further are valued at approximated net realizable values at split-off. However, using a mixed base is unnecessary in this case because all products will be processed further. Scrumptious Turkey's $5,400,000 joint cost is allocated among the products as in Exhibit 11–8.

Scrumptious Turkey can process some or all of the breast meat, ground turkey, and whole turkeys further to create additional types of output (Exhibit 11–9). This further processing does not change the allocation of joint cost previously made to

EXHIBIT 11–8

SCRUMPTIOUS TURKEY'S JOINT COST ALLOCATION BASED ON APPROXIMATED NET REALIZABLE VALUE AT SPLIT-OFF

Joint Product	Tons Produced	NRV per Ton	Approximated Total NRV	Proportion	Joint Cost	Amount Allocated	Cost per Ton
Breast	3,800	$2,900	$11,020,000	0.57	$5,400,000	$3,078,000	$810.00
Ground	2,400	1,900	4,560,000	0.23	5,400,000	1,242,000	517.50
Whole	2,800	1,390	3,892,000	0.20	5,400,000	1,080,000	385.71
Total	9,000		$19,472,000	1.00		$5,400,000	

the joint products. Assume that Scrumptious Turkey used the allocations from Exhibit 11–8 and decided to further process 1,000 tons of breast meat into deli meat, 900 tons of ground turkey into turkey sausage, and 1,200 tons of whole turkeys into marinated turkeys. The further processing would require assigning to the new products some of the original joint cost as well as the processing cost incurred to specifically manufacture these alternative products, as shown in the following journal entries. For simplicity, we assume that the separate costs of processing the "new" output are the same as those for processing their related joint product counterpart.

```
Work in Process Inventory—Deli (1,000 tons × $810.00)        810,000
Work in Process Inventory—Sausage (900 tons × $517.50)       465,750
Work in Process Inventory—Marinated (1,200 tons × $385.71)   462,852
    Work in Process Inventory—Breast                                   810,000
    Work in Process Inventory—Ground                                   465,750
    Work in Process Inventory—Whole                                    462,852
To transfer allocated costs to new product inventories.

Work in Process Inventory—Deli (1,000 tons × $100)           100,000
Work in Process Inventory—Sausage (900 tons × $100)           90,000
Work in Process Inventory—Marinated (1,200 tons × $60)        72,000
    Various accounts                                                   262,000
To record separate processing costs.
```

Note that the selling costs per ton have not been recorded because the products have not yet been sold.

EXHIBIT 11–9

SCRUMPTIOUS TURKEY'S FURTHER PROCESSING DIAGRAM

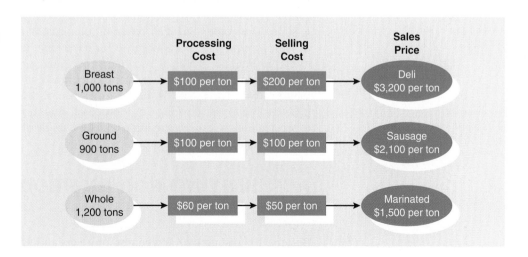

Focus on Quality

Recycling the Railroad

Each year, thousands of old railroad cars reach the point where they are no longer useful except as sources of scrap steel and parts. Companies like Louisville Scrap Material Co. purchase the cars, take them apart, and resell the components. The parts, from the brakes to the axles, may be resold as they are, sent to manufacturers for rework, cut up and sold for scrap, or melted into new bars of steel.

Louisville Scrap's plant, itself, is recycled. In early 1997, the company moved from its previous location at Louisville's busy downtown waterfront to a secure, 14-acre tract at the former Indiana Army Ammunition Plant. Because railroad companies may ship as many as 100 cars per day to the scrap plant, Louisville Scrap needed a site with adequate space.

The Indiana site was not only spacious but contained a vast network of rail track that allowed a large number of cars to be stored. Another nice feature of the site is that it is located in an isolated area that makes it nearly invisible to the local population. That's important because a dismantling facility adds no visual appeal to a neighborhood.

Some of the rail in the facility was built to move army munitions around the site but was too light to handle railroad cars. The owners of Louisville Scrap formed another company, Mid-America Rail, to recycle the light rails. Although too light to accommodate rail cars, the rail was suitable for coal mining operations, moving overhead cranes and other applications. Approximately 40 miles of the light rail were removed and sold. In addition, the cross ties beneath the track were sold to a Kansas company to be turned into landscaping and railroad supports. And the ballasts became reinforcements for concrete parking lots.

Mid-America Rail and Louisville Scrap and their employees are not the only beneficiaries of the recycling effort. By buying the abandoned rail and renting the Indiana facility from the Army, it has put money back into the government's coffers and saved taxpayers the expense of maintaining the train lines. As part of its long-term lease agreement, Mid-America also provides rail-switching services for other commercial tenants at the Army facility, helping turn remote areas of the industrial park into viable sites for new and expanding businesses.

Source: Adapted from Anonymous, "Two Recycling Companies Profit from Army Rail Lines at Facility One," *http://www.pendulumsite.com/fle.htm.*

Each method discussed allocates a different amount of joint cost to the joint products and results in a different per-unit cost for each product. Each method has advantages and disadvantages. For most companies, approximated NRV at split-off provides the most logical joint cost assignment. The most rational joint cost allocation matches the costs of joint processing with its benefits. Approximated NRV is superior to other financial bases of joint cost allocation in measuring "benefits" of joint processing. This is because for each joint product approximated, NRV captures the intended level of separate processing, costs of separate processing, expected selling costs of each joint product, and the expected selling price of each joint product. Thus, NRV is the best measure of the expected contribution of each product line to the coverage of joint costs. It is, however, more complex than the other methods because estimations must be made about additional processing costs and potential future sales values.

ACCOUNTING FOR BY-PRODUCTS AND SCRAP

LO.5
HOW ARE BY-PRODUCTS AND SCRAP ACCOUNTED FOR?

Because the distinction between by-products and scrap is one of degree, these categories are discussed together by presenting several of the treatments found in

How does accounting for by-products and scrap affect joint cost allocation?

practice. The appropriate choice of method depends on the magnitude of the net realizable value of the by-products/scrap and the need for additional processing after split-off. As the sales value of the by-products/scrap increases, so does the need for inventory recognition. Sales value of the by-products/scrap is generally recorded under either (1) the net realizable value approach or (2) the realized value approach. These approaches are discussed in the following sections using additional data for Scrumptious Turkey, which produces fertilizer pellets as a by-product. See Exhibit 11–10 for April 2006 data.

Net Realizable Value Approach

net realizable value approach

Use of the **net realizable value** (or offset) **approach** requires that the NRV of the by-product or scrap be treated as a reduction in the joint cost allocable to joint products. This method is normally used when the NRV of the by-product or scrap is expected to be significant. This approach records an inventory value that equals the selling price of the by-product/scrap produced minus the related processing, storing, and disposal costs. Any income remaining after covering these costs reduces the cost of producing the joint products. Any loss generated by the by-product/scrap is added to joint product cost.

When the by-product is generated and its net realizable value is debited to inventory, one of two accounts may be credited: Work in Process Inventory or Cost of Goods Sold for the joint products. The benefit of using the WIP—Joint Products account is timing: Joint cost is reduced immediately when the by-product or scrap is produced. The disadvantage of this approach is that it is less conservative than waiting to record revenues until the by-product or scrap is actually sold, as does the realized value approach presented in the next section. Additionally, by-products and scrap could have sales potential beyond that currently known by management.

The journal entries to record by-product production and the additional processing, completion, and sale of the by-product follow. Note that in the first journal entry, the alternative credit could have been to the Cost of Goods Sold related to the joint products.

Work in Process Inventory—Fertilizer Pellets (2,000,000 × $0.20)	400,000	
Work in Process Inventory—Joint Products		400,000
To record production of by-product.		
Work in Process Inventory—Fertilizer Pellets (2,000,000 × $0.10)	200,000	
Various accounts		200,000
To record additional processing costs.		
Finished Goods Inventory—Fertilizer Pellets (2,000,000 × $0.30)	600,000	
Work in Process Inventory—Fertilizer Pellets		600,000
To transfer completed by-products to finished goods.		
Cash (or Accounts Receivable) (2,000,000 × $0.30)	600,000	
Finished Goods Inventory—Fertilizer Pellets		600,000
To record sale of by-product.		

EXHIBIT 11–10

APRIL 2006 DATA FOR BY-PRODUCT OF SCRUMPTIOUS TURKEY

Total processing for month: 10,000 tons of turkey, resulting in 9,000 tons of joint products

By-product from joint product production: 1,000 tons (or 2,000,000 pounds) of fertilizer pellet ingredients

Selling price of fertilizer pellets: $0.30 per pound

Processing costs per pound of fertilizer pellets: $0.08 for labor and $0.02 for overhead

Net realizable value per pound of fertilizer pellets: $0.20

Although reducing joint cost by the NRV of by-products/scrap is the traditional method used to account for these goods, it is not necessarily the best method for internal decision making or the management of by-products. By-products can be treated either as having no assignable cost or as having costs equal to their net sales value. However, when management considers by-product to be a moderate source of income, the accounting and reporting methods used should help managers monitor production and further processing of the by-product and make effective decisions regarding this resource.[9] The NRV method does not indicate the sales dollars, expenses, or profits from the by-product/scrap and, thus, does not provide sufficient information to induce management to maximize the inflows from by-product/scrap disposal.

Realized Value Approach

Under the **realized value** (or other income) **approach**, no value is recognized for the by-products/scrap until they are sold. This method is the simplest approach to accounting for by-products/scrap. Several reporting techniques can be used with the realized value approach.

One presentation shows total sales of the by-product/scrap on the income statement under the Other Revenue caption. Costs of additional processing or disposal of the by-product/scrap are included in the cost of producing the main products. This presentation provides little useful information to management because it does not match the costs of producing the by-products/scrap with the revenues generated by those items. The Scrumptious Turkey entries for the incurrence of labor and overhead costs and at point of sale using the Other Revenue method are as follows:

Work in Process Inventory—Joint Products (2,000,000 × $0.08)	160,000	
Manufacturing Overhead (2,000,000 × $0.02)	40,000	
Various accounts		200,000
To record the labor and overhead costs of by-product processing.		
(Note: All costs are included in the cost of joint products.)		
Cash (or Accounts Receivable) (2,000,000 × $0.30)	600,000	
Other Revenue		600,000
To record sale of fertilizer pellets.		

A second presentation for the realized value approach shows by-product/scrap revenue on the income statement net of additional costs of processing and disposal. This method presents the net by-product revenue as an enhancement of net income in the period of sale under the Other Income caption. This presentation allows management to recognize the dollar benefit added to company income by managing the costs and revenues related to by-products/scrap. The entries for Scrumptious Turkey using the Other Income method are as follows for the incurrence of labor and overhead costs and at point of sale:

Work in Process Inventory—Fertilizer Pellets (2,000,000 × $0.10)	200,000	
Various accounts		200,000
To record the labor and overhead costs of by-product processing.		
(Note: All costs are included in the cost of by-products.)		
Cash (or Accounts Receivable)	600,000	
Work in Process Inventory—Fertilizer Pellets		200,000
Other Income		400,000
To record sale of fertilizer pellets net of processing/disposal costs.		

Because the Other Income method matches by-product/scrap revenue with related storage, further processing, transportation, and disposal costs, this method

---

[9] Advances in technology and science have turned many previous "by-products" or "scrap" items into main products. Management should not ignore the significance of such products and should seek new uses or markets for them.

provides detailed information on financial responsibility and accountability for disposition, provides better control, and could improve performance. Managers are more apt to look for new or expanded sales potential because the net benefits of doing so are shown directly on the income statement.

Other alternative presentations include showing the realized value from the sale of by-products/scrap as (1) an addition to gross margin, (2) a reduction of the cost of goods manufactured, or (3) a reduction of the cost of goods sold. The major advantage of these simplistic approaches is clerical efficiency.

Regardless of whether a company uses the net realizable value or the realized value approach, the specific method used to account for by-products/scrap should be established *before* the joint cost is allocated to the joint products. See Exhibit 11–11 for four comparative income statements using different methods of accounting for by-product income for Scrumptious Turkey. Some assumed amounts have been included to provide complete income statements.

By-products, scrap, and waste are created in all types of businesses, not just manufacturing. Managers might not see the need to determine the cost of these secondary types of products. However, with the trend toward more emphasis on cost and quality control, many companies are becoming aware of the potential value of by-products, scrap, and waste as substantial sources of revenue and are devoting time and attention to developing those innovative revenue sources.

BY-PRODUCTS AND SCRAP IN JOB ORDER COSTING

Although joint products normally are not associated with job order costing systems, these systems could have by-products or scrap. Either the realized value approach or the net realizable value approach can be used to recognize the value of by-products/scrap.

In a job order system, by-product or scrap value is appropriately credited to either manufacturing overhead or to the specific jobs in process. The former account is credited if by-products or scrap is typically created by most jobs undertaken. The effect of crediting manufacturing overhead is to reduce the amount of overhead that will need to be applied to all products for the period. In contrast, if only a few or specific jobs generate substantial amounts of by-products or scrap, the individual jobs causing the by-products/scrap should be credited with their value. The effect of crediting specific jobs with the value of by-product or scrap is to reduce the total costs assigned to those jobs.

To illustrate, assume that Scrumptious Turkey occasionally prepares special turkey products for large institutional clients. Every special order job generates scrap meat that is sold to Canine Catering Corporation. In October 2006, Scrumptious Turkey received an order for 20,000 turkey casseroles from the Boone County Public School District. The casseroles are prepared using a combination of breast, thigh, and wing meat. After production of the casseroles, Scrumptious Turkey sold $250 of scrap meat. Using the realized value approach, the entry to record the sale of the scrap is:

Cash	250	
Manufacturing Overhead		250
To record the sale of scrap.		

In contrast, assume that Scrumptious Turkey seldom has salable scrap on its special order jobs. However, during October 2006, the company contracted with Green Cove Convalescent Centers to prepare 25,000 frozen chicken croquettes. Because Scrumptious Turkey normally does not process chicken, it must acquire specific raw material for the job and will charge the cost of all raw material directly to Green Cove. Preparation of the chicken croquettes generates some scrap that can be sold for $375 to Chicken Soup Cannery. Because the raw material cost is

EXHIBIT 11–11

SCRUMPTIOUS TURKEY
COMPARATIVE INCOME
STATEMENTS—
BY-PRODUCT
PRESENTATIONS

(a) Net Realizable Value Approach: Reduce Cost of Goods Sold (CGS)

Sales		$ 6,200,000
Cost of goods sold		
Beginning finished goods	$ 400,000	
Cost of goods manufactured	3,600,000	
CGA	$4,000,000	
Ending finished goods	(380,000)	
Unadjusted CGS	$3,620,000	
NRV of by-product	(400,000)	(3,220,000)
Gross margin		$ 2,980,000
Operating expenses		(2,600,000)
Income from principal operations		$ 380,000
Other income		
Royalties		80,000
Income before income taxes		$ 460,000

(b) Net Realizable Value Approach: Reduce Cost of Goods Manufactured (CGM)

Sales		$ 6,200,000
Cost of goods sold		
Beginning FG	$ 400,000	
CGM ($3,600,000 − $400,000)	3,200,000	
CGA	$3,600,000	
Ending finished goods [assumed to be smaller than under (a)]	(342,000)	(3,258,000)
Gross margin		$ 2,942,000
Operating expenses		(2,600,000)
Income from principal operations		$ 342,000
Other income		
Royalties		80,000
Income before income taxes		$ 422,000

(c) Net Realized Value Approach: Increase Revenue

Sales		$ 6,200,000
Other revenue		
By-product sales		600,000
Total revenue		$ 6,800,000
Cost of goods sold		
Beginning finished goods	$ 400,000	
CGS (main products)	3,600,000	
CGS (processing by-product)	200,000	
CGA	$4,200,000	
Ending finished goods	(380,000)	(3,820,000)
Gross margin		$ 2,980,000
Operating expenses		(2,600,000)
Income from principal operations		$ 380,000
Other income		
Royalties		80,000
Income before income taxes		$ 460,000

(d) Net Realized Value Approach: Present as Other Income

Sales		$ 6,200,000
Cost of goods sold		
Beginning finished goods	$ 400,000	
CGM	3,600,000	
CGA	$4,000,000	
Ending finished goods	(380,000)	(3,620,000)
Gross margin		$ 2,580,000
Operating expenses		(2,600,000)
Loss from principal operations		$ (20,000)
Other income		
Royalties	$ 80,000	
By-product sales (NRV)	400,000	480,000
Income before income taxes		$ 460,000

directly related to this job, the sale of scrap from that raw material also relates to the specific job. Under these circumstances, the production and sale of the scrap are recorded (using the net realizable value approach) as follows:

Scrap Inventory—Chicken	375	
Work in Process Inventory—Green Cove Convalescent Centers		375
To record the production of scrap.		
Cash	375	
Scrap Inventory—Chicken		375
To record sale of the scrap.		

In this case, the net realizable value approach is preferred because of the timing of the recognition. To affect the specific job cost that caused an unusual incidence and amount of scrap, it could be necessary to recognize the by-product/scrap on production; otherwise, the job could be completed before the by-product/scrap can be sold.

Manufacturing processes frequently create the need to allocate costs. However, some costs incurred in service businesses and not-for-profit organizations may be allocated among product lines, organizational locations, or types of activities performed by the organizations.

JOINT COSTS IN SERVICE AND NOT-FOR-PROFIT ORGANIZATIONS

LO.6
HOW SHOULD NOT-FOR-PROFIT ORGANIZATIONS ACCOUNT FOR JOINT COSTS?

Service and not-for-profit organizations can incur joint costs for advertising multiple products, printing multipurpose documents, or holding multipurpose events. For example, not-for-profit entities often issue brochures containing information about the organization, its purposes, and its programs as well as making an appeal for funds.

When do service and not-for-profit organizations have joint costs?

If a service business decides to allocate a joint cost, it can choose either a physical or monetary allocation base. Joint costs in service businesses often relate to advertisements rather than to processes. For example, a local bicycle and lawn mower repair company could advertise a sale and list all store locations in a single newspaper ad. The ad cost could be allocated equally to all locations or be based on sales volume for each location during the period of the sale. In another example, a grocery delivery service could deliver several customers' orders on the same trip. The cost of the trip could be allocated based on the number of bags or pounds of food delivered for each customer.

Service businesses could decide that allocating joint cost is not necessary. However, for financial accounting purposes, not-for-profit organizations are required to allocate joint costs among the activities of fund-raising, offering an organizational program, or conducting an administrative function.[10] A major purpose of this allocation process is to ensure that external users of financial statements are able to clearly determine amounts spent by the organization for various activities—especially fundraising.

---

[10] AICPA Accounting Standards Executive Committee, *Statement of Position 98-2: Accounting for Costs of Activities of Not-for-Profit Organizations and State and Local Governmental Entities That Include Fund Raising* (effective for years beginning on or after December 15, 1998).

Revisiting

Perdue Farms Incorporated

Perdue Farms prides itself on its many customer satisfaction initiatives. These include a "farm-to-fork" food safety program, an Associate Food Safety Pledge for employees, and the use of environmentally friendly, leak-resistant, microwaveable tray packaging.

Quality output has always been Perdue's goal, and the company is noted for many "firsts" in the poultry industry. For example, Perdue Farms was the first poultry company to have a dedicated Environmental Services Department to ensure 100 percent compliance with environmental regulations and was the first to develop an alternative use for poultry litter by converting it into organic fertilizer. It was also the first poul-

try company to include nutritional labeling on its packages, to be awarded an A-grade from the USDA for its broiler boneless breasts, to offer its customers a satisfaction-or-money-back guarantee, and to provide a 1-800 hotline number for comments and questions. In addition, Perdue was the first company to use digital scales to ensure the accuracy of its packaged output and to use satellite tracking of its fleet of trucks to ensure on-time delivery, which is crucial for poultry products because of their short shelf life. These many firsts have helped to make Perdue a top-quality, ecologically aware poultry producer.

Source: *http://www.perdue.com* and *http://www.koami.or.kr/bbs/jck99/sp_3_033.pdf.*

Comprehensive Review Module

Chapter Summary

1. The possible outputs of a joint process include

   - joint products—output with a relative high sales value.

   - by-products—output with a higher sales value than scrap but less than joint products.

   - scrap—output with a low sales value.

   - waste—residual output with no sales value.

2. Joint products

   - are identified at the split-off point.

   - are assigned joint product cost.

   - could have their costs reduced by the net realizable value of by-products and/or scrap.

3. Decisions that must be made in a joint product production process include

   - two that are made before the joint process is started:

     ➤ Do total revenues exceed total (joint and separate) costs?

     ➤ Is this the best use of available facilities?

   - two that are made at the split-off point:

     ➤ Which products will be classified as joint products, by-products, scrap, and waste?

     ➤ Which products will be sold at split-off and which will be processed further?

4. Joint cost is commonly allocated to joint products using one of two common methods:

   - physical measures that provide an unchanging yardstick of output over time and treat each unit of product as equally desirable.

   - monetary measures that consider different valuations of the individual joint products; these valuations can be based on

     ➤ sales value at split-off,

     ➤ net realizable value at split-off, or

     ➤ approximated net realizable value at split-off.

5. By-products and scrap can be accounted for using the

   - net realizable value (offset) approach in which the NRV of the by-products/scrap reduces either the

     ➤ work in process inventory of the joint products when the by-products/scrap are produced

     ➤ cost of goods sold of the joint products when the by-products/scrap are produced

   - realized value (other income) approach in which the NRV of the by-products/scrap is shown on the income statement as either an

     ➤ other revenue item when the by-products/scrap are sold or

     ➤ other income item when the by-products/scrap are sold.

6. Using some reasonable measure, such as percentage of time or space, not-for-profits must allocate the joint cost incurred for a multipurpose advertisement among the categories of

   - fund-raising,

   - program, and/or

   - administrative activities.

Solution Strategies

ALLOCATION OF JOINT COST

Joint cost is allocated only to joint products; however, joint cost can be reduced by the value of by-products/scrap before the allocation process begins.

For physical measure allocations: Divide joint cost by the products' total physical measurements to obtain a cost per unit of physical measure.

For monetary measure allocation:

1. Choose an allocation base.
2. List the values that compose the allocation base for each joint process.
3. Sum the values in step 2.
4. Calculate the percentage of the base value to the total of all values in the base. The sum of all percentages so derived should be 100 percent, or 1.00.
5. Multiply the total joint cost by each percentage to obtain the amount to be allocated to each joint product.
6. Divide the prorated joint cost for each product by the number of equivalent units of production for each product to obtain a cost per EUP for valuation purposes.

Allocation bases, measured at the split-off point, by which joint cost is prorated to the joint products include the following:

Type of Measure	Allocation Base
Physical output	Physical measurement of units of output (e.g., tons, feet, barrels, liters)
Monetary	Currency units of value
Sales value	Revenues of the several products
Net realizable value	Sales value minus incremental processing and disposal costs
Approximated net realizable value	Find sales price minus incremental processing costs

Demonstration Problem

Quazeemo-do Inc. produces two joint products—JP#89-43-A and JP#89-43-B—from a single input. Further processing product JP#89-43-A results in a by-product designated BP#89-43-X. A summary of production and sales for 2006 follows.

- Quazeemo-do Inc. input 600,000 tons of raw material into the Processing Department. Total joint processing cost was $520,000,000. During the joint processing, 90,000 pounds of material were lost.
- After joint processing, 60 percent of the joint process output was transferred to Division 1 to produce JP#89-43-A, and 40 percent of the joint process output was transferred to Division 2 to produce JP#89-43-B.
- Further processing in Division 1 resulted in 70 percent of the input tons becoming JP#89-43-A and 30 percent of the input tons becoming BP#89-43-X. The separate processing cost in Division 1 was $648,000,000.
- Total separate processing costs for JP#89-43-A were $321,300,000. After Division 1 processing and packaging, product JP#89-43-A is salable at $6,000 per ton.
- Each ton of BP#89-43-X can be sold for $120 after total selling cost of $5,000,000. The company accounts for by-products using the net realizable value method and showing the NRV as a reduction in the cost of goods sold of the joint products.
- In Division 2, product JP#89-43-B was further processed at a separate cost of $408,000,000. A completed ton of JP#89-43-B sells for $3,700.
- Selling cost for both products JP#89-43-A and JP#89-43-B is $200 per ton.

Required:

a. Prepare a process diagram similar to the one shown in Exhibit 11–4 or 11–9.
b. Record the journal entry to
  1. recognize incurrence of joint cost.
  2. allocate joint costs to the joint products using tonnage as a physical measure and transfer the products into Divisions 1 and 2.

3. record incurrence of separate processing costs for products JP#89-43-A and JP#89-43-B in Divisions 1 and 2.
4. record incurrence of packaging cost for product JP#89-43-A.
5. transfer completed products JP#89-43-A and JP#89-43-B to finished goods.

c. Allocate the joint cost to products JP#89-43-A and JP#89-43-B using approximated net realizable values at split-off.

d. Quazeemo-do Inc. had no Work in Process or Finished Goods Inventory at the beginning of 2006. Prepare an income statement through gross margin for Quazeemo-do Inc. assuming that:
   - 80 percent of product JP#89-43-A and 90 percent of product JP#89-43-B produced were sold.
   - all the by-product BP#89-43-X that was produced during the year was sold.
   - joint cost was allocated using the physical measurement method in part (b).

Solution to Demonstration Problem

a.

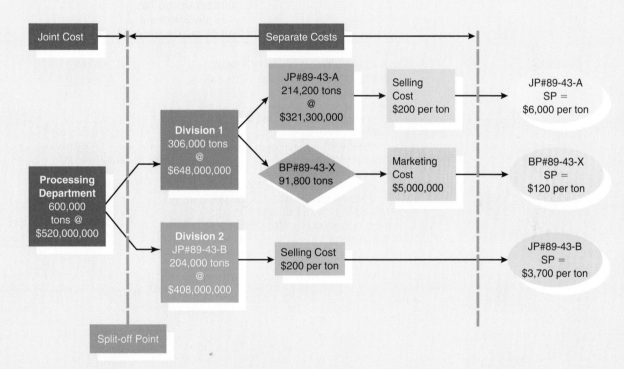

b. 1. Work in Process Inventory—Processing   520,000,000
           Various accounts   520,000,000
         To record 2006 joint processing costs.

    2. Work in Process Inventory—Division 1   312,000,000
        Work in Process Inventory—Division 2   208,000,000
           Work in Process Inventory—Processing   520,000,000
         To allocate joint cost to joint products.

    3. Work in Process—Division 1   648,000,000
        Work in Process—Division 2   408,000,000
           Various accounts   1,056,000,000
         To record separate processing costs.

    4. Work in Process Inventory—Division 1   321,300,000
           Various accounts   321,300,000
         To record packaging costs for JP#89-43-A.

5. Finished Goods Inventory—JP#89-43-A   1,281,300,000
    Finished Goods Inventory—JP#89-43-B   616,000,000
        Work in Process Inventory—Division 1   1,281,300,000
        Work in Process Inventory—Division 2   616,000,000
    To transfer completed production to finished goods.

c. Approximated NRV Method

Product	Tons Produced	NRV per Ton at Split-off*	Total NRV	Proportion	Joint Cost	Allocated Joint Cost
JP#89-43-A	214,200	$1,275	$273,105,000	0.47	$520,000,000	$244,400,000
JP#89-43-B	204,000	1,500	306,000,000	0.53	520,000,000	275,600,000
			$579,105,000	1.00		$520,000,000

	JP#89-43-A	JP#89-43-B
* Selling price/ton	$6,000	$3,700
Separate costs		
Division 1 ($648,000,000 ÷ 214,200)	(3,025)	
Packaging ($321,300,000 ÷ 214,200)	(1,500)	
Division 2 ($408,000,000 ÷ 204,000)		(2,000)
Selling	(200)	(200)
Approximated net realizable value	$1,275	$1,500

d.

QUAZEEMO-DO INC.
Income Statement
For the Year Ended December 31, 2006

Sales		
JP#89-43-A (214,200 × 0.80 × $6,000)	$1,028,160,000	
JP#89-43-B (204,000 × 0.90 × $3,700)	679,320,000	$ 1,707,480,000
Cost of Goods Sold		
Beginning finished goods	$ 0	
Cost of goods manufactured [from part (b5)]		
JP#89-43-A	1,281,300,000	
JP#89-43-B	616,000,000	
Available for sale	$1,897,300,000	
Ending finished goods		
JP#89-43-A ($1,281,300,000 × 0.20)	(256,260,000)	
JP#89-43-B ($616,000,000 × 0.10)	(61,600,000)	
Unadjusted cost of goods sold	$1,579,440,000	
NRV of by-product [(91,800 × $120) − $5,000,000]	(6,016,000)	(1,573,424,000)
Gross margin		$ 134,056,000

Key Terms

approximated net realizable value at split-off allocation *(p. 451)*	net realizable value approach *(p. 455)*	sales value at split-off allocation *(p. 450)*
by-product *(p. 442)*	net realizable value at split-off allocation *(p. 451)*	scrap *(p. 442)*
joint cost *(p. 442)*		separate cost *(p. 442)*
joint process *(p. 441)*	physical measurement allocation *(p. 448)*	split-off point *(p. 443)*
joint product *(p. 442)*		waste *(p. 442)*
net realizable value (NRV) *(p. 451)*	realized value approach *(p. 456)*	

Questions

1. How does management determine how to classify each type of output from a joint process? Is this decided before or after production?

2. In a company that engages in a joint production process, will all processing stop at the split-off point? Discuss the rationale for your answer.

3. By what criteria would management determine whether to proceed with processing at each decision point in a joint production process?

4. Why is cost allocation necessary in accounting? Why is it necessary in a joint process?

5. Compare the advantages and disadvantages of the two primary methods used to allocate joint cost to joint products.

6. Why are approximated, rather than actual, net realizable values at split-off sometimes used to allocate joint cost?

7. Which of the two common approaches used to account for by-products is better? Discuss the rationale for your answer.

8. When are by-product or scrap costs considered in setting the predetermined overhead rate in a job order costing system? When are they not considered?

9. Why must not-for-profit organizations allocate any joint costs incurred among fundraising, program, and administrative activities?

Exercises

10. (Essay; Internet) Use the Internet to find five examples of businesses that have joint processes. For each business, describe:
  a. The various outputs from the processes; using logic, determine whether each output would be classified as a joint product, by-product, scrap, or waste.
  b. Your recommendation of the most appropriate methods of allocating joint cost to the outputs you described in part (a). Express, in nontechnical terms, your justification for each of your recommendations.
  c. For one of the businesses, diagram the flow of costs.

11. (Joint process decision making) Lauren Jackson's aged uncle has asked her to take over the family poultry processing plant. Jackson has learned that you are majoring in accounting—she majored in engineering—and asks you to help her understand the poultry shop business. She would like you to do the following:
  a. Explain, in nontechnical terms, what financial questions about joint processes someone who manages a poultry processing plant must

answer. Also indicate the points in a joint process at which these questions should be answered.

b. Describe, in your own words, the proper managerial use of a joint cost; also describe whether a joint cost can be used inappropriately and the basis on which you think a particular use is inappropriate.

c. Compare and contrast the various categories of outputs generated by a joint process.

12. (Physical and sales value allocations) Holdsclaw Basketball Camp runs two training camps. During 2006, it generated the following operating data:

	High School Leagues	Amateur Adult Leagues
Training hours taught	2,000	1,000
Hourly tuition	$10	$30

The general ledger accounts show $38,000 for direct instructional costs and $4,000 for overhead associated with these two programs. The board of trustees wants to know the cost of each program.

a. Determine each program's cost using a physical measurement base.

b. Determine each program's cost using the sales value at split-off method.

c. Make a case for each allocation method in parts (a) and (b).

13. (Physical measure allocation) Swoopes Timber Company uses a joint process to manufacture two grades of wood: A and B. During October 2006, the company incurred $24,000,000 of joint production cost in producing 36,000,000 board feet of grade A and 12,000,000 board feet of grade B wood. The company allocates joint cost on the basis of board feet of wood produced. Swoopes can sell grade A at the split-off point for $0.50 per board foot or can further process the wood at a cost of $0.75 per board foot and then sell it for $1.60 per board foot. The company has no opportunity to further process grade B wood.

a. What amount of joint cost is allocated to grade A wood and to grade B wood?

b. If grade A wood is processed further and then sold, what is the incremental effect on Swoopes' net income? Should the additional processing be performed?

14. (Allocation of joint cost) T. Catchings Fish Processors produces three products from its fish farm: fish, fish oil, and fish meal. During July 2006, the firm produced the following average quantities of each product from each pound (16 ounces) of fish processed:

Product	Obtained from Each Pound of Fish
Fish	8 ounces
Fish oil	4
Fish meal	2
Total	14 ounces

Of each pound of fish processed, 2 ounces are waste. In July, the firm processed 50 tons of fish (1 ton equals 2,000 pounds). Joint cost amounted to $190,400. On average, each pound of product has the following selling prices: fish, $6; fish oil, $8; and fish meal, $4.

a. Allocate the joint cost using weight as the basis.

b. Allocate the joint cost using sales value as the basis.

c. Discuss the advantages and disadvantages of the answers to parts (a) and (b).

15. (Sales value allocation) S. Cattle produces milk and sour cream from a joint process. During June, it produced 240,000 quarts of milk and 320,000 pints of sour cream. (There are two pints in a quart.) Sales value at split-off point was $100,000 for the milk and $220,000 for the sour cream. The milk was assigned $43,200 of the joint cost.

a. Using the sales value at split-off approach, determine the total joint cost for June.

b. Assume, instead, that the joint cost was allocated based on the number of quarts produced. What was the total joint cost incurred in June?

WebTUTOR Advantage

16. (Net realizable value allocation) D. Staley Communications is a sports-band network and television company with three service groups: Games, News, and Documentaries. In May, the company incurred $12,000,000 of joint product cost for facilities and administration. Revenues and separate production costs of each group for May follow:

	Games	News	Documentaries
Revenue	$18,000,000	$15,000,000	$95,000,000
Separate costs	17,000,000	8,000,000	55,000,000

a. What amount of joint cost is allocated to each service group using the net realizable value approach? Compute the profit for each group after the allocation.

b. What amount of joint cost is allocated to each service group if the allocation is based on revenues? Compute the profit for each group after the allocation.

c. Assume you are head of the Games Group. Would the difference in allocation bases create significant problems for you when you report to the company's board of directors? Develop a short presentation to make to the board if the allocation base in part (b) is used to determine each group's relative profitability. Be certain to discuss important differences in revenues and cost figures for the Games and Documentaries groups.

17. (Approximated net realizable value method) Hammon Perfume Company makes three products that can either be sold at split-off or processed further and then sold. April's joint cost is $240,000.

Product	Bottles of Output	Sales Price at Split-Off	Separate Cost after Split-Off	Final Sales Price
Perfume	15,000	$6.00	$2.00	$8.50
Eau de toilette	20,000	4.00	1.00	6.00
Body splash	25,000	4.00	1.50	6.00

The number of ounces of product in each perfume bottle is 3; eau de toilette is 2; and body splash is 3. Assume that all products are processed further after split-off.

a. Allocate the joint cost based on the number of bottles, weight, and approximated net realizable values at split-off.

b. Assume that all products are additionally processed and completed. At the end of the period, the inventories are as follows: perfume, 500 bottles; eau de toilette, 1,000 bottles; and body splash, 1,500 bottles. Determine the values of the inventories based on answers obtained in part (a).

18. (Processing beyond split-off and cost allocations) Sue Bird Products has a joint process that makes three products from honey for institutional customers. Joint cost for the process is $60,000.

Product	Units of Output	Per Unit Selling Price at Split-Off	Incremental Processing Cost	Final Sales Price
Honey butter	5,000	$2.00	$1.50	$3.00
Honey jam	10,000	1.00	2.00	6.00
Honey syrup	500	1.50	0.20	1.80

A container of honey butter, jam, and syrup includes, respectively, 10 pounds, 6 pounds, and 2 pounds of product.

   a. Determine which products should be processed beyond the split-off point.

   b. Assume honey syrup should be treated as a by-product. Allocate the joint processing cost based on units produced, weight, and approximated net realizable value at split-off. Use the net realizable value method in accounting for any by-products.

19. (Sell or process further) Smith Textiles harvests and processes cotton in a joint process that yields two joint products: fabric and yarn. May's joint cost is $40,000, and the sales values at split-off are $120,000 for fabric and $100,000 for yarn. If the products are processed beyond split-off, the final sales value will be $180,000 for fabric and $140,000 for yarn. Additional costs of processing are expected to be $40,000 for fabric and $34,000 for yarn.

   a. Should the products be processed further? Show computations.

   b. Were any revenues and/or costs irrelevant to the decision? If so, what were they and why were they irrelevant?

20. (Processing beyond split-off) Mabika Cannery makes three apple products from a single joint process. For 2006, the cannery processed all three products beyond split-off. The following data were generated for the year:

Joint Product	Incremental Separate Cost	Total Revenue
Candied apples	$26,000	$620,000
Apple jelly	38,000	740,000
Apple jam	15,000	270,000

Analysis of 2006 market data reveals that candied apples, apple jelly, and apple jam could have been sold at split-off for $642,000, $706,000, and $253,000, respectively.

   a. Based on hindsight, evaluate management's production decisions in 2006.

   b. How much additional profit could the company have generated in 2006 if it had made optimal decisions at split off?

21. (Net realizable value method) Weatherspoon Processing produces fillet, smoked, and canned tuna in a single process. The joint cost is $64,000.

Product	Pounds Produced	Unit Cost at Split-Off	Selling Price
Fillet	9,000	$1.50	$6.00
Smoked	10,000	4.50	6.50
Canned	1,000	0.15	0.75

   a. Assume canned is a by-product, allocate the joint cost based on net realizable value at split-off. Use the net realizable value method to account for by-products.

   b. Determine the value of ending finished goods inventory, assuming that 8,400 pounds of fillets, 9,400 pounds of smoked, and 946 pounds of canned tuna were sold.

22. (By-product accounting method selection) The company you work for engages in numerous joint processes that produce significant quantities and types of by-products. You have been asked to give a report to management on the best way to account for by-products. Develop a set of criteria for making such a choice and provide reasons that each of the criteria has been selected. On the basis of your criteria, along with any additional assumptions you wish to provide about the nature of the company you work for, recommend a particular method of accounting for by-products and explain why you consider it to be better than the alternatives.

23. (Monetary measure allocation) Teasley Realty has two operating divisions: Rental and Sales. In March 2006, the firm spent $25,000 for general company promotions (as opposed to advertisements for specific properties). Lisa Leslie, the corporate controller, now has the task of fairly allocating the promotion costs to the two operating divisions.

Leslie has reduced the potential bases for allocating the promotion costs to two alternatives: expected increase in divisional revenue from the promotions and expected increase in divisional profit from the promotions (before allocated promotion costs). The promotions are expected to have the following effects on the two divisions:

	Rental	Sales
Increase in divisional revenue	$400,000	$800,000
Increase in profit (before allocated promotion costs)	75,000	50,000

a. Allocate the total promotion cost to the two divisions using change in revenue.

b. Allocate the total promotion cost to the two divisions using change in profit before joint cost allocation.

c. Which of the two approaches is more appropriate? Explain.

24. (By-products and cost allocation) Yolanda Salsa has a joint process that yields three grades of tomatoes: premium, good, and fair. Joint cost is allocated to products based on bushels of output. One particular joint process batch cost $240,000 and yielded the following bushels of output:

Product	Output in Bushels
Premium	9,600
Good	26,000
Fair	8,400

The joint process also created by-products that had a total net realizable value of $40,000. The company records by-product inventory at the time of production. Allocate the joint cost to the joint products.

25. (Sell or process further) Penicheiro Clothing produces precut fabrics for three products: dresses, jackets, and blouses from a joint process. Joint cost is allocated on the basis of relative sales value at split-off. Rather than sell the products at split-off, the company has the option to complete each of the products. Information related to these products follows.

	Dresses	Jackets	Blouses	Total
Number of units produced	5,000	8,000	3,000	16,000
Joint cost allocated	$87,000	?	?	$180,000
Sales values at split-off point	?	?	$40,000	$300,000
Additional costs of processing further	$13,000	$10,000	$39,000	$62,000
Sales values after all processing	$150,000	$134,000	$105,000	$389,000

a. What amount of joint cost should be allocated to jackets and blouses?

b. What are the sales values at split-off for dresses and jackets?

c. Which products should be processed further? Show computations.

d. If 4,000 jackets are processed further and sold for $67,000, what is gross profit on the sale?

26. (By-products and cost allocation) Dales-Schumantions Productions produced the movies *Rare Debits & Credits* and *Rare Debits & Credits: The Sequel* from the same original footage that cost $16,000,000. The company, therefore, considers these two movies as joint products. Because of the superb animation in postproduction, however, the sequel was significantly more expensive to produce but was much better received at the box office.

The company also generated what it considers by-product revenue from admissions paid by numerous fans touring the movie production set. Dales-Schumantions accounts for this revenue as a reduction in joint cost before making allocations to the movie output.

The following information pertains to the two movies:

Products	Total Receipts	Separate Costs
Rare Debits & Credits	$ 8,000,000	$ 4,800,000
Rare Debits & Credits: The Sequel	54,000,000	37,200,000
Studio tours	700,000	380,000

a. If joint cost is allocated based on net realizable value, how much of the joint cost is allocated to each movie?

b. How much profit was generated by each movie?

27. (Accounting for by-products) Tamecka Company manufactures various wood products that yield sawdust as a by-product. Selling costs associated with the sawdust are $4 per ton sold. The company accounts for sawdust sales by deducting the sawdust's net realizable value from the major products' cost of goods sold. Sawdust sales in 2006 were 24,000 tons at $21 each. If Tamecka changes its method of accounting for sawdust sales to show the net realizable value as Other Revenue (presented at the bottom of the income statement), how would its gross margin be affected? Show your work.

28. (Accounting for by-products) In making frozen hash browns and potato chips, Azzi Potato Inc. generates potato skins as a by-product. It sells the potato skins to restaurants for use in appetizers. The processing and disposal costs associated with the sales of the by-product are $0.10 per pound of potato skins. During May 2006, Azzi Potato produced and sold 90,000 pounds of potato skins for $11,825. In addition, the joint cost for hash browns and potato chips was $30,000. In May, 80 percent of all joint production was sold for $80,000. Nonfactory operating expenses for May were $3,800.

a. Prepare an income statement for Azzi Potato Inc. assuming that by-product sales are shown as Other Revenue and the processing and disposal costs for the by-product are shown as additional cost of goods sold of the joint products.

b. Prepare an income statement for Azzi Potato assuming that the net realizable value of the by-product is shown as other income.

c. Prepare an income statement for Azzi Potato assuming that the net realizable value of the by-product is subtracted from the joint cost of the main products.

d. Would the presentation in (a), (b), or (c) be most helpful to managers? Why?

29. (Accounting for by-products) Bolton-Holifield EDP provides computing services for its commercial clients. Records for clients are maintained on both computer files and paper files. After seven years, the company sells the paper records for recycling material.

The net realizable value of the recycled paper is treated as a reduction to operating overhead. Data pertaining to operations for 2006 follow:

Budgeted operating overhead	$199,250
Actual operating overhead	$199,750
Budgeted net realizable value of recycled paper	$9,200
Actual net realizable value of recycled paper	$9,794
Budgeted CPU time (hours)	70,000
Actual CPU time	68,400

a. Assuming that CPU time is the allocation base, what was the company's predetermined overhead rate?

b. What journal entry should the company make to record the sale of the recycled paper?

c. What was the company's underapplied or overapplied overhead for 2006?

30. (Accounting for scrap) Renaissance Creations restores antique stained glass windows. On all jobs, it generates some breakage or improper cuts. This scrap can be sold to amateur stained glass hobbyists. Renaissance Creations expects to incur approximately 30,000 direct labor hours during 2006. The following estimates are made in setting the predetermined overhead rate for 2006:

Overhead costs other than breakage		$65,300
Estimated cost of scrap	$3,400	
Estimated sales value of scrap	(1,200)	2,200
Total estimated overhead		$67,500

One job that Renaissance Creations completed during 2006 was a stained glass window of the Soprano family crest that took 126 hours. Direct material cost $210; direct labor is invoiced at $10 per hour. Actual cost of scrap on this job was $27.50; the scrap was sold for $9.

a. What predetermined overhead rate was set for 2006?

b. What was the cost of the family crest stained glass window?

c. What journal entry is made to record the cost and selling value of the scrap from the family crest stained glass window?

31. (Scrap; job order costing) Ruthie Architects offers a variety of architectural services for commercial construction clients. For each major job, architectural models of the completed structures are built for client presentations. The company uses a job order cost system. At the completion of a job, the firm sells the architectural models to an arts and crafts retailer if the clients do not want them. Ruthie Architects uses the realized value method of accounting for sale of the models. The sales value of each model is credited to the cost of the specific job for which the model was built. During 2006, the model for the Stiles building was sold for $2,500.

a. Using the realized value approach, give the entry to record the sale.

b. Independent of your answer to part (a), assume that the sales value of the models is not credited to specific jobs. Give the entry to account for the sale of the Stiles building model.

32. (Net realizable value versus realized value) Indicate whether each item that follows is associated with (1) the realized value approach or (2) the net realizable value approach.

a. has the advantage of better timing

b. ignores value of by-product/scrap until it is sold

c. is easier

d. is used to reduce the cost of main products when by-products are produced

e. credits either cost of goods sold of main products or the joint cost when the by-product inventory is recorded

f. presents proceeds from sale of by-products as other revenue or other income

g. is appropriate if the by-product's net realizable value is small

h. is less conservative

i. is the most clerically efficient

j. should be used when the by-product's net realizable value is large

33. (Not-for-profit program and support cost allocation) Kansas City Jazz Company is preparing a pamphlet that will provide information on the types of jazz, jazz terminology, and biographies of some of the more well-known jazz musicians. In addition, the pamphlet will include a request for funding to support the jazz company. The company has tax-exempt status and operates on a not-for-profit basis.

The 10-page pamphlet cost $180,000 to design and print. Only 200,000 copies of the pamphlet were printed because the director of the company will soon be leaving and the pamphlet will need to be redesigned. One page of the pamphlet is devoted to fund solicitation; however, 98 percent of the design time was spent on developing and writing the jazz information.

a. If space is used as the allocation measure, how much of the pamphlet's cost should be assigned to program activities? To fund-raising activities?

b. If design time is used as the allocation measure, how much of the pamphlet's cost should be assigned to program activities? To fund-raising activities?

34. (Web research) Go to the Web site for **Perdue Farms Incorporated** at *http://www.perdue.com* where the company provides information regarding its philosophies, product lines, strategy, and production systems. Review the information provided and then discuss how an operating environment such as Perdue's, which has many joint production processes, can create unique opportunities for new product innovation. Also discuss employee characteristics that would be important in such an environment.

Problems

35. (Journal entries) Desirable Inc. uses a joint process to make two main products: Forever perfume and Fantasy lotion. Production is organized in two sequential departments: Combining and Heating. The products do not become separate until they have been through the heating process. After heating, the perfume is removed from the vats and bottled without further processing. The residue remaining in the vats is then blended with aloe and lanolin to become the lotion.

The following costs were incurred in the Combining Department during October 2006: direct material, $28,000; direct labor, $7,560; and applied manufacturing overhead, $4,250. Prior to separation of the joint products, costs in the Heating Department for the month were direct material, $6,100; direct labor, $2,150; and applied manufacturing overhead, $3,240. After split-off, the Heating Department incurred separate costs for each product line as follows: bottle for Forever perfume, $2,120; and direct material, direct labor, and applied manufacturing overhead of $1,960, $3,120, and $4,130, respectively, for Fantasy lotion.

Neither department had beginning Work in Process Inventory balances, and all work that started in October was completed in that month. Joint costs are allocated to perfume and lotion using approximated net realizable values at split-off. For October, the approximated net realizable values at split-off were $158,910 for perfume and $52,970 for lotion.

a. Prepare journal entries for the Combining and Heating Departments for October 2006.

b. Determine the joint cost allocated to and the total cost of Forever perfume and Fantasy lotion.

c. Diagram the flow of costs for these two company products.

36. (Physical measure joint cost allocation) Lakeside Dairy began operations at the start of May. The company was founded by local dairy farmers to enhance competition in the market for milk products produced by the farmers.

Lakeside operates a fleet of trucks to gather whole milk from local farmers. The whole milk is then separated into two joint products: skim milk and cream. Both products are sold at the split-off point to dairy wholesalers. For May, the firm incurred the following joint costs:

Whole milk purchase cost	$200,000
Direct labor costs	40,000
Overhead costs	80,000
Total product cost	$320,000

The firm processed 1,000,000 pounds of whole milk and produced 80,000 pounds of cream and 840,000 pounds of skim milk during May. The balance of the whole milk purchased was lost during processing. There were no raw material or work in process inventories at the end of May. Of the products produced, 60,000 pounds of cream were sold for $54,000 and 625,000 pounds of milk were sold for $181,000.

a. Lakeside uses a physical measure (pounds) to allocate joint costs. Allocate the joint cost to production.

b. Calculate the cost of goods sold, cost of ending finished goods inventory, and the gross margin for the month.

c. One farmer who serves on the board of directors at Lakeside noted that the milk fat content of whole milk can vary greatly from farmer to farmer. Because milk fat content determines the relative yields of skim milk and cream from whole milk, the ratio of joint products can be partly determined based on the milk fat content of purchased whole milk. How could Lakeside Dairy exploit information about milk fat content in the whole milk it purchases to optimize the profit realized on its joint products?

37. (Monetary measure joint cost allocation) Refer to the information in Problem 36.

a. Calculate the sales price per pound for skim milk and cream.

b. Using relative sales value, allocate the joint cost to the joint production.

c. Calculate the cost of goods sold, cost of ending finished goods inventory, and the gross margin for the month.

38. (Physical measure joint cost allocation) Midwest Soybeans operates a processing plant in which soybeans are "crushed" to create soybean oil and soybean meal. The company purchases soybeans by the bushel (60 pounds). From each bushel, the normal yield is 11 pounds of soybean oil, 44 pounds of soybean meal, and 5 pounds of waste. For March, Midwest purchased and processed 5,000,000 bushels of soybeans. The yield in March on the soybeans was equal to the normal yield. The following costs were incurred for the month:

Soybeans	$47,500,000
Conversion costs	2,300,000

At the end of March there were no in-process or raw material in inventory. Also, there was no beginning finished goods inventory. For the month, 80 percent of the soybean meal and 60 percent of the soybean oil were sold.

a. Allocate the joint cost to the joint products on the basis of pounds of product produced.

b. Calculate the cost of goods sold for March.

c. Calculate the cost of finished goods inventory at the end of March.

39. (Monetary measure joint cost allocation) Refer to the information in Problem 38.

a. Assume the net realizable value of the joint products is as follows:

Soybean oil $0.339 per pound
Soybean meal $0.169 per pound

Allocate the joint cost incurred in March on the basis of net realizable value.

b. Calculate the cost of goods sold for March using the answer to part (a).

c. Calculate the cost of finished goods inventory at the end of March based on the answer to part (a).

d. Compare the answers to parts (b) and (c) of Problem 38 to the answers to parts (b) and (c) of this problem. Explain why the answers differ.

40. (Joint cost allocation; by-product; income determination) St. Cloud Bank & Trust has two main service lines, commercial checking and credit cards. The firm also generates some revenue from selling antitheft and embezzlement insurance as a by-product of its two main services. Joint costs for producing the two main services include expenses for facilities, legal support, equipment, record keeping, and administration. The joint service cost incurred during June 2006 was $400,000 and is to be allocated on the basis of total revenues generated from each main service.

The following table presents the results of operations and revenues for June:

Service	Number of Accounts	Total Revenues
Commercial checking	6,000	$948,750
Credit cards	14,000	701,250
Theft insurance	13,000	32,500

Management accounts for the theft insurance on a realized value basis. When commissions on theft insurance are received, management presents the proceeds as a reduction to the Cost of Services Rendered for the main services.

Separate costs for the two main services, checking accounts and credit cards, for June were $125,000 and $90,000, respectively.

a. Allocate the joint cost.

b. Determine the income for each main service and the company's overall gross margin for June 2006.

41. (Joint cost allocation; scrap) Kelly's Linens produces cloth products for hotels. The company buys fabric in 60-inch-wide bolts. In the first process, the fabric is set up, cut, and separated into pieces. Setup can be for either robes and bath towels or hand towels and washcloths.

During July, the company set up and cut 6,000 robes and 12,000 bath towels. Because of the irregular pattern of the robes, the process produces scrap that is sold to various prisons and hospitals for rags at $0.65 per pound. July production and cost data for Kelly's Linens are as follows:

Fabric used, 25,000 feet at $1.50 per foot	$37,500
Labor, joint process	$12,000
Overhead, joint process	$11,000
Pounds of scrap produced	3,600

Kelly's Linens assigns the joint processing cost to the robes and towels based on approximated net realizable value at split-off. Other data gathered include these:

	Per Robes	Per Bath Towel
Final selling prices	$40.00	$22.00
Costs after split-off are	16.80	4.60

The selling price of the scrap is treated as a reduction of joint cost.

a. Determine the joint cost to be allocated to the joint products for July.

b. How much joint cost is allocated to the robes in July? To the bath towels? Prepare the journal entry necessary at the point of split-off.

c. What amount of cost for robes is transferred to Finished Goods Inventory for July? What amount of cost for towels is transferred to Finished Goods Inventory for July?

42. (Joint products; by-product) Georgia Peach runs a fruit-packing business in central Georgia. The firm buys peaches by the truckload in season and separates them into three categories: premium, good, and fair. Premium can be sold as is to supermarket chains and specialty gift stores. Good is sliced and canned in light syrup and sold to supermarkets. Fair is considered a by-product and is sold to Yum-Yum Company, which processes it into jelly.

Georgia Peach has two processing departments: (1) Cleaning and Sorting (joint cost) and (2) Cutting and Bottling (separate costs). During the month, the company paid $15,000 for one truckload of fruit and $300 for labor to sort the fruit into categories. Georgia Peach uses a predetermined overhead rate of 50 percent of direct labor cost. The following yield, costs, and final sales value resulted from the month's truckload of fruit.

	Premium	Good	Fair
Yield in pecks	1,500	2,000	500
Cutting and bottling costs	0	$2,000	0
Total packaging and delivery costs	$1,500	$2,200	$500
Total final sales value	$30,000	$15,000	$4,500

a. Diagram the problem similar to diagrams in Exhibits 11–4 and 11–9.

b. Determine the joint cost.

c. Allocate joint cost using the approximated net realizable value at split-off method, assuming that the by-product is recorded when realized and is shown as Other Income on the income statement.

d. Using the allocations from part (c), prepare the necessary entries assuming that the by-product is sold for $4,500 and that all costs were as shown.

e. Allocate joint cost using the approximated net realizable value at split-off method, assuming that the by-product is recorded using the net realizable value approach and that the joint cost is reduced by the net realizable value of the by-product.

f. Using the allocations from part (d), prepare the necessary entries, assuming that the estimated realizable value of the by-product is $4,000.

43. (Process costing; joint cost allocation; by-product) Michelle's Fitness Center provides personal training services and sells a variety of apparel products for its clients. The center also generates some revenue from the sale of used towels, which are periodically sold to a rag-rug manufacturer. The net realizable value of used towels is accounted for as a reduction in the joint cost assigned to the Personal Training Services and Apparel Products. Used towels sell for $0.60 per pound. The cost of bundling the towels is $0.10 per pound, and their selling costs are $0.05 per pound.

The following information is available for 2006 on apparel inventory, which is purchased by the fitness center:

Beginning inventory	$ 35,000
Ending inventory	21,500
Purchases	181,350

Joint cost is to be allocated to Personal Training Services and Apparel Products based on approximated net realizable values (revenues less separate costs). For 2006, total revenues were $753,000 from Personal Training Services and $289,000 from Apparel. The following joint costs were incurred:

Rent $36,000
Insurance   23,800
Utilities   3,000

Separate costs were as follows:

	Personal Training	Apparel
Labor	$431,000	$24,000
Supplies	98,000	700
Equipment depreciation	65,000	1,200
Administration	113,000	3,700

For the year, 2,510 pounds of used towels were collected and sold.

a. Diagram this problem similar to diagrams in Exhibits 11–4 and 11–9.

b. What is the total net realizable value of towels that is applied to reduce the joint cost assigned to Personal Training and Apparel?

c. What is the joint cost to be allocated to Personal Training and Apparel?

d. What is the approximated pre-tax realizable value of each main product or service for 2006?

e. How much joint cost is allocated to each main product or service?

f. Determine the net income produced by each main product or service.

44. (Joint cost allocation; by-product) Muriel Orange Company produces orange juice and orange marmalade from a joint process. In addition, second-stage processing of the marmalade creates a residue mixture of orange pulp as a by-product. The company sells pulp for $0.08 per gallon. Expenses to distribute pulp total $110.

In May 2006, 140,000 pounds of oranges were processed in Department 1; the cost of that input was $44,200. An additional $33,700 was spent on conversion costs. There were 56,000 gallons of output from Department 1. Of that output, 30 percent was transferred as orange juice to Department 2, and 70 percent of the output was transferred to Department 3. Of the input going to Department 3, 20 percent resulted in pulp and 80 percent resulted in marmalade. Joint cost is allocated to orange juice and marmalade on the basis of approximated net realizable values at split-off.

The orange juice in Department 2 was processed at a total cost of $9,620; the marmalade in Department 3 was processed at a total cost of $6,450. The net realizable value of pulp is accounted for as a reduction in the separate processing costs in Department 3. Selling prices per gallon are $5.25 and $3.45 for orange juice and marmalade, respectively.

a. Diagram this problem similar to those in Exhibits 11–4 and 11–9.

b. How many gallons leaving Department 1 were sent to Department 2 for further processing? To Department 3?

c. How many gallons left Department 3 as pulp? As marmalade?

d. What is the net realizable value of pulp?

e. What is the total approximated net realizable value of the orange juice? The marmalade?

f. What amount of joint cost is assigned to each main product?

g. If 85 percent of the final output of each main product was sold during May and Muriel Orange Company had no beginning inventory of either product, what is the value of the ending inventory of orange juice and marmalade?

45. (By-product/joint product journal entries) Kansas Wheat Agricultural is a 5,000-acre wheat farm, which produces two principal products, wheat and straw. It sells wheat for $3.50 per bushel (assume that a bushel of wheat weighs 60 pounds). Without further processing, it sells the straw for $30 per ton (a ton equals 2,000 pounds). If the straw is processed further, it is baled and sold for $45 per ton. In 2006, total joint cost up to the split-off point (harvest) was $175 per acre.

In 2006, the farm produced 70 bushels of wheat and 1 ton of straw per acre. If all straw were processed further, baling costs would be $50,000.

a. Diagram the problem similar to those in Exhibits 11–4 and 11–9.

b. Prepare the 2006 journal entries for straw if it is:

  1. transferred to storage at sales value as a by-product without further processing with a corresponding reduction of wheat's production costs

  2. further processed as a by-product and transferred to storage at net realizable value with a corresponding reduction of the manufacturing costs of wheat

  3. further processed and transferred to finished goods with joint cost being allocated between wheat and straw based on relative sales value at the split-off point

46. (Ending inventory valuation; joint cost allocation) During March 2006, the first month of operations, Nikki Dean's Pork Packing Co. had the operating statistics shown in the following table. Costs of the joint process were direct material, $40,000; direct labor, $23,400; and overhead, $10,000. The company's main products are pork tenderloin, roast pork, and ham; pork hooves are a by-product of the process. The company recognizes the net realizable value of by-product inventory at split-off by reducing total joint cost. Neither the main products nor the by-product requires any additional processing or disposal costs, although management could consider additional processing.

Products	Weight in Pounds	Sales Value at Split-Off	Units Produced	Units Sold
Tenderloin	8,600	$132,000	6,440	5,440
Roast	13,400	86,000	16,740	14,140
Ham	10,800	22,400	8,640	7,600
Hooves	4,600	4,600	9,200	8,000

a. Calculate the ending inventory values of each joint product based on (1) relative sales value and (2) pounds.

b. Discuss the advantages and disadvantages of each allocation base for (1) financial statement purposes and (2) decisions about the desirability of processing the joint products beyond the split-off point.

47. (Essay; ethics) Some waste, scrap, or by-product material have little value. In fact, for many meat and poultry producers, animal waste represents a significant liability because it is considered hazardous and requires significant disposal costs. For example, one environmental group filed a lawsuit against **Smithfield Foods, Inc.**, the largest hog processor in the United States, for "deliberately fouling water, air and soil as part of a strategy to drive competing small farmers out of business." The suit alleges that by ignoring waste treatment, the company can produce pork "so cheaply that independent farmers can't compete."[11]

Alternatively, other companies have found environmentally friendly or inexpensive ways to dispose of animal waste. For example, **Perdue** Farms Incorporated prides itself on quality poultry and environmentally safe waste disposal.

[11] *http://www.mindfully.org/Farm/Smithfield-Foods-RICO.htm*, or see Stephanie Simon, "U.S. Top Hog Processor Accused of Planned Pollution in Lawsuit," *LA Times* (March 1, 2001).

a. Review the Smithfield Foods, Inc., SEC Form 10-K report, especially the sections entitled "Nutrient Management and Other Environmental Issues" and "Regulation," for the year ended April 30, 2000, and comment on whether the company's disposition of industrial waste is a "cheap" alternative.

b. Discuss the ethical and legal implications of disposing of industrial waste in this manner.

c. What actions can people take to reduce this type of incident?

d. Ethically, what obligation does the vendor/manufacturer of these industrial materials have to the consumer of them?

12

Introduction to Cost Management Systems

Objectives

AFTER COMPLETING THIS CHAPTER, YOU SHOULD BE ABLE TO ANSWER THE FOLLOWING QUESTIONS:

LO.1 WHY DO ORGANIZATIONS HAVE MANAGEMENT CONTROL SYSTEMS?

LO.2 WHAT IS A COST MANAGEMENT SYSTEM, AND WHAT ARE ITS PRIMARY GOALS?

LO.3 WHAT MAJOR FACTORS INFLUENCE THE DESIGN OF A COST MANAGEMENT SYSTEM?

LO.4 WHAT THREE GROUPS OF ELEMENTS AFFECT THE DESIGN OF A COST MANAGEMENT SYSTEM, AND WHAT ARE THE PURPOSES OF THESE ELEMENTS?

LO.5 WHAT IS GAP ANALYSIS, AND HOW IS IT USED IN THE IMPLEMENTATION OF A COST MANAGEMENT SYSTEM?

Introducing

Based in Sugar Land, Texas, Imperial Sugar Company is the oldest existing business in Texas. The company has operated continuously from the same site since 1843. In its early years, the company and the community were one and the same. Situated on Oakland Plantation in southeast Texas near the Gulf of Mexico, Imperial Sugar provided for all material needs of its employees. The firm organized a mercantile and other retail stores, paper mill, feed mill, cotton gin, and engaged in meat packing, canning, and processing of various agricultural crops.

Today Imperial Sugar's operations span the country, and the company produces one-sixth of the sugar consumed in the United States. The company markets refined sugar to consumers under familiar brand names such as Holly®, Spreckels®, Dixie Crystals®, Pioneer®, and Imperial®. In addition to these consumer products, the firm markets sugar to the food service industry and to a variety of industrial firms that make consumer products such as soft drinks, doughnuts and pastries, icings, and breakfast cereals.

When it first opened, Imperial Sugar's major raw material was sugar cane. Today the company operates sugar plants that also use sugar beets. Although a significant amount of sugar cane is grown in parts of the South, sugar beets can be grown in many more areas of the United States, particularly in the West. Sourcing raw material and producing finished products near the markets where the products are consumed is important in the industry because of high transportation costs.

Today sugar is regarded as a commodity, which implies that it is difficult for one producer to distinguish its products from those of other manufacturers, and competition is price based. For producers to effectively compete on the basis of price, they must intensely focus on cost management. In the sugar industry, the competition is fierce—so much so that profit has essentially been driven out of the industry. Up to 80 cents of each sales dollar collected by Imperial Sugar Co. goes to pay for one input, raw sugar. The other 20 cents of each dollar must pay for all other operating expenses and provide a profit. Imperial's managers must always focus on ways to contain or reduce costs to maintain a competitive position in the industry.

Sources: *http://www.tsha.utexas.edu/handbook/online/articles/view/II/diicy.html; http://www.imperialsugar.com.*

A fundamental concern managers have in executing their duties is how their actions affect organizational costs and benefits. Ultimately, most models used by managers reduce to a comparative analysis of costs and benefits. Financial experts, especially accountants, bear the primary responsibility for providing managers information about measurements of those costs and benefits.

Chapter 1 discussed the differences and similarities among the disciplines of financial, management, and cost accounting. Cost accounting is described as playing a role in both internal and external reporting. As such, this field of accounting is cast into separate, often competing, roles that the financial reporting role often dominates. Thus, even though directly linked to the managerial functions of planning, controlling, decision making, and performance evaluation, cost accounting information is frequently found to be of limited value to managers because that information is shaped by financial reporting demands.

The problem is that the dictates of financial reporting are very different from those of strategic cost management. For financial reporting purposes, cost information can be highly aggregated and historical and must be consistent with GAAP. In contrast, the cost information required for management purposes may be segmented, current, and relevant for a particular purpose. Consequently, the cost information provided by the financial reporting system is often of little value for cost management purposes.[1] Increasingly, cost accounting practices are being reviewed by financial experts to improve the relevance of the resultant information.

In redesigning cost accounting systems, the general internal use of information and the specific application of information to manage costs are receiving increased attention. The first section of this chapter introduces management information and

LO.1
WHY DO ORGANIZATIONS HAVE MANAGEMENT CONTROL SYSTEMS?

[1] Robin Cooper and Regine Slagmulder, "Strategic Cost Management: Introduction to Enterprisewide Cost Management," *Management Accounting* (August 1998), p. 17.

control systems, thereby offering a foundation and context for understanding the roles of the cost management system. Then the chapter discusses concepts and approaches to designing information systems that support the internal use of accounting and other information to manage costs. A cost management system is presumed to be an integral part of an organization's overall management information and control systems. The discussion emphasizes the main factors that determine the structure and success of a cost management system, the factors that influence the design of such a system, and the elements that compose the system.

INTRODUCTION TO MANAGEMENT INFORMATION AND CONTROL SYSTEMS

management information system
(MIS)

A cost management system is part of an overall management information and control system. Exhibit 12–1 illustrates the types of information needed in an organization to meet the requirements of individuals in performing their managerial functions as well as requirements of external parties in performing their investment and credit-granting functions. A **management information system (MIS)** is a structure of interrelated elements that collects, organizes, and communicates data to managers so they can plan, control, make decisions, and evaluate performance.

EXHIBIT 12–1
INFORMATION FLOWS AND TYPES OF INFORMATION

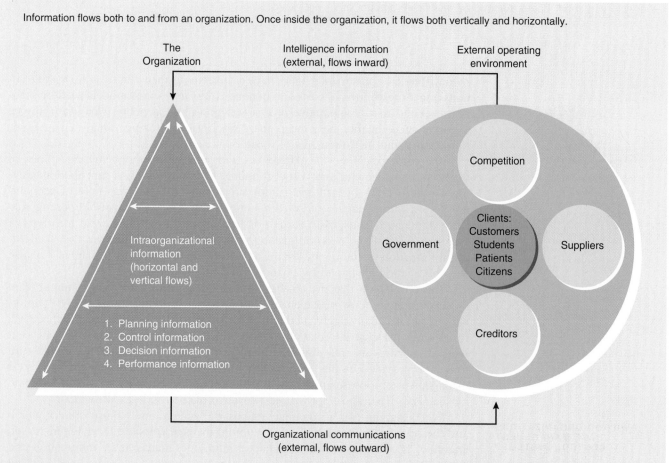

Information flows both to and from an organization. Once inside the organization, it flows both vertically and horizontally.

Source: Adapted from James H. Donnelly, Jr., James L. Gibson, and John M. Ivancevich, *Fundamentals of Management* (Plano, TX: Business Publications, Inc., 1987), p. 565.

An MIS emphasizes satisfying internal demands for information rather than external demands. In most modern organizations, the MIS is computerized for ease of access to information, reliability of input and processing, and ability to simulate outcomes of alternative situations.

The accounting function is charged with the task of providing information to interested external parties such as creditors, the government (for mandatory reporting to the Internal Revenue Service, Securities and Exchange Commission, and other regulatory bodies), and suppliers relative to payments and purchases. External intelligence is also gathered from these parties as well as from competitors. Managers use internally and externally generated information to govern their organizations.

Because one of the managerial functions requiring information is control, the MIS is part of the **management control system (MCS)**. As illustrated in Exhibit 12–2, a control system has the following four primary components:

1. A *detector* or *sensor*, which is a measuring device that identifies what is actually happening in the process being controlled.
2. An *assessor*, which is a device for determining the significance of what is happening. Usually, significance is assessed by comparing the information on what is actually happening with some standard or expectation of what should be happening.
3. An *effector*, which is a device that alters behavior if the assessor indicates the need for doing so. This device is often called *feedback*.
4. A *communications network*, which transmits information between the detector and the assessor and between the assessor and the effector.[2] The arrows in Exhibit 12–2 depict the communication network.

It is through these system components that information about actual organizational occurrences is gathered, comparisons are made against plans, changes are made when necessary, and communications take place among appropriate parties. For example, source documents (detectors) gather information about sales that is compared to the budget (assessor). If sales revenues are below budget, management

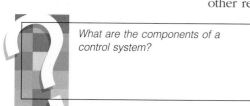

What are the components of a control system?

management control system (MCS)

EXHIBIT 12–2
ELEMENTS OF A CONTROL SYSTEM

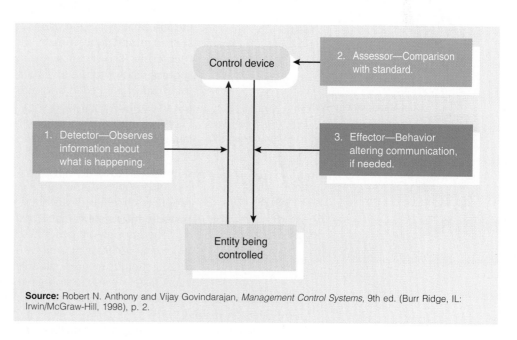

Source: Robert N. Anthony and Vijay Govindarajan, *Management Control Systems*, 9th ed. (Burr Ridge, IL: Irwin/McGraw-Hill, 1998), p. 2.

---

[2] Robert N. Anthony and Vijay Govindarajan, *Management Control Systems*, 9th ed. (Burr Ridge, IL: Irwin/McGraw-Hill, 1998), pp. 1–2.

can issue (communications network) a variance report (effector) to encourage the sales staff to increase volume.

However, different managers could interpret the same information differently and respond differently. In this respect, a management control system is not merely a mechanical process, but it also requires the application of judgment. Thus, a management control system can be referred to as a **black box**, which is defined as an operation whose exact nature cannot be observed.[3] Regardless of the specific actions taken, a management control system should serve to guide organizations in designing and implementing strategies to achieve organizational goals and objectives.

Most businesses have a variety of control systems in place. For example, a control system could reflect a set of procedures for screening potential suppliers or employees, a set of criteria to evaluate potential and existing investments, or a statistical control process to monitor and evaluate quality. Another important part of the management information and control systems is the cost management system.

DEFINING A COST MANAGEMENT SYSTEM

cost management system (CMS)

A **cost management system (CMS)** consists of a set of formal methods developed for planning and controlling an organization's cost-generating activities relative to its short-term objectives and long-term strategies. Business entities face two major challenges: achieving profitability in the short run and maintaining a competitive position in the long run. An effective cost management system must provide managers the information needed to meet both of these challenges.

EXHIBIT 12–3

**THE ORGANIZATIONAL ROLE OF A COST
MANAGEMENT SYSTEM**

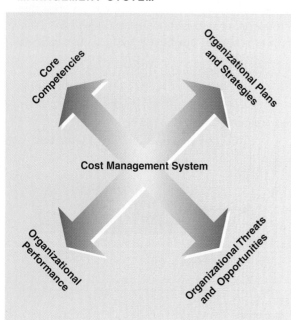

See Exhibit 12–3 for the organizational role of a cost management system. The CMS helps provide information useful to managing an organization's core competencies so the organization can exploit perceived opportunities in the marketplace and develop tactics and strategies to fend off threats. Similarly, the CMS links plans and strategies to actual organizational performance.

Refer to Exhibit 12–4 for a summary of the differences in the information requirements for organizational success in the short run and long run. In the short run, revenues must exceed costs: The organization must make efficient use of its resources relative to the revenues that are generated. Specific cost information is needed and must be delivered in a timely fashion to an individual who is in a position to influence the cost. Short-run information requirements are often described as relating to organizational efficiency.

Meeting the long-run objective of survival depends on acquiring the right inputs from the right suppliers, selling the right mix of products to the right customers, and using the most appropriate channels of distribution. These decisions require only periodic information that is reasonably accurate.

The information generated from the CMS should benefit all functional areas of the entity. Thus, as shown in Exhibit 12–5, a CMS should integrate all areas of the firm and provide managers faster access to an increased quantity of cost information that is more relevant, more detailed, and more appropriate for short-term and long-term decision making.

Crossing all functional areas, a cost management system can be viewed as having six primary goals: (1) to develop reasonably accurate product costs, especially

[3] Ibid., p. 5.

EXHIBIT 12–4
DUAL FOCUS OF A COST MANAGEMENT SYSTEM

	Short Run	Long Run
Objective	Organizational efficiency	Survival
Focus	Specific costs: • manufacturing • service • marketing • administration	Cost categories: • customers • suppliers • products • distribution channels
Important characteristics of information	Timely Accurate Highly specific Short term	Periodic Reasonably accurate Broad focus Long term

Source: Adapted from Robin Cooper and Regine Slagmulder, "Operational Improvement and Strategic Costing," *Management Accounting* (September 1998), pp. 12–13. Copyright by Institute of Management Accountants, Montvale, N.J.

through the use of cost drivers (or activities that have direct cause-and-effect relationships with costs); (2) to assess product/service life-cycle performance; (3) to improve understanding of processes and activities; (4) to control costs; (5) to measure performance; and (6) to allow the pursuit of organizational strategies.

EXHIBIT 12–5
AN INTEGRATED COST MANAGEMENT SYSTEM

Traceability has been made easier by information technology such as bar coding, popularized by Wal-Mart in the early 80's.

GETTY IMAGES

radio frequency identification (RFID)

Primarily, a CMS should provide the means to develop accurate product or service costs; thus, the system must be designed to use cost driver information to trace costs to products and services. The system does not have to be the most accurate, but it should match the benefits of additional accuracy with expenses of achieving such accuracy. Traceability has been made easier by improved information technology, including bar coding and **radio frequency identification (RFID)**. RFID uses exceptionally small "flakes" of silicon to transmit a code for the item to which it is attached. Although available since 1952, bar codes did not become popular until Wal-Mart required all of its suppliers to begin using them in 1984. Now Wal-Mart has said that its top 100 suppliers would be using RFID tags by 2005. Target is currently testing their use.[4]

The product/service costs generated by the cost management system are the inputs to managerial processes. These costs are used to plan, prepare financial statements, assess individual product/service profitability and period profitability, establish prices for cost-plus contracts, and create a basis for performance measurements. If the input costs generated by the CMS are not reasonably accurate, the output of the preceding processes will be inappropriate for control and decision-making purposes.

Although product/service profitability can be calculated periodically as a requirement for external reporting, the financial accounting system does not reflect

What are the organizational roles of a cost management system?

life-cycle information. The cost management system should provide information about the life-cycle performance of a product or service. Without life-cycle information, managers will not have a basis to relate costs incurred in one stage of the life cycle to costs and profitability of other stages. For example, managers might not recognize that strong investment in the development and design stage could provide significant rewards in later stages by minimizing costs of engineering changes and potential quality-related costs. Further, if development/design cost is not traced to the related product or service, managers could be unable to recognize organizational investment "disasters."

A cost management system should help managers comprehend business processes and organizational activities. Only by understanding how an activity is accomplished and the reasons for cost incurrence can managers make cost-beneficial improvements in the production and processing systems. Managers of a company desiring to implement new technology or production systems must recognize what costs and benefits will flow from such actions. Such assessments can be made only if the managers understand how the processes and activities will differ after the change.

A cost accounting system's original purpose was to control costs and, given the current global competitive environment, this is still an important function of a CMS. A cost can be controlled only when the related activity is monitored, the cost driver is known, and the information is available. For example, if units are spoiled in a process, the CMS should provide information on spoilage quantity and cost rather than "burying" that information in other cost categories. Additionally, the

---

[4] Sandy Berger, "RFID, Exciting New Technology," Compu-Kiss (2002); *http://www.compukiss.com/populartopics/print.*

cost management system should allow managers to understand the process so that the underlying causes of the spoilage can be determined. Having this information available allows managers to compare the costs of fixing the process with the benefits to be provided.

Information generated from a cost management system should help managers measure and evaluate performance. The measurements can be used to evaluate human or equipment performance as well as future investment opportunities.

Lastly, to maintain a competitive position in an industry, a firm must generate the information necessary to define and implement its organizational strategies. Strategy is the link between an organization's goals, objectives, and operational activities. In the current global market, firms must be certain that such a linkage exists. Information provided by a CMS enables managers to perform strategic analyses on issues such as determining core competencies and organizational constraints from a cost–benefit perspective and assessing the positive and negative financial and nonfinancial factors of strategic and operational plans. Thus, the CMS is essential to the generation of information for effective strategic resource management.

Because the world of business competition is dynamic and creative managers are constantly devising new business practices and innovative approaches to competition, a cost management system must be flexible. The following section discusses the issues affecting the design and ongoing development of cost management systems in a continually evolving organization.

DESIGNING A COST MANAGEMENT SYSTEM

LO.3
WHAT MAJOR FACTORS INFLUENCE THE DESIGN OF A COST MANAGEMENT SYSTEM?

In designing or revising a cost management system, managers and accountants must be attuned to the unique characteristics of their firms. A generic cost management system cannot be taken "off the shelf" and applied to any organization. Each firm requires a cost management system that is tailored to its situation. However, some overriding factors are important in designing a cost management system. These factors are depicted in Exhibit 12–6 and are described in this section.

Organizational Form, Structure, and Culture

organizational form

Why is an organization's legal form important in designing a CMS?

An entity's legal nature reflects its **organizational form**. Selecting the organizational form is one of the most important decisions business owners make. This choice affects the costs of raising capital, operating the business (including taxation issues), and, possibly, litigating.

The most popular form for large, publicly traded businesses is the corporation. Smaller businesses or cooperative ventures between large businesses use general partnerships, limited partnerships, limited liability partnerships (LLPs), and limited liability companies (LLCs). Both the LLP and LLC provide more protection than a general partnership for a partner's personal assets in the event of litigation that leads to the firm's liquidation. Accordingly, LLPs and LLCs can offer better control for legal costs than general partnerships.

Organizational form also helps determine who has the statutory authority to make decisions for the firm. In a general partnership, all partners are allowed to make business decisions as a mere incidence of ownership unless specified to the contrary. Alternatively, in a corporation, individual shareholders act through a board of directors who, in turn, typically rely on professional managers. This ability to "centralize" authority is regarded as one of the primary advantages of the corporate organizational form and, to some extent, is available in limited partnerships, LLPs, and LLCs.

EXHIBIT 12–6

DESIGN OF A COST MANAGEMENT SYSTEM

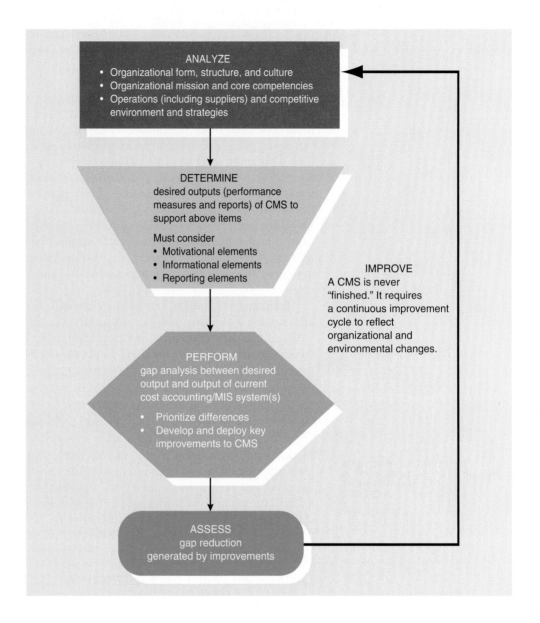

After the organizational form has been selected, top managers are responsible for creating a structure that is best suited to achieving the firm's goals and objectives. Organizational structure, introduced in Chapter 1, refers to how authority and responsibility for decision making are distributed in the entity. Top managers make judgments about how to organize subunits and the extent to which authority will be decentralized. Although the current competitive environment is conducive to strong decentralization, top managers usually retain authority over operations that can be performed more economically centrally because of economies of scale. For example, financing, personnel, and certain accounting functions typically are maintained "at headquarters" rather than being delegated to organizational subunits.

In designing the organizational structure, top managers normally try to group subunits either geographically or by similar missions or natural product clusters. These aggregation processes provide effective cost management because of proximity or similarity of the subunits under a single manager's control.

For example, relative to similarity of mission, business subunits could pursue one of three generic missions (build, harvest, or hold). Subunits pursuing a "build" mission use more cash than they generate. Such subunits invest cash with an expectation of future returns. At the other extreme, subunits pursuing a "harvest" mission are expected to generate excess cash and have a much shorter investment horizon. If one manager were responsible for subunits that represented both build and harvest missions, it would be difficult for top management to design proper incentives and performance evaluation measures for the subunit manager or to evaluate his or her cost management effectiveness and efficiency. Different cost management tools are used for different subunit missions. If a specific cost management tool is to be applied to an entire subunit with a mix of missions across that subunit's components, there is greater potential for making poor decisions.

The extent to which managers decentralize also determines who will be held accountable for cost management and organizational control. An information system must provide relevant and timely information to persons who are making decisions that have cost control implications, and a control system must be in place to evaluate the quality of those decisions.

organizational culture

An entity's culture also plays an important role in setting up a cost management system. **Organizational culture** refers to the underlying set of assumptions about the entity and the goals, processes, practices, and values that its members share. To illustrate the effect of organizational culture on the cost management system, consider AT&T in the early 1980s prior to its divestiture. It was an organization characterized by "bureaucracy, centralized control, nepotism, a welfare mentality in which workers were 'taken care of,' strong socialization processes, [and] little concern for efficiency. . . ."[5] Such a culture would have limited the requirements of a CMS because few individuals needed information, decisions were made at the top of the organization, and cost control was not a consideration because costs were passed on to customers through the rate structure. After divestiture, the company's culture changed to embrace decentralized decision making, cost efficiency, and individual responsibility and accountability. Supporting such a changed culture requires different types, quantities, and distributions of cost management information.

The values-based aspects of organizational culture are also extremely important in assessing the cost management system. For example, two parts of SETECH, Ltd.'s mission statement are to provide "customers with low-cost outsourcing of maintenance, repairs, and operations supply procurement and management" and "ongoing cost savings through technical leadership."[6] Without a well-designed cost management system, SETECH could not evaluate how well it is progressing toward accomplishing that mission. Thus, a CMS is instrumental in providing a foundation for companies with an organizational culture that emphasizes cost savings and continuous improvement.

Organizational Mission and Core Competencies

Knowledge of the organization's mission and core competencies is a key consideration in the design of a cost management system. The mission provides a long-term goal toward which the organization wishes to move. If the entity's mission is unknown, it does not matter what information is generated by the cost management system—or any other information system!

In pursuing the business mission, companies can either avoid or confront competition. For example, companies could try to avoid competition by attempting to be more adept in some way than other entities. The generic paths a company could take to avoid competition include product differentiation and cost leadership as defined in Chapter 1.

In the current global environment, it is often difficult to maintain a competitive advantage under either a differentiation or cost leadership strategy. Competitors are becoming skilled at duplicating the specific competencies that gave rise to the original competitive advantage. For many companies, the key to future success

---

[5] Thomas S. Bateman and Scott A. Snell, *Management Building Competitive Advantage* (Burr Ridge, IL: Irwin, 1996), p. 268.
[6] SETECH, Inc., "About Us: Mission Statement," accessed August 2, 2004; *http://www.setechusa.com/about/mission.html*.

could be to confront competition by identifying and exploiting temporary opportunities for advantage. In a confrontation strategy, companies "still try to differentiate their products by introducing new features, or try to develop a price leadership position by dropping prices, . . . [but, the companies] assume that their competitors will rapidly bring out products that are equivalent and match any price changes."[7] Although it could be necessary, a confrontation strategy is, by its very nature, less profitable for companies than differentiation or cost leadership.

See Exhibit 12–7 for an illustration of how the strategy of the firm, together with the life-cycle stages of products, determines what a firm must do well to be successful at any point in time. This exhibit illustrates how the information requirements of managers change over time as the life cycle evolves and, thus, depend on the strategy being pursued.

The globalization of markets has created, in many industries, competition among equals. Today, many firms are capable of delivering

How does product life cycle influence the focus of a CMS?

EXHIBIT 12–7
STRATEGY AND LIFE-CYCLE STAGE DETERMINE CRITICAL ORGANIZATIONAL ACTIVITIES

Product Strategy	LIFE-CYCLE STAGE			
	Introduction	Growth	Maturity	Decline
Differentiation	Product R&D and design are critical.	Strengthen distinctive product competencies and formalize product support structure.	Exploit competitive advantage.	Divest/spin off operations early.
	Establish presence in market and product distinctiveness.		Maintain heavy product marketing emphasis.	Relate service to new products.
		Marketing is critical.		
Cost Leadership	Process R&D and design are critical.	Quickly determine product cost structure and viability.	Make no major product changes.	Manage, reduce, and control costs.
	Manage high costs coincident with low volume.	Establish or increase market share and/or distribution channels.	Standardization is critical.	Reduce capacity and evaluate low-cost alternatives (e.g., make, outsource, shutdown).
Confrontation	Minimize product development time.	Establish market leadership and reliability.	Refine product manufacturability and process reliability.	Develop existing distribution network for new products.
	Design to facilitate process flexibility.	Provide distribution for quick delivery.	Increase and innovate distribution efforts.	Emphasize exceptional service options.

Source: B. Douglas Clinton and Aaron H. Graves, "Product Value Analysis: Strategic Analysis Over the Entire Product Life Cycle," *Journal of Cost Management* (May/June 1999), p. 23. © 1999 Warren Gorham & Lamont. Reprinted with permission of RIA.

---

[7] Robin Cooper, *When Lean Enterprises Collide* (Boston: Harvard Business School Press, 1995), p. 11.

products and services that are qualitatively and functionally equivalent. Without being able to distinguish one competitor's products from those of another based on quality or functionality, the consumer's focus switches to price. In turn, price-based competition changes the internal focus to costs.

An organization can clarify its mission by identifying core competencies or the operational dimensions that are key to survival. Most organizations would consider timeliness, quality, customer service, efficiency and cost control, and responsiveness to change as five critical competencies. Once managers have gained consensus on an entity's core competencies, the CMS can be designed (1) to gather information related to measurement of those items and (2) to generate output about those competencies in forms that are useful to interested parties.

Operations and Competitive Environment and Strategies

cost structure

Once the organizational "big picture" has been established, managers can assess internal specifics related to the design of a cost management system. A primary consideration is the firm's cost structure. Traditionally, **cost structure** has been defined in terms of relative proportions of fixed and variable costs and, thus, how costs change relative to changes in production or sales volume.[8]

Becoming increasingly dependent on automated technology makes it more difficult for firms to control costs. Many technology costs are associated with plant, equipment, and infrastructure investments that provide the capacity to produce goods and services. Higher proportions of these costs exist in industries that depend on technology for competing on the bases of quality and price. Manufacturing and service firms have aggressively adopted advanced technology.

The cost management implications of this shift in cost structure are significant. Most importantly, because most technology costs are not susceptible to short-run

How have higher fixed costs affected CMSs?

control, cost management efforts are increasingly directed toward the longer term. Also, managing costs is increasingly a matter of capacity management: High capacity utilization (if accompanied by high sales volume) allows a firm to reduce its per-unit costs in pursuing a cost leadership strategy. A second implication of the changing cost structure is the firm's flexibility to respond to changing short-term conditions. As the proportion of costs relating to technology investment increases, a firm has less flexibility to take short-term actions to reduce costs with no long-term adverse consequences.

In pursuing either a differentiation or cost leadership strategy, the management of high technology costs requires beating competitors to the market with new products. Being first to market can enable a company to set a price that leads to a large market share that, in turn, can lead to an industry position of cost leader. Alternatively, the leading-edge company can set a product price that provides a substantial per-unit profit for all sales generated before competitors are able to offer alternative products. Rapid time to market requires fast development of new products and services. Time to market is critical in the high-tech industry because profitability depends on selling an adequate number of units at an acceptable price. Because the price per unit has been falling steadily for years, getting a new product to the market late can be disastrous. Richard O'Brien, an economist for **Hewlett-Packard**, describes the risk: "Product life cycles keep shrinking. If you can't get to market on time, you will have missed your chance because the price point will have moved."[9]

Reducing time to market is one way a company can cut costs. See Exhibit 12–8 for other ways, most of which are associated with the early product life cycle stages. Thus, as has been previously mentioned, product profitability is largely determined by an effective design and development process.

---

[8] An organization's cost structure reflects its operating leverage as discussed in Chapter 9.
[9] Darren McDermott, "Cost Consciousness Beats 'Pricing Power,'" *The Wall Street Journal* (May 3, 1999), p. A1.

EXHIBIT 12–8

ACTIONS TO SUBSTANTIALLY REDUCE PRODUCT COSTS

- Develop new production processes
- Capture learning curve and experience effects
- Increase capacity utilization
- Use focused factory arrangement
  — reduces coordination costs
- Design for manufacturability
  — reduces assembly time
  — reduces training costs
  — reduces warranty costs
  — reduces required number of spare parts
- Design for logistical support
- Design for reliability
- Design for maintainability
- Adopt advanced manufacturing technologies
  — reduces inventory levels
  — reduces required production floor space
  — reduces defects, rework and quality costs

Source: Adapted from Gerald I. Susman, "Product Life Cycle Management," *Journal of Cost Management* (Summer 1989), pp. 8–22. © 1999 Warren Gorham & Lamont. Reprinted with permission of RIA.

Getting products to market quickly and profitably requires a compromise between product innovation and superior product design. Rapid time to market could mean that a firm incurs costs associated with design flaws (such as the costs of engineering changes) that could have been avoided if more time had been allowed for the product's development. Also, if a flawed product is marketed, costs will likely be incurred for returns, warranty work, or customer "bad will" regarding the firm's reputation for product quality. Time to market is important because of the competitive advantages it offers and because of compressed product life cycles. The faster a product gets to market, the fewer competitive products will exist; consequently, a greater market share can be captured (see Exhibit 12–9).

Supplier relationships constitute another aspect of an organization's operating environment. Many companies that have formed strategic alliances with suppliers have found such relationships to be effective cost control mechanisms. For example, by involving suppliers early in the design and development stage of new products, a company should achieve a better design for manufacturability and improve

EXHIBIT 12–9

RELATIONSHIP OF TIME TO MARKET AND MARKET SHARE

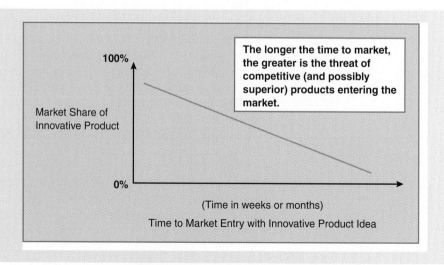

the likelihood of meeting cost targets. Additionally, if the information systems of customers and suppliers are linked electronically, the capabilities and functions of these systems must be considered in designing the CMS.

An internal operating environment consideration in the design of a cost management system is the need to integrate the organization's current information systems. The "feeder" systems (such as payroll, inventory valuation, budgeting, and costing) that are in place should be evaluated to answer the following questions:

- What input data are being gathered and in what form?
- What outputs are being generated and in what form?
- How do the current systems interact with one another, and how effective are those interactions?
- Is the current chart of accounts appropriate for the cost management information desired?
- What significant information issues (such as yield, spoilage, and cycle time) are not currently being addressed by the information system, and could those issues be integrated into the current feeder systems?

With knowledge of the preceding information, management must analyze the cost–benefit trade-offs that relate to the design of the CMS. As the costs of gathering, processing, and communicating information decrease, or as the quantity and intensity of competition increase, more sophisticated cost management systems are required. Additionally, as companies focus on customer satisfaction and expand their product or service offerings, more sophisticated cost management systems are needed. In these conditions, the generation of "better" cost information is essential to long-run organizational survival and short-run profitability.

Even with appropriate information systems in place, there is no guarantee that managers' decisions will be consistent with organizational strategies. Proper incentives and reporting systems must be incorporated into the CMS for managers to make appropriate decisions, as discussed in the following section.

DETERMINE DESIRED OUTPUTS OF CMS

LO.4
WHAT THREE GROUPS OF ELEMENTS AFFECT THE DESIGN OF A COST MANAGEMENT SYSTEM, AND WHAT ARE THE PURPOSES OF THESE ELEMENTS?

A cost management system is composed of three primary elements: motivational elements, information elements, and reporting elements. These elements are detailed in Exhibit 12–10. The elements as a whole must be internally consistent, and the individually selected elements must be consistent with the strategies and missions of the subunits. Different aspects of these elements can be used for different purposes. For example, numerous measures of performance can be specified, but only certain measures will be appropriate for specific purposes.

Motivational Elements

What three sets of elements compose a CMS?

Performance measurements are chosen so as to be consistent with organizational goals and objectives and to motivate or "drive" managers toward designated achievements. These measurements can be quantitative or nonquantitative, financial or nonfinancial, and short term or long term. For example, if a subunit is expected to generate a specified amount of profit for the year, the performance measure has been set to be quantitative, financial, and short term. A longer-term performance measure might be an average increase in profit or change in stock price over a 5-to-10-year period.

Today performance measures and rewards should be designed to support organizational missions and competitive strategies, to motivate employees and managers to act in the best interest of the organization and its subunits, and to help

EXHIBIT 12–10

**COST MANAGEMENT
SYSTEM ELEMENTS**

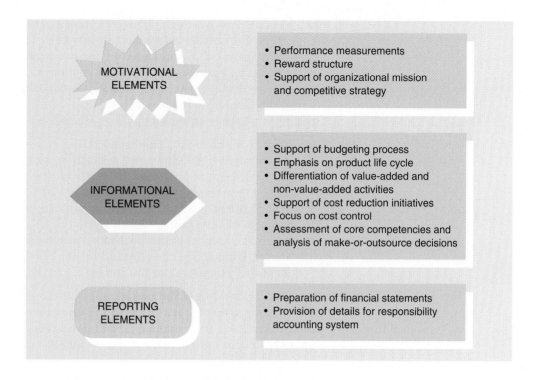

MOTIVATIONAL
ELEMENTS

- Performance measurements
- Reward structure
- Support of organizational mission
  and competitive strategy

INFORMATIONAL
ELEMENTS

- Support of budgeting process
- Emphasis on product life cycle
- Differentiation of value-added and
  non-value-added activities
- Support of cost reduction initiatives
- Focus on cost control
- Assessment of core competencies and
  analysis of make-or-outsource decisions

REPORTING
ELEMENTS

- Preparation of financial statements
- Provision of details for responsibility
  accounting system

recruit and retain qualified employees. Once defined, the criteria used to measure performance should be linked to the organizational incentive system because "you get what you measure." This linkage sends the message to managers that they will be rewarded in line with the quality of their organizational and subunit decisions and, thereby, their contributions to achieving the organizational mission.

In addition to performance measures, different forms of rewards have different incentive effects and can reflect different time orientations. In general, longer-term incentives encourage managers to be more long-term oriented in their decisions while short-term incentives encourage managers to be focused on the near future.

To illustrate, cash is the most obvious reward for short-term performance. All managers receive some compensation in cash for paying living expenses. However, once a manager receives a cash reward, its value does not depend on future performance. In contrast, a stock option that is not exercisable until a future time provides a manager an incentive to be more concerned about long-term performance. The ultimate value of the stock option is determined in the future when the option is exercised rather than on the date it is received. Thus, the option's value is related more to long-term than to short-term organizational performance.

Performance rewards for top management can consist of both short-term and long-term incentives. Normally, a major incentive is performance-based pay that is tied to the firm's stock price. The rewards for subunit managers should be based on the specific subunit's mission. For example, managers of subunits charged with a "build" mission should receive long-term incentives. These managers need to be concerned about long-term success and be willing to make short-term sacrifices for long-term gains. In contrast, managers of subunits charged with a "harvest" mission must be more oriented to the short term. These subunits are expected to squeeze out as much cash and profit as possible from their operations. Accordingly, incentives should be in place to encourage these managers to have a short-term focus in decision making.

Today's companies experiment with a variety of incentives as "carrots" to induce employees and managers to act in the best interest of customers and shareholders. **Profit sharing** refers to compensation that is contingent on the level of

profit sharing

organizational profit generated. This type of pay is a powerful incentive and is now used in virtually every U.S. industry.

Selection of performance measurements and the reward structure is important because managers evaluate decision alternatives based on how the outcomes could impact the selected performance (measurement and reward) criteria.[10] Because higher performance equals a larger reward, the cost management system must have specified performance "yardsticks" and provide measurement information to the appropriate individuals for evaluation purposes. Performance measurement is meaningful only in a comparative or relative sense. Typically, current performance is assessed relative to past or expected performance or relative to customer expectations.

Informational Elements

An organization's accounting function is expected to support managers' abilities to plan, control, make decisions, and evaluate performance. These functions converge in a system designed for cost management. Relative to the planning role, the cost management system should provide a sound foundation for the financial budgeting process.

Budgets provide both a specification of expected achievement and a benchmark against which to compare actual performance. A CMS should both provide the financial information needed for budget preparation and disclose the cost drivers of activities so that more useful simulations of alternative scenarios can be made. The system should be able to highlight any activities that have a poor cost–benefit relationship so that they can be reduced or eliminated and, in turn, reduce organizational costs and improve profits.

As firms find it more difficult to maintain a competitive advantage, they must place greater emphasis on managing the product life cycle. As discussed earlier in this chapter, most actions available to managers to control costs are concentrated in the earliest stages of the product life cycle. Accordingly, information relevant to managing costs must be focused on decisions made during those stages. That information will be provided by a well-designed and integrated cost management system.

Product life cycles are getting shorter as firms become more and more adept at duplicating their competitors' offerings. In the future, managers will confront the fact that products will spend less time in the maturity stage of the product life cycle. Firms will be forced to find ways to continue to "squeeze" cash from their mature products to support new product development. Additionally, the future will place greater emphasis on a firm's ability to adapt to changing competitive conditions. Flexibility will be an important organizational attribute and will cause managers to change the emphasis of control systems (see Exhibit 12–11).

To provide information relevant to product design and development, the CMS must be able to relate resource consumption and cost to alternative product and process designs. Computer simulation models are useful in relating products to activities. In addition to focusing information on the front end of the product life cycle, capital spending is becoming an increasingly important tool in cost management, especially relative to new technology acquisition decisions. Decisions about capital investments affect a firm's future cost structure and, hence, the extent to which short-term actions can effect a change in the level of total costs.

Lastly, the system should produce cost information with minimal distortions from improper or inaccurate allocations or from improper exclusions. Improper exclusions usually relate to the influence of financial accounting, such as the mandate to expense product development and distribution costs. If the system minimizes these cost distortions, cost assignments are more relevant for control purposes and for internal decision making.

---

[10] Performance measurements and rewards are discussed in greater depth in Chapter 19.

EXHIBIT 12–11

SHIFT IN CONTROL EMPHASIS IN FUTURE COMPETITIVE ENVIRONMENTS

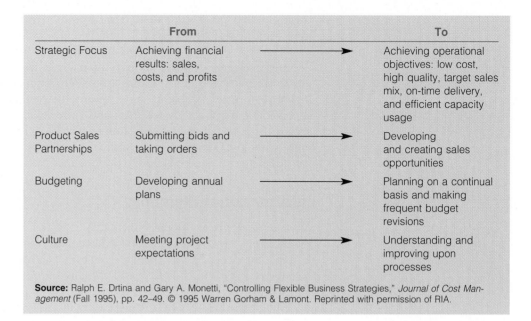

	From		To
Strategic Focus	Achieving financial results: sales, costs, and profits	→	Achieving operational objectives: low cost, high quality, target sales mix, on-time delivery, and efficient capacity usage
Product Sales Partnerships	Submitting bids and taking orders	→	Developing and creating sales opportunities
Budgeting	Developing annual plans	→	Planning on a continual basis and making frequent budget revisions
Culture	Meeting project expectations	→	Understanding and improving upon processes

Source: Ralph E. Drtina and Gary A. Monetti, "Controlling Flexible Business Strategies," *Journal of Cost Management* (Fall 1995), pp. 42–49. © 1995 Warren Gorham & Lamont. Reprinted with permission of RIA.

The information required to support decisions depends on the unique situational factors of the firm and its subunits. The information system must enable the decision maker to evaluate how alternative decision choices would impact the items that are used to measure and evaluate the decision maker's performance. Techniques discussed in other chapters, such as relevant costing, quality cost management, job order and process costing, and cost-volume-profit analysis, relate to the role of cost information in decision making. Many decisions involve comparing the benefit received from some action (such as serving a given customer) to the costs of that action. Only if the cost data contain minimal distortion can managers make valid cost–benefit assessments.

Reporting Elements

The reporting elements of a cost management system refer to methods of providing information to persons in evaluative roles. First and foremost, the CMS must be effective in generating fundamental financial statement information such as inventory valuations and cost of sales. Regardless of whether such information is used for internal planning, control, decision making, or performance evaluation, there should be little difficulty generating an "external" product or service cost if the feeder systems to the CMS have been appropriately integrated and the system itself is designed to minimize distortions.

In addition to financial statement valuations, the reporting elements of the cost management system must address internal needs of a responsibility accounting system. This system provides information to top management about the performance of organizational subunits and their managers.[11] For each subunit, the responsibility accounting system separately tracks costs and, if appropriate, revenues.

Performance reports are useful only to the extent that the actual performance of a given manager or subunit can be compared to a meaningful baseline, such as a measure of expected performance. Expected performance can be denoted in financial terms, such as budgetary amounts, or in nonfinancial terms, such as throughput, customer satisfaction measures, lead time, capacity utilization, and research and development activities. By comparing actual and expected performance, top managers are able to determine which managers and subunits performed ac-

---

[11] Responsibility accounting concepts are discussed in detail in Chapter 13.

cording to expectations and which exceeded or failed to meet expectations. Using this information that has been processed and formulated by the CMS, top managers link decisions about managerial rewards to performance.

The movement toward decentralization has increased the importance of an effective reporting system. With decentralization, top managers must depend on the reporting system to keep all organizational subunits aligned with their subunit missions as well as organizational goals and objectives. A CMS is not designed to "cut" costs. It exists to ensure that a satisfactory yield (revenue) is realized from the incurrence of costs. Accordingly, cost management begins with an understanding that different costs are incurred for different purposes. Some costs are incurred to yield immediate benefits; others are expected to yield benefits in the near or distant future.

Sorting organizational activities according to their strategic roles facilitates effective cost management.

GETTY IMAGES

Only by linking costs to activities and activities to strategies can the yield on costs be understood. Thus, to achieve effective cost management, it is useful to start by sorting organizational activities according to their strategic roles. This logic suggests that organizational management is made easier by breaking down operations into subunits. By so doing, top managers can assign responsibility and accountability for distinct subunit missions to a particular manager. In turn, by creating the proper incentives for each subunit manager, top management will have set the stage for each subunit manager to act in the best interest of the overall organization. This linkage is the start of a process that focuses a specific subunit manager's attention on a set of costs and activities that uniquely relates to the subunit's organizational mission.

Costs can be effectively managed by subunit managers only when they are provided with relevant information. Because the nature and time horizon of decisions made by managers vary across subunits, each manager requires unique information. Accountants face the task of providing information that is tailored to each subunit manager's context. In addition to information about decision alternatives, managers need to know how the alternatives are likely to impact their expected rewards.

The role of a reporting system is to compare actual performance to benchmark performance for each manager. On the basis of this comparison, the relative rewards of subunit managers are determined. Accordingly, this comparison is a key source of motivation for subunit managers to act in the best interest of the organization. Optimal organizational performance is realized only if there is consistency for each subunit across the motivation, information, and reporting elements. Managers of subunits with a "build" mission need information tailored to their competitive strategies and focused on the early stages of the product life cycle. Their incentives to manage costs need to be relatively long term, and their reward structures should emphasize success in the areas of product development and design and market share growth. Alternatively, subunit managers of mature businesses need information that pertains more to short-term competition. Their reward and reporting structures should emphasize near-term profit and cash flow.

One of the evolving challenges in today's business environment is the management of activities across an entire supply chain. Competition is prevalent among supply or "value" chains as well as individual businesses. Thus, future financial specialists will develop cost management systems that include activities not occurring within single firms but occurring within a supply chain and involving several firms.

Because most businesses have some type of CMS in place, most CMS design and implementation issues relate to modifications of the current system. The analysis of existing systems is discussed next.

PERFORM GAP ANALYSIS AND ASSESS IMPROVEMENTS

LO.5

WHAT IS GAP ANALYSIS AND HOW IS IT USED IN THE IMPLEMENTATION OF A COST MANAGEMENT SYSTEM?

gap analysis

How is gap analysis used to improve a CMS?

After the organization and its subunits have been structured and the CMS elements have been determined, the current information system(s) should be evaluated. **Gap analysis** is the study of the differences between two information systems, often a current system and a proposed system. Gap analysis allows a comparison of the information that is currently available with the information that is needed to assess the degree of conformity between the systems. Any differences represent "gaps" or "spaces" to be overcome. In many situations, it is impossible to eliminate all system gaps in the short term potentially because of software or hardware capability or availability. Methods of reducing or eliminating the gaps, including all related technical requirements and changes to existing feeder systems, should be specified in detail. These details should be expressed, qualitatively and quantitatively, in terms of costs and benefits.

In the common circumstance of limited resources, top management can prioritize which gap issues to be addressed and in what order. As system implementation proceeds, management should assess the effectiveness of the improvements and determine the need for others. Once the CMS has been established, previously identified gaps can become irrelevant or can rise in rank of priority. Only through continuous improvement efforts can the cost management system provide an ongoing, viable network of information to users.

Technological impact on cost management system design and implementation is significant. With advancements in technology, it is becoming possible to link a company's feeder systems into a truly integrated cost management system. **Enterprise resource planning (ERP) systems** are packaged business software systems that allow companies to do the following:[12]

enterprise resource planning (ERP) system

- standardize information systems and replace different "legacy" systems;
- integrate information systems and automate the transfer of data among systems;
- improve the quality of information, including purchase preferences of customers; and
- improve the timeliness of information by providing real-time, on-line reporting.

ERP software often involves a large number of separate modules that collect data from individual processes in the firm (sales, shipping, distribution, and so forth) and assemble that data in a form accessible by all managers. ERP is discussed in detail in Chapter 18.

---

[12] Emily Brodeur and Paul Sharman, "ERP Cost and Performance Systems: Risks and Opportunities," *Journal of Cost Management* (March/April 2002), p. 21.

Revisiting

Imperial Sugar Company processes or "refines" raw sugar into the refined sugar purchased and consumed in households across America. Unlike manufacturing firms that typically operate on gross margins of 35 percent to 40 percent of sales, Imperial operates on a razor-thin gross margin of about 8 percent of sales. The company must fund selling and administration expenses and provide for a profit from this 8 percent. Because sugar is a basic commodity consumed in nearly every country and because sugar is produced in 121 countries, the market and the competition in the industry is global.

In its early years, Imperial Sugar Company not only refined raw sugar but also produced raw sugar from processing sugar cane. Today the company has narrowed its focus in the value chain to refining raw sugar into processed sugar and managing the by-products, such as molasses, produced by the refining process.

Until 1988, Imperial Sugar Company was a regional sugar producer but since then, the company has purchased Holly Sugar Corporation, a Colorado-based company producing beet sugar, and Spreckels Sugar Company of California, also a beet sugar producer. The largest acquisition occurred in 1997 when Imperial acquired Savannah Foods & Industries, the second largest sugar refiner in the industry, which manufactured the Dixie Crystals® brand.

Since the late 1990s, Imperial Sugar and the industry have focused on becoming more efficient and cost effective, causing Imperial managers to close some facilities and sell others. By shedding itself of inefficient operations, the company has consolidated operations to obtain a higher rate of utilization of its fixed investment. These changes have allowed Imperial Sugar to endure the relentless pressure on prices and the onslaught of substitute products, such as sugar-free sweeteners and the corn-derived sweeteners that are now widely used in many industries, including soft drinks.

Sources: *http://www.tsha.utexas.edu/handbook/online/articles/view/II/diicy.html; http://www.imperialsugar.com; http://www.sucrose.com.*

Appendix

Cost Management System Conceptual Design Principles

"In 1986, **Computer Aided Manufacturing-International, Inc.** (CAM-I) formed a consortium of progressive industrial organizations, professional accounting firms, and government agencies to define the role of cost management in the new advanced manufacturing environment."[13] One outcome of this consortium was a conceptual framework of principles (listed in Exhibit 12–12) for designing a cost management system. If a CMS provides the suggested information relating to costs, performance measurements, and investment management, that system will be relevant to management's decision-making needs. Although compatible with existing cost accounting systems, the set of principles as a whole suggests a radical departure from traditional practices. The practices focus management attention on organizational activities, product life cycles, integrating cost management and performance measurement, and integrating investment management and strategic management.

[13] Callie Berliner and James A. Brimson, eds., *Cost Management for Today's Advanced Manufacturing* (Boston: Harvard Business School Press, 1988), p. vii.

EXHIBIT 12–12

**CMS CONCEPTUAL
DESIGN PRINCIPLES**

Cost Principles

- Identify costs of non-value-added activities to improve use of resources.
- Recognize holding costs as a non-value-added activity traceable directly to a product.
- Significant costs should be directly traceable to management reporting objectives.
- Separate cost centers should be established for each homogeneous group of activities consistent with organizational responsibility.
- Activity-based cost accumulation and reporting will improve cost traceability.
- Separate bases for allocations should be developed to reflect causal relations between activity costs and management reporting objectives.
- Costs should be consistent with the requirement to support life-cycle management.
- Technology costs should be assigned directly to products.
- Actual product cost should be measured against target cost to support elimination of waste.
- Cost-effective approaches for internal control should be developed as a company automates.

Performance Measurement Principles

- Performance measures should establish congruence with a company's objectives.
- Performance measures should be established for significant activities.
- Performance measures should be established to improve visibility of cost drivers.
- Financial and nonfinancial activities should be included in the performance measurement system.

Investment Management Principles

- Investment management should be viewed as more than the capital budgeting process.
- Investment management decisions should be consistent with company goals.
- Multiple criteria should be used to evaluate investment decisions.
- Investments and attendant risks should be considered interrelated elements of an investment strategy.
- Activity data should be traceable to the specific investment opportunity.
- Investment management decisions should support the reduction or elimination of non-value-added activities.
- Investment management decisions should support achieving target cost.

Source: Callie Berliner and James A. Brimson, eds., *Cost Management for Today's Advanced Manufacturing* (Boston: Harvard Business School Press, 1988), pp. 13–18. Reprinted by permission of Harvard Business School Press. Copyright 1988 by CAM-1. All rights reserved.

Comprehensive Review Module

Chapter Summary

1. Organizations have management control systems to

    *   implement strategic and operating plans.

    *   provide a means for comparison of actual to planned results for management control purposes.

2. A cost management system (CMS)

    *   is a set of formal methods developed for planning and controlling an organization's cost-generating activities relative to its short-term objectives and long-term strategies.

    *   has a short-term goal of making efficient use of organizational resources.

    *   has a long-term goal of ensuring the organization's survival.

3. The design of a CMS is influenced by the

    *   organizational form through, for example, laws that determine who within the organization is entitled to be a decision maker.

    *   organizational structure because it

        ➢   determines how authority and responsibility are distributed in an organization.

        ➢   indicates who is accountable, what they are accountable for, and the nature of information needed by each decision maker.

    *   organizational culture because it determines

        ➢   how people interact with each other in the organization.

        ➢   the extent to which individuals take authority and assume responsibility for organizational outcomes.

    *   organizational mission.

    *   organizational core competencies.

    *   external environment because it determines the

        ➢   nature and extent of competitive pressures bearing on the organization.

        ➢   industry's competitive dimensions and the bases on which organizations compete.

    *   organizational strategies that influence the

        ➢   organizational cost structure.

        ➢   managerial preferences in responding to competitive pressures.

4. Elements that affect the design of a CMS are

    *   motivational, which is used to influence managers and employees to exert high effort and to act in the organization's interests.

    *   informational, which is selected to provide the appropriate information to managers who are responsible for making decisions and for making the organization effective and efficient in its operations.

    *   reporting, which is selected to provide feedback to, and to provide consequences for, managers and employees.

5. Gap analysis

    *   is a tool that can help identify and prioritize necessary changes in a CMS.

    *   assesses differences between an organization's ideal CMS and the organization's existing CMS.

Key Terms

black box *(p. 484)*
cost management system (CMS)
    (p. 484)
cost structure *(p. 491)*
enterprise resource planning (ERP)
    system *(p. 498)*

gap analysis *(p. 498)*
management control system (MCS)
    (p. 483)
management information system
    (MIS) *(p. 482)*
organizational culture *(p. 489)*

organizational form *(p. 487)*
profit sharing *(p. 494)*
radio frequency identification
    (RFID) *(p. 486)*

Questions

1. How can a company evaluate whether it is effectively managing its costs?

2. What is a control system? What purpose does a control system serve in an organization?

3. Why does a cost management system necessarily have both a short-term and long-term focus?

4. Why is it not possible simply to take a cost management system "off the shelf"?

5. How does the choice of organizational form influence the design of a firm's cost management system?

6. What information could be generated by a cost management system that would help an organization manage its core competencies?

7. How could an organization's culture be used as a control mechanism?

8. How does a product's life-cycle stage influence the nature of information required to successfully manage costs of that product?

9. In the present highly competitive environment, why has cost management risen to such a high level of concern while price management has declined in importance?

10. (*Appendix*) What was CAM-I, and why was it organized?

Exercises

WebTUTOR Advantage

11. (Cost management and strategy) As a financial analyst, you have just been handed a 2006 financial report of Firm Z, a large, global pharmaceutical company. Firm Z competes in both traditional pharmaceutical products and in evolving biotechnology products. The following data (in billions) on Firm Z and the pharmaceutical industry are available:

	Firm Z	Industry Average
Sales	$2.00	$0.960
Net income	0.54	0.096
Advertising	0.04	0.160
Research and development	0.16	0.240
New investment in facilities	0.20	0.240

Given these data, evaluate the cost management performance of Firm Z.

12. (Cost management and strategy) Following are descriptions of three businesses. For each, assume that you are the CEO. Identify the most critical information you would need to manage the strategic decisions of that business.

a. Private hospital that competes on the basis of delivering high-quality services to an upscale clientele.

b. Small, high-technology firm that has just developed its first product and will begin marketing it in the coming quarter; five other products are under development.

c. **American Sugar Company**, which is a large competitor of Imperial Sugar Co., the company discussed in the chapter's opening vignette.

13. (Organizational form) Write a paper that compares and contrasts the corporate, general partnership, limited partnership, LLP, and LLC forms of business. At a minimum, discuss issues related to formation, capital generation, managerial authority and responsibility, taxation, ownership liability, and implications for success in mission and objectives.

14. (Cost management and organizational culture) Use Internet resources to gather information on any two firms in the same industry. The following examples are possible pairs to compare.
- **Delta Air Lines** and **Southwest Airlines**
- **ChevronTexaco** and **BP**
- **Nordstrom's** and **Wal-Mart**
- **Oracle** and **Microsoft**
- **Gateway** and **Dell Computer**

In your discussion, address the following questions:

a. Compare and contrast the organizational cultures of the firms.

b. Compare and contrast the operating performance of the firms.

c. Which of the pair is the better operating performer? Discuss the criteria used to make this determination.

b. Do you believe that organizational culture has any relationship to the differences in operations? Why?

15. (Cost management and technology) Many firms now engage in some form of B2B Internet-based commerce. A specific type is B2B buy-side, which is Internet technology that allows firms to solicit bids on inputs that the firms require to support production, sales, and administration. Interested and qualified vendors can view the bid specifications and then electronically submit offers to sell the firms the needed inputs. Search the Internet to learn about B2B buy-side systems, and then discuss how a small firm could use a B2B buy-side system to reduce its supply chain costs.

16. (Organizational strategy) Use Internet resources to find a company (regardless of where it is domiciled) whose managers have chosen to (a) avoid competition through differentiation, (b) avoid competition through cost leadership, and (c) confront competitors head on. Analyze each of these strategies and discuss your perception of how well that strategy has worked.

17. (Cost management and organizational objectives) Prepare an oral presentation discussing how accounting information can (a) help and (b) hinder an organization's progress toward its mission and objectives. Be sure to differentiate between the effects of what you perceive as "traditional" versus "nontraditional" accounting information.

18. (Organizational culture) Write a paper describing the organizational culture at a job you have held or at the college or university that you attend. Be sure to include a discussion of the value system and how it was communicated to new employees or new students.

Problems

19. (Cost management and strategy) You are the product manager at a silicone chip manufacturer. One of your products is a commodity chip that the electronics industry widely uses in cell phones, printers, digital cameras, and so forth. As product manager, you have full profit responsibility for the commodity chip.

The commodity chip is a "cash cow" for your company and enjoys an enviable market share in the industry. Because your company's chip is approximately the same as chips available from competitors, market competition for this product is primarily based on price.

Because of your success in managing the commodity chip, you were recently promoted to product manager of ZX chip, the most innovative chip your company has ever developed. It is innovative because of its data processing speed, miniature size, and incredible functionality. The ZX chip has just completed final testing and will be ready to be presented to the market in two weeks.

You were successful in managing the commodity chip because you kept unit production cost low by achieving high volume and efficient production. Identify and discuss the key variables you will try to manage to make the ZX chip as successful as the commodity chip. Discuss how your efforts to manage costs will be similar to and different from your efforts to manage costs of the commodity chip.

20. (Information and cost management) The price of a product or service is a function of the total costs of producing that product or service. In turn, the total cost of producing a product or service is a function of the aggregate of costs incurred throughout the supply chain.

Higher education is one industry that has been characterized by rapidly rising costs and rapidly rising prices. Study the supply chain of your college or university and prepare a table identifying specific ways in which an improved system of communications with suppliers and customers could result in specific cost savings for the institution, its suppliers, or its customers (students). Organize your table in three columns as follows.

Specific Information to Be Obtained	Information Source	Specific Cost to Be Reduced

21. (Alternative cost management strategies) In 1993, **Procter & Gamble** (P&G) management tried to control costs by eliminating many of its brands' coupons while increasing print advertising. Only a miniscule portion of the hundreds of billions of coupons distributed annually by P&G were ever redeemed by customers. Eliminating coupons allowed P&G to reduce its prices on most brands. After testing a market in the northeastern United States, P&G found that it lost 16 percent of its market share because competitors did not follow P&G in this move. Instead, competitors countered P&G's decrease in price promotions by increasing their price promotions. Although price promotions had been unprofitable, discontinuing them while competitors did not was even more unprofitable for the company. P&G probably anticipated losing some market share in exchange for more profitability and equity for its brands but not to the degree that occurred. Advertising was expected to reverse the damage to penetration.[14]

a. What costs and benefits did P&G likely consider in its discontinuance of coupons?

b. What was P&G's apparent strategy in deciding to lower prices? Explain.

[14] Raju Narisetti, "P&G Ad Chief Plots Demise of the Coupon," *The Wall Street Journal* (April 17, 1996), pp. B1, B5A; and Tim Amber, "P&G Learnt the Hard Way from Dropping Its Price Promotions," *Marketing* (June 7, 2001), pp. 22–23.

22. (Cost management and customer service) Companies sometimes experience difficult financial times, sometimes so drastic that they declare bankruptcy. If a firm either does not conduct sufficient R&D or if its R&D is not sufficiently effective, it will soon find that many of its products are in the decline phase of their life cycles. With the exception of a very few products in the development stages of their product life cycles, **Polaroid Corp.** found itself in this dilemma and was forced to file for Chapter 11 bankruptcy in October 2001. Polaroid had been unable to adequately reduce costs or increase cash flow, and its financial condition had deteriorated to the extent that it was unable to pay some of its debts.

Companies also find themselves in situations that necessitate better cost management for a variety of reasons. A healthy firm can discover that its competitors are taking away market share because they are able to offer customers lower prices by operating with greater efficiencies. If the healthy firm lowers its prices but does nothing to reduce its costs, its operating profits will decline, and stockholders will ultimately experience diminished market values in the company's stock prices.

In highly competitive industries in which many companies are positioned for high volumes of sales, the risk of market downturn exists. In this situation, companies must reduce costs and operations without damaging the company's future. Belt-tightening cannot be excluded from management's responsibilities. Surely, however, managers can go beyond using unimaginative across-the-board cost cutting.

a. What is the implied mission (build, hold, or harvest) for most of the Polaroid Corp. products? Explain.

b. When are across-the-board spending cuts a rational approach to cost management?

c. How could a cost management system help avoid the adverse effects of cost cutting?

23. (Cost management: short term vs. long term) Northwest Metals Co. produces steel products for a variety of customers. One division of the company is Residential Products Division, created in the late 1940s. Since that time, this division's principal products have been galvanized steel components used in garage door installations. The division has been continuously profitable since 1950, and in 2004, it generated $10 million of profits on $300 million of sales.

However, over the past 10 years, divisional growth has been slow; profitability has become stagnant, and few new products have been developed, although the garage door components market has matured. Company president John Stamp has asked his senior staff to evaluate operations of the Residential Products Division and to recommend changes that would improve its operations. The staff uncovered the following facts:

- Tonya Calley, age 53, has been division president for the past 15 years. Her compensation package includes an annual salary of $175,000 plus a cash bonus based on achievement of the budgeted level of annual profit.

- Growth in sales in the residential metal products industry has averaged 12 percent annually over the past decade. Most of the growth has occurred in ornamental products used in residential privacy fencing.

- Nationally, the division's market share in the overall residential metal products industry has dropped from 12 percent to 7 percent during the past 10 years and has dropped from 40 percent to 25 percent for garage door components.

- The division maintains its own information systems, which are essentially the same systems that were in place 15 years ago; however, some of the manual systems have been computerized (e.g., payroll, accounts payable, accounting).

- The division has no customer service department. A small sales staff solicits and takes orders by phone from national distribution chains.
- The major intradivision communication tool is the annual operating budget. No formal statements have been prepared in the division regarding strategies, mission, values, goals and objectives, or identifying core competencies.

Given this information, identify the major problems in the Residential Products Division and develop recommendations to address the problems you have identified.

WebTUTOR Advantage

24. (Cost management and profitability) After graduating last year from an Ivy League university, Jill Young was hired as a stock analyst. Wanting to make her mark on the industry, Young issued a scathing report on a major discount department store retailer, Smart-Mart. The basis of her attack was a comparative analysis between Smart-Mart and Tracy's Department Store, an upscale, full-service department store. Some of the information cited in Young's report follows.

Items as Percent of Sales	Smart-Mart	Tracy's
Cost of goods sold	65%	55%
Gross margin	35	45
Selling and administration	27	33
Profit	8	12

Based on the comparative analysis, Young issued to the firm's clients a "sell" recommendation for Smart-Mart and a "buy" recommendation for Tracy's. The gist of Young's rationale for the recommendations was that Tracy's Department Store was outperforming Smart-Mart in the crucial area of cost management as evidenced by both a higher profit as a percent of sales and a higher gross margin as a percent of sales.

a. Evaluate Young's recommendations given the limited evidence available.

b. Because the two firms contrasted by Young have different strategies, what performance criteria would you use to evaluate their competitiveness in the industry?

25. (Cost management; product life cycle) In May 2004, **Krispy Kreme Doughnuts** issued a profit warning to investors. In the warning, the company indicated full-year earnings would be 10 percent below previous expectations. In the weeks immediately following the profit warning, the stock price of Krispy Kreme (ticker symbol KKD) dropped by more than 33 percent.

a. Using Internet resources, identify the economic reasons cited by Krispy Kreme management for the profit warning issued in May 2004.

b. Applying your understanding of product life cycle, explain why Krispy Kreme's stock price dropped so significantly following the profit warning.

c. Following the profit warning in May 2004, what specific actions did managers take to improve profitability? Do any of these actions suggest that Krispy Kreme had revised its strategy in May 2004?

d. Discuss your evaluation of Krispy Kreme's CMS based on the events occurring in May 2004.

26. (Stakeholders; cost management) Laura Thompson, newly appointed controller of Allied Networking Services Inc. (ANSI), a rapidly growing company, has just been asked to serve as lead facilitator of a team charged with designing a cost management system (CMS) at ANSI. Also serving on the team are Tom Weiss, company president; Susan Turner, vice president of finance; and George Wipple, vice president of marketing.

At the team's organizational meeting, Weiss suggested that the performance measurements to be built into the CMS should have a primary focus based on ANSI's ultimate goal. Thompson advised the team that it would therefore be necessary for the team to work first to gain consensus on the issue of an appropriate goal on which to focus the emphasis for the CMS's primary measurements.

When the team members pressed Weiss for what he thought ANSI's goal should be, he indicated that he believed that maximization of company profits was the most reasonable choice. At this, Wipple chimed in that because sales are the lifeblood of the company, the team should think about making customer satisfaction ANSI's ultimate goal.

Turner, who had been silently listening to the discussion, was prompted by Thompson to give her opinion on the issue. Turner said that much of the professional literature advocates maximization of shareholder wealth as the ultimate goal of business. She did not see why it should not be the same at ANSI. After all, the stockholders provide the financial capital, take the ultimate risk, and are responsible for organizing the company. Therefore, she asserted, the primary emphasis of measurements in the CMS should focus on whether or not stockholder wealth is being maximized.

A heated debate ensued. Wipple said, "Look, without customers, the company has no reason for being in existence—how profitable is a company without customers, and how well off would its managers and stockholders be without revenues?" To this, Turner replied, "Without stockholder funds, you have no company!" Weiss responded, "Unless we manage ANSI profitably, there'll be no company to provide customers with products and services or to provide a basis for stockholder wealth!" The team decided to reconvene after everyone had a chance to assess what had been said.

a. Should the CMS design team be deciding the company's ultimate goal? If not, who should make such a decision?

b. What do you believe should be the ultimate goal for a business? Defend your answer.

c. Can one group of stakeholders effectively be served at the expense of the other stakeholders? Discuss.

27. (CMS; MIS; ethics in reporting) The value of an oil and gas company is tied to two fundamental circumstances. The first is the amount of oil and gas the company is presently producing. This amount, along with unit prices, determines the revenue and cash inflow that the company generates. The second circumstance is the level of oil and gas reserves controlled by the company. Over the long haul, the reserve level is a constraint on the amount and cost of current oil and gas production. Accordingly, the capital markets evaluate the performance of oil and gas companies as much on management of reserves as on management of current production. Because investors use information about reserves to value oil and gas companies, the SEC has developed rules for classifying and reporting reserves.

In a series of several announcements in early 2004, **Shell Oil** (Royal Dutch/Shell Group of Cos.) downgraded its proven oil and gas reserves by more than 20 percent, or about 4.5 billion barrels. Most of the misstatements of reserves, which were revealed to the pubic in 2004, had been booked in the years 1997 to 2000. Following the 2004 disclosures, regulatory bodies, including the SEC and the U.S. Justice Department, opened inquiries into the misreporting of reserves to determine if there had been violations of reporting rules or other laws.

a. Assume that the misreporting of reserves by Shell resulted from the MIS's generation of unintentional but inaccurate information. From a cost management perspective, how might the CMS, built on inaccurate data, have caused managers to take actions that were not in the company's best long-run interests? What actions could managers have taken to ensure the reliability of the data?

b. Assume that Shell intentionally misreported reserves. Discuss how the CMS, if not properly designed, could have contributed to the misreporting.

c. Discuss the ethics of manipulating financial and fundamental data for the purpose of managing (misleading) perceptions of investors and other interested users of company information.

28. (Cost management; social responsibility) Through its three sets of elements (motivational, informational, and reporting), a CMS focuses the attention of a given decision maker on the data and information that are crucial to that decision maker's responsibilities in the organization. However, the nature and scope of information generated by the CMS for that decision maker are often limited by traditions of financial reporting and the imaginations of CMS designers. A common omission from a CMS is information useful in meeting a firm's social responsibility.

Consider the possibility that a CMS could be developed that would be informative relative to organizational performance from the following perspectives: minorities, local community, customers, employees, and the environment. Discuss how this information could be used to manage the following specific expenses.

a. product liability costs

b. local property taxes

c. pollution remediation

d. costs associated with employee turnover

e. warranty expense

13

Responsibility Accounting and Transfer Pricing in Decentralized Organizations

Objectives

AFTER COMPLETING THIS CHAPTER, YOU SHOULD BE ABLE TO ANSWER THE FOLLOWING QUESTIONS:

LO.1 WHICH ORGANIZATIONAL CHARACTERISTICS DETERMINE WHETHER A FIRM SHOULD BE DECENTRALIZED OR CENTRALIZED?

LO.2 HOW ARE DECENTRALIZATION AND RESPONSIBILITY ACCOUNTING RELATED?

LO.3 WHAT ARE THE DIFFERENCES AMONG THE FOUR PRIMARY TYPES OF RESPONSIBILITY CENTERS?

LO.4 WHY AND HOW ARE SERVICE DEPARTMENT COSTS ALLOCATED TO REVENUE-PRODUCING DEPARTMENTS?

LO.5 WHAT TYPES OF TRANSFER PRICES ARE USED IN ORGANIZATIONS, AND WHY ARE SUCH PRICES USED?

LO.6 WHAT DIFFICULTIES CAN BE ENCOUNTERED BY MULTINATIONAL COMPANIES USING TRANSFER PRICES?

Founded in the mid-1880s, **Johnson & Johnson** (J&J) had its beginnings in New Brunswick, New Jersey, as a partnership of brothers having 14 employees. Using Sir Joseph Lister's antiseptic methods, J&J began selling surgical dressings. International growth began in 1919 with the establishment of a Canadian affiliate but, after an around-the-world trip, the sons of one of the company founders convinced the company of the need to establish a true global presence. As of 2004, J&J has operations in 57 countries, sells products in more than 175 countries, is composed of more than 200 operating companies, and has approximately 110,000 employees. The company is the world's most comprehensive and broadly based manufacturer of health care products, as well as a provider of related services for the consumer, pharmaceutical, and professional markets.

Under the leadership of General Wood Johnson, J&J began a policy of decentralization, giving autonomy to the ever-increasing number of divisions to provide them the opportunity to chart their own futures. Additionally, in 1943, General Johnson created the Credo that underlies the company's approach to business conduct. The Credo declares that the company is responsible to its customers, employees, communities, and stockholders. The deliberate ordering of these groups proclaims a bold business philosophy: If the

company meets the first three responsibilities, the fourth will take care of itself.

Each of the company's global affiliates is highly autonomous and accountable for its individual performance; with a few exceptions, local citizens manage international subsidiaries. This structure allows J&J to effectively support its business strategy and helps the affiliates and operating units focus on that part of the business in which their accountability and expertise lie.

The segments and their affiliates are then overlaid with a transparent structure of alignment and shared values. The company's worldwide headquarters provides guidance and services in several critical areas, including human resources, finance, advertising, law, and quality management. This arrangement enables J&J to leverage its size and influence to create outstanding synergy and efficiency. The real key to the success of the J&J organizational structure lies in the way the separate parts are managed so that they function as a single, cohesive entity.

Sources: Adapted from *Johnson & Johnson 2003 Annual Report*; *http://www.jnj.com/our_company/history*; *http://www.jnj.com/careers*; and *http://www.investor.jnj.com.* (*Note:* The company has videos available on its Web site entitled "Johnson & Johnson Today—2004" and "Our Credo—Worldwide" at *http://www.jnj.com/our_company/our_videos/index.htm.*)

An organization's structure typically evolves from highly centralized to highly decentralized as its goals, technology, and employees change. When top management retains the major portion of authority, centralization exists. Decentralization refers to top management's delegation of decision-making authority to subunit managers. **Johnson & Johnson** recognizes the need for decentralization in its corporate structure because the company's global operations demand that managers on location in any particular region be able to most effectively use corporate resources. This chapter describes the accounting methods—responsibility accounting, cost allocations, and transfer pricing—that are appropriate in decentralized organizations.

DECENTRALIZATION

LO.1
WHICH ORGANIZATIONAL CHARACTERISTICS DETERMINE WHETHER A FIRM SHOULD BE DECENTRALIZED OR CENTRALIZED?

decentralization

The degree of centralization can be viewed as a continuum. In a completely centralized firm, a single individual (usually the company owner or president) performs all major decision making and retains full authority and responsibility for that organization's activities. Alternatively, a purely decentralized organization would have virtually no central authority, and each subunit would act as a totally independent entity. **Decentralization** is a transfer of authority, responsibility, and decision-making rights from the top to the bottom of the organization structure. As with any management technique, decentralization has advantages and disadvantages, which are summarized in Exhibit 13–1.

EXHIBIT 13–1

**ADVANTAGES AND
DISADVANTAGES OF
DECENTRALIZATION**

Advantages

- Helps top management recognize and develop managerial talent.
- Allows managerial performance to be comparatively evaluated.
- Can often lead to greater job satisfaction and provides job enrichment.
- Makes the accomplishment of organizational goals and objectives easier.
- Reduces decision-making time.
- Allows the use of management by exception.

Disadvantages

- Can result in a lack of goal congruence or suboptimization by subunit managers.
- Requires more effective communication abilities because decision making is removed from the home office.
- Can create personnel difficulties upon introduction, especially if managers are unwilling or unable to delegate effectively.
- Can be extremely expensive, including costs of training and of making poor decisions.

What are the characteristics of firms that should prefer decentralized rather than centralized management?

A primary advantage of decentralization is that it allows companies to be more adept at employee development, especially in leadership training. For example, Johnson & Johnson's *i*-Lead process model (Exhibit 13–2) illustrates its commitment to the enhancement of employee leadership skills at all organizational levels.

One disadvantage of centralization that became very clear on September 11, 2001, was the consequence of a trend toward corporate centralization of IT workers, operations, and systems. Luckily, **Empire Blue Cross Blue Shield** (headquartered in one of the World Trade Center towers) had not followed that trend: The insurer had built a fully redundant IT architecture that was "designed to guarantee continuous uptime, regardless of catastrophes."[1] This redundancy allowed the company to continue the majority of its services in an uninterrupted fashion.

Either extreme of the centralization–decentralization continuum represents a clearly undesirable arrangement. In the totally centralized company, a single individual could have neither the expertise nor sufficient and timely information to make effective decisions in all functional areas. In the totally decentralized firm, subunits could act in ways that are inconsistent with the organization's goals.

Each organization tends to structure itself according to the pure centralization versus pure decentralization factors in Exhibit 13–3. Most businesses are, to some extent, somewhere in the middle of the continuum. The combination of managers' personal characteristics, nature of decisions required for organizational growth, and types of organizational activities lead a company to find the appropriate degree of decentralization.

Decentralization does not necessarily mean that a unit manager has the authority to make all decisions concerning that unit. Top management selectively determines the types of authority to delegate to and withhold from lower-level managers. As Johnson & Johnson does with legal and advertising, other decentralized companies can choose to organize certain organizational functions, such as cash management and purchasing, centrally.

Top management delegates decision-making authority but retains ultimate responsibility for decision outcomes. Thus, a sophisticated accounting and reporting responsibility accounting system must be implemented to provide top management information about overall subunit accountability as well as the ability to measure it.

[1] Jaikumar Vijayan, "Sept. 11 Attacks Prompt Decentralization Moves," *Computerworld* (December 17, 2001), p. 10.

EXHIBIT 13–2
JOHNSON & JOHNSON'S
***i*-LEAD MODEL**

In the *i*-Lead process:

• The *individual* drives the development process by seeking feedback and by demonstrating commitment to ongoing improvement.

• The *manager* supports the commitment of the individual, leading by example and establishing an effective communication process.

• The *organization* provides a culture that is supportive of leadership development at every level, while providing the systems, processes, tools, and resources necessary to develop leadership skills.

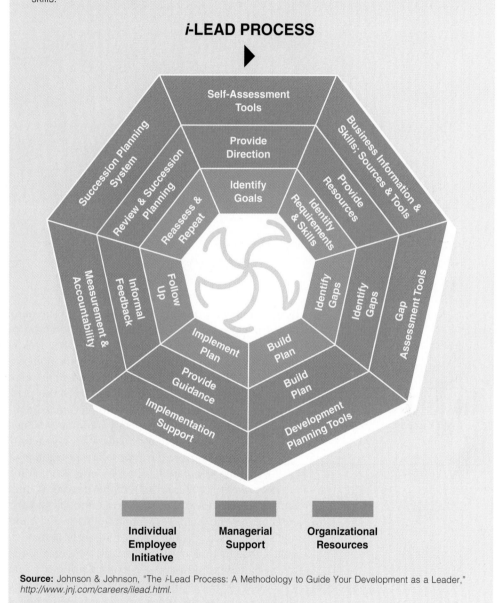

Source: Johnson & Johnson, "The *i*-Lead Process: A Methodology to Guide Your Development as a Leader," *http://www.jnj.com/careers/ilead.html.*

RESPONSIBILITY ACCOUNTING SYSTEMS

LO.2
HOW ARE DECENTRALIZATION AND RESPONSIBILITY ACCOUNTING RELATED?

A responsibility accounting system helps decentralization to work effectively by providing information about the performance, efficiency, and effectiveness of organizational subunits and their managers. Responsibility accounting implies subordinate managers' acceptance of communicated authority from top management.

EXHIBIT 13–3
DEGREE OF DECENTRALIZATION IN AN ORGANIZATIONAL STRUCTURE

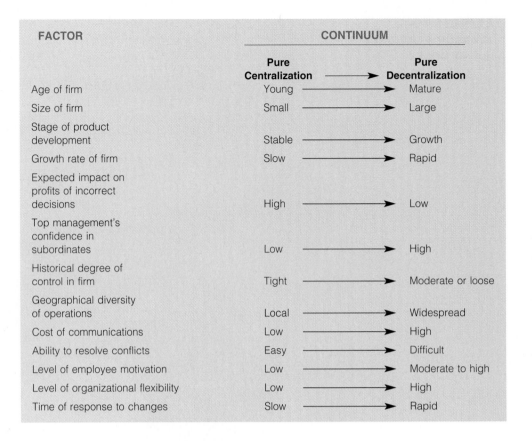

FACTOR	CONTINUUM	
	Pure Centralization ⟶	Pure Decentralization
Age of firm	Young ⟶	Mature
Size of firm	Small ⟶	Large
Stage of product development	Stable ⟶	Growth
Growth rate of firm	Slow ⟶	Rapid
Expected impact on profits of incorrect decisions	High ⟶	Low
Top management's confidence in subordinates	Low ⟶	High
Historical degree of control in firm	Tight ⟶	Moderate or loose
Geographical diversity of operations	Local ⟶	Widespread
Cost of communications	Low ⟶	High
Ability to resolve conflicts	Easy ⟶	Difficult
Level of employee motivation	Low ⟶	Moderate to high
Level of organizational flexibility	Low ⟶	High
Time of response to changes	Slow ⟶	Rapid

Responsibility accounting is consistent with standard costing and activity-based costing because each is implemented for a common purpose: control.

responsibility report

A responsibility accounting system produces **responsibility reports** that assist each successively higher level of management in evaluating the performances of subordinate managers and their respective organizational units. The reports should be tailored to fit the planning, controlling, and decision-making needs of subordinate managers and should include both monetary and nonmonetary information. See Exhibit 13–4 for some examples of important information to be shown in responsibility reports. Depending on the type of responsibility unit for which the report is being generated, all types of information are not necessarily available.

Why are performance data more aggregated for higher-level responsibility centers?

Responsibility should reflect the degree of influence that a unit's manager has on day-to-day operations and costs and should include only the revenues and/or costs under the manager's control. Normally, though, some of an organizational unit's costs are not controlled (or are only partially or indirectly controllable) by the unit manager. In such instances, the responsibility accounting report should separately classify all unit costs as controllable or noncontrollable by the manager. Alternatively, separate reports should be prepared for the organizational unit (showing all costs) and for the unit manager (showing only costs under his or her control).

A responsibility accounting system helps organizational unit managers to conduct the five basic control functions:

1. Prepare a plan (for example, using budgets and standards) and use it to communicate output expectations and delegate authority.
2. Gather actual data classified in accordance with the activities and categories specified in the plan. The responsibility accounting system can be used to record and summarize data for each organizational unit.
3. Monitor the differences between planned and actual data at scheduled intervals. Responsibility reports for subordinate managers and their immediate su-

EXHIBIT 13–4
INFORMATION FOR RESPONSIBILITY REPORTS

Monetary

- Budgeted and actual revenues
- Budgeted and actual costs (computed on a comparable basis)
- Variance computations for revenues and costs
- Asset investment base

Nonmonetary

- Capacity measures (theoretical and that used to compute predetermined overhead rates)
- Target rate of earnings on investment base
- Desired and actual market share
- Departmental/divisional throughput
- Number of defects (by product, product line, supplier)
- Number of orders backlogged (by date, cost, and selling price)
- Number of customer complaints (by type and product); method of complaint resolution
- Percentage of orders delivered on time
- Manufacturing (or service) cycle efficiency
- Percentage of reduction of non-value-added time from previous reporting period (broken down by idle time, storage time, move time, and quality control time)
- Number and percentage of employee suggestions considered significant and practical
- Number and percentage of employee suggestions implemented
- Number of unplanned production interruptions
- Number of schedule changes
- Number of engineering change orders; percentage change from previous period
- Number of safety violations; percentage change from previous period
- Number of days of employee absences; percentage change from previous period

pervisors normally compare actual results with flexible budget figures. In contrast, top management can receive responsibility reports comparing actual performance to the master budget.

4. Exert managerial influence in response to significant differences. Because of day-to-day contact with operations, unit managers should have been aware of any significant variances before they were reported, identified the variance causes, and attempted to correct them. Top management, on the other hand, could not know about operational variances until it receives responsibility reports. By the time top management receives the reports, the problems causing the variances should have been corrected, or subordinate managers should have explanations as to why the problems were not or could not be resolved.

5. Continue comparing data and responding and, at the appropriate time, begin the process again.

Responsibility reports reflect the upward flow of information from operational units to company top management and illustrate the broadening scope of responsibility. Managers receive detailed information on the performance of their immediate areas of control and summary information on all organizational units for which they are responsible. Summarizing results causes a pyramiding of information. Reports at the lowest level of units are highly detailed, whereas more general information is reported to the top of the organization. Upper-level managers desiring more detail than is provided in summary reports can obtain it by reviewing the responsibility reports prepared by their subordinates.

Exhibit 13–5 illustrates a responsibility report for Ganitsky Manufacturing Company. Each area's budget is presented for comparative purposes. Production

EXHIBIT 13–5

GANITSKY
MANUFACTURING
COMPANY
RESPONSIBILITY REPORT
(JUNE 2006)

President's Performance Report

	Budget	Actual	Variance Fav. (Unfav.)
Administrative office—president	$1,192,000	$1,196,800	$ (4,800)
Financial vice president	944,000	936,400	7,600
Production vice president	2,951,984	2,977,600	(25,616)
Sales vice president	1,100,000	1,105,600	(5,600)
Totals	$6,187,984	$6,216,400	$(28,416)

Production Vice President's Performance Report

	Budget	Actual	Variance Fav. (Unfav.)
Administrative office—vice president	$ 720,000	$ 728,800	$ (8,800)
Distribution and storage	498,800	504,000	(5,200)
Production department	1,733,184	1,744,800	(11,616)
Totals	$2,951,984	$2,977,600	$(25,616)

Distribution and Storage Manager's Performance Report

	Budget	Actual	Variance Fav. (Unfav.)
Direct material	$ 144,000	$ 141,600	$ 2,400
Direct labor	218,000	221,200	(3,200)
Supplies	18,800	21,200	(2,400)
Indirect labor	94,400	95,200	(800)
Repairs and maintenance	14,000	14,800	(800)
Other	9,600	10,000	(400)
Totals	$ 498,800	$ 504,000	$ (5,200)

Production Department Manager's Performance Report

	Budget	Actual	Variance Fav. (Unfav.)
Direct material	$ 477,200	$ 490,000	$(12,800)
Direct labor	763,520	752,108	11,412
Supplies	70,624	74,000	(3,376)
Indirect labor	185,152	188,080	(2,928)
Depreciation	154,612	154,612	0
Repairs and maintenance	49,628	51,600	(1,972)
Other	32,448	34,400	(1,952)
Totals	$1,733,184	$1,744,800	$(11,616)

department data are aggregated with data of the other departments under the production vice president's control. (These combined data are shown in the middle section of Exhibit 13–5.) Similarly, the total costs of the production vice president's area of responsibility are combined with other costs for which the company president is responsible (see the top section of Exhibit 13–5).

Variances are individually itemized in performance reports at the lower levels so that the appropriate manager has the necessary details to take any required corrective action related to significant variances.[2] Under the management by exception principle, major deviations from expectations are highlighted under the subordinate manager's reporting section to assist upper-level managers in determining whether they need to become involved in subordinates' operations. In addition, such detailed variance analyses alert operating managers to items that could need to be explained to superiors. For example, the direct material and direct labor amounts in the production department manager's section of Exhibit 13–5 would

---

[2] In practice, the variances presented in Exhibit 13–5 would be further separated into the portions representing price and quantity effects as shown in Chapter 7 on standard costing.

probably be considered significant and require explanations to the production vice president.

Although responsibility reporting generally provides helpful information to managers, the method has some disadvantages. For example, the idea of "rolling up" information to each successively higher level allows potentially important details to be buried. If different units within the responsibility accounting system are competing with each other for resources, managers could try to "promote their own agendas" by blaming other organizational units for problems; alternatively, the competition could lead to a lack of goal congruence between or among organizational units. Additionally, by showing each responsibility unit as a separate part of the report, interdependencies among units might not be visible. As mentioned in Chapter 5, organizational processes are typically horizontal and, thereby, the activities in one unit often impact activities in what might appear to be a totally separate responsibility accounting unit.

responsibility center

Responsibility accounting's focus is on the manager who has control over a particular cost object. In a decentralized company, the cost object is an organizational unit, called a **responsibility center**, such as a division, department, or geographical region.

TYPES OF RESPONSIBILITY CENTERS

LO.3
WHAT ARE THE DIFFERENCES AMONG THE FOUR PRIMARY TYPES OF RESPONSIBILITY CENTERS?

Responsibility accounting systems identify, measure, and report on the performance of people controlling the activities of responsibility centers. Responsibility centers are generally classified according to their manager's scope of authority and type of financial responsibility: costs, revenues, profits, and/or asset base. The four primary types of responsibility centers are illustrated in Exhibit 13–6 and discussed in the following sections.

Cost Centers

cost center

The manager of a **cost center** has the authority only to incur costs and is specifically evaluated on the basis of how well costs are controlled. Cost centers commonly

EXHIBIT 13–6
TYPES OF RESPONSIBILITY CENTERS

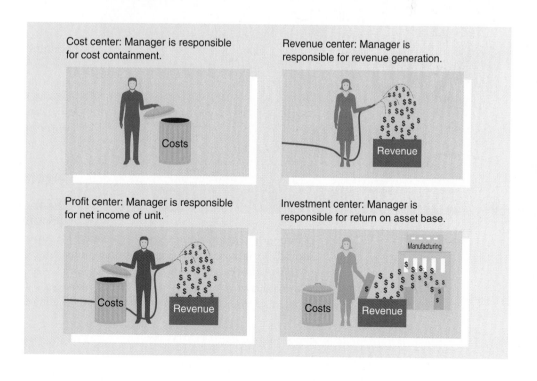

Cost center: Manager is responsible for cost containment.

Revenue center: Manager is responsible for revenue generation.

Profit center: Manager is responsible for net income of unit.

Investment center: Manager is responsible for return on asset base.

include service and administrative departments. For example, the human resources area of Johnson & Johnson can be considered a cost center because it does not generate revenues or charge for its services, but it incurs costs.

In some instances, a cost center can generate revenues, but they are either not under the manager's control or are not effectively measurable. The first situation exists in a community library that is provided a specific proration of property tax dollars but has no authority to levy or collect the related taxes. The second situation could exist in discretionary cost centers, such as a research and development center, in which the outputs (revenues or benefits generated from the cost inputs) are not easily measured.[3] In these two types of situations, the revenues should not be included in the manager's responsibility accounting report.

In the traditional manufacturing environment, the highest priority in a cost center is normally to minimize unfavorable standard cost variances. Top management often concentrates only on the unfavorable variances occurring in a cost center and ignores the efficient performance indicated by favorable variances. However, significant favorable variances should not be disregarded if the management by exception principle is applied appropriately. Using this principle, top management should investigate all variances (both favorable and unfavorable) that fall outside the range of acceptable deviations.

Revenue Centers

revenue center

A retail store may consider each sales department an independent unit in regards to revenue and/or costs.

A **revenue center** is strictly defined as an organizational unit whose manager is accountable only for the generation of revenues and has no control over setting selling prices or budgeting costs. For instance, in many retail stores, each sales department is considered an independent unit, and managers are evaluated based on the total revenues their departments generate. Departmental managers, however, may have no authority to change selling prices to affect volume, and often they do not participate in the budgeting process. Additionally, the departmental managers may have no impact on costs.

In most instances, pure revenue centers do not exist because managers are also involved in the planning and control over some costs incurred in the center. A more appropriate term for such an organizational unit is a *revenue and limited cost center*.

Profit Centers

profit center

The manager of a **profit center** is responsible for generating revenues and planning and controlling expenses related to current activity. Thus, profit centers should be independent organizational units whose managers have the ability to obtain resources at the most economical prices and to sell products at prices that will maximize revenue. A profit center manager's goal is to maximize the center's profit. Expenses not under a profit center manager's control are those related to

---

[3] Discretionary costs are discussed in Chapter 15.

long-term investments in plant assets; such a situation requires that separate evaluations be made of the subunit and the subunit's manager.

Investment Centers

investment center

An **investment center** is an organizational unit whose manager is responsible for generating revenues and planning and controlling expenses. In addition, the center's manager has the authority to acquire, use, and dispose of plant assets to earn the highest feasible rate of return on the center's asset base. Many investment centers are independent, freestanding divisions or subsidiaries of a firm. This independence gives investment center managers the opportunity to make decisions about all matters affecting their organizational units and to be judged on the outcomes of those decisions.

Which type of responsibility center has the broadest span of responsibility?

Because of their closeness to daily divisional activities, responsibility center managers should have more current and detailed knowledge about sales prices, costs, and other market information than top management has. If responsibility centers are designated as profit or investment centers, managers are encouraged, to the extent possible, to operate those subunits as separate economic entities that exist for the same organizational goals. These goals will be achieved through the satisfaction of organizational critical success factors—items that are so important that, without them, the organization would cease to exist. Five of the most commonly embraced critical success factors are quality, customer service, speed, cost control, and responsiveness to change. If these factors are managed properly, the organization should be financially successful; if they are not, sooner or later the organization will fail. Losing sight of the organizational goals while working to achieve an independent responsibility center's conflicting goal results in **suboptimization**, or a situation in which individual managers pursue goals and objectives that are in their own and/or their segments' particular interests rather than in the company's best interests.

suboptimization

In determining the responsibility classification of an organizational unit, top management often makes judgments about the nature and extent of the costs and revenues to include in those responsibility centers. Frequently, rather than attempting to make performance assessments about cost centers, management assigns the costs incurred in cost centers to revenue-producing areas through a process of service department cost allocation. Alternatively, management can attempt to "create" revenues for the cost center by using a system of internal charges for the center's tangible or intangible output that is used by other company units.

SERVICE DEPARTMENT COST ALLOCATION

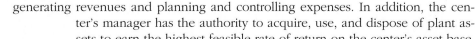

LO.4
WHY AND HOW ARE SERVICE DEPARTMENT COSTS ALLOCATED TO REVENUE-PRODUCING DEPARTMENTS?

service department

administrative department

Organizations incur two types of overhead (OH) costs: manufacturing-related and nonmanufacturing-related OH costs. Typically, as the number of product lines or service types increases, so does the need for additional support activities.

An organization's support areas consist of both service and administrative departments. A **service department** is an organizational unit (such as central purchasing, personnel, maintenance, engineering, security, or warehousing) that provides one or more specific functional tasks for other internal units. **Administrative departments** perform management activities that benefit the entire organization and include the personnel, legal, payroll, and insurance departments, and the organization's headquarters. Costs of service and administrative departments are referred to collectively as service department costs because corporate administration services the rest of the company.

Reasons for Service Department Cost Allocations

All service department costs are incurred to support production or service-rendering activities. Thus, support department costs must be covered in the long run by sales of products and services. These costs can be allocated to production departments to meet the objectives of full cost computation, managerial motivation, and managerial decision making. See Exhibit 13–7 for the reasons for and against allocating service department costs in relationship to each allocation objective.

Allocation Bases

If service department costs are to be assigned to revenue-producing areas, a rational and systematic means by which to make the assignment must be developed. An improper cost allocation base will yield improper information regardless of how

EXHIBIT 13–7

ALLOCATING SERVICE DEPARTMENT COSTS: PROS AND CONS

OBJECTIVE: TO COMPUTE FULL COST

Reasons *for*:

1. Provides for cost recovery.
2. Instills a consideration of support costs in production managers.
3. Reflects production's "fair share" of support costs.
4. Meets regulations in some pricing instances.

Reasons *against*:

1. Provides costs that are beyond production manager's control.
2. Provides arbitrary costs that are not useful in decision making.
3. Confuses the issues of pricing and costing. Prices should be set high enough for each product to provide a profit margin that should cover all nonproduction costs.

OBJECTIVE: TO MOTIVATE MANAGERS

Reasons *for*:

1. Instills a consideration of support costs in production managers.
2. Relates individual production unit's profits to total company profits.
3. Reflects usage of services on a fair and equitable basis.
4. Encourages production managers to help service departments control costs.
5. Encourages the usage of certain services.

Reasons *against*:

1. Distorts production division's profit figures because allocations are subjective.
2. Includes costs that are beyond production manager's control.
3. Will not materially affect production division's profits.
4. Creates interdivisional ill will when there is lack of agreement about allocation base or method.
5. Is not cost beneficial.

OBJECTIVE: TO COMPARE ALTERNATIVE COURSES OF ACTION

Reasons *for*:

1. Provides relevant information in determining corporatewide profits generated by alternative actions.
2. Provides best available estimate of expected changes in costs due to alternative actions.

Reasons *against*:

1. Is unnecessary if alternative actions will not cause costs to change.
2. Presents distorted cash flows or profits from alternative actions since allocations are arbitrary.

Source: Adapted from *Statements on Management Accounting Number 4B: Allocation of Service and Administrative Costs* (June 13, 1985), pp. 9–10. Copyright by Institute of Management Accountants.

complex or mathematically precise the allocation process appears to be. Thus, a valid allocation base should consider the following four criteria:

- Benefit the revenue-producing department receives from the service department
- Causal relationship existing between factors in the revenue-producing department and costs incurred in the service department
- Fairness or equity of the allocations between revenue-producing departments
- Ability of revenue-producing departments to bear the allocated costs

The first two criteria are used most often to select allocation bases because these criteria are reasonably objective and will produce rational allocations. Fairness is a valid theoretical basis for allocation, but its use can cause dissension because everyone does not agree on what is fair or equitable. The ability-to-bear criterion often results in unrealistic or profit-detrimental actions: Managers might manipulate operating data related to the allocation base to minimize service department allocations. Refer to Exhibit 13–8 for some appropriate bases to use to assign various types of service department assets.

Methods of Allocating Service Department Costs

What benefit does each method of service department cost allocation provide?

The allocation process for service department costs is a process of pooling, allocating, repooling, and reallocating costs. When service departments are considered in the pooling process, the primary pools are composed of all costs of both the revenue-producing and service departments. These costs can be gathered and specified by cost behavior (variable and fixed) or in total. Depending on the type of allocation method selected, one or more layers of intermediate pools are then developed in the allocation process; however, the final layer will consist of only revenue-producing departments. Costs of the intermediate pools are distributed to cost objects (such as products and services) using traditional cost drivers (such as direct labor hours or machine hours) or through a process of activity-based costing

EXHIBIT 13–8

APPROPRIATE SERVICE/ ADMINISTRATIVE COST ALLOCATION BASES

Type of Cost	Acceptable Allocation Bases
Research and development	Estimated time or usage, sales, assets employed, new products developed
Personnel functions	Number of employees, payroll, number of new hires
Accounting functions	Estimated time or usage, sales, assets employed, employment data
Public relations and corporate promotion	Sales
Purchasing function	Dollar value of purchase orders, number of purchase orders, estimated time of usage, percentage of material cost of purchases
Corporate executives' salaries	Sales, assets employed, pretax operating income
Treasurer's functions	Sales, estimated time or usage, assets or liabilities employed
Legal and governmental affairs	Estimated time or usage, sales, assets employed
Tax department	Estimated time or usage, sales, assets employed
Income taxes	Pretax operating income
Property taxes	Square feet, real estate valuation

Source: Adapted from *Statements on Management Accounting Number 4B: Allocation of Service and Administration Costs* (June 13, 1985), p. 8. Copyright by Institute of Management Accountants.

using more innovative cost drivers (such as machine throughput time, distance traveled, or number of machine setups).

Pooled service department costs can be allocated to revenue-producing departments using the direct, step, or algebraic method. These methods are listed in order of ease of application, not necessarily in order of soundness of results.

direct method

The **direct method** assigns service department costs straightforwardly to revenue-producing areas. For example, personnel department costs can be assigned to production departments based on number of employees, and purchasing department costs can be assigned to production departments based on number of purchase orders generated.

step method

benefits-provided ranking

The **step method** allows a partial recognition of reciprocal relationships among service departments before assigning costs to revenue-producing areas. This method ranks the quantity of services provided by each service department to other service areas. The **benefits-provided ranking** begins with the service department providing the most service to all other service areas and ends with the service department providing the least service to all other service areas. Then, service department costs are sequentially allocated down the ranking until all costs have been assigned to the revenue-producing areas. For example, the personnel department might be the first department listed in the ranking because it provides services for all company areas; thus, all other areas would receive a proportionate allocation of the personnel department's costs. Although many approaches are used to implement the benefits-provided ranking, the two most common are ranking on the dollar volume of services or the percentage of total services to other service areas.

algebraic method

The **algebraic method** of allocating service department costs considers all departmental interrelationships and reflects these relationships in simultaneous equations. These equations provide for reciprocal allocation of service costs among the service departments as well as to the revenue-producing departments. No benefits-provided ranking is needed. The algebraic method is the most complex of all the allocation techniques, but it is also the most theoretically correct and, if relationships are properly formulated, provides the most accurate allocations.

SERVICE DEPARTMENT COST ALLOCATION ILLUSTRATION

Data for Lewis & Clark Pharmaceuticals (LCP) illustrate the three methods of allocating budgeted service department costs. LCP has two revenue-producing divisions: nutritionals and vision care. The company's service departments are corporate administration, personnel, and maintenance. Budgeted costs of each service department are assigned to each revenue-producing area and are then added to the budgeted overhead costs of those areas to determine an appropriate divisional overhead application rate. See Exhibit 13–9 for an abbreviated 2007 budget of the direct and indirect costs for each department and division of LCP.

EXHIBIT 13–9

LEWIS & CLARK PHARMACEUTICALS BUDGETED DEPARTMENTAL AND DIVISIONAL COSTS

	Administration	Personnel	Maintenance	Nutritionals	Vision Care	Total
Direct departmental costs:						
Material	$ 0	$ 0	$ 0	$1,275,600	$ 669,600	$1,945,200
Labor	1,350,000	150,000	360,000	736,200	864,000	3,460,200
Total	$1,350,000	$150,000	$360,000	$2,011,800	$1,533,600	$5,405,400
Departmental overhead*	1,651,200	69,750	238,200	1,677,000	267,600	3,903,750
Total initial dept'l costs	$3,001,200	$219,750	$598,200	$3,688,800	$1,801,200	$9,309,150

*Would be specified by type and cost behavior in actual budgeting process.

See Exhibit 13–10 for the bases selected for allocating LCP's service department costs. Assume that service departments are listed in a benefits-provided ranking. Management determined that administration provides the most service to all other company areas, personnel provides most of its services to maintenance and the revenue-producing areas, and maintenance provides its services only to the revenue-producing areas (equipment used in other areas is under a lease maintenance arrangement and is not serviced by the company's maintenance department). All product research and development is conducted in a separate subsidiary company.

EXHIBIT 13–10
SERVICE DEPARTMENT ALLOCATION BASES

Administration costs—allocated based on dollars of assets employed

Personnel costs—allocated based on number of employees

Maintenance costs—allocated based on machine hours used

	Dollars of Assets Employed	Number of Employees	Number of Machine Hours Used
Administration	$12,000,000	24	0
Personnel	3,600,000	6	0
Maintenance	6,000,000	18	0
Nutritionals	30,000,000	75	258,000
Vision care	24,000,000	21	64,500

Direct Method Allocation

In the direct method of allocation, service department costs are assigned using the specified bases only to the revenue-producing areas. The direct method cost allocation for Lewis & Clark Pharmaceuticals is in Exhibit 13–11.

EXHIBIT 13–11
DIRECT ALLOCATION OF SERVICE DEPARTMENT COSTS

	Base	Proportion of Total Base	Amount to Allocate	Amount Allocated
Administration costs				
(dollars of assets employed)				
Nutritionals	$30,000,000	30 ÷ 54 = 56%	$3,001,200	$1,680,672
Vision care	24,000,000	24 ÷ 54 = 44	3,001,200	1,320,528
Total	$54,000,000	100%		$3,001,200
Personnel costs				
(number of employees)				
Nutritionals	$75	75 ÷ 96 = 78%	$ 219,750	$ 171,405
Vision care	21	21 ÷ 96 = 22	219,750	48,345
Total	$96	100%		$ 219,750
Maintenance costs				
(number of machine hours used)				
Nutritionals	$258,000	258,000 ÷ 322,500 = 80%	$ 598,200	$ 478,560
Vision care	64,500	64,500 ÷ 322,500 = 20	598,200	119,640
Total	$322,500	100%		$ 598,200

Use of the direct method of service department allocation produces the total budgeted costs for nutritionals and vision care (see Exhibit 13–12). If budgeted revenues and costs equal actual revenues and costs, nutritionals would show a 2007 profit of $1,730,563, or 22.3 percent on revenues, and vision care would show a profit of $1,210,287, or 26.9 percent.

EXHIBIT 13–12
DIRECT METHOD ALLOCATION TO REVENUE-PRODUCING AREAS

	Nutritionals	Vision Care	Total
Total (assumed) budgeted revenues (a)	$7,750,000	$4,500,000	$12,250,000
Allocated overhead			
From administration	$1,680,672	$1,320,528	$ 3,001,200
From personnel	171,405	48,345	219,750
From maintenance	478,560	119,640	598,200
Subtotal	$2,330,637	$1,488,513	$ 3,819,150
Departmental overhead	1,677,000	267,600	1,944,600
Total overhead (for OH application rate determination)	$4,007,637	$1,756,113	$ 5,763,750
Direct costs	2,011,800	1,533,600	3,545,400
Total budgeted costs (b)	$6,019,437	$3,289,713	$ 9,309,150
Total budgeted pretax profits (a − b)	$1,730,563	$1,210,287	$ 2,940,850

VERIFICATION OF ALLOCATION TO

	Administration	Personnel	Maintenance	Nutritionals	Vision Care	Total
Initial costs	$3,001,200	$219,750	$598,200			$3,819,150
Costs from						
Administration	(3,001,200)			$1,680,672	$1,320,528	
Personnel		(219,750)		171,405	48,345	
Maintenance			(598,200)	478,560	119,640	
Totals	$ 0	$ 0	$ 0	$2,330,637	$1,488,513	$3,819,150

Step Method Allocation

To apply the step method allocation, a benefits-provided ranking must be specified. This ranking for Lewis & Clark Pharmaceuticals was given in Exhibit 13–10. Costs are assigned using an appropriate, specified allocation base to the departments receiving service. After costs have been assigned from a department, no costs are charged back to that department. Step method allocation of LCP service costs is shown in Exhibit 13–13.

In this case, the amount of service department costs assigned to each revenue-producing area differs only slightly for the step and direct methods. However, in many situations, the difference can be substantial. If budgeted revenues and costs equal actual revenues and costs, the step method allocation process will cause nutritionals and vision care to show the following profits:

EXHIBIT 13–13
STEP METHOD ALLOCATION TO REVENUE-PRODUCING AREAS

	Base	Proportion of Total Base	Amount to Allocate	Amount Allocated
Administration costs				
(dollars of assets employed;				
000s omitted)				
Personnel	$ 3,600	3,600 ÷ 63,600 = 6%	$3,001,200	$ 180,072
Maintenance	6,000	6,000 ÷ 63,600 = 9	3,001,200	270,108
Nutritionals	30,000	30,000 ÷ 63,600 = 47	3,001,200	1,410,564
Vision care	24,000	24,000 ÷ 63,600 = 38	3,001,200	1,140,456
Total	$ 63,600	100%		$3,001,200
Personnel costs				
(number of employees)				
Maintenance	18	18 ÷ 114 = 16%	399,822[a]	$ 63,972
Nutritionals	75	75 ÷ 114 = 66	399,822	263,882
Vision care	21	21 ÷ 114 = 18	399,822	71,968
Total	114	100%		$ 399,822
Maintenance costs				
(number of machine hours used)				
Nutritionals	258,000	258,000 ÷ 322,500 = 80%	932,280[b]	$ 745,824
Vision care	64,500	64,500 ÷ 322,500 = 20	932,280	186,456
Total	322,500	100%		$ 932,280

[a]Personnel costs = Original cost + Allocated from administration = $219,750 + $180,072 = $399,822
[b]Maintenance costs = Original cost + Allocated from administration + Allocated from personnel = $598,200 + $270,108 + $63,972 = $932,280

VERIFICATION OF ALLOCATION TO

	Administration	Personnel	Maintenance	Nutritionals	Vision Care	Total
Initial costs	$ 3,001,200	$ 219,750	$ 598,200			$3,819,150
Costs from						
Administration	(3,001,200)	180,072	270,108	$1,410,564	$1,140,456	
Personnel		(399,822)	63,972	263,882	71,968	
Maintenance			(932,280)	745,824	186,456	
Totals	$ 0	$ 0	$ 0	$2,420,270	$1,398,880	$3,819,150

	Nutritionals	Vision Care
Revenues	$ 7,750,000	$ 4,500,000
Direct costs	(2,011,800)	(1,533,600)
Indirect departmental costs	(1,677,000)	(267,600)
Allocated service department costs	(2,420,270)	(1,398,880)
Profit	$ 1,640,930	$ 1,299,920

These profit figures reflect rates of return on revenues of 21.2 percent and 28.9 percent, respectively.

The step method is a hybrid between the direct and algebraic methods. This allocation approach is more realistic than the direct method in that the step method partially recognizes relationships among service departments, although it does not recognize the possible two-way exchange of services between service departments.

Under the step method allocation process, a service department is "eliminated" once its costs have been assigned outward. If a service department further down the ranking sequence provides services to departments that have already been eliminated, these benefits are not recognized.

Algebraic Method Allocation

The algebraic method of allocation eliminates the two disadvantages of the step method because it recognizes all interrelationships among departments and no decision must be made about a ranking order of service departments. The algebraic method involves formulating a set of equations that reflect reciprocal service among departments. Solving these equations simultaneously recognizes the fact that costs flow both into and out of each service department.

The starting points of the algebraic method are the allocation bases and their respective amounts for each department (shown in Exhibit 13–10). A schedule is created to show the proportionate usage by each department of the other departments' services. These proportions are then used to develop equations that, when solved simultaneously, give cost allocations that fully recognize the reciprocal services provided.

The allocation proportions for all departments of LCP are shown in Exhibit 13–14. The personnel department allocation is discussed to illustrate the derivation of these proportions. The allocation basis for personnel cost is number of employees. LCP has 138 employees, excluding those in the personnel department. Personnel employees are ignored because costs are being removed from that department and assigned to other areas. Because maintenance has 18 employees, the proportionate amount of personnel services used by maintenance is $18 \div 138$, or 13 percent.

By using the calculated percentages, algebraic equations representing the interdepartmental usage of services can be formulated. The departments are labeled A, P, and M in the equations for administration, personnel, and maintenance, respectively. The initial costs of each service department are shown first in the formulas:

$$A = \$3,001,200 + 0.18P + 0.00M$$
$$P = \$219,750 + 0.06A + 0.00M$$
$$M = \$598,200 + 0.09A + 0.13P$$

EXHIBIT 13–14
INTERDEPARTMENTAL PROPORTIONAL RELATIONSHIPS

	ADMINISTRATION (DOLLARS OF ASSETS EMPLOYED[a])		PERSONNEL (NUMBER OF EMPLOYEES)		MAINTENANCE (NUMBER OF MACHINE HOURS USED)	
	Base[a]	Percent[b]	Base	Percent[b]	Base	Percent[b]
Administration	n/a	n/a	24	18%	0	0%
Personnel	$ 3,600	6%	n/a	n/a	0	0
Maintenance	6,000	9	18	13	n/a	n/a
Nutritionals	30,000	47	75	54	258,000	80
Vision care	24,000	38	21	15	64,500	20
Total	$63,600	100%	138	100%	322,500	100%

[a]000s omitted.
[b]Percentages rounded to total 100 percent.

These equations are solved simultaneously by substituting one equation into the others, gathering like terms, and reducing the unknowns until only one unknown exists. The value for this unknown is then computed and substituted into the remaining equations. This process is continued until all unknowns have been eliminated.

1. Substituting the equation for A into the equation for P gives the following:

$$P = \$219,750 + 0.06(\$3,001,200 + 0.18P)$$

Multiplying and combining terms produces the following results:

$$P = \$219,750 + \$180,072 + 0.01P$$
$$P = \$399,822 + 0.01P$$
$$P - 0.01P = \$399,822$$
$$0.99P = \$399,822$$
$$P = \$403,861$$

2. The value for P is now substituted in the formula for administration:

$$A = \$3,001,200 + 0.18(\$403,861)$$
$$A = \$3,001,200 + \$72,695$$
$$A = \$3,073,895$$

3. Substituting the values for A and P into the equation for M gives the following:

$$M = \$598,200 + 0.09(\$3,073,895) + 0.13(\$403,861)$$
$$M = \$598,200 + \$276,651 + \$52,502$$
$$M = \$927,353$$

The amounts provided by these equations are used to reallocate costs among all the departments; costs will then be assigned only to the revenue-producing areas. These allocations are shown in Exhibit 13–15.

The $3,073,895 of administration costs is used to illustrate the computation of the amounts in Exhibit 13–15. Administration costs are assigned to the other areas based on dollars of assets employed. Exhibit 13–15 indicates that personnel has 6 percent of LCP's total asset dollars; thus, $184,434 (0.06 × $3,073,895) is assigned to that area. A similar proration process is used for the other departments. Allocations from Exhibit 13–15 are used in Exhibit 13–16 to determine the reallocated costs and finalize the total budgeted overhead of nutritionals and vision care.

EXHIBIT 13–15
ALGEBRAIC SOLUTION OF SERVICE DEPARTMENT COSTS

Costs are allocated based on percentages computed in Exhibit 13–14.

	ADMINISTRATION		PERSONNEL		MAINTENANCE	
	Percent	Amount	Percent	Amount	Percent	Amount
Administration	n/a	n/a	18%	$ 72,695	0%	$ 0
Personnel	6%	$ 184,434	n/a	n/a	0	0
Maintenance	9	276,650	13	52,502	n/a	n/a
Nutritionals	47	1,444,731	54	218,085	80	741,882
Vision care	38	1,168,080	15	60,579	20	185,471
Total*	100%	$3,073,895	100%	$403,861	100%	$927,353

*Total costs are the solution results of the set of algebraic equations.

EXHIBIT 13–16

ALGEBRAIC METHOD ALLOCATION TO REVENUE-PRODUCING AREAS

	Total Service Department Cost (from equations)	Administration	Personnel	Maintenance	Nutritionals	Vision Care
Administration	$3,073,895	$ 0	$184,434	$276,650	$1,444,731	$1,168,080
Personnel	403,861	72,695	0	52,502	218,085	60,579
Maintenance	927,353	0	0	0	741,882	185,471
Total costs	$4,405,109	$72,695	$184,434	$329,152	$2,404,698	$1,414,130
Less reallocated costs	(586,281)	(72,695)	(184,434)	(329,152)		
Budgeted costs	$3,818,828	$ 0	$ 0	$ 0		
Departmental OH costs of revenue-producing areas					1,677,000	267,600
Total budgeted cost for OH application rate determination					$4,081,698	$1,681,730

By allocating costs in this manner, total costs shown for each service department have increased over the amounts originally given. For example, the administration department now shows total costs of $3,073,895 rather than the original amount of $3,001,200. These added "costs" arise from the process of service reciprocity. As shown on the line "Less reallocated costs" in Exhibit 13–16, these additional double counted costs are not recognized in the revenue-producing areas for purposes of developing an overhead application rate.

When a company has few departmental interrelationships, the algebraic method can be solved by hand. If a large number of variables are present, however, this method must be performed by a computer. Because computer usage is now prevalent in all but the smallest organizations, the results obtained from the algebraic method are easy to generate and provide the most rational and appropriate means of allocating service department costs.

Regardless of the method used to allocate service department costs, the final step is to determine the overhead application rates for the revenue-producing areas. After service department costs have been assigned to production, they are included as part of production overhead and allocated to products or jobs through normal overhead assignment procedures.

As shown in Exhibit 13–16, the total allocated overhead costs of $4,081,698 and $1,681,730 for nutritionals and vision care, respectively, will be divided by an appropriate allocation base to assign both manufacturing and nonmanufacturing overhead to products. For example, assume that LCP has chosen total ounces of eye products as the overhead allocation base for vision care. If the division expects to produce 2,250,000 ounces of eye produces in 2007, the overhead cost assigned to each ounce of product would be $0.75, or ($1,681,730 ÷ 2,250,000).

For simplicity, cost behavior in all departments has been ignored. A more appropriate allocation process would specify different bases in each department for the variable and fixed costs. Such differentiation would not change the allocation process but would change the results of the three methods (direct, step, or algebraic). Separation of variable and fixed costs would provide more accurate allocation; use of the computer makes this process more practical than otherwise.

Before making any allocations, management should be certain that the allocation bases are reasonable. Allocations are often based on the easiest available measure, such as number of people employed or number of documents processed. Use of such measures can distort the allocation process.

Allocating service department costs to revenue-producing areas makes managers more aware of, and responsible for, controlling service usage. However, if such allocations are made, the income figures derived from using these amounts are inappropriate for evaluating the revenue-area managers' performance. The revenue-area managers can control their usage of services, but cannot control the actual incurrence of service department costs. The financial performance of a revenue-producing department manager should use an incremental, rather than full allocation, approach. For example, the vision care products manager's performance should be evaluated using a predetermined overhead rate of approximately $0.12 per unit ($267,600 ÷ 2,250,000 ounces of product) rather than the $0.75 rate discussed earlier.

The next section discusses the concept of setting transfer prices for products or services between two organizational units. To properly evaluate segments and their managers, useful information about performance must be available. When the various segments of a firm exchange goods or services among themselves, a "price" for those goods or services must be set so that the "selling" segment can measure its revenue and the "buying" segment can measure its costs. Such an internal price is known as a **transfer price**.

transfer price

TRANSFER PRICING

For an organization to be profitable, revenue-producing areas must cover service department costs. These costs can be allocated internally to user departments based on the methods shown earlier in this chapter, or services can be "sold" to user departments using transfer prices. In either case, service department costs are included in the costs of revenue-producing departments so that those departments' sales can cover the service departments' costs. The decision as to the most useful information is at the discretion of top management.

Transfer prices are internal charges established for the exchange of goods or services between responsibility centers within a company. Such prices are always eliminated for external reporting purposes, leaving only the actual cost of the items on balance sheets or income statements. The practice of using transfer prices for products is well established; using transfer prices for services is becoming more prevalent. A **pseudo-profit center** is created when one responsibility center uses a transfer price to artificially "sell" goods or services to another responsibility center: The selling center has artificial revenues and profits, and the buying center has an artificially inflated product or service cost.[4]

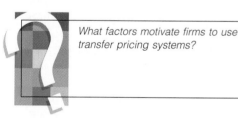

What factors motivate firms to use transfer pricing systems?

pseudo-profit center

Various reasons exist to use transfer prices between responsibility centers. Transfer prices can be established to promote goal congruence, make performance evaluation among segments more comparable, and/or "transform" a cost center into a profit center. A typical reason includes the desire to motivate center managers and to make them more entrepreneurial. If they are used, transfer prices should ensure optimal resource allocation and promote operating efficiency. Using transfer prices for services between organizational units has several advantages (see Exhibit 13–17).

Transfer prices for goods or services can be calculated in a number of ways, but the following general rules are appropriate.

---

[4] Pseudo-profit centers have been discussed for many years. One article by Ralph L. Benke, Jr., and James Don Edwards, "Should You Use Transfer Pricing to Create Pseudo-Profit Centers?" appeared in *Management Accounting* (now *Strategic Finance*) in February 1981. Such centers (though termed *mircroprofit centers*) were also discussed at great length by Robin Cooper in *When Lean Enterprises Collide* (Boston: Harvard Business School Press, 1995).

EXHIBIT 13–17

ADVANTAGES OF TRANSFER PRICES FOR SERVICES

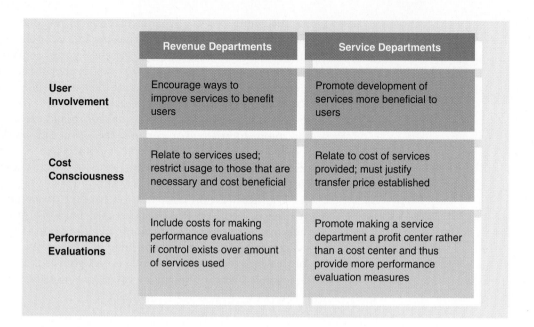

	Revenue Departments	Service Departments
User Involvement	Encourage ways to improve services to benefit users	Promote development of services more beneficial to users
Cost Consciousness	Relate to services used; restrict usage to those that are necessary and cost beneficial	Relate to cost of services provided; must justify transfer price established
Performance Evaluations	Include costs for making performance evaluations if control exists over amount of services used	Promote making a service department a profit center rather than a cost center and thus provide more performance evaluation measures

- The maximum price should be no higher than the lowest market price at which the buying segment can acquire the goods or services externally.
- The minimum price should be no less than the sum of the selling segment's incremental costs associated with the goods or services plus the opportunity cost of the facilities used.

To illustrate the use of these rules, assume that a product is available from external suppliers at a price below the lower limit. The immediate short-run decision might be for the selling division to stop production and for the purchasing division to buy the product from the external suppliers. This decision can be reasonable because, compared with the external suppliers, the selling division does not appear to be cost efficient in its production activities. Stopping production would release the facilities for other, more profitable purposes. A longer run solution could be to have the selling division improve its efficiency and reduce the internal cost of making the product. This solution could be implemented without stopping internal production, but some external purchases might be made until costs are under control.

After establishing the transfer price range limits, one criterion for selecting a specific price within the range is ease of determination. Managers are most comfortable using a transfer price that is uncomplicated to compute and knowing what impact that price will have on their responsibility centers' profits. In addition, from a cost standpoint, simple transfer pricing systems require less time and effort to administer and account for than complicated ones.

The difference between the upper and lower transfer price limits is the corporate "profit" (or savings) generated by producing internally rather than buying externally. Transfer prices act to "divide the corporate profit" between the buying and selling segments. For external statements, such "divided profits" are irrelevant because they are eliminated. For internal reporting, these "profits" can be extremely important. If managerial performance is evaluated on a competitive basis, both buying and selling segment managers want to maximize their financial results in the responsibility accounting reports. The supplier-segment manager tries to obtain the highest transfer (selling) price, whereas the buying-segment manager tries to acquire the goods or services at the lowest transfer (purchase) price. Thus, transfer prices should be agreed on by the company's selling and buying segments.

There are three traditional types of transfer prices: cost based, market based, and negotiated (see Exhibit 13–18). A discussion of each method and its advantages and disadvantages follows. Numerical examples of transfer price calculations are given in the Demonstration Problem at the end of the chapter.

Cost-Based Transfer Prices

A cost-based transfer price is, on the surface, an easily understood concept until one realizes that many definitions of the term *cost* are available, ranging from variable production cost to absorption cost plus additional amounts for selling and administrative costs (and, possibly, opportunity cost) of the selling unit. If only variable costs are used to set a transfer price, the selling division has little incentive to sell products or services to another internal division because no contribution margin to help cover fixed costs is being generated by the transfers. Transfer prices based on absorption cost at least provide a contribution toward covering the selling division's fixed production overhead. Although an absorption cost transfer price provides a reasonable coverage of costs to the selling segment, that same cost could create a suboptimization problem because of the effects on the buying segment.

Modifications can be made to reduce the problems of cost-based transfer prices. When variable cost is used as a base, an additional amount can be added to cover some fixed costs and provide a measure of profit to the selling division. This adjustment is an example of a cost-plus arrangement. Some company managers think cost-plus arrangements are acceptable substitutes for market-based transfer prices,

EXHIBIT 13–18
TYPES OF TRANSFER PRICES AND RELATED QUESTIONS OF USE

Cost Based

1. What should be included in cost?
   Variable production costs
   Total variable cost
   Absorption production costs
   "Adjusted" absorption production costs

2. Should cost be actual or standard?

3. Should a profit margin for the selling division be included?

Market Based

1. What if there is no exact counterpart in the market?

2. What if internal sales create a cost savings (such as not having bad debts) that would not exist in external sales?

3. What if the market price is currently depressed?

4. Which market price should be used?

Negotiated

1. Do both parties have the ability to bargain with autonomy?

2. How will disputes be handled?

3. Are comparable product substitutes available externally?

especially when market prices for comparable substitute products are unavailable. Absorption cost can be modified by adding an amount equal to an average of the nonproduction costs associated with the product and/or an amount for profit to the selling division. In contrast, a transfer price could be set at less than absorption cost if there is no other use for the idle capacity or if there are estimated savings (such as reduced packaging) in production costs on internally transferred goods.

Another consideration in a cost-based transfer price is whether actual or standard cost is used. Actual costs can vary according to the season, production volume, and other factors, whereas standard costs can be specified in advance and are stable measures of efficient production costs. Thus, standard costs provide a superior basis for transfer pricing. Any variances from standard are borne by the selling segment; otherwise, the selling division's efficiencies or inefficiencies are passed on to the buying division.

Market-Based Transfer Prices

To eliminate the problems of defining "cost," some companies simply use a market price approach to setting transfer prices. Market price is believed to be an objective, arm's-length measure of value that simulates the selling price that would be offered and paid if the subunits were independent, autonomous companies. If a selling division is operating efficiently relative to its competition, it should be able to show a profit when transferring products or services at market prices. Similarly, an efficiently operating buying division should not be troubled by a market-based transfer price because that is what would have to be paid for the goods or services if the alternative of buying internally did not exist.

Several problems can exist, however, with the use of market prices for intracompany transfers. First, transfers can involve products having no exact counterpart in the external market. Second, market price is not entirely appropriate because internal sales can provide cost savings by reducing bad debts and/or packaging, advertising, or delivery expenditures. Third, if the external market is experiencing a temporary reduction in demand for the product, there is a question of whether the current "depressed" price or the expected long-run market price should be used as the transfer price. Fourth, different prices, discounts, and credit terms are allowed to different buyers; which market price is the "right" one to use?

Negotiated Transfer Prices

negotiated transfer price

Because of the problems associated with both cost- and market-based prices, **negotiated transfer prices** are often set through a process of bargaining between the selling and purchasing unit managers. Such prices are typically below the normal market purchase price of the buying unit but above the sum of the selling unit's incremental and opportunity costs. If internal sales would eliminate any variable selling costs, these costs are not considered. If external sales do not exist or a division cannot downsize its facilities, no opportunity cost is involved.

Ability to negotiate a transfer price implies that segment managers have the autonomy to sell or buy products externally if internal negotiations fail. Because such extensive autonomy could lead to dysfunctional behavior and suboptimization, top management can provide a means of arbitrating a price in the event that the units cannot agree.

Negotiated transfer prices are often used for services because their value—expertise, reliability, convenience, or responsiveness—is often qualitative and can be assessed only judgmentally from the perspective of the parties involved. The transfer price should depend on the cost and volume level of the service as well as whether comparable substitutes are available. Examples follow:

Pricing for temporary office help generally reflects cost-based or dual transfer pricing.

GETTY IMAGES

■ Market-based transfer prices are effective for common high-cost and high-volume standardized services such as storage and transportation.

■ Negotiated transfer prices are useful for customized high-cost and high-volume services such as risk management and specialized executive training.

■ Cost-based or dual transfer prices are generally chosen for low-cost and low-volume services such as temporary maintenance and temporary office staff assistance.

To encourage cooperation between the transferring divisions, top management can consider joint divisional profits as one performance measurement for both the selling and buying unit managers. Another way to reduce difficulties in establishing a transfer price is simply to use a dual pricing approach.

Dual Pricing

dual pricing arrangement

A **dual pricing arrangement** provides different transfer prices for the selling and buying segments by allowing the seller to record the transfer of goods or services at a market or negotiated market price and the purchaser to record the transfer at a cost-based amount.[5] This arrangement provides a profit margin on the goods transferred from the selling division but a minimal cost to the buying division. Dual pricing eliminates the problem of having to artificially divide the profits between the selling and buying segments and allows managers to have the most relevant information for decision making and performance evaluation. However, an internal reconciliation (similar to that used in preparing consolidated statements when intercompany sales are made between the consolidated entities at an amount other than cost) is needed to adjust revenues and costs when company external financial statements are prepared.

Selecting a Transfer Pricing System

Setting a reasonable transfer price is not an easy task. Everyone involved in the process must be aware of the positive and negative aspects of each type of transfer price and be responsive to suggestions for change. Determination of the type of transfer pricing system to use should reflect the organizational units' characteristics as well as corporate goals. No single method of setting a transfer price is best in all instances. Also, transfer prices are not intended to be permanent; they are frequently revised in relation to changes in costs, supply, demand, competitive forces, and other factors. Flexibility by the selling segment to increase a transfer price when reduced productive capacity is present or to decrease a transfer price when excess productive capacity exists is a strong management lever. Regardless of what method is used, a good transfer price provides

■ an appropriate basis for the calculation and evaluation of segment performance,

■ the rational acquisition or use of goods and services between corporate divisions,

---

[5] Typically, the cost-based amount used by the buying division reflects only the variable costs of the selling division.

■ the flexibility to respond to changes in demand or market conditions, and
■ a means of motivation to encourage and reward goal congruence by managers in decentralized operations.

In contrast, transfer prices can also have the following potential problems:

■ Disagreement between organizational unit managers as to how the transfer price should be set.
■ Additional organizational costs and employee time.
■ The inability to work equally well for all departments or divisions. For example, service departments that do not provide measurable benefits or cannot show a distinct cause-and-effect relationship between cost behavior and service use by other departments should not attempt to use transfer prices.
■ Dysfunctional behavior among organizational units or underutilization or overutilization of services.
■ Complicated tax planning in multinational companies.

A company should weigh the advantages and disadvantages of transfer prices before instituting such a system.

TRANSFER PRICES IN MULTINATIONAL SETTINGS

LO.6
WHAT DIFFICULTIES CAN BE ENCOUNTERED BY MULTINATIONAL COMPANIES USING TRANSFER PRICES?

Because of the differences in tax systems, customs duties, freight and insurance costs, import/export regulations, and foreign-exchange controls, setting transfer prices for products and services becomes extremely difficult when the company is engaged in multinational operations. In addition, as shown in Exhibit 13–19, the internal and external objectives of transfer pricing policies differ in multinational entities.

Multinational companies can use one transfer price when they send a product to or receive it from one country and a totally different transfer price for the same product when it is sent to or received from another country. However, the company should set guidelines on transfer pricing policies that are followed on a consistent basis. For example, a company should not price certain parent company services to foreign subsidiaries in a manner that would send the majority of those costs to the subsidiary in the country with the highest tax rate unless that method of pricing is reasonable and equitable to all subsidiaries. The general test of reasonableness is that a transfer price should reflect an arm's-length transaction.

EXHIBIT 13–19
MULTINATIONAL COMPANY TRANSFER PRICING OBJECTIVES

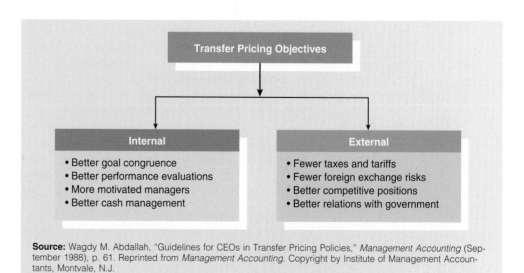

Source: Wagdy M. Abdallah, "Guidelines for CEOs in Transfer Pricing Policies," *Management Accounting* (September 1988), p. 61. Reprinted from *Management Accounting*. Copyright by Institute of Management Accountants, Montvale, N.J.

Tax authorities in both the home and host countries carefully scrutinize multinational transfer prices because such prices determine which country taxes the income from the transfer. The U.S. Congress is concerned about both U.S. multinationals operating in low-tax-rate countries and foreign companies operating in the United States. In both situations, Congress believes that companies could avoid paying U.S. corporate income taxes because of misleading or inaccurate transfer pricing. Thus, the Internal Revenue Service (IRS) can be quick to investigate U.S. subsidiaries that operate in low-tax areas and suddenly have unusually high profits.

Why do income taxes affect transfer pricing strategies in multinational companies?

According to the *Ernst & Young Transfer Pricing 2003 Global Survey*, transfer pricing is the most important international tax issue for multinational enterprises (MNEs), and audits by tax authorities are becoming the rule rather than the exception.[6] More countries are adopting transfer pricing legislation and, as MNEs begin doing business in a new country, they must comply with that country's tax requirements relative to transfer pricing. The Organization for Economic Cooperation and Development has been actively involved in helping to establish internationally accepted procedures for **advance pricing agreements (APAs)**. An APA is a binding contract between a company and one or more national tax authorities that provides details of how a transfer price is to be set and establishes that no adjustments or penalties will be made if the agreed-upon methodology is used. These agreements usually run for three to five years and may be renewed if no major changes occur. APAs also help eliminate the possibility of double taxation on the exchange of goods or services. Information from the U.S. IRS Web site indicates that the majority of transfer pricing methods used in APAs for tangible and intangible property as well as services are based on cost plus a profit margin.[7] One disadvantage of seeking an APA is that several years typically pass before it acquires approval from the IRS.

advance pricing agreement (APA)

Similar to those in international settings, multi-state firms can employ transfer pricing strategies to move profits from state to state. Firms can take advantage of not only different income tax rates across states using transfer pricing arrangements but also can take advantage of the fact that a few states impose no income taxes at all!

---

[6] Carlos Casanovas et al., "Ernst & Young 2003 Global Survey: Transfer Pricing Is Once Again #1 with a Bullet," *Journal of International Taxation* (April 2004), pp. 10ff.
[7] Internal Revenue Service, "2003 APA Statutory Report (Announcement 2004-26)" (March 30, 2004); *http://www.irs.gov/pub/irs-utl/apa03.pdf.*

Revisiting

The atmosphere in each operating unit of Johnson & Johnson characterizes a small company that has the ability to adapt and respond easily to market changes. Because each operating unit has few management layers and little bureaucracy, critical decisions can be made quickly. Thus, J&J's decentralized structure provides a small-company environment and culture, along with big-company opportunities for career development, advancement, and impact.

Overseeing each business segment (Consumer, Pharmaceutical, and Medical Devices & Diagnostics) is a Group Operating Committee, which makes relative investment decisions among and within unit members, selects lead geographic markets, and ensures that product portfolios are strategically aligned. The next level of business segment leadership is the global management of the affiliates within the segment. The management of each affiliate has responsibility for market positioning strategy and for selecting the product categories in which that affiliate will compete. In addition, these managers establish relative pricing, deal with critical issues affecting product technology, identify success models whose accounts will be documented, and track the vitality of the franchise over time. The foundation of each business segment is its autonomous operating unit where the people are closest to the customer and the business. Each operating unit is responsible for helping to grow profitable brands. It develops and implements all activities within its scope, such as business plans, budgets, forecasts, resource allocations, product launches, and performance tracking. Above all, the operating units are responsible for employee development.

The success of Johnson & Johnson's operational structure can be seen in the following statistics: As of 2003, the company had 71 years of continuous sales increases, and dividends (raised each year for 41 consecutive years) have been issued to shareowners every quarter since 1944. Not only is the company considered one of the top performers financially, but also Johnson & Johnson continually appears on *Fortune* magazine's Most Admired Companies list and *Working Mother* magazine's Best Companies for Working Mothers. Equally important in the current period of corporate scandals, Johnson & Johnson has been cited by Harris Interactive's The Reputation Institute for best corporate reputation every year from 2000 through 2004.

Sources: Adapted from *Johnson & Johnson 2003 Annual Report; http://www.jnj.com/our_company/history; http://www.jnj.com/careers;* and *http://www.investor.jnj.com.*

Comprehensive Review Module

Chapter Summary

1. Decentralization is generally appropriate for companies that

   - are mature.

   - are large.

   - are in a growth stage of product development.

   - are expanding operations rapidly.

   - can financially withstand incorrect decisions.

   - have high confidence in the employees' decision-making ability.

   - have widespread operations.

   - want to challenge, motivate, and mentor employees.

   - require rapid response to changing conditions or opportunities.

2. Decentralization and responsibility accounting are related in that decentralization

   - is made to work effectively though the use of responsibility accounting which provides information about the performance, efficiency, and effectiveness of organizational responsibility centers and their managers.

   - implies the acceptance of authority by subordinate managers and responsibility reports indicate the "rolling up" of that authority back to upper management.

   - requires each responsibility center to report on the activities under its manager's immediate control.

   - uses the principle of management by exception, which is reflected in the successively aggregated responsibility reports.

   - seeks goal congruence and responsibility reports to help to highlight any suboptimization of resources.

3. The four primary types of responsibility centers and the characteristics of each are

   - cost centers in which managers are primarily responsible for controlling costs.

   - revenue centers in which managers are primarily responsible for generating revenues; in some instances, managers have control over revenues and some costs.

   - profit centers in which managers are responsible for generating revenue, controlling costs, and maximizing their units' incomes.

   - investment centers in which managers are responsible for generating revenue, controlling costs, and producing a satisfactory return on the asset base under their control.

4. Service department costs are allocated to producing departments

   - to meet the objectives of full cost computation, managerial motivation, or managerial decision making.

   - by using the direct, step, or algebraic method.

     ➢ The direct method assigns service department costs only to revenue-producing departments but does not consider services that can be provided by one service department to another.

     ➢ The step method uses a benefits-provided ranking that lists service departments from the one providing the most service to other departments to the one providing service primarily to the revenue-producing areas. Costs are assigned from each department in order of the ranking.

     ➢ The algebraic method recognizes the interrelationships among all departments through the use of simultaneous equations. This method provides the best allocation information and is readily adaptable to computer computations.

5. Transfer prices, or intracompany charges for goods or services bought and sold between segments of a decentralized company, are

   - typically cost based, market based, or negotiated; a dual pricing system can also be used to assign different transfer prices to the selling and buying units.

   - set using the lowest market price at which the product/service can be acquired externally for the upper limit and using the incremental cost of production or performance plus the opportunity cost of the facilities used as the lower limit.

- used in organizations to

  ➤ enhance goal congruence.

  ➤ make performance evaluations among segments more comparable.

  ➤ change a cost center into a pseudo-profit center.

  ➤ ensure optimal resource allocations.

  ➤ promote responsibility center autonomy.

  ➤ encourage motivation and communication among responsibility center managers.

6. Multinational companies using transfer prices encounter difficulties including

   - differences in tax systems, customs duties, freight and insurance costs, import/export regulations, and foreign-exchange controls.

   - the ability to determine what transfer price would be considered "reasonable" as though generated in an arm's-length transaction.

   - the increase in transfer pricing audits by tax authorities.

   - the process of having an advanced pricing agreement approved by appropriate tax authorities.

Solution Strategies

TRANSFER PRICES (COST BASED, MARKET BASED, NEGOTIATED, DUAL)

Upper limit: Lowest price available from external suppliers

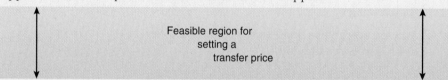

Feasible region for
setting a
transfer price

Lower limit: Incremental costs of producing and selling the transferred goods or services plus the opportunity cost of the facilities used

SERVICE DEPARTMENT COST ALLOCATION

Direct Method

1. Determine rational and systematic allocation bases for each service department.
2. Assign costs from each service department directly to revenue-producing areas using specified allocation bases. No costs are assigned to service areas.

Step Method

1. Determine rational and systematic allocation bases for each service department.
2. List service departments in sequence (benefits-provided ranking) from the one that provides the most service to all other areas (both revenue-producing and non-revenue-producing areas) to the one that provides service to only revenue-producing areas.
3. Beginning with the first service department listed, allocate the costs from that department to all remaining departments; repeat the process until only revenue-producing departments remain.

Algebraic Method

1. Determine rational and systematic allocation bases for each department.
2. Develop algebraic equations representing the services provided by each department to other service departments and to revenue-producing departments using the allocation bases.

3. Solve the simultaneous equations for the service departments through an iterative process or by computer until all values are known.
4. Allocate costs using allocation bases developed in step 2. Eliminate "reallocated" costs from consideration.

Demonstration Problem

RaceFest Inc. has two production divisions. The Ski Division (SD) makes water and snow skis, and the Binding Division (BD) makes rubber boots for water skis. The Binding Division estimates that in the upcoming year, it will produce 800,000 pairs of boots and sell 600,000 pairs internally and 200,000 pairs externally. Managers of the two divisions are in the process of determining a transfer price for a pair of boots. The following information for the Binding Division is available:

Direct material	$27	
Direct labor	12	
Variable overhead	7	
Variable S&A (both for external and internal sales)	4	
Total variable cost		$50
Fixed overhead (rate based on estimated annual production)	$10	
Fixed selling and administrative (rate based on estimated annual sales)	5	
Total fixed cost		15
Total cost per pair of boots		$65
Markup on total variable cost (40%)		20
List price to external customers		$85

Required:
a. Determine a transfer price based on variable product cost.
b. Determine a transfer price based on total variable cost plus normal markup.
c. Determine a transfer price based on full production cost.
d. Determine a transfer price based on total cost per pair of boots.
e. Prepare the journal entries for the selling and buying segments if the transfer is made at the external selling price for the selling division and the full production cost for the buying division.
f. Assume that the Binding Division has no alternative use for the facilities that make the rubber boots for internal transfer. Also assume that the SD can buy equivalent boots externally for $80. Calculate the upper and lower limits for which the transfer price should be set.
g. Compute a transfer price that divides the "profit" between the two divisions equally.
h. In contrast to the assumption in part (f), assume that a large portion of the facilities in which boots are produced can be rented for $600,000 if BD makes boots only for external sale. Determine the lower limit of the transfer price.

Solution to Demonstration Problem

a. | | | |
    |---|---|---:|
    | Direct material | $27 | |
    | Direct labor | 12 | |
    | Variable overhead | 7 | |
    | Transfer price | $46 | |

b. | | | |
    |---|---|---:|
    | Total variable cost | $50 | |
    | Markup (40%) | 20 | |
    | Transfer price | $70 | |

c. | | | |
    |---|---|---:|
    | Variable production cost | $46 | |
    | Fixed production cost | 10 | |
    | Transfer price | $56 | |

d. | | | |
    |---|---|---:|
    | Total variable cost | $50 | |
    | Total fixed cost | 15 | |
    | Transfer price | $65 | |

e.   SD: A/R—BD (600,000 × $56)   33,600,000

            Intracompany Profits* (600,000 × $29)   17,400,000

                 Intracompany Sales* (600,000 × $85)   51,000,000

            Intracompany CGS* (600,000 × $56)   33,600,000

                 Finished Goods (600,000 × $56)   33,600,000

Note: When company income statements are prepared, these amounts would be eliminated as follows:

            Intracompany Sales   51,000,000

                 Intracompany CGS   33,600,000

                 Intracompany Profits   17,400,000

In addition, any remaining amounts of intracompany Accounts Receivable and Accounts Payable shown by the two divisions would be eliminated.

     BD: Inventory (600,000 × $56)   33,600,000

            A/P—SD   33,600,000

f.   Upper limit: Ski Division's external purchase price = $80

    Lower limit: Total variable cost of Binding Division = $50

g.   (Lower limit + Upper limit) ÷ 2 = ($50 + $80) ÷ 2 = $65

h. $600,000 ÷ 600,000 pairs of boots = $1 opportunity cost per pair

    Lower limit: Incremental variable cost of Binding Division + Opportunity cost = $50 + $1 = $51

Key Terms

administrative department *(p. 519)*
advance pricing agreement (APA)
    (p. 535)
algebraic method *(p. 522)*
benefits-provided ranking *(p. 522)*
cost center *(p. 517)*
decentralization *(p. 511)*

direct method *(p. 522)*
dual pricing arrangement *(p. 533)*
investment center *(p. 519)*
negotiated transfer price *(p. 532)*
profit center *(p. 518)*
pseudo-profit center *(p. 529)*
responsibility center *(p. 517)*

responsibility report *(p. 514)*
revenue center *(p. 518)*
service department *(p. 519)*
step method *(p. 522)*
suboptimization *(p. 519)*
transfer price *(p. 529)*

Questions

1. Bill Barnes is the president and chief operating officer of Barnes Electronics. He founded the company and has led it to its prominent place in the electronics field. He has manufacturing plants and outlets in 40 states. Barnes is finding, however, that he cannot "keep track" of things the way he did in the past. Discuss the advantages and disadvantages of decentralizing the firm's decision-making activities among the various local and regional managers. Also discuss what functions Barnes might want to be performed centrally and why he would choose these functions.

2. Why are responsibility reports prepared? Is it appropriate for a single responsibility report to be prepared for a division of a major company? Why or why not?

3. What is suboptimization, and what factors contribute to it in a decentralized firm?

4. Why are service department costs often allocated to revenue-producing departments? Is such an allocation process always useful from a decision-making standpoint? How might service department cost allocation create a feeling of cost responsibility among managers of revenue-producing departments?

5. "The four criteria for selecting an allocation base for service department costs should be applied equally." Discuss the merits of this statement.

6. Compare and contrast the direct, step, and algebraic methods of allocating service department costs. What are the advantages and disadvantages of each method?

7. When the algebraic method of allocating service department costs is used, total costs for each service department increase from what they were prior to the allocation. Why does this occur, and how are the additional costs treated?

8. What are transfer prices, and why do companies use them? How could the use of transfer prices improve or impair goal congruence?

9. Would transfer prices be used in each of the following responsibility centers: cost, revenue, profit, and investment? If so, how would they be used?

10. What problems might be encountered when attempting to implement a cost-based transfer pricing system? A market-based transfer price system?

11. What is dual pricing? What is the intended effect of dual pricing on the performance of each division affected by the dual price?

12. How can service departments use transfer prices, and what advantages do transfer prices have over cost allocation methods?

13. Explain why the determination of transfer prices could be more complex in a multinational setting than in a domestic setting.

Exercises

14. (Centralization versus decentralization) Indicate whether a firm exhibiting each of the following characteristics would more likely be centralized (C) or decentralized (D).
a. Two years old
b. Growth stage of product development
c. Tight management control
d. Widely dispersed operating units
e. Wary of financial impacts of incorrect subordinate management decisions
f. Subordinates highly trained and mentored in decision-making skills
g. Low level of organizational flexibility
h. Few employees
i. Slow growth rate
j. Rapidly changing market environment
k. Large number of employees who telecommute

15. (Decentralization advantages and disadvantages) Indicate whether each of the following is a potential advantage (A) or disadvantage (D) of decentralization. If an item is neither an advantage nor a disadvantage, use N.
a. Provision of increased job satisfaction
b. Development of leadership qualities
c. Promotion of goal congruence
d. Placement of decision maker closer to time and place of problem
e. Use of management by exception principle by top management
f. Support of training in decision making
g. Complication of communication process
h. Delegation of ultimate responsibility
i. Cost of developing the planning and reporting system
j. Speed of decisions

16. (Decentralization; Internet) Search the Internet to identify three decentralized companies. Based on the information you find on each, either determine directly or infer from the information given the types of responsibility centers used by these companies. Also, determine or speculate about whether the companies use transfer prices or allocation of costs for intracompany transfers of services. Prepare a report on your findings and inferences. In cases for which you had to infer, explain what information or reasoning led you to that inference. Why is decentralization appropriate for some companies but not for others?

17. (Centralization vs. decentralization) Many companies are trying to determine the best organizational structure for information technology (IT) operations. In the 1980s, the reduced cost of computing technology and personnel caused many companies to decentralize the IT operations; this trend began to shift back to centralization during the past 10 years. Gather research to compare and contrast the advantages and disadvantages of centralized and decentralized IT operations. What other important information would you need to make a decision on such an organizational structure?

18. (Profit centers and allocations) Multiple-doctor medical practices are often structured with each doctor acting as a profit center.
a. Discuss why such an organizational structure would be useful.
b. Go to the Web and find some software packages that could be used to account for such an organizational structure.
c. List some costs of a medical practice that would be directly traceable to each physician.

d. List some costs of a medical practice that might not be directly traceable to each physician. Provide possible allocation bases for such costs.

19. (Direct method) Adelaide Corporation uses the direct method to allocate service department costs to production departments (Fabricating and Finishing). Information for June 2006 follows:

	Human Resources	Administration
Service department costs	$210,000	$150,000
Services provided to other departments		
Human resources		10%
Administration	15%	
Fabricating	40%	55%
Finishing	45%	35%

a. What amounts of human resource and administration costs should be assigned to fabricating for June?

b. What amounts of human resource and administration costs should be assigned to finishing for June?

20. (Direct method) Imbornone Bank has three service areas (administration, personnel, and accounting) and three revenue-generating areas (checking accounts, savings accounts, and loans). Monthly direct costs and the interdepartmental service structure are shown in the following benefits-provided ranking.

Department	Direct Costs	PERCENTAGE OF SERVICE USED BY					
		Admin.	Personnel	Accounting	Checking	Savings	Loans
Administration	$180,000		10%	10%	30%	40%	10%
Personnel	120,000	10%		10	30	20	30
Accounting	180,000	10	10		40	20	20
Checking	280,000						
Savings	150,000						
Loans	300,000						

Compute the total cost for each revenue-generating area using the direct method.

21. (Step method) Use the information in Exercise 20 to compute total cost for each revenue-generating area if the bank allocates costs under the step method of cost allocation.

22. (Step method) Rapp Company has three service departments (human resources, administration, and maintenance) and two revenue-generating departments (assembly and finishing). It uses the step method to allocate service department costs to operating departments. In October 2006, human resources incurred $120,000 of costs, administration incurred $270,000, and maintenance incurred $90,000. Proportions of services provided to other departments for October 2006 follow:

	HR	Administration	Maintenance
Human resources		10%	5%
Administration	15%		10
Maintenance	10	15	
Assembly	45	50	50
Finishing	30	25	35

a. Assuming that the departments are listed in a benefits-provided ranking, what amount of cost should be assigned to each of the other departments from human resources? From administration? From maintenance?

b. What total service department cost was assigned to assembly in October? To finishing?

(continued)

c. Explain why the cost allocation is affected by the order in which costs are assigned.

23. (Algebraic method) Use the information for Imbornone Bank in Exercise 20 to compute the total cost for each revenue-generating area using the algebraic method.

24. (Algebraic method) The following chart indicates the percentage of service department services used by other departments. Service departments are designated S1, S2, and S3; revenue-producing departments are designated RP1 and RP2.

| Department | SERVICES USED | | | | |
	S1	S2	S3	RP1	RP2
S1	n/a	10%	20%	30%	40%
S2	40%	n/a	30	20	10
S3	20	30	n/a	40	10

Costs of the period were $112,000, $240,000, and $360,000 for S1, S2, and S3, respectively. Allocate the service department costs to the revenue-producing departments using the algebraic method.

25. (Transfer pricing in service departments) Indicate whether each of the following statements constitutes a potential advantage (A), disadvantage (D), or neither (N) of using transfer prices for service department costs.
a. Can increase resource waste
b. Can make a service department into a profit center
c. Can cause certain services to be under- or overutilized
d. Can put all service departments on an equal footing
e. Can require additional organizational data and employee time
f. Can reduce goal congruence
g. Can increase communication about what additional services are needed and which can be reduced or eliminated
h. Can make users and providers more cost conscious
i. Can improve ability to evaluate performance
j. Can increase disagreements among departments

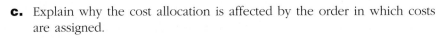

26. (Transfer pricing) Irmela Division, a subsidiary of Siberia Ltd., manufactures computer chips with the following costs:

Direct material	$10.00
Direct labor	17.50
Variable overhead	8.50
Fixed overhead	12.00
Total	$48.00

Some of the chips are sold externally for $108.75; others are transferred internally to the Gerhardt Division. Irmela Division's plant manager wants to establish a reasonable transfer price for chips transferred to Gerhardt. The purchasing manager of Gerhardt Division has informed the plant manager that comparable chips can be purchased externally in a price range from $75 to $115.
a. Determine the upper and lower limits for the transfer price between Irmela Division and Gerhardt Division.
b. If Irmela Division is presently selling all the chips it can produce to external buyers, what minimum price should be set for transfers to Gerhardt Division?

27. (Transfer pricing) Electronics and Appliances are two investment centers of At-Home Company. Electronics produces a microprocessor used by Appliances to manufacture several of its products; the microprocessor is also sold externally for $102.40. The following information is available about the microprocessor:

Total production annually (0.75 sold internally; 0.25 sold externally)	800,000 units
Variable production costs	$41.00
Variable selling costs (includes $4 per unit in advertising cost)	$12.00
Fixed overhead (allocated on the basis of units of production)	$1,200,000
Fixed selling costs	$1,600,000

Determine the transfer price under each of the following methods:

a. Total variable cost
b. Full production cost
c. Total variable production cost plus necessary selling costs
d. Market price

28. (Transfer pricing) Lafayette Co., a profit center of Creole Enterprises, manufactures brake pads to sell internally to other company divisions and externally. A set of Lafayette brake pads normally sells for $36. Production and selling costs for a set of brake pads follow:

Direct material	$4.50
Direct labor	5.70
Variable overhead	2.40
Fixed overhead (based on production of 700,000 sets)	8.25
Variable selling expense	1.50

Hammond Co., another division of Creole Enterprises, wants to purchase 50,000 sets of brake pads from Lafayette Co. during next year. No selling costs are incurred on internal sales.

a. If Lafayette's manager can sell all the brake pads it produces externally, what should the minimum transfer price be? Explain.
b. Assume that Lafayette Co. is experiencing a slight slowdown in external demand and will be able to sell only 600,000 sets of brake pads externally next year at the $36 selling price. What should be the minimum selling price to Hammond Co. under these conditions? Explain.
c. Assume that Ms. El-Deeb, the manager of Hammond Co., offers to pay Lafayette Division's production costs plus 25 percent for each set of brake pads. She receives an invoice for $1,303,125 but was planning on a cost of $787,500. How were these amounts determined? What created the confusion? Explain.

29. (Transfer pricing and management motivation) Yummy's Food Stores operates 20 large supermarkets in the Midwest. Each store is evaluated as a profit center, and store managers have complete control over their purchases and inventory policy. Company policy is that transfers between stores will be made at cost if a store runs short of an item and another store has a sufficient supply.

During a recent period of rapid increases in food prices, company managers noticed that interstore transfers had decreased sharply. Store managers indicated that it was almost impossible to find another store with sufficient inventory to make a transfer when one store ran short of inventory. However, more in-depth checking revealed that many of the other stores did actually have the inventory items on hand.

a. Why would the store managers be reluctant to make the interstore transfers?
b. How could the transfer pricing policy be changed to avoid this type of situation?

30. (Transfer pricing for services) Walsdorf Company's information technology department is developing a service department transfer price based on minutes of computer time. For 2006, its expected capacity was 350,000 minutes, and theoretical capacity was 500,000 minutes. Costs of the IT department for 2006 were expected to total $332,500.

a. What is the transfer price based on expected capacity?

b. What is the transfer price based on full capacity?

c. Actual operating costs in the IT department for 2006 were $350,000, and actual capacity usage was 365,000 minutes. What were the total variances from budget if the IT department used a transfer price based on expected capacity? On full capacity? What are some possible causes of that variance?

31. (Web research) Use the Internet to identify a multinational company encountering tax problems related to transfer pricing between its organizational units in different countries. Prepare a brief discussion of the issues and the actual or potential consequences.

Problems

32. (Decentralization; ethics) A large U.S. corporation participates in a highly competitive industry. Company management has decided that decentralization will best allow the company to meet the competition and achieve profit goals. Each responsibility center manager is evaluated on the basis of profit contribution, market penetration, and return on investment. Failure to meet the objectives established by corporate management for these measures is not acceptable and usually results in demotion or dismissal of a center manager.

An anonymous survey of company managers showed that they felt extreme pressure to compromise their personal ethical standards to achieve corporate objectives. For example, managers at certain plants felt it necessary, for cost control purposes, to reduce quality control to such a level that it was uncertain whether all unsafe products were being rejected. Also, sales personnel were encouraged to use questionable tactics to obtain orders, including offering gifts and other incentives to purchasing agents.

The chief executive officer is disturbed by the survey findings. In her opinion, the company cannot condone such behavior. She concludes that the company should do something about this problem.

a. Discuss what might be the causes for the ethical problems described.

b. Outline a program that could be instituted by the company to help reduce the pressures on managers to compromise personal ethical standards in their work.

(CMA adapted)

33. (Profit center performance) Mitchell Hardy, head of the accounting department at Hill Country College, has felt increasing pressure to raise external funds to compensate for dwindling state financial support. He decided to offer a three-day accounting workshop on income taxation for local CPAs in late February 2007. Jane Bennett, a tenured tax professor, offered to supervise the seminar's planning process. In mid-January, Bennett presented to Hardy the following profit budget:

Revenues ($2,000 per participant)		$200,000
Expenses		
Speakers ($5,000 each)	$110,000	
Rent on facilities	3,600	
Advertising	4,100	
Meals and lodging	19,800	
Departmental overhead allocation	51,000	(188,500)
Profit		$ 11,500

The following explains the budget: The $3,600 facilities rent is a fixed rental, which is to be paid to a local hotel for the use of its meeting rooms. Advertising is also a fixed cost. Meal expense is budgeted at $7 per person per meal (a total of nine meals to be provided for each participant); lodging is budgeted at the rate of $45 per participant per night. The departmental overhead includes a $10 charge per participant for supplies as well as a general allocation of 25 percent of revenues for use of departmental secretarial and production resources. After reviewing the budget, Hardy gave Bennett approval to proceed with the seminar.

a. Recast the budget in a segment margin income statement format.

b. The seminar's actual financial results were as follows:

Revenues (120 participants)		$216,000
Expenses		
Speakers ($5,450 each)	$119,900	
Rent on facilities	4,200	
Advertising	4,500	
Meals and lodging	23,760	
Departmental overhead allocation	55,200	(207,560)
Profit		$ 8,440

Because signups were below expectations, the seminar fee was reduced from $2,000 to $1,800 and advertising expense was increased. In budgeting for the speakers, Bennett neglected to include airfare, which averaged $450 per speaker. With the increased attendance, a larger meeting room had to be rented from the local hotel. Recast the actual results in a segment margin income format.

c. Compute variances between the budgeted segment margin income statement and the actual segment income statement. Identify and discuss the factors that are primarily responsible for the difference between the budgeted and actual profit on the tax seminar.

34. (Responsibility accounting reports) Hendrix Inc. manufactures industrial tools and has annual sales of approximately $3.5 million with no evidence of cyclical demand. R&D is very important to Hendrix because its market share expands only in response to product innovation.

The company controller has designed and implemented a new annual budget system divided into 12 equal segments for use for monthly performance evaluations. The vice president of operations was upset upon receiving the following responsibility report for the machining department for October 2006:

MACHINING DEPARTMENT
Responsibility Report
For the Month Ended October 31, 2006
(in $000s)

	Budget	Actual	Variance
Volume in units	3,000	3,185	185 F
Variable manufacturing costs			
Direct material	$24,000	$ 24,843	$ 843 U
Direct labor	27,750	29,302	1,552 U
Variable factory overhead	33,300	35,035	1,735 U
Total	$85,050	$ 89,180	$4,130 U
Fixed manufacturing costs			
Indirect labor	$ 3,300	$ 3,334	$ 34 U
Depreciation	1,500	1,500	0
Property tax	300	300	0
Insurance	240	240	0
Other	930	1,027	97 U
Total	$ 6,270	$ 6,401	$ 131 U
Corporate costs			
Research and development	$ 2,400	$ 3,728	$1,328 U
Selling and administration	3,600	4,075	475 U
Total	$ 6,000	$ 7,803	$1,803 U
Total costs	$97,320	$103,384	$6,064 U

a. Identify the weaknesses in the responsibility report for the machining department.

b. Prepare a revised responsibility report for the machining department that reduces or eliminates the weaknesses indicated in part (a).

c. Deviations in excess of 5 percent of budget are considered material and worthy of investigation. Should any of the machining department's variances be investigated? Regardless of materiality, is there any area that the vice president of operations might wish to discuss with the manager of the machining department?

(CMA adapted)

35. (Responsibility reports) To respond to increased competition and a reduction in profitability, a nationwide law firm, U.S. Law, recently instituted a responsibility accounting system. One of the several responsibility centers established was the Civil Litigation Division. This division is treated as a cost center for control purposes. In the first year (2006) after the new system was established, the responsibility report for the Civil Litigation Division contained the following comparisons:

	Budget	Actual	Variance
Variable costs			
Professional labor	$1,000,000	$ 940,000	$60,000 F
Travel	50,000	40,000	10,000 F
Supplies	100,000	90,000	10,000 F
Fixed costs			
Professional labor	400,000	405,000	5,000 U
Facilities	250,000	265,000	15,000 U
Insurance	80,000	78,000	2,000 F
Total	$1,880,000	$1,818,000	$62,000 F

For 2006, the division projected it would handle 1,000 cases, but its actual case load was 990.

a. What are the major weaknesses in the preceding responsibility report?

b. Recast the responsibility report in a more meaningful format for cost control evaluation.

c. If U.S. Law uses a management by exception philosophy, which costs are likely to receive additional investigation? Explain.

36. (Evaluating performance) On January 1, 2006, fast-tracker Michael Malicon was promoted to production manager of Salmon Company. The firm purchases raw fish, cooks and processes it, and then cans it in single-portion containers. It sells the canned fish to several wholesalers that specialize in providing food to school lunch programs in the northwest United States and western Canada. All processing is conducted in the firm's highly automated plant in Seattle, Washington. The production manager's performance is evaluated on the basis of a comparison of actual costs to standard costs. Only variable costs that the manager controls are included in the comparison. The cost of fish is noncontrollable. Standard costs per pound of fish for 2006 follow:

Direct labor	$0.25
Repairs	0.05
Maintenance	0.30
Indirect labor	0.05
Power	0.10

For 2006, the company purchased 5 million pounds of fish and canned 3 million pounds. There were no beginning or ending inventories of raw, in-process, or canned fish for the year. Actual 2006 costs were:

Direct labor	$600,000
Repairs	160,000
Maintenance	650,000
Indirect labor	155,000
Power	315,000

a. Prepare a responsibility report for Michael Malicon for 2006.

b. As his supervisor, evaluate Malicon's performance based on the report in part (a).

c. Malicon believes his 2006 performance is so good that he should be considered for immediate promotion to vice president of operations. Do you agree? Discuss the rationale for your answer.

d. Do you believe that all of the costs shown on Malicon's responsibility report are truly under his control? Discuss the rationale for your answer.

37. (Responsibility centers; research) According to Cutting Edge Information, Inc. ("Managing Financial Services Call Centers," August 2003, *http://www. mindbranch.com*), call center spending went from $717 million in 1998 to approximately $1.6 billion in 2003. Call centers are critical to organizational success because these units often have primary responsibility for interactions with customers. In some companies, the call centers are established primarily for customer support; in other companies (especially in the financial services sector), these centers not only provide customer support but also sell additional services to customers who call.

Use library, Web, or interview research to gather information on call centers. A starting point might be Alice Dragoon's, "Put Your Money Where Your Mouthpiece Is," *Darwin Magazine* (February 2002), *http://www. darwinmag.com/read/020102/mouthpiece.html*

a. Call centers often have a large responsibility for customer relationship management (CRM). What is CRM, and why is it so important to companies?

b. List five well-known companies that use call centers and indicate the primary purpose of those call centers.

c. For each company identified in part (b), do you think that its call center would primarily be considered a cost or profit center? Discuss the rationale for your answers.

d. For each company in part (b), list three possible methods of allocating the costs of call centers to revenue-producing departments. Discuss the rationale for your answers.

38. (Direct method) Management of Dekalb Community Hospital has decided to allocate the budgeted costs of its three service departments (administration, public relations, and maintenance) to its three revenue-producing programs (surgery, in-patient care, and out-patient services). Budgeted information for 2006 follows:

Budgeted costs

Administration	$2,000,000
Public relations	700,000
Maintenance	500,000

Allocation bases:

Administration	Dollars of assets employed
Public relations	Number of employees
Maintenance	Hours of equipment operation

	EXPECTED UTILIZATIONS		
	Dollars of Assets Employed	**Number of Employees**	**Hours of Equipment Operation**
Administration	$ 740,090	4	1,020
Public relations	450,100	7	470
Maintenance	825,680	5	1,530
Surgery	1,974,250	10	12,425
In-Patient care	1,229,250	18	8,875
Out-Patient services	521,500	22	14,200

Using the direct method, allocate the expected service department costs to the revenue-producing areas.

39. (Step method) Rodderick Properties classifies its operations into three departments: commercial sales, residential sales, and property management. The owner, Sandy Rodderick, wants to know the full cost of operating each department. Direct departmental costs and several allocation bases associated with each follow:

		AVAILABLE ALLOCATION BASES		
	Direct Costs	Number of Employees/ Salespersons	Dollars of Assets Employed	Dollars of Revenue
Administration	$ 750,000	10	$1,240,000	n/a
Accounting	495,000	5	682,000	n/a
Promotion	360,000	6	360,000	n/a
Commercial sales	5,245,000	21	500,000	$4,500,000
Residential sales	4,589,510	101	725,000	9,500,000
Property management	199,200	13	175,000	500,000

The service departments are shown in a benefits-provided ranking. Rodderick has selected the following allocation bases for each department: number of employees/salespersons for administration, dollars of assets employed for accounting, and dollars of revenue for promotion.

a. Use the step method to allocate the service department costs to the revenue-generating departments.

b. Which department is apparently the most profitable?

40. (Algebraic method) Leyh Press has two service departments (administration and editorial) and two revenue-producing divisions (college textbooks and professional publications). Following are the direct costs and allocation bases for each of these areas:

		ALLOCATION BASES	
Department	Direct Costs	Dollars of Assets Employed	Number of Employees
Administration	$ 450,000	$ 620,000	10
Editorial	350,000	10,000	5
College textbooks	2,250,000	1,200,000	50
Professional publications	950,000	1,050,000	30

Company management has decided to allocate administration and editorial costs using dollars of assets employed and number of employees, respectively. Use the algebraic method to allocate the service department costs and determine the total operating costs of college textbooks and professional publications.

41. (Comprehensive service department allocations) Yolanda Company's annual budget for its three service departments (administration, legal/accounting, and maintenance/engineering) and its two production departments (processing and finishing) follows:

	ANNUAL BUDGET ($000 omitted)					
	Admin.	Legal/ Acctg.	Maint./ Eng.	Proc.	Finish.	Total
Direct labor	$ 700	$500	$ 900	$2,800	$2,000	$ 6,900
Direct material	70	200	90	400	1,200	1,960
Insurance	175	50	75	300	220	820
Depreciation	90	70	80	200	150	590
Miscellaneous	30	20	40	60	30	180
Total	$1,065	$840	$1,185	$3,760	$3,600	$10,450
Sq. ft. of floor space	400	300	300	800	1,000	2,800
Number of employees	40	25	30	200	150	445
Maint./Eng. hours	10	20	15	80	75	200

a. Prepare a cost distribution that allocates service department costs using the step method. Assume the benefits-provided ranking is the order in which the departments are listed. The allocation bases for the service department are (1) administration: number of employees, (2) legal/accounting: floor space, and (3) maintenance/engineering: number of hours. Calculate the factory overhead rates using 400,000 direct labor hours in processing and 300,000 direct labor hours in finishing.

b. Calculate the factory overhead rates per direct labor hour using the direct method.

c. Calculate the factory overhead rates per direct labor hour using the algebraic method.

42. (Comprehensive service department allocations) As the controller for Reed Newspapers, you have been asked to allocate the costs of the paper's two service departments, administration and human resources, to the two revenue-generating departments, advertising and circulation. Administration costs are to be allocated on the basis of dollars of assets employed; human resources costs are to be allocated on the basis of number of employees. The following costs and allocation bases are available:

Department	Direct Costs	Number of Employees	Dollars of Assets Employed
Administration	$ 781,500	10	$ 387,100
Human resources	492,700	7	291,700
Advertising	957,800	12	762,400
Circulation	1,352,600	25	1,870,300
Totals	$3,584,600	54	$3,311,500

a. Using the direct method, allocate the service department costs to the revenue-generating departments.

b. Using your answer to part (a), what are the total costs of the revenue-generating departments after the allocations?

c. Assuming that the benefits-provided ranking is the order shown in the table, use the step method to allocate the service department costs to the revenue-generating departments.

d. Using your answer to part (b), what are the total costs of the revenue-generating departments after the allocations?

e. Using the algebraic method, allocate the service department costs to the revenue-generating departments.

43. (Transfer prices) In each of the following cases, the Speaker Division can sell all of its production of audio speakers externally or some internally to the Sound System Division and the remainder to outside customers. Speaker Division's production capacity is 200,000 units annually. The data related to each independent case are as follows:

Speaker Division	Case 1	Case 2
Selling price to outside customers	$75	$60
Production costs per unit		
Direct material	30	20
Direct labor	10	8
Variable overhead	3	2
Fixed overhead (based on capacity)	1	1
Other variable selling and delivery costs per unit*	6	4
Sound System Division		
Number of speakers needed annually	40,000	40,000
Current unit price being paid to outside supplier	$65	$52

*In either case, $1 of the selling expenses will *not* be incurred on intracompany transfers.

a. For each case, determine the upper and lower limits for a transfer price for speakers.

b. For each case, determine a transfer price for the Speaker Division that will provide a $10 contribution margin per unit.

c. Using the information developed for part (b), determine a dual transfer price for case 1 assuming that Sound System will be able to acquire the speakers from the Speaker Division at $10 below Sound System's purchase price from outside suppliers.

44. (Transfer price) Miranda Company comprises the Engine Division and the Mobile Systems Division. The Engine Division produces engines used by both the Mobile Systems Division and a variety of external industrial customers. External sales orders are generally produced in 50-unit lots. Using this typical lot size, the cost per engine is as follows:

Variable production cost	$2,100
Fixed manufacturing overhead	900
Variable selling expense	300
Fixed selling expense	420
Fixed administrative expense	640
Total unit cost	$4,360

An engine's external selling price is $5,232, providing the Engine Division with a normal profit margin of 20 percent. Because a significant number of sales are being made internally, Engine Division managers have decided that the external selling price should be used to transfer all engines to Mobile Systems.

When the Mobile Systems Division manager learned of the new transfer price, she became very upset because it would have a major negative impact on her division's profit figures. Mobile Systems has asked Engine Division to lower its transfer price so that it earns a profit margin of only 15 percent. Mobile Systems' manager has asked corporate management whether the division can buy engines externally. Tom Hawkins, Miranda's president, has gathered the following information on transfer prices to help the two divisional managers negotiate an equitable transfer price:

Current external sales price	$5,232
Total variable production cost plus a 20% profit margin ($2,100 × 1.2)	2,520
Total production cost plus a 20% profit margin ($3,000 × 1.2)	3,600
Bid price from external supplier (if motors are purchased in 50-unit lots)	4,640

a. Discuss advantages and disadvantages of each of these transfer prices to both the selling and buying divisions and to Miranda Company.

b. If the Engine Division could sell all of its production externally at $5,232, what is the appropriate transfer price and why?

45. (Journal entries) Corporate Travel Division makes top-of-the-line computer bags and sells them to external buyers and to the Travel America Division in luggage sets sold. During the month just ended, Travel America acquired 4,000 bags from Corporate Travel Division, whose standard unit costs follow:

Direct material	$20
Direct labor	6
Variable factory overhead	8
Fixed factory overhead	12
Variable selling expense	4
Fixed selling and administrative expense	6

Travel America can acquire comparable bags externally for $80 each. Give the entries for each division for the past month if the transfer is to be recorded

a. at Travel America's external purchase price.

b. at a negotiated price of variable cost plus 15 percent of full production cost.

c. by Corporate Travel at Travel America's external price, and by Travel America at Corporate Travel's variable production cost.

d. at Corporate Travel's absorption cost.

46. (Internal versus external sale) Providence Products Inc. consists of three decentralized divisions: Park, Quayside, and Ridgetop. The president of Providence Products has given the managers of the three divisions the authority to decide whether to sell externally or internally at a transfer price the division managers determine. Market conditions are such that internal or external sales will not affect market or transfer prices. Intermediate markets will always be available for Park, Quayside, and Ridgetop to purchase their manufacturing needs or sell their product. Division managers attempt to maximize their contribution margin at the current level of operating assets for their divisions.

The Quayside Division manager is considering the following two alternative orders.

- Ridgetop Division needs 3,000 units of a motor that Quayside Division can supply. To manufacture these motors, Quayside would purchase components from Park Division at a transfer price of $600 per unit; Park's variable cost for these components is $300 per unit. Quayside Division would further process these components at a variable cost of $500 per unit.

  If Ridgetop cannot obtain the motors from Quayside, it will purchase the motors from Essex Company for $1,500 per unit. Essex Company would also purchase 3,000 components from Park at a price of $400 for each motor; Park's variable cost for these components is $200 per unit.

- Saxon Company wants to buy 3,500 similar motors from the Quayside Division for $1,250 per unit. Quayside would again purchase components from Park Division, in this case at a transfer price of $500 per unit; Park's variable cost for these components is $250 per unit. Quayside Division would further process these components at a variable cost of $400 per unit.

Quayside Division's plant capacity is limited, and therefore the company can accept either the Saxon contract or the Ridgetop order but not both. The president of Providence Products and the manager of Quayside Division agree that it would not be beneficial in the short or long run to increase capacity.

a. If the Quayside Division manager wants to maximize short-run contribution margin, determine whether Quayside Division should (1) sell motors to Ridgetop Division at the prevailing market price or (2) accept Saxon Company's contract. Support your answer with appropriate calculations.

b. Without prejudice to your answer to part (a), assume that Quayside Division decides to accept the Saxon contract. Determine whether this decision is in the best interest of Providence Products Inc. Support your answer with appropriate calculations.

(CMA adapted)

47. (Transfer prices) Green & Marshand LLC has three revenue departments: litigation (Lit.), family practice (FP), and legal consulting (LC). In addition, the company has two support departments, administration and EDP. Administration costs are allocated to the three revenue departments on the basis of number of employees. EDP's fixed costs are allocated to revenue departments on the basis of peak hours of monthly service expected to be used by each revenue department. EDP's variable costs are assigned to the revenue departments at a transfer price of $40 per hour of actual service. Following are the direct costs and the allocation bases associated with each of the departments:

	Direct Costs (before transfer costs)	ALLOCATION BASES: NUMBER OF		
		Employees	Peak Hours	EDP Hours Used
Administration	$450,000	4	30	290
EDP—Fixed	300,000	2	n/a	n/a
EDP—Variable	90,000	2	n/a	n/a
Lit.	200,000	10	80	1,220
FP	255,000	5	240	650
LC	340,000	3	25	190

a. Was the variable EDP transfer price of $40 adequate? Explain.

b. Allocate all service department costs to the revenue-producing departments using the direct method.

c. What are the total costs of the revenue-producing departments after the allocation in part (b)?

48. (Interdivisional transfers; deciding on alternatives) Amy Keeler, a management accountant, has recently been employed as controller in the Fashions Division of Deluxe Products, Inc. The company is organized on a divisional basis with considerable vertical integration.

Fashions Division makes several luggage products, including a slim leather portfolio. Its sales have been steady, and the marketing department expects continued strong demand. Keeler is looking for ways the Fashions Division can contain its costs and thus boost its earnings from future sales. She discovered that Fashions Division has always purchased its supply of high-quality tanned leather from another division of Deluxe Products, the LeatherWorks Division. LeatherWorks has been providing the 3 square feet of tanned leather needed for each portfolio for $9 per square foot.

Keeler wondered whether it might be possible to purchase Fashions' leather needs at comparable quality from an external supplier at a lower price. Top management at Deluxe Products reluctantly agreed to allow Fashions Division to consider purchasing outside the company.

Fashions Division will need leather for 100,000 portfolios during the coming year. Its management has requested bids from several leather suppliers. The two best bids are $8 and $7 per square foot from Koenig and Thompson, respectively. Keeler has been informed that another subsidiary of Deluxe Products, Barrows Chemical, supplies Thompson the chemicals that are an essential ingredient of Thompson's tanning process. Barrows Chemical charges Thompson $2 for enough chemicals to prepare 3 square feet of leather. Barrows' profit margin is 30 percent.

LeatherWorks Division wants to continue supplying Fashions' leather needs at the same price per square foot as in the past. Tom Reed, LeatherWorks' controller, has made it clear that he believes Fashions should continue to purchase all its needs from LeatherWorks to preserve LeatherWorks' healthy profit margin of 40 percent of sales.

As Deluxe Products' vice president of finance, you have called a meeting of the controllers of Fashions and LeatherWorks. Keeler is eager to accept Thompson's bid of $7. She points out that Fashions' earnings will show a significant increase if the division can buy from Thompson.

Reed, however, wants Deluxe Products to keep the business within the company and suggests that you require Fashions to purchase its needs from LeatherWorks. He emphasizes that LeatherWorks' profit margin should not be lost to the company.

From whom should the Fashions Division buy the leather? Consider both Fashions' desire to minimize its costs and Deluxe Products' corporate goal of maximizing profit on a companywide basis.

(IMA adapted)

49. (Transfer prices; discussion) Biloxi Products Inc. is a decentralized company. Each division has its own sales force and production facilities and is operated as an investment center. Top management uses return on investment (income divided by assets) for performance evaluation. Jackson Division has just been awarded a contract for a product that uses a component manufactured by Walters Division and by outside suppliers. Jackson used a cost figure of $7.60 for the component when the bid was prepared for the new product. Walters supplied this cost figure in response to Jackson's request for the average variable cost of the component.

Walters has an active sales force that is continually soliciting new customers, and sales of the component are expected to increase. Walters's regular selling price is $13 for the component that Jackson needs for the new product. Walters management has the following costs associated with the component:

Standard variable manufacturing cost	$ 6.40
Standard variable selling and distribution cost	1.20
Standard fixed manufacturing cost	2.40
Total	$10.00

The two divisions have been unable to agree on a transfer price for the component. Corporate management has never established a transfer price because interdivisional transactions have never occurred. The following suggestions have been made for the transfer price:
- regular selling price,
- regular selling price less variable selling and distribution expenses,
- standard manufacturing cost plus 15 percent, or
- standard variable manufacturing cost plus 20 percent.

a. Compute each suggested transfer price.

b. Discuss the effect that each of the transfer prices might have on the attitude of Walters Division management toward intracompany business.

c. Is the negotiation of a price between the Jackson and Walters Divisions a satisfactory method to solve the transfer price problem? Explain your answer.

d. Should the corporate management of Biloxi Products Inc. become involved in this transfer controversy? Explain your answer.

(CMA adapted)

50. (Effect of service department allocations on reporting and evaluation) Kendra Corporation is a diversified manufacturing company with corporate headquarters in Eagan, Minnesota. The three operating divisions are Kennedy Division, Plastic Products Division, and Outerspace Products Division. Much of Kennedy Division's manufacturing activity is related to work performed for the government space program under negotiated contracts.

Kendra Corporation headquarters provides general administrative support and computer services to each of the three operating divisions. The computer services are provided through a computer time-sharing arrangement. The central processing unit (CPU) is located in St. Paul, and the divisions have remote terminals connected to the CPU by telephone lines. One standard from the Cost Accounting Standards Board provides that the cost of general administration may be allocated to negotiated defense contracts. Furthermore, the standards provide that, in situations in which computer services are provided by corporate headquarters, the actual costs (fixed and variable) of operating the computer department may be allocated to the Kennedy division based on a reasonable measure of computer usage.

The general manager of each of the three divisions is evaluated based on the division's before-tax performance. The November 2006 performance evaluation reports (in millions of dollars) for each division follow:

	Kennedy Division	Plastics Products Division	Outerspace Products Division
Sales	$ 23	$ 15	$ 55
Cost of goods sold	(13)	(7)	(38)
Gross profit	$ 10	$ 8	$ 17
Selling and administrative			
Division selling and administration costs	$ 5	$ 5	$ 8
Corporate general administration costs	1	0	0
Corporate computing	1	0	0
Total	$ 7	$ 5	$ 8
Profit before taxes	$ 3	$ 3	$ 9

Without a charge for computing services, the operating divisions might not make the most cost-effective use of the Computer Systems Department's resources. Outline and discuss a method for charging the operating divisions for use of computer services that would promote cost consciousness by the operating divisions and operating efficiency by the Computer Systems Department.

(CMA adapted)

51. (Transfer prices) Schmidt Industries consists of eight divisions that are evaluated as profit centers. All transfers between divisions are made at market price. Precision Regulator is a division of Schmidt that sells approximately 20 percent of its output externally. The remaining 80 percent of Precision Regulator's output is transferred to other divisions within Schmidt. No other Schmidt Industries division transfers internally more than 10 percent of its output.

Based on any profit-based measure of performance, Precision Regulator is the leading division within Schmidt Industries. Other divisional managers always find that their performance is compared to that of Precision Regulator. These managers argue that the transfer pricing situation gives Precision Regulator a competitive advantage.

a. What factors could contribute to any advantage that the Precision Regulator Division might have over the other divisions?

b. What alternative transfer price or performance measure might be more appropriate in this situation?

52. (Transfer prices; research) Go to the Ernst & Young Web site or to the *Journal of International Taxation* (April, May, and June 2004) to find information on the E&Y 2003 Global Survey on Transfer Pricing. (Should a more recent survey be available, use its information.) Choose five countries and compare and contrast the transfer pricing survey results for those countries, including APAs.

14

Capital Budgeting

Objectives

AFTER COMPLETING THIS CHAPTER, YOU SHOULD BE ABLE TO ANSWER THE FOLLOWING QUESTIONS:

LO.1 WHY DO MOST CAPITAL BUDGETING METHODS FOCUS ON CASH FLOWS?

LO.2 HOW IS PAYBACK PERIOD COMPUTED, AND WHAT DOES IT MEASURE?

LO.3 HOW ARE THE NET PRESENT VALUE AND PROFITABILITY INDEX OF A PROJECT MEASURED?

LO.4 HOW IS THE INTERNAL RATE OF RETURN ON A PROJECT COMPUTED? WHAT DOES IT MEASURE?

LO.5 HOW DO TAXATION AND DEPRECIATION METHODS AFFECT CASH FLOWS?

LO.6 WHAT ARE THE UNDERLYING ASSUMPTIONS AND LIMITATIONS OF EACH CAPITAL PROJECT EVALUATION METHOD?

LO.7 HOW DO MANAGERS RANK INVESTMENT PROJECTS?

LO.8 HOW IS RISK CONSIDERED IN CAPITAL BUDGETING ANALYSIS?

LO.9 HOW AND WHY SHOULD MANAGEMENT CONDUCT A POSTINVESTMENT AUDIT OF A CAPITAL PROJECT?

LO.10 *(APPENDIX 1)* HOW ARE PRESENT VALUES CALCULATED?

LO.11 *(APPENDIX 2)* WHAT ARE THE ADVANTAGES AND DISADVANTAGES OF THE ACCOUNTING RATE OF RETURN METHOD?

According to the American Pharmaceutical Association, the estimated cost in 2003 to develop a new drug was almost $900 million.* Furthermore, the average time of the development process is almost 12 years.[†] This product development cycle is likely the longest of any major industry, and pharmaceutical firms invest more money in research and development (R&D) than do firms in other industries. In this industry, current revenues are derived from the efforts of previous years' R&D spending, and future revenues are derived from current R&D spending. Thus, R&D spending is a key revenue driver for the industry.

In 2003, Merck & Co., a major global pharmaceutical company, spent in excess of $3 billion on R&D, which represented more than 13 percent of revenue for the year and an increase of 19 percent over 2002 R&D spending. Merck's R&D spending is targeted at common global medical ailments such as asthma, arthritis, cardiovascular disorders, diabetes, infectious diseases, neurological problems, obesity, and osteoporosis. Merck, like other large pharmaceutical companies, maintains an R&D pipeline that is filled with products and ideas at various levels of development.

One major obstacle in the pharmaceutical product development process is clearing the many regulatory hurdles that exist to protect consumers. In the United States, the Food and Drug Administration (FDA) is charged with the responsibility of protecting consumers and maintaining regulatory oversight over new drug development. Similar agencies fulfill comparable roles in other countries.

Significant stages of development and testing precede any involvement by the regulatory authorities in approving potential drugs for the marketplace. Only about 1 in 5,000 potential drugs that are synthesized is eventually marketable.[‡] Hence, managing the risks of product development and carefully choosing how to spend R&D funds are activities that are critical to the success of pharmaceutical companies such as Merck.

Source: Merck & Co. 2003 Annual Report.
*American Pharmaceutical Association, *http://www.aphanet.org/APRS/03enewsedit.html.*
[†]National Center for Policy Analysis, "Costs to Develop New Drugs Soar," *Health Policy Digest*, December 03, 2001; *http://www.ncpa.org/iss/hea/pd120301b.html.*
[‡]American Pharmaceutical Association, *http://www.aphanet.org/APRS/03enewsedit.html.*

capital asset

Choosing the assets in which an organization will invest is one of the most important business decisions for managers. In almost every organization, investments must be made in some short-term working capital assets, such as merchandise inventory, supplies, and raw material. Organizations must also invest in **capital assets**, which are used to generate future revenues or cost savings or to provide distribution, service, or production capabilities. A capital asset can be a tangible fixed asset (such as a piece of machinery or a building) or an intangible asset (such as a capital lease or drug patent). For example, in addition to spending in excess of $3 billion in 2003 on R&D, Merck & Co. spent $788 million to build production facilities, $764 million to build research facilities, and $364 million on other long-term projects.[1]

Providing information about the estimated financial returns of potential capital projects is one of the important tasks of cost accountants. This chapter discusses a variety of techniques that managers use to evaluate the potential financial costs and contributions of proposed capital projects. Several of these techniques are based on an analysis of the amounts and timing of project cash flows.

CAPITAL ASSET ACQUISITION

Capital asset acquisition is often part of the solution to many of the issues discussed in this text. For example, product quality improvement and business process reengineering often depend on the acquisition of new technology or investment in training programs. Creating strategic alliances can involve decisions to invest in other companies.

[1] Merck & Co. 2003 Annual Report.

capital budgeting

Financial managers, assisted by cost accountants, are responsible for analyzing the appropriateness of capital asset acquisitions through a process of capital budgeting. **Capital budgeting** involves the evaluation of future long-range projects or courses of activity to effectively and efficiently allocate limited resources. The process includes planning for and preparing the capital budget as well as reviewing past investments to assess and enhance the success of the decision process. Planned annual expenditures for capital projects for the near term (less than 5 years) and summary information for the long term (6 to 10 years) are shown in the capital budget, which is a key instrument in implementing organizational strategies.

Capital budgeting involves comparing and evaluating alternative projects within a budgetary framework. Managers and accountants apply various criteria to evaluate the feasibility of alternative projects. Although financial criteria are used to assess virtually all projects, firms now also use nonfinancial criteria to critically assess activities that have benefits that are difficult to monetarily quantify. For example, high-technology and R&D investments are often difficult to evaluate using only financial criteria.

One firm in the biotechnology industry uses the nine criteria shown in Exhibit 14–1 to evaluate the feasibility of its R&D projects. By evaluating potential capital projects using a portfolio of criteria, managers can be confident that they have considered all possible costs and contributions of projects. Additionally, multiple criteria allow for a balanced evaluation of short-term and long-term benefits, investment compatibility with existing technology, and project roles in both marketing and cost management. For this biotechnology company, the use of multiple criteria ensures that projects will be considered from the perspectives of strategy, marketing, cost management, quality, and technical feasibility. Note that criterion 4 in Exhibit 14–1 reflects a financial perspective by means of calculating the rate of return on investment, which is one cash flow technique used in capital budgeting.

EXHIBIT 14–1

PROJECT EVALUATION CRITERIA—R&D PROJECTS

1.　Potential for proprietary position

2.　Balance between short-term and long-term projects and payoffs

3.　Potential for collaborations and outside funding

4　Financial rate of return on investment

5.　Need to establish competency in an area

6.　Potential for spin-off projects

7.　Strategic fit with the corporation's planned and existing technology, manufacturing capabilities, and marketing and distribution systems

8.　Impact on long-term corporate positioning

9.　Probability of technical success

Source: Suresh Kalahnanam and Suzanne K. Schmidt, "Analyzing Capital Investments in New Products," *Management Accounting* (January 1996), pp. 31–36. Reprinted from *Management Accounting.* Copyright by Institute of Management Accountants, Montvale, N.J.

USE OF CASH FLOWS IN CAPITAL BUDGETING

LO.1
WHY DO MOST CAPITAL BUDGETING METHODS FOCUS ON CASH FLOWS?

Any investment made by an organization is expected to earn some type of return. Investments in bonds are expected to earn interest, and investments in other companies are expected to earn dividends. In general, such interest and dividends are cash amounts. Investments in capital assets, however, help to earn operating income, which is accrual based rather than cash based. Thus, to compare the returns

Focus on Quality

Vehicle Downtime Can Equal Customer Dissatisfaction

Vehicle-centric businesses (such as distribution companies) understand fleet management and generally have the in-house expertise to do it well. Most other businesses are focused on their core competencies and may not have the talent or energy to engage in good fleet management techniques. But a transportation fleet is, in fact, a business tool that is no different from manufacturing equipment.

The acquisition of the fleet involves a capital budgeting process that must focus on both the obvious direct costs of buying and maintaining the fleet as well as the indirect costs. Indirect costs are more difficult to track than direct costs, but they are certainly no less important. Three important indirect costs are those of driver pay during vehicle downtime, lost revenue from vehicle downtime, and the potential revenue side effects related to customer service and quality issues because of missed appointments caused by vehicle downtime or maintenance.

Many times the vehicle fleet in an organization is used by employees such as sales representatives and service technicians who use vehicle transportation to make critical contributions to generating revenue and assuring customer satisfaction. It is essential that such

employees' transportation needs are effectively supported. Good fleet management can ensure that workers get the transportation they need and sometimes deliver $1 million in cost savings for a typical mid-to-large size enterprise.

In fleet applications where drivers are directly responsible for revenue inflows and customer service, unscheduled vehicle downtime can be far more costly in lost revenue than the cost of the fleet. In some cases, a missed appointment or uncompleted work order can be viewed simply as a "defect" that can be reworked by rescheduling for another day and only the driver's time is lost. In other situations, that missed appointment can result in major revenue loss or customer disruption and the cost of downtime is far higher than lost productivity. The economic benefit of a good fleet management strategy, which should be reflected in the original capital budgeting process, must be weighed against all incremental costs of the transportation process— including the quality of service being provided to organizational customers.

Source: Scott Pattullo, "Save $1 Million with Better Fleet Management," *Strategic Finance* (May 2004). Reprinted with permission.

---

on various investments, operating income must be converted to a cash basis. Remember that accrual accounting recognizes revenue when it is earned rather than when cash is received, and it recognizes expenses when they are incurred rather than when cash is paid. Converting operating income to cash flow information puts all investment returns on an equivalent basis.

Capital budgeting investment decisions can be made using a variety of techniques including payback period, net present value, profitability index, internal rate of return, and accounting rate of return. All of these methods, except the accounting rate of return, focus on the amounts and timing of **cash flows** (receipts or disbursements of cash). Cash receipts include revenues from a capital project that have been earned and collected, savings generated by the project's reductions in existing operating costs, and any cash inflow from selling the asset at the end of its useful life. Cash disbursements include asset acquisition expenditures, additional working capital investments, and costs for project-related direct material, direct labor, and overhead.

Interest cost is a cash outflow associated with debt financing and is *not* part of the project selection process. Project funding is a financing, not an investment, decision. A **financing decision** is a judgment regarding the method of raising capital to fund an investment. Financing is based on an entity's ability to issue and service debt and equity securities. On the other hand, an **investment decision** is

cash flow

financing decision

investment decision

a judgment about which assets to acquire to achieve an entity's stated objectives. Cash flows generated by the two types of decisions should not be combined. Company management must justify the acquisition and use of an asset prior to justifying the method of financing that asset.

Including financing receipts and disbursements with other project cash flows conceals a project's true profitability because financing costs relate to all projects of an entity rather than to a specific project. The assignment of financing costs to a specific project is often arbitrary, which causes problems in comparing projects that are acquired with different financing sources. In addition, including the financing effects in an investment decision creates a problem in assigning responsibility. Divisional managers, or top managers with input from divisional managers, make investment decisions. An organization's treasurer in conjunction with top management typically makes financing decisions.

Cash flows from a capital project are received and paid at different points in time over the project's life. Some cash flows occur at the beginning of a period, some during the period, and others at the end. To simplify capital budgeting analysis, most analysts assume that all cash flows occur at a specific, single point in time—typically, either at the beginning or end of the time period in which they actually occur. The following example illustrates how cash flows are treated in capital budgeting situations.

CASH FLOWS ILLUSTRATED

Assume that various capital projects are being considered by Farm Pharm, a small company in the biotechnology sector of the pharmaceutical industry. One investment that it is considering is the acquisition of a competitor's patent that stands as a barrier to market Farm Pharm's newly developed product.

The expected patent purchase cost and expected cash income and expenses appear in Exhibit 14–2. This detailed information can be simplified to a net cash flow for each year. For Farm Pharm, the project generates a net negative flow in the first year and net positive cash flows thereafter. This cash flow information can be illustrated through the use of a time line.

EXHIBIT 14–2

FARM PHARM'S PATENT ACQUISITION DECISION INFORMATION

Cash Outflows (000s)	
Year 0	$11,500
Year 1	400
Year 2	300
Year 3	200
Cash Inflows (000s)	
Cash receipts less cash operating costs:	
Year 1	$3,700
Year 2	3,500
Year 3	3,400
Year 4	2,900
Year 5	2,400
Year 6	2,100
Year 7	1,000

Note: After year 7, it is expected that competitors will have superior products available that will render the patent worthless.

Time Lines

How are time lines used in evaluating capital investment proposals?

time line

A **time line** visually illustrates the points in time when projected cash flows are received or paid, making it a helpful tool for analyzing cash flows of a capital investment proposal. Cash inflows are shown as positive amounts on a time line and cash outflows are shown as negative amounts.

The following time line represents the cash flows (in millions) from Farm Pharm's potential patent investment.

End of period	0	1	2	3	4	5	6	7
Inflows	$ 0	$3,700	$3,500	$3,400	$2,900	$2,400	$2,100	$1,000
Outflows	(11,500)	(400)	(300)	(200)	(0)	(0)	(0)	(0)
Net cash flow	$(11,500)	$3,300	$3,200	$3,200	$2,900	$2,400	$2,100	$1,000

On a time line, the date of initial investment represents time point 0 because the investment is made immediately. Each year after the initial investment is represented as a full time period; periods serve only to separate the timing of cash flows. Nothing is presumed to happen during a period. Thus, for example, cash inflows each year from product sales are shown as occurring at the end of, rather than during, the time period. A less conservative assumption would show the cash flows occurring at the beginning of the period.

Payback Period

LO.2
HOW IS PAYBACK PERIOD COMPUTED, AND WHAT DOES IT MEASURE?

payback period

Why are managers interested in estimating the payback period of a proposed investment project?

Information on the timing of net cash flows is an input to a simple and often used capital budgeting technique called **payback period**. This method measures the time required for a project's cash inflows to equal the original investment. At the end of the payback period, a company has recouped its investment.

In one sense, payback period measures a dimension of project risk by focusing on the timing of cash flows. The assumption is that the longer it takes to recover the initial investment, the greater is the project's risk because cash flows in the more distant future are more uncertain than relatively current cash flows. Another reason for concern about long payback periods relates to capital reinvestment. The faster that capital is returned from an investment, the more rapidly it can be invested in other projects.

Payback period for a project having unequal cash inflows is determined by accumulating cash flows until the original investment is recovered. Thus, using the information shown in Exhibit 14–2 and the time line presented earlier, the patent investment payback period is calculated using a yearly cumulative total of inflows (in millions) as follows:

Year	Annual Amount	Cumulative Total
0	$(11,500)	$(11,500)
1	3,300	(8,200)
2	3,200	(5,000)
3	3,200	(1,800)
4	2,900	1,100
5	2,400	3,500
6	2,100	5,600
7	1,000	6,600

At the end of the third year, all but $1,800 of the initial investment of $11,500 has been recovered. The $2,900 inflow in the fourth year is assumed to occur evenly throughout the year. Therefore, it should take approximately 62 percent ($1,800 ÷ $2,900) of the fourth year to cover the rest of the original investment, giving a payback period for this project of 3.62 years (or 3 years and 7.5 months).

annuity

When the cash flows from a project are equal each period (an **annuity**), the payback period is determined as follows:

$$\text{Payback Period} = \text{Investment} \div \text{Annuity}$$

Assume that another investment being considered by Farm Pharm requires an initial investment of $50,000 and is expected to generate equal annual cash flows of $8,000 in each of the next 10 years. In this case, the payback period would equal the $50,000 net investment cost divided by $8,000, or 6.25 years (6 years and 3 months).

Company management typically sets a maximum acceptable payback period as one of the financial evaluation criteria for capital projects. If Farm Pharm has set six years as the longest acceptable payback period, the patent investment would be considered acceptable, but the second investment project would be considered unacceptable.

Most companies use payback period as only one way to judge an investment project quantitatively. After being found acceptable in terms of payback period, a project is then subjected to evaluation by other financial capital budgeting techniques. A second evaluation is usually performed because the payback period method ignores three things: inflows occurring after the payback period has been reached, the company's desired rate of return, and the time value of money. These issues are incorporated into the decision process using discounted cash flow techniques.

DISCOUNTING FUTURE CASH FLOWS

In evaluating capital investments, why are discounted cash flow methods desirable?

A time value is associated with money because interest is paid or received on money.[2] For example, $1 received today has more value than $1 received one year from today because money received today can be invested to generate a return that will cause it to accumulate to more than $1 over time. This phenomenon encourages the use of discounted cash flow techniques in most capital budgeting situations to account for the time value of money.

discounting

Discounting means reducing future cash flows to their present value amounts by removing the portion of the future values representing interest. This "imputed" amount of interest is based on two considerations: the length of time until the cash flow is received or paid and the rate of interest assumed. After discounting, all future values associated with a project are stated in a common base of current dollars, also known as their **present values (PV)**. Cash receipts and disbursements occurring at the beginning of a project (time 0) are already stated in their present values and are not discounted.

present value (PV)

Capital project information involves the use of estimates. It is extremely important, therefore, to have the best possible estimates of all potential cash inflows and outflows. To appropriately discount cash flows, managers must estimate the rate of return on capital required by the company in addition to the project's cost and cash flow estimates. This rate of return, called the **discount rate**, is used to determine the imputed interest portion of future cash receipts and expenditures. The discount rate should equal or exceed the company's **cost of capital (COC)**, which is the weighted average cost of the various sources of funds (debt and equity) that compose a firm's financial structure.[3] For example, if a company has a COC of 10 percent, it annually costs an average of 10 percent of each capital dollar to finance investment projects. To determine whether a capital project is a worthwhile

discount rate

cost of capital (COC)

---

[2] The time value of money and present value computations are covered in Appendix 1 of this chapter. These concepts are essential to understanding the rest of this chapter; be certain they are clear before continuing.

[3] All examples in this chapter use an assumed discount rate or cost of capital. The computations required to find a company's cost of capital rate are discussed in any principles of finance text.

investment, this company should generally use a minimum rate of 10 percent to discount its projects' future cash flows.

A distinction must be made between cash flows representing a return *of* capital and those representing a return *on* capital. A **return of capital** is the recovery of the original investment (or the return of principal), whereas a **return on capital** is income and equals the discount rate multiplied by the investment amount. For example, $1.00 invested in a project that yields a 10 percent rate of return will grow to a sum of $1.10 in one year. Of the $1.10, $1.00 represents the return of capital and $0.10 represents the return on capital. The return on capital is computed for each period of the investment life. For a company to be better off by making an investment, a project must produce cash inflows that exceed the investment made and the cost of capital. To determine whether a project meets a company's desired rate of return, one of several discounted cash flow methods can be used.

return of capital

return on capital

DISCOUNTED CASH FLOW METHODS

LO.3
HOW ARE THE NET PRESENT VALUE AND PROFITABILITY INDEX OF A PROJECT MEASURED?

Three discounted cash flow techniques are the net present value method, the profitability index, and the internal rate of return. Each of these methods is defined and illustrated in the following subsections.

Net Present Value Method

If the projected NPV of a proposed project is $0, is the project acceptable?

net present value method

net present value (NPV)

The **net present value method** determines whether a project's rate of return is equal to, higher than, or lower than the desired rate of return. Each cash flow from the project is discounted to its present value using the company's desired rate of return. Subtracting the total present value of all cash outflows of an investment project from the total present value of all cash inflows yields the project's **net present value (NPV)**. Exhibit 14–3 uses a 10 percent discount rate to illustrate the net present value calculations for the cash flow data shown in Exhibit 14–2.

The factors used to compute the net present value are obtained from the present value tables provided in Appendix A at the end of the text. Each period's cash flow is multiplied by a factor obtained from Table 1 (PV of $1) for 10 percent and the appropriate time period designated for the cash flow.

The net present value represents the net cash benefit (or, if negative, the net cash cost) of acquiring and using the proposed asset. If the NPV is zero, the project's actual rate of return is equal to the required rate of return. If the NPV is positive,

EXHIBIT 14–3

NET PRESENT VALUE CALCULATION FOR PATENT INVESTMENT (IN $000s)

			DISCOUNT RATE = 10%		
		a ×		b =	c
Cash Flow	Time	Amount		Discount Factor	Present Value
Initial investment	t_0	$(11,500)		1.0000	$(11,500)
Year 1 net cash flow	t_1	3,300		0.9091	3,000
Year 2 net cash flow	t_2	3,200		0.8265	2,645
Year 3 net cash flow	t_3	3,200		0.7513	2,404
Year 4 net cash flow	t_4	2,900		0.6830	1,981
Year 5 net cash flow	t_5	2,400		0.6209	1,490
Year 6 net cash flow	t_6	2,100		0.5645	1,185
Year 7 net cash flow	t_7	1,000		0.5132	513
Net present value					$ 1,718

the actual rate is more than the required rate. If the NPV is negative, the actual rate is less than the required rate of return. Note that the exact rate of return is not indicated under the NPV method, but its relationship to the desired rate can be determined. If all estimates about the investment are correct, the patent investment being considered by Farm Pharm has an NPV of $1,718,000 and will provide a rate of return of more than 10 percent.

If Farm Pharm chose any rate other than 10 percent and used that rate in conjunction with the same facts, a different net present value would have resulted. For example, if Farm Pharm set 12 percent as the discount rate, a NPV of $997,000 would have resulted for the project (see Exhibit 14–4, which gives net present values at other selected discount rates). The computations for these values are made in a manner similar to those at 10 and 12 percent. (To confirm your understanding of the NPV method, you may want to prove these computations.)

The information in Exhibit 14–4 indicates that the NPV is not a single, unique amount, but is a function of several factors. First, changing the discount rate while holding the amounts and timing of cash flows constant affects the NPV. Increasing the discount rate causes NPV to decrease; decreasing the discount rate causes NPV to increase. Second, changes in estimated amounts and/or timing of cash inflows and outflows affect a project's net present value. Effects of cash flow changes on NPV depend on the changes themselves. For example, decreasing the estimate of cash outflows causes NPV to increase; reducing the stream of cash inflows causes NPV to decrease. When amounts and timing of cash flows change in conjunction with one another, the effects of the changes can be determined only by calculation.

The NPV method, although not providing a project's actual rate of return, provides information on how that rate compares with the desired rate. This information allows managers to eliminate from consideration any project producing a negative NPV because such a project would have an unacceptable rate of return. This method can also be used to select the best project when choosing among investments that can perform the same task or achieve the same objective. However, this method should *not* be used to compare independent projects requiring different levels of initial investment. Such a comparison favors projects having higher net present values over those with lower net present values without regard to the capital invested in the project.

To illustrate, assume that Farm Pharm could spend $400,000 on investment A or $80,000 on investment B. The net present values of investment A and B are

EXHIBIT 14–4

NET PRESENT VALUE CALCULATION FOR PATENT INVESTMENT (IN $000s)

| | | DISCOUNT RATE = 12% | | |
| | | a $\times$ | b = | c |
Cash Flow	Time	Amount	Discount Factor	Present Value
Initial investment	t_0	$(11,500)	1.0000	$(11,500)
Year 1 net cash flow	t_1	3,300	0.8929	2,947
Year 2 net cash flow	t_2	3,200	0.7972	2,551
Year 3 net cash flow	t_3	3,200	0.7118	2,278
Year 4 net cash flow	t_4	2,900	0.6355	1,843
Year 5 net cash flow	t_5	2,400	0.5674	1,362
Year 6 net cash flow	t_6	2,100	0.5066	1,064
Year 7 net cash flow	t_7	1,000	0.4524	452
Net present value				$ 997

Net present value with a 5% discount rate: $3,853
Net present value with a 15% discount rate: $29
Net present value with a 20% discount rate: $(1,330)

$8,000 and $4,000, respectively. If only NPVs were compared, the company would conclude that Investment A was a "better" investment because it has a higher NPV. However, investment A provides an NPV of only 2 percent ($8,000 ÷ $400,000), whereas investment B provides a 5 percent ($4,000 ÷ $80,000) NPV. Logically, organizations should invest in projects that produce the highest return per investment dollar. Comparisons of projects requiring different levels of investment are made using a variation of the NPV method known as the *profitability index*.

Profitability Index

profitability index (PI)

The **profitability index (PI)** is a ratio comparing the present value of a project's net cash inflows to the project's net investment. The PI is calculated as

$$PI = \text{Present Value of Net Cash Flows} \div \text{Net Investment}$$

The present value (PV) of net cash flows equals the PV of future cash inflows minus the PV of future cash outflows. The PV of net cash inflows represents an output measure of the project's worth, whereas the net investment represents an input measure of the project's cost. By relating these two measures, the profitability index gauges the efficiency of the firm's use of capital. The higher the index, the more efficient is the capital investment.

The following information illustrates the calculation and use of profitability index. Farm Pharm is considering two investments: a distribution warehouse costing $1,720,000 and production management software costing $850,000. Corporate managers have computed the present values of the investments by discounting all future expected cash flows at a rate of 12 percent. Present values of the expected net cash inflows are $2,100,000 for the distribution warehouse and $1,180,000 for the software. Dividing the PV of the net cash inflows by initial cost gives the profitability index for each investment. Subtracting asset cost from the present value of the net cash inflows provides the NPV. Results of these computations follow.

	PV of Inflows	Cost	Profitability Index	NPV
Warehouse	$2,100,000	$1,720,000	1.22	$380,000
Production software	1,180,000	850,000	1.39	330,000

Although the warehouse's net present value is higher, the profitability index indicates that the production software is a more efficient use of corporate capital.[4] The higher PI reflects a higher rate of return on the software than on the warehouse. The higher a project's PI, the more profitable that project is per investment dollar.

If a capital project investment is to provide a return on capital, the profitability index should be equal to or greater than 1.00. This outcome is the equivalent of an NPV equal to or greater than zero. Like the net present value method, the profitability index does not indicate the project's expected rate of return. However, another discounted cash flow method, the internal rate of return, provides the expected rate of return to be earned on an investment.

Internal Rate of Return

LO.4
HOW IS THE INTERNAL RATE OF RETURN ON A PROJECT COMPUTED? WHAT DOES IT MEASURE?

internal rate of return (IRR)

A project's **internal rate of return (IRR)** is the discount rate that causes the present value of the net cash inflows to equal the present value of the net cash outflows. The IRR is the project's expected rate of return. If the IRR is used as the discount rate to determine a project's NPV, the NPV will be zero. Data in Exhibit 14–4

[4] Two conditions must exist for the profitability index to provide better information than the net present value method. First, the decision to accept one project must require that the other project be rejected. The second condition is that the availability of funds for capital acquisitions is limited.

indicate that Farm Pharm's patent investment would generate an IRR very close to 15 percent; using a discount rate of 15 percent resulted in an NPV of only $29,000 on an investment of $11.5 million.

The following formula can be used to determine net present value:

$$\text{NPV} = -\text{Investment} + \text{PV of Cash Inflows} - \text{PV of Cash Outflows}$$
$$\text{Other than Investment}$$
$$= -\text{Investment} + \text{Cash Inflows (PV Factor)} - \text{Cash Outflows}$$
$$\text{(PV Factor)}$$

Capital project information should include amounts for the investment, cash inflows, and cash outflows. Thus, the only missing data in the preceding formula are the present value factors. By inserting the known amounts into the formulas, the missing PV factors can be calculated and then can be found in the present value tables. The interest rate with which the factors are associated is the internal rate of return.

The IRR is most easily computed for projects having equal annual net cash flows. When an annuity exists, the NPV formula can be restated as follows:

$$\text{NPV} = -\text{Net Investment} + \text{PV of Annuity Amount}$$
$$= -\text{Net Investment} + (\text{Cash Flow Annuity Amount} \times \text{PV Factor})$$

The investment and annual cash flow amounts are known from the expected data, and the NPV is known to be zero at the IRR. The IRR and its present value factor are unknown. To determine the internal rate of return, substitute known amounts into the formula, rearrange terms, and solve for the unknown (the PV factor):

$$\text{NPV} = -\text{Net Investment} + (\text{Annuity} \times \text{PV Factor})$$
$$0 = -\text{Net Investment} + (\text{Annuity} \times \text{PV Factor})$$
$$\text{Net Investment} = (\text{Annuity} \times \text{PV Factor})$$
$$\text{Net Investment} \div \text{Annuity} = \text{PV Factor}$$

The solution yields a present value factor for the number of annuity periods corresponding to the project's life at an interest rate equal to the internal rate of return. Finding this factor in the PV of an annuity table and reading the interest rate at the top of the column in which the factor is found provides the internal rate of return.

To illustrate an IRR computation for a project with a simple annuity, assume that Farm Pharm is considering the purchase of an electronic data interchange (EDI) system. The system would cost $1,500,000, be installed immediately, and generate cost savings of $300,000 per year over its seven-year life. The system has no expected salvage value.

The NPV equation is solved for the present value factor.

$$\text{NPV} = -\text{Net Investment} + (\text{Annuity} \times \text{PV Factor})$$
$$\$0 = -\$1,500,000 + (\$300,000 \times \text{PV Factor})$$
$$\$1,500,000 = (\$300,000 \times \text{PV Factor})$$
$$\$1,500,000 \div \$300,000 = \text{PV Factor}$$
$$5.0000 = \text{PV Factor}$$

The PV of an ordinary annuity table (Appendix A, Table 2) is examined to find the internal rate of return. In the table, find the row representing the project's life (in this case, seven periods) and find the PV factor resulting from the equation solution. In row 7, a factor of 5.0330 appears under the column headed 9 percent. Thus, the internal rate of return for this machine is very near 9 percent. By using interpolation, a computer program, or a programmable calculator, the exact IRR can be found.[5] A computer program indicates that the IRR of the EDI system is 9.2 percent.

Refer to Exhibit 14–5 for a plot of the net present values that result from discounting the EDI system cash flows at various rates of return. For example, the NPV at 7 percent is $109,146 and at 11 percent is ($77,785). (These computations are not provided here but can be performed by discounting the $300,000 annual cash flows and subtracting $1,500,000 of investment cost.)

The internal rate of return is located on the graph's horizontal axis at the point where the NPV equals zero [9.2 percent (rounded)]. Note that the graph reflects an inverse relationship between rates of return and NPVs. Higher rates yield lower present values because, at the higher rates, fewer dollars need to be currently invested to obtain the same future value.

Manually finding the IRR of a project that produces unequal annual cash flows is more complex and requires an iterative trial-and-error process. An initial estimate is made of a rate believed to be close to the IRR and the NPV is computed. If the resulting NPV is negative, a lower rate is estimated (because of the inverse relationship mentioned earlier), and the NPV is computed again. If the NPV is positive, a higher rate is tried. This process is continued until the net present value equals zero, at which time the internal rate of return has been found.

hurdle rate

The project's internal rate of return is then compared with management's preestablished **hurdle rate**, which is the rate of return specified as the lowest acceptable return on investment. Like the discount rate mentioned earlier, this rate should generally be at least equal to the cost of capital. In fact, the hurdle rate is commonly the discount rate used in computing net present value amounts. If a project's IRR is equal to or greater than the hurdle rate, the project is considered viable from a financial perspective.

The higher the internal rate of return, the more financially attractive is the investment proposal. In choosing among alternative investments, however, managers cannot look solely at the internal rates of return on projects, because the rates do not reflect the dollars involved. An investor would normally rather have a 20 percent return on $1,000 than a 100 percent return on $10!

Using the internal rate of return has three drawbacks. First, when uneven cash flows exist, the iterative process is inconvenient. Second, unless present value tables that provide factors for fractional interest rates are available, finding the precise

EXHIBIT 14–5
NPV BY VARIOUS DISCOUNT RATES

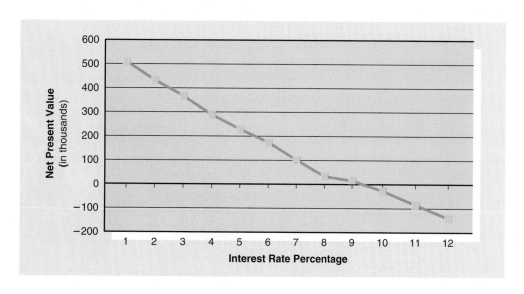

---

[5] *Interpolation* is the process of finding a term between two other terms in a series.

IRR on a project is difficult. These two problems can be eliminated with the use of a computer or a programmable calculator. The last problem is that sometimes it is possible to find several rates of return that will make the net present value of the cash flows equal zero. This phenomenon usually occurs when there are net cash inflows in some years and net cash outflows in other years of the investment project's life (other than at time 0).

In performing discounted cash flow analyses, accrual-based accounting information generally must be converted to cash flow data. One accrual that deserves special attention is depreciation. Although it is not a cash flow item, depreciation has cash flow implications because of its deductibility for income tax purposes.

THE EFFECT OF DEPRECIATION ON AFTER-TAX CASH FLOWS

LO.5
HOW DO TAXATION AND DEPRECIATION METHODS AFFECT CASH FLOWS?

Income taxes are an integral part of the business environment and the managerial planning and decision-making processes. Tax considerations have a large impact on overall business profitability. Managers typically make decisions only after examining how those decisions will affect company taxes. In evaluating capital projects, managers should use after-tax cash flows to determine project acceptability.

Depreciation expense is not a cash flow item: No funds are paid or received for it. However depreciation on capital assets, similar to interest on debt, affects cash flows by reducing a company's tax obligation. Thus, depreciation provides a **tax shield** against the payment of taxes. The tax shield produces a **tax benefit** equal to the amount of taxes saved (the depreciation amount multiplied by the tax rate). The concepts of tax shield and tax benefit are shown on the following income statements. The tax rate is assumed to be 30 percent.

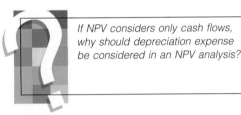

If NPV considers only cash flows, why should depreciation expense be considered in an NPV analysis?

tax shield

tax benefit

No Depreciation Deduction Income Statement		Depreciation Deduction Income Statement	
Sales	$ 500,000	Sales	$ 500,000
Cost of goods sold	(350,000)	Cost of goods sold	(350,000)
Gross margin	$ 150,000	Gross margin	$ 150,000
Expenses other than depreciation	(75,000)	Expenses other than depreciation	(75,000)
Depreciation expense	0	Depreciation expense	(75,000)
Income before taxes	$ 75,000	Income before taxes	$ 0
Tax expense (30%)	(22,500)	Tax expense (30%)	0
Net income	$ 52,500	Net income	$ 0

The tax shield is the $75,000 depreciation expense amount. The tax benefit is $22,500, or the difference between $22,500 of tax expense on the first income statement and $0 of tax expense on the second income statement. The tax benefit also equals the 30 percent tax rate multiplied by the depreciation tax shield of $75,000. Because taxes are reduced by $22,500, the pattern of cash flows is improved.

It is the depreciation taken for income tax purposes rather than the depreciation taken for financial accounting purposes that is relevant in discounted cash flow analysis. Income tax laws regarding depreciation deductions are subject to frequent revision. For example, in recent years, Congress has allowed very rapid depreciation of certain assets to stimulate economic growth in the United States. In making analyses of capital investments, managers should use the most current tax regulations for depreciation. Different depreciation methods can have significant impacts on after-tax cash flows. For a continuously profitable business, an accelerated method of depreciation, such as the modified accelerated cost recovery system (MACRS) allowed for U.S. tax computations, will produce higher tax benefits in the early years of an asset's life than will the straight-line method. These higher tax benefits will translate into a higher net present value for the investment's cash flows.

The depreciation methods and asset depreciable lives that are available for tax purposes could dramatically affect projected after-tax cash flows, net present value, profitability index, and internal rate of return expected from a capital investment. Because capital projects are analyzed and evaluated before investments are made, managers should be aware of the inherent risk of tax law changes. Original assumptions made about the depreciation method or asset life could be invalid by the time an investment is actually made and an asset is placed into service. However, an asset can generally be depreciated using the method and tax life allowed when the asset was purchased and placed into service regardless of the tax law changes occurring after that time.

Relatively unpredictable changes may also occur in the tax rate structure. For example, the Tax Reform Act of 1986 lowered the maximum federal corporate tax rate from 46 percent to 34 percent; the present top U.S. tax rate is 35 percent.[6] With state income taxes added to the federal income tax, the combined rate for large U.S. corporations is approximately 40 percent.[7] A tax rate reduction lowers the tax benefit provided by depreciation because it lessens the impact on cash flow. Tax law changes (such as asset tax-life changes) can cause the expected outcomes of the capital investment analysis to vary from the project's actual outcomes.[8]

To illustrate such variations, assume that Farm Pharm is considering a $12 million investment in new research equipment that will have a 10-year economic life and produce expected net annual cash operating savings of $1.7 million. Assume the company's after-tax cost of capital is 5 percent. Further assume that corporate assets are depreciated on a straight-line basis for tax purposes.[9] Recent tax law changes have dramatically accelerated the rate of cost recovery for many types of assets. Under current law, the cost of some assets can be deducted entirely in the year of acquisition.

In late 2006, prior to making the research equipment investment, Farm Pharm's cost accountant, Ted Tilson, calculated the project's net present value. At the time of Tilson's analysis, Farm Pharm's tax rate was 30 percent, and the tax laws allowed a 10-year depreciable life on this property. See Exhibit 14–6 for the results of his calculations under situation A. Note that depreciation is added to income after tax to obtain the amount of after-tax cash flow. Even though depreciation is deductible for tax purposes, it is still a noncash expense. The present value amounts are obtained by multiplying the after-tax cash flows by the appropriate PV of an annuity factor from Table 2 in Appendix A at the end of the text. The NPV evaluation technique indicates the acceptability of the capital investment

Because Tilson was concerned about proposed changes in the U.S. tax rate, he also analyzed the project assuming that tax rates changed. See Exhibit 14–6 for the different after-tax cash flows and net present values that result if the same project is subjected to either a 25 percent (situation B) or 40 percent (situation C) tax rate. Based on the net present value criterion, a decrease in the tax rate makes the research equipment a more acceptable investment; an increase has the opposite effect.

Understanding how depreciation and taxes affect the various capital budgeting techniques allows managers to make the most informed decisions about capital investments. If they can justify the substantial resource commitment required, managers are more likely to have confidence in capital investments made by the company. Justification is partially achieved by determining whether a capital

---

[6] Surtaxes that apply to corporations can drive the top marginal rate above 35 percent for certain income brackets.

[7] *http://www.kpmg.com.sg/services/intl_tax_pub/corprorate_tax_survey2004.html.*

[8] Additionally, managers should be careful to consider effects of both applicable foreign and state tax laws.

[9] To simplify the presentation, the authors have elected to ignore a tax rule requirement called the *half-year* (or *mid-quarter*) *convention* that applies to personal assets and a mid-month convention that applies to most real estate improvements. Under tax law, only a partial year's depreciation may be taken in the year an asset is placed into service. The slight difference that such a tax limitation would make on the amounts presented is immaterial for purposes of illustrating these capital budgeting concepts.

EXHIBIT 14–6

RESEARCH EQUIPMENT INVESTMENT ANALYSES

Assumed Facts	
Initial investment	$12,000,000
Expected annual before-tax cash flows	1,700,000
Straight-line depreciation (10 years)	1,200,000
Expected economic life	10 years

Situation A: Tax rate of 30% (actual rate in effect)
Situation B: Tax rate of 25%
Situation C: Tax rate of 40%

	SITUATION		
Years 1–10	A	B	C
Before-tax cash flow	$ 1,700,000	$ 1,700,000	$ 1,700,000
Depreciation	(1,200,000)	(1,200,000)	(1,200,000)
Income before tax	$ 500,000	$ 500,000	$ 500,000
Tax	(150,000)	(125,000)	(200,000)
Net income	$ 350,000	$ 375,000	$ 300,000
Depreciation	1,200,000	1,200,000	1,200,000
Cash flow after tax	$ 1,550,000	$ 1,575,000	$ 1,500,000

SITUATION A—NPV CALCULATIONS ASSUMING A 5% DISCOUNT RATE

Cash Flow	Time	Amount	Discount Factor	Present Value
Investment	t_0	$(12,000,000)	1.0000	$(12,000,000)
Annual inflows	t_1–t_{10}	1,550,000	7.7217	11,968,635
Net present value				$ (31,365)

SITUATION B—NPV CALCULATIONS ASSUMING A 5% DISCOUNT RATE

Cash Flow	Time	Amount	Discount Factor	Present Value
Investment	t_0	$(12,000,000)	1.0000	$(12,000,000)
Annual inflows	t_1–t_{10}	1,575,000	7.7217	12,161,677
Net present value				$ 161,677

SITUATION C—NPV CALCULATIONS ASSUMING A 5% DISCOUNT RATE

Cash Flow	Time	Amount	Discount Factor	Present Value
Investment	t_0	$(12,000,000)	1.0000	$(12,000,000)
Annual inflows	t_1–t_{10}	1,500,000	7.7217	11,582,550
Net present value				$ (417,450)

project fits into an organization's strategic plans. To be confident of their conclusions, managers must also comprehend the assumptions and limitations of each capital budgeting method.

ASSUMPTIONS AND LIMITATIONS OF METHODS

LO.6
WHAT ARE THE UNDERLYING ASSUMPTIONS AND LIMITATIONS OF EACH CAPITAL PROJECT EVALUATION METHOD?

As summarized in Exhibit 14–7, each financial capital budget evaluation method has its own underlying assumptions and limitations. To maximize benefits of the capital budgeting process, managers should understand the similarities and differences of the various methods and use several techniques to evaluate a project.

All methods in Exhibit 14–7 have two similar limitations. First, except to the extent that payback indicates promptness of investment recovery, none of the

EXHIBIT 14–7
ASSUMPTIONS AND LIMITATIONS OF CAPITAL BUDGETING METHODS

ASSUMPTIONS	LIMITATIONS
Payback Method	
■ Speed of investment recovery is the key consideration. ■ Timing and size of cash flows are accurately predicted. ■ Risk (uncertainty) is lower for a shorter payback project.	■ Cash flows after payback are ignored. ■ Cash flows and project life are treated as deterministic without explicit consideration of probabilities. ■ Time value of money is ignored. ■ Cash flow pattern preferences are not explicitly recognized.
Net Present Value	
■ Discount rate used is valid. ■ Timing and size of cash flows are accurately predicted. ■ Life of project is accurately predicted. ■ If the shorter lived of two projects is selected, the proceeds of that project will continue to earn the discount rate of return through the theoretical completion of the longer lived project.	■ Cash flows and project life are treated as deterministic without explicit consideration of probabilities. ■ Alternative project rates of return are not known. ■ Cash flow pattern preferences are not explicitly recognized. ■ IRR on project is not reflected.
Profitability Index	
■ Assumptions are the same as NPV. ■ Size of PV of net inflows relative to size of present value of investment measures efficient use of capital.	■ Assumptions are the same as NPV. ■ A relative answer is given but dollars of NPV are not reflected.
Internal Rate of Return	
■ Hurdle rate used is valid. ■ Timing and size of cash flows are accurately predicted. ■ Life of project is accurately predicted. ■ If the shorter lived of two projects is selected, the proceeds of that project will continue to earn the IRR through the theoretical completion of the longer lived project.	■ The IRR rather than dollar size is used to rank projects for funding. ■ Dollars of NPV are not reflected. ■ Cash flows and project life are treated as deterministic without explicit consideration of probabilities. ■ Cash flow pattern preferences are not explicitly recognized. ■ Multiple rates of return can be calculated on the same project.
Accounting Rate of Return (Presented in Appendix 2 of this chapter)	
■ Effect on company accounting earnings relative to average investment is key consideration. ■ Timing and size of increase in company earnings, investment cost, project life, and salvage value can be accurately predicted.	■ Cash flows are not considered. ■ Time value of money is not considered. ■ Earnings, investment, and project life are treated as deterministic without explicit consideration of probabilities.

Are NPV assumptions or IRR assumptions more likely to be satisfied?

methods provides a mechanism to include management preferences with regard to the timing of cash flows. This limitation can be partially overcome by discounting cash flows occurring further in the future at higher rates than those in earlier years, assuming that earlier cash flows are preferred. Second, all methods use single, deterministic measures of cash flow amounts rather than probabilities. This limitation can be minimized through the use of probability estimates of cash flows. Such estimates can be input into a computer program to determine a distribution of answers for each method under various conditions of uncertainty.

THE INVESTMENT DECISION

Management must identify the best asset(s) to acquire to fulfill the company's goals and objectives; to do so requires answers to the following four subhead questions.

Is the Activity Worthy of an Investment?

A company acquires assets when they have value in relation to specific activities in which the company is engaged. For example, Amazon.com invests heavily in product and service development because that (the activity) is the primary path to new revenues. Before making asset acquisition decisions, company management must be certain that the activity for which the assets will be needed is worthy of an investment.

An activity's worth is measured by cost–benefit analysis. For most capital budgeting decisions, costs and benefits can be measured in monetary terms. If the dollars of benefits exceed the dollars of costs, the activity is potentially worthwhile. In some cases, though, the benefits provided by capital projects are difficult to quantify. Difficulty in quantification is no reason to exclude such benefits from capital budgeting analyses. Often surrogate quantifiable measures can be obtained for qualitative benefits. For example, benefits from investments in day care centers for employees' children could be estimated through the reduction in employee time off and turnover. At a minimum, managers should attempt to subjectively include qualitative benefits in the analytical process.

In other circumstances, management could know in advance that the monetary benefits of the capital project will not exceed the costs but that the project is essential for other reasons. For instance, a company could consider renovating the employee workplace with new carpet, furniture, paint, and artwork. The renovation would not make the employees' work any easier or safer but would make the workplace more comfortable. Such a project could be deemed "worthy" regardless of the results of a cost–benefit analysis. Companies could also invest in unprofitable products to maintain market share of a product group and, therefore, protect the market position of profitable products.

Which Assets Can Be Used for the Activity?

Determination of available and suitable assets to conduct the intended activity is closely related to an evaluation of the activity's worth. Management must have an idea of how much the needed assets will cost to determine whether the activity should be pursued. Management should gather the following specific monetary and nonmonetary information (see Exhibit 14–8) for each asset to make this determination: initial cost, estimated life and salvage value, raw material and labor requirements, operating costs (both fixed and variable), output capability, service availability and costs, maintenance expectations, and revenues to be generated (if any). As mentioned in the previous section, information used in a capital project analysis may include surrogate, indirect measures. Management must have both quantitative and qualitative information on each asset and recognize that some projects are simply more crucial to the firm's future than others.

Of the Available Assets for Each Activity, Which Is the Best Investment?

Using all available information, management should select the best asset from the candidates and exclude all others from consideration. In most instances, companies have committees that discuss, evaluate, and approve capital projects. In judging capital project acceptability, a committee should recognize that two types of capital budgeting decisions must be made: screening and preference decisions. A **screening decision** determines whether a capital project is desirable based on some previously established minimum criterion or criteria. A project that does not meet the minimum standard(s) is excluded from further consideration. The second decision is a **preference decision** in which projects are ranked according to their impact on the achievement of company objectives.

screening decision

preference decision

EXHIBIT 14–8
CAPITAL INVESTMENT
INFORMATION

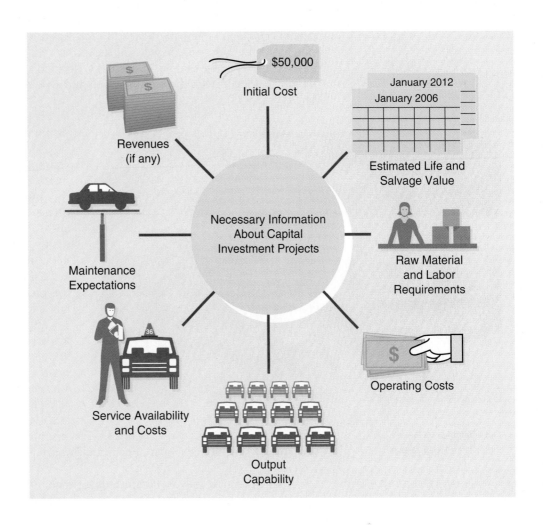

Deciding which asset is the best investment requires the use of one or more of the evaluation techniques discussed previously. Some techniques are used to screen the projects as to acceptability; other techniques are used to rank the projects in order of preference. Although different companies use different techniques for screening and ranking purposes, payback period is commonly used only for screening decisions because payback focuses only on the short run and does not consider the time value of money. The remaining techniques can be used to screen or rank capital projects.

Of the "Best Investments" for All Worthwhile Activities, in Which Ones Should the Company Invest?

Although many worthwhile investment activities exist, each company has limited resources available and must allocate them in the most profitable manner. Therefore, after choosing the best asset for each activity, management must decide which activities and assets to fund. Investment projects are classified as mutually exclusive, independent, or mutually inclusive.

mutually exclusive project

Mutually exclusive projects fulfill the same function. One project will be chosen from such a group, excluding all others from further consideration because they would provide unneeded or redundant capability. A proposal under consideration could be to replace a current asset with one that provides the same basic capabilities. If the company keeps the old asset, it will not buy the new one; if it purchases the new one, it will sell the old asset. Thus, the two assets are mutually exclusive. For example, if a bakery decided to buy a new delivery truck, it would no longer need the existing truck and would sell it to help finance the new one.

Delivery trucks can be considered mutually exclusive in that if you buy a new one, you're likely selling the old one.

GETTY IMAGES

independent project

mutually inclusive project

Other investments could be **independent projects** because they have no specific bearing on one another. For example, the acquisition of an office microcomputer system is not related to the purchase of a factory machine. These project decisions are analyzed and accepted or rejected independently of one another. Although limited resources can preclude the acquisition of all acceptable projects, the projects themselves are not mutually exclusive.

Management may consider certain investments that are all related to a primary project, or **mutually inclusive projects**. In a mutually inclusive situation, if the primary project is chosen, all related projects are also selected. Alternatively, rejection of the primary project dictates rejection of the others. For example, when a firm chooses to invest in new technology, investing in an employee training program for the new technology could also be necessary.

Refer to Exhibit 14–9 for a typical investment decision process in which a company is determining the best way to provide transportation for its sales force. Answers to the four questions asked in the subheadings to this section are provided for the transportation decision.

To ensure that capital funds are invested in the best projects available, managers must carefully evaluate all projects and decide which ones represent the most effective and efficient use of resources—a difficult determination. The evaluation process should consider activity priorities, cash flows, and project risk. Projects should then be ranked in order of acceptability. Ranking could be required for both independent and mutually exclusive projects. Ranking independent projects is required to efficiently allocate scarce capital to competing uses. Ranking mutually exclusive projects is required to select the best project from the set of alternatives.

RANKING MULTIPLE CAPITAL PROJECTS

LO.7
**HOW DO MANAGERS RANK
INVESTMENT PROJECTS?**

When managers must make an accept/reject decision for a single asset, all time value of money evaluation techniques normally point to the same decision alternative. A project is acceptable under the NPV method when it has a zero or positive net present value. Acceptability of a capital asset is also indicated by a profitability index (PI) of 1.00 or more. Because the PI is an adaptation of the NPV method, these two evaluation techniques always provide the same accept/reject decision. To be acceptable using the IRR model, a capital acquisition must have an internal rate of return equal to or greater than the specified hurdle rate. The IRR method gives the same accept/reject decision as the NPV and PI methods if the hurdle rate is used as the discount rate.

More often, however, managers must choose among multiple, mutually exclusive projects. Multiple project evaluation decisions require that a ranking be made, generally using net present value, profitability index, and/or internal rate of return

EXHIBIT 14–9
TYPICAL INVESTMENT
DECISION PROCESS

Activity—Provide transportation for a sales force of 10 people.

1.   Is the activity worthy of an investment?
     Yes; this decision is based on an analysis of the cost of providing transportation in relationship to the dollars of gross margin to be generated by the sales force.

2.   Which assets can be used for the activity?
     Available: Bus passes, bicycles, motorcycles, automobiles (purchased), automobiles (leased), automobiles (currently owned), small airplanes.
     Infeasible: Bus passes, bicycles, and motorcycles are rejected as infeasible because of inconvenience and inability to carry a reasonable quantity of merchandise; airplanes are rejected as infeasible because of inconvenience and lack of proximity of landing sites to customers.
     Feasible: Various types of automobiles to be purchased (assume asset options A through G); various types of leasing arrangements (assume availability of leases 1 through 5); current fleet.
     Gather all relevant quantitative and qualitative information on all feasible assets (assets A–G; leases 1–5; current fleet).

3.   Of the available assets of each activity, which is the best investment?
     Compare all relevant information and choose the best asset candidate from the purchase group (assume asset D) and the lease group (assume lease 2).

4.   Of the "best investments" for all worthwhile activities, in which ones should the company invest?
     Comparing the best asset candidate from the purchase group (asset D) and the lease group (lease 2) represents a mutually exclusive, multiple-candidate project decision. The best candidate is found to be type D assets. Comparing the type D assets to current fleet is a mutually exclusive, replacement project. The best investment is the purchase of a new fleet of 10 type D automobiles concurrently with the sale of the old fleet.

techniques. Payback period also can be used to rank multiple projects. However, the payback method does not provide as much useful information as do NPV, PI, and IRR because it ignores cash flows beyond the payback period.

Managers can use results from the evaluation techniques to rank projects in descending order of acceptability. For the NPV and PI methods, rankings are based on the magnitude of the NPV and PI index, respectively. Although based on the same figures, the NPV and PI methods do not always provide the same order of ranking because the former is a dollar measure and the latter is a percentage. When the internal rate of return is used, rankings of multiple projects are based on expected rate of return. Rankings provided by the IRR method are not always in the same order as those given by the NPV or PI methods.

reinvestment assumption

Conflicting results arise because of differing underlying **reinvestment assumptions** among the three methods. The reinvestment assumption presumes that cash flows released during a project's life are reinvested until the end of that project's life. The NPV and PI techniques assume that released cash flows are reinvested at the discount rate, which should be set at least at the cost of capital (COC) rate. The IRR method assumes that released cash flows can be reinvested at the expected internal rate of return, which could be substantially higher than the COC. In such a case, the IRR method could provide a misleading indication of project success because additional projects that have such a high return might not be found.

In addition to ranking projects based on financial criteria, managers must evaluate whether there are differences in risks across potential projects.

COMPENSATING FOR RISK IN CAPITAL PROJECT EVALUATION

risk

When choosing among multiple projects, managers must consider the risk or uncertainty associated with each project. In accounting, **risk** reflects uncertainty about differences between the expected and actual future returns from an investment.

How can evaluation techniques be adjusted for a proposed project's high level of risk?

LO.8
HOW IS RISK CONSIDERED IN CAPITAL BUDGETING ANALYSIS?

For example, the purchase of a $100,000, 10 percent Treasury note would provide a virtually risk-free return of $10,000 annually because such notes are backed by the full faith and credit of the U.S. government. If the same $100,000 were used to purchase stock, the returns could range from −100 percent (losing the entire investment) to an abnormally high return. The potential for extreme variability makes the stock a much riskier investment than the Treasury note.

Managers considering a capital investment should understand and compensate for the degree of risk involved in that investment. A manager can use three approaches to compensate for risk: the judgmental method, the risk-adjusted discount rate method, and sensitivity analysis. These methods do not eliminate risk, but they do help managers understand and evaluate risk in the decision-making process.

Judgmental Method

judgmental method

The **judgmental method** of risk adjustment allows decision makers to use logic and reasoning to decide whether a project provides an acceptable rate of return in relation to its risk. The decision maker is presented all available information for each project, including the payback period, NPV, PI, and IRR. After reviewing the information, the decision maker chooses from among acceptable projects based on personal judgment of the risk-to-return relationship. The judgmental approach provides no formal process for adjusting data for the risk element. Although such a method sounds a little unorthodox, managers having significant business experience are generally able to use this method with a high level of reliability.

Risk-Adjusted Discount Rate Method

risk-adjusted discount rate method

A more formal method of taking risk into account requires making adjustments to the discount or hurdle rate. Under the **risk-adjusted discount rate method**, the decision maker increases the rate used for discounting future cash inflows and decreases the rate used for discounting future cash outflows to compensate for increased risk. As the discount rate is increased (decreased), the present values of the cash flows are reduced (increased). Therefore, larger cash inflows are required to "cover" the investment and provide an acceptable rate of return. Changes in the discount rate should reflect the degree of cash flow variability and timing, other investment opportunities, and corporate objectives. If the internal rate of return were used for higher risk project evaluation, the risk-adjusted discount rate method would increase the hurdle rate against which the IRR is compared.

Assume that Farm Pharm management is considering the purchase of an automated product-packaging system. The $4,500,000 system would be used for 10 years and then would be sold and replaced with new technology. Refer to Exhibit 14–10 for estimates of the development cost and annual cash savings for the automated packaging system. Farm Pharm management generally uses its 5 percent cost of capital as the discount rate in evaluating capital projects under the NPV method. However, Rachel Schmidt, a capital projects committee member, believes that this project has substantially above-normal risk. First, the cost savings realized from the system could be significantly less than planned. Second, the system's salvage value in 10 years could vary substantially from the $1,000,000 estimate. Schmidt wants to compensate for these risk factors by using a 12 percent discount rate rather than the 5 percent rate. Determining the adjustment of the discount rate (from 5 to 12 percent, for example) is most commonly an arbitrary one. Thus, even though a formal process is used to compensate for risk, the process still involves a degree of judgment on the part of the project evaluators. See Exhibit 14–10 for the NPV computations using both discount rates. When the discount rate is raised to 12 percent, the project's NPV is lowered and shows the project to be unacceptable.

EXHIBIT 14–10
AUTOMATED PACKAGING
SYSTEM ANALYSES

Initial installation cost	$4,500,000	
After-tax net cash flows		
Years 1–5	800,000	
Years 6–10	600,000	
Year 10 (sale)	1,000,000	

NPV USING 5% DISCOUNT RATE

Cash Flow	Time	Amount	Discount Factor	Present Value
Investment	t_0	$(4,500,000)	1.0000	$(4,500,000)
Annual inflows	$t_1–t_5$	800,000	4.3295	3,463,600
Annual inflows	$t_6–t_{10}$	600,000	3.3922[a]	2,035,320
Final inflow	t_{10}	1,000,000	0.6139	613,900
Net present value				$ 1,612,820

NPV USING 12% DISCOUNT RATE

Cash Flow	Time	Amount	Discount Factor	Present Value
Investment	t_0	$(4,500,000)	1.0000	$(4,500,000)
Annual inflows	$t_1–t_5$	800,000	3.6048	2,883,840
Annual inflows	$t_6–t_{10}$	600,000	2.0454[b]	1,227,240
Final inflow	t_{10}	1,000,000	0.3220	322,000
Net present value				$ (66,920)

[a]Factor at 10 Periods at 5% − Factor at 5 Periods at 5% = Factor for Periods 6–10 at 5%

7.7217 − 4.3295 = 3.3922

[b]Factor at 10 Periods at 12% − Factor at 5 Periods at 12% = Factor for Periods 6–10 at 12%

5.6502 − 3.6048 = 2.0454

The same type of risk adjustment can be used for payback period or accounting rate of return (Appendix 2). If the payback method is used, managers can choose to shorten the maximum allowable payback period to compensate for increased risk. This adjustment assumes that cash flows occurring in the more distant future are riskier than those occurring in the near future. If the accounting rate of return (ARR) method is used, managers can increase the hurdle rate against which the ARR is compared to compensate for risk. Another way in which risk can be included in the decision process is through the use of sensitivity analysis.

Sensitivity Analysis

sensitivity analysis

Sensitivity analysis is a process of determining the amount of change that must occur in a variable before a different decision would be made. In a capital budgeting situation, the variable under consideration could be the discount rate, annual net cash flows, or project life. Sensitivity analysis questions what happens if a variable is different from that originally expected. Except for the initial purchase price, all information used in capital budgeting is estimated. Use of estimates creates the possibility of introducing errors, and sensitivity analysis identifies an "error range" for the various estimated values over which the project will still be acceptable. The following sections consider how sensitivity analysis relates to the discount rate, cash flows, and asset life.

RANGE OF THE DISCOUNT RATE

A capital project providing a rate of return equal to or greater than the discount or hurdle rate is considered an acceptable investment. The net present value of the project will change, however, if the discount rate changes. Because the discount and hurdle rates should be set minimally at the organization's cost of capital, an increase in the cost of capital should cause an increase in the discount rate—and a corresponding decrease in the NPV of the project's cash flows. The cost of capital, for instance, can increase because of increases in interest rates on new issues of debt.

Sensitivity analysis allows a company to determine what increases could occur in the estimated cost of capital (and, therefore, the related discount rate) before a project becomes unacceptable. The upper limit of increase in the discount rate is the project's internal rate of return. At the IRR, a project's net present value is zero; therefore, the present value of the cash inflows equals the present value of cash outflows. As long as the IRR for a project is equal to or greater than the cost of capital, the project is acceptable.

To illustrate the use of sensitivity analysis, assume that Farm Pharm has an opportunity to invest $540,000 in new production machinery that has a 10-year life and will generate cost savings of $93,200 per year. Using a 5 percent cost of capital rate for Farm Pharm, the machinery's NPV is computed as follows:

After-tax cash flows for 10 years	
discounted at 5% ($93,200 × 7.7217)	$719,662
Initial investment	(540,000)
Net present value	$179,662

The project provides a positive net present value and is considered an acceptable investment candidate.

Farm Pharm management wants to know how high the discount rate can rise before the project would become unacceptable. To find the upper limit of the discount rate, the present value factor for an annuity of 10 periods at the unknown interest rate is computed as follows:

$$\text{Cash flow} \times \text{PV factor} = \text{Investment}$$
$$\$93,200 \times \text{PV factor} = \$540,000$$
$$\text{PV factor} = 5.7940$$

Using the PV factor, the IRR is found to be 11.39 percent. As long as Farm Pharm's cost of capital is less than or equal to 11.39 percent, this project is acceptable. As the discount rate increases and approaches the project's IRR, the project becomes less desirable. These calculations assume that the cash flows and project life have been properly estimated.

RANGE OF THE CASH FLOWS

Another factor sensitive to changes in estimation is the investment's projected cash flows. Farm Pharm's data for the production machinery investment project are also used to illustrate how to determine the range of acceptable cash flows. Company management wants to know how small the net cash inflows can be and still have the project remain desirable. This determination requires that the present value of the cash flows for 10 periods, discounted at 5 percent, be equal to or greater than the investment cost. The PV factor for 10 periods at 5 percent is 7.7217. The equation from the preceding section can be used to find the lowest acceptable annuity:

$$\text{Cash flow} \times \text{PV factor} = \text{Investment}$$
$$\text{Cash flow} \times 7.7217 = \$540,000$$
$$\text{Cash flow} = \$540,000 \div 7.7217$$
$$\text{Cash flow} = \$69,933$$

As long as the net annual after-tax cash flow equals or exceeds $69,933, the production machinery project will be financially acceptable.

RANGE OF THE LIFE OF THE ASSET

Asset life is related to many factors, some of which, such as the amount and timing of maintenance on equipment, are controllable. Other factors, such as technological advances and actions of competitors, are noncontrollable. An error in the estimated life will change the number of periods from which cash flows are to be derived. This change could affect the accept/reject decision for a project. The Farm Pharm production machinery example is used to demonstrate how to find the minimum length of time the cash flows must be received from the project for it to be acceptable. The solution requires setting the present value of the cash flows discounted at 5 percent equal to the investment. This computation yields the PV factor for an unknown number of periods:

$$\text{Cash flow} \times \text{PV factor} = \text{Investment}$$
$$\$93,200 \times \text{PV factor} = \$540,000$$
$$\text{PV factor} = 5.7940$$

Review the present value of an annuity table in Appendix A under the 5 percent interest column to find the 5.7940 factor. The project life very slightly exceeds seven years. If the project cash flows were to stop at any point before seven years, the project would be unacceptable.

Sensitivity analysis does not reduce the uncertainty surrounding the estimate of each variable. It does, however, provide management a sense of the tolerance for estimation errors by providing upper and lower ranges for selected variables. The preceding presentation simplistically focuses on single changes in each of the variables. If all factors change simultaneously, this type of sensitivity analysis is useless. More advanced treatments of sensitivity analysis, which allow for simultaneous ranging of all variables, can be found under the topic of simulation in an advanced mathematical modeling text.

POSTINVESTMENT AUDIT

LO.9
HOW AND WHY SHOULD MANAGEMENT CONDUCT A POSTINVESTMENT AUDIT OF A CAPITAL PROJECT?

postinvestment audit

In a **postinvestment audit** of a capital project, information on actual project results is gathered and compared to expected results. This process provides a feedback or control feature to both the persons who submitted the original project information and those who approved it. Comparisons should be made using the same technique or techniques used originally to determine project acceptance. Actual data should be extrapolated to future periods in which such information would be appropriate. In cases when significant learning or training is necessary, start-up costs of the first year may not be appropriate indicators of future costs. Such projects should be given a chance to stabilize before making the project audit.

As the size of the capital expenditure increases, a postinvestment audit becomes more crucial. Although an audit cannot change a past investment decision, it can pinpoint areas of project operations that are out of line with expectations so that problems can be corrected before they get out of hand.

Second, an audit can provide feedback on the accuracy of the original estimates for project cash flows. Sometimes project sponsors are biased in favor of their own projects and provide overly optimistic forecasts of future revenues or cost savings. Project sponsors should be required to explain all major variances. Knowing that postinvestment audits will be made could cause project sponsors to provide realistic cash flow forecasts in their capital requests.

Performing a postinvestment audit is not an easy task. The actual information might not be in the same form as the original estimates, and some project benefits could be difficult to quantify. Project returns fluctuate considerably over time, so results gathered at a single point might not be representative of the project. Regardless of the difficulties involved, however, postinvestment audits provide management information that can help to make better capital investment decisions in the future.

Revisiting

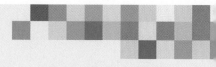

Research and development (R&D) is the foundation of growth for **Merck & Co.** and the pharmaceutical industry. The success of Merck's control over the R&D function is evident in the company's recent financial performance. For 2003 Merck generated nearly $7 billion of net income on sales of $22.5 billion—or a return on sales of over 30 percent! Merck's sales were not concentrated in a limited number of product lines but were spread among the company's wide range of products. The single largest product line generated only slightly more than $5 billion of revenues.

The key for Merck to sustain high sales and profits is to properly manage the R&D pipeline. A dilemma currently facing the pharmaceutical industry is managing the relationship between product prices and the extent of R&D activities conducted. Many governments, such as Canada, have enacted laws to regulate pharmaceutical prices. Such laws have caused the pharmaceutical companies to raise prices in un-

regulated markets, principally the United States, to maintain a sufficient level of gross margin to finance necessary R&D spending. However, some U.S. consumers have responded to the higher prices by purchasing drugs from outlets in countries (e.g., Canada) that regulate prices.

Many federal legislators believe that the high prices in the United States must be addressed. However, legislators are split between the options of opening the U.S. market to greater foreign competition so that downward pressure is placed on prices and of protecting the U.S. market from foreign competition while creating pressure on foreign markets to raise prices so that consumers in those markets share in the cost burden of conducting R&D. No matter which legislative path is chosen, legislators are likely to demand more transparency of the relationship between R&D and product pricing.

Source: Merck & Co. 2003 Annual Report.

Appendix 1

Time Value of Money

LO.10
HOW ARE PRESENT VALUES
CALCULATED?

future value

The time value of money can be discussed in relationship to either its future or its present value. **Future value** (FV) refers to the amount to which a sum of money invested at a specified interest rate will grow over a specified number of time periods. Present value (PV) is the amount that future cash flows are worth currently given a specified rate of interest.[10] Thus, future and present values depend on three things: (1) amount of the cash flow, (2) rate of interest, and (3) timing of the cash flow. Future and present values are related: A present value is a future value discounted back the same number of periods at the same rate of interest. The rate of return used in present value computations is called the discount rate.

simple interest

compound interest

compounding period

In computing future and present values, simple or compound interest is used. **Simple interest** means that interest is earned only on the original investment or principal amount. **Compound interest** means that interest earned in prior periods is added to the original investment so that, in each successive period, interest is earned on both principal and interest. The time between each interest computation is called the **compounding period**. The more often interest is compounded, the higher is the actual rate of interest being received relative to the stated rate.

---

[10] Interest can be earned or owed, received or paid. To simplify the discussion, the topic of interest is viewed only from the inflow standpoint.

The following discussion is based on the use of compound interest because most transactions use this method. Additionally, only present values are discussed because they are more relevant to the types of management decisions discussed in this text.

Interest rates are typically stated in annual terms. To compensate for more frequent compounding periods, the number of years is multiplied by the number of compounding periods per year, and the annual interest rate is divided by the number of compounding periods per year.

Present Value of a Single Cash Flow

Assume that Karen Jones's bank pays interest at 10 percent per year. She wants to accumulate $50,000 in five years to attend graduate school and wants to know what amount to invest now to achieve that goal. The formula to solve for the present value is

$$PV = FV \div (1 + i)^n$$

where PV = present value of a future amount
FV = future value of a current investment
i = interest rate per compounding period
n = number of compounding periods

Substituting known values into the formula gives the following:

$$PV = \$50,000 \div (1 + 0.10)^5$$
$$PV = \$50,000 \div 1.61$$
$$PV = \$31,056$$

In capital budgeting analyses, many future value amounts need to be converted to present values. Rather than using the formula $[1 \div (1 + i)^n]$ to find PVs, a table of factors for the present value of $1 (Table 1) for a variety of "i" and "n" values is provided in Appendix A at the end of the text for ease of computation. Such factors are also available in programmable calculators, making the use of tables unnecessary.

Present Value of an Annuity

ordinary annuity

annuity due

Recall that an annuity is a cash flow (either positive or negative) that is repeated over consecutive periods. For an **ordinary annuity**, the first cash flow occurs at the end of each period. In contrast, the cash flows for an **annuity due** occur at the beginning of each period.

To illustrate the computation of the present value of an annuity, consider the following situation. Billy and Billie Bigwell are planning for their daughter's college education. Their daughter, Bobbie, will need $20,000 per year for the next four years. The Bigwells want to know how much to invest currently at 8 percent so that Bobbie can withdraw $25,000 per year. The following diagram presents the situation:

Time period	t_0	t_1	t_2	t_3	t_4
Future value		$25,000	$25,000	$25,000	$25,000
Present value	?				

The present value of each single cash flow can be found using 8 percent factors in Table 1 as follows:

PV of first receipt: $25,000 × 0.9259	$23,148
PV of second receipt: $25,000 × 0.8573	21,433
PV of third receipt: $25,000 × 0.7938	19,845
PV of fourth receipt: $25,000 × 0.7350	18,375
Total present value of future cash flows	$82,801

The present value factor for an ordinary annuity can also be determined by adding the present value factors for all periods having a future cash flow. Table 2 in Appendix A provides present value of ordinary annuity factors for various interest rates and time periods. From this table, the factor of 3.3121 can be obtained and multiplied by $25,000 to yield $82,803, or approximately the same result as just calculated. (The difference is caused by decimal-fraction rounding.)

Appendix 2

Accounting Rate of Return

LO.11
**WHAT ARE THE ADVANTAGES
AND DISADVANTAGES OF THE
ACCOUNTING RATE OF
RETURN METHOD?**

accounting rate of return (ARR)

The **accounting rate of return (ARR)** measures the rate of earnings obtained on the average capital investment over a project's life. This evaluation method is consistent with the accounting model and uses profits shown on accrual-based financial statements. It is the one evaluation technique that is not based on cash flows. The formula to compute the accounting rate of return is

$$ARR = \text{Average Annual Profits from Project} \div \text{Average Investment in Project}$$

Investment in project refers to project cost and any other costs needed for working capital items (such as inventory) to support the project. Investment cost, salvage value, and working capital released at the end of the project's life are summed and divided by 2 to obtain the average investment over the life of the project.[11] The cost and working capital needed represent the initial investment and the salvage value and working capital released represent the ending investment.

The following information pertains to a new vitamin line being considered by Farm Pharm. The information is used to illustrate after-tax calculation of the ARR.

Beginning investment	
Initial cost of equipment and software	$40,000,000
Additional working capital needed for the product line	20,000,000
Return over life of project	
Average increase in profits after taxes	10,000,000
Return at end of project	
Salvage value of investment in 10 years (end of life of product line)	10,000,000
Working capital released at the end of 10 years	20,000,000

Solving the formula for the accounting rate of return gives

$$
\begin{aligned}
ARR &= \$10,000,000 \div [(\$60,000,000 + \$30,000,000) \div 2] \\
&= \$10,000,000 \div \$45,000,000 \\
&= 22.22\%
\end{aligned}
$$

The 22.22 percent ARR on this project can be compared with a preestablished hurdle rate set by management. This hurdle rate need not be the same as the desired discount rate because the data used in calculating the accounting rate of return do not represent cash flow information. The ARR hurdle rate can be set higher than the discount rate because the discount rate automatically compensates for the time value of money. In addition, the 22.22 percent ARR for this project should be compared with ARRs on other projects under investment consideration by Farm Pharm to see which projects have the higher accounting rates of return.

[11] Sometimes ARR is computed using initial cost rather than average investment as the denominator. Such a computation ignores the return of funds at the end of the project life and is less appropriate than the computation shown.

Comprehensive Review Module

Chapter Summary

1. Most capital budgeting techniques focus on cash flows because

   - evaluation of capital projects requires comparing the return on such projects with the cost of capital, which is calculated using actual net cash flows rather than accounting accruals.

   - cash flows from a capital project can be compared with the cash returns provided from debt investments (in the form of interest) and stock investments (in the form of dividends).

2. The payback period

   - is computed by summing the annual net cash flows until they total the original investment.

   - is the length of time required for cash inflows to recoup the initial cost of a capital project.

3. Net present value and profitability index use discounted cash flows to measure the expected returns on potential capital projects.

   - Net present value (NPV) is the present value of cash inflows minus the present value of cash outflows.

      ➤ To be acceptable, a project must generate an NPV of $0 or more.

   - Profitability index (PI) is the present value of cash inflows divided by the present value of cash outflows.

      ➤ To be acceptable, a project must generate a PI of at least 1.

4. The internal rate of return (IRR) of a project is the discount rate that causes the NPV to equal zero.

   - IRR can be calculated by trial and error. Using the NPV framework, a discount rate can be arbitrarily selected and an NPV calculated.

      ➤ If the resulting NPV is positive, select a higher discount rate and again calculate the NPV.

      ➤ If the resulting NPV is negative, select a lower discount rate and again calculate the NPV.

      ➤ Repeat the process until the discount rate selected causes the NPV to equal zero.

   - IRR can also be calculated by many handheld calculators and computers.

   - If the only cash inflow is an annuity, the IRR can be found by using the present value of an ordinary annuity table.

5. Taxation and depreciation impact a project's cash flows because

   - operating income is subject to income tax, which reduces the cash inflows from the capital project.

   - depreciation reduces the amount of taxes paid since depreciation is deducted in determining the taxable income from a project.

6. Each capital project evaluation method has certain underlying assumptions and limitations.

   - Payback method

      ➤ Assumptions

         ❖ The speed of investment recovery is the most important investment criterion.

         ❖ The timing and amounts of cash flows can be accurately predicted.

         ❖ The risk is lower for projects with shorter paybacks.

      ➤ Limitations

         ❖ Cash flows after payback are ignored.

         ❖ All cash flows are treated as deterministic.

         ❖ The time value of money is ignored.

         ❖ Any managerial preferences in the pattern of cash flows are ignored.

         ❖ This method should be used in conjunction with another method because it ignores both the cash flows after the payback period is reached and the time value of money.

   - Net present value method

      ➤ Assumptions

         ❖ The discount rate used is valid for that project.

         ❖ The timing and amounts of cash flows can be accurately predicted.

         ❖ Cash flows received from projects can be reinvested at the discount rate for the life of the project. When comparing projects with unequal lives, the NPV method assumes that the cash inflows from the shorter project can be reinvested at the discount rate for the life of the longer project.

➤ Limitations

❖ All cash flows are treated as deterministic.

❖ The actual rate of return for projects is not revealed.

❖ Any managerial preferences in the pattern of cash flows are ignored.

• Profitability index

➤ Assumptions

❖ The discount rate used is valid for that project.

❖ The timing and amounts of cash flows can be accurately predicted.

❖ Cash flows received from projects can be reinvested at the discount rate for the life of the project. When comparing projects with unequal lives, the NPV method assumes that the cash inflows from the shorter project can be reinvested at the discount rate for the life of the longer project.

❖ The present value of cash inflows relative to the present value of the investment measures an efficient use of capital.

➤ Limitations

❖ All cash flows are treated as deterministic.

❖ The actual rate of return for projects is not revealed.

❖ Any managerial preferences in the pattern of cash flows are ignored.

❖ Actual dollars of net present value are ignored.

• Internal rate of return method

➤ Assumptions

❖ The hurdle rate used is a valid return benchmark.

❖ The timing and amounts of cash flows can be accurately predicted.

❖ The life of the project can be accurately predicted.

❖ Cash flows received from projects can be reinvested at the internal rate of return for the life of the project. When comparing projects with unequal lives, the IRR method assumes that the cash inflows from the shorter project can be reinvested at the internal rate of return for the life of the longer project.

➤ Limitations

❖ All cash flows are treated as deterministic.

❖ The actual rate of return for projects is not revealed.

❖ Any managerial preferences in the pattern of cash flows are ignored.

❖ The dollar magnitude of return on a project is ignored.

❖ Multiple IRRs can be generated on the same project.

7. Managers can rank capital projects using the following guidelines:

• Shorter payback period is preferred to longer payback period.

• Higher net present value is preferred to lower net present value.

• Higher profitability index is preferred to lower profitability index.

• Higher internal rate of return is preferred to lower internal rate of return.

8. Capital budgeting analysis considers risk by

• requiring a shorter payback period for riskier projects.

• applying a higher discount rate for riskier projects when the NPV or PI method is used.

• applying a higher discount rate for riskier cash flows when the NPV or PI method is used.

• requiring a higher internal rate of return for riskier projects.

• applying sensitivity analysis to the original analyses.

9. Postinvestment audits of projects should be conducted

• after the project has stabilized rather than shortly after start-up.

- to compare actual project performance against expected performance to

  ❖ evaluate the accuracy of original projections.

  ❖ diagnose problems with implementation.

❖ assess credibility of project sponsors' information.

- in greater depth for high-value investment projects.

- using the same technique or techniques originally used to determine project acceptance.

Solution Strategies

Prepare a time line to illustrate all moments in time when cash flows are expected. The minimum discount rate used should be the cost of capital.

PAYBACK PERIOD

1. For projects with an equal annual cash flow:

$$\text{Payback Period} = \text{Investment} \div \text{Annuity}$$

2. For projects with unequal annual cash flows:

    Sum the annual cash flows until investment is reached to find the payback period.

If the payback period is equal to or less than a preestablished maximum number of years, the project is acceptable.

NET PRESENT VALUE

```
−  Investment made currently (always valued at a factor of 1.0000)
+  PV of future cash inflows or cost savings
−  PV of future cash outflows
=  NPV
```

If NPV is equal to or greater than zero, the project is expected to return a rate equal to or greater than the discount rate, and it is acceptable.

PROFITABILITY INDEX

```
+  PV of future cash inflows or cost savings
−  PV of future cash outflows
=  PV of net cash flows
```

$$\text{PI} = \text{PV of Net Cash Flows} \div \text{Net Investment}$$

If PI is 1.00 or higher, the project is expected to return a rate equal to or greater than the discount rate, and the project is acceptable.

INTERNAL RATE OF RETURN

1. For projects with equal annual cash flows:

$$\text{PV Factor} = \text{Net Investment} \div \text{Annuity}$$

    Find the PV factor (or the one closest to it) in the table on the row for the number of periods of the cash flows. The percentage at the top of the column where this factor is found will approximate the IRR. (*Note:* For projects with equal annual cash flows, this factor also equals the payback period.)

2. For projects with unequal annual cash flows: Make an estimate of the rate provided by the project; compute NPV. If NPV is positive (negative), try a

higher (lower) rate until the NPV is zero. Compare IRR to the preestablished hurdle rate. If the IRR equals or is greater than the hurdle rate, the project is acceptable.

TAX BENEFIT OF DEPRECIATION

$$\text{Tax Benefit} = \text{Depreciation Amount} \times \text{Tax Rate}$$

ACCOUNTING RATE OF RETURN

$$\text{ARR} = \text{Average Annual Profits from Project} \div \text{Average Investment in Project}$$

$$\text{Average Investment} = (\text{Beginning Investment} + \text{Recovery of Investment at End of Project Life}) \div 2$$

Compare calculated ARR to hurdle ARR. If the calculated ARR is equal to or greater than the hurdle ARR, the project is acceptable.

BASIC CONCEPTS OF CAPITAL BUDGETING TECHNIQUES

	Payback	NPV	PI	IRR	ARR
Uses time value of money?	No	Yes	Yes	Yes	No
Indicates a specific rate of return?	No	No	No	Yes	Yes
Uses cash flow?	Yes	Yes	Yes	Yes	No
Considers returns during life of project?	No	Yes	Yes	Yes	Yes
Uses discount rate in calculation?	No	Yes	Yes	No*	No*

*Discount rate is not used in the calculation, but it can be used as the hurdle rate.

Demonstration Problem

Midwest Housing Concepts is considering an investment in a B2B system for purchasing office supplies and nonoperating inputs. The project would require an initial investment of $400,000 and have an expected life of six years with no salvage value.

At the end of the fourth year, the firm anticipates it would spend $70,000 to update some hardware and software. This amount would be fully deductible for tax purposes in the year incurred. Management requires that investments of this type be recouped in five years or less. The pre-tax increase in income, resulting from cost savings, is expected to be $95,000 in each of the first four years and $80,000 in each of the next two years. The company's discount rate is 8 percent, its tax rate is 30 percent, and the investment would be depreciated for tax purposes using the straight-line method with no consideration of salvage value over a five-year period.

Required:
a. Prepare a time line for displaying cash flows. Be certain to consider the effects of taxes.
b. Calculate the after-tax payback period.
c. Calculate the after-tax net present value on the project.
d. Discuss the appropriateness of making such an investment.

Solution to Demonstration Problem

a.

End of period	0	1	2	3	4	5	6
Investment	$(400,000)						
Operating inflows[a]		$66,500	$66,500	$66,500	$66,500	$56,000	$56,000
Depreciation[b]		24,000	24,000	24,000	24,000	24,000	
Operating outflows[c]					(49,000)		

[a]$95,000 × (1 − 0.30) = $66,500
  $80,000 × (1 − 0.30) = $56,000
[b]($400,000 ÷ 5) × 0.30 = $24,000
[c]$70,000 × (1 − 0.30) = $49,000

b.

Year	Annual Flow	Cumulative Flow
0	$(400,000)	$(400,000)
1	90,500	(309,500)
2	90,500	(219,000)
3	90,500	(128,500)
4	41,500	(87,000)
5	80,000	(7,000)
6	56,000	49,000

The payback is complete in 5.125 years or in the middle of February in the last year. The portion of the sixth year (0.125) required to complete the payback equals $7,000 ÷ $56,000.

c.

Cash Flow	Time	Amount	Discount Factor	Present Value
Investment	t_0	$(400,000)	1.0000	$(400,000)
Annual flow	t_1–t_3	90,500	2.5771	233,228
Annual flow	t_4	41,500	0.7350	30,503
Annual flow	t_5	80,000	0.6806	54,448
Annual flow	t_6	56,000	0.6302	35,291
Net present value				$ (46,530)

d. The project is unacceptable based on the payback period and fails to qualify based on the NPV criterion as well. Accordingly, from strictly a financial perspective, the project is not acceptable. However, nonquantitative factors, such as effects on competitive position and ability to adopt future technological advances, must be considered.

Key Terms

accounting rate of return (ARR) *(p. 584)*

annuity *(p. 564)*

annuity due *(p. 583)*

capital asset *(p. 559)*

capital budgeting *(p. 560)*

cash flow *(p. 561)*

compound interest *(p. 582)*

compounding period *(p. 582)*

cost of capital (COC) *(p. 564)*

discounting *(p. 564)*

discount rate *(p. 564)*

financing decision *(p. 561)*

future value *(p. 582)*

hurdle rate *(p. 569)*

independent project *(p. 576)*

internal rate of return (IRR) *(p. 567)*

investment decision *(p. 561)*

judgmental method (of risk adjustment) *(p. 578)*

mutually exclusive project *(p. 575)*

mutually inclusive project *(p. 576)*

net present value (NPV) *(p. 565)*

net present value method *(p. 565)*

ordinary annuity *(p. 583)*

payback period *(p. 563)*

postinvestment audit *(p. 581)*

preference decision *(p. 574)*

present value (PV) *(p. 564)*

profitability index (PI) *(p. 567)*

reinvestment assumption *(p. 577)*

return of capital *(p. 565)*

return on capital *(p. 565)*

risk *(p. 577)*

risk-adjusted discount rate method *(p. 578)*

screening decision *(p. 574)*

sensitivity analysis *(p. 579)*

simple interest *(p. 582)*

tax benefit (of depreciation) *(p. 570)*

tax shield (of depreciation) *(p. 570)*

time line *(p. 563)*

Questions

1. What is a capital asset? How is it distinguished from other assets?

2. Why do capital budgeting evaluation methods use cash flows rather than accounting income?

3. How are time lines helpful in evaluating capital projects?

4. What does the payback method measure? What are its major weaknesses?

5. What is the distinction between a return *of* capital and a return *on* capital?

6. What is measured by the net present value of a potential project? If the net present value of a project equals zero, is it an acceptable project? Explain.

7. Will the NPV amount determined in the capital budgeting process be the same amount as that which actually occurs after a project is undertaken? Why or why not?

8. How is the profitability index (PI) related to the NPV method? What does the PI measure?

9. What is measured by the internal rate of return? When is a project considered acceptable using this method?

10. Because depreciation is not a cash flow, why is it important in capital budgeting evaluation techniques that use discounted cash flows?

11. What four questions should managers ask when choosing the investment proposals to fund?

12. How is risk defined in capital budgeting analysis? List several aspects of a project in which risk is involved and how risk can affect a project's net present value.

13. How is sensitivity analysis used in capital budgeting?

14. Why are postinvestment audits performed? When should they be performed?

15. *(Appendix 1)* What is meant by the term *time value of money?* Why is a present value always less than the future value to which it relates?

16. *(Appendix 2)* How is the accounting rate of return computed? How does this rate differ from the discount rate and the internal rate of return?

Exercises

17. (Payback period) Apex Industries is considering the purchase of new production technology that would require an initial investment of $375,000 and have an expected life of 10 years. At the end of its life, the equipment would have no salvage value. By installing the new equipment, the firm's annual labor and quality costs would decline by $75,000.

a. Compute the payback period for this investment.

b. Assume instead that the annual cost savings would vary according to the following schedule:

Years	Annual Cost Savings
1–5	$37,500
6–10	50,000

Compute the payback period under the revised circumstances.

18. (Payback) Cottonwood Department Store is considering a new product line that would require an investment of $80,000 in equipment and $90,000 in working capital. Store managers expect the following pattern of net cash inflows from the new product line over the life of the investment.

Year	Amount
1	$35,000
2	39,000
3	36,000
4	28,000
5	25,000
6	24,000
7	22,000

a. Compute the payback period for the proposed new product line. If Cottonwood requires a four-year pre-tax payback on its investments, should the company invest in the new product line? Explain.

b. Should Cottonwood use any other capital project evaluation method(s) before making an investment decision? Explain.

19. (NPV) Fullerton Iron Works is considering the installation of an $800,000 automated product handling system that would generate the following labor cost savings over its 10-year life:

Years	Annual Labor Cost Savings
1–2	$140,000
3–5	170,000
6–8	144,400
9–10	130,000

The system will have no salvage at the end of its 10-year life, and the company uses a discount rate of 12 percent. What is the pre-tax net present value of this potential investment?

20. (NPV) Jason's Designs has been approached by one of its customers about producing 200,000 special-purpose parts for a new home product. The parts would be produced at a rate of 25,000 per year for eight years. To provide these parts, Jason's would need to acquire new production machines costing a total of $250,000. The new machinery would have no salvage value at the end of its 8-year life.

The customer has offered to pay Jason's $30 per unit for the parts. Jason's managers have estimated that, in addition to the new machines, the company would incur the following costs to produce each part:

Direct labor	$ 4
Direct material	5
Variable overhead	4
Total	$13

In addition, annual fixed out-of-pocket costs would be $20,000.

a. Compute the net present value of the machinery investment, assuming that the company uses a discount rate of 9 percent to evaluate capital projects.

b. Based on the NPV computed in part (a), is the machinery a worthwhile investment? Explain.

c. In addition to the NPV, what other factors should Jason's managers consider when making the investment decision?

21. (PI) Callie's Carpet is interested in purchasing a computer and software that would allow its salespeople to demonstrate to customers how a finished carpet installation would appear. Managers have estimated the cost of the computer, software, and peripheral equipment to be $60,000. Based on this cost, managers have determined that the net present value of the investment is $6,000. Compute the profitability index of the investment.

22. (PI) Bellingham Bus Company (BBC) is considering adding a new bus route. To do so, BBC would be required to purchase a new bus, which would cost $500,000, have a 10-year life, and have no salvage value. If it purchases the new bus, BBC managers expect that net cash inflows from bus ridership would rise by $78,000 per year for the life of the new bus. The BBC uses an 8 percent required rate of return for evaluating capital projects.

a. Compute the profitability index of the bus investment.

b. Should the BBC buy the new bus?

c. What is the minimum acceptable value for the profitability index for an investment to be acceptable? Explain.

WebTUTOR Advantage

23. (IRR; sensitivity analysis) Padre Yacht Club is considering adding a new dock to its marina facilities to accommodate larger yachts. The dock would cost $340,000 and would generate $72,000 annually in new cash inflows. Its expected life would be eight years, and it would have no salvage value. The firm's cost of capital and discount rate are 8 percent.

a. Calculate the internal rate of return for the proposed dock addition (round to the nearest whole percent).

b. Based on your answer to part (a), should the company add the new dock?

c. How much annual cash inflow would be required for the project to be minimally acceptable?

24. (Depreciation; PV) Caldwell Consulting operates three offices in the Midwest. The firm is considering an investment in a new mainframe computer and communications software. The computer and software would cost $2,000,000 and have an expected life of eight years. For tax purposes, the investment will be depreciated using the straight-line method over five years, with no salvage value expected at the end of its life. The company's cost of capital and tax rates are 10 percent and 40 percent, respectively.

a. Compute the present value of the depreciation tax benefit.

b. Assume instead that Caldwell uses the double-declining-balance method of depreciation with a five-year life. Compute the present value of the depreciation tax benefit.

c. Why is the depreciation tax benefit computed in part (b) larger than that computed in part (a)?

25. (Alternative depreciation methods; NPV; sensitivity analysis) Allison West Coast Design Co. is considering an investment in computer-based production technology as part of a business reengineering process. The necessary equipment, installation, and training will cost $30,000,000, have a life of eight years, and generate annual net before-tax cash flows of $6,200,000 from operations. The technology will have no salvage value at the end of its eight-year estimated life. The company's tax rate is 30 percent, and its cost of capital is 6 percent.

a. If Allison uses straight-line depreciation for tax purposes, is the project acceptable using the net present value method?

b. Assume that the tax law allows the company to take accelerated annual depreciation on this asset in the following manner:

Years 1–2	23% of cost
Years 3–8	9% of cost

What is the net present value of the project? Is it acceptable?

c. Recompute parts (a) and (b), assuming the tax rate is increased to 40 percent.

26. (Tax effects of asset sale) Three years ago, Joe Dirt Co. purchased a material conveyor system. The company has decided to sell the system and acquire more advanced technology. Data relating to this system follow:

Current market value	$37,000
Original cost	95,000
Current book value for tax purposes	18,000
Current book value for financial accounting purposes	35,000
Corporate tax rate	40%

a. How much depreciation has been taken on the conveyor system for (1) tax and (2) financial accounting purposes?

b. What will be the after-tax cash flow from the sale of this asset?

c. What will be the after-tax cash flow from the sale of the asset if its market value is $9,000 rather than $37,000?

27. (Uncertain annual cash flow) Central City Consulting is considering the installation of a new system for electronically filing tax returns. The system has an initial cost of $60,000 and an expected life of five years.

a. If the company's cost of capital is 10 percent, how much annual increase in cash flows is necessary to minimally justify the investment?

b. Based on your answer to part (a), what would be the payback period for this investment?

28. (Application of discounting methods) Several capital budgeting techniques depend on discounted cash flow concepts, which are applied in business in a variety of settings. Select a business that relies on discounted cash flow analysis, such as a bond investor, and prepare a brief report on how the firm applies discounting methods to manage the business.

29. (Application of discounting methods) In recent years, stock price averages (e.g., the Dow Jones Industrial Average) have shown sensitivity to changes in interest rates. Based on your understanding of the factors that determine stock prices and of how future cash flows are discounted, prepare a brief report in which you explain why stock prices should be sensitive to changes in interest rates.

30. (Financing decision) Although they should be considered independently, often the investing and financing decisions are considered together.

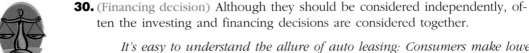

It's easy to understand the allure of auto leasing: Consumers make lower monthly payments; dealers gain volume, move expensive inventory—and keep customers. So it's not surprising to find that one of every three new cars on the road today is leased.

The truth is, dealers have profited more from leasing than from selling. An Atlanta-based leasing expert says, "On a sale a dealer makes about $1,200 to $1,500 in profit. On a lease, it might be $2,500 or $3,000." That's fine, he notes, "unless it's done deceptively."

Source: Deanna Oxender Burgess, "Buy or Lease: The Eternal Question," *Journal of Accountancy* (April 1999), p. 25. Reprinted with permission from the *Journal of Accountancy.* Copyright (2000) by American Institute of CPAs. Opinions of the authors are their own and do not necessarily reflect policies of the AICPA.

Complex lease contracts combined with hidden costs complicate the decision to lease or buy. Only recently have key lease terms such as the cost of the car been disclosed to consumers. Laws in a handful of states, as well as Federal Reserve Board Regulation M (effective in October 1997), and leasing data available on the Internet are prompting dealers to make increased disclosures. Unfortunately, some fees, including the interest rate the dealer uses to calculate the lease payment, known in the industry as the *money factor,* still remain unknown to the consumer.

a. Discuss why some consumers might find leasing a car to be more appealing than purchasing one.

b. Even if not required by law, is the practice of not disclosing lease information ethical? Discuss.

c. As an accountant, how could you aid a client in a car-buying situation?

31. (Appendix 1) You have just invested $7,000 in a bank account that guarantees to pay you 10 percent interest, compounded annually. At the end of five years, how much money will have accumulated in your investment account? (Ignore taxes.)

32. (Appendix 1) You have just purchased a new car, making a down payment of $6,000 and financing the balance of the purchase cost on an installment credit plan. According to the credit agreement, you will pay $900 per month for a period of 60 months. If the credit agreement is based on a monthly interest rate of 1 percent, what is the cost of the car?

33. (Appendix 1) Use the tables in Appendix A to determine the answers to the following questions. Ignore taxes in all circumstances.

a. Jim wishes to have $40,000 in six years. He can make an investment today that will earn 6 percent each year, compounded annually. What amount of investment should he make today to achieve his goal?

b. Jill is going to receive $200,000 on her 50th birthday, 25 years from today. She has the opportunity to invest money today in a government-backed security paying 5 percent compounded annually. How much would she be willing to receive today instead of the $200,000 in 25 years?

c. Tara has $60,000 today that she intends to use as a down payment on a house. How much money did Tara invest 20 years ago to have $60,000 now if her investment earned 8 percent compounded annually?

d. Matt is the host of a television game show that gives away thousands of dollars each day. One prize on the show is an annuity, paid to the winner, in equal installments of $100,000 at the end of each year for the next five years. If a winner has an investment opportunity to earn 8 percent, annually, what present amount would he or she take in exchange for the annuity?

e. Keri is going to be paid modeling fees for the next 10 years as follows: year 1, $50,000; year 2, $55,000; year 3, $60,000; years 4–8, $100,000; year 9, $70,000; and year 10, $45,000. She can invest her money at 7 percent compounded annually. What is the present value of her future modeling fees?

f. Your friend has just won the lottery that will pay her $200,000 per year for the next five years. If this is the only asset your friend owns, is she a millionaire (one who has a net worth of $1,000,000 or more)? Explain.

34. (Appendix 2) Ellis & Associates operates a rehabilitation center for individuals with physical disabilities. The company is considering the purchase of a $1,200,000 piece of equipment that has a five-year life and no salvage value. The company depreciates assets on a straight-line basis. The expected annual cash flow on a before-tax basis for this equipment is $400,000. Ellis requires that an investment be recouped in less than five years and have a pre-tax accounting rate of return of at least 18 percent.

    a. Compute the payback period and accounting rate of return for this equipment.

    b. Is the equipment an acceptable investment for Ellis? Explain.

35. (Appendix 2; comprehensive) Fashion Foto is evaluating the purchase of a state-of-the-art desktop publishing system that costs $40,000, has a six-year life, and has no salvage value at the end of its life. The company's controller estimates that the system will annually generate $14,000 of cash receipts and create $2,000 of cash operating costs. The company's tax rate is expected to be 30 percent during the life of the asset, and the company uses straight-line depreciation.

    a. Determine the annual after-tax cash flows from the project.

    b. Determine the after-tax payback period for the project.

    c. Determine the after-tax accounting rate of return for the project. (Assume tax and financial accounting depreciation are equal.)

Problems

36. (Time line; payback; NPV) Raleigh Retail is considering expanding its building so it can stock additional merchandise for travelers and tourists. Store manager Ralph Lauren anticipates that building expansion costs would be $190,000. Lauren's suppliers are willing to provide inventory on a consignment basis so he would have no additional working capital needs upon expansion. Annual incremental fixed cash costs for the store expansion are expected to be as follows:

Year	Amount
1	$20,000
2	27,000
3	27,000
4	27,000
5	30,000
6	30,000
7	30,000
8	33,000

Lauren estimates that annual cash inflows could be increased by $240,000 from the additional merchandise sales. The firm's contribution margin is typically 25 percent of sales. Because of uncertainty about the future, Lauren does not want to consider any cash flows after eight years. The firm uses an 8 percent discount rate.

    a. Construct a time line for the investment.

    b. Determine the payback period. (Ignore taxes.)

    c. Calculate the net present value of the project. (Ignore taxes.)

37. (Time line; payback; NPV) East Side Delivery is considering the purchase of a new van to replace an existing truck. The van would cost $35,000 and would have a life of seven years with no salvage value. The truck could be sold currently for $4,000, but if it is kept, it will have a remaining life of seven years with no salvage value. By purchasing the van, East Side's managers would anticipate operating cost savings as follows:

Year	Amount
1	$6,800
2	7,100
3	7,300
4	7,000
5	7,000
6	7,100
7	7,200

East Side's cost of capital and capital project evaluation rate is 10 percent.

a. Construct a time line for the purchase of the van.

b. Determine the payback period. (Ignore taxes.)

c. Calculate the net present value of the van. (Ignore taxes.)

38. (NPV; PI; sensitivity analysis) Norton Industries is considering reengineering its manufacturing operations to replace certain manual operations with automated equipment. The new equipment would have an initial cost of $5,000,000 including installation. The vendor has indicated that the equipment has an expected life of seven years with an estimated salvage value of $400,000. Estimates of annual labor savings and incremental costs associated with operating the new equipment follow:

Annual labor cost savings (14 workers)	$950,000
Annual maintenance costs	40,000
Annual property taxes	28,000
Annual insurance costs	44,000

a. Assuming the company's cost of capital is 8 percent, compute the NPV of the investment in the automated equipment. (Ignore taxes.)

b. Based on the NPV, should the company invest in the new equipment?

c. Compute the profitability index for this potential investment. (Ignore taxes.)

d. Assume that of the estimates its management has made, Norton is least confident of the labor cost savings. Calculate the minimum annual labor savings that must be realized for the project to be financially acceptable.

e. What other qualitative factors should the company consider in evaluating this investment?

39. (Payback; IRR) Alley's Accounting Service prepares tax returns for individuals and small businesses. The firm employs four tax professionals. Currently, all tax returns are prepared on a manual basis. The firm's owner, Anne Alley, is considering purchasing a computer system that would allow the firm to service all its existing clients with only three employees. To evaluate the feasibility of the computerized system, Alley has gathered the following information:

Initial cost of the hardware and software	$96,000
Expected salvage value in 4 years	$0
Annual depreciation	$24,000
Incremental annual operating costs	$7,500
Incremental annual labor savings	$37,500
Expected life of the computer system	4 years

Alley has determined that she will invest in the computer system if its pretax payback period is less than 3.5 years and its pre-tax IRR exceeds 12 percent.

a. Compute the payback period for this investment. Does the payback meet Alley's criterion? Explain.

b. Compute the IRR for this project to the nearest percent. Based on the computed IRR, is this project acceptable to Alley?

c. What qualitative factors should Alley consider in evaluating the project?

40. (NPV; PI; payback; IRR) Paul's Paving provides custom paving of sidewalks and driveways. One of the most labor-intensive aspects of the paving operation is preparing and mixing materials. Learned Hand, corporate engineer, has found new computerized equipment to mix (and monitor the mixing of) materials. According to information received by Hand, the equipment's cost is $290,000 and has an expected life of eight years. If purchased, the new equipment would replace manually operated equipment. Data relating to the old and new mixing equipment follow:

	Old Equipment
Original cost	$28,000
Present book value	$16,000
Annual cash operating costs	$75,000
Current market value	$6,000
Market value in 8 years	$0
Remaining useful life	8 years

	New Equipment
Cost	$290,000
Annual cash operating costs	$15,000
Market value in 8 years	$0
Useful life	8 years

a. Assume that the company's cost of capital is 12 percent, which is to be used in discounted cash flow analysis. Compute the net present value and profitability index of investing in the new equipment. Should Paul's Paving purchase the machine? Why or why not? (Ignore taxes.)

b. Compute the payback period for the investment in the new machine. (Ignore taxes.)

c. Rounding to the nearest whole percentage, compute the internal rate of return for the equipment investment.

41. (NPV; taxes; sensitivity analysis) The owner of Frank's Fridge is considering a $390,000 installation of a new refrigerated storage room. The storage room has an expected life of 20 years with no salvage value. The storage room is expected to generate net annual cash revenues (before tax, labor, utility, and maintenance costs) of $86,000 and would increase annual labor, utility, and maintenance costs by $37,500. The firm's cost of capital is 10 percent, and its tax rate is 30 percent.

a. Using straight-line depreciation, calculate the after-tax net present value of the storage room.

b. Based on your answer to part (a), is this investment financially acceptable? Explain.

c. What is the minimum amount by which net annual cash revenues must increase to make this an acceptable investment?

42. (After-tax cash flows; payback; NPV; PI; IRR) Forrester Fashions is considering the purchase of computerized clothes-designing software. The software is expected to cost $160,000, have a useful life of five years, and have no salvage value at the end of its useful life. Assume that tax regulations permit the following depreciation patterns for this software:

Year	Percent Deductible
1	20
2	32
3	19
4	15
5	14

The company's tax rate is 30 percent, and its cost of capital is 8 percent. The software is expected to generate the following cash savings and cash expenses:

Year	Cash Savings	Cash Expenses
1	$61,000	$ 9,000
2	67,000	8,000
3	72,000	13,000
4	60,000	9,000
5	48,000	5,000

a. Prepare a time line presenting the after-tax operating cash flows.

b. Determine the following on an after-tax basis: payback period, net present value, profitability index, and internal rate of return.

43. (NPV; project ranking; risk) Ellsworth Engineering is expanding operations, and the firm's president, Jimmy James, is trying to make a decision about new office space. The following are James' options:

Maple Commercial Plaza	5,000 square feet; cost, $800,000; useful life, 10 years; salvage, $400,000
High Tower	20,000 square feet; cost, $3,400,000; useful life, 10 years; salvage, $1,500,000

If the company purchases Maple Commercial Plaza, it will occupy all of the space. If it purchases High Tower, it will rent the extra space for $620,000 per year. Both buildings will be depreciated on a straight-line basis. For tax purposes, the buildings will be depreciated using a 25-year life. Purchasing either building will save the company $210,000 annually in rental payments. All other costs of the two options (such as land cost) are expected to be the same. The firm's tax rate is 40 percent.

a. Determine the before-tax net cash flows from each project for each year.

b. Determine the after-tax cash flows from each project for each year.

c. Determine the net present value for each project if the cost of capital for Ellsworth Engineering is 11 percent. Which purchase is the better investment based on the NPV method?

d. James is concerned about the ability to rent out the excess space in High Tower for the 10-year period. To compute the NPV for that portion of the project's cash flows, he has decided to use a discount rate of 20 percent to compensate for risk. Compute the NPV and determine which investment is more acceptable.

44. (Capital rationing) Management of Wilson Studios is considering the following capital projects:

Project	Cost	Annual After-Tax Cash Flows	Number of Years
Build new film studios	$20,000,000	$3,100,000	15
Cameras and equipment	3,200,000	800,000	8
Land improvement	5,000,000	1,180,000	10
Motion picture #1	17,800,000	4,970,000	5
Motion picture #2	11,400,000	3,920,000	4
Motion picture #3	8,000,000	2,300,000	7
Corporate aircraft	2,400,000	770,000	5

Assume that all projects have no salvage value and that the firm uses a discount rate of 10 percent. Management has decided that only $25,000,000 can be spent in the current year for capital projects.

a. Determine the net present value, profitability index, and internal rate of return for each of the seven projects.

b. Rank the seven projects according to each method used in part (a).

c. Indicate how you would suggest to the management of Wilson Studios that the money be spent. What would be the total net present value of your selected investments?

45. (Sensitivity analysis) Baldwin Property Management is considering a 50-room motel for sale in Valdosta as an investment. The current owners state that the motel's occupancy rate averages 80 percent each of the 300 days per year the motel is open. Each room rents for $60 per day, and variable cash operating costs are $10 per occupancy day. Fixed annual cash operating costs are $250,000.

Baldwin is considering acquiring the motel for an acquisition price of $1,500,000. The company would keep the motel for 14 years and then dispose of it. Because the market for motels is difficult to predict, Baldwin estimates a zero salvage value at the time of disposal. Depreciation will be taken on a straight-line basis for tax purposes. In making the following computations, assume that there will be no tax consequences of the sale in 14 years. Baldwin's tax rate is estimated at 25 percent for all years.

a. Determine the after-tax net present value of the motel to Baldwin, assuming a cost of capital rate of 11 percent.

b. What is the highest discount rate that will allow this project to be considered acceptable to Baldwin?

c. What is the minimum amount the net after-tax cash flows must be to allow the project to be considered acceptable by Baldwin, assuming a cost of capital rate of 11 percent?

d. What is the fewest number of years for which the net after-tax cash flows can be received and still consider the project acceptable?

46. (Postinvestment audit) Ten years ago, based on a before-tax NPV analysis, Carson Leisure Ware decided to add a new product line. The data used in the analysis were as follows:

Discount rate	10%
Life of product line	10 years
Annual sales increase:	
Years 1–4	$125,000
Years 5–8	$175,000
Years 9–10	$100,000
Annual fixed cash costs	$20,000
Contribution margin ratio	40%
Cost of production equipment	$135,000
Investment in working capital	$10,000
Salvage value	$0

Because the product line was discontinued this year, corporate managers decided to conduct a postinvestment audit to assess the accuracy of their planning process. Actual cash flows generated from the product line were found to be as follows:

Actual Investment

Production equipment	$120,000
Working capital	17,500
Total	$137,500

Actual Revenues

Years 1–4	$120,000
Years 5–8	200,000
Years 9–10	103,000

Actual Fixed Cash Costs

Years 1–4	$15,000
Years 5–8	17,500
Years 9–10	25,000

Actual contribution margin ratio	35%
Actual salvage value	$6,000
Actual cost of capital	12%

a. Determine the original projected NPV on the product line investment.

b. Determine the actual NPV of the project based on the postinvestment audit.

c. Identify the factors that are most responsible for the differences between the projected NPV and the actual postinvestment audit NPV.

47. (Payback; NPV; Appendix 2) Indiana Industrial Tools is considering adding a new product line that has an expected life of eight years. The product manufacturer would require the firm to incur setup costs of $3,200,000 to handle the new product line. All product line revenues will be collected as earned. Variable costs will average 65 percent of revenues. All expenses, except for the amount of straight-line depreciation, will be paid in cash when incurred. Following is a schedule of annual revenues and fixed operating expenses (including $400,000 of annual depreciation on the investment) associated with the new product line.

Year	Revenues	Fixed Expenses
1	$1,500,000	$740,000
2	1,600,000	640,000
3	1,860,000	640,000
4	2,560,000	720,000
5	3,200,000	640,000
6	3,200,000	640,000
7	2,240,000	640,000
8	1,360,000	560,000

The company's cost of capital is 9 percent. Management uses this rate in discounting cash flows for evaluating capital projects.

a. Calculate the payback period. (Ignore taxes.)

b. Calculate the net present value. (Ignore taxes.)

c. Calculate the accounting rate of return. (Ignore taxes.)

d. Should Indiana Industrial Tools invest in this product line? Discuss the rationale, including any qualitative factors, for your answer.

48. (Comprehensive; Appendix 2) The management of Syracuse Steel is evaluating a proposal to buy a new turning lathe as a replacement for a less efficient piece of similar equipment that would then be sold. The new lathe's cost, including delivery and installation, is $710,000. If the lathe is purchased, Syracuse Steel will incur $20,000 to remove the present equipment and revamp service facilities. The present equipment has a book value of $400,000 and a remaining useful life of 10 years. Technical advancements have made this equipment outdated, so its current resale value is only $170,000.

The following comparative manufacturing cost tabulation is available:

	Present Equipment	New Equipment
Annual production in units	390,000	500,000
Cash revenue from each unit	$1.20	$1.20
Annual costs		
Labor	$130,000	$100,000
Depreciation (10% of asset book value or cost)	$40,000	$71,000
Other cash operating costs	$192,000	$80,000

Management believes that if it does not replace the equipment now, the company must wait seven years before the replacement is justified. The company uses a 10 percent discount or hurdle rate in evaluating capital projects and expects all capital project investments to recoup their costs within five years.

Both pieces of equipment are expected to have a negligible salvage value at the end of 10 years.

a. Determine the net present value of the new equipment. (Ignore taxes.)

b. Determine the internal rate of return on the new equipment. (Ignore taxes.)

c. Determine the payback period for the new equipment. (Ignore taxes.)

d. Determine the accounting rate of return for the new equipment. (Ignore taxes.)

e. Determine whether the company should keep the present equipment or purchase the new lathe. Provide discussion of your conclusion.

49. (NPV) Minneapolis Machinery is considering the acquisition of new manufacturing equipment that has the same capacity as the current equipment. The new equipment will provide $150,000 of annual operating efficiencies in direct and indirect labor, direct material usage, indirect supplies, and power during its estimated four-year life

The new equipment costs $300,000 and would be purchased at the beginning of the year. Given the time of installation and training, the equipment will not be fully operational until the second quarter of the year it is purchased. Thus, only 60 percent of the estimated annual savings can be obtained in the year of purchase. Minneapolis Machinery will incur a one-time expense of $30,000 to transfer the production activities from the old equipment to the new. No loss of sales will occur, however, because the plant is large enough to install the new equipment without disrupting operations of the current equipment.

Although the current equipment is fully depreciated and carried at zero book value, its condition is such that it could be used an additional four years. A salvage dealer will remove the old equipment and pay Minneapolis Machinery $5,000 for it.

Minneapolis Machinery currently leases its manufacturing plant for $60,000 per year. The lease, which will have four years remaining when the equipment installation would begin, is not renewable. The company must remove any equipment in the plant at the end of the lease term. Cost of equipment removal is expected to equal the salvage value of either the old or the new equipment at the time of removal.

The company uses the sum-of-the-years'-digits depreciation method for tax purposes. A full-year's depreciation is taken in the first year an asset is put into use. The company is subject to a 40 percent income tax rate and requires an after-tax return of at least 12 percent on an investment.

a. Calculate the annual incremental after-tax cash flows for Minneapolis Machinery's proposal to acquire the new manufacturing equipment.

b. Calculate the net present value of Minneapolis Machinery's proposal to acquire the new manufacturing equipment using the cash flows calculated in part (a) and indicate what action Minneapolis Machinery's management should take. Assume all recurring cash flows occur at the end of the year.

(CMA adapted)

50. (Postinvestment audit) Karnes Group has formal policies and procedures to screen and approve capital projects. Proposed capital projects are classified as one of the following types:

1. expansion requiring new plant and equipment

2. expansion by replacement of present equipment with more productive equipment

3. replacement of old equipment with new equipment of similar quality

All expansion and replacement projects that will cost more than $50,000 must be submitted to the top management capital investment committee for approval. The investment committee evaluates proposed projects considering the costs and benefits outlined in the supporting proposal and the long-range effects on the company.

The projected revenue and/or expense effects of the projects, once operational, are included in the proposal. After the committee accepts a project, it approves an expenditure budget from the project's inception until it becomes operational. The expenditures required each year for the expansions or replacements are also incorporated into Karnes Group's annual budget procedure. The budgeted revenue and/or cost effects of the projects for the periods in which they become operational are incorporated into the five-year forecast.

Karnes Group does not have a procedure for evaluating projects once they have been implemented and become operational. The vice president of finance has recommended that Karnes establish a postinvestment audit program to evaluate its capital expenditure projects.

a. Discuss the benefits a company could derive from a postinvestment audit program for capital expenditure projects.

b. Discuss the practical difficulties in collecting and accumulating information that would be used to evaluate a capital project once it becomes operational.

(CMA adapted)

15

Managing Costs
and Uncertainty

Objectives

AFTER COMPLETING THIS CHAPTER, YOU SHOULD BE ABLE TO ANSWER THE FOLLOWING QUESTIONS:

LO.1 WHAT ARE THE FUNCTIONS OF AN EFFECTIVE COST CONTROL SYSTEM?

LO.2 WHAT ARE THE GENERIC APPROACHES TO COST CONTROL?

LO.3 WHAT FACTORS CAUSE COSTS TO CHANGE FROM PERIOD TO PERIOD OR TO DEVIATE FROM EXPECTATIONS?

LO.4 WHAT ARE THE TWO PRIMARY TYPES OF FIXED COSTS, AND WHAT ARE THE CHARACTERISTICS OF EACH?

LO.5 WHAT ARE THE TYPICAL APPROACHES TO CONTROLLING DISCRETIONARY FIXED COSTS?

LO.6 WHAT ARE THE OBJECTIVES MANAGERS STRIVE TO ACHIEVE IN MANAGING CASH?

LO.7 HOW IS TECHNOLOGY REDUCING COSTS OF SUPPLY CHAIN TRANSACTIONS?

LO.8 WHY IS UNCERTAINTY GREATER IN DEALING WITH FUTURE EVENTS THAN PAST EVENTS?

LO.9 WHAT ARE THE FOUR GENERIC APPROACHES TO MANAGING UNCERTAINTY?

PHOTO: GETTY IMAGES

Introducing

In February 1999, David Neeleman announced that he intended to start a new airline. Shortly thereafter, he placed an order for $4 billion of airplanes from Airbus Industries and arranged to lease an additional eight aircraft. By late 1999, the first of the new airplanes began to arrive and the necessary regulatory approvals had been received. In early 2000, the airline now known as JetBlue Airways was launched with its inaugural flight between New York City and Ft. Lauderdale, Florida.

Critics scoffed at Neeleman's vision of an airline that would combine elements of premium service with a discounted-fare pricing model. For example, JetBlue's planes are equipped with leather seats, have live satellite TV with DirectTV programming and individual television monitors for every passenger, and are the newest in the industry. Unlike competitor Southwest Airlines, which uses a seating policy of "first come, first served," JetBlue uses the industry convention of assigned seating. As for fares, when JetBlue enters a new market, its fares are often 30 to 40 percent below those existing in that market.

The company's financial results have proved that critics were wrong. JetBlue is one of the most profitable airlines, and even in the turbulent year of 2001, when most established airlines had record losses and were able to survive only with the help of a huge government bailout, JetBlue posted a profit. In July 2004, it reported profitable results for the fourteenth consecutive quarter. Another paradox of the company relative to the industry is the unusual circumstance of high profitability and high growth. For example, at year-end 2000, it was operating only 10 planes but by mid-2004 it operated more than 60. From employing less than 1,200 people at year-end 2000, 2004 company employment was more than 5,400.

The obvious question is how these results occurred. How can an airline offer premium services to its customers while selling the seats at fares significantly below competitors' "full-coach" fares? How can a new airline consistently report healthy and increasing profits while most older, larger airlines operate significantly in the red? How can profitability be maintained while high double-digit growth is achieved? How can all this be accomplished while flying one of the newest fleets in the industry?

Source: *http://www.jetblue.com/learnmore/index.html.*

This chapter presents a variety of topics that explain some of the key contributions of accounting and finance personnel to business organizations. The discussion begins with a description of cost control systems and general cost management strategies. Then the discussion turns to the responsibilities and tools of the treasury function including cash management, financial risk management, and supply chain management. The chapter concludes with a presentation of methods and tools for dealing with uncertainty in budgeting and cost management.

COST CONTROL SYSTEMS

**LO.1
WHAT ARE THE FUNCTIONS
OF AN EFFECTIVE COST
CONTROL SYSTEM?**

cost control system

An integral part of the overall organizational decision support system is the **cost control system**, which is the formal and/or informal activities designed to analyze and evaluate how well costs are managed during a period. This system focuses on intraorganizational information and contains the detector, assessor, effector, and network components discussed in Chapter 12. Relative to the cost management system, the cost control system provides information for planning and for determining the efficiency of activities while they are being planned and after they are performed, as indicated in Exhibit 15–1.

Managers alone cannot control costs. An organization is composed of many individuals whose attitudes and efforts should help determine how an organization's costs can be controlled. Cost control is a continual process that requires the support and involvement of all employees at all times.

EXHIBIT 15–1

FUNCTIONS OF AN EFFECTIVE COST CONTROL SYSTEM

Control Point	Reason	Cost Control Method
Before an event	Preventive; reflects planning	Budgets; standards; policies concerning approval for deviations; expressions of quantitative and qualitative objectives; ethical guidelines
During an event	Corrective; ensures that the event is being pursued according to plans; allows management to correct problems as they occur	Periodic monitoring of ongoing activities; comparison of activities and costs against budgets and standards; avoidance of excessive expenditures
After an event	Diagnostic; guides future actions	Feedback; variance analysis; responsibility reports (discussed in Chapter 13)

LO.2
WHAT ARE THE GENERIC APPROACHES TO COST CONTROL?

The general planning and control model in Exhibit 15–2 illustrates that control is part of a management cycle that begins with planning. Without first preparing organizational plans (such as those discussed in Chapter 10), control cannot be achieved because no operational targets and objectives have been established. The planning phase establishes performance targets that become the inputs to the control phase.

Exhibit 15–3 depicts a more specific cost control model. A good control system encompasses not only the managerial functions shown in Exhibit 15–2 but also the ideas about cost consciousness shown in Exhibit 15–3. **Cost consciousness** refers to a companywide employee attitude toward the topics of understanding cost changes, cost containment, cost avoidance, and cost reduction. Each of these topics is important at a different stage of control.

cost consciousness

EXHIBIT 15–2

GENERAL PLANNING AND CONTROL MODEL

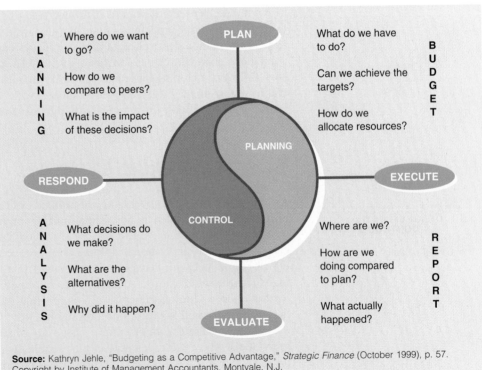

Source: Kathryn Jehle, "Budgeting as a Competitive Advantage," *Strategic Finance* (October 1999), p. 57. Copyright by Institute of Management Accountants, Montvale, N.J.

EXHIBIT 15-3
COST CONTROL SYSTEM

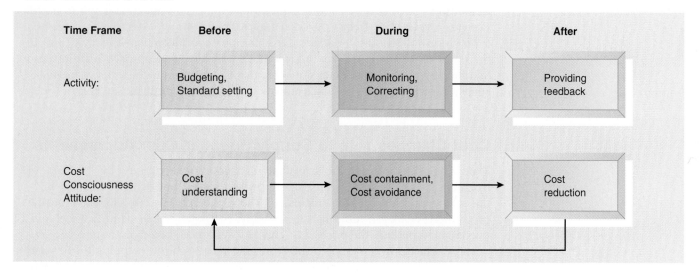

Time Frame	Before	During	After
Activity:	Budgeting, Standard setting	→ Monitoring, Correcting	→ Providing feedback
Cost Consciousness Attitude:	Cost understanding	→ Cost containment, Cost avoidance	→ Cost reduction

UNDERSTANDING COST CHANGES

LO.3
WHAT FACTORS CAUSE COSTS TO CHANGE FROM PERIOD TO PERIOD OR TO DEVIATE FROM EXPECTATIONS?

Control requires that a set of expectations exist. Thus, cost control is first exercised when the budget is prepared. However, budgets cannot be prepared without an understanding of the reasons underlying period cost changes, and cost control cannot be achieved without understanding why costs may differ between periods or from the budgeted amounts.

Cost Changes Due to Cost Behavior

Why is an understanding of cost behavior important in controlling costs?

Some costs change because of their underlying behavior. Total variable or mixed cost increases or decreases with, respectively, increases or decreases in activity. If the current period's actual activity differs from that of a prior period or the budgeted activity level, total actual variable or mixed cost will differ from that of the prior period or the budget. A flexible budget can compensate for such differences by providing expected costs at any activity level. By using a flexible budget, managers can make valid budget-to-actual cost comparisons to determine whether costs were properly controlled.

In addition to the reactions of variable and mixed costs to changes in activity, other factors such as inflation/deflation, supply/supplier cost adjustments, and quantity purchased can cause costs to differ from those of prior periods or the budget. In considering these factors, remember that an external price becomes an internal cost when a good or service is acquired.

Cost Changes Due to Inflation/Deflation

Fluctuations in the value of money are called general price-level changes, which cause the prices of goods and services to change. If all other factors are constant, general price-level changes affect almost all prices approximately equally and in the same direction. In the United States, the Consumer Price Index (CPI) is the most often cited measure of general price-level changes. Inflation and deflation indexes by industry or commodity can be examined to obtain more accurate information about inflation/deflation effects on prices of particular inputs, such as jet fuel.

Some companies include price-escalation clauses in sales contracts to cover the inflation occurring from order to delivery. Such escalators are especially prevalent in industries having production activities that require substantial time. For instance, Congress passed the Debt Collection Improvement Act of 1996, which contained a provision to periodically adjust the Environmental Protection Agency's fines in the event of inflation. The law allows EPA's penalties to keep pace with inflation and thereby maintain the deterrent effect that Congress intended when it originally specified penalties. The first adjustments to penalties were made in 1997.[1]

Cost Changes Due to Supply/Supplier Cost Adjustments

The relationship between the availability of a good or service and the demand for that item affects its selling price. If supply is reduced but demand remains high, the selling price of the item increases. The higher price often stimulates greater production, which, in turn, increases supply. In contrast, if demand falls but supply remains constant, the price falls. This reduced price should motivate lower production, which lowers supply. Therefore, the relationship of supply and demand consistently and circularly influences price. Price changes resulting from independent causes are specific price-level changes, which can move in the same or opposite direction as a general price-level change.

Specific price-level changes are also caused by advances in technology. As a general rule, as suppliers advance the technology of producing a good or performing a service, the cost of that product or service to producing firms declines. Assuming competitive market conditions, such cost declines are often passed along to consumers of that product or service in the form of lower prices. Consider that an inexpensive greeting card that plays "Happy Birthday" contains more computer processing power than existed in the entire world before 1950.[2] This simple example illustrates the interaction of increasing technology and decreasing selling prices and costs.

Alternatively, additional production or performance costs are typically passed on by suppliers to their customers as part of specific price-level changes. Such costs can be within or outside the supplier's control. For example, an increase in fuel prices in the first half of 2004 caused the prices of many products and services to rise, especially those having a high freight or energy content.

The number of suppliers of a product or service can also affect selling prices. As the number of suppliers increases in a competitive environment, price tends to fall. Likewise, a reduction in the number of suppliers will, all else remaining equal, cause prices to increase. A change in the number of suppliers is not the same as a change in the quantity of supply. If the supply of an item is large, one normally expects a low price; however, if there is only one supplier, the price can remain high because of supplier control. Consider that combating illnesses commonly requires the use of various medications. When drugs are first introduced under patent, the supply can be readily available, but the selling price is high because it comes from only a single source. As patents expire and generic drugs become available, selling prices decline because more suppliers can produce the medication.

Sometimes, cost increases are caused by higher taxes or additional regulatory requirements. For example, airlines continually face more stringent noise abatement and safety legislation. Complying with these regulations increases airline costs. The companies can (1) pass along the costs to customers as price increases to maintain the same income level, (2) decrease other costs to maintain the same income level, or (3) experience a decline in net income.

---

[1] *http://www.epa.gov/docs/fedrgstr/EPA-GENERAL/1996/Dece.../pr-23925.htm* (July 9, 2000).
[2] John Huey, "Waking Up to the New Economy," *Fortune* (June 27, 1994), p. 37.

Cost Changes Due to Quantity Purchased

Supplies normally give buying firms quantity discounts, up to some maximum level, when bulk purchases are made. Therefore, a cost per unit can change because quantities are purchased in lot sizes differing from those of previous periods or those projected. Involvement in group purchasing arrangements can make quantity discounts easier to obtain.

The preceding discussion indicates why costs change. Next, the discussion addresses actions firms can take to contain (control) costs.

COST CONTAINMENT

What general strategies can companies apply to control costs?

cost containment

To the extent possible, period-by-period increases in per-unit variable and total fixed costs should be minimized through a process of **cost containment**. Cost containment is not possible for inflation adjustments, tax and regulatory changes, and supply and demand adjustments because these forces occur outside the organization.

In some circumstances, a significant exchange of information occurs among members of the supply chain, and members of one organization can actually be involved in activities designed to reduce costs of another organization. For example, **Citizen Watch Company** has long set target cost reductions for external suppliers. If suppliers could not meet the target, they would be assisted by Citizen engineers in efforts to meet the target the following year.[3]

Costs that rise because of reduced supplier competition, seasonality, and quantities purchased are, however, subject to cost containment activities. A company should look for ways to cap the upward changes in these costs. For example, purchasing agents should be aware of new suppliers for needed goods and services and determine which, if any, of those suppliers can provide needed items in the quantity, quality, and time desired. Comparing costs and finding new sources of supply can increase buying power and reduce costs.

If bids are used to select suppliers, the purchasing agent should remember that a bid is merely the first step in negotiating. Although a low bid may eliminate some competition from consideration, additional negotiations between the purchasing agent and the remaining suppliers could result in a purchase cost even lower than the bid amount, or concessions (such as faster and more reliable delivery) could be obtained. Purchasing agents must also remember that the supplier offering the lowest bid is not necessarily the best supplier to choose. Other factors such as quality, service, and reliability are important.

A company can circumvent seasonal cost changes by postponing or advancing purchases of goods and services. However, such purchasing changes should not mean buying irresponsibly or incurring excessive carrying costs. Economic order quantities, safety stock levels, and materials requirements planning as well as the just-in-time philosophy should be considered when making purchases.

As to services, employees could repair rather than replace items that have seasonal cost changes. For example, maintenance workers might find that a broken heat pump can be repaired and used during the spring and replaced in the summer when the purchase cost is lower.

COST AVOIDANCE AND REDUCTION

cost avoidance

Cost containment can prove very effective if it can be implemented. In some instances, although cost containment is not possible, cost avoidance might be. **Cost avoidance**

---

[3] Robin Cooper, *Citizen Watch Company, Ltd.* (Boston: Harvard Business School Case No. 194-033).

involves finding acceptable alternatives to high-cost items and/or not spending money for unnecessary goods and services. Avoiding one cost may require incurring an alternative, lower cost. For example, some companies have decided to self-insure for many workers' compensation claims rather than pay high insurance premiums. **Gillette** avoids substantial costs by warehousing and shipping Oral-B toothbrushes, Braun coffeemakers, Right Guard deodorant, and Paper Mate ballpoint pens together because all of them share common distribution channels.[4]

cost reduction

Closely related to cost avoidance, **cost reduction** refers to lowering costs. Benchmarking is especially important in this area so that companies can become aware of costs that are in excess of what is necessary. Companies can reduce costs by outsourcing rather than maintaining internal departments. Data processing and the financial and legal functions are prime targets for outsourcing in many companies. Distribution is also becoming a highly viable candidate for outsourcing because "for many products, distribution costs can be as much as 30 percent to 40 percent of a product's cost."[5]

Sometimes money must be spent to generate cost savings. Accountants may opt to use taped rather than live presentations to reduce the cost of continuing education programs. Some of the large accounting firms (such as **Pricewater-houseCoopers**) have their own in-house studios and staffs and provide customized web-based training to their new employees. Although the cost of producing a tape is high, the firms believe the cost is justified because the presentation can be played over and over at very low cost

Some companies are also beginning to look outside for information about how and where to cut costs. Consulting firms, such as Dallas-based **Ryan & Company**, review files for overpayment of state and local taxes. The firm often works on a contingent fee basis: It gets paid only if it can find tax overpayments.

Managers can adopt the five-step method of implementing a cost control system shown in Exhibit 15–4. First, the type of costs incurred by an organization must be understood. Are the costs under consideration fixed or variable, product or period? What cost drivers affect those costs? Second, the need for cost consciousness must be communicated to all employees for the control process to be effective. Employees must be aware of which costs need to be better controlled and why cost control is important to both themselves and the company. Third, employees must be educated in cost-control techniques, encouraged to suggest ways to control costs, and motivated by incentives to embrace the concepts. Incentives can range from simple verbal recognition to monetary rewards to time off with pay. Managers must also be flexible enough to allow for changes from the current method of operation. Fourth, reports that indicate actual results, budget-to-actual comparisons, and variances must be generated. Management must evaluate these costs to determine why costs were or were not controlled in the past. Such analysis can provide insight about cost drivers so that activities causing costs can be better controlled in the future. Last, the cost control system should be viewed as a long-run process, not a short-run solution. "To be successful, organizations must avoid the illusion of short-term, highly simplified cost-cutting procedures. Instead, they must carefully evaluate proposed solutions to ensure that these are practical, workable, and measure changes based on realities, not illusions."[6]

Following these five steps will provide an atmosphere conducive to controlling costs to the fullest extent possible and to deriving the most benefit from the costs that are incurred. Costs to be incurred should have been compared to the benefits expected to be achieved before costs were incurred took place. The costs should also have been incorporated into the budgeting system because costs cannot be controlled after they have been incurred. Future costs, on the other hand,

---

[4] Pablo Galarza, "Nicked and Cut," *Financial World* (April 8, 1996), p. 38.
[5] Rita Koselka, "Distribution Revolution," *Forbes* (May 25, 1992), p. 58.
[6] Mark D. Lutchen, "Cost Cutting Illusions," *Today's CPA* (May/June 1989), p. 46.

EXHIBIT 15–4
IMPLEMENTING A COST CONTROL SYSTEM

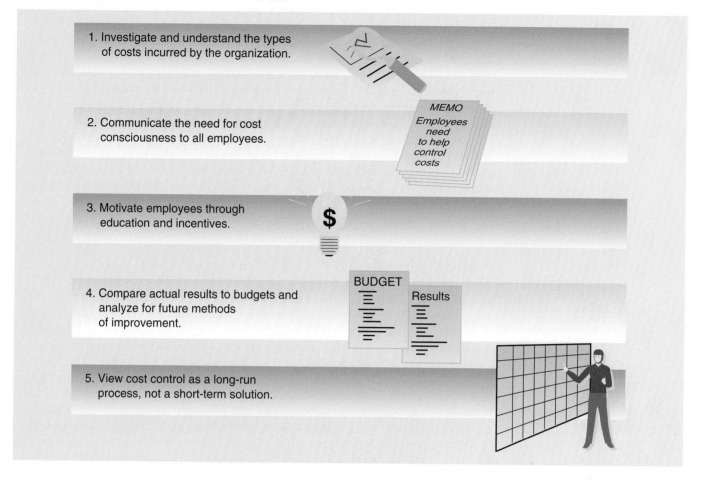

1. Investigate and understand the types of costs incurred by the organization.

2. Communicate the need for cost consciousness to all employees.

MEMO
Employees need to help control costs

3. Motivate employees through education and incentives.

$

4. Compare actual results to budgets and analyze for future methods of improvement.

BUDGET

Results

5. View cost control as a long-run process, not a short-term solution.

can be controlled based on information learned about past costs. Cost control should not cease at the end of a fiscal period or because costs were reduced or controlled during the current period. However, distinct differences exist in the cost control system between committed and discretionary costs. Managers are charged with planning and controlling the types and amounts of costs necessary to conduct business activities. Many activities required to achieve business objectives involve fixed costs. All fixed costs (and the activities that create them) can be categorized as either committed or discretionary. The difference between the two categories is primarily the time period for which management obligates itself to the activity and the cost.

COMMITTED FIXED COSTS

LO.4
WHAT ARE THE TWO PRIMARY TYPES OF FIXED COSTS, AND WHAT ARE THE CHARACTERISTICS OF EACH?

committed cost

Costs associated with basic plant assets and the personnel structure that an organization must have to operate are known as **committed costs**. The amount of committed costs is normally dictated by long-run management decisions involving the desired level of operations. Committed costs include depreciation, lease rentals, property taxes, and staff, which cannot be reduced easily even during temporarily diminished activity.

One method of controlling committed costs involves comparing expected benefits of having plant assets (or human resources) with expected costs of such investments. Managers must decide what activities are needed to attain company

How do committed and discretionary fixed costs differ?

objectives and what (and how many) assets are needed to support those activities. Once assets have been acquired, managers are committed to both the activities and their related costs for the long run. However, regardless of how good an asset investment appears to be on the surface, managers must understand how committed fixed costs could affect income in the event of changes in operations.

A second method of controlling committed costs involves comparing actual and expected results from plant asset investments. During this process, managers are able to see and evaluate the accuracy of their cost and revenue predictions relative to the investment. This comparison is called a postinvestment audit and is discussed in Chapter 14.

An organization cannot operate without some basic levels of plant and human assets. Considerable control can be exercised over the process of determining how management wishes to define *basic* and what funds will be committed to those assets. The benefits from committed costs generally can be predicted and commonly are compared with actual results in the future.

DISCRETIONARY COSTS

LO.5
WHAT ARE THE TYPICAL APPROACHES TO CONTROLLING DISCRETIONARY FIXED COSTS?

discretionary cost

Why is discretionary cost control more challenging than committed cost control?

Discretionary costs, such as employee air travel, are more easily reduced than are committed fixed costs.

In contrast to a committed cost, a **discretionary cost** is one "that a decision maker must periodically review to determine if it continues to be in accord with ongoing policies."[7] A discretionary fixed cost reflects a management decision to fund a particular activity at a specified amount for a specified period of time. Discretionary costs relate to company activities that are important, but the level of funding is subject to judgment. Discretionary cost activities are usually service-oriented and include employee travel, repairs and maintenance, advertising, research and development, and employee training and development. There is no "correct" amount at which to set funding for discretionary costs, and there are no specific activities whose costs are always considered discretionary in all organizations. In the event of cash flow shortages or forecasted operating losses, discretionary fixed costs can be more easily reduced than committed fixed costs.

Discretionary costs, then, are generated by unstructured activities that vary in type and magnitude from day to day and whose benefits are often not measurable in monetary terms. Just as discretionary cost activities vary, performance quality can also vary according to the tasks involved and skill levels of the persons performing them. Because of these two factors—varying activities and varying quality levels—discretionary costs are not usually susceptible to the precise measures available to plan and control variable production costs or the cost-benefit evaluation techniques available to control committed fixed costs. Because the benefits of discretionary cost activities cannot be assessed definitively, these activities are often among the first to be cut when profits are lagging. Thus, proper planning for discretionary activities and costs can be

GETTY IMAGES

[7]Institute of Management Accountants (formerly National Association of Accountants), *Statements on Management Accounting Number 2: Management Accounting Terminology* (Montvale, N.J.: June 1, 1983), p. 35.

more important than subsequent control measures. Control after the planning stage is often restricted to monitoring expenditures to ensure conformity with budget classifications and preventing managers from overspending budgets.

Controlling Discretionary Costs

appropriation

Described in Chapter 10 as both planning and controlling devices, budgets serve to officially communicate a manager's authority to spend up to a predetermined amount (**appropriation**) or rate for each budget item. Budget appropriations serve as a basis for comparison with actual costs. Accumulated expenditures in each budgetary category are periodically compared with appropriated amounts to determine whether funds have been under- or overexpended.

BUDGETING DISCRETIONARY COSTS

Before top management can address the issue of discretionary costs, it must translate company goals into specific objectives and policies that management believes will contribute to organizational success. Then, management must budget the types and funding levels of discretionary activities that will accomplish those objectives. Funding levels should be set only after discretionary cost activities have been prioritized, and cash flow and income expectations for the coming period have been reviewed. Management tends to be more generous about making discretionary cost appropriations during periods of strong economic outlook for the organization than in periods of weak economic outlook.

Discretionary costs are generally budgeted on the basis of three factors: (1) the related activity's perceived significance to the achievement of objectives and goals, (2) the upcoming period's expected level of operations, and (3) managerial negotiations in the budgetary process. For some discretionary costs, managers are expected to spend the full amount of their appropriations within the specified time frame. For other discretionary cost activities, the "less-is-better" adage is appropriate.

As an example of "less is *not* better," consider the cost of preventive maintenance. This cost can be viewed as discretionary, but reducing it could result in diminished quality, production breakdowns, or machine inefficiency. Although the benefits of maintenance expenditures cannot be precisely quantified, most managers believe that incurring less maintenance cost than budgeted is not a positive type of cost control. In fact, spending (with supervisory approval) more than originally appropriated could be necessary or even commendable—assuming that positive results (such as a decline in quality defects) are obtained. Such a perspective illustrates the perception mentioned earlier that cost control should be a long-run process rather than a short-run concern.

Alternatively, spending less than the amount budgeted on travel and entertainment (while achieving the desired results) would probably be considered positive performance, but requesting travel and entertainment funds in excess of budget appropriations could be considered irresponsible.

If revenues, profits, or cash flows are reduced, funding for discretionary expenditures should be evaluated, not simply in reference to reduced operations but also relative to activity priorities. Eliminating the funding for one or more discretionary activities altogether could be possible if other funding levels are maintained at the previously determined amounts. For instance, if a company experiences a downturn in demand for its product, it often reduces the discretionary cost budget for advertising—a potentially illogical reaction. Instead, increasing the advertising budget and reducing the corporate executives' travel budget could be more appropriate.

Discretionary cost activities involve services that vary significantly in type and magnitude from day to day. The output quality of discretionary cost activities can also vary according to the tasks and skill levels of the people performing the activities. Because of varying service levels and quality, discretionary costs are generally not susceptible to the precise planning and control measurements that are available for variable production costs or to the cost-benefit evaluation techniques available for committed fixed costs.

Part of the difference in management attitude between committed and discretionary costs has to do with the ability to measure the benefits provided by those costs. Whereas benefits of committed fixed costs can be measured on a "before" and "after" basis (through the capital budgeting and postinvestment audit processes), the benefits from discretionary fixed costs are often not distinctly measurable in monetary terms.

MEASURING BENEFITS FROM DISCRETIONARY COSTS

Because benefits from some activities traditionally classified as discretionary cannot be adequately measured, companies often assume that the benefits—and, thus, the related activities—are unimportant. Many of the activities previously described as discretionary (repairs, maintenance, R&D, and employee training) are, however, critical to a company's position in a world-class environment. In the long run, these activities produce quality products and services; therefore, before reducing or eliminating expenditures in these areas, managers should attempt to more appropriately recognize and measure the benefits of these activities.

The value of discretionary costs should be estimated using nonmonetary, surrogate measures. Devising such measures often requires substantial time and creativity. Exhibit 15–5 presents some useful surrogate measures for determining the

EXHIBIT 15–5
NONMONETARY MEASURES OF OUTPUT FROM DISCRETIONARY COSTS

Discretionary Cost Activity	Surrogate Measure of Results
Preventive maintenance	• Reduction in number of equipment failures • Reduction in unplanned downtime • Reduction in frequency of production interruptions caused by preventable maintenance activities
Advertising	• Increase in unit sales in the two weeks after an advertising effort relative to the sales two weeks prior to the effort • Number of customers referring to the ad • Number of coupons clipped from the ad and redeemed
University admissions recruiting trip	• Percentage of students met who requested an application • Number of students from area visited who requested to have ACT/SAT scores sent to the university • Number of admissions that year from that area
Prevention and appraisal quality activities	• Reduction in number of customer complaints • Reduction in number of warranty claims • Reduction in number of product defects discovered by customers
Staffing law school indigent clinic	• Number of clients served • Percentage of cases effectively resolved • Percentage of cases won
Executive retreat	• Proportion of participants still there at end of retreat • Number of useful suggestions made • Values tabulated from an exit survey

effectiveness of various types of discretionary costs. Some of these measures are verifiable and can be gathered quickly and easily; others are abstract and require a longer time horizon before they can be obtained.

Amounts spent on discretionary activities reflect resources that have been used and should provide some desired monetary or surrogate output. Comparing input costs and output results can help to determine whether a reasonable cost-benefit relationship exists between the two. Managers can judge this cost-benefit relationship by how efficiently inputs (represented by costs) were used and how effectively those resources (again represented by costs) achieved their purposes. These relationships can be seen in the following model:

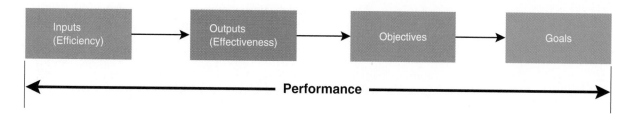

The degree to which a satisfactory relationship occurs when comparing outputs to inputs reflects the activity's efficiency. Efficiency is a yield concept and is usually measured by a ratio of output to input. For instance, one measure of automobile efficiency is miles driven per gallon of fuel consumed. The higher is the number of miles per gallon, the greater is the car's fuel efficiency.

Comparing actual output results to desired results indicates the effectiveness of an activity or how well the activity's objectives were achieved. When a valid output measure is available, efficiency and effectiveness can be determined as follows:

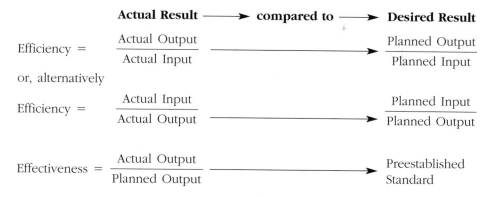

A reasonable measure of efficiency can exist only when inputs and outputs can be matched in the same period and when a credible causal relationship exists between them. These two requirements make measuring the efficiency of discretionary costs very difficult. First, several years could pass before output occurs from some discretionary cost expenditures. Consider, for example, the length of time between expenditures made for research and development or a drug rehabilitation program and the time at which results of these expenditures are visible. Second, there is frequently a dubious cause-and-effect relationship between discretionary inputs and resulting outputs. For instance, assume that you clip and use a cents-off coupon for breakfast cereal from the Sunday paper. Can the manufacturer be certain that it was the advertising coupon that caused you to buy the product, or might you have purchased the cereal without the coupon?

Effectiveness, on the other hand, is determined for a particular period by comparing results achieved with results desired. Determination of an activity's effectiveness is unaffected by whether the designated output measure is stated in monetary or nonmonetary terms. Management can only subjectively attribute some or all of the effectiveness of the cost incurrence to the results. Subjectivity is required because comparison of actual to planned output does not indicate a perfect causal relationship between activities and output results. Measurement of effectiveness does not require the consideration of inputs, but measurement of efficiency does.

Assume that last month Cumberland Airline increased its customer service training expenditures and, during that period, customer satisfaction ratings improved by 12 percent. The planned increase in customer satisfaction was 15 percent. Although management was 80 percent effective ($0.12 \div 0.15$) in achieving its goal of increased customer satisfaction, that result was not necessarily related to the customer service training expenditures. The increase in customer satisfaction could have resulted partially or entirely by such factors as less severe weather disrupting flight service or delays in arrivals and departures, or a reduction in fares. Therefore, management does not know for certain whether the customer service training program was the most effective way in which to increase customer satisfaction.

The relationship between discretionary costs and desired results is inconclusive at best, and the effectiveness of such costs can only be inferred from the relationship of actual to desired output. Because many discretionary costs result in benefits that must be measured on a nondefinitive and nonmonetary basis, exercising control of these costs during activities is difficult. Therefore, planning for discretionary costs can be more important than subsequent control measures. Control after the planning stage is often relegated to monitoring discretionary expenditures to ensure conformity with budget classifications and preventing managers from overspending budgets.

CONTROL USING ENGINEERED COSTS

engineered cost

Some discretionary activities are repetitive enough to allow the development of standards similar to those for manufacturing costs. Such activities result in **engineered costs**, which are costs that have been found to bear observable and known relationships to a quantifiable activity base. Such costs can be treated as either variable or fixed. Discretionary cost activities that can fit into the engineered cost category are usually geared to a performance measure related to work accomplished. Budget appropriations for engineered costs are based on the static master budget level. However, control can be exerted through the use of flexible budgets if the expected level of activity is not achieved.

To illustrate the use of engineered costs, assume that Cumberland Airlines has found that routine daily aircraft inspections can be treated as an engineered cost. Because Cumberland Airlines flies only one type of aircraft, inspections are similar enough to allow management to develop a standard inspection time. Cumberland managers have found that inspection of each plane averages slightly less than 30 minutes. Thus, each inspector should be able to perform approximately two inspections per hour. From this information, the company can obtain a fairly valid estimate of what inspection costs should be based on a particular activity level and can compare actual cost against the standard cost each period. The activity base of this engineered cost is the number of inspections performed.

In May, Cumberland management predicts that 2,500 inspections will be performed and, thus, 1,250 inspection hours should be provided. If the standard average hourly pay rate for inspectors is $70, the May budget for this activity is $87,500. In May, 2,675 inspections are made at a cost of $91,120 for 1,340 actual hours. Using the generalized cost analysis model for variance analysis presented in Chapter 7, the following calculations can be made:

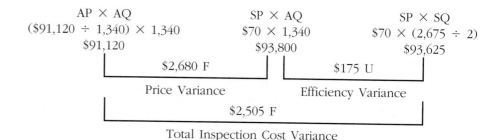

The price variance shows that, on average, Cumberland Airlines paid $2 less per hour [$70 − ($91,120 ÷ 1,340) = $70 − $68] for inspectors during May than was planned. The small unfavorable efficiency variance results from using 2.5 hours more than standard [(2,675 ÷ 2) − 1,340] for May.

The preceding analysis is predicated on the company's willingness and ability to hire the exact number of inspection hours needed and a continual availability of planes to inspect. If Cumberland Airlines can employ only full-time employees on a salary basis, analyzing inspection costs in the preceding manner is not very useful. In this instance, quality inspection cost becomes a discretionary fixed cost, and Cumberland Airlines could prefer the following type of fixed overhead variance analysis:

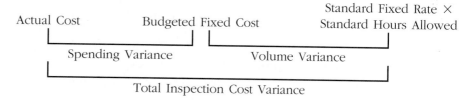

The method of variance analysis and, thus, cost control must be appropriate to the cost category and management information needs. Regardless of the variance levels or the explanations provided, managers should always consider whether the activity itself and, therefore, its cost incurrence were sufficiently justified. Postincurrence audits of discretionary costs are often important in determining an expenditure's value.

CONTROL USING THE BUDGET

After discretionary cost budget appropriations have been made, monetary control is provided through the use of budget-to-actual comparisons in the same manner as for other budgeted costs. Actual results are compared to expected results, and explanations should be provided for variances. Such explanations can often be found by recognizing cost consciousness attitudes. The following illustration involving two discretionary cost activities provides a budget-to-actual comparison that demonstrates employee cost consciousness.

Cumberland Airlines is one of many companies that outsources payroll processing activities to Payroll Financial Services (PFS), which has prepared the condensed budget shown in Exhibit 15–6 for the first quarter of 2006. Allison James, the controller for PFS, estimates 1,200,000 paychecks will be processed during that period; the company charges clients $0.75 per check processed.

In pursuing a strategy of total quality and continuous improvement, PFS's management has chosen to fund employee training to improve employee and customer satisfaction. It also considers maintenance a discretionary cost and budgets it at $1.20 per 50 checks processed. Office costs include utilities, phone service, supplies, and delivery. These costs are variable and are budgeted at $100 for each hour that the firm's office is open. PFS expects to operate at 600 office hours in

EXHIBIT 15–6
PAYROLL FINANCIAL
SERVICES BUDGET—
FIRST QUARTER 2006

Revenues		
Processing fees (1,200,000 × $0.75)		$ 900,000
Expenses		
Employee training	$ 80,000	
Maintenance	28,800	
Office	60,000	
Wages and fringe benefits	240,000	
Salaries and fringe benefits	120,000	
Depreciation	75,000	(603,800)
Operating income before tax		$ 296,200

the budget quarter. Wages are for 10 employees, each of whom is paid $40 per hour. Salaries and fringe benefits are for management level personnel and, like depreciation, are fixed amounts.

Ms. James collected the revenue and expense data shown in Exhibit 15–7 during the first quarter of 2006. Because of computer downtime during the quarter, Payroll Financial Services stayed open five extra hours on four different workdays. Additional contracts were responsible for the majority of the increase in checks processed.

After reviewing the actual results, PFS's board of directors requested a budget-to-actual comparison from James and explanations for the cost variances. Because every cost was higher than budgeted, the board believed that costs had not been properly controlled. She prepared the comparison presented in Exhibit 15–8 and provided the following explanations for the variances. Each explanation is preceded by the related budget item number.

EXHIBIT 15–7
PAYROLL FINANCIAL
SERVICES ACTUAL
RESULTS—FIRST
QUARTER 2006

Revenues		
Processing fees (1,300,000 × $0.75)		$ 975,000
Expenses		
Employee training	$ 70,000	
Maintenance	26,300	
Office	63,860	
Wages and fringe benefits	254,200	
Salaries and fringe benefits	116,450	
Depreciation	85,000	(615,810)
Operating income before tax		$ 359,190

1. The discretionary cost for employee training decreased because the vendor providing training services announced a new, higher price for its services. PFS chose to decrease training services while researching the pricing structure of other training service vendors. *Comment: This explanation reflects a cost containment approach to short-term management of training costs. In the long term, the company must provide at least the original level of training to avoid an eventual decline in quality and customer service.*

2. Maintenance cost decreased because managers obtained a favorable price on maintenance supplies obtained from a new Internet vendor. *Comment: This explanation reflects an understanding of how to reduce costs without adversely affecting quality. The company has found a way to reduce costs without decreasing levels of maintenance or the quality of service delivered to clients. Costs have been reduced by obtaining the maintenance inputs at a lower unit cost.*

EXHIBIT 15-8

PAYROLL FINANCIAL SERVICES BUDGET-TO-ACTUAL COMPARISON FOR FIRST QUARTER 2006

	Budget Item No.	Original Budget	Budget for Actual Results	Actual	Variances
Revenues					
Processing fees		$900,000	$975,000	$975,000	$ 0
Expenses					
Training	(1)	$ 80,000	$ 80,000	$ 70,000	$10,000
Maintenance	(2)	28,800	29,760	26,300	3,460
Office	(3)	60,000	63,860*	63,860	0
Wages and fringe benefits	(4)	240,000	248,000	254,200	(6,200)
Salaries and fringe benefits	(5)	120,000	120,000	116,450	3,550
Depreciation	(6)	75,000	75,000	85,000	(10,000)
Total expenses		$603,800	$616,620	$615,810	$ 810
Operating income before tax		$296,200	$358,380	$359,190	

*This amount is based on the assumption that the higher hourly rate was attributable to an unforeseen utility rate increase: 620 hours × $103 = $63,860

3. Office expenses were influenced by two factors: the additional 20 hours of operation and an increase in local utility rates, which caused PFS's costs to rise $3 per operating hour. *Comment: The first part of the explanation reflects an understanding of the nature of variable costs: Additional hours worked caused additional costs to be incurred. The second part of the explanation reflects an understanding of the nature of specific price-level adjustments. The increase in utility rates was caused by an increase in fuel prices paid by the utility company and passed along to customers through a higher rate.*

4. The increase in wages was caused by two factors: 20 additional operating hours, and a $1 increase in the hourly cost of fringe benefits because of an increase in health insurance premiums.

10 employees × 620 hours × $40 per hour	$248,000
Increase in cost of fringe benefits (10 × 620 × $1.00)	6,200
Total wages cost	$254,200

Comment: These cost changes reflect the nature of variable costs and an unavoidable increase caused by a vendor cost adjustment.

5. A new purchasing agent, hired at the beginning of the quarter, is being paid $14,200 less per year than the previous agent. *Comment: Salaries are usually higher for more experienced managers. Because the new manager is less experienced than the previous manager, the new manager is paid a lower salary.*

6. The depreciation increase was related to the purchase and installation of a new EDI system. The purchase was made with board approval when a competitor went bankrupt during the quarter and had a distress liquidation sale. The purchase of this technology had been included in the capital budget for the end of 2006, not during the first quarter. *Comment: Acquiring the EDI technology is a good example of the cost containment concept. PFS wanted to buy the software and equipment and had an opportunity to buy it at a substantial savings but earlier than anticipated. This purchase created an unfavorable cost variance for depreciation in the first quarter, but it shows an instance of planning, foresight, and flexibility. The long-run benefits of this purchase are twofold. First, the capital budget will show a favorable variance when the cost of this equipment is compared to the expected cost. Second, in future periods, the budgeted committed cost for depreciation will be less than it would have been had the purchase not been made at this time.*

Note that the variance computations in Exhibit 15–8 are based on comparisons between a revised budget that uses actual checks processed as the cost driver and the actual revenues and costs incurred. When comparing budgeted and actual expenditures, managers must be careful to analyze variances using an equitable basis of comparison. These variance computations illustrate the use of flexible budgeting. Comparisons between the original budget and actual results for the variable cost items would not have been useful for control purposes because variable costs automatically rise with increases in cost driver activity.

Suppose that the board of PFS also wanted a better understanding of why the original budget indicated an operating income before tax of $296,200, but the actual results showed $359,190, an increase of $62,990. A set of comparisons of each cost line of the original budget with its counterpart actual cost indicates an increase in expenses of $12,010. Revenue can be analyzed in the following manner:

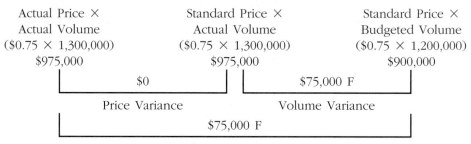

Actual Price ×	Standard Price ×	Standard Price ×
Actual Volume	Actual Volume	Budgeted Volume
($0.75 × 1,300,000)	($0.75 × 1,300,000)	($0.75 × 1,200,000)
$975,000	$975,000	$900,000

| $0 | $75,000 F |
| Price Variance | Volume Variance |

$75,000 F

Total Revenue Variance

The $75,000 favorable variance for revenue is assigned completely to the 100,000 unit increase in checks processed over budget because there was no change in the per-check price. Thus, the increase in income from the original budget is ($75,000 − $12,010), or $62,990. The standard costing models presented in Chapter 7 can be adapted if further analysis of expenses is desired. For the immediate purpose of explaining the increase in operating income before tax, the report shown in Exhibit 15–8 coupled with the previous explanations should suffice. Payroll Financial Services was more profitable by $62,990 than originally planned. With the explanations presented to the board of directors, it does appear that costs were relatively well controlled.

In addition to effectively controlling costs, management also must develop tools that are effective in managing a resource that is crucial to the survival of any organization: cash.

CASH MANAGEMENT

Why is cash management critical to organizational survival?

Of all organizational resources, cash is one of the most important and challenging to manage. Two key cash management tools were introduced in Chapter 10: the cash budget and cash flow statement. This section provides an overview of cash management objectives and tools.

An organization's liquidity depends on having enough cash available to retire debts and other obligations as they come due. However, holding too much cash reduces a firm's profitability because the return on idle cash is below the return that can be earned on other productive assets.

Firms hold cash to liquidate transactions, to cover unexpected events, and for speculation. Objectives of managing cash are similar to objectives of managing inventories. Cash levels should be sufficient to cover all needs (such as avoiding stockouts) but low enough to constrain opportunity costs associated with alternative uses of the cash (carrying costs). Models useful in managing inventory are also useful for managing cash levels. Optimal cash management requires answers to three questions.

What Variables Influence the Optimal Level of Cash?

The cash budget and pro forma cash flow statement provide managers information about the amounts and timing of cash flows. These data are the primary inputs to the determination of the "inventory" of cash that should be available at a specific point in the budget year. However, the actual level of cash maintained can differ from that necessary to meet the cash flow requirements in the cash budget.

The level of confidence that managers have in the cash budget is a subjective factor that influences the desired cash balance. For example, the less certain managers are of either the amount or timing of cash inflows or outflows, the more cash managers will hold. If actual cash flows fail to match budgetary amounts, more cash could be required to satisfy all transactions. Similarly, the greater the variability in cash requirements throughout the year, the more conservative managers must be in managing cash. To avoid liquidity problems, managers of firms with high variability in the operating cycle must hold more cash than managers of firms with very stable, predictable operating cycles. Firms that would have difficulty arranging for short-term credit to cover unexpected cash shortages are forced to carry extra cash to cover contingencies.

Also, securities ratings, particularly bond ratings, can induce firms to hold larger cash balances than is justified based on all other considerations. A favorable bond rating is contingent on the organization's having an ability to pay interest and principal. Security rating agencies encourage organizations to demonstrate conservative practices in managing cash. Related to bond ratings, firms with debt may be obligated by loan covenants to maintain minimum levels of cash.

What Are the Sources of Cash?

There are three usual sources for cash. It is generated by the sale of equity or debt securities and other shorter term instruments. Second, assets no longer necessary or productive are liquidated to provide cash. Last, cash is generated in the normal production/sales cycle assuming goods are sold above their costs of production. The capital budget is the key control tool for the first two sources of cash (Chapter 14).

working capital

Management of cash consumed by and derived from the operating cycle is integral to the management of working capital. **Working capital** equals total current assets minus current liabilities. In the operating cycle, cash is first invested in material and conversion costs, then finished goods inventory, followed by marketing and administrative activities, and finally accounts receivable. The cycle is completed when the accounts receivable are collected. Exhibit 15–9 illustrates the cash collection cycle.

Effective management of the cash collection cycle can both reduce the demand for cash and increase its supply. For example, if the cash invested in the operating cycle (such as inventories and receivables) can be reduced by speeding up the cycle, the cash balance will increase. In the utopian case, raw material would be instantly obtained when a customer placed an order. That material would then be instantly converted into a finished product that would instantly be transferred to the customer who would instantly pay in cash. Even without achieving the utopian ideal, any reduction in the length of the operating cycle will reduce inventory and accounts receivable balances and increase the cash balance. A late 2003 survey of corporate treasurers by Treasury Strategies, Inc., indicated that liquidity was the most significant issue facing corporate treasurers.[8]

---

[8] Mark Prysock, "Top Issues Facing Corporate Treasurers Today," *Financial Executive* (November 2003), p. 60.

EXHIBIT 15–9

THE CASH COLLECTION CYCLE—BALANCE SHEET: CURRENT ASSETS

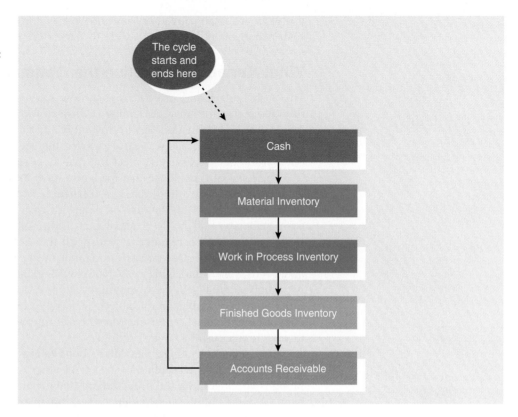

Managers can take explicit measures to accelerate inventory turnover. For example, inventory levels can be reduced if products can be manufactured more quickly after customer orders are received. Just-in-time and other inventory management practices that serve this objective are discussed in Chapter 17.

In addition to reducing inventory, cash collections can be accelerated to increase cash levels. Accounts receivable turnover can be directly influenced by terms given on credit sales, policies governing credit approval, discounts given for early payment, and use of the services of financial intermediaries that specialize in purchasing or factoring accounts receivable. Other practices can be developed to accelerate customer payments including using electronic payments, customer debit cards, lock boxes, and bank courier services. Centralizing cash collection functions will also allow accounts receivable to be converted to cash more quickly.

Alternatively, the cash balance can be increased by slowing down payments for inputs. Managers can search among alternative vendors for the most desirable credit terms and policies. Credit cards rather than cash can be used to purchase inputs. Rather than paying factory employees weekly, a bimonthly or monthly pay plan can be instituted. Also, decentralizing cash disbursement functions will increase the interval from when a check is issued until it clears.

What Variables Influence the Cost of Carrying Cash?

The cost of carrying cash varies over time and there are two classes of costs to manage. One is the cost of borrowing or issuing equity capital. For example, short-term borrowing costs will rise and fall with changes in inflation rates, creditworthiness of the borrower, and availability of funds for lending. The higher these costs, the greater the incentive to minimize idle cash balances.

Second, there is the opportunity cost of holding cash. Excess cash can be invested in productive projects or returned to investors. The more investment opportunities available to a firm, the greater the incentive to convert idle cash to other assets. Even if few investment opportunities are available, managers can always return cash to investors by reducing debt or repurchasing shares. The higher a firm's capital costs, the greater the opportunity cost of holding idle cash.

Banking Relationships

The aspect of trust is key to a good relationship between banker and borrowers.

Managers depend on banks for much of their short-term liquidity and long-term loans. In turn, bankers depend on financial information from creditors to measure risk and determine eligibility for loans. Accounting and cash flow information are key determinants of loan eligibility, loan limits, and credit terms.

From the bank's perspective, credit risk is a primary concern in determining whether, and how much, a bank will lend to an entity. Credit risk also is a key input to determining the borrower's interest rate. To assess credit risk, banks examine the borrower's credit history, ability to generate cash flow, quality of collateral, character of senior officers, and operational plans and strategies. The loan agreement will include covenants or restrictions that prescribe minimal financial thresholds that the borrower must maintain for the life of the loan. For instance, covenants can stipulate minimum acceptable ratios for debt to assets, current assets to current liabilities, and interest coverage.

Accountants must monitor the firm's compliance with loan agreement covenants. By projecting revenues, expenses, and cash flows, accountants can identify potential problems before they are encountered and help develop plans to avoid covenant violations. If a covenant violation is inevitable, accountants can work with the bank to negotiate a solution to the situation. Furthermore, accountants should understand the bank's standard lending policies, such as margin requirements for short-term assets, and manage the firm's compliance with those policies.

Trust is the important key to a good relationship between a bank and a borrower. The development of trust depends on accountants providing accurate, conservative financial data to the bank as well as timely information about operating results. Accountants have the responsibility to prepare the reports provided to the bank and to provide interpretations of the data to help bank personnel understand the financial and operating results.

Bankers do not like surprises. If a firm is facing bad news, such as the potential for bankruptcy, the bank should be kept informed about the circumstances and efforts being made to overcome the challenge. By maintaining a trusting relationship with a bank and its officers, a firm will have a valuable partner in weathering financial storms.

In addition to building relationships with banks and other lenders, the trend is to build stronger ties to suppliers of other necessary inputs as well.

SUPPLY CHAIN MANAGEMENT

Today, competition in markets is as much between supply chains as between individual firms; thus, there is greater joint dependency among firms and their suppliers than existed in earlier eras. This dependency creates an incentive to share information and to manage costs across customers and suppliers. Exhibit 15–10

EXHIBIT 15–10
SUPPLY CHAIN
RELATIONSHIPS

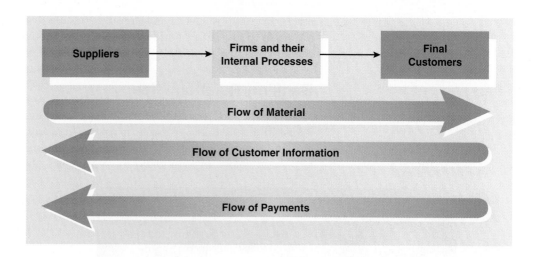

depicts three significant supply chain interactions and dependencies. The most obvious interaction is the downstream flow of goods and services. However, many supply chain costs are associated with the other two arrows: the upstream flow of information and the upstream flow of payments.

Information Technology and Purchasing

LO.7
HOW IS TECHNOLOGY REDUCING COSTS OF SUPPLY CHAIN TRANSACTIONS?

Until recently, a significant amount of time and other resources were spent ordering parts and materials from suppliers and issuing payments for those inputs. The downstream firm typically prepared a material requisition form, purchasing order, and receiving report. The upstream firm issued documents to control the production, shipping, and billing of the ordered goods. Collectively, these control processes and documents created significant supply chain costs.

Why do purchasing transactions create significant supply chain costs?

Today, firms increasingly use electronic exchanges of information and payments to reduce purchasing transaction costs. These exchanges are generally of two types. First, the exchange can involve the acquisition of significant operating needs such as direct materials. These acquisitions can be governed by long-term supply agreements that involve major negotiations and a detailed exchange of product specifications and engineering data. For these transactions, documents such as purchase orders, invoices, and payments are transferred electronically through electronic data interchange (EDI) systems.

The other general type involves the purchase of indirect materials or nonoperating inputs such as office supplies.

Advances in Authorizing and Empowering Purchases

In a traditional purchasing system, buying a box of paper clips might require the same set of documents and procedures as required for buying $1,000,000 of raw materials. Today, however, firms are increasingly using e-procurement systems to purchase nonoperating inputs. **e-procurement** systems are electronic B2B (business-to-business) buy-side applications controlling the requisitioning, ordering, and payment functions for inputs.

e-procurement

One common configuration of such a system involves a large purchaser or a consortium of smaller purchasers, creating an electronic marketplace. Typically, the purchasing organization allows suppliers to make their electronic catalogs of products and materials available on-line. The e-procurement system then allows authorized personnel to order inputs from those catalogs and pay for the purchases electronically. Other systems allow competing vendors to bid for the right to sell inputs to the purchasing firm. Although the early versions of e-procurement systems were unable to support the interfirm collaboration that is often necessary for operating inputs such as direct materials, the latest editions are including more collaborative functionality.

Future versions of these systems will facilitate the exchange of information, such as product specifications or drawings, with an expanded group of potential suppliers to increase competition for both operating (direct materials) and nonoperating (supplies) inputs.

COPING WITH UNCERTAINTY

LO.8
WHY IS UNCERTAINTY GREATER IN DEALING WITH FUTURE EVENTS THAN PAST EVENTS?

The world of the management and cost accountant is split into two spheres separated by time. The first sphere is history. In this sphere, the accountant is concerned with accounting accurately and fairly for events and activities that have already occurred; examples include determining the cost of production for the period, determining the cost of equipment purchased, and ascertaining the cost of operating a department or division.

uncertainty

In the second sphere, accountants deal with events and activities yet to unfold; for example, budgeting cost of goods to be produced, estimating the cost of equipment to be purchased, and preparing operating budgets for departments and divisions. Effectiveness of accountants in this second realm is determined in part by their abilities to cope with and manage uncertainty. **Uncertainty** is doubt or lack of precision in specifying future outcomes. Uncertainty arises from lack of complete knowledge about future events and is the reason accountants are less accurate in assigning costs to future events and activities than to historical events and activities.

What are the sources of uncertainty for future events?

The Nature and Causes of Uncertainty

Before discussing specific strategies for dealing with effects of uncertainty in cost management, it is first necessary to understand the nature of uncertainty and its causes.

UNDERSTANDING CAUSE AND EFFECT

Uncertainty in cost management has two main sources. First, it arises from a lack of identification or understanding of cost drivers. To estimate and budget future costs, accountants exploit the relationship between a cost and its cost driver. In a simple and utopian world, each organizational cost would have a single driver that would perfectly explain every fluctuation in the related cost. However, in the real world, some costs may be predicted with accuracy based on the relationship of the cost to the cost driver, but rarely is the cost predicted perfectly. There is almost always a portion of the cost that is related randomly to the cost driver. In the context of cost prediction and cost understanding, **random** refers to the fact that some portion of the cost is not predictable based on the cost driver or the cost is stochastically, rather than deterministically, related to the cost driver.

random

For example, a factory controller may use machine hours as the basis for predicting factory utility costs. Although changes in volume of machine hours may account for nearly all of the change in utility cost, other factors, such as weather and number of employees, may account for another portion of the cost. If machine hours alone is used as the basis for predicting utility costs, the prediction might be close to the actual cost, but the prediction will contain some error. This error is evidence that part of the utility cost is only randomly related to the machine hour cost driver. Furthermore, logic suggests that while machine hours may explain with relative accuracy the quantity of kilowatt-hours of electricity consumed, machine hours may have no relationship to the price the utility company charges for each kilowatt-hour consumed.

OCCURRENCE OF UNFORESEEN EVENTS

A second source of uncertainty is unforeseen events. For example, the events of September 11, 2001, dealt a severe economic blow to most industries in the United States. However, for the airline industry, the impact of 9/11 was nearly fatal. This industry is characterized by high operating leverage, which is a source of significant risk for firms in the industry. In the immediate aftermath of 9/11, the airlines lost 100 percent of revenues for a brief period and a large portion of revenues for an extended period. Without significant aid from the U.S. government, this entire industry, at least as it existed prior to 9/11, may have been lost from the economy along with thousands of jobs and total disruption of the U.S. transportation system.

When firms plan for unforeseen events, it is impossible to know the severity of all contingencies that could occur. Accordingly, no reasonable plan to deal with unforeseen events will provide solutions for all possible occurrences. Even so, managers must develop strategies for reducing the level of uncertainty to which their firms are exposed.

Four Strategies for Dealing with Uncertainty

LO.9
WHAT ARE THE FOUR GENERIC APPROACHES TO MANAGING UNCERTAINTY?

There are four generic strategies applicable to cost management in the face of uncertainty. First, uncertainty can be explicitly factored into estimates of future costs. Second, costs can be structured to automatically adjust to uncertain outcomes. Third, options and forward contracts can be used to mitigate effects of uncertainty. Fourth, insurance can be purchased to reimburse the firm in the event of unexpected occurrences.

EXPLICITLY CONSIDERING UNCERTAINTY WHEN ESTIMATING FUTURE COSTS

Typically the historical relationship between a cost and its cost driver is used as a basis for assessing the extent to which the cost is only randomly related to the cost driver. Statistical tools are often used in this type of analysis. In Chapter 3, ordinary least squares regression was introduced as a statistical tool to predict costs. In the following equation, y is the cost or other item to be predicted (dependent variable); a and b are, respectively, the intercept and slope in the prediction equation; and X is the predictor variable (independent variable). The least squares method is used to develop estimates of the values for a and b in the prediction equation:

$$y = a + bX$$

When alternative independent variables exist, least squares regression can help select the independent variable that is the best predictor of the dependent variable. For example, managers can use least squares to decide whether machine hours, ambient temperature, factory production hours, or another variable best explains and predicts changes in factory utility expense.

coefficient of determination

Statistical software packages are often used to develop ordinary least squares estimates of the *a* and *b* values. These packages typically produce a variety of statistical information in addition to the estimates of *a* and *b*. For example, nearly all statistical packages as well as spreadsheet software produce a statistic called the **coefficient of determination**, which is the portion of the variance in the dependent variable explained by the variance in the independent variable. The value of this statistic ranges between 0 and 1. A value of 0 indicates the relationship between the predictor variable and the dependent variable is completely random. A value of 1 signifies that the variance of the independent variable explains completely the variance of the dependent variable. More importantly, a coefficient of determination value of 0 means the predictor variable is of no value in predicting the dependent variable, and a value of 1 means the predictor variable is ideal.

How can one measure the strength of the correlation between a predictor variable and a dependent variable?

Although the calculation of the coefficient of determination is beyond the scope of this text, the use of this measure in selecting predictor variables is straightforward and is readily available with even elementary statistical packages. Exhibit 15–11 illustrates the hypothetical relationship of utility costs in a factory to candidate predictor variables: machine hours and plant production hours. The exhibit features the relationships between dependent and independent variables based on six months of recent data. Ordinary least squares has been used to estimate the regression lines that appear in the exhibit. If the coefficient of determination is 1, all data points will fall on the ordinary least squares regression line. This is not the case for either candidate predictor variable. However, the data points for the machine hour regression are much closer to the line than are the data points for the plant production hours regression. The calculated coefficient of determination reflects the proximity of the data points to the fitted regression line and it follows that the coefficient of determination is higher for the machine hours regression (0.91) than the plant production hours regression (0.59).

Using the coefficient of determination as a tool to select the best among candidate predictor variables will reduce the uncertainty regarding estimated costs or revenues. All other things being equal, the higher the coefficient of determination, the lower the uncertainty regarding the resulting prediction or forecast.

Other statistical techniques such as computer simulations and more elaborate regression models, which can include multiple independent variables as well as

EXHIBIT 15–11

HISTORICAL RELATIONSHIP BETWEEN UTILITY COSTS AND ALTERNATIVE EXPLANATORY VARIABLES

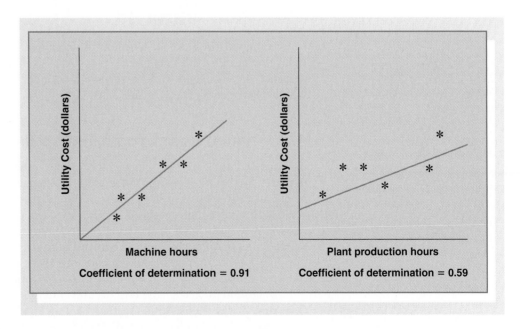

nonlinear relationships between independent and dependent variables, can also be used to select predictor variables. The goal in using more elaborate models is to reduce the prediction error and thereby the effects of uncertainty on accuracy of predictions.

The alternative approach to explicitly considering the effects of uncertainty in cost estimates is to examine the sensitivity of costs and/or revenues to estimation errors. Because tools such as ordinary least squares regression provide predictions of a single value, it is useful to examine effects of errors in estimates. Sensitivity analysis, introduced in Chapter 14, is a tool commonly used for this purpose. To illustrate, assume that Cumberland Airlines predicts its airline maintenance costs (y) as a function of air miles flown (X). Assume the monthly estimation equation is as follows:

$$\text{Monthly airline maintenance cost function: } y = \$300{,}000 + \$5X$$

If Cumberland expects to fly 1,000,000 air miles in the coming month, the predicted cost of airline maintenance would be $300,000 + $5(1,000,000) = $5,300,000. Further assume that, although Cumberland Airlines expects to fly 1,000,000 air miles, the possible range of activity is 900,000 to 1,100,000. Plugging the minimum and maximum values of X into the airline maintenance equation yields a range for the cost of airline maintenance costs.

$$\text{Minimum expected airline maintenance cost} = \$300{,}000 + \$5(900{,}000)$$
$$= \$4{,}800{,}000$$

$$\text{Maximum expected airline maintenance cost} = \$300{,}000 + \$5(1{,}100{,}000)$$
$$= \$5{,}800{,}000$$

This approach yields very useful information in instances where there is uncertainty about volume of operations, perhaps because of customer demand. For example, the three Cumberland Airlines' airline maintenance cost estimates could reflect three possible levels of customer demand:

Most likely customer demand	$5,300,000
Pessimistic scenario of customer demand	4,800,000
Optimistic scenario of customer demand	5,800,000

If Cumberland Airlines' managers are confident of the relationship between air miles flown and airline maintenance costs, as well as their estimates of customer demand, the managers can be relatively confident that airline maintenance cost will fall between $4,800,000 and $5,800,000.

STRUCTURING COSTS TO ADJUST TO UNCERTAIN OUTCOMES

As discussed earlier in the chapter, the events of September 11, 2001, were disastrous for the airline industry. There are few other industries that could be harmed as dramatically by a drop in service/product demand. The airline industry is characterized by very high levels of fixed costs. Hence, in the short run, the level of costs is very insensitive to the level of customer demand. The result is that if demand spikes, profits soar, and if demand falters, profits drop rapidly and quickly turn into losses. The greater the uncertainty about demand, the greater is the risk of allowing fixed costs to comprise a high proportion of total costs.

To illustrate, consider the cost and revenue graphs, A and B, in Exhibit 15–12. Company A has a cost structure that is entirely variable, and Company B has a cost structure that is entirely fixed. The space between the revenue and total cost

EXHIBIT 15–12

RELATIONSHIP BETWEEN UNCERTAINTY AND COST STRUCTURE

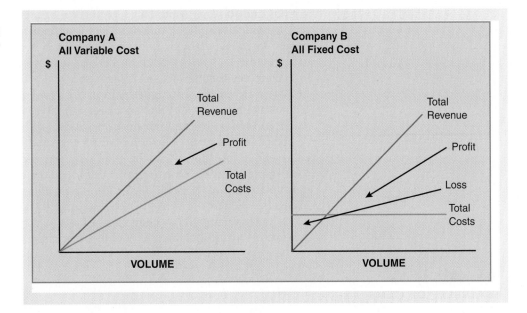

lines in the graphs represent profits or losses and are so labeled. Note how the amount of profit varies greatly with small changes in volume for Company B. Alternatively, Company A's profits change slowly as volume changes. Accordingly, Company A's profits are less exposed to the effects of uncertainty. General relationships between cost structure and profits are discussed in detail in Chapter 9.

Although in most companies, fixed and variable costs are not completely substitutable, most companies have substantial opportunities to change their cost structures. For example, in the airline industry, managers could choose to lease rather than purchase airlines. The shorter the term of the lease, the more the cost of airplanes can approximate a variable cost. That is, as demand changes, leases can be added or cancelled.

USING OPTIONS AND FORWARD CONTRACTS TO MITIGATE PRICE RISK

Uncertainty of the cost of inputs arises from two sources: the quantity of the inputs consumed and the price per unit of those inputs. Although the quantity of inputs consumed is typically highly correlated with customer demand and the volume of production, the price of inputs can be influenced by many other factors. Accordingly, even though machine hours may, on a long-term basis, prove to be highly correlated with utilities cost, machine hours is more highly correlated with the quantity component of cost rather than the price component. Thus, although the uncertainty surrounding quantity of input usage may be best resolved by an improved understanding of volume drivers, other strategies will be necessary to deal with price uncertainty.

Some companies operate in industries that are intensely competitive, and if prices of inputs unexpectedly increase, the companies may be unable to increase prices sufficiently to cover the increase in costs. These companies in particular need effective strategies for dealing with input price uncertainty. Two tools used in such strategies are options and forward contracts.

option

forward contract

hedging

Options and **forward contracts** are agreements that give the holder the right to purchase a given quantity of a specific input at a specific price. Generically, the use of options and forward contracts to manage price risk is known as **hedging**. To illustrate, fuel prices generally increased throughout 2004. Companies, such as airlines, that are heavily exposed to risks of price changes for fuel can use options and forward contracts as protection against such price increases. The extent to which specific companies in the airline industry used these tools varied widely in 2004. Although **Southwest Airlines** hedged approximately 80 percent of its fuel needs, **Delta** placed no hedges against price increases.[9] With no hedges to protect against the fuel price increase, Delta's fuel costs in the second quarter of 2004 were 54 percent higher than in the same quarter for 2003. Although some airlines attempted to add fuel surcharges to fares, this strategy generally failed because consumers resisted the price increases.

Forward contracts or options can be executed between a company and a specific vendor, or options can be purchased on organized exchanges such as the **Chicago Mercantile Exchange**, **Chicago Board of Trade**, and **New York Mercantile Exchange**. Exhibit 15–13 lists items commonly traded on the organized exchanges. Just as the consumer of a commodity such as diesel fuel can use a forward contract or option to hedge against cost uncertainty, a producer of diesel fuel can use a forward contract or option to hedge against revenue uncertainty.

EXHIBIT 15–13
EXAMPLES OF ITEMS COMMONLY HEDGED

Energy	Metals	Interest Rates
heating oil	gold	short-term
crude oil	silver	long-term
gasoline	copper	
natural gas	aluminum	**Agricultural**
electricity	platinum	livestock
coal		meats
propane	**Currencies**	grains
		cotton

INSURING AGAINST OCCURRENCES OF SPECIFIC EVENTS

insurance

The final strategy for coping with uncertainty involves use of insurance contracts. **Insurance** involves a contract in which one party (an insurer) in exchange for a payment (premium) agrees to reimburse a second party (an insured) for the costs of certain occurrences. The nature of the occurrences can include events limited only by the imagination of the contracting parties. Common types of occurrences for which insurance protection is sought include events often described as "acts of nature" such as tornados, hail storms, floods, and earthquakes. Other types of common events covered by insurance include fire, theft, vandalism, accidental death of a key employee, and product failure.

Whereas the other strategies for dealing with uncertainty largely address uncertainty about costs deriving from quantity and price variability, insurance is purchased to cope with uncertainty about occurrences of specific events. Events usually insured against are those that, in the absence of insurance, would dramatically increase costs (e.g., to rebuild a factory following a fire) or decrease revenues (e.g., business is interrupted by a labor strike in a company's only factory).

[9] James F. Peltz, "Companies Look to Cushion Fuel Costs," *The Bryan-College Station Eagle* (August 21, 2004), p. A6.

Revisiting

So how has JetBlue Airways accomplished the two unlikely feats of high profitability and high growth during such a turbulent period in the airline industry? The short answer is that, as of 2004, JetBlue Airways had the lowest cost per passenger mile of all its major competitors. In 2003, JetBlue's cost was only $0.0607 compared to an industry average cost of $0.0985 per available seat mile—a remarkable cost advantage. That lower cost allows the airline to sustain lower fares and maintain profitability.

The new airplanes are actually a key component of the lower cost structure JetBlue enjoys. Part of the cost advantage of the new planes derives from the use of a single model of plane: the Airbus A320. Operating only one model of plane reduces the costs of maintenance, training, parts inventory, and scheduling flights. Also, these planes are designed to provide for only one class of service; there are not separate accommodations for first class, business class, and coach. Thus, every passenger can be accommodated identically. Furthermore, because new planes require fewer repairs and are better designed for maintainability, costs for items such as repairs, maintenance, and downtime are greatly reduced. Some of this cost advantage will erode as JetBlue's fleet ages.

The company applies other cost management strategies that also create a competitive advantage. For example, in 2003, the company operated its aircraft for 13 hours each day. JetBlue managers believe that this level of utilization is highest in the industry and spreads the fixed cost of operating the airline across more passengers and more flights.

Another key variable in airline cost management is the load factor, or the number of available seats that are actually occupied by passengers. The higher the load factor, the lower the fare that must be charged to cover the cost of a flight. For 2003, the airline operated with an average load factor of 84.5 percent, which is well above its break-even load factor of only 72.5 percent. By concentrating on achieving a high load factor, JetBlue can maintain low prices because cost per passenger, or cost per passenger mile, will be minimized.

At least for now, David Neeleman has silenced his critics. His vision of operating an airline that can offer premium services for discounted fares is proving to be a success. This airline strategy relies on maintaining cost advantages over competitors. The new, one-model planes are the key to this strategy along with achieving a high load factor. Perhaps unexpected in the execution of this strategy is how frequently JetBlue is recognized for the superior quality of service delivered to passengers. JetBlue is consistently ranked highly in quality and performance by external rating services. And, as every consumer knows, high quality and low price make an unbeatable combination.

Source: *http://www.jetblue.com/learnmore/index.html; http://www.curran-connors.com/jb2003/financials.html.*

Comprehensive Review Module

Chapter Summary

1. An effective cost control system controls costs

   - prior to an event through

     ➤ establishment of budgets and standards.

     ➤ other stated expectations of performance outcomes.

   - during an event by

     ➤ correcting deviations from plans or budgets.

     ➤ monitoring other aspects of operations relative to expectations.

   - following an event by providing feedback on performance.

2. Three generic approaches to cost control include

   - cost containment, which is an approach to minimize cost increases.

   - cost avoidance, which means finding ways to avoid high cost inputs by substituting lower cost inputs.

   - cost reduction, which involves finding alternative ways to execute operations to lower costs.

3. Costs can change from one period to the next, or deviate from expectations, as a result of

   - variable costs moving with changes in volume.

   - inflation or deflation of prices.

   - supplier-changed prices

     ➤ in response to changes in demand.

     ➤ due to changes in cost of production.

   - purchase volume changes, which affect purchase discounts related to volume.

4. Two primary types of fixed cost are

   - committed fixed costs, which are associated with an organization's basic infrastructure and are determined by long-run strategy; examples include depreciation, lease payments, and property taxes.

   - discretionary fixed costs, which are incurred for activities for which the level and nature are de-

termined by management judgment; examples include research and development, advertising, and employee training.

5. Control of discretionary costs can be effected

   - before an event by the use of budgets or by treating them as engineered costs if they are associated with repetitive activities.

   - during an event by comparing budgets to actual expenditures.

   - after an event by calculating variances for engineered costs.

6. The objectives in managing cash are to

   - maintain an organization's liquidity by making certain there is enough cash to cover cash expense and to retire debt.

   - invest any idle cash so that a return is generated on cash balances exceeding liquidity needs.

7. Technology is reducing costs within supply chains by

   - reducing the need to generate paper documents for purchasing transactions.

   - automating payment transactions.

   - enhancing the exchange of information within the value chain.

   - enhancing competition among alternative suppliers.

8. Uncertainty is greater for future events than for past events because

   - cause and effect relationships are incompletely understood.

   - events that are unforeseen can alter outcomes.

9. Four generic strategies for dealing with uncertainty are to

   - explicitly consider uncertainty when estimates are generated by

     ➤ using best predictor variables in generating estimates.

> analyzing effects of estimation errors on estimates using sensitivity analysis.

• structure costs to adjust to uncertain outcomes.

• use options and forward contracts to manage price risks.

• use insurance to indemnify against occurrences of specific events such as

> acts of nature.

> fire, theft, and liability risks.

Solution Strategies

Efficiency: Relationship of input and output

Actual Yield Ratio = Actual Output ÷ Actual Input

or

Actual Input ÷ Actual Output

Desired Yield Ratio = Planned Output ÷ Planned Input

or

Planned Input ÷ Planned Output

Effectiveness: Relationship of actual output and desired output

Efficiency + Effectiveness = Performance

COST VARIANCES

Comparison of actual costs with budgeted costs: allows management to compare discrepancies from the original plan

Comparison of actual costs with budgeted costs at actual activity level: allows management to determine how well costs were controlled; uses a flexible budget

Variance analysis using standards for discretionary costs: allows management to compute variances for routine, structured discretionary costs

For discretionary costs susceptible to engineered cost treatment:

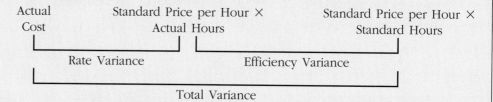

For discretionary costs that are managed as lump-sum fixed costs:

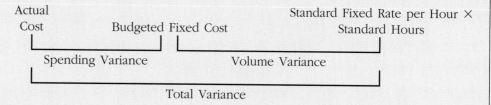

For discretionary costs involving both fixed and variable elements:

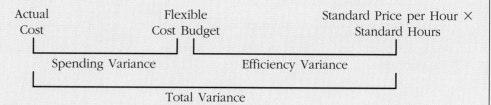

Demonstration Problem

Bullworth Mfg., a firm with global operations, has developed a training program for compliance with company policy and law regarding sexual harassment. The company believes it can treat the cost of this training as an engineered cost. The following data are extracted from documents addressing the training plan and from records regarding actual performance:

Planned volume of training	5,400 employees
Total budgeted trainer days	60
Actual volume of training	6,200 employees
Actual trainer days	65

Required:

a. Calculate the degree of effectiveness of the training relative to number of employees trained.
b. Calculate planned efficiency for the trainers.
c. Calculate the actual efficiency of the trainers.
d. Comment on the performance of the sexual harassment trainers.

Solution to Demonstration Problem

a. Degree of effectiveness = Actual employees trained ÷ Budgeted employees trained
$$= 6,200 ÷ 5,400$$
$$= 1.148, \text{ or } 114.8\%$$

b. Planned efficiency = Planned output ÷ Planned input
$$= 5,400 \text{ employees} ÷ 60 \text{ trainer days}$$
$$= 90 \text{ employees per trainer day}$$

c. Actual efficiency = Actual output ÷ Actual input
$$= 6,200 \text{ employees} ÷ 65 \text{ trainer days}$$
$$= 95.4 \text{ employees per trainer day}$$

d. The performance of the trainers is better than expected because they exceeded both effectiveness and efficiency expectations.

Key Terms

appropriation *(p. 613)*	cost control system *(p. 605)*	hedging *(p. 629)*
coefficient of determination *(p. 627)*	cost reduction *(p. 610)*	insurance *(p. 630)*
committed cost *(p. 611)*	discretionary cost *(p. 612)*	option *(p. 629)*
cost avoidance *(p. 609)*	engineered cost *(p. 616)*	random *(p. 625)*
cost consciousness *(p. 606)*	e-procurement *(p. 624)*	uncertainty *(p. 625)*
cost containment *(p. 609)*	forward contracts *(p. 629)*	working capital *(p. 621)*

Questions

1. How does the cost control system interact with the overall cost management system?

2. Why does the general control model begin with planning activities?

3. At what points in time is cost control for any specific organizational activity exercised? Why are these points of cost control important?

4. What factors can cause costs to change? Which of these factors are subject to cost containment and which are not? What creates the difference in controllability?

5. Differentiate between committed and discretionary costs. Could a cost be considered discretionary by one firm and committed by another? If so, discuss and give an example. If not, discuss why not.

6. Why is it often difficult to measure the output of activities funded by discretionary costs?

7. Define *efficiency* and *effectiveness* and distinguish one from the other. Why is measuring the efficiency of discretionary costs often difficult? Explain how the effectiveness of discretionary cost activities can be measured.

8. What types of discretionary costs are subject to control as engineered costs? Provide several examples.

9. Why do firms hold cash balances? Why do some firms require larger cash balances than other firms?

10. How is technology affecting supply chain purchasing practices and transaction costs?

11. What are the four generic approaches to reducing uncertainty?

12. What factors create uncertainty when estimating future costs and revenues?

Exercises

13. (Cost control activities) The firm of Xtreme Accountants hires full- and part-time professional employees. Full-time experienced staff can be hired for $57,000 per year; fringe benefit costs for each full-time employee amount to 20 percent of base salary. Xtreme Accountants pays part-time professional employees $40 per hour but does not provide any fringe benefits. If a part-time employee has worked for the firm for more than 1,600 hours by year-end, however, he or she receives a $4,000 bonus.

    a. Does the firm's policy of hiring part-time professional staff represent an example of cost containment, cost avoidance, or cost reduction? Explain.

b. For a given professional position, at what level of annual hours worked should the firm consider hiring full-time professional staff rather than part-time?

14. (Cost control activities) Callie Swoosh has just been appointed the new director of Youth Hot-Line, a not-for-profit organization that operates a phone bank for individuals experiencing emotional difficulties. The phones are staffed by qualified social workers and psychologists who are paid on an hourly basis. Swoosh took the following actions in the first week on her new job. Indicate whether the actions represent cost understanding, cost containment, cost avoidance, or cost reduction. Some actions may have more than one implication; if they do, indicate the reason.

a. Increased the advertising budget appropriation for the hot line.

b. Exchanged the more expensive push-button, cream-colored designer telephones for regular push-button desk telephones.

c. Eliminated the call-forwarding feature installed on all telephones because Youth Hot-Line will now be staffed 24 hours a day.

d. Eliminated two paid clerical positions and replaced these individuals with volunteers.

e. Ordered blank notepads for the counselors to keep by their phones; the old notepads (stock now depleted) had the Youth Hot-Line logo and address printed on them.

f. Negotiated a new contract with the telephone company. Youth Hot-Line will now pay a flat rate of $100 per month regardless of the number of telephones Hot-Line has installed. The previous contract charged the organization $10 for every telephone. At the time that contract was signed, Youth Hot-Line had only 10 telephones. With the increased staff, Swoosh plans to install at least five additional telephones.

15. (Committed versus discretionary costs) A list of committed and discretionary costs follows:

Annual audit fees	Internal audit salaries
Annual report preparation and printing	Marketing research
Building flood insurance	Preventive maintenance
Charitable contributions	Property taxes
Corporate advertising	Quality control inspection
Employee continuing education	Research and development salaries
Equipment depreciation	Research and development supplies
Interest on bonds payable	Secretarial pool salaries

a. Classify each of the above costs as normally being either committed (C) or discretionary (D).

b. Which of these costs can be either committed or discretionary based on management philosophy?

c. For the expenses marked discretionary in part (a), provide a monetary or nonmonetary surrogate output measure. For each output measure, briefly discuss any objections that could be raised to it.

16. (Committed versus discretionary costs) Choose letter C (for committed cost) or D (for discretionary cost) to indicate to which type of cost each of the sentences below best relates. Explain the rationale for your choice.

a. Control is first provided during the capital budgeting process.

b. Typical examples include advertising, research and development, and employee training.

c. This type of cost cannot be easily reduced even during temporary slowdowns in activity.

d. There is usually no "correct" amount at which to set funding levels.

e. Typical examples include depreciation, lease rentals, and property taxes.

f. This type of cost often provides benefits that are not monetarily measurable.

g. Temporary reductions can usually be made without impairing the firm's long-range capacity or profitability.

h. This cost is primarily affected by long-run decisions regarding desired capacity levels.

i. It is often difficult to ascribe outcomes as being closely correlated with this type of cost.

j. This cost usually relates to service-type activities.

17. (Effectiveness measures) Williams Wellness Clinic has used funds during 2006 for the following purposes. Provide nonmonetary, surrogate measures that would help evaluate the effectiveness of the monies spent.

a. Sent two cost accounting staff members to seminars on activity-based costing.

b. Installed a kidney dialysis machine.

c. Built an attached parking garage for the hospital.

d. Redecorated the main lobby.

e. Placed a full-page advertisement in the local Yellow Pages.

f. Acquired new software to track patient charges and prepare itemized billings.

18. (Effectiveness and efficiency measures) The president at Northern State University has formed a new department to recruit top out-of-state students. The department's funding for 2006 is $400,000, and the department was given the goal of recruiting 300 new nonresident students. By year-end 2006, the department had been credited with recruiting 330 new students. The department actually consumed $468,600 in its recruiting efforts.

a. How effective was the newly formed department? Show calculations.

b. How efficient was the department? Show calculations.

19. (Engineered cost variances) Fast Freight employs three drivers who are paid an average of $16 per hour for regular time and $24 for overtime. A pickup and delivery requires, on average, one hour of driver time. Drivers are paid for a 40-hour week because they must be on call all day. One driver stands by for after-hour deliveries. Analyze the labor costs for one week in which the company made 105 daytime deliveries and 12 after-hour deliveries. The payroll for drivers for that week was $2,280. The employees worked 120 hours of regular time and 15 hours of overtime.

20. (Engineered cost variances) Management at Datong Industries has estimated that each quality control inspector should be able to make an average of 12 inspections per hour. Retired factory supervisors are excellent quality control inspectors because of their familiarity with the products and processes in the plant. Datong management has decided to staff the quality control program with these individuals and has set $18 as the standard hourly rate. During the first month of the new program, 12,560 inspections were made, and the total pay to the inspectors was $20,928 for 1,030 hours of work.

a. Perform a variance analysis for management on the quality control labor cost.

b. Assume that management could hire four full-time inspectors for a monthly salary of $5,000 each and hire part-timers for the overflow. Each full-time inspector would work 170 hours per month. How would the total cost of this alternative compare to the cost of a 1,030-hour month at the standard rate of $18 per hour?

21. (Revenue variances) The manager of a lumber mill has been asked to explain to the company president why sales of scrap firewood were above budget by $4,200. He requests your help. On examination of budget documents, you discover that budgeted revenue from firewood sales was $75,000 based on expected sales of 1,875 cords of wood at $40 per cord. Further investigation reveals that 1,800 cords were actually sold at an average price of $45. Prepare an analysis of firewood sales and explain what happened.

WebTUTOR Advantage

22. (Revenue variances) "Snippets" is a videotape series that is marketed to day care centers and parents. The series has been found to make babies who watch it extremely contented and quiet. In 2005, Jaklo Ltd., maker of the tapes, sold 400 of the series for $60 per package. In preparing the 2006 budget, company management estimated a 15 percent increase in sales volume because the price was to be reduced by 10 percent. At the end of 2006, company management is disappointed that actual revenue is only $24,440 although 470 packages of the series were sold.
   a. What was the expected revenue for 2006?
   b. Calculate the price and volume variances for Jaklo Ltd.

23. (Variance analysis) Cost control in the Personnel Office of Johnson Robotics is evaluated based on engineered cost concepts. The office incurs both variable and fixed costs. The variable costs are largely driven by the amount of employee turnover. For 2006, budgeted costs in the Personnel Office were:

Fixed $200,000
Variable   400,000 (based on projected turnover of 1,000 employees)

For 2006, actual costs in the Personnel Office were:

Fixed $220,000
Variable   450,000 (actual turnover of 1,050 employees)

Using traditional variance analysis, evaluate the control of fixed and variable costs in the Personnel Office of Johnson Robotics. Does this method of evaluation encourage the Personnel Office managers to hire low-quality workers? Explain.

24. (Cost consciousness; team activity) All organizations seek to be aware of and control costs. In a three- or four-person team, choose one of the following industries and do Web research to identify methods that have been used to control costs.
   - Internet e-tailers
   - Automobile manufacturers
   - Hospitals
   - Software companies
   - Government entities
   Prepare a written presentation that discusses the various methods of cost control, dollars of costs saved (if available), and your perceptions of the positive and negative implications of each of the cost control methodologies. You may choose a particular company within the industry should you so desire.

25. (Cost control) *Hello! This communication lays out new guidelines for the spending of money while on Company time. Please look them over. Keep in mind that they are just suggested procedures to help us keep spending in line for the benefit of all. Each individual's needs and requirements are different, we know that, so please report any breach that you spot in these voluntary guidelines to the Controller's office immediately.*
   - *Travel: Except for Entertainment, with which it is usually paired, Travel is the single biggest expense in the budget. Control in this area will make it less necessary for us to get medieval on you later. Therefore, all trips, be they short or long, must be cleared by the Company, specifically by Barry*

Barber in the Controller's office. A word about Barry. He's been selected because he doesn't care about you or what you need to get your job done. All he cares about is cost. Later, when this downturn is over, we're going to fire him. Until then, you belong to him.

- Booking: *All trips must be booked through Zippy Travel, a division of the company dedicated to providing the very finest in service as long as it's cheap. Book through www.zippy4U.com, or the touchtone system that is most convenient between the hours of 3 A.M. and 6 A.M. when fewer people are there to load it up with stupid demands. Register any complaints with your Human Resources representative, who will take care of you right away.*

- Meals: *All business food expense is hereby capped at 20 percent of what it will cost you in the real world. The rest must come out of your pocket. No breakfasts will be approved that include bacon, and any employing cutlery (except small teaspoons) are forbidden. Luncheons will be capped at $12.50 a person in New York and Los Angeles and $5 elsewhere. Dinners will be limited to $15.50 in major cities with populations over 6 million, and $6.50 everywhere else in the world, except in China, Eastern Europe, South America, and portions of Indiana, where you can get a complete meal for under $1. Doggie bags must be presented to a dog approved by Barry Barber in the Controller's office. Please note that expense caps on meals are not transferable and may not be stockpiled. Just because you do not spend your $12.50 on Monday, Tuesday, Wednesday, and Thursday doesn't mean you can spend $60 on Friday. And don't try to buy each other drinks, either! We know that's what you've been up to! Stop it!*

- Hotels: *Cost of hotel rooms is limited to $49 a night, or no more than 50 percent of their actual price. Those who heretofore have rated a suite will now be booked into a double. All king-size beds will now be downgraded to queens, except in the borough of Queens, where pull-out cots will now be the rule. Things no longer covered during your hotel stay include:*
  - *Room service.*
  - *Anything from the minibar.*
  - *In-room movies.*
  - *Phone calls from the room.*
  - *Closet space that could be used by another executive to sleep standing up.*

That's it for now. Your Company is sure that if these simple rules are followed, we'll survive this temporary reversal in our economy with everybody, not just the little people, suffering for the good of us all. Oh, and turn off your lights when you leave a room, for heaven's sake! What do you think we are—made of money?

Source: Adapted from Stanley Bing, "Cold Cuts for Hard Times," *Fortune* (November 26, 2001), pp. 65–66. Copyright © 2001, Time Inc. All rights reserved.

a. Explain the cost control strategy presented by the author of the preceding tongue-in-cheek communication.

b. What do you think the author of the communication was trying to accomplish?

26. (Cost control; financial records) Minnesota Metals is a medium-size manufacturing corporation in a capital-intensive industry. Its profitability is currently very low. As a result, investment funds are limited and hiring is restricted. These consequences of the corporation's problems have placed a strain on the plant's repair and maintenance program. The result has been a reduction in work efficiency and cost control effectiveness in the repair and maintenance area.

The assistant controller proposes the installation of a maintenance work order system to overcome these problems. This system would require a work order to be prepared for each repair request and for each regular maintenance activity. The maintenance superintendent would record the estimated time to complete a job and send one copy of the work order to the department in which the work would be done. The work order would also serve as a cost sheet for a job. Actual cost of parts and supplies used on the job as well as actual labor costs incurred in completing the job would be recorded directly on the work order. A copy of the completed work order would be the basis for the charge to the department in which the repair or maintenance activity occurred.

The maintenance superintendent opposes the program because the added paperwork will be costly and nonproductive. The superintendent states that the departmental clerk who now schedules repairs and maintenance activities is doing a good job without all the extra forms the new system would require. The real problem, in the superintendent's opinion, is that the department is understaffed.

a. Discuss how such a maintenance work order system would aid in cost control.

b. Explain how a maintenance work order system might assist the maintenance superintendent in getting authorization to hire more mechanics.

(CMA adapted)

27. (Cash management) Indianapolis Tire Company manufactures tires that are sold to both car manufacturers and tire wholesalers. The following data have been taken from a recent balance sheet.

Current assets (in millions)

Cash	$ 10
Accounts receivable	140
Finished goods inventory	25
Work in process inventory	170
Raw materials inventory	90

Current liabilities

Accounts payable	$ 22
Other	7

Discuss recommendations that Indianapolis Tire Company managers could use to improve its cash position. Focus your discussion on the operating cycle rather than on other means of raising cash.

28. (e-procurement) You are employed by a firm engaging in heavy manufacturing. Its direct materials are sourced globally, but its nonoperating inputs are sourced from a variety of U.S. vendors. You have been charged with making a presentation to the CFO about the benefits of e-procurement for nonoperating inputs. Outline the benefits your firm could expect to realize if it replaced its paper controls with a state-of-the-art e-procurement system.

29. (Coping with uncertainty) You have been assigned the task of projecting the cost of 2008 employee fringe benefits for your firm and have identified number of employees, total labor hours and total labor cost as candidate independent variables for use in the estimation equation. Using historical data and ordinary least squares regression, you calculate the coefficient of determination for each of the candidate variables. You get the following results:

Variable	Coefficient of Determination
Number of employees	0.87
Total labor hours	0.95
Total labor cost	0.81

Discuss how you would use the coefficient of determination to select the best predictor variable.

30. (Coping with uncertainty) Metalworks, Inc., manufactures a variety of industrial products from sheet metal. The firm is engaged in its annual process of budgeting costs and revenues for the coming year. The cost of metal consumes approximately 50 percent of total revenues. Discuss which strategies for dealing with uncertainty would be appropriate for Metalworks to use in estimating and managing its metal costs for the coming year.

31. (Coping with uncertainty) Callahan Corp. operates in an industry in which the demand for products is cyclical. The cycles in the industry are often unpredictable. Discuss a strategy to deal with uncertainty associated with the cycles that would be appropriate for Callahan Corp. to employ to maintain its profitability throughout the cycles.

Problems

32. (Cost consciousness) Lynn and Tim Robinson are preparing their household financial budget for December. They have started with their November budget and are adjusting it to reflect the difference between November and December in planned activities. The Robinsons are expecting out-of-town guests for two weeks over the holiday season. The following list describes the budgetary changes from November to December that are contemplated by the Robinson family:
  a. Increase the grocery budget by $135.
  b. Decrease the commuter transportation budget by $50 to reflect the days off from work.
  c. Change food budget to reflect serving pizza rather than steak and lobster each weekend.
  d. Budget an extra $70 for utilities.
  e. Reduce household maintenance budget by $60 to reflect the fact that outside maid services will not be used over the holiday period.
  f. Buy generic breakfast cereal rather than name brand due to the quantity the guests will consume.
  g. Use paper plates so as not to need to run the dishwasher as often.
  h. Buy the institutional-size packages of paper plates rather than smaller size packages.
  i. Budget the long-distance phone bill at $50 less because there will be no need to call the relatives who will be visiting.
  j. Budget movie costs at $3 per rental tape rather than $7 per person to go to the movies.
  k. Postpone purchasing needed work clothes until the January sales.
  l. Budget funds to repair the car. Lynn plans to use part of her vacation time to make the repairs herself rather than take the car to a garage in January.
  Indicate whether each of these items indicates cost understanding (CU), cost containment (CC), cost avoidance (CA), or cost reduction (CR). Some items may have more than one answer.

33. (Cost control) The following graph indicates where each part of the dollar that a student pays for a new college textbook goes.

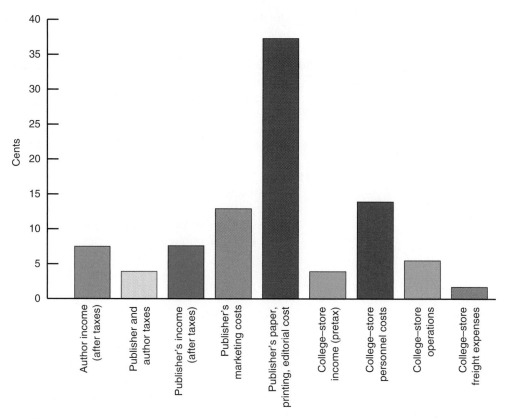

Source: Association of American Publishers and National Association of College Stores, "Where Does the Text-book Dollar Go?" *The Chronicle of Higher Education* (September 22, 1995), p. A51. Reprinted with permission.

Students are frustrated with the cost of their textbooks, but most publishers would say that the selling prices have merely kept pace with inflation. Buying used books is an option, but publishers say that used books simply drive up the cost of future texts: If the publisher cannot sell as many of the new edition as are printed, the price is raised "to compensate for decreased sales volume, and the cycle starts again." Publishers also must cover the costs of many nonsalable faculty supplements such as instructor manuals, solutions manuals, transparency acetates, videos, and test banks (hard copy and electronic). Additionally, as the books become "fancier" with multiple colors, photographs, and periodical cites, costs also increase. Write a paper that does the following:

a. Provides suggestions for ways the college/university bookstore could control costs.

b. Provides suggestions for ways the publisher could control costs.

c. Provides suggestions for ways students can legally control textbook expenditures (remember that substantial reproduction of the text is illegal).

d. Talk to someone who went to college 20 years ago and discuss how today's college textbooks differ from the textbooks he or she used. Are the current differences cost beneficial from your perspective?

34. (Cost control) Temporary or part-time employees may be used rather than full-time employees in each of the following situations:

a. To teach undergraduate accounting courses at a university.

b. To serve as security guards.

c. To staff a health clinic in a rural area.

d. To write articles for a monthly technical magazine.

e. To clean the house when the regular maid is ill.

f. To answer questions on a tax help-line during tax season.

g. To work in department stores during the Christmas rush.

h. To do legal research in a law firm.

i. To perform quality control work in a car manufacturing plant.

j. To do seamstress work in a custom dress shop.

k. To work as a clerk/cashier in a small retail store. The store is a mom-and-pop operation, and the clerk is the only employee in the store when he or she works.

Indicate the potential advantages and disadvantages of the use of temporaries in each of these situations. These advantages and disadvantages can be viewed from the standpoint of the employer or the user of the employer's products or services.

35. (Efficiency standards) Do Little has been asked to monitor the efficiency and effectiveness of a newly installed machine. The specialized machine has been guaranteed by the manufacturer to package 7,800 engine gaskets per kilowatt hour (kWh). The rate of defects on production is estimated at two percent. The machine is equipped with a device to measure the number of kWhs used. During the first month of use, the machine packaged 1,390,000 gaskets, of which 17,900 were flawed, and it used 175 kWhs.

a. What is the efficiency standard for flawless output?

b. Calculate the achieved efficiency for the first month and briefly comment on it.

c. Determine the achieved effectiveness and briefly comment on it.

d. Assume that the company was charged $3.20 per kWh during the first month this machine was in service. Estimate the company's savings or loss in power costs because of the machine's efficiency level in the first month of operations.

e. If you were a customer buying this company's gaskets for use in automobile production, what level of quality control would you want the company to have and why?

36. (Effectiveness/efficiency) Top management of Merlin Magic Stores observed that the budget for the EDP department had been growing far beyond what was anticipated for the past several years. Each year, the EDP manager would demonstrate that increased usage by the company's non-EDP departments would justify the enlarged appropriations. The administrative vice president commented that she was not surprised because user departments were not charged for the EDP department services and EDP department personnel were creative and eager to continue expanding services. A review of the current year's statistics of the EDP department revealed the following:

Budgetary appropriation	$500,000, based on 2,000 hours of run time; $400,000 of this appropriation is related to fixed costs
Actual department expenses	Variable, $87,750 (incurred for 1,950 hours of run time) Fixed, $402,000

a. Did the EDP manager stay within his appropriation? Show calculations.

b. Was the EDP department effective? Show calculations. Comment.

c. Was the EDP department efficient? Show calculations. (*Hint:* Treat variable and fixed expenses separately.)

d. Using the formulas for analyzing variable and fixed costs, calculate the variances incurred by the EDP department.

e. Propose a rate per hour to charge user departments for EDP services. Do you think charging users will affect the demand for services by user departments? Why or why not?

37. (Effectiveness versus efficiency) *The founder and president of the Institute for Healthcare Improvement, Donald Berwick, is convinced that the U.S. health care system can reduce costs by 30 percent while improving overall quality—*

just by getting health care professionals to adopt improvements others already have discovered.

- *Many children, possibly up to 30 percent, are being treated with new, broad spectrum, expensive, and potentially unsafe antibiotics despite national research and expert guidelines urging use of simple, inexpensive antibiotics as far better initial treatment.*
- *MRI scans in the first week of back pain rarely produce useful information compared with "watchful waiting," but many doctors order MRIs for such patients.*
- *Simple, inexpensive medications such as aspirin and beta blocker drugs can significantly reduce the likelihood of dying from heart attacks, but only one in five eligible patients currently receives such medications.*
- *Inhaled steroid medications can prevent disability and complications among asthmatic patients, but fewer than one-third of eligible patients receive such medication.*
- *One HMO-based study showed an 80 percent decrease in hospital days and emergency room visits for asthma care among patients trained to avoid asthma triggers, measure their own lung function, follow a consistent treatment plan, and make adjustments in their own medications.*

Source: Ed Egger, "Best Outcomes May Be Salvation for Shriveling Managed Care Cost Savings," *Health Care Strategic Management* (March 1999), pp. 12–13.

Indicate whether each selected finding mentioned represents effectiveness, efficiency, or both. If the finding represents either efficiency or both, indicate whether you consider it to be primarily cost understanding, cost containment, cost avoidance, or cost reduction. Justify each of your answers.

38. (Budget-to-actual comparison) Buzz Beverages evaluates performance in part through the use of flexible budgets. Selling expense budgets at three activity levels within the relevant range are shown below.

Activity Measures

Unit sales volume	15,000	17,500	20,000
Dollar sales volume	$15,000,000	$17,500,000	$20,000,000
Number of orders processed	1,500	1,750	2,000
Number of salespersons	100	100	100

Monthly Expenses

Advertising and promotion	$1,500,000	$1,500,000	$1,500,000
Administrative salaries	75,000	75,000	75,000
Sales salaries	90,000	90,000	90,000
Sales commissions	450,000	525,000	600,000
Salesperson travel	200,000	225,000	250,000
Sales office expense	445,000	452,500	460,000
Shipping expense	650,000	675,000	700,000
Total	$3,410,000	$3,542,500	$3,675,000

The following assumptions were used to develop the selling expense flexible budgets:

- The average size of the company's sales force during the year was planned to be 100 people.
- Salespersons are paid a monthly salary plus commission on gross dollar sales.
- The travel costs have both a fixed and a variable element. The fixed portion is related to the number of salespersons, and the variable portion tends to fluctuate with gross dollars of sales.
- Sales office expense is a mixed cost with the variable portion related to the number of orders processed.
- Shipping expense is a mixed cost with the variable portion related to the number of units sold. (An order consists of 10 units.)

A sales force of 90 persons generated a total of 1,600 orders, resulting in a sales volume of 16,000 units during November. The gross dollar sales amounted to $14.9 million. The selling expenses incurred for November were as follows:

Advertising and promotion	$1,450,000
Administrative salaries	80,000
Sales salaries	92,000
Sales commissions	460,000
Salesperson travel	185,000
Sales office expense	500,000
Shipping expense	640,000
Total	$3,407,000

a. Explain why the selling expense flexible budget would not be appropriate for evaluating the company's November selling expense, and indicate how the flexible budget would have to be revised.

b. Determine the budgeted variable cost per salesperson and variable cost per sales order for the company.

c. Prepare a selling expense report for November that the company can use to evaluate its control over selling expenses. The report should have a line for each selling expense item showing the appropriate budgeted amount, the actual selling expense, and the monthly dollar variation.

d. Determine the actual variable cost per salesperson and variable cost per sales order processed for the company.

e. Comment on the effectiveness and efficiency of the salespersons during November.

(CMA adapted)

39. (Cash management) As the economy entered the new millennium, Internet companies were competing head-to-head in many markets with established, traditional retailers for the consumer's dollar. In comparing the financial statements of "e-tailers" relative to traditional retailing firms such as Wal-Mart, one interesting difference is the comparatively large amount of cash held by the Internet firms. Using concepts presented in this chapter, discuss the most plausible explanations for the Internet companies holding such large sums of cash.

40. (Analyzing cost control) The financial results for the Continuing Education Department of BusEd Corporation for November 2006 are presented in the schedule at the end of this problem. Mary Ross, president of BusEd, is pleased with the final results but has observed that the revenue and most of the costs and expenses of this department exceeded the budgeted amounts. Barry Stein, vice president of the Continuing Education Department, has been requested to provide an explanation for any amount that exceeded the budget by 5 percent or more.

Stein has accumulated the following facts to assist in his analysis of the November results:

- The budget for calendar year 2006 was finalized in December 2005, and at that time, a full program of continuing education courses was scheduled to be held in Chicago during the first week of November 2006. The schedule allowed eight courses to be run on each of the five days during the week. The budget assumed that there would be 425 participants in the program and 1,000 participant days for the week.

- BusEd charges a flat fee of $150 per day of course instruction, so the fee for a three-day course would be $450. BusEd grants a 10 percent discount to persons who subscribe to its publications. The 10 percent discount is also granted to second and subsequent registrants for the same course from the same organization. However, only one discount per registration is allowed.

Historically, 70 percent of the participant day registrations is at the full fee of $150 per day, and 30 percent of the participant day registrations receives the discounted fee of $135 per day. These percentages were used in developing the November 2006 budgeted revenue.

- The following estimates were used to develop the budgeted figures for course-related expenses.

Food charges per participant day (lunch/coffee breaks)	$ 27
Course materials per participant	8
Instructor fee per day	1,000

- A total of 530 individuals participated in the Chicago courses in November 2006, accounting for 1,280 participant days. This number included 20 persons who took a new, two-day course on pension accounting that was not on the original schedule; thus, on two of the days, nine courses were offered, and an additional instructor was hired to cover the new course. The breakdown of the course registrations were as follows:

Full fee registrations	704
Discounted fees	
Current periodical subscribers	128
New periodical subscribers	128
Second registrations from the same organization	320
Total participant day registrations	1,280

- A combined promotional mailing was used to advertise the Chicago program and a program in Cincinnati that was scheduled for December 2006. The incremental costs of the combined promotional price were $5,000, but none of the promotional expenses ($20,000) budgeted for the Cincinnati program in December will have to be incurred. This earlier-than-normal promotion for the Cincinnati program has resulted in early registration fees collected in November as follows (in terms of participant days):

Full fee registrations	140
Discounted registrations	60
Total participant day registrations	200

- BusEd, which continually updates and adds new courses, includes $2,000 in each monthly budget for this purpose. The additional amount spent on course development during November was for an unscheduled course that will be offered in February for the first time.

Stein has prepared the following quantitative analysis of the November 2006 variances:

BUSED CORPORATION
Statement of Operations
Continuing Education Department
For the Month Ended November 30, 2006

	Budget	Actual	Favorable (Unfavorable) Dollars	Favorable (Unfavorable) Percent
Revenue Course fees	$145,500	$212,460	$ 66,960	46.0
Expenses				
Food charges	$ 27,000	$ 32,000	$ (5,000)	(18.5)
Course materials	3,400	4,770	(1,370)	(40.3)
Instructor fees	40,000	42,000	(2,000)	(5.0)
Instructor travel	9,600	9,885	(285)	(3.0)
Staff salaries and benefits	12,000	12,250	(250)	(2.1)
Staff travel	2,500	2,400	100	4.0
Promotion	20,000	25,000	(5,000)	(25.0)
Course development	2,000	5,000	(3,000)	(150.0)
Total expenses	$116,500	$133,305	$(16,805)	(14.4)
Revenue over expenses	$ 29,000	$ 79,155	$ 50,155	172.9

BUSED CORPORATION
Analysis of November 2006 Variances

Budgeted revenue		$145,500
Variances		
Quantity variance [(1,280 − 1,000) × $145.50]	$40,740 F	
Mix variance [($143.25 − $145.50) × 1,280]	2,880 U	
Timing difference ($145.50 × 200)	29,100 F	66,960 F
Actual revenue		$212,460
Budgeted expenses		$116,500
Quantity variances		
Food charges [(1,000 − 1,280) × $27]	$ 7,560 U	
Course materials [(425 − 530) × $8]	840 U	
Instructor fees (2 × $1,000)	2,000 U	10,400 U
Price variances		
Food charges [($27 − $25) × 1,280]	$ 2,560 F	
Course materials [($8 − $9) × 530]	530 U	2,030 F
Timing differences		
Promotion	$ 5,000 U	
Course development	3,000 U	8,000 U
Variances not analyzed (5% or less)		
Instructor travel	$ 285 U	
Staff salaries and benefits	250 U	
Staff travel	100 F	435 U
Actual expenses		$133,305

After reviewing Stein's quantitative analysis of the November variances, prepare a memorandum addressed to Ross explaining the following:

a. The cause of the revenue mix variance.
b. The implication of the revenue mix variance.
c. The cause of the revenue timing difference.
d. The significance of the revenue timing difference.
e. The primary cause of the unfavorable total expense variance.
f. How the favorable food price variance was determined.
g. The impact of the promotion timing difference on future revenues and expenses.
h. Whether or not the course development variance has an unfavorable impact on the company.

(CMA adapted)

41. (Cost control) *The managers and partners that were interviewed listed reduced manpower costs as the major advantage for utilizing paraprofessionals [in CPA firms]. It seems that these savings were realized in a number of ways. First, there were significant savings in the salaries of paraprofessionals when compared with new staff professionals. Furthermore, since a large number of paraprofessionals were employed for less than 40 hours, many firms were realizing a significant savings in fringe benefit cost. As one manager indicated, "When we want to review inventory, we always try to get our paraprofessional because of his experience in the use of the audit guide, insights on inventory procedures, and level of training." Partners and managers indicated that the part-time nature of the employment agreement for most paraprofessionals offered the firm greater flexibility in scheduling work around peak business periods and aided in reducing hours that cannot be billed.*

Certainly, the savings discussed above can have a significant impact on dwindling profit margins or can be passed on to the client in the form of reduced fees. As indicated [in this article], the billing rate for accounting paraprofessionals seems to be around $60 per hour (for both large and small firms).

Most managers reported that the billing rate for accounting paraprofessionals was 10–15 percent below that of new professional staff personnel. One *manager from a [large] firm indicated that the standard billing rate for para-professionals was $68 per hour and up to $115 per hour for those with more experience.*

For the same firm, the standard billing rate for beginning staff professionals was $115 per hour.

Quality of work, especially on job assignments that require a large amount of detailed and repetitive tasks, was also cited on several occasions as a major consideration when employing accounting paraprofessionals. The fact that paraprofessionals are able to spend longer periods of time on jobs and their willingness to do repetitive tasks may explain the improved quality of work of paraprofessionals.

As one manager stated, "The quality of work of our paraprofessionals far exceeds that of our new staff professionals." Some of the practitioners who were interviewed still expressed concerns about utilizing paraprofessionals and the legal implications of using "less than qualified" individuals on audits. When considering using paraprofessionals on audit engagements, an argument could be advanced that the use of "less than competent audit personnel" is a violation of auditing standards. Of course the basic question is: Do these individuals possess the technical attributes one would normally expect of individuals working in that capacity?

Source: Ted R. Compton, "Staffing Issues for the New Millennium—The Emerging Role of the Accounting Paraprofessional," *Ohio CPA Journal* (July–September 2000), pp. 56ff.

a. Discuss the use of part-timers and paraprofessionals from the perspective of controlling costs.

b. How could the use of part-timers and paraprofessionals impair the quality of work performed by public accounting firms?

c. How could the use of part-timers and paraprofessionals affect the effectiveness and efficiency with which work is performed in public accounting firms?

42. (Supply chain management) Your employer, Southeast Industrial, implemented an e-procurement system last year for purchasing nonoperating inputs. The installation has been such a success that the firm is now considering using the same system to acquire operating inputs (e.g., direct material and product components).

However, some executives in the firm are reluctant to implement such a system for operating inputs because it does not support the rich collaboration that is necessary for effective supply chain cost management. Current systems support exchange of only basic transactional information: price, product availability, shipping terms and dates; and routine transaction processing including electronic ordering and electronic payments.

a. Assume that you are the firm's controller. Would you support the use of the e-procurement system for purchasing operating inputs? Why or why not?

b. Assume that you are vice president of product development. Would you support installation of the e-procurement system? Why or why not?

43. (Coping with uncertainty) After reviewing financial results for 2005, Midtown Industrial's President sent the following e-mail to his CFO and Controller, Jason Sharp.

Dear Jason:

I'm disappointed in the financial results for the year just completed. As you know, profits were $2 million below budget. In comparing the actual results to the budget, I note that the cost of natural gas exceeded budget by almost $1.3 million, and that cost alone accounts for 65% of the profit deficiency. This is the second year in a row that energy costs have dramatically reduced *profits. I am calling a meeting on Tuesday to review our financial results, and I would like you to offer a presentation on the following topics:*

1. *Why our estimates of energy costs have been dramatically below actual costs.*

2. *What actions you intend to take to improve our ability to estimate these costs.*

3. *What actions the company could take to better manage these costs.*

As the most recent hire in the Financial Department of Midtown Industrial, Sharp has asked you for help.

a. What suggestions will you give Sharp to improve the estimates of energy costs for future budgeting cycles?

b. What suggestions will you give Sharp to improve the management of energy costs in the future?

44. (Coping with uncertainty) Stanton Industries manufactures Christmas ornaments in its sole plant located in Wisconsin. Because the demand for the company's products is very seasonal, the company builds inventory throughout the first nine months of the year and draws down inventory the last three months of the year as demand in those months greatly exceeds production capacity. The company recently designated a member of management to be Chief Risk Officer (CRO). This individual has been charged with developing strategies to manage the effects of uncertainty on the business. The CRO has identified the following major sources of uncertainty:

1. Financing costs of inventory.

2. The cost of resin, which is the main material used in production.

3. "Acts of Nature" which could harm or destroy the production facility.

4. The price to be realized for products.

5. The level of demand for the company's products.

As a risk consultant, you have been retained by the CRO to develop strategies to deal with each of these major sources of uncertainty. In a report, outline your recommendations for each of the five major sources of uncertainty.

16

Implementing
Quality Concepts

Objectives

AFTER COMPLETING THIS CHAPTER, YOU SHOULD BE ABLE TO ANSWER THE FOLLOWING QUESTIONS:

LO.1 WHAT IS QUALITY, AND FROM WHOSE VIEWPOINT SHOULD IT BE EVALUATED?

LO.2 WHAT IS BENCHMARKING, AND WHY DO COMPANIES ENGAGE IN IT?

LO.3 WHY IS TOTAL QUALITY MANAGEMENT A SIGNIFICANT MANAGEMENT PHILOSOPHY, AND WHAT CONDITIONS ARE NECESSARY TO YIELD ITS BENEFITS?

LO.4 WHAT TYPES OF QUALITY COSTS EXIST, AND HOW ARE THOSE COSTS RELATED?

LO.5 HOW IS COST OF QUALITY MEASURED?

LO.6 HOW CAN THE BALANCED SCORECARD AND COST MANAGEMENT SYSTEM BE USED TO PROVIDE INFORMATION ON QUALITY IN AN ORGANIZATION?

LO.7 HOW CAN QUALITY BE INSTILLED AS PART OF AN ORGANIZATION'S CULTURE?

LO.8 *(APPENDIX)* WHAT INTERNATIONAL QUALITY STANDARDS EXIST?

Introducing

The song "Puttin' on the Ritz," written by Irving Berlin in the late 1920s, referred to the posh hotels developed by César Ritz and established the terms *ritz* and *ritzy* as referring to society's upper echelon. Ritz's hotels achieved such a renowned reputation in the marketplace that they attained what was often referred to as "The Ritz Mystique." The current-day **Ritz-Carlton Hotel Company** originated in 1983 with William B. Johnson's purchase of The Ritz-Carlton, Boston and the rights to the Ritz-Carlton name. The standards of the Boston hotel became the norms for all hotels in the newly formed chain. The company, with 58 hotels and resorts worldwide in 2004, is 99 percent owned by **Marriott International Inc.** but is independently operated.

The Ritz-Carlton is the only hotel company to twice (1992 and 1999) win the Malcolm Baldrige National Quality Award (MBNQA) in the service category. In addition to the MBNQA, The Ritz-Carlton ranked tops in the JD Power and Associates 2003 North American Hotel Survey in the luxury segment, and numerous Ritz-Carlton lodging and restaurant locations are included in the 2004 American Automobile Association Five-Diamond and Mobil Five-Star awards. The company also received the best overall ratings in the luxury category in the July 2004 Consumer Reports survey.

The Credo of the hotel chain amplifies its promise of high-quality service: "The Ritz-Carlton Hotel is a place where the genuine care and comfort of our guests is our highest mission. We pledge to provide the finest personal service and facilities for our guests who will always enjoy a warm, relaxed, yet refined ambience. The Ritz-Carlton experience enlivens the senses, instills well-being, and fulfills even the unexpressed wishes and needs of our guests." The Ritz-Carlton's Motto indicates the importance of its employees in that process by stating, "We are ladies and gentlemen serving ladies and gentlemen." Additionally, the company has an employee promise that "our Ladies and Gentlemen are the most important resource in our service commitment to our guests. . . . [W]e nurture and maximize talent to the benefit of each individual and the company." The idea of encouraging employee potential can be seen by the fact that the company's chief operating officer, Simon Cooper, began his career working at the front desk at his family-owned hotel in England. Former receptionists and servers can be found on the Executive Committees of many of The Ritz-Carlton Hotels.

Cooper and his team chose to "manage for quality." In 1989, former COO and president, Horst Schultze, selected the Baldrige criteria to optimize Ritz-Carlton's performance. One important part of this pursuit of excellence was that people had to be involved in planning the work that affects them. Thus, training and employee empowerment are essential. In a highly competitive industry that is typically characterized by excess capacity, cost reduction pressures, and high staff turnover, the company's ultimate goals are 100 percent employee pride in job; zero customer difficulties, and 100 percent customer loyalty—a tall order, but one that is fundamentally achievable by a company that is uncompromising in its continued pursuit of "The Ritz Mystique." After all, the company's vision is "to be the premier worldwide provider of luxury travel and hospitality products and services."

Sources: © 1999 The Ritz-Carlton Hotel Company, LLC. All rights reserved. Reprinted with permission of The Ritz-Carlton Hotel Company, LLC. "Consumer Reports Taps Top Brands," *Lodging Hospitality* (July 2004), p. 10; Jonathan Friedland, "Ritz-Carlton Tops Four Seasons; Survey Puts Marriott Unit Ahead of Big Competitor in Luxury-Hotel Category," *The Wall Street Journal* (August 27, 2003), p. D6; "The Ritz-Carlton," *http://www.callcenterejournal.com/Featured.lasso* (accessed August 6, 2004); and Tony Mosely, "Customer Focused Empowerment Pays at Ritz-Carlton," *http://www.serviceexcellence.co.uk/ritz.shtm* (accessed August 6, 2004).

Managers at The Ritz-Carlton and many other entities recognize that high quality is a fundamental organizational strategy for competing in a global economy. Businesses, both domestic and foreign, are scrambling to attract customers and to offer more choices to satisfy customer wants and needs. Competition usually brings out the best in companies, and international competition has evoked even higher quality in company products and services.

Consumers desire a variety of product choices. Because companies have limited funds, they make trade-offs among price, quality, service, and promptness of delivery—providing customers with a limited set of purchase options. However, customers' ready access to multinational vendors, which is now being geometrically accelerated by the Internet, has motivated producers to improve quality and customer service. Vendors are constantly adopting more dynamic approaches to continuously improving products, processes, and customer service interactions.

This chapter discusses issues including quality, benchmarking, total quality management, quality costs, quality cost measurement, and the use of a balanced scorecard and a cost management system to support quality initiatives. Because quality affects costs, accountants understand the long-run trade-offs involved between higher and lower product/service quality.

Many managers have realized that current expenditures on quality improvements can be more than regained through future cost reductions and sales volume increases. These improvements will benefit the firm now and in the future; thus, their costs should not be viewed as expenses or losses but as recoverable investments with the potential for profit generation.

WHAT IS QUALITY?

To improve its product or service quality, an organization must agree on a definition of the word. Originally, after the Industrial Revolution helped manufacturers to increase output and decrease costs, quality was generally defined as conformity to designated specifications. Conformity determination was left to quality control inspectors. The late Dr. W. Edwards Deming, famous expert on quality control, defined quality as "the pride of workmanship."[1] On a less individualized basis, Philip Crosby (another noted quality expert) defines quality as "conformance to requirements."[2] This definition was adopted by the American Society for Quality Control, which defines requirements as measurable written or verbal "specifications, product descriptions, procedures, policies, job descriptions, instructions, purchase/service orders, etc."[3] Thus, a fairly inclusive definition of **quality** is the summation of all characteristics of a product or service that influence its ability to meet the stated or implied needs of the person acquiring it.

quality

Production View of Quality

The responsibility for quality is not simply a production issue; it has become a company profitability and longevity issue. All entity processes (for example, production, procurement, distribution, finance, and promotion) are involved in quality improvement efforts. Therefore, two related perspectives of quality are (1) the totality of internal processes that generate a product or service and (2) the customer satisfaction with that product or service.

What are some non-value-added activities that hinder quality?

Productivity is measured by the quantity of good output generated from a specific amount of input during a time period. Any factor that either slows down (or stops) a production process or causes unnecessary work hinders productivity. Activity analysis can be used to highlight such factors. As discussed in Chapter 5, the various repetitive actions performed in making a product or providing a service can be classified in value-added (VA) and non-value-added (NVA) categories. Value-added activities increase the worth of the product or service to the customer; non-value-added activities consume time and costs but add no value for the consumer. Minimizing or eliminating non-value-added activities increases productivity and reduces costs.

Three important NVA process activities include storing products for which there is little immediate demand, moving materials unnecessarily, and having unscheduled production interruptions. Another non-value-added activity, inspecting incoming components, is caused by potential quality problems at the supplier. To minimize or eliminate this NVA activity, some companies have contracts that require their suppliers to provide only zero-defect components. To ensure compliance with this requirement, companies often perform quality audits of their vendors.

Costs incurred to reprocess, rework, replace, and repair those items that do not conform to specifications create production redundancies that can be reduced

[1] Rafael Aguayo, *Dr. Deming* (New York: Simon & Schuster, 1990), p. xi.
[2] Philip B. Crosby, *Quality Is Free* (New York: New American Library, 1979), p. 15.
[3] American Society for Quality Control, *Finance, Accounting and Quality* (Milwaukee, WI: ASQC, 1990), p. 3.

through quality product design, use of conforming materials, and value-added production processes. These efforts will reduce the product's failure rate and breakage tendencies, and increase product longevity. Furthermore, the elimination of redundancies generated by production efforts—such as rework, waste, and scrap—will enhance production process quality.

Production technology, worker skill and training, and management programs can also help to significantly control production process quality. If impediments to good production are reduced or eliminated, increases in productivity and higher quality products can be expected. Some techniques that increase productivity and enhance quality include having suppliers preinspect materials for conformity to specifications, having employees monitor and be responsible for their work output, and fitting machinery for mistake-proof operations.

Many companies focus on a "six sigma" production view of quality, which means that a process produces no more than 3.4 defects per million "opportunities" or chances for failure or not meeting required specifications. All attempts to reduce variability and product defects reflect the implementation of **quality control (QC)**. QC places the primary responsibility for product or service quality at the source: the maker or provider. Many companies use **statistical process control (SPC)** techniques to analyze where fluctuations or variations occur in the process. SPC is based on the theory that a process has natural (common cause) variations over time and that these variations can cause "errors" resulting in defective goods or poor service. These errors are typically produced at points of uncommon (nonrandom or special cause) variations. Often these variations are eliminated after the installation of computer-integrated manufacturing systems, which have internal controls to evaluate deviations and sense production problems.

To analyze the process variations, various types of **control charts** have been developed to record the occurrence of specified measure(s) of performance at preselected points in a process. Control charts, such as the one in Exhibit 16–1, graph actual process results and indicate upper and lower control limits. For example, a process is considered to be "in" or "out of" control (i.e., stable or unstable) depending on whether the results remain within established limits and do not form telltale patterns that reflect some nonrandom or special-cause variation. In effect, SPC charts use the management by exception principle by requiring that workers respond to occurrences that are outside of some predetermined limit or that form nonrandom, telltale patterns.

quality control (QC)

statistical process control (SPC)

control chart

EXHIBIT 16–1
CONTROL CHART

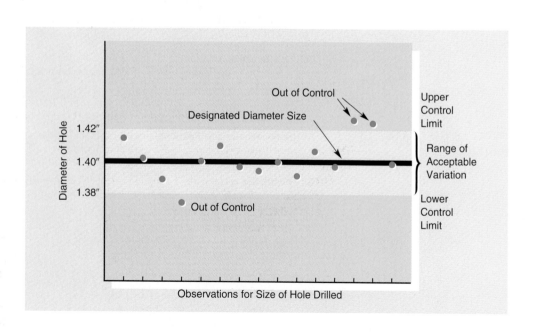

Control charts must be prepared consistently and accurately for an intelligent analysis of out-of-control conditions to be made. Although development and use of such charts is outside the scope of this text, the management accountant is directly involved in selecting appropriate performance measures and helping to interpret the charts. Often the measures selected to prepare control charts are nonfinancial, such as number of defective parts, amount of waste created, and time taken to complete a task. Selection of performance measures to investigate quality is further discussed in Chapter 19. In effect, using SPC causes a process to "talk" to workers about what is occurring in the process. If workers "listen," they can often prevent potential product defects and process malfunctions from ever occurring.

Consumer View of Quality

Every customer who acquires a product or service receives a set of characteristics encompassing a range of features, such as convenience, promptness in delivery, warranty, credit availability, and packaging. The consumer's view of quality reflects more than whether the product or service delivers what was intended, its rate of failure, or the probability of purchasing a defective unit. The customer perceives quality as the ability of a product or service to meet and satisfy all specified needs at a reasonable cost: In other words, from a customer's perspective, quality relates to both performance and value. This quality perspective arose because of increased competition, public interest in product safety, and litigation relative to products and product safety. When high-quality producers dominate a market, entering companies must understand both their own customers' quality expectations and their competitors' quality standards.

See Exhibit 16–2 for eight characteristics that would commonly be included in any customer's definition of product quality. An important difference exists between the first six and the last two characteristics: level of objectivity. Characteris-

EXHIBIT 16–2

CHARACTERISTICS OF QUALITY

A. **Performance** refers to the operating features and relative importance of multiple characteristics such as ease of use and speed. Performance at The Ritz-Carlton might include comfortable beds, fax machines, and speedy Internet connections within each room.

B. **Features** are the extras needed to customize a product. The Ritz-Carlton might include flowers and a fruit basket in a customer's room at check-in and provide guests with spacious hotel rooms and fully equipped health club facilities.

C. **Reliability** refers to the likelihood that a product/service will perform on time as expected without a glitch. Ritz-Carlton customers expect on-time room cleanups and evening turn-down service with quality chocolates on the pillows.

D. **Conformance** is the extent to which products comply with prespecified standards. Ritz-Carlton guests may expect granite countertops on vanities and bathtubs with spa jets.

E. **Durability** refers to expected product life before deterioration and the need for replacement. Ritz-Carlton guests might expect hotel rooms to be refurbished every five years or a fresh fruit basket to be placed in their room every third day of their stay.

F. **Serviceability and Responsiveness** reflect the convenience, ease, and speed with which courteous and competent service staff complete work. Ritz-Carlton customers expect prompt responses to room service and maintenance requests.

G. **Aesthetics** refers to the environmental ambiance required of the discerning customer. The Ritz-Carlton might provide designer towels in the bathrooms and robes and slippers for in-room use.

H. **Perceived Value** is a customer's opinion of the product based on perceptions formed from advertising or product/service reputation. When customers stay at The Ritz-Carlton, they may expect "royal" treatment.

Source: Adapted from David Garvin "Eight Dimensions of Product Quality," *http://www.1000ventures.com/ business_guide/crosscuttings/bizsys_customer.html* (accessed July 20, 2004); and David Garvin, "What Does 'Product Quality' Really Mean?" *Sloan Management Review* (Fall 1984), pp. 25–43.

tics A through F can be reasonably evaluated through objective methods, whereas G and H are strictly subjective. Thus, the first six are much more susceptible to control by an organization than are the other two.

Most, if not all, of the quality characteristics in Exhibit 16–2 apply equally to companies that provide services and those that make tangible products. For example, The Ritz-Carlton might consider providing in-room high-speed Internet access and luxury spas as "features." Additionally, the company might consider providing quiet rooms for guests as high "performance."

Service quality reflects the manner in which an output is delivered to a customer. Some firms use outside assessors to evaluate the level of service provided. For example, an undercover hotel "spy" could put a nonperforming light bulb in a room lamp at an exclusive hotel to determine whether housekeeping immediately detects the bulb outage. In addition to the quality characteristics listed in Exhibit 16–2, the following additional quality characteristics apply to service organizations:

- *assurance*, in that customers expect employees to be knowledgeable, courteous, and trustworthy,
- *tangibles*, in that customers expect quality physical facilities, equipment, and appearance of personnel,
- *empathy*, in that customers expect a high degree of caring and attention from employees.

grade

Not all customers can afford the same grade of product or service. **Grade** refers to one of the many quality levels that a product or service has relative to the inclusion or exclusion of characteristics to satisfy customer needs, especially price. Customers try to maximize their satisfaction within the context of their willingness

value

and ability to pay. They view a product or service as a **value** when it meets the highest number of their needs at the lowest possible total cost (which includes an item's purchase price plus its operating, maintenance, and disposal costs). Thus, although customers may have a collective vision of what constitutes "high quality," some of them may choose to accept a lower grade of product or service because it satisfies their functional needs at a lower cost. Note that "high quality" is a more encompassing concept than "high grade." Someone with 20 minutes left for lunch can find more "value" in a fast-food hamburger than a sit-down restaurant's sirloin steak.

To illustrate the difference between quality and grade, assume that Sally Smith is in the market for a new car in which to travel to and from work, run errands, and go on vacation. She has determined that reliability, gas mileage, safety, and comfort are the most important features to her. She may believe the **Mercedes-Benz** to be the highest quality of car available, but her additional needs are that the price of the car be within her price range and that repair and maintenance services be readily available and within her budget. Thus, she will search for the highest quality product that maximizes her set of quality-characteristic preferences within the grade she can afford.

Customers often make quality determinations by comparing a product or service to an ideal rather than to an actual product or service of the same type or in the same industry. For example, Jerry Dauterive frequently stays at Ritz-Carlton hotels on business trips. On a recent trip, he called a car rental agency to arrange for a car. Jerry could compare the quality of service he received from the car rental agency with the high-quality service he typically receives from The Ritz-Carlton rather than how well the current car rental company served him in comparison to the service from companies he had used in the past. Dauterive is unconcerned that car rental agency employees may not have had the same customer satisfaction training as Ritz-Carlton employees or that The Ritz-Carlton corporate culture is dedicated to high quality while the car rental agency may not have yet made such a quality commitment. When formalized, the process of comparing quality levels of one organization to another's is called competitive benchmarking.

BENCHMARKING

LO.2
WHAT IS BENCHMARKING, AND WHY DO COMPANIES ENGAGE IN IT?

benchmarking

What are the three types of benchmarking?

Benchmarking means investigating, comparing, and evaluating a company's products, processes, and/or services against either those of competitors or companies believed to be the "best in class." Such comparisons allow a company to understand another's production and performance methods so that the interested company can identify its strengths and weaknesses. See Exhibit 16–3 for some reasons for benchmarking.

Because each company has its own unique philosophy, products, and people, "copying" such elements is neither appropriate nor feasible. Therefore, a company should attempt to imitate those ideas that are readily transferable but, more importantly, to upgrade its own effectiveness and efficiency by improving on methods used by others. Codes of conduct have been established for benchmarking activities. These codes address issues such as equal exchange of information, restricted use of learned data, avoidance of antitrust issues and illegalities, and interorganizational courtesy.[4]

results benchmarking

The three types of benchmarking are results (or performance), process, and strategic. In **results benchmarking**, the end product or service is examined using a process called reverse engineering. Its focus is on product/service specifications and performance results. Results benchmarking helps companies determine which other companies are "best in class" in this category. For example, companies such as **Cyrix Corp.** and **Advanced Micro Devices Inc.** have successfully reverse-engineered **Intel Corp.** microprocessors to make less expensive Intel-compatible chips.[5] However, if benchmarking involves making an exact replica of another's product, ethical and legal considerations exist.

Although benchmarking against direct competitors is necessary, it creates the risk of becoming stagnant. To illustrate, **General Motors**, **Chrysler**, and **Ford** historically competitively benchmarked among themselves and, over time, their processes became similar. But then foreign competitors such as **Toyota** entered the U.S. market with totally different, and better, processes that required U.S. companies to change and improve their quality systems. Recently, however, Toyota faced quality problems: Rapid growth had "spread thin the company's famed Japanese quality gurus;" thus, it launched a global campaign to simplify its production systems.[6]

EXHIBIT 16–3

REASONS TO BENCHMARK

1. To increase awareness of the competition
2. To understand competitors' production and performance methods
3. To identify areas of competitors' internal strengths and weaknesses
4. To identify external and internal threats and opportunities
5. To justify a suggested plan for continuous process improvement and change
6. To create a framework for program and process assessment and evaluation
7. To establish a focus for mission, goals, and objectives
8. To establish performance improvement targets

[4] Barbara Ettorre, "Ethics, Anti-Trust and Benchmarking," *Management Review* (June 1993), p. 13.
[5] Mathew Schwartz, "Reverse Engineering," *Computerworld* (November 20, 2001), *http://www.computerworld.com/softwaretopics* (accessed August 6, 2004).
[6] Norihiko Shirouzu and Sebastian Moffett, "As Toyota Closes In on GM, It Develops a Big Three Problem," *The Wall Street Journal* (August 4, 2004), pp. A1, A2.

process benchmarking

Because of the potential for stagnation, comparisons should also be made against companies that are the best in a specific characteristic rather than just the best in a specific industry. Focusing on how best-in-class companies achieve their results is called **process benchmarking**. It is in this arena that noncompetitor benchmarking is extremely valuable. For example, many companies have benchmarked **L. L. Bean**'s world-class warehousing and distribution operations because many organizations, regardless of product type, engage in such activities. Company call centers often use the six Ritz-Carlton centers as a process benchmark; they have an average answer time speed of 20 seconds, a 92 percent customer satisfaction rate, and handle 1,500,000 calls per year.[7] After one stay at The Ritz-Carlton in San Francisco, a credit union vice president suggested that all credit unions should benchmark the personal service provided by The Ritz-Carlton.[8] The widespread applicability of process benchmarking is no better illustrated than when employees from a **General Mills** plant in California decided to go to a NASCAR track, videotape pit crews, study the tapes, and apply the principles of that process to reduce production changeover processes. Doing so enabled them to reduce changeover processes from three hours to 17 minutes![9]

Disney has long been viewed as "best-in-class" in equipment maintenance. Other organizations, regardless of the industry they are in, can use process benchmarking to compare their maintenance activities against this world-class leader.

Strategic benchmarking is also nonindustry specific and focuses on how companies compete, "seeking to identify the winning strategies that have enabled high performing companies to be successful in their marketplaces."[10] This type of benchmarking is most important at many Japanese companies because their managers focus more on long-run performance than the short-run benefits that can be gained from process and results benchmarking.

The process of implementing benchmarking is detailed in Exhibit 16–4. Some companies have more steps and others have fewer, but all have a structured approach. After the negative gap analysis is completed, everyone in the firm is expected to work toward

© JONATHAN BLAIR/CORBIS

strategic benchmarking

both closing that gap and becoming a best-in-class organization. Through benchmarking, companies are working to improve their abilities to deliver high-quality products from the perspectives of how products are made and how customers perceive those products. Integrating these two perspectives requires involvement of all organizational members in the implementation of a total quality management system.

The Ritz-Carlton benchmarks to the industry (**Four Seasons**), outside the industry (best-in-class companies for processes), and within the company (best-in-chain locations). All comparisons are made so that the company can increase both customer and employee satisfaction, improve process development of new hotel locations, and learn and share best practices internally. In addition, benchmarking is used in The Ritz-Carlton Leadership Center training program for external corporate leaders who wish to improve their own organizations.

[7] "The Ritz-Carlton," *http://www.callcenterejournal.com/Featured.lasso* (accessed August 6, 2004).
[8] Mike Miller, "Is Your CU Puttin' on the Ritz?" *Credit Union Magazine* (November 2003), p. 17.
[9] John Hackl, "New Beginnings: Change Is Here to Stay," *Quality Progress* (February 1998), p. 5.
[10] Christopher Bogan and Mike English, *Benchmarking for Best Practices: Winning through Innovative Adaptation* (New York: McGraw-Hill, 1994), p. 8.

EXHIBIT 16–4
STEPS IN BENCHMARKING

 1. Determine the specific area in which improvements are desired and/or needed.

 2. Select the characteristic that will be used to measure quality performance.

 3. Identify the best-in-class companies based on quality characteristics. Remember that these companies do not have to be industry, product, or service specific.

 4. Ask for cooperation from the best-in-class companies. This may be handled directly or through a consulting firm. Be prepared to share information and respect requests for confidentiality.

 5. Have the people who are associated with the specific area being analyzed collect the needed information.

 6. Analyze the "negative gap" between the company's product, process, or service and that of the best-in-class firm.

 7. Act on the negative gap analysis and make improvements.

 8. Do not become complacent. Strive for continuous improvement.

TOTAL QUALITY MANAGEMENT

LO.3
WHY IS TOTAL QUALITY MANAGEMENT A SIGNIFICANT MANAGEMENT PHILOSOPHY, AND WHAT CONDITIONS ARE NECESSARY TO YIELD ITS BENEFITS?

total quality management (TQM)

Total quality management (TQM) is a "management approach of an organization, centered on quality, based on the participation of all its members and aiming at long-term success through customer satisfaction, and benefits to all members of the organization and to society."[11] Thus, TQM has four important tenets:

1. To dictate continuous improvement for an internal managerial system of planning, controlling, and decision making for continuous improvement.
2. To require participation by everyone in the organization.
3. To focus on improving goods and services from the customer's point of view.
4. To value long-term partnerships with suppliers.

The Quality System

The total quality movement requires the implementation of a system to provide information about process quality so managers can plan, control, evaluate performance, and make decisions for continuous improvement. Consideration of quality has not historically been part of the planning process. More often, it involved an after-the-fact measurement of errors because a certain level of defects was tolerated as part of the "natural" business process. Action was not triggered until a predetermined error threshold was exceeded.

In contrast, a total quality system should be designed to promote a reorientation of thinking from an emphasis on inspection to an emphasis on prevention, continuous improvement, and building quality into every process and product. This reorientation should indicate any existing quality problems so that managers can

[11] ISO 8402, *Total Quality Management* (Geneva: ISO, 1994), definition 3.7.

set goals and identify methods for quality improvements. The system should also be capable (possibly through the use of statistical methods) of measuring quality and providing feedback on quality improvements. Last, the system should encourage teamwork in the quality improvement process. In other words, the system should move an organization away from product inspection (finding and correcting problems at the end of the process) to proactive quality assurance (building quality into the process so that problems do not occur).

Employee Involvement

TQM recognizes that all organizational levels share the responsibility for product/service quality. Interactions among employee levels are changing the way managers do their jobs. Upper-level management must be involved in the quality process, develop an atmosphere that is conducive to quality improvements, set an example of commitment to TQM, provide constructive feedback about opportunities for improvement, and provide positive feedback when improvements are made. Workers should be viewed as part of the process of success, not the creators of problems. Encouraging employee suggestions and training workers to handle multiple job functions help improve efficiency and quality. At The Ritz-Carlton, for example, 2 of the 20 basics principles are that "all employees have the right to be involved in the planning of the work that affects them" and "when a guest has a problem or needs something special [an employee] should break away from [his/her] regular duties, address and resolve the issue."[12] To make certain that employees can succeed in their empowerment, any "employee can spend up to $2,000 to immediately correct a problem or handle a complaint" and 250 to 310 hours of training are provided to first-year managers and employees to ensure that they have the skills, knowledge, and standards needed to succeed.[13]

Product/Service Improvement

Total quality management focuses attention on the relationship between the internal production/service process and the external customer. This approach has designated consumer expectations as the ultimate arbiter of satisfaction. Therefore, TQM requires that companies first know who their customers are.

In analyzing their customers, companies must recognize that they may need to stop serving some groups of customers based on the results of cost-benefit analyses. Some customers simply cost more than they add in revenues and/or other benefits. Each revenue dollar does not contribute equally to organizational profitability because the cost to serve different customers can be unequal. The concept that shedding one or more sets of customers would be good for business is difficult to believe at first, but most organizations have some clients who drain, rather than improve, those organizations' ability to provide quality products and service. Managers should be attuned to customers that are not cost-beneficial and send them elsewhere. By doing this, the company can focus its attention on its worthy customers and make itself attractive to new, worthwhile customers.

After identifying its value-adding customers, a company must then understand what those customers want. The primary characteristics currently desired by customers appear to be quality, value, and good service. "Good" service is an intangible; it means different things to different people. But most customers would agree

[12] The Ritz-Carlton, "Gold Standards: 20 Basics" *http://www.ritzcarlton.com/corporate/about_us/gold_standards.asp* (accessed August 5, 2004).

[13] "Malcolm Baldrige National Quality Award 1999 Award Recipient, Service Category: The Ritz-Carlton Hotel Company, L.L.C.," *http://www.nist.gov/public_affairs/bald99/ritz.htm* (accessed August 4, 2004).

that it reflects the interaction between themselves and organizational employees. Frequently, only service quality separates one product from its competition.

The need for information is essential to organizations embracing TQM because poor service can be disastrous. Data indicate that most businesses lose 50 percent of their customers every five years; 68 percent of customers leave because of an employee's "attitude of indifference" versus only 14 percent because of product or service dissatisfaction.[14]

Instituting customer service programs is often useful; for example, The Ritz-Carlton has installed its CLASS database to record information on its returning customers. The system, which holds approximately 1 million files, records recency/frequency of use (by hotel and in total); lifetime purchases; customer likes/dislikes; personal and family interests; preferred credit cards; and any previous difficulties encountered by a customer at a hotel. This RFM (which stands for recency, frequency, and monetary value) database is one common way to sort customers and is often used to decide whether a customer relationship merits additional investment. However, customer service programs should not be "taken to the extreme." Some customers, such as those who demand exorbitant service but are not willing to pay the related price, are not cost beneficial.

Long-Term Supplier Relationships

Adopting a TQM philosophy encourages companies to review their entire supply chain and establish long-term relationships with preferred suppliers. TQM philosophy sees suppliers as a distinct part of a company's ability to satisfy customers—or create extreme dissatisfaction. Consider, for example, the problems faced by **Ford Motor Company** in 2000 when its tire supplier, **Bridgestone/Firestone North America**, recalled 6.5 million potentially defective tires, most of them on Ford Explorers.[15] In total, quality problems cost Ford more than $1 billion in profits for 2000.[16] Additional problems occurred when, in early 2004, Bridgestone/Firestone North America had to recall and replace tires used on about 80,000 Ford Excursion SUVs; the tires were linked to accidents that had caused five deaths.[17]

Given the substantial amount of outsourcing that is now being used, companies need to be certain that they are "linking up" with suppliers that will enhance product quality and customer satisfaction. Many of these relationships will result in single sourcing or certification of suppliers. The Ritz-Carlton uses a semiannual survey of its purchasing personnel to rate company suppliers on factors such as on-time delivery and service, and its suppliers' products on factors such as fitness for use and freedom from defects. Suppliers that rate 80 percent or better on the survey can be certified as "Key Suppliers" for The Ritz-Carlton. Additionally, while suppliers can indirectly enhance customer satisfaction, The Ritz-Carlton is always looking for more direct ways to accommodate customers. Thus, in 2002, the company launched a marketing agreement with **Mercedes-Benz USA** so that selected locations could offer guests the use of a new Mercedes vehicle during their stays. The two companies see this agreement as "a perfect fit

---

[14] "An Executive View of CRM," *http://www.asd.net/library/ba_executiveView.pdf* (accessed August 6, 2004); Larry Galler, "Customer Defections—68 Percent Attitude Problems," *nwitimes.com* (February 2, 2003); *http://www.thetimesonline.com/articles/2003/02/02* (accessed August 6, 2004).

[15] James Healey and Chris Woodyard, "Tire Concerns Go Back 1 1/2 Years Before Recall," *USA Today* (September 11, 2000), p. 1B.

[16] Gregory White and Karen Lundegaard, "Ford Admits Last Year's Quality Snafus Took Big Toll—Over $1 Billion in Profit," *The Wall Street Journal* (January 12, 2001), p. A3.

[17] Danny Hakim, "Another Recall Involving Ford, Firestone Tires and S.U.V.'s," *The New York Times* (February 27, 2004); *www.nytimes.com*.

because both companies' customers share the same high expectation of service and quality."[18]

THE BALDRIGE AWARD

The embodiment of TQM in the United States is the Malcolm Baldrige National Quality Award, which focuses attention on management systems, processes, consumer satisfaction, and business results as the tools required to achieve product and service excellence. There are five categories of entrants: manufacturing, service, small business, education, and health care organizations. To win the award, applicants like The Ritz-Carlton must show excellence in seven categories:

1. *Leadership* requires that the organization's senior managers value, clearly communicate, and inspire customer-focused directions to empowered employees in achieving quality goals ethically, given adequate systems and knowledge resources. The ethics would be documented in the organization's corporate governance.

2. *Strategic planning* requires that the organization develop strategic objectives and plans that are constantly monitored for progress toward achievement.

3. *Customer and market focus* require that the organization set requirements, expectations, and preferences for its customers and markets. This focus includes building customer relationships, establishing key factors that lead to customer acquisition, satisfaction, and loyalty, and developing business expansion.

4. *Measurement, analysis, and knowledge management* requires that the organization select, collect, analyze, manage, and continuously improve its information system and intellectual capital.

5. *Human resource focus* requires the organization empower its employees and utilize their full potential in developing and implementing organizational goals and objectives. This focus requires a work environment that promotes high morale among employees who seek personal and organizational performance excellence as one.

6. *Process management* requires organizations examine the key components of their product/service and business processes developed to satisfy customers and create organizational values that support these processes.

7. *Business results* require organizations improve their key business areas including customer satisfaction, product/service performance, human resource results, financial and marketplace performance, operations performance, corporate governance, and social responsibility. Moreover, organizations should benchmark and compare their performance relative to that of competitors.

Exhibit 16–5 illustrates the relationships among the Baldrige criteria performance categories. To achieve at least 70 percent of the points allocated within a category, the National Institute of Standards and Technology (which manages the Baldrige Award) must determine that the organization is effective and systematic in deploying and achieving the multiple requirements within each category and is innovative in continuously seeking improvement.

Corporate America has accepted the Baldrige award because it represents excellence. Products and services of companies winning the award are regarded as some of the best in the world. Such recognition invigorates workers, pleases all stakeholders, and has caused the entire national economy to be strengthened by the enhanced awareness of and attention to quality and its benefits. Winning companies are asked to provide information about their performance excellence strategies so

---

[18] The Ritz-Carlton, "The Key to Luxury—Mercedes and The Ritz-Carlton Sign Three-Year Marketing Agreement," Press Release; *http://www.ritzcarlton.com/corporate/press_room/releases/mercedes.html* (accessed August 5, 2004).

EXHIBIT 16–5

2004 BALDRIGE AWARD CRITERIA

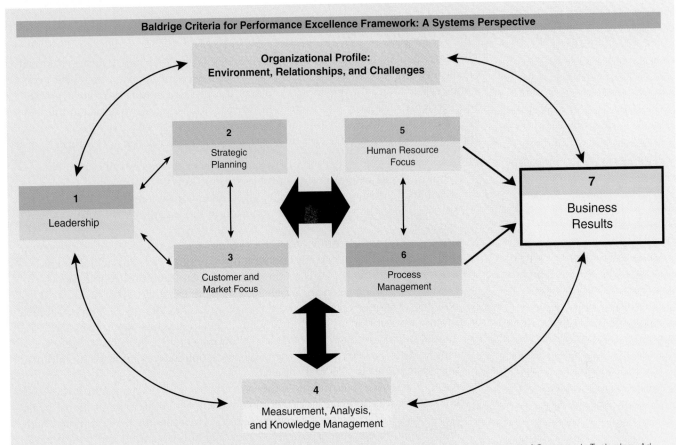

Baldrige Criteria for Performance Excellence Framework: A Systems Perspective

Organizational Profile:
Environment, Relationships, and Challenges

2 Strategic Planning

5 Human Resource Focus

1 Leadership

3 Customer and Market Focus

6 Process Management

7 Business Results

4 Measurement, Analysis, and Knowledge Management

Source: Baldrige National Quality Program, National Institute of Standards and Technology, and United States Department of Commerce's Technology Administration, *2004 Criteria for Performance Excellence* (Gaithersburg, MD: 2004) p. 5.

that other organizations can benchmark to those strategies and adapt them to suit their own needs.

Japan's equivalent of the Baldrige Award is the Deming Prize, named for the late Dr. W. Edwards Deming. Globally, the quality movement has progressed to the point that certain quality standards have been set, although these are not at the level of either the Baldrige Award or the Deming Prize. Some international standards are discussed in the Appendix to this chapter.

BENEFITS OF TQM

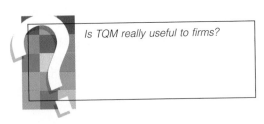

Is TQM really useful to firms?

Some critics of TQM have called it nothing more than a management fad that does not work when practical attempts are made to implement its concepts. A rebuttal to such criticisms is that it is "poor management, not poor ideas, [that] may be responsible for the inconsistency of TQM or other managerial interventions."[19] However, most companies using TQM have cited many positive outcomes and benefits, such as those included in Exhibit 16–6.

Putting TQM into practice in an organization can be very costly given the length of time needed to introduce and permeate the philosophy and concepts through-

[19] David Lemak, Neal Mero, and Richard Reed, "When Quality Works: A Premature Post-Mortem on TQM," *Journal of Business and Management* (Fall 2002), pp. 391ff.

EXHIBIT 16–6
BENEFITS OF TQM

Internal

- Improved response time to change
- Increased ability to compete profitably in the marketplace
- Decreased cost through reduction/elimination of non-value-added activities and waste
- Increased profitability through reduced costs
- Improved products, services, and customer relations
- Increased employee morale, motivation, and retention
- Improved internal communications and organizational focus
- Enhanced employee decision-making abilities and teamwork
- Increased innovation and acceptance of new ideas
- Reduced number of errors
- Increased benchmarks for evaluating employee performance

External

- Increased customer trust and loyalty
- Enhanced customer satisfaction
- Improved response time to customer requests
- Decreased prices resulting from reduced internal costs

out the company. Evidence indicates, however, that firms' operating performances during the process of implementing TQM are comparable to those of other companies. A 2001 study of quality award-winning firms found that, on average, it takes about five years for a company to implement TQM and another five years before its benefits are fully realized. The Baldrige experienced a 20 percent increase in average stock prices compared to a 25 percent decrease in stock price for the benchmarked firms (Exhibit 16–7). This means that stock price increases can be traced back to the operating performance of the TQM firms during five years after the initial implementation of TQM. The study was able to trace these stock price changes to such operating performance measures as operating income, sales, total assets, number of employees, return on sales, and return on assets.[20] All of these operating performance measures were higher for the Baldrige winners during the five years after receiving the Baldrige award than those of the control sample firms.

TYPES OF QUALITY COSTS

LO.4
WHAT TYPES OF QUALITY COSTS EXIST, AND HOW ARE THOSE COSTS RELATED?

prevention cost

appraisal cost

failure cost
internal failure cost
external failure cost

Instituting total quality management in an organization causes a different focus on costs and their incurrence. A company can increase its product and service quality by investing in **prevention costs**, which preclude product defects that result from dysfunctional processing. Amounts spent on improved production equipment, training, and engineering and product modeling are considered prevention costs. Complementary to prevention costs are **appraisal costs**, which represent costs incurred for monitoring and compensating for mistakes not eliminated through prevention activities.   Both of these types of costs will cause a reduction in internal and external **failure costs**. **Internal failure costs** are expenditures, such as scrap or rework, incurred on defective units before being shipped to the customer. **External failure costs** are expenditures for items such as warranty work, customer

[20] Kevin B. Hendricks and Vinod R. Singhal, "Don't Count TQM Out," *Quality Progress* (April 1999), pp 35–42.

EXHIBIT 16–7

STOCK PERFORMANCE OF
MALCOLM BALDRIGE
FIRMS

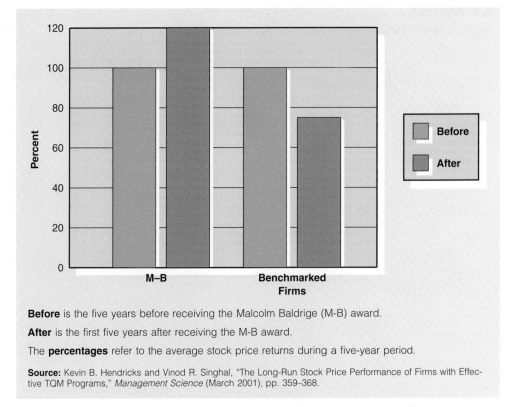

Before is the five years before receiving the Malcolm Baldrige (M-B) award.

After is the first five years after receiving the M-B award.

The **percentages** refer to the average stock price returns during a five-year period.

Source: Kevin B. Hendricks and Vinod R. Singhal, "The Long-Run Stock Price Performance of Firms with Effective TQM Programs," *Management Science* (March 2001), pp. 359–368.

complaints, litigation, and defective product recalls incurred after a faulty unit of product has been shipped to the customer.

The results of TQM indicate that increasing the amounts spent on prevention should decrease the amounts spent on or incurred for appraisal and failure costs—resulting in an overall decline in costs. Also, eliminating non-value-added activities and installing technologically advanced equipment should increase productivity and quality. Lower costs mean that the company can contain (or reduce) selling prices; customers, pleased with the higher quality at the same (or lower) price, perceive they have received value and will buy more. These factors create higher company profits that can be reinvested in research and development or customer satisfaction activities to generate new high-quality products or services. The profits also can be used to train workers to provide even higher quality products and services than are currently available. This cycle of benefit will continue in a company that is profitable and secure in its market share—two primary goals of any organization.

Thus, because the TQM philosophy indicates that total costs will decline rather than increase as an organization makes quality improvements, it appears that the *lack* of high quality rather than the *pursuit* of high quality is expensive. Understanding the types and causes of quality costs can help managers prioritize improvement projects and provide feedback that supports and justifies improvement efforts.

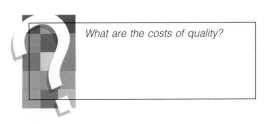

What are the costs of quality?

Total quality costs can also be classified into two rather than four categories: (1) cost of quality compliance or assurance and (2) cost of noncompliance or quality failure. The cost of compliance equals the sum of prevention and appraisal costs. Compliance cost expenditures are incurred to reduce or eliminate the present and future costs of failure; thus, they are proactive on management's part. Furthermore, effective investments in prevention costs can even minimize the costs of appraisal. The cost of noncompliance results from production imperfections and is equal to internal and external failure costs. See Exhibit 16–8 for specific examples of each type of quality cost.

Inspection reports, SPC control charts, and customer returns or complaints contain information about production quality or lack thereof. Information about quality costs, on the other hand, is only partially contained in the accounting records and supporting documentation. Historically, quality costs have not been given separate recognition in the accounting system. For example, the effects and costs of customer complaints that are overheard by potential customers are unknown.

In most instances, the cost of quality is "buried" in a variety of general ledger accounts. For instance, the amounts included in Work in Process Inventory and Finished Goods Inventory contain costs for rework, scrap, preventive maintenance, and other overhead items; marketing and advertising expenses contain costs for product recalls, image improvements after poor products were sold, and surveys to obtain customer information; personnel costs include training dollars; and engineering department costs include funds spent for engineering design change orders

EXHIBIT 16–8
TYPES OF QUALITY COSTS

COSTS OF COMPLIANCE		COSTS OF NONCOMPLIANCE	
Prevention Costs	**Appraisal Costs**	**Internal Failure Costs**	**External Failure Costs**
Employees:	*Before Production:*	*Product:*	*Organization:*
■ Hiring for quality	■ Receiving inspection	■ Reworking	■ Staffing complaint
■ Providing training and		■ Creating waste	departments
awareness	*Production Process:*	■ Storing and disposing of	■ Staffing warranty claims
■ Establishing participation	■ Monitoring and inspecting	waste	departments
programs	■ Keeping the process	■ Reinspecting rework	
	consistent, stable, and		*Customer:*
Customers:	reliable	*Production Process:*	■ Losing future sales
■ Surveying needs	■ Using procedure verification	■ Reprocessing	■ Losing reputation
■ Researching needs	■ Automating	■ Creating unscheduled	■ Losing goodwill
■ Conducting field trials		interruptions	
	During and After Production:	■ Experiencing unplanned	*Product:*
Machinery:	■ Conducting quality audits	downtime	■ Repairing
■ Designing to detect defects			■ Replacing
■ Arranging for efficient flow	*Information Process:*		■ Reimbursing
■ Arranging for monitoring	■ Recording and reporting		■ Recalling
■ Incurring preventive	defects		■ Litigating
maintenance	■ Measuring performance		
■ Testing and adjusting			*Service:*
equipment	*Organization:*		■ Providing unplanned
■ Fitting machinery for	■ Administering quality control		service
mistake-proof operations	department		■ Expediting
			■ Serving after purchase
Suppliers:			
■ Arranging for quality			
■ Educating suppliers			
■ Involving suppliers			
Product Design:			
■ Developing specifications			
■ Engineering and modeling			
■ Testing and adjusting for			
conformity, effective and			
efficient performance,			
durability, ease of use,			
safety, comfort, appeal, and			
cost			

and redesign. When quality costs are buried, managers have no idea how large or pervasive these costs are and, therefore, have little incentive to reduce them.

Because accounting records are commonly kept primarily to serve the requirements of financial accounting, the behavior of quality costs relative to changes in activity as well as the appropriate drivers for these costs must be separately developed or estimated for quality management purposes. The need to estimate quality costs makes it essential for the management accountant to be involved in all activities from system design to accumulation of quality costs. A system in which quality costs are readily available or easily determined provides useful information to managers trying to make spending decisions by pinpointing areas having the highest cost-benefit relationships. Additionally, quality cost information will indicate how a shift in one or more curves will affect the others.

Refer to Exhibit 16–9 for points in the production–sales cycle that quality costs are usually incurred. An information feedback loop should be in effect to link the types and causes of failure costs to future prevention costs. Alert managers and employees continuously monitor failures to discover their causes and adjust prevention activities to close the gaps that allowed the failures to occur. These continuous rounds of action, reaction, and action are essential to continuous improvement initiatives.

EXHIBIT 16–9

TIME-PHASED MODEL FOR QUALITY COSTS

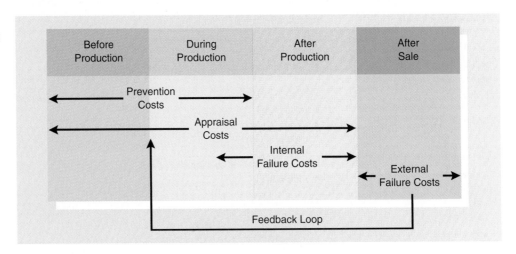

MEASURING THE COST OF QUALITY

LO.5

HOW IS COST OF QUALITY MEASURED?

Theoretically, if prevention and appraisal costs were prudently incurred, failure costs would become zero. However, because prevention and appraisal costs are still incurred to achieve zero failure costs, total quality costs can never actually be zero. If, however, the benefits of increased sales and greater efficiency in an organization exceed all remaining compliance quality costs, the cost of quality is free. Management should analyze the quality cost relationships and spend money for quality in ways that will provide the greatest benefit. Such an analysis requires measuring the cost of quality to the extent possible and practical and estimating the benefits of quality costs.

As discussed in Chapter 5, Pareto analysis is used to separate the "vital few" from the "trivial many." This technique has repeatedly shown that approximately 20 to 30 percent of the items in a set of items (such as inventory, donors to charity, or sources of defects) accounts for 70 to 80 percent of the cost or values. It is also one technique management can use to decide where to concentrate its quality prevention cost dollars. This technique classifies the causes of process problems according to impact on an objective. For example, a company that makes computers might subclassify its warranty claim costs for the past year according to the type of product failure as follows:

Cost by Type of Failure

Model	Monitor	CPU	Printer	Keyboard	Total Dollars
PCs	$15,000	$16,000	$12,000	$ 3,000	$ 46,000
Notebooks	10,000	15,000	7,000	3,000	35,000
All others	6,000	9,000	3,000	5,000	23,000
Total	$31,000	$40,000	$22,000	$11,000	$104,000

Model	Dollars	Percent of Total	Cumulative Percent of Total
PCs	$ 46,000	44%	44%
Notebooks	35,000	34	78
All others	23,000	22	100
Total	$104,000	100%	

Listing the total failure costs of all models in descending order of magnitude indicates that PCs and Notebooks account for 78 percent of total warranty cost claims. Also, the largest single source of warranty claims cost is caused by problems with CPUs. Therefore, management should focus efforts on determining what causes the CPUs on all models to generate the largest warranty claims costs. This information allows management to devote the appropriate portion of its prevention efforts to minimizing or eliminating these specific problems. This analysis should be conducted sufficiently often to detect trends quickly and make adjustments rapidly. For example, The Ritz-Carlton could use Pareto analysis to prioritize service problems and, thus, focus on where to devote the majority of its problem-solving efforts.

A company desiring to engage in TQM and continuous improvement should record and report its quality costs separately so that managers can plan, control, evaluate, and make decisions about the activities that cause those costs. However, just having quality cost information available does not enhance quality. Managers and workers must consistently and aggressively use the information as a basis for creatively and intelligently advancing quality.

A firm's chart of accounts can be expanded to accommodate either separately tracing or allocating quality costs to new accounts. See Exhibit 16–10 for some suggested accounts that will help management focus on quality costs. Opportunity costs, including lost future sales and a measure of the firm's loss of reputation, are also associated with poor quality. Although opportunity costs are real and may be

EXHIBIT 16–10
NEW QUALITY ACCOUNTS

Prevention Costs	Appraisal Costs
Quality Training	Quality Inspections
Quality Participation	Procedure Verifications
Quality Market Research	Measurement Equipment
Quality Technology	Test Equipment
Quality Product Design	

Internal Failure Costs	External Failure Costs
Reworking Products	Complaint Handling
Scrap and Waste	Warranty Handling
Storing and Disposing of Waste	Repairing or Replacing Returns
Reprocessing	Customer Reimbursements
Rescheduling and Setup	Expediting

estimated, they are not recorded in the accounting system because they do not result from specific transactions.

If a firm has a database management system, transactions can be coded so that reports can be generated without expanding the chart of accounts. Coding permits quality transaction types and amounts to be accessible and the generation of a cost of quality report such as the one shown in Exhibit 16–11 (which uses assumed numbers). Two important assumptions underlie this report: stable production and a monthly reporting system. If wide fluctuations in production or service levels occur, period-to-period comparisons of absolute amounts may not be appropriate. Amounts might need to be converted to percentages to have valid meaning. Additionally, in some settings (such as a just-in-time environment), a weekly reporting system is more appropriate because of the need for continuous monitoring.

See Exhibit 16–12 for formulas for calculating an organization's total quality cost, using the prevention, appraisal, and failure categories. Some amounts used in these computations are by necessity estimates. It is better for businesses to use reasonable estimates than to ignore the costs because of a lack of verifiable or precise amounts. Consider the following April 2006 operating information for Southbeach Company:

EXHIBIT 16–11
COST OF QUALITY REPORT

	Cost of Current Period	Cost of Prior Period	Percent Change from Prior Period	Current Period Budget	Percent Change from Budget
Prevention Costs					
Quality training	$ 5,800	$ 5,600	+4	$ 6,000	−3
Quality participation	8,200	8,400	−2	8,000	+3
Quality market research	9,900	7,700	+29	11,000	−10
Quality technology	9,600	10,800	−11	15,000	−36
Quality product design	16,600	12,200	+36	16,500	+1
Total	$ 50,100	$ 44,700	+12	$56,500	−11
Appraisal Costs					
Quality inspections	$ 3,300	$ 3,500	−6	$ 3,000	+10
Procedure verifications	1,200	1,400	−14	1,500	−20
Measurement equipment	2,700	3,000	−10	3,200	−16
Test equipment	1,500	1,200	+25	1,500	0
Total	$ 8,700	$ 9,100	−4	$ 9,200	−5
Internal Failure Costs					
Reworking products	$ 8,500	$ 8,300	+2	N/A*	
Scrap and waste	2,200	2,400	−8	N/A	
Storing and disposing of waste	4,400	5,700	−23	N/A	
Reprocessing	1,800	1,600	+13	N/A	
Rescheduling and setup	900	1,200	−25	N/A	
Total	$ 17,800	$ 19,200	−7		
External Failure Costs					
Complaint handling	$ 5,800	$ 6,200	−6	N/A	
Warranty handling	10,700	9,300	+15	N/A	
Repairing or replacing returns	27,000	29,200	−8	N/A	
Customer reimbursements	12,000	10,700	+12	N/A	
Expediting	1,100	1,300	−15		
Total	$ 56,600	$ 56,700	+0		
Total quality costs	$133,200	$129,700	+3	$65,700	+103

*TQM advocates planning for zero defects; therefore, zero failure costs would be included in the budget.

EXHIBIT 16–12

FORMULAS FOR CALCULATING TOTAL QUALITY COST

Calculating Lost Profits

Profit Lost by Selling Units as Defects = (Total Defective Units − Number of Units Reworked) × (Profit for Good Unit − Profit for Defective Unit)

$$Z = (D − Y)(P_1 − P_2)$$

Calculating Total Internal Costs of Failure

Rework Cost = Number of Units Reworked × Cost to Rework Defective Unit

$$R = (Y)(r)$$

Calculating Total External Costs of Failure

Cost of Processing Customer Returns = Number of Units Returned × Cost of a Return

$$W = (D_r)(w)$$

Total Failure Cost = Profit Lost by Selling Units as Defects + Rework Cost + Cost of Processing Customer Returns + Cost of Warranty Work + Cost of Product Recalls + Cost of Litigation Related to Products + Opportunity Cost of Lost Customers

$$F = Z + R + W + PR + L + O$$

Calculating the Total Quality Cost

Total Quality Cost = Total Compliance Cost + Total Failure Cost

$$T = (\text{Prevention Cost} + \text{Appraisal Cost}) + \text{Total Failure Cost}$$

$$T = K + A + F$$

Prevention and appraisal costs are total estimated amounts; no formulas are appropriate. As the cost of prevention rises, the number of defective units should decline. Additionally, as the cost of prevention rises, the cost of appraisal should decline; however, appraisal cost should never become zero.

Source: Adapted from James T. Godfrey and William R. Pasewark, "Controlling Quality Costs," *Management Accounting* (March 1988), p. 50. Reprinted from *Management Accounting.* Copyright by Institute of Management Accountants, Montvale, N.J.

Defective units (D)	2,500	Units reworked (Y)	1,200
Profit for good unit (P_1)	$25	Profit for defective unit (P_2)	$15
Cost to rework defective unit (r)	$5	Units returned (Dr)	400
Cost of return (w)	$8	Prevention cost (K)	$40,000
Appraisal cost (A)	$7,200		

Substituting these values into the formulas in Exhibit 16–12 provides the following results:

$$Z = (D − Y)(P_1 − P_2) = (2,500 − 1,200)(\$25 − \$15) = \$13,000$$
$$R = (Y)(r) = (1,200)(\$5) = \$6,000$$
$$W = (D_r)(w) = (400)(\$8) = \$3,200$$
$$F = Z + R + W = \$13,000 + \$6,000 + \$3,200 = \$22,200 \text{ total failure cost}$$
$$T = K + A + F = \$40,000 + \$7,200 + \$22,200 = \$69,400 \text{ total quality cost}$$

Of the total quality cost of $69,400, Southbeach Company managers will seek to identify the causes of the $22,200 failure costs and work to eliminate them. The results can also affect the planned amounts of prevention and appraisal costs for future periods.

High quality allows a company to improve current profits, either through lower costs or, if the market will bear, higher prices. Management is often more interested, however, in business objectives other than short-run profits. An example of an alternative, competing objective is that of increasing the company's market share.

Indeed, if increasing market share were an objective, management could combine the strategies of increasing quality and lowering prices to obtain a larger market share. Giving more attention to prevention and appraisal activities increases quality, resulting in declining overall costs and increased productivity. Lower costs and higher productivity support lower prices that, in turn, often stimulate demand. Increased market share, higher long-run profits, and, perhaps, even greater immediate profits result.

OBTAINING INFORMATION ON QUALITY FROM THE BALANCED SCORECARD AND CMS

LO.6

HOW CAN THE BALANCED SCORECARD AND COST MANAGEMENT SYSTEM BE USED TO PROVIDE INFORMATION ON QUALITY IN AN ORGANIZATION?

Where can information on quality be found?

Today's business strategy of focusing on customers and quality requires a firm to manage organizational costs so that a reasonable value-to-price relationship can be achieved. Although prices are commonly set in reference to the competitive market rather than to costs, companies lacking appropriate cost management skills cannot expect to succeed in the long run. Thus, organizations need to engage in cost management.

As discussed in Chapter 12, cost management can be viewed as the use of management accounting information for the purpose(s) of setting and communicating organizational strategies; establishing, implementing, and monitoring the success of methods to accomplish the strategies; and assessing the level of success in meeting the promulgated strategies.[21] An organization's management accounting system should accumulate and report information related to organizational success in meeting or exceeding customer needs and expectations as well as quality-related goals and objectives. Managers can analyze and interpret such information to plan and control current activities and to make decisions about current and future courses of action.

One management accounting tool that is useful in implementing strategy is a balanced scorecard (BSC), which can be used to view the total quality management strategy from four perspectives: learning and growth, internal business, customers, and finance. These perspectives can be integrated with the seven categories of the Malcolm Baldrige National Quality Award (MBNQA). For example, the learning and growth perspective of the BSC is compatible with and reflective of information shown in the MBNQA human resource focus category. The internal business perspective is compatible with the process management category. The customer perspective reflects the award's customer and market focus category. The financial perspective can be seen in the financial and market results category. Also, the BSC and the MBNQA criteria both emphasize the use of nonfinancial performance measurements as indicators of progress toward organizational goals.

To illustrate the potential use of the balanced scorecard in providing information on quality, the Telecommunications Products Division (TPD) of DalTEX, an illustrative company, is used. Assume that TPD wants to fully automate its fiber-optic production line by year-end to reduce the number of product defects. The learning and growth perspective of the BSC focuses on using the organization's intellectual capital to adapt to changing customer needs through automated production. Employees would have to be trained to use new technologies and then evaluated on their abilities while managers focus on employee satisfaction, retention, and productivity. The BSC's internal business perspective addresses empow-

---

[21] The term *strategic cost management* was coined by Professors John K. Shank and Vijay Govindarajan of Dartmouth College. A full discussion of the concept is provided in their book, *Strategic Cost Management* (New York: The Free Press, 1993).

ering employees so that they learn how to troubleshoot production problems before they result in numerous defective units. For example, TPD might allow production line employees to stop the assembly line to correct a newly evolving production process problem. This empowerment reduces wait time because employees do not have to wait while production problems continue to seek supervisor approval before taking action to remedy a problem. The BSC's customer value perspective addresses how well the organization is doing relative to important customer criteria such as speed (lead time), quality, service, and price (both before and after purchase). TPD may allow its sales staff to satisfy customers by offering discounts and allowances when production time is longer than expected or by servicing a product one day after the end of the warranty period. This sales-staff-employee empowerment allows for some delays in lead time and some product defects without resulting in customer complaints. Finally, the BSC's financial perspective addresses the perceptions held by stockholders and other stakeholders as to issues of profitability and organizational growth. TPD seeks to increase customer loyalty through quality production. If customers are more satisfied with TPD's products after the automation change is made, those customers are more likely to be retained and, thus, increase divisional and corporate revenues and market share. Goals and measurements for the BSC perspectives are shown in Exhibit 16–13; Chapter 19 provides more discussion of the balanced scorecard.

In designing a management accounting system, consideration must be given to cost accumulation and process measurement activities. Costs that are accumulated

EXHIBIT 16–13
QUALITY MEASURES OF A BALANCED SCORECARD

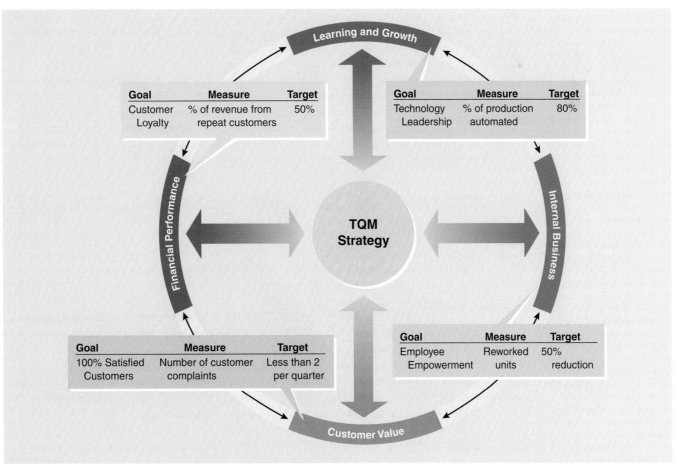

for financial accounting purposes can be inadequate for strategy-based decisions. For example, financial accounting requires that research and development costs be expensed as incurred, but a product's cost is largely determined during the design stage. Design has implications for perceived product value, necessary production technology, ease of product manufacturability, product durability, and likelihood of product failure. Consequently, a strategic cost management system would accumulate design costs as part of product cost. This cost need not appear on the financial accounting statements, but it must exist for decision-making purposes in the management accounting system.

In contrast to its treatment of R&D costs, financial accounting requires all production costs to be inventoried and does not distinguish whether they add customer value or not. A strategic CMS differentiates between costs that add value and those that do not so that managers and employees can work to reduce the non-value-added costs and enhance continuous improvement.

Another example of the functions of a strategic CMS is in the area of process. Financial accounting is monetarily based and, therefore, does not directly measure nonfinancial organizational activities. For example, the percent of automated production, percent of reworked units, number of customer complaints, and percent of repeat customers are not recorded in financial accounting. Additionally, many activities critical to success in a quality-oriented, global marketplace are related to time—a nonmonetary characteristic. A useful cost management accounting system ensures availability of information related to nonmonetary occurrences (such as late deliveries or defect rates) and incorporates that information into a balanced scorecard so that management can achieve total quality management and profitability goals.

Finally, financial accounting reflects a short-term perspective of operating activity. Continuous improvement is a long-term organizational goal, not a short-term one. Gathering monetary information and forcing it into a particular annual period of time does not necessarily clearly indicate to managers how today's decisions will affect the organization's long-run financial success. For example, not investing in research and development would cause a company's short-run profitability to improve but could be disastrous in the long run.

Thus, a strategic cost management accounting system reports more of the costs and benefits of organizational activities than do financial accounting reports. Having strategy-based information included in a balanced scorecard allows managers to make informed assessments of the company's performance in the value chain, its position of competitive advantage (or disadvantage), and its progress toward achieving the organization's mission.

QUALITY AS AN ORGANIZATIONAL CULTURE

**LO.7
HOW CAN QUALITY BE
INSTILLED AS PART OF AN
ORGANIZATION'S CULTURE?**

Quality, propelled by changing customer needs and better competition, must be viewed as a moving target; therefore, TQM is inseparable from the concept of continuous improvement. Continually higher performance standards must be set for everyone in the organization (not just people in the production area) to provide the sense of working toward a common goal. This philosophy provides a new focus: In the future, it will not be the company with the "best" products or the "lowest" costs that will be successful; it will be the company that is the best at learning to do things better.[22]

The behavior of managers and employees composes the basis for TQM. Consistent and committed top management leadership is the catalyst for moving the company culture toward an *esprit de corps* in which all individuals, regardless of rank or position, are obsessed with exceeding customer expectations. Such an attitude should also permeate everything a company does, including customer relations, marketing, research and development, product design, production, distribution,

---

[22] Tom Richman, "What Does Business Really Want from Government?" *The State of Small Business* (1995), p. 96.

and information processing. Management can effectively induce change in its organizational culture by providing an environment in which employees know that the company cares about them, is responsive to their needs, and will appreciate and reward excellent results. This knowledge goes a long way in motivating em-

Team relationships and working together to solve problems is part of the new corporate culture.

ployees to increase cooperation and make them feel trusted, respected, and comfortable. Such employees are more likely to treat customers in a similar manner.

The firm must empower employees to participate fully in the quest for excellence by providing the means by which employees gain pride, satisfaction, and substantive involvement. Managers must provide encouragement, training, job enhancement, and the proper working environment and tools. The new corporate culture work environment involves the effective and appropriate use of teams. Employees should be recognized with praise and rewarded for being involved in team problem solving, contributing ideas for improvement, monitoring their own

work, and sharing their knowledge and enthusiastic attitudes with their colleagues. The true importance of empowerment increases the value of employees "not only to the organization, but also to themselves and to society as a whole."[23]

With its focus on process and customers, TQM is founded on one very obvious and simple principle: Do the right things right the first time, all the time, on time, and continuously improve. The heart of this principle is zero defects now and in the future. For example, a non-TQM production policy statement might read: "Do not allow defective production to be greater than 1 percent of total production." In contrast, total quality management would have the policy statement: "We will achieve zero-defect production." It follows that management's responsibility is to provide employees with the training, equipment, quality of materials, and other resources to meet this objective.

Exhibit 16–14 depicts the quality continuum along which companies move toward achieving world-class status. This continuum indicates that, at the most basic level of quality assurance, a company simply inspects to find defective products

EXHIBIT 16–14
QUALITY CONTINUUM

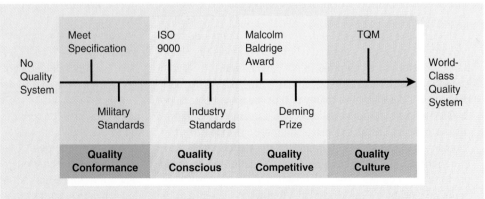

Source: Reprinted by permission from Grant Thornton, *Survey of American Manufacturers* (New York, 1992), p. 20. Copyright 1992.

[23] Cecily Raiborn and Dinah Payne, "TQM: Just What the Ethicist Ordered," *Journal of Business Ethics* (1996), p. 969.

or monitors employees and surveys customers after the fact to find poor service. Implementing a variety of quality control techniques to eliminate the possibilities of defective products or poor service means that the company has become quality conscious.

When a company's (or a division's) quality system has progressed to a high level of development, the company (or division) may choose to compete against others for formal quality recognition as did The Ritz-Carlton when it received the Malcolm Baldrige National Quality Award. Finally, when the concept of quality has become a distinct element of the organizational culture and tolerances for defective products or poor service are set at zero percent, the company has achieved world-class status and can be viewed as the benchmark for others.

Achieving world-class status does not mark an ending point. TQM is not a static concept; when one problem has been solved, another one is always waiting for a solution. For example, after The Ritz-Carlton received the Malcolm Baldrige National Quality Award in 1992, the company reviewed its processes and procedures, sought additional improvements throughout the organization, and reapplied and received the award in 1999. Other companies have sought international quality recognition by earning ISO 9000 certification. This standard, discussed in the Appendix, recognizes a company's quality documentation and implementation practices as well as its ability to make products that comform to ISO 9000 requirements.

Revisiting

The Ritz-Carlton Hotel Company, LLC

Headquartered in Chevy Chase, Maryland, The Ritz-Carlton competes in the "luxury" and "upscale" hotel categories. After receiving the Baldrige Award in 1992, management raised its standards for customer satisfaction to "top of the box" with defect-free experiences for guests. The company made the strategic planning process more systematic and more deeply integrated the TQM system into the organization. The Ritz-Carlton provides each employee a copy of its "Greenbook" as a reference source for quality processes.

To help establish a clear direction for continuous improvement and align actions at all operating levels, the company developed a pyramid that begins with its vision statement and flows to broader, shorter-term tiers. At the foundation are the company's values and philosophy that include its Credo, Motto, three steps of service, 20 "Basics," and employee promise. After extensive internal and external environmental scans, a new pyramid is developed each year during the strategic planning process. Output of the planning process provides the "vital few objectives" for the next three years as well as the measurements that will be used to track performance toward these objectives.

The Ritz-Carlton documents all of its quality improvement steps and problem-solving processes. Third-party experts review the company's data collection methods and its data analyses. Key processes are analyzed to pinpoint where errors could occur. For instance, The Ritz-Carlton has found that there are 970 posssible instances for a problem to occur when interacting with overnight guests and 1,071 possible instances when interacting with meeting event planners. It is easier to prevent a problem from occuring when all possible problem points have already been identified.

The 1999 Baldrige application summary is included on the company's Web site under Quality Philosophy. That application includes a Business Excellence Roadmap, which uses the traditional plan, do, check, and act approach to TQM, leading up to the final "act" section for business results: "continuously and forever improve." Given its attention to detail, employee care, and legendary customer service, The Ritz-Carlton provides the benchmark to which all great hotels will aspire but few will attain.

Appendix

Assessing Quality Internationally

Most large companies view their markets on an international rather than a domestic basis. To compete effectively in a global environment, companies must recognize the need for and be willing to initiate compliance with a variety of standards outside their domestic borders. Standards are essentially the international language of trade; they are formalized agreements that define the various contractual, functional, and technical requirements to assure customers that products, services, processes, and/or systems do what they are expected to do.

ISO

ISO 9000

A primary international guideline for quality standards is the **ISO 9000** series. In 1987, the International Organization for Standardization, based in Geneva, Switzerland, developed a comprehensive list of quality standards known as the ISO 9000 series. The series of three compliance standards (ISO 9001, 9002, and 9003) and two guidance standards (ISO 9000 and 9004) resulted from discussions among the quality standards boards of 91 countries. These directives are written in a general manner and prescribe the generic design, material procurement, production, quality control, and delivery procedures necessary to achieve quality assurance. These directives are not product standards and do not imply that companies using them have better products than competitors. The standards articulate what must be done to ensure quality, but management must decide how to meet the standards.

Because conformity is in the definition of quality, Principle 1 in the ISO 9000 international quality standard stresses that conformity must be judged by customers: "Organizations depend on their customers and therefore should understand current and future customer needs, should meet customer requirements and strive to exceed customer expectations."[24] As mentioned in the introduction to the chapter, The Ritz-Carlton Credo emphasizes the importance of the customer perspective. **Corning, Inc.**, another previous winner of the Baldrige Award, defines quality in its 2003 annual report as what is done "individually and in teams to understand, anticipate and surpass the expectations of customers and markets without error, on time, every day."[25]

ISO 9000 registration is required for regulated products sold in the European Union. Unfortunately, there is no international organization to administer the program. Thus, companies seeking ISO certification must qualify under an internationally accepted registration program that is administered by a national registrar. Examples of such registrars in the United States and Great Britain are Underwriters Laboratories and the British Standards Institution, respectively.

After an internal review, a company deciding that it can meet the standards may apply for ISO registration. To be registered, a company must first submit to a **quality audit** by a third-party reviewer which encompasses a review of product design activities, manufacturing processes and controls, quality documentation and records, and management quality policy and philosophy. After registration, teams visit the company biannually to monitor compliance.

Although registration costs are high, certified companies believe the benefits are even higher. Internally, certification helps ensure higher process consistency and quality and should help to reduce costs. Externally, ISO 9000 certified companies have an important distinguishing characteristic from their noncertified competitors. Additionally, certified companies are listed in a registry of "approved"

quality audit

---

[24] International Organization for Standardization, *ISO 9000, Quality Management Principles, http://www.iso.ch* (downloaded on June 15, 2004).
[25] Corning Inc., *2003 Annual Report*, p. 116.

suppliers, which should increase business opportunities. The cost-benefit relationships of the quality system must be measured, documented, and reported under ISO 9000—all jobs for management accountants.

ISO certification is not required to do business in the United States but should be explored for possible implementation even by companies that do not sell overseas because of the operational and competitive benefits. If a company's competitors are in compliance with and registered under ISO standards, good business sense would recognize the necessity of becoming ISO certified.

EFQM

EFQM was founded in 1988 by the presidents of 14 major European companies with the endorsement of the European Commission to develop a European framework for quality improvement similar to the U.S. Malcolm Baldrige National Quality Award and Japan's Deming Prize. As of August 2004, this management network had more 700 members. The EFQM Excellence Model (shown in Exhibit 16–15) was introduced in 1992 as the basis of assessing applications for the European Quality Award. The model has also become the framework for many national and regional quality awards across Europe.

The model is based on the premise that leadership is delivered through people, policy and strategy, and partnerships and resources, which all impact organizational processes. These factors enable achieving excellent results relative to people, customers, society, and performance. Thus, enablers describe what an organization does, whereas results describe what an organization achieves. Enablers cause results; feedback from results allows innovation and learning to take place that, in turn, improve the enablers.

The EFQM model's effectiveness is indicated by its widespread use as a management system and a means of organizational self-assessment. It helps indicate the gaps between where companies are and where they want to be so that management can determine the necessary activities to minimize those gaps. The model

EXHIBIT 16–15
EFQM EXCELLENCE MODEL

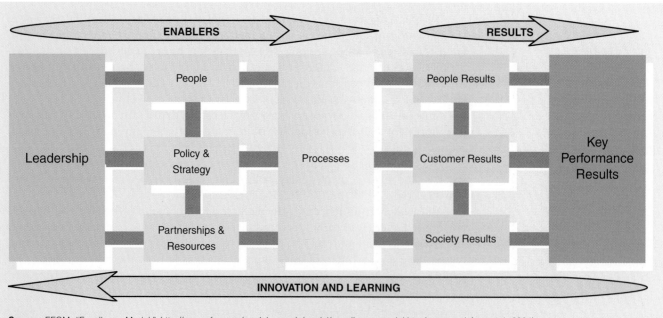

Source: EFQM, "Excellence Model," *http://www.efqm.org/model_awards/model/excellence_model.htm* (accessed August 4, 2004).

is nonprescriptive in that it does not provide a roadmap for the path to organizational excellence. However, the following fundamental concepts provide the model's foundation. These concepts are not listed in a particular order, and the listing is seen as flexible and subject to change as companies develop and improve.[26]

- *Results orientation:* Excellence is achieving results that delight all of the organization's stakeholders.
- *Customer focus:* Excellence is creating sustainable customer value.
- *Leadership and constancy of purpose:* Excellence is visionary and inspirational leadership, coupled with constancy of purpose.
- *Management by processes and facts:* Excellence is managing the organization through a set of interdependent and interrelated systems, processes, and facts.
- *People development and involvement:* Excellence is maximizing the contribution of employees through their development and involvement.
- *Continuous learning, innovation, and improvement:* Excellence is challenging the status quo and effecting change by using learning to create innovation and improvement opportunities.
- *Partnership development:* Excellence is developing and maintaining value-adding partnerships.
- *Corporate social responsibility:* Excellence is exceeding the minimum regulatory framework in which the organization operates and striving to understand and respond to the expectations of their stakeholders in society.

These underpinnings of the model can be seen to relate to both the Baldrige criteria and the balanced scorecard perspectives.

---

[26] "EFQM Excellence Model," *http://www.efqm.org/model_awards/model/excellence_model.htm* (accessed August 4, 2004).

Comprehensive Review Module

Chapter Summary

1. Quality

   - is the sum of all characteristics of a product or service that influence its ability to meet the needs of the person acquiring that product or service.

   - is defined as conformity with customer requirements from a production viewpoint and can be improved by

     ➤ increasing the good output generated from a specific amount of input during a period.

     ➤ reducing variability, often by adding automation in the process.

     ➤ reducing the product's or service's failure rate.

     ➤ conforming with customers' requirements.

   - should be properly evaluated from a consumer viewpoint by

     ➤ making certain that the product or service delivers what was intended.

     ➤ fulfilling consumer needs relative to a grade versus value perspective.

2. Benchmarking

   - refers to investigating, comparing, and evaluating a company's products, processes, and/or services against those of competitors or companies believed to be "best in class."

   - is engaged in by a company to obtain an understanding of another's production and performance methods so that the company can identify its strengths and weaknesses.

   - may be of one of three types:

     ➤ results benchmarking, in which an end product or service is examined using "reverse engineering" with a focus on product/service specifications and performance results; this type of benchmarking is performed on competitors.

     ➤ process benchmarking, in which a specific process is examined to determine how a "best in class" company achieves its results; this type of benchmarking is often performed

   on noncompetitors although competitors may also be used.

     ➤ strategic benchmarking, in which the focus is on understanding how successful companies compete.

3. Total quality management

   - is a significant management philosophy because it involves all organizational employees and places the customer at the center of focus.

   - is defined as seeking continuous improvement in processes so as to exceed customer expectations.

   - requires the following conditions to yield full benefits:

     ➤ sharing planning and decision making among personnel.

     ➤ eliminating non-value-added activities.

     ➤ enhancing technology in hardware, production processes, and management systems that increase productivity.

     ➤ increasing consumer awareness of the numerous types and grades of products available.

     ➤ using competitive benchmarking to close any performance gaps.

   - may lead a U.S. company to pursue attainment of the Malcolm Baldrige National Quality Award.

4. The types of quality costs include the costs of

   - compliance (or assurance), which are incurred to reduce or eliminate the current costs of quality failure and to continuously improve in the future. Compliance costs include

     ➤ prevention costs that are incurred to minimize or eliminate the production of nonconforming products and services. The incurrence of prevention costs tend to reduce the costs of appraisal and failure.

     ➤ appraisal costs that are incurred to determine which units of output do not conform to product specifications. The incurrence of appraisal costs tend to reduce the costs of external failure.

- noncompliance (or quality failure), which comprise

    ➤ internal failure costs that were incurred to identify a nonconforming product that is detected before being shipped to the customer. The incurrence of internal failure costs tend to reduce external failure costs.

    ➤ external failure costs that were incurred to remediate a nonconforming product that is not detected until after being shipped to the customer.

- compliance and noncompliance costs are inversely related.

5. The cost of quality is measured as the sum of the

- total cost of prevention,

- total cost of appraisal, and

- total cost of failure, which reflects the

    ➤ cost of profits lost by selling units as defects,

    ➤ cost of rework for defective goods,

    ➤ cost of processing customer returns,

    ➤ cost of warranty work,

    ➤ cost of product recalls,

    ➤ cost of litigation related to products, and

    ➤ opportunity cost of lost customers.

6. Information on the quality of an organization's products and services can be obtained from the

- balanced scorecard through the computation of

    ➤ manufacturing cycle efficiency.

    ➤ time to market for new products.

    ➤ customer satisfaction levels.

    ➤ on-time deliveries.

    ➤ defect rates.

    ➤ success rates of research and development activities.

- cost management system through the computation of

    ➤ quality costs incurred for production/service activities.

    ➤ costs of non-value-added activities.

    ➤ product/service life cycle costs.

    ➤ rework costs.

7. Quality can be instilled as part of an organization's culture by

- having committed and consistent top management leadership.

- developing an *esprit de corps* among all employees so that they are eager to meet and exceed customer expectations.

- making certain that a work environment is provided in which employees know that the company cares about and will reward efforts to achieve high quality.

- empowering employees.

- providing job and quality training.

- encouraging the pursuit of quality awards.

Solution Strategies

Total Cost of Quality = Cost of Compliance + Cost of Noncompliance

Prevention Costs	Appraisal Costs	Internal Failure Costs	External Failure Costs

Costs of noncompliance are inversely related to the costs of compliance and are a direct result of the number of defects.

Dimensions of product quality include:

- Conformity to specifications
- Effective and efficient performance

- Durability
- Ease of use
- Safety
- Comfort of use
- Appeal

COST OF QUALITY FORMULAS

Profit Lost by Selling Units as Defects =   (Total Defective Units − Number of Units Reworked) × (Profit for Good Unit − Profit for Defective Unit)

$$Z = (D - Y)(P_1 - P_2)$$

Rework Cost = Number of Units Reworked × Cost to Rework Defective Unit

$$R = (Y)(r)$$

Cost of Processing Customer Returns = Number of Defective Units Returned × Cost of a Return

$$W = (D_r)(w)$$

Total Failure Cost = Profit Lost by Selling Units as Defects + Rework Cost + Cost of Processing Customer Returns + Cost of Warranty Work + Cost of Product Recalls + Cost of Litigation Related to Products + Opportunity Cost of Lost Customers

$$F = Z + R + W + PR + L + O$$

Total Quality Cost = Total Compliance Cost + Total Failure Cost

$$T = (\text{Prevention Cost} + \text{Appraisal Cost}) + \text{Total Failure Cost}$$
$$T = K + A + F$$

Demonstration Problem

Telecommunications Inc.'s quality report for October 2006 showed the following information:

Profit for a good unit	$38
Profit for a defective unit	$22
Cost to rework a defective unit	$7
Cost to process a returned unit	$10
Total prevention cost	$27,000
Total appraisal cost	$16,000
Litigation related to product failure	$70,000
Opportunity cost of lost customers while litigation is being settled	$50,000
Total defective units	2,000
Number of units reworked	1,400
Number of customer units returned	650

Required:

Compute the following:

a. Profit lost by selling unreworked defects
b. Total rework cost
c. Cost of processing customer returns
d. Total failure cost
e. Total quality cost

Solution to Demonstration Problem

a. $Z = (D - Y)(P_1 - P_2) = (2,000 - 1,400)(\$38 - \$22) = \underline{\$9,600}$

b. $R = (Y)(r) = (1,400)(\$7) = \underline{\$9,800}$

c. $W = (D_r)(w) = (650)(\$10) = \underline{\$6,500}$

d. $F = (Z + R + W + L + O) = \$9,600 + \$9,800 + \$6,500 + \$70,000 + \$50,000 = \underline{\$145,900}$

e. $T = (K + A + F) = \$27,000 + \$16,000 + \$145,900 = \underline{\$188,900}$

Key Terms

appraisal cost *(p. 663)*
benchmarking *(p. 656)*
control chart *(p. 653)*
external failure cost *(p. 663)*
failure cost *(p. 663)*
grade *(p. 655)*
internal failure cost *(p. 663)*

ISO 9000 *(p. 675)*
prevention cost *(p. 663)*
process benchmarking *(p. 657)*
quality *(p. 652)*
quality audit *(p. 675)*
quality control (QC) *(p. 653)*
results benchmarking *(p. 656)*

statistical process control (SPC)
   (p. 653)
strategic benchmarking *(p. 657)*
total quality management (TQM)
   (p. 658)
value *(p. 655)*

Questions

1. What is meant by the term *quality?* In defining quality, from what two consumer perspectives can a definition be formulated? Why are both important?

2. In conducting activity analyses, the presence of certain activities indicates low production process quality. List five of these activities.

3. Compare and contrast the eight characteristics that compose overall quality from the customer's perspective with the three additional characteristics that compose service quality from the customer's perspective.

4. Locate a well-described product on the Internet. Discuss how that product exemplifies the eight overall quality characteristics. Prepare a balanced scorecard for this product assuming that its manufacturer has a total quality management strategy.

5. Describe three types of benchmarking. Use the Internet to find a company that has engaged in benchmarking. Describe the type of benchmarking used and the benefits and costs of the company's experience.

6. What is TQM? What are the four important tenets of TQM, and why are they important? What is the Malcolm Baldrige National Quality Award? What are the categories of entrants? What are the award criteria categories?

7. In the production-sales cycle, what are the four time phases in which quality costs are incurred? How are these costs interrelated through the phases?

8. How can Pareto analysis help focus managerial efforts on reducing the costs of quality-related problems?

9. How does strategic cost management link information to corporate strategies?

10. What are the four stages or levels on the quality continuum? Where is TQM located on the continuum?

11. *(Appendix)* Why might a common set of global quality standards be needed or desirable?

12. *(Appendix)* What is a quality audit?

13. *(Appendix)* Compare and contrast the EFQM Excellence Model with the Malcolm Baldrige National Quality Award criteria.

Exercises

14. (Essay; quality defined) Use the Internet to find four definitions of quality.
   a. Compare and contrast each of the four definitions with specific emphasis on whether the definition includes conformity or customer orientation.
   b. Assume that you are the manager of (1) a copy store and (2) a kitchen blender manufacturer. Prepare definitions of quality to distribute to your employees and discuss how you would measure service/product adherence to those definitions.

15. (True/False) Mark each of the following statements as true or false and explain why the false statements are incorrect.
   a. The total quality cost is the sum of prevention cost plus failure cost.
   b. Traditional accounting systems have separate accounts to capture quality costs.
   c. Pareto analysis is used to help managers identify areas in which to focus quality-improvement efforts.
   d. As the number of defective products manufactured rises, internal failure costs also rise, but external failure costs are expected to decline.
   e. Higher quality yields lower profits but higher productivity.
   f. Total quality management focuses on production processes rather than customer satisfaction.
   g. Results benchmarking relies only on comparisons to firms within the same industry.
   h. SPC control charts are used to plot the costs of quality over time.
   i. Appraisal cost is used to monitor and correct mistakes.
   j. Quality is free.

16. (Essay; statistical process control) Find the Web page for **Western Digital Corporation** in Santa Clara, California. What products does this company make? How does the company use statistical process controls to control the quality of output? Go to the following Web page: *http://www.nwasoft.com/press/mag_westdig.htm.* Explain how Western Digital has implemented statistical process controls to control the quality of output.

17. (Control chart) Clinton Pizza recently hired several college students to work part-time making pizzas. Robert Clinton, the owner, has the policy to put 36 slices of pepperoni on a pizza, but (given diversity in size) he sometimes puts on between 34 and 38. After observing the students for a few days, Robert gathered the following data on number of pepperoni slices:

11:00 A.M. to 5:00 P.M.
   13 pizzas were made containing the following number of pepperoni slices: 35, 37, 41, 33, 36, 36, 35, 39, 44, 37, 36, 36, 35

5:00 P.M. to 11:00 P.M.
   25 pizzas were made containing the following number of pepperoni slices: 35, 37, 41, 42, 36, 39, 44, 43, 44, 37, 48, 36, 35, 40, 39, 41, 29, 36, 36, 42, 45, 44, 37, 36, 36

   a. Prepare a control chart for pepperoni slices.
   b. What information does the chart provide to Clinton?

18. (Quality characteristics) Choose one product and one service with which you are well acquainted. Indicate how the product and service each meets (or does not meet) the eight overall quality characteristics. For the service, indicate how it meets (or does not meet) the three additional characteristics for service quality.

19. (Definition of quality; quality characteristics) In a three-person team, role-play the following individuals who are visiting a car dealership in your community: (1) a 19-year-old college student, (2) a young married person with two children, and (3) a person of postretirement age. Each person is interested in purchasing a new automobile.

    a. How does each person define quality in an automobile? Explain the reasons for the differences.

    b. What vehicle characteristics are important to all three individuals? Which vehicle characteristics are unique to each individual?

WebTUTOR Advantage

20. (Cost of quality) Dorothy's Sandal Works has gathered the following data on its quality costs for 2006 and 2007:

Defect Prevention Costs	2006	2007
Quality training	$ 9,000	$10,500
Quality technology	7,500	10,000
Quality production design	4,000	9,000

External Failure Costs		
Warranty handling	$15,000	$10,000
Customer reimbursements	11,000	7,200
Customer returns handling	7,000	4,000

    a. Compute the percentage change in the two quality cost categories from 2006 to 2007.

    b. Write a brief explanation for the pattern of change in the two categories.

WebTUTOR Advantage

21. (Cost of quality) Electronia Components' accounting system reflected the following costs related to quality for 2006 and 2007:

	2006	2007
Customer refunds for poor product quality	$ 48,000	$ 36,000
Fitting machines for mistake-proof operations	18,800	27,600
Supply-line management	16,000	20,000
Disposal of waste	88,000	72,000
Quality training	56,000	60,000
Litigation claims	144,000	112,000

    a. Which of these are costs of compliance, and which are costs of noncompliance?

    b. Calculate the percentage change in each cost and for each category.

    c. Discuss the pattern of the changes in the two categories.

22. (Essay; benefits of quality) Sometimes a company, in its efforts to reduce costs, might also reduce quality.

    a. What kinds of costs could an organization reduce that would almost automatically lower product/service quality?

    b. If quality improvements create cost reductions, why would cost reductions not create quality improvements?

    c. Are there instances in which cost reductions would create quality improvements?

23. (Cost of quality) Edwin Engines wants to determine its cost of quality. The company has gathered the following information from records pertaining to August 2006:

Defective units	6,000
Units reworked	1,200
Defective units returned	400
Appraisal costs	$13,600
Cost per unit for rework	$12
Prevention costs	$50,000
Profit per good unit produced and sold	$60
Profit per defective unit sold	$40
Cost per unit for customer returns	$10
Cost of warranty work	$5,000

Compute the following:
a. Lost profits from selling defective work
b. Total costs of failure
c. Total quality cost

24. (Cost of quality) Chelsea Sunglasses Company has gathered the following information pertaining to quality costs of the production of heavy-duty sunglasses for skiing for June 2006:

Total defective units	580
Number of units reworked	380
Number of units returned	100
Total prevention cost	$24,000
Total appraisal cost	$12,000
Per-unit profit for defective units	$20
Per-unit profit for good units	$56
Cost to rework defective units	$16
Cost to handle returned units	$10

Using these data, calculate the following:
a. Total cost to rework
b. Profit lost from not reworking all defective units
c. Cost of processing customer returns
d. Total failure costs
e. Total quality cost

25. (Essay; cost and benefit of quality) Hillary College has a variety of internal and external customers. Use a team of three or four individuals to answer the following.
a. Who are three internal and two external customers of a college or university?
b. How would each of the customers from part (a) define product or service quality at a college or university? Do any of these views conflict and, if so, how?
c. Are a college or university's internal customers as important as external customers? Explain the rationale for your answer.

26. (Essay; cost of quality) By building quality into a process rather than making quality inspections at the end of the process, certain job functions (such as that of quality control inspector) can be eliminated. Additionally, the installation of automated equipment to monitor product processing could eliminate some line worker jobs.

In a nation with fairly high unemployment, would employers attempting to implement valid quality improvements that resulted in employee terminations be appreciated or condemned? Discuss your answer from the standpoint of a variety of concerned constituencies, including the consumers who purchase the company's products.

27. (Cost of quality) Quick Computers is evaluating its quality control costs for 2006 and preparing plans and budgets for 2007. The 2006 quality costs incurred in the CPU Division follow:

Prevention costs	$300,000
Appraisal costs	100,000
Internal failure costs	350,000
External failure costs	100,000
Total	$850,000

Prepare a memo to the company president on the following issues:

a. Which categories of quality costs would be affected by the decision to spend $1,500,000 on new computer chip–making equipment (to replace older equipment)? Why?

b. If projected external failure costs for 2007 can be reduced 60 percent (relative to 2006 levels) by spending either $50,000 more on appraisal or $80,000 more on prevention, why might the firm opt to spend the $80,000 on prevention rather than the $50,000 on appraisal?

28. (Control of quality costs; team activity) The following summary numbers have been taken from a quality cost report of British Furniture Company for 2006. The firm manufactures a variety of English furniture products.

Prevention costs	$ 6,000,000
Appraisal costs	3,000,000
Internal failure costs	3,000,000
External failure costs	2,000,000
Total quality costs	$14,000,000

The company is actively seeking to identify ways to reduce total quality costs. Its current strategy is to increase spending in one or more quality cost categories in hope of achieving greater spending cuts in other quality cost categories. In a team of three or four individuals, prepare an oral presentation to answer the following questions:

a. Which spending categories are most susceptible to control by managers? Why?

b. Why is it more logical for the company to increase spending in the prevention cost and appraisal cost categories than in the failure cost categories?

c. Which cost category is the most likely target for spending reductions? Explain.

d. How would the adoption of a TQM philosophy affect the focus in reducing quality costs?

29. (Quality information system; team activity) Your company is interested in developing information about quality but has a traditional accounting system that does not provide such information directly. In a three- or four-person team, prepare a set of recommendations about how to improve the company's information system to eliminate or reduce this deficiency. In your recommendations, also explain in what areas management would have the most difficulty satisfying its desire for more information about quality and why these areas were chosen.

30. (Supplier quality) Assume that **Honda Motor Co., Ltd.** paid for a full-page advertisement in *The Wall Street Journal*. The ad did not tout Honda products, nor was it in reference to year-end earnings or a new stock issuance. Instead, the ad informed readers that "buying quality parts is not a foreign idea to us." Suppose the ad named Honda suppliers and identified their locations. Prepare a brief essay to answer the following questions.

a. Why would Honda want other companies to know what suppliers it uses?

b. Do you think this advertisement would have any benefit for Honda itself? Discuss the rationale for your answer.

31. (Differences from benchmarks) For a benchmark, assume that the average firm incurs quality costs in the following proportions:

Prevention	25%
Appraisal	25
Internal failure	25
External failure	25
Total costs	100%

With a partner, explain why the following industries might be inclined to have a spending pattern on quality costs that differs from the benchmark:

a. Pharmaceutical company

b. Department store

c. Computer manufacturer

d. Used car retailer

e. Lawn service company

32. (Essay; balanced scorecard) Find The **Benchmarking Exchange** on the Internet. What are five business processes that are currently the focus of its members? Why do you think benchmarking processes related to managing human resources rank highly on the benchmarking interest list of companies? Explain how benchmarking can be used to implement balanced scorecard goals and targets for each of its four perspectives for a company with a total quality management strategy.

Problems

33. (Essay; quality) Pharmeceutical companies **Pfizer** and **Schering-Plough** had quality problems at their prescription drug manufacturing plants. [See Scott Hensley, "Pfizer Is Warned by FDA to Fix Plant's Manufacturing Problems," *The Wall Street Journal* (February 12, 2002), p. B10; and Reuters, "Schering-Plough Inquiry Ends," *The New York Times* (October 2, 2003).]

a. Find information on the Web about problems in the pharmaceutical industry, including those of the above mentioned companies incurred by these companies. Be certain to review annual report footnote information related to contingencies for the companies. Discuss your findings.

b. Compare Pfizer and Schering-Plough's profits with those of other firms in the industry.

c. Discuss why a total quality management system would be more important in pharmaceutical companies than in most companies.

34. (Essay; quality and strategy) Three possible goals for a business are to (1) maximize profits, (2) maximize shareholder wealth, and (3) satisfy customer wants and needs. If goals (1) or (2) are chosen, the primary measurements of "success" are organizational profitability or stock price.

a. Do you believe that one of these three goals can be chosen to the exclusion of the others? Discuss the rationale for your answer.

b. How can total quality management help an organization meet all of these goals?

c. How might the selection of goals (1) or (2) lead to earnings management in an organization? Would the selection of goal (3) be likely to lead to earnings management? Explain.

35. (Essay; external failure cost) Many companies' products have had flaws; some of these companies have been more forthcoming than others in publicly acknowledging such flaws.
   a. Do you think admitting that a product is defective hurts or helps a company's reputation?
   b. Discuss the costs and benefits of halting sales when product flaws are discovered.
   c. Use the Internet to find an example of a company that has continued to sell its product in spite of complaints and other negative feedback about quality. What have been the results?

36. (Baldrige Award) Go to the Web site for the Malcolm Baldrige National Quality Award and find the answers to the following questions.
   a. When and why were the health and education categories established?
   b. How many applications were made in these two categories in each of the past three years?
   c. How do the criteria for the health, education, and manufacturing categories differ? Why are such differences necessary?

37. (Baldrige Award) Go to the Web site for the Malcolm Baldrige National Quality Award. On this site, you will find a questionnaire entitled "Are We Making Progress?"
   a. Download the questionnaire and answer the questions relative to your place of employment or university. Ask four of your colleagues to independently do the same.
   b. Compare and contrast the five sets of answers. How would you rank your organization's "progress" solely based on the information from these questionnaires?

38. (Pareto analysis) Rodham Computers identified the following failure costs during 2006:

COST OF FAILURE BY TYPE

Model	CPU	Internal Drive	External Drive	All Other	Total Dollars
Laptop	$ 8,000	$ 7,000	$ 5,000	$ 3,000	$23,000
Desktop	7,000	6,000	12,000	5,000	30,000
Mini	3,000	1,000	8,000	3,000	15,000
Total	$18,000	$14,000	$25,000	$11,000	$68,000

   a. Rearrange the rows in descending order of magnitude based on the Total Dollars column, and prepare a table using Pareto analysis with the following headings:

Model	Dollars	% of Total	Cumulative % of Total

   b. Which models account for almost 80 percent of all failure costs?
   c. Focusing on the models identified in part (b), prepare a table using Pareto analysis to identify the types of failure causing the majority of failure costs. (*Hint:* Rearrange the cost of failure types in descending order of magnitude.) Use the following headings for your table:

Failure Type	Dollars	% of Total	Cumulative % of Total

   d. Describe the problem areas for which to seek preventive measures first. How, if at all, does this answer reflect the concept of leverage?

39. (Pareto analysis) Cool-It Refrigerators has identified the following warranty costs during 2006 according to the type of product failure as follows:

Model	Electrical	Motor	Structural	Mechanical	Total Dollars
Chic	$25,000	$27,000	$15,000	$ 5,000	$ 72,000
Elegant	28,000	32,000	26,000	6,000	92,000
All others	8,000	15,000	6,000	9,000	38,000
Total	$61,000	$74,000	$47,000	$20,000	$202,000

a. Rearrange the rows in descending order of magnitude based on the Total Dollars column, and prepare a table using Pareto analysis with the following headings:

Model	Dollars	% of Total	Cumulative % of Total

b. Which model(s) account for the vast proportion of all failure costs? Discuss.

c. Devise a plan to address prioritizing projects regarding development of preventive measures based on the findings in the Pareto analysis you just conducted for Cool-It Refrigerators.

40. (Cost of quality) Howell Electronics manufactures hand-held palm pilots for the discriminating business person. The firm produced 3,000 palm pilots during its first year of operations. At year-end, it had no inventory of finished goods. The company sold 2,700 units through regular market channels (some after rework), but 300 of them were so defective that they had to be sold as scrap. For this first year, the firm spent $60,000 on prevention costs and $30,000 on quality appraisal. There were no customer returns. An income statement for the year follows.

Sales		
Regular channel	$540,000	
Scrap	24,000	$564,000
Cost of goods sold		
Original production costs	$300,000	
Rework costs	44,000	
Quality prevention and appraisal	90,000	(434,000)
Gross margin		$130,000
Selling and administrative expenses (all fixed)		(180,000)
Net loss		$ (50,000)

a. Compute the total profit lost by the company in its first year of operations by selling defective units as scrap rather than selling the units through regular channels.

b. Compute the total failure cost for the company in its first year.

c. Compute total quality cost incurred by the company in its first year.

d. What evidence indicates that the firm is dedicated to manufacturing and selling high-quality products?

41. (Cost of quality) E. Hugh-Phones makes portable telephones and produced 20,000 of them during 2006, its first year of operations. It sold all it produced that first year except 500 phones that had a particular defect. Of these, 200 were reworked and sold through regular channels at the original price; the rest were sold as "seconds" without rework. In 2006, E. Hugh-Phones spent $25,000 for prevention measures and $18,000 on appraisal. Following is E. Hugh's 2006 income statement. It is a partnership; thus, no income taxes are presented on the income statement.

E. HUGH-PHONES
Income Statement
For Year Ended December 31, 2006

Regular sales (19,700 units)	$3,940,000	
Sales of seconds (300 units)	42,000	$3,982,000
Cost of goods sold		
Original production costs	$1,600,000	
Rework costs (200 units)	4,000	
Prevention and appraisal costs	86,000	(1,690,000)
Gross margin		$2,292,000
Selling and administrative expenses (all fixed)		(1,200,000)
Net income		$1,092,000

a. Compute the total profit lost by E. Hugh-Phones in its first year of operations by selling defective units as seconds rather than reworking them and selling them at the regular price.

b. Compute the company's total failure cost in 2006.

c. Compute the company's total quality cost in 2006.

d. What evidence indicates that the firm is dedicated to manufacturing and selling high-quality products?

42. (Cost of quality) Golf courses are demanding in their quest for high-quality carts because of the critical need for lawn maintenance. Smooth Bill manufactures golf carts and is a recognized leader in the industry for quality products. In recent months, company managers have become more interested in trying to quantify the company's cost of quality. As an initial effort, the company identified the following 2006 costs by categories that are associated with quality:

Prevention Costs

Quality training	$15,000
Quality technology	50,000
Quality circles	32,000

Appraisal Costs

Quality inspections	$18,000
Test equipment	14,000
Procedure verifications	9,000

Internal Failure Costs

Scrap and waste	$ 6,500
Waste disposal	2,100

External Failure Costs

Warranty handling	$ 9,500
Customer reimbursements/returns	7,600

Managers were also aware that in 2006, 250 of the 8,000 carts produced had to be sold as scrap. These 250 carts were sold for $80 less profit per unit than "good" carts. Also, the company incurred rework costs amounting to $6,000 to sell 200 other carts through regular market channels.

a. Using these data, find Smooth Bill's 2006 expense for the following:

1. Lost profit from scrapping the 250 units

2. Total failure cost

3. Total quality cost

b. Assume that the company is considering expanding its existing full 5-year warranty to a full 7-year warranty in 2007. How would such a change be reflected in quality costs?

43. (Cost of quality) Smooth Sailing is very aware that its scuba diving tanks must be of high quality to maintain its reputation of excellence and safety. The company has retained you as a consultant and you have suggested that quantifying the costs that would be important to the understanding and management of quality. Your experience as a cost accountant helped you determine year 2006 costs of quality from the company's accounting records as follows:

Prevention Costs

Foolproofing machinery	$10,000
Quality training	30,000
Educating suppliers	22,000

Appraisal Costs

Quality inspections	$12,000
Recording defects	9,000
Procedure verifications	6,000

Internal Failure Costs

Waste disposal	$ 4,500
Unplanned downtime	1,400

External Failure Costs

Warranty handling	$ 6,400
Customer reimbursements/returns	5,100

You also determined that 1,200 of the 100,000 tanks made in 2006 had to be sold as scrap for $70 less profit per tank than the nondefective tanks. Smooth Sailing also incurred $4,000 of rework costs that had been buried in overhead (in addition to the failure costs listed) in producing the tanks sold at the regular price.

a. Smooth Sailing's management has asked you to determine the 2006 "costs" of the following:
   1. Lost profit from scrapping the 1,200 units
   2. Total failure cost
   3. Total quality cost

b. Assume that the company is considering expanding its existing full 2-year warranty to a full 3-year warranty in 2007. How would such a change be reflected in quality costs?

44. (Essay; balanced scorecard) Assume that you are in charge of University Physicians Social Service Agency, which provides counseling services to low-income families. The agency's costs have been increasing with no corresponding increase in funding. In an effort to implement some cost reductions, you took the following actions:

- Empowered counselors to make their own decisions about the legitimacy of all low-income claims.
- Told counselors not to review processed claims a second time to emphasize the concept of "do it right the first time."
- Set an upper and lower control limit of 5 minutes on a standard 15-minute time for consultations to discourage "out-of-control" conditions.

a. Discuss the ethics as well as the positive and negative effects of each of the ideas listed.

b. Develop a balanced scorecard for University Physicians Social Service Agency that incorporates the three changes listed.

45. (Essay; balanced scorecard) In mid-2004, a study of German accident data indicated that vehicles made by **Porsche AG** broke down twice as often during 2003 as cars made by **Mazda**. The top European performer was **Volkswagen AG** unit **Audi**. [Source: Chris Reiter and Stephen Power, "Data

Show Porsches Broke Down Twice as Much as Mazda Vehicles," *The Wall Street Journal* (June 1, 2004), p. D2.]

a. What do you perceive to be Porsche's strategy relative to value and grade of its automobiles? How might Porsche modify its strategy to compete better against Japanese vehicles? Do you think such a change in strategy would be profitable for Porsche? Explain.

b. If Porsche were to change its strategy, develop a balanced scorecard that would provide measurements of the new strategy.

46. (Appendix; ISO) Many companies are becoming ISO certified because of customer requests and because of the need to compete in the global marketplace.

a. Why do you think customers are insisting that suppliers meet ISO 9000 standards?

b. Does meeting ISO 9000 standards mean that a supplier's products or services are superior to those of competitors? Elaborate on what conformance to the standards means.

c. Why would the fact that a supplier's industry is moving toward ISO 9000 motivate the supplier to seek registration?

d. How would complying with ISO 9000 help a company improve quality?

47. (Appendix; EFQM Award) Go to the EFQM Web site and find the case studies archive. Choose one of the companies listed for the past two years. Prepare a synopsis of the company, and gather additional information about it to make a brief presentation on why it received an award or was a finalist.

17

Inventory and Production Management

Objectives

AFTER COMPLETING THIS CHAPTER, YOU SHOULD BE ABLE TO ANSWER THE FOLLOWING QUESTIONS:

LO.1 WHAT ARE THE MOST IMPORTANT RELATIONSHIPS IN THE VALUE CHAIN?

LO.2 WHY IS MANAGEMENT OF INVENTORY COSTS IMPORTANT TO MOST FIRMS?

LO.3 HOW DO PUSH AND PULL SYSTEMS OF PRODUCTION CONTROL WORK?

LO.4 WHY DO PRODUCT LIFE CYCLES AFFECT PROFITABILITY?

LO.5 WHAT IS TARGET COSTING, AND HOW DOES IT INFLUENCE PRODUCTION COST MANAGEMENT?

LO.6 WHAT IS THE JUST-IN-TIME PHILOSOPHY? WHAT MODIFICATIONS DOES JIT REQUIRE IN ACCOUNTING SYSTEMS?

LO.7 WHAT ARE FLEXIBLE MANUFACTURING SYSTEMS?

LO.8 HOW CAN THE THEORY OF CONSTRAINTS HELP IN DETERMINING PRODUCTION FLOW?

LO.9 *(APPENDIX)* HOW ARE ECONOMIC ORDER QUANTITY, REORDER POINT, AND SAFETY STOCK DETERMINED AND USED?

Introducing

Al and Frank Jezek in Newark, New Jersey, founded Jezek Tool & Machine in 1953. Early in its history, the company employed about 30 people and used manual technology to manufacture parts and custom machinery for large marquis companies such as IBM, Pitney Bowes, Singer, Johnson & Johnson, Schering-Plough, Owens-Illinois, and for the airlines at nearby Newark International Airport.

In the 1980s, to remain competitive in the industry, the company began replacing manually operated equipment with automated technology including computer-controlled machinery. With this new equipment, the company could manufacture a larger volume of products and do so with less labor input. In addition to the automated equipment, the firm built a "clean room" in which to make high-precision parts for the world-famous Sikorsky Helicopters. Additionally, Jezek Tool built the first plastic extruding machine. With the new equipment and facilities, the company developed the ability to make unique, customized products in small quantities at very high quality for its customers.

The ability to make limited quantities of high-precision parts and products has allowed Jezek to become a preferred supplier to firms that have adopted lean manufacturing practices. These firms demand prompt delivery of parts and equipment on short lead times and in small quantities. Because these firms maintain minimal inventories, the ability of vendors to deliver high-quality inputs on time is crucial to satisfying customers. Jezek has been able to distinguish itself from its competitors in satisfying the rigorous demands of lean manufacturers because it has invested in the equipment and trained its employees to deliver the highest quality products at a competitive price with fast turnarounds.

Source: *http://www.jezektool.com* (accessed August 24, 2004).

Firms such as Jezek have discovered that their customers' views about inventory have changed over the past 25 years. No longer do firms want to hold inventory until a customer decides to make a purchase; they fervently strive to avoid investing cash in inventory until customers actually place orders. These efforts to avoid inventory investment are captured in the following quote.

> *People who believe you can't have too much of a good thing obviously haven't worked with inventory! Operations managers know inventory dispels this adage and face the constant challenge of keeping inventory levels as low as possible without increasing overall costs or negatively impacting product availability. This isn't an easy job, especially since inventory rears its head throughout any organization—from raw materials, to work-in-process, to finished goods.*[1]

Other than plant assets, inventory is often the largest investment a company makes although this investment yields no return until the inventory is sold. This chapter deals with ways companies minimize their monetary commitments to inventory while still satisfying customer demands. The chapter Appendix covers the concepts of economic order quantity (EOQ), order point, safety stock, and Pareto inventory analysis.

IMPORTANT RELATIONSHIPS IN THE VALUE CHAIN

LO.1
WHAT ARE THE MOST IMPORTANT RELATIONSHIPS IN THE VALUE CHAIN?

Every company has a set of upstream suppliers and a set of downstream customers. In a one-on-one context, these parties can be depicted by the following model:

---

[1] Scott W. Hadley, "A Modern View of Inventory," *Strategic Finance* (July 2004), pp. 31–35.

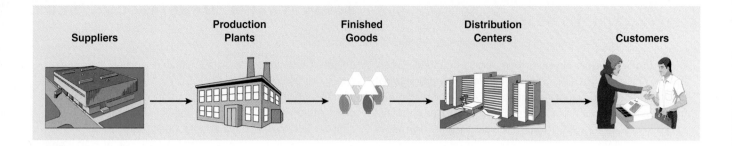

Suppliers **Production Plants** **Finished Goods** **Distribution Centers** **Customers**

How can sharing information within the value chain make firms in the value chain more profitable?

The interfaces of these relationships indicate where the real opportunities for inventory cost management exist. By building improved cooperation, communication, and integration, entities within a value chain can treat each other as extensions of themselves and, thereby, enjoy gains in quality, throughput, and cost efficiency. Entities can reduce or eliminate non-value-added activities and enhance the performance of value-added activities. Shared expertise and problem solving can be very beneficial in the process. These firms can provide products and services faster and with fewer defects as well as perform activities more effectively and reliably with fewer errors and less redundancy. Consider the following areas in which opportunities for improvement between entities exist:

- communication of requirements and specifications,
- clarity in requests for products or services,
- feedback regarding unsatisfactory products or services,
- planning, controlling, and problem solving, and
- sharing managerial and technical expertise, supervision, and training.

These opportunities are also available to individuals and groups within an organization. Each employee or group of employees has both an upstream supplier and a downstream customer that form the context of an intraorganizational value chain. When employees see their internal suppliers and customers as extensions of themselves and work to exploit the opportunities for improvement, teamwork is significantly enhanced. Improved teamwork helps companies in their implementation of pull systems, which are part of a just-in-time work environment and are discussed in the next section. Increased productivity benefits all company stakeholders by

- reducing investment in inventory,
- improving cash-to-cash cycle time,
- generating higher asset turnover,
- generating higher inventory turnover, and
- reducing inventory risk.

BUYING OR PRODUCING AND CARRYING INVENTORY

LO.2
WHY IS MANAGEMENT OF INVENTORY COSTS IMPORTANT TO MOST FIRMS?

In manufacturing organizations, production begins with the acquisition of raw material. Although possibly not the largest production cost, raw material purchases cause a continuous cash outflow each period. Similarly, retailers invest a significant proportion of their assets in merchandise purchased for sale to others. Profit margins in both types of organizations can benefit from reducing or minimizing inventory investments, assuming that the demand for products can still be met. The word *inventory* is used in this chapter to refer to raw material, work in process, finished goods, indirect material (supplies), and merchandise inventory.

Efficient inventory management relies largely on cost-minimization strategies. As indicated in Exhibit 17–1, significant costs associated with inventory are (1) purchasing/production, (2) ordering/setup, and (3) carrying/not carrying goods in stock. The **purchasing cost** for inventory is the quoted purchase price minus any discounts allowed, plus shipping charges. Purchasing/production cost is the amount to be recorded in the appropriate inventory account (Raw Material Inventory, Work in Process Inventory, Finished Goods Inventory, or Merchandise Inventory).

For a manufacturer, *production cost* refers to the costs associated with purchasing direct material, paying for direct labor, incurring traceable overhead, and absorbing allocated fixed manufacturing overhead. Of these production costs, fixed manufacturing overhead is the least susceptible to cost minimization in the short run. An exception is that management is able to somewhat control the fixed component of unit product cost by managing production capacity utilization relative to demand in the short run. Most efforts to minimize fixed manufacturing overhead costs involve long-run measures.

purchasing cost

EXHIBIT 17–1
CATEGORIES OF INVENTORY COSTS

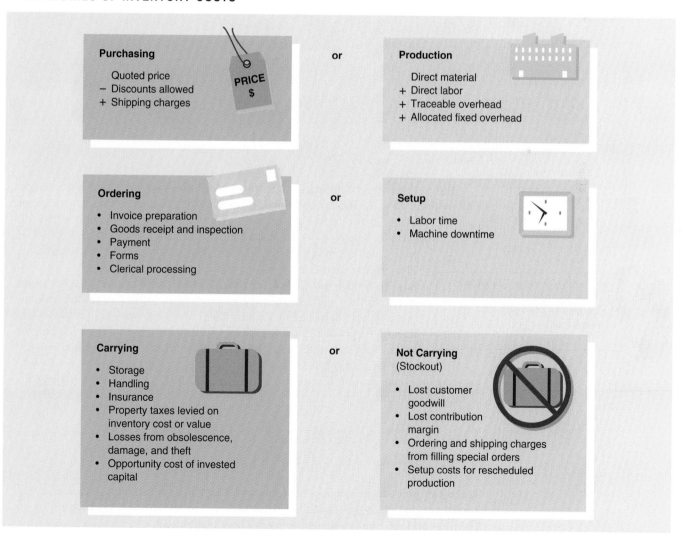

Purchasing

  Quoted price
− Discounts allowed
+ Shipping charges

PRICE $

or

Production

  Direct material
+ Direct labor
+ Traceable overhead
+ Allocated fixed overhead

Ordering

- Invoice preparation
- Goods receipt and inspection
- Payment
- Forms
- Clerical processing

or

Setup

- Labor time
- Machine downtime

Carrying

- Storage
- Handling
- Insurance
- Property taxes levied on inventory cost or value
- Losses from obsolescence, damage, and theft
- Opportunity cost of invested capital

or

Not Carrying
(Stockout)

- Lost customer goodwill
- Lost contribution margin
- Ordering and shipping charges from filling special orders
- Setup costs for rescheduled production

EXHIBIT 17–2
PUSH SYSTEM OF PRODUCTION CONTROL

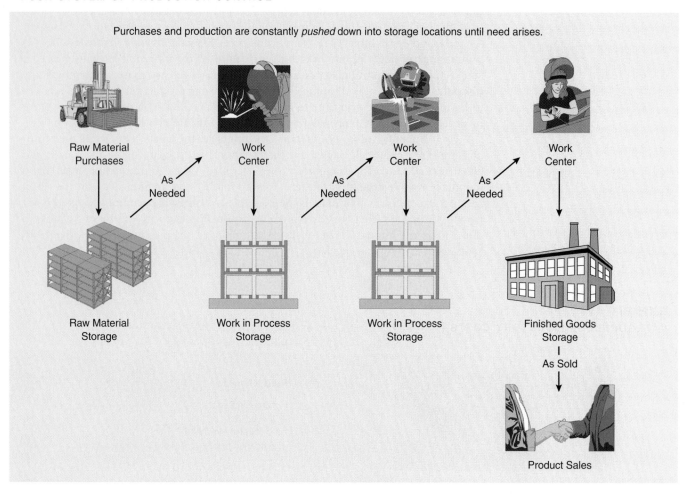

Purchases and production are constantly *pushed* down into storage locations until need arises.

HOW DO PUSH AND PULL SYSTEMS OF PRODUCTION CONTROL WORK?

push system

Is the push or the pull production system the more conventional approach to inventory management?

pull system

The two theoretical approaches to producing inventory are push systems and pull systems. In a traditional approach, production is conducted in anticipation of customer orders. In this approach, known as a **push system** (illustrated in Exhibit 17–2), work centers buy or produce inventory not currently needed because of lead time, economic order size, or production quantity requirements. This excess inventory is stored until it is needed by other work centers. To reduce the cost of carrying inventory until needed at some point in the future, many firms have implemented **pull systems** of production control (depicted in Exhibit 17–3). In these systems, parts are delivered or produced only as they are needed by the work center for which they are intended. Although by necessity some minimal storage must exist, work centers do not produce to compensate for lead times or to meet some economic production run model. Matters such as managing inventory levels and optimum order size are discussed in the chapter Appendix.

UNDERSTANDING AND MANAGING PRODUCTION ACTIVITIES AND COSTS

Managing production activities and costs requires an understanding of product life cycles and the various management and accounting models and approaches to effectively and efficiently engage in production planning, controlling, decision making, and evaluating performance.

EXHIBIT 17–3
PULL SYSTEM OF PRODUCTION CONTROL

Product sales dictate total production. Purchases and production are *pulled* through the system on an as-needed basis.

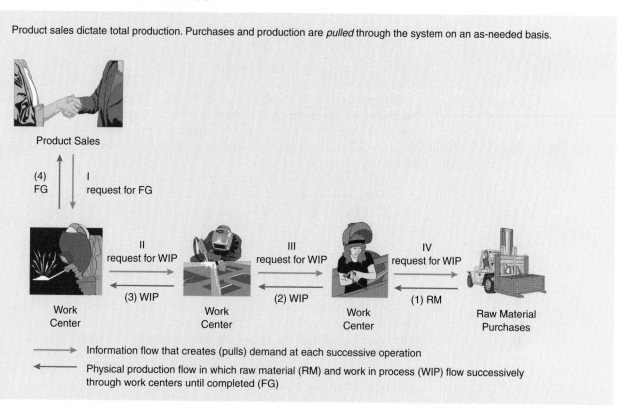

Product Sales

(4) FG   I request for FG

Work Center   II request for WIP   Work Center   III request for WIP   Work Center   IV request for WIP   Raw Material Purchases

(3) WIP   (2) WIP   (1) RM

→ Information flow that creates (pulls) demand at each successive operation

← Physical production flow in which raw material (RM) and work in process (WIP) flow successively through work centers until completed (FG)

Product Life Cycles

LO.4
WHY DO PRODUCT LIFE CYCLES AFFECT PROFITABILITY?

Product profit margins are typically judged on a period-by-period basis without consideration of the product life cycle. However, products, like people, go through a series of sequential life-cycle stages. The product life cycle is a model depicting the stages through which a product class (not each product) passes from the time that an idea is conceived until production is discontinued. Those stages are development (which includes design), introduction, growth, maturity, and decline. A sales trend line through each stage is illustrated in Exhibit 17–4. Companies must

EXHIBIT 17–4
PRODUCT LIFE CYCLE

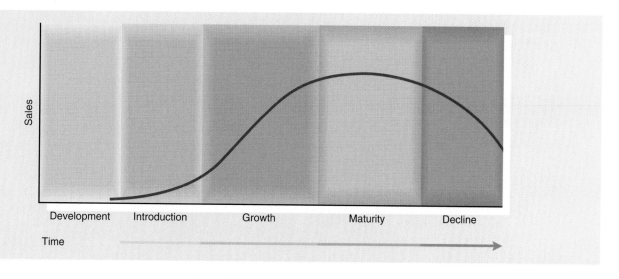

Sales

Development   Introduction   Growth   Maturity   Decline

Time

be aware of where products are in their life cycles because, in addition to the sales effects, the life-cycle stage can have a tremendous impact on costs and profits.

Life Cycle and Target Costing

From a cost standpoint, the development stage is an important one that the traditional financial accounting model almost ignores. Financial accounting requires that development costs be expensed as incurred—even though most studies indicate that decisions made during this stage determine approximately 80 to 90 percent of a product's total life-cycle costs. The materials and manufacturing process specifications made during development generally affect production costs for the remainder of the product's life.

Although technology and competition have tremendously shortened the time spent in the development stage, effective development efforts are critical to a product's profitability over its entire life cycle. Time spent in the planning and development process often results "in lower production costs, reduced time from the design to manufacture stage, higher quality, greater flexibility, and lower product life cycle cost."[2] All manufacturers are acutely aware of the need to focus attention on the product development stage, and the performance measure of time to market is becoming more critical.

One technology that is increasingly used in the design stage is virtual reality. **Virtual reality** is an artificial, computer-generated environment in which the user has the impression of being part of that environment and has the ability to navigate and manipulate objects (such as products) behaving like real-world objects. With virtual reality, much of the testing of new products can focus on a virtual prototype rather than a real prototype.

Once a product or service idea has been formulated, the market is typically researched to determine the features that customers desire. Because many products can now be built to specifications, companies can further develop the product to meet customer tastes once it is in the market. Alternatively, flexible manufacturing systems allow rapid changeovers to other designs.

After a product is designed, manufacturers have traditionally determined product costs and set a selling price based, to some extent, on costs. If the market will not bear the resulting selling price (possibly because competitors' prices are lower), the firm either makes less profit than desired or attempts to lower production costs.

In contrast, since the early 1970s, some companies (especially Japanese companies) have used a technique called target costing to view the costing process differently. As expressed in the following formula, **target costing** develops an "allowable" product cost by analyzing market research to estimate what the market will pay for a product with specific characteristics.

$$TC = ESP - APM$$

$$
\begin{aligned}
\text{where}\quad TC &= \text{target cost}\\
ESP &= \text{estimated selling price}\\
APM &= \text{acceptable profit margin}
\end{aligned}
$$

Subtracting an acceptable profit margin from the estimated selling price leaves an implied maximum per-unit target product cost, which is compared to an expected product cost.

If the expected cost is higher than the target cost, the company has several alternatives. First, the product design and/or production process can be changed

margin notes:

virtual reality

LO.5
WHAT IS TARGET COSTING, AND HOW DOES IT INFLUENCE PRODUCTION COST MANAGEMENT?

target costing

---

[2] James A. Brimson, "How Advanced Manufacturing Technologies Are Reshaping Cost Management," *Management Accounting* (March 1986), p. 26.

cost table

to reduce costs. Preparation of cost tables helps determine how to make such adjustments. **Cost tables** are databases that provide information about the impact on product costs of using different input resources, manufacturing processes, and design specifications. Second, a less-than-desired profit margin can be accepted. Third, the company can decide that it does not want to enter this particular product market at the current time because it cannot make the profit margin it desires. If, for example, the target costing system at **Olympus** (a Japanese camera company) indicates that a product's life-cycle costs are too high to make an acceptable profit, "the product is abandoned unless there is a strategic reason, such as maintaining a full product line or creating a 'flagship' product, for keeping the product."[3]

value engineering

An important step in successful product development is the process of **value engineering**, which involves a disciplined search for various feasible combinations of resources and methods that will increase product functionality and reduce costs. Multidisciplinary teams using various problem-solving tools such as brainstorming, Pareto analysis, and engineering tools seek an improved product cost-performance ratio considering such factors as reliability, conformance, and durability. Cost reduction is considered the major focus of value engineering.[4]

Target costing can be applied to services if they are sufficiently uniform to justify the modeling effort required. Assume that a print shop wants to offer its customers the opportunity to buy personalized picture calendars and other similar items personalized with photographs. A market survey indicates that the metropolitan area could sustain an annual 500-order volume and that customers believe $18 is a reasonable fee per service. The print shop manager believes that a reasonable profit for this service is $8 per customer order. Thus, the shop has an allowable target cost of $10 per order ($18 − $8). The manager will invest in the equipment necessary to provide the new service if he or she believes that the indicated volume suggested by market research is sufficient to support the effort.

If a company decides to enter a market, the target cost computed at the beginning of the product life cycle does not remain the final focus. Over the product's life, the target cost is continuously reduced in an effort to spur a process of continuous improvement in actual production cost. **Kaizen costing** involves ongoing efforts for continuous improvement to reduce product costs, increase product quality, and/or improve the production process after manufacturing activities have begun. These cost reductions are designed to keep the profit margin relatively stable as the product price is reduced over the product life cycle. Exhibit 17–5 compares target and kaizen costing.

kaizen costing

At **Kodak**, both suppliers and customers are included in kaizen initiatives. The following quote from Leslie Barker, Kodak Operating System Director, describes the company's point in surveying customers. "From a customer perspective, we get a better idea of how they use our products, at what rate they're using them, things that work well for them, things that don't—we try to get down to the base functions that we need to drive our operations."[5]

In designing a product to meet an allowable cost, engineers strive to eliminate all nonessential activities from the production process. Such reductions in activities will, in turn, reduce costs. The production process and types of components to be used should be discussed among appropriate parties (including engineering, management, accounting, and marketing) in recognition of the product quality and cost desired. Suppliers also can participate in the design phase by making suggestions for modifications that would allow regularly stocked components to be used rather than more costly special order items.

---

[3] Robin Cooper, *When Lean Enterprises Collide* (Boston: Harvard Business School Press, 1995), p. 159.
[4] Eric Meng, "The Project Manager's Toolbox," *PM Network* (1999), pp. 52ff.
[5] Duff McCutcheon, "Photo Finish," *Advanced Manufacturing* (September/October 2003), *http://www.advancedmanufacturing.com/October03/coverstory.htm*.

EXHIBIT 17–5

COMPARISON OF TARGET AND KAIZEN COSTING

	Target Costing	Kaizen Costing
What?	A procedural approach to determining a maximum allowable cost for an identifiable, proposed product assuming a given target profit margin	A mandate to reduce costs, increase product quality, and/or improve production processes through continuous improvement efforts
Used for?	New products	Existing products
When?	Development stage (includes design)	Primary production stages (introduction and growth; possibly, but not probably, maturity)
How?	Works best by aiming at a specified cost reduction objective; used to set original production standards	Works best by aiming at a specified cost reduction objective; reductions are integrated into original production standards to sustain improvements and provide new challenges
Why?	Extremely large potential for cost reduction because 80% to 90% of a product's lifelong costs are embedded in the product during the design and development stages	Limited potential for reducing cost of existing products, but may provide useful information for future target costing efforts
Focus?	All product inputs (material, labor, and overhead elements) as well as production processes and supplier components	Depends on where efforts will be most effective in reducing production costs; generally begins with the most costly component and (in more mature companies) ends with overhead components

Properly designed products should require only minimal engineering changes after being released to production. Each time an engineering change is issued, one or more of the following problems can occur and create additional costs: Production documents must be reprinted, workers must relearn tasks, machine dies or setups must be changed, and parts in stock or currently ordered can be made obsolete. If costs are to be affected significantly, any design changes must be made early in the process—preferably before production begins.

Using target costing requires a shift in the way managers think about the relationships among cost, selling price, and profitability. The traditional attitude has been that a product is developed, production cost is identified and measured, a selling price is set (or a market price is met), and profits or losses result. Target costing takes a different perspective: A product is developed, a selling price and desired profit amount are determined, and maximum allowable costs are calculated. When costs being incurred rely on an up-front determination of selling price, all costs must be justified. Unnecessary costs should be eliminated without reducing quality.

During the product introduction stage, costs can be substantial and are typically related to engineering changes, market research, advertising, and promotion. Sales are usually low and prices are often set in relationship to the market price of similar or substitute goods if such goods are available.

The growth stage begins when the product has been accepted by the market and begins to show increased sales. Product quality also can improve during this life-cycle stage, especially if competitors have improved on original production designs. Prices are fairly stable during the growth stage because many substitutes exist or because consumers have become "attached" to the product and are willing to pay a particular price for it rather than buy a substitute.

In the maturity stage, sales begin to stabilize or slowly decline, and firms often compete on the basis of selling price. Costs are often at their lowest level during this period, so profits can be high. Some products remain at this stage for a very long time.

The decline stage reflects waning sales. Prices can be cut dramatically to stimulate business. Production cost per unit generally increases during this stage because fixed overhead is spread over a smaller production volume.

JUST-IN-TIME SYSTEMS

LO.6
WHAT IS THE JUST-IN-TIME PHILOSOPHY? WHAT MODIFICATIONS DOES JIT REQUIRE IN ACCOUNTING SYSTEMS?

What advantages are there in manufacturing a product only after a customer has expressed the intention to purchase?

just-in-time

kanban

just-in-time manufacturing system

Just-in-time (JIT) is a philosophy about when to do something. The "when" is as needed and the "something" is a production, purchasing, or delivery activity. The JIT philosophy is applicable in all departments of all types of organizations. JIT's three primary goals are as follows:

1. elimination of any production process or operation that does not add value to the product/service,
2. continuous improvement in production/performance efficiency, and
3. reduction in the total cost of production/performance while increasing quality.

These goals are totally consistent with and supportive of the total quality management program discussed in Chapter 15. The elements of the JIT philosophy are outlined in Exhibit 17–6. Because JIT is most commonly discussed with regard to manufacturing or production activities, this is a logical starting point. Just-in-time manufacturing originated in Japan where a card, or **kanban** (pronounced "kahn-bahn"), was used to indicate a work center's need for additional components. A **just-in-time manufacturing system** attempts to acquire components and produce inventory units only as they are needed, minimize product defects, and reduce cycle/setup times for acquisition and production.

Production has traditionally been dictated by the need to smooth operating activities over time. Although allowing a company to maintain a steady work force and continuous machine utilization, smooth production often creates products that must be stored until they are sold. Traditionally, companies filled warehouses with products that were not currently in demand, often while failing to meet promised customer delivery dates. One cause of this dysfunctional behavior was management preoccupation with spreading overhead over a maximum number of products being produced. This obsession unwittingly resulted in much unwanted inventory, huge inventory carrying costs, and other operations problems to be discussed subsequently.

EXHIBIT 17–6
ELEMENTS OF A JIT PHILOSOPHY

- Quality is essential at all times; work to eliminate defects and scrap.
- Employees often have the best knowledge of ways to improve operations; listen to them.
- Employees generally have more talents than are being used; train them to be multiskilled and increase their productivity.
- Ways to improve operations are always available; constantly look for them, being certain to make fundamental changes rather than superficial ones.
- Creative thinking doesn't cost anything; use it to find ways to reduce costs before making expenditures for additional resources.
- Suppliers are essential to operations; establish and cultivate good relationships with suppliers and, if possible, use long-term contracts.
- Inventory is an asset that generates no revenue while it is held in stock. Thus, it can be viewed as a "liability"; eliminate it to the extent possible.
- Storage space is directly related to inventories; eliminate it in response to the elimination of inventories.
- Long cycle times cause inventory buildup; keep cycle times as short as possible by using frequent deliveries.

Thus, historically, raw material and work in process inventories were maintained at levels considered sufficient to cover up inefficiencies in acquisition and/or production. Exhibit 17–7 depicts these inefficiencies or problems as "rocks" in a stream of "water" that represents inventory. The traditional philosophy is that the water level should be kept high enough for the rocks to be so deeply submerged

EXHIBIT 17–7

DEPICTION OF TRADITIONAL AND JIT PRODUCTION PHILOSOPHIES

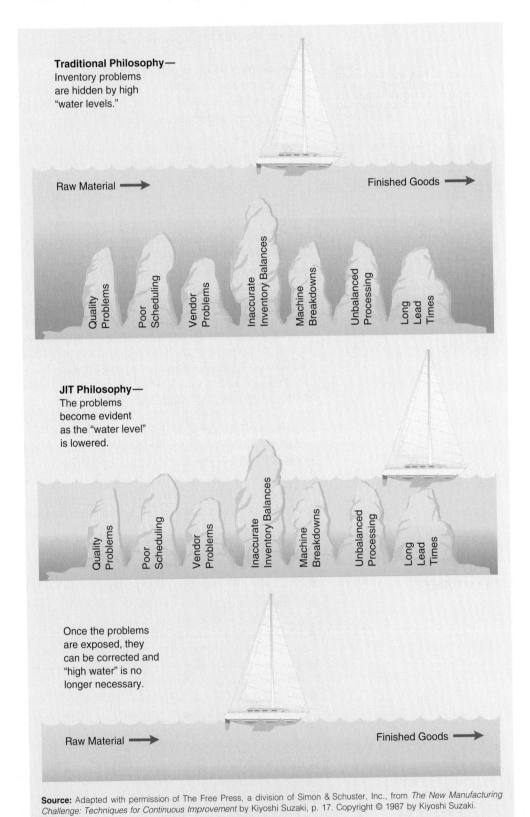

Traditional Philosophy— Inventory problems are hidden by high "water levels."

Raw Material ➞   Finished Goods ➞

Quality Problems · Poor Scheduling · Vendor Problems · Inaccurate Inventory Balances · Machine Breakdowns · Unbalanced Processing · Long Lead Times

JIT Philosophy— The problems become evident as the "water level" is lowered.

Quality Problems · Poor Scheduling · Vendor Problems · Inaccurate Inventory Balances · Machine Breakdowns · Unbalanced Processing · Long Lead Times

Once the problems are exposed, they can be corrected and "high water" is no longer necessary.

Raw Material ➞   Finished Goods ➞

Source: Adapted with permission of The Free Press, a division of Simon & Schuster, Inc., from *The New Manufacturing Challenge: Techniques for Continuous Improvement* by Kiyoshi Suzaki, p. 17. Copyright © 1987 by Kiyoshi Suzaki.

that there will be "smooth sailing" in production activity. This technique is intended to avoid the original problems, but in fact, it creates a new one. By covering up the problems, the excess "water" adds to the difficulty of making corrections. The JIT manufacturing philosophy is to lower the water level, expose the rocks, and eliminate them to the extent possible. The shallower stream will then flow more smoothly and rapidly than the deep river.

CHANGES NEEDED TO IMPLEMENT JIT MANUFACTURING

Implementation of a just-in-time system in a manufacturing firm does not occur overnight. It took Toyota more than 20 years to develop the system and realize significant benefits from it. JIT techniques are becoming more common and more easily implemented, however, and it is now possible for a company to have a system in place and recognize benefits in a fairly short time. In a world where managers work diligently to produce improvements of a percentage point or two, some numbers simply do not look realistic but are. One success story involves Johnson Controls Automotive Systems Group, which successfully adopting just-in-time manufacturing in its Lexington, Tennessee, plant. The company achieved 100 percent on-time delivery for three years—during which sales rose 55 percent!

> *The key to Johnson Controls JIT program is process standardization. John Rog, purchasing manager of supplier manufacturing development at JCI, says that all [the company's] plants rely heavily on such Toyota-inspired strategies as visual management, kanban, and poka-yoke. JCI has also adopted the Japanese idea of the "five S's," namely, sort, stability, shine, standardize, and sustain, which intend to bring order and uniformity to the plant floor. Finally, JCI has created a training program to help its supply base enforce JIT, kaizen, lean manufacturing, and other manufacturing strategies.[6]*

The most impressive benefits from JIT, though, are normally reached only after the system has been operational for 5 to 10 years. Implementing JIT takes time and perseverance. Furthermore, a JIT philosophy must have strong backing and resource commitment from top management. Without these ingredients, considerable retraining, and support from all levels of company personnel, JIT implementation will not succeed.

For just-in-time production to be effective, certain modifications must be made to supplier relationships, distribution, product design, product processing, and plant layout. JIT depends on the ability of employees and suppliers to compress the time, distance, resources, and activities and to enhance interactions needed to produce a company's products and services. The methods currently being used successfully by many companies are discussed next.

Supplier Relationships and Distribution

The optimal JIT situation is to have only one vendor for any given item. Such an ideal, however, creates the risk of not having alternative sources (especially for critical parts) in the event of vendor business failure, production strikes, unfair pricing, or shipment delays. Thus, it is often more realistic to limit the number of vendors to a selected few that are company certified as to quality and reliability. The company then enters into long-term relationships with these suppliers, who become "partners" in the process. Vendor certification is becoming more and more popular. For example, Allen-Bradley, a world-class electronics manufacturer, has been named the preferred automation controls supplier to Ford's Automotive Components Group network of more than 30 manufacturing plants worldwide.

[6] Tim Minahan, "JIT Moves Up the Supply Chain," *Purchasing* (September 1, 1998), pp. 46ff.

Vendor certification requires substantial efforts by the purchasing company, such as obtaining information on the supplier's operating philosophy, costs, product quality, and service. People from various areas must decide on the factors by which to rate the vendor and then must weigh those factors as to relative importance. Rapid feedback should be given to potential vendors/suppliers so that they can, if necessary, make changes prior to the start of the relationship or understand why the relationship will not occur.

Factors commonly considered in selecting suppliers include a vendor's reliability and responsiveness, delivery performance, ability to provide service, personnel qualifications, research and development strength, and production capacity. Evaluations of new and infrequent vendors are more difficult because of the lack of a track record by which the purchaser's vendor analysis team can make informed judgments.

Forming partnerships with fewer vendors on a long-term basis provides the opportunity to continuously improve quality and substantially reduce costs. Such partnerships involve formal agreements in which both the vendor and the buying organization commit to specific responsibilities to each other for their mutual benefit. These agreements usually involve long-term purchasing arrangements according to specified terms and can provide for the mutual sharing of expertise and information. Such partnerships permit members of the supply chain to eliminate redundancies in warehousing, packaging, labeling, transportation, and inventories.

Product Design

Products should be designed to use the fewest number of parts and to minimize production steps and risks. For example, a company found that it used 29 different types of screws to manufacture a single product. Downtime was excessive because screwdrivers were continuously being passed among workers. Changing to all of the same type screws significantly reduced production time.

In another example, fresh produce poses a problem for restaurant chains because unwashed lettuce poses safety hazards if the restaurant does not wash it properly. Prewashed, precut lettuce solves that problem; it simplifies in-house operations and reduces contaminant threats.[7]

Parts standardization does not necessarily result in identical finished products. Many companies are finding that they can produce a larger number of variations in finished products from just a few basic models. The production process is designed so that the vast proportion of parts and tasks can be standardized and added or performed prior to beginning variation work, which comes near the end of the process. Such differentiation is aided by flexible manufacturing systems and computer-integrated manufacturing, which are discussed later in this chapter.

Products should be designed for the quality desired and should require only a minimal number of engineering changes (ENCs) after the design is released for production. Approximately 80 to 90 percent of all product costs have been established by the time the production design team has completed only 25 to 50 percent of its work. An effective arrangement for a vendor–purchaser partnership is to have the vendor's engineers participate in the design phase of the purchasing company's product; an alternative is to provide product specifications and allow the vendor company to draft the design for approval.

If costs are to be significantly affected, any design changes must be made early in the process. As discussed earlier, engineering changes often create significant costs for non-value-added activities. Regardless of whether a company embraces JIT, time that is spent doing work that adds no value to the production process should be viewed as wasted. Effective activity analysis eliminates such non-value-added work and its unnecessary cost.

---

[7] Nancy Backus, "The Changing Face of Fast Food," *Food Product Design* (June 2004), *http://www.foodproductdesign.com/current/0604FFOC.html.*

From another point of view, good product design should address all concerns of the intended consumers, even the degree of recyclability of the product. For example, an automobile plant can be equipped to receive and take apart used-up models, remanufacture various parts, and then send them back into the marketplace. Thus, companies are considering remanufacturing as part of their design and processing capabilities.

Product Processing

In the production processing stage, one primary JIT consideration is the reduction of machine setup time so that processing can shift between products more often and at a lower cost. Costs of reducing setup time are more than recovered by the savings derived from reducing downtime, in-process inventory, and material handling as well as by increasing safety, flexibility, and ease of operation.

Most companies implementing rapid tool-setting procedures have been able to obtain setup times of 10 minutes or less. Such companies use a large number of low-cost setups rather than the traditional approach of a small number of more expensive setups. Under JIT, setup cost is considered almost purely variable rather than fixed as it was in the traditional manufacturing environment. One way to reduce machine setup time is to have workers perform as many setup tasks as possible while the machine is on-line and running. All unnecessary movements by workers or of material should be eliminated. Teams similar to pit-stop crews at auto races can be used to perform setup operations, with each team member handling a specialized task. Based on past results, it appears that with planning and education, setup times can be reduced by 50 percent or more.

Another essential part of product processing is the institution of high-quality standards because JIT has the goal of zero defects. Under just-in-time systems, quality is determined on a continual basis rather than at quality control checkpoints.

Building in quality checks, such as optical scanners, into product processing helps reduce the costs of obtaining high quality.

GETTY IMAGES

Continuous quality is achieved by first ensuring the quality of vendors' products at purchase point. Workers and machines (such as optical scanners) monitor quality during production. Controlling quality on an ongoing basis significantly reduces the cost of obtaining high quality. The JIT philosophy recognizes that it is less costly *not* to make mistakes than to correct them after they have been made. Unfortunately, quality control and scrap costs are often buried in production cost standards, making such costs hard to identify.

The ability to standardize work so that every worker performs according to stated procedures without variation, on time, every time is important in any process. Standard procedures indicate the most efficient way to conduct a particular task as well as to allow planning, supervising, and training tasks to be more efficiently and effectively conducted. Standardization also provides the ability to improve processes because tasks are performed with consistency. It is nearly impossible to improve an unstable process because it contains too much variation to be able to identify cause-and-effect relationships so that modifications can be made.

Plant Layout

Traditionally, manufacturing plants were designed to conform with functional areas; machines of like type and workers of similar specialized skills were placed together. For JIT to work effectively, the physical plant must be conducive to the

manufacturing cell

flow of goods and the organization of workers and to increasing the value added per square foot of plant space. Manufacturing plants should be designed to minimize material handling time, lead time, and movement of goods from raw material input to completion of the finished product. This goal often requires that machines or workers be arranged in S-shaped or U-shaped production groupings, commonly referred to as **manufacturing cells** (see Exhibit 17–8), to generate the most efficient and effective production process for a particular product type. This streamlined design allows for more visual controls to be instituted for problems such as excess inventory, production defects, equipment malfunctions, and out-of-place tools. It also allows for greater teamwork and quicker exchange of vital information.

The informational arrows in Exhibit 17–8 indicate how production is "pulled" through the system as successive downstream work centers issue their kanbans to acquire goods or services needed from their upstream suppliers to produce the goods or services demanded by their downstream "customers." Many pull systems today use electronic methods such as computer networks (rather than cards) to send requests for goods or services to upstream workstations.

Exhibit 17–9 illustrates the flow of three products through a factory before and after the redesign of factory floor space. In the "before" diagram, processes were grouped together by function, and products flowed through the plant depending on the type of processing needed to be performed. If the company uses JIT and a cellular design, substantial storage is eliminated because goods should be ordered only as needed. Products also flow through the plant more rapidly. Product 2 can use the same flow as Product 1 but skips the grinding process. When plant layout is redesigned to incorporate manufacturing cells, an opportunity arises for workers to broaden their skills and deepen their involvement in the process because of multiprocess handling. Workers are multiskilled, trained to monitor numerous machines, and more flexible and less bored because they are performing a variety of tasks. The ability to oversee an entire process can prompt employee

EXHIBIT 17–8
DEPICTION OF A MANUFACTURING CELL

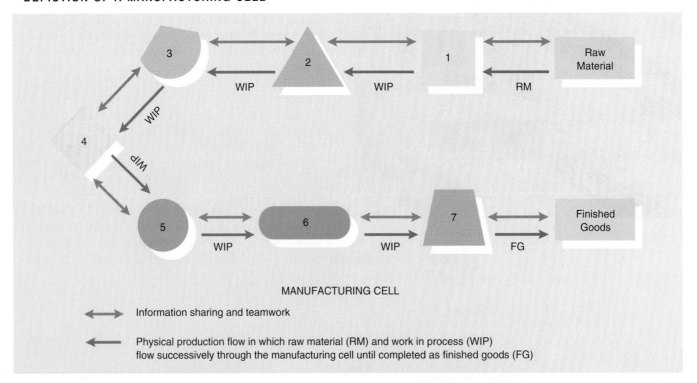

MANUFACTURING CELL

⟷ Information sharing and teamwork

⟵ Physical production flow in which raw material (RM) and work in process (WIP) flow successively through the manufacturing cell until completed as finished goods (FG)

EXHIBIT 17–9
FACTORY FLOOR SPACE REDESIGN

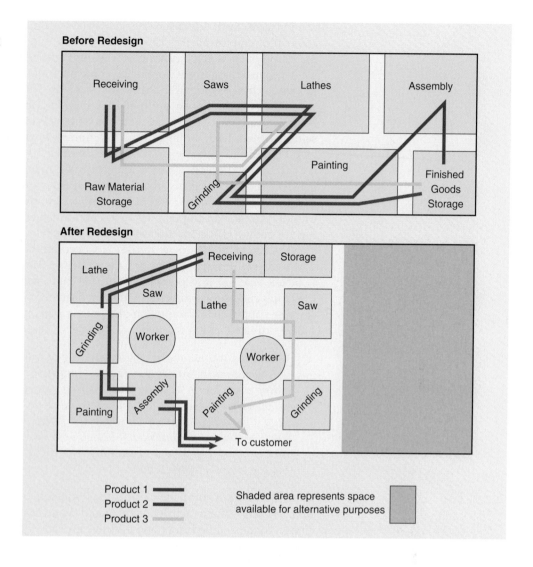

suggestions on improvement techniques that would not have been visible had the employee been working on a single facet of the process.[8]

Although highly automated equipment can run without direct labor involvement, it still requires monitoring. Employees must be available for oversight if an automated piece of equipment is programmed to stop when a given situation arises. The "situation" can be positive (a specified quantity of production has been reached) or negative (a quality defect has been indicated). The use of such programmed factory equipment is referred to as **autonomation** to distinguish it from automated factories in which the machinery is not programmed to stop when specified situations arise. Because machines "know" the certain conditions they are expected to sense, one worker is able to oversee several machines in a single manufacturing cell concurrently.

autonomation

LOGISTICS OF THE JIT ENVIRONMENT

In a JIT environment, a certain degree of logistical assistance is developing in the areas of information technology (IT), new support services, and new value-chain

[8] The average U.S. company receives about one suggestion per year from every six eligible employees. On the other hand, Japanese companies receive an average of 32 suggestions. See John Tschohl, "Be Bad: Employee Suggestion Program Cuts Costs, Increases Profit," *The Canadian Manager* (Winter 1998), pp. 23–24.

relationships. Such advancements can enhance the effectiveness and efficiency of companies employing JIT. These can be viewed in overriding support systems, in the preproduction stage, during production, and after production.

JIT can be employed within the context of more comprehensive management models such as TQM and the six-sigma method. The **six-sigma method** is a high-performance, data-driven approach to analyzing and solving the root causes of business problems. There are four steps for a successful application of the six-sigma method. First, an initial team determines what the organization knows about its customers and competitors; second, an executive action-planning workshop is conducted to develop a vision of how six-sigma can assist the organization to achieve its business goals; third, improvement workshops are held to familiarize personnel with methods and strategy and how they will be combined into the unit's business plan to push improved performance; and fourth, team-leader training is conducted for application of just-in-time.[9]

The **Internet business model** has become the new orthodoxy, transforming cost and service equations across the corporate landscape. This model refers to a business with (1) few physical assets, (2) little management hierarchy, and (3) a direct pipeline to customers. In this environment, electronic commerce is transforming supply-chain integration and delivering cost savings.[10] The benefits of this model are cited in the following quote:

Web-based technology allows the sharing of information, not just one-to-one—but one-to-many—and even many-to-many. . . . It is not simply a case of providing access to a Web site, but creating "extranets" where key customers and suppliers have access to "virtual private networks" that enable collaborative planning, forecasting, and replenishment. It is like traditional one-to-one customer/supplier scheduling, but now it has gone to one-to-many—and the supplier can turn around and do the same thing with all of its suppliers. It is basically linking the entire supply chain.[11]

Supply-chain management is the cooperative strategic planning, controlling, and problem solving activities conducted by a company and its vendors and customers to generate efficient and effective transfers of goods and services within the supply chain. Three levels of business-to-business (B2B) relationships exist in e-commerce: transactional, information-sharing, and collaboration:

Transactional relationships include the use of EDI to automate such things as purchase orders and invoices. At the information-sharing level, firms might exchange production schedules or details on the status of orders. At the highest level—collaboration—information is not just exchanged and transmitted, but the buyer and seller also jointly develop it. Generally this information deals with future product plans and needs. . . . However, unlike an information-sharing relationship, information is not shared on an FYI-basis, since either trading partner may change it until both parties agree.[12]

The use of e-commerce has advanced more rapidly for the acquisition of certain types of inputs than for others. For example, travel arrangements and office supplies and equipment are acquired much more frequently than manufacturing inputs, which are still most frequently acquired through traditional long-term supplier relationships.[13]

(margin notes) six-sigma method | Internet business model | supply-chain management

---

[9] Jerome A. Blakeslee, Jr., "Implementing the Six Sigma Solution," *Quality Progress* (July 1999), pp. 77ff.

[10] Nuala Moran, "E-Commerce Based Procurement Solutions for the Chemical Industry Eliminating Paper Trail," *Chemical Week* (August 18, 1999), pp. S9ff.

[11] John H. Sheridan, "Pushing Production to New Heights," *Industry Week* (September 21, 1998), pp. 43ff. Reprinted with permission from *Industry Week*. Copyright Penton Media, Inc., Cleveland, Ohio.

[12] Ibid.

[13] Kip R. Krumwiede, Monte R. Swain, and Kevin D. Stocks, "10 Ways E-Business Can Reduce Costs," *Strategic Finance* (July 2003), pp. 25–29.

GETTY IMAGES

Simulation software can improve processes by reducing inventory levels, run time, and setup time.

focused factory arrangement

In addition to the IT improvements in product design for manufacturability, simulation software is available to develop production systems that can enhance financial performance. The benefits of improving processes based on such simulations include greater throughput, reduced inventory levels, and further cost savings from reduced run time and setup time. Analyzing the important interaction and dependence that exist in production systems through software simulation can help answer questions such as these: (1) How many items can the system produce? (2) What will result if the equipment is rearranged? (3) Can delivery dates be met?[14] Additionally, real-time information processing software for finished goods inventory management can better serve the customer, minimize errors, and yield savings in labor, transportation, capital, and carrying costs.[15]

JIT companies often adopt **focused factory arrangements** to connect a vendor more closely to production operations. In such an arrangement, a vendor agrees to provide a limited number of products according to specifications or to perform a limited number of unique services for the JIT company. The vendor can be another division of the same organization or a separate, nonrelated company. Focused factory arrangements can also involve relocation or plant modernization by the vendor, and financial assistance from the JIT manufacturer can be available to recoup such investments. In addition, the vendor benefits from long-term supply contracts. One downside, especially for small vendors, of focused factory arrangements is that they could create overreliance on a single customer. A decline in the business of the primary customer or demands by that customer for lower prices can be disastrous for the focused factory.

ACCOUNTING IMPLICATIONS OF JIT

How does JIT provide an opportunity to simplify the accounting system?

Companies adopting a just-in-time inventory and/or flexible manufacturing system must be aware of the significant accounting implications such a system creates. A primary accounting impact occurs in variance analysis. Because a traditional standard cost accounting system is primarily historical in nature, its main goal is variance reporting so that variances can be analyzed for cause-and-effect relationships to eliminate future similar problems.

Variance reporting and analysis in JIT systems essentially disappear. Because most variances first appear physically (rather than financially), JIT mandates immediate recognition of variances so that causes can be ascertained and, if possible, promptly removed if unfavorable or exploited if favorable. JIT workers are trained to monitor quality and efficiency during, rather than at the end of, production. Further, if the firm is using statistical process controls, workers can predict the potential for production defects and take measures to prevent the defects from ever actually occurring. Therefore, the number and monetary significance of end-of-period variances being reported for managerial control should be limited.

Under a JIT system, long-term price agreements have been made with vendors, so material price variances should be minimal. The JIT accounting system should be designed so that purchase orders cannot be issued without manager approval for an amount higher than the designated price.[16] In this way, the variance amount and its cause are known in advance, providing an opportunity to eliminate the excess expenditure before it occurs. Calls can be made to the vendor to negotiate the price, or other vendors can be contacted for quotes.

---

[14] Mike C. Patterson, "A Simulation Analysis of Production Process Improvement," *Journal of Business Education* (November 1998), pp. 87ff.

[15] "Improving Productivity and Customer Service: Real Time Intelligent Information Processing Reaps Gains from Warehouse Inventory Management," *Plant* (October 23, 1995), pp. 16–17.

[16] This same procedure can be implemented under a traditional standard cost system as well as under a JIT system. However, it is less commonly found in a traditional system, but it is a requirement under JIT.

The ongoing use of specified or certified vendors also provides the ability to control material quality. It is becoming relatively common for companies to require that their vendors, regardless of global location, maintain quality standards and submit to quality assurance audits. Because better control of raw material quality is expected, few if any material quantity variances should be caused by substandard material. If usage standards are accurate based on established machine-paced efficiency, there should be virtually no favorable usage variance of material during production. Unfavorable use of material should be promptly detected because of ongoing machine and/or human observation of processing. When an unfavorable variance occurs, the manufacturing process is stopped to correct the error causing the unfavorable material usage variance to be minimized.

One type of quantity variance is not caused by errors but by engineering changes (ENCs) made to the product specifications. A JIT system has two comparison standards: an annual standard and a current standard. Design modifications would change the current standard but not the annual one. The annual standard is one of the bases for the preparation and execution of the company's master budget and is ordinarily kept intact because all of the financial plans and arrangements for the year covered by the master budget are predicated on the standards and plans used to prepare the master budget.

Such a procedure allows comparisons to be made that indicate the cost effects of engineering changes implemented after a product has begun to be manufactured. Exhibit 17–10 shows the calculation of a material quantity variance caused by an ENC. The portion of the total quantity variance caused by the engineering change ($2,700 U) is shown separately from that caused by efficiency ($540 F). Labor, overhead, and/or conversion can also have ENC variances.

Labor variances in an automated just-in-time system should be minimal if standard rates and times have been set appropriately. Labor time standards should be carefully evaluated after the implementation of a JIT production system. If the plant is not entirely automated, redesigning the physical layout and minimizing any non-value-added labor activities should decrease the direct labor time component.

EXHIBIT 17–10

MATERIAL VARIANCES UNDER A JIT SYSTEM

Annual standard	
8 feet of material M × $3.05	$24.40
5 feet of material N × $3.35	16.75
	$41.15
Current standard	
7 feet of material M × $3.05	$21.35
6 feet of material N × $3.35	20.10
	$41.45
Production during month	9,000 units
Usage during month	
64,800 feet of material M × $3.05	$197,640
52,200 feet of material N × $3.35	174,870
Total cost of material used	$372,510
Material quantity variance	
9,000 × 7 × $3.05	$192,150
9,000 × 6 × $3.35	180,900
Material cost at current standard	$373,050
Actual material cost	(372,510)
Material quantity variance	$ 540 F
Engineering change variance for material	
9,000 × 8 × $3.05	$219,600
9,000 × 5 × $3.35	150,750
Material cost at annual standard	$370,350
Material cost at current standard	(373,050)
ENC variance	$ 2,700 U

An accounting alternative that could occur in a JIT system is the use of a "conversion cost" category for purposes of cost control rather than the use of separate labor and overhead categories. This category becomes more useful as factories reduce the direct labor cost component through continuous improvements and automation. A standard departmental or manufacturing cell conversion cost per unit of product (or per hour of production time per manufacturing cell) can be calculated rather than individual standards for labor and overhead. Denominators in each case would be practical or theoretical capacity measured by an appropriate activity base.[17] If time were used as the base, the conversion cost for a day's production would equal the number of units produced multiplied by the standard number of production hours multiplied by the standard cost per hour. Variances would be determined by comparing actual cost to the designated standard. However, direct labor is a very small part of production in such an environment. Use of efficiency variances to evaluate workers can cause excess inventory because these workers are trying to "keep busy" to minimize this variance. Therefore, direct labor efficiency variances in this setting could be counterproductive.

In addition to minimizing and adjusting the variance calculations, a JIT system can have a major impact on inventory accounting. Companies employing JIT production processes would no longer require a separate raw material inventory classification because material would be acquired only when and as production occurs. Instead, JIT companies could use a Raw and In-Process (RIP) Inventory account.

The focus of accounting in a JIT system is on the plant's output to the customer.[18] Each sequential activity in a production process depends on the previous activity; thus, any problems will quickly cause the system to stop the production process. Individual daily accounting for the costs of production will no longer be necessary because all costs should be at standard, and variations will be observed and corrected almost immediately.

Additionally, fewer costs need to be allocated to products because more costs can be traced directly to their related output in a JIT system. Costs are incurred in specified cells on a per-hour or per-unit basis. In a comprehensive JIT system, energy is considered a direct production cost because there should be a minimum of machine downtime or unplanned idle time for workers. Virtually the only costs still being allocated are costs associated with the structure (building depreciation, rent, taxes, and insurance) and machinery depreciation. The reduction of allocations provides more useful measures of cost control and performance evaluation than have been traditionally available.

backflush costing

Backflush costing is a streamlined cost accounting method that speeds up, simplifies, and minimizes accounting effort in an environment that minimizes inventory balances, requires few allocations, uses standard costs, and has few variances from standard. During the period, this costing method records purchases of raw material and accumulates actual conversion costs. Then, at a predetermined trigger point such as (1) at completion of production or (2) upon the sale of goods, an entry is made to allocate the total costs incurred to Cost of Goods Sold and to Finished Goods Inventory using standard production costs.

Cranberry Manufacturing makes high-tech ceramic products and is used to illustrate just-in-time system backflush entries. To establish a foundation set of transactions from which to illustrate subsequent alternative recordings in a backflush costing system, entries for one of Cranberry Manufacturing's products are presented in Exhibit 17–11. The product's standard production cost is $65.25. A long-term contract with Cranberry's direct material supplier indicates a cost of $19.25 per unit, so no material price variance exists at point of purchase. Beginning inventories for July are assumed to be zero. Standard conversion cost per unit is $46.00.

---

[17] Practical or theoretical capacity is the appropriate measure because the goal of JIT is virtually continuous processing. In a highly automated plant, these capacities more closely reflect world-class status than does expected annual capacity.
[18] A company may wish to measure output of each manufacturing cell or work center rather than plant output. Such measurements can indicate problems in a given area but do not correlate with the JIT philosophy of the team approach, plantwide attitude, and total cost picture.

EXHIBIT 17–11

BASIC ENTRIES USED TO ILLUSTRATE BACKFLUSH COSTING

Cranberry Manufacturing's standard production cost per unit:

Direct material	$19.25
Conversion	46.00
Total cost	$65.25

No beginning inventories exist.

(1) Purchased $392,500 of direct material in July:

Raw and In-Process Inventory	392,500	
Accounts Payable		392,500

To record material purchased at standard cost under a long-term agreement with supplier.

(2) Incurred $921,750 of conversion costs in July:

Conversion Costs	921,750	
Various accounts		921,750

To record conversion costs; various accounts include Wages Payable for direct and indirect labor, Accumulated Depreciation, Supplies, etc.

(3) Applied conversion costs to RIP for 20,000 units completed:

Raw and In-Process Inventory (20,000 × $46.00)	920,000	
Conversion Costs		920,000

To apply labor and overhead to units completed.

(4) Transferred 20,000 units of production in July:

Finished Goods Inventory (20,000 × $65.25)	1,305,000	
Raw and In-Process Inventory		1,305,000

To transfer completed goods from WIP.

(5) Sold 19,800 units on account in July for $110 each:

Accounts Receivable (19,800 × $110)	2,178,000	
Sales		2,178,000

To record goods sold on account.

Cost of Goods Sold (19,800 × $65.25)	1,291,950	
Finished Goods Inventory		1,291,950

To record cost of goods sold.

Ending inventories:

Raw and In-Process Inventory ($1,312,500 − $1,305,000)	$7,500
Finished Goods Inventory ($1,305,000 − $1,291,950)	$13,050

In addition, there are underapplied conversion costs of $1,750 ($921,750 − $920,000).

The following selected T-accounts summarize the activity presented in Exhibit 17–11.

Raw and In Process Inventory

(1)	392,500	(4)	1,305,000
(3)	920,000		
Bal.	7,500		

Conversion Costs

(2)	921,750	(3)	920,000

Finished Goods Inventory

(4)	1,305,000	(5)	1,291,950
Bal.	13,050		

Cost of Goods Sold

(5)	1,291,950		

Accounts Receivable

(5)	2,178,000	

Sales

		(5)	2,178,000

Four alternatives to the entries presented in Exhibit 17–11 follow. First, if production time were extremely short, Cranberry Manufacturing might not journalize raw material purchases until completion of production. In such a case—in addition to recording entries (2) and (5) in Exhibit 17–11—the entry to replace entries (1), (3), and (4) follows. Completion of the finished goods is the trigger point for this entry.

Raw and In-Process Inventory	7,500	
Finished Goods Inventory (20,000 × $65.25)	1,305,000	
Accounts Payable		392,500
Conversion Costs (20,000 × $46.00)		920,000
To record completed production and accounts payable, and adjust RIP inventory account valuation.		

Second, if goods were shipped immediately to customers on completion, Cranberry Manufacturing could use another alternative in which the entries to complete and sell would be combined. Doing so would replace entries (3), (4), and the first element in (5) in Exhibit 17–11. Entries (1), (2), and the second element in (5) in Exhibit 17–11 would still be needed. Sale of the products is the trigger point for this entry.

Finished Goods Inventory (200 × $65.25)	13,050	
Cost of Goods Sold (19,800 × $65.25)	1,291,950	
Raw and In-Process Inventory (20,000 × $19.25)		385,000
Conversion Costs (20,000 × $46.00)		920,000
To record sale of products and adjust RIP and FG inventory account valuations.		

The third alternative reflects the ultimate JIT system, in which only one entry is made—other than recording entry (2) in Exhibit 17–11. Sale of the products is the trigger point for this entry. For Cranberry Manufacturing, this entry would be

Raw and In-Process Inventory (minimal overpurchases)	7,500	
Finished Goods Inventory (minimal overproduction)	13,050	
Cost of Goods Sold	1,291,950	
Accounts Payable		392,500
Conversion Costs		920,000
To adjust inventory account valuations and record accounts payable.		

A fourth alternative charges all costs to the Cost of Goods Sold account, with a subsequent backflush of costs to the Raw and In-Process Inventory and the Finished Goods Inventory accounts at the end of the period. The following entries replace entries (1), (3), (4), and (5) shown in Exhibit 17–11. Entry (2) in Exhibit 17–11 would still be made; product sale is the trigger point for this entry.

Cost of Goods Sold	1,312,500	
Accounts Payable		392,500
Conversion Costs		920,000
To charge all material, labor, and overhead costs to CGS.		

Raw and In-Process Inventory	7,500	
Finished Goods Inventory	13,050	
Cost of Goods Sold		20,550
To adjust inventory account valuations.		

Implementation of the just-in-time philosophy can cause significant cost reductions and productivity improvements. Even within a single company, however, all inventory situations do not necessarily have to be on a just-in-time system. Management should consider the costs of and benefits provided by any inventory control system before making an installation decision. One qualitative benefit that must be quantified in the decision process is that the use of JIT allows workers as well as managers to concentrate on providing quality service to customers.

Flexible Manufacturing Systems and Computer-Integrated Manufacturing

LO.7
WHAT ARE FLEXIBLE MANUFACTURING SYSTEMS?

Many manufacturers have changed their manufacturing philosophy in the past few decades. Causes of change include (1) automated equipment and a cellular plant layout, (2) computer hardware and software technology, and (3) new manufacturing systems and philosophies such as JIT and activity-based management.

Traditionally, most manufacturing firms employed long production runs to make thousands of identical models of the same products; this process was encouraged by the idea of economies of scale. After each run, the machines would be stopped and a slow and expensive setup would be made for the next massive production run to begin. Now, many companies are using a new generation of manufacturing known as **flexible manufacturing systems (FMSs)**.

flexible manufacturing system (FMS)

An FMS involves a network of robots and material conveyance devices monitored and controlled by computers that allows for rapid production and responsiveness to changes in production needs. Two or more FMSs connected via a host computer and an information networking system are generally referred to as **computer-integrated manufacturing (CIM)**. Exhibit 17–12 contrasts the dimensions of a traditional manufacturing system with an FMS. Although an FMS is typically associated with short-volume production runs, many companies (such as **Werthan Packaging**, **Allen-Bradley**, and **Cummins Engine**) use CIM for high-volume lines.

computer-integrated manufacturing (CIM)

FMSs are used in modular factories and can customize output upon request by customers because the systems have the ability to introduce new products quickly, produce in small lot sizes, make rapid machine and tool setups, and communicate and process large amounts of information. Information is transferred through an electronic network to computers that control the robots performing most of the production activities. The system functions with on-line, real-time production flow control using fiber optics and local-area networks. Companies are able to operate at high speeds and can quickly and inexpensively stop producing one item and start producing another, making it possible to minimize product costs while building a large assortment of high-quality products to offer its customers.

The system can operate in a "lights-out" environment and never tire; thus, the need for direct labor is diminished. However, because they handle a greater variety of tasks than the narrowly specialized workers of earlier manufacturing eras, workers in a company employing an FMS must be more highly trained than those working in traditional manufacturing environments. Persons with greater authority and responsibility manage the manufacturing cells. This increase in control occurs

EXHIBIT 17–12

COMPARISON OF TRADITIONAL MANUFACTURING AND FLEXIBLE MANUFACTURING SYSTEM

Factor	Traditional Manufacturing	Flexible Manufacturing System
Product variety	Limited	Extensive
Response time to market needs	Slow	Rapid
Worker tasks	Specialized	Diverse
Production runs	Long	Short
Lot sizes	Massive	Small
Performance rewards basis	Individual	Team
Setups	Slow and expensive	Fast and inexpensive
Product life-cycle expectations	Long	Short
Work area control	Centralized	Decentralized
Production activity	Labor intensive	Technology intensive
Information requirements	Batch based	On line, real time
Worker knowledge of technology	Low to medium	High

because production and production scheduling changes happen so rapidly on the shop floor that an FMS relies on immediate decisions by persons who "live there" and have a grasp of the underlying facts and conditions.

Lean Enterprises

lean manufacturing

Lean manufacturing refers to making only those items in demand by customers and making those items without waste. Lean manufacturing originated in post-World War II Japan when many manufacturing resources such as materials, factory equipment, and warehouse space were scarce. Thus, managers of Japanese enterprises were compelled to develop practices that minimized waste and consumption of resources. The lean enterprise wields many of the management tools discussed earlier in this chapter such as cellular manufacturing, JIT, six sigma, TQM, and team-based production. One of the major themes in lean enterprises is the same as that of just-in-time: Inventory needs to be eliminated as much as possible because it hides production problems and wastes resources.

Lean enterprises, such as Jezek Machine & Tool Co., put pressure on the entire value chain to minimize waste, maximize quality, eliminate activities that add costs but not value to products, and shorten the lead time for delivering products and services. Central to the success of the lean enterprise and its value chain are leveraging technology and training employees. Technology allows for short cycle times, high-quality products, and quick changeovers of production lines. Well-trained employees manage the technology, identify ways to become more efficient, and focus on satisfying the needs of customers. Lean enterprises have raised the competitive bar in many industries through their abilities to quickly develop and sell high-quality products having minimal defects. For some industries, these competitive pressures have led to reduced product life cycles and dramatically reduced time to market for new products.

The theory of constraints is another important production management tool that is used by lean enterprises.

THEORY OF CONSTRAINTS

LO.8
HOW CAN THE THEORY OF CONSTRAINTS HELP IN DETERMINING PRODUCTION FLOW?

theory of constraints (TOC)
constraint

The **theory of constraints (TOC)** can help management reduce cycle time. This theory indicates that the flow of goods through a production process cannot be at a faster rate than the slowest constraint in the process.[19] A **constraint** is anything that confines or limits the ability of a person or machine to perform a project or function.

Production limitations in a manufacturing environment are caused by human, material, and machine constraints. Some constraints relate to process speed, while others relate to absolute production limits such as availability of materials or machine hours. Still other constraints relate to humans and any inabilities they have to understand, react, or perform at some particular rate of speed. These constraints cannot be totally overcome (because humans will never be able to work at the speed of an automated machine) but can be reduced through proper hiring and training. Because the labor content contained in products is declining rapidly as automation increases, constraints caused by machines are often of more concern than human constraints in reducing cycle time.

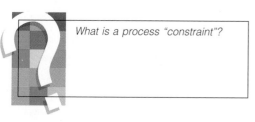
What is a process "constraint"?

bottleneck

Machine constraints, also called **bottlenecks**, are points at which the processing levels are sufficiently slow to cause the other processing mechanisms in the network to experience idle time. Bottlenecks cause the processing of an activity to be impeded. Even a totally automated, "lights-out" process will have some

---

[19] The theory of constraints was introduced to business environments by Eliyahu Goldratt and Jeff Cox in the book *The Goal* (New Haven, CT: North River Press, Inc./Spectrum Publishing Company, 1986).

constraints because all machines do not operate at the same speed or handle the same capacity. Therefore, the constraints must be identified and worked around.

See Exhibit 17–13 for a simplified illustration of a constraint in a production process. Although Machine 1 can process 90,000 pounds of raw material in an hour, Machine 2 can handle only 40,000 pounds. Of the 70,000 pounds of input, 30,000 pounds of processed material must wait at the constraining machine after an hour of processing. The constraint's effect on production is obvious, but the implications are not quite as clear. Managers have a tendency to want to see machines working, not sitting idle. Consider what this tendency would mean if the desired output were 450,000 pounds rather than 70,000. If Machine 1 were kept in continual use, all 450,000 pounds would be processed through Machine 1 in five hours. However, a backlog of 250,000 pounds [450,000 − 5(40,000)] of processed material would now be waiting at Machine 2! All of this material would require storage space and create an additional cost of a non-value-added activity.

Machine constraints also impact quality control. Managers normally choose quality control points to follow the completion of some particular process. When constraint points are known, quality control points should *always* be placed in front of constrained processes. "If you scrap a part before it reaches the bottleneck, all you have lost is a scrapped part. But if you scrap the part after it's passed through the bottleneck, you have lost time that cannot be recovered."[20]

As soon as constraints are known, a company should make the best use of the time or productive capacity the constrained processes provide and limit the constraints' impacts on performance. Options to reduce limitations, such as adding more machines to perform the constrained activity or processing material through other machines, should be investigated. Managing constraints is a process of continuous improvement.

EXHIBIT 17–13
PRODUCTION CONSTRAINT

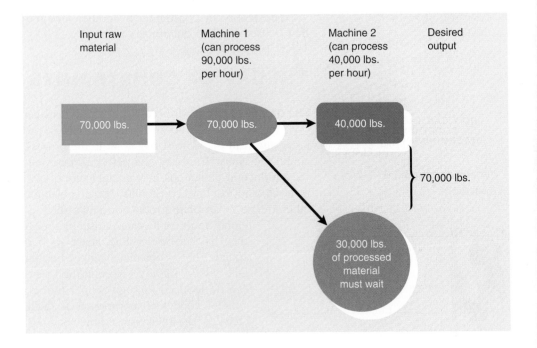

[20] Ibid., p. 156.

Revisiting

The philosophy of firms regarding inventory has changed remarkably in the past 25 years. No longer is inventory thought to be an asset; rather, it is thought to be a nonproductive use of precious working capital. With the change in attitude have come changes in the interactions of firms within supply chains. Coordination of the activities of each link in the supply chain have become much tighter and more interdependent. Competition is now as much between supply chains as between individual firms. In addition, each complete supply chain is now exposed to the frailties of the weakest link—as is the final customer.

Because manufacturing firms are adopting practices that reduce investment in inventory, the buffers in the supply chain have been reduced or eliminated. Without such buffers, firms that seek to be vendors of choice to lean manufacturing firms must develop the capability to deliver flawless products on

time, in small quantities, and with short lead times. Failure of parts and materials to arrive on the production floor as scheduled interrupts production and delays deliveries to customers. Even among lean manufacturers, Jezek Tool & Machine has been designated as a preferred provider by many of its world-class customers.

Jezek's competitive position has been achieved by managing two key variables. First, the company has invested heavily in technology to quickly develop and produce high-quality products. Second, the company has maintained a loyal and well-trained group of employees. Many of the skilled machinists and operators of the computer-controlled machinery have been with the firm for 25 years or more. In fact, in 2002, the company was purchased from the Jezek family by Al Muschiatti, an employee who had worked for the company for 40 years and had served as the plant manager.

Source: *http://www.jezektool.com; http://www.nceo.org/library/obm_albums.html* (accessed August 24, 2004).

Appendix

Economic Order Quantity and Related Issues

LO.9
**HOW ARE ECONOMIC ORDER
QUANTITY, REORDER POINT,
AND SAFETY STOCK
DETERMINED AND USED?**

The concepts of economic order quantity and economic production run are used, respectively, for purchasing and manufacturing decisions.

Economic Order Quantity

economic order quantity (EOQ)

Companies making purchasing (rather than production) decisions often compute the **economic order quantity (EOQ)**, which represents the least costly number of units to order. EOQ indicates the optimal balance between ordering and carrying costs by mathematically equating total ordering costs to total carrying costs. EOQ is a tool that is used in conjunction with traditional "push" production and inventory management systems. Because EOQ implies acquiring and holding inventory before it is needed, it is incompatible with "pull" systems such as JIT.

Purchasing managers should first determine which supplier can offer the appropriate quality of goods at the best price in the most reliable manner. After the supplier is selected, the most economical inventory quantity to order—at a single time—is determined. The EOQ formula is

$$EOQ = \sqrt{\frac{(2QO)}{C}}$$

where EOQ = economic order quantity in units
        Q = estimated annual quantity used in units
              (can be found in the annual purchases budget)
        O = estimated cost of placing one order
        C = estimated cost to carry 1 unit in stock for one year

Note that unit purchase cost is not included in the EOQ formula. Purchase cost relates to the question of from whom to buy, which is considered separately from the question of how many to buy at a single time. Inventory unit purchase cost does not affect the other EOQ formula costs except to the extent that opportunity cost is calculated on the basis of investment.

All inventory-related costs must be evaluated when purchasing or production decisions are made. The costs of ordering and carrying inventory offset each other when estimating the economic order quantity.

Cranberry Manufacturing uses 64,000 pounds of a particular material in producing ceramic products. The cost associated with placing each order is $40. The carrying cost of 1 pound of the material is $2 per year. Therefore, Cranberry Manufacturing's EOQ for this material is calculated as follows:

$$EOQ = \sqrt{\frac{(2 \times 64{,}000 \times \$40)}{\$2}} = 1{,}600 \text{ kilos}$$

Economic Production Run

economic production run (EPR)

In a manufacturing company, managers are concerned with how many units to produce in a batch in addition to how many units (of raw material) to buy. The EOQ formula can be modified to calculate the appropriate number of units to manufacture in an **economic production run (EPR)**. This estimate reflects the production quantity that minimizes the total costs of setting up a production run and carrying a unit in stock for one year. The only change in the EOQ formula is that the terms of the equation are redefined as manufacturing rather than purchasing costs. The formula is

$$EPR = \sqrt{\frac{(2QS)}{C}}$$

where EPR = economic production run quantity
        Q = estimated annual quantity to be produced in units
              (can be found in annual production budget)
        S = estimated cost of setting up a production run
        C = estimated cost to carry 1 unit in stock for one year

One product manufactured by Cranberry Manufacturing is a ceramic sink. A total of 183,750 units of this product are made each year. The setup cost for a ceramic sink run is $240, and the annual carrying cost for each sink is $5. The economic production run quantity of 4,200 sinks is determined as

$$EPR = \sqrt{\frac{(2 \times 183{,}750 \times \$240)}{\$5}} = 4{,}200$$

The cost differences among various run sizes around the EPR might not be significant. If such costs were insignificant, management would have a range of acceptable, economical production run quantities.

The critical element in using either an EOQ or EPR model is to properly identify costs, especially carrying costs. This process is often very difficult, and some costs (such as those for facilities, operations, administration, and accounting) traditionally viewed as irrelevant fixed costs could, in actuality, be long-term relevant variable costs. Also, the EOQ model does not provide any direction for managers attempting to control all of the separate costs that collectively compose ordering and carrying costs. By considering only the trade-off between ordering and carrying costs, the EOQ model does not lead managers to consider inventory management alternatives that can simultaneously reduce both categories of costs.

Additionally, as companies significantly reduce the necessary setup time (and thus cost) for operations and move toward a "stockless" inventory policy, a more comprehensive cost perspective will indicate a substantially smaller cost per setup and a substantially larger annual carrying cost. These changes will reduce the EOQ and EPR.

Order Point and Safety Stock

order point

usage

lead time

safety stock

The economic order quantity or production run model indicates how many units to order or produce, respectively. Managers are also concerned with the **order point**, which reflects the level of inventory that triggers the placement of an order for additional units. Determination of the order point is based on three factors: usage, lead time, and safety stock. **Usage** refers to the quantity of inventory used or sold each day. The **lead time** for an order is the time in days it takes from placing an order to obtaining or producing the goods. Many times companies can project a constant, average figure for both usage and lead time. The quantity of inventory kept on hand by a company in the event of fluctuating usage or unusual delays in lead time is called **safety stock**.

If usage is entirely constant and lead time is known with certainty, the order point equals daily usage multiplied by lead time:

$$\text{Order Point} = \text{Daily Usage} \times \text{Lead Time}$$

As an example, assume that Cranberry Manufacturing produces ceramic art objects for sale to a chain of department stores. Cranberry Manufacturing uses 5,000 pounds of silica sand per day, and the supplier can have the material to Cranberry Manufacturing in 2 days. When the stock of silica sand reaches 10,000 pounds, Cranberry Manufacturing should reorder.

The order point formula minimizes the dollars a company has invested in its inventory. Orders would arrive at precisely the time the inventory reached zero. This formula, however, does not take into consideration unusual events such as variations in production schedules, defective products being provided by suppliers, erratic shipping schedules of the supplier, and late arrival of units shipped. To provide for such events, managers carry a "buffer" safety stock of inventory to protect the company from being out of stock. When a safety stock is maintained, the order point formula becomes:

$$\text{Order Point} = (\text{Daily Usage} \times \text{Lead Time}) + \text{Safety Stock}$$

Safety stock size should be determined based on how crucial the item is to production or to retail sales, the item's purchase cost, and the amount of uncertainty related to both usage and lead time.

One way to estimate the quantity of safety stock is to allow one factor to vary from the norm. For example, either excess usage during normal lead time or normal usage during an excess lead time can be considered in the safety stock calculation. Assume that Cranberry Manufacturing never uses more than 8,000 pounds of silica sand in one day. One estimate of the necessary safety stock is 6,000 pounds, computed as follows:

Maximum daily usage	8,000 pounds
Normal daily usage	(5,000) pounds
Excess usage	3,000 pounds
Lead time	× 2 days
Safety stock	6,000 pounds

Using this estimate of safety stock, Cranberry Manufacturing would reorder silica sand when 16,000 pounds (10,000 original order point + 6,000 safety stock) were on hand.

Pareto Inventory Analysis

Pareto inventory analysis

Unit cost commonly affects the degree of control that should be maintained over an inventory item. As unit cost increases, internal controls (such as inventory access) are typically tightened and a perpetual inventory system is more often used. Recognition of cost-benefit relationships can result in a **Pareto inventory analysis**, which separates inventory into three groups based on annual cost-to-volume usage.

Items having the highest value are referred to as A items; C items represent the lowest dollar volume of usage. All other inventory items are designated as B items. See Exhibit 17–14 for the results of a typical Pareto inventory analysis: 20 percent of the inventory items (A items) accounts for 80 percent of the cost; an additional 30 percent of the items (B items), taken together with the first 20 percent (the A items), accounts for 90 percent of the cost; and the remaining 50 percent of the items (C items) accounts for the remaining 10 percent of the cost.

Once inventory is categorized as A, B, or C, management can determine the best inventory control method for items in each category. A-type inventory should require a perpetual inventory system and would be a likely candidate for just-in-time purchasing techniques that minimize the funds tied up in inventory investment. The highest control procedures would be assigned to these items. Such a treatment reflects the financial accounting concept of materiality.

EXHIBIT 17–14
PARETO INVENTORY ANALYSIS

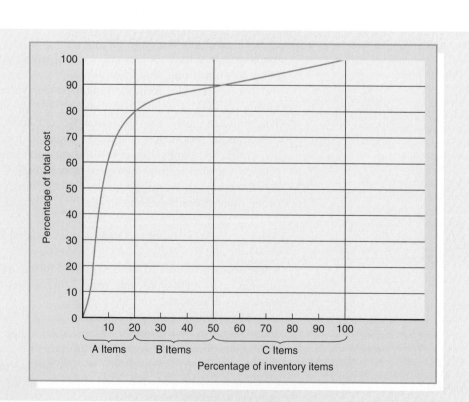

Items falling into the C category need only periodic inventory control procedures and can use a two-bin or red-line system. Under a **two-bin system**, two containers (or stacks) of inventory are available for production needs. When production begins to use materials in the second container, a purchase order is placed to refill the first container. In a **red-line system**, a red line is painted on the inventory container at the point at which to reorder. Both systems require that production needs and estimates of receipt time from suppliers be fairly accurate.

Having the additional container or stack of inventory on hand is considered to be reasonable based on the insignificant dollar amount of investment involved with C category items. The control placed on C items is probably minimal also because of the lack of materiality of the inventory cost. The type of inventory system (perpetual or periodic) and the level of internal control associated with items in the B category depend on management's judgment. Such judgment is based on the significance of the item to the production process, speed of response time of suppliers, and estimates of benefits to be gained by increased accounting or access controls. Computers have made additional controls over inventory easier and more cost beneficial.

Comprehensive Review Module

Chapter Summary

1. The most important value chain relationships for a firm are those

   - with suppliers in order to get the highest quality inputs, on time, at a competitive price.

   - with customers in order to deliver the features, quality, and value that lead to customer satisfaction.

   - within the firm in order to coordinate production activities.

2. Managing inventory costs is important to the firm because inventory

   - produces no value for the firm until it is sold.

   - can hide inefficiencies in production activities.

   - is a significant investment.

3. Two systems for managing inventory and controlling production are the "push" and "pull" systems:

   - push systems produce goods to satisfy a production schedule based on economic production run concepts.

   - pull systems produce goods only in response to current customer demand.

4. Product life cycles affect profitability because

   - costs vary across the product life cycles, although most costs are determined in the development stage of the life cycle.

   - sales volume and prices vary across the life-cycle stages.

5. Target costing

   - is calculated as estimated selling price minus acceptable profit margin.

   - is a tool to manage production costs

     ➤ in the development stage of the product life cycle.

     ➤ by developing an estimate of an "allowable" production cost (target cost) based on the estimated sales price of the product.

   - forces managers to align the expected production cost with the target cost.

   - is continually reduced over a product's life cycle so as to spur continuous improvement.

6. Just-in-time (JIT) is a philosophy that states production should not occur until a customer demands the product.

   - Successful implementation of JIT requires

     ➤ elimination of non-value-adding activities.

     ➤ a focus on continuous improvement.

     ➤ persistent efforts to reduce inventory.

     ➤ a focus on improving quality of processes.

     ➤ high-quality inputs from vendors.

   - JIT can cause modifications to the accounting system to recognize

     ➤ variances immediately upon occurence rather than at period-end.

     ➤ that inventories can be sufficiently small to no longer justify separate accounting for raw, in-process, and finished goods. Simpler systems, such as backflush costing, can be adopted.

7. Flexible manufacturing systems

   - integrate computer systems with automated production equipment.

   - are often used in plants organized for cellular manufacturing.

   - minimize the time required to set up for production.

   - are ideal for low-volume, high-quality products.

8. The theory of constraints is a tool to reduce cycle time by

   - maximizing the flow of products through production bottlenecks.

   - overcoming constraints in the flow of goods through a production system.

Solution Strategies

TARGET COSTING

Target Cost = Expected Long-Range Selling Price − Desired Profit

Compare predicted total life-cycle cost to target cost; if life-cycle cost is higher, determine ways to reduce it.

Material and Labor Variances under JIT

Two standards can exist:

1. an annual standard (set and held constant for the year) and
2. a current standard (based on design modifications or engineering changes).

Generally, firms have minimal, if any, material price variances because prices are set by long-term contracts. A labor rate variance can exist and is calculated in the traditional manner.

Material Quantity Variance

Actual material cost
− Material cost at current standard
Material quantity variance

Engineering Change Variance for Material

Material cost at annual standard
− Material cost at current standard
ENC variance

Labor Efficiency Variance

(Actual labor hours × current standard rate)
− (Standard labor hours × current standard rate)
Labor efficiency variance

Engineering Change Variance for Labor

(Exists only if a change occurs in the mix of labor used to manufacture the product or through the automation of processes.)

(Standard labor hours × annual standard rate)
− (Standard labor hours × current standard rate)
ENC variance

(*APPENDIX*) ECONOMIC ORDER QUANTITY

$$EOQ = \sqrt{\frac{(2QO)}{C}}$$

where EOQ = economic order quantity in units
Q = estimated annual quantity to be used in units
O = estimated cost of placing one order
C = estimated cost to carry one unit in stock for one year

(*APPENDIX*) ECONOMIC PRODUCTION RUN

$$EPR = \sqrt{\frac{(2QS)}{C}}$$

where EPR = economic production run quantity

Q = estimated annual quantity to be produced in units

S = estimated cost of setting up a production run

C = estimated cost to carry one unit in stock for one year

(APPENDIX) ORDER POINT

Order Point = (Daily Usage × Lead Time) + Safety Stock

Demonstration Problem 1

Topaway Mfg. has designed a new consumer product, a floor cleaner and wax, that is expected to have a five-year life cycle. Based on its market research, Topaway's management has determined that the new product should be packaged in 32 ounce containers, with a selling price of $6 in the first three years and $4 during the last two years. Unit sales are expected as follows:

Year 1	300,000 units
Year 2	400,000
Year 3	600,000
Year 4	400,000
Year 5	250,000

Variable selling costs are expected to be $1 per package throughout the product's life. Annual fixed selling and administrative costs are estimated to be $500,000. Topaway management desires a 25 percent profit margin on selling price.

Required:

a. Compute the life-cycle target cost to manufacture the product. (Round to the nearest cent.)

b. If Topaway anticipates the new product will cost $3 per unit to manufacture in the first year, what is the maximum that manufacturing cost can be in the following four years? (Round to the nearest cent.)

c. Suppose that Topaway engineers determine that expected manufacturing cost per unit over the product life cycle is $2.25. What actions might the company take to reduce this cost?

Solution to the Demonstration Problem 1

a. Step 1—Determine total product life revenue:

Year 1	300,000 × $6 =	$ 1,800,000
Year 2	400,000 × $6 =	2,400,000
Year 3	600,000 × $6 =	3,600,000
Year 4	400,000 × $4 =	1,600,000
Year 5	250,000 × $4 =	1,000,000
Total revenue		$10,400,000

Step 2—Determine average unit revenue during product life (AR):

$$AR = \text{Total Revenue} \div \text{Total Product Life Units}$$
$$= \$10,400,000 \div 1,950,000 \text{ units}$$
$$= \$5.33$$

Step 3—Determine average total fixed selling and administrative cost (ATFS&A):

$$\text{ATFS\&A} = (5 \text{ years} \times \$500,000) \div 1,950,000 \text{ units} = \$1.28$$

Step 4—Determine unit selling and administrative cost (US&AC):

$$US\&AC = ATFS\&A + \text{Variable Selling Cost}$$
$$= \$1.28 + \$1.00$$
$$= \$2.28$$

Step 5—Calculate target cost (TC):

$$TC = AR - 0.25(AR) - US\&AC$$
$$= \$5.33 - \$1.33 - \$2.28$$
$$= \$1.72$$

b.　Step 1—Determine total allowable cost over product life:

$$1{,}950{,}000 \text{ units} \times \$1.72 = \$3{,}354{,}000$$

Step 2—Determine expected total production cost in first year:

$$\$3 \times 300{,}000 \text{ units} = \$900{,}000$$

Step 3—Determine allowable unit cost in last four years:

$$(\$3{,}354{,}000 - \$900{,}000) \div 1{,}650{,}000 \text{ units} = \$1.49$$

c.　The following actions are potential options for the company:
- Product design and/or production processes can be changed to reduce costs. Cost tables can be used to provide information on the impact of using different input resources, processes, or design specifications.
- The 25 percent acceptable profit margin can be reduced.
- Topaway can suspend consideration of the project at the present time.

Demonstration Problem 2

Hondo Corp manufactures home-improvement products in a JIT environment. The annual and current material standards for one of the company's products follows.

Annual Material Standards

4 pounds of material 1 × $3.75	$15.00
12 pounds of material 2 × $2.25	27.00
	$42.00

Current Material Standards

8 pounds of material 1 × $3.75	$30.00
8 pounds of material 2 × $2.25	18.00
	$48.00

The current material standards differ from the original because an engineering change was made near the end of August. During September, the company manufactured 1,000 units of product and used 7,500 pounds of Material 1 and 8,200 pounds of Material 2. All material is acquired at the standard cost per pound.

Required:
a.　Calculate the material variance and the ENC material variance.
b.　Explain the effect of the engineering change on product cost.

Solution to Demonstration Problem 2

a.

Actual Material Usage

Material 1: 7,500 × $3.75	$28,125
Material 2: 8,200 × $2.25	18,450
Total material cost	$46,575

Material Cost at Current Standards

Material 1: 1,000 × 8 × $3.75	$30,000
Material 2: 1,000 × 8 × $2.25	18,000
Total material cost	$48,000

Material Cost at Annual Standards

Material 1: 1,000 × 4 × $3.75	$15,000
Material 2: 1,000 × 12 × $2.25	27,000
Total material cost	$42,000

Material cost at current standard	$48,000
Actual material cost	(46,575)
Material quantity variance	$ 1,425 F

Material cost at annual standard	$42,000
Material cost at current standard	(48,000)
ENC variance	$ 6,000 U

b. The effect of the engineering change was to substitute higher-priced material 1 for lower-priced material 2. The financial effect of that change was to increase expected production costs for August by $6,000. However, the increase in costs could have been offset by an increase in price, assuming the change in mix of materials increased product quality.

Key Terms

autonomation *(p. 707)*
backflush costing *(p. 711)*
bottleneck *(p. 715)*
computer-integrated manufacturing
　(CIM) *(p. 714)*
constraint *(p. 715)*
cost table *(p. 699)*
economic order quantity (EOC)
　(p. 717)
economic production run (EPR)
　(p. 718)
flexible manufacturing system
　(FMS) *(p. 714)*
focused factory arrangement
　(p. 709)

Internet business model
　(p. 708)
just-in-time *(p. 701)*
just-in-time manufacturing system
　(p. 701)
kaizen costing *(p. 699)*
kanban *(p. 701)*
lead time *(p. 719)*
lean manufacturing *(p. 715)*
manufacturing cell *(p. 706)*
order point *(p. 719)*
Pareto inventory analysis
　(p. 720)
pull system *(p. 696)*
purchasing cost *(p. 695)*

push system *(p. 696)*
red-line system *(p. 721)*
safety stock *(p. 719)*
six-sigma method *(p. 708)*
supply-chain management
　(p. 708)
target costing *(p. 698)*
theory of constraints (TOC)
　(p. 715)
two-bin system *(p. 721)*
usage *(p. 719)*
value engineering *(p. 699)*
virtual reality *(p. 698)*

Questions

1. What are the three costs associated with inventory? Explain each and give examples.

2. Differentiate between the push and pull systems of production. Is JIT a push or a pull system?

3. How does a product's life-cycle stage have a bearing on production cost management?

4. What is target costing, and how is it useful in assessing a product's total life-cycle costs?

5. Why does the development stage have such a significant influence on the profitability of a product over its life cycle?

6. What is kaizen costing, and how does it differ from target costing?

7. What are the primary goals of the JIT philosophy, and how does JIT attempt to achieve these goals?

8. What kinds of changes need to occur in a production environment to effectively implement JIT? Why are these changes necessary?

9. How would switching from a traditional manufacturing system to a flexible manufacturing system affect a firm's inventory and production control systems?

10. What is meant by the theory of constraints? How is this concept appropriate for manufacturing and service companies?

11. *(Appendix)* How are ordering costs and carrying costs related?

12. *(Appendix)* What is Pareto inventory analysis? Why do A items and C items warrant different inventory control methods? What are some methods that can be employed to control C items?

Exercises

13. (Cost classification) Indicate whether each of the following costs would be considered an ordering cost (O), a carrying cost (C), or a cost of not carrying (N) inventory. For any costs that do not fit these categories, indicate N/A for "not applicable."

a. Telephone call to supplier
b. Stationery and purchase order forms
c. Purchasing agent's salary
d. Purchase price of product
e. Goodwill of customer lost due to unavailability of product
f. Postage on purchase order
g. Freight-in cost on product
h. Insurance for products in inventory
i. Wages of receiving clerks
j. Preparing and issuing checks to suppliers
k. Contribution margin lost due to unavailability of product
l. Storage costs for products on hand
m. Quantity discounts on products ordered
n. Opportunity cost of funds invested in inventory
o. Property taxes on warehouses
p. Handling costs for products on hand
q. Excess ordering and shipping charges for rush orders of standard product lines
r. Spoilage of products awaiting use

14. (Carrying costs) Determine the carrying costs for an item costing $6.80, given the following per-unit cost information:

Storage cost	$0.12
Handling cost	0.14
Production labor cost	0.85
Insurance cost	0.22
Opportunity cost	8% of investment

15. (Target costing) Capricorn Tools has developed a new kitchen utensil. The firm has conducted significant market research and estimated the following pattern for sales of the new product:

Year	Expected Volume	Expected Price per Unit
1	38,000 units	$19
2	48,000	18
3	90,000	16
4	40,000	12

If the firm desires to net $4.50 per unit in profit, what is the target cost to produce the new utensil?

16. (Target costing) The marketing department at Cellton Production Company has an idea for a new product that is expected to have a life cycle of six years. After conducting market research, the company has determined that the product could sell for $350 per unit in the first four years of life and for $275 per unit for the last two years. Unit sales are expected as follows:

Year 1	4,000
Year 2	3,600
Year 3	4,700
Year 4	5,000
Year 5	1,500
Year 6	1,000

Per-unit variable selling costs are estimated at $80 throughout the product's life; total fixed selling and administrative costs over the six years are expected to be $1,750,000. Cellton Production Company desires a profit margin of 20 percent of selling price per unit.

a. Compute the life-cycle target cost to manufacture the product. (Round to the nearest cent.)

b. If the company expects the product to cost $225 to manufacture in the first year, what is the maximum that manufacturing cost can be in the following five years? (Round to the nearest cent.)

c. Assume that Cellton Production Company engineers indicate that the expected manufacturing cost per unit is $210. What actions might the company take to reduce this cost?

17. (Target costing) Buggin Corporation is developing a propane-powered mosquito zapper for campers. Market research has indicated that potential purchasers would be willing to pay $225 per unit for this product. Company engineers have estimated that first-year production costs would amount to $230 per unit. On this type of product, Buggin would normally expect to earn $20 per unit in profits. Using the concept of target costing, write a memo that (1) analyzes the prospects for this product and (2) discusses possible organizational strategies.

18. (JIT benefits) Choose a fast-food restaurant and prepare a report showing how it could use JIT to improve operations.

19. (JIT benefits) Everyone in your company seems excited about the suggestion that the firm implement a JIT system. Being a cautious person, however, your company president has asked you to write a report describing situations in which JIT will not work. Prepare such a report.

20. (Manufacturing cells) Research the topic of manufacturing cells on the Internet, and write a brief report on company experiences using them.

21. (Value engineering) Research the topic of value engineering on the Internet, and write a brief report on a company or an organization's experiences using this technique.

WebTUTOR Advantage

22. (JIT variances) Lazlow Company uses a JIT system. The following standards are related to Materials A and B, which are used to make one unit of the company's final product:

Annual Material Standards

3 pounds of material A @ $2.25	$ 6.75
4 pounds of material B @ $3.40	13.60
	$20.35

Current Material Standards

2 pounds of material A @ $2.25	$ 4.50
5 pounds of material B @ $3.40	17.00
	$21.50

Current material standards differ from the original because of an engineering change made near the end of June. During July, the company produced 3,000 units of its final product and used 11,000 pounds of Material A and 10,000 pounds of Material B. All material is acquired at the standard cost per pound.

a. Calculate the material variance and the ENC material variance.

b. Explain the effect of the engineering change on product cost.

23. (JIT variances) Laura Dawn uses a JIT system in her manufacturing firm, which makes pots for plants. She provides you the following standards for a typical 1 gallon pot:

Annual Material Standards

32 ounces of component X @ $0.01	$0.32
2 ounces of component Y @ $0.05	0.10
	$0.42

Current Material Standards

22 ounces of component X @ $0.01	$0.22
4 ounces of component Y @ $0.05	0.20
	$0.42

In-house experiments indicated that this material change would make the pots stronger, so the company issued an engineering change order for the product. March production was 8,000 pots. Usage of raw material (all purchased at standard costs) was 184,000 ounces of Component X and 31,000 ounces of Component Y.

a. Calculate the material quantity variance.

b. Calculate the engineering change variance.

c. Summarize the company's effectiveness in managing March production costs.

d. Comment on the circumstances in which a company would institute an engineering change that results in the expected product cost being unchanged.

24. (Backflush costing) Consider the following data pertaining to March 2006 for a firm that has adopted JIT.

Production	4,000 units
Sales ($20 per unit)	3,950 units
Standard production costs	
Direct material	$4
Conversion costs	$8

Assume that there were no cost or usage variances for March, and the amount of materials used equaled the quantity purchased. All materials are purchased on account, and all units started were completed.

a. Assuming that the company uses a traditional costing system, record the journal entries to recognize the following:

  1. purchase of materials.

  2. incurrence of conversion costs.

  3. completion of the month's production.

  4. sale of the month's production.

b. Assuming that the company initially charges all costs to Cost of Goods Sold and then uses backflush costing to assign costs to inventories at the end of the period, record the journal entries to recognize the following:

  1. incurrence of conversion costs.

  2. completion of production.

  3. backflushing of costs to inventories.

25. (Backflush costing) Refined Products uses backflush costing to account for production costs of its clothing line. During August 2006, the firm produced 160,000 garments and sold 159,000. The standard cost for each garment is

Direct material	$2
Conversion costs	4
Total cost	$6

The firm had no inventory on August 1. The following events took place in August:

• Purchased $322,000 of direct material.

• Incurred $648,000 of conversion costs.

• Applied $640,000 of conversion costs to Raw and In-Process Inventory.

• Finished 160,000 garments.

• Sold 159,000 garments for $10 each.

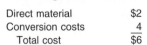
WebTUTOR Advantage

a. Prepare journal entries using backflush costing with a minimum number of entries.

b. Post the amounts in part (a) to T-accounts.

c. Explain any inventory account balances.

26. (Production constraints) Xcaliber manufactures high-end flatware. One of the crucial processes in flatware production is polishing. The company normally operates three polishing machines to maintain pace with the upstream and downstream production operations. However, one of the polishing machines broke yesterday, and management has been informed that the machine will not be back in operation until repairs are completed in three weeks. Two machines cannot keep pace with the volume of product flowing to the polishing operation. You have been hired as a consultant to improve the throughput of the polishing operation. Discuss the tactics you would recommend Xcaliber employ to deal with the capacity limitation.

27. (Production constraints) Office Provisions produces commercial calendars in a two-department operation: Department 1 is labor intensive and Department 2 is automated. The average output of Department 1 is 45 units per hour. Units from Department 1 are transferred to Department 2 to be completed by a robot. The robot can finish a maximum of 45 units per hour. Office Provisions needs to complete 180 units this afternoon for an order that has been backlogged for four months. The production manager has informed the people in Department 1 that they are to work on nothing else except this order from 1 P.M. until 5 P.M. The supervisor in Department 2 has scheduled the same times for the robot to work on the order. Department 1's activity for each hour of the afternoon follows:

Time	1:00–2:00 P.M.	2:00–3:00 P.M.	3:00–4:00 P.M.	4:00–4:58 P.M.
Production	44 units	40 units	49 units	47 units

Each unit moves directly from Department 1 to Department 2 with no lag time. Did Office Provisions complete the 180 units by 5 P.M.? If not, explain and provide detailed computations.

28. (Appendix; carrying cost) Gidget Gourmet manufactures a variety of animal food products from alfalfa "pellets." The firm has determined that its EOQ is 40,000 pounds of pellets. Based on the EOQ, the firm's annual ordering costs for pellets is $6,700. Given this information, what is the firm's annual carrying cost of pellets? Explain.

29. (Appendix: multiproduct EOQs) A retail cosmetics chain carries three types of skin products: face cream, lotion, and powder. Determine the economic order quantity for each, given the following information:

Product	Order Cost	Carrying Cost	Demand
Face cream	$2.25	$2.00	2,000 units
Lotion	3.25	1.45	1,000 units
Powder	1.70	1.25	900 units

30. (Appendix: product demand) Compute annual estimated demand for a product if the economic order quantity is 800 units, carrying cost is $0.35 per unit, and ordering cost is $140.00 per order.

31. (Appendix: EPR) UpTown Mfg. custom makes machine parts used by other companies. The following data relate to production of Part 23:

Annual quantity produced in units	1,600
Cost of setting up a production run	$400
Cost of carrying one unit in stock for a year	$2

Calculate the economic production run for Part 23.

32. (Appendix: EPR) Danielle Steele has taken a job as production superintendent in a plant that makes, among other products, jewelry cases. She is trying to determine how many cases to produce on each production run.
Discussions reveal that last year the plant made 7,500 such cases, and this
level of demand is expected for the coming year. The setup cost of each
run is $400, and the cost of carrying a case in inventory for a year is esti-
mated at $2.50.

   a. Calculate the economic production run (EPR) and the total cost associated with it.

   b. Recalculate the EPR and total cost if the annual cost of carrying a case
in inventory is $10 and the setup cost is $100.

   c. Based on your answer to part (a), how many production runs should
Steele expect for the coming year?

   d. Based on your answers to parts (a) and (c), estimate the total setup
costs to be incurred for the year.

Problems

33. (Identification of carrying, ordering costs) Bama Steel management has been
evaluating company policies with respect to control of costs of metal tubing,
one of the firm's major component materials. The firm's controller has gathered the following financial data, which may be pertinent to controlling
costs associated with the metal tubing:

Ordering Costs

Annual salary of purchasing department manager	$41,500
Depreciation of equipment in purchasing department	22,300
Cost per order for purchasing department supplies	0.30
Typical phone expense per order placed	3.02
Monthly expense for heat and light in purchasing department	400

Carrying Costs

Annual depreciation on materials storage building	$15,000
Annual inventory insurance premium (per dollar of inventory value)	0.05
Annual property tax on materials storage building	2,500
Obsolescence cost per dollar of average annual inventory	0.07
Annual salary of security officer assigned to the materials storage building	18,000

   a. Which of the ordering costs should Bama's controller consider in performing short-run decision analysis? Explain.

   b. Which of the carrying costs shyould Bama's controller consider in performing short-run decision analysis? Explain.

34. (Target costing) The Products Development Division of Fast Foods has just
completed its work on a new microwave entrée. After consumer research
was conducted, the marketing group has estimated the following quantities
of the product can be sold at the following prices over its life cycle:

Year	Quantity	Selling Price	Year	Quantity	Selling Price
1	100,000	$2.50	5	600,000	$2.00
2	250,000	2.40	6	450,000	2.00
3	350,000	2.30	7	200,000	1.90
4	500,000	2.10	8	130,000	1.90

Initial engineering estimates of direct material and direct labor costs are
$0.85 and $0.20, respectively, per unit. Variable overhead per unit is expected to be $0.25, and fixed overhead is expected to be $100,000 per year.
Fast Foods' management strives to earn a 20 percent gross margin on products of this type.

   a. Estimate the target cost for the new entrée.

   b. Compare the estimated production cost to the target cost. Discuss this comparison and how management might use the comparison to manage costs.

c. Based on your answer in part (b), should Fast Foods begin production of the new entrée? Explain.

35. (Target costing) Donna Dierks has just been presented the following market and production estimates on Product Ninja-Z that has been under development in her company.

Projected market price of Ninja-Z	$430 (based on 180,000 life cycle unit sales over 5-year life)
Projected profit per unit	70
Estimated selling and administrative costs per unit	80

Estimated production costs
Direct material	$140
Direct labor	80
Variable overhead	30
Fixed overhead	$10,000 annually

Use the concept of target costing to integrate the marketing and engineering information and interpret the results for Dierks.

36. (Just-in-time features) Indicate by letter which of the three categories apply to the following features of just-in-time systems. Use as many letters as appropriate.

D = desired intermediate result of using JIT
U = ultimate goal of JIT
T = technique associated with JIT

a. Reducing setup time
b. Reducing total cost of producing and carrying inventory
c. Using focused factory arrangements
d. Designing products to minimize design changes after production starts
e. Monitoring quality on a continuous basis
f. Using manufacturing cells
g. Minimizing inventory stored
h. Measuring variances caused by engineering changes
i. Using autonomation processes
j. Pulling purchases and production through the system based on sales demand

37. (JIT journal entries) Tanawak Industries recorded the following transactions for its first month of operations.

(1)	Direct Material Inventory	12,000	
	Accounts Payable		12,000
	To record purchase of direct material.		
(2)	Work in Process Inventory	12,000	
	Direct Material Inventory		12,000
	To record distribution of material to production.		
(3)	Conversion Costs	20,000	
	Various accounts		20,000
	To record incurrence of conversion costs.		
(4)	Work in Process Inventory	20,000	
	Conversion Costs		20,000
	To assign conversion cost to WIP.		
(5)	Finished Goods Inventory	32,000	
	Work in Process Inventory		32,000
	To record completion of products.		
(6)	Accounts Receivable	58,000	
	Sales		58,000
	To record sale of products.		
	Cost of Goods Sold	31,000	
	Finished Goods Inventory		31,000
	To record cost of goods sold.		

Because Tanawak Industries employs JIT, the company's CEO has asked how the accounting system could be simplified.

a. Prepare the journal entries, assuming that no transactions are recognized until goods are completed.

b. Prepare the journal entries, assuming that good are shipped to customers as soon as they are completed and that no journal entries are recorded until goods are completed.

c. Prepare the journal entries, assuming that sale of product is the trigger point for journal entries.

d. Prepare the journal entries, assuming that sale of product is the trigger point for journal entries and that the firm uses backflush costing.

38. (JIT journal entries; advanced) Hanson Products has implemented a just-in-time inventory system for the production of its insulated wire. Inventories of raw material and work in process are so small that Hanson uses a Raw and In-Process account. In addition, almost all labor operations are automated, and Hanson has chosen to cost products using standards for direct material and conversion. The following production standards are applicable at the beginning of 2006 for one roll of insulated wire:

Direct material (100 yards @ $2.00)	$200
Conversion (4 machine hours @ $35)	140
Total cost	$340

The conversion cost of $35 per machine hour was estimated on the basis of 500,000 machine hours for the year and $17,500,000 of conversion costs. The following activities took place during 2006:

1. Raw material purchased and placed into production totaled 12,452,000 yards. All except 8,000 yards were purchased at the standard price of $2.00 per yard. The other 8,000 yards were purchased at a cost of $2.06 per yard due to the placement of a rush order. The order was approved in advance by management. All purchases are on account.

2. From January 1 to February 28, Hanson manufactured 20,800 rolls of insulated wire. Conversion costs incurred to date totaled $3,000,000. Of this amount, $600,000 was for depreciation, $2,200,000 was paid in cash, and $200,000 was on account.

3. Conversion costs are applied to the Raw and In-Process account from January 1 to February 28 on the basis of the annual standard.

4. The Engineering Department issued a change in the operations flow document effective March 1, 2006. The change decreased the machine time to manufacture one roll of wire by 5 minutes per roll. However, the standard raised the amount of direct material to 100.4 yards per roll. The Accounting Department requires that the annual standard be continued for costing the Raw and In-Process Inventory for the remainder of 2006. The effects of the engineering changes should be shown in two accounts: Material Quantity Engineering Change Variance and Machine Hours Engineering Change Variance.

5. Total production for the remainder of 2006 was 103,200 rolls of wire. Total conversion costs for the remaining 10 months of 2006 were $14,442,000. Of this amount, $4,000,000 was depreciation, $9,325,000 was paid in cash, and $1,117,000 was on account.

6. The standard amount of conversion cost is applied to the Raw and In-Process Inventory for the remainder of the year.

Note: Some of the journal entries for the following items are not explicitly covered in the chapter. This problem challenges students regarding the accounting effects of the implementation of a JIT system.

a. Prepare entries for items 1, 2, 3, 5, and 6.

b. Determine the increase in material cost due to the engineering change related to direct material.

c. Prepare a journal entry to adjust the Raw and In-Process Inventory account for the engineering change cost found in part (b).

d. Determine the reduction in conversion cost due to the engineering change related to machine time.

e. Prepare a journal entry to reclassify the actual conversion costs by the savings found in part (d).

f. Making the entry in part (e) raises conversion costs to what they would have been if the engineering change related to machine time had not been made. Are conversion costs under- or overapplied and by what amount?

g. Assume that the reduction in machine time could not have been made without the corresponding increase in material usage. Is the net effect of these engineering changes cost beneficial? Why?

39. (Inventory control) Larson Company manufactures various electronic assemblies that it sells primarily to computer manufacturers. Larson's reputation has been built on quality, timely delivery, and products that are consistently on the cutting edge of technology. Larson's business is fast paced. The typical product has a short life; the product is in development for about a year and in the growth stage, with sometimes spectacular growth, for about a year. Each product then experiences a rapid decline in sales as new products become available.

Larson's competitive strategy requires a reliable stream of new products to be developed each year, which is the only way that the company can overcome the threat of product obsolescence. Larson's products go through the first half of the product life cycle similar to products in other industries; however, differences occur in the second half of their life cycles. Larson's products never reach the mature product or declining product stage. Near the end of the growth stage, products just "die" as new ones are introduced.

a. In the competitive market facing Larson Company, what would be key considerations in production and inventory control?

b. How would the threat of immediate product obsolescence affect Larson's practices in purchasing product components and materials?

c. How would the threat of product obsolescence affect the EPR for a typical product produced by Larson Company?

(CMA adapted)

40. (Essay) The director of supply management at Karlie Tool & Die has contracted for $1 million of spare parts that are currently unneeded. His rationale for the contract was that the parts were available for purchase at a significantly reduced price. The company just hired a new president who, on learning about the contracts, stated that the parts contracts should be canceled because the parts would not be needed for at least a year. The supply management director informed the president that the penalties for canceling the contracts would cost more than letting the orders go through. How would you respond to this situation from the standpoint of the president? From the standpoint of the supply management director?

41. (Essay) A plant manager and her controller were discussing the plant's inventory control policies one day. The controller suggested to the plant manager that the ordering policies needed to be reviewed because of new technology that had been put in place in the purchasing department. Among the changes that had been implemented in the plant were installation of

(1) computerized inventory tracking, (2) electronic data interchange capabilities with the plant's major suppliers, and (3) in-house facilities for electronic fund transfers.

a. As technology changes, why should managers update ordering policies for inventory?

b. Write a memo to the plant manager describing the likely impact of the changes made in this plant on the EOQ of material input.

42. (Essay) William Manufacturing Company began implementing a just-in-time inventory system several months ago. The production and purchasing managers, however, have not seen any dramatic improvements in throughput. They have decided that the problems are related to their suppliers. The company's three suppliers seem to send the wrong materials at the wrong times. Prepare a discussion of the problems that might exist in this situation. Be certain to address the following items: internal and external communications; possible engineering changes and their impacts; number, quality, and location of suppliers; and length of system implementation.

43. (Appendix: EOQ) Frank Chone operates a health food bakery that uses a special type of ground flour in its products. The bakery operates 365 days a year. Chone finds that he seems to order either too much or too little flour and asks for your help. After some discussion, you find that he has no idea of when or how much to order. An examination of his records and answers to further questions reveal the following information:

Annual usage of flour	14,000 pounds
Average number of days delay between initiating and receiving an order	12
Estimated cost per order	$16.00
Estimated annual cost of carrying a pound of flour in inventory	$0.50

a. Calculate the economic order quantity for flour.

b. Assume that Chone desires a safety stock cushion of seven days' usage. Calculate the appropriate order point.

44. (Appendix: EPR) Funky Flower grows and sells a variety of indoor and outdoor plants and garden vegetables. One of the more popular vegetables grown by the firm is a red onion. The company sells approximately 30,000 pounds of red onions per year. Two of the major inputs in the growing of onions are seeds and fertilizer. Due to the poor germination rate, two seeds must be purchased for each onion plant grown (a mature onion plant provides 0.5 pound of onion). Also, 0.25 pound of fertilizer is required for each pound of onion produced. The following information summarizes costs for onions, seeds, and fertilizer. Carrying costs for onions are expressed per pound of onion; carrying costs for seeds are expressed per seed; and for fertilizer, carrying costs are expressed per pound of fertilizer. To plant onions, the company incurs a cost of $50 to set up the planter and the fertilizing equipment.

	Onions	Seeds	Fertilizer
Carrying cost	$0.25	$0.01	$0.05
Ordering cost	—	$4.25	$8.80
Setup cost	$50.00	—	—

a. What is the economic production run for onions?

b. How many production runs will Funky Flower make for onions annually?

c. What are the economic order quantities for seeds and fertilizer?

d. How many orders will be placed for seeds? For fertilizer?

e. What is the total annual cost of ordering, carrying, and setting up for onion production?

f. How is the planting of onions similar to and different from a typical factory production run?

g. Are there any inconsistencies in your answers to parts (a) through (c) that need to be addressed? Explain.

18

Emerging Management Practices

Objectives

AFTER READING THIS CHAPTER, YOU SHOULD BE ABLE TO ANSWER THE FOLLOWING QUESTIONS:

LO.1 HOW DOES BUSINESS PROCESS REENGINEERING CAUSE RADICAL CHANGES IN THE WAY FIRMS EXECUTE PROCESSES?

LO.2 WHY ARE COMPETITIVE FORCES DRIVING DECISIONS TO DOWNSIZE AND RESTRUCTURE OPERATIONS?

LO.3 IN WHAT WAYS AND WHY ARE OPERATIONS OF MANY FIRMS BECOMING MORE DIVERSE? HOW DOES THE INCREASING DIVERSITY AFFECT THE ROLES OF THE FIRMS' ACCOUNTING SYSTEMS?

LO.4 WHY ARE FIRMS ADOPTING ENTERPRISE RESOURCE PLANNING SYSTEMS, AND WHAT ARE THEIR PURPOSES?

LO.5 WHAT ARE STRATEGIC ALLIANCES, WHAT FORMS DO THEY TAKE, AND WHY DO FIRMS ENGAGE IN THEM?

LO.6 WHAT ARE THE CHARACTERISTICS OF OPEN-BOOK MANAGEMENT, AND WHY DOES ITS ADOPTION REQUIRE CHANGES IN ACCOUNTING METHODS AND PRACTICES?

LO.7 WHAT ARE THE THREE GENERIC APPROACHES THAT FIRMS CAN TAKE IN CONTROLLING ENVIRONMENTAL COSTS?

Introducing

In 1975, Howard Schuman and two colleagues founded Albums, Inc., in Middleburg Heights, Ohio. The firm serves the photography industry, and its slogan is "everything after the photography." In other words, the firm sells a diverse set of products to store and display photographs including products for digital photographs.

Within a few months after its founding, the firm had outgrown its space and moved to Brook Park, Ohio. From there, the company continued to expand and, in 2004, occupied seven facilities around the United States. In 1989, the company set up an employee stock ownership program (ESOP) in which each employee was given ownership in the company. Peter Cardello, who was serving as general manager of the firm's Atlanta operations, was promoted to CEO a few years later. Immediately, Cardello had to confront new challenges. With the economic recession of the late 1980s, the company for the first time in its history was operating at a loss.

Financial pressures of the recession, coupled with stock ownership now being widely distributed across employees, caused Cardello to seek a much more participative management style than had been used by the founder. Because employees were owners, they had a right to have their say in the company's management. Additionally, the employees' collective organizational knowledge was so extensive that Cardello needed to find ways to drive the organization with that knowledge. However, of the roughly 150 employees, most were only high-school educated and in their 20s. Thus, few employees had the necessary training to be effective managers and most did not understand basic financial information. The challenge faced by Cardello was to find a way to share decision making with a workforce that was not well prepared to participate. Conventional approaches to decentralizing authority were unlikely to work in this setting. The solution would require a revolution in thinking.

Sources: *http://www.albumsinc.com/, http://www.nceo.org/library/obm_albums.html.*

The experience of Albums, Inc., is typical of many firms today. The trend is to push the authority and responsibility for making decisions down to the level of teams and individuals. This trend has created opportunities and challenges for the accounting functions. To be effective, decision makers must have the skills to interpret a variety of information, including financial. However, as with Peter Cardello's experience, not all employees are adequately trained to understand financial information. This circumstance has created some innovative approaches to developing the information skills used by managers.

This chapter's theme is innovation in management practices and the impact of innovation on accounting. The "age of change" is an apt description for the current environment in which managers and financial professionals must function. Although, some changes have been driven by the fast pace of evolution in management practices and techniques, many changes have been driven by the even faster evolution of technology. The discussion begins with dramatic structural changes occurring in the workplace that are affecting many employers and employees.

THE CHANGING WORKPLACE

The forces of global competition and technological advancements have caused profound changes in business organizations. To survive, managers must develop ways to achieve needed competitive changes in their organizations. In general, change can be achieved in two ways: immediately or gradually. Managers seek both types of change.

Some overriding change implementation principles that managers should follow when implementing changes are presented in Exhibit 18–1. Note that principles 5 through 8 involve major roles for financial professionals within the firm. These roles are explained further as the chapter unfolds. When major operational

EXHIBIT 18-1

MANAGERIAL PRINCIPLES FOR SUCCESSFULLY MANAGING CHANGE

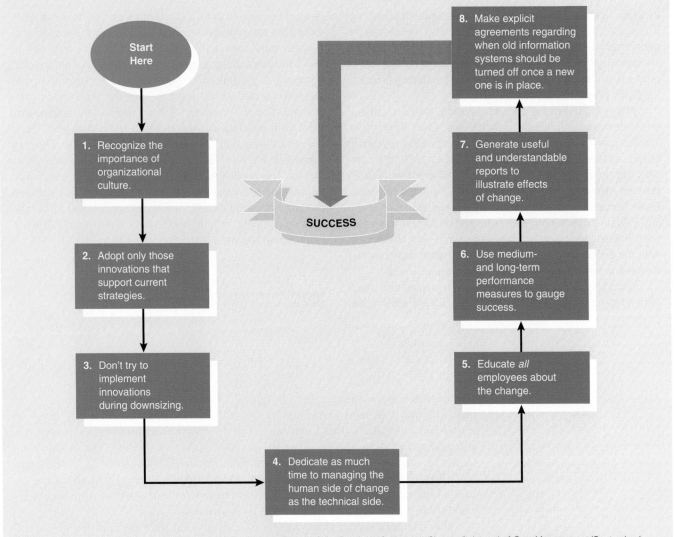

Start Here

1. Recognize the importance of organizational culture.

2. Adopt only those innovations that support current strategies.

3. Don't try to implement innovations during downsizing.

4. Dedicate as much time to managing the human side of change as the technical side.

5. Educate *all* employees about the change.

6. Use medium- and long-term performance measures to gauge success.

7. Generate useful and understandable reports to illustrate effects of change.

8. Make explicit agreements regarding when old information systems should be turned off once a new one is in place.

SUCCESS

Source: S. Mark Young, "Implementing Management Innovations Successfully: Principles for Lasting Change," *Journal of Cost Management* (September/ October 1997), pp. 16–20. © 1997, Warren Gorham & Lamont. Reprinted with permission of RIA.

improvements are mandated, managers completely revise the way activities are performed. Business process reengineering is a tool to achieve large, quick gains in effectiveness or efficiency through redesigning the execution of specific business functions.

BUSINESS PROCESS REENGINEERING

LO.1
HOW DOES BUSINESS PROCESS REENGINEERING CAUSE RADICAL CHANGES IN THE WAY FIRMS EXECUTE PROCESSES?

business process reengineering (BPR)

Business process reengineering (BPR) is a method of examining processes to identify and then eliminate, reduce, or replace functions and processes that add little customer value to products or services. The focus of BPR is on discrete initiatives to improve specific processes. Examples of processes include handling or storing purchased materials and components, issuing checks to pay labor and other production expenses, packaging finished products for shipment to customers, recording journal entries, and developing an organizational strategic plan. BPR initiatives

How does business process reengineering achieve dramatic changes in operations?

in a global enterprise could extend to the entire firm or to only a single subunit. Thus, the initiatives can originate with managers at different organizational levels.

BPR is designed to bring radical changes to operations and is often associated with employee layoffs, outsourcing initiatives, and technology acquisition. Three major business trends are promoting the increased use of BPR in the twenty-first century. The first trend is the advancement of technology. Neither the electronic remittance of accounts payable nor the use of robotic equipment to move and assemble components in a manufacturing facility were possible 50 years ago. Both of these practices are common today, even in small companies. Because BPR focuses on alternative ways to execute required organizational functions, it is useful in automating processes that cannot be eliminated. Technology advancements have improved efficiencies throughout the supply chain. The feasibility of automating processes is constantly changing because technology is constantly evolving. For example, in mid-2004, the Federal Reserve announced that its Boston check-processing facility would transfer or lay off more than 100 employees. The staff reductions were attributed to the reduction in check-clearing volume, following the increased use of credit and debit cards for store purchases.[1]

The second trend leading toward increased use of BPR is the pursuit of increased quality. As discussed in Chapter 16, global competition allows consumers to purchase products and services from the highest quality providers in the world. In many product and service markets, quality has become one of the most important criteria applied by consumers in purchasing decisions. Because BPR focuses attention on processes associated with poor quality, this methodology can help indicate ways in which quality can be improved by replacing, changing, or eliminating those processes.

The third trend resulting in expanded BPR usage is the increase in price competition caused by globalization. To successfully compete on the basis of price, firms must identify ways to become more efficient and, thus, reduce costs. BPR can be used to improve efficiency, particularly when a process needs a major overhaul or a new generation of technology is needed. Because BPR methodically revolutionizes business practices, formal steps can be defined; however, creativity is an important element of the method. See Exhibit 18–2 for the steps for implementing BPR.

Objectives of a BPR project represent the potential benefits to be realized from reengineering. All relevant technological innovations must be known so that all technological constraints and opportunities are considered. Because process reengineering is much more involved than merely automating or upgrading existing processes, creativity and vision are needed to design a prototype of the revised process.

EXHIBIT 18–2

STEPS TO BUSINESS PROCESS REENGINEERING

1. Define the objectives of the BPR project.
2. Identify the processes that are to be reengineered.
3. Determine a baseline for measuring the success of the BPR project.
4. Identify the technology levers. These are the potential sources of innovation, increased quality, increased output, and decreased costs.
5. Develop initial prototypes of the reengineered processes and then, through subsequent iterations, develop incremental improvements to the prototypes until satisfactory results are achieved.

Source: Adapted from Yogesh Malhotra, "Business Process Redesign: An Overview," *http://www.brint.com/ papers/ bpr.htm* (1996).

[1] Robert Gavin, "Fed to Cut Hub Jobs as Fewer Use Checks [Third Edition]," *Boston Globe* (August 3, 2004), p. D1.

Accountants are important participants in the BPR process because they can provide baseline performance measurements, help determine BPR objectives, and measure the achieved performance of the redesigned process. Accountants must also be aware of potential applications for newly developed software and hardware that may lead to BPR innovations. The following keys to a successful BPR implementation highlight the importance of involving customers, suppliers, and top-level managers in the process:

- Set "stretch" goals for the reengineered process, expressing them in the most appropriate performance measure, such as financial, time, or defective production.
- Make certain that the reengineering efforts have a "champion" and are supported by top management.
- To the extent possible, involve all constituents of the value chain, especially customers and suppliers, in the regineering project.
- Assign both the authority and responsibility for the project to a single person.
- Use a pilot project to identify problems that might arise during full implementation.[2]

Involvement of customers ensures that their perspective drives the process redesign. Involvement of top managers signals the project's importance to the organization and secures the resources necessary to execute the project.

The focus of BPR is on improvement of organizational operations. Whether the issue is quality, cost, or customer value, BPR can help effect organizational improvements and change. Because BPR is designed to achieve radical changes, its impacts—downsizing and restructuring—on organizational employees are potentially profound.

DOWNSIZING, LAYOFFS, AND RESTRUCTURING

LO.2
WHY ARE COMPETITIVE FORCES DRIVING DECISIONS TO DOWNSIZE AND RESTRUCTURE OPERATIONS?

Global competition is a fact of life in many industries, and survival requires firms to continually improve product quality while maintaining competitive prices. Not all firms are able to adapt and survive under the pressures of global competition. Just as global competition has driven firms to higher levels of quality and efficiency, competitive pressures drive some businesses out of competition altogether. Firms are now forced to evaluate which businesses they want to defend and which they are willing to sacrifice to the competition.

Many methods discussed in this chapter, including the use of automated technology to replace manual labor or equipment run by humans, have proven useful in improving process efficiency and effectiveness as well as product quality. However, in realizing improvements, firms also realize additional problems. Foremost among these problems is the handling of excess personnel. Both businesses that are striving to remain viable and those that are retreating from the competition are forced into restructuring operations and reducing the workforce.

One of the grim realities of ever-improving efficiency is that ever fewer workers are required to achieve a given level of output. Using business practices such as business process reengineering, firms are constantly restructuring operations to maintain or gain competitive advantages. Each successful restructuring leverages the work of employees into more output. At higher levels of efficiency, fewer workers are needed and a reduction in workforce is required. **Downsizing** is any management action that reduces employment upon restructuring operations in response to competitive pressures. The Laborforce 2000 survey of more than 400 American-

downsizing

[2] Gene Hall, Jim Rosenthal, and Judy Wade, "How to Make Reengineering Really Work," *Harvard Business Review* (November–December 1993), pp. 119–131.

based business managers gave insight into how downsizing related to competitive pressures facing businesses. The following three strategic issues were said to be of greatest concern to their companies: global competitiveness; economic concerns, such as a need to cut costs and improve profitability; and core competency issues of quality, productivity, and customer service.[3]

The most common organizational response to these three strategic issues has been downsizing. Of the survey respondents, 64 percent downsized plants and facilities, and slightly more than 50 percent sold off some business units. The primary reason cited for downsizing was the need to reduce costs and improve profits. Seventy-five percent of the firms surveyed also made substantial investments in advanced technology in conjunction with downsizing.

KB Toys illustrates downsizing caused by competitive pressures. In January 2004, KB Toys filed for bankruptcy protection under Chapter 11. To cut costs and remain price-competitive with discounters such as **Wal-Mart**, KB Toys eventually may close 500 of its 1,200+ stores. Prior to closing any stores, the company employed about 13,000 employees.[4]

Downsizing as a response to competitive pressures can result in many risks and dangers. First, firms can find that layoffs have depleted the in-house talent pool. The collective workforce knowledge or organizational memory may have been reduced to the point that the ability to solve problems creatively and generate innovative ideas for growth has been greatly diminished. Also, after downsizing, many firms have found that positions that once served as feeder pools for future top management talent have been eliminated.

Second, to survive in the presence of global competition, trust and effective communication must exist between workers and managers. Successive rounds of layoffs diminish worker morale, cause worker trust in managers to wane, and lead to a decrease in communication between workers and managers. Workers often fear that sharing information could provide insights to management about how to further increase productivity and reduce costs by eliminating more of the workforce. Many management methods discussed in this chapter depend heavily on cooperation among all employees of a firm. Firms that are downsizing should not concurrently attempt to implement other innovative practices.

Third, downsizing can destroy a corporate culture that embraced lifetime employment as a key factor in attracting new employees or that was perceived as "nurturing" by employees. Significant negative change in an organization's culture is likely to have a similar negative impact on employee morale and trust.

Downsizing is an accounting issue because of its implications for financial reporting and its role in cost management. The financial consequences of downsizing can be high. When restructuring and downsizing occur in the same year, the firm often reports in that year large, one-time losses caused by sales of unprofitable assets and severance costs connected with employee layoffs. From a cost management perspective, accountants must understand the full consequences, both monetary and nonmonetary, of downsizing. Before recommending downsizing to improve organizational efficiency, accountants should examine the likely impacts on customer service, employee morale and loyalty, and future growth opportunities.

See Exhibit 18–3 for impacts of supply chain decisions, including downsizing. The exhibit demonstrates that strategic decisions affect the manner in which inputs, such as labor, technology, purchased material, and services, are converted into outputs for customers. Downsizing changes the mix of inputs used to produce outputs. Downsizing also increases the emphasis on technology-based

---

[3] Philip H. Mirvis, "Human Resource Management: Leaders, Laggards, and Followers," *Academy of Management Executive* (May 1997), pp. 43–56.

[4] Chris Reidy, "KB Toys Files for Chapter 11 Protection; Action May Mean Closing 500 Stores," *Boston Globe* (January 15, 2004), p. E4.

EXHIBIT 18–3

**THE VALUE CHAIN AND
COST MANAGEMENT**

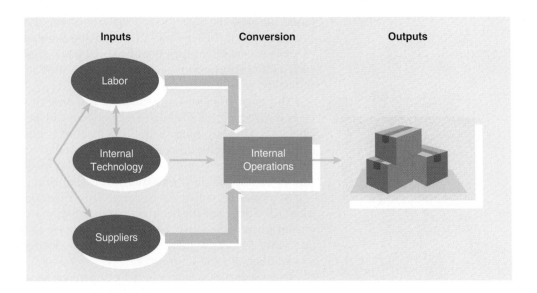

conversion processes and reduces the emphasis on manual conversion processes and, thus, the labor requirement. The two-directional arrow shows increased outsourcing from suppliers and increased dependence on technology as substitutes for labor.

The financial analysis of the downsizing decision is complex. The decision relies on comparing cost savings from reduced labor costs to be generated in the future to the current outlay for restructuring and acquiring additional technology. The capital budgeting methods discussed in Chapter 13 should be applied to this decision. If downsizing involves asset sales, the financial analysis must compare the cash to be realized from such sales to the annual net revenues or net cash flows that will *not* be realized in the future because of the reduced asset base. Capital budgeting tools provide managers information about how downsizing is likely to affect profitability and the return on invested capital.

WORKFORCE DIVERSITY

LO.3

IN WHAT WAYS AND WHY ARE OPERATIONS OF MANY FIRMS BECOMING MORE DIVERSE? HOW DOES THE INCREASING DIVERSITY AFFECT THE ROLES OF THE FIRMS' ACCOUNTING SYSTEMS?

Why is diversity increasingly important in businesses?

Under the pressure of global competition, many firms have expanded operations geographically. By sourcing and marketing worldwide, firms are able to develop new markets, reduce input costs, and manage the effects of peaks and valleys in local economies. The globalization of operations presents managers with new opportunities and challenges.

With widespread manufacturing and other operations, companies find that their employees have divergent religions, races, values, work habits, cultures, political ideologies, and education levels. The diversity across countries is evident within companies that operate globally. Corporate policies and information systems must adapt to the changing workforce and greater diversity of operations, which often results in the accounting function having a larger role in managing operations. Although different languages and cultures can impede communications within globally dispersed operations, accounting information can be a powerful coordinating mechanism. The interpretation of accounting information need not depend on local culture or language.

Accounting concepts, tools, and measurements can be the medium through which people of diverse languages and cultures communicate. Accounting provides an ideal international technical language because it is a basic application of another universal language—mathematics. Managing a global business, as opposed to one that operates in a single country, involves many considerations in addition to coordinating employees. Global businesses must consider country differences in currency values, labor practices, political risks, tax rates, commercial laws, and infrastructure such as ports, airports, and highways. These considerations require development of new systems and controls to manage risks and exploit opportunities.

Diversity across countries is evident in global businesses.

Within the United States, there is a trend to increase workplace diversity. The trend is driven partly by legal requirements and business initiatives to increase opportunities for minorities and partly by organizational self-interest. Refer to Exhibit 18–4 for reasons, other than legal requirements, that firms may seek a more diverse workforce. Unfortunately, this trend can be problematic in light of other business practices discussed in this chapter. Business process reengineering and downsizing diminish the opportunity to diversify and become more responsive to the marketplace.

Technology plays a major role in the communications that are necessary to harmonize employee actions to manufacture products and serve customers. Often, the integration of information systems is accomplished with enterprise systems.

EXHIBIT 18–4
WHY SELF-INTERESTED FIRMS SEEK A DIVERSE GROUP OF EMPLOYEES

1. *Increase market share.* A more diverse workforce connects to a more diverse market.
2. *Decrease costs.* Increased diversity leads to lower employee turnover.
3. *Increase productivity.* A heterogeneous group is more creative than a homogeneous group.
4. *Improve management quality.* A more diverse employee pool yields more management talent.
5. *Improve recruiting efforts.* Fewer worker/talent shortages affect firms that recruit from the broadest possible future employee pools.

Source: Ann Morrison, *The New Leaders: Guidelines on Leadership Diversity in America* (San Francisco: Jossey-Bass, 1992), pp. 20–27.

ENTERPRISE RESOURCE PLANNING (ERP) SYSTEMS

LO.4
WHY ARE FIRMS ADOPTING ENTERPRISE RESOURCE PLANNING SYSTEMS, AND WHAT ARE THEIR PURPOSES?

Firms commonly use networked personal computers (PCs) and minicomputers to handle the information management requirements of specific functions, such as finance, marketing, and manufacturing. PCs allow maximum user flexibility in accessing and manipulating data in real time. However, the increased use of PCs and local-area networks has resulted in the decentralization of information. As data management and storage have become more decentralized, firms have often lost the ability to integrate information across functions and to quickly access information that spans multiple functions. See Exhibit 18–5 for a presentation of how internal processes and functions are distributed across the supply chain and the types of information that may reside in isolated databases.

enterprise resource planning (ERP) system

Enterprise resource planning (ERP) systems are packaged software programs that allow companies to (1) automate and integrate the majority of their

EXHIBIT 18–5
INTERNAL SUPPLY CHAIN AND TRADITIONAL INFORMATION MANAGEMENT

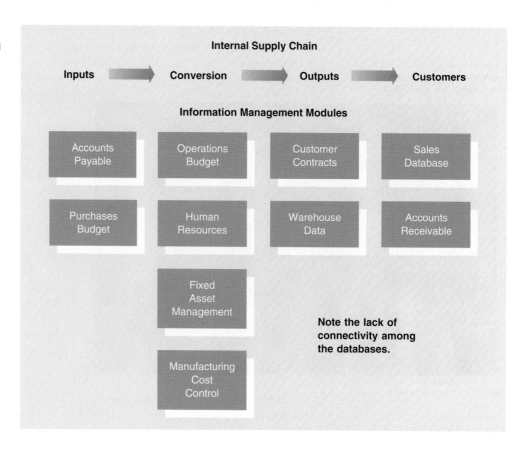

business processes, (2) share common data and practices across the entire enterprise, and (3) produce and access information in a real-time environment.[5] Implementing an ERP system should help a company to provide customers the highest quality products and best possible service; see Exhibit 18–6 for an illustration of an integrated, centralized information system. In theory, the ERP system should link the customer end of the supply chain with all functional areas responsible for the production and delivery of a product or service all the way upstream to suppliers. Increasingly, businesses will allow customers to access all necessary data about their orders through the Internet.

Why do firms implement ERP systems?

The following quote describes the benefits from ERP implementation for the whole business, its marketing function, and its customers:

The benefits of an ERP package to a business are in reduced overheads, improved customer service and better quality, and more timely management information. Reduced overheads should be achieved through the elimination of duplication of effort in duplicate keying and reconciliation of independent systems. Better management information becomes available when all company information is held in one database which can be queried to provide quality reports on margins broken down by customer, product, rep, area, etc. E-commerce has the potential to offer a quantum leap in customer service by giving the customer direct access to your systems.[6]

ERP's key concept is a central repository for all organizational data so that they are accessible in real time by and in an appropriate format for a decision maker. Data are entered into the central depository through a series of modules. Usually 30 or more modules are required to complete an ERP installation.[7] Exhibit 18–7 provides a list of typical modules included in an ERP system.

---

[5] Win G. Jordan and Kip R. Krumwiede, "ERP Implementers Beware!" *Cost Management Update* (March 1999), p. 1.
[6] Paddy White, "ERP: The Big Company Solution for Small Companies," *Accountancy Ireland* (August 1999), p.4. Reprinted with permission.
[7] Ibid.

EXHIBIT 18–6
ENTERPRISE RESOURCE PLANNING INFORMATION MANAGEMENT

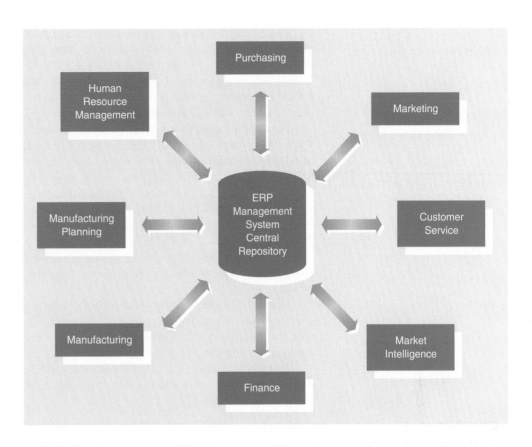

EXHIBIT 18–7
TYPICAL MODULES IN AN ERP INSTALLATION

Finance Function (bookkeeping, paying bills, collecting cash)

General ledger: Keeps centralized charts of accounts and corporate financial balances

Accounts receivable: Tracks payments due to the company

Accounts payable: Schedules bill payments

Fixed assets: Manages costs related to property, plant, and equipment

Treasury management: Monitors and manages cash holdings and investment risks

Cost control: Analyzes costs related to overhead, products, and customers

Human Resources Management (personnel-related tasks)

Human resources administration: Automates processes such as recruitment, business travel management, and vacation allotments

Payroll: Handles accounting and preparation of checks to employees for salary and bonuses

Self-service HR: Lets workers select benefits and manage their personal information

Manufacturing and Logistics

Production planning: Performs capacity planning and creates a daily production schedule

Materials management: Controls materials purchasing and manages inventory

Order entry and processing: Automates entry of customer orders and tracks their status

Warehouse management: Maintains records of stored goods and follows their movement through warehouses

Transportation management: Arranges, schedules, and monitors delivery of products to customers

Project management: Monitors costs and work schedules on a project-by-project basis

Plant maintenance: Sets plans and oversees upkeep of facilities

Customer service management: Administers service agreements and checks contracts and warranties when customers contact the company

Source: *Computerworld, http://www.computerworld.com.*

Results from a survey of international company managers about their motivations for implementing an ERP system and the perceived benefits gained from the implementation are shown in Exhibit 18–8. Timeliness of information and having information to support decision making are the two most commonly cited reasons for implementing an ERP system. The perceived benefits of implementing ERP appear to align with these motivations.

Installation of an ERP system impacts the financial function in three significant ways. First, financial and system specialists become responsible for selecting and installing the software. ERP software includes brand names such as SAP, R/3, PeopleSoft, and Baan. Installing an ERP system in a large company involves thousands of hours of labor and millions of dollars of capital.

Second, financial specialists will be responsible for analyzing the data repository to support management decisions. Data analysis often involves "drilling down" from aggregate data (such as total sales for the firm) to detailed data (such as sales by store) to identify market opportunities and to better manage costs. Such analysis can explain why a certain product moves well at some stores but not at others.

data mining

Analysis can also involve **data mining**, which uses statistical techniques to uncover answers to important questions about business operations.[8] Data mining is useful to uncover quality problems, study customer retention, determine which promotions generate the greatest sales impact, and identify cost drivers.

ERP installation places a burden on financial specialists to maintain the integrity of the data depository. Fulfilling this obligation requires accountants and other spe-

EXHIBIT 18–8

SURVEY OF REASONS FOR ADOPTING ERP AND PERCEIVED BENEFITS FROM ADOPTION

Reasons for Adopting ERP Systems	Percentage of Respondents Answering Affirmatively
Increased demand for real-time information	96
Information for decision making	92
Integration of applications	77
Business process reengineering	54
Cost reduction	50
Taxation requirements	35
Increase sales	31
Application of new business plan	27

Perceived Benefits of ERP Implementation in Rank Order

Increased flexibility in information generation

Increased integration of accounting applications

Improved quality of [financial] reports

Improved decisions based on timely and reliable accounting information

Reduction of time for annual closing of books

Improved decision making process

Increased use of financial ratio analysis

Reduction in time for issuance of [financial] reports

Improved internal audit function

Reduction of time for transaction processing

Improved working capital control

Source: Charalambos Spathis and Sylvia Constantinides, "Enterprise Resource Planning Systems' Impact on Accounting Processes," *Business Process Management Journal* 10: 2 (2004), pp. 234–247.

[8] Ibid.

cialists to monitor the ERP modules and be confident that the system successfully converts raw data into the standardized format required for the main repository.

Also, finance specialists are accountable for integrating externally purchased data (such as industry sales data and other external intelligence) with internally generated data. ERP systems represent a generational leap in the gathering, processing, and analysis of information. As ERP systems become increasingly integrated into Internet-based technology, customers will have ease of access to a worldwide marketplace.

In turn, customer-driven competition will cause firms to continually seek innovative ways to attract potential customers. These innovations are often obtained through strategic efforts that combine the talents and capabilities of two or more firms.

STRATEGIC ALLIANCES

LO.5
WHAT ARE STRATEGIC ALLIANCES, WHAT FORMS DO THEY TAKE, AND WHY DO FIRMS ENGAGE IN THEM?

strategic alliance

What challenges do strategic alliances create for the accounting function?

The usual supply chain structure has clear distinctions between supplier and customer firms—no "fuzzy boundaries" create an inability to determine where one firm ends its contribution to the supply chain and another begins its contribution. In some instances, however, companies have incentives to develop interorganizational agreements that go beyond normal supplier/customer arrangements. Generically, these agreements are called **strategic alliances**: agreements involving two or more firms with complementary core competencies to jointly contribute to the supply chain.

Strategic alliances can take many forms including joint ventures, equity investments, licensing, joint R&D arrangements, technology swaps, and exclusive buyer/seller agreements.[9] A strategic alliance differs from the usual interactions among independent firms in that the output produced reflects a joint effort between (or among) the firms and the rewards of that effort are split between (or among) the allied firms. An unusual illustration of a strategic alliance is a recent agreement between the Georgia Ports Authority and the Panama Canal Authority. In the agreement, the two parties committed to jointly promote shipping routes between Asia and the Port of Savannah. The agreement also calls for sharing data, technology, and information as well as executing a joint marketing program.[10]

The strategic alliance is typical of many other business arrangements: It involves the exploitation of partner knowledge, has partners with access to different markets, and allows sharing of risks and rewards. The use of strategic alliances to exploit or create business opportunities is pervasive and economically significant, although the following quote indicates the challenges in measuring the frequency in use of alliances.

> *In Hollywood and Silicon Valley, alliances are old hat: in a sense, almost every movie is an ad-hoc alliance, as is the development of every new computer chip. But, as in so much else, these two fashionable places are proving models for older industries. The most obvious change is in the sheer number of alliances.*
>
> *Mergers, like marriages, can be legally defined and therefore readily counted. Alliances are more like love affairs: they take many forms, may be transient or lasting, and live beyond the easy reach of statisticians.[11]*

A typical strategic alliance involves the creation of a new entity. In structuring the new entity, the contributions required of the parent organizations must be determined. Beyond simply contributing cash, many new ventures will require inputs

[9] T. K. Das and Bing-Sheng Teng, "Resource and Risk Management in the Strategic Alliance Making Process," *Journal of Management* (January–February 1998), p. 21.
[10] "Georgia Ports Authority, Panama Canal Sign Agreement," *Journal of Commerce* (June 20, 2003), p. 1.
[11] "Mergers and Alliances," *The Economist* (May 15, 1999), p. 73.

of human capital, technology, access to distribution channels, patents, and supply contracts. Furthermore, a governing board or set of directors must be established for the entity, and agreement must be reached as to how many directors can be appointed by each parent. Composition of the governing board determines which of the parent entities is more influential in managing the new entity. Simultaneous agreements must be executed to express the rights of the parents in sharing gains and to specify obligations for bearing losses. Such agreements will have significant implications for the risks borne by the parent organizations.

An overriding concern in designing a strategic alliance is aligning the interests of the parent organizations with the new entity. The alliance is likely to work only if both parent organizations believe they are receiving adequate value for their contributions. This caveat is especially true today when many strategic alliances involve agreements between competitors.

Establishing strategic alliances involves a series of complex decisions that are based on inputs from many specialists. For example, financial professionals must assess risk and develop strategies for parent company management. These experts must also design a financial structure, develop management control systems, and install accounting and other information systems. The execution of a strategic alliance is as involved as the establishment of any new business. The process of managing an alliance requires the use of virtually every tool and concept discussed in this text including cost management systems, product costing systems, cost allocation, inventory management, decision making, and performance evaluation.

The technology evolution has been shown to have a significant impact on management practices and the activities of the financial professional. The next section discusses how technological and other organizational changes affect nonprofessional workers and how financial professionals have been pressured to develop ways to convey information to those without technical finance and accounting expertise.

OPEN-BOOK MANAGEMENT

open-book management

LO.6
WHAT ARE THE CHARACTERISTICS OF OPEN-BOOK MANAGEMENT, AND WHY DOES ITS ADOPTION REQUIRE CHANGES IN ACCOUNTING METHODS AND PRACTICES?

Open-book management is a philosophy about increasing a firm's performance by involving all workers and by ensuring that all workers have access to operational and financial information necessary to achieve performance improvements. Although no specific definition of open-book management exists, it has some defined principles, as shown in Exhibit 18–9. Firms practicing open-book management typically disclose detailed financial information to all employees, train them to interpret and use the information, empower them to make decisions, and tie a portion of their pay to the company's bottom line.[12] Application of this philosophy is appropriate in decentralized organizations that have empowered employees to make decisions. Proponents of open-book management argue that the approach helps employees understand how their work activities affect the firm's costs and revenues. With this understanding, employees can adopt or change work practices to either increase revenues or decrease costs.

However, merely opening the financial records to a firm's employees will not necessarily solve any problems or improve anyone's performance. Most employees, particularly nonmanagerial workers, neither have developed skills to interpret business financial information nor understand accounting concepts and methods. Even many highly educated functional specialists have little knowledge of how profits are generated and performance is measured in financial terms. The key to understanding is training. **Springfield Remanufacturing**, a recession-era spin-off

---

[12] Edward J. Stendardi and Thomas Tyson, "Maverick Thinking in Open-Book Firms: The Challenge for Financial Executives," *Business Horizons* (September–October 1997), p. 35.

EXHIBIT 18–9

TEN COMMON PRINCIPLES OF OPEN-BOOK MANAGEMENT

1. Turn the management of a business into a game that employees can win.
2. Open the books and share financial and operating information with employees.
3. Teach the employees to understand the company's financial statements.
4. Show employees how their work influences financial results.
5. Link nonfinancial measures to financial results.
6. Target priority areas and empower employees to make improvements.
7. Review results together and keep employees accountable. Regularly hold performance review meetings.
8. Post results and celebrate successes.
9. Distribute bonus awards based on employee contributions to financial outcomes.
10. Share the ownership of the company with employees. Employee stock ownership plans (ESOPs) are routinely established in firms that practice open-book management.

Source: Tim Davis, "Open-Book Management: Its Promises and Pitfalls," *Organizational Dynamics* (Winter 1997), pp. 6–20. Copyright © 1997, with permission from Elsevier Science.

of General Motors, first introduced the concept of open-book management. Gary Brown, human resources director at Springfield Remanufacturing, provides some insights about the learning curve for nonfinancial workers to become financially literate.

> *Brown estimates that it generally takes two years for people to become financially literate (two iterations of the planning cycle). However, formal financial education and training is not the major expense, nor does training consume the most time, according to Brown. He emphasizes that the most valuable learning takes place in the "huddles" and when employees study the figures by themselves. An exceptionally motivated employee who does a great deal of self-study may become financially literate in six months.[13]*

If financial information is to be the basis of employee decision making, the information must be structured with the level of sophistication of the decision maker in mind. Providing such information requires accountants to become much more creative in the methods used to compile and present financial data.

Why does the use of open-book management often involve "games"?

Effective open-book management requires sharing accounting and financial information with employees who have little knowledge of accounting concepts. Games can be used to teach these concepts to financially unsophisticated employees.

Games People Play

Games make learning both fun and competitive and can simplify complex financial practices. To illustrate how games can be used in open-book management, assume that Newway Manufacturing, a manufacturer of portable buildings, has decided to implement open-book management concepts. One of its key departments is Assembly, which is responsible for combining building components of various models into finished products. Most components that are required for assembly are manufactured in other departments of the company.

Assembly employs one manager and 10 workers. Although highly skilled in the technical aspects of assembling wall, door, and frame components, workers do not know anything about financial management or accounting techniques. For these

---

[13] Tim Davis, "Open Book Management: Its Promises and Pitfalls," *Organizational Dynamics* (Winter 1997), p. 13.

workers, the game must begin with very simple accounting principles. The outcomes of the game, as determined by financial and nonfinancial performance measurements, must be easy to comprehend and must be easily related to the motivation for establishing the game—for example, to maximize firm profit, maximize customer satisfaction, and maximize shareholder value.

Data in Exhibit 18–10 pertain to one product of the firm: an economy building. These data have been gathered from the most recent month's production and accounting records and have been provided by Newway's controller.

The starting point in designing a system to provide information to Assembly employees is to determine the system's objectives. Reasonable initial design objectives include the following:

- enabling Assembly employees to understand how their work affects the achievement of corporate objectives; to this end, it is important to measure what you want employees to do well;
- helping Assembly workers understand how their work affects upstream and downstream departments; and
- generating demand from the employees for information and training that leads to improvements in performance in Assembly.

Because overhead cost is more difficult to comprehend than direct material and direct labor cost, information on overhead costs can be excluded from the initial system developed for Assembly employees. Direct material and direct labor will be the information focus. Furthermore, employees cannot exert control over the price paid for materials or labor, thus these data could be presented at budgeted or standard, rather than actual, cost. If actual costs are used, variations in purchase prices occurring throughout the year could disguise other more important information from the financially unsophisticated workers (such as quantities of materials consumed). If desirable, a more sophisticated system can be developed once the workers fully understand the initial system.

One motivation for providing information to Assembly workers is to cause them to understand how their actions affect achievement of the overall corporate objectives. To initiate this understanding, management can establish a sales price for Assembly output so that a measure of the department's contribution to corporate profits can be established. Assume that the initial price for the assembled

EXHIBIT 18–10

NEWWAY MANUFACTURING ASSEMBLY DEPARTMENT COST DATA

Item	Quantity	Unit Cost	Total Cost
Door panels	2	$ 5.00	$ 10.00
Wall panels (sides)	2	28.00	56.00
Wall panels (ends)	2	19.00	38.00
Structural frame	1	90.00	90.00
Roofing panels	8	7.00	56.00
Door frame			
Top	2	7.00	14.00
Bottom	2	8.00	16.00
Sides	4	4.00	16.00
Door hinges	4	3.00	12.00
Fasteners	1 package	4.50	4.50
Total direct material cost			$312.50
Direct labor cost	4 hours	15.00	60.00
Total direct cost			$372.50

portable building is set at $475; it is not necessary for the established sales price to represent actual market value. The per-unit profit calculation for Assembly workers follows:

Sales price	$ 475.00
Total direct cost (from Exhibit 18–10)	(372.50)
Profit contribution	$ 102.50

Total profit equals per-unit profit multiplied by the number of units produced. By analyzing this simple profit calculation, workers quickly realize that they can increase profits by decreasing costs or increasing the units produced. However, some elementary quality information should be added so that the implication of defective production can be seen. For example, quality defect costs could be charged to Assembly for products that are not of the quality specified. An income statement for the Assembly Department for a period would then appear as follows:

Sales	$ XXXXXX
Total direct cost	(XXXXXX)
Rework and defects	(XXXX)
Profit contribution	$ XXXX

With this profit calculation, workers will see that profit maximization requires maximization of output, minimization of direct costs, and minimization of quality defects.

One Japanese company, **Higashimaru Shoyu**, a maker of soy sauce, has gone so far as to create its own internal bank and currency.[14] Each department purchases its required inputs from other departments using the currency and established transfer prices. In turn, each department is paid in currency for its outputs. The flow of currency reinforces the profit calculations applying to each department.

To exploit the financial information they are given, workers should be trained in ways to improve profits. The "game" of trying to increase profits serves as motivation for workers to learn about cost and operational management methods. Relating training to the game allows workers to see the relevance of training, and they will seek training to help them understand how to read and comprehend a simple income statement and to identify approaches that can be used to improve results.

Motivating Employees

It cannot be assumed that the Assembly workers at Newway are internally motivated to play the game well. Instead, upper management should promote the game. The obvious way to motivate workers to use the game information to improve profits is to link their compensation to profits. Assembly workers could be paid bonuses if profits are above a target level. Alternatively, the workers could be paid a percentage of profits as a bonus. In either case, linking compensation to profits is a necessary step to motivate workers to have an interest in the game and to improve their performance. The positive effects of a good bonus program are described as follows:

> *Open-book management works only if it is accompanied by adequate incentives. "People start to back away if they don't have some sort of reward. In effect, you are asking people to take on ownership behaviors, but not treating them*

---

[14] Robin Cooper, *When Lean Enterprises Collide (Competing Through Confrontation)* (Boston: Harvard Business School Press, 1995).

*like owners. That's like getting to smell lunch, but not being allowed to taste it,"
says [Corey] Rosen of the National Center for Employee Ownership. "If people
don't have a stake in the company, why should they care?"[15]*

Some companies offer performance-based bonuses to motivate employees and
some offer employee stock ownership plans (ESOPs). Other companies, such as
Album, Inc., do both. Pay and performance links can also be based on more specific data. For example, measures can be devised for on-time delivery rates (to the
next downstream department), defect rates, output per labor hour, and other performance areas to make workers aware of how their inputs and outputs affect other
departments and financial outcomes. All critical dimensions of performance including costs, quality, and investment management can be captured in performance
measurements.

As soon as workers have become accustomed to receiving financial and other
information to manage their departments, more elaborate information systems can
be developed as the sophistication of the information consumers (workers) evolves.
For example, once the direct material, direct labor, and quality costs are understood, workers in Newway's Assembly Department can learn to evaluate overhead
cost information.

Implementation Challenges

Open-book management can be difficult to implement. Characteristics of firms that
are best suited to a successful implementation include small size, decentralized
management, a history of employee empowerment, and the presence of trust between employees and managers. In small firms, employees can more easily understand how their contributions influence the organization's bottom line. Firms
with decentralized structures and empowered employees have workers who are
accustomed to making decisions. Trust among employees and managers is necessary for games to be devised that result in higher pay and greater job satisfaction
for all employees.

Accountants face unique challenges in implementing open-book management
in even the most favorable environments. The challenges are present in both the
obstacles to be overcome and the innovations in reporting to be designed and implemented. One significant organiza-
tional obstacle in many firms is a
history of carefully guarding financial
information. Even in publicly owned
companies that are required to release
certain financial information to the general public, top managers have historically limited employee access to
financial data that the top managers regard as sensitive. Accountants have
typically viewed themselves as the cus-
todians of this sensitive information
rather than its conveyors. To successfully implement open-book management, accountants must develop an
attitude about information sharing that
is as enthusiastic as the traditional attitude of information guarding.

*Open-book management means
literally opening the books to
share accounting information.*

GETTY IMAGES

---

[15] Julie Carrick Dalton, "Between the Lines," *CFO: The Magazine for Senior Financial Executives* (March 1999), p. 61. © 1999
CFO Publishing Corporation. Reprinted with permission.

Having been grounded in higher education courses and other appropriate training, accountants have generally operated under the assumption that financial information users have an adequate understanding of the rules used to compile financial data. However, open-book management requires the provision of accounting data to users who have little understanding of accounting conventions and rules. Thus, accountants must develop ways to convey accounting information so that unsophisticated users will understand it. Furthermore, by teaching users to have a better understanding of financial data, accountants help facilitate better organizational decision making.

Accountants must also be innovative to implement open-book management. One significant requirement is the development of information systems that are capable of generating information for an organizational segment in a format that the segment's employees can understand. Thus, the information system must be designed to be sensitive to the user's financial sophistication.

Similarly, performance measures that employees can understand must be devised. The measures must capture the actual performance relative to the objectives of organizational segments and the organization as a whole. Objectives can be stated in terms of competitors' performance or industry norms. For example, a firm's objective can be to surpass the average product quality level of the industry. Measurement of actual achievement relative to this objective requires accountants to develop information systems that are focused on gathering nontraditional types of information—in this instance, quality level of output in the industry. The primary principle of measurement is to measure what is important. "The 'what' to measure comes from your mission statement, strategic business plan and the things that drive your business. If customer satisfaction is vital, measure customer satisfaction. If profit is vital, measure profit."[16]

Finally, because principles of open-book management include involving all employees and evaluating and rewarding their performance, measures that can be integrated across segments and functional areas must be devised. For example, if one of a firm's major objectives is to increase profitability, performance measures must be devised for engineers, accountants, production workers, administrators, janitors, and so forth that cause all of these functional groups to work toward a common end: increased profits.

An emerging area of concern for managers in nearly all entities is the impact of their operations on the environment. The concerns have arisen as a result of an increased consciousness of environmental issues and new governmental regulations enacted to protect the environment.

ENVIRONMENTAL MANAGEMENT SYSTEMS

LO.7
WHAT ARE THE THREE GENERIC APPROACHES THAT FIRMS CAN TAKE IN CONTROLLING ENVIRONMENTAL COSTS?

What is the least risky strategy for managing pollution?

Impact of businesses on the environment is of increasing concern to governments, citizens, investors, and managers. Accountants are increasingly concerned with both measuring business performance in regard to environmental issues and managing environmental costs. In the future, investors are likely to evaluate a company's environmental track record along with its financial record when making investment decisions.

Management of environmental costs requires the consideration of environmental issues in every aspect of operations. For example, environmental effects are related to the amount of scrap and by-products produced in manufacturing operations, materials selected for product components (recyclable or not), actions of suppliers that produce necessary inputs, and habits of customers in consuming and disposing of products and packaging. In short, environmental issues span the entire

[16] Matt Plaskoff, "Measure What You Want to Improve," *Professional Builder* (June 2003), p. 93.

value chain. In addition to voluntary intentions to reduce pollution, under the 1997 Kyoto Protocol, many countries, not including the United States, agreed to reduce the pollution (particularly greenhouse gases) generated by their industries.

Although some companies are striving to voluntarily reduce pollution because of a social consciousness, other companies are trying to do so to reduce the financial risks associated with generation of pollution. By avoiding these risks, companies may lower their cost of capital as suggested in the following quote.

> *A group of analysts at Innovest contend that a company's strategic response to environmental risk is a window into the company's management ability. The more "eco-efficient" a company is, the better its stock performance is likely to be compared with others in its industry—and that's true, apparently, whether the industry is oil, mining, or solar energy.[17]*

There are three generic strategies for dealing with environmental effects of operations, and each has unique financial implications. First, an "end-of-pipe strategy" may be employed. With this approach, managers "produce the waste, or pollutant, and then find a way to clean it up."[18] Common tools used in this approach are wastewater cleaning systems and smokestack scrubbers, but this strategy can be ineffective in reducing the generation of greenhouse gases. A second strategy involves process improvements, which include changes to "recycle wastes internally, reduce the production of wastes, or adopt production processes that generate no waste."[19] A third strategy is pollution prevention, which involves "complete avoidance of pollution by not producing any pollutants in the first place."[20]

Although minimizing the environmental impact of operations can be a reasonable goal, some impact on the environment is unavoidable. For example, energy must be consumed to manufacture products; similarly, materials must be consumed as goods are produced. Without energy and material consumption, no goods can be manufactured.[21] In the management of environmental costs, accountants must analyze the environmental dimensions of investment decisions:

> *In the capital investment area, accountants can help managers by including quality and environmental benefits in the analysis. If a proposed project is more energy efficient or produces less pollution than an alternative, those factors should be included in the analysis. The financial data should include any cost savings from lower energy usage. If the company must control pollution, the financial impact should be recognized.[22]*

Other managerial concerns related to the management of environmental costs include managing quality, research and development, and technology acquisition. Although the relationship between quality costs and environmental costs is not fully understood, many examples can be cited suggesting that quality and environmental costs are highly related. For instance, the reduction in scrap and waste production (quality improvements) serves to reduce environmental costs and concerns (waste disposal).

Research and development identifies new products and new production processes, and develops new materials. New product design influences the (1) types and quantities of materials produced, (2) types and quantities of waste, scrap, and by-products produced, (3) amount of energy consumed in the production

---

[17] Abrahm Lustgarten, "Lean, Mean and Green?" *Fortune* (July 26, 2004), p. 210.

[18] Germain Böer, Margaret Curtin, and Louis Hoyt, "Environmental Cost Management," *Management Accounting* (September 1998), p. 28ff.

[19] Ibid.

[20] Ibid.

[21] For more information on this concept, see Frances Cairncross, *Costing the Earth* (Boston: Harvard Business School Press, 1992), p. 26.

[22] Harold P. Roth and Carl E. Keller, Jr., "Quality, Profits, and the Environment: Diverse Goals or Common Objectives?" *Management Accounting* (July 1997), pp. 50–55.

process, and (4) potential for gathering and recycling products when they reach obsolescence.

Technology acquisition also has many environmental impacts. For instance, technology affects energy consumption and conservation; environmental emissions; the quantity, types, and characteristics of future obsolete equipment (for instance, whether it is made of recyclable materials); the rate of defective output produced; the quantities of scrap, waste, and by-products produced; and the nature and extent of support activities necessary to keep the technology operating.

Exhibit 18–11 provides considerations for the financial professional to evaluate whether a firm's information systems provide relevant information for managing environmental costs. An analysis of the checklist shows that the financial professional must effectively gather both quantitative and nonquantitative data both within and outside of the firm.

EXHIBIT 18–11

CONSIDERATIONS FOR ENVIRONMENTAL COST CONTROL

Cost Management Systems

How much does each of our divisions spend on environmental management?

Do we have consistent and reliable systems in place to measure environmental costs?

How does our cost management system support good environmental management decisions?

How do we track compliance costs?

How do we connect line management decisions to the environmental costs they create?

Which divisions manage environmental costs the best?

How do we compare with competitors in managing environmental costs?

What kinds of waste do we produce?

What are the proposed regulations that will affect our company?

Cost Reporting Systems

Who receives reports on environmental costs in our company?

Does our bonus plan explicitly consider environmental costs?

How do we charge internal environmental costs to managers?

How does the financial system capture environmental cost data?

Do our managers have all necessary tools to measure total costs of the wastes generated?

Do our systems identify environmental cost reduction opportunities?

Source: Germain Böer, Margaret Curtin, and Louis Hoyt, "Environmental Cost Management," *Management Accounting* (September 1998), p. 32.

Revisiting

Albums, Inc.

Peter Cardello selected open-book management as the innovation to build the skills of his employees so they could assume more responsibility in operating the organization. Albums, Inc., created games for each department to teach financial management concepts. For example, the sales department plays "The Sales Game." The metaphor used in this game is a gas pump in which the "price per gallon" is the proxy for average unit sales price. The focus of the game is on increasing average daily sales and its payoff is a free lunch. The receiving department plays "The Receiving Game" in which the aim is to keep the shelves stocked so that orders can be filled promptly. The metaphor in this game is a climber ascending steps up a mountain. The climber advances on days when there are no stockouts and retreats on days when stockouts occur. The object is to get the climber to the top of the mountain; when that occurs, the employees are allowed to leave work two hours early. "The Recycling Game" was organized to induce employees to reuse boxes received from vendors when sending products to customers.

In this game, the employees set goals for the number of boxes to be recycled each month, and if they attain the goal, the employees receive a free lunch.

Some of the principles applied to the games at Album are as follows: (1) games should encourage "friendly" competition; (2) when goals are met, everyone in the department shares in the reward, not just a single person or team; (3) employees rather than managers design the game; and (4) games should add both fun and rewards to the work experience.

Album management now shares all financial information except salaries with employees each month in regularly scheduled meetings. In the meetings, financial rewards are given to employees who can answer financial questions. Employees can choose to either "pass" or "play" in a game. When the games were first introduced, most employees passed; now most play. The benefits have been tangible: Employee turnover has been reduced, employee trust in management has increased, profits are strong, and employees are sharing in the higher profits.

Sources: *http://www.albumsinc.com/, http://www.nceo.org/library/obm_albums.html.*

Comprehensive Review Module

Chapter Summary

1. Business process reengineering causes radical changes in ways firms execute processes by

   - using fewer employees.

   - making better use of technology.

2. Global competition is forcing firms to downsize and restructure operations to

   - defend core competencies.

   - remain cost competitive.

3. Many organizations are becoming more diverse

   - as measured by the religion, race, values, work habits, cultures, political ideologies, and education level of employees.

   - because of globalization and proactive diversification programs.

   - and are placing more pressure on the accounting system

     > for communicating among employees.

     > for measuring performance.

4. Many firms are adopting enterprise resource planning (ERP) systems

   - which consist of a number of modules (such as payroll, fixed assets, accounts receivable, and cash management), each of which accounts for specific activities.

   - which facilitate data mining and the integration of financial and nonfinancial information across functional areas of the business.

   - to automate accounting processes.

   - to share data across the enterprise.

   - to provide real-time access to company data.

5. Strategic alliances

   - are agreements involving two or more firms to jointly contribute to the supply chain.

   - often blur traditional boundaries between supplier/customer.

   - take many different forms such as

     > joint ventures.

     > equity investments.

     > licensing arrangements.

     > joint R&D arrangements.

     > technology swaps.

     > exclusive buy/sell agreements.

   - allow the sharing of risks and rewards between/among firms.

6. Open-book management

   - increases the transparency of information within an organization, which often requires accountants to change from a mind-set of guarding to sharing information.

   - creates challenges and opportunities for accountants to make information understandable to financially unsophisticated employees, which frequently involves the creation of games and meetings.

   - decentralizes both authority to make decisions and responsibility for decision results, which can be implemented by tying rewards to performance.

7. The three generic approaches to controlling environmental costs include

   - cleaning up pollutants are dealt with after they are produced (end-of-pipe strategy).

   - improving processes to reduce the amount of waste produced.

   - preventing pollution by never producing polluting materials.

Key Terms

business process reengineering (BPR) *(p. 740)*
data mining *(p. 748)*

downsizing *(p. 742)*
enterprise resource planning (ERP) system *(p. 745)*

open-book management *(p. 750)*
strategic alliance *(p. 749)*

Questions

1. What is business process reengineering? Does it lead to radical or modest changes in business practices? Discuss.

2. Business process reengineering and downsizing often occur together. Why?

3. Describe "downsizing," its causes, and its primary risks.

4. How has the globalization of firms affected the diversity of their employees? Why has increased diversity put an additional burden on accounting systems?

5. Besides increasing globalization, what trends within the United States are causing firms to seek more diversified workforces?

6. What is an enterprise resource planning (ERP) system? How do ERP systems improve on prior generations of information systems?

7. New strategic alliances are formed every day. What are they, and why are they increasingly being used by businesses?

8. Open-book management is a relatively new philosophy about the use of information in organizations. Describe open-book management and how it differs philosophically from the traditional view of the management of financial information in an organization.

9. How does the implementation of open-book management require an organization's accountants to change their traditional practices?

10. Describe the three generic strategies for dealing with the environmental effects of operations. Is one of the strategies always preferred to the others? Discuss.

Exercises

11. (Technology acquisition) Acquisition of new technology is often a perilous event for firms. The successful acquisition and implementation of new systems require much more than merely purchasing hardware and software. For example, expenditures for a typical installation of a new financial system are split as follows:

Presales consultancy and advice	11.74%
Software	37.64
Implementation	28.27
Training	14.12
Other services	8.23

Source: Anonymous, "An Overview of Accounting Software Packages," *Management Accounting* (London; March 1999), pp. 50–53.

    a. Why should training be included as a cost of technology acquisition?

    b. How can the financial function of a business improve the internal process of technology acquistion?

12. (Technological change) Financial professionals are at the forefront in adopting new technologies, many of which are at the core of business strategies. Discuss how the increasing reliance of business on technology coupled with the responsibility of the financial professional to manage technology has changed the skills required of corporate accountants.

13. (Business process reengineering) Business process reengineering (BPR) can be an effective tool to achieve breakthroughs in quality improvement and cost management. Total quality management (TQM) is another philosophy about achieving organizational change. Conduct a library or Internet search to identify articles that discuss BPR and TQM, and write a report in which you compare and contrast the two methodologies.

14. (Business process reengineering) Process mapping and value analysis are tools often used in business process reengineering. As discussed in Chapter 5, a process map is a flowchart of the set of activities that compose a process. Value (or activity) analysis examines each of the activities identified in the flowchart and determines to what extent it provides "value" to the customer. Those activities that add no value are targets to be designed out of the process.

    Select a process at your college or university such as admissions or enrollment. Prepare a process map, and conduct a value analysis of the process map. Then develop a plan (using Exhibit 18–2 as a guide) to design out of the process activities that add no value to the student customer.

15. (Downsizing) In the past decade, the Japanese economy has fallen from its lofty levels of the 1980s. As a consequence, many Japanese companies have been forced to downsize. In most companies, one of two strategies can be pursued in downsizing. First, a company can lay off employees. Second, a company can cut employment through natural attrition and by reducing future hiring.

    Conduct a library or Internet search of "Japanese management culture" to identify attitudes of Japanese managers about employees. Then prepare a report in which you explain why Japanese companies might prefer one of these downsizing strategies to the other.

16. (Downsizing) During the late 1990s and the early 2000s, the financial press reported story after story regarding downsizing and layoffs. Often the stories involved companies that had multiple rounds of downsizing events.

    Assume that you are a stock market analyst and are responsible for interpreting the economic significance of corporate layoffs. In general, would you interpret the layoffs as good news or bad news? Explain the rationale for your answer.

17. (Diversity) The issue of whether diversity is positive or negative for an organization has been hotly debated for many years. Some people argue that, because of its homogeneous workforce, Japan has an inherent advantage in competing with the United States. The benefits of a homogeneous workforce result from a common language, religion, work ethic, and so forth. Prepare a two-minute oral report in which you take a position and persuasively present an argument on whether diversity aids or hinders an organization.

18. (Diversity and discrimination) **Boeing Co.** settled a lawsuit for $15 million brought by its own African-American workers claiming discrimination in promotions. On the heels of that decision, a group of Asian workers, also claiming discrimination in promotions, filed suit against Boeing. Similar stories make headlines in the financial press nearly every day.

Discuss the contributions that can be made by the accounting and finance professionals in an organization to actively promote diversification of the workforce while managing real and perceived discrimination in promotion of workers and managers.

19. (Enterprise resource planning) With an ERP system, a company can develop a "storefront" on the Internet. Through its storefront connection with customers, the company can gather much information about the market and the demand for specific products.

Assume that you are employed by an automaker. How could you use the Internet storefront and data mining to learn more about the purchasers of your vehicles to improve the market share of future generations of your company's autos?

WebTUTOR Advantage

20. (Enterprise resource planning) ERP software programs allow tighter linkages within a supply chain than were possible with earlier generations of software. Consider the possibility of a tighter link between the marketing and engineering functions within a firm that makes consumer electronics. Discuss how the link between these two functions could improve
   a. customer satisfaction.
   b. time to bring new products to market.
   c. cost management.

21. (Enterprise resource planning) ERP software can facilitate the sharing of information throughout the supply chain. For example, an Internet storefront can be used to interact downstream with the final customer. Sales data gathered from the storefront can then be used as a basis for determining the quantity and mix of products to be produced. From this information, a production schedule can be prepared. Discuss how posting the production schedule on the Internet could result in improved coordination with the upstream (vendor) side of the supply chain.

22. (Strategic alliances) In their annual reports, companies provide brief descriptions of their most important contracts, including strategic alliances. Select a large publicly traded company and obtain a copy of its most recent annual report (in hard copy, on the company's Web site, or on the EDGAR portion of the SEC's Web site). Review the portions of the annual report that discuss strategic alliances. Based on your review, prepare an oral report in which you discuss the following points:
   a. motivations for establishing strategic alliances.
   b. extent to which strategic alliances are used to conduct business.
   c. relative financial success of the strategic alliances.

23. (Strategic alliances) Assume you are employed by a technology company that is considering entering into a strategic alliance with a communications company to provide certain innovative services delivered via the Internet. As a financial professional, how could you contribute to the organization and management of the strategic alliance?

24. (Open-book management) "Monopoly" by **Parker Brothers** has been a popular board game for many years. Assume that you have just been hired by a company in the steel industry. The company manufactures a variety of products from stock steel components. The management of your new employer is examining the potential use of open-book management techniques. Prepare a written report for the top managers in your company discussing your recommendations for implementing open-book management. In your report, discuss how you would use "Monopoly" as a training tool for workers who have little knowledge of accounting concepts.

25. (Open-book management) You have been hired as a consultant by a company that manufactures plastic and resin toys. Company management is presently discussing ways to improve product quality. Evidence of quality problems is everywhere: high rates of product defects, many customer returns, poor rate of customer retention, and high warranty costs. Top management has traced virtually all quality related problems to the production department.

Production workers in the company are paid based on a flat hourly rate. No bonuses are paid based on corporate profits or departmental performance measures. As the outside consultant, prepare an oral report to present to your client's top management discussing how open-book management could be applied to address the quality problems. At a minimum, include in your report how quality information would be conveyed to workers, how workers would be trained to understand the information, and how incentives would be established for improved quality performance.

26. (Environmental costs) Following are descriptions of environmental waste situations. Identify the environmental strategy you would select to deal with each situation and discuss your logic.
  a. A relatively small amount of low toxicity waste is produced. This waste is not easily recycled, nor is technology available to avoid its production. Disposal costs are relatively modest.
  b. The waste produced is highly toxic and is associated with several lethal diseases in humans. The cost of disposal is extraordinarily high.
  c. A moderate amount of waste, which is nearly identical to a chemical purchased and used in an etching operation, is produced. The waste differs from the purchased chemical only because of a small amount of contaminants introduced in the production process.

WebTUTOR Advantage

27. (Environmental costs) Galveston Products produces a variety of chemicals that are used in an array of commercial applications. One popular product, a chemical solvent, contains two very caustic acids, A and B, which can present a very serious environmental hazard if not disposed of properly. For every ton of chemical produced, 500 pounds of acid A and 300 pounds of acid B are required. Because of inefficiencies in the present production process, 40 pounds of acid A and 20 pounds of acid B remain as waste from each ton of chemical manufactured. Because of impurities in the waste acids, they cannot be used in the production of future batches of product. The company incurs a cost of $2 per pound to dispose of the waste acid produced.

Recently, the company has become aware of new technology that reduces the amount of waste acids produced. This technology would generate only 1 pound of acid A and 5 pounds of acid B as waste from each ton of chemical manufactured. Corporate management has estimated that the new technology could be acquired and installed at a cost of $500,000. The technology would have a life expectancy of six years. The new technology would not otherwise affect the cost of producing the chemical solvent.
  a. Which environmental cost management strategy is Galveston Products considering in this example?

b. Why would the application of discounted cash flow methods (see Chapter 13) be appropriate to evaluate the new technology?

28. (Environmental cost management) Firms' increasing awareness of their impacts on the environment has led to the establishment of companies that specialize in all aspects of managing the environmental effects of operations. Search the Internet using the term "environmental cost management." Review the Web pages of the vendors of environmental services identified by the search, and then write a brief report in which you describe the types of services that can be purchased to manage environmental costs.

Problems

29. (Accounting; downsizing; BPR) Most accounting professionals would agree that the accounting profession has developed effective tools for measuring and reporting events involving tangible assets. Most might also agree that the profession has miles to travel to report as effectively on events involving intangible assets. Examples of intangible assets are patents developed rather than purchased; customer and supplier relationships; and employee knowledge, skills, and abilities.

Assume that a U.S.-based manufacturing company implemented a BPR that resulted in the layoff of 20 percent of production workers.

a. How would the layoff impact the company's intangible assets?

b. How would the BPR event be reflected in the company's financial statements?

c. Given your answer to (a), do you think the financial reports reflect all significant effects of the layoffs? Explain.

30. (Downsizing) *"Most experienced CEOs have seen command-and-control management come and go. They've been through downsizing and rightsizing. Now they're seeing most companies (their own included) working to recast themselves as 'high-performing' organizations, with streamlined, non-hierarchical, fast moving teams of 'knowledge workers' trying to generate the greatest possible return on 'human capital.' The New Economy has put that capital in high demand and short supply, particularly in IT and other high-tech fields. As a result, CEOs and their top executives find themselves facing a broad spectrum of new challenges: competing for top talent, designing jobs consistent with business goals, communicating strategy, sharing information, earning employees' trust and commitment, measuring and improving employee performance, moving them up and leading them onward."*

Source: Hannele Rubin, "How CEOs Get Results," *Chief Executive* (February 2001), p. 8ff.

What can the accounting function in an organization do to help identify potential top management talent from internal operations?

31. (Open-book management) Kathy Townsend, Technical Instruments Division manager of Bigelow Electronics, attended a 30-minute seminar on open-book management recently. As a result of the seminar, she decided to implement some open-book management practices in her division. She began the process today when she received the latest quarterly results for her division.

Gary Robinson, the production supervisor of the finishing department in Townsend's division, was surprised to receive the following note in his afternoon mail.

Dear Gary:

I've just finished reviewing the financial results for the last quarter. I am including some data from the financial reports below. Because our firm must identify ways to become more cost competitive, I intend to share data from the financial reports with you each quarter. I want you to use the information as the basis for making your department more efficient. By early in the coming year, I intend to put in place an incentive pay system that will replace your current salary. Accordingly, your income in the future will depend on your ability to manage the costs of your department.

To begin reducing costs, I suggest you concentrate on the cost items which I have circled below. Please give me a call if you have any questions.

Regards,
KT

FINISHING DEPARTMENT COST ANALYSIS

	This Quarter	This Quarter Last Year	Last Quarter
Direct material	$ 95,000	$ 75,000	$ 90,000
Direct labor	925,000	840,000	940,000
Material-based overhead	27,000	22,000	23,000
Labor-based overhead	413,000	382,700	396,500
Machine-based overhead	657,000	589,000	617,000

As corporate controller of Bigelow Electronics, you are surprised when Robinson calls your office and asks to meet with your staff to discuss the financial report and to discuss the meaning of "overhead." As you consider how to deal with him, you begin to contemplate the memo that you are going to write to Townsend. Before any decisions are implemented, you realize that she can use your expertise to design and implement open-book management practices. As you write the memo, you know that your suggestions must be specific, positive, and informative.

32. (Various) Karen Krackle, CEO of Kar Komponents, sat dejected in her chair after reviewing the 2006 first-quarter financial reports on one of the company's core products: a standard, five-speed transmission (product number 2122) used in the heavy equipment industry in the manufacture of earth-moving equipment. Some of the information in the report follows.

MARKET REPORT, PRODUCT NUMBER 2122, QUARTER 1, 2006

Sales Data

Total sales (dollars), Quarter 1, 2006	$4,657,500
Total sales (dollars), Quarter 1, 2005	$6,405,000
Total sales (units), Quarter 1, 2006	3,450
Total sales (units), Quarter 1, 2005	4,200

Market Data

Industry unit sales, Quarter 1, 2006	40,000
Industry unit sales, Quarter 1, 2005	32,000
Industry average sales price, Quarter 1, 2006	$1,310
Industry average sales price, Quarter 1, 2005	$1,640

MARKET REPORT, PRODUCT NUMBER 2122, QUARTER 1, 2006

Profit Data

Miltown average gross profit per unit, Quarter 1, 2006	$ 45
Miltown average gross profit per unit, Quarter 1, 2005	160
Industry average gross profit per unit, Quarter 1, 2006	75
Industry average gross profit per unit, Quarter 1, 2005	140

Kar Komponents' strategy for this transmission is to compete on the basis of price. The transmission offers no features that allow it to be differentiated from those of major competitors. Kar Komponents' level of quality is similar to the average of the industry.

Also on Krackle's desk was a report from her business intelligence unit, on which she underlined the following key pieces of information.

- Commodity transmission components (nuts, bolts, etc.), which all major transmission producers acquire from specialty vendors, decreased in price by approximately 5 percent from January 2005 to January 2006.
- Two major competitors moved their main assembly operations from the United States to China in early 2005. These competitors are believed to have the lowest unit production cost in the industry.
- A third major competitor ceased manufacturing of major gear components and began outsourcing these parts from a Mexican firm in mid-2005. This firm increased its market share in 2005 from 10 to 14 percent following a major decrease in sales price.
- Kar Komponents' production operations did not change in any material respect from 2005 to 2006.
- Kar Komponents manufactures approximately 83 percent of the components used in the heavy industrial transmission. The industry norm is to make 57 percent of the components.
- For the balance of 2006, industry experts agree that quarterly demand for the heavy industrial transmission will be even higher than the levels posted for the first quarter of 2006.

a. Examine the information Krackle has gathered. Analyze the data to identify as specifically as possible the problems that have led to Kar Komponents' loss of profit and market share in the heavy industrial transmission market.

b. Based on your analysis in part (a) and the information given to Krackle, suggest specific alternatives that she should consider to make her firm more competitive in its market. Use concepts presented in the chapter as the basis of your recommendations.

33. (Enterprise resource management) **Borders** and **Amazon.com** are competitors in vending books and other consumer items. The two are differentiated to an extent by their marketing strategies. Although Amazon.com relies exclusively on Internet marketing, Borders operates both retail stores and an Internet outlet.

Assume that you work for a financial services firm that specializes in ERP installations. Your personal specialty involves ERP solutions that link the marketing function to the "back end" of businesses. Write a report in which you discuss the benefits that could be realized by Borders and Amazon.com from purchasing ERP software from you. In your report, discuss how the ERP solution that you would design for Borders would differ from the solution you design for Amazon.com.

34. (Environmental cost management) Classic Plastics has experienced serious problems as a result of attempts to manage its impacts on the environment. To illustrate the problems, consider the following events, which occurred during the past five years:

- Classic was assessed $75 million in fines and penalties for toxic emissions. These amounts related to several separate regulatory investigations.
- Classic received reprimands from several regulatory bodies for failing to maintain required records regarding hazardous waste.
- Classic is currently facing a class-action lawsuit filed by former employees of a subsidiary in Mexico alleging that management failed to disclose information to employees about the toxicity of certain materials. As a consequence, the health of the former employees has been permanently harmed.
- Classic must submit bids to obtain most of its business. Managers have casually observed that the company is successful more frequently when it bids on jobs that require handling the most toxic chemicals.
- Classic has a very basic accounting system that tracks costs on a job order basis but is not sensitive to quality or environmental costs.

Assume that you are an employee of the consulting firm that Classic has hired to improve management of all environmental effects. As the financial expert on the consulting team, you are expected to make recommendations as to how the information systems should be modified to reduce environmental costs. Prepare a report discussing your recommendations for Classic.

35. (Ethics) *"Employees expect that all parties will honor their explicit and implicit obligations. Distrust occurs when these obligations are not met or when the parties have different expectations regarding the obligations. When downsizing is employed as an organizational strategy, it focuses on economic goals over the promotion of commitment, and, as a result, the employees view the strategy with distrust.*

"John A. Challenger notes, 'It may be unrealistic to expect intense loyalty on the part of the worker when in many instances the employer cannot promise loyalty in return. The current spate of mergers in the banking, media, utilities, and other industries, major re-engineering efforts, and downsizings all have weakened the ties that spur employee commitment and productivity.' Frederick Reichheld states, 'The great betrayal of American workers is the failure of companies to let them know how much value they are creating, versus how much they are costing.'"

Source: Adapted from Larry Gross, "Downsizing: Are Employers Reneging on Their Social Promise?" *CPCU Journal* (Summer 2001), p. 112ff.

a. In your opinion, does the achievement of high-quality operations mandate that a firm treat its employees ethically? Discuss.

b. Discuss how employee perceptions of their employers mesh with the open-book management requirement to have honest exchanges of information between employees and managers.

36. (Strategic alliances) Strategic alliances and joint ventures are being used with increasing frequency to exploit market opportunities. Virtually all larger firms are involved in several to many strategic alliances.

a. From the perspective of controlling the quality of production, discuss how a strategic alliance is significantly different from a typical vendor/customer relationship.

b. How can the accounting function contribute to the management of quality for strategic alliances?

37. (Restructuring and outsourcing) Automakers provide an interesting study in cost management strategies. **General Motors** often provides a contrast to other U.S. manufacturers. For example, **DaimlerChrysler** and **Ford** have opted to outsource many product components, but GM continues to manufacture a much higher percentage of the parts needed to produce its cars.

One of the variables driving GM's strategy is its high level of unionization. The unions have resisted attempts made by General Motors to restructure operations and outsource more components.

a. From the perspective of price-based competition, why would GM want the flexibility to outsource more of its parts and components?

b. From the perspective of managing quality, how could outsourcing positively or negatively affect GM's ability to manage quality relative to its competitors?

c. What ethical responsibility does GM bear to the union in seeking to restructure and outsource more of its parts manufacturing?

38. (Environmental management) John Vickers was reprimanded by the home office for recommending a pollution abatement project because the project did not meet the standard financial criterion of a 10 percent rate of return. However, John had concluded that the $60,000 piece of equipment was necessary to prevent small amounts of arsenic from seeping into the city's water system. No EPA warnings had been issued to the company.

a. Discuss the company requirement of a 10 percent rate of return on all projects.

b. What might be the ultimate consequence to Vickers' company if it fails to prevent arsenic seepage into the groundwater system?

c. How should (or can) Vickers justify the purchase of the equipment to the home office?

39. (Environmental management) The chapter discusses three approaches to managing environmental costs. Some strategies deal with hazardous waste only after it has been produced.

a. Does a firm have any ethical obligations *not* to produce hazardous waste regardless of how successfully it is dealt with by the firm?

b. Assume that you are a key financial adviser in a firm that produces a large amount of toxic waste and that faces severe financial pressures and risks bankruptcy. By improperly disposing of certain waste materials, your firm could save millions of dollars, avoid bankruptcy, and preserve 10,000 local jobs. What action would you recommend your firm take? Explain the rationale for your answer.

19

Performance Measurement, Balanced Scorecards, and Performance Rewards

Objectives

AFTER COMPLETING THIS CHAPTER, YOU SHOULD BE ABLE TO ANSWER THE FOLLOWING QUESTIONS:

LO.1 WHY IS A MISSION STATEMENT IMPORTANT TO AN ORGANIZATION?

LO.2 WHAT ROLES DO PERFORMANCE MEASURES SERVE IN ORGANIZATIONS?

LO.3 WHAT GUIDELINES OR CRITERIA APPLY TO THE DESIGN OF PERFORMANCE MEASURES?

LO.4 WHAT ARE THE COMMON SHORT-TERM FINANCIAL PERFORMANCE MEASURES, AND HOW ARE THEY CALCULATED AND USED?

LO.5 WHY SHOULD COMPANY MANAGEMENT FOCUS ON LONG-RUN PERFORMANCE?

LO.6 WHAT FACTORS SHOULD MANAGERS CONSIDER WHEN SELECTING NONFINANCIAL PERFORMANCE MEASURES?

LO.7 WHY IS IT NECESSARY TO USE MULTIPLE MEASURES OF PERFORMANCE?

LO.8 HOW CAN A BALANCED SCORECARD BE USED TO MEASURE PERFORMANCE?

LO.9 WHAT DIFFICULTIES ARE ENCOUNTERED IN TRYING TO MEASURE PERFORMANCE FOR MULTINATIONAL FIRMS?

LO.10 WHAT IS COMPENSATION STRATEGY, AND WHAT FACTORS MUST BE CONSIDERED IN DESIGNING THE COMPENSATION PLAN?

Introducing

Founded in 1968 to build semiconductor memory products, Intel introduced the world's first microprocessor in 1971. Today, with 84,000 employees and almost 300 offices and facilities around the world, Intel supplies the computer and communications industries with essential chips, boards, systems, and software products. The company manufactures hundreds of millions of CPUs, chipsets, and flash memory products every year. For 2003, Intel recorded $30.1 billion in revenues, up 13 percent from 2002; company net income for 2003 was $5.6 billion, up a whopping 81 percent from 2002! Spending during 2003 was $4.4 billion on research and development, and $3.7 billion on capital assets, mostly factories and equipment.

Intel uses performance measures to drive performance; the company uses measures from the traditional monetary ones such as return on investment and cash flow to the more innovative, nonmonetary ones such as throughput time and good output yield from production. The company uses a balanced scorecard approach to performance measurement, setting targets for each of the four perspectives and comparing actual results to targets with an eye toward continuous improvement. The balanced scorecard perspectives align with Intel's mission statement: Do a great job for our customers (*customers*), employees (*learning and growth*), and stockholders (*financial*) by being the preeminent building block supplier (*internal processes*) to the worldwide Internet economy.

One key metric in the fabrication sector at Intel is cost per wafer and the direct material in computer wafers is silicon. The more computer chips that can be obtained from a wafer, the lower the direct material cost per chip; hence, Intel strives to maximize the yield of chips from a silicon wafer. Direct labor cost per chip is small because the fabrication processes are highly automated. Overhead cost per chip is

high, so one effort made by Intel to lower this cost created a $2 billion construction expenditure! The company decided to convert its 200mm Arizona wafer fabrication facility so that it would produce 300mm wafers. The "new" wafers provide a 225 percent surface area increase, allowing significantly more computer chips to be put on each wafer and causing a lower overhead depreciation cost per unit. Additionally, larger wafers reduce utilities overhead cost per unit because production of each chip requires 40 percent less energy and water. The reduction in the depreciation and utilities overhead cost per unit justified the $2 billion facility renovation expenditure.

The cost per unit measurement should be "normalized" for comparison purposes among facilities for at least two reasons. First, when a new fabrication facility opens, the first wafers produced very expensive because only a limited number of wafers are manufactured until output quality is confirmed; allocating the extremely high facility depreciation charges over limited output creates a skewed overhead charge per unit. Second, per unit cost differentials may be created by facility location. For example, the fabrication plants in Ireland and Israel receive government-sponsored investment incentives that reduce total production overhead charges and, therefore, overhead cost per unit. It would be inequitable to compare the cost per chip produced in California with one produced in Ireland or Israel. However, the various fabrication facilities can benchmark against the "best in class" internal fabrication facility to gain perception on how well each facility is doing in a key performance measurement.

Note: To see how computer chips are made, go to *http://www.intel.com/education/makingchips/index.htm*.

Sources: Intel, *2003 Annual Report* (*http://www.intel.com/intel/annual03/ar03.pdf*) (accessed August 8, 2004); Intel Web site, *www.intel.com*; and conversations with Tim Pebworth, Components Cost Team Manager, and Suri Iyer, CPU Cost Manager, Intel Corporation.

Today's managers recognize that, to achieve profitability in the face of global competition, the single most important variable is to attract and satisfy customers. Historically, managers focused almost exclusively on short-run financial performance measures while ignoring the long-run and critical nonfinancial activities. Such tunnel vision was partially created by two circumstances: (1) managers were commonly judged on a short-term basis and (2) long-run and nonfinancial performance data were often unavailable from the accounting system. Note that many of the recent accounting scandals resulted from intense pressure on managers to achieve short-term performance targets. Because more managers are beginning to recognize the need for a longer horizon to gauge performance and the ability of new technology to implement strategic cost management systems, world-class companies such as Intel have started to adopt multiple types of performance measures.

An organization's performance evaluation and reward systems are key tools to align worker, management, and owner goals.[1] The expressed primary function of managers is to maximize stockholder value or stockholder wealth. When workers help control costs and profits increase, stockholders benefit through increased dividends and/or stock market prices. One of the most important ways of motivating employees to maximize stockholder wealth is through the design and implementation of the employee performance measurement and reward system.

ORGANIZATION MISSION STATEMENTS

LO.1
WHY IS A MISSION STATEMENT IMPORTANT TO AN ORGANIZATION?

Organizations have reasons or missions for which they exist. The mission statement expresses an organization's purpose and should identify how the organization will meet its targeted customers' needs through its products or services. The mission statement must be communicated to employees. For example, at Intel, the mission statement is "Do a great job for our customers, employees and stockholders by being the preeminent building block supplier to the worldwide Internet economy." This mission is communicated throughout the organization in numerous ways, including being posted in every conference room and being printed on cards that employees can add to their identification badges.

How does a values statement complement a mission statement?

values statement

In addition to a mission statement, many companies have developed a **values statement** that reflects the organization's culture by identifying fundamental beliefs about what is important to the organization. These values may be objective (such as profitability and increased market share) or subjective (such as ethical behavior and respect for individuals). Intel's values statement contains six primary items: (1) risk taking, (2) quality, (3) great place to work, (4) discipline, (5) results orientation, and (6) customer orientation. All new employees are required to take a class on company values.

Mission and values statements are two of the underlying bases for setting organizational goals (abstract targets to be achieved) and objectives (quantified targets with expected completion dates). Goals and objectives can be short term or long term, but they are inexorably linked. Without achieving at least some short-run success, there will never be long-run success. Without engaging in long-run planning, short-run success will rapidly fade.

ORGANIZATIONAL ROLES OF PERFORMANCE MEASURES

LO.2
WHAT ROLES DO PERFORMANCE MEASURES SERVE IN ORGANIZATIONS?

In fulfilling organizational missions, managers design and implement strategies that apply organizational resources to activities. The organizational structure reflects the manner in which a firm assigns and coordinates its people in deploying strategies. Subunits can be created and charged with making specific contributions to the business strategy. The extent to which each subunit succeeds in its mission can be assessed using carefully designed performance measures that capture the subunit's important performance dimensions.

Management talent and time are dedicated to planning, decision making, controlling, and evaluating performance with respect to these activities to maximize the efficiency and effectiveness of resources used. For an organization to be successful, managers must devise appropriate information systems to track and gauge the effective and efficient use of resources. Two conditions must exist to make such determinations: (1) the terms *effective* and *efficient* must be defined within

---

[1] The authors use the term *employees* to refer to all personnel of an organization. The terms *workers* and *managers* are used to identify mutually exclusive groups of employees.

the context of the organization, and (2) measures consistent with those definitions must be formulated. Definitions of effective and efficient could relate to historical organizational performance, competitive benchmarking, or stakeholder expectations. Once defined, effectiveness and efficiency can be assessed by comparing measures of actual performance with defined and targeted performance goals.

As indicated in Exhibit 19–1, performance measures should exist for all elements that are critical to an organization's success in a competitive market. Management must recognize that progress toward a goal can be achieved only if the goal is specified and communicated to the organization's members. Thus, not setting performance measures for any of an organization's critical elements is tantamount to stating that the ignored element is unimportant. All elements are linked because high performance in one element should lead to high performance in the others.

What organizational elements need performance measurements?

EXHIBIT 19–1

CRITICAL ELEMENTS FOR PERFORMANCE MEASUREMENT AND EXAMPLES OF MEASUREMENTS

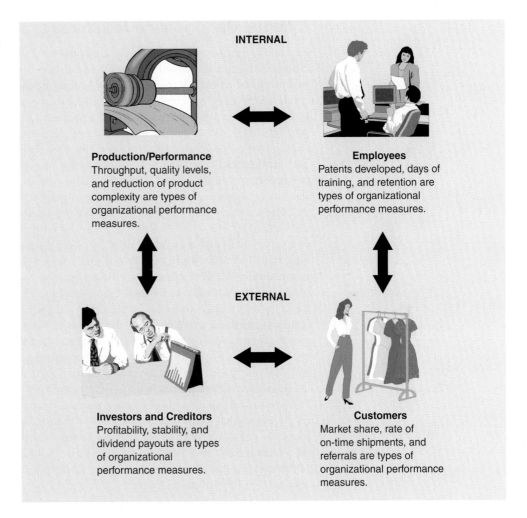

Internal Performance Measures

Internal measures that provide a focus on the efficiency and effectiveness of production processes must be developed. Inadequate processes make it more difficult for a company to manufacture a product or perform a service that will engender both employee pride and customer satisfaction. Internal process measures must reflect concern for streamlined production, high quality, and minimization of product complexity. Products and services compete with others on the dimensions of price, quality, and product features. Superior performance in any of these three areas can provide the competitive advantage needed for success. Developing performance measures for each competitive dimension can identify alternative ways to leverage a firm's competencies.

Employee performance is also a critical element of organizational success. Each successive level of management establishes target measures for subordinates. These measures are used to communicate organizational mission, goals, and strategies and to motivate subordinates to strive to accomplish the stated targets. Measures are also used to implement organizational control over activities, such as comparing actual to budgeted results in responsibility accounting reports. Performance measures also compare individuals' work to make judgments about promotions and retention. A firm searching for new ways to provide customers with more value at less cost must develop an organizational culture that promotes employee learning, job satisfaction, and production efficiency.

External Performance Measures

Externally, performance measures must reflect an organization's ability to satisfy customers better than rival firms do. The quality and quantity of firms competing in the global market have placed consumers at the center of attention. Although profit levels may be viewed as the ultimate measure of success in serving customers, other measures that indicate relative success in specific areas of market performance can be developed. For example, performance measures must reflect characteristics that customers highly value, such as product/service reliability, value, and on-time delivery. Meeting or exceeding the performance targets set for customers should result in the increased likelihood of meeting or exceeding the performance targets set for investors and creditors.

The most common performance measure used for all organizations is a financial one. The effective and efficient use of capital resources is the performance measurement domain of financial accounting. Generally accepted accounting principles are formulated to provide information that is comparable across firms. This comparability facilitates investor/creditor judgments about which firms are worthy of capital investments and which firms can provide appropriate returns relative to the investment risks assumed. Additionally, stockholders are very interested in performance measures that indicate the firm's ability to generate profits that, in turn, create stock price appreciation and dividend distributions. Financial performance measures typically determine whether top management is retained or dismissed. Although management can establish internal performance measures for profitability, it is the market that will ultimately judge the acceptability of such measures. However, meeting or exceeding the market's expectations of performance should create the capital inflows that will result in improved processes, more qualified employees, and more satisfied customers. Management must be careful to realize, after recent accounting scandals in the business community, that "good" financial performance should not be sought by improper accounting—whether managing revenues or expenses.

DESIGNING A PERFORMANCE MEASUREMENT SYSTEM

LO.3
WHAT GUIDELINES OR
CRITERIA APPLY TO THE
DESIGN OF PERFORMANCE
MEASURES?

Measurement is important in all critical elements of an organization, but the measurement used for each element must differ. In any performance measurement system, it is important to remember that people focus on the things that are measured. Thus, an essential question to address in implementing a performance measurement system is: What actions will this metric encourage? The performance measurement system should be designed to encourage behaviors that will result in outcomes that generate organizational success. Additionally, the system should be developed as a unified and cohesive structure rather than a patchwork of "old" performance measurements that the company has used in the past.

Is there any commonality among performance measurement systems?

General Criteria

Regardless of which performance element is being measured, the employee level at which the measurement is occurring, or the type (monetary or nonmonetary) of measure that is being used, five general criteria (Exhibit 19–2) should be considered in designing a performance measurement system:

1. The measures should be established to assess progress toward the organizational mission and its related goals and objectives.
2. The persons being evaluated should be aware of the measurements used and have had some input in developing them.
3. The persons being evaluated should have the appropriate skills, equipment, information, and authority to be successful under the measurement system.
4. Feedback of accomplishment should be provided in a timely and useful manner.
5. The system should be flexible to adapt to new conditions in the organizational environment.

Assess Progress toward Mission

Organizations have a variety of objectives, including the need to be financially viable. Therefore, financial performance measures must be relevant for the type of

EXHIBIT 19–2

CRITERIA FOR DESIGNING A PERFORMANCE MEASUREMENT SYSTEM

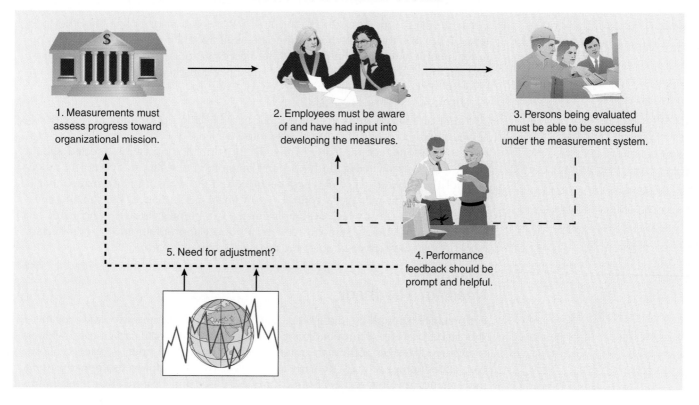

1. Measurements must assess progress toward organizational mission.

2. Employees must be aware of and have had input into developing the measures.

3. Persons being evaluated must be able to be successful under the measurement system.

4. Performance feedback should be prompt and helpful.

5. Need for adjustment?

organization or subunit being evaluated and must reflect an understanding of accounting information and its potential for manipulation. In addition to financial success, many companies are now establishing operational targets of total customer satisfaction, zero defects, minimal lead time to market, and environmental and social responsibility. These goals generally cannot be defined directly using traditional, short-term financial terms. Alternative measures are needed to capture the nonfinancial dimensions of performance. Nonfinancial performance measures that indicate progress—or lack thereof—toward the achievement of a world-class company's critical success factors can be developed.

Awareness of and Participation in Performance Measures

Regardless of the number or types of measures chosen, top management must set high performance standards and communicate them to others. The measures should promote harmonious operations rather than suboptimization among organizational units. Because people normally act in accordance with the way they are measured, they must be aware of and understand the performance measures used. Withholding measurement information does not allow people to perform at their highest level, which is frustrating for them and does not foster feelings of mutual respect and cooperation.

If standard or budget comparisons are used as performance measures, people should be involved in setting those standards or the budget. Participation results in a "social contract" between participants and evaluators because it generates an understanding and acceptance of the reasonableness of the standards or budget. Also, people who have participated in setting targets generally attempt to achieve the results to affirm that the plans were well founded.

Appropriate Tools for Performance

For performance measures to be fair, it is first necessary for people to either possess or be able to obtain the appropriate skills for their jobs. Given job competence, people must then be provided the necessary tools (equipment, information, and authority) to perform their jobs in a manner consistent with the measurement process. If the appropriate tools are unavailable, people cannot be presumed to be able to accomplish their tasks.

In decentralized firms in which there may be little opportunity to directly observe subordinates' actions, managers must evaluate the outcomes that are captured by performance measures. Thus, the performance measures selected should (1) be highly correlated with the subunit mission, (2) be fair and complete reflections of the subunit manager's performance, and (3) measure performance that is under the subunit manager's control. To evaluate performance, benchmarks must be established against which accomplishments can be measured. A benchmark can be monetary (such as a standard cost or a budget appropriation) or nonmonetary (such as zero defects or another organization's market share).

Need for Feedback

Performance should be monitored, and feedback (both positive and negative) should be provided on a continuing basis to the appropriate individuals. Waiting to give feedback on performance until a known evaluation point is reached allows employees no opportunity for early adjustment. Thus, if employees know that their performance reviews and evaluations are to be performed annually at their hiring anniversary dates, feedback on performance should be provided periodically during the year so that employees are aware of how they are doing, have ample opportunities to maximize positive results and correct negative results, and are not negatively "blindsided" during their performance reviews.

The ultimate feedback is that organizational stakeholders exhibit belief in the firm's viability. The primary determinant of this belief is typically provided by short-run financial performance measures.

SHORT-TERM FINANCIAL PERFORMANCE MEASURES FOR MANAGEMENT

LO.4
WHAT ARE THE COMMON SHORT-TERM FINANCIAL PERFORMANCE MEASURES, AND HOW ARE THEY CALCULATED AND USED?

As discussed in Chapter 13 relative to responsibility centers and responsibility accounting, each manager in a firm is expected to make some level of organizational contribution. Measurements selected to ascertain managerial performance must be appropriate for the type of responsibility assigned and behavior desired. Traditionally, managerial performance was primarily judged on monetary measures such as profits, achievement of and variations from budget objectives, and cash flow.

What financial performance measures are appropriate for responsibility centers?

The ability to use monetary measures is, however, affected by the type of responsibility center being evaluated because managers should be evaluated only with metrics that reflect authority and responsibility. In a cost center, the primary financial performance measurements are the variances from budgeted or standard costs. Performance in a pure revenue center can be primarily judged by comparing budgeted revenues with actual revenues. Profit and investment center managers are responsible for revenues, expenses, and return on investment; thus, a variety of measures are appropriate.

Divisional Profits

The segment margin of a profit or investment center is a frequently used measure of divisional performance.[2] This amount is compared with the center's budgeted income objective, and variances are computed to determine where objectives were exceeded or not achieved. Thus, segment margin does not include allocated common costs.

One problem with using segment margin to measure performance is that its individual components (like any other accounting income-based amounts) are subject to manipulations, such as the following:

- If a cost flow method other than FIFO is used, inventory purchases can be accelerated or deferred at the end of the period to manage the period's Cost of Goods Sold.
- Replacement of workers who have resigned or been dismissed can be deferred to minimize salary expense for the period.
- Routine maintenance can be delayed or eliminated to reduce perceived expenses for the short run.
- If fixed overhead is being allocated to inventory, production can be increased so that cost per unit declines.
- Sales recognition can be delayed or accelerated.
- Advertising expenses or other discretionary costs can be delayed or accelerated.
- Depreciation methods can be changed to affect depreciation expense.

---

[2] The term *segment margin* is defined in Chapter 10 as segment sales minus (direct variable expenses and avoidable fixed expenses).

These tactics can be used to "cause" reported segment margin to conform to budget expectations, but such manipulations are normally not in the center's long-run best interest and could even be improper accounting.

Cash Flow

For an entity or an investment center to succeed, it must meet two requirements: (1) long-run profitability and (2) continuous liquidity. The statement of cash flows (SCF) provides information about the sources and uses of cash from operating, investing, and financing activities. Such information can assist in judging the entity's ability to meet current fixed cash outflow commitments, to adapt to adverse changes in business conditions, and to undertake new commitments. Furthermore, because the cash flow statement identifies the relationships between segment margin (or net income) and net cash flow from operations, the SCF assists managers in judging the reliability of the entity's earnings. Analysis of the SCF in conjunction with budgets and other financial reports provides information on cost reductions, collection policies, dividend payout, impact of capital projects on total cash flows, and liquidity position. Many useful financial ratios (such as the current ratio, quick ratio, and number of days' collections in accounts receivable) involve cash flow that is available to assist managers to effectively conduct their responsibilities.

Return on Investment

return on investment (ROI)

Return on investment (ROI) is a ratio relating income generated by an investment center to the resources (or asset base) used to produce that income. The return on investment formula is

$$\text{ROI} = \text{Income} \div \text{Assets Invested}$$

> *Why are specific definitions needed for the ROI terms?*

Before ROI can be used effectively, both terms in the formula must be specifically defined as indicated in Exhibit 19–3. Once definitions have been assigned to the terms, ROI can be used to evaluate individual investment centers and to make intracompany, intercompany, and multinational comparisons. However, managers making these comparisons must consider differences in the entities' characteristics and accounting methods. **Intel** uses return on investment as an important performance measure for each operating unit.

Data for Attaya Corporation (Exhibit 19–4) are used to illustrate return on investment computations. The company has investment centers in Reno, Sioux Falls, and Allentown. All three divisions operate in the same industry, offer the same types of services to customers, and are charged with similar missions. Similarity in business lines and missions allows for comparisons among the three centers.

See Exhibit 19–5 for returns on investment rates (using a variety of bases) for Attaya Corporation investment centers. The results vary because different definitions are used in each case for the numerator and denominator. These variations demonstrate why the income and assets involved must be precisely specified before making computations or comparisons.

The ROI formula can be restated to provide useful information about two individual factors that compose the rate of return: profit margin and asset turnover. This restatement, called the **Du Pont model**, is

Du Pont model

$$\text{ROI} = \text{Profit Margin} \times \text{Asset Turnover}$$
$$= (\text{Income} \div \text{Sales}) \times (\text{Sales} \div \text{Assets})$$

profit margin

Profit margin is the ratio of income to sales. It indicates what proportion of each sales dollar is *not* used for expenses and, thus, becomes profit. Profit margin can be used to judge the center's operating leverage by indicating management's effi-

EXHIBIT 19–3
ROI DEFINITIONAL QUESTIONS AND ANSWERS

Question	Preferable Answer
Is income defined as segment or operating income?	Segment income Because the manager does not have short-run control over unavoidable fixed expenses and allocated corporate costs.
Is income on a before-tax or after-tax basis?	Before-tax Because investment centers might pay higher or lower tax rates if they were separated from the organization.
Should assets be defined as ■ total assets utilized; ■ total assets available for use; or ■ net assets (equity)?	Total assets available for use Because if duplicate or unused assets were eliminated from the formula, there would be no encouragement for managers to dispose of those assets and gain additional cash flow that could be used for more profitable projects. Alternatively, if the objective is to measure how well the segment is performing, given the funds provided for that segment, then net assets should be used to measure return on equity.
Should plant assets be included at ■ original cost; ■ depreciated book value; or ■ current value?	Current value Because as assets age and net book value declines, an investment center earning the same income each year would show a continuously increasing ROI. Although more difficult to obtain and possibly subjective, current values measure the opportunity cost of using the assets.
Should beginning, ending, or average assets be used?	Average assets Because the numerator income amount is for a period of time, the denominator base should be calculated for the same time frame.

asset turnover

ciency with regard to the relationship between sales and expenses. **Asset turnover** measures asset productivity and shows the number of sales dollars generated by each dollar of assets. This metric can be used to judge marketing's effective use of assets relative to revenue production.

See Exhibit 19–6 for the calculations of the ROI components using Attaya Corporation's segment margin and total historical cost as the income and asset base definitions. Thus, these computations provide the same answers as those given in the third calculation of Exhibit 19–5.

Reno enjoys both the highest profit margin and highest turnover. Reno may be benefiting from economies of scale relative to the other divisions, which could partially account for its superior performance. Additionally, Reno is better at leveraging its assets, as shown in Exhibit 19–4, the center's assets are 100 percent utilized.

The Sioux Falls investment center is performing very poorly compared to the other two divisions. Based on the amount of accumulated depreciation, the Sioux Falls center appears to be the oldest, which could be related to its poor performance. Sioux Falls's manager might want to purchase more modern facilities to generate more sales and greater profits. Such an investment could, however, cause ROI to decline because the asset base would be increased. Rate of return computations can encourage managers to retain and use old plant assets (especially when

EXHIBIT 19–4

DATA FOR ATTAYA CORPORATION

	IN THOUSANDS			
	Reno	Sioux Falls	Allentown	Total
Revenues	$ 3,200,000	$ 675,000	$ 430,000	$ 4,305,000
Direct costs				
Variable	(1,120,000)	(310,000)	(172,000)	(1,602,000)
Fixed (avoidable)	(550,000)	(118,000)	(60,000)	(728,000)
Segment margin	$ 1,530,000	$ 247,000	$ 198,000	$ 1,975,000
Unavoidable fixed				
and allocated costs	(372,000)	(78,000)	(50,000)	(500,000)
Operating income	$ 1,158,000	$ 169,000	$ 148,000	$ 1,475,000
Taxes (34%)	(393,720)	(57,460)	(50,320)	(501,500)
Net income	$ 764,280	$ 111,540	$ 97,680	$ 973,500
Current assets	$ 48,500	$ 33,120	$ 20,000	
Fixed assets	6,179,000	4,610,000	900,000	
Total asset cost	$ 6,227,500	$ 4,643,120	$ 920,000	
Accumulated				
Depreciation (b)	(1,232,500)	(1,270,000)	(62,500)	
Total asset book value	$ 4,995,000	$ 3,373,120	$ 857,500	
Liabilities	(2,130,000)	(600,000)	(162,500)	
Net assets	$ 2,865,000	$ 2,773,120	$ 695,000	
Proportion of total				
assets utilized	100%	93%	85%	
Current value of				
fixed assets	$ 5,500,000	$ 2,400,000	$ 780,000	
Market value of				
invested capital (for EVA)	$18,250,000	$ 2,400,000	$ 500,000	

Note: A summarized corporate balance sheet would not balance with the investment center balance sheets because of the existence of general corporate assets and liabilities.

EXHIBIT 19–5

ROI COMPUTATIONS

	Reno	Sioux Falls	Allentown
Operating Income	$1,158,000	$169,000	$148,000
Assets Utilized	$4,995,000	$3,137,002	$728,875
ROI	23.2%	5.4%	20.3%
Operating Income	$1,158,000	$169,000	$148,000
Asset Current Value	$5,500,000	$2,400,000	$780,000
ROI	21.1%	7.0%	19.0%
Segment Margin	$1,530,000	$247,000	$198,000
Total Asset Cost	$6,227,500	$4,643,120	$920,000
ROI	24.6%	5.3%	21.5%
Segment Margin	$1,530,000	$247,000	$198,000
Asset Book Value	$4,995,000	$3,373,120	$857,500
ROI	30.6%	7.3%	23.1%
Segment Margin	$1,530,000	$247,000	$198,000
Asset Current Value	$5,500,000	$2,400,000	$780,000
ROI	27.8%	10.3%	25.4%
Segment Margin	$1,530,000	$247,000	$198,000
Net Assets	$2,865,000	$2,773,120	$695,000
ROI	53.4%	8.9%	28.5%

EXHIBIT 19–6
ROI COMPONENTS—
DUPONT FORMULA

Reno Investment Center

ROI = (Income ÷ Sales) × (Sales ÷ Assets)

$\quad$ = ($1,530,000 ÷ $3,200,000) × ($3,200,000 ÷ $6,227,500)

$\quad$ = 0.478 × 0.514

$\quad$ = 24.6%

Sioux Falls Investment Center

ROI = (Income ÷ Sales) × (Sales ÷ Assets)

$\quad$ = ($247,000 ÷ $675,000) × ($675,000 ÷ $4,643,120)

$\quad$ = 0.366 × 0.145

$\quad$ = 5.3%

Allentown Investment Center

ROI = (Income ÷ Sales) × (Sales ÷ Assets)

$\quad$ = ($198,000 ÷ $430,000) × ($430,000 ÷ $920,000)

$\quad$ = 0.460 × 0.467

$\quad$ = 21.5%

accumulated depreciation is deducted from the asset base) to keep ROIs high as long as those assets can keep revenues up and expenses down.

The Allentown investment center appears to be the newest of the three based on its low level of accumulated depreciation relative to its investment. With increased asset utilization, the Allentown investment center should generate a higher asset turnover and raise its ROI.

Sales prices, volume and mix of products sold, expenses, and capital asset acquisitions and dispositions affect ROI. Return on investment can be increased through various management actions including (1) raising sales prices if demand will not be impaired, (2) decreasing expenses, and (3) decreasing dollars invested in assets, especially nonproductive ones. Actions should be taken only after considering all interrelationships that determine ROI. For instance, a price increase could reduce sales volume if demand is elastic with respect to price.

Profit margin, asset turnover, and return on investment can be assessed as favorable or unfavorable only if each component is compared with a valid benchmark. Comparison bases include expected results, prior results, or results of other similar entities.

Residual Income

residual income (RI)

An investment center's **residual income (RI)** is the profit earned that exceeds an amount "charged" for funds committed to the center. The "charged" amount is equal to a specified target rate of return multiplied by the asset base and is comparable to an imputed rate of interest on divisional assets used.[3] The rate can be changed to compensate for market rate fluctuations or for risk. The residual income computation is as follows:

$$\text{Residual Income} = \text{Income} - (\text{Target Rate} \times \text{Asset Base})$$

Residual income yields a dollar figure rather than a percentage. Expansion (or additional investments in assets) should occur in an investment center as long as

[3] This target rate is similar to the discount rate used in capital budgeting (discussed in Chapter 14). For management to invest in a capital project, that project must earn at least a minimum specified rate of return. In the same manner, the ROI of an investment center must be equal to or higher than the target rate used to compute residual income.

positive residual income (dollars of return) is expected on the dollars of additional investment. Continuing the Attaya Corporation example, see Exhibit 19–7 for the calculation of each investment center's RI. Attaya has established a 15 percent target return on total assets and has defined income as segment margin and assets as total historical cost. Reno and Allentown show positive residual incomes, but Sioux Falls' negative RI indicates that income is significantly low relative to asset investment.

EXHIBIT 19–7

ATTAYA CORPORATION RESIDUAL INCOME CALCULATIONS

Reno

RI = $1,530,000 − (0.15 × $6,227,500) = $1,530,000 − $934,125 = $595,875

Sioux Falls

RI = $247,000 − (0.15 × $4,643,120) = $247,000 − $696,468 = $(449,468)

Allentown

RI = $198,000 − (0.15 × $920,000) = $198,000 − $138,000 = $60,000

Economic Value Added

economic value added (EVA®)

One of the most well-known measures that has been developed to more directly align the interests of common shareholders with managers' is **economic value added (EVA®)**.[4] Conceptually similar to RI, EVA is a measure of the profit produced above the cost of capital. However, EVA applies the target rate of return to the market value of the capital invested in the division rather than the book value of assets used for RI. Furthermore, EVA is calculated on net income or the after-tax profits available to stockholders. The EVA calculation is:

$$EVA = \text{After-Tax Profits} - (\text{Cost of Capital \% } \times \text{Market Value of Invested Capital})$$

Using information on net income and market values given in Exhibit 19–4, calculations of EVA for each Attaya Corporation investment center are given in Exhibit 19–8. The after-tax cost of capital is assumed to be 13 percent.

EXHIBIT 19–8

ATTAYA CORPORATION'S ECONOMIC VALUE ADDED CALCULATIONS

Reno

EVA = $764,280 − (0.13 × $18,250,000) = $764,280 − $2,372,500 = $(1,608,220)

Sioux Falls

EVA = $111,540 − (0.13 × $2,400,000) = $111,540 − $312,000 = $(200,460)

Allentown

EVA = $97,680 − (0.13 × $500,000) = $97,680 − $65,000 = $32,680

As the difference between the market value of invested capital (total equity and interest-bearing debt) and the book value of assets increases, so do the relative benefits of using EVA rather than RI as a performance measure. The results given in Exhibit 19–8 show a different portrayal of performance than those given by ROI and RI. EVA shows the Allentown center to be the stellar performer. By failing to capture the large difference between the market and book values of the Reno investment center, ROI and RI significantly overstate Reno's performance. Sioux Falls still appears to be performing poorly, although better than Reno.

[4] EVA is a registered trademark of Stern Stewart & Co. It was first discussed by Alfred Marshall, an English economist, in about 1890. More information about EVA can be found at *http://www.sternstewart.com/evaabout/whatis.php.*

Despite its growing popularity, EVA cannot measure all dimensions of performance and is short-term focused. Accordingly, the EVA measure can discourage investment in long-term projects because such investments cause an immediate increase in the amount of invested capital but increase after-tax profits only at some future point. For greatest benefit, EVA should be supplemented with longer term financial and nonfinancial performance measures.

Limitations of Return on Investment, Residual Income, and Economic Value Added

Each financial measure of performance discussed has certain limitations. For example, the limitations of divisional profit and cash flow are their potential for income and cash flow manipulation.

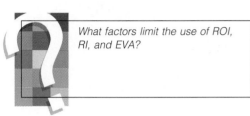

What factors limit the use of ROI, RI, and EVA?

ROI, RI, and EVA have three primary limitations. The first limitation reflects the use of accounting income. Income can be manipulated or managed in the short run, depending on the accounting methods selected to account for items such as inventory or depreciation. For valid comparisons to be made, all investment centers must use the same accounting methods. Because neither cash flows nor the time value of money is considered, income may not always provide the best basis for evaluating performance.

The second limitation of ROI, RI, and EVA relates to the asset investment base used. Asset investment can be difficult to properly measure and assign to center managers. Some investments (such as research and development costs) have value beyond the accounting period but are not capitalized and, thus, create an understated asset base. Previous managers could have acquired assets; thus, current managers can potentially be judged on investment decisions over which they had no control. If fixed assets and inventory are not restated for price level increases, net income could be overstated (or understated, in the event of price level decreases) and the investment base could be understated (or overstated). Managers who keep and use older assets can report much higher ROIs than managers using new assets. For EVA, this situation exists for the income measure but not for asset measurement because EVA focuses on market value of capital employed.

The third limitation of these measures is a single, potentially critical problem: They direct attention to how well an investment center performs in isolation rather than relative to company-wide objectives. Such focus can result in suboptimization of resources so that the firm is not maximizing its operational effectiveness and efficiency. Assume that the Allentown Division of Attaya Corporation (shown in Exhibit 19–6 to have an ROI of 21.5 percent) has an opportunity to increase income by $40,000 by installing a new $200,000 computer network. This separate investment with a ROI of 20 percent ($40,000 ÷ $200,000) would cause Allentown's ROI to decline. If Attaya Corporation evaluates investment center managers based only on ROI, the Allentown center manager will not accept this investment opportunity. If, however, Attaya Corporation has a 15 percent target rate of return on investment, the Allentown manager's decision to reject the new opportunity suboptimizes companywide returns. This venture should be accepted because it provides a return higher than the firm's target rate. Top management should be informed of such opportunities, made aware of the effects that acceptance might have on divisional performance measurements, and be willing to reward such acceptance based on the impact on company performance.

DIFFERENCES IN PERSPECTIVES

LO.5
WHY SHOULD COMPANY MANAGEMENT FOCUS ON LONG-RUN PERFORMANCE?

Concentrating solely on financial results is similar to a basketball player focusing solely on the game score. Both the financial measures and the score are lagging indicators, or reflections of the results of past decisions. Succeeding in business or sports requires that considerable attention be placed on actionable steps for effectively competing, whether in the global marketplace or on the court. Measurements for improving performance should involve tracking **leading indicators** or statistical data about the actionable steps that will create the results desired. Thus, as illustrated in Exhibit 19–9, leading indicators reflect causes and lagging indicators reflect effects or outcomes.

EXHIBIT 19–9
LEADING AND LAGGING INDICATORS

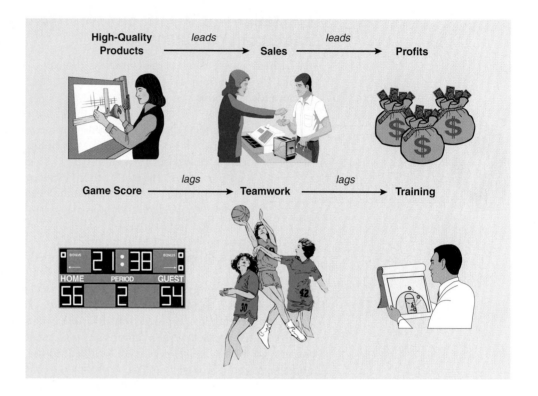

Managing for the long run has commonly been viewed as managing a series of short runs. Theoretically, if a firm performs well in each of its short runs, its future is secure. Although appealing, this approach fails when the firm does not keep pace with long-range technical and competitive improvement trends. Thinking only of short-run performance and ignoring the time required to make long-term improvements can doom a firm in the global competitive environment.

Short-run objectives generally reflect a focus on the effective and efficient management of current operating, investing, and financing activities. A firm's long-term objectives generally involve resource investments and proactive efforts to enhance competitive position, such as customer satisfaction issues of quality, delivery, price, and service. Because competitive position results from the interaction of a variety of factors, a firm must identify the most important drivers (not just predictors) of the achievement of a particular long-run objective. For example, predictors of increased market share might include increased spending on employee training or capital improvements. The true drivers of increased market share for a firm, however, are likely to be product and service quality, speed of delivery, and reputation relative to the competitors. Measurements of success in these areas would be leading indicators of increased market share and profitability.

NONFINANCIAL PERFORMANCE MEASURES

Performance can be evaluated using both qualitative and quantitative measures. Qualitative measures are often subjective; for example, a manager could be evaluated using simple low-to-high rankings on job skills such as knowledge, quality of work, and need for supervision. Rankings can be given for an individual on a stand-alone basis, in relationship to other managers, or on a group or team basis. Although such measures provide useful information, at some point and in some way, performance should also be compared to a quantifiable—but not necessarily financial—standard. People are generally more comfortable with and respond better to quantitative, rather than qualitative, measures of performance because such measures provide a defined target at which to aim. Quantifiable performance measures are of two types: financial and nonfinancial.

Selection of Nonfinancial Measures

LO.6
WHAT FACTORS SHOULD MANAGERS CONSIDER WHEN SELECTING NONFINANCIAL PERFORMANCE MEASURES?

What nonfinancial performance measures are frequently used?

Nonfinancial performance measures (NFPMs) use information contained in the strategic cost management system rather than that in the financial accounting system. Thus, NFPMs are based on nonmonetary details, such as time (e.g., manufacturing cycle time or setup time), quantities (e.g., number of patents generated or pounds of material moved), and ratios (e.g., percentage of good units to total units produced or percentage of sales generated by repeat customers). Appropriate nonfinancial metrics are those that can be clearly articulated and defined, are relevant to the objective, can trace responsibility, rely on valid data, have set target objectives, and have established internal and/or external benchmarks. As indicated in Exhibit 19–10, NFPMs have many distinct advantages over financial performance measures.

Using a very large number of NFPMs is counterproductive and wasteful. Additionally, there may be considerable interdependence among some of the measures. For example, increased product quality should increase customer satisfaction or increased levels of worker training should decrease poor service performance. An organization must determine which factors are essential to long-term success and develop short-run and long-run metrics for these areas to steer the company toward success. A short-run measure of success for quality is the number of customer complaints in the current period; a long-range success measure for quality is the number of patents obtained for quality improvements of company products.

EXHIBIT 19–10

ADVANTAGES OF NONFINANCIAL OVER FINANCIAL PERFORMANCE MEASURES

Compared to financial measures, nonfinancial performance measures are more

- **relevant** to nonmanagement employees who are generally more familiar with nonfinancial items (such as times and quantities) than financial items (such as costs or profits)
- **timely** than historical financial data and, thus, more apt to indicate where problems lie or where benefits can be obtained
- **reflective** of the leading indicators of activities that create shareholder wealth, such as manufacturing and delivering quality goods and services and providing service for the customer
- **causative** of goal-congruent behavior (rather than suboptimization) because they promote long-term success rather than the short-term success promoted by financial measures
- **integrated** with organizational effectiveness because they can be designed to focus on processes rather than simply outputs
- **indicative** of productive activity and the direction of future cash flows
- **appropriate** for gauging teamwork because they can focus on outputs that result from organizational effort (such as quality) rather than inputs (such as costs)
- **cross functional** than financial measures, which are generally related to one function
- **comparable** for benchmarking externally than financial measures (which can be dramatically affected by differences in accounting methods)
- **aligned** with the reward system because they are more likely to be under the control of lower-level employees than are financial measures

Choosing appropriate performance measures can also help a company focus on the activities that cause costs to be incurred and, thus, control costs and improve processes. As discussed in Chapter 5 on activity-based management, if the activity is controlled, the cost resulting from that activity is controlled.

Establishment of Comparison Bases

Once the NFPMs are selected, benchmark performance levels should be established as bases of comparison against which actual data can be compared. These levels can be developed internally (such as from another world-class division) or determined from external sources (such as competitors or companies in other industries). In addition, a system of monitoring and reporting comparative performance levels should be established at appropriate intervals. Typically, lower-level results are monitored more frequently (continuously, daily, or weekly) than upper-level results (monthly, quarterly, and annually). Measures used by middle management are intermediate links between the lower- and upper-level performance measures and require monitoring at intermediate points (weekly, monthly, and annually). Annual measurements can be plotted to reveal long-run trends and progress toward long-run objectives.

A general model for measuring the relative success of an activity compares a numerator representing number of successes with a logical and valid denominator representing total outcome volume. For example, delivery success could be measured for a period based on success or failure information. Assume that Attaya Corporation made 1,000 deliveries during a period; of those, 922 were on time and 78 were late. The company's measurement of delivery success is 92.2 percent (922 ÷ 1,000), or its delivery failure rate is 7.8 percent (78 ÷ 1,000). Determination of how well or poorly the company performed for the period would require comparison with previous periods, a target rate of success (such as 100 percent on-time deliveries), or a benchmark with a world-class competitor. Analysis of the types and causes of the 78 late deliveries should allow management to consider actions to take to eliminate these causes in the process of continuous long-term improvement.

Use of Multiple Measures

LO.7
WHY IS IT NECESSARY TO USE MULTIPLE MEASURES OF PERFORMANCE?

A performance measurement system should encompass a variety of measures, especially those that track factors considered necessary for mission achievement and long-run success. Although internal measures of performance are useful, only a company's customers can truly assess organizational performance. Good performance is typically defined as providing a product or service that equals or exceeds a customer's quality, price, and delivery expectations. This definition of good performance is totally unrelated to internal measurements such as standard cost variances or capacity utilization. Companies that cannot meet quality, price, and delivery expectations will find themselves at some point without customers and without any need for financial measures of performance.

Knowing that performance is to be judged using external criteria should cause companies to implement concepts such as just-in-time inventory management, total quality management, and continuous improvement. Two common themes of these concepts are to make the organization, its products, and its processes (production as well as customer responsiveness) better and to provide higher value through lower costs.

Exhibit 19–11 provides ideas for judging managerial performance in four areas. Some of these measures should be monitored for both short-run and long-run implications. For example, a short-run measure of market improvement is the growth rate of sales. A long-run measure is the growth rate of the repeat customer pool. Brainstorming about both short-run and long-run measures can be an effective ap-

EXHIBIT 19–11
EXAMPLES OF PERFORMANCE MEASUREMENTS

| | | Quantitative | |
	Qualitative	Nonfinancial	Financial
PERSONNEL	Acceptance of additional responsibility Increased job skills Need for supervision Interaction with upper- and lower-level employees	Proportion of direct to indirect labor (low or high depending on degree of automation) Diversity of ethnic background in hiring and promotion Scores on standardized examinations	Comparability of personnel pay levels with those of competitors Savings from using part-time personnel
MARKET	Addition of new product features Increased product durability Improved efficiency (and/ or effectiveness) of product	Number of sales transactions Percentage repeat customers Number of new ideas generated Number of customer complaints Delivery time	Increase in revenue from previous period Percent of total market revenue Revenue generated per advertising dollar (by product or product line)
COSTS	Better traceability of costs Increased cost consciousness Better employee suggestions for cost reductions Increased usage of automated equipment for routine tasks	Time to design new products Number of engineering change orders issued Length of process time Proportion of products with defects Number of different product parts Number of days of inventory Proportion of material generated as scrap/waste Reduction in setup time since prior period	Reduction in production cost (DM, DL, & OH and in total) since prior period Reduction in distribution and scrap/waste cost since prior period Variances from standard Cost of engineering changes
RETURNS (PROFITABILITY)	Customer satisfaction Product brand loyalty	Proportion of on-time deliveries Degree of accuracy in sales forecasts of demand	Change in market price per share Return on investment Change in net income

proach to identifying measurements. Because measures should reflect the organization's mission and culture in addition to management's expectations and philosophies, changes in any of these factors should also create changes in performance measures.

THROUGHPUT

throughput

One nonfinancial performance indicator that is becoming widely accepted is **throughput**, or the number of good units or quantity of services that are produced and sold or provided by an organization within a specified time. Because its primary goal is to earn income, a for-profit organization must sell inventory (not simply produced) for throughput to be achieved.

Throughput can be analyzed as a set of component elements (in a manner similar to the way the Du Pont model includes components of ROI). Components of throughput include manufacturing cycle efficiency, process productivity, and process quality yield.[5] Throughput can be calculated as follows:

[5] These terms and formulas are based on the following article: Carole Cheatham, "Measuring and Improving Throughput," *Journal of Accountancy* (March 1990), pp. 89–91. One assumption that must be made with regard to this model is that the quantity labeled "throughput" is sold. Another assumption is that the units started are always completed before the end of the measurement period.

$$\frac{\text{Manufacturing}}{\text{Cycle Efficiency}} \times \frac{\text{Process}}{\text{Productivity}} \times \frac{\text{Process}}{\text{Quality Yield}} = \text{Throughput}$$

$$\frac{\text{Value-Added}}{\substack{\text{Processing Time} \\ \text{Total Time}}} \times \frac{\text{Total Units}}{\substack{\text{Value-Added} \\ \text{Processing Time}}} \times \frac{\text{Good Units}}{\text{Total Units}} = \text{Throughput}$$

process productivity

process quality yield

Manufacturing cycle efficiency (defined in Chapter 5) is the proportion of value-added processing time to total processing time. Value-added processing time reflects activities that increase the product's worth to the customer. Total units produced during the period divided by the value-added processing time determines **process productivity**. Production activities can produce both good and defective units. The proportion of good units resulting from activities is the **process quality yield**. An example of these calculations is given in Exhibit 19–12.

Management should strive to increase throughput by decreasing non-value-added activities, increasing total unit production and sales, decreasing the per-unit processing time, increasing process quality yield, or a combination of these. Some companies have increased throughput significantly by the use of flexible manufacturing systems and, in some cases, by reorganizing production operations. At Intel, throughput is enhanced by the technicians' ability to monitor automated operations from centralized locations, which allows for faster reaction time to production circumstances that might create downtime. Computer technologies such as bar coding, computer-integrated manufacturing, and electronic data interchange have also enhanced throughput at many firms. Improved throughput means a greater ability to respond to customer needs and demands, to reduce production costs, and to reduce inventory levels and, therefore, the non-value-added costs of moving and storing goods.

COST OF QUALITY

Companies operating in the global environment are also generally concerned with high product and service quality and the need to develop quality measurements such as those presented in Exhibit 19–13. For example, if a performance measure-

EXHIBIT 19–12

THROUGHPUT CALCULATION EXAMPLE

Total processing time	40,000 hours
Total value-added processing time	10,000 hours
Total quantity of product HD#240 manufactured	50,000 tons
Total quantity of good production manufactured and sold	44,000 tons

Manufacturing Cycle Efficiency = VA Processing Time ÷ Total Processing Time
        = 10,000 ÷ 40,000 = 25%
                (means that 75% of processing time is non-value-added)

Process Productivity = Total Units ÷ VA Processing Time
        = 50,000 ÷ 10,000 = 5
                (means that 5 units can be produced per hour)

Process Quality Yield = Good Units ÷ Total Units
        = 44,000 ÷ 50,000 = 88%
                (means that 12% of the yield was defective)

Throughput = MCE × PP × PQY
        = 0.25 × 5 × 0.88 = 1.1
                (means that 1.1 good units are produced per hour of total processing time, compared with the 5 units actually produced per value-added hour)

    or

Throughput = Good Units ÷ Total Time
        = 44,000 ÷ 40,000 = 1.1

EXHIBIT 19–13

NONFINANCIAL QUALITY MEASUREMENTS

Element	Measure
Prevention	Design review (number of hours) Preventive maintenance (number of hours) Employee training (number of hours) Quality circles (number of hours) Quality engineering (number of hours)
Appraisal	Material inspection (number of inspections) Work in Process inspection (number of inspections) Finished Goods inspection (number of inspections) Sample preparation (number of samples) Product simulation (number of simulations)
Internal failure	Scrap (number of units) Rework (number of units) Spoilage (number of units) Quality related downtime (number of hours) Reinspection of rework (number of units)
External failure	Warranty claims (number of claims) Complaint processing (number of complaints) Loss of goodwill (percentage of nonreturning customers*) Liability suits (number of suits) Product recalls (number of recalls)

*Not as originally listed in article.

Source: Ronald C. Kettering, "Accounting for Quality with Nonfinancial Measures: A Simple No-Cost Program for the Small Company," *Management Accounting Quarterly* (Spring 2001), p. 17.

ment is the cost of defective units produced during a period, the expectation is that defects will occur and management will accept some stated or understood defect cost. If, instead, the performance measurement is zero defects, the expectation is that no defects will occur and such a measurement would create an atmosphere more conducive to eliminating defects than would the first. As quality improves, management's threshold of "acceptable" performance becomes more demanding and performance is evaluated against progressively more rigorous benchmarks.

LEAD TIME

A nonfinancial measure of customer service is lead time, or how quickly customers receive their goods. Measuring lead time should cause products to be available to customers more rapidly. In addition, using fewer parts, interchangeable parts, and parts that require few or no engineering changes after the start of production shortens lead time. Lead time measurement could also provide an incentive to revise a building layout to speed work flow, to increase workforce productivity, and to reduce defects and rework. Last, lead time measurement should cause managers to observe and correct any non-value-added activities or constraints that are creating production, performance, or processing delays. Some companies are implementing activity-based management (ABM) techniques to remove any implied acceptance of non-value-added activities. ABM can provide information on the overhead impact created by reengineered processes to streamline activities and minimize nonquality work.

USING A BALANCED SCORECARD FOR MEASURING PERFORMANCE

LO.8
HOW CAN A BALANCED SCORECARD BE USED TO MEASURE PERFORMANCE?

In recognition of the multiple facets of performance, some companies have begun to use a balanced scorecard (BSC) approach to performance measurement. The balanced scorecard provides a set of business measurements that "complements financial measures of past performance with measures of the drivers of future performance."[6] The scorecard should reflect an organization's mission and strategy and typically includes performance measures from four perspectives: financial, internal business, customer, and learning and growth. Managers choosing to apply the balanced scorecard demonstrate a belief that traditional financial performance measures alone are insufficient to assess how the firm is doing and identify specific actions that must be taken to improve performance.

Each company will adapt the balanced scorecard approach to fit its own structure and environment. The 2002 balanced scorecard for **Futura Industries** is shown in Exhibit 19–14; the actual BSC includes specific targets for each measurement which are compared to actual results at specific measurement dates during the year. Futura is an international company that is engaged in aluminum extruding, finishing, fabrication, machining, and design.

Are all balanced scorecards the same?

EXHIBIT 19-14
2002 BALANCED SCORECARD FOR FUTURA INDUSTRIES

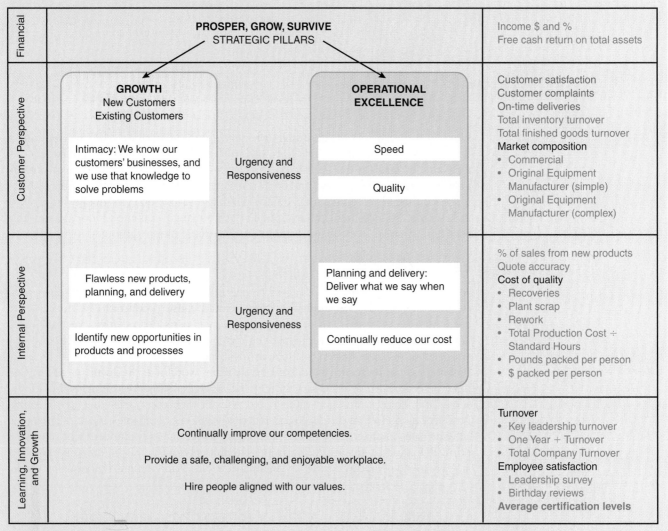

Source: Andra Gumbus and Susan D. Johnson, "The Balanced Scorecard at Futura Industries," *Strategic Finance* (July 2003), p. 38.

---

[6] Robert S. Kaplan and David P. Norton, *The Balanced Scorecard* (Boston: Harvard Business School Press, 1996), p. 8.

Financial measures of the balanced scorecard should reflect stakeholder-relevant issues of profitability, organizational growth, and market price of stock. Such measures are lag indicators of the other perspectives and can include subunit operating income, bottom-line net income, cash flow, change in market share, and return on assets. Customer measures lead financial perspective measures and should indicate how the organization is faring relative to customer issues of speed (lead time), quality, service, and price (both at purchase and after purchase). Internal process measures should focus on things the organization needs to do to meet customer needs and expectations. Measures in this area are usually quantitative and could include process quality yields, manufacturing or service cycle efficiency, time to market on new products, on-time delivery, and cost variances. Learning and growth measures lead customer perspective measures and should focus on using the organization's intellectual capital to adapt to changing customer needs or influence new customer needs and expectations through product or service innovations. Learning and growth measures tend to be quantitative, long-term targets. These measures might include number of patents or copyrights applied for, percentage of research and development projects resulting in patentable products, average time of R&D project from conception to commercialization, and percentage of capital investments on "high-tech" projects. Learning and growth measures can help an organization ascertain its ability to learn, grow, improve, and survive.

First introduced in the early 1990s, balanced scorecards are now being used in some organizations at multiple levels: top management, subunit, and even individual employees. When a BSC is implemented at lower levels of the organization, care should be taken to make certain that the measurements used can "roll up" into higher level measurements that will ultimately provide the organizational results desired. Regardless of the managerial level at which the scorecard is used or the type of organization using the scorecard, this technique allows measurement data to be compiled to reflect the organizational mission. "Taken together, the measures provide a holistic view of what is happening both inside and outside the organization or level, thus allowing all constituents of the organization to see how their activities contribute to attainment of the organization's overall mission."[7]

No single BSC, measurement system, or set of performance measurements is appropriate for all organizations or, possibly, even all responsibility centers within the same company. Although some performance measurements, such as financial viability, zero defects, and customer service, are important regardless of the type of organization or its location, foreign operations may require some additional considerations in performance measurement and evaluation compared to domestic operations.

PERFORMANCE EVALUATION IN MULTINATIONAL SETTINGS

LO.9
WHAT DIFFICULTIES ARE ENCOUNTERED IN TRYING TO MEASURE PERFORMANCE FOR MULTINATIONAL FIRMS?

Many large companies have overseas operations whose performance must be measured and evaluated. Use of a singular measurement criterion such as income is even less appropriate for multinational segments than it is for domestic responsibility centers.

The investment cost necessary to create the same type of organizational unit in different countries can differ substantially. For example, because of exchange rates and legal costs, it is significantly more expensive for a U.S. company to open a Japanese subsidiary than an Indonesian one. If performance were measured using residual income calculated with the same target rate of return, the Japanese unit would be placed at a distinct disadvantage because of its larger investment base. However, the company could believe that the possibility of future Japanese

---

[7] Chee W. Chow et al., "The Balanced Scorecard: A Potent Tool for Energizing and Focusing Healthcare Organization Management," *Journal of Healthcare Management* (May–June 1998), pp. 263–280.

Exchange rates and legal costs make it more costly for a U.S. company to start a Japanese subsidiary than it would to open an Indonesian subsidiary.

GETTY IMAGES

joint ventures or market inroads justifies the larger investment. One method of handling such a discrepancy in investment bases is to assign a lower target rate to compute residual income for the Japanese subsidiary than for the Indonesian one. This type of differential might also be appropriate because of the lower political, financial, and economic risks.

Income comparisons between multinational units could be invalid because of differences in trade tariffs, income tax rates, currency fluctuations, and the possibility of restrictions on the transfer of goods or currency from a country. Income earned by a multinational unit can also be affected by conditions totally outside its control, such as protectionism of local companies, government aid, or varying wage rates caused by differing standards of living, levels of industrial development, and/or the amount of socialized services. If the multinational subunit adopts the local country's accounting practices, differences in international standards can make income comparisons among units difficult and inconvenient even after the statements are translated to a single currency basis.

Firms with multinational profit or investment centers (or subsidiaries) need to establish flexible systems of measuring performance for those units. Such systems should recognize that differences in sales volumes, accounting standards, economic conditions, and risk might be outside the control of an international subunit's manager. Qualitative performance measures such as market share increases, quality improvements (defect reductions), improvement of inventory management with the related reduction in working capital, and new product development could become significantly more useful.

Regardless of location, the measurement of performance is the measurement of people. Because people are unique and have multiple facets, the performance measurement system must reflect those characteristics. By linking performance measures to an organization's mission and reward structure, employees are given an incentive to improve performance that will result in long-run organizational viability.

COMPENSATION STRATEGY

LO.10
WHAT IS COMPENSATION STRATEGY, AND WHAT FACTORS MUST BE CONSIDERED IN DESIGNING THE COMPENSATION PLAN?

compensation strategy

How should an organization determine employee compensation?

The many changes (technological advances, globalization, customer and quality orientation) that have occurred in business in the recent past have created opportunities and challenges in establishing responsibility and rewarding individuals for organizational performance. Each organization should determine a **compensation strategy** that addresses the role that compensation should play in the firm. The foundation for the actual compensation plan should tie organizational goals, mission, and strategies to performance measurements and employee rewards. The relations and interactions among these elements are shown in Exhibit 19–15.

The traditional U.S. compensation strategy differentiates among three employee groups: top management, middle management, and workers. Top managers usually receive compensation containing a salary element and significant incentives that are provided for meeting or exceeding targeted objectives such as companywide net income or earnings per

EXHIBIT 19–15
PLAN–PERFORMANCE–
REWARD MODEL

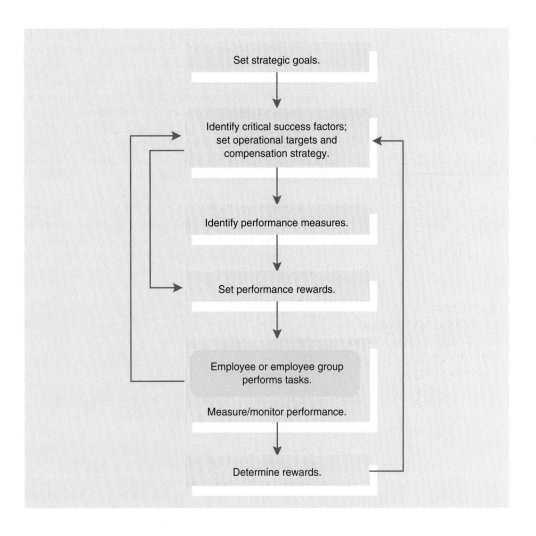

share. Middle managers are typically given salaries with the opportunity for future raises (and possibly bonuses) based on some performance measure such as segment income or divisional return on investment. Workers are paid wages (usually specified by union contract or tied to the minimum wage law) for the number of hours worked or production level achieved; current or year-end bonuses can arise when performance exceeds some specified quantitative measure.

The most basic reward plan consists of hourly, weekly, monthly, or other periodic compensation, which is based on time spent at work rather than on tasks accomplished. Different workers command different periodic pay rates/amounts because of seniority, skill, or education level. However, this type of compensation provides no immediate link between performance and reward. The only motivational aspects of periodic compensation are the prospects for advancement to a higher periodic pay rate/amount, demotion to a lower pay rate/amount, or dismissal.

PAY-FOR-PERFORMANCE PLANS

Compensation plans should encourage higher levels of employee performance and loyalty while lowering overall costs and raising profits. Such plans must encourage behavior essential to achieving organizational goals and maximizing stockholder value.

In a pay-for-performance plan, the defined performance measures must be highly correlated with the organization's operational targets. Otherwise, suboptimization could occur, and workers could earn incentive pay even though the organization's broader objectives were not achieved. More than any other goal or objective, maximization of shareholder wealth (a long-term goal) drives the design of reward systems.

A second important consideration when designing a performance-based system is that the measures should not focus solely on the short run. Short-run measures are not necessarily viable proxies for the long-run wealth maximization that is the primary objective of U.S. businesses. Pay-for-performance criteria should encourage workers to adopt a long-run perspective. Many financial incentives now involve shares of corporate common stock or stock options. Employees (regardless of level) who become stockholders in their employing company tend to develop the same perspective as other stockholders: long-run wealth maximization.

Because each organizational subunit has a unique mission and possesses unique competencies, the performance measurement system and reward structure should be crafted with the subunit's mission in mind. What is measured and rewarded affects the focus of the subunit employees, and the focus of the employees should be specifically on factors that determine the success of each subunit's operations. Exhibit 19–16 indicates how the form of reward is influenced by the subunit mission.

EXHIBIT 19–16

DIFFERENT STRATEGIC MISSIONS: IMPLICATIONS FOR INCENTIVE COMPENSATION

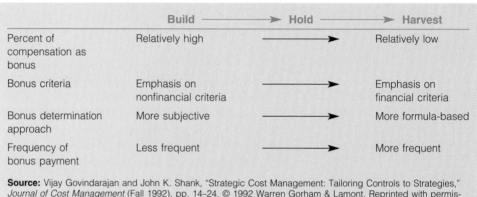

	Build ——————→ Hold ——————→ Harvest		
Percent of compensation as bonus	Relatively high	——————→	Relatively low
Bonus criteria	Emphasis on nonfinancial criteria	——————→	Emphasis on financial criteria
Bonus determination approach	More subjective	——————→	More formula-based
Frequency of bonus payment	Less frequent	——————→	More frequent

Source: Vijay Govindarajan and John K. Shank, "Strategic Cost Management: Tailoring Controls to Strategies," *Journal of Cost Management* (Fall 1992), pp. 14–24. © 1992 Warren Gorham & Lamont. Reprinted with permission of RIA.

Employee age is also an important factor in designing employee incentive plans. Younger employees, for natural reasons, may have a longer term perspective than older employees who expect to retire from the firm within a few years. In designing employee incentives, this difference in perspective between younger and older employees should be given due regard. Older employees could suboptimize to see short-run, rather than long-run, benefits of investment projects.

Another consideration in designing worker incentives is balancing the incentives provided for both individuals and groups (or teams). In automated production systems, workers devote more time to indirectly monitoring and controlling machinery and are less involved in hands-on production. At the same time, many organizational and managerial philosophies stress group or team performance. Group incentives are necessary to encourage cooperation among workers. However, if *only* group incentives are offered, the incentive system could be ineffective because the reward for individual effort goes to the group. The larger the group size, the smaller the individual's share of the group reward becomes. Eventually, some workers could decide to take a "free ride" on the group because they perceive their proportional shares of the group reward to be insufficient to compensate for their efforts.

CONSIDERATIONS IN SETTING PERFORMANCE MEASURES

When the compensation strategy and target objectives are known, performance measures for individual employees or employee groups can be determined based on their required contributions to the operational plan. Performance measures should, directly or indirectly, link individual actions with the basic business strategies. Rewards in a performance-based compensation plan should be based on both monetary and nonmonetary, short-term and long-term measures. "When many things are measured but only financial results are rewarded, it is obvious which measures will be regarded as most important."[8]

Degree of Control over Performance Output

Actual performance is a function of employee effort, employee skill, and random effects. The random effects include performance measurement error, problems or inefficiencies created by coworkers or adjacent workstations, illness, and weather-related production problems. After the actual performance is measured, determining the contributions of the controllable and noncontrollable factors to the achieved performance is impossible in many instances. Using performance-based pay systems causes employees to bear more risk than does the use of less comprehensive input–output measurements to determine compensation. Efforts should be made to identify performance measures that minimize the risk borne by employees.

At the worker level, performance measures should be specific and typically have a short-run focus—usually on cost and/or quality control. Each higher level in the organizational hierarchy should include increasingly more elements related to the critical success factors under an individual's control and responsibility. As the level of responsibility increases, performance measures should, by necessity, become less specific, focus on a longer time horizon, and be more concerned with organizational longevity rather than short-run cost control or income. When the compensation strategy, operational targets, and performance measurements have been determined, appropriate target rewards can be specified. Rewards should motivate employees to contribute in a manner congruent with the operational objectives, and employees must be able to relate their performance to the reward structure.

Incentives Relative to Organizational Level

As with performance measures, employees' organizational levels and current compensation should affect their rewards. Individuals at different organizational levels typically view monetary rewards differently because of the relationship of pay to standard of living. Relative pay scales are essential to recognizing the value of monetary rewards to different employees. At lower employee levels, most incentives should be monetary and short term (to enhance current lifestyles), but some nonmonetary and long-term incentives should also be included so these individuals will take a long-run organizational ownership view. At higher levels, most incentives should be nonmonetary and long term (such as stock and stock options) so that top management will be more concerned about the organization's long-term well-being rather than short-term personal gains.[9]

Performance Plans and Feedback

As employees perform their required tasks, performance related to the measurement standards is monitored. The two feedback loops in the model shown in Exhibit 19–15 exist so that problems identified in one period can be corrected in future periods. The first feedback loop relates to monitoring and measuring performance, which must be considered in setting targets for the following periods.

[8] Robert G. Eccles and Phillip J. Pyburn, "Creating a Comprehensive System to Measure Performance," *Management Accounting* (October 1992), p. 44.
[9] Two Web sites useful for benchmarking salary information are *www.salary.com* and *www.salaryexpert.com*.

The second feedback loop relates to the rewards given and the compensation strategy's effectiveness. Both loops are essential in the managerial planning process.

Worker Pay and Performance Links

The competitive environment in many industries has undergone substantial changes that have, among other effects, led companies to use more automation and fewer labor-intensive technologies. Also, evolving management philosophies are now emphasizing the need for workers to perform in teams and groups. An interesting paradox has been created by these changes. Workers are more detached from the production function and more involved with higher technology tasks. Thus, the trend is to rely more on performance-based evaluation and less on direct supervision to control worker behavior. This trend is consistent with the movement to empower workers and decrease levels of supervision and layers of management.

Promoting Overall Success

Many performance-based plans have the expressed goal of getting common stock into the hands of employees. One popular arrangement is profit sharing, which provides incentive payments to employees. These current and/or deferred incentive payments are contingent on organizational performance and can be in the form of cash or stock. Allocation of the total profit-sharing payment among individual employees is made on the basis of personal performance measurements, seniority, team performance, managerial judgment, and/or specified formulas. One popular profit-sharing compensation program is the **employee stock ownership plan (ESOP)**, in which investments are made in the employer's securities. An ESOP conforming to Internal Revenue Code rules offers both tax and incentive advantages. Under an ESOP, the employer makes tax-deductible payments of cash or stock to a trust fund. If cash is contributed, it is used by the trust to purchase shares of the employing company's stock. Trust beneficiaries are the employees, and their wealth grows with both the employer contributions and advances in the stock price. Of course, as was so dramatically illustrated at **Enron**, employees are at risk of losing some or all of these benefits if the employing company goes bankrupt.

employee stock ownership plan (ESOP)

Nonfinancial incentives, such as awards, can be used to motivate employees.

GETTY IMAGES

Nonfinancial Incentives

Besides various forms of monetary compensation, workers can also be motivated by nonfinancial factors. Although all employees value and require money to satisfy basic human needs, other human needs cannot necessarily be fulfilled with monetary wealth. Employees are typically more productive in environments in which they think their efforts are appreciated. Supervisors can formally recognize contributions of subordinates through simple gestures such as compliments and small awards; Intel has spontaneous recognition of employee contributions as well as quarterly department events. Allowing employees to participate in decisions affecting their own and the firm's welfare also contributes to making employment socially fulfilling and lets employees know that superiors are attentive to, and appreciative of, their contributions.

TAX IMPLICATIONS OF COMPENSATION ELEMENTS

tax deferral

tax exemption

Differences in tax treatments of employee compensation are important because they affect the after-tax income received by employees and the after-tax employer cost of the pay plan. There are three different tax treatments for employee compensation: full and immediate taxation, deferral of taxation, and exempt from taxation. **Tax deferral** indicates that taxation occurs at a future, rather than current, date. **Tax exemption** is the most desirable form of tax treatment because the amount is never subject to income taxation.

When analyzing the compensation plan, employers and employees must consider the entire package—not simply one element of the package. For the employer, compensation beyond wages and salaries will create additional costs; for employees, such compensation creates additional benefits. Fringe benefits can include employee health insurance, child care, physical fitness facilities, and pension plans. However, different types of fringe benefits have different tax consequences. Certain employee fringe benefits are not treated as taxable income to the employee but are fully and currently deductible by the employer.

ETHICAL CONSIDERATIONS OF COMPENSATION

A major issue of discussion and contention involves perceptions of disparity between the pay of ordinary workers and top managers. Plato argued that no one should earn more than five times the income earned by the lowest-paid worker. In the early 1900s, however, J. P. Morgan stated that the differential should be no more than 20 times. Today, there are numerous examples of CEOs earning many times the pay of the average worker.[10]

A new, major conflict between workers and managers surfaced in the 1990s. As more bonus plans of upper managers were revised to make them more sensitive to stockholder issues, top managers became more aggressive in controlling costs to generate profits. Simultaneously, technological advantages allowed firms to increase their productivity, generating more output using fewer workers. These two forces combined to create a historically rare circumstance: firms reporting record levels of profits while firing hundreds or thousands of workers.[11]

The greatest ethical compensation dilemmas involve circumstances that pit the welfare of employees against that of stockholders or the welfare of managers against the welfare of workers. Only if there is a perception of equity across the contributions and entitlements of labor, management, and capital will the organization be capable of achieving the efficiency to compete in global markets.

GLOBAL COMPENSATION

As more companies engage in multinational operations, compensation systems must be developed that reward all employees and managers on a fair and equitable basis. Intel, for example, even includes a benefits and compensation comparison on its Web site.

---

[10] In April of each year, *The Wall Street Journal* provides a special report on executive pay.

[11] Interestingly, one study that has been on-going for 18 years has concluded that downsizing does not necessarily help improve organizational profitability. In fact, the study (conducted by Professor Wayne Cascio of the University of Colorado at Denver) found that the companies that outperform others are the ones that create new assets, find new sources of revenue, and innovate. Adrianna Huffington, *Pigs at the Trough* (New York: Crown Publishers, 2003), pp. 69–70.

expatriate

A very important issue related to global compensation is the manner in which expatriates are compensated. **Expatriates** (expats) are parent-company and third-country nationals assigned to a foreign subsidiary or foreign nationals assigned to the parent company. Relocating individuals in foreign countries requires consideration of compensation. A fair and reasonable compensation package in one locale might not be fair and reasonable in another.

The compensation package paid to expats must reflect labor market factors, cost-of-living considerations, and currency fluctuations as well as recognize tax consequences. Typically, an expatriate's base salary and fringe benefits should reflect what he or she would have been paid domestically—adjusted for reasonable cost-of-living factors. These factors could be quite apparent (such as obtaining housing, education, and security needs similar to those that would have been obtained in the home country or compensating for a spouse's loss of employment), or they could be less obvious (such as a need to hire someone in the home country to care for an elderly relative or to handle real estate investments).

Expats can be paid in the currency of the country in which they reside, in their home currency, or in a combination of both. Frequently, price-level adjustment clauses are built into the compensation system to counteract any local currency inflation or deflation. Regardless of the currency makeup of the pay package, the fringe benefits related to retirement must be related to the home country and should be paid in that currency.

Tying compensation to performance is essential because everyone in business recognizes that what gets measured and rewarded is what gets accomplished. Businesses must focus their reward structures to motivate employees to succeed at all activities that will create shareholder and personal value. In this highly competitive age, the new paradigm of success is to provide quality products and services at a reasonable price while generating a reasonable profit margin. Top management compensation has traditionally been tied to financial measures of performance; more and more companies are beginning to tie compensation to nonfinancial performance measures.

Revisiting

Intel seeks to always be one generation ahead of the competition. It has established its competitive advantage in large degree because of the company's scale of operations, agility of its factory network, high product quality, and consistent execution worldwide. Company engineers are currently designing chips that will better support everything from multimedia applications to the consumer's "digital home." CEO Craig Barrett wants to put Intel's chips in all types of digital devices: cell phones, flat-panel televisions, wireless home networks, and medical diagnostic equipment. Digital is where it's at, and if it's digital, it's Intel. "Once photos, music, and video take digital form, they become the bits that Intel's chips can process, store, and zap across the Web."

Intel pursues new products because it believes that those products will add to shareholder value through corporate profitability. Intel is also concerned with the communities in which it has a significant presence and, therefore, invests in educational programs that advance science, math, and technology education.

Intel carefully designed its performance reward system so that it was aligned with the performance measurement system. In addition to hourly or monthly compensation, all employees are recommended for a stock option grant when they are hired; additional stock options are based on performance levels and anticipated future contributions. Employees also receive three bonuses per year. One bonus is determined based on an employee's bonus target, the financial performance of the corporation, and the performance of his or her business group against preset goals; the other two bonuses are tied to corporate pre-tax profits. These bonuses instill a message that employee efforts are correlated to shareholder

value creation and corporate income. Additionally, after each seven years of full-time service, employees receive eight weeks of full-pay and a vacation sabbatical so that they can return to work refreshed and recharged. These types of benefits make it easy to understand why, as of 2004, Intel had been named one of Fortune's "100 Best Companies to Work For" for seven consecutive years.

Additionally, Intel's concern for the environment has led to plans to eliminate approximately 95 percent of the lead used in its processors and chipsets beginning in 2004. The transition will require a massive effort with numerous technological, logistical, and economic challenges. New production materials have been developed to meet the performance and reliability requirements of lead but are more environmentally friendly. These changes will create some new overhead charges that will be reflected in capital asset depreciation. The company is certain that the benefits will be well worth the costs.

Cost control and profitability are important in any business, even one that was sitting on almost $8 billion in cash at the end of 2003. The concept of spreading fixed costs over more and more products is innate to Intel corporate accountants—capacity increases are always applauded as long as product demand exists. The company wants to make sure that it gets the most "bang" for each of its bucks, which will translate to lower product costs. In turn, consumers buying products with "Intel Inside" will be able to get faster access to many of the things that make life fun—digitally speaking, of course. After all, customer satisfaction is another one of Intel's many important performance measurements.

Sources: Cliff Edwards and Olga Karif, "This Is Not the Intel We All Know," *BusinessWeek* (August 16, 2004), p. 32; Cliff Edwards, "Intel," *Business Week* (March 8, 2004), pp. 56ff; Robert Levering and Milton Moskowitz, "2004 Special Report: The 100 Best Companies to Work For," *Fortune* (January 12, 2004); Intel Web site (*www.intel.com*); Intel Press Release, "Intel Working to Get the Lead Out" (April 7, 2004); and conversations with Tim Pebworth, Components Cost Team Manager, and Suri Iyer, CPU Cost Manager, Intel Corporation.

Comprehensive Review Module

Chapter Summary

1. A mission statement is important to an organization because it

   - expresses the organization's purpose.

   - identifies how the organization intends to meet its customers' needs through its products/services.

   - communicates organizational purpose and intentions to employees.

   - acts as a basis for setting organizational strategy.

2. Performance measures in organizations serve to

   - assess organizational performance.

   - relate organizational goals and missions to managerial performance.

   - foster growth of subordinate managers.

   - motivate managers.

   - enhance organizational communication.

   - evaluate comparative managerial performance.

   - implement organizational control.

3. The design of performance measures should be guided by

   - assessing progress toward organizational mission, goals, and objectives.

   - allowing the people being evaluated to participate in the development of the measures.

   - hiring people who have the appropriate skills and talents (or training people to have such) and providing them with the necessary equipment, information, and authority to be successful.

   - providing feedback to people in a timely and useful manner.

   - establishing a set of multiple measures that will provide a variety of information about performance.

4. Common short-term financial performance measures include

   - divisional profits or segment margin, which is

     - calculated as segment sales minus (direct variable expenses and avoidable fixed expenses).

     - used to assess whether segmental profitability goals were achieved.

   - cash flow (by segment or responsibility unit), which is

     - calculated as cash provided (used) from operating activities, investing activities, and (if appropriate) financing activities.

     - used to assess the ability of the responsibility unit to be profitable, have sufficient liquidity to pay debts as they arise, adapt to adverse conditions, and undertake new commitments.

   - return on investment, which is

     - calculated as profit margin multiplied by asset turnover.

     - used to assess the generation of income relative to the resources used to producte that income.

   - residual income, which is

     - calculated as income earned above a target rate on the unit's asset base.

     - used to assess the generation of income relative to the resources used to produce that income.

   - economic value added, which is

     - calculated as after tax-profits above the market value of capital invested multiplied by the cost of capital percentage.

     - used to assess the generation of income relative to the market value of the resources used to produce that income.

5. Company management should focus on long-run performance because such a perspective reflects

   - usage of leading, rather than lagging, indicators.

   - technical and competitive trends.

   - a more intensive investigation of resource allocations.

   - proactive efforts to enhance competitive position.

6. When selecting nonfinancial performance measures, managers should consider that

- people are more comfortable with quantitative rather than qualitative measures.

- the measures need to be clearly specified and communicated to those who will be evaluated by the measures.

- the measures must be relevant to the objective, trace responsibility, and benchmark internally and/or externally.

- the measures use valid data that can be obtained in a cost-beneficial manner.

- too many measures are counterproductive.

7. Multiple measures of performance should be used because an organization's success depends on a variety of factors, each of which should be reviewed for progression toward the organization's mission, goals, and objectives.

8. A balanced scorecard can be used to measure performance by providing a set of measurements that reflect the organization's mission and strategy from a

- financial perspective.

- customer perspective.

- internal process perspective.

- learning and growth perspective.

9. Measuring performance for multinational firms often creates difficulties because of differing

- labor and tax laws.

- employee work ethics.

- market and political stability.

- inflation, exchange, and labor rates.

- consumer wealth and purchasing power.

- financing costs.

- accounting practices.

10. Compensation strategy

- addresses the role compensation should play in an organization.

- forms the underlying structure for the compensation plan, including consideration of

  ➤ employees' control over performance output.

  ➤ employees' level in the organization.

  ➤ employees' opportunities to gain feedback and adapt performance.

  ➤ alignment of organizational mission, goals, and objectives with the performance measurements and employee rewards.

  ➤ tax and ethical implications of compensation.

Solution Strategies

PERFORMANCE MEASURES FOR RESPONSIBILITY CENTERS

- **Cost Center**

  Budgeted costs
  − Actual costs
  Variances (consider materiality)

- **Revenue Center**

  Budgeted revenues
  − Actual revenues
  Variances (consider materiality)

- **Profit Center**

  Budgeted profits
  − Actual profits
  Variances (consider materiality)

  Cash inflows
  − Cash outflows
  Net cash flow (adequate for operations?)

- **Investment Center**

  Budgeted profits
  − Actual profits
  Variances (consider materiality)

  Cash inflows
  − Cash outflows
  Net cash flow (adequate for operations?)

Return on Investment = Income ÷ Assets (high enough rate?)

Du Pont Model ROI = Profit Margin × Asset Turnover
= (Income ÷ Sales) × (Sales ÷ Assets) (high enough rate?)

Residual Income = Income − (Target Rate × Asset Base)
(positive or negative? amount?)

Economic Value Added = Income − (Cost of Capital % × Market Value of Capital Invested)
(positive or negative? amount?)

THROUGHPUT

$$\frac{\text{Manufacturing}}{\text{Cycle Efficiency}} \times \frac{\text{Process}}{\text{Productivity}} \times \frac{\text{Process}}{\text{Quality Yield}} = \text{Throughput}$$

$$\frac{\text{Value-Added}}{\text{Processing Time}} \times \frac{\text{Total Units}}{\frac{\text{Value-Added}}{\text{Processing Time}}} \times \frac{\text{Good Units}}{\text{Total Units}} = \text{Throughput}$$

REWARD SYSTEM

The design of an effective reward structure depends heavily on each organization's unique characteristics. It is impossible to design a generic incentive model that would be effective in all firms. However, affirmative answers to the following questions provide guidance as to the applicability of a proposed incentive and reward plan for a particular organization.

1. Will the organizational objectives be achieved if the proposed compensation structure is implemented?
2. Is the proposed structure consistent with organizational design and culture as well as management philosophy?
3. Are there reasonable and objective performance measures that are good surrogates for the organizational objectives and subunit missions?
4. Are factors beyond employee/group control minimized under the performance measures of the proposed compensation structure?
5. Is there minimal ability of employees to manipulate the performance measurements tied to the proposed compensation structure?
6. In light of the interests of managers, workers, and stockholders, is the proposed reward structure fair, and does it encourage and promote ethical behavior?
7. Is the proposed reward structure arranged to take advantage of potential employee/employer tax benefits?
8. Does the proposed reward structure promote harmony among employee groups?
9. Is there an adequate balance between group and individual incentives?

Demonstration Problem 1

Phoenix Offices is a division of Strategic Technologies. The division had the following performance targets for 2006:

Asset turnover	2.2
Profit margin	7%
Target rate of return on investments for RI	13%
Cost of capital	10%
Income tax rate	30%

Actual information concerning the company's performance for last year follows:

Total assets at beginning of year	$ 7,200,000
Total assets at end of year	10,600,000
Average FMV of invested capital	16,000,000
Sales	18,000,000
Variable operating costs	7,300,000
Direct fixed costs	9,530,000
Allocated fixed costs	1,350,000

Required:

a. Compute the 2006 segment margin and average assets for Phoenix Offices.

b. Based on segment margin and average assets, compute the profit margin, asset turnover, and ROI.

c. Evaluate the ROI performance of Phoenix Offices.

d. Using your answers from part (b), compute the residual income for Phoenix Offices.

e. Compute the EVA for Phoenix Offices using segment margin as pre-tax income. What causes EVA and RI to differ?

f. Based on the data given in the problem, discuss why ROI, EVA, and RI could be inappropriate measures of performance for Phoenix Offices.

Solution to Demonstration Problem 1

a.
Sales	$18,000,000
Variable operating costs	(7,300,000)
Direct fixed costs	(9,530,000)
Segment margin	$ 1,170,000

Average assets = ($7,200,000 + $10,600,000) ÷ 2 = $8,900,000

b. Profit margin = $ 1,170,000 ÷ $18,000,000 = 6.5%
Asset turnover = $18,000,000 ÷ $8,900,000 = 2.02
ROI = 6.5% × 2.02 = 13.13%

c. The target ROI for the division was 15.4% (7% × 2.2). The division generated a ROI of only 13.13 percent. The division did not achieve either its target rate of return or asset turnover. However, the ROI fell short of the target level primarily because the profit margin was below its target level.

d. RI = $1,170,000 − (0.13 × $8,900,000)
= $1,170,000 − $1,157,000
= $13,000

e. After-Tax Profits = Pre-tax segment Income − Taxes
= $1,170,000 − ($1,170,000 × 0.30)
= $1,170,000 − $351,000
= $819,000

EVA = $819,000 − ($16,000,000 × 0.10)
= $819,000 − $1,600,000
= $(781,000)

EVA and RI differ for three reasons. First, RI is based on pre-tax, rather than after-tax, income; RI is based on the book value of investment whereas EVA is based on the market value of investment; and the target rates of return differ between the methods.

f. ROI, RI, and EVA are measures of short-term performance. These measures may be particularly inappropriate for divisions that have long-term missions (such as high growth). In this case, the relatively large growth in assets of Phoenix Offices from the beginning to the end of the period could indicate that this division is oriented to growth. If so, the ROI, RI, and EVA measures will provide an incentive contrary to the growth mission.

Demonstration Problem 2

Alicia Company makes cell phone casings. During November 2006, managers compiled the following data:

Total casings manufactured	744,800
Good casings produced and sold	707,560
Total processing time	7,600
Value-added processing time	2,660

Required:

a. Calculate the manufacturing cycle efficiency.
b. Calculate the process productivity.
c. Calculate the process quality yield.
d. Calculate throughput using one ratio.
e. Confirm your answer to part (d) using the results of parts (a), (b), and (c).

Solution to Demonstration Problem 2

a. $\dfrac{\text{Value-Added Processing Time}}{\text{Total Time}} = \dfrac{2,660}{7,600} = 0.35$

b. $\dfrac{\text{Total Casings Produced}}{\text{Value-Added Processing Time}} = \dfrac{744,800}{2,660} = 280$

c. $\dfrac{\text{Good Casings Produced}}{\text{Total Casings Produced}} = \dfrac{707,560}{744,800} = 0.95$

d. $\dfrac{\text{Good Casings Produced}}{\text{Total Time}} = \dfrac{707,560}{7,600} = 93.1$

e. $(0.35 \times 280 \times 0.95) = 93.1$ casings per hour (rounded)

Key Terms

asset turnover *(p. 779)*
compensation strategy *(p. 792)*
Du Pont model *(p. 778)*
economic value added (EVA®) *(p. 782)*
employee stock ownership plan (ESOP) *(p. 796)*

expatriate *(p. 798)*
lagging indicator *(p. 783)*
leading indicator *(p. 784)*
process productivity *(p. 788)*
process quality yield *(p. 788)*
profit margin *(p. 778)*
residual income (RI) *(p. 781)*

return on investment (ROI) *(p. 778)*
tax deferral *(p. 797)*
tax exemption *(p. 797)*
throughput *(p. 787)*
values statement *(p. 772)*

Questions

1. What are the benefits of an organizational mission and values statement? How are organizational missions and strategies related to performance measures?

2. Why is performance measurement important to the success of businesses? Should performance measures be qualitative, quantitative, or both? Justify your answer. For performance measurements to be meaningful, why is it necessary to establish benchmarks?

3. What benefits can be gained by allowing a manager to participate in developing the performance measures that will be used to assess that manager's performance?

4. On what basis should the performance of a responsibility center be measured? What are the traditional financial performance measures for each type of responsibility center? Why can the same quantitative measures of performance not be used for all types of responsibility centers?

5. How can cash flow be used as a performance measure? In what ways is cash flow a relatively stronger or weaker performance measure than accrual measures such as segment income?

6. The president of Toys for Boys evaluates the performance of Annie and Andy, the divisional managers, on the basis of a variety of net income measures. Drew, the controller, informs the president that such measures could be misleading. What are the major concerns in defining the "income" measures? Are internal or external measures more susceptible to manipulation? Explain.

7. What is residual income, and how is it used to measure divisional performance? How is it similar to, and different from, the return on investment measure? How is residual income similar to, and different from, economic value added? How is economic value added superior to residual income as a performance measure?

8. In designing a performance measurement system, why should managerial rewards be linked to the performance measures? Why would an effective compensation strategy treat top managers, middle managers, and other workers differently?

9. What is the balanced scorecard? What perspectives are considered in selecting performance measures for the balanced scorecard?

10. Why is the trend in U.S. business away from automatic pay increases and toward increased use of incentive compensation plans?

11. If worker performance measures used in a pay-for-performance plan are not highly correlated with corporate goals, what is the likely result for the organization? For the workers?

12. How does the time perspective of a performance-based plan affect the selection of performance measures?

13. Why should different missions for two subunits result in different performance reward structures for the managers of those subunits? How does the mission of an organizational subunit affect the mix of financial and nonfinancial, and short-term and long-term, rewards?

14. How can feedback, both positive and negative, be used to improve managerial performance? How is feedback used in a performance-based reward system?

15. Many pay structures involve compensation that is both cash and stock based. Why do firms want employees to be holders of the firm's common stock? Why are additional performance measurement and reward issues created when managers are not shareholders in the firms they manage?

16. What are some of the important equity issues in designing reward structures? Why is the achievement of equity in the reward structure important?

Exercises

17. (ROI) Data for the three autonomous divisions of Leopold Corporation for fiscal year 2006 follow:

	Division 1	Division 2	Division 3
Segment income	$ 750,000	$ 250,000	$ 2,000,000
Asset investment	5,000,000	1,000,000	20,000,000

Compute the return on investment for each division.

18. (ROI) For the most recent fiscal year, the Withers Division of Lang Corporation generated an asset turnover ratio of 4 and a profit margin (as measured by the segment margin) ratio of 8 percent on sales of $3,600,000.
a. Compute the average assets employed.
b. Compute the segment margin.
c. Compute the ROI.

19. (ROI) The following 2006 information is available for Crandall Industries: average assets invested, $7,200,000; revenues, $26,400,000; and expenses, $24,600,000.
a. Calculate return on investment.
b. Calculate profit margin.
c. Calculate asset turnover.
d. Using parts (b) and (c), prove your answer to part (a).

20. (RI) Weston Corp. has established a 10 percent target ROI for 2006 for its Jamestown Division. The following data have been gathered for the division's operations for 2006: average total assets, $22,400,000; revenues, $60,000,000; and expenses, $56,000,000. What is the division's residual income? Did the division successfully meet the target ROI?

21. (RI) Parkson Ltd. operates its two divisions as investment centers. Information about these divisions is shown below.

	Division 1	Division 2
Sales	$2,100,000	$1,200,000
Total variable costs	1,260,000	300,000
Total fixed costs	250,000	700,000
Average assets invested	3,050,000	1,100,000

WebTUTOR Advantage

a. What is the residual income of each division if the "charge" on invested assets is 12 percent? Which division is doing a better job?

b. If the only change expected for next year is a sales increase of 22 percent, what will be the residual income of each division? Which division will be doing a better job financially?

c. Why did the answers to the second questions in parts (a) and (b) differ?

22. (ROI, RI) Corporate headquarters set a 14 percent target rate of return for the division located in Sacramento. For 2006, the Sacramento division generated $39,000,000 of revenue on average assets of $25,000,000. The division's variable costs were 45 percent of sales, and fixed costs were $6,750,000. Compute the following items for the Sacramento Division for 2006:

a. ROI

b. Residual income

c. Profit margin

d. Asset turnover

WebTUTOR Advantage

23. (EVA) Arguello Inc.'s cost of capital is 11 percent. In 2006, one of the firm's divisions generated an EVA of $3,270,000. The fair market value of the capital investment in that division was $26,500,000. How much after-tax income was generated by the division in 2006?

24. (EVA) EVA is used by top management at Denver Technologies to measure and evaluate the performance of segment managers. The company's cost of capital is 13 percent. In 2006, its Schnepel subsidiary generated after-tax income of $13,260,000, with $8,900,000 fair market value of invested capital.

a. Compute the subsidiary's EVA.

b. As the controller of Denver Technologies, how would you determine the fair value of capital investment for a particular division?

25. (Selecting performance measures) Jorja Property Management provides management services for commercial real estate development projects. The firm recently started a new division to market video game services to existing clients. The new division will purchase and maintain the video equipment placed in client buildings. Clients will be paid 20 percent of gross video equipment revenues.

Jorja Property Management has hired you to report on recommended performance measures to be used to monitor and evaluate the success of the new division and its manager. Begin your report with a discussion of your perception of the new division's strategic mission.

26. (Performance measurement manipulation) Following is a list of transactions that affected one division within a multiple-division company. Indicate, for the current fiscal year, whether each transaction would increase (I), decrease (D), have no effect (N), or have an indeterminate (?) effect on asset turnover, profit margin, ROI, and RI. Each transaction is independent.

a. In September, the division fired its R&D manager; the position will not be filled during the current fiscal year.

b. At mid-year, the division manager increased scheduled annual production by 5,000 units. This decision has no effect on scheduled sales.

c. Equipment with an original cost of $680,000 was sold for $139,000. At the time of sale, the book value of the equipment was $170,000. The equipment sale had no effect on production or sales activities.

d. The division wrote down obsolete finished goods by debiting Cost of Goods Sold and crediting Finished Goods Inventory for $96,000.

e. The division manager automated a previously labor-intensive operation. The action had no effect on sales, but total annual operating expenses declined by 17 percent.

f. Because of significant changes in its cost of capital, the company lowered the division's target rate of return from 12 to 10 percent.

g. A special overseas order was accepted at a selling price significantly less than that for domestic business. The selling price, however, was sufficient to cover all traceable costs of the order.

h. During the year, the division manager spent an additional $165,800 on advertising, which sparked an immediate increase in sales.

27. (Time perspective) Choose a company that has either gone out of business or is currently in poor financial condition. Use the Web to research that company's history. Prepare a report on your findings, concentrating on indicators that might have provided a perspective of failure. Describe these indicators as short-term or long-term and as leading or lagging.

28. (Throughput) A-Bit-Nutty, a macadamia nut cannery, is analyzing its throughput for September. The following statistics are obtained for the month:

WebTUTOR Advantage

Cans packed and sold	360,000
Total cans packed	391,020
Value-added processing time	343 hours
Total processing time	2,450 hours

a. Calculate the manufacturing cycle efficiency.
b. Calculate the process productivity.
c. Calculate the process quality yield.
d. Calculate the throughput using only good units and total time.
e. Verify your answer to part (d) by using your answers to parts (a), (b), and (c).

29. (Throughput) Kishiyama Corp. wants to compute its throughput for August 2006. The following production data are available:

Good units produced and sold	2,923,200
Total units produced	3,360,000
Total processing time	288,000 hours
Value-added time	100,800 hours

a. Determine the manufacturing cycle efficiency.
b. Determine the process productivity.
c. Determine the process quality yield.
d. Determine the throughput.
e. What can company management do to raise hourly throughput?

30. (Throughput) Management at Hanks Corp. has decided to begin using throughput as a divisional performance measure. The Eleanor Division is a job shop that makes carefully crafted furniture to customer specifications. The following first quarter information is available for the division:

Good units started, completed, and sold	24,800
Total units completed	26,112
Total value-added hours of processing time	7,680
Total hours of divisional time	12,000

a. What is the division's manufacturing cycle efficiency?
b. What is the division's process productivity?
c. What is the division's process quality yield?
d. What is the total hourly throughput?
e. Discuss whether throughput is as useful a performance measurement in a job shop as in an automated plant. Why would you expect process quality yield to be high in a job shop? Why might a job shop such as Eleanor Division have low manufacturing cycle efficiency?

31. (Pay plan and suboptimization) Pierre Wilke is a division manager of English Manufacturing Inc. He is in the process of evaluating a $2,000,000 investment. The following net annual increases, before depreciation, in divisional income are expected during the investment's five year life:

Year 1	$ 200,000
Year 2	300,000
Year 3	380,000
Year 4	1,600,000
Year 5	1,600,000

All company assets are depreciated using the straight-line method. Wilke receives an annual salary of $300,000 plus a bonus of 2 percent of divisional pre-tax profits. Before consideration of the potential investment project, he anticipates that his division will generate $4,000,000 annually in pre-tax profit.

a. Compute the effect of the new investment on the level of divisional pre-tax profits for years 1 through 5.

b. Determine the effect of the new project on Wilke's compensation for each of the five years.

c. Based on your computations in part (b), will Wilke want to invest in the new project? Explain.

d. Would upper management likely view the new investment favorably? Explain.

32. (Variable pay and incentives) In recent years, salaries for chief financial officers (CFOs) of large U.S. corporations averaged only about 20 percent of the total compensation package; the other 80 percent is performance-based, variable compensation that includes mostly stock options and short-term and long-term incentive bonuses. Among major corporate officers, typically, only CEOs have a higher percentage of pay that is variable.

a. What does the high portion of variable CFO pay indicate about the importance of CFOs to their organizations?

b. Discuss any concerns investors might have about such a high percentage of CFO pay being variable.

Problems

33. (Divisional profit) The Executive Consulting Division (ECD) of Global Financial Services is evaluated by corporate management based on a comparison of budgeted and actual pre-tax income. For 2007, ECD's budgeted income statement was as follows:

Sales	$ 18,000,000
Variable costs	(12,600,000)
Contribution margin	$ 5,400,000
Fixed costs	(3,600,000)
Pre-tax income	$ 1,800,000

At the end of 2007, ECD's actual results were as follows:

Sales	$ 19,500,000
Variable costs	(14,625,000)
Contribution margin	$ 4,875,000
Fixed costs	(3,615,000)
Pre-tax income	$ 1,260,000

a. Based on the preceding information, evaluate ECD's performance. What was the principal reason for the poor profit performance?

b. Why do complete income statements provide a more complete basis for evaluating the profit performance of a manager than mere comparisons of the bottom lines of the budgeted and actual income statements?

34. (Statement of cash flows) Ramagos System's controller prepared the following cash flow statements (in thousands of dollars) for the past two years, the current year, and the upcoming year (2007):

	2004	2005	2006	Budget 2007
Net cash flows from operating activities				
Net income	$ 41,700	$ 39,200	$ 43,700	$ 45,100
Add net reconciling items	2,200	4,300	3,000	4,000
Total	$ 43,900	$ 43,500	$ 46,700	$ 49,100
Net cash flows from investing activities				
Purchase of plant and equipment	$(18,700)		$(12,200)	$ (4,600)
Sale (purchase) of investments	8,700	$ (3,600)	(12,600)	(15,800)
Other investing inflows	1,200	800	600	2,400
Total	$ (8,800)	$ (2,800)	$(24,200)	$(18,000)
Net cash flows from financing activities				
Payment of notes payable	$(12,000)	$(24,000)	$(15,000)	$ (7,000)
Payment of dividends	(20,000)	(7,000)	(13,300)	(20,000)
Total	$(32,000)	$(31,000)	$(28,300)	$(27,000)
Net change in cash	$ 3,100	$ 9,700	$ (5,800)	$ 4,100

After preparation of the budgeted cash flow statement for 2007, Arnie Maine, the company president, asked you to recompile it based on a separate set of facts. He is evaluating a proposal to purchase a local-area network (LAN) computer system for the company at a total cost of $50,000. The proposal has been deemed to provide a satisfactory rate of return. However, he does not want to issue additional stock and he would prefer not to borrow any more money to finance the project.

Projecting the market value of the accumulated investments for the previous two years ($3,600 and $12,600) reveals an estimate that these investments could be liquidated for $18,400. Maine said the investments scheduled for 2007 did not need to be purchased and that dividends could be reduced to 40 percent of the budgeted amount. These are the only changes that can be made to the original forecast.

a. Evaluate the cash trends for the company during the 2004–2007 period.
b. Giving effect to the preceding changes, prepare a revised 2007 budgeted statement of cash flows and present the original and revised in a comparative format.
c. Based on the revised budgeted SCF, can the LAN computer system be purchased if Maine desires an increase in cash of at least $1,000?
d. Comment on the usefulness of the report prepared in part (b) to Maine.

35. (Cash flow) Shannon O'Leary, the controller of Rosepetal Co., is disillusioned with the company's system of evaluating the performance of divisional profit centers and their managers. The present system focuses on a comparison of budgeted to actual income from operations. Ms. O'Leary's major concern with the current system is the ease with which profit center managers can manipulate the measure income from operations. Most corporate sales are made on credit and most purchases are made on account. The profit centers are organized according to product line. Following is Limerick Division's second quarter 2007 income statement:

Sales	$ 31,500,000
Cost of goods sold	(25,500,000)
Gross profit	$ 6,000,000
Selling and administrative expenses	(4,500,000)
Income from operations	$ 1,500,000

O'Leary has suggested that company management replace the accrual-based income from operations evaluation measure with a cash flow from operations measure. She believes this measure will be less susceptible to manipulation by profit center managers. To defend her position, she compiles a cash flow income statement for the same profit center:

Cash receipts from customers	$ 26,400,000
Cash payments for production labor, materials, and overhead	(21,600,000)
Cash payments for selling and administrative activities	(4,200,000)
Cash flow from operations	$ 600,000

a. If O'Leary is correct about profit center managers manipulating the income measure, where are manipulations likely taking place?

b. Explain whether the proposed cash flow measure would be less subject to manipulation than the income measure.

c. Explain whether manipulation would be reduced if both the cash flow and income measures were utilized.

d. Do the cash and income measures reveal different information about profit center performance? Explain.

e. How could the existing income statement be used more effectively in evaluating performance?

36. (ROI) Tywanda Enterprises operates a chain of lumber stores. In 2006, corporate management examined industry-level data and determined the following performance targets for lumber retail stores:

| Asset turnover | 2.7 |
| Profit margin | 7.0% |

The actual 2006 results for the company's lumber retail stores follow:

Total assets at beginning of year	$10,200,000
Total assets at end of year	12,300,000
Sales	28,250,000
Operating expenses	25,885,000

a. For 2006, how did the lumber retail stores perform relative to their industry norms?

b. Where, as indicated by the performance measures, are the most likely areas to improve performance in the retail lumber stores?

c. What are the advantages and disadvantages of setting a performance target at the start of the year compared with one that is determined at the end of the year based on actual industry performance?

37. (ROI, RI) Elysian Togs sells clothing to specialty retail and department stores. For 2006, the company's Bradley Division had the following performance targets:

| Asset turnover | 1.8 |
| Profit margin | 8.0% |

Actual information concerning the performance of the Bradley Division in 2006 follows:

Total assets at beginning of year	$ 9,400,000
Total assets at end of year	14,900,000
Sales	24,000,000
Operating expenses	22,560,000

a. For 2006, did the Bradley Division achieve its target objectives for ROI, asset turnover, and profit margin?

b. Where, as indicated by the performance measures, are the most likely areas to improve performance?

c. If the company has an overall target return of 12 percent, what was the Bradley Division's residual income for 2006?

38. (Adjusting income for ROI purposes; advanced) Imelda Sanchez, manager of the Arias Division of Poncé Chemical, is evaluated based on the division's return on investment and residual income. Near the end of November 2006, she was reviewing the division's financial information as well as some activities projected for the remainder of the year. The information she was reviewing follows.

1. Annual sales were projected at 100,000 units, each with a selling price of $30. Sanchez has received a purchase order from a new customer for 5,000 units. The purchase order states that the units should be shipped on January 3, 2007, for arrival on January 5.

2. The division's 2006 beginning inventory was 500 units, each with a cost of $11. Purchases of 99,500 units have been made steadily throughout the year, and the per-unit cost has been constant at $10. Sanchez intends to make a purchase of 5,200 units before year-end, providing a 200-unit balance in inventory after making the shipment to the new customer. Carrying costs for the units are quite high, but ordering costs are extremely low. The division uses a LIFO cost flow assumption for inventory.

3. Shipping expenses are $0.50 per unit sold.

4. Sanchez has just received a notice from her primary supplier that he is going out of business and is selling his remaining stock of 15,000 units for $9 each. She makes a note to herself to place her final order for the year from this supplier.

5. Division advertising is $5,000 per month for newspaper inserts and television spots. No advertising has yet been purchased for December, but Sanchez intends to have her sales manager call the paper and TV station early next week.

6. Salaries through the end of the year are projected at $700,000. This amount assumes that the position to be vacated by the division's personnel manager will be filled on December 1. The personnel manager's job pays $66,000 per year. Sanchez has an interview on Monday with an individual who appears to be a good candidate for the position.

7. Other general and administrative costs for the full year are estimated to total $590,000.

8. As Sanchez was reviewing the divisional information, she received a phone call from the division's maintenance supervisor. He informed her that $10,000 of electrical repairs to the office heating system is necessary. When asked if the repairs were essential, the supervisor replied, "No, the office won't burn down if you don't make them, but they are advisable for energy efficiency and long-term operation of the system." Sanchez tells the supervisor to see her on Monday at 8:00 A.M.

Using her information, Imelda prepared a pro forma income statement and was fairly pleased with the division's results. Although providing the 13 percent rate of return on investment desired by corporate management, the results did not reach the 16 percent rate needed for Sanchez to receive a bonus for the year.

a. Prepare a 2006 pro forma income statement for the Arias Division. Determine the division's residual income, assuming that the division has an asset investment base of $4,500,000.

b. Sanchez's less-than-scrupulous friend, Juan Greer, walked into the house at this time. When he heard that she was not going to receive a bonus, Greer said, "Here, let me take care of this for you." He proceeded to re-compute the pro forma income statement and showed Imelda that, based on his computation of $723,000 in income, she would receive her bonus. Prepare Greer's pro forma income statement.

c. What future difficulties might arise if Sanchez acts in a manner that will make Greer's pro forma income statement figures a reality?

39. (ROI, RI; advanced) Anderson Industries produces stamping machinery for manufacturers. The company expanded vertically in 2001 by acquiring a supplier, DuCharm Company. To manage the two separate businesses, DuCharm is now operated as a divisional investment center.

Anderson monitors its divisions on the basis of both unit contribution and return on average investment (ROI), with investment defined as average operating assets employed. Management bonuses are determined based on ROI. All investments in operating assets are expected to earn a minimum return of 11 percent before income taxes.

DuCharm's cost of goods sold is entirely variable, whereas the division's administrative expenses are totally fixed. Selling expenses are a mixed cost with 40 percent attributed to sales volume. DuCharm's ROI has ranged from 11.8 percent to 14.7 percent since 2001. During the fiscal year ended November 30, 2006, DuCharm contemplated a capital acquisition with an estimated ROI of 11.5 percent; however, division management decided that the investment would decrease DuCharm's overall ROI.

The division's operating assets employed were $15,750,000 at November 30, 2006, a 5 percent increase over the 2005 year-end balance. The division's 2006 income statement follows.

DUCHARM DIVISION
Income Statement
For the Year Ended November 30, 2006
($000 Omitted)

Sales revenue		$ 25,000
Less expenses		
Cost of goods sold	$16,500	
Administrative expenses	3,955	
Selling expenses	2,700	(23,155)
Income from operations before income taxes		$ 1,845

a. Calculate the segment contribution for the DuCharm Division: 1,484,000 units were produced and sold during the year ended November 30, 2006.

b. Calculate the following performance measures for 2006 for the DuCharm Division:
  1. pre-tax return on average investment in operating assets employed (ROI), and
  2. residual income calculated on the basis of average operating assets employed.

c. Explain why the management of the DuCharm Division would have been more likely to accept the contemplated capital acquisition if residual income rather than ROI were used as a performance measure.

d. The DuCharm Division is a separate investment center within Anderson Industries. Identify several items that DuCharm should control if it is to be evaluated fairly by either the ROI or residual income performance measures.

(CMA adapted)

40. (Decisions based on ROI, RI) Destin Marine uses ROI to evaluate the performance of its two division managers. The following estimates of relevant measures have been made for the upcoming year:

	Powerboats	Sailboats	Total Company
Sales	$18,000,000	$48,000,000	$66,000,000
Expenses	16,200,000	42,000,000	58,200,000
Divisional assets	15,000,000	30,000,000	45,000,000

Both division managers have the autonomy to make decisions regarding new investments. The Powerboats division manager is considering investing in a new asset that would generate a 14 percent ROI; the Sailboats division manager is considering an asset investment that would generate an 18 percent ROI.

a. Compute the projected ROI for each division, disregarding the contemplated new investments.

b. Based on your answer in part (a), which of the managers is likely to actually invest in the additional assets under consideration?

c. Are the outcomes of the investment decisions in part (b) likely to be consistent with overall corporate goals? Explain.

d. If the company evaluated the division managers' performances using a residual income measure with a target return of 17 percent, would the outcomes of the investment decisions be different from those described in part (b)? Explain.

41. (EVA) As a division manager of Camden Projects Corp., your performance is evaluated primarily on one measure: after-tax divisional segment income less the cost of capital invested in divisional assets. The fair value of invested capital in your division is $37,500,000, the required return on capital is 10 percent, and the tax rate is 35 percent. Current income projections for 2007 follow:

Sales	$ 60,000,000
Expenses	(52,500,000)
Segment income	$ 7,500,000
Taxes	(2,625,000)
After-tax segment income	$ 4,875,000

You are considering an investment in a new product line that would, according to projections, increase 2007 pre-tax segment income by $600,000. The investment cost is not yet determinable because negotiations about several factors are still underway.

a. Ignoring the new investment, what is your projected EVA for 2007?

b. In light of your answer in part (a), what is the maximum amount that you would be willing to invest in the new product line?

c. Assuming that the new product line would require an investment of $2,100,000, what would be the revised projected EVA for your division in 2007 if the investment were made?

42. (Long-run performance) The company president has asked you, as the new controller, to comment on any deficiencies of the firm. After saying you believe that the firm needs long-run performance measurements, the president says that the long run is really just a series of short runs. He says that if you do a good job of evaluating these short-run performances, the long run will take care of itself. He sees that you are unconvinced and agrees to keep an open mind if you can make a good case for measuring and evaluating long-run performance. He suggests that you prepare a report stating your case. Do so.

43. (Throughput) Miguel Prieto manages the Springfield Division of Wilson Corporation. Prieto is concerned about the amount of the division's production. The following production data are available for April 2006:

Total units completed	423,360
Total good units completed and sold	359,856
Total value-added hours of processing time	15,680
Total hours of processing time	56,000

Determine each of the following for this division for April.

a. What is the manufacturing cycle efficiency?

b. What is the process productivity?

c. What is the process quality yield?

d. What is the total throughput per hour?

e. If only 280,000 of the units produced in April had been sold, would your answers to any of the preceding questions differ? If so, how? If not, why not?

f. If Prieto can eliminate 20 percent of the non-value-added time, how would throughput per hour for these data differ?

g. If Prieto can increase quality output to a yield of 90 percent and eliminate 20 percent of the non-value-added time, how would throughput per hour for these data differ?

h. How would Prieto determine how the non-value-added time was being spent in the division? What suggestions do you have to decrease non-value-added time and increase yield?

44. (Balanced scorecard) You have been elected president of your university's newly chartered accounting honor society. The society is a chapter of a national organization that has the following mission: "To promote the profession of accountancy as a career and to imbue members with high ethical standards."

a. Determine the balanced scorecard categories that you believe would be appropriate for the honor society.

b. Under each category, determine between four and six important performance measures.

c. How would you choose benchmarks against which to compare your chapters to others of the national organization?

45. (Balanced scorecard) One of the fundamental performance measurements in an organization's balanced scorecard learning and growth perspective is number of patents obtained. The following information from the U.S. Patent & Trademark Office [and cited in Cecily Fluke and Lesley Kump, "Innovation," *Forbes* (July 5, 2004), p. 44] indicates the total U.S. patents issued for five years prior to July 2004:

Company	Total Patents
IBM	15,756
Canon	9,447
NEC	8,818
Micron Technology	7,420
Samsung Electronics	7,007
Matsushita	6,947
Sony	6,903
Hitachi	6,809
Fujitsu	6,018
Toshiba	5,895

In a team of three or four people, research these companies on the Web and prepare a written report on their financial performance, customers' perceptions of their service and product quality, and manufacturing operations (such as level of automation in plants).

46. (Performance evaluation; ethics) In September 2006, Helpful Corporation decided to launch an expansion plan for some new product lines. To finance this expansion, the firm has decided to issue $200,000,000 of new common stock in November 2006.

Historically, the firm's personal digital assistant (PDA) was a significant contributor to corporate profits. However, a competitor has recently introduced a PDA that has rendered Helpful Corporation's PDA obsolete. The controller has informed Helpful's president that the inventory value of the PDAs needs to be reduced to its net realizable value. Because Helpful Corporation has a large inventory of the PDAs in stock, the write-down will have a very detrimental effect on both the balance sheet and income statement.

The president, whose compensation is determined in part by corporate profits and in part by stock price, has suggested that the write-downs be deferred until January 2007. He argues that, by deferring the write-down, existing shareholders will realize more value from the shares to be sold in November because the stock market will not be informed of the pending write-downs.

a. What effects are the performance evaluation measures of the president likely to have on his decision to defer the write-down of the obsolete inventory?

b. Is the president's decision to defer the write-down of the inventory an ethical treatment of existing shareholders? Of potential new shareholders?

c. If you were the controller of Helpful Corporation, how would you respond to the president's decision to defer the write-down until after issuance of the new stock?

47. (Performance measurement) Research suggests that as people work over a certain number of hours, productivity goes down, stress goes up, and work is not as good. You have taken this observation to heart and want to establish some performance measures in your accounting firm to help indicate that there is a balance between work and leisure for employees. Use all resources available to research this topic and prepare your list of performance measures. How will you benchmark these measures? How will you react to employees who are "workaholics"?

48. (Performance measurement) Recall the various ways in which your academic performance has been measured and rewarded. Have the ways that your class grades have been determined always provided the best indications of performance? Provide at least two positive and two negative examples. What would you have done to change the measurement system in the negative examples?

49. (Performance measurement; BSC) For each of the following items, indicate two performance measurements that could be obtained from a strategic cost management system. Classify each item into one of the four balanced scorecard perspectives.

a. Quality
b. Cost
c. Production line flexibility
d. People productivity and development
e. Inventory management
f. Lead time
g. Responsive after-sale service
h. Customer satisfaction and retention
i. Product and process design
j. Manufacturing planning process
k. Procurement process
l. Manufacturing process

    m. Management accomplishments

    n. Marketing/Sales and customer service

    o. Delivery performance

    p. Financial accounting services

50. (Providing feedback on performance) Terry Travers is the manufacturing supervisor of the Aurora Manufacturing Company, which produces a variety of plastic products. Some of these products are standard items that are listed in the company's catalog, whereas others are made to customer specifications. Each month, Mr. Travers receives a performance report displaying the budget for the month, the actual activity for the period, and the variance between budget and actual. Part of Mr. Travers' annual performance evaluation is based on her department's performance against budget. Aurora's purchasing manager, Bob Christensen, also receives monthly performance reports and is evaluated in part on the basis of these reports.

    The most recent monthly reports were just distributed when Terry met Bob in the hallway outside their offices. Scowling, Terry began the conversation, "I see we have another set of monthly performance reports hand delivered by that not very nice junior employee in the budget office. He seemed pleased to tell me that I was in trouble with my performance again."

    Bob: "I got the same treatment. All I ever hear about are the things I haven't done right. Now, I'll have to spend a lot of time reviewing the report and preparing explanations. The worst part is that the information is almost a month old, and we spend all this time on history."

    Terry: "My biggest gripe is that our production activity varies a lot from month to month, but we're given an annual budget that's written in stone. Last month, we were shut down for three days when a strike delayed delivery of the basic ingredient used in our plastic formulation, and we had already exhausted our inventory. You know that, of course, since we had asked you to call all over the country to find an alternate source of supply. When we got what we needed on a rush basis, we had to pay more than we normally do."

    Bob: "I expect problems like that to pop up from time to time—that's part of my job—but now we'll both have to take a careful look at the report to see where charges are reflected for that rush order. Every month, I spend more time making sure I should be charged for each item reported than I do making plans for my department's daily work. It's really frustrating to see charges for things I have no control over."

    Terry: "The way we get information doesn't help, either. I don't get copies of the reports you get, yet a lot of what I do is affected by your department, and by most of the other departments we have. Why do the budget and accounting people assume that I should be told only about my operations even though the president regularly gives us pep talks about how we all need to work together as a team?"

    Bob: "I seem to get more reports than I need, and I am never getting asked to comment until top management calls me on the carpet about my department's shortcomings. Do you ever hear comments when your department shines?"

    Terry: "I guess they don't have time to review the good news. One of my problems is that all the reports are in dollars and cents. I work with people, machines, and materials. I need information to help me solve this month's problems—not another report of the dollars expended last month or the month before."

    a. Based on the conversation between Terry Travers and Bob Christensen, describe the likely motivation and behavior of these two employees resulting from the Aurora Manufacturing Company's performance reporting system.

b. 1. When properly implemented, both employees and companies should benefit from performance reporting systems. Describe the benefits that can be realized from using a performance reporting system.

2. Based on the situation presented here, recommend ways for Aurora Manufacturing Company to improve its performance system to increase employee motivation.

(CMA adapted)

51. (Balanced scorecard) Lone Star Enterprises manufactures a variety of glass products having both commercial and household applications. One of its newest divisions, BellClear, manufactures fiber optic cable and other high-tech products. Recent annual operating results (in millions) for BellClear and two older divisions follow:

	BellClear	Industrial Glass	Kitchenware
Sales	$250	$900	$750
Segment income	25	92	85

Lone Star Enterprises uses economic value added (EVA) as its only segment performance measure. Claudia Levy, CEO of Lone Star, posed some serious questions in a memo to the controller, Jim Mullins, after studying the operating results.

> *Dear Jim:*
>
> *I'm concerned about BellClear. Its key competitor's sales and market share are growing at about twice the pace of BellClear. I'm not comforted by the fact that BellClear is generating substantially more profits than the competitor. The mission we have established for BellClear is high growth. Do you think we should use EVA to measure the division's performance and as a basis to compensate BellClear's divisional management? Do we need to change our performance criteria?*
> *Claudia*

After pondering the memo and studying the operating results, Mullins passed the memo and operating results to you, his newest employee in the controller's office and asked you to respond to the following questions.

a. Why would the use of EVA discourage a high-growth strategy?

b. Could the concept of the balanced scorecard be used to encourage a higher rate of growth in BellClear? Explain.

52. (Balanced scorecard) As the cost of health care continues to increase, hospital and clinic managers need to be able to evaluate the performance of their organizations. Numerous articles have been written on performance measurements for health care organizations. Obtain some of these articles and prepare a report on what you believe to be the best set of balanced scorecard measures for such an organization.

53. (Compensation) Relative to worker compensation, no topic is more hotly debated than the minimum wage law. Using concepts from this chapter, prepare a report in which you explain why increases in the minimum wage are not desirable and how alternative mechanisms could be used to increase the compensation of low-paid workers.

54. (Pay plans and goal congruence) In 2006, the lead story in your college newspaper reports the details of the hiring of the current football coach.

The previous football coach was fired for failing to win games and attract fans. In his last season, his record was 1 win and 11 losses. The news story states that the new coach's contract provides for a base salary of $200,000 per year plus an annual bonus computed as follows:

Win less than 5 games	$ 0
Win 5 to 7 games	25,000
Win 8 games or more	75,000
Win 8 games and conference championship	95,000
Win 8 games, win conference, and get a bowl bid	150,000

The coach's contract has essentially no other features or clauses.

The first year after the new coach is hired, the football team wins three games and loses eight. In the second year, the team wins six games and loses five. In the third year, the team wins nine games, wins the conference championship, and is invited to a prestigious bowl. Shortly after the bowl game, articles appear on the front page of several national sports publications announcing that your college's football program has been cited by the National Collegiate Athletic Association (NCAA) for nine major rule violations including cash payoffs to players, playing academically ineligible players, illegal recruiting tactics, illegal involvement of alumni in recruiting, and so on. The national news publications agree that the NCAA will disband your college's football program. One article also mentioned that during the past three years, only 13 percent of senior football players managed to graduate on time. Additional speculation suggests that the responsible parties, including the coaching staff, athletic director, and college president, will be dismissed by the board of trustees.

a. Compute the amount of compensation paid to the new coach in each of his first three years.

b. Did the performance measures in the coach's contract foster goal congruence? Explain.

c. Would the coach's actions have been different if other performance measures had been added to the compensation contract? Explain.

d. What performance measures should be considered for the next coach's contract, assuming the football program is allowed to continue?

55. (Compensation; ethics) Chalmette Manufacturing has just initiated a formula bonus plan that rewards plant managers for various achievements. One of the current criteria for bonuses is the improvement of asset turnover. The plant manager of the Violet Plant asked Sam Jensen, his assistant, to meet him Saturday when the plant is closed. Without explanation, the plant manager specified that certain raw materials were to be loaded on one of the plant's dump trucks. When the truck was loaded, the plant manager and Jensen drove to a secluded mountain road where, to Jensen's astonishment, the plant manager flipped a switch and the truck dumped the raw materials down a steep ravine. The plant manager grinned and said that these raw materials were obsolete and the company would run more smoothly without them. For the next several weekends, Jensen observed the plant manager do the same thing. The following month, the plant manager was officially congratulated for improving asset turnover.

a. How did the dumping improve asset turnover?

b. What are the ethical problems in this case?

c. What are Jensen's options? Which should he choose and why?

Appendix A

Present Value Tables

TABLE 1 *Present Value of $1*

Period	1.00%	2.00%	3.00%	4.00%	5.00%	6.00%	7.00%	8.00%	9.00%	9.50%	10.00%	10.50%	11.00%
1	0.9901	0.9804	0.9709	0.9615	0.9524	0.9434	0.9346	0.9259	0.9174	0.9132	0.9091	0.9050	0.9009
2	0.9803	0.9612	0.9426	0.9246	0.9070	0.8900	0.8734	0.8573	0.8417	0.8340	0.8265	0.8190	0.8116
3	0.9706	0.9423	0.9151	0.8890	0.8638	0.8396	0.8163	0.7938	0.7722	0.7617	0.7513	0.7412	0.7312
4	0.9610	0.9239	0.8885	0.8548	0.8227	0.7921	0.7629	0.7350	0.7084	0.6956	0.6830	0.6707	0.6587
5	0.9515	0.9057	0.8626	0.8219	0.7835	0.7473	0.7130	0.6806	0.6499	0.6352	0.6209	0.6070	0.5935
6	0.9421	0.8880	0.8375	0.7903	0.7462	0.7050	0.6663	0.6302	0.5963	0.5801	0.5645	0.5493	0.5346
7	0.9327	0.8706	0.8131	0.7599	0.7107	0.6651	0.6228	0.5835	0.5470	0.5298	0.5132	0.4971	0.4817
8	0.9235	0.8535	0.7894	0.7307	0.6768	0.6274	0.5820	0.5403	0.5019	0.4838	0.4665	0.4499	0.4339
9	0.9143	0.8368	0.7664	0.7026	0.6446	0.5919	0.5439	0.5003	0.4604	0.4419	0.4241	0.4071	0.3909
10	0.9053	0.8204	0.7441	0.6756	0.6139	0.5584	0.5084	0.4632	0.4224	0.4035	0.3855	0.3685	0.3522
11	0.8963	0.8043	0.7224	0.6496	0.5847	0.5268	0.4751	0.4289	0.3875	0.3685	0.3505	0.3334	0.3173
12	0.8875	0.7885	0.7014	0.6246	0.5568	0.4970	0.4440	0.3971	0.3555	0.3365	0.3186	0.3018	0.2858
13	0.8787	0.7730	0.6810	0.6006	0.5303	0.4688	0.4150	0.3677	0.3262	0.3073	0.2897	0.2731	0.2575
14	0.8700	0.7579	0.6611	0.5775	0.5051	0.4423	0.3878	0.3405	0.2993	0.2807	0.2633	0.2471	0.2320
15	0.8614	0.7430	0.6419	0.5553	0.4810	0.4173	0.3625	0.3152	0.2745	0.2563	0.2394	0.2237	0.2090
16	0.8528	0.7285	0.6232	0.5339	0.4581	0.3937	0.3387	0.2919	0.2519	0.2341	0.2176	0.2024	0.1883
17	0.8444	0.7142	0.6050	0.5134	0.4363	0.3714	0.3166	0.2703	0.2311	0.2138	0.1978	0.1832	0.1696
18	0.8360	0.7002	0.5874	0.4936	0.4155	0.3503	0.2959	0.2503	0.2120	0.1952	0.1799	0.1658	0.1528
19	0.8277	0.6864	0.5703	0.4746	0.3957	0.3305	0.2765	0.2317	0.1945	0.1783	0.1635	0.1500	0.1377
20	0.8195	0.6730	0.5537	0.4564	0.3769	0.3118	0.2584	0.2146	0.1784	0.1628	0.1486	0.1358	0.1240
21	0.8114	0.6598	0.5376	0.4388	0.3589	0.2942	0.2415	0.1987	0.1637	0.1487	0.1351	0.1229	0.1117
22	0.8034	0.6468	0.5219	0.4220	0.3419	0.2775	0.2257	0.1839	0.1502	0.1358	0.1229	0.1112	0.1007
23	0.7954	0.6342	0.5067	0.4057	0.3256	0.2618	0.2110	0.1703	0.1378	0.1240	0.1117	0.1006	0.0907
24	0.7876	0.6217	0.4919	0.3901	0.3101	0.2470	0.1972	0.1577	0.1264	0.1133	0.1015	0.0911	0.0817
25	0.7798	0.6095	0.4776	0.3751	0.2953	0.2330	0.1843	0.1460	0.1160	0.1034	0.0923	0.0824	0.0736
26	0.7721	0.5976	0.4637	0.3607	0.2812	0.2198	0.1722	0.1352	0.1064	0.0945	0.0839	0.0746	0.0663
27	0.7644	0.5859	0.4502	0.3468	0.2679	0.2074	0.1609	0.1252	0.0976	0.0863	0.0763	0.0675	0.0597
28	0.7568	0.5744	0.4371	0.3335	0.2551	0.1956	0.1504	0.1159	0.0896	0.0788	0.0693	0.0611	0.0538
29	0.7493	0.5631	0.4244	0.3207	0.2430	0.1846	0.1406	0.1073	0.0822	0.0719	0.0630	0.0553	0.0485
30	0.7419	0.5521	0.4120	0.3083	0.2314	0.1741	0.1314	0.0994	0.0754	0.0657	0.0573	0.0500	0.0437
31	0.7346	0.5413	0.4000	0.2965	0.2204	0.1643	0.1228	0.0920	0.0692	0.0600	0.0521	0.0453	0.0394
32	0.7273	0.5306	0.3883	0.2851	0.2099	0.1550	0.1147	0.0852	0.0634	0.0058	0.0474	0.0410	0.0355
33	0.7201	0.5202	0.3770	0.2741	0.1999	0.1462	0.1072	0.0789	0.0582	0.0500	0.0431	0.0371	0.0319
34	0.7130	0.5100	0.3660	0.2636	0.1904	0.1379	0.1002	0.0731	0.0534	0.0457	0.0391	0.0336	0.0288
35	0.7059	0.5000	0.3554	0.2534	0.1813	0.1301	0.0937	0.0676	0.0490	0.0417	0.0356	0.0304	0.0259
36	0.6989	0.4902	0.3450	0.2437	0.1727	0.1227	0.0875	0.0626	0.0449	0.0381	0.0324	0.0275	0.0234
37	0.6920	0.4806	0.3350	0.2343	0.1644	0.1158	0.0818	0.0580	0.0412	0.0348	0.0294	0.0249	0.0210
38	0.6852	0.4712	0.3252	0.2253	0.1566	0.1092	0.0765	0.0537	0.0378	0.0318	0.0267	0.0225	0.0190
39	0.6784	0.4620	0.3158	0.2166	0.1492	0.1031	0.0715	0.0497	0.0347	0.0290	0.0243	0.0204	0.0171
40	0.6717	0.4529	0.3066	0.2083	0.1421	0.0972	0.0668	0.0460	0.0318	0.0265	0.0221	0.0184	0.0154
41	0.6650	0.4440	0.2976	0.2003	0.1353	0.0917	0.0624	0.0426	0.0292	0.0242	0.0201	0.0167	0.0139
42	0.6584	0.4353	0.2890	0.1926	0.1288	0.0865	0.0583	0.0395	0.0268	0.0221	0.0183	0.0151	0.0125
43	0.6519	0.4268	0.2805	0.1852	0.1227	0.0816	0.0545	0.0365	0.0246	0.0202	0.0166	0.0137	0.0113
44	0.6455	0.4184	0.2724	0.1781	0.1169	0.0770	0.0510	0.0338	0.0226	0.0184	0.0151	0.0124	0.0101
45	0.6391	0.4102	0.2644	0.1712	0.1113	0.0727	0.0476	0.0313	0.0207	0.0168	0.0137	0.0112	0.0091
46	0.6327	0.4022	0.2567	0.1646	0.1060	0.0685	0.0445	0.0290	0.0190	0.0154	0.0125	0.0101	0.0082
47	0.6265	0.3943	0.2493	0.1583	0.1010	0.0647	0.0416	0.0269	0.0174	0.0141	0.0113	0.0092	0.0074
48	0.6203	0.3865	0.2420	0.1522	0.0961	0.0610	0.0389	0.0249	0.0160	0.0128	0.0103	0.0083	0.0067
49	0.6141	0.3790	0.2350	0.1463	0.0916	0.0576	0.0363	0.0230	0.0147	0.0117	0.0094	0.0075	0.0060
50	0.6080	0.3715	0.2281	0.1407	0.0872	0.0543	0.0340	0.0213	0.0135	0.0107	0.0085	0.0068	0.0054

11.50%	12.00%	12.50%	13.00%	13.50%	14.00%	14.50%	15.00%	15.50%	16.00%	17.00%	18.00%	19.00%	20.00%
0.8969	0.8929	0.8889	0.8850	0.8811	0.8772	0.8734	0.8696	0.8658	0.8621	0.8547	0.8475	0.8403	0.8333
0.8044	0.7972	0.7901	0.7832	0.7763	0.7695	0.7628	0.7561	0.7496	0.7432	0.7305	0.7182	0.7062	0.6944
0.7214	0.7118	0.7023	0.6931	0.6839	0.6750	0.6662	0.6575	0.6490	0.6407	0.6244	0.6086	0.5934	0.5787
0.6470	0.6355	0.6243	0.6133	0.6026	0.5921	0.5818	0.5718	0.5619	0.5523	0.5337	0.5158	0.4987	0.4823
0.5803	0.5674	0.5549	0.5428	0.5309	0.5194	0.5081	0.4972	0.4865	0.4761	0.4561	0.4371	0.4191	0.4019
0.5204	0.5066	0.4933	0.4803	0.4678	0.4556	0.4438	0.4323	0.4212	0.4104	0.3898	0.3704	0.3521	0.3349
0.4667	0.4524	0.4385	0.4251	0.4121	0.3996	0.3876	0.3759	0.3647	0.3538	0.3332	0.3139	0.2959	0.2791
0.4186	0.4039	0.3897	0.3762	0.3631	0.3506	0.3385	0.3269	0.3158	0.3050	0.2848	0.2660	0.2487	0.2326
0.3754	0.3606	0.3464	0.3329	0.3199	0.3075	0.2956	0.2843	0.2734	0.2630	0.2434	0.2255	0.2090	0.1938
0.3367	0.3220	0.3080	0.2946	0.2819	0.2697	0.2582	0.2472	0.2367	0.2267	0.2080	0.1911	0.1756	0.1615
0.3020	0.2875	0.2737	0.2607	0.2483	0.2366	0.2255	0.2149	0.2049	0.1954	0.1778	0.1619	0.1476	0.1346
0.2708	0.2567	0.2433	0.2307	0.2188	0.2076	0.1969	0.1869	0.1774	0.1685	0.1520	0.1372	0.1240	0.1122
0.2429	0.2292	0.2163	0.2042	0.1928	0.1821	0.1720	0.1625	0.1536	0.1452	0.1299	0.1163	0.1042	0.0935
0.2179	0.2046	0.1923	0.1807	0.1699	0.1597	0.1502	0.1413	0.1330	0.1252	0.1110	0.0986	0.0876	0.0779
0.1954	0.1827	0.1709	0.1599	0.1496	0.1401	0.1312	0.1229	0.1152	0.1079	0.0949	0.0835	0.0736	0.0649
0.1752	0.1631	0.1519	0.1415	0.1319	0.1229	0.1146	0.1069	0.0997	0.0930	0.0811	0.0708	0.0618	0.0541
0.1572	0.1456	0.1350	0.1252	0.1162	0.1078	0.1001	0.0929	0.0863	0.0802	0.0693	0.0600	0.0520	0.0451
0.1410	0.1300	0.1200	0.1108	0.1024	0.0946	0.0874	0.0808	0.0747	0.0691	0.0593	0.0508	0.0437	0.0376
0.1264	0.1161	0.1067	0.0981	0.0902	0.0830	0.0763	0.0703	0.0647	0.0596	0.0506	0.0431	0.0367	0.0313
0.1134	0.1037	0.0948	0.0868	0.0795	0.0728	0.0667	0.0611	0.0560	0.0514	0.0433	0.0365	0.0308	0.0261
0.1017	0.0926	0.0843	0.0768	0.0700	0.0638	0.0582	0.0531	0.0485	0.0443	0.0370	0.0309	0.0259	0.0217
0.0912	0.0826	0.0749	0.0680	0.0617	0.0560	0.0509	0.0462	0.0420	0.0382	0.0316	0.0262	0.0218	0.0181
0.0818	0.0738	0.0666	0.0601	0.0543	0.0491	0.0444	0.0402	0.0364	0.0329	0.0270	0.0222	0.0183	0.0151
0.0734	0.0659	0.0592	0.0532	0.0479	0.0431	0.0388	0.0349	0.0315	0.0284	0.0231	0.0188	0.0154	0.0126
0.0658	0.0588	0.0526	0.0471	0.0422	0.0378	0.0339	0.0304	0.0273	0.0245	0.0197	0.0160	0.0129	0.0105
0.0590	0.0525	0.0468	0.0417	0.0372	0.0332	0.0296	0.0264	0.0236	0.0211	0.0169	0.0135	0.0109	0.0087
0.0529	0.0469	0.0416	0.0369	0.0327	0.0291	0.0258	0.0230	0.0204	0.0182	0.0144	0.0115	0.0091	0.0073
0.0475	0.0419	0.0370	0.0326	0.0289	0.0255	0.0226	0.0200	0.0177	0.0157	0.0123	0.0097	0.0077	0.0061
0.0426	0.0374	0.0329	0.0289	0.0254	0.0224	0.0197	0.0174	0.0153	0.0135	0.0105	0.0082	0.0064	0.0051
0.0382	0.0334	0.0292	0.0256	0.0224	0.0196	0.0172	0.0151	0.0133	0.0117	0.0090	0.0070	0.0054	0.0042
0.0342	0.0298	0.0260	0.0226	0.0197	0.0172	0.0150	0.0131	0.0115	0.0100	0.0077	0.0059	0.0046	0.0035
0.0307	0.0266	0.0231	0.0200	0.0174	0.0151	0.0131	0.0114	0.0099	0.0087	0.0066	0.0050	0.0038	0.0029
0.0275	0.0238	0.0205	0.0177	0.0153	0.0133	0.0115	0.0099	0.0086	0.0075	0.0056	0.0043	0.0032	0.0024
0.0247	0.0212	0.0182	0.0157	0.0135	0.0116	0.0100	0.0088	0.0075	0.0064	0.0048	0.0036	0.0027	0.0020
0.0222	0.0189	0.0162	0.0139	0.0119	0.0102	0.0088	0.0075	0.0065	0.0056	0.0041	0.0031	0.0023	0.0017
0.0199	0.0169	0.0144	0.0123	0.0105	0.0089	0.0076	0.0065	0.0056	0.0048	0.0035	0.0026	0.0019	0.0014
0.0178	0.0151	0.0128	0.0109	0.0092	0.0078	0.0067	0.0057	0.0048	0.0041	0.0030	0.0022	0.0016	0.0012
0.0160	0.0135	0.0114	0.0096	0.0081	0.0069	0.0058	0.0049	0.0042	0.0036	0.0026	0.0019	0.0014	0.0010
0.0143	0.0120	0.0101	0.0085	0.0072	0.0060	0.0051	0.0043	0.0036	0.0031	0.0022	0.0016	0.0011	0.0008
0.0129	0.0108	0.0090	0.0075	0.0063	0.0053	0.0044	0.0037	0.0031	0.0026	0.0019	0.0013	0.0010	0.0007
0.0115	0.0096	0.0080	0.0067	0.0056	0.0046	0.0039	0.0033	0.0027	0.0023	0.0016	0.0011	0.0008	0.0006
0.0103	0.0086	0.0077	0.0059	0.0049	0.0041	0.0034	0.0028	0.0024	0.0020	0.0014	0.0010	0.0007	0.0005
0.0093	0.0077	0.0063	0.0052	0.0043	0.0036	0.0030	0.0025	0.0020	0.0017	0.0012	0.0008	0.0006	0.0004
0.0083	0.0068	0.0056	0.0046	0.0038	0.0031	0.0026	0.0021	0.0018	0.0015	0.0010	0.0007	0.0005	0.0003
0.0075	0.0061	0.0050	0.0041	0.0034	0.0028	0.0023	0.0019	0.0015	0.0013	0.0009	0.0006	0.0004	0.0003
0.0067	0.0054	0.0044	0.0036	0.0030	0.0024	0.0020	0.0016	0.0013	0.0011	0.0007	0.0005	0.0003	0.0002
0.0060	0.0049	0.0039	0.0032	0.0026	0.0021	0.0017	0.0014	0.0011	0.0009	0.0006	0.0004	0.0003	0.0002
0.0054	0.0043	0.0035	0.0028	0.0023	0.0019	0.0015	0.0012	0.0010	0.0008	0.0005	0.0004	0.0002	0.0002
0.0048	0.0039	0.0031	0.0025	0.0020	0.0016	0.0013	0.0011	0.0009	0.0007	0.0005	0.0003	0.0002	0.0001
0.0043	0.0035	0.0028	0.0022	0.0018	0.0014	0.0012	0.0009	0.0007	0.0006	0.0004	0.0003	0.0002	0.0001

TABLE 2   *Present Value of an Ordinary Annuity of $1*

Period	1.00%	2.00%	3.00%	4.00%	5.00%	6.00%	7.00%	8.00%	9.00%	9.50%	10.00%	10.50%	11.00%
1	0.9901	0.9804	0.9709	0.9615	0.0524	0.9434	0.9346	0.9259	0.9174	0.9132	0.9091	0.9050	0.9009
2	1.9704	1.9416	1.9135	1.8861	1.8594	1.8334	1.8080	1.7833	1.7591	1.7473	1.7355	1.7240	1.7125
3	2.9410	2.8839	2.8286	2.7751	2.7233	2.6730	2.6243	2.5771	2.5313	2.5089	2.4869	2.4651	2.4437
4	3.9020	3.8077	3.7171	3.6299	3.5460	3.4651	3.3872	3.3121	3.2397	3.2045	3.1699	3.1359	3.1025
5	4.8534	4.7135	4.5797	4.4518	4.3295	4.2124	4.1002	3.9927	3.8897	3.8397	3.7908	3.7429	3.6959
6	5.7955	5.6014	5.4172	5.2421	5.0757	4.9173	4.7665	4.6229	4.4859	4.4198	4.3553	4.2922	4.2305
7	6.7282	6.4720	6.2303	6.0021	5.7864	5.5824	5.3893	5.2064	5.0330	4.9496	4.8684	4.7893	4.7122
8	7.6517	7.3255	7.0197	6.7327	6.4632	6.2098	5.9713	5.7466	5.5348	5.4334	5.3349	5.2392	5.1461
9	8.5660	8.1622	7.7861	7.4353	7.1078	6.8017	6.5152	6.2469	5.9953	5.8753	5.7590	5.6463	5.5371
10	9.4713	8.9826	8.5302	8.1109	7.7217	7.3601	7.0236	6.7101	6.4177	6.2788	6.1446	6.0148	5.8892
11	10.3676	9.7869	9.2526	8.7605	8.3064	7.8869	7.4987	7.1390	6.8052	6.6473	6.4951	6.3482	6.2065
12	11.2551	10.5753	9.9540	9.3851	8.8633	8.3838	7.9427	7.5361	7.1607	6.9838	6.8137	6.6500	6.4924
13	12.1337	11.3484	10.6350	9.9857	9.3936	8.8527	8.3577	7.9038	7.4869	7.2912	7.1034	6.9230	6.7499
14	13.0037	12.1063	11.2961	10.5631	9.8986	9.2950	8.7455	8.2442	7.7862	7.5719	7.3667	7.1702	6.9819
15	13.8651	12.8493	11.9379	11.1184	10.3797	9.7123	9.1079	8.5595	8.0607	7.8282	7.6061	7.3938	7.1909
16	14.7179	13.5777	12.5611	11.6523	10.8378	10.1059	9.4467	8.8514	8.3126	8.0623	7.8237	7.5962	7.3792
17	15.5623	14.2919	13.1661	12.1657	11.2741	10.4773	9.7632	9.1216	8.5436	8.2760	8.0216	7.7794	7.5488
18	16.3983	14.9920	13.7535	12.6593	11.6896	10.8276	10.0591	9.3719	8.7556	8.4713	8.2014	7.9452	7.7016
19	17.2260	15.6785	14.3238	13.1339	12.0853	11.1581	10.3356	9.6036	8.9501	8.6496	8.3649	8.0952	7.8393
20	18.0456	16.3514	14.8775	13.5903	12.4622	11.4699	10.5940	9.8182	9.1286	8.8124	8.5136	8.2309	7.9633
21	18.8570	17.0112	15.4150	14.0292	12.8212	11.7641	10.8355	10.0168	9.2922	8.9611	8.6487	8.3538	8.0751
22	19.6604	17.6581	15.9369	14.4511	13.1630	12.0416	11.0612	10.2007	9.4424	9.0969	8.7715	8.4649	8.1757
23	20.4558	18.2922	16.4436	14.8568	13.4886	12.3034	11.2722	10.3711	9.5802	9.2209	8.8832	8.5656	8.2664
24	21.2434	18.9139	16.9355	15.2470	13.7986	12.5504	11.4693	10.5288	9.7066	9.3342	8.9847	8.6566	8.3481
25	22.0232	19.5235	17.4132	15.6221	14.0939	12.7834	11.6536	10.6748	9.8226	9.4376	9.0770	8.7390	8.4217
26	22.7952	20.1210	17.8768	15.9828	14.3752	13.0032	11.8258	10.8100	9.9290	9.5320	9.1610	8.8136	8.4881
27	23.5596	20.7069	18.3270	16.3296	14.6430	13.2105	11.9867	10.9352	10.0266	9.6183	9.2372	8.8811	8.5478
28	24.3164	21.2813	18.7641	16.6631	14.8981	13.4062	12.1371	11.0511	10.1161	9.6971	9.3066	8.9422	8.6016
29	25.0658	21.8444	19.1885	16.9837	15.1411	13.5907	12.2777	11.1584	10.1983	9.7690	9.3696	8.9974	8.6501
30	25.8077	22.3965	19.6004	17.2920	15.3725	13.7648	12.4090	11.2578	10.2737	9.8347	9.4269	9.0474	8.6938
31	26.5423	22.9377	20.0004	17.5885	15.5928	13.9291	12.5318	11.3498	10.3428	9.8947	9.4790	9.0927	8.7332
32	27.2696	23.4683	20.3888	17.8736	15.8027	14.0840	12.6466	11.4350	10.4062	9.9495	9.5264	9.1337	8.7686
33	27.9897	23.9886	20.7658	18.1477	16.0026	14.2302	12.7538	11.5139	10.4664	9.9996	9.5694	9.1707	8.8005
34	28.7027	24.4986	21.1318	18.4112	16.1929	14.3681	12.8540	11.5869	10.5178	10.0453	9.6086	9.2043	8.8293
35	29.4086	24.9986	21.4872	18.6646	16.3742	14.4983	12.9477	11.6546	10.5668	10.0870	9.6442	9.2347	8.8552
36	30.1075	25.4888	21.8323	18.9083	16.5469	14.6210	13.0352	11.7172	10.6118	10.1251	9.6765	9.2621	8.8786
37	30.7995	25.9695	22.1672	19.1426	16.7113	14.7368	13.1170	11.7752	10.6530	10.1599	9.7059	9.2870	8.8996
38	31.4847	26.4406	22.4925	19.3679	16.8679	14.8460	13.1935	11.8289	10.6908	10.1917	9.7327	9.3095	8.9186
39	32.1630	26.9026	22.8082	19.5845	17.0170	14.9491	13.2649	11.8786	10.7255	10.2207	9.7570	9.3299	8.9357
40	32.8347	27.3555	23.1148	19.7928	17.1591	15.0463	13.3317	11.9246	10.7574	10.2473	9.7791	9.3483	8.9511
41	33.4997	27.7995	23.4124	19.9931	17.2944	15.1380	13.3941	11.9672	10.7866	10.2715	9.7991	9.3650	8.9649
42	34.1581	28.2348	23.7014	20.1856	17.4232	15.2245	13.4525	12.0067	10.8134	10.2936	9.8174	9.3801	8.9774
43	34.8100	28.6616	23.9819	20.3708	17.5459	15.3062	13.5070	12.0432	10.8380	10.3138	9.8340	9.3937	8.9887
44	35.4555	29.0800	24.2543	20.5488	17.6628	15.3832	13.5579	12.0771	10.8605	10.3322	9.8491	9.4061	8.9988
45	36.0945	29.4902	24.5187	20.7200	17.7741	15.4558	13.6055	12.1084	10.8812	10.3490	9.8628	9.4163	9.0079
46	36.7272	29.8923	24.7755	20.8847	17.8801	15.5244	13.6500	12.1374	10.9002	10.3644	9.8753	9.4274	9.0161
47	37.3537	30.2866	25.0247	21.0429	17.9810	15.5890	13.6916	12.1643	10.9176	10.3785	9.8866	9.4366	9.0236
48	37.9740	30.6731	25.2667	21.1951	18.0772	15.6500	13.7305	12.1891	10.9336	10.3913	9.8969	9.4449	9.0302
49	38.5881	31.0521	25.5017	21.3415	18.1687	15.7076	13.7668	12.2122	10.9482	10.4030	9.9063	9.4524	9.0362
50	39.1961	31.4236	25.7298	21.4822	18.2559	15.7619	13.8008	12.2335	10.9617	10.4137	9.9148	9.4591	9.0417

11.50%	12.00%	12.50%	13.00%	13.50%	14.00%	14.50%	15.00%	15.50%	16.00%	17.00%	18.00%	19.00%	20.00%
0.8969	0.8929	0.8889	0.8850	0.8811	0.8772	0.8734	0.8696	0.8658	0.8621	0.8547	0.8475	0.8403	0.8333
1.7012	1.6901	1.6790	1.6681	1.6573	1.6467	1.6361	1.6257	1.6154	1.6052	1.5852	1.5656	1.5465	1.5278
2.4226	2.4018	2.3813	2.3612	2.3413	2.3216	2.3023	2.2832	2.2644	2.2459	2.2096	2.1743	2.1399	2.1065
3.0696	3.0374	3.0056	2.9745	2.9438	2.9137	2.8841	2.8850	2.8263	2.7982	2.7432	2.6901	2.6386	2.5887
3.6499	3.6048	3.5606	3.5172	3.4747	3.4331	3.3922	3.3522	3.3129	3.2743	3.1994	3.1272	3.0576	2.9906
4.1703	4.1114	4.0538	3.9976	3.9425	3.8887	3.8360	3.7845	3.7341	3.6847	3.5892	3.4976	3.4098	3.3255
4.6370	4.5638	4.4923	4.4226	4.3546	4.2883	4.2236	4.1604	4.0988	4.0386	3.9224	3.8115	3.7057	3.6046
5.0556	4.9676	4.8821	4.7988	4.7177	4.6389	4.5621	4.4873	4.4145	4.3436	4.2072	4.0776	3.9544	3.8372
5.4311	5.3283	5.2285	5.1317	5.0377	4.9464	4.8577	4.7716	4.6879	4.6065	4.4506	4.3030	4.1633	4.0310
5.7678	5.6502	5.5364	5.4262	5.3195	5.2161	5.1159	5.0188	4.9246	4.8332	4.6586	4.4941	4.3389	4.1925
6.0698	5.9377	5.8102	5.6869	5.5679	5.4527	5.3414	5.2337	5.1295	5.0286	4.8364	4.6560	4.4865	4.3271
6.3406	6.1944	6.0535	5.9177	5.7867	5.6603	5.5383	5.4206	5.3069	5.1971	4.9884	4.7932	4.6105	4.4392
6.5835	6.4236	6.2698	6.1218	5.9794	5.8424	5.7103	5.5832	5.4606	5.3423	5.1183	4.9095	4.7147	4.5327
6.8013	6.6282	6.4620	6.3025	6.1493	6.0021	5.8606	5.7245	5.5936	5.4675	5.2293	5.0081	4.8023	4.6106
6.9967	6.8109	6.6329	6.4624	6.2989	6.1422	5.9918	5.8474	5.7087	5.5755	5.3242	5.0916	4.8759	4.6755
7.1719	6.9740	6.7848	6.6039	6.4308	6.2651	6.1063	5.9542	5.8084	5.6685	5.4053	5.1624	4.9377	4.7296
7.3291	7.1196	6.9198	6.7291	6.5469	6.3729	6.2064	6.0472	5.8947	5.7487	5.4746	5.2223	4.9897	4.7746
7.4700	7.2497	7.0398	6.8399	6.6493	6.4674	6.2938	6.1280	5.9695	5.8179	5.5339	5.2732	5.0333	4.8122
7.5964	7.3658	7.1465	6.9380	6.7395	6.5504	6.3701	6.1982	6.0342	5.8775	5.5845	5.3162	5.0700	4.8435
7.7098	7.4694	7.2414	7.0248	6.8189	6.6231	6.4368	6.2593	6.0902	5.9288	5.6278	5.3528	5.1009	4.8696
7.8115	7.5620	7.3257	7.1016	6.8889	6.6870	6.4950	6.3125	6.1387	5.9731	5.6648	5.3837	5.1268	4.8913
7.9027	7.6447	7.4006	7.1695	6.9506	6.7429	6.5459	6.3587	6.1807	6.0113	5.6964	5.4099	5.1486	4.9094
7.9845	7.7184	7.4672	7.2297	7.0049	6.7921	6.5903	6.3988	6.2170	6.0443	5.7234	5.4321	5.1669	4.9245
8.0578	7.7843	7.5264	7.2829	7.0528	6.8351	6.6291	6.4338	6.2485	6.0726	5.7465	5.4510	5.1822	4.9371
8.1236	7.8431	7.5790	7.3300	7.0950	6.8729	6.6629	6.4642	6.2758	6.0971	5.7662	5.4669	5.1952	4.9476
8.1826	7.8957	7.6258	7.3717	7.1321	6.9061	6.6925	6.4906	6.2994	6.1182	5.7831	5.4804	5.2060	4.9563
8.2355	7.9426	7.6674	7.4086	7.1649	6.9352	6.7184	6.5135	6.3198	6.1364	5.7975	5.4919	5.2151	4.9636
8.2830	7.9844	7.7043	7.4412	7.1937	6.9607	6.7409	6.5335	6.3375	6.1520	5.8099	5.5016	5.2228	4.9697
8.3255	8.0218	7.7372	7.4701	7.2191	6.9830	6.7606	6.5509	6.3528	6.1656	5.8204	5.5098	5.2292	4.9747
8.3637	8.0552	7.7664	7.4957	7.2415	7.0027	6.7779	6.5660	6.3661	6.1772	5.8294	5.5168	5.2347	4.9789
8.3980	8.0850	7.7923	7.5183	7.2613	7.0199	6.7929	6.5791	6.3776	6.1872	5.8371	5.5227	5.2392	4.9825
8.4287	8.1116	7.8154	7.5383	7.2786	7.0350	6.8060	6.5905	6.3875	6.1959	5.8437	5.5277	5.2430	4.9854
8.4562	8.1354	7.8359	7.5560	7.2940	7.0482	6.8175	6.6005	6.3961	6.2034	5.8493	5.5320	5.2463	4.9878
8.4809	8.1566	7.8542	7.5717	7.3075	7.0599	6.8275	6.6091	6.4035	6.2098	5.8541	5.5356	5.2490	4.9898
8.5030	8.1755	7.8704	7.5856	7.3193	7.0701	6.8362	6.6166	6.4100	6.2153	5.8582	5.5386	5.2512	4.9930
8.5229	8.1924	7.8848	7.5979	7.3298	7.0790	6.8439	6.6231	6.4156	6.2201	5.8617	5.5412	5.2531	4.9930
8.5407	8.2075	7.8976	7.6087	7.3390	7.0868	6.8505	6.6288	6.4204	6.2242	5.8647	5.5434	5.2547	4.9941
8.5567	8.2210	7.9090	7.6183	7.3472	7.0937	6.8564	6.6338	6.4246	6.2278	5.8673	5.5453	5.2561	4.9951
8.5710	8.2330	7.9191	7.6268	7.3543	7.0998	6.8615	6.6381	6.4282	6.2309	5.8695	5.5468	5.2572	4.9959
8.5839	8.2438	7.9281	7.6344	7.3607	7.1050	6.8659	6.6418	6.4314	6.2335	5.8713	5.5482	5.2582	4.9966
8.5954	8.2534	7.9361	7.6410	7.3662	7.1097	6.8698	6.6450	6.4341	6.2358	5.8729	5.5493	5.2590	4.9972
8.6058	8.2619	7.9432	7.6469	7.3711	7.1138	6.8732	6.6479	6.4364	6.2377	5.8743	5.5502	5.2596	4.9976
8.6150	8.2696	7.9495	7.6522	7.3754	7.1173	6.8761	6.6503	6.4385	6.2394	5.8755	5.5511	5.2602	4.9980
8.6233	8.2764	7.9551	7.6568	7.3792	7.1205	6.8787	6.6524	6.4402	6.2409	5.8765	5.5517	5.2607	4.9984
8.6308	8.2825	7.9601	7.6609	7.3826	7.1232	6.8810	6.6543	6.4418	6.2421	5.8773	5.5523	5.2611	4.9986
8.6375	8.2880	7.9645	7.6645	7.3855	7.1256	6.8830	6.6559	6.4431	6.2432	5.8781	5.5528	5.2614	4.9989
8.6435	8.2928	7.9685	7.6677	7.3881	7.1277	6.8847	6.6573	6.4442	6.2442	5.8787	5.5532	5.2617	4.9991
8.6489	8.2972	7.9720	7.6705	7.3904	7.1296	6.8862	6.6585	6.4452	6.2450	5.8792	5.5536	5.2619	4.9992
8.6537	8.3010	7.9751	7.6730	7.3925	7.1312	6.8875	6.6596	6.4461	6.2457	5.8797	5.5539	5.2621	4.9993
8.6580	8.3045	7.9779	7.6752	7.3942	7.1327	6.8886	6.6605	6.4468	6.2463	5.8801	5.5541	5.2623	4.9995

Glossary

ABC see activity-based costing

ABM see activity-based management

abnormal loss a decline in units in excess of normal expectations during a production process

absorption costing a cost accumulation and reporting method that treats the costs of all manufacturing components (direct material, direct labor, variable overhead, and fixed overhead) as inventoriable or product costs; it is the traditional approach to product costing; it must be used for external financial statements and tax returns

accounting rate of return (ARR) the rate of earnings obtained on the average capital investment over the life of a capital project; computed as average annual profits divided by average investment; not based on cash flow

accretion an increase in units or volume caused by the addition of material or by factors inherent in the production process

activity a repetitive action performed in fulfillment of business functions

activity analysis the process of detailing the various repetitive actions that are performed in making a product or providing a service, classifying them as value-added and non-value-added, and devising ways of minimizing or eliminating non-value-added activities

activity-based costing (ABC) a process using multiple cost drivers to predict and allocate costs to products and services; an accounting system collecting financial and operational data on the basis of the underlying nature and extent of business activities; an accounting information and costing system that identifies the various activities performed in an organization, collects costs on the basis of the underlying nature and extent of those activities, and assigns costs to products and services based on consumption of those activities by the products and services

activity-based management (ABM) a discipline that focuses on the activities incurred during the production/performance process as the way to improve the value received by a customer and the resulting profit achieved by providing this value

activity center a segment of the production or service process for which management wants to separately report the costs of the activities performed

activity driver a measure of the demands on activities and, thus, the resources consumed by products and services; often indicates an activity's output

actual cost system a valuation method that uses actual direct material, direct labor, and overhead charges in determining the cost of Work in Process Inventory

ad hoc discount a price concession made under competitive pressure (real or imagined) that does not relate to quantity purchased

administrative department an organizational unit that performs management activities benefiting the entire organization; includes top management personnel and organization headquarters

advance pricing agreement (APA) a binding contract between a company and one or more national tax authorities that provides details of how a transfer price is to be set and establishes that no adjustments or penalties will be made if the agreed-upon methodology is used

algebraic method a process of service department cost allocation that considers all interrelationships of the departments and reflects these relationships in simultaneous equations

algorithm a logical step-by-step problem-solving technique (generally requiring the use of a computer) that continuously searches for an improved solution from the one previously computed until the best answer is determined

allocate assign based on the use of a cost driver, a cost predictor, or an arbitrary method

allocation the systematic assignment of an amount to a recipient set of categories

annuity a series of equal cash flows (either positive or negative) per period

annuity due a series of equal cash flows being received or paid at the beginning of a period

applied overhead the amount of overhead that has been assigned to Work in Process Inventory as a result of

productive activity; credits for this amount are to an overhead account

appraisal cost a quality control cost incurred for monitoring or inspection; compensates for mistakes not eliminated through prevention activities

appropriation a budgeted maximum allowable expenditure

approximated net realizable value at split-off allocation a method of allocating joint cost to joint products using a simulated net realizable value at the split-off point; approximated value is computed as final sales price minus incremental separate costs

asset turnover a ratio measuring asset productivity and showing the number of sales dollars generated by each dollar of assets

authority the right (usually by virtue of position or rank) to use resources to accomplish a task or achieve an objective

autonomation the use of equipment that has been programmed to sense certain conditions

backflush costing a streamlined cost accounting method that speeds up, simplifies, and reduces accounting effort in an environment that minimizes inventory balances, requires few allocations, uses standard costs, and has minimal variances from standard

balanced scorecard (BSC) an approach to performance measurement that weighs performance measures from four perspectives: financial performance, an internal business perspective, a customer perspective, and an innovation and learning perspective

batch-level cost a cost that is caused by a group of things being made, handled, or processed at a single time

benchmarking the process of investigating how others do something better so that the investigating company can imitate, and possibly improve upon, their techniques

benefits-provided ranking a listing of service departments in an order that begins with the one providing the most service to all other corporate areas; the ranking ends with the service department providing service primarily to revenue-producing areas

bill of materials a document that contains information about the product materials components and their specifications (including quality and quantities needed)

black box a term for a management control system whose exact nature of operation cannot be observed

bottleneck any object or facility having a processing speed sufficiently slow to cause the other processing mechanisms in its network to experience idle time

break-even chart a graph that depicts the relationships among revenues, variable costs, fixed costs, and profits (or losses)

break-even point (BEP) the level of activity, in units or dollars, at which total revenues equal total costs

budget a financial plan for the future based on a single level of activity; the quantitative expression of a company's commitment to planned activities and resource acquisition and use

budget manual a detailed set of documents that provides information and guidelines about the budgetary process

budget slack an intentional underestimation of revenues and/or overestimation of expenses in a budgeting process for the purpose of including deviations that are likely to occur so that results will occur within budget limits

budget variance the difference between total actual overhead and budgeted overhead based on standard hours allowed for the production achieved during the period; computed as part of two-variance overhead analysis; also referred to as the controllable variance

budgeting the process of formalizing plans and committing them to written, financial terms

build mission a mission of increasing market share, even at the expense of short-term profits and cash flow; typically pursued by a business unit that has a small market share in a high-growth industry; appropriate for products that are in the early stages of the product life cycle

business process reengineering (BPR) the process of combining information technology to create new and more effective business processes to lower costs, eliminate unnecessary work, upgrade customer service, and increase speed to market

business-value-added activity an activity that is necessary for the operation of the business but for which a customer would not want to pay

by-product an incidental output of a joint process; it is salable, but the sales value of by-products is not substantial enough for management to justify undertaking the joint process; it is viewed as having a higher sales value than scrap

capacity a measure of production volume or some other activity base

capital asset an asset used to generate revenues or cost savings by providing production, distribution, or service capabilities for more than one year

capital budget management's plan for investments in long-term property, plant, and equipment

capital budgeting a process of evaluating an entity's proposed long-range projects or courses of future activity for the purpose of allocating limited resources to desirable projects

capital rationing a condition that exists when there is an upper-dollar constraint on the amount of capital available to commit to capital asset acquisition

carrying cost the total variable cost of carrying one unit of inventory in stock for one year; includes the opportunity cost of the capital invested in inventory

CASB see Cost Accounting Standards Board

cash flow the receipt or disbursement of cash; when related to capital budgeting, cash flows arise from the purchase, operation, and disposition of a capital asset

centralization a management style that exists when top management makes most decisions and controls most activities of the organizational units from the company's central headquarters

Certified Management Accountant (CMA) a professional designation in the area of management accounting that recognizes the successful completion of an examination, acceptable work experience, and continuing education requirements

charge-back system a system using transfer prices; see transfer price

coefficient of correlation a measure of dispersion that indicates the degree of relative association existing between two variables

coefficient of determination a measure of dispersion that indicates the "goodness of fit" of the actual observations to the least squares regression line; indicates what proportion of the total variation in y is explained by the regression model

coefficient of variation a measure of risk used when the standard deviations for multiple projects are approximately the same but the expected values are significantly different

committed cost a cost related either to the long-term investment in plant and equipment of a business or to the organizational personnel whom top management deem permanent; a cost that cannot be changed without long-run detriment to the organization

compensation strategy a foundation for the compensation plan that addresses the role compensation should play in the organization

competence the notion that individuals will develop and maintain the skills necessary to practice their profession

compound interest a method of determining interest in which interest that was earned in prior periods is added to the original investment so that, in each successive period, interest is earned on both principal and interest

compounding period the time between each interest computation

computer-integrated manufacturing (CIM) the integration of two or more flexible manufacturing systems through the use of a host computer and an information networking system

concurrent engineering see simultaneous engineering

confidentiality the notion that individuals will refrain from disclosing company information to inappropriate parties, such as competitors, that could be specifically defined in the company's code of ethics

confrontation strategy an organizational strategy in which company management decides to confront, rather than avoid, competition; an organizational strategy in which company management still attempts to differentiate company products through new features or to develop a price leadership position by dropping prices, even though management recognizes that competitors will rapidly bring out similar products and match price changes; an organizational strategy in which company management identifies and exploits current opportunities for competitive advantage in recognition of the fact that those opportunities will soon be eliminated

constraint a restriction inhibiting the achievement of an objective

continuous budgeting a process in which there is a rolling twelve-month budget; a new budget month (twelve months into the future) is added as each current month expires

continuous improvement an ongoing process of enhancing employee task performance, level of product quality, and level of company service through eliminating non-value-added activities to reduce lead time, making products (performing services) with zero defects, reducing product costs on an ongoing basis, and simplifying products and processes

continuous loss any reduction in units that occurs uniformly throughout a production process

contribution margin the difference between selling price and variable cost per unit or in total for the level of activity; it indicates the amount of each revenue dollar remaining after variable costs have been covered and going toward the coverage of fixed costs and the generation of profits

contribution margin ratio the proportion of each revenue dollar remaining after variable costs have been covered; computed as contribution margin divided by sales

control chart a graphical presentation of the results of a specified activity; it indicates the upper and lower control limits and those results that are out of control

controllable cost a cost over which a manager has the ability to authorize incurrence or directly influence magnitude

controllable variance the budget variance of the two variance approach to analyzing overhead variances

controller the chief accountant (in a corporation) who is responsible for maintaining and reporting on both the cost and financial sets of accounts but does not handle or negotiate changes in actual resources

controlling the process of exerting managerial influence on operations so that they conform to previously prepared plans

conversion the process of transformation or change

conversion cost the total of direct labor and overhead cost; the cost necessary to transform direct material into a finished good or service

core competency a higher proficiency relative to competitors in a critical function or activity; a root of competitiveness and competitive advantage; anything that is not a core competency is a viable candidate for outsourcing

correlation analysis an analytical technique that uses statistical measures of dispersion to reveal the strength of the relationship between variables

cost the cash or cash equivalent value necessary to attain an objective such as acquiring goods and services, complying with a contract, performing a function, or producing and distributing a product

cost accounting a discipline that focuses on techniques or methods for determining the cost of a project, process, or thing through direct measurement, arbitrary assignment, or systematic and rational allocation

Cost Accounting Standards Board (CASB) a body established by Congress in 1970 to promulgate cost accounting standards for defense contractors and federal agencies; disbanded in 1980 and reestablished in 1988; it previously issued pronouncements still carry the weight of law for those organizations within its jurisdiction

cost allocation the assignment, using some reasonable basis, of any indirect cost to one or more cost objects

cost avoidance the practice of finding acceptable alternatives to high-cost items and/or not spending money for unnecessary goods or services

cost-benefit analysis the analytical process of comparing the relative costs and benefits that result from a specific course of action (such as providing information or investing in a project)

cost center a responsibility center in which the manager has the authority to incur costs and is evaluated on the basis of how well costs are controlled

cost consciousness a company-wide attitude about the topics of cost understanding, cost containment, cost avoidance, and cost reduction

cost containment the practice of minimizing, to the extent possible, period-by-period increases in per-unit variable and total fixed costs

cost control system a logical structure of formal and/or informal activities designed to analyze and evaluate how well expenditures are managed during a period

cost driver a factor that has a direct cause-effect relationship to a cost; an activity creating a cost

cost driver analysis the process of investigating, quantifying, and explaining the relationships of cost drivers and their related costs

cost leadership a company's ability to maintain its competitive edge by undercutting competitor prices

cost leadership strategy a plan to achieve the position in a competitive environment of being the low cost producer of a product or provider of a service; it provides one method of avoiding competition

cost management a reflection of management's concern for continuously reducing costs while concurrently improving customer satisfaction

cost management system (CMS) a set of formal methods developed for planning and controlling an organization's cost-generating activities relative to its goals and objectives

cost object anything to which costs attach or are related

cost of capital (COC) the weighted average cost of the various sources of funds (debt and stock) that comprise a firm's financial structure

cost of goods manufactured (CGM) the total cost of the goods completed and transferred to Finished Goods Inventory during the period

cost of production report a process costing document that details all operating and cost information, shows the computation of cost per equivalent unit, and indicates cost assignment to goods produced during the period

cost-plus contract a contract in which the customer agrees to reimburse the producer for the cost of the job plus a specified profit margin over cost

cost pool a collection of monetary amounts incurred either for the same purpose, at the same organizational level, or as a result of the occurrence of the same cost driver

cost presentation the approach to product costing that determines how costs are shown on external financial statements or internal management reports

cost reduction the practice of lowering current costs, especially those that may be in excess of what is necessary

cost structure the relative composition of an organization's fixed and variable costs

cost table a database providing information about the impact on product costs of using different input resources, manufacturing processes, and design specifications

cost-volume-profit (CVP) analysis a procedure that examines changes in costs and volume levels and the resulting effects on net income (profits)

critical success factor (CSF) any item (such as quality, customer service, efficiency, cost control, or responsiveness to change) so important that, without it, the organization would cease to exist

customer value perspective a balanced scorecard perspective that addresses how well an organization is doing relative to important customer criteria such as speed (lead time), quality, service, and price (both purchases and after purchase)

CVP see cost-volume-profit analysis

cycle time the time between the placement of an order to the time the goods arrive for usage or are produced by the company; it is equal to value-added time plus non-value-added time

data bits of knowledge or facts that have not been summarized or categorized in a manner useful to a decision maker

data mining a form of analysis in which statistical techniques are used to uncover answers to important questions about business operations

decentralization a management style that exists when top management grants subordinate managers a significant degree of autonomy and independence in operating and making decisions for their organizational units

decision making the process of choosing among the alternative solutions available to a course of action or a problem situation

decision variable an unknown item for which a linear programming problem is being solved

defect a unit that has been rejected at inspection for failure to meet appropriate quality standards or designated product specifications but that can be reworked and sold

defective unit a unit that has been rejected at a control inspection point for failure to meet appropriate standards of quality or designated product specifications; can be economically reworked and sold through normal distribution channels

degree of operating leverage a factor that indicates how a percentage change in sales, from the existing or current level, will affect company profits; it is calculated as contribution margin divided by net income; it is equal to (1 ÷ margin of safety percentage)

dependent variable an unknown variable that is to be predicted using one or more independent variables

design for manufacturability (DFM) a process that is part of the project management of a new product; concerned with finding optimal solutions to minimizing product failures and other adversities in the delivery of a new product to customers

differential cost a cost that differs in amount among the alternatives being considered

differentiation strategy a technique for avoiding competition by distinguishing a product or service from that of competitors through adding sufficient value (including quality and/or features) that customers are willing to pay a higher price than that charged by competitors

direct cost a cost that is distinctly traceable to a particular cost object

direct costing see variable costing

direct labor the time spent by individuals who work specifically on manufacturing a product or performing a service; the cost of such time

direct material a readily identifiable part of a product; the cost of such a part

direct method a service department cost allocation approach that assigns service department costs directly to revenue-producing areas with only one set of intermediate cost pools or allocations

discounting the process of reducing future cash flows to present value amounts

discount rate the rate of return used to discount future cash flows to their present value amounts; it should equal or exceed an organization's weighted average cost of capital

discrete loss a reduction in units that occurs at a specific point in a production process

discretionary cost a cost that is periodically reviewed by a decision maker in a process of determining whether it continues to be in accord with ongoing policies; a cost that arises from a management decision to fund an activity at a specified cost amount for a specified period of time, generally one year; a cost that can be reduced to zero in the short run if necessity so dictates

distribution cost a cost incurred to warehouse, transport, or deliver a product or service

downsizing any management action that reduces employment upon restructuring operations in response to competitive pressures

downstream cost a cost related to marketing, distribution, or customer service

dual pricing arrangement a transfer pricing system that allows a selling division to record the transfer of goods or services at one price (e.g., a market or negotiated market price) and a buying division to record the transfer at another price (e.g., a cost-based amount)

Du Pont model a model that indicates the return on investment as it is affected by profit margin and asset turnover

economic order quantity (EOQ) an estimate of the number of units per order that will be the least costly and provide the optimal balance between the costs of ordering and the costs of carrying inventory

economic production run (EPR) an estimate of the number of units to produce at one time that minimizes the total costs of setting up production runs and carrying inventory

economic value added (EVA) a measure of the extent to which income exceeds the dollar cost of capital; calculated as income minus (invested capital times the cost of capital percentage)

economically reworked when the incremental revenue from the sale of reworked defective units is greater than the incremental cost of the rework

effectiveness a measure of how well an organization's goals and objectives are achieved; compares actual output results to desired results; determination of the successful accomplishment of an objective

efficiency a measure of the degree to which tasks were performed to produce the best yield at the lowest cost from the resources available; the degree to which a satisfactory relationship of outputs to inputs occurs

electronic data interchange (EDI) the computer-to-computer transfer of information in virtual real time using standardized formats developed by the American National Standards Institute

employee stock ownership plan (ESOP) a profit-sharing compensation program in which investments are made in the securities of the employer

employee time sheet a source document that indicates, for each employee, what jobs were worked on during the day and for what amount of time

empowerment the process of giving workers the training and authority they need to manage their own jobs

engineered cost a cost that has been found to bear an observable and known relationship to a quantifiable activity base

engineering change order (ECO) a business mandate that changes the way in which a product is manufactured or a service is performed by modifying the design, parts, process, or even quality of the product or service

enterprise resource planning (ERP) system a packaged software program that allows a company to (1) automate and integrate the majority of its business processes, (2) share common data and practices across the entire enterprise, and (3) produce and access information in a real-time environment

environmental constraint any limitation on strategy options caused by external cultural, fiscal, legal/regulatory, or political situations; a limiting factor that is not under the direct control of an organization's management; tend to be fairly long-run in nature

e-procurement a system that is an electronic B2B (business-to-business) buy-side application controlling the requisitioning, ordering, and payment functions for inputs

equivalent units of production (EUP) an approximation of the number of whole units of output that could have been produced during a period from the actual effort expended during that period; used in process costing systems to assign costs to production

ethical standard a standard representing beliefs about moral and immoral behaviors

expatriate a parent company or third-country national assigned to a foreign subsidiary or a foreign national assigned to the parent company

expected capacity a short-run concept that represents the anticipated level of capacity to be used by a firm in the upcoming period, based on projected product demand

expected standard a standard set at a level that reflects what is actually expected to occur in the future period; it anticipates future waste and inefficiencies and allows for them; is of limited value for control and performance evaluation purposes

expired cost an expense or a loss

external failure costs expenditures for items such as warranty work, customer complaints, litigation, and defective product recalls incurred after a faulty unit of product has been shipped to the customer

failure cost a quality control cost associated with goods or services that have been found not to conform or perform to the required standards as well as all related costs (such as that of the complaint department); it may be internal or external

feasible region the graphical space contained within and on all of the constraint lines in the graphical solution to a linear programming problem

feasible solution a solution to a linear programming problem that does not violate any problem constraints

FIFO method (of process costing) the method of cost assignment that computes an average cost per equivalent unit of production for the current period; keeps beginning inventory units and costs separate from current period production and costs

financial accounting a discipline in which historical, monetary transactions are analyzed and recorded for use in the preparation of the financial statements (balance sheet, income statement, statement of owners'/stockholders' equity, and statement of cash flows); it focuses primarily on the needs of external users (stockholders, creditors, and regulatory agencies)

financial budget a plan that aggregates monetary details from the operating budgets; includes the cash and capital budgets of a company as well as the pro forma financial statements

financial perspective a balanced scorecard perspective that addresses the concerns of stockholders and other stakeholders about profitability and organizational growth

financing decision a judgment made regarding the method of raising funds that will be used to make acquisitions; it is based on an entity's ability to issue and service debt and equity securities

finished goods the stage in the production or conversion process where units are fully completed

fixed cost a cost that remains constant in total within a specified range of activity

fixed overhead spending variance the difference between the total actual fixed overhead and budgeted fixed overhead; it is computed as part of the four-variance overhead analysis

fixed overhead volume variance see volume variance

flexible budget a presentation of multiple budgets that show costs according to their behavior at different levels of activity

flexible manufacturing system (FMS) a production system in which a single factory manufactures numerous variations of products through the use of computer-controlled robots

focused factory arrangement an arrangement in which a vendor (which may be an external party or an internal corporate division) agrees to provide a limited number of products according to specifications or to perform a limited number of unique services to a company that is typically operating on a just-in-time system

Foreign Corrupt Practices Act (FCPA) a law passed by Congress in 1977 that makes it illegal for a U.S. company to engage in various "questionable" foreign payments and makes it mandatory for a U.S. company to maintain accurate accounting records and a reasonable system of internal control

forward contract see option

full costing see absorption costing

functional classification a separation of costs into groups based on the similar reason for their incurrence; it includes cost of goods sold and detailed selling and administrative expenses

future value the amount to which one or more sums of money invested at a specified interest rate will grow over a specified number of time periods

gap analysis the study of the differences between two information systems, often a current and a proposed system

goal a desired abstract achievement

goal congruence a circumstance in which the personal and organizational goals of decision makers throughout a firm are consistent and mutually supportive

grade (of product or service) the addition or removal of product or service characteristics to satisfy additional needs, especially price

harvest mission a mission that attempts to maximize short-term profits and cash flow, even at the expense of market share; it is typically pursued by a business unit that has a large market share in a low-growth industry; it is appropriate for products in the final stages of the product life cycle

hedging the use of options and forward contracts to manage price risk

high-low method a technique used to determine the fixed and variable portions of a mixed cost; it uses only the highest and lowest levels of activity within the relevant range

historical cost a cost incurred in the past; the recorded purchase price of an asset; a sunk cost

hold mission a mission that attempts to protect the business unit's market share and competitive position; typically pursued by a business unit with a large market share in a high-growth industry

hurdle rate a preestablished rate of return against which other rates of return are measured; it is usually the cost of capital rate when used in evaluating capital projects

hybrid costing system a costing system combining characteristics of both job order and process costing systems

ideal capacity see theoretical capacity

ideal standard a standard that provides for no inefficiencies of any type; impossible to attain on a continuous basis

idle time the amount of time spent in storing inventory or waiting at a production operation for processing

imposed budget a budget developed by top management with little or no input from operating personnel; operating personnel are then informed of the budget objectives and constraints

incremental analysis a process of evaluating changes that focuses only on the factors that differ from one course of action or decision to another

incremental cost the cost of producing or selling an additional contemplated quantity of output

incremental revenue the revenue resulting from an additional contemplated sale

independent project an investment project that has no specific bearing on any other investment project

independent variable a variable that, when changed, will cause consistent, observable changes in another variable; a variable used as the basis of predicting the value of a dependent variable

indirect cost a cost that cannot be traced explicitly to a particular cost object; a common cost

information a bit of knowledge or a fact that has been carefully chosen from a body of data and arranged with others in a meaningful way

input-output coefficient a number (prefaced as a multiplier to an unknown variable) that indicates the rate at which each decision variable uses up (or depletes) the scarce resource

inspection time the time taken to perform quality control activities

Institute of Management Accountants (IMA) an organization composed of individuals interested in the field of management accounting; it coordinates the Certified Management Accountant program through its affiliate organization (the Institute of Certified Management Accountants)

insurance a contract in which one party (an insurer) in exchange for a payment (premium) agrees to reimburse a second party (an insured) for the costs of certain occurrences

integer programming a mathematical programming technique in which all solutions for variables must be restricted to whole numbers

integrity the notion that individuals will not participate in activities that would discredit their company or profession

intellectual capital the sum of the intangible assets of skill, knowledge, and information that exist in an organization; it encompasses human, structural, and relationship capital

internal business perspective a balanced scorecard perspective that addresses those things an organization needs to do well to meet customer needs and expectations

internal control any measure used by management to protect assets, promote the accuracy of records, ensure adherence to company policies, or promote operational efficiency; the totality of all internal controls represents the internal control system

internal failure costs expenditures, such as scrap and rework, incurred on defective unites before those units are shipped to the customer

internal rate of return (IRR) the expected or actual rate of return from a project based on, respectively, the assumed or actual cash flows; the discount rate at which the net present value of the cash flows equals zero

Internet business model a model that involves (1) few physical assets, (2) little management hierarchy, and (3) a direct pipeline to customers

interpolation the process of finding a term between two other terms in a series

intranet a mechanism for sharing information and delivering data from corporate databases to the local-area network (LAN) desktops

inventoriable cost see product cost

investment center a responsibility center in which the manager is responsible for generating revenues and planning and controlling expenses and has the authority to acquire, dispose of, and use plant assets to earn the highest rate of return feasible on those assets within the confines and to the support of the organization's goals

investment decision a judgment about which assets will be acquired by an entity to achieve its stated objectives

ISO 9000 a comprehensive series of international quality standards that define the various design, material procurement, production, quality-control, and delivery requirements and procedures necessary to produce quality products and services

ISO 14000 a series of international standards that are designed to support a company's environmental protection and pollution prevention goals in balance with socioeconomic needs

JIT see just-in-time

job a single unit or group of units identifiable as being produced to distinct customer specifications

job cost record see job order cost sheet

job order cost sheet a source document that provides virtually all the financial information about a particular job; the set of all job order cost sheets for uncompleted jobs composes the Work in Process Inventory subsidiary ledger

job order costing system a method of product costing used by an entity that provides limited quantities of products or services unique to a customer's needs; focus of recordkeeping is on individual jobs

joint cost the total of all costs (direct material, direct labor, and overhead) incurred in a joint process up to the split-off point

joint process a manufacturing process that simultaneously produces more than one product line

joint product one of the primary outputs of a joint process; each joint product individually has substantial revenue-generating ability

judgmental method (of risk adjustment) an informal method of adjusting for risk that allows the decision maker to use logic and reason to decide whether a project provides an acceptable rate of return

just-in-time (JIT) a philosophy about when to do something; the when is "as needed" and the something is a production, purchasing, or delivery activity

just-in-time manufacturing system a production system that attempts to acquire components and produce inventory only as needed, to minimize product defects, and to reduce lead/setup times for acquisition and production

kaizen the Japanese word for continuous improvement

kaizen costing a costing technique to reflect continuous efforts to reduce product costs, improve product quality, and/or improve the production process after manufacturing activities have begun

kanban the Japanese word for card; it was the original name for a JIT system because of the use of cards that indicated a work center's need for additional components during a manufacturing process

key variable a critical factor that management believes will be a direct cause of the achievement or nonachievement of the organizational goals and objectives

labor efficiency variance the number of hours actually worked minus the standard hours allowed for the production achieved multiplied by the standard rate to establish a value for efficiency (favorable) or inefficiency (unfavorable) of the work force

labor mix variance (actual mix × actual hours × standard rate) minus (standard mix × actual hours × standard rate); it presents the financial effect associated with changing the proportionate amount of higher or lower paid workers in production

labor rate variance the actual rate (or actual weighted average rate) paid to labor for the period minus the standard rate multiplied by all hours actually worked during the period; it is actual labor cost minus (actual hours × standard rate)

labor yield variance (standard mix × actual hours × standard rate) minus (standard mix × standard hours × standard rate); it shows the monetary impact of using more or fewer total hours than the standard allowed

lag indicator an outcome assessed by historical financial data that has resulted from past actions

lagging indicators reflections of the results of past decisions

lead indicator a future financial and nonfinancial outcomes, including opportunities and problems, which helps assess strategic progress and guide decision making before lag indicators are known

lead time see cycle time

leading indicators statistical data about the actionable steps that will create the results desired

lean manufacturing a concept that refers to making only those items in demand by customers and making those items without waste

learning and growth perspective a balanced scorecard perspective that focuses on using an organization's intellectual capital to adapt to changing customer needs or to influence new customers' needs and expectations through product or service innovations

learning curve a model that helps predict how labor time will decrease as people become more experienced at performing a task and eliminate the inefficiencies associated with unfamiliarity

least squares regression analysis a statistical technique that investigates the association between dependent and independent variables; it determines the line of "best fit" for a set of observations by minimizing the sum of the squares of the vertical deviations between actual points and the regression line; it can be used to determine the fixed and variable portions of a mixed cost

life cycle costing the accumulation of costs for activities that occur over the entire life cycle of a product from inception to abandonment by the manufacturer and consumer

line employee an employee who is directly responsible for achieving the organization's goals and objectives

line manager a manager who works directly toward attaining organizational goals

linear programming a method of mathematical programming used to solve a problem that involves an objective function and multiple limiting factors or constraints

long-term variable cost a cost that was traditionally viewed as a fixed cost

loss an expired cost that was unintentionally incurred; a cost that does not relate to the generation of revenues

make-or-buy decision a decision that compares the cost of internally manufacturing a component of a final product (or providing a service function) with the cost of purchasing it from outside suppliers (outsourcing) or from another division of the company at a specified transfer price

management accounting a discipline that includes almost all manipulations of financial information for use by managers in performing their organizational functions and in assuring the proper use and handling of an entity's resources; it includes the discipline of cost accounting

Management Accounting Guidelines (MAGs) pronouncements of the Society of Management Accountants of Canada that advocate appropriate practices for specific management accounting situations

management control system (MCS) an information system that helps managers gather information about actual organizational occurrences, make comparisons against plans, effect changes when they are necessary, and communicate among appropriate parties; it should serve to guide organizations in designing and implementing strategies so that organizational goals and objectives are achieved

management information system (MIS) a structure of interrelated elements that collects, organizes, and communicates data to managers so they may plan, control, evaluate performance, and make decisions; the emphasis of the MIS is on internal demands for information rather than external demands; some or all of the MIS may be computerized for ease of access to information, reliability of input and processing, and ability to simulate outcomes of alternative situations

manufacturer a company engaged in a high degree of conversion that results in a tangible output

manufacturing cell a linear or U-shaped production grouping of workers or machines

manufacturing cycle efficiency (MCE) a ratio resulting from dividing the actual production time by total lead time; reflects the proportion of lead time that is value-added

margin of safety the excess of the budgeted or actual sales of a company over its breakeven point; it can be calculated in units or dollars or as a percentage; it is equal to (1 ÷ degree of operating leverage)

mass customization personalized production generally accomplished through the use of flexible manufacturing systems; it reflects an organization's increase in product variety from the same basic component elements

master budget the comprehensive set of all budgetary schedules and the pro forma financial statements of an organization

material mix variance (actual mix × actual quantity × standard price) minus (standard mix × actual quantity × standard price); it computes the monetary effect of substituting a nonstandard mix of material

material price variance total actual cost of material purchased minus (actual quantity of material × standard price); it is the amount of money spent below (favorable) or in excess (unfavorable) of the standard price for the quantity of materials purchased; it can be calculated based on the actual quantity of material purchased or the actual quantity used

material quantity variance (actual quantity × standard price) minus (standard quantity allowed × standard price); the standard cost saved (favorable) or expended (unfavorable) due to the difference between the actual quantity of material used and the standard quantity of material allowed for the goods produced during the period

material requisition form a source document that indicates the types and quantities of material to be placed into production or used in performing a service; it causes materials and their costs to be released from the Raw Material Inventory warehouse and sent to Work in Process Inventory

material yield variance (standard mix × actual quantity × standard price) minus (standard mix × standard quantity × standard price); it computes the difference between the actual total quantity of input and the standard total quantity allowed based on output and uses standard mix and standard prices to determine variance

mathematical programming a variety of techniques used to allocate limited resources among activities to achieve a specific objective

method of least squares see least squares regression analysis

method of neglect a method of treating spoiled units in the equivalent units schedule as if those units did not occur; it is used for continuous normal spoilage

mission statement a written expression of organizational purpose that describes how the organization uniquely meets its targeted customers' needs with its products or services

mix any possible combination of material or labor inputs

mixed cost a cost that has both a variable and a fixed component; it varies with changes in activity, but not proportionately

modified FIFO method (of process costing) the method of cost assignment that uses FIFO to compute a cost per equivalent unit but, in transferring units from a department, the costs of the beginning inventory units

and the units started and completed are combined and averaged

multiple regression a statistical technique that uses two or more independent variables to predict a dependent variable

multiprocess handling the ability of a worker to monitor and operate several (or all) machines in a manufacturing cell or perform all steps of a specific task

mutually exclusive projects a set of proposed capital projects from which one is chosen, causing all the others to be rejected

mutually inclusive projects a set of proposed capital projects that are all related and that must all be chosen if the primary project is chosen

negotiated transfer price an intracompany charge for goods or services set through a process of negotiation between the selling and purchasing unit managers

net present value (NPV) the difference between the present values of all cash inflows and outflows for an investment project

net present value method a process that uses the discounted cash flows of a project to determine whether the rate of return on that project is equal to, higher than, or lower than the desired rate of return

net realizable value approach a method of accounting for by-products or scrap that requires that the net realizable value of these products be treated as a reduction in the cost of the primary products; primary product cost may be reduced by decreasing either (1) cost of goods sold when the joint products are sold or (2) the joint process cost allocated to the joint products

net realizable value at split-off allocation a method of allocating joint cost to joint products that uses, as the proration base, sales value at split-off minus all costs necessary to prepare and dispose of the products; it requires that all joint products be salable at the split-off point

noncontrollable variance the fixed overhead volume variance; it is computed as part of the two-variance approach to overhead analysis

non-negativity constraint a restriction in a linear programming problem stating that negative values for physical quantities cannot exist in a solution

non-value-added (NVA) activity an activity that increases the time spent on

a product or service but that does not increase its worth or value to the customer

normal capacity the long-run (5–10 years) average production or service volume of a firm; it takes into consideration cyclical and seasonal fluctuations

normal cost system a valuation method that uses actual costs of direct material and direct labor in conjunction with a predetermined overhead rate or rates in determining the cost of Work in Process Inventory

normal loss an expected decline in units during the production process

normal spoilage spoilage that has been planned or foreseen; is a product cost

objective a desired quantifiable achievement for a period of time

objective function the linear mathematical equation that states the purpose of a linear programming problem

objectivity the notion that individuals will provide full and fair disclosure of all relevant information

offshoring an outsourcing of jobs formerly performed in the home country to foreign countries

open-book management a philosophy about increasing a firm's performance by involving all workers and by ensuring that all workers have access to operational and financial information necessary to achieve performance improvements

operating budget a budget expressed in both units and dollars

operating leverage the proportionate relationship between a company's variable and fixed costs

operational plan a formulation of the details of implementing and maintaining an organization's strategic plan; it is typically formalized in the master budget

operations flow document a document listing all operations necessary to produce one unit of product (or perform a specific service) and the corresponding time allowed for each operation

opportunity cost a potential benefit that is foregone because one course of action is chosen over another

opportunity cost of capital the highest rate of return that could be earned by using capital for the most attractive alternative project(s) available

optimal solution the solution to a linear programming problem that provides the best answer to the objective function

option an agreement that gives the holder the right to purchase a given quantity of a specific input at a specific price

ordering cost the variable cost associated with preparing, receiving, and paying for an order

order point the level of inventory that triggers the placement of an order for additional units; it is determined based on usage, lead time, and safety stock

ordinary annuity a series of equal cash flows being received or paid at the end of a period

organization chart a depiction of the functions, divisions, and positions of the people/jobs in a company and how they are related; it also indicates the lines of authority and responsibility

organizational culture the set of basic assumptions about the organization and its goals and ways of doing business; a system of shared values about what is important and beliefs about how things get accomplished; it provides a framework that organizes and directs employee behavior at work; it describes an organization's norms in internal and external, as well as formal and informal, transactions

organizational form an entity's legal nature (for example, sole proprietorship, partnership, corporation)

organizational-level cost a cost incurred to support the ongoing facility or operations

organizational structure the manner in which authority and responsibility for decision making is distributed in an entity

outlier an abnormal or nonrepresentative point within a data set

outsourcing the use, by one company, of an external provider of a service or manufacturer of a component

outsourcing decision see make-or-buy decision

overapplied overhead a credit balance in the Overhead account at the end of a period; when the applied overhead amount is greater than the actual overhead that was incurred

overhead any factory or production cost that is indirect to the product or service; it does not include direct material or direct labor; any production cost that cannot be directly traced to the product

overhead application rate see predetermined overhead rate

overhead efficiency variance the difference between total budgeted overhead at actual hours and total

budgeted overhead at standard hours allowed for the production achieved; it is computed as part of a three-variance analysis; it is the same as variable overhead efficiency variance

overhead spending variance the difference between total actual overhead and total budgeted overhead at actual hours; it is computed as part of three-variance analysis; it is equal to the sum of the variable and fixed overhead spending variances

Pareto analysis a method of ranking the causes of variation in a process according to the impact on an objective

Pareto inventory analysis an analysis that separates inventory into three groups based on annual cost-to-volume usage

Pareto principle a rule which states that the greatest effects in human endeavors are traceable to a small number of causes (the *vital few*), while the majority of causes (the *trivial many*) collectively yield only a small impact; this relationship is often referred to as the 20:80 rule

participatory budget a budget that has been developed through a process of joint decision making by top management and operating personnel

payback period the time it takes an investor to recoup an original investment through cash flows from a project

perfection standard see ideal standard

performance evaluation the process of determining the degree of success in accomplishing a task; it equates to both effectiveness and efficiency

period cost a cost other than one associated with making or acquiring inventory

phantom profit a temporary absorption costing profit caused by producing more inventory than is sold

physical measurement allocation a method of allocating a joint cost to products that uses a common physical characteristic as the proration base

planning the process of creating the goals and objectives for an organization and developing a strategy for achieving them in a systematic manner

postinvestment audit the process of gathering information on the actual results of a capital project and comparing them to the expected results

practical capacity the physical production or service volume that a firm could achieve during normal working

hours with consideration given to ongoing, expected operating interruptions

practical standard a standard that can be reached or slightly exceeded with reasonable effort by workers; it allows for normal, unavoidable time problems or delays and for worker breaks; it is often believed to be most effective in inducing the best performance from workers, since such a standard represents an attainable challenge

predetermined overhead rate an estimated constant charge per unit of activity used to assign overhead cost to production or services of the period; it is calculated by dividing total budgeted annual overhead at a selected level of volume or activity by that selected measure of volume or activity; it is also the standard overhead application rate

predictor an activity measure that, when changed, is accompanied by consistent, observable changes in another item

preference decision the second decision made in capital project evaluation in which projects are ranked according to their impact on the achievement of company objectives

present value (PV) the amount that one or more future cash flows is worth currently, given a specified rate of interest

present value index see profitability index

prevention cost a cost incurred to improve quality by preventing defects from occurring

prime cost the total cost of direct material and direct labor for a product

process a series of activities that, when performed together, satisfy a specific objective

process benchmarking benchmarking that focuses on practices and how the best-in-class companies achieved their results

process complexity an assessment about the number of processes through which a product flows

process costing system a method of accumulating and assigning costs to units of production in companies producing large quantities of homogeneous products; it accumulates costs by cost component in each production department and assigns costs to units using equivalent units of production

process map a flowchart or diagram indicating every step that goes into making a product or providing a service

process productivity the total units produced during a period using value-added processing time

process quality yield the proportion of good units that resulted from the activities expended

processing time the actual time consumed performing the functions necessary to manufacture a product

product complexity an assessment about the number of components in a product

product contribution margin the difference between selling price and variable cost of goods sold

product cost a cost associated with making or acquiring inventory

product differentiation a company's ability to offer superior quality products or more unique services than its competitors

product- (or process-) level cost a cost that is caused by the development, production, or acquisition of specific products or services

product life cycle a model depicting the stages through which a product class (not necessarily each product) passes

product line margin see segment margin

product variety the number of different types of products produced (or services rendered) by a firm

productive capacity the number of total units that could be produced during a period based on available equipment time

productive processing time the proportion of total time that is value-added time; also known as manufacturing cycle efficiency

profit center a responsibility center in which managers are responsible for generating revenues and planning and controlling all expenses

profit margin the ratio of income to sales

profit sharing an incentive payment to employees that is contingent on organizational or individual performance

profit-volume graph a visual representation of the amount of profit or loss associated with each level of sales

profitability index (PI) a ratio that compares the present value of net cash flows to the present value of the net investment

project the purchase, installation, and operation of a capital asset

pseudo-profit center a center created when one responsibility center uses a transfer price to artificially "sell" goods or services to another responsibility center

pull system a production system dictated by product sales and demand; a system in which parts are delivered or

produced only as they are needed by the work center for which they are intended; it requires only minimal storage facilities

purchasing cost the quoted price of inventory minus any discounts allowed plus shipping charges

push system the traditional production system in which work centers may produce inventory that is not currently needed because of lead time or economic production/order requirements; it requires that excess inventory be stored until needed

quality the condition of having all the characteristics of a product or service to meet the stated or implied needs of the buyer; it relates to both performance and value; the pride of workmanship; it is conformance to requirements

quality assurance the process of determining that product or service quality conforms to designated specifications usually through an inspection process

quality audit a review of product design activities (although not for individual products), manufacturing processes and controls, quality documentation and records, and management philosophy

quality control (QC) the implementation of all practices and policies designed to eliminate poor quality and variability in the production or service process; it places the primary responsibility for quality at the source of the product or service

radio frequency identification (RFID) advanced information technology that uses exceptionally small "flakes" of silicon to transmit a code for the item to which it is attached

random the concept that some portion of a cost is not predictable based on the cost driver or the cost is stochastically, rather than deterministically, related to the cost driver

raw material the stage in the production or conversion process where work has not yet been started

realized value approach a method of accounting for byproducts or scrap that does not recognize any value for these products until they are sold; the value recognized upon sale can be treated as other revenue or other income

red-line system an inventory ordering system in which a red line is painted on the inventory container at a point deemed to be the reorder point

regression line any line that goes through the means (or averages) of the set of observations for an independent variable and its dependent variables; mathematically, there is a line of "best fit," which is the least squares regression line

reinvestment assumption an assumption made about the rates of return that will be earned by intermediate cash flows from a capital project; NPV and PI assume reinvestment at the discount rate; IRR assumes reinvestment at the IRR

relevant cost a cost that is logically associated with a specific problem or decision

relevant costing a process that compares, to the extent possible and practical, the incremental revenues and incremental costs of alternative decisions

relevant range the specified range of activity over which a variable cost per unit remains constant or a fixed cost remains fixed in total; it is generally assumed to be the normal operating range of the organization

replacement cost an amount that a firm would pay to replace an asset or buy a new one that performs the same functions as an asset currently held

residual income (RI) the profit earned by a responsibility center that exceeds an amount "charged" for funds committed to that center

responsibility the obligation to accomplish a task or achieve an objective

responsibility accounting system an accounting information system for successively higher-level managers about the performance of segments or subunits under the control of each specific manager

responsibility center a cost object under the control of a manager

responsibility report a report that reflects the revenues and/or costs under the control of a particular unit manager

results benchmarking benchmarking in which an end product or service is examined; the focus is on product/service specifications and performance results

return of capital the recovery of the original investment (or principal) in a project

return on capital income; it is equal to the rate of return multiplied by the amount of the investment

return on investment (ROI) a ratio that relates income generated by an investment center to the resources (or asset base) used to produce that income

revenue center a responsibility center for which a manager is accountable only for the generation of revenues and has no control over setting selling prices, or budgeting or incurring costs

risk uncertainty; it reflects the possibility of differences between the expected and actual future returns from an investment

risk-adjusted discount rate method a formal method of adjusting for risk in which the decision maker increases the rate used for discounting the future cash flows to compensate for increased risk

Robinson-Patman Act a law that prohibits companies from pricing the same products at different amounts when those amounts do not reflect related cost differences

rolling budget see continuous budgeting

routing document see operations flow document

safety stock a buffer level of inventory kept on hand by a company in the event of fluctuating usage or unusual delays in lead time

sales mix the relative combination of quantities of sales of the various products that make up the total sales of a company

sales value at split-off allocation a method of assigning joint cost to joint products that uses the relative sales values of the products at the split-off point as the proration basis; use of this method requires that all joint products are salable at the split-off point

scarce resource a resource that is essential to production activity, but is available only in some limited quantity

scrap an incidental output of a joint process; it is salable but the sales value from scrap is not enough for management to justify undertaking the joint process; it is viewed as having a lower sales value than a by-product; leftover material that has a minimal but distinguishable disposal value

screening decision the first decision made in evaluating capital projects; it indicates whether a project is desirable based on some previously established minimum criterion or criteria (see also preference decision)

segment margin the excess of revenues over direct variable expenses and avoidable fixed expenses for a particular segment

sensitivity analysis a process of determining the amount of change that must occur in a variable before a different decision would be made

separate cost a cost following incurrence of joint cost that can be incurred in later stages of production that is assignable to a specific primary product

service company a firm engaged in a high or moderate degree of conversion that results in service output

service department an organizational unit that provides one or more specific functional tasks for other internal units

service time the actual time consumed performing the functions necessary to provide a service

setup cost the direct or indirect cost of getting equipment ready for each new production run

shrinkage a decrease in units arising from an inherent characteristic of the production process; it includes decreases caused by evaporation, leakage, and oxidation

simple interest a method of determining interest in which interest is earned only on the original investment (or principal) amount

simple regression a statistical technique that uses only one independent variable to predict a dependent variable

simplex method an iterative (sequential) algorithm used to solve multivariable, multiconstraint linear programming problems

simultaneous engineering an integrated approach in which all primary functions and personnel contributing to a product's origination and production are involved continuously from the beginning of a product's life

six-sigma method a high-performance, data-driven approach to analyzing and solving the root causes of business problems

slack variable a variable used in a linear programming problem that represents the unused amount of a resource at any level of operation; it is associated with less-than-or-equal-to constraints

Society of Management Accountants of Canada the professional body representing an influential and diverse group of Certified Management Accountants; this body produces numerous publications that address business management issues

special order decision a situation in which management must determine a sales price to charge for manufacturing or service jobs outside the company's normal production/service market

split-off point the point at which the outputs of a joint process are first identifiable or can be separated as individual products

spoilage a unit that has been rejected at inspection for failure to meet appropriate quality standards or designated product specifications and that cannot be reworked and sold

spoiled unit a unit that is rejected at a control inspection point for failure to meet appropriate standards of quality or designated product specifications; it cannot be economically reworked to be brought up to standard

staff employee an employee responsible for providing advice, guidance, and service to line personnel

standard a model or budget against which actual results are compared and evaluated; a benchmark or norm used for planning and control purposes

standard cost a budgeted or estimated cost to manufacture a single unit of product or perform a single service

standard cost card a document that summarizes the direct material, direct labor, and overhead standard quantities and prices needed to complete one unit of product

standard cost system a valuation method that uses predetermined norms for direct material, direct labor, and overhead to assign costs to the various inventory accounts and Cost of Goods Sold

standard overhead application rate a predetermined overhead rate used in a standard cost system; it can be a separate variable or fixed rate or a combined overhead rate

standard quantity allowed the quantity of input (in hours or some other cost driver measurement) required at standard for the output actually achieved for the period

Statement on Management Accounting (SMA) a pronouncement developed and issued by the Management Accounting Practices Committee of the Institute of Management Accountants; application of these statements is through voluntary, not legal, compliance

statistical process control (SPC) the use of control techniques that are based on the theory that a process has natural variations in it over time, but uncommon variations are typically the points at which the process produces "errors," which can be defective goods or poor service

step cost a cost that increases in distinct amounts because of increased activity

step method a process of service department cost allocation that assigns service department costs to cost objects after considering the interrelationships of the service departments and revenue-producing departments

stockout the condition of not having inventory available upon need or request

strategic alliance an agreement between two or more firms with complementary core competencies to jointly contribute to the supply chain

strategic benchmarking a type of benchmarking that is nonindustry-specific and focuses on how companies compete, seeking to identify the winning strategies that have enabled high performing companies to be successful in their marketplaces

strategic planning the process of developing a statement of long-range (5–10 years) goals for the organization and defining the strategies and policies that will help the organization achieve those goals

strategy the link between an organization's goals and objectives and the activities actually conducted by the organization

strict FIFO method (of process costing) the method of cost assignment that uses FIFO to compute a cost per equivalent unit and, in transferring units from a department, keeps the cost of the beginning units separate from the cost of the units started and completed during the current period

suboptimization a situation in which an individual manager pursues goals and objectives that are in his/her own and his/her segment's particular interests rather than in the company's best interests

substitute good an item that can replace another item to satisfy the same wants or needs

sunk cost a cost incurred in the past and not relevant to any future courses of action; the historical or past cost associated with the acquisition of an asset or a resource

supply-chain management the cooperative strategic planning, controlling, and problem solving by a company and its vendors and customers to conduct efficient and effective transfers of goods and services within the supply chain

surplus variable a variable used in a linear programming problem that represents overachievement of a minimum requirement; it is associated with greater-than-or-equal-to constraints

tactical planning the process of determining the specific means or objectives by which the strategic plans of the organization will be achieved; it is short-range in nature (usually 1–18 months)

target costing a method of determining what the cost of a product should be based on the product's estimated selling price less the desired profit

tax benefit (of depreciation) the amount of depreciation deductible for tax purposes multiplied by the tax rate; the reduction in taxes caused by the deductibility of depreciation

tax deferral a tax treatment in which income is subject to tax in a future period

tax exemption a tax treatment in which income is never subject to income taxation

tax shield (of depreciation) the amount of depreciation deductible for tax purposes; the amount of revenue shielded from taxes because of the depreciation deduction

theoretical capacity the estimated maximum production or service volume that a firm could achieve during a period

theory of constraints (TOC) a method of analyzing the bottlenecks (constraints) that keep a system from achieving higher performance; it states that production cannot take place at a rate faster than the slowest machine or person in the process

throughput the total completed and sold output of a plant during a period

time line a representation of the amounts and timing of all cash inflows and outflows; it is used in analyzing cash flow from a capital project

total contribution margin see contribution margin

total cost to account for the sum of the costs in beginning inventory and the costs of the current period

total overhead variance the difference between total actual overhead and total applied overhead; it is the amount of underapplied or overapplied overhead

total quality management (TQM) a structural system for creating organization-wide participation in planning and implementing a continuous improvement process that exceeds the expectations of the customer/client; the application of quality principles to all company endeavors; it is also known as total quality control

total units to account for the sum of the beginning inventory units and units started during the current period

total variance the difference between total actual cost incurred and total standard cost for the output produced during the period

transfer price an internal charge established for the exchange of goods or services between organizational units of the same company

transfer time the time consumed by moving products or components from one place to another

treasurer an individual in a corporation who handles the actual resources of the organization but who does not have access to the accounting records

two-bin system an inventory ordering system in which two containers (or stacks) of raw materials or parts are available for use; when one container is depleted, the removal of materials from the second container begins and a purchase order is placed to refill the first container

uncertainty the doubt or lack of precision in specifying future outcomes

underapplied overhead a debit balance in the Overhead account at the end of a period; when the applied overhead amount is less than the actual overhead that was incurred

unexpired cost an asset

unit-level cost a cost caused by the production or acquisition of a single unit of product or the delivery of a single unit of service

units started and completed the difference between the number of units completed for the period and the units in beginning inventory; it can also be computed as the number of units started during the period minus the units in ending inventory

upstream cost a cost related to research, development, or product design

usage the quantity of inventory used or sold each time interval

value the characteristic of meeting the highest number of customer needs at the lowest possible price

value-added (VA) activity an activity that increases the worth of the product or service to the customer

value chain the set of processes that converts inputs into products and services for the firm's customers; it includes the processes of suppliers as well as internal processes

value chart a visual representation indicating the value-added and non-value-added activities and time spent in those activities from the beginning to the end of a process

value engineering a disciplined search for various feasible combinations of resources and methods that will increase product functionality and reduce costs

values statement an organization's statement that reflects its culture by identifying fundamental beliefs about what is important to the organization

variable cost a cost that varies in total in direct proportion to changes in activity; it is constant on a per unit basis

variable costing a cost accumulation and reporting method that includes only variable production costs (direct material, direct labor, and variable overhead) as inventoriable or product costs; it treats fixed overhead as a period cost; is not acceptable for external reporting and tax returns

variable cost ratio the proportion of each revenue dollar represented by variable costs; computed as variable costs divided by sales or as (1 − contribution margin ratio)

variable overhead efficiency variance the difference between budgeted variable overhead based on actual input activity and variable overhead applied to production

variable overhead spending variance the difference between total actual variable overhead and the budgeted amount of variable overhead based on actual input activity

variance a difference between an actual and a standard or budgeted cost; it is favorable if actual is less than standard and is unfavorable if actual is greater than standard

variance analysis the process of categorizing the nature (favorable or unfavorable) of the differences between standard and actual costs and determining the reasons for those differences

vertex a corner produced by the intersection of lines on a graph

virtual reality an artificial, computer-generated environment in which the user has the impression of being part of that environment and has the ability to navigate and manipulate objects (such as products) behaving like real-world objects

vision a conceptualization of a future state for the organization that is better than the current state

volume variance a fixed overhead variance that represents the difference between budgeted fixed overhead and fixed overhead applied to production of the period; is also referred to as the noncontrollable variance

waste a residual output of a production process that has no sales value and must be disposed of

weighted average method (of process costing) the method of cost assignment that computes an average cost per equivalent unit of production for all units completed during the current period; it combines beginning inventory units and costs with current production and costs, respectively, to compute the average

work in process the stage in the production or conversion process where work has been started but not yet completed

working capital total current assets minus total current liabilities

yield the quantity of output that results from a specified input

yield ratio the expected or actual relationship between input and output

Name Index

Organization Index

Subject Index